Volume 9

# EARLY CREATIONIST JOURNALS

# CREATIONISM IN TWENTIETH-CENTURY AMERICA

Volume 9

# EARLY CREATIONIST JOURNALS

# EARLY CREATIONIST JOURNALS

Edited by
## RONALD L. NUMBERS

Routledge
Taylor & Francis Group

LONDON AND NEW YORK

First published in 1995 by Garland Publishing, Inc.

This edition first published in 2022
by Routledge
4 Park Square, Milton Park, Abingdon, Oxon OX14 4RN
605 Third Avenue, New York, NY 10017

*Routledge is an imprint of the Taylor & Francis Group, an informa business*

*British Library Cataloguing in Publication Data*
A catalogue record for this book is available from the British Library

ISBN: 978-0-367-43553-0 (Set)
ISBN: 978-1-00-314991-0 (Set) (ebk)
ISBN: 978-0-367-43796-1 (Volume 9) (hbk)
ISBN: 978-0-367-43802-9 (Volume 9) (pbk)
ISBN: 978-1-00-300590-2 (Volume 9) (ebk)

DOI: 10.4324/9781003005902

**Publisher's Note**
The publisher has gone to great lengths to ensure the quality of this reprint but
points out that some imperfections in the original copies may be apparent.

**Disclaimer**
The publisher has made every effort to trace copyright holders and would welcome
correspondence from those they have been unable to trace.

# New Preface to the Re-issue of 2021

This anthology of primary documents related to the early history of creationism in the United States first appeared a quarter century ago, in 1995. My interest in the topic had been aroused by my years of research on creationism, which resulted in *The Creationists* (New York: Alfred A. Knopf, 1992). In the meantime, a former student of mine, Edward J. Larson, had published an excellent legal survey, *Trial and Error: The American Controversy over Creation and Evolution* (New York: Oxford University Press, 1985). The philosopher of science Michael Ruse had published the edited volume *But Is It Science? The Philosophical Question in the Creation/Evolution Controversy* (Amherst, NY: Prometheus Books, 1988); and the anthropologist Christopher P. Toumey had just released *God's Own Scientists: Creationists in a Secular World* (New Brunswick, NJ: Rutgers University Press, 1994). Led by Willard B. Gatewood's *Preachers Pedagogues and Politicians: The Evolution Controversy in North Carolina, 1920–1927* (Chapel Hill: University of North Carolina Press, 1966), local studies had also begun to appear. Nevertheless, few, if any, research libraries had begun collecting creationist literature; and not one, to my knowledge, possessed even a complete run of the *Creation Research Society Quarterly*, launched in 1964.

During the past quarter century the landscape of creationism has changed dramatically. Since 1995 the institutional heart of creationism has shifted from the Institute for Creation Research, founded by Henry M. Morris in southern California in 1972, to Ken Ham's Answers in Genesis, headquartered in northern Kentucky. In 2007 the charismatic Australian-born Ham opened a $27-million Creation Museum in Petersburg, Kentucky, across the Ohio River from Cincinnati. Forty-five miles away, in Williamstown, Kentucky, Ham in July 2016 opened an Ark Encounter featuring a "life-size" replica of Noah's ark, at a projected cost of $150 million.

Such growth has attracted considerable attention, such as Susan L. Trollinger and William Vance Trollinger Jr., *Righting America at the Creation Museum* (Baltimore: Johns Hopkins University Press, 2016), and James S. Bielo, *Ark Encounter: The Making of a Creationist Theme Park* (New York: New York University Press, 2018).

The literature on the general history of creationism in the twentieth century has exploded, symbolized most dramatically by Edward J. Larson's Pulitzer Prize-winning volume *Summer for the Gods: The Scopes Trial and America's Continuing Debate over Science and Religion* (New York: Basic Books, 1997). Other significant contributions include Michael Lienesch, *In the Beginning: Fundamentalism, the Scopes Trial, and the Making of the Antievolution Movement* (Chapel Hill: University of North Carolina, 2007); Adam Laats, *Fundamentalism and Education in the Scopes Era: God, Darwin, and the Roots of America's Culture Wars* (New York: Palgrave Macmillan, 2010); Jeffrey P. Moran, *American Genesis: The Evolution Controversies from Scopes to Creation Science* (New York: Oxford University Press, 2012); and Adam R. Shapiro, *Trying Biology: The Scopes Trial, Textbooks, and the Antievolution Movement in American Schools* (Chicago: University of Chicago Press, 2013).

Still, access to creationist sources before the early 1960s remains patchy. To help remedy this condition, Routledge has agreed to reissue the 10-volume set of *Creationism in Twentieth-Century America*. I thank them for their continuing interest.

Ronald L. Numbers
April 2021

VOLUME

# 9

# EARLY CREATIONIST JOURNALS

Edited with introductions by

## RONALD L. NUMBERS

*University of Wisconsin—Madison*
*William Coleman Professor of the*
*History of Science and Medicine*

GARLAND PUBLISHING, Inc.
New York & London
1995

**Library of Congress Cataloging-in-Publication Data**

Early creationist journals / edited with introductions by Ronald L.
Numbers.
    p.   cm. — (Creationism in twentieth-century America ;
v. 9)
    Includes bibliographical references.
    ISBN 0-8153-1810-3 (alk. paper)
    1. Creationism.  2. Bible and evolution.  3. Evolution—
Religious aspects—Christianity.  4. Evolution (Biology)—
Religious aspects—Christianity.  I. Numbers, Ronald L.
II. Series.
BS651.E27  1995
231.7'65—dc20                           94-45522
                                            CIP

Printed on acid-free, 250-year-life paper
Manufactured in the United States of America

# CONTENTS

# Contents

# SERIES INTRODUCTION

In recent years creationism has enjoyed a stunning renaissance both in the United States and around the world. Public opinion polls show that 47 percent of Americans, including one quarter of college graduates, believe that "God created man pretty much in his present form at one time within the last 10,000 years." In the early 1980s two states, Arkansas and Louisiana, passed laws mandating the teaching of "creation science" whenever "evolution science" was taught in the public schools. The United States Supreme Court subsequently overturned these laws, but creationists actively—and often successfully—continue to promote their cause in local schools and churches.

Since the early 1960s creationism has become increasingly identified with a particular nonevolutionary belief known as "scientific creationism" or "creation science." Scientific creationists believe that all life on earth originated no more than 10,000 years ago, and some argue that the entire universe is equally young. To explain the appearance of age suggested by the fossil record, they typically invoke Noah's flood, which, they claim, deposited virtually the entire geological column in the span of a year or so.

Before the 1960s relatively few Americans, including religious fundamentalists, subscribed to such restrictive views of earth history. At the height of the antievolution controversies of the 1920s, for example, most creationists who expressed themselves on the subject embraced interpretations of the book of Genesis that allowed them to accept the evidence of historical geology for the antiquity of life on earth. They generally did so in one of two ways: either by assuming that the "days" of Genesis 1 really meant "ages" or by interposing a gap of perhaps hundreds of millions of years between the creation "in the beginning" and the relatively recent Edenic creation (or restoration, as some would call it) associated with Adam and Eve. Only a few fundamentalists at the time, mostly Seventh-day Adventists, insisted on the recent appearance of life and on the geological significance of the deluge. In recent years, however, through the influence of books such as John C. Whitcomb, Jr. and Henry M. Morris's *The Genesis Flood* (1961), organizations such as the Creation Research Society (1963) and institutions such as the Institute for Creation Research (1972), the so-called flood geologists, now known as scientific creationists, have co-opted the very name creationist for their once peculiar views.

Despite the undeniable importance of antievolutionism in American cultural history, few libraries, academic or otherwise, have collected more than the odd book or pamphlet on creationism, and early creationist periodicals are almost impossible to find. Whether the result of prejudice or indifference, such neglect has made it difficult for students and scholars to explore the development of creationist thought in the twentieth century. This collection of reprinted documents from the first six decades of the century makes available some of the most widely read works on creationism by such stalwarts as Arthur I. Brown, William Bell Riley, Harry Rimmer, Byron C. Nelson, George McCready Price, Harold W. Clark, and Frank Lewis Marsh. It also reprints, for the first time, three of the earliest and rarest creationist journals in America: the *Creationist*, the *Bulletin of Deluge Geology*, and the *Forum for the Correlation of Science and the Bible*.

# INTRODUCTION

In 1906 George McCready Price announced the appearance of a new creationist monthly, undoubtedly the first of its kind, called *The Modern Heretic: A Magazine of Primal Orthodoxy*. He himself served as both editor and publisher. The journal, he promised, would "try to give the most recent discoveries in geology, biology, physiology and archaeology, and to discuss their bearings on the Christian religion." Subscriptions could be purchased for 50 cents a year. It is impossible to say with certainty whether any issues actually appeared. Over twenty years later Price referred to it as "a short-lived journal." No copies seem to have survived in either libraries or archival collections, including Price's own personal papers. In 1908 Price tried unsuccessfully to convince the Seventh-day Adventist church to back the publication of a magazine he proposed calling *The Creationist*.[1]

During the antievolution movement of the 1920s creationists with a scientific bent, still without a journal of their own, typically published their articles in fundamentalist periodicals. Perhaps the leading antievolution paper of the time was the *Bible Champion,* published by the Bible League of North America, which in 1928 began listing Price as a contributing editor. Three years later, when it merged with another journal to form *Christian Faith and Life*, he became editor of a department called "Current Scientific Discoveries." For a brief period in 1927 Harry Rimmer published monthly newsletters from his largely one-man Research Science Bureau in *The Defender*, a right-wing, fundamentalist magazine edited by Gerald B. Winrod in Kansas. The *Sunday School Times, Christian Faith and Life*, *Moody Monthly* (Moody Bible Institute), and *The King's Business* (Bible Institute of Los Angeles) all gave a platform to the antievolutionists.[2]

On occasion enterprising creationsts proposed periodicals to air their views, but nothing seems to have become of them. In 1927 Price declined an invitation from E. S. Ballenger, a dissident Seventh-day Adventist minister and editor, to serve as editor-in-chief of a proposed antievolution magazine, to be called *The Monkey Magazine*. Price claimed to have grown "tired of ephemeral and abortive attempts to turn the world upside down." The creationist cause, he argued, deserved nothing less than "a dignified, scholarly presentation of facts and arguments" and would only be discredited by something that featured the "'Jocko-Homo,' 'Puddle-to-Paradise' style of argument," a reference to the titles of two antievolution pamphlets published in the 1920s by B. H. Shadduck, a minister in the Pilgrim Holiness Church.[3]

But Price did not let his dream of a creationist journal die. In 1935 he broached the idea to one of the earliest and most enthusiastic non-Adventist converts to his distinctive flood-geology brand of creationism: an eccentric California rancher and sometime farm-journal editor named Dudley Joseph Whitney. Whitney countered with the suggestion that they first form a society to sponsor the magazine. Thus was born in 1935 the Religion and Science Association, apparently the first antievolution organization in America aimed at resolving scientific and hermeneutical problems rather than restricting the teaching of evolution. At a time when most fundamentalists still read the first chapter of Genesis as allowing for the antiquity of life on earth, either by interpreting the Mosaic "days" as geological ages or by postulating the existence of a pre-Adamic world before the creation in the Garden of Eden, Price called for the Religion and Science Association to create a united front against evolution by placing itself on record as supporting only his ultraliteralistic theory of flood geology, which allowed for no life on earth before the Edenic creation. He expected that the association would condemn and repudiate "the only other possible alternatives about the fossils: (a) The Day-Age theory, which is false scientifically and cannot be made to harmonize with the record of Genesis I; and (b) The Pre-Adamic Ruin Theory, which makes nonsense of the scientific facts and is utterly fantastic theologically."[4]

The experiment foundered within two years when the leaders of the association fell to squabbling over the age of life on earth. "A swell gang we are," Whitney noted ironically, "trying to fight evolution when we can agree on nothing among ourselves except that evolution is wrong." But Whitney refused to concede failure. As the association drew its last breaths in 1937, he revived Price's idea of publishing *The Creationist*, launching the venture single-handedly as a mimeographed sheet nominally associated with the Religion and Science Association. By this means he hoped to lay "the ground work for something more elaborate" in the future. Except for letters to the editor, Whitney wrote all copy himself, mostly defending Price's flood geology against rival interpretations of Genesis. With the start of the second volume in 1938, he dropped all mention of the parent organization, and by the spring of that year he was referring to "the late Religion and Science Association." *The Creationist* itself did not survive the year, although Whitney apparently issued a second series from 1950 to 1953, and from 1963 to at least 1965 C. William Anderson of the Christian Evidence League, Malverne, New York, published a little magazine called *The Creationist*, which carried Whitney's last essays.[5]

With the demise of the Religion and Science Association, Price set about to create a new creationist society in his own image. In 1938 he and a nucleus of Adventist associates in the Los Angeles area, where he had retired, formed the Society for the Study of Creation, the Deluge, and Related Science, better known as the Deluge Geology Society. To avoid the dissension that had rent the Religion and Science Association, the founders of this professedly nonsectarian organization limited membership to persons who believed that the week of creation lasted no more than "six literal days, and that the Deluge should be studied as the cause of the major geological changes since creation." In other words, creationists who subscribed to the day-age theory or to the notion of a pre-Edenic world were not welcome.[6]

The spark plug of the new society was a Whitney-like refugee from the Religion and Science Association named Benjamin Franklin Allen, a lawyer turned evangelist who believed that Price's creationist works had been written "under the guidance of the Holy Spirit." Most of the organizational and promotional work of the new society fell to Allen and several Seventh-day Adventists physicians associated with the College of Medical Evangelists (now Loma Linda University). Among the most active medics were the nationally known neurologist Cyril B. Courville and the young Dutch-born dermatologist Molleurus Couperus. In addition to holding monthly meetings, the members circulated a mimeographed newsletter and published a journal, the *Bulletin of Deluge Geology and Related Sciences*, which in both content and appearance put *The Creationist* to shame. By 1942 membership stood at about four hundred, and just three years later Allen was claiming "a band of more than 600 loyal and sacrificing" supporters. "In no other part of this round globe," bragged Price, "could anything like the number of scientifically educated believers in Creation and opponents of evolution be assembled, as here in Southern California."[7]

Though Adventists constituted by far the largest contingent within the society, Allen thought it wise to "avoid having so many

Adventists that it could be called an Adventist group." Thus the society actively sought to attract persons of other faiths, especially individuals suspected of having sympathy for flood geology. The popular creationist lecturer Dr. Arthur I. Brown reportedly kept "in constant touch" with the society and spoke to the group in June 1943. Henry M. Morris, the leading creationist of the second half of the century, early signed on as a member, as did the two biologists who later took the lead in organizing the Creation Research Society in 1963, William J. Tinkle and Walter E. Lammerts. Lammerts, a horticulturalist then with the University of California at Los Angeles, drummed up interest in the society among fellow Missouri Synod Lutherans, assuring them that though most members of the society were Adventists, they included "some fine students of nature." In contrast to the Religion and Science Association, which had squandered all of its energies on internecine disputes, the Deluge Geology Society undertook some of the earliest collective field research connected with creationism, including investigations of allegedly human fossil footprints and an abortive search for Noah's ark.[8]

For a society ostensibly bound together by a common commitment to flood geology, the Deluge Geology Society enjoyed a surprisingly short honeymoon. Within a few years, members were wrangling over everything from hermeneutics to tectonics, angrily denouncing one another with a freedom usually reserved for family disputes. The divisiveness stemmed in part from the members' ultra-Protestant insistence on the right of private interpretation, but a new factor had also come into play: the presence of younger university-trained scientists unwilling to accept the dictatorial pronouncements of armchair savants like Price or intellectual bullies like Allen.

The most contentious debates in the society focused on the question of "pre-Genesis time for the earth," the same issue, noted Allen, that had destroyed the old Religion and Science Association. As early as 1943 Allen was complaining of disruptions resulting from "the theory of radioactive time which would place 1 billion 600 million years between verses 1 and 2 of Genesis I." Largely to accommodate new evidence from radioisotope dating, some of the younger, better-educated members of the society were pushing for acceptance of an ancient earth and solar system, with most denying the existence of *life* on earth until the Garden of Eden. In this way they could salvage a literal six-day creation and fossil-burying flood while accepting the latest scientific findings about the age of the solar system. At times even Price himself embraced the notion of a lifeless earth before Eden.[9]

By mid-1945 Allen had grown so obstreperous over the age of the earth that the society's board of directors removed him as secretary and installed Couperus in his place. This action only enraged the combative creationist, who made life miserable for his perceived enemies. To rid themselves of Allen once and for all, before the end of the year the board changed the name of the organization to the Natural Science Society and transferred all of the assets of the Deluge Geology Society to the new entity. They also discontinued the old *Bulletin of Deluge Geology* and began a new journal, the *Forum for the Correlation of Science with the Bible*, edited by Couperus. The *Forum* survived for two volumes before dying in 1948.[10] The next year the American Scientific Affiliation began publishing its journal, which for years served as the periodical of choice for discussing creationism.[11]

## NOTES

1 W. W. Prescott to G. M. Price, November 6, 1908, and C. C. Lewis to G. M. Price, October 23, 1908, both in George McCready Price Papers, Adventist Heritage Center, Andrews University. For a description of *The Modern Heretic*, see the back cover of George McCready Price, *Illogical Geology: The Weakest Point in the Evolution Theory* (Los Angeles: Modern Heretic Co., 1906).

2 Ronald L. Numbers, *The Creationists* (New York: Alfred A. Knopf, 1992), pp. 63, 100, 104. Regarding Price's appointment as a contributing editor, see *Bible Champion* 34 (1928): 126.

3 G. M. Price to E. S. Ballenger, April 20, 1927, and January 30, 1928, Ballenger Papers, courtesy of Donald F. Mote.

4 G. M. Price to B. C. Nelson, July 8, 1935, Byron C. Nelson Papers, Institute for Creation Research. On the Religion and Science Association, see Numbers, *The Creationists*, pp. 102-117.

5 D. J. Whitney to G. M. Price and B. C. Nelson, card postmarked February 17, 1937, and D. J. Whitney to Fellow Directors, February 26, 1937, both in the Nelson Papers. *The Creationist* 2 (April 1938): 2, refers to the late Religion and Science Association. On a second series of *The Creationist*, see Henry M. Morris, *A History of Modern Creationism* (San Diego: Master Book Publishers, 1984), p. 138. Parts of this paragraph are taken from Numbers, *The Creationists*, pp. 114-15, and are used with the permission of the publisher.

6 On the Deluge Geology Society, see Numbers, *The Creationists*, pp.

118-39, from which parts of this account are taken with the permission of the publisher. In the *Creation-Deluge Society Newsletter,* September 16, 1944, members were instructed to refer unofficially to the organization as the Creation-Deluge Society, not the Deluge Society, but the most frequently used name was the Deluge Geology Society.

7   B. F. Allen to G. M. Price, March 9, 1929, and G. M. Price to H. W. Clark, October 23, 1944, both in the Price Papers; Ben F. Allen, "Deluge Geology Society," *Ministry* 12 (August 1939):40. The society's journal began in 1941 as the *Bulletin of Deluge Geology and Related Sciences;* in 1943 it became the *Bulletin of Creation, the Deluge and Related Science;* in 1945 it reverted (almost) to its original title, *Bulletin of Deluge Geology and Related Science.*

8   W. E. Lammerts to Theodore Graebner, November 8, 1941, Box 1, Theodore Graebner Papers, Concordia Historical Institute. In his first book, *That You Might Believe* (Chicago: Good Books, 1946), Henry M. Morris cited over a dozen articles from the *Bulletin of Deluge Geology.*

9   B. F. Allen to Board of Directors, August 12, 1945, and B. F. Allen, "The Question of a Second Society," circular letter dated April 26, 1943, both in the Couperus Papers.

10  Numbers, *The Creationists,* pp. 135-36.

11  On creationism in the American Scientific Affiliation, see ibid., pp. 158-83. In the late 1930s the Pennsylvania botanist Arthur Pierson Kelley attempted to start a Creationist Society of America. He also briefly edited a creationist quarterly called the *Landenberg Review of Natural History.*

THE CREATIONIST

olume 1.                    Exeter, California                    Number 1.
                              May, 1937.

Sent out by Dudley Joseph Whitney, Secretary of the Religion
                   and Science Association.

The organization of the Religion and Science Association came
about as a result of the expression of a wish by George McCready Price
that a magazine could be published, called the CREATIONIST, to discuss
the many questions connected with the problem of creation and to provide various kinds of information which a well informed Christian
should know.

There were many obstacles toward starting such a paper, the
greatest being the expense of bringing it into a self-supporting condition, and as a substitute for the paper the Religion and Science
Association was organized.

Certain great difficulties have arisen in the operation of this
association and the directors have authorized the Secretary-Treasurer
to send out a circular letter to the members and friends of the organization, and perhaps to send out a series of such letters.   In
doing this the Secretary-Treasurer has chosen to put them in the
form of a periodical with the name Professor Price suggested.   There
is no idea of turning these letters into a periodical, although this
might be done if the demand was great enough for it and financial
conditions justified the step.  Meanwhile the officers of the Asso-
iation hope that readers may be given some very necessary informa-
.on.

The expense of this letter is small and there is enough money
in the treasury to send out two or three similar letters later, provided it seems well to do so.  Until a definite request is given for
contributions to continue these letters we ask no financial assistance.  If the series is to be continued, the expense will probally
be small.  This statement is made in reply to requests from certain
members about further dues.  No further dues are required now or
until formal notice is given.

------

### The Election.

The last circular letter dealt in part with the election of
directors.  There were no votes for any one except the old board of
directors and all replies dealing with the subject were in favor of
the reelection of the old board.  They therefore have been elected
to serve another term.

------

### Opinions about Creation.

Members will recall a request by the secretary for the views
of the nature of the creation of the earth as given in the first
chapter of Genesis.  Three ways to take this account were mentioned:
1. The six periods of Creation Week were geological ages.  2, They
were literal days of an original ordering of the earth and
the fossils came from the Flood.  3. They were literal days of the

recordering of a ruined earth.

All that was asked was an expression of opinion, without a statement of the reasons for the belief, and a number of the replies were of this nature. However, certain members undertook to give a statement of the reasons for their belief. These were intensely interesting and if they could be published members of our association and all others interested in the problem of creation would profit much by seeing what was said. Unfortunately, space does not permit their publication. Readers will, however, wish to know the results of this straw vote about creation.

In the report of this vote the Secretary does not include the views of any of the officers or of various members whose views he knows, but who did not make a formal reply to the inquiry. This report includes only the replies made definitely in answer to the request for information.

One member said that he was undertain as to what should be believed. Only two members, and both of these were associate, not active members, believed that the days of creation were geological ages. (There are, however, active members who hold this view, but none of these submitted their views in answer to the letter.) A clear majority of members reporting stated that they believed that the periods of creation were literal days and that the fossils came from the Flood. Therefore if we decide that the replies made indicate the views of members about creation, we find that a clear majority reject the text book theories of creation and believe in a real creation of the earth in literal days, and that the fossils came from the Flood. (More comments on this will be given below.)

About a third of the members replying stated that they believed in a literal day creation, but they believed that this creation was the re-ordering of an earth which had been brought to ruin.

This view is a very common "Fundamentalist" view, but it can be seen that among the members of this organization only a minority believe this, and not a large minority either. However, by correspondence the Secretary can report that the view is held fairly extensively among the membership, both among the active and associate members.

Here, however, is a very interesting feature of this: at least one of the members reporting belief in a pre-Adamic ruin and reconstruction stated that he believed that the fossils came from the Flood. Therefore as far as geology is concerned he lines up with the members who accept literal day creation and Flood geology; he rejects the geological ages. Other members voting on the matter did not say what their opinion on the history of the earth was. Perhaps they believed in Flood geology, and perhaps they believed in the geological ages with a ruin toward their end. This matter should be clarified.

Readers may have noticed a few paragraphs above that more comments were to be made regarding belief that the fossils came from the Flood. Two or three members said that although they believed in Flood geology, they questioned whether all the fossils came from the Flood. This actually demoralizes the whole program, as it leaves uncertain the origin of the fossils and therefore the history of the earth.

The simple fact of the case is that creationists as a whole are confused in their belief about creation. Many of them are clear about certain phases of creation, but others who are equally clear, or positive, in their beliefs have different views entirely. Although the position may not be represented in our Association, certain vigorous defenders of the general proposition of creation even believe in what can be called theistic evolution. This is to say, they believe in the course of events put forth by the evolutionists, but they believe that these were caused by the wish and plan of the Deity.

As far as the Secretary knows every officer of this Association, with the far larger part of the members, is emphatic in the conviction that what the evolutionists assert is the origin and history of this earth is inconsistent with the Bible narrative and is in addition bad science. If we fulfill our obligations as a scientific organization we must show clearly that what is asserted to be the history of the earth and of mankind by the evolutionists is not the real history, and we should decide fairly well what the real history of the earth has been.

However, it should be clear to every thinking man that when one creationist believes in geological ages, another believes that the ages did not occur, but that the fossils came by the Flood, and when others believe in a pre-Adamic ruin and are uncertain what the history of the earth was before and after that ruin, creationist belief is little better than chaos and no effective work can be done against evolution or for Bible science. We should know what we believe before we condemn the evolutionists very vigorously.

### Difficulties of the Association.

The officers of the Religion and Science Association, as is fitting, were not chosen to represent any one school of thought about creation, but hold different views about certain features of creation just as the members hold different views.

In the nature of the case this has hindered and in fact almost prevented certain activities which seemed very desirable. Even when majority held a certain view it felt unwilling to override the views of the minority and certain activities which were planned and approved by one or more officers could not be carried through without overriding the wishes of one or more of the other officers, and this would not be done.

The decision was finally made to have the Secretary notify the friends and members of our organization regarding these conditions and see what could be accomplished. This letter, and perhaps other letters to follow, is the result. This letter is prepared by the Secretary alone, on his judgment and responsibility, though with the authorization and approval of the directors. They may not, however, agree with much that is said. Readers will therefore consider what is said here as the views, not of the officers individually or as a group, but of the Secretary.

Certain very important features of the problem of creation have been the subject of extensive correspondence among different officers, but no material change in the opinions of any officer seems to have resulted by such correspondence. If much of this correspondence could be made public and given a wide circulation, certainly several features of the problem of creation would be clarified.

The president of one of the Fundamentalist colleges has asked that such correspondence be mimeographed and circulated. What is essentially the same request has been made by several others. Unfortunately, however, nearly all of this correspondence was rather informal and not prepared for public circulation and in addition the expense of doing this would be considerable. Perhaps if this series of letters can be continued, discussions can be carried along in it. There are several ways in which it seems possible to accomplish much work by our Association, but it remains to be seen how well these can be carried out.

As an example of what might be done two discussions can be referred to.

One of the biggest problems of creation, and of geology in general, is the extent of the geological work done by the Flood. For instance, the geologist should decide how much difference was made in the face of the earth by the Flood and how many fossils were deposited by it. Three of our direcotrs believe that if any fossils came by the Flood, all 'ld, except a few which are clearly recent. Certain of our members o not believe this. One who wished to thresh the matter out had an extensive correspondence with the Secretary, which was submitted to three members of the faculty of Wheaton College for a report. This has not yet been given. If a discussion like this, well conducted by both parties, could be published, with comments by capable scholars, these persons who wanted to study the subject would certainly be helped.

Also, although fixity of species is a present rule of nature and by some is held to be almost synonymous with the doctrine of special creation, the conviction is almost unanimous that there has been considerable change since creation. The extent of such change, or more accurately, the method creationists should use to decide the extent of such change, was also the subject of correspondence between two officers. This correspondence is also in the hands of the gentlemen at Wheaton, but no report has yet been received from them.

If various great problems of creation like the ones named could be discussed thoroughly and given publication, much progress might be made.

As a matter of news the Secretary might mention that he participated in a debate on the creation or the evolution of man which was published this spring in The Truth Seeker, the official organ of the atheist association. He hoped that the type could be utilized for getting the debate published in good form, but he so convinced of the intentional lack of good faith by the evolutionist that he decided that the debate was not worth publishing. Unless the case for evolution is honestly set forth, its overthrow is valueless.

-----

### A Possible Program.

If the program of discussing important parts of the problem of creation seems good to our members a possible method of making excellent progress seems apparent.

Say that there is an important question upon which many creationists disagree. Two capable men discuss this question, one taking one side and one the other. If it seems well to do so, a committee is chosen to give its views upon the matter after considering the evidence submitted. Such a discussion should have enough sale to justify its printing by a reputable publisher. Being an official publication of our Association, it should have far more standing than a book prepared by an individual on his own responsibility.

If such a discussion were prepared and several members would subscribe $_ each to underwrite its publication, any publisher would doubtless be glad to publish it and the sale should be large enough so that the money advanced would all be returned.

It is just possible that some such discussions can be conducted briefly in letters like this.

Some of the problems which can well be discussed are: 1. How many fossils, if any, were left by the Flood? The answer to this question will to a great extent indicate what should be believed regarding the whole history of the earth. 2. Where the six periods of Creation Week an original ordering of the earth, or the reordering of a ruined earth? 3. How much change took place in the descendents of the animals and plants of the Edenic earth? 4. How long ago was the creation of Adam?

Now there are many questions like this. Any one who attempts to do systematic worken creation meets them everywhere. On practically nothing of importance in the whole problem of creation is there anything resembling general agreement. Yet there ought to be. Unanimous agreement is impossible while men's minds are as fantastic in their operation as they are, but there is no good excuse for differences as great as exist to continue to exist as extensively as they do.

Just one thing will serve as an example of the helplessness of creationists to oppose evolution effectively under the present conditions. In my discussion on the creation of man my opponent cited some of the so-called fossil men as being of great antiquity and connecting modern men with the apes.

Ussher's chronology which on the appearance of things seems not far from correct and which is accepted, with moderate modification, by more than a few good scholars would make man not more than about 6,000 years old. Then if one accepts the Flood as being responsible for the fossils there remain only two possibilities: first, all these fossil men are postdiluvial, or the descendents of Noah; second, some are the descendents of Noah and some may be antediluvian.

On the other hand, if one accepts the geological ages, some of these would appear to be pre-Adamic and a good deal of difficulty would develop in getting an Adam who was made in the image of God created thousands of years after brute-like men lived. If one tries to place some of these men as pre-Adamic by the ruin and reconstruction theory, he also appears to be in difficulty, as the Secretary looks at it. Certain valiant defenders of the faith have even called some of these presumed fossil men apes.

As long as such conditions exist creationists certainly are like
abes in the woods in their attempts to oppose evolution. They may
feel pleased with their intelligence as long as do not realize the
problems they are up against, but such a condition is something more
than unfortunate.

### What About Fossil Men?

Merely as a matter of news, it may be worth stating that a recent
pronouncement of the anthropologists regarding certain fossil men
seems to demoralize their whole case; at least it would do so if they
awoke to the implications of their decision.

They have been greatly interested for several years in some
ancient human remains found in certain caves in northern China and
have termed the men whose bones were found Peking Man, or Sinanthropus.
These men are said to have been low skulled and very primitive, and
the oldest men known.

However, the announcement is also made that these men were early
Mongolians. Now, the Chinese are recognized by historians as having
originated in the district north of the Persian Gulf (where the early
descendents of Noah are said to have lived) and to have migrated
from there in the 23rd century before Christ. (See "China", by Sir
Rober K. Douglas, Part of Lodge's "History of Nations"). It is plain
as can be that if the greatest branch of the Mongolian race, the
Chinese, came from southwestern Asia only about 4,000 years ago, another branch of the Mongolian race did not live in China nearly a
million years ago, or materially earlier than the Chinese started
their migration. Therefore these supposedly most ancient men were not
very ancient nor were they semi-brutes.

The writer has, by request, written upon this matter more in detail for a widely circulated Fundamentalist magazine.

### A Creed of Creation.

Further discussion of the reasons for being clear about the great
parts of the problem of creation is not needed now, but the Secretary
will make a suggestion to every reader of this who is really interested in this great subject. Write down for yourself your creed of creation, with particular relation to the Genesis narrative and see how it
looks.

Here is a very brief creed submitted by the Secretary. There is
not one part of it which has not been denied as fact by one or more
creationists. Few will agree with it entirely. Several of the directors will, I think, agree with the for larger part of it, but I believe that not more than one of the other officers will accept it with
not more than trivial amendment and perhaps he will disagree with it
more than I expect.

The Creed. I believe that God has created the whole universe, but
possibly there was never a time when there was not substance in the
universe which He controlled. As to the time of the creation of the
material composing this earth I know nothing, but I believe that this
was ordered and plants and animals created upon it in six literal
days, and this ordering occurred not far from 4,004 B. C. I believe
that this was a perfect earth and that both plants and animals

have in the main changed greatly for the worse since such creation. In other words, I believe that change among plants and animals since creation has often passed what can reasonably be called the species limits.

I believe that the whole face of the earth was changed greatly by the Flood and that the geography of the present earth is completely different from the geography of the antediluvian earth, and that the fossils came by the Flood. I also believe that Usshor's chronology is substantially correct.

------

### Two Criticisms.

One of the great obstacles toward the successful operation of our Association is that this is a great country and our officers are widely seperated and correspondence between a group of five or six people is difficult. One of the best ways therefore to clarify some of the difficulties before creationists may be for the Secretary to state his views about one or two things which he considers very important and perhaps these views, or criticisms, may be answered.

Two of the greatest obstacles toward offective opposition to evolution, in the view of the Secretary, are: 1. The commonly stated doctrine that a perfect pre-Adamic earth was brought to ruin and reconstructed in six litoral days. 2. The common emphasis upon fixity of species as being a presumed proof of special creation. As the Secretary sees it, the usual offect of both of those things has been to drive intelligent men to believe that of course evolution was a fact and anti-evolution nonsense. (I use vigorous language for the sake of getting as strong a reaction as possible to these statements.)

However, there are qualifications to both of these statements. Let us consider the pre-Adamic ruin theory first. The main fault with this, as the Secretary sees it, is that it is used as a substitute for thought. One of our outstanding members accepts this theory, but he believes that the fossils came from the Flood. (At least a public writing indicates this.) He knows what he thinks; he does not dodge the problem of geology, but faces it. He is not to be criticized.

One of our directors accepts the pre-Adamic ruin theory, but he rejects the geological ages and has a system of geology which pleases him. He does not dodge the issue. Others seem to be uncertain whether there were geological ages or not, and whether the fossils came from the geological ages, a pre-Adamic ruin, or the Flood, or in part from all three. They dodge the whole issue, which is all wrong.

Any person who tries to get his science and theology in harmony should do two things: he should <u>know</u> what he believes regarding the actual history of the earth and how that fits the Genesis account; and he should not only know what he believes, but should investigate the problem sufficiently to decide that what he believes is what should be believed. In general holders of this pre-Adamic ruin theory are sadly at fault in this. They are not all at fault, but the majority seem to be. Of course others believe in geological age "days" of creation and are very indefinite upon the subject. They merit criticism. Others have thought the thing through, perhaps correctly and perhaps incorrectly, and are not to be criticized.

The trouble with the emphasis upon fixity of species is that there has clearly been much change since creation. If one reads the Genesis account of creation intelligently, he will see that an ideal earth was provided for mankind, but after sin came the whole terrestrial creation degenerated and went wrong. The mere fact that the races of men differ so greatly indicates that fixity of species has operated with limitations. Then when an orator on the platform insists on fixity of species, the obvious conclusion of a biologist is that he does not know what he is talking about. The cause of creation has received inestimable injury in this way.

If creationists would make the fact clear that they do not insist upon absolute fixity of species, this harm would be prevented.

As far as the Secretary knows every outstanding proponent of special creation agrees that there has been considerable change since creation and has written to that effect. George McCready Price, for example, has pointed out the resemblances between various felines and the interbreeding of certain of those felines, as an indication that all felines are probably related. Although Byron C. Nelson takes "After Its Kind" as the name of a very meritorious book on creation, he also gives examples of change within the type since creation.

The Secretary, however, thinks that possibly he goes farther than any other out-and-out creationist in believing in extensive change since creation. Right or wrong, he has from school days lamented the desire of creationists to emphasize fixity of species as being an injury to the cause of creation. He now wishes to ask every interested person to read the creation account carefully and see the implications that the Edenic creation was perfect, then to consider how far from perfect nearly every living thing is--and how far from perfect most of the fossil animals were.

A consideration of certain questions like this may indicate what a great field there is for the careful study of creation, with particular reference to the Scriptures.

--------

Some very interesting correspondence has come to the Secretary and if these letters can be continued, some of this may be published. Within the last week a special request has come that another meeting be held, like the one held a year ago in Chicago. An attempt was made to have the papers given there published, but the expense seemed too great. It is probable that another letter will follow this, possibly next September, but a decision on this will be reached later.

Dudley Joseph Whitney, Secretary-Treasurer,<br>The Religion and Science Association.<br>Exeter, California; May, 1937.

########

# T H E   C R E A T I O N I S T
## Exeter, California
Volume 1.                                     October, 1937                                     Number 2
Dudley Joseph Whitney, Secretary of the Religion and Science Associa-
tion, Editor.

---

Two kinds of comments greeted the first issue of the CREATIONIST.
One can be summarized by "Let us avoid points of disagreement and
present a united front to the public on those things in which we can
agree". The other was in effec, "You are on the right line, stay
with it".

From Massachusetts came this: "Your valued MS, The Creastionist,
has been received, and, after prayer for wisdom (which was not mentioned in the MS) I feel led to point out a similar situation that
faced young Count Zinzendorf at Herrnhut in the year of our Lord
1727. After prayer, the young Count had thrown open Herrnhut as an
asylum to the pious but disputatious followers of Huss, Luther,
Calvin, Zwingle, etc., but to unite them in a common doctrine was
superhuman wisdom guided the young Count to draw up a Brotherly
Covenant, which sought out and emphasized the points in which they
agreed, rather than their differences..."

After citing paragraph 3 of our Constitution this gentleman writes,
"Discussion of further details of God's creation will only lead to
confusion and disagreement among ourselves... We stand on holy
ground when we as scientists state that we believe the plain facts
given in the Bible. But to conjecture on details which God has expressly kept out of the Bible, takes us off holy ground into the
changing quicksands of human opinion, which changes with every
development..."

In some ways there is more approval than disapproval here. So
many fantastic theories about creation and the assumed early history
of the earth are put forth by creationists that the need to cease from
fanciful conjecture is very apparent.

-----

This comes from Douglas Dewar, England. "I most emphatically disagree with Mr. D. J. Whitney that there ought to be complete agreement among creationists. The present state of scientific knowledge
is utterly inadequate for any one to determine which of some twenty
(thirty would be more like it. D.J.W.) different interpretations of
the first two chapters of Genesis is the correct one. We cannot hope
to interpret these correctly until our knowledge of geology, palaeontology and biology is far greater than it now is...

"They, (the creationists) ought to concentrate on exposing the
fallacies of evolutionism, and when challenged by the evolutionists
to state a theory, say,'The evidence is insufficient to set forth a
scientific account of creation. We have not yet nearly sufficient
knowledge to assert what the units of creation were, or whether
there have been successive creations, or the length of time life or
man has existed on the earth, and we are not going to copy you
evolutionists by setting forth theories as facts, or even formulat-
ing more than tentative hypotheses at present'".

Dan Gilbert writes from California, "I think you have struck off the right lines. We need, not so much to demolish evolutionist arguments --the demolition of the evolutionary theory is already an accomplished fact. What we need is to do is to formulate a constructive and complete position regarding Creation. We need to reinforce and publicize the proofs of Creation.... But the main emphasis, I feel, should be put where you have put it--upon the sound exposition of our own position. I really believe that a magazine, expanded along the lanes that you have set out upon, would be a 'sensation'

"If we are to stop the evolutionist advance--working slyly through our schools and churches--we must have a widely circulating organ which will not only expose it, but rally Christian opinion to a recognition of the infallable proofs of the case for Creation".

The Very Apparent Situation for any person to see who is not willfully blind is that the things which are set forth in schools, newspapers, many pulpits, and elsewhere, about the origin of the earth and its history, the origin of living things on the earth and their history, and the origin and history of man is in flat conflict with what the Bible teaches. We can shut our eyes to this if we wish, which is and has been the standard policy of the Church for about a century and a half, or we can face the issue and see it through. We have the choice of showing that what is being taught is wrong, of )as nou) ignoring the whole problem while our children are being lost. To say that the teaching of evolution is false, while we do not know what to believe about Genesis is ridiculous.

Can we achieve agreement? Which r. Dewar says the Editor wants? Not until He comes w ose right it is to reign. Any one who knows of the multitude of fantastic theories about details of creation will know that there is no prospect for complete agreement. The human mind is so constituted that the more fantastic the idea, the more the holder is convinced of its perfection, and these freakish theories will never be completely discarded. However, if after much evidence has been presented upon the different problems of creation the great majority of intelligent creationists do not become in substantial agreement upon the leading features of the subject we should cease to oppose evolution and leave the field to the enemy. These freakish theories about creation shame us before the evolutionists, and if we also allow, as Mr. Dewar suggests, that we do not know what we ought to believe upon important parts of the problem of creation we ought also to be ashamed.

Sir George Darwin made the statement that science was only comon sense used in a mathematical manner. Except for the freakishness of the human intellect there is no more excuse for scientists to differ among themselves than there is for mathematicians differ upon the answer to a problem in mathematics. We could well use more information about creation than is available, but we still have enough to reach valid conclusions, provided we use that evidence in a reasonable manner.

When one gets down to examine these twenty to thirty different views about the meaning of Genesis one finds that nearly all of them are based upon the idea that creation did not occur in the way Genesis evidently states, but that the account should be warped more or less so as to fit the assumed findings of science. The more the account is warped, the worse it becomes. I have no respect for that kind of science and theology. The Scriptures should be taken in a simple, direct and natural manner, or not at all.

The science better in that way than in any other way.

### The First Problem to study.

Our most important problem in deciding about creation is unquestionably to decide how the fossils came into being and therefor to determine what was the history of the earth. The most important single point in this problem is to determine the relation of the Flood to the fossils.

The fossils, with some related phenomena, are used by the evolutionists to overthrow the Genesis account of creation. They assert that these were formed during long ages and that the ordering of the earth and the creation of man was not 6,000 years ago, although the Bible indicates that it was not far from then. Pictures of gigantic reptiles are displayed and their bones are shown in museums. The assertion is made that these lived long before man and the common warm blooded animals.

Fossils are also shown of extinct types of mammals which are asserted to have lived long before the creation of Adam. Low browed, brute-like men are asserted to have lived tens of thousands of years before God is said to have made man in his own image.

We creationists must have some reasonable explanation for the existence of these fossils or cease to oppose evolution; there is no sense in accusing the evolutionists of being wrong without having a course of history which is both good science and in harmony with the Scriptures.

There is just one system of geologic history to account for these fossils contrary to ages geology which has any substantial following, and that is FLOOD GEOLOGY, the doctrine that the fossils came from the Flood and that there were no long ages before then ad far as the evidence shows. When we believe that the fossils came by the Flood belief in the origin of the first plants and animals by creation immediately before the creation of Adam is natural and inevitable. This doctrine of Flood Geology therefore makes the Flood the earth-devasting event which the Genesis account indicates and allows the full and normal acceptance of the Genesis account of Creation. There is no forcing of any detail of the Genesis record once this doctrine of Flood Geology is accepted. It is the only one of the twenty to thirty ways of taking Genesis to which Mr. Dewar refers which requires no warping of either Genesis or reason.

On the other hand every other system of belief about Creation is forced in at least some manner, and not one is satisfactory. They all have a foundation of disbelief that the earth was put in order and living things created upon it six thousand years ago and that the fossils came since then and not--at least in part--earlier than then.

### "Age Days" of Creation Week.

The old way of "reconciling science and Genesis" was to consider the evolutionary geologists right and to make the six periods of creation geologic ages. However, the six periods of creation cannot be harmonized with geology without doing violence to reason, and in addition evolutionary geology allows no place for the Flood. A person may, if he so desires, force his mind to make evolutionary geology fit the Genesis account of creation, but when he does this he has to discard the account of the Flood, to which is given more space than the account of creation itself. There is no gain in this; it brings discredit upon the Scriptures.

There is another way of attempting to reconcile Genesis with evolutionary geology, and that is to assume that the ages took place as the geologists assert, but that there was a ruin and reconstruction of the earth just before the creation of Adam. This is a very popular doctrine, but unfortunately it is used as a means of avoiding ruin and restitution difficulties rather than facing them. Of course, some holders of the theory accept Flood Geology and so accept the Flood as a satisfactory solution for the origin of the fossils.

The situation, however, is that there is a numerous and influential group of Christian scholars who accept Flood Geology, but with very few exceptions those creationists who reject Flood Geology are uncertain what was the actual history of the earth, what was the extent and effect of the Flood, and what was the cause of the fossils. Few Christian scholars can investigate evolutionary geology and have much more respect for it then they can have for the theory of organic evolution; nevertheless those persons who reject Flood Geology in nearly every instance accept to a greater or less extent the teachings of the evolutionary geologists about the history of the earth. This certainly shows that a study of the Flood, and particularly of the merits (and possible faults) of Flood Geology is of prime importance in any thorough study of Creation.

## Opposition to Flood Geology.

Flood Geology is nevertheless anathema to many influentail creationists. The writer has often been condemned for his support of the theory. He has received numerous criticisms of other upholders of the theory. Also many persons approve certain features of Flood Geology, but reject and condemn the theory as a whole.

Following the publication of the first issue of the CREATIONIST; but in referring to another matter, a teacher in a prominent Fundamentalist college wrote:
"The incubus of Flood Geology is a dead weight on fundamentalism. No fundamentalist is opposed to a man having strange interpretations of an individual preference, but fundamentalism can never withstand any attempt to add to the generally accepted fundamental contentions any pet theory which a group may be inclined to compell others to accept as fundamental". The writer of this is a member of The Religion and Science Association. It may be presumed that students in his classes at such times, if any, as Flood Geology is mentioned, get no favorable impression of it.

"The incubus of Flood Geology". If Flood Geology is bad science, we had better decide so as soon as possible. If it is good science, those thousands of pastors and hundreds of teachers who are as yet uncertain whether it is right or wrong, or who believe it to be wrong, had better bestir themselves to find what should be believed about it.

Therefore The CREATIONIST is going to take as its first task the problem of the Flood. Among the members of The Religion and Science Association the problem of the Flood must first be discussed on the basis that the Genesis record is authentic and good history. The geology of a member of our Association must fit the account of the Flood, and of Creation.

Geologists in general may deny the validity of Genesis and with them we must discuss the subject upon a purely scientific basis, without demanding belief in the Scriptures. However, among ourselves, for the first step in an analysis of the subject, Genesis must be held true and our geology must correspond with it.

Nearly four chapters of Genesis are given to an account of this great event. Everything which had breath is said to have been destroyed by the Flood, except those creatures saved in the Ark. More than a full year passed between the outbreak of the Flood and the time that the earth was habitable again. All the mountains upon the earth were covered with water and remained covered for six months or thereabouts. When the Ark grounded it grounded, not on a sand bar near the mouth of a river, or along a sea shore, but upon land which rose to be a high mountain. Such a great disturbance to the face of the earth must have inevitably accomplished an enormous amount of geologic work. Since fossils were buried, it certainly is reasonable to assume that a cataclysmic event like the Flood would bury many fossils. We who have studied the subject (I speak for others also) find no reasonable stopping place between the conclusion that the Flood formed some of the fossils and the conclusion that it formed them all--except of course a few which are clearly recent in origin.

This thesis has been put forth in private correspondence several times, that if the Flood formed some of the fossils it was responsible for them all. It can now be discussed in some detail.

The response has come several times (using my own words to express it), "To say that because the Flood caused some of the fossils it must have caused all, is silly".

Please note, however, that I have not said that all of the fossils came from the Flood because some came in that way. I do not remember any effort whatever being made by any critic of this position to point out what fossils came by the Flood and what did not. (Note. Some human artifacts under ancient Ur have been asserted to have been antediluvian, but this is in effect saying that no fossils came from the Flood.)

### A Classification of the Fossils.

The sedimentary rocks and the fossils therein are classified by the evolutionary geologists as belonging to different systems, supposedly laid down in a series of geological ages. These rocks and the fossils therein are called Cambrian, Silurian, Devonian, Cretaceous, and a list of other names. The fossils supposedly formed immediately preceding the present geological epoch are termed Pleistocene; the ones preceding those Pliocene, and so on backward.

We will await the word of some critic of Flood Geology, of some one perhaps who holds Flood Geology to be an incubus upon Fundamentalism in the war against evolution to say whether Pleistocene fossils are the result of the Flood and Pliocene earlier in origin, or just how the fossils are to be divided as a result of the Flood, before making a systematic analysis of this part of the problem.

However, there are certain points which can well be stated now. These sedimentary formations are given different names, which supposedly indicate difference in age and time of origin. Cambrian rocks are said to contain the oldest true fossils. However, certain Cambrian rocks are surface rocks, just the same as certain Pleistocene rocks are surface rocks. Every last one of these systems is represented by extensive suface rocks, and if the fossils in Pleistocene sediments were laid down by the Flood, the fossils in those other surface formations show just as much signs of having been laid down in the Flood.

There is certainly no material distinction between the Pliocene fossils and the Pleistocene; there is no material distinction is far as location is concerned, and not much in the way of classification, as far as Pliocene and Miocene fossils are concerned.

Going back through what are called the Tertiary formations (Pliocene, Miocene and Eocene) and coming to the Cretaceous formations, there is a marked difference in the animal fossils, but the Cretaceous plants are definitely modern, and Cretaceous sediments as far as location is concerned cannot well be called pre-Flood, or antediluvian, if Tertiary deposits are caused from the Flood. And so we can go right down the line to the Cambrian sediments and certain pre-Cambrian deposits and find no dividing line which can rightly serve as a division between Flood-formed and pre-Flood fossils.

Not only this, but many instances occur when so-called "older" formations rest above so-called younger deposits. Instances can be cited where Mesozoic rocks rest on top of Tertiary rocks, although the Mesozoic rocks are said to be older. Certainly therefore no reasonable man can rightly assert that the Tertiary rocks in these instances are younger than the rocks which rest upon them, both showing all signs of having been laid down in water one upon the other.

This "upside down" condition occurs not only with Mesozoic and Tertiary rocks, but with all the formations from certain so-called pre-Cambrian rocks onward. It is a condition which utterly and positively discredits the whole system of "ages geology" and it certainly prohibits the development of any reasonable system of classifying the fossils which would make some the result of the Flood and some the result of earlier geologic activity.

I therefore set forth first in this analysis of the problem of the fossils the thesis that: If we allow that any appreciable amount of the fossils were laid down by the flood, all were laid down in that way. Since the Flood Geology is vigorously criticized by certain creationists and is even held an "incubut" in our battle for Creation, and since scores and hundreds of fundamentalists hesitate to accept Flood Geology, I therefore call upon critics of this position to say what fossils came by the Flood and what came earlier that than the Flood. The Creationist is not designed as an agency for compelling belief in any theory. Let us hear from critics of Flood Geology on this point.

### The Uplift of the Mountains.

There is much more to the subject than this. The mountains that are formed partly or wholly from sedimentary rocks were certainly uplifted from below sea level, or at least from below lake level. The sedimentary rock composing them (or part of them) was laid down in water. It was not laid down as part of a mountain, but as low lying material. Later it was uplifted. This is evolutionary geology as well as Flood geology. The evolutionist asserts that these sedimentary mountains came by uplift; the Flood geologist asserts the same thing. They agree on this point. However, the Flood geologists have them uplifted recently, right after the Flood. The evolutionist would have some of them uplifted long ago, but with erosion as rapid as it is, he has a puzzle in front of him to explain while they were not eroded to nothingness long ago if they are millions of years old, as he asserts some of them to be.

The Flood account, if one will read it with understanding, shows that these mountains must be recent in origin; they could not be old. During the early part of the Flood--after the ruin of the antediluvian earth was complete, which may have taken 40 days or more--the waters covered everything.

Present mountains could not have existed then; otherwise the water would not have covered them; it would have drained off in a few hours or days into ocean beds. The gradual emergence of the Ark from the mountains of Ararat was not therefore the gradual drainage of water from previously existing mountains, but the gradual uplift of land into a mountain mass. This is as plain as anything could be.

If therefore, the mountains were uplifted during the latter part of the Flood period, it seems perfectly reasonable to decide that the fossils which they contain were formed in the great cataclysm which brought the face of the antediluvian earth to ruin.

The face of the earth was also made over in Creation Week. The account indicated that early in Creation Week the waters covered everything. They could not well do so if there were mountains. In fact the account indicates clearly that land arose from water in the Third Day of creation. Existing fossils, therefore, would hardly be the remains of creatures which lived long before Adam, withstanding the mountain building of Creation Week, the destruction of the Deluge, and the remaking of the face of the earth. And they cannot be classified so as to make some pre-Adamic, some post-Adamic but antedluvian, and some the result of the Flood.

If we take the record in a simple, natural manner, we must therefore decide that the fossils came from the Flood. The Scriptures do not come out with the statement, "The fossils came from the Flood", but the inference is clearly to that effect.

Or are we wrong on this? We who uphold Flood geology, have been accused by our critics of bringing disrepute upon creationism by our bad science. Let our critics now speak up and show how we are wrong. If there is a single other point in the whole problem of creation as important as this one matter of the relation of the Flood to the fossils I do not know what it is. I call for criticism of our position, but with the proviso that the critics accept the Genesis record as correct.

Criticism is easy; any one can criticize. I therefore make one demand of the critics of Flood geology. They must say what fossils, if any, they believe came from the Flood and they must say how they believe the others originated. Particularly I wish to know their belief about ages geology. I also wish to know whether they think existing mountains existed before the Flood or not.

When we get these matters settled there are many other questions which must be taken up. I am ready to defend Flood Geology from the standpoint of pure geology, aside altogether from the Genesis record, but when we creationists start to put our house in order we must begin by real belief in the Scriptures. So let us hear without delay from critics of Flood Geology who are willing also to take Genesis as true.

One very important feature which has been slighted by critics of Flood Geology should be noted here. Without a single exception as far as the experience of the writer goes every critic of Flood Geology who substitutes for it some kind of ages geology warps that ages geology into a form in which the geologists would refuse to own it. The Flood geologists are therefore between two fires. Our main task is certainly to show that ages geology is bad science and this we can easily do, and while doing this we give good evidence for Flood Geology. However, our enemies are those of our own household; those who feel that Flood Geology is an incubus on fundamentalism, but use some "strange interpretations of individual preference in opposition to it.

These critics have no system of history to put in its place when they warp ages geology out of shape. True, they have many systems of history, but none of these systems agrees with the others or has any real following. A few of them can be mentioned.

A noted British creationist, an outstanding man in many ways, accepts the ages, with the idea that a series of pre-Adamic ruins took place during them, and believes that a final pre-Adamic ruin came about when the sun became dark and cold, so that the earth became waste and lifeless. Later he thinks the sun was made to shine again and give heat during Creation Week, starting the earth off anew without showing any material signs of this ruin and reconstruction. I can imagine the geologists accepting that as preferable to Flood Geology!

The canopy theory still has some followers who appear to believe that the fossils were buried by the collapse of successive series of canopies over the earth. Let us try to imagine that being accepted as reasonable!

Another believes that gigantic meteorites hit the earth and provided the agencies by which assumed earth movements of geologic ages could develop, and as the means of destroying pre-Adamic life.

One outstanding defender of the faith in America asserts that the moon flew off from the earth in the Permian period, which he says was part of the fourth period of creation. That is the way he accepts ages geology!

Many others simply assert a pre-Adamic ruin sometime near the end of the ages, although they point out no definite signs of such a ruin and the geologists refuse to allow that such a ruin occurred or that all life was destroyed not long ago so that things had to be created all over again. These people either have no geologic work to show as the result of the Flood, or they have some theory of the Flood which the geologists do not accept.

All of this simply shows that these people who are as they think opposing Flood Geology in favor of ages geology of some type actually warp that geology into some fantastic shape which geologists refuse to accept. Then they assert that they are more scientific than we who believe in Flood geology and know why we believe it.

We Flood geologists ought bot to be called upon to meet this kind of opposition; until ages geology is either routed or sustained we sho ld have to battle it alone,

Let me quote again the words of the critic referred to earlier: "No fundamentalist is opposed to a man having strange interpretations of an individual preference, but fundamentalism can never withstand any attempt to add to the generally accepted fundamental contentions any pet theory which a group may be inclined to compell others to accept as fundamental". This is fine; let us set there pet theories of individual preference aside.

Rememver, Flood Geology has been indicted; it is now on trial. Critics are invited to submit their charges provided they accept the Genesis account as given and provided they meet the requirements I announced earlier. But remember also they certainly ought not to demand that fundamentalists accept as the alternative to Flood Geology some pet theory of their own. Our pages are open to the critics.

------------
## The Future of the Creationist

Some urgent requests have come in to make the Creationist a regularly printed journal. A great deal of money would be required to do this and it is very doubtful if such a paper would be self supporting even after a fair subscription list had been built up. The money to start such a paper is not available and I would hesitate to spend the money if it were available for a venture which would not be self supporting.

There certainly is an urgent need that this problem of creation be clarified and that a paper be provided to discuss the subject and other problems connecting science and religion. The Creationist ought to be able to serve that purpose and can do so if it gets reasonable moral support and some slight financial support.

At present the expense of publishing is nominal, but there are expenses. If it is to be continued on the present basis contributions from a few of our readers of a dollar or two will be needed. A few contributions per issue will be sufficient to keep it going on the present basis.

The mimeographing is now done gratis as practice for students in a near-by school. This reduces the cost, but it has certain disadvantages. Second class mailing privileges could be secured from the post office if a genuine subscription list of 200 or more persons were secur d. I believe I could then get out about ten issues a year and have them mimeographed by a commercial concern. The subscription would be $1.00 per year and the number of free copies would have to be greatly reduced. Arrangement, however, could be made so that the paper could be sent at a reduced price to certain institutions which should get it.

Will each of our readers who approves the idea of developing a regular subscription list kindly drop me a post card to that effect or send a dollar or more for expenses to keep the paper going on the present basis, with the understandin that this will pay for a subscription if the Creationist is to be made a mimeographed journal. Progress will be reported in the next issue. God willing, there will be one more issue.

If not another cent comes in for expenses, but that will be the end.

Pleas also do this: if you are not particularly interested in getting this paper, kindly send me a card to that effect so that you may be dropped from the mailing list. Please pass your copy along to some one who ought to see it too. Send me the name of persons who should get this paper; let us make it as well known as possible at a minimum cost. If it is worth while it c n keep going; if not, it ought to die.

---

## Odds and Ends.

A number of interesting things have developed in the world of science since the last issue, but space will permit the mention of only a few.

Word comes from the Evolution Protest Movement, 24 Essex St., London, W.C.2, that the British British Broadcasting Corporation "has flatly refused to allow the scientific case against the theory organic evolution to be broadcast by scientists of the highest attainments".

That is the open minded attitude of evolutionists for you.

The following list of new books is also given, with the price, postage extra. They can be ordered from the address named.

"The Intersecting Spheres of Religion and Science" By Sir Ambrose Fleming

"A Challenge to Evolutionsts"   By Douglas Dewar   2/6
"Organic Evolution Provably False" By Major H.R.Kindersley  1/-
"The Story of Creation"        By ..H.Molesworth      6d.

The writer has read only the second and third of these and found them interesting. Listing the others therefore is not necessaryily an endorsement of the conditions set forth in them.

## "A Challenge to Evolutionists"

This booklet is worth telling about. The Protest Movement challenged the British Rationalists to debate organic evolution, but they would not at first meet the challenge. Finally Joseph McCabe, a noted Rationalist, well known in America as well as Great Britain, agreed to debate organic evolution with Mr. Dewar.

The debate was held and a stenographic report made by a stenographer hired by the Rationalists. Mr. Dewar and the Protest Movement went ahead to arrange for publication of the debate. Mr. McCabe, however, flatly refused to allow any statements of his to be published. We can guess what he thought about the effect it would have on readers. As a result the publication of the debate had to be made with nothing more than the case given by Mr. Dewar, the remarks of the chairman, and a few necessary notes. This is like the play of Hamlet with Hamlet missing. Otherwise the booklet is a delight to read. Students in the American universities who are taught that evolution is a fact ought to profit by seeing this book, although it would make the professors lose face".

In contrast to the backwardness of the British Rationalists to meet the issue as described above I wish to absolve the American Rationalists as a group from the use of such tactics. They have opened the columns of their Truth Seeker to a debate on evolution and to

papers from Christian writers and they are at present running a three
cornered discussion on the question, Does God work naturally, super-
naturally, or not at all?  The participants are Charles Smith,
atheist; Dr. T. Darley Allen, president of the Anti-Atheist Association; and the editor of the Creationist.

## Flood Geologists Please Note.

One of our charter members who is a well known writer on creation
has prepared a mimeographed bulletin on the different features of
Flood Geology which call for special study.  A full hundred topics
are named. Persons particularly interested may write to the author
for copies, of which a few extra are available.  The address:  Mr.
Ben F. Allen, 219 N. Grand Avenue, Los Angeles, Calif.

What Mr. Allen is driving at is to have these subjects
discussed thoroughly by Flood Geologists so as to get the benefit
of having many minds working on the subject.  This is a very fine
piece of work and a fine program.


## A Suggestion

Dr. Alfred C. Lane, chairman of the committee on the measurement
of geologic time for the National Research Council, a former
president of the Geological Society of America, and of course a geolo
-gist of the highest rank, in a personal letter to the editor of
the Creationist some weeks ago told of an automobile tour in which
he participated with a number of oil geologists this summer and
mentioned, casually, that he should like to see a trip something
like this in which both Fundamentalists and evolutionary geologists
participated.  Would that not be a fine thing for next summer, if
it could be arranged?  Perhaps no evolutionary geologists would come
along, but a trip like that would provide grand instruction for such
Fundamentalists as are interested in geology, and we might know
better what was what at the end of the trip than we knew at the
beginning.

The writer would like to see such a tour in California next
year.  We have all kinds of geology. We have the highest  mountain
and the lowest valley in the continental United States.  We also
have the only active volcano in America, and we have about everything else one could ask in geology except coal, and there is
even a little of that.

If the idea of such a trip appeals to you, please write and
tell me.  I have an idea that if such a trip was made Dr. Lane
might be induced to go along, though I have no assurance that he
would.  I trust that I am not out of order in saying that he and
I have exchanged a great many letters, that he has given me many
helpful suggestions and I believe he has had some thoughts from me
which have made the correspondence worth while to him.

## "A History of Evolutionary Thought"

This is the title of the presidential address of Sir Edward B.
Poulton reported in Science of September 3, 1937 and given before
the British Association for the Advancement of Science.  Space
permits mention of more than one feature of the address, comments
upon the way evolution works--if it does work.  The two possibilities

are: the inheritance of acquired characters as set forth by Lamarck
and the natural selection of Charles Darwin.

Herbert Spencer insisted that there had been inheritance of acquired characters or there had been no evolution. The weight of evidence
has been against this, however, and now this theory is officially
buried by Sir Edward. He describes the theory as holding that "a
past of indefinite duration is powerless to control the present,
while the brief history of the present can readily control the future". That is the present status to the theory: Peace be to its
ashes.

Meanwhile nearly every great biologist agrees that a detailed examination of Darwin's theory of natural selection finds it incompetent to accomplish more than trivial changes in organisms. This
leaves organic evolution with mighty claims but no power to sustain
them.

But please, Creationists, do not say that this knocks out evolution. Evolution is not knocked out until creationists know what
they believe about creation and until they are right in said belief.
As a group--or many groups-- they do not know this and they are as
helpless as babes in the woods to know how to make progress. Until
they get the beam out of their own eye they have little cell to act
as oculists for prospect there will be to make some progress.

## The Possible Antediluvian Origin of Coal Vegetation.

This is a memorandum I made some week ago: Persons who have
thought that the great amounts of coal and oil found in the earth
could not have accumulated in the period between Adam and the Flood
might well note a statement made in the Science Supplement of July
30, 1937, that the plants of the world each year return a thousand
times as much carbon dioxide to the air as all the mined fuel burned
during the past 50 years. "A thousand times as much carbon dioxide";
this is to say, a thousand times as much carbon as was contained in
the coal and petroleum supplies of the earth during the last half
century, and since the Edenic creation was evidently far finer than
the present creation and Flood, perhaps the task of accumulating the
organic material from which the coal and petrolerm was derived was
not as great as the men of little faith seem to have believed. Think
it over.

## Another Flood Tradition

Accounts of primitive peoples contain numerous items of Flood
traditions. The National Geographic Magazine often mentions these.
In the issue of May, 1937, there is an account of certain Indians of
Michoacan, Mexico, and the statement is made: "Among their native
legends is the tale of a great flood, from which a Noah-like god
escaped in a boat filled with birds and animals". Perhaps such
traditions would endure if the Flood of Genesis was merely a spring
freshet on Chaldean plains from which some Sumerian patriarch escaped
on a raft; and perhaps not. No system of geology is worthy of confidence which ignores this Flood. If geologists do not like that
Flood they have to reject, not only Genesis, but the traditions of almost every race on earth.

The editor may seem to give too much importance to the Flood and
Flood Geology, but in the condition of fundamentalist thought this
is the subject which has to be clarified before any true progress can
be made. The subject of special study next issue will be evolutionary
geology.

# THE CREATIONIST

Volume 1     Exeter, California -- November, 1937     Number 3

D.J. Whitney, Secretary of The Religion and Science Association, Editor.

✦✦✦

Attention, Members of the Religion and Science Association: The annual election of officers will soon be held and nominations for the Board of Directors are in order. For further information, kindly turn to page L1.

✦✦✦

## Further Study of the Problem of Creation

The condition of belief about creation among Christians is unquestionably in a state of chaos, the situation being to some extent indicated by a postscript to a letter written to the editor by a gentleman who had received a copy of the first number of The Creationist: "I have certainly enjoyed reading The Creationist, but one needs about a month to think it through". This is to say, although this gentleman had been interested in certain features of the problem of creation, he needed a good deal of time to think over a statement of the general view of the problem.

One of the main causes of this situation, which is general, in the presumed necessity to fit the Genesis account of creation to the course of history of this earth which is set forth by scholars as having happened.

Thus this gentleman in the body of his letter wrote, "I am inclined believe that to obtain a clear insight into and a full knowledge of ιε cryptic first and second chapters of Genesis, one would need to ιave a direct revelation; in lieu of which, the illumination of St. Paul and Augustine on spiritual lines, and on scientific lines the penetrative intellect of Copernicus and Newton, plus the grip on astrophysics of Jeans, and in geology of LeConte". Why call these chapters cryptic? They are not hard to understand.

Looking over this list of names, Augustine's views about creation were influenced in an unfortunate way by Greek philosophy, which was the science of that day, and the astrophysics of Jeans and the geology of LeConte are both almost purely evolutionary. LeConte's geology, which is the geology of today, except for minor details, is definitely in conflict with Genesis; though Jeans' astrophysics is not necessarily in conflict with Genesis, and like most great astronomers and physicists, he sees the need of creation in the establishment of the universe.

The observation of this gentleman is made on the assumption that to have a true understanding of the Genesis account of creation, standard beliefs about the origin and history of the earth should be held, yet the two, being in conflict, cannot be harmonized by a person with as much genius as that of all the men named, unless perchance such genius be used to reach an unreasonable conclusion. Much genius is used for that purpose.

On the other hand, no genius is required to understand the Gensis account of creation if it be taken in a simple, direct manner, without preconceived views of what occurred. There may be a few details upon which there can reasonably be some difference of opinion, but nothing more serious than that.

To begin with, the account is devoted primarily to the ordering of ιne earth rather than the making of the universe. The earth, being part

ᴼf the
solar system and being in existence before the start of Creation
Week, the account does not deal with the origin of the solar system,
or even of the earth itself. It could have any origin the Creator
saw fit to give it, save that the first verse indicates clearly that
creation by divine fiat was used in the making of everything.

At the start of Creation Week the surface of the earth was dark
and covered with water. This is shown by the fact that darkness was
over the face of the deep and the first act of the ordering of the
earth was a moving of the Spirit of God over the waters. Whether
the darkness was due to a cloudy covering over the earth or to the
absence of light in the universe may be open to question. Viewing
the thing in a simple, natural way, the presumption is in favor of
a cloudy covering over the earth, perhaps because the globe then was
very hot, causing most of the water to be part of atmosphere or in
the form of dense clouds. Otherwise the sun, though presumably
existing because the earth existed, would be dark, and the stars,
far removed from the earth, would also be dark, and there is no
occasion to call for such conditions in the ordering of a single
planet.

Under the usual assumption that the surface of the earth was
dark on account of a cloudy covering over it, the events of the first
day would be a partial clearing of the atmosphere so that light from
the sun could penetrate the clouds in diffused form. The earth
would rotate then as now, allowing the six periods of Creation Week
to be literal days, as the Jews believed them to be and as nearly
all Christian scholars believed them to be until they thought they
had to reconcile Genesis with evolutionary geology.

The whole account of Creation is that of fiat creation, not of
evolutionary processes, and fiat creation could be accomplished as
well in literal days as in millions of years; for a day with the Lord
is as a thousand years, and a thousand years as one day.

The work of the fourth day would simply be the clearing of the
atmosphere sufficiently so that the light from the heavenly bodies
would then shine directly upon the surface of the earth for the first
time.

The making of the "firmament" on the second day would be the
clearing of the atmosphere to a condition in which life could exist.
The term firmament was poorly chosen in translating the Hebrew.
It means the expanse above us. By the word translated firmament is
not meant a solid, bowl-like covering over the earth. This is shown
by a later statement that the birds were to fly in the firmament.
They do not fly in a solid medium, but in the air. There is an interesting problem in the events of the second day in connection with
the term "the waters above the earth" but that is a matter of detail,
worthy of special study some time, but not having to be studied in
order to get a clear view of the problem of creation in general.

Until the third day the surface of the earth was evidently
covered with water, since that was the original condition, and land
was not made until then. Upon the third day land was elevated and
plants were created upon it. The evident meaning is that a great
variety of vegetation was formed, including fruit-bearing trees.
Without mention of animal life at this time, but with the definite
mention of the creation of different kinds of animals during two
the - ᵢ

final days of creation week, the natural assumption is that no animal
life was created until the last two days.

The creation of animals occurred in two periods; water animals
of very diverse kinds, together with birds, being first created, and

the land animals, including "creeping things," in which category
would seem to be included the insects and other lowly forms of air-
breathing creatures. Man, by the first chapter of Genesis, was
created before or after them is not stated. In the second chapter
mention of man before the beasts does not necessarily indicate his
earlier creation.

The whole account is that of a divine ordering of the earth
and a fiat creation of the living things. Parts of the creation
account show clearly that this was an ideal earth at the time;
plants did not have thorns, neither did animals devour one another.
One of the greatest mistakes men have made about creation is to
visualize the Edenic earth as being populated by beasts and other
creatures of the same dispositions and habits as those of the present
disordered earth, or as being pupulated by animals such as those
whose fossil remains are found in the rocks.

If therefore a person takes the account of creation in a simple,
direct and natural way, there is not difficulty in understanding it;
the combined genius of a Copernicus, Newton and LeConte is not required. Genius may be used to force the account of creation into
a course of history with which it will not truly harmonize, but
nothing more than ordinary common sense is needed to understand
what the writer of the account evidently meant. The trouble during
the last century and a half has been through trying to force Genesis
into a kind of history the earth never had, or at least with which
it will not harmonize.

This direct, natural meaning will never be universally accepted.
There will always be men who have a bent for seizing some word or
phrase and applying to it some hard and fast meaning, and forcing
the account of creation or some other matter to fit the meaning
they adopt. Since this trait is often found in men, no natural,
direct acceptance of the Genesis account of creation will ever be
universal. Otherwise something very similar to the above summary
should unquestionably be standard, unless men think that science
indicates another kind of history and they believe that they have to
stick to science. The writer of the above summary does not insist
that it is correct in all details, but it seems to him to show what
Genesis is intended to indicate.

### Bound by Evolutionary Theory.

Part of a personal letter to a friend may show why Christian
leaders refuse to agree upon the Genesis account of creation, or even
to decide in their own minds what it means. They are convinced, like
the correspondent first quoted, that they must accept the astrophysics
of Jeans and the geology of LeConte and the biology of the biologists.
I quote myself.

"I think that I can put my finger exactly on the reasons why
Christian leaders refuse even to consider the problem of creation and
why there is so little progress in the war against evolution, they
simply will not believe that the scientists are wrong. The scientists
say that the earth is old and has gone through the ages; therefore it
has. Evidence to the contrary is meaningless. To say that the Flood
did everything that the ages are said to have done is too insane a concept for a minute's serious consideration; therefore they will not consider it. They believe in Creation; Yes, and they think that evolution
is wrong, but still they accept the system of facts which the

## 3 Con't.

scientists assert and merely try to interpret them in a different
way than the evolutionists; the basic conclusions of scientists are
not questioned by them in spite of Genesis. All they will do is to
give kind of a theistic slant to the presumed facts and they try to
work Christianity and creation on the assumption.

26

that the scientists are right. If what the scientists teach is in flat
contradiction with the Genesis accounts of Eden, Adam, Eve and the Flood
--well, there may be some way to reconcile the two, but it is beyond
the capacity of man to do so, therefore the best thing is to avoid the
problem until we reach the next state of consciousness. A man who
tries to present facts to people like that might as well try to plunge
head first through a stone wall.

"Of course these Christian leaders do not know science. I cannot
say that I blame them from the science standpoint, but I feel that they
are at fault from a spiritual standpoint: when the Scripture is flatly
against what science teaches it is up to them as men of authority in
the church to face the music and find what is right, and particularly
they should have an answer for the young people whose faith is being
overturned by science falsely so-called. Weighed in the balances, they
are found wanting. They have an obligation and they avoid it.

"The ones most at fault are the ones with the highest scholarship
and the highest standing. They are the ones most convinced that science
is right, and the ones most fearful of being shamed before scholars
for holding to some fanciful, unscientific dogma (as they view it)
just because their religion demands it. They feel that this brings
shame to their religion. As long as the overwhelming majority of
Christian scholars take this position progress is almost hopeless; the
case is surrendered to the evolutionists.

"The whole proposition simmers down to the question whether a person
will base his opinion upon evidence or upon authority; that is to say,
upon the conclusions of others. No. 1 is the right way; No. 2 is the
semi-universal system. Christian scholars with the rarest of exceptions
follow policy 2. I think that this explains the apparently hopeless
condition of the battle for creation and Genesis against false scholarship."

An illustration of the backwardness of Christian leaders may be
given by citing part of a letter from a member of the faculty of a
Fundamentalist institution of learning, a man widely know. In a letter
to him I had pointed out that in the faculty of which he was a member
there were, to my knowledge, three or four distinct and conflicting
ways of taking the Genesis account of creation, and said that this
ought to be remedied.

Part of his reply was, "I really think your emphasis upon the
question of the length of the creative days is disproportionate. The
question of baptism, for example, is much more important but nevertheless Fundamentalists can get along together gloriously while disagree-
ing on even that point."

The question is not the length of the creative days, for a person
might think them not literal days without violating reason or altering
the general nature and history of the events of creation--or so it seems
to me--provided he realized that this was a fiat and not an evolutionary ordering of the earth. It is a question of understanding Genesis,
for if Genesis falls, the rest of the Scriptures are built upon sand.
A Christian youth, confused by the teaching of the universities against
Genesis, could not go to such a Christian school and find what Genesis
meant. If the faculty members could not decide this among themselves,
they could hardly help a puzzled Christian youth. That is the situation
among all but a few of the Christian theological seminaries, colleges,

Bible Institutes in America today.   We should admit it to our own shame
A contrast to the position of this Christian educator is shown in
a letter from a gentleman in Canada who has been doing public work
against evolution:

"I have received a copy of the 'Creationist' which I welcome very
much.   It is quite evident that the time is long overdue for definite
pronouncement of the scientific facts of Genesis so that a concrete
stand may be taken instead of offering different theories.   When this
has been done the creationists will have scored one of the greatest
triumphs over the evolutionists and rationalists in the realms of
science and religion".  Well, I would not say that a decision by creationists on what should be believed about Genesis and creation would
be a triumph against evolutionists, but it certainly would be a gigantic stride in that direction and give quick hope of victory.   Since
the children of this world are wiser in their generation than the
children of light, the children of light can generally be expected
to do the wrong thing rather than the right in a matter of this nature
and importance.   Pardon my misanthropy.

### What Evolutionary Geology Demands.

Well, we have talked long enough about the general situation, and
possibly too long, and the task now should be to get down to some
more study of the problem of creation.

We have seen approximately what the Genesis account of creation
calls for in the history of the earth.   We have noted that many
Christian scholars feel obliged to string along with the scientists
in their belief on this matter, though trying to give a theistic slant
to the conclusions of scientists.   The third thing to do is to notice
what the scientists say happened in the origin and ordering of the
earth.   This will show whether or not a Christian scholar can keep
hold of Genesis with one hand and modern science with the other.

In the first place by evolutionary geology--the standard belief of
scholars--the earth is assumed to have originated by an evolutionary
process.   Just how it evolved is stumping the astronomers and geologists; nevertheless it is assumed to have evolved.

The time of origin is held to be about 2,000 million years ago.
Two decades ago the usual figure adopted was 60 million years.   One
time of origin is about as much in conflict with Genesis as another.
Standard belief now is that for about 1,500 million years nothing except some very simple kinds of marine organisms lived.

About 500 million years ago shell fish are believed to have been
abundant in the ocean, their remains being found in what are termed
Cambrian and later sediments.   No land plants are believed to have
lived then, except possibly some very simple kinds of which only traces
have been found.   About 100 million years later the first true fishes
are supposed to have lived, these being of "primitive" kinds, of the
shark, and later, the ganoid type.   Primitive amphibians are also
believed to have appeared a little later, as the land areas became
covered luxuriently with various kinds of non-flowering plants.

Somewhat later, standard belief goes, the first true reptiles
made their appearance, and later flying reptiles, then primitive birds,
and possibly a few primitive kinds of mammals.   Still later, the large

reptiles mostly perishing, appeared "archaic" mammals; then mammals
of the tiles mostly perishing, appeared modern type, and lastly, men.
The remains of the first men, some of them

mammals of the modern type, and lastly, man. The remains of
the first men, some of them

Brute-like, are supposed to go back for hundreds of thousands
of years.

This is what modern geology sest forth. Fit it to Genesis
if you can. Christian scholars have tried to do so for many
decades and have had such poor success that now, unless they
accept Flood geology, they mostly avoid the problem of creation
instead of trying to solve it. One wonders how there could be
an Eden and an Adam as Genesis records on an earth which was
always filled with violence, as far as the living creatures on
it was concerned, and how Eve could be the mother of all living
when bruteplike men lived, presumably, long before the creation
of Adam.

Those who fit this system of geologic history to Genesis
have two or three ways of doing so. One is to say that the
six periods of Creation Week were geologic ages. Another way
is to assert that there was an immense period of time between
the first and second verses of Genesis in which there was, as
Bartoli expresses it, "scope for the geological ages". A third
method is to warp both Genesis and evolutionary geology out of
shape and so to tie them together. There are so many ways of
doing this that they cnnot be examined in detail.

### "Age Days of Creation"

The original way of harmonizing Genesis and geology after
evolutionagy geology became standard belief was to say that the
six periods of creation were geologic ages. This was the position
of Gladstone in his historic debate with Huxley; it was the position of the older Christian theologians.

Even a brief examination of the teachings of Genesis and
of evolutionary geology should convinne the most cautious
Christian scholar that the two cnnot be harmonized. This can
perhaps best be shown by presenting side by side twolists of
the ovents of creation: those of Genesis, and those of evolutionary geology.

| Time. | Genesis | Place in Modern Gelolgy |
|---|---|---|
| Before the First Day | Dark and Unordered | Earth in Astronomical Condition. |
| Day Two | Making of Light | AS soon as earth cooled, or earlier. |
| Day Three | Making (Clearing) of Atmosphere | Archaen period for origin of land. Plants from Devonian |
| Day Four | Sun, Moon and Stars Appear | As soon as earth cooled, or earlier. |
| Day Five | Water Creatures and Bird Created | From Cambrian to Jurassic Periods |
| Day Six | Beasts and Creeping Things Created | At intervals from Devonian period onward. |

********

The inconsistency between Genesis and evolutioary geology
is by this comparison seen to be almost as great as it well
could be. (The periods mentioned in the order in which they
occur in evolutionary grology are: Archaen, Cambrian, Dvonian,
Jurassic, Cretaceous, intermediate periods not being listed.)

Years ago there were some reasons for thinking that the two systems of creation might be harmonized. It was believed that if the earth was very hot in the beginning the presence of immense quantities of water vapor in the atmosphere would make the earth dark--darkness would be on the face of the deep. Next was the fact that in both evolutionary geology and Genesis the higher animals were later in appearing than the more simple animals. In the nature of things plants must precede animals, to give the latter food, though in evolutionary geology the seas swarmed with life before anything more than the most simple kinds of land plants existed. Other inconsistencies are too many to mention.

The only real excuse for believing in a harmony between Genesis and evolutionary geology by "age days" of creation seems to be the assumption that the harmony exists, without examining the record. In view of the actual lack of harmony between them the conservative opinion that the six periods of creation were geologic ages seems absolutely unpardonable.

Then, too, the Genesis account of creation seems to be truly a fiat creation, not an evolutionary process, and midern geology is based purely upon the assumption of evolution.

The ruin and restitution people are also inconsistent if they try to fit that theory to evolutionary geology. Think of the inconsistency of believing that the earth took form through a long series of evolutionary ages, then reached a complete ruin in which all living things perished, to be later reconstructed by fiat in six days. If holders of this theory wish to hold it, rejecting evolutionary geology and adopting some other scheme of geologic history, I do not know that any one can criticize their position very seriously. However, as the writer sees it, they are entirely out of order if they accept evolutionary geology with that ruin and reconstruction theory.

I will also say this: any person who accepts evolutionary geology, warped or unwarped, and then thinks that he can oppose organic evolution effectively, simply does not know what he is talking about. To accept those geologic ages is to surrender about four fifths of one's case to the evolutionists. I assert without hesitation that I can take the case for ages and get by far the better of the argument. In fact if the Creationist continues I may use the most of some issue in giving the case for evolution. It might cause wails of anguish from many creationists, but most of them--particularly those who accept those geologic ages--, seem to have little understanding of the case for evolution anyway.

And so let me repeat, when a person accepts those evolutionary ages he has no right to assert belief in creation rather than evolution. He might, it is true, believe in a kind of theistic evolution, but the biologists can only laugh at the person who asserts belief in creation when all he means is some indefinite kind of theistic evolution.

(There I am with my misanthropy again. I simply cannot think of the way most creationists try to believe in creation without becoming misanthropic.)

### The Mountains and the Flood.

The one group of persons who are--as I see it--consistent in their belief about creation are the Flood geologists, who believe that the fossils came in a great ruin and reconstruction of the earth during the time of Noah. We can believe in a fiat creation of the earth itself and then in its fiat ordering in six literal days. We can believe that the Edenic plants and animals were ideal, not preying upon one another as those of the geologic ages were. We can believe in their degeneration during the time between Creation Week and the Flood, so that their descendents were the fossils which are found in the rocks, and the living things which now live. We can accept Ussher's chronology, amended perhaps in some details as is fitting with the Scriptures.

Some features of Flood geology have been discussed in earlier issues. Other features of the problem should be taken up now; particularly features which have been criticized.

One of the great problems of the Flood through the centuries has been how the water could cover the mountains as long as the Genesis account states. To lighten this part of the discussion a bit a little poem on the matter may be given. It will be seen that the author is a Rationalist, disbelieving in the Genesis account of creation and the Flood.

## Twenty Nine Thousand Feet Speaking

I once was a hollow, down under the sea,
And little lime conches oft fell into me.
Till one day a sun-spot shook up baby earth,
And Dionne volcanoes had violent birth.

I'm lonely and homesick, up high in the air
And back--as a hollow, I wish I were there!
A person named Whitney--he means well, I know--
Says water once covered this region of snow.

Some people who lived on a plain, flat as flat,
Once wrote an Account of Big Water like that;
They started a tower at 200 feet!
Los Angeles, even, has not got that beat.

Why Whitney believes Romances written by those--
Why anybody does it--well, nobody knows.
But I'm here to witness, who always was there,
We've had no "Big Water" up here in the air--
29,000 feet!
Barbara Kaywood Rogers
Written Oct. 13 as (Rationalist Correspondence College)
Compliment to D. J. Whitney.
1937
***

This is the argument which is so often advanced against the Deluge. A Mountain rises 29,000 feet high and if the water could cover that it would have to stand an equal height above normal sea level the earth over. That it could do so seems impossible--except by most astounding miracle. Therefore it is argued that the water did not stand over the mountains. The argument is a valid one and it should be met.

In practically every great mountain range on earth, save those made almost exclusively by volcanic action, there are great quanities of sedimentary rocks, many of which contain sea shells or the remains of other creatures of sea or land. The material was evidently laid down in water at or near sea level. Now it is part of a mountain, as the poem indicates.

A critic asks us how water could cover such material during the Flood. We point out ot him that water certainly did cover that material and that he agrees that it did. How does he account for this condition?

"Oh", he replies, "This was not mountain when the water covered it and buried the fossils. It was down near sea level, or below sea level at the time. The material was later elevated so as to become part of a mountain."

"Exactly so, Brother", we reply. "That is the position we Flood geologists take. During the Flood this was not mountain, but part of the ruins of the antediluvian earth. The mountains were elevated during the later part of the Flood period, or even later." Our explanation is exactly that of the geologists, as far as having sedimentary rocks laid down in water and later elevated into mountains is concerned. In addition certain features of the problem are far more simple for us than for the evolutionary geologists.

The evolutionary geologists require twenty or more times of mountain uplift. They have mountain masses lifted and then worn away by the action of wind and rain during long ages; then they have new mountains uplifted, and they require that this occur time after time. The Flood geologists creation, and next at the time of the ruin and reconstruction of the Flood. If the geologists criticize us for our difficulty in making mountains, they have far and away more difficulty because they have about ten times as many periods of mountain building.

This is only a small part of the comparison in which they get the worst of it. They not only need uplift, but they require parts of the surface of the earth to slide sideways for many miles, and Flood geologists need none of that except for the crushing movements which naturally would occur in any great uplift. In the making of Chief Mountain in Montana and the asserted "overthrusting" of which it is a part, there would have to be thousands of feet of uplift, followed by side shoving of 15 miles or more. (See the writings of Directors Price and Nelson on this, also several standard textbooks of geology.) To form the Alps would be needed about 100 miles of movement sideways, or telescoping, of the upper layers of the earth's crust. Similar great movements are absolutely in explicable and the solid interior and rigidity of the earth deny that they could take place. They are a thousand times as difficult to explain as mere uplift, yet we Flood geologists need only uplift, and far less of it than the evolutionists, while they need this inexplicable side shoving also. (The plain evidence is that there was no such side shoving; 'which nobody can deny'.)

Through past centuries Christians have been floundering around in all sorts of confusion at the problem how water could cover the mountains, yet the answer was plain before them all the time. Mankind has been noted for its inability to see what is plain before its eyes, and this is a fine example of such a case. Of course the mountains came by uplift from sea level or below, but few Christians could think of such a thing, though they exercised amazing ability to figure how possibly the breaking of an ice cap or some such phenomenon might make water splash over the mountains and cause a very different kind of flood from what Genesis records.

The dilemma of creationist critics of Flood geology in this matter is indeed pitiful, or would be if they realized their situation in the case. They progess full belief in the Scriptures. The Scriptures tell explicetly that the waters covered the whole earth, and that all the high mountains were covered and that everything that had breath died, save what was preserved in the Ark. The account indicated that the land was covered for months. The Ark itself rested high on the mountains of Ararat (not necessarily on Mt. Ararat itself, which is a volcanic mountain). Where it rested must have been many thousands of feet above sea level, provided those mountains were antediluvian, and water covering them would cover mountains of similar height the earth over. Thus the Flood could not have been merely a local event.

To say, therefore, that these mountains existed before the time of Noah, to say nothing of before the time of Adam, would make the Flood, as it is described in Genesis, impossible, save by astounding miracle. The only thing left is Flood geology--belief that the first part of the Flood swept away the face of the antediluvian earth and that the mountains were then uplifted. Plainly creationist critics of Flood geology cannot reject that geology without rejecting Genesis too. That is a definite chalenge to critics of Flood geology, many of whom will read this--provided they will take the time to do so. Opportunity is hereby offered them to reply to this charge against their disbelief in Flood Geology. In the next Creationist they can, if they will, explain how they can believe Genesis and still reject Flood Geology. I assert that they cannot do this. We will wait and see.

## The Time of Mountain Uplift

An important question relates to the time of mountain uplift. Fortunately geology provides us with an answer to this. J. Claude Jones, geologist at the University of Nevada, studied the increase of saline matter in shallow lakes in the Lahontan Basin, which covers a large area in Northwestern Nevada. Streams continually carry various salts into those shallow lakes, which have no outlet, and as the water evaporates they become more and more saline. Comparing the amount in the lakes and the rate of increase of the saline matter from stream flow, the length of time the streams have run is indicated. Jones found this to be from 4,000 to 5,000 years. This is to say, the mountains around the basin were uplifted only about 5,000 years ago. That is about as near the time Ussher figured for the Flood as could be asked.

Remember this is not fantasy by some Fundamentalist, but the findings of a reputable geologist. A detailed report on it is given in Publication 352 of the Carnegie Institution. Dr. Alfred C. Lane also refers to this in his paper on Rating the Geologic Clock in the Report on the XVI International Geological Congress, held in Washington in 1933. Critics of Flood geology should know of things like this.

Certain rivers also show that the continents were formed not long ago. The Colorado River rises in the country east of the Lahontan Basin and carries enormous quantities of silt into the Gulf of Mexico. If the continent is tens and hundreds of thousands--to say nothing of millions--of years old, the burden of silt deposited at the mouths of rivers should be enormous; yet it is not, considering the assumed

age. According to the Scientific American of September, 1937, there
was so much less silt in the delta of the Colorado something more than
500 years ago that the mouth of the river was then 60 miles north of
its present location. This is to say, only a few hundred years ago,
say 800 for good measure, about 60 miles of delta was formed. This
is about one-fifth of the time since the Flood by Ussher's chronology,
and, apparently, not far from one fifth of the delta. Look it up.
Since the stream flow and the burden of silt was undoubtedly far greater when the continent was new and the rainfall greater than it is now,
as it admittedly was, delta building was doubtless far more rapid in
the beginning than now. North America as a continent can hardly be
much older than the time the Bible gives for the Flood.

Look also at a map of the continent. The Mississippi discharges
at what seems to be the natural edge of the continent, but if the land
were hundreds of thousands of years old, the delta by this time should
project far out into the Gulf of Mexico. Since it does not, the continent is evidently not old.

There is an abundance of evidence like this for taking the Genesis
account of the early history of this earth for just what it appears to
mean, yet when we try to do so we are opposed vigorously by those of
our own household, and seemingly the overwhelming majority of church
leaders, and leaders of education in the church, seem to think it safer
to ignore the problem of creation than to study it and find out what
they should believe. Truly, the children of this world are wiser in
their generation than the children of light.

## The Coming Election

Space does not permit further discussion of evidence for creation
and against evolution, and a few remarks on the coming election seem
to be in order.

The majority of the present board of directors seems to favor the
program followed in the Creationist. Certain members of the Association do not favor this policy, but are greatly opposed to it. Possibly
it would be an excellent idea to have two tickets of directors in the
field, one favoring the present policy and the other a more conservative policy. I suggest that members approving this idea write to the
president, Dr. L. Allen Higly, Wheaton College, Wheaton, Ill. I believe that if sufficient wish is expressed for a change of policy, he
will see that nominations are offered which will suit persons who
disapprove of the present policy. A member can, of course, nominate
any candidate or set of candidates he wishes, though the secretary
has not made public the list of members and a nominating committee
would probably be best. At all events I suggest that members write
Dr. Higley their wishes for the future of the Association. I might
say that the majority of the present directors feel that little can be
done by the Association as long as there is so much disagreement about
the nature and history of creation, except to continue the Creationist.

As to the future of the Creationist, the editor has to report some
very hearty commendation for it; also some vigorous disapproval from
certain members. The financial support has been small. Only a little
more than half enough money has come in to get out a single issue.
Nearly half of that came from non members, one contributor being not
far from an agnostic. Unless more support comes the next issue will
have to be the last; so you folks who think that what is being done
in analyzing the problem of creation should be done, kindly back up
such belief by sending in a dollar or so. If even $5 per issue comes
in the editor will make up the deficit from his own pocket.

The election will be called in our next issue, which will probably
not appear until January. In it I expect to discuss the ruin and

not appear until January. In it I expect to discuss the ruin and
reconstruction theory, the relation of evolutionary geology to organic
evolution and a few other matters. And to you who dislike my ideas,
let me say that these columns are open to you to show where I am
wrong and you are right.

36

T H E C R E A T I O N I S T
volume 1.   Exeter, California -- December, 1937 Issue 4.

Important Announcement.  Plans are being worked out for
the continued publication of the Creationist, either as a mimeographed
bulletin as heretofore, or as a printed monthly.  Which of the two will
be issued depends upon the response of our readers.  There is an urgent
demand to make the Creationist a printed journal.  This will b done
if sufficient subscriptions are sent in by our readers; otherwise
mimeographed bulletins will be sent out as soon as possible.

The present issue is sent out now so that arrangements may be
made for the future Creationist to start as soon as possible after the
first of the year.  The mimeographing and mailing of the Creationist
No. 3 was unfortunately delayed greatly, so this will following rather
quickly--unless it also is delayed.  There has not been time since its
mailing to receive nominations for officers of The Religion and Science
Association, so formal announcement of the election in that organization
will come later.

Further information about the possible future of the Creationist
will be given in the last few pages of this issue.

On the editorial policy, let it suffice to say now that it will
be devoted primarily to two purposes: to established a firm faith in
in Genesis and the other scriptures, and to show the falsity of the
system of belief which is based upon the dogma of evolution.

The Creationist thus far and including most of the present issue
has been devoted mainly to the task of showing what system of geologic
history is most in harmony with Genesis.  Little space has been given
to the falsity of the theory of evolution, which will be, God willing,
the subject most discussed in the future Creationist, although a definite
creed of creation will be put forth as the correct alternative to the
creed of modern science.  If this creed of creation requires amendment,
it will be amended.  The present issue should wind up the systematic
discussion of the subject, Genesis and Creation.

To complete this systematic discussion the topic which seems to
demand special attention now is

The Geologic Ares and Their Bearing upon the Genesis Account
of Creation.

The thing that makes this whole problem of creation so important
is that Christians are confronted with the situation that Genesis calls
for belief in a very different kind of origin and early history of the
earth than is set forth in the textbooks and taught in our schools .
Christians have too often avoided the task of examing the teachings of
science in the light of Genesis, or they have tried to reconcile the
two systems of teachings when in fact they are beyond reconciliation.

In our last bulletin we have shown that evolution and Genesis
apparently cannot be harmonized.  The fact was shown that the six
periods of Creation Week as outlined in Genesis were definitely not

amphibians and lizards; and so for nearly every great group of living
things.  The sequence of fossils in the rocks, provided ages geology
is valid science, either demands this belief or it simply does not
make sense.  Then accept it and think that

geologic ages of the kind described in textbooks of geology. They should no longer be asserted to be so. On the other hand many of us believe from what we think is valid evidence that the fossils came from the Flood, not by geologic action during long ages. If we are right, true science is in full accord with Genesis.

Others refuse to accept Flood Geology; many of them because they think that what the geologists assert must be so; others because they think that they have found some bad science in Flood geology. These latter either have some strange interpretation of individual preference in geologic history which no one else will accept or they adapt ages geology to Genesis in some way or other.

The thesis to be set forth here is that no one can believe in both ages geology and true creation as set forth in Genesis and still be consistent. I do not care whether they use evolutionary geology with assumed age days of creation or whether they have evolutionary geology proceed for millions of years and wind it up by a supposed ruin and reconstruction of the face of the earth: evolutionary geology is still inconsistent with a sound belief in creation. I wish that Christian leaders could awake to that fact!

One of the parts of this problem which calls for special attention is the relation of evolutionary geology to the theory of organic evolution.

Discussions of the merits of special creation as opposed to organic evolution have usually been centered around Darwin's theory of natural selection, whether species were fixed or unchangable, and whether man could have been descended from ape or monkey. All of these subjects are of very trivial importance as far as the great problem of creation is concerned. When men try to oppose evolution by centering their attacks on features of very secondary importance like the ones named, and at the same time have directly or tacitly allowed the probable truth of evolutionary geology, they have in fact surrendered their case to the evolutionists whether they realize it or not! No one can oppose evolution while accepting evolutionary geology and do other but convice evolutionists that he does not know what he is talking about. Let us see if this is so.

In the first place evolutionary geology demands belief that very simple plants and animals lived on this earth long before the higher plants and animals, and that change was an almost universal rule with all living things. It also demands belief that the earth is many scores or hundreds of millions of years old and that for the first part of this time nothing lived at all. Supposedly there were, by evolutionary geology, a long series of geologic ages, during all of which the plants--if any--and the animals--if any--were different to a notable extent from the plants and animals in the other ages.

Most special creationists have fixity of species as one of their cardinal doctrines, but evolutionary geology is based largely upon the belief in great change in nearly every kind of living thing. The first crustaceans were supposedly far different from present crustaceans; the first sea snails far different from present sea snails; the first amphibians and lizards far different from the present amphibians and lizards; and so for nearly every great group of living things. The sequence of fossils in the rocks, provided ages geology is valid science, either demands this belief or it simply does not make sense. Then accept it and think that you can oppose evolution! Deny both ages geology and Flood geology and get a system of geologic history which any one but you will believe, or which can possibly harmonize with Genesis! It cannot be done.

A few illustrations will show how the supposed sequence of life in evolutionary geology implies the action of organic evolution and denies the probability of a sane system of special creation.

When the history of the organic creation (according to evolutionary geology) first got a good start in the supposed Cambrian period the most notable fossils were trilobites: crustceans comparable to shrimps or crabs, but different in form from either. Trilobites were not of one kind, but many. Their fossils (if we allow evolutionary geology) were found in sediments deposited through a series of scores of millions of years and the earliest trilobites were very different-- though still clearly trilobites--in the early and later sediments. Thus the Creator either made numerous trilobite species as separate creations, no more related to one another than to sharks, or he allowed much change to take place in species and genera, the failure of Darwin's natural selection no twithstanding.

Kindly permit a diversion just now to consider the relation of Darwinism to changes like this which seem to have occurred with trilobites, and by that token, with nearly every other kind of creature.

### Darwinism and Species Change.

Charles Darwin about three-fourths of a century ago set forth a theory by which he assumed that transformation of species could occur. If there was transformation of species "evolution" was assumed proved. Careful examination of Darwin's theory by which transformation of species could occur has proved it faulty: it does not work, except perhaps for trivial changes within a species. Certain creationists have pointed out this and shouted (I paraphrase, of course): "Hurrah, Darwin was wrong; evolution is licked!" The evolutionists have asserted, "Even if Darwin was wrong in the agency by which evolution (a false use of the term) worked; we nevertheless see that is has worked". The change amond trilobites is an example of transformation of species. Creationists must--if they are logical demand that each separate species of ancient trilobite be a separate and distinct special creation, or allow that there has been transformation of species. (Transformation of species is not evolution, but this is a truth that seems not to have dawned on either evolutionists or the big majority of creationists yet.

Now in the nature of the case belief in transformation of species among the trilobites (all continuing to be trilobites) is far and away more reasonable than believing that all the early trilobite species would die and later trilobite species would be specially created.

One of the outstanding champions of creation among the fundamentalists a decade and more ago once wrote me about the distinction between species change and real evolution or something, like this: (I quote as accurately as I can) "Most Fundamentalists are still shaking puny fists and mouthing impotent threats against a kind of evolution which has been descredited by the evolutionists themselves, years ago." Of course I agreed with him, even though my language about creationist policy, strong as it is, is seldom as strong as he used.

-4-

Suppose instead of studying trilobites we study plants. For the earliest ages there were, as far as is known, no land plants whatever, except of the most simple sorts, and only traces of those. Later there were plants like ferns and others reproducing by spores; then simple flowering plants of the coniferous type, and only late in geologic time the higher flowering plants. Here would be creation by degrees in evolutionary geology.

Among birds the first known, if evolutionary geology is a fact, had long vertebrated tails, also teeth, which no existing birds have.

Among the mammals, the first known were largely "archaic" or "primitive" in their organization. Thus three and four toe horses are said to have preceded true horses; primitive elephants are said to have preceded true elephants of the existing type. The vertebrate fishes are said to have come in an evolutionary-appearing series; and the same thing is said to have occurred with the amphibians and reptiles.

In all of these the first appearing would--with rare exceptions-die off before the later appearing lived.

Think what kind of CREATION this would be: the Creator, instead of making a complete and perfect earth, which was the kind of earth he had at the end of Creation Week, would create some great kinds of organisms--like the trilobites--and have them perish completely from the earth before the first of other great kinds were created. Thus the trilobites would all die before the first warm blooded beasts were made or before there were any flowering plants. Early kinds of trilobites would die as unfit for their environment before the late ones were created, and so for the other types of living things.

This kind of creation will not make sense. The only kind of thing which will make sense with this kind of history is evolution, although a person may call it theistic evolution if he wants God to operate it. I do not care whether a person has that life sequence in supposed age-days of creation, or whether he has it coming before a supposed ruin and reconstruction of the earth, it is not sound creation theory.

As far as the pre-Adamic ruin theory is concerned, think how absurd it would be to allow evolutionary geology, with that kind of creation of living things, or any other kind of creation that will fit evolutionary geology and still make sense, but to assert that all kinds of living things were destroyed completely and then re-created by special creation in three literal days! If one wants the ruin and reconstruction theory, let him have the first creation a true and perfect creation, not an evolutionary geology. As far as I can see Flood Geology is the only system of geology that can properly be fitted to this ruin and struction theory.

Evolutionary Geology and the Pre-Adamic Ruin Theory.

Evolutionary geology is particularly unfitted to the pre-Adamic ruin theory since one of the foundation features of this theory is that the earth, when it was created, was not "without form and void", but evolutionary geology has it so. At least it has the earth presumably so hot that no life could exist upon it and no true ocean or no solid land.

40

The only kind of primal earth which will suit the ruin theory is a perfect earth, an earth like that at the close of the six days of creation, where no plants had thorns or were otherwise harmful, and no animal lived by preying upon another animal.

The fossils then would have to be explained either as all having come in the Deluge ruin; or in one pre-Adamic ruin or a series of such ruins; or partly by the Deluge ruin and partly by one or more pre-Adamic ruins. It would seem unfitting to deny that the Deluge was responsible for none of the fossils, but pre-Adamic ruins were responsible for all, but it also seems impossible to assert that some fossils came by the Deluge and some earlier. At least, no system of classification of the fossils has yet been advanced which would make some the result of the Deluge and some the result of earlier action. Therefore the only reasonable way to fit the pre-Adamic ruin theory to geologic history seems to be to make the fossils came by the Deluge. At least one outstanding champion of the theory accepts Flood Geology. The others if they think the thing through, evidently should do so.

## The Theology of the Ruin Theory

An unfortunate thing about this theory is that it was adopted to go with evolutionary geology.

The Jews, in whose language Genesis was written, seem never to have thought that any ruin and reconstruction occurred before Creation Week. In the Christian Church through the centuries the idea has no standing and was not even thought of, except perhaps by an occasional theologian who gave undue weight to the supposed science inherited from the Greek philosophers. It was only adopted the birth of modern geology, or at least, after the earth was believed to be very old.

Theologians thought that their theology should fit science; therefore when scientists decided that the earth was not created about 4,000 B.C. the theologians first decided that the days of creation were long periods of time; and later some who felt that the six periods of creation were certainly literal days overcame the assumed discrepancy between Genesis and geology by deciding that the earth became waste and void and was then reconstructed in six literal days. Belief in evolutionary geology was therefore kind of a step farther to the ruin and reconstruction theory, and we have seen how poorly evolutionary geology fits and sound theroy of creation.

As far as the writer is concerned he has no criticism of any person who adopts this ruin and reconstruction theory provided he believes it is demanded by the Scriptures and provided he gets his geology clear and reasonable too. There are, however, certain objections to this theory from the standpoint of theology, and these merit attention before the subject is dropped.

For one thing, the theory is based mainly on the idea that the passage reading, "And the earth was without form and void", should read, "And the earth became without form and void". Nevertheless standard translations, which should be followed unless very strong evidence exists that they are wrong, have been without exception "was" and not "became". Of the many translations by individuals, only a few read "became" and this reading seems to have been adopted more because geology is believed to demand such reading than because the Hebrew demanded it. This does not give the theory a very favorable start.

Again, of necessity the existence of Satan as the great foe of God is required for such a ruin; otherwise nothing would destroy the works of God; but a noted passage in Ezekiel 28 seems to indicate strongly that the change of an angel of light to Satan, the destroyer, did not occur until after the founding of Eden, and therefore until after Creation Week. There was, therefore, no Satan until after the work of Creation week had been accomplished. Let us look at the passage.

Only parts of verses 12 to 15 need be quoted: "Thou sealest up the sum, full of wisdom and perfect in beauty. Thou hast been in Eden, the garden of God;... Thou wast the anointed cherub that covereth; and I have set thee so;... Thou wast perfect in thy ways from the day that thou was created, till iniquity was found in thee..."

The intimation is clearly that the being who became Satan was set as the cherub over "Eden, the garden of God" and at the founding of Eden, was full of wisdom and perfect, but rebelled and became Satan, the destroyer. If this was actually the Eden of Genesis, there was no pre-Edenic ruin.

Two arguments are offered by the holders of the ruin and reconstruction theory to show that this was not the Eden of Genesis. They are inconsistent with one another, but both are used with satisfaction by their holders. One is that the Eden mentioned was not the Eden of Genesis, for this Eden of Ezekiel's vision was Eden, the garden of God, and the home of Adam in the Edenic earth was a garden in Eden.

To me this seems like hair splitting. The only Eden of a perfect earth of which the Hebrews knew was that in which their first parents lived, yet God would have his prophet refer to a perfect Eden, the garden of God, which was not the Eden of Genesis at all, but a pre-Edenic eden of which they had never heard! There are several other allusions to Eden in the Old Testament, some of which will be mentioned anon, and all others seem to refer to the Eden of Genesis. That being the case, it would be surprising if this alone referred to a different Eden. Yet if it refers to the Eden of Genesis, Satan at the time of its founding was not Satan, but an angel who was set over that garden of God. He could hardly have brought the earth to a condition of ruin earlier than then.

The other explanation or argument is that the Eden of Ezekiel 28 was not a garden of plants, but of minerals and fire. Of course this is different from the argument just mentioned.

An examination of a few Scriptures should be helpful in this whole matter. Take Ezekiel 31:9: "All the trees of Eden, that were in the garden of God envied him." This seems to be both the Eden of Genesis and of Ezekiel 28. Isaiah 51:3 is to the same effect: "For the Lord will comfort Zion,...and he will make her wilderness like Eden, and her desert like the garden of the Lord." There is an identity between Eden and the garden of God, or of the Lord, even if God is said to have prepared a garden for Adam in Eden. The matter should not require more discussion, although more could be said on it if necessary.

However, as I have said before, I am not concerned particularly with the opinion of a person about a ruin before Creation Week, but I am concerned with the kind of geology which a holder of that theory has.

he can merely tell a college youth who is troubled by the teaching
of evolutionary geology that there was a ruin and reconstruction of
the earth some time during the history of the earth, leaving the
work of the Flood undetermined and the general geologic history of
the earth unsettled, I feel that he is greatly at fault, but if he
sees the thing through and accepts Flood geology with the ruin theory,
I cannot see that I can criticize him any more than I can criticize
a person for differing with me on some other problem in theology of
secondary importance. Let the holders of the theory examine it again,
particularly in relation to evolutionary geology which ought not to
be believed and which gave the doctrine standing in the first place.

In future issues of the Creationist I should like to give the
holders of the theory space to discuss it among themselves, to decide in what form, if any, it should be held.

## What is the Right Theory of Creation?

This problem of creation should be looked at in one good
birdseye view as well as being studied in detail. When we read the
Genesis account carefully, with an open, believing mind, we should
believe that the Edenic earth was ideal. No plants then had thorns
or were poisonous; no creature was then a destroyer, either on land
or sea. Fossils of destroying animals from both land and sea must
have been the degenerated and greatly altered descendents of perfect
created animals. The present killers of both land and sea but also
have been changed greatly from their Edenic ancestors.

This whole idea of creatures developing through long ages by
having to fight to survive is all wrong. There are only these
possible ways which make sense, as far as I know, to explain the
existence of this present evil earth. These are:

1. The position of atheism; in fact this provides the greatest
and most commonly used argument for atheism. God, so say the
atheists, would create an evil earth and have conditions as bad
as they now are and as they have been; therefore there is no God;
everything has been operating by purely natural processes, like an
eternally existing self-winding clock.

2. The position of theistic evolution and of modernism generally: God works by natural law and has creation improve by experience until it finally reaches an ideal state. This is one way,
in philosophy, to account for evil and yet believe in God. Evolution, of course, is believed to be the motive power by which Nature
operates.

3. God made an ideal creation, but, allowing the freedom of
will of certain of his creatures—man and woman—their transgression
caused such part of the creation as was connected with them to go
wrong and brought conditions into their present evil state. The
Creator has, however, provided a Savior for the world and will
ultimately restore it to a condition of perfection.

This third kind of explanation for Nature being as it is fits
Genesis and the other Scriptures. I also assert that only on this
basis can the organic creation be explained in a reasonable and
scientific way. Position No. 1 is bad science, since Nature could
never have become established as we find it except by acts of a
Creator.

such as the origin of matter, the organization of the earth, the creation of life, of various organs, and so on. The second position is equally faulty for the same reason, however attractive it may be as a matter of philosophy. I hope to have this fundamental problem, The Relation of God to Nature, taken up in the next issue.

************

## The Future Creationist.

Formal announcement is hereby made that the Creationist will hereafter be issued as a printed monthly, provided sufficient sub-scriptions come in and there is good promise of its ability to pay its way. Otherwise it will be continued as a mimeographed bulletin. There is certainly a great need for it and sufficient urgent de-mands for its continuance have come in to justify the promise of its continued publication in some form.

A modest paper can apparently be published without financial assistance provided a good subscription list is provided. To get this several persons should provide funds for from 20 to 40 subscrip-tions each and if possible the names of the subscribers, and readers in general should subscribe not only for themselves, but for a friend or two also. A gross income of $500 for a year will allow the printing of 1,000 copies of the Creationist as a four page paper, country newspaper style.

The subscription will be 50¢ a year, but without guarantee of publication for more than half a year for college students in groups of five or more, or for other groups of ten or more. To each reader who sends in a dollar bill for a subscription I ask that you have the paper sent also to a friend or to a public library, so as to get as wide a circulation as possible. The writer will simply be taking over a lot of work without expectation of remuneration, but unless he sees a strong probability that a printed paper will pay its way in dollars and cents, he will not undertake its printed publication. If only five persons would guarantee the costs of such a paper for a only five persons would guarantee the costs of such a paper for a half year up to $50 each, its publication could be undertaken. All the money that came in would reduce by so much the possible deficit.

I will make no appear for financial support. There is the case. With even half a year publication some mighty blows for cre-ation and against evolution can be achieved. If the response is favorable printed publication will be undertaken as soon as possible. Without it, mimeographed bulletins will be continued. In sending subscriptions kindly state whether they will hold good for a mimeographed bulletin. If sufficient funds come in future bulletins will be mimeographed by a commercial concern, instead of gratis.

## Testimonials.

One of the whole trubles in this antirevolution fight has been the lack of appreciation by christian theologians of the scientific problems involved, and a lack of knowledge of the difficulties not by Cristian students in universities and colleges. Illustrations of this developed in letters after the first and second Creationists were mailed: "Just oppose evolution; do not try to get creationists to believe alike". As if we could oppose evolution without knowing what to believe about creation!

The best answer to this is some letters which have come in. The first is from an associate member of our association who is a botany student in a prominent university in Pennsylvania. I quote only part of the letter:

"Received the Creationist" last week. I find it extremely helpful and a necessary balance-wheel to the biological environment here at------U. Keep up the good work. I'm heartily endorsing your stand on the fundamental biblical account. I certainly want to see the Creationist become a monthly periodical. It needs a wide circulation to combat the periodical Evolution. (Evolution has died. D.J.W.) My copy is always passed on to other students, even though it may jeopardize my department fellowship. If you know of any other botanist, struggling with the problems of evolutionary morphology and phylogeny, please drop me a card with their address.

"Here's a dollar to heep along. I'll try to send one occasionally to help the work. There's a great work ahead of us."

You who do not know much natural science see how the Creationist fills the need of a student who is being taught in evolutionary natural science, as is standard in universities. He even risks his reputation for intelligence and his future as a botanist by passing his copy along. Pass your copy along to some Christian science student in a university and get his reaction to it and thus see whether the progress of the Kingdom will be helped by the Creationist.

---

Here is another letter, written not by a student in a public university, but by the head of the department of organic Science in a denominational college in Michigan. He had received only Creationist No. 2.

"At the last meeting of our "Nature and Scripture Study Club" I read Vol. 1, No. 2, of the Creationist, which had come to my hand. The Club expressed intense interest in the paper. Our group was very sympathetic to "Flood Geology". (That does not look as if it was an "incubus" to Fundamentalism, does it? D.J.W.)

"Our Club is composed of fifteen selected Christian men and women who hold a college degree and have majored in natural science. As indicated by its name, this club seeks the light of Scripture for interpreting nature. It is convinced that nature and Scripture must be correlated.

"In order to give you some idea of our attitude toward our problems, I shall request that a copy of"------" to be published soon be sent to you. This "------" (evidently the college paper) will contain a review of "--------" ( a certain book on Genesis. D.J.W.) and it will explain why we are not at all satisfied with the restitution theory."

That illustrates the view of a group of men who have majored in natural science and who also believe the Scriptures, take about creation. If they are right, the more promotion the Creationist can get and the more Christian scholars who will study it, the better.

God willing, at least mimeographed publication will be continued. and as many subscribers as possible are asked for that. If the response is sufficient and the financial risk is not too great, a printed publication will be undertaken. The future of the Creationist is in the hands of those who read this..

Dudley Joseph Whitney, Editor.

**************

45

# THE CREATIONIST

Volume 2          Exeter, California--March, 1938          Number 2
Dudley Joseph Whitney, Editor

*******

## Do Variations Indicate Evolution?

Our challenge to debate organic evolution with the ditor of
EVOLUTION or any person he wished to select for the task has been
unanswered. These evolutionists are very certain of the truth of
evolution, but we notice that whenever the issue is put squarely
before them they seem to have business elsewhere. Our challenge is
still open. Our case was presented in the February issue of The
Chreationist. Is any evolutionist anywhere brave enough to answer the
challenge?

As a substitute for a reply by an evolutionist we wish to copy
a letter from the Truth Seeker, the Organ of the American Association
for the Advancement of Atheism, referring to some writings of the
editor of The Creationist. An answer to the points this gentleman
brought up will then be given.

Letter to the Truth Seeker of March 20, 1937

"After reading D. J. Whitney's articles against evolution, there
are three questions I should like to ask the writer.

"1st. He admits that changes in plants and animals by natural
variation have occurred 'very limited in amount'. Admitting that
these variations can and have occurred, by what right or authority
does he limit them? If a certain variation can take place in one
century, why cannot an equal amount take place in the same direction
during the next century, and so continue indefinitely, so long as
the same natural laws are in operation?

2nd. He says that no type of ape, living or fossil, has been
discovered that can be considered as man's ancestor. Accepting that
as true, which would have no weight as evidence anyway. does he apply
that statement to all other species? Huxley has said in the Encyclopedia Britannica that 'On the evidence of palaeontology, the evolution
of many existing forms of animal life from their predecessors is no
longer an hypothesis but an historical fact'.

3rd. What evidence is there in support of special creation?
Hitherto your argument merely attempts to discredit evolution. If,
at some time, God really created a new species out of dust, or out
of nothing, or whatever material he is supposed to use, you could
have no proof of it unless by direct revelation, and God might not
take the trouble to inform you. If every particle of scientific
evidence in favor of evolution could be destroyed the evolution theory
would stand just where the balance of probability would still be in
favour of evolution because the evolution theory merely applies to
the spedividual, the only method of production ever yet discovered
in nature.--W. P. Lawrence, Nova Scotia."

1st. Admitting that changes, very limited in amount have occured by natural variation, by what authority do I limit them? Answer. I limit them for several reasons. For one thing, persistence of type is one of the plainest laws of biology, so change within the type is one thing and change to a creature of a different type of organization is a different thing entirely: it would be contrary to this biological law. For example, the fern is very different type of organization from the poppy; some changes may occur among ferns, but they will still be poppies; in fact, we see that there are numerous species of poppies. However, evolution demands that poppies descend, naturally, from ferns. This would be contrary to nature and there is no evidence that it occurred; therefore it should not be believed.

Among animals evolution demands that whales descend, naturally, from shrews or somewhat somewhat similiar animals. A change from shrew to whale is too great altogether for nature to bring about; therefore it should not be believed. Also, even if we should accept; apes geology, which I assert is bad science, we find whales among the earliest of mammal fossils. This would have them live about as early as their hypothetical shrew ancestors, which is out of the question considering the untold millions of years which would be required to alter shrews to whales by natural variation, even if evolution did work. A little change from shrew to whale in one century could hardly be followed by similar change in that direction century after century until true whales evolved. Neither could a little change of eyeless creatures toward the development of an eye be continued century until finally an eye evolved. The Creator might make an eye that way, but evolution could not do so, and I think that a far more reasonable kind of creation would be for the creator to make the complete animal by a single act. I hope this answers question one.

2nd. Would the absence of any known ape, living or fossil, which could well be an ancestor of man have no weight as evidence anyway'? Well, I wonder why the anthropologists have been so eager to find missing links? Would their presence be evidence for evolution, but their absence be nothing against the theory? I wish they would tell the public that this is a case. Can they rightly assert the descent of man from apes or monkeys, without having any ancestor for him?

Do I say that what is true of man is true of all other species? Yes. Present bears, felines, crabs and elephants were evidently descended from bears; felines, crabs and elephants whose fossils we find, and so for other kinds of living things. There has been some change, mostly along the lines of decadence and specialization, in nearly every kind of creature: the fossil ancestors of living things are mostly of a larger and finer type than their descendents. However, change has been within the type and not of the change to a very different type of organization. Huxley's statement was true in a way, but was meaningless as far as the theory of evolution is concerned as evidence of change of one kind of creature to a very different kind of creature.

3rd. How does evidence against evolution help the theory of special creation? Would the balance of probability still favor evolution even if there were no evidence for it? Well, we ought to decide about this, particularly since on this point we are getting close to the heart of the whole proposition. Evolutionists seem to think that the failure to find how evolution could accomplish the work it is assumed to have done is no evidence for creation. How much reason is there to this argument?

This is very bad science. George Darwin said that scientific reasoning was only common sense used in a mathematical way. By mathematics if there are certain ways to explain a certain result and all ways but one are proved faulty, that one way is proved true. Common sense shows that if there are five paths to a cabin in the woods and one can reach it only by those paths, proof positive is given that a person came by a certain path provided he is at the cabin and did not come by any of the other paths. Or if a man can reach an island only by swimming or by boat or raft and he did not come by boat or raft, he must have got there by swimming.

Thus in the organic world the first whales, birds, dinosaurs and men originated either by evolution or special creation, which is to say, either by the operation of natural processes or by some supernatural process, which by the meaning of words, would be by creation. Every possible line of evidence is examined for the operation by evolution and failure is shown in every case. By elimination, all that is left is creation. I ask every person who disagrees with this reasoning to point out its error, if it be error. I know there is the theoretical possibility that some way for evolution to work in changing shrews to whales and in developing eyes where no eyes have been might some time be discovered, but certainly it would be a delight to creationists to have the evolutionists admit that their support for evolution was actually nothing more than the possibility that in some unknown way, in some unknown time in the future, evolutionary explanations for problems now apparently inexplicable may be found; yet that is the best that evolutionists now can do.

Mr. Lawrence says in his last sentence that the evolution theory merely applies to the species the same natural law of growth which applies invariably to the individual, the only method of production yet discovered in nature. He is wrong. The law of growth in the individual is that it is controlled by heredity: a beast has eyes and hair and a certain type of organization because its parents and other ancestors had the same kind of organization; this denies that eyes and other organs could originate naturally, without inheritance, or that fishes could alter into shrews and shrews into whales. So to nature therefore and nature testifies against evolution and consequently for creation.

If the denial of evolution does not indicate creation I shall have to confess myself defeated, for if creation actually occurred, and there would be no way in science to prove that it did occur science would be impotent indeed. Speak up, scientists, and let us know if you are arguing that creation must be denied, no matter how badly evolution fails.

I hope Mr. Lawrence is satisfied with my reply.

*****

### "Go Make a Fossil."

One of our most vigorous critics of Flood Geology--a man who professes belief in creation rather than evolution--has written us several times saying that Flood geologists should be able to explain just how the

fossils were formed in Flood Geology and saying that he could build Equipment which
would reproduce the formation of sedimentary strata as these were supposedly
formed during ages geology. One of his letters was sent to Major E. C. Wren of
Devonshire, England, who wrote the gentleman the following letter, to which
we request special attention:

"Dear Sir:

I have been permitted to see your letter, to Mr. Whitney, dated 12th
July, 1937.

"You claim that, given sufficient time and money, you could build a model
of any geological formation using only such forces of erosion, sedimentation,
crustal deformation, etc., as are now observable in various parts of the world.

"I would suggest that you make such a model, using only the forces you
suggest, which will show a fossil fish such as the common herring.

"The expense would be very small and the time required for the experiment
would be limited, probably, to one summer season anywhere outside the Arctic
Regions.

"It would not be necessary to make a complete fossil, there would be no
time for that; all you will have to do would be to subject a number of those
fishes to your proposed processes and to dig up one at intervals to see the
progress made.

"It seems to me that you will find in a very short time that instead of
starting to become fossils those fish have rotted.

"I mention a fish as it is so common and there must be millions becoming
fossils at the mouths of rivers if the theory of continuity is true.

"Yours sincerely,

"E. C. Wren"

---

Now there is a real suggestion. Why did not some one think of it earlier?
The geologists point out the way they believe the fossils prove a series of
ages. Surely a very simple thing would be to demonstrate the way fossils were
formed. We Flood geologists have pointed out time after time that erosion and
sedimentation do not cause fossils to form similar to those found in the rocks.
Why did we not tell the geologists to make some fossils experimentally? Why did
they not think of it themselves and in teaching students geology; why did they
not run some experiments in making fossils?

But wait; perhaps they tried this and found that the experiments did not work.
Perhaps they found that the safest thing was to ignore this part of the problem.
They need dodge it no longer, since the Creationist hereby challenges them to go
make some fossils. As Major Wren points out, the experiments need not continue
until true fossils are made. It needs to continue long enough to show that, the
way continuity buries things, decay will not occur nor will worms devour the
bodies of the organisms buried.

49

All right then, take a lot of fishes or guinea pigs, or dead horses; place them on a mud flat or some convenient place and wash a layer of mud over them; then go back at intervals and dig up a specimen. If decay occurs, the experiment will show that the fossils were not made that way; if decay does not occur and a fine impression of the body is being left in the mud, the experiment may show that a fossil can be made in this manner.

I will say one thing very flatly: if bird, beast or fish is buried in sediment so that it will fossilize--and I think it very probable that burial can be made so that a fossil can be made experimentally--that burial will indicate catastrophe, which is to say, Flood conditions. It will not indicate <u>continuity</u>, or the kind of geologic history which ages geology demands. That is an out-and-out statement which no orthodox geologist can deny and no creationist critic of Flood Geology will deny. If any one makes such a denial, I can simply say, "Go make a fossil". Thank you for the suggestion, Major Wren.

I had once written this gentleman on his claim that he could reproduce the geological formations by means of processes such as occur now that he surely could not reproduce the "upside-down" conditions of many formations: that is to say, where assumed "older" formations lie smoothly and without sign of disturbance on what is called "younger" formations, requiring side movements of parts of the surface of the globe for scores of miles. This is on a rigid, unyielding globe. If he made some equipment to reproduce these formations, he would have to cause side movements which the earth does not have. This did not disturb the gentleman; inconsistencies in ages geology do not seem to influence the views of critics of Flood Geology. However, perhaps the challenge to make a fossil experimentally will have better success. This challenge is given to all critics of Flood Geology and believers in the laying down of fossil-bearing sediments by gradual action.

----------------

A personal letter from Major Wren to the editor also contains a striking bit of information.

"Of course you have heard of the discovery of minute crystals of calcium citrate at the bottom of the Weddell sea.—I got a full report of this discovery from the author, as I have an idea that the only way to account for the presence of calcium citrate, a vegetable product, is by the Flood. It seems to me that a district where lemons were growing was suddenly swept away and buried and went through some process which, as I am no chemist, am not able to suggest."

No, I had not heard of this, but I am glad to hear of it now. Certainly calcium citrate--a combination of calcium (lime) with citric acid, produced in citrus fruits--could hardly occur on sea bottom by processes such as operate now. The catastrophic burial of citrus products and the combination of lime with the citric acid is a far more probable explanation for the presence of the calcium citrate.

Major Wren sent the editor a typewritten manuscript on certain features of the problem of creation which are very interesting, and permission has been given to tell of these in future issues of The Creationist.

## Answering Criticisms of Flood Geology.

In justification for the use of so much space on geology, let us say again that no clear view of creation can be held without being clear about the geologic history of the earth; next, standard teachings about the earth being very old and going through a long series of ages are inconsistent with Genesis and we have given much evidence that they are contrary to true science; also, evidence shows that the fossils really came by the Deluge. Nevertheless many creationists refuse to believe Flood Geology, making this without any question the most important part of the whole problem of creation for Christians to study.

As a result of what The Creationist has said upon the subject Douglas Dewar, one of the outstanding defenders of creation in England, has written us the following letter, to which we should make reply:

"You ask for objections to what is known as flood geology. I attach this letter a short list of objections, the examples could be greatly increased and the list greatly extended.

"A feature of the geological record is that the greater number of both land and water animals and plants of which fossils have been found are not only a species that have become extinct, but of extinct families. How and when, according to flood geology, did this vast multitude of plants and animals become extinct?"

Here are his

### "Objections to Flood Geology"

"1. Not a single fossil of any living species or genus of bird or placental mammal has been found in the same beds as any fossil of any of the following extinct families of mamals: Mixodectidae, Pantolestidae (and 18 other names), or the following extinct orders of reptiles: Pterodactyls, Dinosaurs, (and 12 other names)." (We are taking the liberty of omitting these lists of names, save for one or two at the beginning of each list.)

"2. Although fossils of the marine Trilobites and Graptolites have been found all over the world not a single fossil of a graptolite or a trilobite has been found in the same deposit as that of a crab, lobster, shrimp, whelk, mussel, cowrie, oyster, cockle, winkle, or a bony fish (Teleost) although fossils of these have been found in all parts of the world.

"3. Why is no fossil of a frog or toad ever found in the same deposit as that of a stegocephalian amphibian?

"4. Why is no fossil of any of the families of fish in list A below ever found in the same bed as fossil of any of the families of fish in list B?

"List A. Birkeniidae, Pterolepidae (and 24 other names). List B. Alopidae, (and 27 other names; with which the following common names are given in brackets: eels, mullets, cod fishes, flat fish, perches, horse mackerels, sea breams, wrasses, mackerels, sword fishes, gobies, blennies, angler fishes, gunards).

"Until it can be explained how the flood sorted out the animals in this extraordinary way, it is folly to adopt flood geology even as a working hypothesis.

"Douglas Dewar".

## Answer to Objections to Flood Geology.

Let us get things straight in our reply to these points. Instead of calling for objections to Flood Geology I specifically and definitely called upon such persons as had objections to this theory to say what geological work the Flood did and to say what fossils, if any, the critic believed were laid down by the Flood and I made several other requirements. The purpose of these was to block criticism by Fundamentalists (using that term to designate all who accept the Scriptures as being inspired) who did not know or who would not say what they believed about the Flood and about geologic history generally. I will point out to Mr. Dewar and others that in his communication these requirements are ignored, though from other letters by Mr. Dewar I can gather something of his beliefs.

I have stated that what I want is almost more than anything in the whole realm of creationist discussion to get some geologist to defend ages geology against Flood Geology. I assert that ages geology cannot stand a minute against Flood Geology, and if after a discussion of the two, both are found wrong and some third system of geology is found better we can decide upon it. Meanwhile two things are most lamentable: first, the great mass of Christian leaders seem unable or unwilling to decide upon the subject; second, numerous creationists oppose Flood Geology most vigorously, although it certainly is in full harmony with Genesis, and ages geology, which is its only alternative, is in definite conflict with Genesis.

I am not asking critics for their objections to Flood Geology; I am asking that some qualified believer in ages geology have the courage to debate the subject with me in these pages. I will venture to say that after such a debate and the utter rout of ages geology Fundamentalist critics will be a little less free in their criticism of Flood Geology. Please, readers, try to arrange a debate on this subject for me. However, I will reply to Mr. Dewar's letter.

My answer to 3, 4 and 5 is , I do not know. There is no question to 1 and 2, which are statements of fact, presumably correct. Since no questions are asked, no answers seem needed. However, I have found a number of instances where fossils of things living only late in time were discovered in sediments supposedly far older. Perhaps none of the kinds of fossils mentioned by Mr. Dewar have been found associated with fossils of the opposing groups, although discoverids equally inconsistent with the ages have been found. I was looking up the fossil history of plants once and found where palms had been discovered in Triassic sediment, long before any were supposed to exist; an angiosperm seed ball in Carboniferous coal, and there were other glaring inconsistencies in the fossil record. If some of these are needed I am sure that George McCready Price, Byron Nelson or B.F. Allen can provide readers of The Creationist with a nice list.

The answer, "I do not know" ought to be given to numerous questions about how things came to be as they are. There are numerous phenomena which men cannot explain and they do not cease to exist because men cannot explain them. The ages geologists are also helpless to explain almost every fundamental feature of their theory. If one points the finger of scorn at the Flood Geologists for being too conservative to try to explain certain facts, shall we point the finger of scorn at the ages geologists because there are many things inexplicable by their theory? Shall I alter Mr. Dewar's last sentence to make it read, "Until it can be explained how continuity formed the coal beds, petroleum beds, beds of fish fossils and terrestrial fossils, how it admitted mountains and kept volcanoes operating for long ages, it is folly to believe in ages geology?" That position is just as reasonable as the position of Mr. Dewar.

I assert that the geologists cannot explain any one of the features I have named. For example, many of them allow that great beds of lignite came into place by drift, not by the vegetation growing where it is now lignite. That was catastrophic deposit, the kind of thing the Flood might do; it is not continuity and cannot be explained on the basis that the present is the key to the past. If it can, some one please explain it, (See U.S.G.S. Bulletin 770, page 758.) Although I cannot explain how the Deluge or any other catastrophe could form a great bed of lignite, such beds of lignite exist in spite of my inability to see just how they were formed. There is the FACT, admitted by geologists. Evidence is also conclusive for the catastrophic formation of beds of fish fossils, of the petroleum deposits, and of coal beds. If we are to deny the implications of all these things because we do not understand the mechanism of the Deluge and because we do not understand how the fossils came to be sorted the way they are, we should bury the whole problem of geology in the depths of the sea, ages geology included.

On the problem of the segregation of fossils from one another there are certain things to be said, even though explanations are somewhat difficult. For example, California covers lots of territory and there are many fossils in certain parts, yet for years not a single "Mesozoic" dinosaur had been found here. Then about two years ago a school boy found some dinosaur bones in a hillside about 80 miles northwest of the home of the editor of The Creationist. I think one other dinosaur has also been found since then. They therefore lived when certain extensive formations were laid down. Judging by the number of dinosaur fossils found elsewhere, they must have been very abundant upon the earth at that time, yet only two were found here. Numerous kinds of dinosaurs have not been found here at all. Shall I therefore be reasonable if I say, "Unless you explain why fossils of those creatures were not found here, the theory for the formation of fossils which you assert, be it ages geology or anything else, is folly?" This is essentially what Mr. Dewar says.

A plain condition exists: tens of thousands of different kinds of land and water animals were evidently living when (or just before) the dinosaur and certain other fossils were buried. They are not mixed in one jumble, but they are segregated from one another to a very considerable extent. Why they are so segregated we do not know, though we might hazzard a few guesses. The problem of how they segregated is just as difficult in ages geology as in Flood Geology and no critic of Flood Geology can use this fact unless he also rejects ages geology and has some good third system of geologic history which he is willing to sponser. Where is such theory?

Also, I have seen numerous masses of sedimentary rock twisted and distorted so that the task of arranging the fossils in a systematic order for

for the time of burial would be difficult. I have seen photographs
and diagrams in textbooks and government bulletins of sediments laid
down, so it is asserted, millions of years apart in time, yet in one
hillside the contours of the different formations were like a crazy
quilt. Sometimes the older fossils were above the younger and only
a few feet distant and it seemed very irregular to say that they were
laid down in different ages and not together. I can cite numerous
examples of formations where the overlying fossils are said to be
older than the ones in the underlying rock. Price's "New Geology"
and other works give many examples of this; so does Nelson's "The
Deluge Story in Stone", all of which are allowed by the ages geologists

Take dinsaur and mammal fossils: they may be segregated in different rocks, but in one place rock of the "Age of Mammals" is above
rock of the "Age of Reptiles" and in another place the reverse condition exists. Also, this reverse condition is not uncommon and it
indicates as strongly as anything could that the dinosaur fossils were
not buried earlier than the mammal fossils, but all were buried in the
same general period. Mr. Dewar's criticisms are as much against ages
geology as against Flood Geology. I wish that Christians who hesitate
to accept Flood Geology would recognize that fact. Men can criticize
Flood Geology on the basis that they cannot understand just how it
operated, but that is the only real criticism that they have of it
which I have yet found.

Please remember hereafter, everybody, that I want Christian critics
of Flood Geology to commit themselves to some beliefs about the Flood
and geologic history generally, as itemized in Volume 1 of The Creationist.

Also, in all discussion of Flood Geology, or geologic history generally two features should be decided: first, were many sediments deposited by catastrophe, or quickly; or did they form by continuity, by
processes such as operate now? Second, is there a true classification
of the geologic formations, as given in standard textbooks of geology?
If not, what about this alleged order of formations? Please critics,
tell me what you think of these two important points when you submit
your criticisms. If we allow the catastrophic formation of many of
these sediments, standard beliefs of geologists must be rejected. If
we allow also that there is no true order for the geologic formations,
Flood Geology is certainly implied. Flood Geologists have irrefutable
evidence in abundance on both of these features. When did extinct
families of animals become extinct? On the question, I answer:
Evidently at the time of the Flood.

*****

### An Important Point of Fact.

Closely connected with what has just been written is a criticism
which has come in private correspondence from a geologist, not a
Fundamentalist, but a geologist by profession, a man of national
standing in his profession.

He writes: "One recent statement you made is away off--we do not
find mammal's teeth as far down as reptile remains." (Italics his.)
I think this refers to a statement I made somewhere that teeth of
elephants (mastodons or mammoths) were taken from the Coast Range
mountains almost due west of here in a comparable location to reptile
remains found in that range 40 to 60 miles to the north.

THE CREATIONIST

Volume 2          Exeter, California----April, 1938          Number 3

\*\*\*\*\*\*\*

## Our Creed of Creation

We believe that behind the operations of what is called Nature is the power of a Creator and Controller of the universe. Although the different parts of the universe normally act according to what may be termed natural law, the Creator can originate matter by divine fiat and cause it to take form in ways transcending the normal processes of nature, and we believe that he has done so. The creation of matter, of living things, or of other objects, was in its nature different from the normal processes of such matter or of living forms after creation.

We believe that the creation of different parts of the universe may have taken place at different times and probably did so.

In our study of nature we believe in examining the normal processes of nature according to their causes and effects; but we follow the postulate that when normal processes of nature seem incompetent to account for a certain phenomenon, like the origin of a star, the origin of life, or of organs of plants and animals, creation should be believed to have been used. We believe that creation was used in the origin of the objects named.

We believe that the Genesis account of creation and the early history of the earth is true and that the record should be taken in a direct and natural way. Without deciding about the time of the creation of the earth and the rest of the solar system, we believe that this was much more recent than astronomers and geologists assert and that the ordering of the earth and the creation of living things upon it was done by divine fiat in six literal days not far fr m 4,004 B. C. We believe that this creation was of an ideal earth and that conditions on the earth now are due to the demoralization of the ideal earth as the result of the sin of our first parents.

We believe that the fossils, ———————————————————————— through the ruin and reconstruction of the face of the earth at the time of the Noachian Deluge and that existing races of men are descended from the three sons of Noah. We furthermore believe that all of these things are in full harmony with true science.

Our fundamental break with standard beliefs of modern scientists is that they attempt to explain all things solely by the operation of natural processes, with the possibility of there having been one great act of fiat creation in the distant past, while we assert that divine fiat should be allowed whenever the operation of natural processes seem incompetent to account for some certain condition. On the history of the earth we break with the standard belief of geologists that the earth is hundreds of millions of years old and has reached its present condition by the operation of evolutionary processes, and we believe that it was ordered by divine fiat only a few thousand years ago.

Our purpose is to examine available evidence carefully and with an open mind on the points mentioned and to alter the creed of creation just given to accord with the evidence, provided evidence demands such alteration.

\*\*\*\*\*\*\*\*

## Remarks on the Creed.

Several reasons exist for the presentation of this creed.
1. If we are to study Creation, we should have some starting point,
and it is far better to put down some definite points of belief and
then to correct them if they need correction than to be hazy and indefinite about the whole problem; which, unfortunately, is the situation among many Christian scholars.

2. Note particularly that this creed starts the earth as the
home of man and other living things as an ideal earth, not as an
earth developed by long evolutionary processes, not as an earth
oppressed by glacial ages, or an earth which, before the creation
of men with saber-toothed tigers or savage dinosaurs.
If we start all living things on an ideal earth, evolutionary
geology, which is the geology of the text books, must be rejected.
Wake up, Christian scholars, and recognize this fact. The position
that present conditions came about through the demoralization of
a perfect earth also produces a far sounder and more scientific
system of thinking than does the theory of organic evolution.

3. Christians are under the obligation to accept one or
other of these two positions of a perfect initial creation, or
else of a system thoroughly tied to the theory of evolutionary
geology, or they should set forth an alternative Creed of Creation.
Most of them refuse to do this; they have no real belief on the matter. "How long halt ye between two opinions? If God be God, fear
him; but if Baal, fear him".

4. Notice also the great difference in our interpretation of
Nature and that of scientists in general, and decide which of the
two is correct. When scientists fail utterly in accounting for
a condition by evolution they nevertheless assume that evolution
worked in some unknown way; their philosophy of nature absolutely
debars the concept of creation, except in some rather hazy kind of
an initial creation, and any Christian scholar who is convinced
that he must stick with the evolutionary history or other speculative
conclusions of modern science, by that fact rejects the creative
power of God. He may not realize this, but that will not make it
any less true.

## What Others Think.

Four directors of the late Religion and Science Association have
given their opinion of the creed. George McCready Price endorses
it "100 percent". Dr. Harold W. Clark accepts it fully, with the
understanding that perhaps some corals or other fossils of the
antediluvian earth remain in the sediments laid down by the Flood.
Both Prof. Price and the editor accept this as a matter of course.

Byron C. Nelson has made no statement for publication on the
creed but by correspondence he seems to endorse its leading features
with one marked exception: he believes evidence exists that the
Flood was much farther back than Ussher's chronology would indicate
and that Creation Week was therefore much earlier than 4,004 B.C.
When there are differences of opinion on matters like this they
should be mentioned and the problems studied: we are not giving
a hard and fast creed which must be accepted; we are giving a
statement of belief which can be, and should be amended if evidence
demands such amendment.

Dr. L. Allen Higley, president of our late association, believes
the creed at fault in many ways, since he holds a view of the history
of the earth which is contrary to both evolutionary geology and
Deluge geology. The editor, however, is not informed about this
belief or the reasons for holding it. So far

3

volutionary geology and Flood geology form the basis of the only systems of geologic history known by the editor.

Douglas Dewar of England wrote some time ago in a personal letter: "In the present state of knowledge it is premature to propound a constructive theory of a scientific kind. We have got to go a long way before this can be done with any hope of success. Similarly, in the present state of knowledge we cannot hope to interpret correctly the Genesis narrative." I assume that Mr. Dewar will not object to my use of his statement. His is a very common viewpoint among Christian scholars, though men who hold it almost invariably have a very strong tendency toward belief in evolutionary geology.

Here is a question for every one: What kind of a creed of creation can you prepare for yourself? I venture to say that if you try to prepare a creed which you can accept, you will find it a very profitable exercise. I venture also to say that any creed of creation will be better than none; state a creed, even if you are doubtful about parts of it; then correct such parts as you find to be faulty. If our creed as given is faulty, let us correct it; however, a system of belief which can be amended whenever it is found at fault should be a help in attaining a clear view of what Genesis teaches and how nature came to be as nature is.

*****

## Why the Waste of Energy in the Universe?

"At its last meeting our Nature and Scripture Study Club discussed a paper on the effects of various forms of radiant energy upon plants. From the paper and the discussion it seemed probable that mutations are merely hereditary injuries. Much of the discussion of the evening centered around the decreasing availability of energy as the result of its radiation. The significance of this loss of energy availability could not be correlated with any Scriptural statement.

"Such a situation seems unsatisfactory to me. If you can give us any light on the relation between this universal process and the world picture of the Bible, we will appreciate it." Rapids, Mich.

At the time this question arrived the Truth Seeker, organ of the Atheist Association, was running a series of articles by one of the officers of that organization on the Atheism of Astronomy, and one of the arguments for atheism was the great dissipation of energy in space from the stars. The question which has been asked and the argument for atheism can be considered together.

The situation is that the sun sends out an enormous amount of energy each second, each day, each year. If the sun were composed of anthracite coal and there was a way for it to burn quickly, all of the coal would be exhausted in a year in the production of the heat which the sun sends out. A very, very small amount of the sun's heat comes to the earth, providing it with necessary warmth, giving energy for growth, and making life possible. None of the rest of the heat of the sun, as far as is known, helps out life anywhere in the universe, and only an infinitesimally small fraction is caught by other stars. For all that can be seen, most of it is simply dissipated into space.

Other stars are much like the sun; some are larger and some are smaller; some are hotter and some are cooler; some appear to be older and some younger. All that are visible send out immense quantities of heat into space, nearly all of it being "wasted" as far as evidence shows, or put to no known useful

57

ppose. The theoretical life of a star is for it to begin in a highly expanded and rarefied condition and to shrink and shrink as it gives out heat, its ultimate fate being to be cold, dense and dead. The question the Club asks is in effect, Why should this be according to the Scripture? The argument of the atheist is that a deity would not permit such a "waste" of energy, and since the dissipation of energy continues, there is no God. As evidence of the non-existence of God the atheist also cites the immensity of unoccupied space and the apparent uselessness of many stars.

The answer to these questions which the writer offers is that God does not give his reasons for what he does: "Who hath known the mind of the Lord, and who hath been his counsellor?" To the atheist we may point out that the nature of stars shows conclusively the fact of God: since the energy is not preserved or self-sustaining, "Nature" could not keep it going; therefore only God could do that. Why he should have the stars operate as they do we do not need to know.

Certain Scriptures point out the limited life of the stars in contrast to the eternal life of God: "The heavens are the work of thy hands; they shall perish, but Thou shalt endure; Yea, all of them shall wax old like a garment; as a gesture shalt thou change them and they shall be changed; but Thou art the same and thy years shall have no end." Thus the Scriptures do speak of the dissipation of energy from the stars; they at least point out their limited existence and the permanence of God.

The evidence of God's creative power on account of the limited life of the stars should be plain. If heat was not lost into space; if it simply passed without loss from one star to another, or to one body from another so that the universe was like an eternally-existing, self-winding clock, a philosopher might have some excuse for saying that the universe was eternal and self-existing, just as physicists used to say that matter was eternal, but the continual dissipation of heat and energy from the stars and their continual cooling, without any hint of a way by which their life could be renewed, indicates creation, and the need for creation is scientific evidence of God.

Space, distant from a star, is exceedingly cold, but the gigantic "now" stars, being highly expanded and composed of matter as tenuous as "thin air" and yet being very hot, could not come into being naturally in cold space. Also, they do not continue in that condition, but gradually become smaller and smaller and more dense. They "wax old" and are changed. Nothing but creation can account for them.

Why God should have so many stars and should have them so distant, as a rule, from one another; why he should have some stars without planets and without life, we know not. Human philosophy may provide answers to the Why of nature, but human philosophy is very helpless, faulty guide. We do not need answers to these problems. However, since God has created those stars and provided the energy with which they shine, surely he can afford to have them send out their energy into space and the dissipation of that energy will do him no injury. Perhaps when the new heavens and the new earth come into being we will understand why the universe acts as it does. Until then we need not philosophize about those things, but only recognize the clear evidence that without creation there could be no stars: the very nature of the stars proclaims the fact of creation: "The heavens declare the glory of God"

One other observation on the subject may be made: the ancient philosophers of Egypt and Greece apparently did not realize the magnitude of the heavens and the number of the stars. Certainly Ptolemy did not when he set forth the geocentric system of cosmology which was believed by scholars until the time of Copernicus and Galileo. The old-time scholars believed that there were only a few hundred stars, for the haze of the milky way and certain other parts of the heavens was not known to be composed of untold millions of stars, yet far back as the time of Abraham God told him that his descendents should be as numerous as the sands of the sea and as the stars of heaven, making the number of the stars comparable with the sands of the sea. This was 2,000 years before Ptolemy and on record long before the days of Ptolemy. The Scriptures were right; Ptolemy and the philosophers which followed him were wrong.

The Scriptures fare well in astronomical matters and the heavens declared the glory of God instead of indicating atheism.

*********

## Fixity of Species and Change after Creation.

Outside of the question of the history of the earth, which seems to be resolved into the problem of evolutionary geology versus Flood geology, there is probably no other problem of creation so important as that of the changes which have occurred among living things since creation. This is particularly the case on account of the lamentable and ill advised emphasis upon fixity of species by most anti-evolutionists. Let us undertake a brief study of the problem and make an attempt of clarify the subject.

Certain facts seem fairly plain. 1. As nature now operates "fixity of species" seems a rule of nature. "Like father, like child". There are variations within species, but no splitting up of a species to make two or more new species. 2. The number of so-called species run up to about the million mark, and even though it be agreed that many groups counted as distinct species are merely different races in the same species, the number of true species will run into the tens of thousands. By true species is meant a group of plants or animals between which there is fertility, the off-spring also being fertile with others of the group. 3. A very great number of species are killers, or otherwise injurious to other living things. Many others show strong evidences of having degenerated from a finer condition of their remote ancestors. 4. Genesis records a perfect creation, for on the Edenic earth nothing but ideal creatures lived. There has therefore been a great deal of change among living things since Eden. 5. Various features of nature make a determination of the extent of change since creation hard to determine, but certainly the problem should be studied.

A particular reason for a study of the problem and for a public pronouncement upon the matter is, that the evolutionists and the public in general believe that opposition to evolution requires belief in fixity of species. However, if a person believes Genesis when it records a perfect Edenic creation and then sees that the present creation is not perfect--"the whole creation groaneth and travaileth together in pain"--he cannot reasonably hold to fixity of species. Evolutionists who assert that some transformation of species--even in the line of degeneracy--is "evolution", and anti evolutionists who seem to make transformation of species practically synonymous with evolution are both casting a smoke screen over the whole problem of creation and making it almost impossible for Bible creationists to get their case over to the public.

Let us therefore take the thesis that there was a perfect creation to begin with, and much change since creation, and see how it works out. Let us assume the possibility that change after creation has often passed species boundaries, so that certain animal groups which now are distinct species still have descended from common ancestors.

An illustration will show what is meant. We know that there are many kinds of monkeys and that there are many monkey species: groups which will not mate with certain other monkey groups, or if they do mate, as in a zoo, there is no progeny as a result of such mating. Some monkeys are native to Asia and Africa; others are natives of America. Zoologists classify Old World monkeys into ten genera with about 185 species and American monkeys into nine genera and about 89 species. Some of these species will probably cross with individuals of a different species in the same genus, but there are certainly many different monkey species, no matter how elastic the term 'species' is made and still to remain reasonable. A question is whether or not there is relationship between different monkey species by descent from common ancestors. If there has been, change since creation has passed species limits and undue emphasis has often been laid upon fixity of species.

Instead of examining monkeys for change since creation, we might study clovers, poppies, crabs, spiders, butterflies, humming birds, or almost every other type of plant and animal which lives. With few exceptions we will find all kinds of living things classified into families, genera, species and races. Some relationship is indicated most strongly in many cases between different species, and often between genera in a family. Under any conditions the line of relationship by descent among certain groups is very hard to determine.

The seriousness of the whole problem develops mainly from the practice of many creationists in making fixity of species the foundation of their attack upon evolution, and "If the foundation be destroyed, what can the righteous do?"

Illustrating the ~~emphasis laid upon fixity of species~~, two citations can be given from a booklet opposing evolution which was published not long ago in England. To avoid embarassment the title of the booklet will not be given. One quotation is by an evolutionist; the other by an outstanding champion of creation.

From J.B.S. Haldane, a noted biologist, this quotation is given, being taken from his book, "Science and the Supernatural": "The barrier of interspecific sterility is the most serious argument against Darwin's 'Organic Evolution'". (The impossibility of originating eyes and other organs by evolution, or of changing shrews to whales, does not seem to have occurred to this scientist. Evolutionists seem to think that if one parent monkey species could be ancestral to two or more monkey species, or if generalized rabbit could be ancestral to both jackrabbit and cottontail, little things like the problem of originating eyes, wings and milk glands can be overlooked.)

As expressing the view of creationists, the other gentleman writes in a foreword to the booklet mentioned, speaking of the case made by its author: "He is on sound ground in his premises that organic evolution and the mutability of species stand or fall together. I know of no biologist so illogical as to question this."

Please notice the last sentence particularly. All biologists agree that organic evolution is good science if transformations of species have taken place. We could point out the seeming impossibility of the naturalistic origin of eyes and the wings of insects, and the seeming impossibility of the descendents of shrews becoming whales, but the evolutionists need only point out evidences of transformation of species and evolution would have to be admitted, because 'organic evolution and the mutability of species stand or fall together! What a desperate condition! We simply cannot oppose evolution effectively while both evolutionists and leading anti-evolutionists take this view of the way the subject should be studied.

## The Real Place of Fixity of Species.

Remember now that present-day fixity of species has a real place in the war against evolution. Persistence of type is a barrier to evolution which the evolutionist should be made to face; only too much importance should not be given--the whole problem should not be made to hang upon this one feature. Nevertheless evidences of degeneracy are so abundant among many living things, both plants and animals, that some transformation of species during the progress of such degeneracy seems positive. However, degeneracy is not evolution.

The biological limits of a species should be determined by the inter-fertility of members. If one kind of a deer will mate with an individual of another kind and produce fertile progeny, the two should be held to be of one species, not members of two different species. Thus the caribou and the reindeer mate freely and thus prove to be one species. On the other hand if two monkeys will not mate, or if they will produce no progeny by mating, they are of distinct species, even though they may have had the same original ancestors.

However, inter-fertility does not provide a satisfactory guide to species limits, since all degrees of inter-fertility can be found from natural mating up to almost full sterility and full sterility. The horse and the ass will hybridize and produce a sterile mule. The bison and the ox will hybridize and the males of such a mating will be sterile, though the females will breed back to both bison and ox. Bantams and pheasants give very similar results when hybridized. Among cultivated plants there has been an immense amount of hybridizing, some of it natural, and all degrees of inter-fertility can be found. One can read the writings of Luther Burbank for some striking illustrations of this. If a person wishes to take sterility of partial sterility of the progeny when hybridizing can occur, as a measure of species, he simply cannot make that system apply well: there are too many instances where the sterility is too little, and others where it is almost, but not quite, complete.

But aside from the problem of hybridizing, or mating individuals of two groups or plants or animals, the classification of plants and animals indicates relationship so strongly that it should evidently be believed, though it cannot perhaps be proved in this manner. Mention of monkeys has been made in this connection and the classification of monkeys certainly indicates relationship in cases where there is complete sterility between groups as far as is known.

The American monkeys all resemble one another in certain respects in which they differ from Old World monkeys and the Old World monkeys all resemble one another in certain ways in which they differ from American monkeys. Thus American monkeys have 36 teeth. Surely it would be surprising if the Creator made numerous American monkeys, no more related to one another than to spiders, although they all had 36 teeth, when none of the Old World monkeys had more than 32 teeth. Then many American monkeys can hang by their tails and no Old World monkeys can do so, and this would be surprising coincidence if no relationship were indicated by the fact. Then there are certain other very important ways in which the two great

divisions of the monkey world differ from one another, although all
members of each division resemble other monkeys of that division in
the ways in question. This certainly implies descent of all American
monkeys from some common ancestral stock, and descent of all Old World
monkeys come from common parents.

Think about the deer. There are many kinds of deer, all clearly
deer, though of distinct species. Surely it is more reasonable to
allow a probable relationship between these than to insist that each
is a separate creation. There are numerous antelope species, resembling deer in some ways, but very distinct from them in others. Surely
the different antelope species can be held to be related to one another.
The reasonable conclusion seems to be that there has been creation and
change after creation in those groups.

The biologist can hardly examine any kind of plants and animals
without finding them divided into races, species, genera and families
in a way which indicates relationship by descent from common ancestors,
and it seems a big mistake to deny the probability of relationship just
because fixity of species now operates so strongly. The battle against
evolution can be fought so much more effectively on other grounds that
it is a big mistake to take a line of attack where evolutionists have
so strong a case and then to assert that our whole case depends upon
the merits of this one feature.

On the question of the origin of organs and of extreme transformations in certain theoretical lines of evolutionary descent evolutionists are helpless. Even such transformations of species as appear to
have occurred are shown by genetics to be mostly in the way of loss
rather than gain; it is change after creation, as Genesis indicates,
not change as a substitute for creation. Let us get this question
settled and not make our attack on the one feature where we invite
defeat. Let us particularly not say "that organic evolution and the
mutability of species must stand or fall together".

Again, unless evolutionary geology is true, organic evolution is
ruined. Eyes, wings, and numerous other organs are not going to originate naturally, nor are fishes going to change to lizards, eagles and
so on, unless there were untold millions of years for evolution to operate
--provided it could operate. Once men recognize the unanswerable evidences in favor of flood geology and against evolutionary geology,
organic evolution falls into ruin. Two things creationists
should do are: to recognize the folly of evolutionary geology, substituting flood geology for it unless some better system of geology can
be shown; and, to put the biological side of the fight against evolution on the other grounds than to put the biological side of the fight
against evolution on other grounds than fixity of species. Remember:
Genesis asserts that the Bible creation was perfect. This inevitably
implies the falsity of the doctrine of evolutionary geology and of
other branches of evolution.

### Miscellaneous

The last issue of the Creationist had two misadventures. Copy
was ready in due time, but sufficient paper was not available then at
the high school to get it out, and a shipment which was ordered was
delayed greatly. This delayed preparation of the paper. Then, through
a mistake too few copies were run off and a few American subscribers
and most of our foreign subscribers had to go without their papers.
If any of our readers have copies they can spare, we should appreciate
their return to us. The postage should not be more than 1½ cents per
copy.

-------

The editor was not particularly pleased with the last issue, but
some readers liked it very much. Thus a card from our friend B. F.
H. reads in part:

"...I feel that your last Creationist is among your best. To my
mind one way to make fossil segregation a boon to flood geology is to
consider it on a basis of modern ecology. We should parallel living
ecology with fossil ecology. Prof. Harold W. Clark is perhaps our
best man to tackle that problem, as he is a biologist and ecologist,
and is teaching both, doing fine work in the latter."

"The whole fossil world can be gone over and given a new setting, and offered to the world from a new, natural and reasonable viewpoint. We can make fossil ecology one of our very strongest points if we will only give it concentrated research."

For our non-technical readers we can say that ecology is a study of the relation of environment to the form and nature of living things. Personally, the editor has always felt that we are still very far from explaining how the fossils came into being in the way they are. The thing which the evolutionary geologists should be made to recognize is that they are more stumped in this connection than we are: we Flood geologists have the catastrophic burial of fossils buried in the first favor, but evolutionary geologists cannot get their fossils buried in the first place. Still, the concentrated research which Mr. Allen suggests is sorely needed.

---

### Sinanthropus Again.

Once more "Peking Man", alleged to be the oldest group of human beings known, comes to the attention of anthropologists, making said Peking Man decidedly human and increasing the gap between man and any hypothetical ape ancestors. It has long been a practice to depict Neanderthal men as hunched over as if they had not gotten the back bone of their ape ancestors (?) fully human; but Peking Man is asserted to be earlier than Neanderthal Man and therefore nearer the apes at least in time.

However, the reconstruction of his thigh bone eliminates this imaginary semi-ape stoop. Franz Weidenreich, writing from the Peiping Union Medical College to SCIENCE, says, "My recently stated conclusion that Sinantropus must have already adopted a completely upright posture has now been confirmed by the discovery of the femur".

Since Sinanthropus is allowed to have been a Mongolian and therefore descended from the same original human group which was ancestral to the Nordics, Semites, Sumerians, negroes and Polynesians one would think that his completely human characteristics of both form and mind would have been known to begin with and the finding of some thigh bones would not be necessary to show that fact. Or so it seems to the Creationist. However, it is nevertheless interesting to note that as science advances evolution fares worse and worse and creation better and better.

---

### Jonah and the Whale.

Some lively discussions have been conducted in New York recently about the account of Jonah and the whale, and the editor has been asked to discuss the subject. He cares to say very little upon it:

1. That a man could be swallowed by a whale and remain in the stomach of the animal for any length of time without dying seems impossible. This feature favors the skeptics. 2. Evidence seems to exist that one or more men were swallowed by whales and then rescued. 3. By the Hebrew language a whale would be a fish, so there is no valid excuse for quibbling over the fact that in our system of classification a whale is not a fish. 4. If God so willed a whale could swallow Jonah without killing him, just as well as God could create a star or a fern. If "natural law" is insisted upon as a universal process, there was no creation and no healings or other miracles by Jesus, and there was no creation. However, since creation has been proved by science, no one in the name of science has the slightest justification for asserting disbelief in the account of Jonah and the whale. Admit God as Creator, and the validity of the Scriptures must inevitably be allowed.

# THE CREATIONIST

Volume 2          Exeter, California--May, 1936          Number 4

******

## "Given time enough, anything may happen."

This is one of the famous sayings of the ancients which has been taken over by those scientists who are committed to the dogma of evolution. Without unlimited amounts of time, every feature, almost without exception, in the whole realm of evolutionary theory falls into ruin. Unless the evolutionists can have almost unlimited amounts of time for the operation of evolution, there can be no real evolution.

A few illustrations will show this: first among living things, then in the assumed evolutionary history of the earth.

By the theory of evolution once nothing lived on the earth and the first living things came into being, not by any real act of God, but by some purely natural combination of circumstances. Those first living things would have to be very simply organized, but from them evolution would have to cause endently in several distinct kinds of living things: crustaceans, molluscs, and bats must have evolved. The descendents of water creatures must have become land creatures, and the descendents of some of those land creatures must have returned 'or mightly to the water. Every organ of every living thing must have come into being, naturally by the struggle of its first owners to survive. The amount of time required for evolution to accomplish these things would certainly be a rather large piece of eternity.

In the evolutionary life of the earth as it is now asserted to have been about 100 miles' thickness of sedimentary rock would have to be deposited; mountain masses would have to be uplifted and eroded away, to give place to new mountains; great beds of coal would have to form by gradual accumulation--unless the geologists will agree, as many of them do agree, that coal came by catastrophic deposit, though once they allow this, evolutionary geology is ruined. Then the land where the coal vegetation accumulated would have to sink so that the vegetation could be buried; and following this it would have to rise for the accumulation of a mass of vegetation which in turn would have to be buried. This process would have to be repeated time after time on a solid, unyielding earth, until every bed or series of beds was formed.

Later the process would have to be repeated somewhere else for the making of coal beds of other assumed ages.

We hear mention of a series of ice epochs preceding the epoch in which we live. Actually a number of series of such epochs are asserted in the history of the earth. To get ice epochs, the earth would have to cool--after warm climates had endured for millions of years at the poles-- and great ice caps would have to form, not only in parts of the temperate regions, but even in the present tropics; then the earth would have to warm up and stay warm for millions of years only to have other glacial and warm epochs come.

This postulate, "Given time enough and anything may happen" is therefore demanded by both organic evolution and evolutionary geology.

Our thesis in connection with this is simply: The earth is not old;
it is not old enough for more than a very tiny fraction of the evolutionary processes which the evolutionists assert took place. Conse-
uently, if the earth is not old, both evolutionary geology and organic
evolution are **nonsense**. They can be and have been proven to be nonsense
by other evidence than that of time; however, they can be proven to be
nonsense by nothing more than the evidence of **time**.

### "Till the Sun Grows Cold"

One of the great reasons for believing that the earth is not any-
tin like as old as evolutionists assert it to be is that--as far as
physics can show--the sun could not provide heat to the earth for many
millions of years.

This is as plain as can be. The earth depends upon the sun for
heat, and unless the sun sent out the heat that it does, life could not
exist on the earth in its present form. Lord Kelvin pointed out this
fact several decades ago and showed that contraction could only give
an age of from 20 to 40 million years for the sun; consequently the
earth could be no older than that. Now, 20 to 40 million years was all
too little for both the organic evolutionists and the evolutionary geologists, although the geologists could use a lot of catastrophe and
still keep their age. The organic evolutionists could only ignore
the difficulties which this limited amount of time gave them in evolving the organs of plants and animals, in changing invertebrates into
fishes, and the fishes into eagles, whales and men.

Then radioactivity was discovered, giving new light on the nature
of matter and allowing speculative theories to replace Kelvin's evidence on the production of heat in the sun. By radioactivity the earth is
figured to be 2000 million years or more old, and whenever an evolutionist wants a few score million years to accomplish a difficult task
all he has to do is to assume them. Belief that the earth is old is
considered evidence that the sun is also old, whether there is any
way to explain the production of the sun's heat or not.

Some form of radioactivity, ~~or of the destruction of matter, has~~
been assumed as the agency for the production of heat in the sun for
thousands of millions of years. Like certain other theories, this
stood approved only as long as it was not studied too closely. With
the increase of knowledge about the nature of matter it has been found
that the destruction of matter evidently gives little heat in the sun.
Now a favored theory for the production of the solar heat is that atoms
of hydrogen are uniting to form heavier atoms, while these unite to
form still heavier atoms. Just how hydrogen is going to be available
to produce heat for untold millions of years and how it is going to be
available to produce heat for untold millions of years and how it is
going to go in the interior of the sun in material amounts when it is
a light, gaseous element, is one of those things which are hard to
explain. Evolutionists continue to talk of the production of heat
within the sun for thousands of millions of years when actually the
only source of the energy of which they know to give this heat is contraction, which can give a maximum age for the sun of only about two
score million years. It is like their references to the birth of the
solar system as the result of a star passing near the sun long ago, when
this theory has been examined carefully and found terribly at fault.
(See The Solar System and Its Origin, by H. N. Russell.) There is too
much of this in evolution: referring to some theory as if it were fact,
when actually the greatest scientists examine those theories and find
that they are wrong. Kelvin's figures still stand as the only explanation which will endure inspection for the possible life of the

sun. If any one doubts this assertion I request that he look up recent reports on the matter. The subject has been discussed several times in SCIENCE during the last year or two. One theory after another for ... ... ..... of heat in the sun has had to be discarded, and only contraction remains.

Some one may ask, "Is not even 20 millions years far too long for anything but evolutionary geology"? Possibly so, but the point is this: If the geologists are finally compelled by the pressure of evidence to discard their theories of a very old earth and to undertake a renewed study of the subject, they will find their whole system of geologic theory demoralized, and the organic evolutionists will be in still a worse fix. That theory is fantastic enough at the best, with unlimited time at its disposal, but if eyes and wings and organs galore have to be originated, and if natural selection has to turn ameba into men and algae into apples with only about 20 million years at its disposal--providing an analysis of the subject will justify belief that the earth is that old--it will become too fantastic altogether for any but the most hardshell evolutionists.

### The Salts of the Ocean.

There are numerous other evidences that the earth cannot be old enough for either evolutionary geology or organic evolution, but only one or two of these will now be mentioned, and the one of these which has bothered geologists most is the salt content of the ocean.

The writer's particular attention to this came by reading Osborn's "The Origin and Evolution of Life" soon after its publication. Osborn showed how, by the rate that sodium was being carried into the ocean in the rivers as the rocks were disintegrating and the land being leached from materials dissolved in the water, the earth could be (as he figured it) only about 60 million years old. (Figures from U.S.G.S. Bulletin 770, "The Data of Geochemistry" shows that at the present rate of increase of sodium in the ocean a little more than 89 million years would be enough to supply all the sodium in the ocean, even if there were none there at the beginning.)

On reading Osborn's argument, the writer said to himself, "Goodness gracious, Man, what kind of figuring are you doing? Don't you realize that the primal ocean of necessity would be a salt water ocean? Don't you realize that only a small part of the sodium of the ocean would originate by leaching of the land? The rest would be there from the beginning, and far less than 60 million years would be sufficient to give the ocean its present sodium content."

That was the argument the writer used to himself. The words in which his thoughts were expressed were much more violent, as he had a great disrespect for folly when it is perpetrated in the name of science. That argument still stands and every geologist must give it a wide berth or reject evolutionary geology.

Because this sodium theory of estimating the age of the earth was standard two decades ago, geologists are compelled to give it some attention and to discredit if they can, since they now say that the earth is 30 to 40 times as old as their sodium estimates allowed, extravagant as they were. They therefore sometimes point out reasons for believing that the figures in "The Data of Geochemistry" are too high, and they assert that the land stands higher and the rivers run faster now than during most of geologic time. They do not give, and cannot give, any real attention to the fact that the ocean must have been rich in saline matter from the beginning.

Even their argument about sodium being leached from the land more rapidly now than during most of geologic time--as they figure the geologic ages--is nonsense. They agree that in their theory of ages up until the Devonian period the land was bare of more than the most simple and primitive kinds of vegetation. Until then practically nothing in the way of land vegetation existed to protect the land from erosion or leaching, but now plants protect the land from both erosion and leaching, and much of the water which falls and sinks into the soil is drawn up into the plants and evaporated into the air. Then it would simply run off the surface or sink into the land and in time find its way to the ocean, carrying dissolved matter from the land with it. If 60 or 90 millions of years would supply all the sodium of the ocean as thorough now operates, far and away less would be required with the kind of ages the geologists assert, and who of them can deny it, giving valid reasons for such denial? Yet by their present scheme of ages rivers would have to run into the ocean for say 30 times as long as would supply all the sodium of the ocean at the rate of increase which was 'official' a few years ago! And this is without making any allowance for

## The Salts of the Primal Ocean!

This certainly is a most important matter. No reasonable explanation for the ocean can be given which would make it other than very salty at the start. For instance, the standard assumption now (to which some few geologists take exception) is that the earth was once molten with heat. Under those conditions nearly all the water of the earth would be part of the atmosphere as water vapor. Certainly much of the chlorine would be vaporized too, the sulphur also, and carbon dioxide. This would give a very acid rain upon the surface of the earth as the temperature fell, the acids dissolving the sodium, calcium, magnesium and potassium of the land and making a very saline ocean.

At the present time the ocean is so salty that for 47 parts of water there is one part of chlorine. Occasional geologists, without stopping to think of the facts of the case, say that the chlorine of the ocean comes, or came, from volcanoes, yet the figures in "The Data of Geochemistry", which are admittedly official and presumably not far from correct, show that chlorine is emitted in very small amounts from volcanoes in comparison with water, carbon dioxide, sulphur and some other substances. Volcanoes do not emit chlorine in sufficient amounts to make the ocean contain appreciably more. The only scientific conclusion is that the chlorine of the ocean must have been abundant from the beginning, and with it would be great amounts of sodium, magnesium, potassium and sulphur ($SO_4$). Very, very little time would therefore be needed to give the ocean its present sodium content.

In this connection the sulphur, potassium and magnesium content is very significant in connection with the possible age of the ocean. Like sodium, when these go into solution in the ocean, they stay in solution, although some magnesium may be withdrawn by shell fish or by base exchange, and very small amounts of the sulphur and potassium may also be withdrawn from sea water. One cannot figure a primal ocean which was not rich in sulphates, but these increase at such a rate by river flow that in a little more than ten million years the ocean would be fully supplied with them, even if there were none there at the beginning. All the potassium would be supplied by this flow in ten million years and all the magnesium in 19 million years (by figures from "The Data of Geochemistry"). If any geologist does not like these conclusions, let him decide that the ocean could be 20 millions years old, and then let him try to figure how rivers could run to the ocean for 2,000 million years, or 100 times as long!

These facts confront all geologists who will accept them. How they are going to get 100 miles of sediment laid down by uniformity and coal beds galore made by uniformity in the time facts will allow, neither they not I know, and they certainly will not say. How the organic evolutionists are toing to evolve worms from nothing and insects from worms, how they are going to evolve fishes from invertebrates and the higher vertebrates from fishes in the time available, they refuse to state. All they can do is to assume that the earth is old, without meeting evidence that the earth is not old. This is modern science as set forth by evolutionists.

Geologists assert that the earth is very old. The so-called evidence they give is in flat conflict with what they thought was good evidence for a much younger earth a couple of decades ago, and it it definitely inconsistent with such evidence. There are also fundamental flaws in their alleged evidence for an old earth. If any person wishes to deny this statement, our columns are open for such denial. Give your reasons for believing that the earth is old and we will show that those reasons are wrong.

Meanwhile I ask that all persons who read this, evolutionists and creationists alike, remember that both evolutionary geology and organic evolution go to ruin if the earth is not many scores of millions of years old; yet it is not that old and cannot be. Tell how the sun could give heat so long if the earth is very old; tell how the moon came into existence and why it is not farther from the earth if the earth-moon system is really old; explain why there is not more helium in the atmosphere; tell how volcanic activity could operate for long ages; tell how water could be emitted from within the earth for 2,000 million years without covering every mountain on earth; tell how frivers could run into the sea for long ages without making the ocean more salty than it is. If you cannot do this, be a true scientist and agree that the earth is not old.

### "Go Make a Fossil"

Delight has been expressed from several persons with Major Wren's challenge to evolutionary geologists to go make a fossil. One correspondent wonders how they will wiggle out of it.

The answer to this is easy: they will not try to wiggle out of it; they will simply ignore the challenge. That has been a foundation principle of evolution from the beginning: whenever there is a difficulty, skip it. They know they cannot make fossils experimentally in a manner which will fit the geology of uniformity: therefore they will not try to do so.

One former science teacher, an author of certain pro-evolution books, did write making the intentional quibble that to make a true fossil would take perhaps a thousand years, which is too long a for an experiment. He realized fully the fact that Major Wren pointed out: that with the normal burial in mud which might possibly happen now, a fish or other soft bodied creature would rot so quickly that in a few weeks, or months, or a year, there would be no distinct trace of it and proof would be given that such burial would NOT result in a fossil. If I am wrong, it will be easy to prove me wherg in this statement: go bury some fish in the mud, or bury a depth of rabbit, then dig it up in a few months if you can.

In this connection there is one point I wish to bring up. Frequently we see mention of footprints in slabs of rocks, or ripple marks, or mud cracks, as proving that the rocks were long in the making. This is evidence against unformity, not for it. I wrote to a geologist, telling him he could never such things forming now so as to be preserved. He replied that he has seen them often. So have I: ripple marks on the beach, cracks in soft mud, tracks of things in the mud. A tide has come in and swept away the ripple marks, making new ones, obliterating the tracks of creatures which walked over mud or sand. A river has risen and destroyed completely marks of rain drops or cracks in the mud.

Go the world over, along ocean shore or river side and find footprints, cracks or ripple marks made a year earlier and on the way to be preserved to future generations, and you will find something which no one else has seen since geology became a so-called science. We can add to the challenge: Go make a fossil, the challenge: Go find the ripple marks of a year ago. When one gets down to chases it is striking how many of the arguments for evolution prove to be arguments against it.

### ***

### Submarine Canyons, Glacial Phenomena and the Flood.

SCIENCE of April 15, 1938, contains a condribution from A. H. Fretz of Lehigh University which seems very speculative but which has some striking ideas in connectionwith the phenomena upon which the theory of an ice ages immediately preceding the present epoch are based. The subject is important to creationists since this theory of an ice age provides a stumbling block to Bible chronology and to the acceptance of the Flood account.

There are on the continental shelves of North America and in other parts of the earth "submarine canyons" that resemble closely canyons cut out by streams on land. Their form suggests that they were made by streams, but how this could be when they are below sea level puzzles geologists. If they were not formed by stream flow, they probably are fissures which formed when the continents were uplifted after the Flood. If they were much older than that sedimentation should have filled them by now . However, there is no agreement regarding their origin.

Prof. Fretz believes that they came by erosion and suggests the possibilitity that some asteroid or other celestial body passed close to the earth thousands of years ago and drew water from the ocean in the Tay that some geologists believe a passing star may have drawn matter from the sun to cause the solar system to form. This would lower the ocean level and give stream flow the opportunity to cut the submarine canyons. Prof. Fretz thinks that this water was held for a while in the form of salty ice over the earth something as the rings of Saturn are held over that planet, but that these rings changed into icy mist which was recipated upon the earth and did much to cause the phenomena which are responsible for the theory of the ice age.

Since space is not available here to give Prof. Fretz paper, I suggest that persons particularly interested in the matter look it up in SCIENCE. Let it be understood that his views are given as a speculative hypothesis, not as a proved theory, or a theory which should be adopted without careful study and investigation. The writer does not believe that it will endure such study, particularly in that feature demanding the removal of water from the ocean by the passing of some celestial body.

However, certain other features seem significant. The presence of such water in the form of ice high above the earth suggests strongly "the waters above the firmament" mentioned in the first chapter of Genesis, the precipitation of which helped cause the Flood as "the windows of heaven were opened". The fall of a large part of this moisture as ice in the higher latitudes might cause "ice age phenomena" to come by catastrophe and not by accumulation during long ages. These "ice age phenomena" could therefore have a basis in fact, but they would originate by catastrophe as an incident to the Flood and not by any real ice age. In fact, careful investigation of the ice age theory shows it to be nonsense.

The hypothesis of Prof. Fretz may be faulty in places, but it at least is very striking in its indication of the possibility of the catastrophic nature of 'ice age' phenomena and in its resemblance in certain ways to the canopy theory of the Flood. If SCIENCE, the leading news magazine of the scientists of America, can present an hypothesis like this, certainly it would seem that Flood geologists could believe in the possibility of the catastrophic origin of the so-called glacial phenomena of the alleged ice ages.

On the canopy theory itself, there seem to be in it features worthy of respect, though like some other theories which are worthy of respect, much nonsense seems to have been tied to it too. In some other issue we may discuss the theory at greater length.

\*\*\*

## The Nature and Scripture Study Club of Grand Rapids.

(From Philadelphia comes a request from a theological student on some way to organize a society there, and at the request of The Creationist Dr. John P. Van Haitsma, Professor of Organic Sciences at Calvin College, Grand Rapids, tells of the activity of the Club named above, or which he is president. Surely similar societies could be organized elsewhere and be of great value in showing the harmony between Scripture and true science.)

This club is composed of men and women who avowedly accept the infallibility of the Bible. They are all college graduates who have revealed more that an ordinary interest in natural science. The membership includes a minister, a doctor of medicine, a dentist, several high school or college teachers of biology, of physic, and of chemistry, a teacher of philosophy, a nature writer, and several grade school teachers. There are nineteen members in all. The minister in our club, the Reverend William Hendriksen, has the respect of all of our members not only because he has studied natural science and is interested in it, but also because he is an able and a cautious exegete of Scripture.

The club has adopted a program of studies which will require several years for their completion. During the past two years the Reverend Hendriksen has introduced most of the topics for discussion at our meetings. The topics were subdivisions of the Biblical description of the origin of the universe. These topics were known to the members at least a month before the meeting at which they were discussed. When a topic has been introduced the members of the club discuss the ideas presented and try to apply them to the data of the various sciences. In this way we have had very interesting and profitable meetings.

At times we learned that Scripture does not actually teach what we had supposed. The importance of a knowledge of the Bible as a criterion for science has become much clearer and therefore more vital to us. To form a truly integrated world view we found that it is necessary to distinguish carefully between fact and conclusion in science. For this purpose the check of one member upon another has proved invaluable. We have faced problems which we could not solve satisfactorily. This was to be expected, for our knowledge of nature and Scripture is confessedly imperfect. However, we have also discovered some very striking agreements between science and the Bible. They confirm our faith in our method of study and they stimulate us to increase our efforts. Our evenings always seem altogether too short.

From the foregoing description it will be evident that small, local groups of interested students are better adapted for the study of the concordances between nature and Scripture than larger organizations whose members live far apart. Our club holds seven meetings a year. For the sake of a more sociable atmosphere we meet at the homes of the members. Small groups are apt to be more congenial and therefore promote more intimate discussions. Sometimes one member will loan a book to another to help to explain some problem. If several local groups like ours could be formed in different parts of the country they might cooperate for each other's benefit. Our club would encourage the organization of such groups.

The secretary of our club is Dr. E. Y. Monsma, 1236 Allerton Avenue, Grand Rapids, Michigan.

****

## A Mixture of Fossils

An item in SCIENCE for April 29, 1938, has an important bearing on the recent discussion in The Creationist about the way that fossils were segregated in the different formations. Near Cumberland, Md., has been found "an ancient cavern death-trap, where Ice-Age beasts perished and left their bones in great masses.... Remains of nothern creatures like wolverine and marten are mingled with those of southern animals like tapir and alligator. The West is represented with fossils of such prairie or plains animals as wild horses and coyotes. No table were some enormous cats, as big as lions or tigers..." Of course, explanations can be devised for the mingling of creatures whose natural habitats were as different as the ones named, but the trouble with such explanations is that they do not explain, they develop more difficulties than they resolve. Any Flood geologist who devises an explanation of the manner by which these fossils came to be where they are is likely to be badly mistaken, and any ages geologist who tries for such an explanation is certain to be wrong. We had better be careful about trying to explain certain conditions until we are pretty sure that we have all the data we need for them.

*****

## Announcements

This issue of The Creationist will probably be the last until after the summer vacation. How much longer it will continue then remains to be seen. The expenses of publication, though small, are still well above the income. However, certain problems on creation should be threshed out, and our purpose is to continue publication until these issues are clarified. Here and there thinking men are waking up as a result of reading The Creationist and their influence is bound to be felt. We have two great problems: 1. To arouse Christian leaders to recognize the need of interest, knowledge and action on creation. This seems to be a hopeless task. 2. To get the scientists to face the issue in a formal discussion of either evolutionary geology or organic evolution. Corespondence on how this

THE

# BULLETIN

OF

# DELUGE GEOLOGY

## AND RELATED SCIENCES

| Volume I | June, 1941 | Number I |
|---|---|---|

## CONTENTS

## FOREWORD

" . . . all the fountains of the great deep (were) broken up, and the windows of heaven were opened. . . . And the waters prevailed exceedingly upon the earth; and all the high hills . . . and the mountains . . . And all flesh died that moved upon the earth, . . . and every man . . . and Noah only remained alive, and they that were with him in the ark. . . . And the waters returned from off the earth, going and returning (margin). Gen. 7:11, 19, 20, 21, 23; 8:3.

There are two current explanations for the geologic formations of the crust of the earth as they are found today. One accounts for these features as a result of natural processes which have been operating through countless ages of the past. The other holds that such formations are the result of a catastrophe of world magnitude. The theory of uniformitarianism (that nature has always proceeded as at present), as elaborated by modern geologists, is a little more than a century old. The belief in a universal Deluge is as old as written history.

Since there are no other admitted possibilities, and since the two accounts are mutually contradictory, one or the other of them must be wrong. Putting aside the authority of the Old Testament Scriptures for the moment, and viewing the situation purely on a scientific basis, which of the two accounts is in closest agree-

The BULLETIN is published by, and is the official organ of the "Society For the Study of Deluge Geology and Related Sciences." The Editorial Board is comprised of Professor George McCready Price and Dr. Cyril B. Courville. It is printed at the Collegiate Press, Arlington, California. For members the BULLETIN is free, and extra copies 30 cents each (each number priced according to size); for non-members it is $2.00 per year; and this number is 40 cents. All correspondence should be directed to the Managing Editor, Mr. Ben F. Allen, 219 North Grand Avenue, Los Angeles, California.

73

ment with the facts of geology? The truth must lie in the testimony of the rocks, if this source of information can be correctly read and rightly interpreted. To this source of information, every scientist, every honest seeker after truth, must submit his thesis.

Even to the superficial student of Geology, certain fundamental facts seem to be self evident. It is agreed generally that the very uniform strata of the earth's crust imply the action of water. The disruption of the earth's crust which is evidently responsible for mountain formation indicates the action of some tremendous superimposed force, effecting its influence in great lines and extensive areas of the several continents. A study of the fossils, moreover, indicates a profound change sometime in the past in the types and distribution of the fauna and flora of the earth, a change which has evidently been accompanied by a climatic change of no small degree. Upon these data, which all geologists can accept as basic, a study of the two conceptions may be undertaken.

It is worth while to canvass the field in an effort to see whether, on the face of things, there is any good reason whatever to believe that a Deluge may have occurred. We believe there is. The sudden disappearance of families of gigantic reptiles and of many mammals, the formation of great coal fields, often hundreds of miles in extent, the formation of great deserts by recedence of great inland lakes, the abrupt change of climate at the poles from warm to cold as well as the unique universal lamination of the sedimentary layers of the earth's crust can better be explained by a universal Flood than by any long-continued process known to man. This superficial evidence is sufficiently substantial to warrant a more critical investigation of the details.

On the other side, the facts which weigh heavily against the doctrine of uniformitarianism are the universal stratification of the earth's crust without any locally complete record of the "geologic ages"; the reversal of these layers and other irregularities in a number of extensive areas; the occurrence of fossil "graveyards" which indicate sudden destruction of animals in large numbers (without historical counterpart) ; the testimony of fossil trees standing through many laminations of coal thus refuting the theory that coal has been ages in the making, the absence of even a solitary example of an imperfect transitional fossil form of the countless failures which must have lived and died if organic evolution were true, and finally a failure to account for the radical change in climate which evidently occurred at some time in the past.

With much evidence in favor of a universal deluge and a number of facts which militate against the acceptance of the long-age theory of the formation of the earth's crust, it would seem as though any fair minded individual would be compelled to recognize the possibility, and to admit the likelihood, of a Deluge at least seriously enough for scientific consideration. The critical testing of any theory which has any merits is legitimate. It is now proposed that the Deluge "theory" be put to the crucial test, not only as to the general geologic phenomena, but as to the details of the various related sciences.

Many biological and botanical features of plants and animals in the past as compared to those of the present, together with the principles of geography, climatology, ecology, paleontology, oceanography, hydrology, geophysics, chemistry, mineralogy, archeology, ethnology, philology and certain phases of astronomy, as well as other sciences, are necessary in developing the history of the earth and its life. Research is going forward in all of these sciences to construct, if possible, a more reasonable and scientific history of the earth and its life than current theories afford. If the Bible statements are true, only by developing the facts underlying them can this be done.

This is the object of the *Society for the Study of the Deluge Geology and Related Sciences*, organized some three years ago under the encouragement and stimulation of Professor George McCready Price. The Society is non-denominational and has for its only essential thesis, the literal interpretation of the Book of Genesis and other Scriptures relating thereto. If the Deluge did occur, it is believed that the scientific facts now available, or easily discoverable, will abundently prove it.

This BULLETIN is published by the Society to record for the use of resident and distant members and other interested individuals, worthwhile source material which has been presented before the organization. In this way it is hoped to accumulate material which will be useful to Christian workers and Bible Students. This publication must of necessity be small at first. It has no endowment and therefore its continued existence depends upon the support of those interested in its message. As the number of members and subscribers increases, the BULLETIN will be correspondingly enlarged. The support of believers everywhere is therefore earnestly solicited.

*The Editorial Staff*

---

## THE FATE OF THE DINOSAURS

"Fate cropped him short, for be it understood
He would have lived much longer, if he could."—*IV. B. Rhodes*

"The great race [the dinosaurs] entrenched on earth for so many million years, widespread over the six continents, and consisting of forms which were certainly majestic for their time, silently passed away, leaving the reptilian field to a few relatively unimportant orders, but having no descendants of its own. . . . Then, almost suddenly, at the end of the Cretaceous, and for no obvious cause, the candle flame of their life was extinguished; the wind of some unknown circumstance had blown over it and it was gone. So closed one of the most memorable chapters in the history of life on earth."

"The main problem before us, then, is why towards the close of the Cretaceous period, there were numerous forms of dinosaurs alive and apparently comfortably settled in their respective habits and environments, yet, when the Tertiary era dawned, none was left and the mammals were assuming the dominant position among the land-living forms. Was the cause some world-wide cataclysm of a physical nature, or some widespread epidemic whose ravages have left no trace upon the bones?

"Now, the period of the extinction of the dinosaurs was coincident with the world-wide Lamaride revolution which must have brought profound changes in its train, and which must have supplied the basic geological cause of extinction."

" . . . It is generally agreed, however, that considerable uplift-movements of the land, and a consequent diminution in the extent of the seas, followed, and there was very probably a decrease in the temperature, though this was not so marked as that accompanying other great revolutions."

"The career of the dinosaurs was far from brief, and far from a futile or vain attempt to snatch a permanent hold on the chain of life. Their passing was comparable with, and no less dramatic than, that of a mighty empire of world-wide extent." —Swinton, W. E.: *The Dinosaurs. A Short History of a Great Group of Extinct Reptiles*, London, 1934, pp. 176-187.

# DINOSAURS AND THE DELUGE*

## Prof. George McCready Price

"One of the most inexplicable of events," declares Dr. Charles Schuchert, a well known geologist, speaking of dinosaurs, "is the dramatic extinction of this mighty race."[1]

A "dramatic extinction," as here used, means an extinction which came suddenly, and was universal over the entire globe; while the word "inexplicable" means that this extinction cannot be explained in the terms of the accepted theories of natural science.

The late Henry Fairfield Osborn also expressed surprise at the sudden and universal extinction of these animals, for he said: "The cutting off of this giant dinosaur dynasty was nearly, if not quite, simultaneous the world over."[2]

The question naturally arises, What was it that killed them all off? We all know that reptiles are notoriously tough and hard to kill. This applies to all the various kinds of reptiles still living, whether snakes, alligators, lizards, or turtles, all of which are included in the class reptiles. They are not much subject to diseases, nor to external or internal parasites. And many of them today are among the longest lived animals now living, some turtles or tortoises being known to live for more than two hundred years. All these facts add to the mystery of the sudden and complete extinction of that mighty race, the ancient dinosaurs. What but a universal Flood could possibly have killed them all off, and "simultaneously the world over"? And this conclusion is rendered even more inevitable when we learn that their bones or skeletons are universally found

where they must have been buried by vast currents of flowing water, often in regions like the high plateaus of Wyoming and other parts of Western America, or the dry tablelands of central Asia, where large volumes of water are now unknown.

### GIANT LIVING TANKS

The dinosaurs comprised some of the most gigantic animals which ever walked on dry land. Several fairly complete skeletons have been recovered which are 70 or more feet long, with a body that must have weighed 30 or 40 tons, or as much as ten full grown elephants. James D. Dana says that, if we did not have the positive evidence of the bones themselves, we might have thought that such masses of living flesh would be too gigantic for muscles to move on dry land. But any one who has visited any of the larger museums in this country or in Europe has seen the actual bones themselves, these bones being sometimes fairly fresh-looking, and not at all highly mineralized.

Of course, they were not all such monstrous brutes. Some were no bigger than an ordinary alligator, while others were even smaller. But they were among the most bizarre or odd-looking creatures imaginable.

For instance, the *Stegosaurs* were covered with a complete coat of mail, like a modern crocodile, the hide of which will resist a rifle bullet. But the Stegosaurs were as heavy as an ordinary elephant, with fairly long and sturdy legs, and a body flattened laterally, with two rows of large plates of horny material along the ridge of the back from the head to the tail, the latter being armed with massive

*Presented before the Deluge Society on Dec. 21, 1940.

[1] Shuchert, Charles: *"A Text Book of Geology,"* 1915, p. 842.
[2] Osborne, H. F.: in *Century Magazine,* 68: 608-694, 1904, cited by Mathew in *Dinosaurs,* 1915, p. 150.

spokes several inches in length. Some of the dorsal plates were nearly two feet in size. In the museum in Berlin, Germany, I was shown a specimen of one of these creatures from East Africa which had massive spikes instead of the flat plates along the back. These Stegosaurs had very small heads, and diminutive brains. They were probably vegetable feeders, and harmless enough; but their massive armor rendered them like living, traveling citadels, almost immune to attack.

*Triceratops* is the name of another kind of massive animal weighing several tons, with a strong horn over the nose, like a rhinoceros, but with an additional horn over each eye. The skull had a massive extension backward over the entire neck, making the skull sometimes six or seven feet long. They were evidently formidable fighters, as is evidenced by fractured and healed jaws and horns, with neck-crests and even skulls that have been pierced and healed again. Two of these old warriors charging at each other like infuriated rhinoceroses or wild bulls must have been a terrifying spectacle.

### EXTINCTION "DRAMATIC" AND "SIMULTANEOUS"

There were also monstrous carnivorous dinosaurs, with sturdy hind legs and massive tail, like a kangaroo, but with diminutive front legs which must have been of little use except for assisting in eating. The body was stout and strong, weighing several tons; the head was massive with a large mouth and a formidable array of teeth; and the creature when standing erect on its tripod of tail and hind feet must have reached a height of twenty-five or thirty feet. Then if we may suppose it to have been as active accordingly as a modern "skidoo lizard," it must have been able to travel with amazing speed, probably faster than any modern automobile. Alto-

gether it must have been a very formidable animal. One of these carnivorous monsters has been named *Tyrannosaurus rex,* meaning king of the tyrant monsters, a name which seems very appropriate.

A very interesting kind of flying reptile was the *Pterodactyl,* which though having a long tail might be supposed to resemble somewhat a modern bat; for its long wings had a spread of fifteen or twenty feet, and must have enabled it to fly with ease and rapidity. Its head had a long beak, somewhat like a bird; but unlike most of the other reptiles its brain was large, probably indicating an active habit of life. The pictures which have been made to indicate what it looked like may be very misleading; for one cannot help thinking that it may have been of a beautiful appearance. And when one remembers the reptile in the tree of the Garden of Eden, one cannot help wondering whether or not this charmer resembled these Pterodactyls, whose skeletons are now to be seen in several of our modern museums.

Men and all the higher vertebrates have a fixed size at maturity. But reptiles (and also fishes) continue to grow as long as they live; so that the size of a turtle or crocodile or dinosaur tells us something of the duration of its life. Of course, each type of animal even among the reptiles and fishes has its own regular standard of size; but the fact that they keep on growing as long as they live, is to be taken into account when we see the monstrous skeletons of these ancient creatures, some of which probably kept on growing for many centuries.

It is certainly better for us that they are now all gone. And yet their "dramatic extinction" cannot well be accounted for except on the basis of a world-wide cataclysm, such as the Bible describes under the name of the Flood. Marine reptiles have been found as fossils in Australia and the extreme end of South America; while the gigantic land reptiles occur not only throughout much of the Great Plains region of North America, but also Belgium and England, East Africa, Madagascar, and in many places in Eastern Asia. And throughout all these regions, these ancient reptiles seem to have disappeared at one time, even on the testimony of the evolutionists. Note again the words of Osborn, who certainly could not be accused of being prejudiced in favor of a world-catastrophe:

"The cutting off of this giant dinosaur dynasty was nearly if not quite simultaneous the world over."

## How Separate the Fossils?

But we need to remember that there were also gigantic mammals, like the titanothers, the megatheriums, the balucitharium, and the mastodons, which also became extinct in a very unaccountable way, their skeletons also being found in almost all parts of the world. And no reliable scientific reasons can be advanced for separating the extinction of these warm-blooded mammals from that of the reptiles, nor indeed for separating any of these from the burial and extinction of the countless invertebrates, like the crustaceans and shell fish whose remains are found in the rocks of the entire globe. Only a fantastic theory which cannot stand critical examination prompts the evolutionists to put some of these extinctions and burials in one age and some in another. There is no shadow of a scientific reason for putting their extinction in a serial order.

A multitude of good, sound, scientific reasons tell us that all these destructions of former living things took place *at one time,* and that this time corresponds to that time spoken of in the Bible, when "the world that then was, being overflowed with water, perished." (II Peter 3:6).

### DISCUSSION

Many questions were asked Prof. Price, and much additional information was brought out.

One student of Deluge Geology raised the point as to the proper objective of Deluge Geology research in connection with Dinosaur remains. He suggested that excavations be conducted wherever the remains are found with a view of finding Mammal bones mingled with those of the Dinosaur, thus proving that Mammals and Dinosaurs were contemporary, and were both destroyed by the same catastrophe.

Another stated that he had two locations in mind where the foot-prints of man are reported by unscientific observers to be mingled with those of the Dinosaur, reports which he intends to investigate. He said that evolutionary geology now puts some ninety-five million years between mammals and Dinosaurs. The still unexplained etching on the wall of the Hava Supai Canyon, a branch of the lower Grand Canyon, of a Man and an Elephant fighting, and the plain etching of a Dinosaur, was brought up also.

Prof. Price reminded the Society that these data would, if found to be fully authentic, upset the whole theory of the geologic ages and evolution.

References on man's foot-prints even two-hundred and fifty million years before man entered the supposed evolutionary picture are as follows: Science News Letter, Oct. 29, 1938; Signs of the Times, Apr. 25 and May 2, 1939, and Sept. 3, 1940. Scientific American, Jan. 1940. In the last reference the geologist says that "If these foot-prints are human (and no objective facts are given to the contrary) "we may as well quit and get a job driving a truck."

# DELUGE ICE DATA FROM OCEAN DEPTHS*

## Benjamin Franklin Allen

The gigantic frozen animals in the frigid north, still saving in perfect refrigeration even the food in their stomachs, are still unexplained by current science. Fossil palms, breadfruit, and other tropical vegetation in those same lands, with these and the superabundance of cool plants in both Arctic and Antarctic lands, undeniably give those frozen animals a tropical environment and prove a tropical climate for all present frigid regions.

But what about the living things in the ocean waters, especially the microscopic forms and various corals and shells, which leave their remains in the ooze on the bottom and in coral and other formations? They are amazingly d e l i c a t e and accurate self-recording thermometers, far more accurate than life on the lands. Better still, they make *a continuous record from the very beginning to the present day,* without the slightest interruptions, thus "covering" the whole episode of the sudden chill of the world, including both prior and subsequent conditions.

In this study we shall reveal the record made by these ocean-bottom thermometers. Then we shall compare it with the better-known records made by the land-living fossils. Finally we shall present evidence that many of these tropical ocean-bottom formations were upheaved upon the lands, where we find them today in all climates. If it can be shown that the sudden chilling of the oceans coincided with the general upheaval of the ocean bottoms containing tropical remains, with similar upheavals on land, and that these movements are substantially related to the overdashing of the oceans over the lands, this will dovetail into other constructive evidence of the universal Deluge.

### CORES FROM THE NORTH ATLANTIC OCEAN

Dr. C. S. Piggot, of the Carnegie Geophysical Laboratory, invented a torpedo tube ten feet long which he shoots straight downward in the ooze.[1] It is open at both ends and of course fills with a cross-section of the ooze. Later, in the laboratory, it is examined chemically, microscopically, and biologically. About a dozen soundings were made between Newfoundland and the coast of Ireland, and the tubes were examined by Dr. Wilmott H. Bradley, the director of the U. S. Geological Survey, and a staff of specialists.[2]

In several of the cores the top layer is about a foot thick, and is composed of the remains of microscopic plants and animals, some of which live in the surface waters and some on the bottom. In the U. S. Geological Survey Professional Paper cited here, enlarged photographs of these microscopic forms are shown. In this top layer are found all the forms now living in those waters, and they are classed as belonging in moderately cold waters. Some fine windblown, or atmosphere volcanic dust was found near the bottom of this layer.

Below this layer were found in several of the cores three or four feet of the remains of life forms belonging to frigid waters. Mixed with these, and forming a large part of the whole, are silt, sand, and gravel, and some

---

*Read before the Deluge Society, September 21, 1940.

[1] Piggot, Charles S.: Core Samples of the Ocean Bottom and Their Significance, *Scientific Monthly,* March, 1938, p. 201.

[2] Bradley, Wilmot H.: Geology and Climatology from the Ocean Abyss, *Scientific Monthly,* February, 1940, p. 97.

*Ibid:* Deep Sea Core Samples, *U. S. G. S. Professional Paper,* 196-A, 1940, p. 39.

of the gravel is as large as a half inch in size. But interspersed, are two or three layers or streaks of ooze of life-forms belonging to waters much warmer than even the present, and containing none of the inorganic material as found in the cold-water zone, but the higher one contained a mingling of glacial remains and life remains of the colder sort. Dr. Bradley stresses the latter gradation.[3]

Dr. W. Schott (1925-27) used a tube about a yard long in sounding the muds of the tropical Atlantic, and found the same cold water life remains, but with no sand, silt, or gravel. Dr. Bradley cites data from dredgings in the far southern frigid and temperate waters, (mentioning boulders and rocks, which of course Dr. Biggot's small 2½-inch tube could not get), indicating a similar approach northward of cold waters at one time, though this evidence is not yet as well developed as that now in hand from the North Atlantic.

Below the cold water zone, the more representative cores, of which Dr. Bradley takes number seven as an example, the cold forms and the sand, silt, and gravel cease. The remainder of these cores is composed of very pure remains of warm water life. The two biologists, specialists in marine life, who examined these forms declared them to be tropical. The cores did not reach to the bottom of these tropical oozes.

DR. BRADLEY'S INTERPRETATION

The top layer as representing the present moderately cool era, with its pumice perhaps from the volcanic Azores or Iceland; and middle layer of colder water forms in a liberal mass of sand, silt, and gravel from floating land ice, this layer representing the Ice Age or some part thereof; and

the two or three streaks of warm water remains within the glacial zone and the lower mass of pure remains of warm water life of unknown depth as representing possible inter-glacial periods—these are Dr. Bradley's leading views.

Of the geologic periods and the rate of deposit of these layers, he said, "In our interpretation of the deposits penetrated by the cores, we have followed the principle long ago laid down by Lyell." His estimate is one inch to a thousand years, but he says: "Sedimentation is ten times more rapid in the blue mud zone off the Newfoundland Banks than it is at the site of the core just west of the mid-Atlantic ridge, and it is the slowest on the crest of the mid-Atlantic ridge."[4]

VIEWS OF THE BIOLOGISTS

Dr. A. J. Cushman and L. S. Henbest said, in discussing climate changes: "The globigerinides characteristic of very warm surface waters were not found in abundance in the top samples of the cores, but in some of the lower zones, in several cores warm water species were present in great abundance. . . ."[5] They postulate a shifting of the warm Gulf Stream to account for this.

Note their statements, in part, on the tropical part of the cores: (1). "It is evident from these charts (many charts showing marked climatic changes) that several alternations of periods of colder and warmer than the present have occurred during the time represented by the sediments in these cores."[6] (2) A certain life form "globigerinoides conglobata (H. B. Brady) is a characteristic tropical Gulf Stream form . . . observed in several net hauls of the Meteor Expedition in the Tropical Atlantic . ." (3) Another form "globorotalia men-

---

[3] Bradley, W. H., et al.: Scientific Monthly, February, 1940, pp. 8, 10.
[4] Bradley, W. H., et al.: loc. cit., February, 1940, pp. 98, 101.
[5] Bradley, W. H., et al.: U. S. G. S. Professional Paper, 196-A, 1940, p. 39.
[6] Bradley, W. H., et al.: loc. cit., p. 46.

ardii (D'Orbigny) is reported as abundant in the Pacific around the Hawaiian and Philippine Islands . . . in the tropical Indian Ocean. . . . Schott used this form as an indicator of surface water temperatures comparable to those now prevailing in the tropical part of the Atlantic."[7]

## SOME VIEWPOINTS OF DELUGE GEOLOGY

In the main, little comment is needed by students of Deluge Geology.

1. Of course the idea of "uniformity," that the past was like the present, is to us a doubtful and discredited time-scale all around, but most especially as applied to such radically different deposits as the glacial layer here. Why should a scale worked out for ooze stand for silt, sand, and gravel? Especially do we question this point, because only two cores reached the bottom, the shortest of all, less than two feet long, one striking a submarine lava flow and one on the high mid-Atlantic ridge where Dr. Bradley admits the accumulation is the slowest. The Newfoundland Banks core did not get through even the top layer (showing its extremely irregular thickness) and we see no basis for a comparison there. Again, if Dr. Bradley allows that the Newfoundland Banks bottom is building up ten times as fast as farther out, why couldn't the terrific amount of floating land ice which he pictures deposit material many times that fast? We see light in the very rapid formation of this glacial layer, especially as we are willing to allow perhaps a thousand years before the floating ice ceased. But Dr. Bradley makes no allowance for these features.

2. While some students suggest that this silt, sand, and gravel may be the sedimentation of the agitated and

moving waters of the Deluge ocean, rather than from floating ice, the lack of this inorganic material in the tropical Atlantic, as reported by Dr. W. Schott, seems to halt that interpretation for the present. The waters should have been as much in motion in one place as another. Besides, the very light ooze deposited uniformly throughout this zone seems opposed to that view, as moving waters would have sifted and drifted this light and microscopically fine material. However, Dr. Bradley finds that in the one core from the mid-Atlantic ridge, the finer material is actually missing, but that is in shallow water. What remains, however, is far too fine for swift water.

3. The interfingering of the warm water streaks within the cold water or glacial zone might be laid to the unbalanced condition of the ocean due to rotational disturbance during the Deluge period. Dr. Bradley says that large numbers of warm species would be killed by the sudden intrusion of the colder waters. And these variations can perhaps be laid to variation in the intensity of the ice period during its entire duration, which we allow may have lasted a thousand years, on the well-known theory of the "ice ages" being caused by volcanic dust screening out the Sun's heat from the Earth. A terrific outburst of volcanism would seemingly result from the gigantic crustal convulsions and mountain upheavals postulated for the Deluge period, and the volcanics would dwindle slowly and irregularly.

4. Another item under this head is the number of life forms oddly out of place in the various layers, and some shallow water forms that do not belong there at all. To us, these microscopic "erratics" seem to suggest irregular movements of the ocean.

---

[7] Bradley, W. H.: *U. S. G. S. Professional Paper,* 196-A, 1940, p. 46.

5. One might object: "Where were the cold water life forms before the Deluge, during the world-wide tropical climate?" But Dr. Cushman and Dr. Henbest answer this by citing certain Globigerina bulloides that thrive in both cold and warm waters.[8] Speaking much more broadly, the whole realm of fossils apparently demanding a tropical climate, certain forms identical to them are now thriving in cold climates, while others are found only in the tropics. Adaption to climatic change has differed widely, and apparently is mostly responsible for extinction of forms.

6. In 1883 Krakatoa's smoke and dust lowered the temperature of the whole world 12 per cent (15-20 degrees) for many months, and 3 to 6 per cent (4-8 degrees) for several years, and Katmai in 1912 lowered the temperature as much as 18 per cent (20-30 degrees) in the northern hemisphere for some weeks. Scientists say even one degree lower would finally produce a mild ice age.[9] Yet Dr. Bradley and his staff failed to find any trace of those or even the many greater volcanic outbursts within historic times. Even a trace of the modern great eruption in near-by Iceland, they also failed to find. This leads us to the idea that the dust they did find stands for far more tremendous outbursts than we might casually expect if we did not mention these late explosions and their marked climatic effects. These matters call for more attention. They seem to mean more than was at first apparent.

7. As we shall presently show, there are many masses of rock and countless beds of ocean fossils now on land, even in the coldest climates, which could only have been formed in tropical waters. Can the pure chalky remains of tropical ocean life found in the lower part of some of the Piggot cores be identified with any of the great beds of chalk so widely distributed on land? Were any of the chalk beds tropical? This should be easy to determine. If they were, we would consider them of the pre-Deluge period to which we propose to assign the tropical ooze in the bottom of the Piggot cores, and postulate the crustal upheavals which raised them out of the oceans as one feature of the dynamics of the Deluge period. Practically all other ocean-bottom life-forms are to be seen abundantly in geologic strata on land. Why not these Piggot core strata, especially the pre-Deluge parts thereof?[10] But, according to our theory, we should not generally find counterparts on land of the Deluge and post-Deluge features of these strata, because we hold that there has been no occasion since the Deluge for extensive upheavals of ocean bottom. We are only too anxious for a factual showdown on all these points.

CONCLUSIONS AND POSSIBLE SEQUENCE OF EVENTS

From our viewpoint of the rather incomplete facts, the approximate sequence of events may have been: (1) the original ocean bottom when life first started in the waters; (2) the warm water life in those waters; (3) the sudden chilling of the waters to frigid; (4) the chilling accompanied by rapid droppings of land glacial sand, silt, and gravel, (with even large boulders and rocks dredged up in former years by other means), with a somewhat prevalent sprinkling of volcanic dust indicating at least some obscuration of the Sun; (5) then the gradual warming up of the waters to the present temperature, much as Dr. Bradley suggests, with a thin streak of

---

[8] Bradley, W. H.: *U. S. G. S. Professional Paper,* 196-A, 1940, p. 46.
[9] Griggs, Robert F.: *The Valley of Ten Thousand Smokes,* pp. 32-44.
[10] In a recent letter to the writer, Dr. Bradley admits basic facts supporting this conclusion.

local pumice low in the streak, but no more glacial droppings.

Dr. Bradley is hopeful that with the Piggot device we may learn when the Sahara began blowing dust into the Mediterranean, and he hopes for other interesting investigations. The possibilities are very promising.

However, there are further facts of an entirely different nature in the depths which to us mean practically the same thing which the Piggot cores mean. In fact, these cores give them new significance and reinforce their message as interepreted in terms of Deluge Geology.

### THE FACTS FROM FUNAFUTI

What further deposits do we find in the ocean, and on the land, which could only have been formed while the ocean was much warmer than it is today? And do these deposits also indicate a much colder period than the present, as do the Piggot cores? Our object is to show that our great atolls and coral reefs, those now living, those now dead in waters far too cold for them, and those which were raised out on land, all tell a connected story of one event, the Deluge, and of that which followed after.

A well was drilled 1114 feet deep on the tropical Atoll Island of Funafuti, South Pacific Ocean.[11] Core samples were taken about every ten feet, and these were studied chemically and microscopically. The following table shows a few representative cores all the way down. The key to this data is mainly the sharp differences in the amounts of magnesium in the rock as the bit went down. A vast number of chemical experiences have proved that the warmer the water the more the lime in this rock is dissolved out and the more the magnesium from the sea water takes its place. Therefore, the more magnesium, the warmer the water indicated. Technically, the animal remains forming this atoll are mostly not corals, but we need not go into that much detail. Ocean life in all warm oceans exceed the same kinds living in colder waters in the amount of magnesium their bodies contain.

James G. Dana in 1843 reported 38.07 per cent of magnesium carbonate in a rock from a coral island in the Pacific, and suggested it had been enriched from the water by replacing the lime. "Since Dana's observations were made, many other investigators have recorded similar enrichments of coral reefs, and the synthetic experiments of various chemists, as cited in the preceeding pages, have shown that the indicated reaction can actually take place." In all, Clarke gives fifteen pages of experiments and data, and these experiments indicate that this special form of magnesium rock is an alteration resulting from warm water.[12]

| Depth in feet | Enrichment in magnesium oxide. % | |
|---|---|---|
| 4 | 4.23 | |
| 13 | 7.62 | Present |
| 15 | 6.40 | surface water |
| 20 | 11.99 | cooler than |
| 26 | 16.00 | formerly? |
| 55 | 5.85 | |
| 110 | 2.11 | Sudden cold, |
| 159 | .70 | much colder |
| 200 | 2.70 | than at |
| 250 | 4.90 | present? |
| 400 | 3.10 | |
| 500 | 2.70 | |
| 598 | 1.66 | |
| 640 | 26.33 | |
| 698 | 40.04 | Originally |
| 795 | 38.92 | much warmer |
| 1000 | 40.56 | than at |
| 1114 | 41.05 | present? |

The rows from 13 to 26 are bracketed and marked "13 ft."; the rows from 640 to 1114 are bracketed and marked "474 ft."

Notice that about 13 feet of the rock near the surface is richer in magnesium than that immediately below. The reason is that the surface waters are much warmer than

---

[11] Sollas, W. J.: *The Age of the Earth*, pp. 86-132.
[12] Clarke, F. W.: Data of Geo-Chemistry, *U. S. G. S. Bulletin* No. 770, 1924.

those below, and just warm enough now to deposit that much magnesium. The sudden drop in magnesium from there down represents also all that these colder waters could deposit. But now see how, below 640 feet, it is *suddenly more than twenty times as rich, and finally forty times richer, and nearly three times richer than near the surface.*

This rich bottom rock is called dolomite, because of its high magnesium content. Clarke says: "These figures are remarkable. They show, first, the enrichment in magnesium carbonate near the surface, then irregular rising and falling in much smaller amounts, while below 700 feet the approach to a dolomite ratio is apparent." But, to account for it geologically, he confesses that "What different conditions have existed to account for these differences is not known."[13]

CAN DELUGE GEOLOGY EXPLAIN IT?

Little explanation seems necessary for students of Deluge Geology. Though these facts are old, yet, in the light of the new data from the Piggot cores from the bottom ooze of the North Atlantic, they take on new significance. They seem to tell the same story in a totally different tongue. But after all, haven't we long been ammassing overwhelming fossil evidence of the tropical or sub-tropical climate of the whole world from the beginning till its sudden chill at the Deluge? What could we expect but a very much warmer ocean than at present? And didn't the chill last a long time, finally warming to our present mild "ice age" as compared to the Edenic climate of the fossil world?

These data from Funafuti[14] are accompanied by much more from other coral formations in different parts of the world. In the first place,

these temperatures and their radical changes could not have been local, as the ocean is too deep and mobile to permit that. And you might submerge this island, slowly or rapidly, as you wish, but still these facts do not change their meaning. Other atoll islands were elevated as much as this one was submerged, and have hills and mountains of dolomite of the same richness as at the bottom of this well. Other atolls and reefs were similarly tested in different parts of the world, and though not of the same chemical composition, lacking sufficient magnesium to be dolomite because of differences in the kinds of animals that made the atolls and reefs, they tell the same chemical story. We only wish Piggot's device could test out the oozes in the ocean bottoms around them.

"FOSSIL" REEFS AND ATOLLS ON LAND

Not only have dolomite atoll *islands* and other reefs of different composition been uplifted, but, as Deluge Geology could only expect, we find similar masses on land far from oceans or other waters and even in cold climates. Dr. A. W. Grabau[15] tells about them, showing pictures, and describing how they were formed, and shows fossil reefs, some of which are dolomite, explaining how dolomite formed from limestone. During pre-Deluge time, from this evidence, it appears that it made no difference where in the oceans the dolomite-forming reefs were growing, there was warmth enough to form dolomite in those rocks which had been made from certain marine animals.

Additional Deluge Geology features of these land remnants of pre-Deluge atolls and reefs are, (1), they are all small as compared to their brothers still growing in the present warm

---

13 Clarke, F. W.: *loc. cit.*, pp. 576, 577.

14 Judd, J. W.: The Atoll of Funafuti, *Journal of the Royal Soc.*, London, 1904, pp. 363-389.

15 Grabau, A. W.: *Principles of Stratigraphy*, pp. 417-444, 445, 759, 762.

oceans which were not raised out on land, and (2), because some of these on land are dolomatic.[16] (3) A question for current Geology to answer is: If "geologic time" ever existed, and the lands have been under water for billions of years, why do we not find the same gigantic atolls and reefs on land that we find still growing in the warmest of the oceans? (4). Do we find the dead reefs in the frigid zones and other colder waters no larger than those small ones now high and dry on the lands? Did they grow under the same conditions? There seems to be a correlation here worthy of deeper research. (5). Perhaps an approximation of both pre-Deluge and post-Deluge time can be roughly computed by comparing these "fossil" land reefs with those which were not interrupted in their growth. We have other geologic time checks which we are developing, entirely apart from these.

It is common knowledge that the Artic Ocean contains dead coral reefs, and that they, with other warm-ocean life remains, crop out in it and around it. One authority says: "Silurian coral rocks are plentiful in Siberia and they contain the same kinds of corals as are found in the Artic regions of North America. A chain coral (*Halysites*) and a honeycomb coral (*Favosites*) occur in these rocks on both sides of the Artic Ocean, occurring in one instance at Polaris Bay, 81 degrees north latitude.[17]

Near the South Pole, at Snow Hill Island, remains of corals are abundant, which admittedly prove a warm climate for that region in the past. But proof on this point is uncalled for.

## How Warm Must Corals Be?

At present the farthest north of any living reef coral is the one near the Bermudas, and that only by virtue of the special intensity of the Gulf Stream at that point. But the reef-forming corals of the kinds fossilized in the Frigid zones required waters that never go below 68 degrees F. They thrive up to 78 degrees F., and can live up to 88 degrees F., actual water temperatures. But that takes account only of surface temperatures. Then what about the depths to which they once grew? Why do they not grow in deeper water today? They are now seldom able to grow deeper than 150 feet on account of the increase of cold with depth. But once they grew at many times that depth.

Look again now at the Funafuti record. See the 474 feet of dolomite at the base, with no indication of decline at the bottom of the well, and no one knows how much deeper it runs. And this material not only was formed by atoll-forming animals requiring warm water, but was transformed afterwards to dolomite by waters warmer, perhaps, than the animals needed. We see no way to avoid this except to postulate that this island sank at just the right rate to allow the organisms and the surface warmth to form this dolomite, which seems rather a freak idea in view of the large number of such rock masses in and out of the ocean.

The Great Barrier Reef northeast of Australia is 1250 miles long and it raises in places from a depth of 1800 feet below sea level. New Caledonia Reef is 400 miles long, and some parts very deep. Some atolls are known to be as much as mile from bottom. Of course the reefs grow outward and waves break off fragments which build up the floor of the ocean, but still that does not seem to answer the data as to the former temperature of the waters.

---

[16] Sollas, W. J.: *The Age of the Earth*, pp. 131, 132.
[17] Price, George McCready: *The New Geology*, pp. 396, 397.

## ONLY ONE EVENT RECORDED

Answering to the ocean records of a sudden freeze-up at the start of the Deluge are the still frozen animals and plants of the far north, many buried in what we consider major Deluge strata in contrast to deposits of present superficial drainage. These animals would have decayed at the least delay, and at any subsequent thaw, and the same is true of the hibernating forms being discovered by Russian scientists.[18]

F. W. Clarke emphasizes the sudden change saying: "In short, within three feet the rock changed from almost non-magnesium limestone to one that was strongly dolomitic—."[19] He says it represents an old reef surface, but why isn't that dolomite forming *now* at the surface?

Surely no one would expect that such a change as the world-wide land fossil beds indicate could be recorded otherwise than thus in the oceans. If these things were done repeatedly and by piecemeal over billions of years in scattered localities, why do we find such a one-event record? Even if such temperature changes could be local, which is beyond our comprehension, the many changes over such long periods would have over-lapped many times, and jumbled this one-event record. And if the writer's history is straight, it was partly the tendency among geologists to split up the Deluge ice period into a number of separate events that delivered Geology into the camp of the evolutionists.

## SUMMARY AND CONCLUSIONS

The facts from the Piggot cores, first the ocean bottom and tropical water when life in the water first began, representing the Edenic climate; then the sudden chill of the waters indicated by only colder water life-forms, mingled with sand, silt and gravel droppings from land-ice, representing the Deluge and its ice-period debris; the volcanic pumice therein representing a probable cause of the ice by obscuring the rays of the Sun; and finally the moderately cold layer representing the present climate; these are our main conclusions in adapting the facts of the Piggot cores to Deluge Geology.

Of the facts from Funafuti, which to us tell the same story in different terms, the main features are the lower reaches of the atoll which is of dolomite about three times richer in magnesium than the temperature of those waters can concentrate at the surface today, indicating a very much warmer ocean of old than at present; then a sudden change to very much colder water than at present, as indicated by the very small magnesium content of the rock; finally the surface now moderately cold, yet warmer than the cold period, but able to concentrate only about one-third the magnesium possible during the tropical period which in our view was before the Deluge. Further important facts are the old reefs and atolls of the same dolomite rock, requiring tropical waters for their formation, which we find today upheaved out of the pre-Deluge ocean on the continents in all climes, and the dead reefs in the waters of the Frigid zones which required tropical waters for their formation. To us, these fossil "land" atolls identify the dynamic upheavals of the crust of the earth with the Deluge and the sudden change of climate.

To us these records tell of only one event, because otherwise, they would have overlapped and jumbled and destroyed each other.

---

[18] Allen, B. F.: "The Ten Frozen Horses," *Signs of the Times,* Nov. 28, 1939.
[19] Clarke, F. W.: *loc. cit.,* pp. 576, 577.

# A CHEMIST'S VIEW OF GENESIS[*]

## O. L. Brauer, Ph.D.

(Professor of Chemistry, San Jose State College, San Jose, California)

"The very foundation of our science (geology) is only an inference; for the whole of it rests on the unprovable assumption that, all through the inferred lapse of time which the inferred performance of inferred geological processes involve, they have been going on in a manner consistant with the laws of nature as we know them now. We seldom realize the magnitude of that assumption. . . ."

"The more clearly the immensely speculative nature of geological science is recognized, the easier it becomes to remodel our concepts of any inferred terrestrial conditions and processes in order to make outrages upon them not outrageous."[1]

The members of this society realize the speculative nature of geological science as now taught and I take it we are here to make "outrages" upon it. What a tragedy it is that a theory built on such an unstable foundation has been so widely taught and allowed to do such irreparable damage?

In the first place, we prefer the Christian philosophy based on the Bible as the Word of God because it gives us a logically and scientifically complete and satisfying picture, which the evolutionary and materialist cannot have. We believe that there are many mysteries which the human mind cannot fathom, but which are understood by the Infinite mind of God.

### THE CHEMISTRY OF LIFE

Since the title of this talk suggests the chemist's point of view, let us consider one of the outstanding chemical facts of the earth—life. The evolutionist must assume that somehow the stream of life got started out of non-living matter embodied in compounds or elements that were in no way related to or formed by living organisms. Let us survey the magnitude of the task of preparing a cell of living protoplasm out of non-living substances. Let us kill a living cell and analyze it into its constituents. In these we find fats, carbohydrates, and proteins.

Fats are the simplest of the three kinds of substances. They are composed of the three elements: Carbon, hydrogen, and oxygen. Today these three elements can be confined together in a vessel to themselves, but they show not the slightest tendency to form fats. The chemist making use of the accumulated knowledge of chemistry, could prepare fats from the elements, but it would require twenty separate chemical reactions to prepare the fat, palmitin, the principal fat in the olive. Most of these reactions would be slow, and would have to be carefully controlled.

Chemists are not able to synthesize most of the carbohydrates occurring in the food and in living protoplasm. However, glucose, the simplest and most important of the carbohydrates, can be built up from the elements carbon, hydrogen, and oxygen, but only through a series of twenty-three individual reactions which would have to be intelligently planned and carefully controlled. It is unthinkable that the unguided force of nature could possibly bring about the conditions necessary to reproduce any of these reactions, let alone all of them.

### CAN LIVING PROTEIN BE SYNTHESIZED?

The largest part and the most important part of protoplasm is the proteins. Every living cell must contain several proteins, each one much more complex than anything chem-

---

[*]Presented before the Society for the Study of Deluge Geology, March 15, 1941.

[1] Davis, W. N.: *Science*, May 7, 1926, p. 465.

ists have ever been able to duplicate in the laboratory. Proteins when boiled in acid solution hydrolyse or re-act with water to separate into a group of about eighteen simpler substances known as amino acids, together with a few other substances not so simple.

The chemist knows how to build these amino acids up from their constituent elements, carbon, hydrogen, nitrogen, oxygen, and in a few cases sulpher, if he had occasion to do so. Probably on an average it would require twenty separate reactions to build each of the eighteen amino acids, which would be 360 more or less difficult chemical reactions. One of the other products of some proteins is nucleic acid which is so complex chemists know little about preparing it.

Chemists have never yet been able to unite the amino acids into any of the naturally occuring proteins. Emil Fisher at the University of Berlin, helped by about 300 graduate chemists, combined eighteen molecules of amino acids into a protein-like substance which had a molecular weight of 1818. Some of the simplest naturally occurring proteins have molecular weights around 17,000 which is approximately ten times that of Fisher's substance. The problem of synthesizing a naturally occuring protein is so difficult that no chemist or group of chemists since Fisher's time has had the courage to attempt it.

## CARBON IN THE LIVING CELL, A CHEMICAL MIRACLE

The problem of originating a living cell is infinitely more complex than anything we have hinted at thus far. Take the most learned chemist living today and give him the right amount of proteins, fats and carbohydrates to make a living cell, still he cannot make it take on life. To postulate the formation of anything as simple as the simplest living cell without the conscious planning of an Intelligence infinitely superior to that of man is unthinkable.

To get carbon activated, so that it could take its place in the protein molecule in the living cell, the carbon would have to be heated to at least 300° C., which would of course kill the protein, as the living protein could stand not over 80° C. at the most. This blocks all artificial methods at the outset.

Then to extend the complexity to that of a living human being, automatically regulated within narrow bounds, self healing and able to regenerate many worn-out parts, invites still more confidence in the supreme Intelligence. A universe without God as conceived by the atheist is impossible chemically. Chemistry constantly demands this Intelligence and Power back of the laws of nature.

## GEOLOGIC TIME VERSUS THE DELUGE

Time is the essence of the geologist's religion. Processes which he cannot explain, and which are not taking place now, he accounts for by allotting a few million years for their accomplishment. To illustrate how speculative some of the geologist's million year time expanses are, let me relate a personal experience. Several years ago my family and I went through the Oregon Caves with a group. One statement of the guide to emphasize the greatness of the stalactites was that it took three million years to form a stalactite eight inches long. Several years ago the City of San Francisco in order to deliver water from Hetch Hetchy dug a tunnel through the hills between Livermore and Mission San Jose. This tunnel required approximately twenty years to complete. In this tunnel there grew stalactites five inches long. There is a decided difference between eight inches in three million years, and five inches in twenty years. About twenty years ago there was described in

*Science* a wooden flume in Southeastern United States from which were hanging stalactites several inches long.

Another instance when fancied time shrinks, when confronted with facts, is recorded in the Science Counsellor Magazine:

"Formerly the oldest cave residents at Four Corners (juncture of Arizona, New Mexico, Colorado and Utah) were dated from 1000–3000 B. C.

"Tree rings have demanded a revision of this guess and it can now be said with reasonable security that these cave remains must be dated in the early centuries after Christ."[2]

## GOLD CONCENTRATION AND THE DELUGE

Bible believers are now confronted with the inspiring task of reinterpreting the accumalated facts of geology, paleontology, and biology in the light of Creation and the Biblical Flood. This Society has begun the task of putting to a scientific test the harmony of nature with the teachings of the Bible. Many of the outstanding facts of geology are apparently explainable only by the Deluge as related in the Bible. A phase of this subject which I shall now discuss is the occurrence of gold.

Gold is widely distributed over all the continents of the world. Generally in the crust of the earth gold occurs in almost a negligible percentage. However, it has been concentrated into pure pieces from the size of fine flour to the weight of a man. When this gold is found in the original quartz or rock where it has been concentrated, it is always connected with a ledge or a dyke which is either a crack or hole in the fundamental crust of the earth. These ledges, veins, and dykes are usually quartz and related rocks. At the time when the earth's crust was cracked, molten rock or water solutions flowed up through the cracks or holes. The gold was probably

dissolved in this quartz in very small concentration. When the quartz came in contact with iron compounds, and organic materials buried by the Deluge, the gold was precipitated out of solution and concentrated at that point. The result was that at the top of the dyke or fissure was a pocket and the ledge was rich in gold where it reached the vegetable or iron compounds. In other places, molten rock swelled up under limestone or other organic surface material filling it full of cracks. The heat and hot water caused the metallic compounds, being more volatile and soluble than the silicates, to distill and dissolve up into the cracks, making a mineralized region at the top of the magmatic intrusion.

If all the gold fields of the earth were formed by the forces that are now operating under the conditions that now exist, it would indeed require a long time to account for them. Actually, the opposite is going on now, by eroding and downward seepage, with no increase. No doubt only the easily accessible outcropping gold pockets and veins have been discovered. On the other hand, they could easily have been formed simultaneously at the time of the Deluge and the period soon afterward, with mostly wastage since then.

We have earthquakes today due to the shifting of weight by erosion and the readjustment of stresses in the earth's crust. With a disturbance as violent as the universal Deluge, block would be grinding against block, cracking would be taking place everywhere. Simultaneously the world over, lava, quartz, or granite, and other magmas would be boiling up from the interior. Anything of a geological nature could happen in a very short time. It would also be very probable that after a violent disturbance on the

---

[2] Henry, Emil H.: published by Duquesne University, Dec., 1940, p. 95.

earth's surface of the magnitude of the Deluge, that there would be unusual volcanic and magmatic activity and readjustment of stresses for several centuries.

## UNBELIEF'S MAIN WEAKNESS

The greatest weakness in the position of our unbelieving biological and geological friends is that they try to create this extremely complex world without an Intelligence to have planned it. If a savage in Africa should find a running watch in the jungle and should take the position that it evolved under the long time action of the forces of nature, wind, rain, gravity, electricity, light, sound, etc., we would say, "Ridiculous." Any living organism is a thousand times more involved than the watch, yet our atheist biological friends will have the living organism evolving without any previous intelligent planning. Many evolutionists pretend to believe in some sort of a god, but when pinned down to it, their god is nature. Because of the inconsistency of their position, the theistic evolutionists are the laughing stock of their agnostic brothers, because they have neither science nor the Bible to back their theism.

The present chaotic condition of mankind is the outcome of teaching the evolutionary theory in the schools of the civilized world. Religion having lost its hold on mankind, they are rapidly running amuck unrestrained. Their actions are now guided by the anti-Christian philosophies of Hegel and Nietzsche. As admitted by the leaders in geology, the modern understanding of geology is built on a very shaky foundation. The geologist has not a single theory to account for the the origin of matter, no conception as to how time began, and no picture of the outer bounds of space.

Chemically, the creation of a single living cell without an Intelligence far greater than that of any man is unthinkable. In many cases the long-time scale of the geologists shrinks into insignificance as in the case where a stalactite five inches long formed in less than twenty years instead of the supposed several million. The occurrence of gold concentrated in many places all over the globe can readily be explained in the terms of the Flood. The most necessary foundation of any scheme of things is to assume a divine Intelligence as having planned it all and guided the processes. We hope to demonstrate that scientific discoveries superior to any yet seen can be developed under this conception.

## DISCUSSION

The lecture was short, but it stimulated many questions and discussions which were not concluded until a late hour.

The theory of the age of the earth on a basis of the decomposition of the electron, especially that of uranium, was brought up. Prof. Brauer said, in part: "The radio-active series from uranium to lead contain several steps of very long duration. Any measurements that have been made during the short time radio-activity has been known are valueless. For instance, the first change in the series requires 4,560,000,000 years for half the sample to change; the fourth change requires 120,000,000 years for half to change; the fifth change, 74,300 years. Since radio-activity has only been known 45 years, measurements based on such long changes are only guesses.

"Moreover, the whole scheme is based on the assumption that all lead occurring with uranium is the result of decomposition of uranium. But what about lead deposits free from uranium? Since lead is more abundant than uranium, the chances of lead being laid down simultaneously with the uranium is greater than those of uranium being laid down alone and then decomposing to lead.

"With the multiplicity of radio-active elements formed artificially by the cyclotron, we find that radio-activity is a far more common phenomenon and far more involved than we thought it was. When order is fully restored in the present confusion about radio-activity, I predict that the radio time clock will have faded away."

Mr. Allen cited the excellent discussion by Dr. F. W. Clarke ("Data of Geo-Chemistry," U. S. G. S. Bulletin 770, 1924, pp. 315-323,) where some fifteen objections to the time theory based on radio-activity are recorded. He also described how a similar theory was once proposed concerning the supposed time of depositing the various mineral salts in the oceans, which gained great popularity, till the fact that each mineral gave such a radically different period of time put an end to the whole theory. Mr. Allen put the question as to why we should take only uranium, merely because it is the slowest to disintegrate, when we could just as reasonably take radium itself, with a period of less than 2000 years for half of it to disintegrate to the next lower element in atomic number.

Dr. Brauer was next asked about the chemistry of gem-quality wood petrifaction. He said this is not understood as yet, but that in his opinion the facts should be sought for by placing wood for some days or weeks in hot water and alkali mud strong with sodium and calcium salts with some sulphur, and with abundant silicon dioxide or silicic acid, chemically combined or in solution; and carbon dioxide under perhaps 200 pounds to the square inch pressure, providing both intake and outlet for hot water solutions and gases to pass slowly through so as to drain off the dissolved carbonaceous material and keep up the supply of silica.

He was asked if he would undertake to discover the processes and chemistry of wood putrefaction in his laboratory. He said he was planning to do so. With unleached clay now contacting Arizona petrified woods, and with waters now in Yellowstone Park capable of petrifying wood, he will experiment.

The possibility of dating the Deluge by the annual tree rings in petrified wood was asked and referred to Mr. H. L. Transtrom of Glendale, who has developed a microcamera and other means of reducing tree-ring study to a science. Mr. Transtrom then gave the main basic facts of tree-ring study, and it was mentioned that he and Mr. Allen are planning to make such a study of the trees of the Arizona Petrified Forest. They plan to read the rings from the bark of the trees inward, to find out if they are all of the same weather cycle, and if so, they may have lived at the same time and died the same year, whereas evolutionary geology has set forth three different ages for those trees, separated by several million years. However, it will be impossible to date the Deluge from tree rings, owing to the world-wide break in the life of trees all over the world at that time. No trees today go back to the Deluge.

Much interest was aroused by Dr. Brauer's mention of the rate of growth of stalagmites and stalactites. Mr. Allen drew on the blackboard a sketch of Prof. Kitto's six-inch thick stalagmite which he had cut and polished. He illustrated that it has no rings except near the surface, but is made up of pure amber-colored calcite with crystals radiating from the center, indicating a rapid and uninterrupted growth from a constant supply of fairly pure calcite. Toward the outside he showed that two or three rings formed, indicating interruptions in the supply, and that the rings then rapidly became thinner toward the surface, where no rings at all, but only thin scales, were the last to form. He said that these surface scales are now erroneously used to estimate the age of the whole growth, and this is the false basis for their supposed great age.

He said that, by the principles of Deluge Geology, the caves were eroded out while the overlaying layers were still somewhat soft, wet, and full of unleached lime, still in solution. The much more abundant rainfall after the deluge, together with the water still in the sediments, made for very much more rapid growth of all travertine formation than is possible now. As the rocks leached and dried out, and the rains declined, the rate greatly slowed down, as proven by the final appearance of rings marking dry periods, which finally gave way to thin scales only, and of mineral so impure that seldom any crystalline structure is found.

Dr. Brauer was asked if he would perform experiments in his laboratory on the manner and rate of these travertine formations, (such as stalactites and stalagmites) and he said he would do so. When asked to describe how he would proceed, he said, "I would crush up limestone which has never been leached; put it in containers with waters containing some carbon dioxide and other organic acids; and let this water run out below at a controlled rate, under controlled temperatures and humidities."

Prof. Price very interestingly referred to Dr. Brauer's mention of the evolutionary theories of the eternal nature of matter which have now been abandoned, the whole view of science now being that matter is disintegrating off into heat, and primarily is truly a form of energy. He spoke of this as being acceptable by Bible believers, in that matter is a form of the power of the Creator, the power of His Word, who spoke, and it was, and that He upholds all things, and in Him all things consist. Prof. Price expressed his appreciation of Dr. Brauer's lecture and of the profitable discussion following it which he led.

## NATURAL LAW AND THE MIRACULOUS

"Most evolutionists indignantly deny atheism. And faith in God, whether it be the idol of the barbarian, the Inscrutable Power of Spencer or Fiske, or the Divine Spirit of the Christian or Jew, carries with it the conviction of a Power which instituted natural law and the self-consciousness of the human spirit. To admit the existence of God in any sense of the word is to admit the possibility of the miraculous.

"To say that natural law was instituted by a Power, and to deny that natural law may be suspended or changed, is to accept the greater mystery and to deny the less. If God instituted the laws by which the solar system moves, then I see no reason, so far as physics is concerned, why the sun may not have stood still at the command of God

through Joshua. To say it would have changed the solar system is an argument which should have no more weight than to say that a man who had made a machine could not stop it and start it again without deranging its mechanism. The disbelief in such miracles comes from the conviction of so steadfast a reign of law that the purpose ascribed to the miracles is not commensurate with the infraction of the law. But believing, as I do, in free will, which is contrary to scientific law, and that man can comprehend imperfectly the laws of the universe, it seems reasonable to assume that he can also, to the same extent, comprehend the Creator of the laws."—More, Louis T., *The Dogma of Evolution*, pp. 556, 557.

## PHILOSOPHY OF NIETZSCHE VS. LIFE OF CHRIST

"I can find in the doctrine of evolution no guide to such a standard of life. . . . I can find no symbol and no law to satisfy our spiritual nature in the quasi-Christianity of the humanitarian application of evol-

ution. The real tendency of evolution is to be found in the philosophy of Nietzsche and not in the life of Christ."—More, Louis T., *The Dogma of Evolution*, p. 383.

## THE UNIVERSE A CLOCK RUNNING DOWN

"The universe is like a clock which is running down, a clock which, so far as science knows, no one winds up, which cannot wind itself up, and so must stop in time. It is at present a partially wound up clock, which must at some time in the past have been wound up in some manner unknown to us."

"Everything points with overwhelming force to a definite event, or series of events, of creation at some time or times, not infinitely remote. The universe cannot have originated by chance out of its present ingredients, and neither can it have always been the same as now."—Sir James H. Jeans, *"Eos,"* pp. 52, 55.

## WHAT IS BEHIND CELLULAR PROTOPLASM?

"Once the elements or units of either living or non-living matter are thus taken apart, not all the king's horses nor all the king's men can put them together again." (489)

"The physical procedure by which the ordinary substances of soil, air and water drawn into the cell and transformed into the colloidal states of protoplasm are not to be regarded as understood until they are capable of being expressed in mathe-

matical equations the minor factors of which are being diligently sought. The power by which these operations are carried out is derived by oxidation of organic substances the formulae of which are yet to be found satisfactorily. Still more remote is the fundamental capacity of protoplasm by which bonding in nitrogen and carbon is carried out in its colloidal mechanism."—D. T. MacDougal, "Trends in Plant Science," *Scientific Monthly*, June, 1941, pp. 489, 495.

THE

# BULLETIN

OF

# DELUGE GEOLOGY

AND RELATED SCIENCES

| Volume I | August, 1941 | Number 2 |

## THE RECAPITULATION THEORY

### Some Notes on Its History and Present Status

### Cyril B. Courville

The history of the recapitulation theory, otherwise known as the "biogenetic law" (Haeckel), the "law of morphogenesis" (Hyatt), the "doctrine of parallelism" (Cope), the "morphogenetic theory" (Hatschek) or the "repetition theory" (Morgan), is one of the most important of the many biologic concepts which have been proposed in modern times. Because of its far-reaching implications, this theory has perhaps done more to stimulate scientific thought than any other biologic postulate, presuming as it does to account for the history of the evolution of animal life. This position it shares alone with Paleontology, as the only possible sources of information as to the steps taken in the ascent of animal life as proposed in the larger theory of Organic Evolution. Since there are many who are still convinced that the theory of recapitulation is valid and contributes strong supportive evidence as to the mechanics in the ascent of man, it is entirely

The BULLETIN is published by, and is the official organ of the "Society For the Study of Deluge Geology and Related Sciences." The Editorial Board is comprised of Professor George McCready Price and Dr. Cyril B. Courville. It is printed at the Collegiate Press, Arlington, California. For members the BULLETIN is free, and extra copies 60 cents each (each number priced according to size); for non-members it is $2.00 per year; and this number is 75 cents. All correspondence should be directed to the Managing Editor, Mr. Ben F. Allen, 219 North Grand Avenue, Los Angeles, California.

93

fitting to re-investigate briefly the entire story, bringing it up-to-date with a survey of recent opinions and critically reviewing the theory in the light of late developments in Embryology.

Simply stated, the theory of recapitulation intimates that the various stages in the development of the individual animal embryo (ontogeny) constitutes a brief, condensed, though somewhat distorted review or summary of the evolution of the race (phylogeny). To properly orient the problem, nothing more to the point can here be presented than a quotation from Arey, the well-known contemporary embryologist:

"In accordance with this so-called *law of recapitulation,* the fertilized ovum is compared to a unicellular organism like the Ameba; the blastula is supposed to represent an adult Volvox type; the gastrula, a simple sponge or hydroid; the segmented embryo a worm-like stage; the embryo with gill slits, a fish-like stage. Moreover, most of the organs of the human embryo pass through progressive stages, roughly characteristic of the fish, amphibian, and reptile, before the mammalian condition is attained. Outstanding examples are the brain, heart, kidneys, blood-vessels and skull."

Stated more simply, this indicates according to the same author that: ". . . The individual in its development seems to repeat hastily and imperfectly its own evolutionary history."[1] The essential problem, therefore, is to determine whether, in the minds of those best able to deal with available evidence, the stages of the human embryo really represent a history of the evolution of man. Since, as Arey again so correctly states that:

". . . However unsatisfactory the developmental review (of phylogeny, or the history of the race) may be, the fact remains that the embryological changes encountered constitute the only record which supplies any information as to how the human species may have reached its present state, . . ."

an adequate and final conclusion as to the essential truth of this theory is naturally of tremendous scientific importance.

## THE PRE-EVOLUTIONARY HISTORY OF RECAPITULATION

Critical students of the developing embryo have for centuries recognized its orderly progress from the simple to the complex, the roughly paralleled resemblance of its earliest stages to the lower forms of animal life. It is not surprising, therefore, that references to this similarity were made long before any evolutionary significance was attributed to these phenomena. Of the numerous contributions on this point by pre-evolutionary writers, Meyer[2] has written a scholarly commentary. He does not agree with Needham[3] that Aristotle suggested the essence of recapitulation in his remarks about the growing embryo. It is indeed difficult to say that the theory is foreshadowed in: "For an animal does not become at the same time an animal and a man or a horse or any other particular animal,"[4] although Meckel, too, referred to this same passage as anticipating this theory.

While William Harvey[5] (1628) expressed the thought more definitely, it is likewise very doubtful that he had any concise idea of causality in his remarks: "By the same steps in development of every animal, passing through the structural stages, I might say, of egg, worm, and fetus, it obtains perfection in each."

[1] Arey, L. B.: *Developmental Anatomy,* Philadelphia, 1934, pp. 10, 11.
[2] Meyer, A. W.: Some Historical Aspects of the Recapitulation Idea, *Quart. Rev. Biol.,* (Dec.) 1935, 10:379-396.
[3] Needham, J.: *History of Embryology,* Cambridge, 1934, p. 37.
[4] Aristotle: *De generatione animalium,* Book II, 3, c. 9.
[5] Harvey, William: *De motu cordis,* trans. by C. Leake, 1931, p. 127.

It was over a century later that John Hunter (*circa* 1755) ,[6] after some personal dissections on chick embryos, wrote:

" . . . If we were to take a series of animals, from the more imperfect to the perfect, we should probably find an imperfect animal, corresponding with some stage of the most perfect."

While again, it is doubtful that Hunter had any more clear conception of recapitulation than did Harvey, the idea of p a r a l l e l i s m between the embryonic stages of the embryo and a d u l t  a n i m a l s is quite clearly expressed.

It is Kielmeyer (1793) [7] who is credited with being the first to really suggest the concept of recapitulation, although Meyer is by no means convinced that this is so. Attention was called to the resemblance of a tadpole to a fish and of the resemblance of the embryos of higher forms to adult forms of lower ones. These, the most suggestive of his remarks, no more than generally indicate the concept of parallelism. Oken (1805, 1810-11) seems to be the first to state definitely that the human embryo passes through all those stages through which other animals pass, a worm, a mollusk, and so on up the biological ladder.

"Each animal metamorphoses itself through all animal forms. The frog appears first under the form of a mollusk in order to pass from this stage to a higher one, . . . The metamorphosis of an insect is a repetition of the whole class, scolopendra, oniscus, julus, spider, crab."[8]

Shortly after this statement was made, von Walther (1808) wrote in a similar vein:

"The human foetus passes through its metamorphosis in the cavity of the uterus in such a way that it repeats all classes of animals, but, remaining permanently in none, develops more and more into the innate human form. First the embryo has the form of a worm. It reaches the insect stage just before its metamorphosis. The origin of the liver, the appearance of the different secretions, etc., show clearly an advance from the class of the worm into that of the mollusk."[9]

It remained for Meckel (1808, 1811, 1821), a contemporary embryologist, to review the opinions of his predecessors and to crystallize their concepts in a concrete form. He believed that embryos of higher forms pass through stages at which lower animals appear to be checked throughout their lives, and that this rule applies to individual organs as well as to the body as a whole. To this point Meckel wrote:

"In fact, embryos of higher animals, especially the mammals and particularly man, come to occupy more or less completely a place of the lower animals standing below them, in respect to separate organs as well as the entire body, in the number, position and relative size of organs as well as tissues, combinations (s y s t e m s) and capabilities through external transformations."[10]

Had the theory of evolution then been well developed, Meckel would no doubt have been its prophet, a place which Haeckel came to fill half a century later. As it was, he and his antecedents had gone far in endowing parallelism with something more than similarity. He helped sow the seed of a crop that Haeckel watered and saw come to full fruitage in the summertime of Organic Evolution, warmed by the sun of Darwinism.

---

[6] Hunter, John, Progress and Pecularities of the Chick in *Essays and Observations*, p. 203, Reprinted in 1861.

[7] Kielmeyer, C. F.: (Cited by Meyer[2]) .

[8] Oken, L.: *Die Zeugung*, Frankfurt bey Wesche, translation by Morgan in *Evolution and Adaptation*, 1903, p. 59.

[9] von Walther, P. F.: *Physiologie des Menschen mit durchganiger Ruchsecht auf die comparative Physiologie der Thiere*, 1808.

[10] Meckel, J. F.: *System der vergleichendden Anatomie*, 1821, (Cited by Meyer[2]) .

Time need not be taken to discuss individually the opinions of the bevy of contemporary writers on this problem of parallel embryological development, of Autenrieth, Carlisle, Blumenbach, Tiedmann, Swammerdam, Carus, de Blainville and of Serres (he of the "law of Meckel and Serres"). Suffice it to say that "parallelism" already had an extensive background with leanings toward causal implications before it was finally christened as the "biogenetic law." But we cannot close the period without reference to the misunderstood von Baer.

In 1828, Karl von Baer[11] published the first comprehensive treatise on the subject of embryology. In this work he reviewed the problem of parallelism and formulated not one law but four, which have come to bear his name. These "laws" were (1) general forms of embryos of a large group of animals appear earlier than special forms; (2) from the most general structure, less general structures develop until the most special finally appear; (3) the embryo of each animal, instead of passing through the forms of simpler animals, tends to distinguish itself from them; and (4) the embryo of a higher form is never like another adult form but resembles only its embryo.

In closing this first period of the history of recapitulation, two facts need to be made clear. In the first place, as Meyer[2] so emphatically states, von Baer "clearly rejected the theory as formulated before his time and made no claim to authorship of another." His objections to the implications of identity as included in the current theory were that (1) no adult animal ever had a yolk sac, that (2) no animal is ever surrounded by embryonic fluids, that (3) there is no close correspondence between embryonic forms of higher animals and adult forms of lower ones, that (4) structural relationships in the embryo are different from those found in an adult, and that (5) parts appearing only in the highest forms of animal life do not necessarily appear latest in embryonic life. Davidson[12] furthermore emphasizes the fact that von Baer was not responsible for the evolutionary implications of the "law of recapitulation" which has quite generally and erroneously been credited to him.

"It is important to remember that von Baer had reference in his statements to likenesses among animals, and not to ancestral relationships. Von Baer did not accept evolution, although the issues between the two theories had been well drawn before his death. Later Herbert Spencer pointed out that a thorough going application of von Baer's law in filial and ancestral relationships implied the recapitulation of Oken, that is, the idea that the embryogeny 'repeated the story of creation of the animal groups.'"

It may therefore be concluded that, while von Baer clearly showed that the earlier investigations had often mistaken resemblances for identity, those who followed him continued to place a causal significance on this observation and "the older view of recapitulation continued to dominate the thoughts of embryologists throughout the whole of the nineteenth century."[13]

## EVOLUTIONARY IMPLICATIONS OF RECAPITULATION

While the idea that the growing embryo repeats its evolutionary history may have been growing on pre-Darwin biologists, full acceptance of this notion was very slow. It was Darwin himself who gave impetus to the

11 von Baer, Karl Ernst: *Uber Entwicklungsgechichte der Thiere,* Konigsberg, 1828, (Cited by Meyer[2]).

12 Davidson, Percy E.: *The Recapitulation Theory and Human Infancy,* 1914, p. 9, 15.

13 Morgan, T. H.: *Evolution and Adaptation,* New York, 1903, p. 61.

concept of phylogenetic significance although he himself feared to make much of it at the outset. It was not until the sixth edition of his famous *Origin of Species* that h i s ideas seemed to be expressed in any clear form. In the meantime, Fritz Müller had risen to the defense of Darwin in Germany, and in his thesis the recapitulation theory was put to the specific test in the case of the *Crustacea*. His conclusions, therefore, could be expressed with more precision than Darwin was able to do in his first edition of the *Origin*. Müller concludes:

"Descendants, therefore, reach a new goal, either by deviating sooner or later whilst still on the way towards the form of their parents, or by passing along this course without deviation, but then instead of standing still, advance still further.

"In the second case the entire development of the progenitors is also passed through by the descendants, and, therefore, so far as the production of a species depends upon this second mode of progress, the historical development of the species will be mirrored in its developmental history."[14]

In short, Müller concluded that there are two possibilities as far as the development of the *Crustacea* is concerned and in only one, the second, is recapitulation to be considered as an explanation.

With the work of Müller now available, together with the early statements of Haeckel, Darwin was able to set forth his views on recapitulation in the following statements:

"On the other hand, it is highly probable that with many animals the embryonic or larval stages show us, more or less completely, the condition of the progenitor of the whole group in its adult state. . . . So again it is probable, from what we know of the embryos of mammals, birds, fishes, and reptiles, that these animals are the modified descendants of some ancient progenitor, which was furnished in its adult state with branchiae, a swim-bladder, four fin-like limbs, and a long tail, all fitted for aquatic life.

" . . . On this view we can understand how it is that in the eyes of most naturalists, the structure of the embryo is even more important for classification than of the adult. In two or more groups of animals, however much they differ from each other in structure and habits in their adult condition, if they pass through closely similar embryonic stages, we may feel assured that they all are descended from one parent-form, and are therefore closely related."[15]

It can thus be seen that Darwin's interest in embryology and recapitulation was due primarily to their possibilities as an aid in the explanation of ancestral history and the classification of animals.

It remained for Haeckel to push the "biogenetic law" (as he designated it) to its ultimate limits. As Davidson[12] has so well expressed it:

"Haeckel was not content to limit himself to a study of the causes of descent. At once speculative and intrepid, he carried the doctrine in every direction his system-loving mind pointed, and ultimately built a complete natural philosophy upon it. He would not demonstrate the kinship within one class only, as had Fritz Müller. Nothing less than a genealogical tree of the entire animal world became his object."

It was through the works of Haeckel that the modern version of the recapitulation theory has come down to us. But let Haeckel speak for himself:

"These two branches of our science—on the one side ontogeny or embryology, and on the other phylogeny, or the science of race evolution—are the most vitally connected. The one cannot be understood without the other. It is only when the two branches fully cooperate and supplement each other that 'Biogeny' (or the science of the genesis of life in the widest sense) attains to the rank of a philosophic science. The connection between them is not external and superficial, but profound, intrinsic and causal. This is a discovery made by recent research, and it is most clearly and correctly expressed in the comprehensive law which I have called 'the fundamental law of organic evolution,' or 'the fundamental law of biogeny.' This general law . . . may be briefly expressed in

---

[14] Müller, Fritz: *Facts and Arguments for Darwin*, English ed., 1864, pp. 111-114.
[15] Darwin, C.: *Origin of the Species*, 6th ed., 1872, p. 395.

the phrase: 'The history of the foetus is a recapitulation of the history of the race;' or, in other words, 'Ontogeny is a recapitulation of phylogeny.' It is surprising that the fact that recapitulation is quite out of harmony with development in the plant world did not impress Haeckel more than it apparently did. The universal law of biogenesis was therefore not universal having an assumed implication only in animals."[16]

It is in this reduced and simplified form that the theory is remembered by the average college student. What is not remembered, if learned at all, is Haeckel's statement that recapitulation and evolution are inseparable, which intimates that if one falls, so falls the other. The majority of college graduates still cling to the shibboleth that "ontogeny recapitulates phylogeny," not realizing that their current faith is entirely unfounded in the minds of most critical contemporary students of embryology. But this remains to be proved.

It is important at this point to make clear what Haeckel meant by his theory. He at first proposed twenty-two separate s t a g e s (later increased to thirty) in the evolution of man and for which counterparts were to be sought in the developing embryo. With due criticism of Haeckel's over-emphasis of his "l a w," it must be agreed that he did attempt to fit the law to some sort of scheme of evolution. This position, illogical as it has proven to be, was infinitely more consistant than has been the attitude of neo-recapitulationists who seem satisfied with the general acceptance of the theory, apparently unable or unwilling to put it to the crucial test of detailed embryological investigation.

EARLY DEFLECTIONS FROM THE BASIC
CONCEPT OF RECAPITULATION

Herbert Spencer[16] saw the philosophical weaknesses in the theory which was then taking shape even before it had been crystallized into the "biogenetic law." He again called attention to the premise of von Baer that it was gross resemblances only that were being dealt with in this law of embryologic parallelism.

"The resemblances which hold together great groups of embryos in their earlier stages, and which hold together smaller and smaller groups in their later and later stages are not special or exact but general or approximate; and in some cases, the conformity to this general law is very imperfect. . . . Hence, remembering the perpetual intrusions of organisms on one another's modes of life, often widely different: and on remembering that these intrusions have been going on from the beginning, we shall be prepared to find that the general law of embryological parallelism, is qualified by irregularities that are mostly small, in many cases considerable, and occasionally great."

This statement of Spencer, who was not in any sense a professional embryologist, was prophetic of the defects in the recapitulation theory. Not only did he point out the fact that irregularities in the law did exist, but he also indicated what these irregularities were, pointing out deviations from the straight r e c o r d, deviations for which Haeckel and his school had already begun to coin words to describe. Included among these irregularities were: (1) *retrogressive* rather than progressive development (suppression of the fetal teeth in whales) ; (2) *substitution* of one organ for another with the same function (replacement of lungs for the gill mechanism of the fish; (3) *loss of structures* (as the loss of limbs in certain parasites in their adult stage) ; and (4) *substituted modes of development*, directly from egg to adult in higher forms of life, while only indirectly through stages of metamorphosis as in insects.

While, to be sure, Spencer later became convinced that von Baer's law did indeed imply some form of recapitula-

---

[16] Haeckel, E.: *The Evolution of Man,* trans. by McCabe from the 5th German ed., New York. 1906, pp. 2, 228.

tion, neither he nor anyone else has adequately explained away the objections which he raised against the law of biogenesis, the deviations from the presumed regular course of phylogeny which have become the rule rather than the exception the more deeply the superficial r e s e m b l a n c e s were probed and put to the critical test. But the disposition of these "irregularities" in the law at the hands of its most devout adherents remains yet to be seen.

The ink was scarcely dry on Haeckel's *Generelle Morphologie der Organismen* (1866), when other criticisms of his new born "biogenetic law" were forthcoming. Vogt had already said:

"The embryo of the higher animal to be sure passes in its development through the developmental movements which are analogous to those of lower forms of the same type, but its transitory organization is never perfectly similar to that of lower animals in their mature condition. It is still more opposed to the truth when one a s s e r t s, founding upon inaccurate observations, that the higher animals pass in their development through conditions that are analogous to the adult animals of other fundamental types."[17]

Haeckel himself came to realize that all was not what it seemed from superficial observation, and that the history of the race was not a simple and direct story if the evident facts in the embryological record were to be considered at their face value. Disturbing deviations in the form of subtractions and additions, accelerations and retardations as well as complete reversal of the chronological story had somehow to be accounted for. It seemed that Nature in her attempt to evolve man had "destroyed" parts of the record, "confused," or in some instances, actually "falsified" the phylogenetic record.

This question had already been raised by Müller who found in his study of Crustacea that recapitulation could be made to apply in only one of two large groups. Müller laid down some premises to account for these deviations from the normal record which came to be quite generally accepted:

"The historical record contained in development becomes gradually wiped out, in that the embryology takes an always more direct path from the egg to the adult animal, and it becomes frequently falsified through the struggle for existence that the free-living larvae have to meet. The genealogy of the species becomes the more fully retained in its embryology the longer is the line of immature conditions, which species traverse at equal pace, and the more accurately, the less the mode of life of the young differs from that of the adults, and the less the peculiarities of the several immature conditions may be conceived as pushed back into earlier periods or as independently acquired."[18]

To get Haeckel's own explanation of the exceptions to the "law" which he re-evaluated, let us note his conclusion in the matter of the distorted record, a conclusion written sufficiently long afterwards to permit of prolonged and careful reflection.

"In order to appreciate this important feature, we have distributed the embryological phenomena in two groups, *palingenetic* and *cenogenetic*. Under palinogenesis we count those facts of embryology that we can directly regard as a faithful synopsis of the corresponding stem-history. By cenogenesis we understand those embryonic processes which we cannot directly correlate with corresponding evolutionary processes, but must regard as modifications or falsifications of them. With this careful discrimination be-

---

[17] Vogt, C.: Cited by Montgomery, *Analysis of Racial Descent in Animals*, New York, 1906. This crucial objection to the current earlier belief in the law of Meckel and Serres is to be considered as a continuation of the stand taken by von Baer himself (that gross similarities were not to be confused with identity), rather than an objection to the yet unstated biogenetic law.

[18] Müller, F.: *loc. cit.*

tween palingenetic and cenogenetic phenomena, our biogenetic law assumes the following more precise shape:—The rapid and brief development of the individual (ontogeny) is a condensed synopsis of the long and slow history of the stem (phylogeny) : this synopsis is the more faithful and complete in proportion as the original features have been preserved by heredity, and modifications have not been introduced by adaptation.

" . . . As a result of the above-mentioned cenogenetic processes—those of disturbed and curtailed heredity—whole series of lower stages have dropped out in the embryonic development of man and the other animals, especially from the earliest periods, or been falsified by modification. . . . They (fishes) represent the transition to the higher vertebrates, in which the middle and older stages of ancestral development have been either distorted or curtailed, but in which we find the more recent stages of the phylogenetic process well preserved in ontogeny."[19]

Contemporary with this attempt to account for the acceleration, retardation, addition, subtraction, reversal and interpolation of the record of evolution was an effort to apply the theory to current researches on the Crustacea already begun by Müller. This investigator had c o n c l u d e d, with one group of exceptions that

" . . . the Nauplius, the Zoea, and other crustacea represent phylogenetic states in the history of the higher crustacea, and that from these we can see today what the ancestors of these modern crustacea were like."

This was a start in the right direction, for if it could be proved that the theory could be accurately applied to one animal group, there was some reason to continue the investigation. The entire problem is too involved to go into any detail in a survey such as this, but a brief summary of this situation is in order. The Nauplius is a larval form of the lower crustaceans having six legs and which was thought to be an ancestor of the entire group of crustacea. The Zoea was a larval

form of one of the group of higher crustacea represented by the crabs and lobsters, which in turn was supposed to be an ancestor of the still higher group of decapods. Morgan's comment on the final outcome of this supporting theory is pertinent:

"It is generally admitted now that the Zoea does not represent an original ancestral form at all, but a highly modified new form, as new perhaps as the group of the decapods themselves. We are forced to conclude, then, that the presence of a larval form throughout an entire group cannot be accepted as evidence that it represents an ancestral stage. . . .

"The fate of the Zoea theory cast a shadow over the nauplius theory, since the two rested on the same sort of evidence. The outcome was, in fact, that the nauplius theory was also abandoned, and this was seen to be the more necessary, since a study of the internal anatomy of the lowest group of crustaceans, the phyllopods, showed that they have probably come directly from many segmented, annelidian ancestors."[20]

Thus terminated a somewhat prolonged investigation of what was hoped to be a strong support of the recapitulation theory.

No discussion of the deficiencies in the recapitulation theory would be complete without a statement from Balfour who was perhaps the outstanding comparative embryologist of his day. Since as Locy[21] has so aptly put it, "The recapitulation theory was a dominant one in all Balfour's speculations," his impressions are worth recording. It is to be regretted that his untimely death prevented our knowing what his more mature reflections on the theory might have been. Balfour explained that:

" . . . the law (of recapitulation) above enunciated is, like all physical laws, the statement of what would occur without interfering conditions. Such a state of things is not found in nature, but development as it actually occurs is the resultant of a

---

19 Haeckel: loc. cit. pp. 179, 180.
20 Morgan, T. H.: Evolution and Adaptation, New York, 1903, pp. 58-90.
21 Locy, Wm. A.: Biology and Its Makers, 2nd ed., New York, 1910, pp. 230, 232.

series of influences of which that of heredity is only one. As a consequence of this, the embryological record, as it is usually presented to us, is both imperfect and misleading. It may be compared to an ancient manuscript with many of the sheets lost, others misplaced, and with spurious passages interpolated by a later hand. The embryological record is almost always abbreviated in accordance with the tendency of nature (to be explained on the principle of survival of the fittest) to attain her ends by the e a s i e s t means. The time and sequence of the development of parts is often modified, and finally, secondary structural features make their appearance to fit the embryo or larva for special conditions of existence. When the life history of a form is fully known, the most difficult part of his task is still before the scientific embryologist. Like the scholar with his manuscript, the embryologist has by a process of careful and critical examination to determine where the gaps are present, to detect the later insertions, and to place in order what has been misplaced."[22]

The contemporary zoologist, Marshall expressed himself in a similar vein, apparently unable to convince himself that so many and devious exceptions to the rule of recapitulation did not cast some doubt as to the truth of the whole theorem. He writes:

"Although it is undoubtedly true that development is to be regarded as a recapitulation of ancestral phases, and that the embryonic history of an animal presents to us a record of the race-history, yet it is also an undoubted fact, recognized by all writers in embryology, that the record so obtained is neither a complete nor straightforward one. It is indeed a history, but a history of which entire chapters are lost, while in those that remain many pages are misplaced and others are so blurred as to be illegible; words, sentences, or entire paragraphs are omitted, and, worse still, alterations or spurious additions have been freely introduced by later hands, and at times so cunningly as to defy detection."[23]

Such statements intimating that nature had "distorted," or "falsified"

her own history of the race, as though, with tongue-in-cheek she had smeared the record to make it difficult to understand, are more the language of fiction than of science. This sort of analogy was bound to provoke a reaction on the part of embryologists who saw in the orderly course of development of the embryo some design and purpose other than an effort at confusing the record. T y p i c a l of such a reaction is the statement of Gegenbauer.

"But if we are compelled to admit that cenogenetic characters are intermingled with palingenetic then we cannot regard onto-geny as a pure source of evidence regarding phyletic relationships. Ontogeny, accordingly, becomes a field in which an active imagination may have full scope for its dangerous play, but in which positive results are by no means everywhere to be attained. To attain such results the palingenetic and the cenogenetic phenomena must be sifted apart, an operation which requires more than one critical *granum salis*. If it is once admitted that not everything in development is palingenetic, and that not every ontogenetic fact can be accepted, so to speak, at its face value, it follows that nothing in ontogeny is immediately available for the critique of embryological development. This conclusion cannot be escaped."[24]

The more serious objections to the theory naturally came from the embryologists themselves who were in a better position to find flaws in the argument. It is especially significant that serious objections to the philosophy came from His and Roux, the two men who gave Embryology its great impetus along analytical lines, an impetus which ultimately led to the epoch-making work of Speman on "organizers." His wrote in 1874:

"In the entire series of forms which a developing organism runs through, each form is the necessary antecedent of the fol-

---

[22] Balfour, F. M.: *A Treatise on Comparative Embryology*, London, 1880. Vol. I, p. 3.
[23] Marshall, A. M.: The Recapitulation Theory in *Biological Lectures and Addresses*, London, 1894, p. 306.
[24] Gegenbauer: Cited by E. B. Wilson, *Biological Lectures*, Woods Hole, 1894, p. 104.

lowing. If the embryo is to reach the complicated end-forms, it must pass step by step, through the simpler ones. Each step of the series is the physiological consequence of the preceding stage and the necessary condition of the following. Jumps, or short cuts of the d e v e l o p m e n t process, are unknown in the physiological process of development. If embryonic forms are the inevitable precedents of the mature forms, because the more complicated forms must pass through the simpler, we can understand the fact that paleontological forms are so often like the embryonic forms of today. The paleontological forms are embryonic, because they have remained at a lower stage of development, and the present embryos must pass also through lower stages in order to reach the higher. But it is by no means necessary for the later, higher forms to pass through embryonal forms because their ancestors have once existed in this condition."[25]

His was looking forward to a physiological investigation of the embryo rather than limiting himself as others had done to structure. He had thus far been able to perceive that similarity of form did not signify ancestry, a conclusion which modern experimental embryology has s e r v e d to strengthen. It is now shown experimentally that similar structures in related types of animals may be constructed of tissues from different sources indicating a different life history for a homologous part. This lesson was already being learned by embryologists, being foreshadowed by the "irregularities" in the ontogenetic record.

It was about this time that Hatschek introduced an argument against recapitulation, the full significance of which he himself could not fully realize. He wrote:

"We must consider it as a general law, derivable from the principle of causality, that with the phylogenetic modification of an animal form never only the end stage becomes changed, but always the whole row from the egg cell to the end stage. Each modification of the end stage or the addition of new stages necessitates a change of the egg itself."[26]

In his textbook appearing eight years later, this concept was somewhat amplified.

"When one premises that the modifications, which the developed individual inherits directly through outer influences, become hereditary in the descendants, then the explanation shapes itself very simply. The new acquisitions of the adults bring about immediately a prolongation, very insignificant in a single generation but increasing in the course of generations, of the ontogenetic row of forms in the descendants. But when one holds fast to the view that only those newly occurring characters become inherited, which have arisen through variation of the reproductive glands, another explanation seems necessary. One must pre-suppose 'overstepping varieties' with which name I would call such varieties as consist in a prolongation of the ontogenetic row of forms."[27]

In other words, Hatschek insisted that if a new stage was added in ontogenesis, this would call for a change in all the potentialities of the egg cell. This simple addition of stage to stage ('overstepping') might not be so difficult if transmission of acquired characteristics were assumed. The difficulties would become infinitely increased when reversal or interpolation of stages occurred, when a complete re-shuffling of all the potentialities leading to various stages of development would become necessary. From a genetic standpoint this seems a hopeless situation to evaluate. But more of this later.

By this time, conclusions as to the recapitulation t h e o r y had become fairly well crystallized in the minds of embryologists with some t h i r t y years of experience on which to base

---

[25] His, W.: *Unserer Korperform und das physiologische Problem ihrer Enstehung,* Leipzig, 1874.
[26] Hatschek: Cited by Montgomery, *Analysis of Racial Descent,* 1906, p. 184.
[27] Hatschek: (Cited by Montgomery).

their opinions. Hurst in particular was rather outspoken:

"Ontogeny is not an epitome, is not a record, either perfect or imperfect, of past history, is not a recapitulation of the course of evolution."[28]

Hertwig, an outstanding contemporary embryologist, in his early work on the coelom theory, had leaned toward Haeckel's gastrea theory and its recapitulatory implications. These beliefs he ultimately came to retract, recognizing similarity in external form did not necessarily imply similarity in structure: "Ontogenetic studies give us, therefore, only greatly changed copies of phylogenetic stages. The two correspond not according to their actual contents but only as to their form."[29] Morgan objects to this last expression of Hertwig's by asking, "Can we be asked to believe for instance that a young chick repeats the ancestral adult fish form but not the contents of the fish?" This seems to be merely a matter of translation or at worst of choice of words. Hertwig simply stated that only the general form of the embryonic stage of the chick resembled that of the fish, a resemblance which did not extend to anatomic detail, a conclusion reached by others before him.

"Our doctrine is, that the species-cell, even as the adult, many-sided representative of the species, has passed through a progressive, and indeed a general, a corresponding development in the course of phylogeny. This view appears to stand in contradiction to the biogenetic law. . . . We must drop the expression 'repetition of form of extinct forefathers,' and put in its place the repetition of forms which are necessary for organic development, and lead from the simple to the complex. . . . The egg-cell of the present time, and its one-celled predecessor in the phylogenetic theory, the amoeba, are only comparable in so far as they fall under the common definition of the cell, but beyond this they are extraordinarily different from each other. . . . Undoubtedly there exists in a certain sense a parallel between the phylogenetic, and the ontogenetic development. . . . "

In his outstanding study on the problems of evolution, Morgan presented a fairly comprehensive study on the history and essential basis of the recapitulation theory which he rechristened the "theory of embryonic repetition." He further writes:

"In conclusion, then, it seems to me that *the idea that adult ancestral stages have been pushed back into the embryo, and that the embryo recapitulates in part these ancestral adult stages is in principle false.* The resemblance between embryos of higher forms and the adults of lower forms is due, as I have tried to show, to the presence in the embryos of the lower groups of certain organs that remain in the adult forms of this group. It is only the embryonic stages of the two groups that we are justified in comparing; and there has been an ancestral adult form having these embryonic stages in its development and these stages have been handed down to the divergent lines of its descendants."[30]

Montgomery also takes a decided position in regard to the recapitulation theory as a possible source of information in the descent of animals. He concludes:

" . . . An analysis of the stages during the life of one individual can in no way present a knowledge of its ancestry; and the method of comparing non-correspondent stages of two species is entirely wrong in principle."

"The recapitulation hypothesis is scientifically untenable, and where there has been transmutation of species, the embryogeny, neither in whole nor in part, exactly parallels the racial history. The relation between the two is always that of inexact parallelism. Considerations based upon any such idea of recapitulation are erroneous, and therefore of no help in determining racial descent."[31]

---

[28] Hurst, C. H.: (Cited by Wilson, 1896).

[29] Hertwig, O.: (Cited by Morgan in *Evolution and Adaptation*, pp. 78-82).

[30] Morgan, T. H.: *loc. cit.*

[31] Montgomery, T. H.: *The Analysis of Racial Descent in Animals*, New York, 1906, pp. 194, 203.

This phase of discussion may be concluded by the deductions of Sedgwick, one of the outstanding embryologists of his period, who once more emphasizes the essential question of similarity versus identity, which in the last analysis is the only real basis the theory has to rest on.

"The generalization (recapitulation) undoubtedly had its origin in the fact that there is what may be called a family resemblance between embryos and larvae, but this resemblance which is by no means exact, is largely superficial and does not extend to anatomic detail."

"It must, therefore, be admitted that one outcome of the progress of the embryological and palaeontological research for the last 50 years is negative. The recapitulation theory originated as a deduction from the evolution theory and as a deduction it still remains."[32]

## GEOLOGY AND THE DOCTRINE OF PARALLELISM

The full story of recapitulation would not be told unless it included a consideration of the relationship of this theory to Paleontology. The early proponents of the concept hoped that a study of fossil forms would establish recapitulation by showing a close correspondence between some of the primitive forms and the various stages of the embryo. This was a reasonable supposition, for if evolution had actually occurred by means of gradual transition from one form to another and if the development of the individual were any sort of a history of that process, some degree of confirmation should be forthcoming. It was in this fond hope that the paleontologist, who believed he held the only other key to the problem of the history of evolution, so gladly welcomed

recapitulation and has held so tenaciously to it. In fact so enthusiastic was the paleontologist's acceptance of the theory, that Bather insisted that:

"If the embryologists had not forstalled them, the paleontologists would have had to invent the theory of recapitulation."[33]

At any rate, these two sciences are both concerned in any consideration of the theory and the arguments of both must be heard.

It is Agassiz who is given credit for first applying the recapitulation concept to extinct animal forms, but Carl Vogt had already suggested in 1842 that fossil species pass through changes similar to those which the embryos of living forms undergo.[34] In 1848 Agassiz proposed for the first time that the embryo of higher forms resembled the lower forms of animals of past ages more than they did living ones. In his subsequent work, he attempted to classify both living and extinct species. Perhaps with conscious effort to coordinate the embryonic "l a w s" of von Baer and the "theory of types" of contemporary biologists (Cuvier, Mueller and Owen) into a philosophy consistent with his own views of creation, Agassiz again compared the embryonic stages with extinct animals. This scheme formed the basis of his "Essay on Classification."[35]

Darwin hoped that "the universal law of nature" proposed by Agassiz would prove helpful to his thesis, although, because of variations in the embryo and imperfections in the fossil record, he was uncertain whether this could ever be done.[36] It was Haeckel who specifically tied up the

---

[32] Sedgwick, A.: The Influence of Darwin on the Study of Animal Embryology, in *Darwin and Modern Science*, New York, 1909, pp. 175, 176.

[33] Bather, F. A.: The Recapitulation Theory in Paleontology, *Nat Sci.*, 1893, (Cited by Cumings, *loc. cit.*).

[34] See Morgan, T. H.: *loc. cit.*, footnote p. 62.

[35] Agassiz, L.: *Essay on Classification*, Boston, 1857.

[36] Darwin, C.: *Origin of Species*, New York, 1925, Vol. 2, p. 254.

biogenetic law with Geology and Paleontology as he had with Organic Evolution. He made relatively small point of the combination, however, even in his later books with the plea that the evidence was incomplete and might always be.[37] Such an assumption on any basis was covering a lot of territory, at least so it appeared to Déperet who wrote:

"Bolder than Darwin, the learned German zoologist did not hesitate to set about reconstituting by the embryonic method, the general pedigree of organized beings, animal and vegetable, commencing with the appearance of life on the globe down to the present day. At the head of his system stands a primary and inevitable hypothesis, the apparition of the first germ of life by spontaneous generation."[38]

Haeckel suggested that, in view of the various stages of development of the human embryo, there were some twenty-two stages (his early view) in the evolution of man. In commenting on these stages Déperet later said:

"If these twenty-two stages of the human geneology of Haeckel are submitted to the paleontological checks it must at once be noted that the first nine stages are entirely unknown to us in the fossil state. The tenth or Monorhine stage is perhaps represented by some small isolated dental organs, the *Conodontes* of the lower Silurian in Russia, but at the same epoch we already know some veritable Placodermal Ganoid fish in the limestone of Canyon City (Colorado).

"No paleontological fact authorizes us to consider the eleventh or Selachian stage as having given birth to the Dipneuston stage, this latter being already clearly characterized as the lower Devonian by the genera *Coccosteus* and *Dipterus*.

"The fourteenth, or Triton stage, is observed it is true, in the Labyrinthodous of the Coal and of the Permian periods, but it is already accompanied by reptilian types of a high organization."[39]

By further elaboration Déperet showed that the hypothetical stages of human evolution were either missing entirely from the fossil record or, when present in any similar form, older fossil forms were also present in the same period. To-day geologists limit themselves to certain groups and make no serious effort to run the whole gamut of Haeckel's 22 (or 30) stages.

Haeckel had not yet appeared in print with his earlier concepts of the relationship of the "biogenetic law" with Paleontology when contemporary doubts as to the validity of this association were voiced. Huxley, for example, wrote in 1862:

"An impartial survey of positively ascertained truth then negatives the common doctrines of progressive modification, or as a necessary progress from more or less embryonic forms . . . it either shows us no evidence of any such modification or demonstrates it to have been very slight."[40]

To this same point von Zittel writes:

"If we consult paleontology, it shows that these surmises are by no means confirmed. There are, indeed, a great number of fossil genera which retain throughout life the embryonic, or, rather, the youthful characters of their existing allies, but it is only among the mammals, and to some extent among the reptiles, that I could name a complete series of forms following one another in time and belonging to the same line of development. The Eocene, Oligocene, and, in part also, even the Miocene Mammalia stand to their now existing allies, for the most part in the relation of youthful forms, while they, almost without exceptions, exhibit at least some characters which are quickly passed through by their geologically younger successors in the embryonic or youthful stage. The ontogeny of organisms now living would, for the rest, afford but an unsafe basis for the reconstruction of ancient faunas and floras, since experience teaches that the biogenetic law is frequently veiled or completely obscured owing to various causes."[41]

[37] Haeckel, E.: *loc. cit.* p. 208.
[38] Déperet, C.: *The Transformations of the Animal World*, New York, 1909, pp. 43-60.
[39] Déperet, C.: *loc. cit.*
[40] Huxley, T.: *Scientific Memoirs*, Vol. II, p. 528 (Cited by Davidson, *loc. cit.* p. 29).
[41] von Zittel, K. A.: Palaeontology and the Biogenetic Law, *Nat. Sc.*, 1895, 6:305.

The strongholds of the paleontologists in their belief of the recapitulation theory, are to be found in some of the groups of lower animals and in some of the fossil vertebrates, notably the horse. As an example of those who defend this thesis, Cumings stands pre-eminent. He maintained in 1909 that the *Cephalopoda*, the *Pelecypoda*, the *Gastropoda*, the *Brachiopoda*, the *Trilobita*, the *Bryozoa*, the *Graptolites* as well as other groups were examples to prove the truth of the recapitulation theory. He argued that the reason why embryologists had grown cold toward the theory was because they had compared the embryonic stages with adult living forms. He further argues:

"When, however, the entire life history of the individual is considered, instead of only the embryonic period, and when the successive stages of the epembryonic (post embryonic) development are compared with adult characters of related types, in immediately preceeding geologic periods, it will be found that the fundamental principle of recapitulation is sound, and that the individuals do repeat in their own epembryonic development the characters of their immediate ancestry." [42]

Smith had also asserted that the reason why embryologists had lost their enthusiasm was that they had studied only the earlier embryonic stages and therefore did not understand the full ontogeny of animals. He adds: "To this sort of study is due the idea of 'falsification of the record,' a crime of which nature has not yet been guilty, although she at times may not perhaps have told the whole truth." [43] Smith disputes the claim of Wilson and others by stating that not comparative anatomy but paleontology gives the only clue to cenogenetic (newly introduced) characters.

and that paleontology constitutes "a court from which there is no appeal."

Thus we have developed a most unusual situation! The paleontologists defend an embryological theory which the embryologists themselves have largely deserted as untenable, and that on a basis of epembryonic (post embryonic) stages which under no circumstances could have to do with those early forms of life whose counterparts were certainly to be sought *in early* (not late) embryonic stages!

No discussion of the relationship of the recapitulation theory to paleontology would be complete without reference to the problem of the Ammonites, whose fossil shells are found in abundance in many localities. These forms have shells which are flat spirals, one cell being added to another in sequence as the animal grows. This addition of a larger cell to the smaller preceding one was long considered to be a simple but classical example of recapitulation. These views were first presented by Hyatt (1865) and Wurtemberger (1880).

After a more recent study on the A m m o n i t e s in various localities, Spath[44] made the following statement:

"It may be necessary to assume an inverted geological order if our views of the biological order of Ammonites are to continue to be governed by discredited 'laws' of recapitulation. And . . . when the horizons of all these stocks are definitely known, it is hoped to get good additional evidence for a final rejection of the views on Ammonite development connected with the names of Hyatt and Wurtemberger."

After a study on Jurassic Ammonites, Brinkmann concluded that while in some cases a parallelism between phylogeny and ontogeny seemed to exist, in many others this was not so.

---

[42] Cumings, E. R.: Paleontology and the Recapitulation Theory, *Proc. Indiana Acad. Sc.*, 1909, pp. 305-340.

[43] Smith, J. P.: The Biogenetic Law from the Standpoint of Paleontology, *J. Geol.*, (July-Aug.) 1900, 8:413-425.

[44] Spath, L. F.: Cited by DeBeer, *Embryos and Ancestors*, 1940, p. 8.

"Phylogeny," it was decided, "had lost its influence over ontogeny."[45]

The same situation exists when any critical attempt is made to prove recapitulation by any of the other forms of fossil shells. The recent comment of Watson on this group of fossil animals in general and the coral in particular is quite to the point:

"Application of the biogenetic law to the stages so preserved (as fossils) should allow of the construction of a phylogeny which can then be compared with ammonites found in earlier beds . . . This type of evolution, which was investigated by C. E. Beecher, has been supposed to occur not only in ammonites but also in gastropods, lamellibranches and brachipods, in all of which the shell preserves its early growth-stages. It has also been recognized in the development of a colony amongst coelenterates and Bryozoa.

"Out of this vast mass it is difficult to select a single case which can be regarded as conclusively established, perhaps the best are those of the development and evolution of the simple coral *Zaphrentis delanouei*, from the Lower Carboniferous of Scotland." [The proof here rested solely in the decreasing incidence of the "earlier" forms in the ascending horizons of layers of sediment, corresponding with an increasing incidence of "later" forms in these layers.]

"It appears that the biogenetic law, though a useful tool, must be used with caution in the construction of phylogenies, and that genealogical trees made by its aid must not be used as evidence in favour of the hypothesis itself."[46]

If the theory of recapitulation cannot be established in the case of such simple and abundant forms as corals and ammonites, examples in which parallelism in an evolutionary sense seems a most likely possibility, what can be hoped for in the more complex fossil animals? But let us see what the evidence is in such a case.

No genealogical tree seems so well established among the vertebrates, in so far as the paleontological record is concerned, as that of the horse. If recapitulation was really going to prove workable among any higher animal, it should certainly do so in this case. On this point Ewert queries:

"What evidence is afforded by the horse in favor of the recapitulation theory?"

"It is impossible with any degree of accuracy, either to speak of a *Hyrocotherium* or a *Mesohippus* stage, or even of a *Hipparion* stage. . . . To admit that the horse, before assuming its own specific characters, makes, as it were, a deflection toward the not very ancient form *Hipparion*, is hardly going far enough to justify the assertion that the horse during its development assumes, one after another, the characters of its ancestors, or, in other words, except in the most limited sense, 'climbs its own ancestral tree.' "[47]

To summarize the opinions of some of those who have attempted to evaluate the entire role of Paleontology in establishing or dethroning the theory of recapitulation, the conclusions of Déperet and Sedgwick may be taken. Déperet writes:

"Has Paleontology completely confirmed the conclusions thus drawn from the embryology of existing beings? We may approach this important question by two different methods. The first method, which is the oldest and the one most generally employed, consists in finding in geological strata forms which in the adult state reproduce one of the transitory phases through which the development of an existing animal passes. . . .

"But it must be clearly stated that these examples of representation in fossil adult species of the embryonic, or more correctly, of the youthful characteristics of existing animals, cannot be generalized and that they remain up until now in the state of exceptional facts."[48]

Sedgwick concludes:

"If it could be shown, as was stated to be the case by L. Agassiz, that ancient and extinct forms of life present features of structure now only found in embryos, we should have a body of facts of the greatest

[45] Brinkmann, R.: Cited by DeBeer, *loc. cit.*
[46] Watson, D. M. S.: Palaeontology, *Encyclopedia Brittanica*, ed. 14, Vol. 17, p. 110.
[47] Ewart, J. C.: Cited by Davidson.[12]
[48] Déperet, C.: *loc. cit.* pp. 254-256.

importance in the present discussion. But as Huxley (*Scientific Memoirs*, London, Vol. L., p. 303, 1898) has shown and as the whole course of palaeontological and embryological investigation has demonstrated no such statement can be made. The extinct forms of life are very similar to those now existing and there is nothing specially embryonic about them. So that the facts, as we know them, lend no support to the theory."[49]

In spite of these conclusions by contemporary investigators, we find paleontologists such as Schindewold[50] in Germany struggling over the neologisms of Müller and Haeckel, old terms such as *palingenesis* as well as terms more recently added such as *anagenesis* (deviation or prolongation of development) and *katagenesis* (unchanged repetition and abbreviation) and finally *proterogenesis* (an assumption of old characters through young stages). While Needham the embryologist insists that recapitulation and evolution offer no solution to the problems of the developing embryo (*vide infra*), George, a paleontologist from the same University (Cambridge), insists that:

"Examples are provided by phyletic seriation in fossils which appear to furnish conclusive evidence that at least in certain instances there is a more or less complete recapitulation of ancestral skeletal stages in skeletal ontogeny . . . . Recapitulation and the developmental laws of von Baer are not antagonistic to each other."[51]

By thus establishing himself as a defender of the biogenetic law, George can scarcely be accused of trying to discredit it. And yet the best he can possibly say for it is that:

"The application of the law must be tentative rather than final; it is approximate, rather than exact; it suggests and implies rather than fulfills."[52]

The embryologist, by long and critical comparative analysis of embryos, has come to the conclusion that the recapitulation theory is entirely untenable and should therefore be rejected. The paleontologist, in spite of his inability to prove the theory in case of the simplest of animal forms, clings tenaciously and unreasonably to it, because it seems essential in order to prove the evolution of animals. Which, of the two, stands on solid ground?

## TWENTIETH CENTURY ADHERENTS AND THEIR CREDO

It should not be assumed from what has gone before that the biogenetic law or the theory of recapitulation, at least in a somewhat modified form, is no longer held by scientists of the various biological schools. Quite the opposite is true. While the scientific basis of the law has been reduced to simple similarities of form and structure, there are many who still maintain that the essential principle of the law is sound. This fidelity to a law, now definitely discredited by those in best position to know, is apparently due to the fact that its believers cannot escape the original premise of Haeckel that recapitulation and organic evolution are inseparable. A brief survey of the opinions of these faithful recapitulationists is worthy of attention.

As an example of one who lived through this period when embryologists became the most severe critics of the law, Conklin may be cited. As to his beliefs in 1913, he writes:

"Our knowledge of the mechanics of evolution must always depend in large part upon the study of individual development. More than any other science, embryology

---

[49] Sedgwick, A.: *loc. cit.*, p. 174.
[50] Schindewold, O. H.: Ontogenie und Phylogenie, *Palaeontolog. Ztschr.*, 1929, 11:54-67.
[51] George, T. N.: Palingesis and Paleontology, *Biol. Rev. and Bio. Proc. Cambridge Philos. Soc.*, 1933, 8:107-135.
[52] George, T. N.: *loc. cit.*

holds the keys to the *method of evolution*. If ontogeny (life history of the individual) is not a true recapitulation it is at least a true type of evolution, and the study of the causes of development will go far to determine the factors of phylogeny or race development."[53]

Woodruff writes in a similar vein:

"One cannot avoid the fact that the organs of higher animals pass through developmental stages which correspond with the adult condition of similar organs in lower forms. The correspondence is not exact, to be sure, but it is not an exaggeration to say that embryological development is parallel to that which anatomical study leads us to expect. A knowledge of the anatomy of an animal actually gives a sound basis of facts from which to predict in broad outlines its embryological development.

"But when one considers the widespread general correspondence of the developmental stages in higher forms with conditions as they exist in the adults of lower forms, the facts almost overwhelmingly force us to go further and conclude that the similarity has its basis in inheritance, in actual blood relationship between the higher and lower forms, in descent with modification—evolution."[54]

To these opinions that of Dendy may be added:

"In short, the embryological investigation of both animal and vegetable organisms leaves no doubt as to the general truth of the recapitulation hypothesis, and must convince any unbiased observer that, however much modified it may be by abbreviation and by the superposition of secondary features, the life-history of the individual is essentially a condensed epitome of the ancestral history of the race. The law of recapitulation, indeed, may be regarded simply as a local extension of the law of heredity, for every organism tends to inherit the characters not only of its immediate progenitors but of all its ancestors, and these characters appear in the individual life-history in the same order as that in which they first appeared in the ancestral history—in other words, ontogeny is a repetition of phylogeny and can only be explained in terms of organic evolution."[55]

Thus after sixty years, it would appear from this statement of Dendy, that biologists as a group have finally gotten around once more to the concepts of Haeckel whose exact conclusions have simply been paraphrased. Vernon Kellogg, the next year (1924), makes almost exactly the same statements:

"In the development of any individual plant or animal we can find a swift, much condensed and often much modified but, on the whole, very enlightening recapitulation of the general evolutionary history of the species to which the individual belongs. Embryonic stages occur which are essentially similar to stages in the embryology of other animals, and also stages are passed through, rapidly and incompletely but cognizably, which repeat and thus represent, in many characteristics, the adult stages of other lower animals or plants. The 'recapitulation theory' is one of the greatest generalizations that has been made in biological study. . . . But it contains, without any doubt, a large residuum of truth, and is one of the strongest evidences of evolution. The human body in its growth and development from a single fertilized egg cell to complex trillion-celled adult condition, with its many differentiated tissues and its elaborate systems or organs, tells us much of the history of the evolution of man."[56]

Of even greater significance is the relatively recent statement of Thomas Hunt Morgan, he who almost thirty years before had expressed himself to the effect that *"The idea that adult ancestral stages have been pushed back into the embryo and that the embryo recapitulates in part these ancestral adult stages is in principle false."* In what seems to be at least a partial recantation of his former view of the falsity of the *principle* of the recapitulation theory, he elaborates:

"While it is admitted on all sides today that a strain too great to bear was put on the facts of descriptive embryology, never-

[53] Conklin, E. G.: The Factors of Evolution from the Standpoint of Embryology, in *Foot-notes to Evolution*, by David Starr Jordan, New York, 1913, pp. 100-117.

[54] Woodruff, L. L.: *Foundations of Biology*, New York, 1922, pp. 364-366.

[55] Dendy, A.: *Outlines of Evolutionary Biology*, New York, 1923, p. 292.

[56] Kellogg, Vernon: *Evolution the Way of Man*, New York, 1924, pp. 53-64.

theless hosts of cases were discovered which are contributory to the evolution theory in the sense that they find their simplest interpretation of that theory. The facts almost speak for themselves: The gill-slits found in the embryos of birds and mammals; the appearance of a notocord in the embryo and its replacement by the vertebral column; the sequence of the blood systems in the higher vertebrates; the development accessively of the head-kidney, mid-kidney, and permanent kidney in the mammals; the embryonic history of the reproductive system, etc. These and many similar facts find their simplest and, I think, a satisfactory interpretation in the evolution theory as representing the past history of the embryonic development of the higher groups."[57]

Still another opinion in a similar vein is that of Pycraft:

"According to the recapitulation theory, with which I have no quarrel, every animal climbs its own ancestral tree. That is to say, it repeats in the course of its development, from the embryonic to the adult stage, the successive stages which marked the development of its ancestory, near and remote. Many objections have been raised to this conception, but these were largely based on too narrow interpretation of its terms.

"In its essential features there can be no escape from 'recapitulation.' "[58]

To carry the point further would only be to pile Pelion on Ossa. To read any general discussion on the Evolution theory, it seems conclusive that we must hark back to Haeckel's "biogenetic law," with modifications, to find "the strongest evidence in favor of evolution." This may be due, as Haeckel himself charged, to the fact that "no opponent of the principle has been able to set up anything better in its place."[59] It is noteworthy, nevertheless, that critical and analytical embryologists continue today to deny any significance to this theory, and yet those who have had little to do with studying out the details of

embryology, either structural or experimental, cannot "escape" from the significance of recapitulation. For these neo-recapitulationists, a new survey of the entire problem is therefore once more in order.

## FUNDAMENTAL WEAKNESSES OF THE RECAPITULATION CONCEPT

The reason for this tendency in some scientific circles to cling to the theory of recapitulation long after those who gave it birth have given it up, needs some elucidation. Is this true because the similarities clearly recognized for a century and a half are too significant to ignore, or is it because the newer findings in experimental embryology have nullified the arguments set forth by the leaders in the field years ago? It is certainly worth while to reinvestigate the concept since so many biologists "cannot escape" the conclusion that somehow these similarities signify blood relationships. The chief objections to the theory will now be taken in what seems to be a logical order.

1. *The recapitulation theory should be discarded because it is based on a false system of logic.*

It must be granted that the recapitulation theory had its beginnings in a proper scientific atmosphere. The early observers noted a parallelism in the morphology of early stages of vertebrate embryos. They assumed that these similarities must have some significance and concluded that these similarities indicated causal relationships. It was perfectly legitimate scientifically to formulate a theory based upon a series of observations, even though these observations were limited in extent. It is noteworthy that von Baer, who in his time was best

[57] Morgan, T. H.: *The Scientific Basis of Evolution,* New York, 1932, p. 174.
[58] Pycraft, W. P.: Some New Aspects of Evolution, *Ann. Rep. Smithsonian Inst.,* 1936, pp. 217-241.
[59] Haeckel, E.: Cited by Wilson, R. V.: The Recapitulation Theory or Biogenetic Law in Embryology, *Am. Nat.,* 1941, 75:26.

prepared to analyze the situation, denied any causal relationship even with the facts then available, thus anticipating almost a century the final conclusions of embryologists of our day.

It was Darwin who reversed the entire logic of the argument insofar as recapitulation is concerned, thus putting the scientific cart before the horse. In the first place it is very doubtful that he ever critically reviewed the evidence in the then available monograph of von Baer. Not being an embryologist, he was in no position to evaluate the facts within his reach. He needed recapitulation to support his concepts of evolution and the essential principle of parallelism was accepted by him.

Much the same is to be said for Haeckel who started out to prove the thesis of evolution in which he devoutly believed. He marshalled his material to this end. This objective obscured his vision to all other possibilities. Radl emphasizes this background of all Haeckel's endeavors in the following language.

"Evolution is the life-blood of his books. Take away the ideas about evolution and nothing is left but a lifeless husk, a mass of high-sounding words, of dull, descriptions, of many-coloured pictures—all empty and devoid of life. We look in vain for depth of feeling, for fineness of conception, for humour, style, self-distrust—in short, for any spark of humanity."[60]

A similar evaluation of Haeckel's method is given by another reputable historian, Nordenskiöld:

"Haeckel was never a specialist in embryology and its points of detail were of no interest to him in themselves, but only insofar as they could serve as evidence to show the descent of man. His ideas of embryology could in such circumstances only be one-sided and deficient; the professional embryologists

offered serious objections to them, which he either affected to overlook or answered with personal abuse. Complaints were made especially against his illustrations, which, contrary to usual practice, he hardly ever borrowed from monographs of the subject, but drew himself. Being designed exclusively to prove one single assertion, his illustrations were naturally schematic and without a trace of scientific value, sometimes indeed so far divergent from the actual facts as to cause him to be accused of deliberate falsifications—an accusation that a knowledge of his character would have at once refuted."[61]

It is thus evident that it was Haeckel's objective to prove the "law of biogenesis" and the chief attention which he gave to its deficiencies was to coin words to cover them. Thus the usual principle of scientific treatment of theories was reversed. Instead of putting the theory to the critical test at the hands of available facts, it was assumed to be true, simply awaiting verification until all the necessary details could be properly lined up. This conclusion is aptly put by Wallis:

"The recapitulation theory is deductive rather than inductive, the a priori creation rather than the empirical finding of Müller and of Haeckel. Haeckel admits this, and indeed, boasts that the theory is a priori. The facts are forced into this scheme, the evidence is not judiciously weighed, and the other interpretations are not considered. When Haeckel cited von Baer's position he deliberately suppressed the fourth conclusion of von Baer. This was: 'Fundamentally the embryo of a higher animal form never resembles the adult of another animal form, but only its embryo.' "[62]

It was the enthusiasm, personal force and literary effusiveness of Haeckel which carried the biogenetic law far out beyond its scientific depths. As Meyer has so pertinently put it: "Haeckel's formulation made recapitulation into a slogan but this could not make it a law."[63] So effective was

[60] Radl, E.: The History of Biological Theories, trans. by Hatfield, London, 1930, pp. 122-146.

[61] Nordenskiöld, E.: The History of Biology, trans. by L. B. Eyre, New York, 1928, p. 517.

[62] Wallis, W. D.: Human Recapitulation, Sc. Monthly, (Nov.) 1934, 443-448.

[63] Meyer, A. W.: loc. cit.

this effort, that it took embryologists almost half a century to free the science of Embryology from this old man of the sea, a thralldom under which Paleontology is still unconsciously laboring.

In conclusion it may be stated that recapitulation is very likely in error, if for no other reason than for the fact that it has been *assumed* to be true and that the f a c t s have been forced to fit it by its proponents. Scientific effort can hope to arrive at truth only when a given theory is put to the full test, and when exceptions become so strong and so numerous as to be preponderent, all that an honest investigator can do is to reject it and to try another in an effort to find some meaning to the phenomena which he thus investigates.

"Facts are desirable possessions, so are theories, but the two should not be confused. Facts should be kept in one pocket and theories in another. One should never forget that diagram, classification, symbolism, and hypothesis are but temporary expedients. They are good servants but poor masters. Like all man-made things they are imperfect, and as new facts come into view, they must all be revised or discarded. Moreover, those of us who are prudent will be particularly wary of the quick and easy explanation of the processes of living matter. In his classical monograph on comparative embryology von Baer places on the back of his title page the Latin slogan: 'Simplex est sigilum veritatis!'–simplicity is the seal of truth. That may have been a good working hypothesis at the time; but in view of our new knowledge of the remarkable intricacy of nature should we not change it to read: 'Complex est sigilum veritatis!'[64]

. . . . . .

"A consideration of these biological developments, utterly foreign to the biological background of early Haeckelians, taken with the many observational departures from the embryological sequences demanded by the theory of recapitulation, as well as the logical difficulties arising from an examination of the theory itself, seems to demand that the hypothesis be abandoned. Those of us who were reared in the phylogenetic tradition may see it go with a sigh of regret. Those of us charged with the responsibility of expounding the law of evolution to our classes will miss a familiar maxim, easily learned, and a convenient skeleton on which to hang the discrete data of embryology. But there can be no excuse for continuing to impress plastic minds by means of discredited generalizations. Let us return to the laws of von Baer and explain the resemblances which these describe in terms of processes rather than of precedents."[65]

## 2. *The theory of recapitulation is unreliable because the embryonic record is not coordinately condensed.*

While this is the simplest of the possible objections to the theory, it was not the first to be emphasized, for it was necessary to establish some sort of criterion of comparison of animal forms in order to know whether the condensation was proportional to the assumed evolutionary history. This consideration, simple as it seems, is important for it involves the basic concept of the theory, i. e., that the evolutionary history of the individual was "pushed back" into a short space of time in embryonic life. If this was all that had been done, a situation of "exact parallelism" would have existed.

Allowing for deviations in the record (to be considered in subsequent sections) there should be a rough correspondence in the time intervals of embryonic life and assumed evolutionary history. It is evident, even from superficial examination that such is not the case. The earlier embryonic stages evidently are too much condensed, for in man the "fish stage" is attained in relatively few hours in a life destined to be years long. By strict application of the theory, insufficient time is allowed for these stages in the embryo.

64 Streeter, G. L.: Archetypes and Symbolism, *Science,* (Apr. 29) 1927, 65:405-412.
65 Wallis, W. D.: *loc. cit.*

This argument is all the more pertinent in the light of the complaint of Cuming and other paleontologists that in their application of the recapitulation theory, embryologists considered only the embryonic phase of ontogeny and ignored the epembryonic period which lies between birth and adulthood. Conceding this argument, what a problem we have on our hands in considering the evolutionary history of man! If the approximate man-ape stage occurs just prior to birth, it would mean that the evolution of man from an anthropoid took 24 times as long (18 years to 9 months) as it did for the amoeba to develop into an ape-like ancestor, a conclusion with which no evolutionist would possibly agree. The theory works better when limited to the embryonic period.

This difficulty in which comparative embryos failed to maintain proper developmental relationships to each other soon became apparent to embryologists. The point in question is very well stated by Morgan:

"The point to which I wish to draw attention in this connection is that in the higher forms the gill-slits appear at a very early stage; in fact, as early in the mammal as in the salamander or fish, so that if we suppose their appearance in the mammal is a repetition of the adult amphibian stage, then, since this stage appears as early in the development of the mammal as in the amphibians themselves, the conclusion is somewhat paradoxical."[66]

To introduce this concept of condensation, a concept contemporary with the biogenetic law itself, Hyatt wrote that:

"All modifications and variations in progressive series tend to appear first in the adolescent or adult stages of growth, and then to be inherited in successive descendants at earlier and earlier stages according to the law of acceleration until they either become embryonic or are crowded out of the organizations, and replaced in the development by characteristics of later origin."[67]

It will now be argued that nature has tremendously condensed the simpler stages, and that there was an "acceleration" or "retardation" of the rate to suit her altered purpose in the development of the embryo. This subtheory of a variation in rate was recognized almost immediately after an attempt was made to make the various embryos fit into the proper scheme. The concept of "acceleration" was introduced by Hyatt, a paleontologist, who defined the term to mean that the accelerated or earlier appearance of a given character in the embryo was due to the omission or suppression of the earliest or older stages and an addition of characteristics strictly pertinent to the adult stage.

Smith, a contemporary geologist, stated that this change in pace was to be expected particularly

" . . . in the larval and adolescent periods where the shortness of time of development causes throwing together of characters that were not contemporaneous in the ancestry, and where the small size and general habits prevented differentiation of organs that in the correlative adult forms were highly developed. . . ."[68]

Before further consideration is given this general problem which seems to have been supported largely by geologists, a second subtheory of "retardation" should be introduced. Cope, an American naturalist of note, wrote:

"Where characters which appear latest in embryonic history are lost, we have simple retardation, that is, the animal in successive generations fails to grow up to the highest point of completion, falling further and further back, thus presenting an increasingly slower growth in the special direction in question."[69]

This is another way of stating that there are evidences in the embryo of

[66] Morgan, T. H.: loc. cit., p. 64.
[67] Hyatt, A.: Genesis of the Arietidae, Smithsonian Contributions to Knowledge, 1890.
[68] Smith, J. P.: loc. cit.
[69] Cope, E. D.: The Origin of the Fittest, New York, 1887.

retrogressive as well as progressive alteration, *devolution* as well as *evolution*.

In order to fully prove the point of "acceleration" and "retardation", it would be necessary to show that, in the evolutionary history of the individual organism in question, nature had accelerated the development of these coordinate characters which were to prove of special value to the individual or retard those characters which were to be ultimately lost. Unless this accelerated or retarded embryonic character actually met this fate in the evolutionary story, the force of the argument would naturally fall flat. It is obviously beyond the scope of this review to put these subtheories to a full scrutiny. Suffice it to say that such detailed causal interpretations of these variants in the speed of ontogeny have as yet not been made clear.

To pursue the point further and in a slightly different direction, the remarks of Cope on this point are quite in order:

"It is evident that 'exact parallelism' can only exist between ancestor and descendant in the same restricted line. . . . So soon as new subordinate characters are assumed, or a change in the order of appearance of character supervenes, the parallelism becomes 'inexact' and such is the kind of parallelism usually observed. And it is more inexact the more widely removed in relationship are the forms compared. All progressive organic evolution is by acceleration, as here described. Retrogressive evolution may be accomplished by a retardation of the rate of growth of the taxonomic characters, so that instead of adding and accumulating them, those already possessed are gradually dropped; the adults repeating in reversed order the progressive series, and approaching more and more the primitive embryonic stages. This process I have termed 'retardation.' Retardation is not, however, always exact. . . ."[70]

Based on this idea of "acceleration" (otherwise known as "preco-

cious segregation" (Lankester)) and of "retardation," it is not surprising that Morgan concluded that the concept "is in principle false" and that Montgomery opined that the idea was "highly figurative and metaphorical rather than exact."

3. *The theory of recapitulation cannot be correct because the order of the record is too seriously altered to be relied upon.*

If simple "acceleration" and "retardation" render the embryological parallelism inexact to the point where it cannot be depended upon to tell a true story, the interpolation and "falsification" of the record makes it all the more unreliable. As soon as the "biogenetic law" was applied to comparative embryology, it immediately became apparent to both Müller and Haeckel that, while some of the record seemed to be logically consecutive (palingenetic), other characters had obviously been added largely as adaptations to the embryonic existence (cenogenetic). These additions, especially in the presence of dropped characters and retardation, soon confused the "record" to a point where it was impossible to make sure which was what. This became evident to Gegenbauer, an early associate of Haeckel's, who made the following critical commentary:

"But if we are compelled to admit that cenogenetic characters are intermingled with palingenetic, then we cannot regard ontogeny as a sure source of evidence regarding phyletic relationships. Ontogeny, accordingly, becomes a field in which an active imagination may have full scope for its dangerous play, but in which positive results are by no means everywhere to be attained. To attain such results the palingenetic and the ontogenetic (cenogenetic) phenomena must be sifted apart, an operation that requires more than one critical *granum salis*. On what ground shall this critique be based? Assuredly not by the way of a circulus vitio-

---

[70] Cope, E. D.: *The Primary Factors of Organic Evolution*, Chicago, 1896.

sus on the ontogeny again; for if cenogenetic characters are present in one case, who will guarantee a second case used for comparison with the first, does not likewise appear in a cenogenetic disguise? . . . The necessary c r i t i q u e must be drawn from another source."[71]

Wilson, carrying this point to its implied conclusion, writes:

"And thus we are brought to a point of view directly opposed to that which on the whole is, I believe, the prevalent one, to the view, namely, that we must take anatomy as the key to embryology, and not the reverse. Comparative anatomy, not comparative embryology, is the primary standard of the study of homologies, and hence of genealogical descent."[72]

This view, which is now generally accepted, simply means that the embryologic record is so badly mixed up that it can no longer be relied upon and that it must be interpreted in the light of comparative anatomy. Recapitulation fails, therefore, in proving evolutionary sequence.

But this is not all. A more recent consideration of the difficulties provoked by this problem of "heterochrony," or reversal of sequence in development, is that of Shumway. He cited the observation of Keibel who called attention to the fact that, among vertebrates, teeth are structures much "older" than the tongue, but in the development of mammals the tongue appears before the teeth. DeBeer also listed some eight classes of disturbances of sequence with examples of each. To make the picture of heterochrony and its effects on the embryonic history more graphic. Shumway continues:

"Let us see what is left for recapitulation. Assume for the moment that an ideal ontogeny is composed of a series of stages (a, b, c, d, . . .) corresponding to a phylogenetic series of adults (A, B, C, D, . . .). To this we may add new terminal stages (i, ii, iii, iv, . . .) corresponding to new types of adults arising in evolution (I, II, III, IV, . . . ). Unless the period of ontogeny is lengthened, the series must be reduced by shortening the period allowed to each of its stages and eventually to the omission of some, e. g., c; and h. The series now takes the form (a, b, d, f, g. . . . z, i, ii, iii, iv).

"But new characters may also appear by interpolation and without corresponding adult types. The caenogenetic characters may be represented individually (1, 2, 3, 4, etc.). Their appearance will result in further abbreviations and omissions and we will arrive at such a series as (a, i, d, 2. . . . z, i, 8, vi).

"Now heterochrony comes upon the scene and our original series by reversal of stages may become thoroughly scrambled in the order (a, I, p, 4, 2, d, . . . 8, z, i, vi). It will now require the services of an embryological cryptographer to decipher the evolutionary meaning in terms of A, B, C, and I, II, III."[73]

While "confusion" of the embryonic stages may be overemphasized by this method, the fact remains, from both an experimental and philosophical standpoint, that room is left for considerable difference of opinion as to the significance of any individual stage of the embryo. With Gegenbauer and Wilson, Shumway agrees that the criterion must come from some outside source and that "only the methods of comparative anatomy, itself deductive, or of paleontology, can be used to decipher the record. To carry still further the figure of speech so eloquently used by Balfour, Marshall and others who compared the embryonic record with an abridged and altered manuscript, subsequently "interpolated by another hand," *it now appears that this manuscript has been written in an unknown language, the only clue to which is another language, itself quite susceptible of various interpretations!*

---

[71] Gegenbauer: Cited by Wilson, *loc. cit.*

[72] Wilson, E. B.: The Embryological Criterion of Homology, in *Biological Lectures*, Boston, 1896, p. 104.

[73] Shumway, W.: The Recapitulation Theory, *Quart. J. Biol.*, (March) 1932, 7:93-99.

Under these circumstances, of how much value is ontogeny as an interpretation of the evolutionary record? Is not this interpretation of comparative embryology by comparative anatomy, which in itself is "deductive," reasoning "in a very small circle" as Gegenbauer has charged?

Shumway, in a conclusion of the whole matter, writes:

"It is the function of the embryo to become an adult without looking backward on ancestral history. It is the business of the embryologist to describe the phenomena which he observes in terms of individual development without undue attention to what can be interpreted at most as reminiscences of evolution."[74]

4. *The theory of recapitulation rests on a fundamentally insecure basis since superficial resemblances are shown not to be synonymous with identity.*

Perhaps no other fact so contributes to the greatness of von Baer, unless perchance it is his discovery of the mammalian ovum, as does his clear distinction between similarity and identity of embryonic structures. Not only did he see this distinction himself, but he also discerned the confusion of others on this point, which confusion was to merge almost imperceptibly with the developing idea of organic evolution to become the full-blown "biogenetic law." On this point von Baer writes:

"Some supporters (of parallelism) are so zealous that they no longer speak of similarity but of complete identity, and act as though the correspondence is proven universally and in each particular. We read a short time ago, in a paper upon the blood circulation of the embryo, that the human embryo does not omit a single animal form."[75]

There can be no doubt but that this evident morphological parallelism in early stages of the embryo did at that time, and still does, impress those who are evolutionary-minded. If one will be content to satisfy himself with these superficial similarities, the subject might be dismissed with the conclusion that such similarities must have some phylogenetic import. Only those who have actually wrestled with the details of a problem in embryological research can fully understand the errors that can be fallen into in this regard. While the various individual structures likely to have recapitulatory significance, namely the "branchial" arches, the aortic arches, the heart, kidneys, and skull cannot be investigated in detail in a general review such as this is, the argument on this point is not to be dismissed lightly. This is particularly so because of a modification of the recapitulation theory proposed by Lillie,[76] and apparently acceded to by Shumway,[77] to the effect that the theory of recapitulation "is not applicable to the embryo as a whole, but only to individual organs or systems of organs."

Attention should first be given to the cervical arches (commonly and erroneously know as "gill-arches" and the associated depressions designated as *gill-slits*), since it is this resemblance which is so often appealed to when dealing with the lay mind. To show the extent to which this error has gone, even the minds of the leaders in biological science, one need only to refer again to the quotation from Thomas Hunt Morgan, renowned embryologist and geneticist, writing within the last decade:

"While it is admitted on all sides today that a strain too great to bear was put on the facts of descriptive embryology, never-

[74] Shumway, W.: *loc. cit.*
[75] von Baer, K.: Cited by Davidson, *loc. cit.*
[76] Lillie, F. R.: The Development of the Chick, The Macmillan Co., New York, 1919.
[77] Shumway, W.: *loc. cit.*

theless hosts of cases were discovered which are contributory to the evolution theory in the sense that they find their simplest interpretation on that theory. The facts almost speak for themselves: The gill-slits found in the embryos of birds and mammals; the appearances of the notochord in the embryo and its replacement by the vertebral column; the sequence of the blood systems in the higher vertebrates; the development successively of head-kidney, mid-kidney, and the permanent kidney in the mammals, the embryonic history of the reproductive system, etc. These and many similar facts find their simplest and, I think, a satisfactory interpretation in the evolution theory as representing the past history of the embryonic development of the higher groups."

"In birds and mammals . . . most of the gill-slits close up and disappear."[78]

It is this sort of inexact terminology which is misleading to less able and less critical minds in dealing with the problem of the branchial arches.[79]

It is difficult to understand this more recent position of Morgan which seems like a reversal of his earlier critical attitude toward the "gill-arch" argument when he had this to say:

"It is useless to say, as Weismann has stated (*The Evolution Theory*, London, vol. II, p. 176, 1904), that 'it cannot be disputed that the rudiments (vestiges his translator means) of gill-arches and gill-clefts, which are peculiar to one stage of human ontogeny, gives us every ground for concluding that we possessed f i s h - l i k e ancestors.

"The question at issue is: did the pharyngeal arches and clefts of mammalian embryos ever discharge a branchial function in an adult ancestor of the mammalia? We cannot, therefore, without begging the question at issue in the grossest manner, apply to them the terms 'gill-arches' and 'gill-clefts.' That they are homologous with the 'gill-arches' and 'gill-clefts' of fishes is true: but there is no evidence to show that they ever discharged a branchial function. Until such evidence is forthcoming, it is beside the point to say that 'it cannot be disputed' that they are evidence of a piscine ancestry."[80]

As still another argument against this position, Morgan writes in this same survey:

"The point to which I wish to draw attention in this connection is that in the higher forms the gill slits appear at a very early stage; in fact as early in the mammal as in the salamander of the fish, so that if we suppose their appearance in the mammal is a repetition of the adult amphibian stage, then since this stage appears as early in the development of the mammal as in the amphibians themselves, the conclusion is somewhat paradoxical."[80]

If one inspects superficially a series of human embryos at various stages in development, he finds an external and superficial resemblance of the cervical arches to the anlage of the gills in the fish embryo. A more critical examination, however, shows the fallacy of this assumption. The first and most prominent of these arches will be found to form the lower jaw of the fetus (which it does not do in the fish) and should, therefore, not be included in the series of arches at all. The next two arches can be traced into the for-

---

[78] Morgan, T. H.: *The Scientific Basis of Evolution*, New York, 1932, p. 174.

[79] It is to be emphasized that "in birds and mammals" no *gill-slits* ever existed. To be sure there are a series of local swellings separated by depressions which superficially resemble the gill-arches of the fish embryo. The fact remains that these depressions or clefts are never open, and therefore do not close, as Morgan has intimated. As a classical example of what this sort of loose thinking will do among those who have never critically looked into the matter, is a short treatise written for high school students by Moore entitled, "The Law of Biogenesis." In it he writes: "There is always a stage in the embryonic development of birds and mammals when they breathe by gills like a fish and have the other general characters of a fish." It is small wonder that under such tutelage our high school students have come to believe the recapitulation theory as a *law*. The advice of Shumway to embryology teachers might well apply to biology teachers as well.

[80] Morgan, Thomas Hunt: *Evolution and Adaptation*, New York, 1903, p. 64.

mation of the external ear by progressive morphological alterations. These cervical elevations are, therefore, no meaningless "gill-arches," hangovers from an ancestral fish stage, but structures which without deviation or hesitation enter into the formation of the outer ear.

Experimental embryology gives further point to the principle of progressive formation of the ear as related to internal structures. Experimental removal of these external arches in the f r o g embryo and replacement with a non-elevated part of the covering of the frog, results in a new formation of these external structures. This has been interpreted to mean that it is the internal endodermal folds which "organize" or lead out in the development of the external structures. In local development the external structures simply conform to i n t e r n a l functional arrangement which have to do with the respiratory function of the fish on the one hand and the formation of the ear of the mammal on the other, two quite different and distinct functions. This establishes a causal significance to these folds, rather than interpreting them on the basis of ancestral influences. Since Morgan reviewed these studies in his monograph in 1927, it is strange that in 1932 he felt still constrained to say that: "These and similar facts find their simplest and, I think, a satisfactory interpretation in the evolution theory as representing the past history of the embryonic development of the higher groups."

Ignoring the far more important fact that the branchial arches in the early vertebrate embryos are indicative of a basic plan of development. that they are the result, not the cause of local structural developments which are to enter into the formation of other structures, having nothing to do with the function of respiration.

a more vital problem as it pertains to evolution should be noted. In his early discussion of the theory of recapitulation, Herbert Spencer called attention to an important objection to it, i. e., that it gives no clue to the cause or the method of substitution of the lungs for the gill mechanism of the fish. If the recapitulation theory is of any significance in this discussion, it should indicate, at least in one of the embryonic stages, just how this transition has taken place. This is particularly vital to the point, because no other cenogenetic (newly developed) character has apparently interfeared at this stage to destroy or distort the embryonic record.

Nothing can serve better to disclose the essential error of superficial similarity in application of the recapitulation theory than this out-worn allusion to the *gill-slits* of avian and mammalian embryos.

Closely related to the problem of the branchial arches is that of the aortic arches which, in the human embryo, are alleged to be recapitulatory of those of the lower forms of life. Streeter, one of the most outstanding embryologists and investigators in this field, has this to say about these arches:

"On studying the blood vessels coursing through them, they (Rathke and von Baer) found a series of aortic arches on each side similar to what had already been observed in the chick. All this seemed to signify the existence of a transitory branchial apparatus throughout the mammals, and pyramiding theory upon theory, it later came to be one of the favorite arguments for the recapitulation theory. . . . To say that they (the aortic arches) are a transitory set of symmetrical and uniform tubes, a symbol of a phase in ancestral history, is no longer an adequate description of them. . . . With this better knowledge of the exact anatomy of the aortic arches, it has become apparent that at no time does Rathke's embryonic type really exist in the embryo—any more than does the Owen archetype vertebrae.

. . . If we start with a diagram of something that does not exist, an infinite number of improvements cannot make it correct. This appears to be the situation in which Rathke's diagram now finds itself."[81]

It is not surprising that Doctor Streeter concludes that "we now have better ways of accounting for the phenomena of embryology than by the recapitulation theory."[82]

One is tempted to enter into a discussion of the significance of comparative morphogenesis of the brain, a subject in which the writer is particularly interested, but space does not permit. As in some other details, it has long been held that the development of the brain is recapitulatory of the phylogenesis of this organ. Sometimes cited as proof of this is the apparent similarity in the development of the three primary brain vesicles. On this point Streeter has this to say:

"In other words, the brain begins to build its definitive parts before the closure of the neural tube without going through the preliminary archetypal indifferent three-vesicle stage. With further experience and additional material this has been abundantly substantiated in the pig as well as in man. There seems to be no evidence that the brain wastes any empty gestures toward the past. With no false moves it proceeds directly with the building of an organ appropriate in all its parts for the respective species. It has taken a long time to find this out. It probably would not have taken so long if we had not been so well satisfied with the diagramatic concept of the three brain vesicles."[83]

In the writer's experience, a comparison of the detailed structures and the stages of development of any portion of the brain soon discloses the fact that there is no real parallelism of phylogenetic significance. The development of the diencephalic floor, for example, which has been assumed to be one of the more "primitive" parts of the brain, undergoes in each

species an individuality in development which extends even to the various cell groups which make up its finer structure. In the brain, too, the recapitulatory concept does not extend to anatomic details.

Perhaps of all the systems of organs which are most suggestive of having recapitulatory import, the urinary system is most significant. The successive occurrence of the fore-kidney or pronephros (which is the only excretory organ as in the hags), the mid-kidney or mesonephros (the pronephros being the provisional, the hind-kidney or mesonephros the permanent kidney as in the selachians and the amphibians) and the metanephros (with the pronephros and the mesonephros as provisional kidneys, as in the birds and mammals). These important details together with the rather "primitive" character of the pronephros in the human embryo makes the biogenetic law a rather strong possibility as an explanation of the development of the urinary system. Three important arguments, however, stand out against this concept and will here be given consideration.

In the first place, *the preservation of all presumed intermediate stages in the formation of a given system is not the plan Nature evidently has used in the ontogeny of an animal.* In fact, the alleged "crowding back" of the evolutionary history in the embryological history has necessitated, so it is said, the omission of many of the stages of phylogeny, touching only the high points of its history. What, then, has made it possible for the entire history of the urinary system to be preserved? There is no cogent argument in favor of preservation of all the stages in the development of the

---

[81] Streeter, G. L.: Archetypes and Symbolism, *Science,* (April 29) 1927, 65:405-412.
[82] Streeter, G. L.: Personal communication to the writer.
[83] Streeter, G. L.: *loc. cit.*

urinary system, when, for example, none of the assumed stages in the transition of the respiratory system from gills to lungs has been preserved. This is particularly significant when it is recognized that the tubules of the first kidney (pronephros) are still present in urogenital ridge, when the tubules of the mesonephros (mid-kidney) begin to develop in an adjacent portion of the same ridge. Moreover, only the tubules of one system r e p l a c e those of the other, all systems use the same excretory duct. In short, only the tubules (ultimately the kidney proper) are recapitulatory, while the excretory duct ultimately the ureter) is not.

To show the inadequacy of this conclusion, we have but to turn to comparative anatomy, which has already been presumed (by some recapitulationists) to be the final court of appeal. In a classical study on the question of urinary secretion in the embryos of mammals, Bremer found that mammalian embryos can be divided into three groups on this basis; (1) in which the primitive kidney (Wolffian body) retains its function until the permanent kidneys are sufficiently developed to take over excretion (reptiles, birds, pigs, sheep, and cats); (2) those in which this body degenerates before the permanent kidney is formed, under which circumstances the placenta must take over the excretory function, (rabbit, guinea pig, and man); and (3) in which urinary excretion takes place entirely through the placenta throughout embryonic and fetal life (rat).[84]

It would thus appear, for example, that among the rodents alone (guinea pigs vs. rats), two entirely different types of urinary execretion occurs during the embryonic and fetal stage.

If so great a difference is found in so restricted a group, how much significance can be placed on conclusions drawn on the entire vertebrate group?

A study of the primate kidney gives still more c o n f u s i n g results when viewed from the phylogenetic standpoint. The various students of the problem have found that there are five different kinds of kidneys among the primates. From these observations, two opposing theories of renal phylogeny have arisen. One group of investigators insist that the "simple, essentially undivided, unipapillate kidney represents the primitive type," while the other school concludes that the multi-papillate kidney represents the primitive type. On this point Straus writes:

"Wood-Jones (1929) was especially concerned with the theory that Man is more primitive in structure than are the extant apes and monkeys. Respecting the kidney, he writes that 'Man retains . . . an earlier ontogenetic stage of kidney development than do the Cynomorpha or the Anthromorpha' (p. 323). This assumption is extremely hazardous in the light of present knowledge. It is based apparently upon the occurrence of external renal lobules in prenatal man. Yet Maresch encountered no increase in number of renal papillae in human foetuses and newborns as compared with adult Man. The external renal lobulation, therefore, may merely be superficial, and not expressive of a fundamental or primitive lobulation."

"One other point of phylogenetic interest concerns certain statements of Weinert (1932). He attempted to show that in the structure of the kidney (i. e., number of papillae), among other points, the chimpanzee more closely approaches Man than does any other Primate. A critical examination of the available evidence, however, shows plainly that neither the chimpanzee nor any other anthropoid ape can be regarded as suggesting the human form of kidney.

"Consideration of Primate kidneys from the phylogenetic aspect merely emphasizes the unique and isolated position of Man. The only approach to the human condition

---

[84] Bremer, J. L.: The Interrelations of the Mesonephros, Kidney and Placenta in Different Classes of Animals, *Am. J. Anat.*, (Mar.) 1916, 19:179.

is made by the spider monkey, and this feature is not a constant one in that animal. Surely no one would seriously claim other than a very remote relationship between *Homo* and *Ateles*. The presence of true primary renal lobulation in the two forms can only be regarded as the product of convergence, a phenomenon which in these two animals is not limited to the kidney alone."

The author concludes:

"The phylogenetic history of the kidney is by no means clear. No existing theory is entirely satisfactory. The chief point of interest lies in the isolated position of Man among Primates in respect to renal form, and the approach to the human condition by the spider monkey."[85]

In the second place, as has already been suggested by the studies cited above, *no satisfactory phylogenetic arrangement of animals can be made on the basis of comparative embryology of the kidney*. Two short citations will suffice to emphasize this point. In the first, Morgan points out that, although the embryogeny of the urinary system seems to be a recapitulation of its phylogeny, the problem is not so simple:

"In the development of the kidneys, or nephridia, we find, perhaps, another parallel, although, owing to recent discoveries, we must be cautious in our interpretation. As yet nothing corresponding to the nephridia of the Amphioxus has ever been discovered in other vertebrates. Our comparison must begin, therefore, higher up in the series."[86]

In other words, the pronephros, which by its simplicity has so often been taken as primitive, fails to give us the starting point in any comparative development of the kidney.

Again, as Felix wrote in his basic study of the development of the human kidney:

"The human pronephros (head- or forekidney, the most 'primitive' one) is by far

the best developed within the group of mammals. It shows its relations more clearly than it does in birds and is at least as distinct as in reptiles."[87]

In other words, the pronephros, the primitive kidney, is better developed in man than in the birds and is equally as well developed as in reptiles. On this basis the reptiles evolved from the birds instead of vice versa, and insofar as the pronephros is concerned, Man has not evolved further than the reptile stage.

Finally, it seems clear from recent histological and chemical investigations, that *the pronephros and mesonephros are functioning organs*, at least in some of the mammals. The better way of accounting for the presence of these organs in Man, therefore, rather than assuming that they have persisted through ontogeny because they are recapitulatory, is to recognize their temporary place as simple excretory organs at a stage when no complex organ for this function has yet had time to develop.

One might also investigate other details of embryonic development which have been alluded to as recapitulatory, such as the heart. ("We find here, then, a sort of parallel, provided we do not inquire too particularly into details"—Morgan), but space does not permit. It may fairly be assumed that if the argument that the "gill-arches," the aortic arches, the brain and the kidney which seem the best examples of recapitulation do not hold water, the remaining examples are less likely to, particularly if scrutinized in the light of the propositions to be considered in the next argument.

5. *The recapitulation theory is to be doubted because the philosophy*

[85] Straus, William L.: The Structure of the Primate Kidney, *J. Anat.*, (Oct.) 1934, 69:94.

[86] Morgan, T. H.: *Evolution and Adaptation*, p. 56.

[87] Felix, W.: The Development of the Urinogenital Organs in *Manual of Human Embryology* (Keibel and Mall), Philadelphia, 1912, Vol. II, p. 770.

*does not extend to anatomic details, even in case of closely allied forms.*

Sedgwick insisted many years ago that the "family resemblance between embryos and larvae, . . . which is by no means exact, is largely superficial and does not extend to anatomical detail."[88] This suggestion carries more weight than the superficial investigator will think. The citation of Montgomery is quite to the point:

"Two closely related species of Nemertine, as in the genus *Lineus*, may show quite different modes of development, the one continuous and the other discontinuous (larval). More than this, individuals of the same species from different localities may show different kinds of larval development, as in the case of certain Crustacea. We are in no way justified in concluding, from the examination of embryology alone, that one of these modes is more ancestral than the other."[89]

The opposite situation is also true that very similar larvae may give rise to quite different adults.

One of the most unusual phenomena among embryologists, particularly those who are convinced that organic evolution is a fact and that certain aspects of comparative embryology have recapitulatory significance, is that so little critical effort is directed to testing the theory by the facts which they elicit from personal study. Almost never can one find any critical deductions from any extensive study of material in this direction. Either such efforts have been found to be fruitless or less faith exists in the theory than one would still presume from general reading in the biologic sciences. This same conclusion is aptly expressed by Shumway:

"It is an interesting sidelight on the status of the recapitulation theory among embryologists that, while many of them have in-vestigated the organogeny of many different animals and have arrived at certain conclusions concerning the phylogeny of these groups, few have made use of their material to prove or disprove the validity of the theory itself. The most ardent advocates of the Haeckelian theory have been found among anatomists and paleontologists, who have not the opportunity of observing how the different embryological stages arise one from the other, nor the problem of analyzing the functions of the different elements associated in each stage."[90]

It was this sort of an attempt which led the writer to take an active interest in the recapitulation theory. As one of his problems, a comparative study of the development of the diencephalic floor in various vertebrates was made. In the material available to both personal study and that found in the literature, the variation in size and detail of this relatively simple portion of the brain as found in early embryos was very striking. As has been the experience of others, any attempt to arrange the various representative mammals on one basis was found to throw the whole series into hopeless confusion on all others.

While it must be recognized that this problem of embryonic detail cannot be applied to animals widely variant in their adult stages, it seems reasonable that two closely allied forms should have closer similarities than two forms not so closely related. But this is not the case. What is even more significant than simple morphology in comparisons is the light shed on the question by experimental embryology. It is found that identical structures in closely allied species may be formed from material from entirely different sources. This fact seems to destroy the very essence of the concept of recapitulation.[91]

---

[88] Sedgwick, A.: *Darwin and Modern Science*, p. 175.
[89] Montgomery, T. H.: *loc. cit.* p. 193.
[90] Shumway, W.: *loc. cit.*
[91] It seems highly significant that the new science of experimental embryology has had no place for the theory of recapitulation. One searches in vain for any serious reference

6. *The recapitulation theory is inconsistent because it ignores certain major details of embryonic development which obviously run counter to the concept.*

From the time of Haeckel to the present, the deficiences in the theory of r e c a p i t u l a t i o n have been excused on the basis that, in the process of "pressing back" into this epitome of the evolution of the race, many of the details have been crowded out of the picture. This in itself is not an unreasonable assumption. On the other hand, it also seems fair to assume that the major features, constant throughout the entire course of development, should retain their full significance.

Perhaps the most important example in point is the development of the head and brain. Throughout the embryonic series, the head end of the embryo is always the most significant in its size. And yet there is a progressive diminution in the relative size of the head as development proceeds. No paleontologist would care to assume that ancestors of either animals or man possessed larger heads and brains than are observed today. This outspoken defect is ignored by the large number of recapitulationists who seem certain that the less impressive and less conclusive "gill-arches" do have ancestral significance.

By applying this logic more particularly in a comparison between the anthropoids and man, where it should theoretically work out in favor of recapitulation if the concept were valid, we find that the theory works the wrong way. Wallis writes to this point:

"This (exaggerated size of the head), of course, is contrary to the general story of evolution, which shows an increase in relative size of the brain from the lower creatures to the higher, from the non-Primates to Primates, and from most of the lower Primates to man . . . Indeed, if one accepts recapitulation, much of the prenatal and early postnatal development implies that man's ancestry developed from a more human to a less human form, that is from humanlike to anthropoid apelike, or in ontogenetic development the human individual acquires relatively less brain, proportionally greater supraorbital prominences and proportionally lower cranial vault."[92]

Wallis elaborates further on this point:

"If we apply the some logic to the anthropoid as to man—and we should extend that charity—the anthropoid recapitulates human ancestry; for the further back one traces anthropoid ontogenetic development, the more human-like are the anthropoid characteristics. The logic which suggests that man recapitulates anthropoid ancestry suggests also that the anthropoid recapitulates human ancestry."

"Indeed, if one accepts recapitulation, much of the prenatal and early postnatal development implies that man's ancestry developed from a more human to a less human form, that is, from humanlike to anthropoid apelike, for in ontogenetic development the human individual acquires relatively less brain, proportionately greater supraorbital prominences and proportionally lower cranial vault. . . . In relative head size in terms of trunk length, the *cebus apella*, one of the lower primates, exceeds man by about 8 units."

'In many respects man is tardy in developing the traits which distinguish the anthropoid apes; that is, he does not acquire until adolescence or adulthood some traits which are found in the anthropoid apes soon after birth or even during prenatal development."[93]

As examples of some of these details in which man recapitulates his primate ancestry rather than vice versa are: (1) Dentition is slower in man

to the subject in the several text-books and articles on the subject which are now available. It would seem almost certain that if the concept had any essential truth to it, the newer discoveries in this field should somehow lend it some visible support.

[92] Wallis, W. D.: Human Recapitulation, *Sc. Monthly*, (Nov.) 1934, 443-448.
[93] Wallis, W. D.: *loc. cit.*

than in the ape. (2) Prognathism is more marked in the adult than in the infant. (3) Adult man has more hair than does the fetus or infant. (4) Especially noticeable in the dark races, pigmentation increases a f t e r birth. (5) The eyebrows and projecting lower jaw are more evident in the adult. (6) The zygomatic arches are wider in the adult. (7) The delayed closure of the suture lines of the skull are reminiscent of the ape. While s u c h examples are not necessarily proof of anything, it cannot be gainsayed that, with so many serious contradictions to the theory in the primate group itself, one is not entitled to accept recapitulation in its wider application without grave misgivings. Certainly the unusual degree of development of the head and brain in the early embryo is far more significant than any consideration of the "branchial" arches can possibly be.

7. *The recapitulation theory is disproven by the failure to reproduce transitional stages by natural or experimental retardation.*

If the theory of recapitulation is tenable, it is reasonable to assume t h a t interference w i t h normal development from whatever cause should, in a certain percentage of cases, result in abnormalities reminiscent of these transitional stages, at least insofar as the affected part is concerned. In the past, there has been some effort to account for some of the congenital malformations and anomalies on a basis of atavism. The resultant deformity was explained in a few isolated cases by a retardation of the development of the embryo or fetus at a given stage. The most conspicuous abnormalities to be accounted for on this basis are the relatively rare human "tails" (which, when present, more nearly resemble a pig's tail than anything else, if they resemble a tail at all), multiple nipples and breasts (whose argument in favor of atavism rests upon the presumed existence of a mythical prehuman ancestor or, more commonly, upon a miscomprehension of the embryology of the lacteal glands on the one hand and of nipples on the other), and the superficial resemblance of the head and brain in certain malformations to those of the apes. This whole problem is of sufficient importance to devote considerable space and time to it, quite out of order in a review. In a subsequent article, particular attention will be given to the details of this subject.

Granting the above rare exceptions as being significant (which they are n o t), the tremendous majority of congenital abnormalities are generally recognized to have no recapitulatory significance whatever. Retardation of development, whether from some naturally acquired disturbance or produced experimentally, completely fails to reproduce any of the presumed ancestral stages. While known to be due to other causes in the past, experimental embryology has thrown new light on the entire problem. Malformations are now accounted for by a disturbance in the hierarchy of organizing factors, a principle entirely foreign to atavism. Recapitulation fails to account for malformations and interference with embryonic growth fails to produce pictures of lower forms of animal life.

## RECENT TRENDS IN EMBRYOLOGY AND THEIR SIGNIFICANCE IN THE LIGHT OF THE RECAPITULATION THEORY

"The Haeckelian recapitulationists knew nothing of modern genetics and very little experimental embryology. They were fancy free in dealing with heredity and the physical forces involved in development. Hence they could refer to a mysterious heredity and conclude that an adult might in some occult sense determine the course of development in the offspring, even though the characters transmitted were acquired in a Lamarckian sense."[94]

So writes Shumway in 1932, sixty odd years after the elaboration of the biogenetic law by Haeckel. Unrestricted by the laws of heredity elaborated by Mendel, then entirely unknown to them, the early recapitulationists did not n e e d to trouble themselves as to how the progressive changes might have taken place.

It was Hatschek who came to recognize that any modification in the new individual had to be preceded by a change in the egg itself, which involved a complete reshuffling of the entire s e r i e s of embryonic stages. While Hatschek later considered this to be possible, it was only by accepting the idea that "newly occurring characters become inherited which have arisen through variation of the reproductive glands."

Today in the light of what is known about genetics and the remarkable mechanism for transmission of characters, there seems to be considerable reluctance to associate recapitulation with genetic variation, even on the part of Thomas Hunt Morgan who is a master in both embryology and genetics. Insofar as the writer knows, Morgan has made no attempt to bring his "repetition theory" (which is a rechristened recapitulation theory) and his work on genetics together. And if this seems difficult for him to do, who shall attempt it? The simple fact remains that the modern science of genetics has needed no help from the recapitulation theory and has done nothing to support or clarify it. Indeed, the present trend against any transmission of acquired characteristics seems only to intone a requiem for recapitulation and its aliases.

Much the same is to be said for experimental or physiological embry-

ology. The attempts on the part of His and Roux to interpret the phenomena of the developing embryo other than by the preconceived and essentially rigid formulary of recapitulation, have resulted finally in a new science of Experimental Embryology which has come to be completely estranged from the older morphological science dominated by the theory of recapitulation. There has been no serious attempt to coordinate experimental embryology with the biogenetic law, and those who still cling to the theory have never evoked the help of this department of the science in an attempt to materialize its departed spirit. While perhaps it is too early to formulate the organizer concepts into laws," the facts again seem to controvert the basic concept of recapitulation. It seems that the great advances in this new territory are to be accounted for by the fact that no handicapping hypothesis has gotten in the way.

Still another branch of embryology, not so sharply separated from its experimental branch, is that of Chemical Embryology which follows its own line of investigation. As the result of extensive studies in this field, Needham, the founder of a n e w school, writes by way of conclusion:

"An account of the present status of the theory of recapitulation is introduced by a discussion of the transitory function of embryonic life: neutral development, hatching enzymes, egg-breakers, the glycogenic functions of blastoderms and yolk-sacs, and yolk hormones. The similarity between the organizer phenomena and the formative stimuli provided by recapitulated structures is pointed out, and it is concluded that recapitulation itself can not be regarded as an explanation of anything. . . . Recapitulation may be regarded as fundamentally the result of the necessary passage from simplicity to complexity, from low to high organization, which is entailed by the metazoal sexual system of reproduction, with its simple egg-

[94] Shumway, W.: loc. cit.

cell. The retention of visible organs and structures from lower ontogenies in a given ontogeny is only a special case of this general rule and probably depends on the presence in them of essential formative stimuli."[95]

Thus it may be seen that the three children of Morphologic Embryology pay no heed to the "fundamental law of biogenesis" which promised so much and provided so little by way of any real help. It, moreover, seems likely that it has been a freedom from the restraints of this law that has accounted for the real progress which has been made. Today these children do not seem to recognize their indolent step-father and are certainly doing nothing to support him in his dotage.

"This evolutional theory is undeniably Haeckel's most brilliant and most important contribution to the history of biology. O. Hertwig was right in saying that for fifty years biological literature was under the influence of this idea; the abundant facts that were amassed on this subject of embryology during this period were mostly intended to confirm the biogenetical principle or the 'recapitulation' theory, as it has also been called, and biologists strained every effort to apply it to every detail in the development of the embryo. And the application was 'strained' in the fullest sense of the word. Haeckel knew from the outset that the gastrula stage of the mammals is not formed through invagination, as the theory claimed, but through delamination, or splitting off; he consoled himself, however, with the thought that in the lancet-fish invagination generally takes place, and from this primitive animal he derives the mammals, with the assertion that their gastrula form is due to later adaptation—to the 'falsification' of documents, of which Fritz Müller had spoken. He also explains a number of other facts of a similar kind according to the same method. . . . But, even apart from this, time has dealt hardly with Haeckel's ontogenetical theories. The gastrula formation by means of invagination has proved far less general than Haeckel believed—inter alia, it is lacking in

most of the Coelenterata — and the far-fetched homologization of the germinal layers has been considerably restricted, the same organs in a number of different animals having been found to possess an entirely different origin. In particular, the mesodermal formation has now been resolved into a number of different processes. In fact, the entire 'biogenetical principle' is nowadays severely challenged, even as a hypothesis; in the vegetable kingdom it has received no confirmation, which is indeed strange for a theory proposed to hold good as a general explanation of life, but even those zoologists who in general give any support at all to the recapitulation theory do so with considerable reservations, called for by the results of modern hereditary research and experimental biology. Nowadays one does not compare without question, as they did in Haeckel's time, the ideas of similarity and affinity; similarity can demonstrably arise through the influence of very different factors, and it is preferred to follow His in seeking for the mechanical conditions governing the development of form instead of seeing therein resemblances to animal life of past ages. But this should not involve our depreciating Haeckel's influence on the development of embryology; it was his theory which evoked that interest in those phenomena that brought about the immense revival of this form of research lasting up to the present day. In this connection we may remember von Baer's words that 'inaccurate but definitely pronounced general results have, through the corrections which they call for and the keener observation of all the circumstances which they induce, almost invariably proved more profitable than cautious reserve.' It is just herein that Haeckel has benefited his science most; here he has made his most important and historically most valuable contribution. But with it he gave all that he had to give; the years that he lived afterwards produced nothing to increase his reputation, but detracted much from it."[96]

Thus is epitomized the history and present day status of the recapitulation theory with which we have been dealing. In no better way can be expressed the present status of the theory than so stated by this outstanding biologist.

---

[95] Needham, J.: The biochemical aspect of the recapitulation theory, *Biol. Rev. & Biol. Proc. Cambridge Phil. Soc.*, 1930, 5:142-158. (Also Abstract. Biol. Rev.)
[96] Nordenskiöld, E.: *loc. cit.*

## RECAPITULATION'S TWO CHALLENGES

But Haeckel and his biogenetic law cannot be finally dismissed until two of his statements are given an airing. The first was written at the outset of his career as a biologist, the second near its close. The first is that:

"These two branches of our science—on the one side ontogeny or embryology, and on the other phylogeny, or the science of race evolution—are most vitally connected. . . . This is a discovery made by recent research, and it is most clearly and correctly expressed in the comprehensive law which I have called 'the fundamental law of organic evolution,' or 'the fundamental law of biogeny.'"

In this statement, Haeckel maintained that embryology and evolution were vitally connected, a connection which was "not external and superficial, but profound, intrinsic, and causal." The remorseless hand of time has indeed "dealt hardly" with his biogenetic law, and today biologists in general and embryologists in particular find little in it to stimulate thought or activity. But what have they done with the theory of evolution which the biogenetic law with its reflections in embryology and paleontology was presumed to support? Has this conclusion of Haeckel been repudiated?

It may be stated that the downfall of the recapitulation theory which was originally elaborated in defense of evolution does not of itself prove that the parent theory is falacious, although it is obviously much weakened by such a failure since embryology professedly presents some of the strongest evidence in its support. But what has been developed to take the place of the theory? If organic evolution has taken place, it would seem as though there must be some significance to certain embryologic phenomena. Is the resemblance that certainly exists, "inescapable" in its reminiscence of evolution?

As far as the writer knows, there has been only one serious attempt to use Embryology to save the day for Organic Evolution, and that a short treatise by DeBeer. In his thesis, he reviews the various expressions which have been used in the past to account for the disturbances in the ontogenetic record, phenomena as have been described in the stages of the embryo,— *heterochrony* (alteration and reversal of the embryonic stages), *neotony* (sexual maturity before adulthood), *caenogenesis* (adaptations characteristic of the embryo itself, *hypermorphosis* (overstepping of one stage by another), *paedomorphosis* (introduction of youthful characters by means of deviation and neotony), *gerontomorphosos* (modification of a d u l t characters by means of variation), *hypermorphosis and acceleration*. In his conclusions DeBeer intimates that evolution has occurred by the transmission of internal factors which were evoked by the action of external factors (evidently the transmission of acquired characteristics), that changes have come about in internal factors by changes in rates of development, and that "evolution is brought about by an acquisition of qualitative novelties, and by the production of novel situations by quantitative alteration of the rate of action of the internal factors." Repetition of ancestral ontogenetic stages is due to transmission of internal factors from ancestor to descendant.

In conclusion DeBeer writes:

"It goes without saying that even if the views set forth here are correct, they do not provide an 'explanation' of evolution, for there remains the problem as to how and why novelties arise, and why heterochrony acts upon them in those cases in which it does. But what is claimed is that after dethroning the theory of recapitulation, we are able to make a better synthesis of our knowledge of embryology and evolution."[97]

It is difficult to see in this book anything other than a re-baptism of recapitulation. While couched in somewhat different words, transmission of acquired characters is demanded, heredity only being required to hand down in ontogenetic stages what somehow has gotten into the egg. All DeBeer has done is to once more resurrect the old "biogenetic law" by the introduction of new definitions brought up to date from a genetic standpoint. With all this he recognizes that his views "do not provide an 'explanation' " of evolution.

A decade after the appearance of this n e w concept of recapitulation (vocabulary and all), DeBeer has rewritten his monograph under a new and more suggestive caption. He changes none of his former ideas, but adds that by discarding the theory of recapitulation:

" . . . we are able to consider possibilities other than the repetition of adult characters by youthful descendants, and . . . we are rid of a mental straight-jacket which has had lamentable effects on biological progress. It is no exaggeration to say that Haeckel's theory of recapitulation has thwarted and delayed the introduction of causal analytic methods into embryology. For instance, when His attempted to analyze ontogenetic processes into s i m p l e r components such as growth, expansion, adhesions, perforation, etc., Haeckel ridiculed them on the grounds that 'each of these simple ontogenetic processes of unfolding is the result of an extremely complicated series of historical events. It is causally determined by the thousands of phylogenetic changes, by the innumerable hereditary and adaptive alterations, which the ancestors of the organism in question have undergone during the course of millions of years.' "

"Clearly, phylogeny does not explain ontogeny at all. Even if we had a complete phylogenetic series of adults ancestral to any given descendant, it would not help us to understand the processes of fertilization, cleavage, differentiation, organogeny, etc., which take place in the ontogeny of that descendant. . . .

"Conversely, if we knew all the processes involved in the events of ontogeny, such knowledge would not of itself provide an explanation of phylogeny. For past phylogeny no method of study other than the historical descriptive is possible. But since phylogeny is but the result of modified ontogeny, there is the possibility of a causal analytic study of present evolution in an experimental study of the variability and genetics of ontogenetic processes."[98]

Thus, seventy-five years after the formulation of the biogenetic law, it is castigated as an obstruction to genuine advance in the science of embryology. According to DeBeer there remains only 'the *possibility* of a causal analytic study of present evolution in an experimental study of the variability and genetics of ontogenetic processes.' In other words, embryology has thus far failed to prove either the theory of recapitulation or to support decisively the parent theory of organic evolution.

This complete absence of any adequate solution to the relationship between Embryology and Evolution has been recognized by Needham who writes five years after DeBeer's original effort to establish his modification of the theory of recapitulation:

"On the other hand, there can be no doubt that a plethora of observation and experiment is also bad for scientific progress. Modern biology is the crowning instance of this fact. What has been well called a 'medly of *ad hoc* hypotheses' is all that we have to show as the theoretical background of a vast and constantly increasing mass of observations and experiments. Embryology in particular has been theoretically threadbare, since the decay of the evolution theory as a mode of explanation. Embryologists of the school of F. M. Balfour thought that their task was accomplished when they had traced a maximum

---

[97] DeBeer, G. R.: *Embryology and Evolution*, London, 1930.
[98] DeBeer, G. R.: *Embryos and Ancestors*, London, 1940, pp. 97, 98.

number of evolutionary analogies in the development of an animal. Wilhelm His, perhaps the first causal embryologist, struggled successfully to end this state of affairs. 'My own attempts,' he wrote in 1888 in a famous passage, 'to introduce some elementary physiological or mechanical explanations into embryology have not been even generally agreed to by morphologists. To one it seemed ridiculous to speak of the elasticity of the germinal layers; another thought that by such considerations we put the cart before the horse; and one recent author states that we have something better to do in embryology than to discuss tensions of germinal layers, etc., since all embryological explanations must necessarily be of a phylogenetic nature.' But this strictly evolutionary dominance did not last on into the twentieth century. The unfortunate thing is that nothing has so far been devised to put in its place. Experimental embryology, Morphological embryology, Physiological embryology and Chemical embryology form today a vast range of factual knowledge, without one single unifying hypothesis, for we cannot dignify the axial gradient doctrines, the field theories, and the speculations on the genetic control of enzymes, with such a position. We cannot doubt that the most urgent need of modern embryology is a series of advances of purely theoretical, even mathematico-logical, nature. Only by something of this kind can we redress the balance which has fallen over to observation and experiment; only by some such effort can we obtain a theoretical embryology suited in magnitude and spaciousness to the wealth of facts which contemporary investigators are accumulating day by day."[99]

We must yet answer the second challenge of Haeckel. After forty-four years of argument over his "biogenetic law," he charged his opponents that they had nothing better to put in its place. Minor changes in the law itself or its redesignations as proposed by Morgan, Patten, or even by DeBeer can scarcely be said to be any better answer to the problem than was the old law of Meckel and Serres. Perhaps in answer to this challenge, Sedgwick thirty-two years ago suggested that:

"If after 50 years of research and close examination of the facts the recapitulation theory is still without satisfactory proof, it seems desireable to take a wider sweep and to inquire whether the facts of embryology cannot be included in a larger category."[100]

The reader of Sedgwick's dissertation is left, however, without learning what this "larger category" might be, although one might interpolate the idea that Evolution itself might be so considered.

But does Evolution in its wider implications account for the phenomena of embryology? DeBeer's effort clearly shows that it does not. He can suggest in conclusion that embryology only points out the possibility of an experimental study of the variability and genetics of ontogenetic processes. Needham had already recognized the fact that Evolution had "decayed" as an explanation of the phenomena of embryology. Genetics, experimental embryology and its allied branches likewise, have as yet supplied no "unifying hypothesis" to substitute for the theory of recapitulation.

Haeckel's second challenge, therefore, remains unanswered. It is, therefore, pertinent to inquire, "What does Embryology propose to put in its place?"

SUMMARY AND CONCLUSIONS

As is usually the case with biological theories, the theory of recapitulation has had a slow evolution. It has been long observed that in their early stages the embryos of different species of animals resemble each other more or less closely. At first this parallelism was more or less taken for granted. About the turn of the 19th century,

---

[99] Needham, Joseph: Limiting Factors in the Advancement of Science as Observed in the History of Embryology, *Yale J. Biol. & Med.*, (Oct.) 1935, 8:1-18.

[100] Sedgwick, A.: In *Darwin and Modern Science*, 1909.

[101] Needham, J.: *loc. cit.*

however, a causal significance came to be applied to these similarities. Biologists were lead to believe that the early stages of the embryo were identical with lower forms of animal life.

By the time von Baer's monograph was published (1828), this view was apparently held by the general run of biologists, although von Baer himself "clearly rejected the theory as formulated before his time and made no claim to authorship of another." It was probably Meckel and Serres who were most responsible of all contemporary students of the problem for the earliest suggestion of specific ancestral implications of the various stages of the embryo, although these concepts did not come to full fruition in their day. These two views are emphasized by Radl who writes (1930):

"It is true that there is a superficial resemblance between the two theories (of von Baer and Meckel). Von Baer said that the embryos of different animals are alike because they are developing on the same plan. Meckel asserted that, as it developes, every animal passes through the (adult) phase of certain of the animals below it in the scale of existance. Von Baer compared embryos with embryos; Meckel compared embryos with adult forms.

"Darwin was probably the first to confuse the two views . . ."

This statement may be giving Darwin too much credit (or blame), but it is generally agreed that it was Darwin who gave the concept of parallelism its first strong evolutionary coloring. Darwin, however, was not an embryologist and therefore was not in a position to be critical on this point and could only make general deductions. Haeckel, on the other hand, encouraged by the observations of Müller on Crustacean larvae, put the concept in its basic form that "ontogeny recapitulates phylogeny."

It was evident, even to the author of the "fundamental law of biogenesis," that it was not all as simple as this,

and words were coined by Haeckel ("as if every word represented a new thought!" (Radl)) and others to express these variations and details of the normal record of evolution—first "palingenesis" and "cenogenesis," then "acceleration" and "retardation" and "overstepping" and finally "neotony," "heterochrony," "paedomorphosis," and "gerontomorphosis." Unfortunately, more than new words were needed to account for the complex situation created by the steadily accumulating exceptions to the "law." It was very evident that the problem of separating the details which differentiated the true part of the record from the false was in itself a major one, and it is small wonder that Lang wanted first to try to eliminate the false details.

The most unusual feature of this history is the relationship of Geology to the recapitulation theory. It seemed clear, as both Darwin and Haeckel suggested, that if evolution had actually taken place, the only two possible sources of information as to its method are the developing embryo and the fossil remains. The embryologist had the advantage of critically surveying his material at first hand, and this may account for the relatively early doubts as to the validity of the law and its ultimate repudiation. The paleontologist had to wait until his material accumulated; meanwhile, in spite of accumulating paleontological proofs against it, he had clung to the "law" which its early sponsors have now repudiated. He has apparently needed some sort of a "yard stick" to evaluate his findings and, on an evolutionary basis, if this support is gone, he has nowhere else to turn. The degree of fidelity to this theory by some contemporary paleontologists is really remarkable, considering the apathy with which it is held by embryologists. Evidently these two sciences have diverged so widely, that their followers are now quite out of touch.

Shortly after the turn of the twentieth century, there came a revival of interest in the theory chiefly on the part of general biologists and schematists who were unable to escape the implications of resemblance which, it had hoped, would prove to be the "strongest evidence in favor of evolution." This accounts for the two horns of the dilemma on which investigators like Morgan found themselves. As an embryologist, Morgan found the theory to be "in principle" false (1903); as a biologist he believed that it provided "facts that spoke for themselves" (1932) as supporting the larger theory of evolution.

While embryologists have largely discarded the idea of recapitulation, many biologists, anatomists and paleontologists, who have not had the opportunity to put the law to the crucial test, "cannot escape" the implications of similarity. It is found, however, that the "facts" of recapitulation resolve themselves into simple analogy and homology, without any proven genetic relationships. These "facts," moreover, do not stand very close scrutiny and are just as apt to prove *devolution* as e v o l u t i o n when applied to what should be close biologic relationships, as between apes and man. It is now believed by modern embryologists that the embryo has more important things to do than to reminisce on its presumed ancestry.

The newer subsciences of chemical embryology, physiological embryology, and genetics have dealt even less kindly with the theory of recapitulation than did morphologic embryology in its later day. Today articles and monographs in these fields are quite completely devoid of any reference to the subject except perhaps in its historical aspect. Needham has gone so far as to say that the theory of recapitulation and evolution itself has "decayed" as a mode of explanation for the phenomena of embryology.

And yet the final challenge of Haeckel himself remains unanswered,— "No opponent of the principle has been able to set up anything better in its place." While this is a poor argument for retention of a theory so completely discredited, the fact remains that Embryology has today "no accepted unifying hypothesis." The similarity of the forms of early embryos, as well as their structure which is indicative of a basic plan, very likely do have some significance. This significance is certainly not indicative of a presumed phylogenetic history.

What, then, does parallelism mean?

## PERSISTENCE OF THE RECAPITULATION THEORY

"Such is the history of the development of thought which has led to the theory of recapitulation. This still has a remarkable sway. It is responsible for the fact that so many biological examination papers answered by schoolboys contain the statement that 'during its life-history an animal climbs up its family tree.' The criticism to which the biogenetic law and theory of recapitulation have been subjected seems to have made but little impression, for the schoolboys' answers do not change, and yet these criticisms have not been unimportant. In the first place it was pointed out (by Agassiz, Keibel, and Mehnert among others) that the order in which characters appeared in phylogeny is not always faithfully reproduced in ontogeny. For instance, teeth were evolved before tongues, but in mammals now tongues develop before teeth. To this alteration and reversal of the sequence of

stages the term *heterochrony* is applied, and it creates the suspicion that the alleged retraction of adult characters into younger states of development (if it really occurs) is not simply due to the piling up of new variations at the end of the life-history, for the order of the pile is not necessarily respected. It also suggests that it is not legitimate to speak of a 'stage' being shifted back to a later or on to an earlier period in the life-history. It is not the 'stage' which is shifted *en bloc,* but certain characters which may be peculiar to the stage. It must also be remembered that what an embryologist calls a 'stage' is merely an arbitrarily cut section through the time-axis of the life of an organism. A 'stage' is thus really an abstraction of the four dimentional space-time phenomenon which a living organism is." —G. R. De Beer in *"Embryos and Ancestors,"* 1940, pp. 6, 7.

## OSKAR HERTWIG AND THE BIOGENETIC LAW

"Oskar Hertwig's criticism of the biogenetic law is especially significant as coming from one so eminent in embryology and is moreover of the highest importance in that it brings out the essentials of whatever has been said against the law in the many discussions of the subject. Hertwig finds that no true picture of an ancestral form can be gained from ontogeny nor from comparative anatomy. The embryonic stages are only outline sketches that tell us nothing of the particulars that go to make up a real animal, and no one would maintain that any existing simpler form, amphioxus, *e. g.,* is in the ancestral line of a higher form. Often too there is such an intermixture of lower and higher characteristics that the

embryonic stage cannot be said to represent an ancestor.

"His objection then is that an embryonic stage is never the repetition, through and through, of an ancestral form or organ. It is only a phase in a continuous change that will end in an animal very different from the hypothetical ancestor. A gastrula, for instance, is never a hydroid polyp, although it may differ externally from one 'only in insignificant features.' 'No fish,' he goes on, 'constructed as is the embryo of a higher vertebrate, could have existed. The notochord of a mammalian embryo is not a replica of the amphioxus notochord since it is not really a supporting organ.'" —Professor H. V. Wilson, The Recapitulation Theory or Biogenetic Law in Embryology, *Amer. Nat.,* 1941, Vol. 85, p. 27.

## THE "LAW" OF RECAPITULATION

"While Haeckel held that embryonic stages represent for the most part ancestral adult types, he was familiar with embryonic adaptations that could never have been adult stages, such as the allantois, amnion, and yolk sac of birds and mammals. He spoke of these as falsifications of phylogenetic ancestral stages. They are embryonic adaptations. This admission was soon found to open the door to skepticism with respect to many larval and embryonic stages that had been interpreted as ancestral, such, for example, as the nauptlius of crustacea, and

the trochophore of annelids, which are now regarded only as specialized larval forms whose widespread occurrence in a group is not sufficient evidence that they are ancestral adult stages. In other words: if the recapitulation theory is a 'law,' it has so many exceptions that it has become useless and often misleading. Moreover, as stated above, it carries an implication with respect to the way in which new characters are 'added' that is inconsistent with a large body of definite information." —Thomas Hunt Morgan in *"Embryology and Genetics,"* 1934, p. 149.

# BULLETIN

OF

# DELUGE GEOLOGY

AND RELATED SCIENCES

| Volume 1 | October, 1941 | Number 3 |
|---|---|---|

## GEOLOGY AND THE RECAPITULATION THEORY

### A STUDY IN CIRCULAR REASONING

#### GEORGE MCCREADY PRICE

#### DEFINITIONS AND ASSUMPTIONS

Two sources of error in scientific work which are more or less common are hasty induction and reasoning in circles.

Hasty induction is also called *incomplete induction*, sometimes called *jumping to a conclusion*. However, since no human being can ever hope to have in hand all the data concerning any large problem, any induction about the larger problems of the world runs the risk of being incomplete. But conclusions from incomplete data may later become justified by additional facts. For example, when Columbus sailed west, he had only very scanty facts on which to base his conclusion that he might find land in that direction. The outcome precludes our blaming him for his incomplete induction; instead we say, "How wonderful; what a brilliant intuition." Similarly, William Harvey,

the discoverer of the circulation of the blood, announced that all animals come from an egg, or an ovum. We now know that he was right. But at that time (1651), nearly three hundred years ago, nobody had ever seen the ovum of any mammal. Harvey was just making a hasty but clever induction and happened to be right. In this case also, we commend him for his shrewd insight, his intelligent grasp of fundamentals. His induction was based on incomplete data, but turned out to be completely correct.

But reasoning in circles is very different. It is identical with trying to lift oneself by one's bootstraps. When used in any line of scientific work, it becomes the one unpardonable, logical sin, the one that hath never forgiveness. It makes one look ridicu-

The BULLETIN is published by, and is the official organ of the "Society for the Study of Deluge Geology and Related Sciences." The Editorial Board is comprised of Professor George McCready Price and Dr. Cyril B. Courville. It is printed at the Collegiate Press, Arlington, California. For members the BULLETIN is free, and extra copies 25 cents each (each number priced according to size); for non-members it is $2.00 per year; and this number is 30 cents. All correspondence should be directed to the Managing Editor, Mr. Ben F. Allen, 219 North Grand Avenue, Los Angeles, California.

lous; it shows a lack of mental clearness, a mental blind spot, an incapacity for seeing and judging evidence.

Circular reasoning can get us nowhere. Not only are all conclusions thus reached absolutely worthless, but they are a disgrace to those who indulge in these mental acrobatics, no matter how the facts may turn out in the end. Even if the same conclusion is afterwards reached in another and perfectly legitimate manner, we still throw away the first method and have nothing but blame for the one who may have reached the right conclusion in this whirligig fashion; because we all instinctively feel that there must be something wrong with one who can indulge in such queer tricks of the mind. He may be merely indulging in wishful thinking, or may be trying to fool us deliberately. Which of these are we to think of in this case?

But let us in this paper start with some fundamentals. All study of the natural sciences involves some assumptions; hence it is highly important that all our assumptions be rigidly sound. In physics and chemistry, for instance, we have to assume that the things which we examine are genuine entities, also that our minds are capable of estimating their "properties" or their behavior. Many other assumptions are made in these basic sciences of physics and chemistry, and we hope they are all sound and correct.

In geology, of course, we have to make all the same assumptions with which we start to study physics and chemistry; but then we go on to make some additional assumptions which

are much more speculative or even contrary to fact. One is that the present behavior of the ocean, the atmosphere, and of all the other features of nature are a true measure of all that has ever happened in the past; whereas the members of this Society believe that there is ample evidence to the contrary. They believe that something must have happened to our earth in the long ago which was radically different from the more or less orderly procedure of nature with which we are acquainted in our modern world.

Another doctrine of geology as commonly taught, which we declare is a pure assumption (or perhaps a wretchedly incomplete induction), is that the various forms of life (plants and animals) have been appearing on the earth in a serial order of increasing size and complexity of organization, the process covering many millions of years, and that geologists have acquired the skill to know the relative ages of these different kinds of plants and animals, so that whenever any of these typical "index fossils" as they are called are discovered, the geologists can immediately assign the rocks in which they occur to their proper stage in the long-drawn-out geological ages. All this, I repeat, is an unfounded assumption; the arrangement of these index fossils in an alleged historical order is a purely artificial process; and the entire scheme is a direct denial of the Bible account of the *absolute contemporaneity* of all the various forms of life from the very beginning.[1]

It will be our task in the present paper to study some of the events in

---

[1] Suppose it were proved that in 60 or 75 per cent of instances, for the world as a whole, Paleozoic fossils occur physically lower in the strata than do the Mesozoic, and that the Mesozoic occur in a similar proportion below the Tertiary, there would be other ways of explaining these facts instead of inferring a geological succession of life. These facts are in no way inconsistant with the Flood as the cause of the fossils.

the history of the rise of this succession-of-life theory of the fossils, to see some of the sad slips in logic made by the early geological pioneers. Were they merely making hasty inductions or were they also indulging in circular reasoning?

## THE EARLY WORK OF AGASSIZ

First we must go back over a hundred years ago, to a time when Louis Agassiz, as a young man, was struggling for his first recognition as a man of science. He had been studying medicine, but in the meantime was even more interested in various lines of natural science. He made his first reputation by his studies of fishes, living and fossil, the opportunity for much of this work having been placed in his hands by no less a person than Baron Cuvier. On January 18, 1830, when young Louis was not yet quite 23 years of age, we find him writing to his brother as follows:

"Add to this that just now there is a real need of this work [on fossil fishes], for the determination of the different geological formations. Once before, at the Heidelberg meeting, it had been proposed to me; the Director of the mines at Strasbourg, M. Voltz, even offered to send me at Munich the whole collection of fossil fishes from their museum."[2]

Here then was a very young man, brilliant and aggressive, who had moved about from one museum and university to another in Switzerland and southwest Germany, and even as far as Paris, who by a comparison of various fossil fishes undertakes to determine the chronology of the geological deposits of the entire world from the comparatively few specimens which were available for him. He was not concerned with the stratigraphic sequence in the field of one bed above another; partly because fossil fishes are usually found in great shoals, as in life, and one has to go to another locality, perhaps many miles away, to find another fish bed. But he was undoubtedly much more influenced by the then prevailing doctrine, as taught by Cuvier, the great leader in all these studies, that *all* the fossils, without exception, belonged to *extinct* species. There had been a great many successive creations and catastrophes, so Cuvier taught, and all the fossils belonged to a long-vanished world, with no natural connection with the animals now living. Hence Agassiz felt quite free to arrange his specimens in any way he thought would best illustrate that scheme of ideal development in the plan of creation which he thought must be the correct one.[2a]

Geology, as we now know it, was just then beginning. The first volume of Lyell's "Principles of Geology" appeared a little later in this same year, 1830, and the second volume two years later. But Lyell himself was not at this time particularly concerned with problems about the relative sequence of the fossils. In fact, no comprehensive scheme about the relative

---

[2] Agassiz, Elizabeth Cary; *Louis Agassiz, His Life and Correspondence*, Boston, 1886, 2 vols., pp. 123, 124.

[2a] It should be carefully remembered that young Agassiz, as well as Cuvier and the other pioneers in this line of geology and biology, thought they were studying out the method of *creation*, instead of the method of the *destruction* of the animals and plants of the world. They all expressly or implicitly denied the Flood as the cause of the fossils; instead they assumed that the fossils would reveal *successive stages in the original creation*. And they then (particularly Agassiz) assumed that they knew *how* an ideal series of creations probably took place, and they arranged the fossils accordingly. This is the whole dominating idea of the life-work of Agassiz, the idea which he industriously taught to the world, and which became the most important mental concept at the foundation of the theory of organic evolution.

sequence of the fossils for the world as a whole had yet been suggested by anybody, though a few very local stratigraphic successions of beds had been worked out in various parts of the British Isles and on the Continent. *Hence Agassiz thought that he had a free hand and a completely open field.* By his study of the various specimens which he could examine in a few museums, he worked out what he regarded as the ideal classification series, though it happened to differ considerably from the classification series then accepted; and on the basis of this *a priori* system of classification he undertakes to place his fossil specimens in their correct geological order. In short, according to Agassiz, the geological series of the fossils is just an old-time classification or taxonomic series, and the one should parallel the other.

Two and a half years later, or in July, 1832, we find him writing from Paris to Alexander von Humboldt the following enthusiastic statement of his work and his methods of reasoning:

"What was my joy and surprise to find that the simplest enumeration of the fossil fishes according to their geological succession, was also a complete statement of the natural relations of the families among themselves; that one might therefore read the genetic development of the whole class [of fishes] in the history of creation, the representation of the genera and species in the several families being therein determined; in one word, that the genetic succession of the fishes corresponds perfectly with their zoological classification, and with just that classification proposed by me. The question therefore in characterizing formations is no longer that of the numerical preponderance of certain genera and species, but of distinct structural relations, carried through all the formations according to a definite direction, following each other in an appointed order, and recog-

nizable in the organisms as they are brought forth. . . . If my conclusions are not overturned or modified through some later discovery, they will form a new basis for the study of fossils."[3]

This new basis for the study of the fossils by making their geological classification correspond with their zoological or taxonomic classification, is very decisively and confidently set forth in a statement in his preface to the large work of five magnificently illustrated volumes entitled, "Researches on Fossil Fishes," issued between 1833 and 1843. I quote the translation given by his wife:

"I have succeeded in expressing the laws of succession and of the organic development of fishes during all geological epochs; and science may henceforth, in seeing the changes in this class from formation to formation, follow the progress of organization in one great division of the animal kingdom, through a complete series of the ages of the earth."[4]

Now let no one say that this is not the recapitulation theory. I admit that it is not a direct and obvious part of that theory; but for anyone who wishes to get at the psychological foundations of this theory, this work by Agassiz will be seen as a prime essential for the building up of the geological series of the fossils, without which there could never have been any thought of the embryo repeating or recapitulating the geological history of its ancestors. Hence this pioneer work by Agassiz, in his purely artificial scheme of arranging the fossil fishes to fit what he regarded as the ideal classification series, is of prime importance both for geology and for that theory of recapitulation which became so large a factor in the work of Darwin and Haeckel in convincing the world about their theory of organic evolution.

---

[3] *Id.*, pp. 203, 204.
[4] *Id.*, p. 243.

## THE WORK OF D'ORBIGNY

But Agassiz had worked only with the fishes, and fishes are after all not the most important of the "index fossils." The shells, both brachiopods and mollusks, together with such other invertebrates as trilobites, are considered more important than the vertebrate fishes in determining the "age" of the strata. What about the methods of Agassiz when applied to these other fossils?

The man who seems to have been the first to apply this same method to the study of certain kinds of mollusks (ammonites) was Alcide d'Orbigny (1802-1857), a contemporary of Agassiz, and ultimately becoming professor of paleontology in the Museum of Natural History in Paris. Like Agassiz, d'Orbigny was a disciple and admirer of the great Baron Cuvier, who was over thirty years their senior and died in 1832. But all three of these men believed in many successive creations and world-destructions as the cause of the fossils. Zittel, the standard historian of geology, says:

"D'Orbigny supposed that organic creation has been completely renewed twenty-seven or twenty-eight times."[5]

The folowing summary of d'Orbigny's methods is given by Henry Fairfield Osborn in an elaborate article in the "Encyclopaedia Britannica":

"He recognized the fact that the shells of mollusks, which grow by successive additions, preserve unchanged the whole series of changes of their individual development so that each shell of a Cretaceous ammonite, for example, represents five stages of progressive modification as follows: the first is the *periode embryonnaire*, during which the shell is smooth; the second and third represent periods of elaboration and ornamentation; the fourth is a period of initial degeneration; the fifth and last a period of degeneration when ornamentation becomes obsolete and the exterior smooth again."[6]

Of course, since he was not an evolutionist, he did not claim that the living pearly nautilus, which is the modern representative of the fossil ammonites, is the lineal representative of the kinds found in the Mesozoic beds. But he did classify the fossil ammonites (and by implication all other shell fossils) according to this scheme of comparison with the individual development of a typical modern specimen, which is the geological aspect of the full recapitulation theory. Neither he nor Agassiz went the whole journey; let us give them the benefit of the doubt and say that they saw the ridiculousness of using the modern embryonic development of the individual to help prove evolution, when this same modern individual development has already been used to arrange the fossil specimens in an alleged chronological order. To put it more briefly, we hope they could have seen the absurdity of using *ontogeny* to prove evolution, after this same ontogeny had been used to construct their *phylogeny*,—though of course we are here using these terms anachronously, for the words had not yet been invented by Haeckel.

## AGASSIZ'S "ESSAY ON CLASSIFICATION"

Here we must consider some of the outstanding teachings of Agassiz in his "Essay on Classification," published first in 1857, though it was the culmination of what he had been teaching in his classes and in popular lectures for several years previously. I have stated that Agassiz started out by dealing with living and fossil fishes, and at that time he had only *two* sets or series of facts to compare, first the classification series (his new

[5] *History of Geology and Paleontology*, London, Walter Scott, 1901, p. 507
[6] Eleventh edition, Vol. XX, p. 583.

scheme being considerably different from the one in ordinary use at that time), and second, the geological series as he then arranged the fossils, Agassiz's theory being that the two series ought to correspond. As his studies continued and enlarged, he wanted to include all other kinds of fossils, and he seems to have been the first to make use of the embryonic development of the individuals of the various groups for comparison with the fossils, though I have been unable to find the exact date at which he began this use of embryology. But it must have been well over twenty-five years before his "Essay on Classification" that he had started his life-time work of comparing the *three* parallelisms, as he termed them, the modern classification series, the geological series of the fossils, and the embryonic series or the successive stages of the "typical" individual in each of the great groups of animals; for now his ambition was to make his comparisons embrace all the animal kingdom.

I shall let Dr. Percy E. Davidson give a summary of the results of Agassiz in his work on classification:

"As his interest broadened to include the systematic classification of the whole animal world, Agassiz relied more and more upon the facts of embryology to make good the deficiencies of fossil remains and to prevent the confusion, inevitable as he believed, from an examination of anatomical differences alone. In 1857 he wrote, 'I satisfied myself long ago that embryology furnishes the most trustworthy standard to determine the relative rank among animals.'

"In the system ultimately evolved by Agassiz, descriptive of what he believed to be the natural order, there were four great parallelisms, or systems of relationship. These were (1) a parallelism between the geological succession of animals and their relative standing or structural gradation; (2) a parallelism between the geological succession of animals and the individual development of their living representatives; (3) a parallelism between the relative rank or gradation of animals and their individual development; and (4) these several series were again related to geographical distribution. Thus—[quoting Agassiz himself]: " '. . .the phenomena of animal life correspond to one another, whether we compare their rank as determined by structural complication with the phases of their growth, or with their succession in past geological ages; whether we compare this succession with their embryonic growth, or all these different relations with each other and with the geographical distribution of animals upon earth. The same series everywhere!' "[7]

Of course, in Agassiz's enthusiastic description of his four parallelisms to his students and in his writings, he never called attention to the fact that *only one* of these four series, the embryonic development of the individual, has an honest-to-goodness objective reality; all the others are artificial, mere constructs of the mind and made by human arrangement and manipulation. How perpetually has the classification system been adjusted to fit the discoveries or the whims of the classifier, and how perpetually has the alleged geological succession of the fossils been adjusted to fit both the classification series and the embryonic, and how constantly may the geographical distribution be arranged to suit any one's fancy! There is only the one, the embryonic development, which cannot be manipulated or "doctored" by human caprice in the interests of some preconceived theory. Unfortunately, even the embryonic development of one group does not always correspond very closely to that of other somewhat related groups, as Haeckel found out to his sorrow, giving occasion for him and his followers to charge nature with confusing or

[7] *The Recapitulation Theory and Human Infancy*, New York, 1914, p. 10.

even falsifying the phylogenic record.[8] Accordingly, what a tangle of confusion was served up before a confiding and admiring world, when Agassiz presented them with these four parallelisms, as he called them, "The same series everywhere!"

No one is likely to question my statement that the geographical distribution of animals is a highly artificial idea. Indeed, any mind that can take seriously such an idea as anything more than a whim or a fancy, must have some mental axe to grind. The classification series seems more like a natural arrangement; but at which end shall we begin? Why must we necessarily begin with the amoeba and run up to man? Why may we not begin with man and arrange all animal life in descending complexity down to the amoeba? Surely there is no finality about the one method as compared with the other,—except in the mind of someone who has long been obsessed with the doctrine of organic evolution.

### THE ARTIFICIAL CHARACTER OF THE GEOLOGICAL SERIES

But many will indignantly resent the idea that the geological series is an artificial one. It is the object of the present paper to prove this proposition, and from this proof to show the circular reasoning in taking this artificially constructed history of life on the earth ("phylogeny") as the backbone of the whole evolution theory, whenever the embryonic series is compared with it.

It is now well over a hundred years since geologists began to follow the lead of William Smith in classifying the strata according to the fossils found in them, instead of according to their mineral content, as previously taught by A. G. Werner. Yet only the very few who are intimately acquainted with the century-long history of geology since that day realize how repeatedly, I might almost say perpetually, during this time the stratigraphic position of certain sets of beds which seemed perplexing in the field has been settled by studies of their fossils. Museum collections of fossils always contain many specimens which have been picked up by local village collectors, who could not always be expected to remember correctly just what locality furnished each of the many individual specimens which they have gathered. Sometimes, indeed, rare specimens which may have been found lying loose on the top of the ground may have found their way into museum collections; for atmospheric weathering of such exposed specimens is a very slow process, and many splendid looking fossils have been found in this way. Thus uncertainties have more than once been injected into collections which have been used in the "momentous" decisions of paleontologists in deciding just how a certain set of beds should be placed in the geological series.

In any clearly defined locality, of course, the relative age of the beds is a simple matter of stratigraphical succession, at least so far as the processes of laying down the materials are concerned. As I have pointed out

---

[8] After quoting some strong statements from the best historian of biology, Nordenskiöld, to the effect that Haeckel's illustrations for this book were always drawn by himself and were designed exclusively to prove one single alleged fact and that they "were naturally schematic and without a trace of scientific value," Dr. Cyril B. Courville, in a recent paper well remarks: "It is thus evident that Haeckel's objective was to prove the 'law of biogenesis,' and the chief attention which he gave to its deficiencies was to coin words to cover them." ("*Bulletin of Deluge Geology*," Vol. 1, 1941, p. 39).

elsewhere,[9] we have no authority to say that the materials in three successive beds, limestone, sandstone, and conglomerate, for example, may not *all* have been in existence *contemporaneously* before any of the beds were deposited. And if this is true concerning the materials composing the beds, it is also just as true concerning the fossils contained in them. If trilobites are found in the limestone, dinosaurs in the sandstone, and elephant bones in the conglomerate, it is nothing but a pure, unfounded assumption to say that all three kinds of animals could *not* have been living contemporaneously before their remains were deposited in this serial order.[10] Hence, while the order of superposition does show the order of deposit, or the sequence in which the beds were laid down, it cannot tell us a thing about the relative age of the materials composing the beds, nor about the relative age of the fossils found within them. *We must first assume something like a succession of life on the globe or a long series of creations on the installment plan, as taught by Cuvier, d'Orbigny, and Agassiz, before we can say that the trilobites actually lived before the dinosaurs and the latter before the elephants.*

Stratigraphy can tell us the relative order of the beds for only a limited area, often for only a *very* limited area. The beds on opposite sides of any mountain range can never be correlated by stratigraphy, not to mention the beds in countries separated by an ocean. In thousands of instances

beds only a mile or two apart can never be traced together by either their lithological structure or their stratigraphy. In all such instances, the fossils contained in the beds are always used to decide the matter. The many notorious cases of "deceptive conformities" and so-called "thrust faults," prove that the fossils are always the final criteria of the age of a set of beds; and when an evolutionary minded geologist is armed with the conviction that he *knows* the true order in which the beds *ought* to be found, and then has at his command such devices as "deceptive conformities" and "thrust faults" to help him out in any difficulty, it must be confessed that it is exceedingly difficult to get him in a logical corner.

It would be tiresome to cite illustrative examples to show how the fossils have constantly been used to decide about the correct position (in the geological series) of any specific set of beds, I mean its position as compared with other beds in distant parts of the world. This would help to show the constructive or artificial character of the geological series, by illustrating how the imposing geological succession of the fossils from all parts of the world has been built up through the years. It may be more in accord with this brief discussion of a very large subject to go back and give a few more facts about the way in which embryology and taxonomy were employed in the work of adjusting the geological succession, and then the way in which the results thus attained were used as propaganda to

---

[9] *The Pan-American Geologist,* March, 1937, pp. 117-128.

[10] If any one feels certain that the trilobites, dinosaurs, and mastodons could not have been living thus contemporaneously, he must have gained this assurance from some other source than their occurance in the strata. What other source of assurance does he have? Obviously, this whole idea is an *evolutionary assumption* pure and simple. It is injected into the study of the rocks and the fossils, it is not derived from them.

help "prove" the general theory of evolution.

We have already seen how Agassiz, in the year 1830, was writing his brother about the great need there was for the work which he was then doing about fossil fishes, "for the determination of the different geological formations." This method of using the classification principles of the various groups of animals for the determination of the ideal order of the different geological formations was, however, soon supplemented by the use of embryology for the same purpose. And we have seen how "Agassiz relied more and more upon the facts of embryology to make good the deficiencies of fossil remains, and to prevent the confusion, inevitable as he believed, from an examination of anatomical differences alone."[11]

We have also seen how d'Orbigny used the embryonic comparisons in the case of mollusk shells for the same purpose. But it was Alpheus Hyatt (1838-1902), an ardent disciple of Agassiz who went further than his master and accepted the theory of evolution, who first (1866) applied this principle to the study of fossil ammonites. As Henry Fairfield Osborn tells us, "He [Hyatt] showed that from each individual shell of an ammonite the entire ancestral series may be reconstructed."[12]

SPLITTING SPECIES

With the modern classification series and the embryonic series both now enlisted in making "good the deficiencies of fossil remains," the work of adjusting the fossiliferous "record" for all the various groups of animals went forward rapidly. Darwin had taught the world that varieties and races are constantly diverging more and more into species and genera, so

that "species" are largely imaginary groups, and anyway they are (so he said) only temporary stages in the transformation of races into the higher categories. Hence, the botanists and zoologists felt themselves justified in splitting up the long recognized species into much smaller units, whenever it seemed convenient to do so. This vogue for splitting species was not long in taking on with the paleontologists and geologists, for in the case of the fossils there are few of the other checks on classification besides mere outward form; and when embryology stands as mentor in the study of fossil fishes, or shells, or what not, it becomes very easy to find a new "species" to fit almost any theory.

Zittel tells us how this tendency toward splitting species has worked out in the case of brachiopods, which are among the oldest known fossils. Thomas Davidson's work dealing with "British Fossil Brachiopods" (1870-1885) set a high standard in the study of this group; but the subsequent workers in this field had come more completely under the influence of the recapitulation theory. And Zittel tells the results as follows:

"Whereas Davidson in his systematic treatment allowed for a considerable extent of variability in his definitions of genera and species, the new direction of research guided by Hall, Clarke, and Beecher in North America, and by Waagen and Bittner in Europe, tries to restrict generic and specific definitions within the narrowest possible limits, in order to enhance the value of fossil brachiopods for the characterization of stratigraphical horizons. A systematic review of all known brachiopods forms an introductory chapter in the comprehensive monograph of Palaeozoic types which has been published by Hall and Clarke. The number of genera has been greatly increased, and in many cases species have been elevated to the rank of genera. A new classification was proposed in 1889 by Beecher.

[11] Davidson, Percy E., The Recapitulation Theory, p. 10.
[12] Encyclo. Brit., Eleventh edition, Vol. XX, p. 583.

in which it has been the author's aim to bring the ontogenetic and phylogenetic development of the group into more apparent correspondence, and to apply the differences in the beak region more often for systematic distinctions."[13]

It is not always that the paleontologists have acknowledged so unashamedly their recapitulation leanings in the matter of their classification of the fossils. In other groups the same methods have been followed, though not so plainly acknowledged.[14] But in this very large and important group of the brachiopods, whose fossils are so frequently used in the naming and classification of the beds of the Paleozoic, these specialists try to restrict "generic and specific definitions within the narrowest possible limits, in order to enhance the value of fossil brachiopods for the characterization of stratigraphical horizons;" and the announced aim has been "to bring the ontogenetic and phylogenetic development of the group into more apparent correspondence."

And when the ontogenetic and the phylogenetic development have been thus brought into more apparent correspondence, the followers of Darwin and Haeckel can then point to these facts as helping to *prove* the general theory of organic evolution. Was there ever a more perfect example of reasoning in a circle?

OPPEL AND BUCKMAN SUBDIVIDING
THE AMMONITES

These principles may be illustrated by the history of the study of fossil ammonites, as carried on by Oppel and Buckman.

Carl Albert Oppel (1831-1865), who preceded Zittel in the chair of Paleontology in the University of Munich, south Germany, and who died at the early age of thirty-four, devoted his life to the study of the various subdivisions of the Jurassic system, as shown by the special guide-fossils or index-fossils in the various museums of Germany, France, and England, all of which localities he visited and compared. He was a careful observer of the details concerning the fossils, and undertook to compare not only the large subdivisions of these localities by means of their fossils, but also the smallest groups of the strata.

"Setting aside all lithological features, Oppel deduced from his observations a series of paleontological horizons which he termed *zones,* each of which represented the definite age-limit of some leading fossil type or types. 'A Zone,' he says. 'is characterized as a definite paleontological horizon by the constant occurrance in it of certain species which do not occur in the preceding or succeeding neighboring zones.' "[15]

And if Oppel had been able to visit the Gondwana beds of India, the Karoo of South Africa, as well as the Jurassic beds of Australia, South America, and Russia, he could doubtless have still further subdivided his "zones," from the slight differences which he would find among the index-fossils in these distant localities. For as William Berryman Scott says, some of the same identical fossils found in Europe are also found occurring in these distant places; and "even the minuter divisions, the substages and

---

[13] Zittel, K. V., *History of Geology and Paleontology*, London, Walter Scott, 1901, p. 400.

[14] Any one acquainted with geology knows that the series of fossil horses, or elephants, or camels, etc., which make such "convincing" displays for evolution in the museums, were never found together in any vertical sequence, but invariably have been assembled from scattered localities and artificially arranged in this alleged historical sequence. Such exhibits are just evolutionary propaganda. They make an "imposing" display in more than one sense of the word.

[16] Zittel, *History, etc.,* p. 509.

zones of the European Jura, are applicable to the classification of the South American beds." Why not? Since this system of index-fossils overrides all other criteria, Zittel himself acknowledging above that under it the paleontologists "set aside all lithological features," and since this system of index-fossils becomes nothing but an old-time taxonomic system of the life of the ancient world, why should it not be just as applicable to South America or Australia or Timbuktu as to Europe?

An Englishman, who lived up until only a few years ago, and who had many increased opportunities for studying the ammonites from wide portions of the globe, has carried the scheme to even greater detail.

Sidney Savory Buckman (1860-1929), became fascinated with the work of making fine subdivisions in both the paleontological and the stratigraphical analysis, as the only effective method of recognizing the genetic relationships between the different grades of fossils. He multiplied greatly the genera and species among the ammonites. I quote from a recent review of his work:

"His paleontological studies soon convinced him that the simple stratigraphical principles of William Smith could be applied with much greater precision than had hitherto been attempted. This led to a great deal of stratigraphic subdivision, so that the thirty-three Jurassic zones of Oppel became elaborated into a system of about four hundred zones."[16]

By the simple device of seeking to separate the sedimentary history from the biological history of the fossils, he was able to devise a dual nomenclature for the subdivisions of geological time, one for the strata *per se* and the other for the fossils, by which

he seemed to avoid the absurdities of minute fossil onion coats for the entire world to correspond to the minute "zones" which he named.

"Working on this principle [of having a two fold nomenclature, one set of names for the strata and another for the fossils], Buckman produced his biological chronology of the Jurassic period, in which the period is divided into forty-five ages and about four hundred *hemerae* or biological time units."[17]

It would exhaust my time and your patience to go into the history of the other important groups which have been used as "index-fossils." The trilobites and graptolites of the Ordovician have been favorite subjects for the making of minute subdivisions, and thus for tracing out alleged evolutionary pedigrees for those groups. As all the trilobites and graptolites are probably extinct, there are no modern kinds with which to check up by their embryology or otherwise on the evolutionary theories proposed for them; in this way paleontologists can avoid the embarrassment which has come to the students of gastropods and pelecypods, in which groups, as one writer remarks, so-called "ancestral forms" "... are all too frequently preceded by their theoretical descendants."[18] Even the ammonites themselves seem to have occasioned difficulties, for L. F. Spath is quoted as saying:

"It may be necessary to assume an inverted geological order, if our views of the biological order [in time] of the ammonites are to continue to be governed by discredited 'laws' of recapitulation."[18a]

## HOW THE GEOLOGICAL SEQUENCE IS ADJUSTED

But these instances of finding "index fossils" in very troublesome positions, or in the "inverted" order of

---

[16] *Science,* July 26, 1929, pp. 87 ,88.
[17] *Science,* July 26, 1929, pp. 87, 88.
[18] *Nature,* March 17, 1928.
[18a] Quoted by G. R. De Beer, *Embryos and Ancestors,* 1940, p. 8.

sequence, take on a familiar look to those who are acquainted with the "pioneer colonies" of Barrande, the "recurrent faunas" of Ulrich, and the notorious "deceptive conformities" and "thrust faults" found almost everywhere, the last-mentioned being known as "nappes" by the Swiss geologists. What a great cloud of witnesses are now arising to refute the theory of an invariable sequence in which the fossils are always found in all parts of the globe!

Two factors of a more general nature, however, need to be kept in mind when dealing with the fossils assembled from various parts of the world for the purpose of comparing evolutionary pedigrees, these two factors tending to show the artificial nature of all such work.

(1) The profuse numbers of some of these creatures (trilobites, ammonites, etc.) which are often found together in a specific locality frequently preclude the possibility of dealing with individual specimens in the matter of classifying or "dating" the beds where they occur; so that the scientist falls back on the average or general aspect of the entire lot, to determine just where the bed should be classed in the geological "column." And we all know how the personal factor always looms very large in work of judging the average or general aspect of any large numbers of specimens.

(2) As deposits of these invertebrate fossils occur in almost every part of the world, the wide separation of these deposits makes correlation by stratigraphy quite out of the question; hence the scientists have to fall back on what they regard as the

general principles of the subject. And since all geologists are already convinced evolutionists, and believe in the correctness of using the embryonic development as more or less of a guide in classifying all animals, living and fossil, it is too much to expect that those who do the classifying of the fossils would not do so in conformity with the general principles of the evolution doctrine. Human nature being what it is, we may regard it as a foregone conclusion that geologists and paleontologists should look at their facts through the colored spectacles of Darwin and Lyell.

The wise words of one of our most thoughtful modern scientific writers are well worthy of consideration in this connection:

"The history of thought shows that false interpretations of observed facts enter into the records of their observation. Thus both theory, and received notions as to fact, are in doubt."[19]

And again by the same writer:

"Every scientific memoir in its record of the 'facts' is shot through and through with interpretation."[20]

Prof. F. C. S. Schiller, of Oxford University, also has emphasized the truth that all reports of scientific "facts" always contain more or less of theory.[21] This is not because the scientists reporting them are unreliable, but because human nature is what it is. No one can escape more or less of bias in every report about what he regards as scientific "facts."

Zittel, who is usually so candid and fair in his judgments, seems to blame some modern paleontologists for not making a freer use of the parallelisms of embryology and taxonomy in their

---

[19] Whitehead, Alfred North; *Process and Reality*, 1929, p. 19.
[20] *Id.*, p. 22
[21] In a personal letter to me about my little book, "The Geological-Ages Hoax," Prof. Schiller wrote: "I found your contention interesting and a beautiful illustration of the possibility of putting an alternative interpretation on even the best established 'facts' (which always contain 'theories')."

studies of the fossils. At least, that is how I understand his statements as given below. He tells how August Schenk (1868-1891) brought in a reform in the study of paleobotany by his sound knowledge of living plants, so that "now," says Zittel, "the author of a paper on any department of paleophytology is expected to have a sound knowledge of systematic botany."

But he immediately goes on to make the following complaint:

"It cannot be said that paleozoology has yet arrived at this desirable standpoint."

He names a large number of eminent men, like Cuvier, Owen, Huxley, and others who were also well acquainted with living animals as well as with the fossils.

"But comparatively few individuals have such a thorough grasp of zoological and geological knowledge as to enable them to treat paleontological researches worthily, and there has accumulated a dead weight of stratigraphical-paleontological literature wherein the fossil remains of animals are named and pigeon-holed solely as an additional ticket of the age of a rock deposit, with a willful disregard of the much more difficult problem of their relationships in the long chain of existence.

"The terminology which has been introduced in the innumerable monographs of special fossil faunas in the majority of cases makes only the slenderest pretext of any connection with recent systematic zoology; if there is a difficulty [regarding genetic relationships], then stratigraphical arguments are made the basis of a solution [that is, new specific or generic names are given to the fossils]. Zoological students are, as a rule, too actively engaged and keenly interested in building up new observations to attempt to spell through the arbitrary paleontological conclusions arrived at by many stratigraphers, or to revise their labors from a zoological point of view."[22]

In this quotation Zittel may be right in condemning the common custom of coining new names for the fossils *just because they are fossils,*

this custom being a hang-over from the days of Cuvier, when all the fossils were always regarded as extinct species, even though they seem identical with certain living forms which look just like them. I have no sympathy with this custom; for it has made mountains of difficulty for those who desire to gain a truthful knowledge of the ancient world which lies buried in the rocks beneath our feet. But he shows his strong evolutionary bias when he chides certain scientists for using their fossils "solely as an additional ticket of the age of a rock-deposit, with a wilful disregard for the much more difficult problem of their [evolutionary] relationships in the long chain of existence." He evidently thinks that one line of evolutionary relationship worked out by means of the very familiar method of comparisons with the taxonomic series and the embryonic series would be worth almost any number of specimens "named and pigeon-holed solely as an additional ticket of the age of a rock-deposit." In other words, he chides these scientists for not using their fossils to help work out the evolutionary evidence for their particular groups of animals.

But in the other quotation given above Zittel has no word of blame for what he calls the new direction of research, in which the paleontologists split up fossil species and genera "within the narrowest possible limits, in order to enhance the value of fossil brachiopods [and presumably other fossils also] for the characterization stratigraphical horizons," in an openly avowed aim of bringing "the ontogenic and [the] phylogenetic development of the group into more apparent correspondence."

Here then we have a peep at the inside story of how the geological

---

[22] Zittel, Karl Alfred von, *History of Geology and Paleontology,* 1901, pp. 375, 376.

series, or the phylogenic series, as the evolutionists like to call it, has been built up. We remember how William Smith and Lyell laid its foundations by dating the rocks according to their fossil contents, which was assuming the succession of life to begin with, that is, was assuming the main outline of the evolution theory. Then we remember how Agassiz taught the world to adjust the fossils by comparisons with both the embryonic series and the taxonomic series. And now we find that modern geologists and paleontologists try to split their fossil species and genera as finely as possible, "in order to enhance the value of fossil brachiopods [and other fossils] for the characterization of stratigraphical horizons." in an openly declared effort "to bring the ontogenetic and the phylogenetic development of the group into more apparent correspondence." [23]

In view of all this, how can anyone object when I say that the geological series is a highly artificial affair, built up by using both the taxonomic and the embryonic series as guides and comparisons? And then, what are we to think of using this constructed geological series as the standard with which to compare the embryonic development of man and other animals, in an attempt to prove the theory of evolution? It almost makes one dizzy to think of the whirligig logic involved in such a performance.

When scientists are on a wrong track entirely in any particular line, about the only way for them to get right is for them to travel on to the very end, to convince them that they are running up a blind alley. The advocates of the recapitulation theory seem now to be at about the end of their blind alley. About the only

recent attempt to save the recapitulation theory is G. R. De Beer's "Embryos and Ancestors" (London, 1940), which is reviewed by Dr. Cyril B. Courville in a comprehensive paper dealing with this subject. Summing up De Beer's book Courville says:

"Thus, seventy-five years after the formulation of the biogenetic law [the recapitulation theory], it is castigated [by De Beer] as an obstruction to genuine advance in the science of embryology. According to De Beer, there remains only 'the *possibility* of a causal analytic study of present evolution in an experimental study of the variability and genetics of ontogenetic processes.' In other words, embryology has thus far failed to prove either the theory of recapitulation or to support decisively the parent theory of organic evolution."[24]

But the main thesis of the present paper is that the geological series has itself been artificially built up partly by comparison with the embryonic development, and hence that it is not legitimate to invoke geology again to prove the main theory of evolution. In order better to understand all this, it will be well to go back again to the early work of Louis Agassiz and see what ideas he really taught and what came out of them.

## HOW AGASSIZ PREPARED THE WAY FOR EVOLUTION

We have seen that Agassiz was the first to use fishes, modern and ancient, for the classification of the various geological horizons. Zittel tells us that he was also the first to use the embryonic development to evaluate or classify the many geological subdivisions or "horizons." Zittel says:

"Agassiz was the first scientist who ,in discussing the genealogy of fishes, pointed out the correspondence between the characters of the different forms succeeding one another in time, and the characters of suc-

---

23 Zittel, *op. cit.*, p. 400.
24 *Bulletin of Deluge Geology*, vol. 1, no. 2, 1941, p. 56.

cessive phases passed through by an organism during embryonic development."[25]

Agassiz could not get the world to adopt his new scheme for classifying fishes largely based on the scaly skeleton; scientists thought the system already proposed by Cuvier was much better. And yet his methods of comparing the parallelisms of the embryonic development with the taxonomic and the geological, made a great hit with the scientific world, and under Haeckel and others these parallelisms became one of the most convincing arguments in support of the theory of organic evolution, which Agassiz always detested and fought to his dying day.[26]

Joseph Le Conte, who had studied under Agassiz at Harvard and later became professor of geology at the University of California, has left us an enthusiastic praise of Agassiz as the man who taught the world many of the most fundamental ideas of the doctrine of evolution, though he himself refused to travel the road to the inevitable end. I shall let Le Conte speak for himself:

"Now, I think it can be shown that to Agassiz, more than to any other man, is due the credit of having *established the laws of succession of living forms* in the geological history of the earth—laws upon which must rest any true theory of evolution. Also, that to him, more than to any other man, is due the credit of having *perfected the method* (method by comparison) by the use of which alone biological science has advanced so rapidly in modern times."[28]

Le Conte proceeds to explain the meaning of the taxonomic or classification series, the embryonic or ontogenetic series, and the geological or phylogenic series. Cuvier was the founder of comparative anatomy; but he worked only with the first of these series, the taxonomic. Von Baer and Agassiz, Le Conte says, added comparison in the embryonic series also, and then compared these two series with each other, and used the facts of embryology to help develop a "correct" classification of animals.

"If Von Baer was the first announcer, Agassiz was the first great practical worker by this method. Last and most important of all, in its relation to evolution, Agassiz added *comparison in the geologic or phylogenic series.* The one grand idea underlying Agassiz's whole life-work, was the essential identity of the three series, and therefore the light which they must shed on one another.... In other words, during his whole life, Agassiz insisted that the laws of embryonic development (ontogeny) are also the laws of geological succession (phylogeny). Surely this is the foundation, the only solid foundation, of a true theory of evolution."[29]

Such is the language of one who wanted to praise Agassiz for doing so much to help lay the foundation of the evolution theory.

## CONCLUSION

In closing this paper let us consider again just what the four series used by Agassiz really mean. They are:

1. The classification series, made by arranging or listing the present-day animals from the amoeba to man, that is, from the simple to the complex.

[25] *History of Geology and Paleontology,* p .411.
[26] Agassiz is reported to have said to Prof. A. S. Packard, one of his former students: "The greatest mistake of my scientific life has been in fighting the theory of evolution. I saw that it was coming for years, and my 'Essay on Classification' was written largely to forestall it. I believed it all wrong, but now I see that it will prevail." (Reported by J. S. Kingsley, of the University of California, *Science,* February 27, 1925, pp. 234-235.) For those who believe that the popularity of a scientific theory is a proof of its truthfulness, this will seem like a recantation by Agassiz in his old age.
[28] *Evolution and Its Relation to Religious Thought,* Appleton, 1899, p. 38. Italics as in the original.
[29] *Evolution,* etc., p. 43. Italics as in the original.

2. The embryonic series, actually made by nature in developing the one-celled ovum into the mature individual, oyster, or horse, or man.

3. The geological series of the "index fossils," or typical fossils, from the Cambrian formation on through the whole list up to the Pleistocene or the Modern.

4. The geographical distribution series.

How can anyone deny that No. 2 is the only series actually made by nature, and that the others are all made by the mind and arrangement of man? True, in the case of No. 1, the animals all really exist; but the arrangement of them in a series from the amoeba to man is an artificial process; it could just as well be reversed, and dozens of different methods have been adopted in arranging the series, for there is no finality about any of them. No. 3, or geological series, is similarly an artificial arrangement. Granting that the fossils exist in the strata, we must still confess that the work of arranging them from widely scattered localities into the so-called geological "column" is an artificial act. When we consider how perpetually the fossils from the various localities have been adjusted in the series by comparisons with both the taxonomic series and the embryonic, and then how frequently other adjustments have had to be made because of such puzzles as "deceptive conformities" and "thrust faults," surely every candid mind must acknowledge that the geological series as we now know it is a highly artificial arrangement. And of course, any series made to illustrate geological distribution is purely artificial and nothing else.

Of course, those who believe in evolution are convinced that the geological series represents an actual historical event or series of events prolonged over long periods of time, and that it is only certain human limitations or difficulties which stand in the way of making the geological series correspond to the reality of earth's history. The members of this Society deny all this, and believe that the fossils represent *contemporary* floras and faunas which were overwhelmed by one gigantic world-disaster. I need not here try to give our reasons for thus affirming the contemporary relationship of the fossils in contradistinction to their historical succession during long periods of time; the evidence for this is scattered through many books by the present writer.

But the vital point which I am trying to make is this: Agassiz had only one series of phenomena, the embryonic, which has an honest-to-goodness reality in nature; all the others are artificial, the work not of nature itself but of the human mind and human planning. Then what circular reasoning, what hasty induction, to take any comparisons of these four series as supposed evidence for the theory of organic evolution.

It all sums up to this: The geological series of the fossils is an artificial arrangement, constructed for the world as a whole largely by the help of comparison with both the taxonomic and the embryonic series. It assumes the evolutionary sequence of life instead of proving it. Accordingly, to compare the embryonic growth of the individual with its supported ancestry in the geological series, as is done in the recapitulation theory, and to use this comparison as evidence for organic evolution, is circular reasoning of the most extreme kind. Clear thinking people cannot be expected to give any heed to such perversions of logic.

Verily, the mills of the logic of science grind slowly, but they grind exceedingly small.

THE

# BULLETIN

OF

# DELUGE GEOLOGY

AND RELATED SCIENCES

| Volume 1 | November, 1941 | Number 4 |

## CONTENTS

---

## SOME EARLY EXPERIENCES WITH EVOLUTIONARY GEOLOGY*
### *With Observations on Fundamental Defects of the Rock-Age Theory*
### GEORGE McCREADY PRICE

About a year ago the Professor of Geology at Pomona College visited me at my home and asked me to address his class. He had met me two or three times previously, for I had been doing some research work in the geological library of that institution, and he had several of my books in this library, including my college textbook, "The New Geology."

I thought it strange that he, a dyed-in-the-wool evolutionist, should ask me to lecture to his students; so I asked him what textbook he used in his class, and why he wanted to hear from me. He said he was using Charles Schuchert's book, but that he wanted his students to hear both sides of the story. With a little more conversation, I agreed to speak to his class, which I found to consist of some twenty-five bright youngsters most of them doing upper-division work and some of them being in their final year. After the lecture, he was more than ever cordial and frank in his conversation, and assured me, "Well, Mr. Price, you certainly did give a good account of yourself."

I mention this incident because I plan to present here much the same

\* Presented to the Deluge Geology Society, June 21, 1941.

The BULLETIN is published by, and is the official organ of the "Society for the Study of Deluge Geology and Related Sciences." The Editorial Board is comprised of Professor George McCready Price and Dr. Cyril B. Courville. It is printed at the Collegiate Press, Arlington, California. For members the BULLETIN is free, and extra copies 50 cents each (each number priced according to size); for non-members it is $2.00 per year; and this number is 65 cents. All correspondence should be directed to the Managing Editor, Mr. Ben F. Allen, 219 North Grand Avenue, Los Angeles, California.

line of study that I gave on that occasion, with this difference, that then I was before a more or less unfriendly audience, while this evening I feel sure I am among friends, among men and women who are at the outset sympathetic to the view that the Flood of the Bible did actually take place and that this great world-wide catastrophe furnishes by far the best and most reasonable explanation of the phenomena of the fossiliferous rocks. In addition, I may say that I have very seldom talked much in public about my early experiences in arriving at my views on these subjects, but I think that in the presence of this friendly and sympathetic audience I may even tell some details which I did not feel free to mention before that class at Pomona College.

EARLY EXPERIENCES IN GEOLOGY

I must first take you back a little over forty-one years ago, when I was acting as the head of a small high school in Eastern Canada. The locality was a French-Acadian village in the extreme northeastern part of New Brunswick, on the somewhat bleak shores of the Gulf of St. Lawrence. There were only a few English-speaking families in the place, which owed its chief importance to a hospital for lepers, I think the only regular lazaretto in all Canada at that time. It was of course run by the Government, and the head physician was a certain Doctor Smith, who was regarded as one of the few experts in leprosy in all America, a man who had medical degrees from Harvard, McGill, and Edinburgh, and who had been medical superintendent of this institution for nearly a generation.

Almost immediately on our first interview he asked me what church I belonged to. I don't think that the name of the particular church registered very distinctly in his mind; the thing that did impress him was that I was a religious man, and another subject for his atheistic missionary work. For he immediately informed me that he was an evolutionist, and by his belief in evolution he had entirely outgrown any belief in revealed religion. He asked me whether I had ever read much on the subject. When he found I had not, he asked me if I were willing to read, and then presented me with three good-sized books, and told me to read this one first, this one next, and the other one last. He evidently had in mind to lead me along through a graded course on the subject.

Within a week or two, I brought his three books all back to him and wanted more. He expressed much surprise that I hadn't become infuriated and refused to read further and that, though unconvinced, I was still anxious to read further on these subjects.

This was the beginning of a new chapter in my life. I told him that his theory of evolution *all turned on its view of geology, and that if its geology were true, the rest would seem more or less reasonable.* I asked him what he had on geology as a separate science, and he showed me one or two small elementary textbooks, and then pointed me to shelves of Canadian Government Geological Survey Reports, which he as a Government officer could have for the asking. To make a long story short, I spent two and one-half years as teacher in that school, and during that interval purchased a number of important geological books of my own, including Zittel's "History of Geology and Palaeontology." I still have in my library James D. Dana's "Manual of Geology," of over a thousand pages, much of it fine print, and there is a note written on the flyleaf that I read it through in one day more then four weeks. I also started my subscription to the English scientific journal, *Nature,* a weekly of the very highest standing, a journal in which all the leading scientists of the world, including those from America, try to report their first announcements of important discoveries. For over thirty years I have continued to read this remarkable journal, and I do not know of any better method of keeping informed on scientific progress.

### Intellectual Background

It may very properly be asked, What were my qualifications for engaging in such a line of research? What was my intellectual background?

When I first began this line of study under the guidance of Doctor Smith, I was only a little over twenty-nine years of age. I had had two years at Battle Creek College, where I was concerned with Greek and Latin, Ecclesiastical History and Theology. I had spent one summer vacation selling books in Pueblo, Colorado, with several more full years in tramping on foot and selling books in various parts of New Brunswick, Nova Scotia, and Prince Edward Island. I had also taken a teacher's training course at the Normal School in New Brunswick at which institution I had had some elementary courses in some of the natural sciences, including some mineralogy.

It will thus be very clear that my preparation for geological research was very slender indeed, so far as any formal scientific training was concerned. As a matter of fact, until I came up face to face with this problem of the theory of evolution, my intellectual interests had been entirely elsewhere. I remember that for years before this episode I used to make it a rule to read a chapter in my Greek New Testament every day and several chapters on the Sabbath. I had accumulated a small library on early Church history, and my entire purpose was to master these subjects as a preparation for what I considered my lifework. I had even conceived an antipathy toward the rising vogue of scientific studies; I had the notion that they offered very little in the way of real culture or opportunities, nothing but the most utilitarian form of education. Why then should I spend time on such matters? But when suddenly and Providentially confronted with the problem of mastering such subjects as organic evolution *and its foundation in geology and the fossils,* I could not evade the conviction that God wanted me to enter this unworked field; accordingly I threw myself into it with all the energy I possessed, constantly asking and receiving special help from the guiding and enlightening Spirit of God.

And yet, as I now look back upon my early life, I can see that in many respects I had *a good preparation for just the kind of work which Providence had planned for me.* It seems to me a great mistake for us to look for God's care and guidance only in the greater or more spectacular crises of our lives; on the other hand, I firmly believe that for those who are fully under the guidance of God, all things, even the most seemingly trivial and unimportant, are superintended by Him "in Whom we live and move and have our being." For one thing, I was born and reared amid the most typical so-called "glacial" surroundings, and was studying geological phenomena even as a child. And my travels to Michigan, Colorado, the New England States and New York in my early twenties, to say nothing of tramping over large areas of all three of the Maritime Provinces of Eastern Canada, gave me plenty of first-hand knowledge of the surface features of these parts of the world. Whenever I read of geological phenomena, even from the beginning, I never had any difficulty in visualizing just about what it all meant. From childhood I had always believed in the Flood as *an actual historical event in the early history of the world;* and as I was already familiar with that very interesting and remarkable book, "Patriarchs and Prophets,"[1] I had become convinced of what that book teaches about the Flood as the cause of the chief geological changes.

And as it is emphatically true that it is far better not to know so much, than to know so many things which aren't so, I am now very thankful that I never had any formal instruction in the theories of geology and its correlated sciences until I met them head on under the urgent impulsion of a man completely obsessed with the atheistic and fanatical zeal of the evolutionists of the latter years of the nineteenth century, when thousands of apostles of Darwin and Lyell, of Huxley, Spencer, and Haeckel, waged a continuous and bitter war against everything that Christianity stands for.

As it was, I almost lost my way. I remember that on three distinct occasions, while I was making my first investigations, determined to get to the very bottom of the entire prob-

lem, I said to myself, "Well, there must be something to this claim that the fossils do occur in a definite sequence, and thus there must be something to the geological ages." Three times this conviction swept over me; and it was only by some very Providential discoveries that I began to see my way through the problem, and to see how the actual facts of the rocks and fossils, *stripped of mere theories,* splendidly refute this evolutionary theory of the invariable order of the fossils, *which is the very backbone of the evolution doctrine.*

## LOGIC VERSUS ILLOGIC

It will now be in order to consider what some of these discoveries really were like, and what they mean in connection with this problem of the Flood *versus* the geological "ages." And I feel confident that if those who have become confused over this subject of the alleged regular order of the fossils had ever gone through the experiences I had to go through, they would today either be out-and-out evolutionists, or would repudiate with the utmost vigor and decision this false and insidious claim that the fossils always occur in a definite order, that trilobites and graptolites always occur below the dinosaurs, and the latter always below the mastodons and the other Tertiary mammals.[2] If this latter idea is true, then the Society

---

[1] Mrs. Ellen G. White, 1890.

[2] Any one familiar with the stratified rocks and the fossils knows that the waters of the Flood did not churn everything up into one indistinguishable mixture. On the contrary, in most places the different kinds of rock materials now composing the limestone, shale, and sandstone, are remarkably distinct from each other, especially in the lower layers, the upper beds showing much more commingling of materials. The same principle is seen in the case of the fossils, which are often quite distinctly separated from one another in the various beds. For instance, those animals which lived habitually on the bottom of the ocean, such as brachiopods, crinoids, and trilobites, seem to have been among the first victims of the disturbed waters of the Flood; for they are now found (usually) in the deeper layers, often with thousands of feet of other deposits above them, these upper deposits containing the fossils of such creatures as fishes or other swimming animals which could longer survive. The land animals are found chiefly in the more superficial beds. In the case of land vegetation, since height above sea level is one of the chief ecological factors

which we here represent is laboring under a serious delusion, and we might as well close up shop and go home.

Man, it is often said, is not a logical but an emotional creature. And it is a fact that great numbers of people live as they do and believe as they do because of other things than cold reason or logic. Nevertheless, most of the great leaders of the world, those who have shaped its thinking and its history other than by conquest and force, have been those who could see through all superficial obscurities and could recognize the reason and the logic of the large facts and principles

which were involved in the great issues which were then confronting the world. And certainly for all those who aspire to think clearly and logically, it is recognized that the alleged history of life on the globe from the protozoa up through the the invertebrates, the reptiles, and the mammals, to man, which grew inevitably into the theory of organic evolution,—I say, that these people always recognize that this theory rests almost entirely on the supposed geological history of the fossils, and the latter idea rests wholly and absolutely upon the alleged fact that the fossils always occur in a definite sequence, and that this definite sequence is never reversed.[3]

in the distribution of modern plants, we often find ferns, equiseta, etc., as fossils in the deeper beds, with such trees as the sequoia, pine, maple, etc., in distinctly different localities, and in what seem to be "later" or more superficial deposits. There are notable exceptions to these general rules; but in probably over fifty per cent of the fossiliferous areas of the world there is a rough approximation to ancient ecological conditions now recognizable in the relative order of the fossils in the various strata. It is *this rough approximation to ancient habitats,* both in the oceans and on the lands which has been so wrongly exploited by the evolutionists and made to seem to prove a genuine historical order of the fossils during uncounted millions of years. I have touched upon this subject here and there in several of my books. But the many and obvious exceptions to these general rules about the relative sequence of the fossils, as shown in the present paper and in the author's published works, completely disprove the arguments of the evolutionists about successive ages.

[3] A hundred years ago, when both geology and all the biological sciences were still in their infancy, a strange twist was given to all of them by the fanciful idea that the embryonic changes of the individual animal, from its one-celled stage of early life to its many-celled stages of later growth, give us the key to the history of all life on the globe during many millions of years. Louis Agassiz was one of the chief exponents of this idea, which was at a later period used with such success by Ernst Haeckel in his propaganda for the evolution doctrine. This idea that the embryonic development of the individual could be used to interpret the past history of the race during the geological "ages," is known as the "recapitulation theory," for it means that the individual recapitulates or repeats on a small scale the long history of the race in its evolutionary development. By Agassiz and the other early geologists, this embryonic development (which can be proved) was used for age-tagging the fossils found in the rocks, and thus for giving relative dates for the rocks themselves. The history of these sciences shows that widely separated fossiliferous deposits were time and time again rearranged in a supposedly *better* order, in accordance with the dictates of this recapitulation theory. See the author's "Evolutionary Geology," pp. 163, 164, 191, etc.

But in the early days, when microscopes were poor, embryologists often made mistakes regarding what they saw. For this and other reasons, embryologists have now largely abandoned this recapitulation theory, though the geologists and embryologists seem unaware of the modern situation. See the recent paper by Dr. Cyril B. Courville, "The Recapitulation Theory, Some Notes on Its History and Present Status," in this *Bulletin* of August, 1941.

In this connection, the writer wishes to emphasize certain major deficiencies in this concept, i. e., that there is no universal rock-age sequence, but that many of the presumed "ages" are missing in all localities; that there is no uniform "bottom" stratum of rocks; and that the strata are not infrequently found in a reversed order. Moreover, the wide divergence in the opinions of geologists themselves should in itself suggest that there is something seriously wrong with the whole philosophy.

## THE MISSING "AGES"

The stratified beds from all over the world are supposed, according to evolutionary interpretation, to present a record of the geological changes which the earth has passed through during many millions of years. And the customary method of dating these deposits depends almost entirely upon the fossils found in the various beds. No single area is regarded as at all sufficient for making this record of the earth's history continuous; selection has to be made from here and there in order to make a continuous record. Also something like a development or progress from the lower or more simply organized forms of life to those higher and more complexly organized must be assumed as the guide in determining which fossils come first and which later. And this assumption, of course, means something like the skeleton or outline of the evolution theory, which is thus taken for granted preliminary to the arrangement of the fossil-bearing strata in a supposed chronological order.

Moreover, in order to have a reliable record of this geological succession of life, as it is commonly called, it is absolutely essential that there be no regions found anywhere around over the earth where the fossils are found occuring in a *reverse order,* or in an order inconsistent with the alleged historical sequence. This standard order of the fossils must never be reversed. Also, where the physical evidence shows a clear case of rapid and continuous deposition, which is called 'conformity of bedding,' it will be clear evidence against the evolutionary theory of the fossils if great *blanks* in the continuity of the fossils occur here and there.

In other words, the evolutionary order of the fossils must be continuous wherever the physical evidence shows a steady and continuous deposition of the sediments; and the evolutionary order must never be found reversed. These are the two leading tests which must be applied to the theory of the evolutionary succession of the fossils.

I think that the first important example which I found tending to refute this idea was in a Canadian Government report of the region near Banff, the well-known resort town on the Canadian Pacific Railway. I shall quote from this document which is an honest and naive description of the actual conditions:

"East of the main divide the Lower Carboniferous is overlaid in places by beds of Lower Cretaceous age; and here again, although the two formations differ so widely in respect to age, one overlies the other without any preceptible break, and the separation of one from the other is rendered more difficult by the fact that the upper beds of the Carboniferous are lithologically almost precisely like those of the Cretaceous [above them]. Were it not for fossil evidence, one would naturally suppose that a single formation was being dealt with."[4]

For the benefit of some of my hearers who may not be very familiar with the scientific names involved, I shall try to explain briefly.

The classification of the fossil-bearing strata is always read from the

---

[4] Canadian "Annual Report," *Geological Survey,* New Series, 2, Part A, 8.

CHART OF THE GEOLOGICAL "AGES"

| Groups | Systems | Series | Typical Fossils |
|--------|---------|--------|-----------------|
| CENOZOIC | Quaternary | (15) Pleistocene | Elephants and Other Mammals |
| | Tertiary | (14) Pliocene<br>(13) Miocene<br>(12) Eocene | Many Extinct Mammals |
| MESOZOIC | Cretaceous<br>(9) Jurassic<br>(8) Triassic | (11) Upper Cretaceous<br>(10) Lower Cretaceous | Chalk, Dinosaurs, Palms, Conifers |
| PALEOZOIC | (7) Permian<br>Carboniferous<br>(4) Devonian<br>(3) Silurian<br>(2) Ordovician<br>(1) Cambrian | (6) Upper Carboniferous<br>(5) Lower Carboniferous | Amphibians<br>Coal Beds<br>Insects<br>Crinoids<br>Fishes<br>Profuse Marine Invertebrates |
| ARCHAEAN or PRIMITIVE | | | Scanty Fossils or None |

This brief outline of the chief geological divisions and subdivisions is to be read from bottom upwards, to conform to the theory of evolutionary geology that the Cambrian etc., are always found at the bottom of the fossiliferous series all over the globe; which of course is not the case. As some names are needed in dealing with the various fossil-bearing strata, the prevailing names and grouping can be retained by those who believe in Deluge Geology; though of course these names must be stripped of all alleged *time values,* and used simply as convenient handles in dealing with the rocks and their fossils. The numbering also is purely arbitrary, and is here adopted for purposes of convenience. They correspond to the numbers used in this paper.

bottom upward. But instead of trying to remember the relative position of all these geological names, Cambrian, Ordovician, Silurian, Carboniferous, Cretaceous, etc., it will be convenient to number them in serial order, 1, 2, 3, 4, 5, etc. Accordingly, in the example given above, it would be that No. 10 is here found occurring on top of No. 5, *with all the other formations missing.* And this Government official honestly tells us that these two, No. 10 and No. 5 are so precisely alike in their make-up, that, "were it not for fossil evidence, one would naturally suppose that a single formation was being dealt with." In other words, if we accept the common evolutionary theory of the historical order of the fossils, we have to believe that after the shaley bed No. 5 was deposited, although many millions of years elapsed with nothing here to show for it either in the way of further deposits or by erosion of the surface, finally another precisely similar bed of mud was deposited all over this old surface, so that now the two look exactly alike, and can only be separated by their respective fossils.

On the basis of common sense, without any theory concerning the historical order of the fossils, the conditions here described would mean that these two beds, No. 5 and No. 10, had followed one another in quick succession, so quick, in fact, that the same kind of mud had been laid down in both, though the fossils embedded in these two mud layers are thought by the evolutionists to have lived in two distinct ages many millions of years apart.

Do you wonder that, when I read this account, and its meaning began to dawn upon my young and unsophisticated mind, I realized that I had made a very important discovery? Obviously, these so-called geological "ages" may not be so considerably apart after all, if these two widely separate strata could thus be telescoped into what appears like just one formation. And then we might say that the fossils in these two beds, No. 5 and No. 10, could easily have been living contemporaneously, the *changing currents merely bringing them here* into a vertical position one above the other, though this relative position would not in any way imply two successive ages, least of all two ages separated by many millions of years. The latter position is untenable, if we take the physical evidence of these beds at their full face value.

Naturally enough, I had next to keep my eyes open to find out how common and how widespread such conditions prevail. In course of time, I learned that examples like this are exceedingly common, and are also often of such wide extent as to prevail over areas of hundreds of square miles. Such exceptions are termed "deceptive conformatives," a name which is quite expressive. A true or ordinary conformity occurs where one bed lies directly upon another and fits it as a glove fits the hand, the upper surface of the lower one having been soft and unconsolidated before the next one was placed upon it, with no erosion and no disturbance, the two having followed one another in quick succession. But the special examples which we are considering are called "deceptive" conformities by geologists, because the fossils which they contain are thought by them to have lived, not contemporaneously, but many millions of years apart. The physical evidence, they say, is deceptive, and the fossils alone are telling us the real truth.

Examples of this sort can be found in great numbers throughout geological literature. I have discussed the subject in one chapter in my "Evolutionary Geology,"[5] which is my most formal and complete discussion of this entire subject of the proposed successive geological "ages." Many years later than the time here spoken of when I first discovered this important fact, I was talking with Dr. E. O. Ulrich, of the U. S. Geological Survey. I asked him whether such conditions are common. He smiled rather impatiently and remarked that he supposed he had seen and examined a thousand such instances. I then asked how widespread they were, and he said that some of them were extensive enough to cover a whole State or two. I met this same accomplished scientist later at the Geological Congress in Madrid, Spain, in the early summer of 1926. Doctor Ulrich has since died, but I mention this testimony because he has written more extensively on this particular topic of "deceptive conformities" than any other writer, so far as I know. He tried the best he could to explain how such conditions might happen, but no attempt at explanation can ever make the theory

[5] Pacific Press Publishing Association, Mountain View, California, 1926.

of the differential ages of the fossils appear very reasonable.

## THE BOTTOM STRATA

As nearly as I can now remember, I think that my next line of inquiry was concerning the Cambrian beds, regarded as the oldest of the series, or formation No. 1, according to the system of numbering which we have been using. Everyone knows that the fossiliferous strata are seldom more than a mile or so in total thickness, often only a few hundred feet, and that below them is the granite or other primitive rocks which contain no fossils and never did contain any signs of life. I wished to know how widespread the Cambrian or formation No. 1 is found over the globe, and whether it is the only set of fossil-bearing beds occuring in this bottom position. In course of time I learned that No. 1 is not the only one to be found at the bottom, or next to the granite. Throughtout much of the Middle West of this country, Nos. 5 and 6 are thus at the bottom of the series. In Georgia and much of the southeastern United States, Nos. 10 and 11 are found next to the granite, and are often highly consolidated and crystalline. In much of Central Europe Nos. 8 and 9 are in a similar situation and condition. In Southern California it is the Tertiary beds, or Nos. 12 and 13, which thus occur and which are often "folded or otherwise altered so that they are as much consolidated as are the formations of the Paleozoic."[6] Extensive examples of these conditions may be found in the Tehachapi Mountains, the Coast Range and elsewhere.

From all this we learn that there are no particular kinds of fossils which always occur in the bottom position, for any of them may be found in this position. Not only so, but any of them may be found in highly crystalline rocks, which resemble both in texture and in position the very "oldest" of the series. *Hence there are no genuine bottom or oldest fossils for the world as a whole.* Any of them may occur in this bottom position. And accordingly the evolutionary concept cannot adequately account for the facts here stated, for no one type of fossil life can be shown to be intrinsically older than all others, and hence none can be fixed upon to start the life on the globe.

## FOSSILS IN REVERSE ORDER

It is further pertinent to ask whether the fossils are ever found in the *reverse* order, that is, with the "older" above and the so-called "younger" underneath, yet obviously having been deposited in this reverse order by the natural operation of the waters. This would seem to be a crucial or decisive test. Perhaps you may think that, in the face of such contradictory evidence, the geologists ought to acknowledge that the fossils cannot represent different "ages." I used to think so but I have learned that man is not a rational creature. Even professors of geology and biology do not seem to be any more governed by cold logic and objective facts than other people. For there are plenty of examples of fossils in the reverse of the evolutionary sequence. But geologists are so completely convinced by their *a priori* theory of how the fossils *ought* to occur, that they invent all kinds of mechanical impossibilities to explain *why* the fossils happen to appear in this reverse order. Even some who profess to believe the Bible record of Creation and the Flood have become so confused in their thinking that they are willing to take at face value these romantic explanations of evolutionary geologists instead of be-

---

[6] Schuchert, Charles; *Textbook of Geology*, 1915, 911.

lieving that the fossils were actually deposited as we find them, in an order which contradicts the alleged evolutionary order.

## THEORY VERSUS PHYSICAL EVIDENCE

But let us retrace our steps somewhat, back to my early experience in trying to find out the actual facts about the fossils as I was studying the subject some forty-one years ago. Very early in my research I ran across the following choice tit-bit of reasoning by an eminent paleontologist of Scotland:

"It may even be said that in any case where there should appear to be a clear and decisive discordance between the physical and the paleontological [fossil] evidence as to the age of a given series of beds, it is the former that is to be distrusted rather than the latter."[7]

This is a candid statement of the settled policy which for over a century has been followed by all evolutionary geologists in dealing with these matters, although their methods of procedure have not always been so openly and candidly acknowledged. When I read it, I began to realize that examples *have* been found where the fossils are seen to be in the reverse of the evolutionary order. It is to be expected that other examples will again be found. But this eminent authority declares that the standard order of the fossils must be maintained at all hazards, and some explanation must be devised as to *how* the beds happened to get into this relative position where we find them, with the so-called "younger" below, the "older" above. The physical evidence of superposition is to be distrusted, our eyesight and common sense is to be denied, in order to save the theory. This sacred cow of an invariable order of the fossils is to be trusted, no matter what the physical evidence may be.

In my further study of this subject I then ran across the big English textbook by Sir Archibald Geikie, for many years the official Director of the Geological Survey of that country. In this textbook I found two important statements. The first is as follows:

"We may even demonstrate that in some mountainous ground the strata have been turned completely upside down, if we can show that the fossils in what are now the uppermost layers ought properly to lie underneath those in the beds below them."[8]

You will notice that it is precisely the same fundamental reasoning as that advocated by Nicholson. The *a priori* theory of the historical order of the fossils must never be doubted; let this theory of the fossils be true, though every physical evidence be false. And a complete inversion of whole mountains can even be "demonstrated" by showing that the fossils contradict the physical evidences of our eyesight and common sense. But modern geologists can go this Englishman one better. For they can even demonstrate similar upside-down conditions deep underground in flat, level country, away from any mountains, as in the coal mines of Belgium and from the oil wells of Oklahoma and Texas, the fossils being the only proof of such a reversal of layers.

The second statement which I promised to give from Geikie is as follows and deals with conditions found in the Alps:

"The strata could scarcely be supposed to have been really inverted, save for the evidence as to their true order of succession supplied by their included fossils. . . . Portions of Carboniferous strata appear as if regularly interbedded among Jurassic rocks, and indeed could not be separated save after a study of their enclosed organic remains."[9]

---

[7] Nicholson, H. Alleyne, *Ancient Life-History of the Earth*, 1877, 40.
[8] Geikie, Sir Archibald, *Textbook of Geology*, 1903, 837.
[9] Geikie, Sir Archibald, *loc. cit.* 678.

I give these quotations from this eminent geologist because of the well-known principle that admissions in favor of the truth from one who opposes it constitute the very highest kind of evidence. And since it is important for us to understand that in all these many examples of this sort which are now known from all parts of the world, *the physical evidence of the strata gives no indication of anything abnormal*, but that the fossils only are found in what is regarded as the wrong order of succession, I shall present one more statement from this same eminent geologist, concerning conditions in the northwest of Scotland, where the strata had been at first described by Murchison, Sedgwick, and others of the most experienced geologists as quite normal in the sequence of the beds. But after index fossils had been discovered in strange, unlooked-for places in these beds, the whole area had to be redescribed in terms of gigantic thrusts.[10]

The thrust planes, says Geikie in an early article in *Nature,* are difficult to be

"distinguished from ordinary stratification planes, like which they have been plicated, faulted, and denuded. Here and there, as a result of denudation, a portion of one of them appears capping a hilltop. One almost refuses to believe that the little outlier on the summit does not lie normally on the rocks below it, but on a nearly horizontal fault by which it has been moved into its place."[11]

And he describes in the following picturesque language the perfectly natural appearance of the contact lines between these contradictory sets of strata:

"Had these sections been planned for the purpose of deception, they could not have been more skillfully devised . . . and no one coming first to this ground would suspect that what appears to be a normal stratigraphical sequence is not really so."

In the presence of such testimony from so eminent a geologist we are not greatly impressed when some guide in the Glacier National Park tells tourists that he has found a place where 'slickensides' can be observed there. On the strength of this flimsy evidence, these tourists are asked to believe this fiction that the entire Rocky Mountain area, including the Glacier Park and running up to the Yellowhead Pass in Alberta, west of Edmonton, an area of 500 miles long and 50 miles wide, was lifted up and pushed bodily eastward into its present position. And this in spite of the fact that some of the most experienced geologists have expressed their astonishment at the apparently natural contact between the upper and lower strata. I well remember talking with one of the leading men in the office

[10] The recapitulation theory, which has been mentioned above (see footnote on page 81) was one of the chief sources of the theory that the fossils always occur in a certain definite order all over the globe. According to this theory of the invariable time-order of the fossils, the trilobites are always to be found below the dinosaurs, and the latter always below the elephants and other mammals. Accordingly, if in any place dinosaur fossils should happen to be found underneath beds containing trilobites, as happens to be the case throughout this immense region of Montana and Alberta, then an anxious hunt is made to find some way of explaining away this very awkward evidence. *This is the entire reason behind the theory of the thrust-faults.* Were it not for this *a priori* theory, no one would ever dream of such a fantastic scheme as that this entire area was lifted up several miles and then pushed bodily for some fifty miles or more across the country to where the Rocky Mountains now stand.

It is such illogical use of the plain, objective evidence that this paper is designed to expose and discredit.

[11] Geike, Sir Archibald, *Nature,* Nov. 13, 1884, 29-35.

of the Geological Survey in Washington, D. C., about this matter. When I asked him if the contact line between the two sets of strata here in the Rockies didn't look perfectly natural, he shrugged his shoulders and said with a quizzical smile: "That's the queer thing about it, they do look perfectly natural."

The writer does not care to herald his achievements in these matters, for he has never claimed to be an expert field geologist or a scientific collector. But he has seen a few of these outcrops of so-called "older" rocks on top of so-called "younger," at some places around Banff and in the Crownest Pass, Alberta, as well as in several places in the Alps. And to him these outcrops look perfectly natural and show no physical signs of abnormal conditions.

The writer also has many photographs by some of the most famous geologists of the world, some of them having been used in his books. We need expert photographers of our own who know what to look for, and who can take close-up photographs of some of these outcrops. We also need our own investigators who can bring us back actual specimens from these contact surfaces. Then we can judge whether the rocks are deceiving us, or whether it is the evolutionists and their appeasers in our own ranks who are misinterpreting the actual facts of nature.

A multitude of statements could be gathered from some of the most eminent geologists testifying to the amazingly natural appearance of what the theory calls the nearly horizontal fault-plane. Here is one from R. G. Mc-Connell who afterwards became the head of the Canadian Geological Survey, regarding one outcrop on the east side of the Rockies near Banff, where the Canadian Pacific Railway enters the foothills:

"The angle of inclination of its plane to the horizon is very low, and in consequence of this its outcrop follows a very sinuous line along the base of the mountains, and acts exactly like the line of contact of two nearly horizontal formations. . . . The fault plane here is nearly horizontal, and the two formations [Paleozoic on Cretaceous], viewed from the valley, appear to succeed one another conformably."[12]

He also adds the revealing information that the underlying Cretaceous shales are "very soft," and appear to "have suffered little by the sliding of the limestone [Rocky Mountain mass] over them."[13]

At my request this same gentleman sent me from the Government office in Ottawa a map of the Alberta part of the Rockies, on which he had marked with pencil some two dozen places where similar outcrop conditions are to be observed. Bailey Willis, R. T. Chamberlain, and others might be quoted to confirm the seemingly natural appearance of the strata on the American side of the international boundary line, for as I have said above, the entire area is a unit, and extends about 500 miles from north to south and nearly 50 miles wide from east to west.

Similarly James D. Dana testifies concerning some similar conditions in the Alps.

"The thrust-planes look like planes of bedding, and were long so considered."[14]

In view of all this testimony, which could be multiplied a hundred fold from all over the world and from the testimony of the most experienced geologists who wonder at the strange naturalness and complete absence of signs

[12] McConnell, R. G., Canadian Geological Survey, *Annual Report*, 1886, Part D, 33-34.
[13] *loc. cit.* 84.
[14] Dana, J. D., *Manual of Geology*, 4th Edition, 534.

of violence in the so-called thrust faults, of what use is some tourist's report that he heard from a ranger in the Glacier Park about a disturbed spot there where slickensides extend for six or seven miles? What has this to do with an area 500 miles long by 50 miles wide, throughout which nine-tenths of the contact planes are as undisturbed and seemingly conformable as the bricks in a new building?

And what are slickensides? They are scratched or polished surfaces due to movement of the rocks, and are seen not only in veins and faults but are very common between stratified beds, or wherever a movement of the parts has taken place. They are found in most coal mines, sometimes at more than one level. A movement of even a few inches may produce slickensides, if the pressure has been sufficient. I doubt if any area of ten miles square exists anywhere on the earth which would not show such evidences of movement, if sufficient search were made, just as no area of this size is without faults and fissures. No, something more substantial than a few slickenside surfaces is demanded in order to make credible the fantastic theory that a district 25,000 square miles in extent was lifted up bodily and pushed along over soft shales for 40 or 50 miles. The real push behind this fancy is the *a priori* theory of the evolutionary succession of the fossils, now so definitely contradicted by the finding of fossils of dinosaurs and other Cretaceous animals in the lower beds and trilobites and other Paleozoic fossils throughout all the mountains standing upon them.

## CONTRADICTORY THEORIES

The last point which time and space permit me to dwell upon is the important fact that the geologists disagree among themselves as to what it really was that happened to put the beds in this allegedly "wrong" position. Many years ago the Swiss and German geologists used to talk of gigantic folds many miles high which had turned the beds over like a gigantic pancake. It was a belief in this theory which induced James D. Dana to say that one of these mythical pancakes "has put the beds upside down over an area of 450 square miles."[15] The late Dr. William Diller Matthew, Professor of Paleontology in the University of California, whose father before him was a writer on geology and lived not far from where I was born in Eastern Canada, once argued with me that these strata such as we have been here discussing must have been turned over, because as he said, many of the fossils are on their backs. But he neglected to add that in all the ordinary or normal beds, the fossils are about as likely to occur upside down as right side up.

Suffice it to say that the Swiss geologists, with many investigators in this country, are now denying these monstrous folds and are saying that flat-lying thrusts will account for the occurrence of these strange "reversed" sequences of the fossils. During the summer of 1926, much of which I spent in the Alps, the geology teachers there gave me dozens of diagrams made by their students, attempting to show the mechanisms by which the strata were pushed into their present positions. The students are encouraged to be original in showing how it all happened, for the idea seemed to prevail that with everybody having a trial at the puzzle, some one will finally hit upon the right solution. Geology is a very interesting subject to the students in Swiss high schools

---

[15] Dana, J. D., *loc. cit.*, 367.

and universities; for all around them are mountains whose strata directly contradict the accepted sequence in which they "ought" to occur. Hence with many clever young people having a hand at these diagrams, it is no wonder that they are fearfully and wonderfully made. I brought away several dozen of these incredible mechanical inventions, no two of them alike for the same mountains.

And anyone in this country who thinks, that the exact method of the formation of the Alps has been solved, because of some diagrams which one finds in such books as those by Emmons, or Schuchert, or others, ought to go and talk with some of the instructors of geology who live and work on the spot. I remember talking to one of these men about Mt. Mythen, a striking peak in the William Tell country, near the edge of Lake Lucerne, with Permo-Carboniferous beds at the top and Tertiary at the bottom. In terms of our numbers, this would be Nos. 6 or 7 on top of 13 or 14. The differences in coloring are very striking and the horizontal bedding line between them can be recognized miles away from a boat on the lake. This professor of geology remarked that he didn't know where the top of this mountain could have come from, unless it dropped down from the moon.

Here in the United States, the district involving Sheep Mountain and Heart Mountain just east of Yellowstone Park is recognized as just a part of the great zone of so-called "overthrusts" to the northwest in Montana and Alberta; and yet the geologists cannot agree about the mechanics of the process. E. H. Stevens, of the Colorado School of mines, writing in 1936, quotes two preced-

ing investigators as saying that the upper rocks, or those in the so-called "thrust plate," are only about 1500 feet thick, and thus are too thin to stand being pushed from behind at a distance of 28 or 30 miles, as the local conditions would demand. The title of his paper is "Inertia as a Possible Factor in the Mechanics of Low-Angle Thrust Faulting."[16] Outlined briefly, the theory which he suggests is that it was the earth which moved suddenly out from under the mountain, leaving the mountain sitting in a strange new position, about as one can jerk a book suddenly from beneath a jar and leave the latter standing on an entirely new foundation. Two years later he renewed his discussion of this problem and candidly acknowledged that a detailed study of this locality "failed to disclose proof of the mechanics of thrusting or of the direction of movement of the thrust mass."[17] Incidently, he mentions three additional theories suggested by other geologists, one to the effect that these mountain remnants may have been transported by glacial ice, or that they are the results of a large volcanic explosion, or that Sheep mountain is the result of "a circular fault that punched the Paleozoic limestone up through the Wasatch [Tertiary] formation."

All of this illustrates the amazed perplexity of contemporary geologists in the face of the actual facts which contradict their theory. Dr. Albert Heim, Professor of Geology in the University of Geneva, Switzerland, with whom I had some correspondence over thirty years ago when I was first studying these subjects, once wrote me that it was as plain as the nose on one's face that the strata are in an order contrary to the evo-

16 Stevens, E. H., *Journal of Geology*, Vol. 44, 1936, 729-736.
17 Bull. Geol. Soc. of Amer., Vol. 49, No. 8, Aug., 1938, pp. 1233-1266.

lutionary sequence,—"only we know not yet how to explain it in a mechanical way." In another communication he revealed the fundamental method of reasoning which always dominates the minds of all evolutionists who study these subjects. He wrote:

"The most incredible mechanical explanation is more probable than that the evolution of organic nature [i.e. the succession of the fossils] should have been inverted in one country as compared with another."

The English geologist, W. W. Watts, also recently expressed the perplexity of the orthodox geologists:

"The problem of the overthrust 'nappes' of mountain regions is one of our greatest difficulties, and all explanations hitherto proposed are so hopelessly inadequate that we have sometimes felt compelled to doubt whether the facts really are as stated. But the phenomena have now been observed so carefully and in so many districts that any real doubt as to the facts is out of the question, and we must still look for some adequate method by which the overthrusting could have been brought about."[18]

The mental attitude shown by these two quotations is that of most modern scientists; it is that of men who implicitly believe in some sort of evolution for the world as a whole, and who never dream that all the fossils could possibly have been living contemporaneously a nd then destroyed by a universal Deluge. This latter possibility has apparently never suggested itself to their minds in any serious way. Hence all their mental processes have been directed toward solving the manifest puzzle of these many examples all over the world where the fossils are found in an order of succession in the strata which obviously contradicts their established notions. There is therefore small wonder at their perplexity in the face of such contradictory facts. Since these difficulties are not so easily dis-

posed of, they are unable to explain the facts as they are shown in the Alps, in Alberta and Montana, and in so many other parts of the world, where the fossils in the rocks are obviously in a position which denies their evolutionary sequence.

The crucial nature of these examples make it extremely important that we develop our field knowledge of them still further, so we can present the facts in even a stronger manner. We have considerable evidence already, but there is much more and even more conclusive evidence which awaits our discovery. We know now where to go and what to look for. Why should we not improve to the utmost every opportunity to gain a better and a more complete knowledge of these crucial facts?

Let no one object that all these evidences against the geological "ages" is merely of a negative character, In one sense they may seem negative, in that they tend to destroy the idea of many long geological "ages." On the other hand, this would imply that the fossils must have all belonged to one age and one condition of the world. If the fossils cannot be proved to have lived in many successive ages, they must be regarded as having lived *contemporaneously*, and that means a positive confirmation of the Bible record of a world which was overwhelmed by the Flood. The establishment of this great fact of a universal Deluge becomes not only the best antidote for all the modern delusions about evolution, but as Peter points out in his second Epistle, this great fact of the former destruction of the world by water, becomes a warning that the next time the Lord deals with a wicked world it will be by fire.

I am also greatly encouraged in my life-work along these lines by the

---

[18] Watts, W. W., Smithsonian Institution; *Annual Report*, 1925, 283-284.

noble purposes of this Deluge Geology Society, in planning to study every phase of this subject, not only those usually grouped with geology, but also all the related sciences. The work of this Society promises wonderful things in the near future, when a whole army of enthusiastic investigators will unite to do research in both field and library along many contributing lines, thus developing a more complete and more convincing picture of that world, "which being overflowed with water, perished."

## CONCLUSION

1. Historical geology, as it is commonly called, in the last analysis is based entirely on the traditional order in which the fossils are conceived to have occured during uncounted millions of years. All other evidence, such as the lithic or mineralogical structure of the strata, their conformity or non-conformity, and even their order of superposition, all are subordinated, or, if necessary, explained away, in order to allow the fossils to testify to a supposed invariable order in which they lived and died.

2. In no place on earth do we find more than a small fraction of the total succession of the fossils. Scattered formations from here and there over several continents have to be assembled together in order to construct the geological column. This of course makes it possible to adjust sequences of the beds from here and there according to the preconceived idea as to how the typical or "index fossils" must have been laid down.

3. Genuine conformity of successive beds furnishes objective physical evidence that no great lapse of time could have taken place between their succesive depositions; they must have followed one another in comparatively quick succession. In other words, *conformity means essential continuity of deposition.* Yet there are hundreds, perhaps thousands of instances, where formations containing fossils allegedly separated by many millions of years occur in complete and perfect conformity over wide areas, some even where both the upper and lower beds are composed of exactly the *same kind and texture of sandstone or limestone,* as the case may be, and where the two formations can only be separated by their fossils. Interbedding of such allegedly incongruous strata is also of frequent occurence. Common sense tells us that the long ages alleged to be missing never occurred in these localities, and hence not in any other part of the world.

4. Plenty of examples are now known from all over the world where the fossils occur in the "wrong" order, or with allegedly "old" fossils in the upper layers and much "younger" fossils in the lower ones. The differences are often strikingly great; for Cretaceous or even Tertiary beds may be below, and Carboniferous or even Cambrian beds above, and these conditions may spread over tens or even hundreds of square miles.

5. So far as the plants and animals found buried in the rocks are concerned, the entire case between the Flood theory and the evolutionary theory turns upon whether these fossil forms lived contemporaneously or during long successive ages. And we now have abundant evidence that the theory of successive geological ages has completely broken down, and the evidence is clear and conclusive that the fossils lived contemporaneously. Thus the record of the Bible is confirmed: "The world that then was, being overflowed by water, perished."

# SIGNIFICANCE OF THE STRATA OF THE EARTH

## A Preliminary Survey

### BENJAMIN FRANKLIN ALLEN

It is the object of this study to introduce, in a preliminary way, some aspects of the strata of the earth other than their sequence, their relative position, or their fossils. These features are offered as constructive and descriptive of the work of the Deluge, as well as in opposition to the theory of the geologic-age system of the strata.

The following propositions are suggested: (1) the possibility that only the present topsoil, and some remnants of only one prior geologic era, ever existed; (2) that only the remains of one river system prior to our present one ever existed; (3) that the transitions between strata of different supposed geologic ages are inconsistent with that theory, but indicate the aqueous catastrophe of Genesis; (4) that the major strata were deposited by oversweeping waters not now operating; (5) that unbroken folds and effects of heat in the sedimentaries indicate that they were all wet and soft at the same time; (6) that there has been only one major period of underground heat and dynamics (plutonics, fissures, faults, mountain-making); and (7) that there has been only one episode of mineralization.

In this brief survey, only a few lines of investigation shall be pointed out. A full discussion of any one of these would call for a much larger discussion than this entire presentation.

### EVIDENCE OF ONLY ONE FORMER TOPSOIL

Roots, root holes, grass, weeds, seeds, trees, and all vegetation, together with worms, worm holes, insects and their borings, and the burrowings of animals, all acting through many centuries or thousands of years in the presence of water in the soil and its dissolved minerals above and below—these almost indelibly mark the surface soil. This topsoil, generally black or darker than that below it because of the carbon of decomposed vegetation, is present where sufficient rain or snow supports its living things and keeps its chemical processes in operation, at least a part of the time.[1]

*Fossil Forms Do Exist.* A leading geologist, in speaking of the rise of the ocean and its transgression over the lands, says:

"Where transgression takes place over an old peneplain surface [an old land surface] on which residual soil has accumulated during the long period of exposure, this ancient soil may be incorporated, without much change, as a basal bed."[2]

This substantiates the proposal that it is possible to find remnants of fossil topsoil. Naturally it would not be expected where land-slopes suffered the unprotected fury of the rising and raging oceans, but only in sheltered areas protected by comparatively small inlets. Here mud-laden waters could cover it deeply and preserve it. But later changes of many sorts could and did wash away and otherwise destroy all but remnants of it. Yet, in places, even considerable fragments may be reasonably expected.

Though some examples of fossil topsoil offered by geologists are questionable, because they lack positive indentification, still these are valuable in this investigation. One such example is suggested in the swamp theory of the origin of coal. The light, soft, watery muds of swamps are many times more destructable by encroach-

---

[1] Grabau, A. W., *Principles of Stratigraphy*, 1924, pp. 693-695.
[2] Grabau, A. W., *loc. cit.*, p. 731.

ing waters than the dryer, tougher, root-filled mat of topsoil. The much more vast areas of topsoil, also, increase the logical expectancy of finding it fossil.

Hardpan, a rock-crust or series of crusts which in some countries forms at a foot or more below the surface,[3] would still further serve to identify the topsoil, and to some extent preserve it. This hardpan results from the cementation of clay or other earthy materials in the chemical battle line between the down-seeping surface acid waters and the upsweeping basic or alkaline waters from below. But the marked differences of the former climate, and perhaps soils also, render uncertain the former existance of the hardpan. Further investigation offers many possibilities.

*Identification of Metamorphic Topsoils.* The writer is making some interesting studies of possible fossil topsoils in various stages of remineralization, all the way to complete petrifactions and even beautiful variegated jaspers, showing that positive identification, at least in the field, may be possible in some cases. The outcome of such investigations should throw light on all features of the problem.

*Significance of the Nampa Image.* More than 335 feet below the bottom of an old filled-up lake bed along the Snake River in Idaho was found a baked clay image, of a woman, about two inches long. It was found on top of a vegetable soil which was so identified by leading geologists. But we reserve judgment, awaiting more details, and we mention this find only as a fair example of investigation.

Dr. Wright[4] described this image as follows:

"This is a miniature image of a female form, beautifully formed, which was found in August, 1889, by Mr. A. M. Kurtz, while boring an artesian well at Nampa, Ada County, Idaho. The strata passed through included, near the surface, fifteen feet of lava. Underneath this, alternating beds of clay and quicksand occurred to a depth of 320 feet, where there appeared indications of a former surface soil lying just below bedrock, from which the clay image was brought up in the sand pump."

Since thousands of feet of solid rock overlie some fossil topsoils, the presence of bedrock *above* this alleged one does not appear extraordinary. This case illustrates the value of human implements in soil identification, and also the value of well logs, especially of oil wells because they are more numerous and deeper. However, only the cores should generally afford positive identification, as a rule.

*The Nature of the "Underclay" in Coal.* Along with the swamp theory of the origin of coal there came the theory that the underclay is the soil in which the coal-forming plants grew. Dr. Arber said of this theory, in part:

". . . Nothing could be more unlike a soil, in the usual sense of the term, than this underclay. . . . Coal seams may occur immediately above a conglomerate sandstone, as in South Wales; above limestone, as in some of the Scotch coal fields; or above igneous rocks as in central France."[5]

As a rule, the underclay is only about two inches thick, which would seem rather thin as a soil for timber or any other rank growth. Many deposits of it are formed far from coal fields, not at all related to any vegetation or supposed topsoil. Underclay being highly silicious, it is used for making fire-brick, and why such sterile clay should underlie swamps is not explained, for it is not formed under modern swamps.

Dr. Arber and others deny that the few upright stumps and trees found in coal formations actually grew there, and point to the one hundred times

[3] Clarke, F. W., "Data of Geo-Chemistry," *U. S. G. S. Bulletin* 770, 1924, pp. 486-489.
[4] Wright, G. F., *Man and the Glacial Period*, 1892, pp. 297, 298.
[5] Arber, E. A. N., *Natural History of Coal*, 1911, pp. 29, 98.

more abundant prone logs without upright stumps. Root systems which should absolutely permeate the underclay, and also the various partings between seams, are without a trace worthy of mention. If these few upright stumps are natural, they should be the rule rather than the very rare exception.

Perhaps some coal beds do rest on the floors of forests, and even on ancient swamps. But in that case only the bottom seam of coal should be of this nature. European geologists have almost unanimously abandoned the swamp theory, and with it goes the underclay theory.

*Summary on Topsoil Evidence.* There seems to be little doubt that fossil topsoil exists, though many destructive processes reduced it and are reducing it in amount. Thorough field study and the examination of well logs and cores should be conducted. The theory of underclay as a former soil labors under many difficulties.

If the Genesis catastrophe actually occurred, and the prior history of the earth therein given is true, only one former topsoil should be found in any locality. But if the long exposed land surfaces of the geologic ages ever occurred, each "age" should be marked by at least some well indentified remnants of its topsoil. Current geologic literature fails to disclose any regular effort to identify any such key topsoils marking the various geologic land horizons.

Thorough search should be made for possible fossil topsoils, because, if they can be identified as of the former geologic era, they may lead to a valuable series of facts. They would serve as a key horizon for geological reference, would perhaps contain fossils identifiable with those in higher beds and elsewhere, and would point out for profitable research the very important pre-flood surface as well as the nature of prior underground conditions of the original surface of the earth.

### ABSENCE OF A RIVER SYSTEM FOR EACH GEOLOGIC AGE

If the geologic ages ever existed, each with its well developed topsoil, (which is generally agreed could have been fossilized), it is reasonable that the horizon of each age would still be marked also by fossil rivers, at least by rare fragments.

*Existance of Fossil Rivers.* Underground water channels in caves, gravel beds, faults, fissures, etc., where there is no positive identification of a former actual surface river, are ruled out. But examples have been described which can be accepted without much question. That many more fossil rivers should be found can scarcely be denied by evolutionary geologists, because, if such vast coal-making swamps existed as are claimed, very much more abundantly could fossil rivers be saved.

Therefore, since several seams of coal are often found superimposed one above the other, and in places more than one hundred, it would seem reasonable to expect that at least as many river systems one above another should be identified in one locality as there are geologic ages represented there.

Parts of rivers which are still running over land surface said to be a billion years old are no more deeply eroded, and do not differ in any physical respect, from geologically "recent" rivers, though extremely marked differences should reasonably be expected.

One geologist says of the rate of river erosion:

"There are many examples on record of gorges hundreds of feet deep which have been cut through solid rock with only two or three hundred years of work. Lyell mentions the case of the Simeto, in Sicily, which was dammed up by a lava eruption in 1603. In a little over two centuries it had excavated a channel from 50 to several hundred feet in depth, and in some places 40 to 50 in width, although the rock through which it was cutting was hard, solid basalt. He describes also a gorge cut through a deep bed of decomposed rock in Georgia, which started at first as a mere mud crack a yard deep, but which in 20 years was 300 yards long, from 20 to 180 feet wide, and 55 feet deep. . . . The action of flowing water when carrying stones or boulders may be illustrated by what happened in the Sill Tunnel, in Austria. The bottom of this tunnel or water channel was provided with a pavement or flooring of granite slabs more than a yard thick. Through this tunnel a strong current of water carrying great quantities of debris was passed at a high velocity; but so rapid was the abrasion of the granite slabs that it was found necessary to renew them after only a single year."[6]

The *rate of erosion* is very variable, yet it can be depended upon, along with the rate of growth of alluvial lands in depth, and of deltas, where present, to give some approach to an estimate of the age of a river. But these estimates seem to bear no relation whatever to the supposed "geologic age," as determined by the age of the land surface through which the rivers run.

*Example of a Possible Fossil River.* Though sufficient field work by the writer in the Mother Lode country of California has not been done to justify a final opinion, some of the old filled-up, lava-capped channels may be of the proposed former river system. Some are now about the highest land in that region, and are called "Table Mountains" because the ice and water cut down deeply on each side and left them there. In the bottom of the old high channels are found placer gold, gravel, human remains, both bones and implements, and the bones of large extinct camels, deer, mammoths, elephants, and other giants of the previous geologic era. With them are

found the fossil trees and plants on which they lived, all tropical or subtropical, and *all of low-altitude types.* The uplift of these mountains *after* these trees and the animal life had been destroyed is therefore necessary. In this case it was "man before the mountains," and the same conditions are pointed to in other parts of the world by competent geologists.

In these river beds very fine volcanic dust and scoriae were deposited as fine muds, laid down in quiet water almost on the level. This was interspersed with layers of gravel, seemingly indicating periods of oversweeping of torrential waters covering the whole country with gravel rather than merely filling up these channels. A river cannot run on a steep enough slope to lay down gravel and also deposit soft muds. This fact seems to demand oversweeping waters periodic in sequence not operating anywhere in the world today. It was not caused by any sloping of the country and it was too widespread to be attributed to those rivers. No delta or shore formations suggest these as the possible causes. There is no evidence of alluvial lands or periodic overflows of rivers. The *one system* of life buried there lends no color to any theory but that of a single episode, because the same fossils are present in the entire formation, except of course the molten lava caps.

The finding of fossil rushes, weeds, reeds, etc., along the shores of these ancient rivers and lagoons is a test that few so-called fossil rivers can stand. Naturally, in the gigantic catastrophe of which the writer speaks, the raging waters would form many short and temporary channels of terrific size, speed, and volume, and of every degree thereof. These are found in abundance, at all depths, in certain areas of the world, but they

[6] Price, George McCready, *New Geology*, 1923, pp. 142, 143.

throw light on our problem rather than confusion. They indicate a single periodically oversweeping overflow *overall,* and serve more to emphasize the real former rivers than to obscure them.

When the Mother Lode fossil rivers were about filled up, having maintained their approximately level state, the whole Sierra region was uplifted many thousands of feet and tilted westward at a grade of about 80 feet to the mile. This is indicated by the molten lava that then ran down these channels at that slope. At once, but not before this elevation had occurred and the lava flowed, ice and water began cutting down on each side of these rivers, through the gold-bearing native slate and schist of the original earth in which these fossil rivers ran. This is still in progress, having concentrated far more gold in the new channels but much more coarsely ground than in the old, and leaving high the old rivers of the "table mountains" the Mother Lode country.[7][8]

No river or rivers lie beneath these old channels. They have beneath them inorganic slate and schist or granite. If the Genesis catastrophe occurred, no fossil river may be found with another above it or below it. But if the geologic ages ever occurred, then it is reasonable to expect remnants of fossil rivers marking the original surfaces of those supposedly long ages. But they are not thus found, except in positions as likely as not in no way related to those ages, but often a serious embarrassment to them.

TRANSITIONS BETWEEN STRATA CONSISTENT WITH DELUGE BUT NOT WITH GEOLOGIC AGES

*Irregular Sequence of Fossil Topsoils and Rivers.* Now that some of soils and rivers have been surveyed, the situation may be more critically examined from quite a different angle. Fossil soils and rivers should be found *marking the transition between* strata of different ages, *but not elsewhere in the strata.* And, unfortunately for the theory, they are formed as often as not where no time interval is permitted on the evolutionary basis.

Again, where strata, having been tilted, worn off, and others laid down upon the edges, the non-conformity thus formed shows no more time or erosion for a billion years than where no time at all is allowed. The same is true where there is no non-conformity at all to mark billion year periods, which is postulated solely on the theory of the evolutionary sequence of the fossils found. This is where two "ages" imperceptibly blend so that no structural transition between them appears, apparently laid down at the same time. Structurally, there is only one stratum. One would get the impression that the strata, structurally, do not have much significance in evolution, there being no consistent rule. The strata are not permitted to have any meaning where they contradict their fossil contents.

*Similarity of "Ancient" and "Young" Topsoils.* It is reasonable to suppose that surface soils exposed a billion years, as in the case of the "still unconsolidated Paleozoic sands and clays of the undisturbed plains of Russia,"[9] should be infinitely more marked, deeper, more decomposed, than surface soils only a few thousand years old. But such is not the case. And it is likewise expected that the peneplains of such billion-year surfaces, which were supposedly all that time being dissected by erosion, should

---

[7] Whitney, J. D., *Auriferous Gravels in California,* 1879, Vol. 1, pp. 133, 233-236.

[8] Allen, Benjamin Franklin, "Man Before the Mountains." *Signs of the Times,* Mountain View, Calif., July 11 to Aug. 22, 1939.

[9] Grabau, A. W., *loc. cit.,* p. 750.

be many times more grooved than "recent" peneplains, but they are not. The two, whether topsoils or peneplains, present the same appearance, the vast difference in age being postulated solely on the theory that the living things in the older appeared on earth that long before those in the younger. These cases should suggest that perhaps there is something wrong with the measuring stick by which these periods have been marked off.

*Uniformity versus Catastrophe in the Strata.* Although the principle of uniformity in the deposition of the strata is strongly upheld by geologists as a doctrine, yet great "revolutions" or upheavals on a continent-wide and even on a world-wide scale are sometimes postulated to explain abrupt transitions from one geologic age to another. To illustrate this point we quote from a well known text.

"*Close of the Mississippian (Ouachita) Revolution.*—The complete emergence of the continent at the close of the Mississippian was brought about largely without folding or tilting of the strata. In certain regions, however, there was actual mountain-making movements, though not on a large scale. . . . "*Close of the Permean (Appalachian) Revolution.*—The Paleozoic era was brought to a close by one of the most profound physical disturbances in the history of North America. It has been called the Appalachian Revolution because at that time the Appalachian Range was brought out of the sea by upheaval and folding of the strata."[10]

Textbooks on historical geology insist on the philosophy that "all things have continued as they were from the beginning," but use these gigantic non-uniform catastrophes to account for abrupt demarcations between the strata where uniformity could not apply.

*Missing Transitions Mean "Missing Links."* To show how these abrupt transitions between strata of different "ages" disrupt the biologic continuity, the writer would like to digress to refer to the fossil record, as it was expressed by one geologic commentator, as follows:

"So we have much the situation of the ancestors of the mammals that we have of the ancestors of the vertebrates. The latter was, apparently, a fresh water form—and we do not have fresh water deposits from the lower Paleozoic [a geologic age supposedly hundreds of millions of years prior to uplands]. The former was an upland creature, and we do not have upland deposits of the Mesozoic. Men can read only the records given them.

"In the same way, we know little about the ancestry of the higher flowering plants, such as now make up our forests and carpet our fields. Most of these nowdays are upland forms. Very few, even now, will grow in salt water. So we do not have their remains and we cannot make out directly what their history has been. They appear suddenly, just as the lower vertebrates did before them, and the higher mammals afterward. But their histories are not in print."[11]

And this is the testimony of one who sets out to contradict the story of the catastrophe of Genesis!

Another example of the biological difficulties of these geological gaps between strata of different "ages" is that one of the highest authorities felt constrained to form a radically new theory of the multiple origins of all the main forms of life. He proposed that all main forms originated separately and independently of each other, and had evolved in a parallel manner, not converging from one original cell. He would postulate a whole "zoo" of origins.[12]

These gaps in the strata, forcing "missing links" in the supposed evolutionary chain of life, are called "skipping." As has been amply pointed out by Price[13] they are one of the most troublesome and vulnerable

---

[10] Miller, Dr. J. W., *Introduction to Historical Geology*, 1928, p. 165.
[11] Brewster, E. T., *This Puzzling Planet*, 1928, pp. 286, 287.
[12] Clark, Dr. Austin H., *The New Evolution, Zoogenesis*, 1930, pp. 180, 181.
[13] Price, George McCready, *Evolutionary Geology and the New Catastrophe*, pp. 196-223.

weaknesses in the whole philosophy of the geologic timetable, and cast grave doubts on the whole scheme of evolution. Some other theory seems necessary to account for these features in the significance of the strata.

*Summary.* Fossil topsoil and fossil rivers are found as often as not where they do not belong, in places in the strata where no time interval is allowed by the geologic timetable. Topsoils and peneplains a billion years exposed are no more marked than "recent" ones. Worn and eroded transitions between strata of different geological age show no more wear than those where no time at all is supposed to have elapsed. Often no physical indication at all marks a *fossil* difference of a billion years. The lack of transitions between the strata mean "missing links" to paleontologists and biologists, and one high authority was apparently driven to invent a theory of multiple origins and parallel evolution of all leading forms of life, in order to avoid the difficulties of the missing links between them. "Skipping" of the strata is one of the greatest weaknesses of the whole theory of evolution.

DEPOSITION OF THE MAJOR STRATA

The crux of the significance of the strata is the manner in which they were formed, and this is a vital point in any philosophy of the history of the earth. Evolutionary geology holds that the major strata were formed as river fans (like those formed where streams rush out of mountain canyons on a flat plain), or by river deltas, river alluvial lands, lake-beds, swamps, estuaries, ocean shores, ocean bottoms, volcanic products, and wind deposits, all of these acting in the past as they do today. This is in accord with the doctrine of uniformity.

But the theory presented here postulates waters in motion over the face

[14] Genesis 8:3, 5.

of the earth ("going and returning," according to the original account [14]), changing in depth, in speed, and somewhat in direction, alternately bringing debris of a different nature from different sources, and, in fairly closed areas, moderately still as compared to other localities, depending upon the convolutions of the surface and changes therein. Quiet periods between major flows are seen in the fine material between major layers. Much ocean sediment was apparently not greatly disturbed, but simply raised up and became a land surface, possibly after much sediment of a land or shore character had buried it and thus protected it. But also, much of the ocean ooze was stirred up, suspended in the waters, mingling itself in all proportions with all other sediments.

*Flood-plain Levels Produced.* These waters thus in motion we present as the only adequate agent in smoothing out large areas like the prairies, the pampas, the llanos, and the steppes. At the present time the action of water is doing quite the reverse, in all the land surface of the earth above flood-plain levels, cutting the smooth surfaces into sharp hills and valleys—destructive rather than creative. These plains are not former ocean bottoms or lake bottoms, because they are not primarily of the proper sediments, and because their strata reveal far too much motion in the waters, as well as alternation in motion and direction. Neither are they deltas, because they are not perfectly level, because they do not contain the meanderings of properly identified rivers, and because no rivers can be imagined of size gigantic enough to form them, not to mention present streams. They have no relation to present alluviation.

*Origin of the Strata of the Great*

171

*Plains.* For brevity, since this discussion is but an introductory survey, only the great plains east of the Rockies and those of southern Germany will be taken up. One of the leading authorities on the strata holds the American plains to be due to fan formations from waters from the Rocky Mountains.[15]

Grabau and others invoke desert conditions for these fans, but do not refer to a single desert fossil found in them to support this position. Instead, they cite the ancient crocodile, the mammoth, the dinosaur, ancient horses and turtles, etc., and such plants as made our coal, plants long ago classed unanimously by botanical experts as tropical or subtropical and which they say demanded humid conditions.[16]

Red beds colored by iron oxide are offered as evidence of the desert or arid origin of these sediments, affirming that only under arid condition could the iron oxidize. However, in another publication[17] Grabau admits that these beds may have been laid down yellow and more thoroughly oxidized later. Just as there are large beds of laterite (red clay rich in iron oxide) today, so there may have been much more in the prior geologic era. As Price[18] has pointed out, the warm humid former climate greatly favored rapid rock decomposition of most rocks rich in iron to red clay, and that in the tropics today this is in progress on a large scale. Therefore, from the geo-chemical facts, as well as from the fossils, we see no necessity of considering the Great Plains of arid origin.

Some geologists disagree with Dr. Grabau as to the origin of these plains,

holding that ocean waters as well as fresh played their part, and this is in line with the theory of the present writer. This difference of opinion he recognizes as follows:

"Not all stratigraphers agree in regarding the formations enumerated below as of unequivocally non-marine origin."[19]

Grabau continues by citing these differences of opinion and gives facts which seem to the writer to overbalance his views, as will be presently shown.

We quote further:

"Among the Tertiary deposits of the Great Plains regions of the western United States are many beds showing stratification, but composed in large part of alternate pebble and sand beds, with cross-bedding structure well marked. [Cross-bedding is proof of torrential water deposit.] These have commonly been classed as 'lake deposits,' but, as Davis has shown, these are more likely deposits made by running water, and represent outwash plains or alluvial fans, formed by the streams from the mountains."

Alternation of land with ocean sediments is of frequent occurrence and suggests the ebb and flow of tidal action. Mixtures of ocean (marine) and land sediments, called "breakish" are often cited. Limestone is generally of ocean origin. In describing the plains sweeping out into Germany from the Alps, Grabau says:

"This is a complex series of light-colored sandstones and conglomerates with occasional limestones. . . . The lower part of the Molasse [the plain] is of Oligocene age, and begins as a marine series. In southern Germany this reaches a thickness of 600 meters (Bavaria) and is followed by an immense series of fresh water sands and conglomerates approaching 1000 meters in thickness. This series shows in part brackish waters and in part river and lake conditions. The brackish water phase contains Cyrena, Cerithium, Cytherea, etc., and the fresh water contains

---

[15] Grabau, A. W., *loc. cit.,* pp. 626-640.

[16] White, David, and Thiessen R., "The Origin of Coal," 1913, *U. S. Bureau of Mines Bulletin* 38, pp. 64-70.

[17] Grabau, A. W., *Text Book of Geology,* Part 2, 1921, p. 509.

[18] Price, George McCready, *New Geology,* 1923, pp. 445, 476-478.

[19] Grabau, A. W., *Principles of Stratigraphy,* 1924, p. 626.

Limnaeus, etc. Numerous leaves and other remains of land plants (Cinnamomum, Juglans, Quercus, Betula, Rhamnus, etc.) are found locally, forming what is known as 'Blattermolasse,' and forming occassional beds of brown coal, which is extensively exploited in the Bavarian fore-alps."

In subsequent pages, Grabau continues his discussion of this alternation of land and ocean and breakish remains, as he takes up the other "ages," and infers that the same conditions apply to the other great plains of the world. It seems evident from this that the ocean waters played a large part in the deposition of these major land strata. The mind seems unable to picture these great plains as mere fans or river deltas, because of their enormous size and their inappropriate changing character from place to place, and because of the absence of rivers at all thinkable as large enough. These lands are almost perfectly preserved, and therefore, if they are deltas, a most fragile land structure, one wonders what became of the much less fragile rivers of such gigantic size. They are not to be found.

*The "Loess" and the Strata.* Dr. Grabau and others refer to windblown material in the strata, known as loess, some of it lying about as it fell, some as it fell in standing water, and some as it has been carried and deposited by water. It reminds the student of the geology of the Genesis catastrophe of the great wind spoken of during the latter part.[20] The convulsed and deluged lands were barren of vegetation, which is in harmony with the special abundance of windblown material at that time. At no other time in the earth's history was there sufficient bare ground. The loess is found on top of the ground or not far below it, indicating its lateness in the catastrophic period. The generally sharp and unworn particles, indicating their original formation and source from fresh decomposition and break-

age, would be expected just then and at no other possible condition of the earth's surface before or since, and is in marked contrast to the smoothed and rounded particles carried by winds today. Perhaps the loess will yet show still better evidence of a single world catastrophe. Lastly, the apparently sudden chill of the air, with the yet warm oceans, could easily have been the natural means used to start and maintain the necessary winds, which would lay down the loess only as those conditions approached normal, if the present could be so designated. The force and direction of these winds should be investigated by physical and mineralogical tests of the loess.

*Volcanic Action and the Strata.* All stratigraphers discuss the influence of volcanism in the formation of the strata. Scoriae in the air, as well as dust, fell widely, and, lava itself being generally easily eroded by water, much of it was deposited in the strata. A special significance is that much of the great volcanic cycle can be read in the strata today, a study of considerable promise in volcanism. The outburst of volcanic and magmatic material was inevitable immediately with the break-up of the crust of the earth and its continued convulsions, which started and maintained the oversweepings of the oceans over the lands.

*Oversweeping Oceans Indicated.* These citations from geologists, who of course hold no brief for the catastrophism of the Genesis record, yet whose data are so easily interpreted in harmony therewith, apparently indicate the conditions necessary for the deposition of the strata of the earth. But original field research from new viewpoints is far more promising. The oscilating motion of the waters is well illustrated by the alternating cycles of

[20] Genesis 8:1.

strata the world over, and as deep down as well-logs go. Every well-log through sedimentaries, and the face of every escarpment of sedimentary layers, all displaying the rythmic cycles, tell the same story.

## SIMULTANEOUS DEPOSIT OF STRATA INDICATED BY FOLDING AND METAMORPHISM

The writer's proposition is that many folds and bends in the entire strata, from top to bottom, taking in all supposed ages, indicate that all of the strata were soft and wet at once, rather than only the top one at a time, with those below hardened. Otherwise one wonders how the great layers of hard brittle rock could be bent like old fashioned ribbon candy without extensive cracking and fragmentation.

*Old Rock-Flow Theory Abandoned.* The theory that any and all rocks could bend and flow if subjected to sufficient pressure persisted for a long while. But in 1938 Griggs[21] demonstrated its fallacy for the Geological Society of America. Working with the equipment of Prof. P. W. Bridgeman, which developed greater pressure than was ever produced by man, Griggs showed that limestone can be compressed 35 percent in length, but will break if the pressure is applied long enough. Quartz was found to remain brittle at all pressures. Therefore, some other explanation for unbroken but crumpled rock-bends is in order.

*Plastic Sediments.* Of the rocks supposedly bent in nature, no regard was shown for the kind of material bent—all was plastic, except quartz and other rocks which were either formed later of were crushed to breccia. The hardest and most brittle but greatly foliated rocks are frequently found interlaminated with the softest shales, with no sign of any more resistance by one than another. There can be but one explanation—bending in the mud stage, and subsequent hardening.

A paper given before the British Association describes the action of earthquake waves in soft sediments.[22] These waves, traveling through one kind of rock and meeting a mass of more solid rock, will "heap up the strata in folds against the obstacle somewhat as where waves break upon the shore." Whole mountains, and even whole ranges of mountains, *now* hard rock of many kinds, apparently moved like the waves of the sea, and "froze" in the act. The large class of molten rocks of course flowed with equal ease when plastic, and these are often found interfolded and otherwise related with sedimentaries, indicating that both were soft at the same time.

*Metamorphism.* Any material transformed by heat, hot water and minerals, or by chemical change, into a different form, is metamorphic. Wood (changed to coal, peat, charcoal, or petrified), bone, mud, shell, sand, granite, or what not may be metamorphosed to a different form. Granite, the most original rock of the earth, upon melting in the presence of the muds, waters, minerals, and gases, became changed to hundreds of different forms.

*Metamorphism and Geo-Chemistry.* Whole mountains and even mountain ranges may consist of metamorphic granites, altered more and more in all directions from their relatively pure cores. Furthermore, whole mountain ranges of metamorphic sedimentaries are observed. The force of these facts lies in the principle that the entire sedimentary mass had to be wet in order to be metamorphosed on such a vast scale, because neither the chemis-

---

[21] *Science News Letter*, Dec. 17, 1938, p. 338.
[22] *Nature*, Nov. 23, 1905, p. 98.

try of the process nor the heat could permeate the mass in the dry state. Water was necessary for both. The dry mass would only insulate itself from the heat, and what little would melt would require fully twice as much heat in the dry state.

Likewise the whole mass of molten granite had to be contacted by waters and corrupting sedimentaries while it was hot enough to absorb and act upon these decomposing agencies, in order to accomplish the evident result. Every sort of inclusion and engulfment points to this conclusion. It is generally agreed that molten rock, especially granite, will absorb water vapor in any quantity. Geo-chemistry abundantly testifies to the truth of these principles.

*Folded Thin Layers Mistaken for Petrified Trees.* In the western part of Little Rock, Arkansas, the writer observed an excellent example of metamorphic rock of very thin layers which had been folded while still soft, and all but the bend washed away. The "tree" was about ten feet thick, and ran through two parallel railroad cuts. It was of very hard and brittle fine sandstone. These "half" trunks or troughs of folds are not uncommon in well folded layers near the top of the ground, which have been left, erosion having truncated the folds. Seldom is a crack found in any of these hard rocks, except weather cracks, which are of course of subsequent and recent origin.

Near one of the water reservoirs of Hot Springs, Arkansas, the writer observed another "half-tree" of gigantic size, actually designated as a petrified tree by a card in a glass frame by a geologist of the U. S. Geological Survey. The poster was there in 1928. That whole region is composed of much the same material. Nearer the city, more within the zone of hydrothermal action, the originally carbon-

aceous thin layers were silicified just to the proper stage and manner to make the world-famous Hot Springs novaculites, the finest natural abrasive stone in the world. The hot springs themselves are remnants of the process, and still carry silica in solution.

*Summary.* The object is to indicate the necessity for the simultaneous deposition of the major strata as one event, in a condition of wet mud. Modern earthquakes cannot completely account for this phenomenon, because they are not accompanied by water or heat for metamorphic action, nor are they in the least sense sufficient for mountain-making.

Therefore the view is maintained that the folded and metamorphic strata indicate such a catastrophe as is herein postulated.

## ONLY ONE PERIOD OF CRUSTAL DYNAMICS

Still dealing with the same general problems and the same line of reasoning, the writer now proposes that major faults, fissures, fractures, dykes, and all remains of crustal dynamics of the deeper sort, were the result of but one episode, and occurred mainly as the molten or wet material began to be sufficiently solid to break and fissure rather than bend.

In a more profound way, the theory postulates crustal dynamics themselves as the major cause of the action of the waters and the upheavals.

*Bending, Then Breakage.* Students in the field can observe what seems to be much greater movements during the mud or plastic stage than later. The preservation of gigantic folds testify to this. During and after the hardening processes, however, breakage certainly occurred. Some of the material that hardened ahead of the general mass was crushed to breccia. The stresses breaking the hardening strata seemed to come from the same sources from which they had been coming during the soft stage, for we find the breakage to have taken place in the same directions in which the bendings had been taking place. Some of the breakage and fissuring was brought about, apparently, not by external forces, but by internal shrinkage incident to dehydration and chemical changes as well as settling and drainage. All of these features can be observed in the field, and also in many polished specimens used in fine buildings, especially black marble, as the white calcite fillings are prominent.

*Breakage Ignored Geologic Ages.* It is true that there are non-conformities between some supposed geologic ages—where the lower beds were upturned, eroded off, and the second "age" laid down level over the upturned edges, (and this perhaps repeated more than once). Evolutionists are wont to emphasize these cases. This feature, however, is spoiled as an exception, because, as often as not, or even more often, the same thing happened where no "age" is allowed, and no time at all is permitted by the geologic timetable. And this principle applies to all sorts of horizontal non-conformities.

Likewise perpendicularly, the fractures, faults and fissures show no respect for "age" horizons any more than for horizons which have no time element attached to them. They extend down through all alike. In fact the latter far outnumber the former, and this goes for all horizontal non-conformities also.

*Major Breaks Extend Down to Convulsed Plutonics.* Carrying the perpendicular features of breakage to its logical conclusion, it is found that the major breaks extend downward through the whole superficial mass, to the plutonics and magmatics. The situation is as though the powers and forces causing the breakage originated in the underlying plutonics and magmatics.

In the Grand Canyon, for instance, the greatly contorted and convulsed plutonics can be seen beneath the uplifted canyon as a whole as well as beneath some individually marked upheavals. The Canyon area was apparently uplifted by the upward expansion of these underlying plutonics into an anticline lengthwise of the Canyon, (in places even the remaining rim is over 2000 feet higher than it was), causing great gaps to appear at the surface, through which the waters rushed. But the uplift nevertheless impounded a very large and deep body of water back of it for a time, as large areas are more than 2000 feet below the south rim. The valley of the Little Colorado River is nearly all less than 5000 feet, and only slightly above that at the border of New Mexico. Possibly the sedimentary layers in the Canyon were then not yet fully consolidated to their present hardness.

This major break occurred, generally speaking, along two parallel lines, or along one main line with parallel breaks. Crosswise of the Canyon occurred eleven cross-faults, thus breaking up the mass into the great blocks which are present, some tilted this way and that, and some settled down.[23] Needless to say, all of the major faults extend downward to the plutonics, as inevitably they should if the powers causing them were exerted by those plutonics. Apparently most of the minor breaks are merely the result of the major ones and cannot be interpreted, as a rule, on any basis of the geologic age theory. Local inequalities in material, texture, degree of solidification at that time, etc., are

[23] La Rue, E. C.; "Water Supply Paper 556," *U. S. Geological Survey*, 1925, Plate 15.

ample to account for local fracturing accompanying the major upheaval. Subsequent movements have been only slight readjustments.

As to the cause of the plutonic and magmatic upheavals, the writer attributes that to dynamic forces affecting the whole earth at that time, but there is no need in this present paper for entering into that subject.

*Summary.* The major part of the displacements appear to have occurred during the plastic stage of the material, whether mud or molten. But, as the material solidified, which seemed to follow the more violent period of upheaval, breakage superseded bending. The same forces from the same directions still seemed to operate, however, but to a far less degree, and shrinkage and uneven settling went on somewhat independently of exterior forces and were responsible for a share of the breakage.

These dynamics ignored the geologic age horizons, both horizontally and perpendicularly.

Therefore it is affirmed that there has been only one period of major dynamics, and that it coincided with the one universal aqueous catastrophe.

## ONE EPISODE OF MINERALIZATION

Whether considered in its broader sense as the process of hardening and cementation of the rocks in general, or in its more restricted sense of the formation of mineral veins and ores of all kinds, the writer's proposition is that there has been but one era of mineralization the world over. Naturally this was inevitable as the result of the previously affirmed single period of dynamics, plutonics, and hydraulics.

*The Heat of Chemical Formation.* Chemically produced heat as a widespread factor in mineralization (the hardening of much rock and the formation of vein materials) is a new suggestion, in the sense and scope offered here. This heat is called the "heat of formation." The writer has estimated the amounts of heat produceable against the amounts required for more than a thousand chemical compounds.[24] It was found that slightly over 53 times more heat is produced by average chemical reactions than is used in the process. In many cases the heat produced is so great that the processes are highly explosive.

To illustrate from nature, it is always deeply impressive to see marcasite (pyrite) blazing up spontaneously when exposed to the air and dumped on the waste pile outside certain coal mines. Both the iron and the sulphur make haste to separate and take on oxygen in the air, hence the fire, a case of spontaneous combustion.

*Chemical Heat in the "Caldron of Chemistry."* The sudden burial of the world full of luxuriant plant and animal life, (judged by the character and abundance of the fossils to have been many times more plentiful than today), intermingling suddenly with inorganic muds and chemical solutions of all kinds, and not only forming its own heat on a grand scale but in certain locations subjected to magmatic heat as well—this is a new suggestion in mineralization. It was a caldron of chemistry worthy of profound study. The geological as well as the mineralogical implications loom large.

Where magmatic heat was not present, or did not approach sufficiently close to the surface to make its influence felt, only the chemical reactions resulting from the sudden burial and decomposition of the organic world of life would cause the milder types of uniform mineralization which are observed. It was the same in

[24] *Handbook of Chemistry and Physics,* Sept., 1931, pp. 650-668.

principle as the demand for water in large-scale metamorphism. And here came into sole play chemically produced heat on a world-wide scale, as well as the all permeating and simultaneous chemical reactions which produced that heat and also the mineralization.

*Plutonists versus Neptunists.* Through the centuries the long controversy has persisted between the Plutonists, who affirmed that mineralization was due alone to heat, and the Neptunists who contended that it was due to water.[25] The conflict has centered round the theory of the formation of mineral ores, has been indulged in by all of the highest authorities, and is still in progress. Prevailing expert opinion has swung back and forth a number of times. But this proposed mineralization, along with that of the more local but greater magmatic sources of heat, with all of the elements of the controversy at its command, and harmonizing them all, may be said to be occupying the no-man's-land with a peaceful settlement. It has entirely adequate sources of heat, water, chemistry, minerals, and dynamics.

*Surface Enrichment.* Miners of gold, silver, copper, lead, zinc, and all other minerals are aware that there is but one system of mineral deposits in any one place. Just at the top, "at the grass roots," the minerals are often especially rich. They are generally enclosed in hard weather-resisting rock which apparently became hardened before the mineral was leached out. Deeper down, in the zones of more steady moisture, decomposition and leaching are faster, but all of these surface leachings are influenced by the warmth and humidity of the climate.

The process of surface enrichment is important in this study of the signi-ficance of the strata because it tends to throw light on the history of the strata since their deposition. The surface became rich in minerals because it was the dumping place of richly mineral-charged waters coming up or out from the interior of the strata. Varying in heat, but always originally hot enough, with the aid of solvents, to dissolve the minerals they carried, the waters approached the surface. The loss of heat and pressure outside forced out of solution much of their mineral content. Furthermore, in addition to the probable influence of freshly deposited organic matter in the depths, fresh organic sediments generally tended to precipitate these minerals on a scale all out of proportion to the present. In fact the process of ore formation has practically ceased, and mostly the reverse is now in progress, wasting away.

*Secondary Enrichment.* Within usually less than 100 feet below the surface of the ground, "the grass-root-riches" too often play out. The greater dampness and decomposing processes, and the present generally down-seeping waters (as contrasted with the former up-seeping of hot solutions) pass the minerals on down or drain them out through openings lower down. At times these minerals may be trapped in their downward course, where they may form a "secondary enrichment." But no geologist has ever maintained that these mark former surface enrichments belonging to any of the previous geologic ages. And not since the complete abandonment of the theory of the geologic ages as marked off by different mineral horizons, (Werner's theory) has any geologist suggested any such thing. Today no one postulates mineral zones as having any time sequence.

These secondary enrichments usually are in the form of sulphates or

---

[25] Crook, Thomas, *History of the Theory of Mineral Ores*, 1933.

carbonates. If still deeper, minerals are found in the form of sulphides, in which form they are thought to have originally come up from the depths, then the mine may be worthy of deeper development.

*Summary of Mineralization.* If there was only one catastrophe of dynamics and water, caused by and mingled with the outpouring or surface-approaching heat from below, the single episode of mineralization necessarily follows. If the whole luxurient world of life was suddenly engulfed in the seething vortex of such a catastrophe, a world-wide chemical activity of great mineralizing possibilities resulted which alone seems to satisfy the requirements.

SUMMARY AND CONCLUSIONS

In this brief survey of the possible significance of the strata of the earth, (other than their sequence, their relative position, and their fossils), only certain main features have been mentioned. Each of the propositions has been introduced only to indicate clearly the broad fields of investigation available and some of the lines of approach. Apparently research from these viewpoints opens up new fields.

The importance of each proposition is seen in that *each alone,* if true, precludes the possibility of the geologic ages, on which evolution depends. But, taken together, their force challenges attention of the highest order. If they are true, a new science is taking form.

Fossil topsoils, for instance, well identified, are to be expected marking the horizons of each of the geologic ages, but they are missing. Only one former topsoil, apparently, has been found fossil in any one locality, presumably that spoken of in Genesis.

The same may be said of fossil rivers, except with even more force. Constructively, a universal flood is indicated. Fossil rivers are far more to be expected than fossil soils, especially the supposed coal-forming swamps.

If the theory of the geologic ages is correct, then some consistency is to be expected in transitions between strata of those ages. Remnants of topsoil and fossil rivers should at least have some place in such transitions as keys. But they do not, and are found as often as not where no time interval at all is allowed by the geologic time-table.

Underground, the most prominent non-conformities are more than likely not transitions between geologic eras at all, and have no time-table significance. But often, in order to maintain the "age" theory on the basis of the fossils, an entirely undisturbed stratum has to be theoretically divided by a line marking a billion years of lapse of time with only a change of fossils to show for it.

However, all of these difficulties are only explanations of the work of the aqueous-dynamic event which is suggested. They are all positive and constructive evidence, because all are in harmony with it and necessary to it.

The manner of the formation of the major strata is deeply fundamental to any history of the earth. But even in the leading evolutionary works on the strata can be found a fair presentation of their catastrophic origin, provided one follows those presentations with catastrophic conceptions in mind. No agency other than continental oversweeping waters, apparently, could have smoothed out the broad plains of the world. They consist of more or less alternating fine and coarse sediments, from both land and ocean, sometimes cross-bedded indicating moving waters. The indications of varying depths, also, and rates of motion, as well as directional shifts, all are totally unlike any present methods of deposition.

The volcanic products and the loess in the strata, as described by stratigraphers, fit well the Biblical account of the disrupted surface of the earth and the strong wind which blew during the latter part of the catastrophe and perhaps long afterward.

Only one episode of major folding and bending of the strata, from top to bottom, seems to have occurred, and that only while the strata were wet and soft and the molten materials still plastic. The old "rock-flow" theory has failed under recent geophysical tests, and there appears to be no explanation of large masses of the strata waving like the waves of the sea and "freezing in the act," *without a crack*, but that they were in a soft and unconsolidated state.

The seeming impossibility of metamorphosing whole mountain ranges, both sedimentary and granitic, except in the wet stage, or under the influence of muds and waters, is another determining factor. The fixed principles of geo-chemistry are well satisfied, and all minor features of local metamorphism like petrifaction, carbonization, etc., are in harmony.

The conception of only one crustal dynamic convulsion, causing the overflowing waters of the oceans, and causing the plutonic and magmatic action, and the upheavals, is fundamental to the Flood theory. But the breakage of the sedimentary strata and of the formerly molten material, as they began to be less plastic, is the feature which is mostly stressed in the effects on the strata. These breaks pay no regard to the supposed geologic ages, but treat the entire sedimentary formations as a unit. They seem to reveal the seat of their origin and power in the convulsed plutonics and magmatics below them.

One period of mineralization would be the inevitable corollary of all of these conditions, and this means both rock hardening in general as well as the origin of mineral veins. The chemical reactions resulting from the engulfed world of living things and the important chemically formed heat and the plutonic from below, constitute a new suggestion as the basis for mineralization. Surface enrichment and secondary enrichment are fully in harmony with and are demanded by these conditions, but they both apparently block evolutionary conceptions.

In a word, it appears that fossil topsoils and rivers may occur only once in any locality, and may represent the original surface of the earth from Creation to the Flood; that they are mostly embarrassing to the geologic-age system; that the transitions between strata not only tend to support these statements, and are themselves descriptive of that catastrophe, but point out special weaknesses of the geologic-age theory; that, resulting from these facts and reinforcing them, there was apparently but one period of bending, while the strata were soft and wet, harmonizing with metamorphic action at the same time; that this condition developed into the one era of breakage and faulting as the strata hardened; and that all of these processes contributed to and coincided with the single episode of universal mineralization.

If these closely related features, suggested as a preliminary survey, can be fairly substantiated by further research, they will be strongly constructive and descriptive evidence that the Flood of Genesis actually occurred.

THE

# BULLETIN

OF

# DELUGE GEOLOGY

## AND RELATED SCIENCES

| Volume I | December, 1941 | Number 5 |

## CONTENTS

## VISIBLE PROOFS OF THE FLOOD

### Its Universality and Its Recency

### George McCready Price

If the earth did really experience a universal Deluge some thousands of years ago, we might reasonably expect to find animals and plants buried in the deposits then made. But we should also expect to find still evident on the surface of the globe visible marks of the last work of the waters as the lands were emerging or the waters receding from off the surface of the lands. It is well known that we do find relics of animals and trees buried deep in the earth; we also find sea shells embedded by the thousands in strata high up on the mountains of every country on the globe; but these tell-tale evidences have been systematically explained away by the evolu-

tionists as having been done a few at a time in a gradual manner, during uncounted millions of years. But in addition to all these things we might expect to find objective evidences around over the surface of the globe of a once universal spread of the ocean.

Three classes of facts will be here considered: (1) the old shore lines around all the continents, which are clear proofs of the time when the ocean waters were retreating from off the lands, or the lands were emerging from the waters, which would be the same thing; (2) ancient high river terraces along the sides of the valleys of all the great river systems of the

The BULLETIN is published by, and is the official organ of the "Society for the Study of Deluge Geology and Related Sciences." The Editorial Board is comprised of Professor George McCready Price and Dr. Cyril B. Courville. It is printed at the Collegiate Press, Arlington, California. For members the BULLETIN is free, and extra copies 35 cents each (each number priced according to size); for non-members it is $2.00 per year; and this number is 45 cents. All correspondence should be directed to the Managing Editor, Mr. Ben F. Allen, 219 North Grand Avenue, Los Angeles, California.

world; (3) vast interior basins on all the continents, which have old shore lines around the inside of the mountains which hem them in, these old shore lines having been formed when these interior basins were full of water to their very brims.

We shall take up these phenomena in regular order; because I believe that every intelligent man or woman ought to become familiar with them, and ought to be able to read from them the message which they proclaim of that ancient time when "the world that then was, being overflowed with water, perished," but was delivered by the Word of the Almighty, to become again the habitation of the various races of mankind. For every person who travels a hundred miles from his home, indeed, almost every person who steps out of his own dooryard, will come face to face with some of these evidences of the retreating waters; and he ought to learn how to interpret what he sees.

### CONTINENTAL SHORE LINES

Along the Atlantic and Pacific Coasts of America, as well as the coasts of Europe and the other continents, are clearly marked old shore lines, rising one above another at various levels. These old shore lines, or old strand lines, as they are also called, are remarkably constant for long distances, though of course here and there they have been obliterated by subsequent erosion. But some of them are also equally spaced on both sides of the Atlantic, showing that the causes which produced them must have been acting simultaneously in Europe and America.

In some instances these ancient beaches may be obscured by a luxuriant growth of forest trees, or partly obliterated by streams which cut across them. But even an untrained eye ought to be able to recognize them, since they are so distinctly visible along many parts of the coasts of the entire world. In form they are exactly like the shore lines of the present day, though of course they are usually covered with grass or other forms of vegetation, and they are at levels above the present shore where one might not be looking for anything of the kind. I shall give a list of the measurements for some of these shore lines on the Atlantic coast south of New York, which may serve as examples of what will be found in other parts of the world. The figures here given are the heights above the present sea level, as given by reliable authorities: — 81 meters (265 feet), 65 meters (213 feet), 49 meters (160 feet), 29 meters (95 feet), 20 meters (65½ feet), 8 meters (26 feet). Others at much higher levels, up to several thousand feet, also occur, but are more widely interrupted by erosion, and can be detected only at widely spaced distances. Several successive old shore lines are plainly visible on San Pedro Hill and at other places here in Southern California, as well as along all the Pacific Coast.

No one can deny that these benchlike marks on the sides of the mountains were made by the ocean as it stood for a while in its downward movement to its present level, or as the lands were emerging from the waters. And no great lapse of time would be necessary to make one of these marks on the mountain side; one good storm of a few hours might easily accomplish all that we now see in any one locality. Whether the lands were being elevated or the waters were being lowered would make no difference in the final result; but the remarkable horizontality of many of these shore lines would seem to suggest that some common movement of the entire ocean was what took place. If large areas of the bottoms of the Atlantic and the Pacific were to drop down a few hundred feet, all the facts would seem to be explained. Slight subsequent warpings of the lands of the coasts would explain all the irregularities which have been observed here and there. There is no sufficient proof that at the present time the ocean level is gradually changing in any part of the world. Douglas Johnson, the highest authority on this subject, declares that the supposed evidences for present-day changes of level "are open to suspicion."[1] The stability of the ocean level in our day is good proof that it is still obeying God's ancient command: "Hitherto shalt thou come, but no further; and here shall thy proud waves be stayed" (Job 38:11).

The present shore line around the oceans differs markedly from the old ones in being many times more deeply cut into the lands, and also greatly extended in its width; for the continental shelves which surround all the continents of the entire world may well be regarded as only parts of the present shore line. Indeed, if all the waters of the oceans should be removed, these gigantic continental shelves, often extending out fifty or a hundred miles, would be seen to be exactly like the old shore lines now found on the sides of the mountains, only the present ones are on a far more enormous scale.

But the very size and strongly marked character of the present shore is a good evidence of the length of time that the ocean has been where it now is. I mean, that the present shores are visible evidence of the *relative stability* of the lands and the ocean for many hundreds or thousands of years.

Long ago, Eduard Suess, that prince of geologists, expressed this same idea:

"Phenomena confront us which testify to the stability of the existing state, which has endured since the remotest period of human tradition, or since a period even earlier still: in hundreds of localities, the sea has graven its mark deep in the rocks at the level of the tide."[2]

More recently we have a modern writer on the subject drawing the same conclusion. F. P. Shepard, in a paper severely critical of many widely held notions about the ocean, its bottom, and the continental shelf, says that the uniform levels around all the continents is plain objective proof that "there has been a long period of stability since any great uplifts and sinkings" have occurred.[3]

All this fits perfectly into the general picture which we have of the Flood and its sequences. For the stages in the subsidence of the waters must have been brief; and when we look at the old elevated shore lines we realize that one or two good storms would have been sufficient to produce any one of them. On the other hand, the modern or present-day shore lines in every part of the world give evidence of having been where they are for thousands of years.

In a few instances the old strand lines on the Atlantic Coast have been found capable of being correlated with somewhat similar shore lines on the other side of the Appalachian Mountains, or in the Mississippi Valley. But modern geologists do not seem to take much interest in such matters; and these problems have not been studied in other parts of the world. However, as we shall see presently, some of the old shore lines in Europe have been followed around to the mouths of such rivers as the Seine, the Elbe, and the Rhone, where they are found to blend with the high

---

[1] Johnson, D.: "Shoreline Investigations on the Atlantic Coast," *Science,* 65:4, Jan. 7, 1927.

[2] Suess, Edward: "The Face of the Earth," Vol. 2, p. 554, 1904-1908.

[3] Shepard, F. P.: "Geological Misconceptions Concerning the Oceans," *Science,* 78:406, Nov. 3, 1933.

river terraces which occur along the banks of these rivers. Undoubtedly similar correlations could be worked out in other parts of the world.

### Ancient River Terraces

All the large rivers of all the continents have strongly marked terraces or old banks high up above their present levels. In the eastern United States, these terraces occur four or five hundred feet above the Ohio and other rivers, while all around the Great Lakes similar terraces, or perhaps old shorelines, occur at various successive levels up to a thousand feet or more. All other rivers show similar phenomena. At such heights these rivers must have been of enormous volume, many times their volume at the present day. All the lower terraces are simply the remains of the old flood plains of the rivers when flowing at former levels; for during the centuries these rivers have been cutting down their channels to their present levels. But the highest terraces of all, which may be at heights of a thousand feet or more, cannot be distinguished from old ocean beaches, which they probably were. Those terraces along the foothills of the Rocky Mountains are clearly phenomena of this nature. They were formed when the Mississippi Valley was full of water; for these water marks are a full mile or so above the present level of the ocean. Anyone who is familiar with the eastern foothills of the Rockies for a distance of several thousand miles up and down, will remember plenty of these marks of the retreating waters which are still visible and indicate the action of water on an enormous scale.

I have mentioned that the high terraces of the Ohio and other eastern rivers occur at elevations of four or five hundred feet. But the higher terraces (or old strand lines) around the Great Lakes and elsewhere often show signs of having been warped or disturbed; for they are often no longer horizontal. The many old beaches which occur throughout the Green Mountains, the White Mountains, and in other parts of New England, as well as in the British Isles and in Switzerland, at levels of half a mile or more above modern sea level, usually occur only in scattered localities; for the great subsequent erosion has largely obliterated the intervening parts of what once existed.

The theory of great sheets of ice of continent-wide extent has greatly obscured the meaning of all these facts. We can readily believe in much larger glaciers in the higher mountains, without feeling any necessity of saying that immense sheets of ice a mile or so in thickness covered the flat plains of America and Europe. And since there are beds of semi-tropical vegetation interbedded with the so-called glacial beds in many places both in America and Europe, modern geologists demand at least four periods of these great ice sheets, separated by a corresponding number of warm periods, when these warm-climate trees could flourish. But all these things would stretch out the total period of the ice to not less than one or two million years. This alone will convince any believer in the Bible that there must be something wrong with this glacial theory. And we need also to remember that it was this glacial theory, first taught by Louis Agassiz about a hundred years ago, which tended finally to discredit the Flood theory, which up until that time had been almost universally accepted. As Richard M. Field of Princeton has expressed it, "The last support of the cataclysmic idea [the Flood theory] was destroyed by the proof [?] of the glacial drift."[4]

---

[4] Field, Richard M.: "Principles of Historical Geology." p. 12, 1933.

And when we remember that today this glacial theory is used as a means of explaining away the surface evidences of a universal deluge which stare at us from all over the northern lands, we properly become suspicious of all alleged work of the glaciers except what can be actually demonstrated.

If we admit that there was once a universal Flood, then these old shore lines and high river terraces were obviously formed as the waters of the universal ocean were being drained off the lands, leaving the rivers to cut down their beds to their present levels during the subsequent centuries.

But it is very interesting to note how very little in the way of cutting down the beds of the rivers is now being done. For the lowest of these river terraces, now but little above the present flood plains of the rivers, are now the sites of important towns and cities, which have occupied these positions since the early settlement of America. Of course, this is not a long period; but in Europe and Asia hundreds of cities have occupied similar situations on the banks of the rivers for many hundreds of years. Yet during all these many centuries the present volumes of the rivers have scarcely cut down their channels to any appreciable extent, though deltas like that of the Po and the upper Rhone flowing into Lake Geneva have built out the lands for several miles.

The evolutionists point to the extremely slow work of the modern rivers as evidence of the enormous lapse of time since the present configuration of the lands took place. But these facts should rather be interpreted as evidence of the extreme rapidity with which the first postdiluvial changes took place. For the rocks of all the lands were then freshly deposited and still soft and unconsolidated; they had absolutely no protecting cover even of grass, to say nothing of forests, to delay the run-off. Moreover, the precipitation for the first centuries must have been enormous beyond anything now known. From all these facts, we conclude that immediately after the emergence of the continents, all the rivers and streams must have cut down their channels at enormous rates. The gorge of the Colorado will illustrate what I mean, though in this instance there is clear evidence that this river began working on the broken crest of a gigantic anticline, thus giving the waters an easy beginning, and the great drainage area and the softness of the rocks in the early days, furnishing the other necessary conditions for the rapid digging out of this which Mark Twain called "the biggest ditch on earth." It is worth noting in passing that many other rivers of the world also started by running along the broken ridges of anticlines, which is good proof that this action began while the universal ocean had scarcely yet subsided from the lands.

Within recent years some study has been made of the river terraces along the streams flowing into the Mediterranean Sea and the Persian Gulf. Five well-marked terraces have been traced along the banks of the old Euphrates, and the ones at fifteen feet, thirty feet, and fifty-five feet are at almost the precisely same levels as similarly situated ones on rivers flowing into the Mediterranean and the Atlantic. These similar conditions from such widely separated localities would indicate that the dropping of the bottom of the ocean would best explain the facts, which I have obtained from a report by Prof. W. J. Sollas, of Oxford University.[5]

[5] Sollas, W. J.: "River Terraces of the Euphrates," *Nature*, 118:692, Nov. 13, 1926.

Singularly enough, these unambiguous marks left by the receding waters have been almost wholly neglected by modern geologists. An inquiry at Science Service, in Washington, D. C., which poses as a clearing house for scientific information, brought the response that they knew of no recorded studies along these lines. However, all those who believe in Flood geology ought to be intensely interested in studying similar facts in other parts of the world.

I remember how, on one of my trips across the continent, I was strongly impressed with the obvious signs of the continental recession of the waters, as seen on the way from Utah down through Wyoming and into Colorado. Everyone knows that this region is now conspicuously arid; and yet terraces and old shore lines are very conspicuous, and could have been made only by waters in enormous volume when receding from off these lands. The continental divide is at Creston, on the Union Pacific Railway, about 146 miles west of Laramie. This point is 7,107 feet, or over a mile and a quarter, above sea level. South of this, on the road to Denver, old bosses of red rock project through the surface at many places, with abundant signs of waters in enormous volume; yet all these evidences are as fresh as if the waters had receded all at once and only a few years ago. But throughout all this region vast open rolling prairies stretch away to the south and east, this whole surface, though over a mile high, being entirely open to the valleys of the Missouri and the Mississippi. And to have enough water to leave these visible marks at this level, the entire Mississippi Valley would have to be full of water. Obviously these water marks must have been made when the Rocky Mountain region was finally emerging from beneath the ocean waters.

## GREAT INTERIOR BASINS

We have next to consider the subject of the great interior basins, and their present condition as arid or desert wastes.

When we look at the earth as a whole, one of its outstanding features is a large number of great depressed areas here and there on all the continents, these sunken or depressed areas having only interior drainage into dried up lakes or salty lakes without any outlet. Ranges of mountains of considerable height usually ring these basins all around or nearly so, and on the interior sides of these mountains we find the same relics of old shore lines, mute evidences of the time when these interior basins were full of water.

Great Salt Lake is only the remnant of a very much larger lake which once occupied this region; and the existence of this ancient lake is so clearly proved by physical evidences around on the hills that it has received a definite name, being known to geographers as Lake Bonneville. This ancient lake was once two-thirds the size of the present Lake Superior, and then occupied parts of three States. Its old shore line can be readily seen from the valley a thousand feet above the present level of Great Salt Lake.

All these ancient lakes show more than one level of old shore lines. In the case of Lake Bonneville, the lowest of three such ancient beaches is about 900 feet above the present lake level, while a higher one at 1000 feet is thought to be younger. From these few facts, which are so easily capable of various interpretations, hasty conclusions about very distinct fluctuations in the ancient climate have been drawn. But some comparatively slight changes in the level of the ancient outlets at the brim of the lake, due to the very sudden action of earthquakes, might easily produce the results which we find recorded here and elsewhere. The same may be said regarding the many instances of rivers like the Niagara, the Missouri, and the Columbia, which have been diverted more than once from the channels in which they once flowed. Earthquake action, which we know is always sudden, offers a far more reasonable explanation for these diversions of rivers from their channels, than does the theory of the gradual growth and gradual diminishing of gigantic glaciers. For it is abundantly evident that the tremendous convulsions in the surface of the earth which accompanied the Flood itself, did not cease abruptly at the close of that event. And sudden earthquake action in producing changes of level is clearly indicated by these fluctuations in the ancient lake shore lines. At least this hypothesis ought to stand until something much better is proved far more clearly and conclusively than has hitherto been done.

Lake Lahontan is the name given to another body of water that formerly existed to the west of Lake Bonneville. Prof. J. Claude Jones of the University of Nevada once made a careful study of the mineral content of many of the shallow lakes within the area of the ancient Lahontan Basin, which includes much of northwestern Nevada and parts of neighboring States. Jones discovered that the drying up of this ancient lake took place not so very long ago. I quote from his summary:

"All of the physical evidence points to the recent existence of the old lake. The terraces, bars, and other lacustrine features are today practically as fresh and unchanged as when they were first formed by the lake waters. . . . With the exception of an occasional scarring of the terraces by cloud bursts, there has been practically no erosion of the beach-lines. . . . In brief, all of the evidence bearing on the age of the former lake seems to clearly indicate that the history of Lake Lahontan has all taken place within the past few thousand years."[6]

Professor Jones makes it plain that he considers that the history of this lake *began as well as ended* only a few thousand years ago. I am not here concerned with his theory of how it began as an incident connected with the immense precipitation at the close of what geologists are pleased to term the "Glacial Period." It is sufficient for our purpose that the entire history of this immense lake, its beginning and its drying up by evaporation, must all have taken place well within the limits of the chronology of the Bible.

But these two immense lakes, Bonneville and Lahontan, are together only parts of a still more enormous area known as the Great Basin, which occupied practically all of Nevada, with large portions of Utah, Idaho, Oregon, and California. Some parts of this district, such as Death Valley, are many feet below the present sea level; and when the Great Basin was full of water, we can understand that at places the water must have been very deep. Any good textbook on physical geography will give maps of this area, for its ancient boundary lines on the east, north, and west are definitely known, although its boundary on the south is not so well preserved.

The Caspian Sea is properly only a lake within an interior basin. The district to the east and south of the Caspian is arid, so that few streams flow into it from those parts; but large rivers flow into it from the north and west, with the result that the water of the Caspian is nearly fresh, though its waters have no outlet. Its present surface is eighty-six feet below ocean level; and its area is about twice that of all the Great

---

[6] Jones, J. Claude: "Geologic History of Lake Lahontan," Pub. Carnegie Institution of Washington, p. 50.

Lakes of North America put together. Large as this area is, however, it is only a part of a still more immense basin, known as the Aralo-Caspian basin, which includes also the Sea of Aral. When this basin was more or less full of water, it formed what is known as the Eurasian Mediterranean, or the Sarmatian Ocean, though its exact boundaries have not been carefully surveyed.

There are considerable areas in Tibet, with only interior drainage, which evidently were once full of water, as old beaches on the hillsides, several hundred feet higher than the present levels, show where the waters once stood. In one of the very old Tibetan histories we have the record of an Indian holy man who visited this region on two separate occasions. When he came there the first time he found the region under water. As the record pictures him as having lived to a great age, it tells us that on his later visit he noticed that the waters had receded, and that patches of brushwood could be seen here and there, with some deer and other animals running about.

This region of Tibet is often called the roof of the world. Hence it is very interesting to note the extreme recency of these conditions of widespread water, when the interior basins of this region were not yet dried up from the waters remaining from the universal Deluge.

There are several large interior basins within the continent of Africa. Lake Chad represents one such area, while the middle region of the Congo would be another; and if the Congo River were dammed to only a moderate height, this Congo basin would then communicate with the Chad basin to the north. Another large lake could be made by a dam on the Zambezi River, this area representing another basin with chiefly interior

drainage. And there are good archaeological evidences that the present races of Africa were acquainted with Albert Nyanza when it stood more than one thousand feet above its present level.

In all parts of the world are found these extremely interesting interior basins. Some of them are not at the present time capable of holding water up to their very brims, as they have some outlets, though at comparatively high points, where the water would drain off to the outside. But all of them have old shore lines still clearly visible on the surrounding hills or mountains, marking the levels at which the water formerly stood.

Now it is as simple as an elementary problem in arithmetic that, in each of these instances, we have indisputable proofs that these basin-like areas were once full of water. And what is more natural than for us to conclude that they were all thus full *contemporaneously*, and that the time indicated was when the waters of the Flood had just recently been drained off the lands? The evolutionary geologists to be sure, are not willing to admit that they were all thus full contemporaneously. For taken together these basin-like areas constitute a total of 20 per cent, or one-fifth, of the entire land surface of the earth; and to admit that they were all full of water at the same time, would be too much like the ghost of Noah's Flood staring them in the face. So they try to evade this point, and try to follow their favorite device of dating some of them in one age and some in another. But this is a mere subterfuge; for there is no proof that they were *not* thus contemporaneous. But if they were all full of water at the same time, they become overwhelming evidence that the record of a universal Deluge must be true. The force of this argument can be appreciated by a child.

But these immense areas have another story to tell us, a story of a gradual change in the earth's climate from damp to dry, and from one of fairly equable temperature to one of great extremes,—at least for large portions of the globe.

For when all these basins were full of water, their extensive surfaces could not fail to saturate much of the surrounding air and render the climate of the neighboring lands moist enough to support a dense vegetation. And the great quantity of water represented in these basins would tend to stabilize the general temperature; for all large bodies of water have this stabilizing influence. The problem of the climate of ancient times, and the other factors which combined with these huge bodies of water to effect a damper climate and yet one much less subject to extremes of heat and cold than at present, is far too large a subject to be discussed here. It must suffice to say that all these ancient interior basins are now more or less areas of arid or semi-desert conditions. And it is important for us to consider briefly what it is that has brought about these modern conditions.

The mountain ranges which ring these basins all around act as barriers to the entrance of moisture-laden air, and thus keep away the natural precipitation which falls on areas differently placed. For all mountains tend to act as condensers of whatever moisture happens to be in the air which blows against them; and by the same method they tend to dry out the air currents which flow over them and drop down their opposite sides. This takes place in two ways. The air which flows against the side of a mountain must rise to pass over it; but in thus rising it expands and thereby becomes cooler, both processes tending to precipitate whatever moisture it may hold. But on this same air rolling down on the opposite side of the elevation, it becomes more condensed and also warmer, thus rendering it drier and eager to take up more moisture. Accordingly, since these interior basins are, as a general rule, surrounded on all sides by moderate sized or even high mountains, the result is that essentially all the winds which blow over these mountains and into the basins are already deprived of their moisture before they cross the mountains, and when they reach the inside of the basin areas they are dry winds, tending to pick up every drop of moisture which they encounter.

Thus it has come about that these basins, once full of water, are now mostly arid wastes, with only a few dried remnants of their former lakes, or in some instances, as Death Valley, and other parts of Arabia and North Africa, they may even be now absolute deserts. And at least in the now arid lands of north Africa and southwestern Asia, there is abundant evidence that not so very many thousands of years ago these areas were well watered and held a luxuriant vegetation and were the homes of settled populations and well built cities. Their desication, such as now prevails, seems to have come about largely since the times of the Caesars, or at least since the time of the early Hebrews.

## METHODS OF GEOLOGIC INTERPRETATION

One more point needs our attention ere closing. It has to do with an inquiry as to which is the best and the most reasonable method of approaching the study of the past history of the earth's surface, that is, whether we ought to begin at some hypothetical point of time in the earth's past, and then work our way up to the present, or whether we might not better begin with the present and try to work our way backward in time, to try to discover what the early condition of our globe really was like. Both methods have been used; both are still being used by different classes of people. Which is the better, the more scientific, the safer and the surer method?

I have discussed this matter at some length elsewhere.[7] It will not be expected that I shall here do more than give an outline of what I mean, so as to make clear the results which will be attained by applying sensible methods to those outstanding surface features which we have been studying, the old strand lines, the high river terraces, and the great interior basins.

For if we may suppose ourselves to have to act as coroners upon the earth as a whole, to determine what physical processes have made the earth what it now is, these surface features just mentioned would naturally be the *very first things* which we would have to consider. And if we do this, and begin the study of the past of our globe by first examining these surface features and leaving aside all *a priori* theories about how the world first began and how life began slowly to develop from the little to the big, which leads to the evolution theory,— I say, if we begin with these visible and undeniable surface features, there can be no doubt about the conclusion which we would be compelled to reach. We should have to acknowledge that the entire surface of the globe must have been completely under water at a period of time which cannot have been very long ago. There would be no possible way of avoiding this conclusion and remain intellectually honest.

Obviously, the common geological custom of beginning with what are called the oldest fossil-bearing rocks, and from them working gradually up towards the present, assigning the fossils to successive ages in the earth's hypothetical history, is a clever device which enables the geologist to avoid the very embarrassing conclusion of a universal Flood. But this common geological method is not a sound method for studying the world as a whole. It is a purely hypothetical method. It is founded not on secure, present-day facts, but on suppositions about what somebody thinks may have been the beginning and the early history of the globe. It is a method of guesswork, an *a priori* method, under which certain facts seem to follow if we make certain assumptions to start with. But these assumptions are always anti-Biblical, and many of them are clearly contrary to everyday facts and common sense.

On the other hand, if we consider first the great surface features of the globe, as we have been doing in the present paper, we are inevitably brought face to face with proofs of a former universal Deluge which cannot possibly be avoided. We then reason that, since this universal Flood actually took place and not so very long ago, *this great fact intervenes between us and any evolutionary scheme about the earth's early history* which is based on a gradual development of life as shown by the fossils. For the Flood, if treated as an actual fact, makes nonsense of every scheme of organic evolution. The two ideas are mutually exclusive. If one is true the other must be false.

But the surface features of the globe, the old strand lines around all the continents, the high river terraces which line the valleys of all the larger watercourses of the world, and the gigantic interior basins which were obviously once full of water to

---

[7] Price, George McCready: "Methodology in Historical Geology," *Pan-American Geologist*, March, pp. 117-128, 1937.

the very brim, all these visible, easily understood facts confirm the record of the Bible, that "the world that then was, being overflowed with water, perished." (II Peter 3:6.)

### DISCUSSION

MR. BEN F. ALLEN: *Are river and lake terraces tilted as much as the old ocean shore lines? Why?*

PROFESSOR PRICE: All such tilting is merely local phenomena. For many, many miles these old terraces and old shore lines have not been disturbed to any noticeable degree. But I do not know of any differences between the two classes, *as classes.* I think their present conditions are about the same for the two classes. I suppose the reason for this is that the two classes of phenomena are about equally ancient, and that the regions around the coasts of the oceans have not changed more than have the interiors of the continents.

MR. ALLEN: *If the long geological ages are true, with all the past agencies acting very much like those of the present, might we not expect to find what might be called old fossil shore lines and old continental shelves buried under subsequent deposits? Have any such submerged continental shelves and shore lines ever been found?*

PROFESSOR PRICE: Continental shelves are on far too large a scale to permit us to identify any of them in buried form, even if any of them should have been buried by diluvial deposits, which probably did not take place. As a matter of fact, evolutionary geologists have long been in the habit of pointing to various sets of beds here and there over the world and claiming that they were formed on ancient continental shelves. This is partly because we now know that no true stratified beds are nowadays being formed at the bottom of the oceans out beyond the continental shelves, and partly because almost all the fossiliferous formations show us more or less of a mixture of land forms and deep-sea forms, or at least an

alternation of the two classes, and they think that no such mixtures of the two classes of fossils could take place anywhere except on something like ancient continental shelves. No typical deep-sea deposits, and very few typical fresh-water or purely continental deposits are found; almost always the beds show an alternation or a blending of the two very different classes of fossils. All this fits the Flood theory perfectly, but is very hard to reconcile with the theory that the deposits of the past were formed as they are being produced today.

MR. ALLEN: *With all the interior basins filled to the brim with water, and with the resulting modification and stabilizing of the world's climate which you suggest, would these conditions not go far toward explaining the many examples of abundant vegetation and abounding animal life which we find in such places as the Sahara desert, and other arid regions all over the surface of the ground, where little or nothing can now live? Might not these conditions also help to explain the many cases where post-diluvian animals have become extinct since then?*

PROFESSOR PRICE: Undoubtedly what you suggest is very true. Many examples of extinct forms of plants and animals occur on various continents, lying around on top of the ground in such a condition that we know they must have lived and died off after the Flood took place. And the surface of most arid regions, like the Sahara, abound with evidences of a former abundant vegetation, which must have flourished soon after the Flood. In the time of Abraham and Lot, they saw a wide stretch of country which was "well watered every where" (Gen. 13:10), but now it is nothing but a desert. Many old abandoned towns and cities may be seen in these regions where there is now no vegetation capable of supporting any such populations. All these facts fit perfectly into the Flood interpretation; in fact there is not a single large or important fact of geology which is inconsistent with the interpretation of the Flood as the cause of the geological changes.

# THE AGE OF THE EARTH

## COMMENTS ON SOME GEOLOGIC METHODS USED IN ITS DETERMINATION

### DUDLEY JOSEPH WHITNEY

For the past century it has been one of the chief objectives of study on the part of geologists to determine the age of the earth. This interest dates from the time of Cuvier, whose philosophy on successive creations and catastrophies obviously demanded more time than Biblical chronology would allow. Cuvier's conjecture as to the age of the earth was some fifty or sixty thousand years, an estimate which must have been arrived at largely by guesswork as far as any available supporting evidence was concerned. On the basis of this same theory of repeated creations and cataclysms, Agassiz increased the length of this period to one hundred thousand years.

With the development of the theory of Organic Evolution with its many problems of transition from simple to more complex forms of animal life, it came to be realized that the earth must be extremely ancient to permit of the evolution of man from some one-celled antecedent. While no definite age is now insisted on, the present estimates vary between one thousand million and ten thousand million years, with the consensus of opinion favoring about two thousand million years. This estimate has been reached by a determination of the apparent age of various rocks through radioactivity, which method will be discussed in due time.

It is the purpose of this study to show that, by certain data worked out by geologists, no such an extreme age of the earth can be established and to show to the contrary the earth cannot be so very old. A study of available data indicates that no adequate time interval sufficient to make organic evolution possible is allowed.

## OCEAN ELEMENTS IN THEIR BEARING ON THE AGE OF THE EARTH

Up to about twenty years ago, the most acceptable way of estimating the probable age of the earth was by a comparison of the amount of the element sodium in the ocean with the amount carried into it each year by the rivers. As rain water falls upon the land, it gathers up the various soluble materials derived from the weathering of the rocks and carries into the rivers, and ultimately into the ocean, great amounts of soluble material which either remains in solution or is precipitated upon the ocean floor. This process is believed to have continued since geologic history began. Assuming that the rate of increase of chemical substances has been fairly uniform throughout geologic time, the time needed to accumulate the sodium in the ocean in this way was once believed to indicate the age of the ocean and hence the approximate age of the earth. By assuming that the ocean was composed of fresh water at the start and that it has increased in salinity at the present rate, geologists estimated that the earth was between 60 and 100,000,000 years old.[1]

The bulletin by Clarke on "The Data of Geo-chemistry" is probably the most comprehensive work on geochemistry available, and the data in it are generally considered quite reliable. In the accompanying table (Table I) the annual increase of the various elements in the ocean is shown as taken

---

[1] Clarke, F. W., "Data of Geo-chemistry," *U. S. G. S. Bulletin No.* 770, 1924, chapter 4, "The Ocean."

from the fifth edition of this work. The figures in the last column are the results of calculation by the writer and not by Clarke. These figures are given in round numbers only.

*Sodium.* Considering the figures for sodium alone, it would seem that the ocean could not be more than 90,000,000 years old, but by making certain allowances, such as the return of small quantities of salt from the ocean to the land, Clarke estimated the ocean to be about 100,000,000 years old. In this estimate, no allowance was made for any initial salinity of the ocean, although it is likely that some allowance should be made.

period, the surfaces of the continental masses (hundreds of millions of years ago) would either have been depleted of their soluble contents, or the ocean would be far more saline than it now is.

By analysis it should be clear that, taking sodium as a basis of computation, the ocean is not more than one-twentieth of its presumed age, now generally believed to be 2,000,000,000 years, and this figure makes no allowance for any original salinity.

*Potassium and Magnesium.* The amounts of magnesium and potassium now in the ocean suggest an outside

TABLE I
*Age-Index Elements in the Ocean*

| Element | Metric Tons In Ocean x 1,000,000,000,000 | Annual Increase in Tons x 1,000 | Years Necessary to Attain this Amount |
|---|---|---|---|
| Sodium (Na) | 14,130.0 | 158,357 | 90,000,000 |
| Potassium (K) | 510.8 | 57,982 | 8,800,000 |
| Magnesium (Mg) | 1,721.0 | 95,264 | 18,400,000 |
| Sulphate (SO₄) | 3,553.0 | 332,030 | 10,600,000 |
| Chlorine (Cl) | 25,538.0 | 155,350 | 164,400,000 |
| Calcium (Ca) | 552.8 | 557,670 | |

To account for the difference between 100,000,000 years and the 2,000,000,000 years now commonly accepted for the age of the earth, some geologists have tried to show that the rivers could run to the sea for many more years than the increase of sodium will allow,[2] but without success.

One insurmountable difficulty which has been largely ignored, is that the land (according to the popular theory) had no covering of vegetation to evaporate the moisture and to protect the rocks from leaching, until well into the Devonian period, or for approximately four-fifths of presumed geologic time. Weathering of the rocks and leaching of soluble material from the land during this interval would obviously be extremely rapid. With this process going on for so long a

limit of from 9 to 19 millions of years as the age of the earth. These figures also make no allowance for any original salinity of the ocean. Geologists argue, however, that sufficient amounts of potassium and magnesium are precipitated out of solution to make these elements useless as indicators of the age of the earth. However, the salts of both these elements in the ocean are extremely soluble, and Clarke's own data on the composition of marine sediments show that such sediments contain too little of these elements in precipitated form (potassium and magnesium) to make up the discrepancy. Therefore, this argument is not valid, and these two elements further testify that the ocean is by no means as old as it has been believed to be.

[2] Holmes, Arthur, "The Age of the Earth," 1927, chapter 3.

*Chlorine.* In some respects chlorine is the most important element in the ocean when it comes to estimating the possible age and history of the ocean. From the figures given by Clarke it is evident that the ocean contains seven times as much chlorine as sulphate, which is the equivalent of 21 times as much of the element sulphur. Yet more than twice as much sulphate as chlorine is being added to the ocean by river flow and in other ways. Unless, therefore, the ocean were very rich in chlorine from the beginning and also contained very little sulphate, the amount of sulphate in the ocean should far surpass the amount of chlorine. And yet the contrary is the case.

There seems to be only three ways to account for the chlorine in the ocean: (1) that it was there from the beginning, (2) that it was added by leaching from the land, or (3) that it had its origin from within the earth, being added to the ocean water through volcanic action. But the rocks contain very little chlorine, so no great amount could have been obtained from that source. Clarke gives the chlorine content of igneous rocks as 0.048 per cent while the sulphur content is 0.052 per cent. There is 55 times as much sodium in these rocks as there is chlorine, so very little chlorine could have been added to the ocean by the disintegration of rocks and their consequent leaching. Neither could volcanic activity have added much chlorine to the ocean. In the analyses of volcanic gases cited by Clarke, time after time chlorine is not even mentioned, and only rarely is it found to occur in notable amounts. Frequently it is given only as a trace. Consequently, most of it must have been in the ocean from the beginning, and there it would be combined, as it is now, with sodium and magnesium, or with other bases.

This is a feature of the utmost importance in studying the possible age of the earth, for no one can properly compute how old the earth may be through the annual increase of sodium, potassium, magnesium and sulphate, without making allowance for the initial content of these materials. Since they were possibly abundant in the ocean in the beginning, a very limited amount of time might suffice to make the ocean as saline as it is now. The rapidity with which the elements named are increasing by the leaching of the land not only suggests that the earlier method of figuring the age of the earth by the increase in sodium was worthless, but also that the earth cannot be extremely old.

*Sulphur and the Sulphates.* From the figures in Table 1 it would seem that sulphur is of greater significance in estimating the possible age of the earth than sodium, for while 90 to 100,000,000 years of river flow would provide all the sodium of the ocean at its present rate of increase, a little more than 10,000,000 years of river flow would account for all the sulphates in the ocean.

But in addition to this source of sulphates, must be considered the important fact that much sulphur is also added to the ocean from the air. Oxides of sulphur exist in considerable quantities in the air, notably so in the vicinity of volcanoes, from which sulphur is emitted in great amounts. When rain falls, these oxides are carried to the ground or fall into the ocean and in combination with calcium or some other bases form sulphates.

As Clarke points out, some 17.26 pounds of sulphuric oxide were added per acre per year to the land by rainfall over a period of five years at Rothamsted, England. This is the equivalent of nearly 21 pounds of sulphates ($SO_4$). Considering the fact that the seas cover more than twice the area of the land, it will be seen that probably more sulphur is added to the ocean from the air than by riverflow. By this method (and still making no allowance for any original sulphates), the maximum possible age of the earth would be five or six, instead of eleven million years.

But there is still another factor to be given consideration in the matter of the sulphur content of ocean water, and that is, volcanic action as the source of this element. The great amount of sulphur emitted from volcanoes is clearly shown by the fact that one volcano in Japan in one period of eight months in 1937 sent forth an estimated 200,000 tons of pure liquid sulphur in addition to enormous unmeasured amounts of sulphur in volcanic gases. From another Japanese volcano in 1936 there was an "outflow of an enormous volume of pure fluidial sulphur from an old explosive crater."[3] Since volcanic activity seems to have been far greater not so long ago than it is at present, and is said to have continued for millions of years, the ocean should contain far more sulphur than it actually does. No long period of time such as has been predicated could possibly have elapsed without overwhelming the earth and the seas with the compounds of sulphur.

From a study of the salts of the ocean it therefore seems clear that the ocean cannot possibly be anywhere near as old as it has been estimated to be on the basis of the geologic timescale.

### DEPLETION OF THE LAND BY LEACHING

The figures given by Clarke contribute in still another way to this problem of the age of the earth. His data regarding the depletion of the land of its soluble salts by leaching are rather significant. It should be noted

that practically as much chlorine is carried into the ocean as sodium, the two evidently being carried largely in combination as sodium chloride or common salt. Sodium has the atomic weight of 23 and chlorine of 35.5. This indicates that almost exactly two-thirds of the sodium goes off as sodium chloride, not by disintegration of rocks. This seems evident since Clarke gives the chlorine content of the upper rocks as only 0.05 per cent, and that of sodium as 2.75 per cent, making sodium 55 times as abundant on land as chlorine. The calcium content of the rocks is given as 3.64 per cent.

Clarke points out that it would take a layer of igneous rock a third of a mile (1,760 feet) thick over the entire globe to provide the sodium that is now present in the ocean. The disintegration of half a mile of rock would probably be required to supply this amount since some of the sodium would remain with the silica and as other insoluble residues. But if all of the land above sea level were spread evenly over the face of the earth, it would make a layer only 660 feet thick, only three-eighths of the required one-third of a mile. Thus if every bit of rock above sea level were completely leached of sodium, it would provide only about one-third of the sodium now present in the ocean. Where, then, did the rest of the sodium come from?

The conclusion demanded by these facts is that most of the sodium of the ocean was there from the beginning, and probably the same can be said for most of the other elements there in solution. By the figures cited above, all the sodium above sea level would be removed from the land at the present rate in about 32 million years, and all the chlorine in about a million years. But since neither of these ele-

[3] Watanabe, T., and Suzuki, J., *Pan-American Geologist*, June, 1939, p. 335.

ments has been completely removed from the land by a considerable amount, it is evident that, whatever the real age of the earth, actually no great expanse of time has elapsed.

### CALCIUM AS AN INDICATOR OF THE AGE OF THE EARTH

While the figures pertaining to the amount of calcium in the ocean are more suggestive of the way the land is being depleted of this element than they are to the age of the ocean, they probably do have some significance in this direction. Although igneous rock contains only about one-third more calcium than sodium, about three and a half times as much calcium is being carried into the ocean as sodium. At this rate the land would lose all its calcium in a little more than 12 million years. One must therefore wonder how the continents could have continued to supply calcium to the ocean for alleged hundreds of millions of years. As a matter of fact, the rocks above sea level in spite of weathering and leaching still contain an abundance of soluble materials. It is therefore inconceivable that the earth has gone through any such long history as the modern concept of geology demands.

### THE TESTIMONY OF THE SEDIMENTARY ROCKS

The increase in the soluble contents of the ocean is not the only means which has been used in determining the possible age of the earth. Another means that is often considered in any study of this problem is the thickness of the sediments in relation to the rate that sedimentary rock is laid down. By dividing geologic history into a series of eras, periods and epochs, and estimating the greatest thickness of rock for each period, geologists have calculated that the age

of the earth is about 60 million years, by adding all these thicknesses together and figuring how long it would take to form them at the rate sediments are now being laid down in river deltas.[4] Subsequent studies on this point have added considerably to this estimate.

There are two fundamental errors in this method of calculation. The first is the obvious error of adding the thickness of sedimentary rock in one locality to that in another and so on for a series of such thicknesses, when there is absolutely no evidence to show that such a series of layers ever existed in any one locality. Moreover, there is no evidence to contradict the conclusion that in any one locality, all such layers were superimposed in a relatively short time, and that over great stretches of the earth's surface. The second defect is that, instead of presuming that these sediments were laid down very slowly as in a river delta, the predominant indications are that they were laid down very quickly by water, one layer succeeding another. This last principle seems to be recognized, at least in some circles. Thus Holmes writes:

"Another difficulty arises from the fact that the thickest formations can never represent a continuous record of all time involved. Individual beds may have been deposited very rapidly, and indeed they must have been to insure the burial and preservation of large fossils."[5]

This last sentence contains a principle of fundamental importance in this problem of rate of deposit of the various strata. If a great mammoth or dinosaur had to be buried with cataclysmic rapidity to be preserved as a fossil, and beds containing hundreds or thousands of such fossils must needs have been buried at the same time, the necessary extent and rapidity

---

[4] Schuchert, Charles, "The Age of the Earth on the Basis of Sediments and Life," Bulletin 80, National Research Council, 1931, "The Age of the Earth," pp. 10-65.

[5] Holmes, Arthur, loc. cit., p. 83.

of such burials can be roughly appreciated.

These self-evident facts should make it clear that any effort to estimate the age of the earth on the basis of rate of deposit of the sediments, as is now being used, can only lead to extremely erroneous conclusions, widely divergent from the true facts.

## ATMOSPHERIC HELIUM AS AN EVIDENCE OF THE RELATIVE YOUTH OF THE EARTH

There are still other lines of evidence which show that the earth is not old, although to be sure, they do not tell us exactly how old it might be. Atmospheric helium is known to be increasing quite rapidly (at an unknown rate), although there are still comparatively small amounts of it present in the air. Unless some of it escapes into space, which is very improbable, this element could not have been added to the atmosphere over any great length of time.

The increase of this element in the air may come about in two ways: (1) by its emission from certain springs, and (2) from the radioactive elements uranium and thorium which are continually changing into helium and lead. These two elements are widely distributed in the granite rocks, and as the rocks disintegrate, the helium passes out into the air. On this point Jeffreys writes:

"If the average age of igneous rocks when denuded was 160 million years, all the helium in the atmosphere would be explained if the average thickness of igenous rocks denuded from the earth's surface was 40 meters. This is an impossible small amount. . . . No satisfactory explanation of why the atmosphere contains so little helium has been offered."[6]

In other words, the atmosphere contains an impossibly small amount of helium for the age of the earth as it is now asserted to be. Jeffreys does not assert that helium escapes into space as the solution of the difficulty. Russell does so, not however, until he has agreed that according to the kinetic theory of gases, it should not be so escaping.[7] The opinion of Walter S. Adams seems to be conclusive on this point and he writes:

"The mass of the earth is sufficient to maintain a hydrogen atmosphere almost indefinitely."[8]

Since helium is several times as heavy as hydrogen the theory of its escape into space seems invalid. On this point of the formation of helium, it may therefore be stated that, while helium is being formed at a fairly rapid rate, there is still very little in the atmosphere. And this is evidently not because it is escaping into space. This conclusion indicates that the process has not been going on for more than a small fraction of the time, which evolutionary geology demands.

## EVIDENCE FROM THE COMETS AND METEORS

Comets provide evidence from an astronomical point of view that the earth is not particularly ancient. This is suggested by the fact that comets waste away and are broken up into streams of meteors without any new comets coming into existence as far as is now known.

The most striking feature of comets which pass close to the sun is their tail, which is composed of material driven from the head by radiant pressure from the sun. This material is permanently lost to the comet as far as is known. Thus each time a comet passes near the sun it loses some of the material which composes it, and in time it is completely destroyed or its orbit so altered that it no longer

---

[6] Jeffreys, Harold, "The Earth", 1924, p. 254.

[7] Russell, Henry Norris, "The Solar System and Its Origin," 1935, pp. 75, 76.

[8] Adams, Walter S., *Scientific Monthly*, July, 1934, p. 13.

approaches the sun and may be lost to observation.

Russell discusses this matter and points out that the force of gravity of Jupiter and other large planets tends to act upon comets which pass near them so that they will be projected out of the solar system, which will make them no longer visible from the earth. This effect is more probable than some change in their orbit, which makes them pass near the sun. Several comets have been known to have been destroyed or changed into streams of meteors in the last century. Halley's comet, the most famous of all, has lost much in size in its last few passages near the sun. In fact, the wasting of comets is so rapid that it strongly suggests that the life of the solar system should be estimated in thousands rather than millions of years.

Still another detail pertaining to meteors which gives one some concept as to the age of the earth is concerned with meteor dust. Meteorites contain much iron and it is likely that meteors do likewise, although they are burned to dust by friction as they pass through our atmosphere. This dust settles upon the earth. The iron of meteorites contains considerable quantities of nickel. Consequently, if there is much meteor dust on the earth, there should be a measurable quantity of nickel in it. This is not the case, for nickel is found in too small quantities to be significant.

Clarke gives the average meteoric iron as being composed of 90.85 per cent iron, 8.52 per cent nickel, and 0.59 per cent cobalt. Copper and chromium are the only other metals abundant enough to be mentioned. Even stony meteorites are said to contain an average of 1.32 per cent nickel and cobalt. It goes without saying that if meteors and meteorites have been falling on the earth for millions of years, an appreciable amount of nickel should be found on the earth's surface, or if dissolved and carried by the rivers to the oceans and there precipitated, it should be found in some quantity on the ocean's floor. It is found in neither place in more than a trace. Clarke does not even list nickel in his record of analyses of marine sediments, and nickel and cobalt together in two analyses of marine clays amount to only .039 and .064 per cent respectively, which amounts could well be derived simply from terrestrial matter.

There is some uncertainty regarding the amount of meteoric matter which falls from the earth, but Nininger estimates that the daily accretion is of the magnitude of 50,000 tons.[9] This would make a layer of about 100 feet thick in the course of two thousand million years. Whether Nininger's estimate is correct or not, after this enormous lapse of time nickel should be found in good quantities over most of the face of the earth and upon the ocean floor. Instead, it is found in such small quantities that the earth by this standard must be extremely young.

Meteorites are unknown in *underground*, supposedly "ancient," sediments, which should not be the case if they had accumulated through uncounted millions of years. They reach the earth fairly frequently today and very likely have done so in the past. But they are all on the surface. The absence of such "fossil" meteorites and of significant amounts of nickel from the surface of the earth is therefore an indication that the earth is not particularly old.

## THE RELATIONSHIP OF VOLCANISM TO GEOLOGIC TIME

Mention has already been made in an earlier section of this paper of the amount of sulphur emitted from vol-

[9] Nininger, H. H., "Our Stone-Pelted Planet," 1933.

canoes in connection with the small amount of this element in the rocks and in solution in the ocean, which suggests that volcanic activity has not existed in the past over a period of millions of years. This is an important point, for volcanic activity is one of the most striking features of geologic history. Briefly, volcanic eruptions may be compared to the operation of a steam boiler.[10] Water and other gases that are dissolved in the hot rock in the crust of the earth act very much like water in a boiler, and the escape of steam and other gases causes eruptions. Explosive eruptions are comparable to the explosion of a boiler. The amount of water and other gases emitted from volcanoes is enormous. Clarke mentions the measurement of water vapor escaping from one of the numerous parasitic vents on Etna. On this point, Dr. Alfred C. Lane has said:

"If Foqué was right in estimating that one of Etna's minor parasitic cones emitted in 100 days 2,100,000 cubic meters of water, in 600 years it would discharge a cubic mile of water. Thus only a hundred such vents would suffice to discharge all the 300 million cubic miles of water in the 1,800 million years or so in which it seems likely that we have had plenty of time to have discharged the ocean."[11]

While Foqué's findings are generally accepted as being reasonably accurate, it must be admitted that certain other factors must be considered in any such estimate, such as the possible return (from the uniformitarian viewpoint) of some of this emitted vapor in the form of water to this underground reservoir. Nevertheless, with due allowances, this statement does have startling implications. The output of 100 such parasitic vents of one volcano would obviously be much

less than the normal output of all active volcanoes (it is estimated that there are now 420 active or recently active volcanoes) at the present time. Furthermore, if the volcanic action were much greater in the past, as is generally assumed, the production of water by this method would be enormous. It must also be remembered that the oceans are presumed to contain an abundance of water from the beginning. This conclusion is inevitable if it is decided that most of the chlorine was there from the beginning.

A few remarks on the activity of Etna itself as well as the amount of water necessary to have within the earth will serve to show the impossibility of this situation. Assuming that the total output of water of Etna came from ten such parasitic vents, about a cubic mile of water would be produced in 60 years. Etna is known to have been active for a period of about 2500 years, which would mean a total output of 40 cubic miles of water. If this volcano had been active since the time of the Flood, it would have produced about 100 cubic miles of water. But geologists estimate from a study of the size of its cone, at its present rate of increase, that this volcano has been active for 300,000 years, which would mean a total water output of 50,000 cubic miles. But this is quite impossible. What is still more incredible is the belief that volcanism has been going on continuously in Italy (and Iceland) "since Miocene time, which Urry's determinations put over 15 million years ago."[12] If Etna or one other volcano of equivalent activity has been active during this long interval, the total amount of

10 Clarke, F. W., loc. cit., p. 229.

11 Lane, Alfred C., Science, Vol. 75, April 15, 1932, p. 396.

12 "Annual Report of the Committee of the National Research Council on the Measurement of Geologic Time," 1936, p. 1.

water produced would be 250,000 cubic miles.

On this basis what would be the combined production of 400 active volcanoes for an interval of 100 million years? Where would this impossible amount of water come from and where would it go?

To look at the other side of the question, what would be the source of all this water, even if all the water in the ocean came from such volcanic activity alone? To supply the water of the ocean from within the earth, there would have to be the equivalent of 8,600 feet deep of water beneath the earth's crust all over the world to begin with, were it all in liquid form. The interior of the earth being hot, however, this would make the crust of the earth like a boiler full of water and heated beyond an explosive temperature. It is incredible, of course, that the earth could have contained so much water. To reach any other conclusion is to ignore the nature of volcanic activity.

### RADIOACTIVITY AS A MEASURE OF THE EARTH'S AGE

In view of these evidences of the youth of the earth, the question arises as to how geologists have arrived at such vast estimates of its age. At first, when the science of geology was young, no such vast periods were offered, estimates being based on the rates of erosion and deposits now in progress as compared to evidences of former erosion and deposit. The method is based on the slow but fixed rates at which radioactive elements, especially uranium and thorium, change to certain elements of lower atomic number, i.e., lead and helium. When the amount of uranium and thorium are known in a rock, and also the amount of lead and helium (of the types known to be derived from the former by radioactive disintegration) the proportions of the amounts present form a mathematical basis for estimating the total amount consumed in the process. The time necessary to accomplish this change is made the basis for estimates of the age of the earth.

The theory is simple, but as in the case of age-estimation on the basis of the various elements in the ocean waters, deficiencies in the method have become evident. To begin with, the results from time estimates from the two elements do not agree. Moreover, to the extent that either uranium or thorium entered or left the rock before or after the process began, or to the extent which the lead or the helium left it, after it was thus produced or was there before the process had begun, the calculations will be at fault. And since these factors cannot always be determined, this difficulty seems permanent. Still greater uncertainties are that the age of a given geologic formation by this new method is usually at variance with the supposed age of that formation as it appears in the geologic timetable, so long and laboriously worked out upon the supposed sequence of the evolution of the fossils. The rocks ordinarily dealt with in these estimations are the inorganic rocks, such as granite, and this again bids fair to raise more questions than it settles, because one of the most difficult things in geological science is the decision as to when these granites and other intrusives were first formed, as well as when the intrusion took place.

In the report of the Committee on Geologic Time for 1939-1940, certain important admissions of serious faults in this method are mentioned on pages 62, 63, 73, and 76. In the 1940-1941 report fundamental flaws in the lead residue method were also pointed out. Often it is found that too much lead is present, so that the estimated age is extravagantly great for that specimen, and vice versa. This uranium-derived lead has a different atomic weight from common lead, which is not so derived, so that the latter must be omitted from the estimate. But even this does not solve the problem; as much of the lead of supposedly uranium derivation is found not to be in fact "radiogenic" (page 55 and elsewhere), thus rendering the calculations worthless.

Looking still deeper into the fundamentals of the problem, the theory is vague as to whether or not these elements originated at the time the rock in which they are now found was formed. If not, then still more uncertainties arise, because it is well-known to mineralogists that many of the ores have been concentrated subsequently to the country rock in which they are now found. It is agreed that such common lead has often been deposited with the uranium and thorium, and if this could occur, naturally the lead of radiogenesis could be so deposited too, making impossible an accurate estimate of what proportions of each type to use in arriving at a final conclusion as to the age of the formation.

It is evident that the radioactive method is the only method that will provide time enough to satisfy present theories of the age of the earth. But if this method were otherwise faultless, the insuperable objections to it would still remain in that (1), the various salts in the ocean water have defied all attempts to work out a consistent estimate of the time required for their accumulation, and (2), all estimates of age are hopelessly too small for the radioactive method. It is evident that they could not possibly have been increased at present rates for more than a small fraction of that length of time, nor could the sulphur have been increased on the surface of the earth at present rates, for so long a time. The ocean salts method, once as popular as a means of estimation of the age of the earth as the radioactive method is now,

at present contradicts the conclusions of its late rival, the radioactive method.

For all of these reasons it would seem necessary to reject as unreliable the radioactive method of calculating the age of the earth. The one fact of the constancy of the process of radioactive disintegration seems to be the only fully scientific certainty there is in it. But this is true for all of the radioactive elements, some of which disintegrate very rapidly. The apparently unsolvable problem of judging when and how the radioactive elements were accumulated with reference to the rocks wherein they are now found, is as difficult as the other problems of the chronology and sequence of ore deposition or infiltration, few if any of which are as yet understood. Added to this are the still more uncertain features of the chronology of the plutonic actions by which most of the rocks used in this method came into being or came to their present location. In addition to all this, there remains the tangled relations which this method has with the already supposedly well-established geologic timetable. Lastly, the wide disagreement of the results of this method with those estimated on the basis of each of the elements in the ocean waters, which are far too small in amount if such vast eons of time have elapsed, seems to prohibit further consideration of the radioactive method of calculating the age of the earth.

SUMMARY AND CONCLUSIONS

One of man's objectives in his search for the history of the past has been to determine the age of the earth. Since the span of years allowed by Biblical chronology is impossibly insufficient to permit of the development of man by the process of evolution designed to replace the story of Creation, it has been necessary first to postulate and then to seek methods to prove an antiquity of the earth consistent with the philosophy of evolutionary origins. The very essence of evolution must have been that of a slow transition from one type to another. To allow of the necessarily long course of the development of man from the primeval ooze, it has been variously estimated that from a thousand to ten thousand million years have elapsed in the process. If some evidence of the age of the earth could be obtained from some source or sources which would bear out this theory of an incredibly old earth, one would have to admit of the possible truth of the theory of evolution. On the other hand, if estimates made on the basis of various suggested methods fall too far short of these long ages, too short to permit of evolution, it may likewise be concluded that the whole philosophy is false. It has been the object of this study to analyze critically some of the methods which have been proposed for the determination of the age of the earth and the results obtained thereby.

The method used most conclusively up to the past decade or two was a study of the sodium content of ocean water. On the basis of present findings, it has been estimated that the ocean is 100 million years old. This conclusion ignores what seems to be a fair assumption that the ocean must have had some degree of original salinity. Moreover, such an estimate demands a relatively uniform addition of sodium to the ocean, a very unlikely occurrence even from the standpoint of evolutionary geology. This leaching process must have been indefinitely more rapid during the period when the earth had no protective covering of vegetation until well into the Devonian period, roughly four-fifths of presumed geologic time. One can only conclude that under these supposed primeval circumstances, the ocean should long ago have attained its present degree of salinity and the land

areas long since impoverished of their sodium content. While objections are raised by evolutionists to the use of other contained elements in the estimation of the age of the ocean, many of these objections are not valid. Such estimates suggest a much shorter history, far too short for evolution to have taken place.

A study of this problem on the basis of rate of depletion of the land of its soluble salts has also been undertaken. It has been estimated that it would require the disintegration of half a mile thick of rock over the face of the globe to provide the sodium now present in the ocean. Since all the land now above sea level spread evenly over the face of the earth would make a layer only 660 feet thick (three-eighths of the required amount) and since the land as yet is by no means depleted of its sodium, it is fair to conclude that the ocean must have had a fair degree of original salinity, and by deduction, must be much younger than the estimate of 100 million years. By figures cited, *all* the sodium above sea level would be removed from the land at the present rate in 32 million years and *all* the chlorine in a million years. But since neither of these elements has been completely removed by a wide margin, even these estimates must be considerably reduced. But they would still disagree with each other in much the same ratio, which renders any conclusion on that basis impossible.

The fallacy of the method of age determination by the rate of deposition of sedimentary rock is obvious when it is realized that there are no uniform stratifications in various localities and the evident fact that thick layers of sediment must have been laid down in a very short time to preserve large animals, often in great numbers, as fossils.

The small amount of helium in the atmosphere also indicates that the earth cannot be as old as has been presumed by evolutionary geologists.

Evidence from comets and meteors also indicates that the earth is not old. The extremely small amount of nickel in the soil, at the present rate of addition from meteoric dust, also suggests that the process has not been going on for any great length of time.

Volcanism as a source of water furnishes another avenue for investigation of the age of the earth. If the earth were anywhere near as old as alleged, volcanic action alone would have produced an impossibly large amount of water. For example, the water output of Etna in Italy alone would be 250,000 cubic miles in its alleged history of 15 million years.

The most recent and most popular method of estimation of the age of the earth is that of radioactivity. The weaknesses in the method consist in the lack of information as to the relative amounts of lead and helium originally present in the given sample of rock, and the amounts of these elements which may have left or which have entered the rock in the meantime. The results obtained by the method are very often inconsistent with the presumed age of the specimen

and with the discredit now being laid at the door of the method, it is likely to be discarded as valueless, even by its most enthusiastic proponents.

As a result of this survey, several facts seem to emerge. In the first place, the results of estimates of the age of the earth as determined by the various methods show too great discrepancies to bring any harmony out of the conflicting conclusions. In the second place, it is evident that the methods are seriously defective in that the original chemical state of affairs in the earth and ocean are unknown, so that one does not know where to begin with the process. Moreover, one cannot be entirely sure that these processes have always proceeded at the same rate as at present. Finally, it is quite certain that, with due consideration of all known factors, the earth has no such a long history as geologists have postulated. In fact, the history of the earth even by these methods is too short to permit of organic evolution having taken place.

Whether from the tangled skein of available evidence, it will be possible to make a more positive approach to the problem, one which can bring some harmony out of the existing confusion, the future alone will tell.

## THE SIGNIFICANCE OF RAISED BEACHES

"It has long been known to those who have paid attention to the superficial features of the earth's crust, that on the lesser elevations of all continents there exist certain phenomena in the way of raised beaches or abandoned shore lines, which testify in the strongest manner that during some very recent geologic period, these lands have been deeply submerged beneath the waters of some long-enduring lake or sea.

"The convincing nature of the evidence as to submergence, to which these ancient coast lines bear witness, has long been recognized and accepted by geologists; but if explanation is requested as to the manner in which these terraces, once necessarily near the water's level, have acquired their present considerable altitudes above sea level, no decisive or satisfactory reply can be given. The subject still remains one of the most perplexing problems in science. . . .

"The theories and beliefs now obtaining in this matter of the raised beaches are in many cases not only inconsistent with the requirements of physics, but are often in opposition with each other. . . ."—Pearson, H. W., The Basis for a New Geology, Raised Beaches and Their Cause, Sc. American Sup. Vol. 65, 1908. pp. 186-188, 202-204, 218-220, 234-236.

## TILTED LAKE BEACHES

"A detailed investigation of the terraces and raised beaches in eastern Wisconsin, with measurements by spirit level, leads to the following conclusions:

"There is a series of warped waterplanes of Lake Algonquin [a former lake more than covering the present Lake Michigan and Lake Huron], which rise at a moderate rate north of Sturgeon Bay, diverging, fan-fashion, until the highest is 90-95 feet above Lake Michigan at Washington Island. The divergence of these planes is interpreted to mean earth-movements contemporaneous with the Lake Algonquin stages. The tilting seems to have decreased greatly in measure south of Sturgeon Bay, dying out in the vicinity of Two Rivers, where the Algonquin beach stands about 26 feet above the lake. South of this point the Algonquin shore-line is thought to be horizontal above Lake Michigan and represented by the highest beach of the 'Toleston' group in the Chicago district, at a height of 20-25 feet, just as in the southern part of Lake Huron basin the Algonquin seems to be horizontal at a 25-foot level."—Goldthwait, James W., Correlation of the Raised Beaches on the West Side of Lake Michigan, Journal of Geology, Vol. 14, pp. 411-424, 1906.

## GEOLOGIC VERSUS RADIOACTIVE TIME

Shortly after the opening of the century the discoveries of radioactivity destroyed the foundations on which the principal physical methods of estimating geologic time had previously rested. These discoveries, however, gave us methods based on atomic disintegration which soon indicated that geologic time is from 10 to 20 times as long as had been deemed probable from the estimates previously considered most trustworthy. . . . Schuchert now finds that the maximum thickness of strata on the North American continent deposited since the beginning of Cambrian time reaches the immense total of 259,000 feet. . . . The aggregate thickness of strata on the other continents has never been assembled, but it is believed that eventually the pile of strata for the world will total 400,000 feet. To translate this thickness into years, even approximately, is still an unsolved problem. A mean rate of deposition that will hold for all strata cannot be ascertained, and the most that can be expected is a mean for each basin of deposition. . . .

"It is therefore impossible in the light of present knowledge to check by means of the sedimentary record the time-determinations that are based on radioactive disintegration." —Knopf, Adolph, The Age of the Earth, Bulletin 80, National Research Council, June, 1931, pp. 3-4.

THE

# BULLETIN

OF

# DELUGE GEOLOGY

## AND RELATED SCIENCES

Volume 2         July, 1942         Number 1

## THE CAUSAL SIGNIFICANCE OF "PARALLELISM"

AN INQUIRY INTO CERTAIN FUNDAMENTAL PRINCIPLES OF
EMBRYONIC DEVELOPMENT

### CYRIL B. COURVILLE

Since the attention of investigators was first directed to a study of animal embryos, their similarity in form and external detail even in the case of embryos of widely divergent species (especially in their early stages) and the general conformity to a basic plan of the various organs and organ systems has been recognized. At first no particular significance was attached to these resemblances, the similarity being taken more or less for granted. About the turn of the 19th century, some of the outstanding biologists of the period, notably Kielmeyer, Oken, Meckel and Serres, for reasons not entirely clear, began to teach that some relationship existed between the embryonic forms of higher animals and the adult forms of lower ones. Evidently because these embryonic forms were not very critically examined, it finally came to be taught that the early worm-like stage of an embryo was identical with the adult form of certain of the worms. By thus associ-

The BULLETIN is published by, and is the official organ of the "Society for the Study of Deluge Geology and Related Sciences." The Editorial Board is comprised of Professor George McCready Price and Dr. Cyril B. Courville. It is printed at the Collegiate Press, Arlington, California. For members the BULLETIN is free, and extra copies 65 cents each (each number priced according to size); for non-members it is $2.00 per year; and this number is 75 cents. All correspondence should be directed to the Managing Editor, Mr. Ben F. Allen, 219 North Grand Avenue, Los Angeles, California.

ating the embryonic stages of complex animals with adult stages of simpler ones, the groundwork was laid for the evolutionary implications of what came to be known as the recapitulation theory.

Von Baer, the most outstanding embryologist of his time, clearly saw the error into which his less observant predecessors and contemporaries had fallen. He insisted, and rightly so, that the embryos of higher animals did not resemble the adult forms of lower ones, although the embryos of both might resemble each other at a given stage. This observation came

however, was an obvious fact, and the possible implications of this fundamental truism came to attract more and more attention. The term "parallelism" was introduced to express this similarity although it was recognized that it was an inexact resemblance both as to structural detail and as to the course of development of external form. Hence the term did not represent the facts correctly, since any two embryonic forms which might resemble each other quite closely at any given stage usually became *progressively unlike* as development proceeded. Moreover, as Sedgwick[2] so

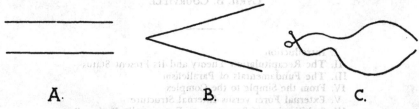

A.                    B.                    C.

FIG. 1. THE SIGNIFICANCE OF "PARALLELISM"

The term "parallelism" (A) implies an exactly comparative development of a given feature (such as external form) of two embryos, which is not actually the case. "Divergent parallelism" (B) indicates a *progressive unlikeness* of two compared forms. The true situation is shown in (C) indicating constantly changing variability depending upon embryos compared (in this case the newt and the lizard which come to resemble each other closely).

to be known as von Baer's "law of embryonic resemblance".[1] The concept of the identity of an embryonic stage with some adult form now seems quite absurd. So clear were the facts of the problem to von Baer that, although he lived to see the rise of the theory of organic evolution and the theory of recapitulation which was a deduction from it, he accepted neither of them. The false premises upon which both were founded were too obvious to permit him to entertain such nebulous conceptions of parallelism.

The similarity of embryo to embryo,

well pointed out, not only racial and special characteristics, but also individual differences became apparent when looked for even in remarkably young embryos. The designation *divergent* or *inexact parallelism* was finally introduced by Cope[3] to express more correctly this progressive unlikeness of embryos. In order to avoid the use of the more bunglesome term, the word *parallelism* will be used in this treatise with this "inexactness" in mind.

Von Baer's statement that embryos should be compared with embryos and

[1] Von Baer, Karl Ernest: (Cited by Davidson, P. E.: *The Recapitulation Theory and Human Infancy*, New York, 1914. p. 8).

[2] Sedgwick, Adam: On the Law of Development, commonly known as Von Baer's Law, and on the Significance of Ancestral Rudiments of Embryonic Development, *Quart. J. Micros. Sc.* 36:35, 1894.

[3] Cope, E. D.: *The Origin of the Fittest*, New York, 1887, p. 142.

not with adult forms was either over-looked or ignored by most subsequent observers. In laying the groundwork for his concept of organic evolution, Darwin harked back to the less accurate observations of earlier biologists and concluded that this crude resemblance of an embryo to some lower form indicated identity of origin. And it was on this assumption that Haeckel reared the complex structure of his *biogenetic law* which has become more widely known and popularized as the recapitulation theory. In short, the phenomenon of parallelism was clothed with a causal significance and it was assumed that because an early mammalian embryo with its relatively prominent digitations produced by the underlying somites roughly resembled a segmented worm, the mammal must therefore have evolved from a worm. Whether this theory supplies a sufficiently satisfactory explanation of the phenomenon of parallelism needs now to be briefly considered.

### THE RECAPITULATION THEORY AND ITS PRESENT STATUS

It is not in the province of this treatise to review *in extenso* the history and the present status of the recapitulation theory, a matter which has already been given consideration in another study.[4] It is necessary, however, to summarize the evidence which shows that this theory is not the correct interpretation of parallelism. Only when this is done will it be legitimate to explore some other possibility.

Radl[5] points out that it was Darwin who first confused the two essential implications of parallelism, assuming that embryos resembled adult animals of lower forms as held by Meckel and Serres instead of the more correct position of von Baer that embryos simply resembled embryos. Darwin seized upon the more suggestive details of such comparison and used these details in support of his philosophy of organic evolution. In this he was later encouraged by the observations of Müller who found that, in some types of crustacea, the embryo seemed to recapitulate the adult forms of simpler types. Darwin concluded that this similarity of the embryo to adult indicated identity of origin, which is the essential principle of the theory of organic evolution.

It remained for Haeckel to carry this idea to its ultimate lengths. On the basis of this similarity of embryonic forms, he attempted to reconstruct the evolutionary history of the entire animal kingdom.[6] He insisted that all embryonic phenomena were to be interpreted in the light of phylogenesis (evolution). He made light of the efforts of Wilhelm His in particular who tried to analyze these developments on a more rational physiologic basis. Haeckel's "law of biogenesis" included two separate concepts: (1) that ontogeny (the stages of embryonic development) was a short, if incomplete and not entirely accurate, history of phylogeny (the evolutionary development of the species or race), and furthermore that (2) phylogeny, or evolution, was actually the cause, or the predetermining factor of ontogeny, or embryonic development, of the individual. In other words, the pro-

---

[4] Courville, C. B.: The Recapitulation Theory. Some Notes on Its History and Present Status, *Bull. Deluge Geol.* 1:21-59, 1941.

[5] Radl, E.: *The History of Biological Theories*, trans. by Hatfield, London, 1930, pp.122-146.

[6] Haeckel contended that his "biogenetic law" was indeed the *fundamental* law of all biology. Whether this assumption was made as a result of his ignorance of botany, or simply as a consequence of his enthusiasm cannot now be stated with certainty. The fact remains that recapitulation has little to support it in plant reproduction. This alone should make one hesitate about accepting it as a fundamental law of *biology*.

gressive development of each individual embryo was not only a review or recapitulation of its evolutionary history, but also that the consecutive steps in this development were a direct result of its evolution.

It soon became evident that all was not as simple as a superficial survey of the problem had suggested. At every turn, serious exceptions to the theory presented themselves, and new words had to be coined to express these exceptions ("as if every word represented a new thought"[7]). In the first place it was obvious that many of the embryonic structures, such as the membranes which envelope the growing embryo, could have no possible evolutionary significance. These features were therefore accounted for as being *cenogenetic* (newly introduced). Some embryonic structures appeared in stages in advance of their proper place in the alleged evolutionary history; these developments were therefore described as having been *accelerated*. Other structures appeared later than they should according to this "history" (*retardation*) while still other structures or even stages were completely missing. Finally some details were observed to occur in reverse order (*heterochrony*) to what they should in their presumed evolutionary sequence. These frequent and manifold exceptions to the rule served to "falsify" the history, as Haeckel so graphically put it. In a delightful bit of prose, Marshall described this jumbled evolutionary record in these words:

"Although it is undoubtedly true that development is to be regarded as a recapitulation of ancestral phases, and that the embryonic history of an animal presents to us a record of the race history, yet it is also an undoubted fact, recognized by all writers in embryology, that the record so obtained

is neither a complete nor straight-forward one. It is indeed a history, but a history of which entire chapters are lost, while in those that remain many pages are misplaced and others are so blurred as to be illegible; words, sentences, or even entire paragraphs are omitted, and worse still, alterations or spurious additions have been freely introduced by later hands, and at times so cunningly as to defy detection."[8]

Thus it was obvious even to the most sanguine evolutionist that something had to be done to straighten out this confused history. It was further recognized that Embryology itself could not be appealed to as an interpretation of this history, for parallelism could not logically serve at the same time as both problem and proof. Recourse was made, therefore, to Paleontology by some students and to Comparative Anatomy by others. Paleontology was recognized to be of doubtful help because it could never be certain that all the fossil forms related to the animal in question were available for study. Because of this and other difficulties it is more than passing strange that so many present-day paleontologists still try to support their evolutionary concepts by the broken reed of recapitulation, while the embryologist who should be most conversant with recent developments has long since given up the use of fossils in an effort to put his phylogenetic house in order. On the other hand, Comparative Anatomy proved to be in no better position to accomplish the task, for, in the last analysis who was to say in what order animals were to be arranged to determine proper evolutionary sequence? As Waddington so correctly described the situation:

"The refutation by modern biology of Victorian ideas of embryonic recapitulation, and the consequent failure of comparative morphology to provide any explanatory con-

---

[7] Radl, E.: *loc. cit.*

[8] Marshall, A. M.: The Recapitulation Theory, in *Biological Lectures and Addresses*, London, 1894, p. 306.

cepts for embryology, has placed the latter on its feet as a definite field of inquiry."[9]

Since, then, the "language" of Comparative Anatomy itself was not fully understood and capable of various interpretations, the writer, in his earlier study on recapitulation, could not desist from carrying the illuminating metaphor of Balfour and of Marshall a step further:

". . . It now appears that this manuscript [of evolutionary history] has been written in an unknown language, the only clue to which is another language, itself quite susceptible of various interpretations."[10]

It is not surprising, then, that Hurst writing in 1893 was already of the opinion that:

"Ontogeny is not an epitome, is not a record, either perfect or imperfect, of past history, is not a recapitulation of the course of evolution."[11]

In 1934, Thomas Hunt Morgan, who throughout his long career has had much to say for and against the theory of recapitulation, was of this mind:

"When Haeckel held that embryonic stages represent for the most part ancestral adult types, he was familiar with embryonic adaptations that could never have been adult stages, such as the allantois, amnion, and yolk sac of birds and mammals. He spoke of these as falsifications of phylogenetic ancestral stages. They are embryonic adaptations. This admission was soon found to open the door to skepticism with respect to many larval and embryonic stages that had been interpreted as ancestral, such for example, as the nauplius of crustacea, and the tocophore of annelids, which are now regarded only as specialized larval forms whose widespread occurrence in a group is not sufficient evidence that they are ancestral adult stages. In other words if the recapitulation theory

is a 'law', it has so many exceptions that it has become useless and often misleading. Moreover, as stated above, it carries an implication with respect to the way in which new characters are 'added' that is inconsistent with a large body of definite information."[12]

It should be clear, on the basis of accumulated evidence, that the recapitulation theory is no longer acceptable to the critical contemporary embryologist as an explanation of the phenomena of development. This is especially true when it is recognized that the theory is strangely out of place in the newer subsciences of Physiological Embryology, Chemical Embryology, and Genetics, which certainly have contributed nothing noteworthy to its support.

But what is even of greater importance is the statement of Needham to the effect that:

"Embryology in particular has been theoretically threadbare, since the decay of the evolution theory as a mode of explanation [of the development of the embryo]."[13]

In other words, not only has the theory of recapitulation failed to account for the developing embryo, but so has the larger theory of evolution. Nevertheless, such an effort has recently been made by DeBeer who, of all contemporary embryologists, has made the most intensive effort in this direction. After a review of the arguments pertaining to his revised theory of recapitulation, he concludes:

"It goes without saying that even if the views set forth here are correct, they do not provide an 'explanation' of evolution, for there remains the problem as to how and why novelties arise, and why heterochrony acts upon them in those cases in which it

---

[9] Waddington, C. H.: Problems of Experimental Embryology, *Brit. M. J.* 2:245 (August 1) 1936.

[10] Courville, C. B.: *loc. cit.*, p. 43.

[11] Hurst, C. H.: Biological Theories—III. The Recapitulation Theory, *Nat. Sc.* 2:194 and 364, (March and May), 1893.

[12] Morgan, T. H.; *Embryology and Genetics*, New York, 1934, p. 149.

[13] Needham, J.: Limiting Factors in the Advancement of Science as Observed in the History of Embryology, *Yale J. Biol. & Med.* 18:1-18 (Oct.) 1935.

does. But what is claimed is that after dethroning the theory of recapitulation, we are able to make a better synthesis of our knowledge of embryology and evolution."[14]

In other words, DeBeer states that since the older theory of recapitulation has been dethroned, it is now possible to see more clearly the relationship between embryology and evolution. But in a revision of his study after ten years' further deliberation on the subject, all that he can contribute to this vital point is that:

"Clearly, phylogeny [evolutionary history] does not explain ontogeny [embryonic development] at all. Even if we had a complete phylogenetic series of adults ancestral to any given descendant, it would not help us to understand the process of fertilization, cleavage, differentiation, organogeny, etc., which take place in the ontogeny of that descendant. . . .

"Conversely, if we knew all the processes involved in the events of ontogeny, such knowledge would not of itself provide an explanation of phylogeny. For past phylogeny no method of study other than the historically descriptive is possible. But since phylogeny is but the result of modified ontogeny, there is the possibility of causal analytic study of present evolution in an experimental study of the variability and genetics of ontogenetic processes."[15]

After three quarters of a century of diligent effort to prove that the phenomena of parallelism have an evolutionary significance, we are now left with the conclusion that we are now in a position to investigate "the possibility of a causal analytic study of present evolution." This is but another way of stating that we have made a complete circle in our philosophic wanderings and have arrived once more at the starting point of the whole problem, for this is precisely the place where Haeckel started.

Perhaps it is time "to inquire whether the facts of embryology cannot be included in a larger category,"[16] one even larger than the theory of evolution itself.

## THE FUNDAMENTALS OF PARALLELISM

As has already been pointed out, even the most superficial observer must agree that there is a roughly divergent parallelism of form and structure in the development of embryos, even when one includes quite widely separated species. Since recapitulation and its parent philosophy evolution have failed to account for this similarity, it is now our privilege to review the facts and to see what other possible significance this fundamental principle might have. As a basis for discussion a series of seven postulates is herewith presented.

1. In embryonic development, there is an obvious parallelism which in each case must pass from the simple to the complex.
2. This parallelism tends to become more and more "inexact" or "divergent" as far as external form is concerned, but may continue to be relatively more exact as far as individual organs or organ-systems are concerned.
3. There is a remarkable identity of structure and function of individual organs and structures of animals widely separated in the scale of life, indicating stabilization on a successful solution of a functional problem.
4. While temporary function and structure are often similar in different embryos, neither are absolutely parallel even in closely related forms of life.
5. In the development of comparative structures or organs the embryo does not always use the same material in accomplishing the task, nor does it utilize the same potencies (organizers) in doing so.
6. Back of all embryonic development, there is a controlling force, a guiding principle, which directs in the formation of each separate part as well as of the coordinated whole.
7. In attainment of their individual goals (i. e., the adult form), comparative embryos take the most efficient course in the development of individual structures and organs.

These simple postulates will serve

[14] DeBeer, G. R.: *Embryology and Evolution,* London, 1930, p. 109.
[15] DeBeer, G. R.: *Embryos and Ancestors,* London, 1940, pp. 97, 98.
[16] Sedgwick, A.: The Influence of Darwin on the Study of Animal Embryology, in *Darwin and Modern Science,* New York, 1909, pp. 175, 176.

as a starting point for a series of more detailed discussions from which some pertinent conclusions may be drawn.

## FROM THE SIMPLE TO THE COMPLEX

There are but two possible methods of reproduction, and Nature uses them both. In the smaller forms of life, simple direct division, or *fission* (asexual reproduction), into two new individuals is the rule. In such cases, development is essentially a moderate enlargement of the parent form, which by division becomes two separate individuals. In sexual reproduction, on the other hand, the potential new creature is contained within an egg which may be very small as in the case of animals, moderately small as in the fish or amphibian, or relatively large in case of the reptiles and birds. In development from a fertilized egg, progressive construction of the new individual must of necessity be a long process, the result of an unfolding of remarkable potentialities within the egg, made possible by the supply of oxygen and nutritive material. As Wallis has so well expressed it, it is inconceivable that life should start in a complex form. Therefore, it is by no means necessary that some similarity of embryos, progressing from the simple to the complex, from the unspecialized to the specialized, should be due to some presumed ancestral influence. It is more simple to explain the situation on the basis of "the logic of necessity."

"Some similarities in early ontogenetic development, therefore, would be present if man and ape had evolved in different solar systems, and had no common ancestry. In so far, then, as such resemblances are inevitable because of the circumstances of development, they must be regarded as similarities due to the operation of similar factors, rather than as due to common influences."[17]

But even this superficial view does not adequately express all of the essentials of the problem. There is a remarkable degree of diversity in the eggs, the starting point of development of various animal forms. The variability, for example, in the forms of spermatozoa and ova indicates that the animals represented by each form have a different starting point. Therefore, while the lines which might be drawn to represent the comparative development of two embryos are divergent, they can not be two radii of a circle, as the implication of the term "divergent parallelism" would suggest. The starting points of lines representing a dogfish, a newt, a lizard, a rabbit and man would be quite widely separated, even when only the external form and structure be considered and the inherent potentialities in each be ignored. And, oddly enough from an evolutionary viewpoint, the dogfish would be more closely related to the mammal than would the reptile. This observation alone should suggest the likelihood that different forms of the eggs are not derived from any ultimate single source.

The early recapitulationists, limited entirely to comparison of forms, fell into errors which are now quite obvious. If all there was to embryology was a slow motion picture of progressive change in the form of the embryo, recapitulation might have retained more of its appeal. But with knowledge of its ever-increasing importance, we have become concerned with the second element of *function*. It was an effort on the part of Wilhelm His and Roux to add the concept of physiology to morphology which resulted in the rejection of the strictly evolutionary interpretation of the phenomena of development. It should furthermore be added that the deeper into the problems of embryonic physiology investigators have gone, the less use they have for the recapitula-

[17] Wallis, W. D.: Human Recapitulation, *Sc. Month.* 37:443-448 (Nov.) 1934.

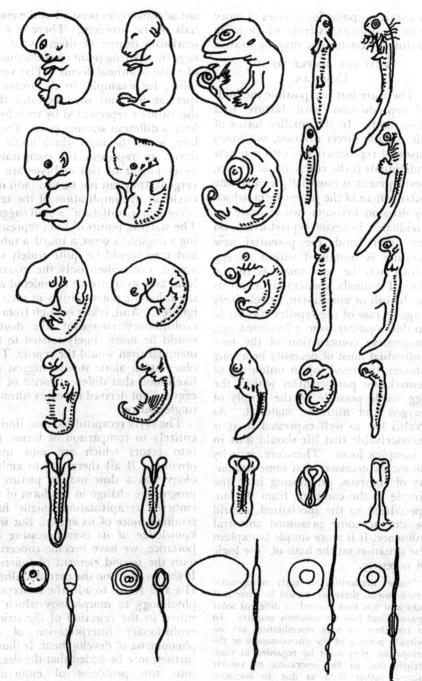

FIG. 2. THE FACT OF "PARALLELISM"

Drawing of early stages of the embryos of man, a rabbit, lizard, newt and dogfish showing similarities in form and structure. The sizes of the egg (or ovum) and spermatozoon are only relative. (Adapted from "The Science of Life," vol. 1, fig. 136).

tion theory as a means of explaining anything.

Because of the great difficulties imposed by the small size of the embryo as well as the peculiar circumstances under which it grows, the approach to the problem of its functions has been necessarily indirect. Some impressions have been gained by a study of chemistry. In this field again, a super-

nificance. The order, carbohydrate, protein, lipid, being the order of selection by the embryo, is also the order of solubility in water of oxygen content, of ease of digestibility of enzymes by the gastrointestinal tract and the ease with which they are sensitized by solar energy. Some significance may also be attached to the order in which the nitrogenous end-products of protein metabolism are produced. The simplest product of deaminization of amino acids is the first to appear; the most complex is last. Ammonia,

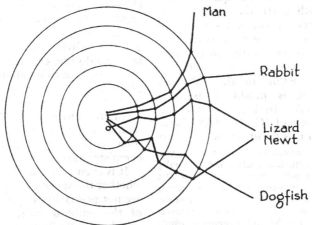

FIG. 3. THE APPLICATION OF "PARALLELISM"

When but one factor, the external shape of the five embryos shown in figure 2 is compared graphically, the myth of parallelism is clearly shown. In this simple diagram, portions of two compared lines may show fairly close true parallelism for a short time in some instances, progressively divergent "parallelism" in others, and continuously varying "parallelism" in still others.

ficial resemblance to recapitulation is at first suggested, but one which fails to hold water on critical scrutiny. As an example of one who has leaned toward the recapitulatory significance of the chemistry of the hen's egg, Calverly may be cited.

"The theory that the development of the individual repeats briefly the evolution of the species has been widely accepted by embryologists. It is based upon the comparison between the embryonic development of the individual and the comparative anatomy of the species to which it belongs. There is little biochemical evidence for such a phenomenon. However, it is possible that the order in which the developing embryo selects its food stuffs may have recapitulatory sig-

the most soluble and highest in nitrogen content, is produced first, while uric acid, the most insoluble and the least in nitrogen content, is produced last and accounts for over 90 per cent of the nitrogen excreted by the chick embryo. Other evidence for recapitulatory phenomenon is that the invertebrate embryo is relatively richer in sodium chloride than the new born, the chick is lower by half at fifteen days than at the beginning, the water content gradually decreases, the enzymes of the adult are gradually formed and the membranes of the eggs of some species are not keratin but resemble a mucin. It may be that the ovomucoid of the hen's egg is phylogenetically reminiscent of the time when it was used as a membrane."[18]

Wilkerson and Gortner likewise imply a recapitulatory significance in

[18] Calverly, H. O.: The Embryological Biochemistry in the Developing Hen's Egg. *Sc. Month.* 31:301 (Oct.) 1930.

the incidence of nitrogenous compounds in the growing pig embryo. They conclude that:

"The recapitulatory significance of the variation of the bases was pointed out, 'arginine' and 'histidine' decreasing while 'lysine' increases. This is exactly as the distributions vary as we go up in the animal evolutionary scale."[19]

A further word may be added on the chemistry of these nitrogenous compounds, with particular attention to the character of the excreta of the embryo. It has been learned that among the invertebrates nitrogenous waste is excreted as ammonia $(NH_4OH)$, while in the fish and amphibia, it is produced as urea $(CO(NH_2)_2)$. In birds it is eliminated as uric acid $(C_5H_4N_4O_3)$. Commenting on this point, DeBeer writes:

"Now the embryo bird excretes first ammonia and then, later, urea, before finally excreting uric acid. But the fact that this parallelism exists between these two series is no evidence that it represents a recapitulatory phenomenon. On the contrary, it seems to represent the order and sequence in which biochemical reactions of increasing degrees of complexity can be performed. Both in ontogeny and phylogeny there is a transition from the simple to the complicated. In addition, Needham has pointed out that the production of urea by the chick embryo (by means of the arginine-arginase system) is not identical with that which occurs in fish and amphibia (by the ornithine cycle). At all events, the failure to recognize the principle of parallelism of increasing degrees of complexity was a grave error in the theory of recapitulation."[20]

While it is not the writer's purpose to wander too far afield in this discussion of progression from the simple to the complex, brief attention must be given to this matter of chemical recapitulation, since the above cited examples are believed to be reminiscent of evolution. In the first place, as Wallis has already pointed out, progression from the simple to the complex, whether considered morphologically or chemically, is not proof of phylogenetic relationships. One without any knowledge whatever of chemical processes in the embryo should be able to anticipate that chemical (as well as other physiological) processes must of necessity be simple in the early stages of the embryo. Only by flying in the face of facts would one expect the forekidney or pronephros to break down complex nitrogenous compounds. "Some similarities in early ontogenetic development, therefore, would be present if man and ape had evolved in different solar systems,"[21] is just as true of chemistry as it is of morphology.

It is even more pertinent to inquire whether the specific chemical reactions are not primarily adapted to the needs of the embryo rather than serving simply as a "reflection" of phylogenesis. This is certainly shown in the early nutrition of the embryo, in which case Calverly concludes that "the embryo and not its food supply controls the situation." In other words, the chemistry of nitrogenous metabolism (and probably of others as well), as its nutrition, has been adapted to the needs of the growing embryo and not the reverse.

As suggested by Calverly[22] it is evident from a recapitulatory viewpoint that much stress has been laid on the salt and water content of the early chick embryo. It is inferred thereby that the original high water and sodium chloride content is evidence that the

[19] Wilkerson, V. A. and Gortner, R. A.: The Chemistry of Embryonic Growth. III. A Biochemical Study of the Embryonic Growth of the Pig with Special Reference to Nitrogenous Compounds, *Am. J. Physiol.* 102:153 (Oct.) 1932.

[20] DeBeer, G. R.: Embryology and Evolution, in *Essays of Evolutionary Biology*, London, 1934, pp. 57-78.

[21] Wallis, W. D.: *loc. cit.*

[22] Calverly, H. O.: *loc. cit.*

egg, phylogenetically speaking, originated in sea water.[23] In the first place, it should be pointed out that while an egg is a one-celled form, it is not a one-celled animal. It would be more logical to compare the chemical constituents of an egg to one-celled animals presumed to arise from sea water. It is less certain that the mammalian ovum or even the eggs of a fish or frog, which would more closely resemble chemically as well as structurally our presumed one-celled ancestors than does the egg of birds, have recapitulatory significance. The large fluid and salt content of the bird's egg is probably necessary to the prolonged development within the shell without further supply of these elements, a physiologic rather than a phylogenetic necessity. This assumption of the sea origin of life further serves to emphasize the essential fault with the entire philosophy of recapitulation, i. e., that organic evolution had to be presumed, and then only those details in the growing embryo which seemed to fit this concept were accepted; *all others were cenogenetic!* This is an easy way to dispose of any features of a theory which cannot be made to fit into it, but it is scarcely the method that characterizes a critical science.

By this time it should be clear from the physiology, and particularly the physiological chemistry of the embryo that there is a second "parallelism" in development, not only between the *structures* of two embryos but also between the structure and function of the various organs of the same embryo, there being a progression from simplicity to complexity in both. The early simple renal epithelium of the bird is to excrete only ammonia, but as the epithelium itself is developed it becomes able to excrete urea, a more complex nitrogenous compound.

But before closing this subject of chemistry and recapitulation, attention should be given to the conclusions of Needham on this point, since Needham is one of the outstanding investigators in this field. In a very scholarly review on the subject of chemistry as it pertains to the recapitulation theory, he deals with some of the transitory chemical functions of the embryo. In the various matters considered, he concludes that hatching enzymes, egg-breakers and sugar-forming functions of blastoderms and yolk sacs are temporary expedients. He explains how the embryo develops these transitory functions which serve only this period of life and often only a part of this period. Such transitory functions, as indicated above, obviously have no recapitulatory significance. He then considers a number of situations which do seem to have such implications as the excretion of increasingly complex nitrogenous compounds (already mentioned), the appearance of the hormones, the ash and water contents of various stages of embryonic life.

---

[23] This emphasis on "sea water" as opposed for example to swamp water, demanded because of the sodium chloride content of the egg, is but a part of the romantic fiction which has grown up around the presumed origin of life. Because protoplasm contains the essential chemicals of nature, it is concluded that in some shallow, sun-warmed Paleozoic sea, by some happy chance, a combination of chemicals resulted in the first living protoplasm. It seems as though "sea water" was necessary, because salt was needed; ordinary swamp water, evidently much more potent in the other requisites of protoplasm, apparently does not fit so closely the demands of the situation.

"Such are the principal attempts of modern biologists to formulate in some concrete way the evolution of matter in the living states from the elements of the earth. Their consideration is valuable in that it indicates the uniformitarian trend which, at the present day, biological thought follows in this field, and also the diversity of results arrived at by the scientific imagination when it is largely untrammeled by facts." (Woodruff, L. L.: The Origin of Life, in *The Evolution of the Earth*, 1924. pp. 106, 107.)

purine metabolism, the increasing efficiency of embryo metabolism, and the progressive use of carbohydrate, protein and fat. In all of these cases there seems to be an increasing ability on the part of the embryo to perform more complex chemical functions, which again is roughly parallel to the situation as found in the ascending order of animal life. To the recapitulationist, these chemical parallelisms are significant as reminiscences of past ancestral stages. Needham reviews the evidence and toward the close of his article draws the following conclusion:

"But on the whole we may conclude that there is more likelihood of recapitulation being explained by physico-chemical causes than of anything in physico-chemical embryology being explained by the theory of recapitulation. As an explanation itself, it is not at all attractive, for it can do no more than appeal to a mysterious and enigmatic force of heredity or evolutionary urge, and cannot explain why the nose of ancestral portrait should repeat itself through endless subsequent generations of portraits, while all other features should fall into oblivion. On this view, 'Oblivion blindly scattereth her poppy', as Sir Thomas Browne said, but if we accept the theory of formative stimuli outlined in the preceding pages, then the phenomena fall into a reasonable order, embryos only recapitulate what they must, and in a word recapitulation is itself explained by the physico-chemical requirements of the developing organism."[24]

Again in his summary, Needham says:

"Recapitulation may be regarded as fundamentally the necessary passage from simplicity to complexity, from low to high organization, which is entailed by the metazoal sexual system of reproduction with its single egg cell. The retention of visible organs or structures from lower ontogenies in a given ontogeny is only a special sense of this general rule and probably depends on the presence in them of essential formative stimuli."

Because of the entire field of Experimental Embryology, the study of the chemistry of the embryo is perhaps the newest subscience of Chemical Embryology and because Needham seems to occupy the position of its prophet, these statements must be carefully analyzed lest an important truth be lost in a maze of high sounding words. As a result of this survey of the entire field of the chemistry of the embryo, two important fundamentals become evident: (1) that in chemical features (as in morphological features), there is simply a "necessary passage from simplicity to complexity, from low to high organization" which is demanded by the system of sexual reproduction. *There is no other way!* Therefore to assume that these similarities in compared embryos, whether chemical or structural, are to be interpreted on a recapitulatory (or evolutionary basis) is simply begging the question. With Needham one must agree "that recapitulation itself cannot be regarded as an explanation of anything." (2) That there is more likelihood of recapitulation (or evolution) being explained by physico-chemical causes than recapitulation explaining these causes. In other words, the *a priori* theory of recapitulation or its parent theory of organic evolution has failed to account chemically (or otherwise) for the phenomena of embryology, and is therefore valueless as a theory. But Needham thinks that a study of the physiochemistry of the embryo might explain evolution. How? By the "presence in them [the embryos] of essential formative stimuli" apparently. This statement simply moves the proof of the theory into a field where proof is not immediately available. But as will be shown in a subsequent section, the presence of these "essential formative stimuli" are certainly no proof of either recapitulation or evolution as far as the embryo is concerned.

[24] Needham, J: The Biochemical Aspect of the Recapitulation Theory, *Biol. Rev.* 4:142-158, 1930.

Before closing this discussion of the principle of progression in the egg and embryo from the simple to the complex, it should be pointed out that the principle applies not only to form and structure and to the chemical and physiologic processes but to inherent powers and potentialities as well. In the early gastrula stage of the embryo but one center of development influence which has come to be known as the "organizer" is sufficient to initiate formation of the central nervous system and its adjacent structures. As development proceeds, there appear other centers of influence, at first a few, then in progressingly increasing numbers, so that the embryo becomes a veritable system of "wheels within wheels." Each center or "organizer" controls the development of a structure or organ in its immediate vicinity, the entire system of organizers being coordinated or integrated by some potency as yet not understood. Moreover, once development of organs has proceeded to a certain point, the organs themselves contribute a certain potency to their own formation. This is a rather strange situation from a mechanistic viewpoint, a machine constructing itself while in operation.

In concluding this point, then, one can say that there is a gradation from the simple to the complex in structure, function and potentialities. While some may be led to believe that the progressive development of structure and function may have some phylogenetic significance, the problem of developmental potencies is not so easily disposed of. The evolutionary significance of such potencies could only be the addition to the evolving animal of some power already existent and somehow acquired by it which would assist it in its upward urge. This sounds too much like vitalism to satisfy the mechanistic evolutionist. But if one is going to use the increasing complexity of structure and func-

tion as proof of phylogenesis, some significance also must be given to those unseen but vital forces which make embryologic development possible. It is a consideration of these unseen forces which makes the phylogenetic concept of parallelism completely illogical.

Therefore, "*the necessary passage from simplicity to complexity*" *of the embryo in its development from egg to adult is a limitation of the sexual metazoal form of reproduction and cannot be taken in any sense as proof of either recapitulation or evolution.* Divergent parallelism in which the form and structure, the chemistry and physiology, the powers and potentialities, begin in the fertilized egg and unfold along roughly divergent lines to the attainment of their final objective is a requisite of the process. Any applied causal interpretation must include all these factors, not all of which, though they were entirely consistent with the recapitulation theory, are helpful to the evolutionary philosophy. This "parallelism" therefore cannot be accepted as proof of identity of origin of two compared embryos.

## PARALLELISM OF EXTERNAL FORM VERSUS THAT OF STRUCTURE

The second theorem in this study of the meaning of parallelism is that *parallelism of form tends to become more and more inexact or divergent while that of development of systems of organs and organs themselves tend to be more exact.* In this discussion, it is proposed to show that the philosophy of either type of parallelism is in itself quite "inexact." As has already been explained, the paths of divergence from the egg to the adult cannot be represented as simple radii of a circle, not only because they have different starting points, but also because the degree of divergence is continuously altered and to a different degree for each structural feature compared. In order to get a clear perspective on this point, it is necessary to correct a common misconception as to the so-called "stages" of the embryo.

It was Haeckel who originally proposed first a series of 22, then 30 stages of the human embryo, which were considered to be typical of a series of antecedents in our human ancestry. These stages were selected solely on the basis of external form. It was obviously necessary for him to select certain arbitrary cross-sections in the development of the embryo for each of these stages. It is also evident that

space-time phenomenon which a living organism is."[25]

This point is a vital one, for it contains two significant considerations. Since, in the first place, the embryo does not develop by abrupt but rather by gradual and continuous alterations, its development cannot describe a line, either straight or broken, but a sinuous curve whose arc is constantly changing. But what is even more important, this curve must be plotted separately for each and every morphologic structure in the compared embryos, not only for those which

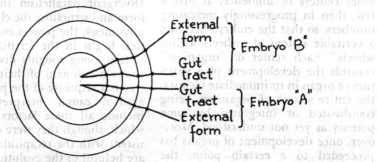

FIG. 4. "PARALLELISM" OF EXTERNAL FORM VERSUS INTERNAL STRUCTURE
Diagrammatic representation of comparison of external form and gut tract of rabbit and dogfish in their early stages.

even a few hours' difference in the age of the embryo would have made considerable difference in its form, for most of these stages had to be taken from early embryos in which changes occurred quite rapidly. The remarks of DeBeer on this matter of "stages" of embryonic life are very much to the point:

"It [the term *heterochromy*, or disturbed alteration in the order of embryonic stages] also suggests that it is not legitimate to speak of a 'stage' being shifted back to a later or to an earlier period in the life-history. It is not the 'stage' which is shifted *en bloc*, but certain characters which may be peculiar to the stage. It must also be remembered that what an embryologist calls a 'stage' is merely an arbitrary cut section through the time-axis of the life of an organism. A 'stage' is thus really an abstraction of the four dimensional

seem most promising. Even then one might plot one curve for size, another for shape, and still another for composition of the part or organ compared. Since such curves could be described only with reference to similar structures in another embryo, it will readily be seen that the sum total of the curves plotted for half a dozen separate details would result in a hopeless tangle of wavy lines composing two irregular wedges which diverge progressively one from the other.

To translate this concept into terms of the second postulate, it will be recalled that parallelism is more exact when comparing organs or systems of organs than when comparing the external forms of the embryo. This

[25] DeBeer, G. R.: *Embryos and Ancestors*, London, pp. 6, 7, 1940.

evident fact led Shumway to conclude that the theory of recapitulation "is not applicable to the embryo as a whole, but only to individual organs or systems of organs."[26] The wedge of curved lines for the various details of external form would diverge much more quickly than would the wedges representing the details of the viscera. Therefore, there would result not two composite wedges but four. The inner ones, representing the organs of the two embryos under comparison, might overlap each other in their proximate margins in the early part of their course, but the outer wedge of external form would very likely diverge widely within a short time.

From these facts an important conclusion can be drawn, i.e., *that Nature, whether producing either external form or internal organ, follows a basic and roughly parallel plan, and that the more nearly the resemblance of ultimate function, the more close the parallelism of structure is likely to be.*

It is tempting to introduce a mechanical comparison in this connection. Two automobiles, which may closely resemble each other in external shape and to a considerable degree in internal details, are produced on entirely different assembly lines with somewhat different systems of construction, yet both give evidence of design and function, based on what is generally recognized as sound engineering principles. The similarity in form and structure are in themselves no proof that they came from the same factory.

## STABILIZATION OF DEVELOPMENT ON FUNCTIONALLY PERFECT PATTERNS

The *third postulate*, the truth of which is self-evident, *makes itself apparent in the remarkable identity of structure of individual organs in animals widely separated in the scale of complexity which indicates stabilization on a successful functional solution of the problem.*

Some years ago there appeared a little volume written by that eminent surgeon, Dr. W. W. Keen, in an attempt to bridge the gulf between organic evolution and the fundamental concepts of Christianity. As an argument for his belief in the evolution of animal life as well as in Omnipotent God as a Creator, Doctor Keen presented an illustration showing the remarkable resemblance in structure of 100 examples of semicircular canals of the ear observed in a great variety of animals. He commented:

"Observe the exact duplication in every apparatus for hearing in every animal, in man and in the bird. If one of these dissections of medium size were presented to an expert zoologist, he would be unable to say whether it was from an animal or a human ear."[27]

On this fact Doctor Keen leaned heavily for support of his belief that organic evolution has taken place. It seems to the writer that a more reasonable conclusion with quite the opposite significance could be drawn from the same example. From this evidence it is quite clear that if evolution did occur, it soon stabilized on but one pattern of labyrinth. Evidently no evolution had taken place in this organ for untold millions of years, for the labyrinth of birds, reptiles and mammals are all constructed on the same design. If Doctor Keen had concluded that the Creator in whom he believed had recognized the one perfect solution of the problem of vestibular function and that the same pattern had been used in all animals in the construction of this particular organ structure, his philosophy would have been easier to follow. But why this Creator who was able to work out

---

[26] Shumway, W.: The Recapitulation Theory, *Quart. J. Biol.* 7:93-99 (March) 1932. Ibid.: *Vertebrate Embryology*, New York, 1927.

[27] Keen, W. W.: *Why I Believe in God and Evolution*, Phila. Rev. 4th ed., p. 44, 1925.

this perfect solution to the problem could find no other way to bring it into being but by the long, fumbling process of evolution is not made clear. At any rate, this illustration of Dr. Keen's will serve as an excellent text for a discussion of the third postulate, which is concerned with the fact that organs and structures of animal life are stabilized on basic designs.

A superficial analysis of the various organ systems of vertebrates will show a remarkable stability of basic plan from the simplest to the most complex forms of life, the obvious fact upon which the entire idea of parallelism has been constructed. The alimentary tract, whose functions demand a long exposure of the digesting food to the various digestive enzymes and to a continuous absorbing surface to allow optimum utilization of the broken down products of digestion, the heart and the circulatory system, the respiratory system, the excretory system, and the central nervous system, all are constructed on a similar basic design. Therefore, it is getting close to the primary question of his study when it is asked, "What is the meaning of this parallelism of organ systems?" We shall review the various possibilities pro and con.

From a *phylogenetic viewpoint* one is obliged to make certain deductions on this basis as follows: (a) that the evolution of external form has continued to progress from fish to man, while the evolution of the internal organs has evidently ceased early in phylogenetic history, a phenomenon for which there is no adequate explanation, and (b) that stabilization of a successful functional pattern of the various organ systems evidently occurred at various "stages" of development without any adequate reason for their having done so.

When viewed from *any other viewpoint*, it seems evident that organogenesis, though demonstrating a closer

parallelism than does external form, is dependent upon certain factors which can have no possible phylogenetic interpretation. In the first place, all development must of necessity be adapted to embryonic situations. For this reason, the heart of animals developing from large eggs, i.e., the reptiles and birds, shows an early development entirely out of proportion to its adult size. Because of the necessarily extensive circulation to carry food material from all parts of the yolk to the embryo, the early chick embryo appears to be "all heart." Again, the rapid early development of the brain in vertebrates is out of all proportion to its use in the lower forms of life. While this precocious development of the brain may have some significance as a center for organizer activity for the construction of its detached parts, this observation is obviously of no help in support of the theory of phylogenesis. As with the brain, the rapid early development of the gut-tract and genital system is more likely indicative of the long road they have to travel to complete their complex structure, as well as the part that each may plan meanwhile in the coordinated development of the whole.

It may therefore be stated that the level of stabilization of a basic plan of the various organ systems differs considerably in the various animals and in the different systems. The linear alimentary system and central nervous system are already found in the worm and the same plan continues to be followed in all vertebrates. The fundamental idea of the eye has not been altered from the insect. On the other hand, the basic design for the excretory system is not laid down so definitely before the vertebrate level, and the same may be said for the sexual system. The final plan for the respiratory system is not established until the level of the air-breathers is reached, i.e., the reptiles, the birds and the mammals (incidentally without leaving any embryonic trace of any connection between the fish and its alleged posterity).

It may thus be concluded that the essential factor which decided the plan for any system was the use to which it was to be put. This implies design and purpose as a forethought, the details of structure being adapted to functional requirements rather than the result of blind fate probing here and there for a chance solution of its problems. And while there have been minor adaptations to suit the individual animal economics, no "improvements" on the basic plan have been shown to have developed or evolved, regardless of the degree of complexity reached in the animal scale. If organic evolution has taken place, is it not strange that chance has not worked out more than one plan for organ systems in all the vertebrate kingdom? And is it not even more strange that organic life became "satisfied" with a successful design and did not wander off to perish with some superdesign? The conclusion seems inescapable that some Force, call it what you will, not only directed the early establishment of a basic plan for the organ systems, but also had intelligence enough to be satisfied with a perfect solution to the problem.[28]

### PRESERVATION OF IDENTITY IN PARALLELISM

Standing out in contrast to the general principle of parallelism is another principle, that with all the conformation of organ-systems to a basic plan *there is a remarkable propensity for each species to preserve certain characteristics which stamp them with an identity all their own.* The characters which establish this identity so cut across all lines of alleged ancestral relationships as to completely nullify the superficial resemblances upon which the philosophy of recapitulation is based. It is to the significance of these hall-marks of the species that we shall now direct attention. But we must first establish the fact.

It is not surprising that early attention was directed to the principle of parallelism since the similarity of early embryos of different animals was obvious even to the most superficial observer. The oft-cited statement of von Baer serves to emphasize this point:

"The embryos of mammals, of birds, lizards, and snakes, and probably also of chelonia, are in their earliest states exceedingly like one another, both as a whole and in the mode of development of their parts: so much so, in fact, that we can often only distinguish the embryos by their size. In my possession are two little embryos in spirit, whose names I have omitted to attach, and at present I am quite unable to say to what class they belong. They may be lizards or small birds, or very young mammals, so complete is the similarity in the mode of formation of the head and trunk in these animals. The extremities of these embryos are, however, absent still. But even if they had existed in the earliest stages of their development we should learn nothing, for the feet of lizards and mammals, the wings and feet of birds, no less than the hands and feet of man, all arise from the same fundamental form."[29]

To this significant statement of parallelism, which is certainly true, Darwin attached the implication of evolution, when he said, "Community of embryonic structure reveals com-

---

[28] There are some in the medical profession who presume to point out that certain organs or structures of the human body are deficient or imperfect in their specific functions. After all, if man *is* a product of chance, perhaps it is legitimate to point out where the finished product might have been improved. While certain allowances may be necessary owing to decadence, the writer has yet to see one of these correctors of nature plan a more efficient organ than the one with which we are now equipped.

[29] Von Baer, K. E.: (Cited by Needham, *loc. cit.*, pp. 26, 27).

munity in descent."[30]  Thus the concept of recapitulation with its evolutionary implications was born. Unfortunately for science, certainly the science of embryology, proper emphasis has never been placed on possible opposing implications. It seems that dissimilarities between embryos did not mean discommunity of descent but rather represented characteristics which had been lost in evolution or which were added to assist in the temporary demands of embryonic life.

What entirely escaped Darwin, because he was in no sense an embryologist, was the fact that it would have been possible to distinguish embryos of different species remarkably early, much earlier in many cases than one would suppose from a phylogenetic viewpoint. It was Sedgwick who called attention to some of these remarkable differences. In comparing the embryos of the chick and dogfish he showed that the differences in color of their yolks, the presence of blastopore in the fish and its absence in the chick, the presence of six gills in the fish and by four rudimentary swellings in the chick, the small head, straight body and long tail of the fish as compared to the large head, the various curvatures and short tail of the chick, etc. He also called attention to the fact that differences between embryos of similar organisms such as the chick and the duck were evident even in very early stages. It is even more significant to know that it is possible to distinguish between human embryos of white and colored parentage at a very early stage in life. This truism will become all the more evident by making a few simple comparisons of closely allied species, from the standpoint of certain details of organs in which parallelism is so much more close.

Perhaps no better place can be found to begin this discussion of the preservation of the identity of embryos of individual species than with the placenta, that portion of the fetal membrane which forms the vital union of the embryo with the maternal circulation in the uterus. In an authoritative survey, Grosser described four types of placenta found in the various mammals, the epitheliochorial, the syndesmochorial, the endotheliochorial and the hemochorial. The first type is found in the pig, the cow, and the lemur, a monkey which is supposed to lie near the stem of human antecedents. The second type is found among the ruminants, the third type among the carnivora and some of the insectivora and the chiroptera, and the fourth type in the rodents, some of the insectivora and chiroptera, and in monkeys and man. From a phylogenetic (evolutionary) standpoint, Grosser writes:

"Obviously the different types of placentation must have originated in some way from one another. Notwithstanding, it does not seem possible to arrange the great groups of mammals according to their placentation into something like a phylogenetic scale. In my opinion, it is probable, or nearly sure, that the epithelio-choral type of placentation must have occurred in the primitive animals."[31]

In other words, Grosser finds it impossible to arrange the mammals in a phylogenetic scale on the basis of the structure of the placenta. With particular attention to the human placenta, he has this to say:

"No doubt the human type of placentation is to be considered as the product of evolution and even as the terminal production of a phylogenetic line, an extreme expression of a structural principle, not to be continued or even to be surpassed. But such extremes have always been, in phylogeny, dangerous to their bearers. . . . There is no doubt that the human species exhibits on one side, many primitive features, whilst on the other it is extremely specialized. . . . we can expect

---

[30] Darwin, C.: *The Origin of Species*, New York, 6th Amer. ed., Vol. ii, p. 253, 1925.

[31] Grosser, O.: Human and Comparative Placentation Including the Early Stages of Human Development, Lancet 224:999-1001 (May 13) and 1053-1058 (May 20) 1933.

disastrous effects from the continuation of growth and specialization of the brain and the placenta—the more so as both already, today, are not free from the troublesome effects on the whole genus. . . . And with growing insight into the forces of development and phylogenetic change, the man of a remote future will, in philosophical stoicism, await the end of humanity when it has accomplished its time on the earth."

This is the bright picture which the placenta (and brain) of man hold out

which has attracted some attention. It has been learned that mammalian embryos can be divided into two types, on this basis, (1) those which retain functional Wolffian bodies (primitive kidneys) until the kidneys are sufficiently developed to secrete urine (bird, reptile, pig, sheep, and cat), and (2) those in which the Wolffian body degenerates before the kidneys

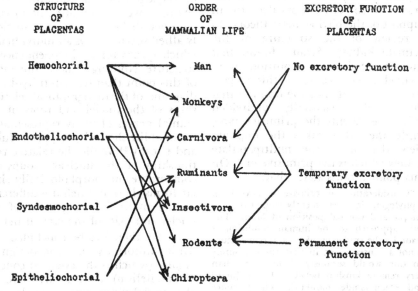

| STRUCTURE OF PLACENTAS | ORDER OF MAMMALIAN LIFE | EXCRETORY FUNCTION OF PLACENTAS |

FIG 5. PRESERVATION OF STRUCTURAL AND FUNCTIONAL IDENTITY IN PARALLELISM
An attempt to compare structural and functional classifications of the placenta with phylogenetic sequence.

for him, the assumed inevitable result of overspecialization (plus the retention of "many primitive features"). While the writer can scarcely hope in his own right to be prophetic, he dares to make the assertion that it is just about as difficult to reconstruct a phylogenetic tree on the basis of any one embryonic detail as it is with the structure of the placenta. But there is more evidence on this point.

The question of the placenta being an excretory organ, as well as having better understood nutritive and respiratory functions, has been one

reach functional ability (rabbit, guinea-pig, and man). In the second class the placenta is provided with an apparatus similar to that found in the adult kidney which takes over the function between the time of disappearance of the Wolffian body and the development of this function by the permanent kidney. On this point Bremer remarks:

"From these facts it appears that embryonic and fetal urinary excretion takes place wholly through the placenta in the rat, at first through the Wolffian body and later through the placenta in the rabbit, guinea pig and man, but never through the placenta in the pig, sheep or cat."[32]

It becomes evident again that this functional classification of the placenta as an excretory organ cuts across all phylogenetic lines, in fact, all taxonomic lines as well. In this classification, man seems to be sandwiched in between the rat and the pig.

Along closely allied lines of excretory function, the structure of the embryonic kidney is of interest since this organ is so often appealed to in support of the phylogenetic theory. In a review of the structure of the primate kidney, Strauss found that students of human evolution were divided into two camps on this subject. The one school is of the opinion that the simple, essentially undivided kidney represents the primitive type, while the other takes the opposite view that it is the multipapillate kidney which is the primitive one. On this point Strauss states that:

"Consideration of primate kidneys from a phylogenetic aspect merely emphasizes the unique and isolated position of Man. The only approach to the human condition is made by the spider monkey, and this feature is not a constant one in that animal. Surely no one would seriously claim other than very remote kinship between Homo [man] and Ateles [spider monkey]. The presence of true primary internal renal lobulation in the two forms can only be regarded as the product of convergence, a phenomenon which in these two animals is not limited to the kidney alone."[33]

One is compelled on this basis of the embryologic development of the kidney to agree with Strauss that "the phylogenetic history of the kidney is by no means clear" and that "no existing theory is entirely satisfactory." Would it not be wiser, as Sedgwick recommends, to review the evidence on some wider category in an effort to solve the problem of the origin of the kidney?

Another organ which has also been frequently cited as evidence of evolutionary development is the brain. The so-called primary brain vesicles (which as Streeter has shown never really exist in the embryonic brain), the gross similarity of the major parts as well as its linear arrangement have been pointed out to support the theory of phylogenetic relationships. Here again, however, any attempt to compare detailed structures, even in closely allied species shows an individuality which speaks for an independence of structure. Nothing is more illustrative of this point than the carefully drawn diagrams of the topographical relationships of the nuclei and roots of the cranial nerves of many representative forms of life shown by Kappers, Huber and Crosby.[34] While the relative relationships of the nuclear groups are comparable, in morphologically similar forms there is a definite difference in the internal arrangement of the nuclei and exits of the cranial nerves.

It may therefore be concluded that while uniformity in basic design of organs (which is the essential concept of parallelism) does occur, there are also special differences in the development of form, structure and function of such organs which preserve the identity of each. When attempts are made to classify animals on the basis of structural details, it is found that such lines often fail to support, and many times categorically deny any possibility of phylogenetic relationships. These special or specific characteristics indicate an hereditary transmission and their relatively early appearance in embryonic life, often far ahead of the time they should appear

---

[32] Bremer, J. L.: The Interrelations of the Mesonephros, Kidney and Placenta in Different Classes of Animals, Am. J. Anat. 19:179-205, 1916.

[33] Strauss, W. L.: The Structure of the Primate Kidney, J. Anat. 69:94-108, 1934.

[34] Ariens Kappers, C. V., Huber, G. C. and Crosby, E. C.: The Comparative Anatomy of the Nervous System of Vertebrates Including Man, New York, 1936, vol. 1, pp. 506-644.

on a phylogenetic basis, demands some interpretation other than the evolutionary one. Before there was an embryo, there was a species, is the only conclusion that can be drawn from this evidence.

## MULTIPLE SOURCES OF MATERIAL IN ORGAN-MAKING

One of the major contributions to modern embryology has been the elaboration of the "organizer" concept of the sequence of causal factors in development. It has been learned in the past few decades that in the fertilized ovum there has been planted an inherent system of powers or faculties which guide step by step in the formation of the various structures, organs and tissues. As a result of experimental studies it has become evident that certain regions of the growing embryo exert a controlling influence over the development of the surrounding parts. In turn these secondary areas come to have control over the development of parts or structures immediately adjacent to them. For example, an area in the head end of the embryo contains elements, chemical, electrical or otherwise, which control the development of structures near the rostral end of the neural tube. As these structures elaborate, they in turn exert a controlling influence on the adjoining head end of the gut tract which results in the formation of oral cavity, etc. Thus throughout the course of development there is an evident control of each step of the process by this graded system, this "hierarchy" of organizers.

As remarkable and significant as this system is (and there is more to be said on this point) there is one important feature which needs to be emphasized in the process of organ-making. Much has been made of *homology*, or structural affinity of parts or organs in various animal forms, as indicative of their community of origin. The recapitulation theory itself has specifically emphasized the homology of similar parts, notably the branchial arches or gillclefts, as some so persistently and erroneously call them. It is now learned that identical (and therefore homologous) organs may develop under the influence of different organizers and may use material from different sources with which to build the given organ. On this point DeBeer writes:

"It might seem, then, that in considering the homology of any given structure it is necessary to consider not only the tissues from which they arise but the organizers which have induced their formation. . . . But the important point to notice is that the *structures can owe their origin to different organizers without forfeiting their homology.*"[35]

DeBeer points out that in the ascidian tadpole, the development of the neural tube is not dependent on the activity of an underlying organizer as is the case in similar forms. In one frog (*Rana esculenta*) the lens of the eye is determined by the gradient-field coordinates of the whole embryo, while in another (*Rana fusca*) the lens is induced by the optic cup. Organ-forming materials for corresponding structures may likewise be taken from different regions as illustrated in the crustacean *Dentalium* and in the tunicates.

Not only in these developmental potencies, commonly designated as "organizers," which initiate and guide in the process of development of individual organs is there great variability which makes homology of doubtful value, but this is true also as to the source of materials in organ-making. While specific details on this point are not available for many organs or many animals yet enough is known to show that it is not legitimate to use struc-

[35] DeBeer, G. R.: Embryology and Evolution, in *Essays of Evolutionary Biology*, London, 1934, pp. 57-78.

tural homology as proof of phylogenetic (or evolutionary) relationships. Individual organs are not only formed from any one or all of the three germ layers (ectoderm, mesoderm and entoderm), but also from different portions of these layers. As examples of this important fact Jenkinson has shown that the gastro-intestinal tract may be formed from the archenteron (original abdominal cavity) as a whole in the *Cyclostomata* (lampreys, etc.), *Cerotodus* (lung fish) and the *Urodela* (salamanders, etc.), from both the roof and floor of this cavity in the *Lepidosiren* (eel-shaped fish) and *Anuria* (frogs), from the yolk cells in the floor of the cleavage cavity in *Gymnophiona* (worm-like amphibian), or from the lower layer of the blastoderm in the *Ammniota* (reptiles, birds and mammals), areas which obviously occupy widely different positions in the egg and early embryo.[36] The ganglion of the trigeminal (or fifth) cranial nerve, usually arising from the neural crest from which all the dorsal root ganglia are derived, has its origin in the frog from an epidermal placode, a skin derivation such as develops into the ear. Similarly, in the frog, the visceral arches arise from the neural crest, an ectodermal structure, rather than from mesoderm. The thymus gland arises from the entoderm of the gill pouches of the salmon (*Salmo*),[37] from both ectoderm and mesoderm in *Trichosurus* (a phalanger),[38] from the ectoderm alone in the mole, and from the entoderm alone in the rabbit and man.

From the relatively small number of the lower animals which have thus far been studied very critically, it seems entirely clear that in detail

embryos of closely related animals may have an entirely different organizer plan, and may use materials in organ-making from entirely different sources, even different germ layers, in the construction of homologous organs. The conclusion of DeBeer is therefore very much to the point:

"The fact is that *correspondence between homologous structures can not be pressed back to similarity of position of cells in the embryo or of parts of the egg out of which the structures are ultimately composed.*"[39]

One can carry this conclusion one step further without doing violence to the facts and state that, not only do these facts completely controvert any possible recapitulatory significance to similar or homologous organs or structures, but it is also impossible to account for them on the "larger category" of evolution. And what is still more vitally important is that the fundamental argument of homology, which has been depended upon so much in establishing alleged evolutionary relationships, is thereby completely nullified! It must be further inferred that whatever the system which has been used or whoever the Mechanic who devised it, the organizer system and selection of material for organ-making displays an individuality characteristic of the species, one which has evidently been transmitted from one generation to another without the slightest evidence of its having ever been transmitted to any other species.

### THE GUIDING PRINCIPLE IN EMBRYONIC DEVELOPMENT

The theory of recapitulation had scarcely been christened until there arose a revolt against this empiricism which threatened to stifle all real advance in scientific investigation in

---

[36] Jenkinson, J. W.: *Vertebrate Embryology*, London, 1925.

[37] Deanesley, R.: *Quart. J. Micros. Sc.* 71:113, 1927 (Cited by DeBeer[35]).

[38] Fraser, E. A. and Hill, J. P.: *Philosoph. Trans.* (Section B) 207:1, 1915 (Cited by DeBeer[35]).

[39] DeBeer, G. R.: *loc. cit.* (italics those of DeBeer's).

so far as embryology was concerned. Haeckel argued that since all phenomena of development were the result of processes set in motion in the dim and distant past, all that remained to be done was to fit the facts of embryology into this presumed evolutionary history. There is probably no truer commentary as to the false basis of this philosophic approach to the problem than this. It is little wonder that critical thinkers began to object to such an *a priori* shackle on all constructive thought, to this mental tether which limited all concepts to the notion that changes in the embryo were but a mirrored reflection of the upward struggle of its ancestors. The early murmurs of disapproval were largely lost, however, in the tumult of enthusiasm for recapitulation. Nevertheless, the "still small voice" of the few dissenters set in motion a movement which has resulted in the greatest advance in the science of embryology. First Wilhelm His, then Wilhelm Roux, ignoring the alleged phylogenetic significance of embryonic processes, made a more positive effort to understand these processes in terms of physiology. Feeble as these early efforts were, the foundation was laid for the experimental method which has profoundly altered the science of embryology. Since Experimental Embryology (which includes Chemical as well as Physiologic Embryology) had its beginnings by a bold departure from the then popular recapitulation theory, it will be interesting to see where such a course has led.

Not only has Experimental Embryology attained its present status by ignoring the "fundamental law of biogeny" which Haeckel and his contemporaries so fondly hoped would establish beyond question the larger concept of evolution, but it has also failed to contribute anything to the support of either theory. In the monographs on the subject of Experimental Embryology by Thomas Hunt Morgan,[40] by Dürken,[41] by Huxley and DeBeer,[42] by DeBeer,[43] by Dalcq,[44] and by Spemann,[45] which the writer has had at his immediate disposal, very little reference to the subject of recapitulation is made. Nevertheless, since any comments from the standpoint of experimental embryology are vitally important, all of these remarks will be reviewed.

In his introduction to a scholarly treatise on the subject, Thomas Hunt Morgan, who had had so much to say in the past on the subject of recapitulation writes:

"The recognition of the advantage of applying the method of experiment to problems of development may be said to have begun with Wilhelm Roux in 1883. Today the need of this procedure seems so obvious that we are apt to forget the strong opposition that the movement at first met from embryologists of the old school, who had already developed a philosophy dealing with the developmental process as a series of historical events. The phylogenetic school had interpreted each stage in development as the survival of ancestral adult form, in line with the then current theories of evolution. The study of development had resolved itself into a quest for ancestors for the successive stages."[46]

The remarks are obviously merely historical comments and say nothing

[40] Morgan, T. H.: *Experimental Embryology*, New York, 1927.

[41] Dürken, B.: *Experimental Analysis of Development*, trans. by H. G. and A. M. Newth, New York, 1932.

[42] Huxley, J. S. and DeBeer, G. R.: *The Elements of Experimental Embryology*, Cambridge, 1934.

[43] DeBeer, G. R.: *An Introduction of Experimental Embryology*, Oxford, 1934.

[44] Dalcq, A. M.: *Form and Causality in Early Development*, Cambridge, 1938.

[45] Spemann, Hans: *Embryonic Development and Induction*, New Haven, 1938.

[46] Morgan, T. H.: *loc. cit.*, p. 1.

of any possible relationship between evolution and experimental embryology.

In their introduction to the subject, Huxley and DeBeer have this to say:

"Even after the discomfiture of the preformationist view at the hands of Wolff and others, and the acceptance of an epigenetic theory of development, the need for an application of the causal postulate was clouded by the unfortunate effects of Haeckel's theory of recapitulation. This view, pushed to its ultimate conclusion, maintained t h a t ontogeny or embryonic development was inevitably a recapitulation of phylogeny or racial evolutionary history, a n d t h a t phylogeny was the mechanical cause of ontogeny, whatever Haeckel may have meant by that statement. If this was true, then clearly there was no need to look for other causes than the evolutionary history in order to explain development. But, as Wilhelm His saw, it was not true.

". . . . On the other hand, Wilhelm His, having overthrown Haeckel's theory of recapitulation, regarded each stage of development as a sufficient cause of the following stage, and so paved the way for a new branch of science: Entwicklungsmechanik or causal embryology, the foundations of which were laid by Wilhelm Roux."[47]

These statements again indicate the divergent courses of those two philosophies, showing their contrasting values, not comparative ones.

Four years later, Dalcq had only this to say about recapitulation:

". . . . The uniformity of this phase (blastomere) induced Haeckel to imagine the ancestral type called *gastraea*. If such a being ever existed, its physiology must have been radically different from that of our actual gastrulae."[48]

With these brief comments on recapitulation, the writers of the monographs mentioned above proceed to their task. It is obvious from their relative silence on the subject of recapitulation and the gross neglect of any reference to its parent theory, evolution, that the biogenetic law is but a strained and discordant note as compared with the newer harmonics of experimental embryology.

In order to lay the groundwork for the seventh and last of our postulates, it will be necessary to cite briefly the newer discoveries made by the experimental method in the field of embryology.

a. From an experimental standpoint, it is now known that there are two essential types of eggs, i.e. *mosaic-eggs* and *regulation-eggs*, although some transitional eggs are also known to exist. This classification is based upon the speeds at which the egg undergoes cleavage and organ-forming substances develop. In the more rapidly developing mosaic eggs, cutting the egg into two parts will result in the formation of half an embryo, while division of the more slowly developing regulation egg at the same stage will result in the formation of two embryos.

b. Most eggs have an *axis* along which the embryo develops, as well as two poles, the *animal pole* which becomes the head end of the embryo, and the *vegetable pole* which marks the position of the yolk when such is present. The axis gives the embryo a bilateral symmetry.

c. Development is dependent upon both internal (hereditary) factors and external (environmental) factors, both of which must be normal to produce a normal embryo. Under ordinary circumstances the internal factors will produce a normal embryo. If the external factors are disturbed it is possible to produce deficits in the embryo which may be transmitted to offspring for several generations.

d. After fertilization of the egg, early development is dependent upon local differences in rate of activity (with different potencies of development) which are arranged along the axis of the organism. This gradation of developmental along one or more axes is called *axial gradient*. The gradient potencies decrease progressively from the head end to the tail end of the embryo.

e. After an early period of development along the axial gradient, further growth results from the presence of certain chemical elements called *organizers*, which exert their effect by contact with the tissues on which they act. The dorsal lip of the blastopore in this way serves as the organizer for the first axial structures, the neuraxis, notochord,

[47] Huxley, J. S. and DeBeer, G. R.: *loc. cit.*, pp. 8, 9.
[48] Dalcq, A. M.: *loc. cit.*, p. 7.

somites, etc. Secondary organizers then assist in the subsequent development of adjacent regions. Thus more detailed construction is dependent upon the elaboration of a system of organizers of increased complexity.

f. When an early embryo is disturbed before chemo-differentiation by organizers sets in, its equilibrium in some cases can be reestablished (regulation), a process which can occur only when the tissues are plastic and capable of adjusting themselves to the original status.

g. Still later in the course of development, differentiation is made possible only by the aid of stimuli produced by function. "During the first period [of structural determination] differentiation determines the function that any particular tissue will perform, in the second, function reacts on the tissue and perfects it (DeBeer)."

While these important discoveries seem complicated in their essence, the basic truths they represent are fairly simple. From these deductions from experimental observations, certain conclusions can be made which may give one some insight into the principles which stand behind all development.

In the first place, *development is the result of a combination of external and internal factors.* The internal factors are the hereditary ones, the external those which are incident to the environment of the embryo. Under normal circumstances and left to its own devices, an embryo will develop into a normal individual, with specific characteristics of structure and function as are transmitted to it by its parents. This development is accomplished by the help of inherent potencies in the egg which (at times) determine its axis and poles. This normal process can be interfered with by alteration of external factors and structural (and probably functional) defects can thus be produced in the embryo. In other words, any disturbance of these external factors, the only mechanism by which changes in the direction of evolution could be produced, will result only in deficits, never additions. These defects may be passed down through three or four generations, inferring that some transitory malign influence on the chromosomes of the injured embryo may exist. It is significant that *defects* may be temporarily transmitted; no additions to the embryo have ever been proved to be transmitted even for one generation. This suggests the impossibility of transmission of acquired characters, either structural or functional.

Pointing very much to the same conclusion is the presence of an *inherent system of development* characteristic of each species. This characteristic system indicates that the fertilized ovum is supplied with a tremendous potency, which if allowed to run its normal course, supplied meanwhile with oxygen and nutritive materials, will carry the individual through an entire life-time. It is difficult to grasp fully the fact that all the complex and far-reaching possibilities of life are enfolded within the fertilized ovum. The first of these potencies is that of self-development, first structurally evident in the formation of the dorsal lip of the blastopore, then invisible and chemical but still exerting its influence on the general structure of the embryo, and finally functional, the essential functions of the part or organ determining its structure. By implication, early structure must be predetermined on the basis of future needs, and before the demands upon structure are present, a mechanism exists to induce them. Only when structure has proceeded far enough to permit some function, does function take over and perfect the structure.

When these general conclusions are reviewed in the light of recapitulation, it is not strange that no adequate attempts have been made to synthesize experimental embryology and evolution. It is clear that there are too many prerequisite and transmitted powers which must exist before embryonic development (ontogeny).

Even if interpreted in the light of evolution, such development can only imply the presence of some pre-existent force which not only decrees the hereditary bounds of the organism, but which also furnishes the mechanism by which development is guided. And more, such a force supplies an inherent life potency, sufficient to carry the organism through its life span. Again, this sounds too much like vitalism to suit the mechanist, who must content himself, therefore, with the determination of the facts of function and structure, perhaps gaining meanwhile some general concepts of the principles upon which development depends. But to the less easily satisfied investigator, there always remains the question: "Has anyone observed a machine that was capable of evolution *without a mechanic?*"[49]

## THE PRINCIPLE OF LEAST ACTION IN EMBRYOLOGY

In 1774, a French scientist by the name of Maupertuis enunciated a fundamental principle of nature which is generally known as the "principle of least action." In his own words Maupertuis described this principle as follows:

"There is a principle truly universal, from which are derived the laws which control the movement of elastic and inelastic bodies, light and all corporeal substances; it is that in all the changes which occur in the universe . . . that which is called the quantity 'action' is always the least possible amount."[50]

By way of explanation of this law, Fee states that "whenever there is more than one conceivable method of operation, nature follows the one in which the product of time multiplied by the energy is the least possible amount."

While the principle of least action was first conceived in its application to physical forces of the universe, it is also applicable to many phases of biology. Evidently very little investigative thought has been directed along these lines in physiology, but it is quite evident that here too nature loses little time or energy in the accomplishment of its purpose. Recognizing the limitations of tissue structure, the speed with which chemical reactions of the body take place indicates genuine efficiency.[51]

The developing embryo is a classical example of the correctness of this principle.[52] While this truism would be difficult to express mathematically in terms of time and energy, it is self-

---

[49] Woodger, J. H.: The "Concept of Organism" and the Relation Between Embryology and Genetics. *Quart. Rev. Biol.* 5:1-22, 1930.

[50] Fee. Jerome: Maupertuis and the Principle of Least Action. *Sc. Month.* 52:487-503 (June) 1941.

[51] Instinct or behavior cannot be interpreted on this basis any more than can volition. The peculiar courses pursued by certain animals, evidencing a distinct change at some time in the past in their habits, obviously do not conform to this principle. An example of this sort called to the writer's attention by Dr. Frank Marsh is the peculiar migration tendency of Bobolinks which fly first to the east before going south, a rather roundabout way of reaching their objective. While there is a good reason for this course, on the basis of habit, such an instinctive behavior is not to be cited as an example of least action. Even the average man with his reasoning powers does not follow the shortest way in the accomplishment of his purposes. When this ability is evident in some superlative individual, he is looked upon as a genius, a benefactor of the race.

[52] In response to a question propounded by the writer, "Is embryological development governed by laws," an outstanding contemporary American embryologist wrote, "When one watches the orderly sequence of events in the development of an embryo one must realize that it is following some sort of "laws." The difficulty is that we still know too little of the controlling factors to formulate these laws satisfactorily. We can get a glimpse here and there of some of the guiding principles, but they interlock and overlap in a manner which

evident to anyone who will take time to observe a growing chick embryo. Development of form and structure evidently takes place with a minimum of "action." As Streeter has so pertinently put it in his comments on the development of the brain:

"In other words the brain begins to build its definite parts before closure of the neural

empty gestures toward the past. With no false moves it proceeds directly with the building of an organ appropriate in all its parts for the respective species."[53]

Not only does the embryo "proceed directly" with the construction of its various structures and organs, but in the process there is no waste of material. In some instances what seems

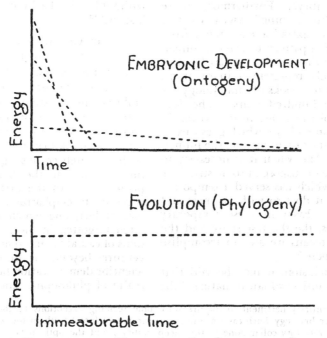

FIG. 6. THE PRINCIPLE OF "LEAST ACTION" IN ONTOGENY AND PHYLOGENY

When the interrelationship of energy X time is diagrammed in ontogeny (embryonic development) it suggests that the principle of "least action" holds good. It is obvious that in organic evolution, aside from waste of energy, almost immeasurable presumed time has elapsed in the making of man.

tube—without going through a preliminary archetypal indifferent three-vesicle stage. With further experience and additional material this has been abundantly substantiated in the pig as well as in man. There seems to be no evidence that the brain wastes any

superficially to be an excessive formation of tissue turns out usually that this material is subsequently utilized for some other purpose. For example, some of the blood cells (mononuclears)

makes the phrasing of them exceedingly difficult."

Another well-known embryologist gave this answer: "No one who has sat and watched for half a day or more the progressive transformations in the living egg or embryo could help being deeply impressed by the orderliness of the procedure. When he sees how much the environment may be changed in certain cases and yet not seriously modify the course of development, he realizes that inner forces are at work and can hardly doubt but that they are governed by fundamental principles or 'laws'."

[53] Streeter, G. L.: Archetypes and Symbolism, *Science*. 65:405-412 (April 29) 1927.

are formed from the solid chords of the primordial blood vessels. Moreover, whenever possible, the same tissue or organ is used for a double purpose. For example, the same tube is used for all three stages of the kidney, although the structure of each individual kidney is evidently not adaptable to the changing excretory needs of the embryo. Furthermore, there is no "tinsnipping" away of the presumed "extra" aortic arches from the fish-like pattern to make a human design of these arches, as has been so suggestively represented in diagrams found in textbooks of embryology for over one hundred years. The fish-pattern of the arches never existed in the human embryo, which goes directly about the task of making the human pattern. And when it is necessary to obliterate or dispose of some structure or part which has served a temporary purpose, it does so with neatness and dispatch. Even in these temporary structures, the shortest route and the simplest means are used to accomplish the purpose.[54]

In conclusion, it may be said that the truly universal law of nature, "the principle of least action," seems to apply in the case of the developing embryo. With directness of effort, economy of material, and in remarkable shortness of time, the complex, full-term fetus develops from a single cell. And withal, there are no "empty gestures to the past." "It is the function of the embryo to become an adult without looking backward on ancestral history."[55]

### THE CAUSAL SIGNIFICANCE OF PARALLELISM

With this analysis of the principles guiding in the development of the embryo, the question may be asked, "How much emphasis can we place on these facts in any evaluation of the origin of living matter? How far can we legitimately go in suggesting causal implications on the basis of these principles?" In the first place, it is necessary to emphasize a most fundamental fact, one which has been so often forgotten in the past in discussions of causality, and that is when one ventures beyond the limits of simple scientific demonstration he invades the realm of philosophy. And in philoso-

---

[54] It is entirely pertinent to inquire into some seeming exceptions to the law of least action in embryology. Such cases as the disappearance of foetal teeth in the whale, the presence of a transitory collar bone in the sheep embryo, and the optic nerves which become atrophic in blind cave fish are suggested as contradictions to this concept. If this disappearance of structures present in the fetus has the same significance in all these forms, the degeneration of the optic nerve in the cave fish would suggest that they were structures which, owing to a change in the animal's habits, are no longer useful during adult life. The absence of these structures represents a *deficit* from some original state. This is in accord with the observations of experimental embryology as exemplified in the malformations produced by X-ray or otherwise which may be transmitted through several generations. These reductions from the original structure do not necessarily negate the essential truth of the principle of "least action" in development. Certainly they are of no value as proof of the theory of evolution, although they are often so used, for this philosophy is based upon the *addition* of structures, potencies and abilities; not their subtraction. This entire problem will be considered *in extenso* in a forthcoming study.

In order to be proposed as a contradiction to the theory of "least action," the development of a given embryonic structure must be shown to be uneconomical of time and material, and in the case of temporary structures, that some good use has not been made of the excess tissue in keeping with its amount and complexity. It is obviously fruitless to say that the placenta, for example, disproves the principle of "least action" because it is finally rejected, any more than to conclude that an oil derrick is evidence of poor engineering, because it is of so little use after the well has been bored. The remarkable thing about the construction of the embryo is the absence of sawdust and chips when the process has been completed.

[55] Shumway, W.: The Recapitulation Theory, *Quart, J. Biol.* 7:99 (March) 1932.

phy one draws conclusions on the basis of pure logic — reasoning from the known to the unknown.

The question therefore first arises, "Is it permissible for one primarily interested in science to step over into the field of philosophy?" Judging from what science has done in the past, this passing from the realm of fact into that of philosophy seems entirely legitimate, for in every branch of science writers have never considered themselves so restricted. In fact, there are those who insist that science and philosophy are not to be separated, that there is no sharp line of division between the two. Of this group, Gengerelli may be taken as an example. He says:

"It is hard to understand what people have in mind when they distinguish so emphatically between science and philosophy. It is certain that the science they are thinking of is not science at all but technology. The very great scientists are all great philosophers in the one and only significant sense in which the term may be used, namely, that

they tried and succeeded in imposing upon the universe the kaleidoscopic perception concepts and principles which make it simpler and more orderly. The illustrious names of Galileo, Newton, Darwin and Einstein come immediately to mind."[56]

As has already been shown in the first article of this series, the recapitulation theory itself is but a philosophical deduction from the fact of "parallelism," and biologists in general and embryologists in particular have shown no particular hesitancy in the past in exploring this philosophy to its limits. Accepting the larger theory of evolution as a fact, Haeckel made the deduction from it that "ontogeny was a recapitulation of phylogeny," a philosophy which proved to be a scientific wilderness in which men wandered for half a century.[57] The original error here was in making a deduction from another deduction, which in itself was still only a theory, a philosophy which likewise had not yet been established as fact.[58] It is therefore not surprising

[56] Gengerelli, J. A.: Facts and Philosophers, Sc. Month. 54:431-440 (May) 1942.

[57] There have been efforts in the past to condone the evil effects of recapitulation on embryologic research by stating that it stimulated a great deal of study and resulted in the investigation of a great many embryos in an effort to prove the theory. While this may all be true, the question may also be raised as to how much more might have been accomplished in the same period by investigations along more fruitful lines. While searching in blind alleys may yield some truth, it doesn't get one very far on the road to ultimate achievement. Most scientists have had this as a personal experience. This seems to be the position reached by Hurst who writes:

"If the value of a theory is to be measured by the number and the extent of the papers written, and by the amount of work done under its inspiration, then the value of the Recapitulation Theory is indeed great: but there is always room for the doubt as to whether an equal amount of work would not have been done without that inspiration: whether, for instance, Hyatt, Buckman, Jackson, and Beecher would not have published researches as great and as brilliant as those referred to by Mr. Bather in his article on 'The Recapitulation Theory in Palaentology' (p. 281), even if they had been inspired by something less fantastic than the theory in question." (C. H. Hurst: The Recapitulation Theory. Nat. Sc. 2:364 (May) 1893.

[58] Many writers have put themselves on record as believing in the "fact" of evolution. It is very doubtful whether there is now available any more certain proof of the origin of life than there was in 1870, when Huxley said, "Looking backward through the prodigious vista of the past, I find no record of the commencement of life, and therefore I am devoid of any means of forming a definite conclusion as to the conditions of its appearance. Belief, in the scientific sense of the word, is a serious matter, and needs strong foundations. To say, therefore, in the admitted absence of evidence that I have any belief as to the mode in which existing forms of life have originated, would be using words in a wrong sense. . . . That is the expectation to which analogical reasoning leads me; but I beg you once more to recollect that I have no right to call my opinion anything but an act of philosophical faith."

that the daughter theory has proven to be so completely false.

Since as so many investigators of the problem have shown (and no modern research embryologist now holds it to be true) that the recapitulation theory as an explanation of parallelism is no longer valid and tenable, it therefore cannot be appealed to as proof of anything. It is therefore necessary to go back to original philosophy of evolution and see whether in its "larger category" there is anything which will shed any light on the fact of parallelism. If Haeckel's contention that,

"These two branches of our science—on the one side ontogeny or embryology, and on the other phylogeny, or the science of race-evolution—are most vitally connected. The one cannot be understood without the other. It is only when the two branches fully cooperate and supplement each other that 'biogeny' (or the science of the genesis of life in the widest sense) attains to the rank of a philosophic science. The connection between them is not external and superficial, but profound, intrinsic, and causal."[59]

is true, then on the strength of his assertions, the fall of his "fundamental law of organic evolution" must carry down with it the parent theory. Of course, Haeckel may have been wrong as to the vital connection between the two philosophies, since he was completely mistaken as to the significance of parallelism. Science at large does not seem to think that this connection is so vital as Haeckel contended, for there is no indication that the philosophy of evolution is now being discarded.

The question now confronting us is whether there remain any deductions from parallelism which would contribute to the support of the theory of organic evolution, or, otherwise expressed, whether one can still find in the phenomena of development some of the "strongest evidence in favor of evolution." If this is not the case it is legitimate to inquire whether some other philosophy might better fit the situation. The facts which have become apparent by this survey of parallelism will now be reviewed *seriatim*.

1. *The similarities in embryologic development (which constitutes the very basis of parallelism) in the passage of embryos from the simple to the complex can best be explained on the "logic of necessity."* As Wallis has said, "Some similarities in early ontogenetic development, therefore, would be present if man and ape had evolved in different solar systems and had no common ancestry."[60] Moreover, his conclusion that these similarities must be regarded "as due to the operation of similar factors, rather than as due to common ancestral influences" cannot be gainsayed. There is no other way for two separate and distinct species to develop when starting from a single cell and aiming for an ultimate goal in which similarities still exist, but to follow a somewhat parallel course. And as will be shown, this is the result of the "operation of similar factors" in each case. Reduced to a comparison of homologous structures, those which seem to favor the philosophy of evolution are apt to be selected as evidence supporting this concept. These comparable similarities have been frequently referred to as the "reminiscences (if not a 'history') of evolution." But is it legitimate scientifically to "pick out all the big strawberries

[Thomas H. Huxley (cited by L. L. Woodruff in *The Evolution of the Earth*, 1924, p. 107).]

[59] Haeckel, E.: *The Evolution of Man*, trans. by J. McCabe from 5th ed., New York, 1906, p. 2.

[60] Wallis, W. D.: *loc. cit.*

and put them on top of the basket,"[61] particularly when there is so much underneath that cannot be construed as "strawberries" at all? *Unless all the evidence of homology can thus be explained or otherwise accounted for, it cannot be used as proof to support any theory.* If one were permitted thus to select his evidence, he could "prove" almost anything.

2. *The parallelism of external form becomes more and more "divergent" while that of the internal organs and structures remains relatively "exact."* To attempt to account for this phenomenon on the basis of evolution, it would be necessary to postulate a double influence in the process. The evolution of the viscera must have stopped, other than for minor details, very early in the process, while evolution of external form has gone on apace throughout presumed uncounted millions of years to result in a tremendous diversity of form and size. Why should this be so? Perhaps someone will explain that the great divergence of external form with its dependence upon the skeletal structure is a response to external influences while the similarity of form and structure of the viscera is due to a response to internal stimuli which remain quite constant. One difficulty with this argument is that it does not apply to many of the simpler forms of invertebrates in which divergence of both external form and internal structure exist. Moreover, it would be necessary to prove that heredity has a more immediate and more persistent control over the internal organs than it does over external form, a theory which would be difficult to establish. This principle, therefore, fails to give any definite support to the theory of evolution.

3. *The various organ systems and organs are established on successful functional solutions of a given problem at various levels of complexity, but the fundamental plan is usually in evidence remarkably low in the animal scale.* If evolution were a hit-or-miss chance process and taking place simultaneously in many different places, it is to be expected that a number of solutions of the various problems of function would have been attempted and evidences of these attempts should be found at least as "reminiscences" in the embryo if not in the fossil remains. It is significant that the embryo has failed to "reminisce" on any of the mistakes which evolution must have made by the legion (if any were made at all). Instead, Nature provided a basic plan for the ingestion and absorption of food, for the circulation of the blood, for the excretion of waste products, and for the transmission of nervous impulses, etc. While modified to suit individual differences, the plan for the intake, digestion and absorption of food and the elimination of digestive waste is the same in the earthworm as for man. There has been no evolution of this plan beyond that point. Wherever there is a demand for a balancing mechanism, an arrangement with one essential principle was provided, and there has been no evolution even in the essentials of this plan from the cyclostomes to man. If one were to grant that evolution had taken place he would also be compelled to admit that somehow the process was stopped when the best solution to the problem was reached. But from the standpoint of logic, it is easier to believe that an Intelligence back of all levels of animal life had established a basic plan for the various functions of life and that a single successful principle was used, whenever possible as far as its adaptation to external morphology was concerned.

4. *In contrast to the general principle of parallelism in structure and*

---

[61]Miall, L. C.: *Trans. Brit. Assn.* 1897, p. 682.

*function, another principle of the establishment of an early identity which preserves the individuality of each species presents itself.* These individualities exist early in the embryo, far too early to be accounted for on the basis of ancestry (therefore they constitute evidence of "acceleration" from the standpoint of phylogeny). As shown in the case of the placenta, the excretory system and the brain, similarities as well as differences cut across all ancestral lines to the disruption of most carefully drawn phylogenetic trees. Certainly the evidence on this point fails to support any concept of evolutionary development and does suggest after all there may be something to the older concept that animals have succeeded one another through the centuries, each "after his kind."

5. *In the construction of an identical organ, the embryos of even closely allied species use cells and tissues from various or different sources.* This observation completely destroys any hope of tracing one's presumed evolutionary ancestry, since the lines formed in organ-making, as far as source of material and the organizers which use it, cut directly across the lines of theoretic phylogenetic trees. As DeBeer puts it:

> "The correspondence between homologous structures cannot be pressed back to similarity of position of cells in the embryo or of parts of the egg out of which the structures are ultimately composed."[62]

This fact destroys the whole significance of homology, the last concept upon which the "reminiscences" of evolution are based. Moreover, without the aid of homology there is very little wood left to construct ancestral trees on any basis.

It is obvious that the embryo gives evidences of an individuality, not only of structures but also of the laws which control the development of that individuality. There is no evidence to the contrary, and there is certainly no reason not to believe that this individuality in the process of organ-making has been transmitted indefinitely from parent to offspring. This is perhaps doubly significant since it is in the matter of organs that the theory of recapitulation finds its closest application. This mechanism of organ-making is evidently transmitted on the same basis of other characteristics and supports more specifically the philosophy of a special creation than of evolution.

6. *Experimental embryology has shown that development is the result of a highly organized reaction of various potentialities inherent in the fertilized egg, which powers set about to reconstruct a new creature in a manner characteristic of the individual species.* Experimental investigations have shown that eggs are to be classified on the speed with which they undergo cleavage and develop organ-forming substances; that development proceeds along certain lines of potencies (axial gradients); that while development is begun along such gradients, it is carried along by the presence of chemical organizers which set up a "hierarchy" controlling the development (as far as it can be traced) to considerable detail; and finally, that the function already begun in an organ plays an important part in its ultimate development. This last fact is very disturbing to any purely mechanistic view of embryology. What machine can assist in its own construction while in the process of operation? It has also been learned that deficits or imperfections in the embryo may be transmitted "even unto the third and fourth generation," but that additions cannot be so transmitted.

The theory of evolution seems completely lost in the newer experimental

---

[62] DeBeer, G. R.: in *Essays on Evolutionary Geology, loc. cit.*

subsciences of embryology. In all the available treatises on the subject, *no effort whatever is put forth to show how this new evidence has come to the aid of evolution.* While this may be considered significant only from a negative standpoint, it is certainly evident that even in the mind of philosophical scientists an "explanation" in terms of evolution has not yet been provided. More than this, with all that has been learned about the embryo in the past few decades, De Beer in his latest effort to synthesize embryology and evolution (1940) states: "But since phylogeny [evolution] is the result of modified ontogeny [embryonic development], there is the *possibility of a causal analytic study of present evolution in an experimental study of the variability and genetics of ontogenetic processes.*"[63] Eighty odd years have passed since the theory of evolution was introduced to the scientific world; almost the same number of years have elapsed since the first effort was made to discover in the embryo evidence to support this evolutionary concept. In the half century and more in which experimental work on the embryo has played an important part in the development of the subject, the greatest emphasis that can be placed on achievement in this direction is shown by DeBeer to the end that we are now open to the possibility of investigating the causal factors in present evolution (evolution going on at the present time?) by an experimental study of the variation of the various processes of development and the genetic factors involved. Gone apparently are the hopes of tracing our ancestry in the dim ages of the past. Passed are all chances of proving the processes on which previous evolution has taken place. DeBeer believes that if evolution is going on today we may discover some of its processes. If it is not going on, where has all this prolonged study of the embryo led us, as far as evolution is concerned?

Because attempts to account for the phenomena of development on the basis of causality have failed "since the decay of the evolution theory as a mode of explanation,"[64] one may be pardoned for making an attempt to see what there is to be learned from recent advances in this field viewed on the basis of some "wider category." In the first place, it is learned that tremendous inherent potentialities must exist in the embryo, powers which are supported by, but not added to, by nutrition and respiration. These potentialities are sufficient to start in motion a machine which is not only capable of constructing itself but also of keeping itself running meanwhile. These powers are manifest (experimentally) by the variable potentialities along the axial gradients, subsequently rearranged by the development of chemical organizers, and ultimately reinforced by the functions of the embryo itself. These powers, as well as the structures resulting from them, cut across all evolutionary concepts which have been advanced thus far. They also suggest, by causal analogy, that not only the characteristics of the adult animal but also the very mechanism which produces it, are transmitted genetically from parent to offspring, and that these inherent qualities are to be traced back to some source which possessed them in the first place and started them on their course through history. The embryo has been able to gather nothing new unto itself. It is able to transmit only what it has, although it may be able temporarily to transmit defects due to injuries it may receive.

7. *A study of the embryo indicates*

---

[63] DeBeer, G. R.: *Embryos and Ancestors*, London, p. 98.
[64] Needham, J.: *Yale J. Biol. & Med.* 18:1-18 (Oct.) 1935.

*that its development occurs in accord with the universal principle of "least action."* Had Haeckel really been interested in a universal law, one which he could have applied to plants as well as animals, to biologic forces as well as to physical ones, he might have gone back about a century and restated the one great principle of all creation, the law of "least action" as proposed by Maupertuis. This law states "that in all the changes which occur in the universe . . . that which is called the quality 'action' is always the least possible amount." In other words, Nature takes the shortest possible route in the accomplishment of her purposes. The resulting product of time multiplied by the energy expended is always the least possible amount. This is an end for which human intelligence is constantly striving in the solution of its mechanical problems. Is there, by any possible chance, some Intelligence at work behind this universal law? Is it possible that the principles which control both the great machine of the universe as well as the small one of the bee indicate the existence of a Reason which constructed them and set them running without any lost motion?

The principle of least action, if truly universal, is fatal to the evolutionary concept of embryology. Organic evolution is quite the antithesis of this principle. The almost incomprehensively slow process of evolution as it is generally understood, made necessary by the tremendous complexity of life, as well as the slowness of change indicated by normal variation, is certainly "the longest way around" to the creation of the world. If evolution is a fact, as some scientific philosophers aver, then Nature cast all discretion to the wind in the making of man. Evolution completely denies the principle of "least action" and, if true, constitutes the solitary exception to the rule in the entire known realm

of nature. It must have worked by laws not now existent.

Since, therefore, evolution has failed to account for the development of the embryo, it is legitimate to seek some other philosophy to replace it. Until Embryology has something better to substitute, is it too much to ask for a critical analysis of the only admitted rival hypothesis of evolution, that "outworn and completely refuted idea of special creation, now retained only by the ignorant, the dogmatic, and the prejudiced?"

## SUMMARY

For centuries man has recognized that embryos of different animals, particularly in their early stages, show some resemblance to one another. This "law of embryonic resemblance," subsequently and generally known as "parallelism," was interpreted by biologists living in the early part of the 19th century as indicating an *identity* of these early embryonic forms with the lower forms of life. This erroneous deduction was the result of imperfect observation. When von Baer set himself to make a critical study of the growing embryo, he found that while an embryo of one species might resemble that of another, there was no reason to say that either was identical to a simpler form of animal life. From this phenomenon of parallelism, Darwin made another deduction, i.e., that community of form and structure indicated community of descent, thereby furnishing strong evidence in favor of the theory of organic evolution. Based upon this postulate of evolution, Haeckel constructed a second theory to the effect that the developing embryo was a recapitulation or review of the history of evolution. The passing years and further studies by embryologists have shown that the recapitulation theory is entirely untenable and useless in accounting for the changes observed in embryonic development.

There remained certain features of the embryo, such as the gill-slits, the urinary system, the heart and central nervous system, which were still considered by some to be "reminiscent" of ancestral relationships, reminiscences which are still clung to with the idea that these aspects of parallelism somehow must have evolutionary significance. In other words, these homologies persist as the last embryologic stronghold, not only of recapitulation, but of evolution itself. This last premise is now destroyed by experimental embryology, which shows that homogous structures in the adult or even in the embryo cannot be pressed back into earlier stages of the embryo or the egg. The embryo uses different material under the influence of different organizers to construct these homogous parts. Therefore, from the standpoint of origins, they are completely without significance. The strength of this conclusion is further reinforced by the fact that attempts at classification of embryonic parts on a structural or functional basis have only resulted in complete phylogenetic confusion.

On the other hand, there is much to be said about the phenomena of development which favors the only admitted rival hypothesis to evolution, that of special creation. Not only the hereditary transmission of adult characters but also a similar transmission of inherent powers in the embryo to develop itself along lines which are peculiarly individualistic suggest that such powers were created in the original progenitor of the series. This seems especially true since there is no experimental evidence to show that the embryo can acquire either structural or functional characteristics, although it can transmit temporarily deficits produced by injury.

Perhaps the most weighty evidence of all on the subject is the fact that the embryo develops in accord with the law of "least action," which indicates that in biology as in the physical universe, all functions are performed with the least expenditure of effort (time $\times$ energy). By this token, the embryo does not represent evolution in any sense, for evolution is the world's most outstanding philosophical contradiction to this universal law. It must therefore be concluded that if evolution ever occurred, it did so under laws and circumstances not now existent. This leaves the philosophy of evolution without any possible embryologic proof as far as known facts and laws are concerned. On the other hand, in so far as one can draw deductions from parallelism, the evidence supports the concept of a special creation with the original placement in each animal of powers and potentialities which are characteristic and inherent within the individual and which have not been altered in transmission by any gradual process of change. By deduction, it may reasonably be assumed that when these processes were initiated, it was done in accord with the principle of "least action."

THE

# BULLETIN

OF

# DELUGE GEOLOGY

## AND RELATED SCIENCES

| Volume 2 | September, 1942 | Number 2 |
|---|---|---|

## THE GEOLOGIC AGE OF THE MISSISSIPPI RIVER
### WITH A PRESENTATION OF BASIC FACTORS PERTAINING TO AGE-ESTIMATES OF RIVER DELTAS

### BENJAMIN FRANKLIN ALLEN

The rivers of the world owe their existence, location, and character to the differences in elevation of the land as expressed in mountains, plains and valleys. That this unevenness of surface was originally caused by up-and-down movements of the earth's crust, is apparent. If these movements were of sufficiently sudden and severe occurrence they would have been of a catastrophic nature, the great bodies of water would have been unbalanced and set in violent motion, overflowing the land and creating a fresh surface for the start of entirely new river systems. If it can be shown by accepted facts of geology that the world's present river systems began simultaneously, then it would seem reasonable to conclude that the cause was just such a cataclysm of a world-wide scope occurring immediately prior to their birth.

The delta of a river, built by its conveyed sediments, is the chief source of information concerning the length of time the river has been flowing. The average volume of solid matter carried annually, the yearly increase in the length of the delta, and its total cubic content can all be measured with a surprising degree of accuracy. These facts form the basis for the calculation of the whole period of the river's existence from its origin to the present time. Thus the approximate date when a river began flowing can be established.

If, by this method, fair age-estimates can be obtained of a sufficiently large number of deltas to be considered as fairly representative of the world's rivers, and the life span is found to be substantially the same for all, the significance of such a result would be striking. Automatically the date would seem to be fixed, not only of the beginning of the world's rivers, but of the original catastrophe itself which must immediately have preceded the origin of the rivers.

If the date of this convulsion is

The BULLETIN is published by, and is the official organ of the "Society for the Study of Deluge Geology and Related Sciences." The Editorial Board is comprised of Professor George McCready Price and Dr. Cyril B. Courville. It is printed at the Collegiate Press, Arlington, California. For members the BULLETIN is free, and extra copies40 cents each (each number priced according to size); for non-members it is $2.00 per year; and this number is 50 cents. All correspondence should be directed to the Managing Editor, Mr. Ben F. Allen, 219 North Grand Avenue, Los Angeles, California.

found to correspond, within reasonable limits, to the chronology of the aqueous catastrophe as recorded in sacred history, supported as it is by archaeology, such coincidence will be of vital importance both to science and to religious faith.

*The Mississippi Delta a Special Study.* Inasmuch as the Mississippi river with its delta has been the subject of more scientific study than any other in the world, and since the main problems are very much the same for all rivers, it has been selected as an example for special study and will be given examination in detail. Basic principles pertaining to age estimates of all deltas will also be presented. Though given at the risk of tiring some readers, this careful attention to detail is indispensable to the main object of establishing a reliable basis for calculating age-estimates of all rivers. While firmly establishing the age of the Mississippi river, the object of this study is also to lay a foundation for age-estimates of other rivers.

It should be borne in mind that the present paper is intended as little more than a suggestive outline of the subject, which it is hoped others may be encouraged to follow in a more comprehensive investigation. In the present paper, only the age of the Mississippi river will be calculated.

THE PROBLEM AND ITS OUTLINE

For more than twenty-five years there was a disagreement between Sir Charles Lyell and General A. A. Humphreys over scientific interpretations with regard to the age of the Mississippi river delta. Sir Charles Lyell, professor in Kings' College, London, and leading English geologist of his day, had estimated its age as 60,910 years.[1] General Humphreys, by different methods, had estimated it as from 4,400 to 5,000 years.

During a large part of that time Humphreys was in charge of the U. S. Army Corps of Engineers working on the river and delta, and, with his staff of experts and the aid of professor E. W. Hilgard, state geologist of Louisiana, and other contemporary geologists, had accumulated a vast array of facts and a thorough knowledge of the whole delta area.

Hilgard quotes Humphreys as saying in an early report: "The river is flowing through the delta region in a channel belonging to an epoch antecedent to the present."[2] Lyell had challenged this statement. The contest was on, and has continued to the present day, into the second or third generation of geologists.

There are seven general features of the problem which should be considered. (1) Is the channel bed of the river antecedent to the river? Could the bed of the river have been an estuary? (2) What is the significance of the layers of gravel beneath the river, the Gulf, and the delta, and do they demand cataclysmic waters for their origin? (3) Shall we accept General Humphreys' data, and the reports of his staff, as the approved basis for the age of the delta? (4) Do the subsequent and latest views on the factors vital to the age of the delta, which sharply oppose each other on certain items, still fairly sustain the originally discovered facts? (5) The main problem being the general theory of deltaic subsidence, does the actually observed subsidence in the Mississippi delta, considered in the light of the established principles of geo-physics, sustain that theory? (6) Is Lyell's estimate of the age of the delta based upon a consistent concep-

---

[1] Lyell, Sir Charles: *Principles of Geology,* 9h Ed. 1853, pp. 271-275.

[2] Hilgard, E. W.: Report on the Geologic Age of the Mississippi River Delta, *Report of U. S. Army Engineers,* 1869-1870, p. 352.

tion of its depth? (7) Do Humphreys' two methods of calculating the age of the delta rest upon a reasonable interpretation of all available facts, and do they properly check with each other?

The most important question of all is the theory of deltaic subsidence. It assumes that deltas, by their increasing weight, depress the crust of the earth, and thus grow downward many times faster than upward. The data given here mainly refer to the Mississippi delta, though the opposing general theories are discussed. In order to make clear first the less technical features in preparation for this problem, and to give an adequate conception of its significance, this discussion of subsidence will be reserved till the last, just before entering upon the final computations of the age of the Mississippi delta.

### THE "ANTECEDENT BED"

Hilgard and the U. S. Army Engineers had discovered what they interpreted to be an ancient "estuary bottom", extending some six hundred miles up the river, as far as to Cairo at the mouth of the Ohio. Into the sediment forming this ancient bed, the river had cut its channel from low water downward through many of its strata.

This same material had been found, so they stated,[3] beneath New Orleans in an artesian well, the log of which had been carefully preserved. In this well the upper stratum, approximately 38 to 41 feet in thickness, was of typical delta alluvial deposits. The bottom of this stratum was marked by a thin layer of white quartz sand at the 41-foot level, which was the beginning of a distinctly different formation, carrying layers of a certain "blue clay" interspersed with other clay and layers of various types of sand and shell fragments—this being the first occurrence of the shells. This formation continued on down to the bottom of the well, a depth of 630 feet.

These men pointed out that the depth of the Gulf on each side of the delta corresponded with the 41-foot level of the well. All along its lower course the river deepens from 150 to 200 feet in places, and in its bed they found the same ocean shells. The supposition of these engineers was that the present river is flowing over the site of an ancient "estuary," its bottom now deeply eroded by the river. Hilgard,[4] in describing it, said: "It is shown that the delta, or alluvial deposits proper, cover the older formations to a comparatively slight depth only, the river running on paludal [marshy] deposits and then on an ancient sea-bottom of corresponding age, from above New Orleans to near its mouth."

Another more recent authority is cited by Trowbridge,[5, 6] who says: "The whole of the immediate valley of the river in the driftless area of Wisconsin, Illinois, Minnesota and Iowa, appears to have been cut out since the close of the Tertiary, and there is no evidence that the river existed in Tertiary time. The Pliocene Citronelle formation, the outcrop of which is crossed by the river above Baton Rouge, is not a part of the delta, and was eroded by the river so that it forms the erosional walls of the valley there."

---

[3] Hilgard, E. W.: loc. cit., p 354.

[4] Hilgard, E. W.: Upper Delta Plain of the Mississippi, American Naturalist, Vol. 4, Nov. 1870, p. 638.

[5] Trowbridge, Arthur C.: Building the Mississippi Delta, Bulletin American Assn. Petroleum Geologists, Vol. 14, pt. 2, 1930, pp. 167-192.

[6] Matson, G. C.: (Special Ref. by Trowbridge) The Pliocene Citronelle Formation of the Gulf Coastal Plain, U. S. G. S. Prof. Paper 98, 1916, pp. 167-192.

Hilgard[7] long before had pointed out the nature and order of the various deposits in this supposedly old sea-bottom beneath the river. First there was found the very thick strata far beneath the bed of the river consisting of ocean sediments containing marine shells, mingled with land sediments. This, as was later discovered, reached to a depth of 3,000 feet, where a layer of coarse gravel was spread out under the river and delta and well out into the Gulf and under all the north Gulf Coast states.

Much nearer the surface were found other layers of similarly wide extent. These layers constitute the "antecedent bed," the first consisting of coarse sediments, pebbles and gravel mixed with sand and clay, which he called "Orange Sand." Next above came the "Bluff," or "Loess," thought to have been originally a wind-blown deposit brought from the north by the supposed estuarian waters, and spread out over the "Orange Sand." Apparently it fell from the atmosphere *in standing water,* by no means river water. Then followed the fine "Yellow Loam" mixed with clay, which seemed more like the deposit of strait-like waters from the glaciated area, but not by river action.

Each of these layers was laid down evenly and, regardless of topography, at much the same thickness all over the bottom of the supposed "estuary." After these came the formation of the "upper terraces," which was pointed out as of ocean origin, and the "lower terraces," the formation of which was attributed to the river.

*The Meaning of the Terraces.* Terraces along river valleys are ancient shore lines, or strand lines, originating from two sources: the lower were cut by rivers and occur only in connection with them, sloping with their gradients in every case. The upper, or higher terraces were cut by the ocean and can be traced for the most part around the continents of the world. They follow their own ocean level, independently of the river terraces, around all ocean embayments, and up all river embayments as well, which proves that the ocean was over all so-called "estuarian" river beds.

Hilgard's view regarding the oceanic character of the Mississippi "antecedent" bed receives strong confirmation in the fact that wherever these higher terraces are found in deltas the world over, they lend themselves only to the interpretation of true ocean terraces, but never as river terraces. Had they been formed by gigantic rivers in a past era, *then in connection with them would be found the remnants of gigantic deltas, and these do not exist anywhere in the world.* There are plenty of gigantic sedimentary plains reaching down into the water, but these are not deltas, and cannot be attributed to rivers.

Professor Price[8] recently reviewed the subject of terraces which in all their aspects bear an important relation to Deluge Geology.

*Significance of Pebbles Beneath River, Delta, and Gulf.* Hilgard[9] described his conceptions of the causes of widespread pebbles and sediments, as follows: "The great torrent which spread the northern drift is seen to have swept over the southern coast with sufficient force to transport pebbles of five or six ounces in weight [one third of a pound] from far distant regions, the nearest being Tennes-

---

[7] Hilgard, E. W.: On the Quaternary Formation of the State of Mississippi, *American Journ. of Science,* Vols. 41, 42, 1866, Sec. Ser., Art. 30, pp. 311-325.

[8] Price, George McCready: Visible Proofs of the Flood, Its Universality and Its Recency, *Bulletin of Deluge Geology and Related Sciences.* 1941. Vol. 1, pp. 109-114.

[9] Hilgard, E. W.: Upper Delta Plain of the Mississippi, *American Naturalist* Vol. 4, 1870, p. 638.

see and Arkansas." Note the recent confirmation of a much deeper bed of gravel by a later geologist: "Gravels below New Orleans, thought to be equivalent in age . . . lie at least 3,000 feet felow sea-level. . . . Pleistocene glaciation caused streams to carry heavy loads of gravel and other debris, overloading them to such an extent that they anastomosed and spread their coarse deposits widely over the Gulf Coast States."[10]

Another recent authority says of the shallow bed: "Littlefield, who made a special study of the bars below the mouth of the Arkansas river and found that between 400 and 700 miles below Cairo there was a gravel bar consisting of pebbles as large as 64 mm. [about two and one-half inches] in diameter just downstream from almost every bend, concluded that most of these gravels were locally derived from a valley fill, probably of Pleistocene age. He said, 'Below the mouth of the Red River the quantity and size of the pebbles decrease, except where the river crosses the Citronelle formation, and no gravel was found in the lower 150 miles of the river.' "[11, 12] This interpretation of a "valley fill" conforms approximately to the findings of Hilgard in the local well at New Orleans, that no gravel was found in the delta, but coarse white quartz sand at a depth of from 38 to 41 feet, and between that and eight inches farther down "chiefly coarse silicious

sand, part sharp, mixed with fragments of shells."[13]

Trowbridge, in describing the gravels out in the Gulf off the delta, said:[14] "The coarsest sediment shown on the map by the oblique lines which lies on the surface of a submarine dome[15] that stands more than 100 feet above its surroundings, did not come to the Gulf through the river, at least not through the river as it is now."[16]

After making every effort to uphold Lyell's view of the depth of the delta, but still expressing doubts, another reputable geologist[17] makes a more recent statement concerning these sediments: "Even more necessary are further offshore investigations, where the pioneer work of Trowbridge has indicated some of the many problems awaiting solution. Glauconite[18] is said to be present 'on the outer steep slope of the Gulf bottom,' and coarse sediments cap mounds well beyond the pass mouths on the floor of the Gulf."

GRAVEL CALLS FOR WATER
CATACLYSM

The utter impossibility of transportation by the river of these great strata of gravel-bearing clay and sand should at once be apparent. Not only is the gradient of the whole valley too slight to admit of it, but our greatest rivers in capacity and power afford no comparison to the magnitude of force, volume and expanse required for such a transcendent accomplishment. Add to this the phenomenon,

---

[10] Russell, R. J., Russell, R. D.: Mississippi River Delta Sedimentation, Recent Marine Sediment, A Symposium, 1939, p. 174.

[11] Trowbridge, Arthur C.: loc. cit., p. 874.

[12] Littlefield, Max: Mississippi Gravels Below the Mouth of the Arkansas River, (Abstract) Bull. Amer. Geol. Soc., Vol. 38, 1927, p. 147.

[13] Hilgard, E. W.: Report on Geologic Age of the Mississippi Delta, U. S. Eng. Rep. 1869, 1870, p. 354.

[14] Trowbridge, Arthur C.: loc. cit., pp. 890, 891.

[15] Perhaps an uplift from a deep salt deposit which occurs abundantly to the westward. One topped with gravel was found on the upper delta.

[16] Gilbert, G. K.: The Transportation of Debris by Running Waters, U. S. Geological Survey, Prof. Paper 86, 1914, pp. 225-227, 246, 247.

[17] Russell and Russell: loc. cit., p. 174.

[18] An ancient ocean-bottom concretionary formation.

impossible to a river, of distinct lay-eration with each layer composed of its own peculiar grade of sand, the differing layers ranging from the finest to the coarsest, with the interspersion between of other layers of the finest clays — clearly, *overspreading waters laid down one kind at a time,* impossible for a river.

Then, capping off the whole series of pre-river formations, is the final overspreading layer of "Yellow Loam," apparently not greatly altered or shifted by the waters. But as though these all were still not convincing enough, the climax of evidence is furnished by the deposits of seashells in the sands and clays of some of these underlying layers. In the face of these astounding facts, Lyell's doctrine of uniformity breaks down completely —and just where it is counted on most heavily.

The gravels and sands are much coarser in the upper regions of the deposits, becoming less coarse as the Gulf is approached. It was perhaps this fact that led the geologists to believe they were dealing with river action, especially since there is a river there now. Even Hilgard, whose more acceptable theory of a "great torrent that produced the northern drift" of coarse gravels, shells and landward fragments, and "swept over the southern coast," did not seem to realize that it could not have been river action. A gradient such as that of the Mississippi, at least from Cairo on down to the Gulf, would be utterly insufficient for the task, much less an estuary such as Hilgard postulated, with its opposing force of ocean waters and the tides opposing the river waters.

Nowhere in operation today can be found an example of such a tremendous feat of transportation. Catastrophic action is apparently demanded.

*General Humphreys on the Foundations Beneath the Mississippi Delta.*

The long and close personal study given to the river and delta by General Humphreys, with his staff of engineers, and Professor Hilgard and other eminent geologists called in for collaboration, lends great weight and authority to his official findings, more than to those of more widely known geologists who visited the area only briefly.

During their practical labors, Humphreys and his associates observed and identified in many localities the same "Blue Clay" as that discovered in the artesian well at New Orleans. In this well the blue clay first appeared at a depth of 41 feet, and frequently from that depth downward.

Following is General Humphreys' summary of the main facts he offered concerning the Blue Clay and the depth of the delta:

### "THE BLUE CLAY"

"*Inferences Respecting the Blue Clay and Facts Bearing Upon Its Probable Age.*

"The facts are very important for they prove either that the peculiar Blue Clay in the bed of the river is alluvial deposit, or that the thickness of the alluvial stratum in the delta region has been greatly over-estimated, and that the river is flowing through it in a channel belonging to a geological epoch antecedent to the present. The following data have been collected:

"1. *Its physical characteristics.* The clay is quite different in appearance, color, etc., from any deposit now made by the river. As long as it remains wet, it seems nearly insoluble, resisting for years the strong current of the river. If it is thoroughly dried, however, and then again placed in water, it rapidly disintegrates into a powder. The clay itself has a somewhat gritty feel between the teeth and a peculiar taste. It effervesces less with acids than the present deposits of the river, judging by the samples of the latter collected by the survey.

"2. *It underlies the Yazoo Bottom* below the great sand stratum, if we may judge from the fact that it constitutes the bottom of the Yazoo and the Sunflower rivers, as well as that of the Mississippi; and all three are on the same level.

"3. *It underlies the Vicksburg Bluff,* which is a Tertiary formation. In this bluff it underlies the stratum which contains marine shell, and which Sir Charles Lyell and Dr. Harper both pronounce Eocene Tertiary; that is, it is the oldest Tertiary stratum. . . . It undoubtedly underlies other of the river bluffs. . . . It is visible only at low water.

"4. *It underlies New Orleans* [below 41 feet] in strata alternating with sand and marine shells for at least 630 feet, as shown by the artesian well which was begun in that city in February 1854 and carried to that depth. Dr. N. B. Benedict, recording secretary of the New Orleans Academy of Sciences, in behalf of a committee of that body, of which he was a member, devoted himself to the study of the well, securing samples of every stratum pierced, and otherwise thoroughly investigating the subject. . . . The geological age of the strata pierced is well established, but it is evident that none below the depth of 41 feet from the surface were deposited by the river. The same must be acknowledged in reference to the channel of the river itself, for it is identical in character with the sample of the very last stratum, which was presented for comparison by Dr. Benedict. . . . [Here follows the log of the well as prepared by the Academy.]

"5. *It crops out under sandstone on the east coast of Texas.* Mr. A. M. Lee, of Knoxville, Tennessee, an engineer of high scientific attainments, formerly of the army, states that this identical clay with which he is familiar, crops out under calcareous sandstone at a depth of 24 feet below the level of the Gulf at Aransas Bay and Lagune Madre on the coast of Texas.

"6. *It possibly underlies the Estacado.* (A well was drilled by Capt. John Pope, Topographical Engineer) . . . . The close analogy between the physical characteristics of such a formation and that underlying the Vicksburg Bluff, together with the similarity of the supposed geological ages, suggest that they may be identical. . . .

"7. *Found in the Missouri River Valley.* Lieutenant S. K. Warren, Topographical Engineer, states that this peculiar Blue Clay very closely resembles a formation which covers a great area in the immediate valley of the Missouri east of the Black Hills. His geological assistant, Dr. Hayden, assigns a place for this formation near the middle Cretaceous, and describes it as follows: 'Bluish and dark-gray plastic clays, contain-

ing *Naubilus De Kayi, Ammonites placenta, Baculites ovatus,* and *B. compussus,* with numerous other marine molusca. . . . remains of *Mosasauras.* Thickness 350 feet'. . . ."[19]

*Gulf Depth Compared.* Humphreys, in a letter to Colonel Theodore Lyman, well summarized his data, saying:

"There can be no misapprehension as to the identity of the clay found below the depth of 41 feet in the artesian well with that in the bluffs at Columbus, Vicksburg, etc., and in the bed and channel-way of the river. There is an unmistakable difference between this clay and that deposited by the river. . . . Further, the original depth of the Gulf of 41 feet at New Orleans is at least as great as that of the Gulf off the coast of Alabama and Mississippi, where the sandy bottom indicates that the original marine bottom has not been covered with the mud of the Mississippi river."[20]

He then refers to maps published in his Professional Paper 13, herein frequently quoted from. These maps give the contours drawn from extensive soundings by the U.S. Coast Survey, showing that there is no reason for supposing the bottom of the delta to be any deeper than the bottom of the Gulf on each side where no river sediments have been deposited upon it.

Concerning this point, he wrote to Sir Charles Lyell, as follows: "When I came here in the fall of 1850, I was familiar with your views upon the subject, but I could not accept them. There was no instance on the whole Tertiary coast of the United States of a sound, or bayou inlet of a sea, with the great depth which you assigned to the ancient sound into which the Mississippi river originally emptied. Nor was there anything in the form

---

[19] Humphreys, General A. A., and Abbott, Major H. L.: Report of the Physics and Hydraulics of the Mississippi River, *Prof. Paper* 13, *U. S. Army Corps of Engineers,* 1876, pp. 92-95.

[20] Humphreys, Gen. A. A.: *U. S. Engineers Report,* 1869-1870, p. 376.

and character of the adjacent coast and country to render such an original depth probable."[21]  The coast country is low and flat.

*Portales' Report of the Coast Survey.*  Portales, a leading authority on shore and ocean geology, dredged samples of the clay formation from the bottom of the lower part of the river and delta from Carrolton to the mouth.  These contained, besides the characteristic clay, corals and marine shells in abundance.  In the summary of his report to General Humphreys, he said: "The most general conclusion which can be drawn from this examination is the confirmation of your opinion that the bed of the river is not composed of recent alluvium, or in other words, that the river has not contributed to any considerable extent to the formation of its bed in the localities examined, but in flowing over a former sea-bottom."[22]

Of the peculiar clay beneath the river and delta, (after over 30 more years of research,) Hilgard says: "This is called the 'Blue Delta Clay' by Humphreys and Abbott; it will here be called Port Hudson Clay, because it is entirely independent of the modern delta formation built up by the river."[23]

Again, at this late date, 1912, speaking of the formations below the Blue Clay, he said: "But these formations, as well as the Port Hudson Clay, have nothing to do with the present problems of the delta, beyond serving *as the floor on which it is built forward.* The depth of the sands and silts of the true delta is from 30 to 40 feet, and rarely reaches 60 feet."  Elsewhere in the same paper he said: "As is well known, a continual shelf covered by a comparatively shallow depth of water,

runs out for 30 miles beyond the present mouth of the river, then breaks off into the deep waters of the Gulf.  The original stratum of this shelf is the Port Hudson Clay, (the 'Blue Clay' of Humphreys and Abbott) : but this is now coming to be gradually covered with the delta deposits and river sediments."

## LATER VIEWS VS. UNDISTURBED ORIGINAL FACTS

The old controversy still has not come to an end. But the basic facts supporting these older views are still acknowledged to a surprising degree, though interpretations may vary.  A study of the late literature discloses that many of the detailed data and thorough observations which determined and supported the older views are now seldom considered. They are lost or ignored beneath the weight of standard geological doctrines that postulate the very slow but continuous general upheaval and subsidence together with other features of uniformitarianism.

Forty years after the appearance of the Humphreys-Abbott report, even as late as 1912, Hilgard, then at the University of California, and still the leading authority on the Mississippi delta, noted that the well-established facts which he and Humphreys had patiently established were being ignored by later men, regardless of the absence of anything new by way of refutation of the original conclusions. Even today their careful and accurate report seems to be among the most valuable of all geological contributions to the subject.

That some still hold to the old view that the river cut its channel through a Tertiary sea-bed is shown by the short statement by Mr. Trowbridge[24]

---

[21] Humphreys and Abbott: *loc. cit.,* pp. 647, 648.
[22] Humphreys and Abbott: *loc. cit.,* pp. 647, 648.
[23] Hilgard, E. W.: The Mississippi Delta, *Popular Science Monthly,* Vol. 80, 1912, pp. 238, 239.
[24] Trowbridge, Arthur C.: *loc. cit.,* p. 868.

given previously and here repeated: "The whole of the immediate valley of the Mississippi river in the Driftless Area of Wisconsin, Illinois, Minnesota, and Iowa, appears to have been cut since the close of the Tertiary, *and there is no evidence that the river existed in Tertiary time.*" He continues, stating that this condition extended down approximately to Baton Rouge. Here, he says, the delta begins, and "does not, as many textbooks teach, extend up to the mouth of the Ohio river and include all of the Tertiary formations of the Mississippi embayment."

Another view, almost opposite to this, yet bearing out some of the main fundamentals of the older view, was expressed as late as 1941. As these late geologists view the size of the delta, instead of its being from 12,500 to 12,600 square miles in area as originally estimated by Lyell, Hilgard, Humphreys, and others, the position is taken that it "extends from Louisiana to central Texas," and begins in southeastern Missouri, progressing 600 miles southward. They say: "More than 200,000 square miles have been filled by the river to depths ranging from something over 100 to more than 12,000 feet; and the river has probably been working several million years to make the deposits."[25] Yet continuing they make the following statement as to the character of the bed on which the river flows, which, after all, is basically not far from the older views: "The 200,000 square miles of the landward part of the delta was once all sub-oceanic, so that, in drilling wells through the delta sediments, most of the material encountered were deposits below the sea. This is determined by fragments of sea shells found in well cuttings."

As to the depth of the river sediments, they wrote: "In drilling wells for oil or water in the delta, drills cut through a few feet to possibly 100 feet of sand and clay deposited above the ocean level. Below this are found a few feet deposited in shallow water, and below that a few thousand feet of clay and fine sand deposited far from shore." The "100 feet deep of sand and clay" coincides with the Hilgard-Humphreys report that the delta is 100 feet deep at the outer part. But that it is "deposited above the ocean level" is questioned, especially if applied anywhere on the real delta, because at its highest point up river it is not over 15 or 20 feet above sealevel and less than that in its lower parts, most of it being only five feet or less. In this report, however, the distinct identity of the bottom of the real delta and the original bottom of the Gulf can be easily seen; though why these geologists should add to the deeper "few thousand feet of clay and fine sand" the words, "deposited far from shore," is not apparent. *Such materials are certainly not being deposited now in any sea "far from shore,"* a fact to which authorities on shore deposits abundantly testify.

Thus we see that Benson and Tarr, while extending the delta to such extreme widths, still constructively admit that it is as shallow as reported by the Humphreys group. Trowbridge, on the other hand, while still clinging to the excessive depth advocated by Lyell, flatly disagrees with Benson and Tarr as to the wide extent of the delta. He would narrow it down even more than the original workers. Though holding opposite opinions on these vital points, these men all agree to excessive age-estimate of the delta involving many millions of years, *and use opposing arguments to sustain it.* Yet none of them offer any newly discovered facts of importance; and no facts at all that in any way invalidate

[25] Benson, E. B., and Tarr, A. W.: *Introduction to Geology*, 2nd Ed. 1941, pp. 116-118.

the careful work of those earlier geologists, but they ignore many basic facts upsetting to their theory. It would seem that the late opinions are governed more by the standard doctrines of uniformity than by any new supporting evidence. The original position of the Humphreys group, the only one ever held with any unanimity, is still apparently the only logical position to hold, as all subsequent discoveries, though meager, seem to harmonize with it.

Dana[26], also one of the former generation of geologists, demonstrates that the Mississippi river alone, with its generally agreed sedimentary load of 1/2600 of the bulk of its water, *could fill the whole Gulf of Mexico with silt in only* 10,400,000 *years.* And this period is not far from the figure vaguely intimated for the delta alone by these later and more doctrinaire geologists than Dana.

Benson and Tarr, as well as Russell and Russell, and also Trowbridge, take the position that the 30 to 100 foot delta of Humphreys, Abbott, and Hilgard is only the "top-set bed" of the real delta, that is, only that part laid down above the ocean water by river overflow. Subsidence, they say, enables a delta to grow downward hundreds of times faster than upward. But, if the delta "has been working several million years to make the deposits", as they claim, why is not this top layer hundreds of times thicker than the bottom layers? Why does it not constitute almost the whole supposed thousands of feet, since only the original shallow depth of the Gulf shore there could form the bottom-set and fore-set beds?[27] This position thus breaks down under mere logic.

It has become clear that the general theory of deltaic subsidence is the most important obstacle to establishing the age of any delta. If true, especially would this apparently forbid the possibility of any two or more rivers being the same age. Lyell insisted that the necessary variation in the rate or amount of subsidence of different deltas renders any general coincidence in the age of the rivers of the world utterly impossible.[28]

## THE SIGNIFICANCE OF DELTAIC SUBSIDENCE

All geologists assume that deltas subside, but they do not agree as to the cause or extent of that subsidence. The main issue is the question of whether the sediments merely settle into more compact form, or the crust of the earth itself actually gives way beneath their weight, or whether both occur.

Obviously, this question is most fundamental, especially in its relation to the depth of deltas. Therefore, because it is so vital in calculating delta age, it has been reserved to the last.

In discussing the general features of the problem, certain questions naturally present themselves. (1) How is the basis of the theory of deltaic subsidence related to uniformitarianism, and how is it applied to the Mississippi delta? (2) What is the relation of the ocean and river terraces to the supposed subsidence of the Mississippi delta, and do they prove the general theory? (3) Does the supposed deep trough or syncline beneath the Mississippi delta agree with field observations, and with the principles of geo-physics involved? (4) Does the relative thickness of the beds of deltas, as compared with that of the beds beneath them, indicate that such subsidence has occurred? (5) Are local earthquakes which are accompanied by sinking of land proof of the general subsidence theory? (6) Do the facts from coal deposits sustain

---

[26] Dana, James G.: *Manual of Geology*, 1896, p. 191.
[27] The beds laid down beneath the water.
[28] Lyell, Sir Charles: *Principles of Geology*, 1853, 9th Ed., pp. 285-286.

the theory that coal was formed in subsiding delta swamps? (7) Can lava flows and extensive erosion cause lands to sink or to rise, or, do the observed conditions defeat the theory of current subsidence and upheaval?

Though to the lay reader these questions may seem extraneous to the main subject and objectives, it will soon become apparent that they go to the most vital parts of the whole problem of the geologic age of the Mississippi delta and other deltas. Nearly all of the data are from the Mississippi delta, and the remainder are pertinent and necessary in establishing the broad general principles of *a long-needed science of delta formation,* on which to base age estimates of the Mississippi river and other rivers of the world.

*The Basis and Implications of the Theory.* The general theory of crustal deformation is based on the supposition that vaguely-defined forces beneath and upon the surface of the earth are continuously exerted to cause changes of level, both of subsidence and emergence. Excepting the work of erosion, these forces are credited with producing the continents, the islands, the mountains, the valleys, and also all irregularities of surface under water. Almost infinitely slow movements, acting through eons of time, are postulated, though certain movements are supposed to be more rapid than others. This is the principal feature of the doctrine of uniformity and one of the main supports of the theory of geological evolution. But it is very vague and vulnerable to attack.

As applied to deltas, it teaches that the crust of the earth is depressed or bent downward by the weight of the increasing delta sediments. The accumulating sediments in all basins are supposed to be depressing the bottoms of these basins so as to make room for more and more of the sediments. The theory teaches that deltas grow downward hundreds of times faster than upward, and that after a billion or more years an extremely thick bed of deltaic sediments results. This body of sediments is called a "lens," because it is supposed to be very much thicker in the central portion than around the edges.

Typical uniformitarian views are expressed by Russell and Russell[29] as follows: "Louisiana and the adjacent areas in Texas and Mississippi have been the theater of deltaic sedimentation for such a long period of time that it is impractical, if not impossible, to assign either date or stratum of rock as marking the beginning of Mississippi river history."

Every sedimentary layer from the surface down to an unknown depth where there is no more mingling of ocean fossils with land fossils, they conceive to be the work of delta-sedimentation. Describing it, they say: "The geo-syncline[30] presumably has been increasing in depth, and the base of the Tertiary is thought to lie possibly as deep as 30,000 to 40,000 feet in the vicinity of New Orleans." Clearly, these men out-Lyell Lyell, doubtless who would have been pleased to know of such a vast increase in the estimated depth of the delta, and therefore of its age.

*The Evidence of the Terraces.* These men report that in the central part of the state of Louisiana, certain of the highest ocean terraces above the alluvial plain of the river slope slightly more than do the lower terraces along the river. They stress this fact in support of their theory, reasoning that in the immense lapse of time between the making of these two sets

[29] Russell and Russell: *loc. cit.*, pp. 156-171.
[30] The supposedly deep and subsiding trough of deltaic sediments.

of terraces, the delta subsided enough to cause this difference, which is only from one to two or three feet per mile.

These isolated terraces are more than 100 miles from the delta and many miles from the river itself, toward the west on the edge of rising land. It would seem that they are too far distant from the delta to bear any particular relation to it.

Professor Price has shown that these upper terraces were not formed by the river at all, as were the lower terraces, but by the ocean itself before the river existed.[31] This view was originally brought out in detail by Hilgard, in presenting his evidence of the supposed estuary of pre-river history; and he voiced the opinion of the entire Humphreys group. Price suggests that all of the ancient ocean beaches may have been only very temporary, the result of a brief halt in the general withdrawal of the oceans from the lands; or that each of these strand lines might have been cut by a single storm. The depth of the ancient beaches cut by the waters is only trivial compared to modern beaches, and this is generally true the world over. He also offers and approves the generally accepted view that because these ancient strand lines as a whole have the same elevation above the oceans all the world over, they mark retrogressive stages by which the oceans, due to some general or very large subsidence somewhere on the ocean floor, sank to their present level. He suggests that the occasional local and irregular tilting of these old ocean beach lines may indicate that while parts of the ocean floor were then undergoing final adjustments, *so also were parts of the land.* Indeed this would be seemingly inevitable.

From the viewpoint of the student of Deluge Geology, these ocean terraces were apparently cut while the sediments were freshly deposited. The sediments were especially deep toward the Gulf where they would settle the most. Therefore, if not disturbed, they might naturally have tilted somewhat in that direction. No doubt there might be found some of these irregular lines that show a northward slope. The ocean terraces often are locally tilted in other parts of the world. In any case, no dependence can be placed in them to shed light on the subsequent formation of the delta. They are too far away from the delta. Besides, the greatest degree of tilting claimed is not worth considering by comparison with the extreme tilting that would be indicated if caused by the enormous delta subsidence (30,-000 to 40,000 feet) which these men postulate.

Russell and Russell further insist:[32] "Evidences of subsidence are so overwhelming in the lower parts of the delta, and agree so closely with the hypothesis that subsidence is the result of sedimentary loading, that escape from the idea that deltaic sedimentation is the most potent factor in the Gulf Coast disastrophism[33] seems impossible." They describe the subsidence of Indian mounds, buildings, streets, and other landmarks, and sum up as follows: "Survey markers near the mouths of the most active passes[34] subside at the rate of nearly eight feet a century. Twenty miles inland the rate is about two feet a century." The facts here brought out are all granted, but they appear directly against the theory propounded.

[31] Price, George McCready: *loc. cit.*, pp. 109-114.
[32] Russell and Russell: *loc. cit.*, pp. 156-171.
[33] Crustal deformation caused by sinking.
[34] Water passages or mouths.

*They merely indicate that the fresher, softer, and deeper the sediments are, the more and faster they settle.*

*The Geophysics of Subsidence.* According to this theory of delta subsidence, not only the immediate site of deposition settles, but the weight of the delta supposedly depresses the crust of the earth in the whole surrounding region, carrying down with it the entire delta and vicinity. The crust of the earth is supposed to be rigid enough to cause this.

Geologists point to certain lakes and embayments on the far flanks of deltas, affirming that these were carried downward by the regional subsidence of the deltas. From the principles of geo-physics, the most rapid subsidence should be *beneath the center of gravity of the delta as a whole.* From this point the subsidence should be less in all directions. This is the theory of the formation of the geo-syncline or deepening trough through the continuous deposit of sediments. But as a matter of fact, the actual subsidence is *most rapid in whatever portion of the delta the deposition happens, for the time being, to be greatest.* Such locations may be many, and the areas of deposition may vary in size, and shift about widely from time to time, each perhaps sinking at a different and changing rate. These facts, seemingly so fatal to the modern interpretation of deltaic subsidence, are ignored by proponents of the theory.

Inasmuch as the theory of deltaic subsidence is thus lacking in the proper geo-physical behavior essential to the theory, the existence of these lakes and bays can be attributed just as well to other causes. Now, as always, they occupy delta areas farthest from the river and have been least affected by sedimentation. River overflows lose most of their sediments within a mile or two after leaving the river. It would seem, therefore, that they merely have not as yet been filled up, or that sedimentation is too slow or has not as yet been sufficient to overcome the local settling of the sediments they have received.

The theory of the deltaic geo-syncline demands a downward dip on all sides toward the delta to indicate the 30,000 to 40,000 feet of thickness claimed for deltaic material by Russell and Russell, the present leading proponents of the theory. If Trowbridge's claim be allowed of a small delta area of about 150 miles long by 50 or 60 miles wide, this great depth within such a small area would call for the strata to dip at an extremely steep angle, causing a syncline that would be nothing but a deep sinkhole. But though these same authorities are also leading oil geologists and as such would never think of drilling into a syncline for oil, and though their sole purpose in recent studies of the delta region has been to understand the relation of modern river deltas to the formation of oil, and though oil is now being produced from beneath parts of the delta, yet, not one stratum has been reported from those wells as actually indicating any syncline.

There is also another very significant fact that stands squarely in the way of this theory. The famous "Blue Clay" that underlies the delta and the Mississippi river above for several hundred miles, instead of dipping steeply underneath the delta as called for by the syncline theory, follows the present Gulf bottom gradient without deviation or break all the way underneath the delta and all the surrounding regions.

*Shallowness of Deltas Misinterpreted as Subsiding Top-set Beds.* Bear in mind how the capping of all of these supposedly deep beds with only the thin top layer from 20 to 100 feet thick is utterly inconsistent with the "deep delta" theory. These men hold that this cap is the top-set bed, the bed formed above the level of the Gulf after the delta had emerged from the ocean, *formed by river overflows on land.* Their theory is that, as it thus formed, it was gradually lowered by regional subsidence. But they say the many thousands of feet of deltaic sediments below it were laid down *under water,* (some say, "far from land"). Now the thing that seems to defeat this theory is *the thousand-fold thickness of those underlying beds as compared to the supposed top layer.* If this top layer has been growing thicker and pressing down the delta for millions of years, *why is it so remarkably thin as compared to the beds below it?*

Could the bottom beds be also thousands of times thicker, by subsidence, than the depth of the Gulf at the cite of the delta? In other words, how could beds 30,000 to 40,000 feet thick be laid down in water only 20 to 60 feet deep? It would seem, also, that the up-river part of the delta, that nearest the original shore, *the oldest part,* in that case, *should have the deepest top layer,* under the theory, *instead of the shallowest, because it has had the longest period above water.* Therefore, logic alone seems to defeat this theory. How does it happen that this supposed top layer is so thin *in all deltas* as compared to the thickness of the theoretically deep deltaic beds below them?

The marvel of geologists (from their viewpoint) is this extreme shallowness of deltas, or what some presume to be the top layer only. It is little wonder that some of them have invented the theory that these thin deltas are only the top-set beds of the supposedly very deep deltas which supposedly "have grown hundreds of times faster downward," by subsidence of the crust of the earth by the mere weight of the sediments. On the shallowness of the deltas, in flat denial of this theory, the following statement is by perhaps the leading authority on the origin of sedimentary strata:

"The depth of delta deposits on modern sea coasts varies greatly, but is, on the whole, comparatively slight. Thus the mud of the Nile delta is not over 10 to 15 meters thick. It rests on loose sand. The delta deposits of the Rhine have a thickness of 60 meters, those of the Rhone over 100 meters. In the Po the depth average is 122 meters, though near Venice 172.5 meters were penetrated without reaching bottom. The delta deposits of the Ganges and Bramaputra rest on the older sediments and average only 20 meters in thickness. The actual delta deposits of the Mississippi range from 9.5 to 16 meters at New Orleans, increasing to 30 meters at the head of the passes."[35]

It is suggested by a co-worker that, inasmuch as deltaic sediments are mostly laid down under water, and therefore displace the water, their downward pressure is thereby so greatly reduced that little weight is left to exert pressure on the bottom. Such sediments being of very light material anyway, he says the added weight is so small that the theory of deltaic subsidence is rendered all the more untenable. The terms of the theory of deltaic subsidence counteract this suggestion largely, however, by the postulation that, through millions of years, sediments many times deeper than the water have gradually subsided, and that, by comparison, the weight of the water is now insignificant. Besides, the claim is made that, after the delta is built up and becomes land, still the subsidence continues by the deposit of alluvium from river overflow. However, suggestions like this are helpful, because, in discussing them, added light is thrown on the subject.

*"The Legerdemain of Local Upheavals."* Trowbridge, strange to say, he being an advocate of the general

[35] Grabau, E. W.: *Principles of Stratigraphy*, 1923, pp. 609, 610.

subsidence theory, very logically rejects general subsidence as applied to the Mississippi delta. He writes as follows:[36] "The total amount and rate of settling have not been determined. The settling is probably due to the compacting of the underlying sediments, rather than to disastrophic[37] subsidence of the delta as a whole, and to superficial drainage and decay of vegetable matter."

So many opposing views existing among these recent delta authorities, reveal a weakness in their theory, and invoke most favorable impressions of the Humphreys group, the only set of workers yet to agree on a mutual interpretation of all the basic facts.

Earthquakes in river valleys which were accompanied by some subsidence, and at least one such occurrence in a delta, have often been strongly urged as examples of subsidence caused by sedimentation. A small area just above the delta of the Indus subsided slightly on the occasion of an earthquake. Another example was the New Madrid earthquake in the Mississippi valley in 1912, though this was some hundreds of miles above the delta. Geologists who endeavor to use such occurrences in support of the subsidence theory seem to forget that deltas and river valleys are no more subject to such phenomena than most any other part of the earth.

Hilgard, in his report to General Humphreys, criticises this theory thus: "Much has been said of the possible effects of earthquakes which so frequently startle, for a moment, the inhabitants of the Mississippi valley; and it is more than likely that the record of such events as those of New Madrid and Reelfoot lake will be found stamped on many dislocated strata hereafter. But there is a wide difference between such effects and the legerdemain machinery of 'local upheavals' which is so readily resorted to by amateurs for the explanation of any unusual phenomenon."[38]

Though there is little likelihood that this was intended as applying to Lyell, yet Lyell was perhaps the originator of the application of these particular earthquakes to the theory of delta subsidence, if not the original proponent of the theory itself. He strongly contended that delta subsidence rendered impossible the accurate estimation of the age of any delta, and for this reason he especially opposed the idea that the rivers of the world could be of the same age.

*Deltaic Subsidence and the Swamp Theory of the Origin of Coal.* In support of the general theory of subsidence or changes in level as applied to deltas, the theory is frequently urged that coal was formed in deltaic swamps or where marine remains are present in estuary swamps.

Not only is coal presumed to have been formed in deltas, as a consequence of their gradual subsidence, but coal formation is also pointed to as proof of the general subsidence theory of deltas. It is used both as proof and as the thing to be proven. Therefore a brief examination of the facts about coal formation and deltas is necessary, and doubly profitable. Coal theories are so closely connected with the whole subject of delta formation that *no adequate conception of the problems and principles of deltas is possible without putting those theories to the test and proving that they are false.*

The veins or seams of coal are said to be buried and carbonized remains of vegetable swamp-mud, principally

---

[36] Trowbridge, Arthur C.: *loc. cit.*, p 874.
[37] Pertaining to the forces which have disturbed or depressed the earth's crust.
[38] Hilgard, E. W.: Report on the Age of the Mississippi Delta, *U. S. Engineers' Report*, 1869, 1870, p. 365.

of timber or other vegetation that has grown in swamps which later have become sunken, and been buried where it grew by deposition of silt; after which other growth has appeared and in its turn been sunken and buried, and so on, endlessly, the process repeating through millions of years on end. Accumulation of vegetation sufficient to produce a single vein of ordinary thickness is supposed to have required a long geologic period.

The kinds of vegetation, so far as identified, that have been converted into coal in supposed estuarian swamps, are the same, generally speaking, as those found in coal fields of supposed deltaic swamps. This means, if this coal-origin theory be true, that the plants which grew in brackish, or saline environment, *are the same kind as plants which grew in fresh water swamps.* Yet today with few exceptions, plants grow only in either one or the other of these two opposing environments, *but not in both. The same is true of fish life.*

Of course, in an ocean delta all degrees of salinity may be found, depending on whether river or ocean water locally predominates. These conditions might change from time to time. But in a coal-mining area, such fluctuations seldom, if ever, occur. At times, fossil deposits known to have come from the deepest parts of the ocean are found interlayered with coal. Frequently coal is interlayered with coarse gravel, and often with coarser conglomerate. Even large rocks, called "erratics," sometimes appear. Yet no delta in the world today contains any sediment coarser than sand. It should be apparent that all of these conditions not only point away from the deltaic and swamp theory of the origin of coal,

but especially oppose the estuarian origin of coal formation.

Sometimes, protruding up through many layers of sediment (representing, so they say, as many geological ages) tall trees, petrified or carbonized, have been found, some in upright position, but most of them oddly slanting.[39] Such trees may appear with tops that have not suffered from weather, wear, or decay, any more than their root ends, before being transformed into their present state. Because of this phenomenon, geologists hesitate about assigning to the layers of these particular formations the millions of years they habitually assign to layers elsewhere exactly the same except for the position of the fossil trees.

In a supposed coal-bearing swamp thus silted up many feet deep, always deeply enough to bury standing trees, why should not large numbers of trees be found in a standing position? Why are they practically all prone as though having drifted to the location? (And bear in mind that this discussion omits consideration of the coal beds themselves.) These questions are still unanswered.

A single coal deposit consisting of many seams, one above another, contains almost exactly the same kinds of plants throughout, *even to the outer edges.* But in the natural swamp forest today, the kinds of plants vary from time to time, not only as to kind, but as to location in the swamp, and may change almost completely within a man's lifetime. Moreover, as to location, they may differ in kind from place to place in the area, especially from the center toward the outer edges. This leads to the next question: How could a swamp subside at the exact rate necessary for the growth of almost identically the same kinds of plants throughout the entire area

---

[39] Lyell, Sir Charles: *Elements of Geology*, 5th Ed., 1868, pp. 481-488.

of the swamp, and do this while it was passing through changes constantly for millions of years? And how could a single standing tree be found extending up through them all?

Of the few instances where coal and peat have been found beneath deltas, Lyell and others have made the most in an effort to bolster up their theory.[40] But they ignore the fact that coal and peat are found also, and much more abundantly, under the rivers themselves farther upstream, and under other rivers and even in far distant hills and mountains, having no relation either to rivers or deltas. Furthermore, the apparent insincerity of the claim that coal is a deltaic swamp product, or the product of any other kind of swamp, is revealed by the fact that there appears to be no record of any modern delta or swamp having produced coal, *or ever having even been prospected for coal.* Why should not *at least a few such swamps* be still in process, with many rich beds of coal beneath as the finished product?

In concluding this discussion on coal and deltas, a sample statement is in order from those who aver the delta-swamp theory, to illustrate the attitude which they take (but also to show their agreement with the writer on the recent age of two great deltas):

"The Ganges annually carries across its delta to the sea sufficient sediment to cover one square mile 221 feet deep; the Mississippi annually discharges into the Gulf of Mexico sufficient to cover one square mile 268 feet deep. Apply these figures to the hypothetical case, and assuming that one half of the discharge goes to make foreset beds by which the delta is built outward, it is seen that the Ganges would completely reclaim this area in 4,524 years and the Mississippi in 3,730 years. These, however, are two of the greatest rivers. But even if the Carboniferous rivers [the supposed Car-boniferous geologic age], discharging across the region of the Appalachian coal fields, delivered but one tenth part of the detritus borne to the sea by the Ganges and the Mississippi, it is seen that the transgressive effect of the supposed subsidence would be completely nullified in periods of 45,240 and 37,300 years."[41]

In other words, Dr. Barrell is so sure that subsidence exactly keeps pace with deposit that he depends upon subsidence to be in exact proportion to the deposit. This is the essence of the doctrine as applied to coal formation. Hence, he infers that, if the supposed carboniferous-age rivers maintaining the great Appalachian coal-making swamps were only one tenth the size of the two large rivers which he names, those ancient deltas would require just ten times as long to subside an equal amount, thus exactly keeping pace with deposit. But the whole theory has been shown to be untenable by abundant data.

For these and many other reasons, the idea that coal is a delta product and therefore affords proof for the subsidence theory is rejected. European geologists, as a rule, do not hold the swamp theory of coal-formation.

*Lava Flows as a Factor in Surface Depression.* There are many hundreds of square miles of lava flows in the world, some of them many thousands of feet thick. The lava habitually sought out and flowed down valleys, often over sedimentary deposits of great thickness. But although lava is a great deal heavier than sediments of any kind, especially deltaic material, in no case did it cause subsidence, at least not enough to be reported by geologists. Why do we not have huge geosynclines of lava layers? The fact is that geologists, in view of their firmly held crustal-depression theory, have

[40] Arber, E. A. N.: *Natural History of Coal,* 1912, pp. 101, 102, 114, 127, 128.
[41] Barrell, Joseph: Relative Geological Importance of Continental, Littoral, and Marine Sedimentation, *Journal of Geology,* Vol. 14, 1906, p. 456.

long marvelled that lava has not depressed the crust of the earth.

As an explanation of this paradox, leading authorities offer the argument that since the lava flow is the result of expansion from beneath, there is no actual addition of load to the earth's crust. This may be granted, but it would seem that the very expansion of the underlying material would render it all the more susceptible to the compression demanded by this theory of depression.

The question still persists, Why may ordinary sediments depress the earth's surface, and yet lava, which is many times heavier, even though it buries these sediments by many thousands of feet, fail to add weight sufficient to cause such depressions?

Again, lava has been known in many instances to flow with great thickness farther than the length of any river delta in the world. In these cases, the transported lava did not represent any expansion of the underlying material, but was an actual addition to the weight upon the crust where it accumulated. Yet no subsidence from this cause has ever been reported. Thus the contention that crustal subsidence is the result of transfer of sediments from one part of the earth to another, in which river flow is distinguished from lava flow, is without foundation. This subject is given a typical geological discussion by Dr. Charles M. Nevin,[42] who takes the usual viewpoint, but who admits there must be something wrong somewhere.

If overloading is the cause of subsidence, then it stands to reason that a condition the reverse of overloading would give a result the reverse of depression, namely, elevation. All geologists admit that the large valleys were formed by erosion. The amount of material eroded out must have been many times greater in weight than that composing deltas. Yet, admitedly, in no case has appreciable elevation resulted from loss of load, another enigma to uniformitarians. Nevin admits this also.

These same geologists who contend so strongly for depression of the crust of the earth by deltaic overloading, admit that many individual mountains standing apart exist as separate units "by reason of rigidity of the earth's crust" to use Nevin's words. Would it not seem rather queer, then, that a few feet of vegetable swamp mud, *nature's lightest sediment*, should be so potent?

*Summary of Delta Subsidence.* Seven lines of evidence have been introduced which apparently disprove the theory that delta sediments depress the crust of the earth:

1. The argument drawn from the slight slope towards the Gulf of some of the upper terraces in central Louisiana is nullified by the fact that these are not river terraces, but ocean terraces having no relation to the delta as such, but maintaining in general a constant level all over the world. Other reasonable causes are assigned for occasional irregular local tilting. Even if they were river terraces they are too distant to be depended upon as guides in delta subsidence. Such isolated cases would require multiplying a hundredfold to provide evidence for the 30,000 to 40,000 feet as claimed.

2. The true principles of geo-physics would require greater subsidence at the center of gravity in the delta as a whole than at other points, whereas actually deltas are found to settle most rapidly at any point where fresh sediments at the time are being deposited.

3. Though recent geological opinion affirms that the Mississippi delta lies in a deep trough, or geo-syncline, yet the Blue Clay that has been shown to

---

[42] Nevin, Charles M.: *Principles of Structural Geology*, 1931, pp. 233, 234, 263-266.

underlie the whole delta, in no instance dips to accommodate such a geo-syncline. Moreover, the drilling of many oil wells throughout the whole region reveals no strata that indicate such a structure.

4. Earthquakes, as a cause of subsidence, are ruled out, being no more frequent in river deltas and alluvial lands than elsewhere; one case only having been reported, that of the Indus.

5. Every attempt to prove that coal formation demands conditions afforded by the theoretically subsiding modern delta or estuary is apparently frustrated by numerous facts regarding coal that disprove the swamp-coal theory, and the subsidence theory as well.

6. Lava flows apparently block the general theory of local flexibility of the earth's crust. Though much heavier than delta sediments, lava flows do not depress even the sediments, much less the crust of the earth.

7. Conversely, no erosion has been enormous enough to relieve the internal pressure sufficiently for the crust to rise; and large outlying mountains are admittedly dependent for their existence on the rigidity of the earth's crust.

In view of the foregoing facts, the theory of general subsidence will be disregarded in the present paper in calculating the age of the delta of the Mississippi river or the age of the delta of any other river.

THE AGE OF THE MISSISSIPPI DELTA

Having thus made clear the main issues in the controversy, the way is now open to deal directly with the mathematics of the age of the Mississippi delta.

*Sir Charles Lyell's Estimate.* Sir Charles Lyell's own account of his calculations on the delta's depth and age follows in part:[43]

"When I visited New Orleans in February, 1846, I found that Dr. Riddell had made numerous experiments to ascertain the proportion of the sediment contained in the waters of the Mississippi; and he concluded that the mean annual amount of solid matter was to the water as 1/1245 in weight, or about 1/3000 in volume. From the observations of the same gentleman, and those of Dr. Carpenter and those of Mr. Forshey, our eminent engineer, the average width, depth, and velocity of the Mississippi, and thence the mean annual discharge of water, were deduced. I assumed 528 feet, or a tenth of a mile, as the probable thickness of the deposit of mud and sand in the delta; founding my conjecture chiefly on the depth of the Gulf between the southern point of Florida and Belize (a city on the lower delta), which equals an average of 100 fathoms, and partly on some borings 600 feet deep in the delta at New Orleans, in which the bottom of the alluvial matter had not been reached. The area of the delta being 13,600 square miles, and the quantity of solid matter annually brought down by the river being 3,702,758,400 cubic feet, it must have taken 67,000 years for the formation of the whole, and if the alluvial matter of the flood-plain above the delta be 264 feet deep, or half that of the delta, it might have required 33,500 years more for its accumulation, even if its area be estimated as only half that of the delta, whereas it is in fact, larger."[44]

Lyell later accepted a slightly higher annual water discharge from Mr. Forshey, the engineer, which, as Lyell said, "would diminish by one eleventh the number of years required to accomplish the task alluded to." This reduces his estimate of the age of the delta to 60,910 years.

The writer questions Lyell's assumption of 528 feet as the depth of the delta, because, first: In the log of the well at New Orleans, at this depth there occurred no change in fossils or other materials from those

---

[43] Lyell, Sir Charles: *Principles of Geology*, 9th Ed., 1853, p. 273.
[44] Note by Lyell: "The calculation here given were communicated to the British Association, in a lecture which I delivered at Southampton in September 1846." (See *Athenaeum Journal*, Sept. 26, 1846, and *Report of British Association* 1846, p. 117.)

immediately preceding, and there was nothing at 528 feet to mark the termination of a stratum. On the other hand, the sediment at that depth was decidedly different from that above the 41-foot level, *which did very definitely mark a geologic horizon* both in fossils and in the character of inorganic materials. Second: the method followed by Lyell involves a great inconsistency. In selecting an average depth, he takes the average depth from the delta to the tip of Florida, which takes in the deepest part of the Gulf, running to 946 feet, and takes no account of the shallow waters that lie along the shore on the site of the delta. Why should he do that? Besides, the bottom of the formation not having been reached at the bottom of the well at New Orleans, the choice of even the bottom would have been illogical. Much more accurate and reasonable appears to have been the method of Humphreys in plotting on his map (published in his Professional Paper 13, already referred to) the contours of the whole Gulf, and then choosing the depth along the coast on each side of the delta corresponding in distance with the delta from the general shore line. This Humphreys found to be approximately 40 feet for the middle part, but 100 feet for the outer edge. Third: Lyell's position that the delta could not start till the river had filled up its flood-plains is seemingly not tenable, as the river is still filling up its flood-plains though it has built its delta; and this is true of all rivers with flood-plains and deltas. Therefore his call for a separate period for that purpose, though seemingly plausible, cannot be granted.

*Hilgard on the Depth of the Delta.* Lyell had not only challenged in Humphreys' former report the state-

ment that "the river is flowing through the delta region in a channel belonging to a geological epoch antecedent to the present," but also had suggested that the log of the New Orleans well be examined by a competent geological observer, not having made such examination himself, apparently having seen only the written account of the log drawn up by non-geologists of the local Academy of Science. General Humphreys, therefore, appointed Professor Hilgard, state geologist of Louisiana, to make the investigation.

But the Civil war interfered and Hilgard's report was not published till 1868. From that report is taken the following statement: "The annual, or in a sense the rather mensual floods of the river ought to cause a much more frequent alteration and change in the character of the deposits than is actually found, especially in the lower portion of the profile."[45] He further reports that an occasional fragment of decomposed or partly lignitized wood is found in the deposits below 41 feet, but that the true river sediments above that depth besides having the larger fragments, are permeated with fine crumbs or grindings of wood, by the wear of the river.

Thus Hilgard points out that the *extreme thickness of the layers below the 41-foot level is incompatable with river action,* and that this view is further supported by the difference in wood fragments, none ground fine by river action appearing below the 41-foot level. In this connection he says: "Sir Charles Lyell still inclines in a measure to the opinion that the strata penetrated in the New Orleans well may be delta deposits. This supposition, however, appears to be incompatible, not only with what we already know of the general geology

---

[45] Hilgard, E. W.: Report on the Geologic Age of the Mississippi River Delta, *U. S. Engineers' Report,* 1869-1870, pp. 352-361.

and geological history of the lower Mississippi valley (as shown in former papers), but with the character of the strata themselves. *They are altogether too prevalently of a marine character, so far as examined.*[46]

The same opinion is given by Trowbridge.[47] He and others admit that the layers beneath the 41-foot level are to a large extent contemporaneous with the shellfish living today in the Gulf. Many authorities place these shells back in the Pliocene; but Hilgard, in his table, comparing the shells found below 41 feet at New Orleans with those thought to be of the Pliocene and post-Pliocene on the coast of South Carolina, and comparing these both with those now living in the Gulf, says that for the most part these shells are apparently of one series. He makes the astonishing statement:[48] "Moreover, not only the leading shells of the New Orleans strata, but the *entire list*, excepting the new species, might be picked up in an hour's time on the beach of any of the islands of the Mississippi Sound." One would conclude that the situation shown by this testimony does not lend consistency to the theory of the geologic ages.

In Hilgard's log, in this same report, no shells are listed till a depth of 41 feet and 8 inches is reached, and then he mentions "a few shell fragments." At 41 to 42 feet, he says he found "coarse rounded sand, with numerous shells, mostly broken, quite hard *Mactra lateralis, M. Sayi, Arca transversa, Cardium magnum, Tellina flexuosa, T. tenta, Lucina costata, Venus crebraria, Astarte lunulata, Pandora trilineata, Oliva literata, Natica pusilla, N. campeaehensis, Acus dislocatum, Marginella limatula, Bullina cassaliculata.*"

Continuing in his report, he described the findings at 543½ to 546 feet, as follows: "Coarse white beach sand, with numerous shells, *Mactra lateralis, Area transversa, A. ponderosa, Lucina costata, L. multilineata, Pholas costata, Artemis concentrica, Cardium N. sp.* [same as at 43 to 56, and at 235 feet]. *Bullina canaliculata, Olive mutica, Pleurotoma carinum, Buccinum acutum, Natica pusilla, Dentalium sp.*"

Notice the similarities between shells found at a depth of from 543 to 546 feet with those at from 41 to 42 feet. One naturally is led to wonder why Lyell, who chose 528 feet as the average depth of the delta, could not just as well have chosen 41 feet, *and better, because it marked the only distinct transition in the whole log.*

Hilgard's report especially shows the changes in the minerals composing the sands and clays below 41 feet to be far too extreme and abrupt to have been laid down from a river channel, where the grains would be mixed and remixed continuously as they were carried along by the river, producing a more homogeneous deposit. These abrupt extremes tend to show that the sediments have been brought in large quantities at a time and from different directions, as by oversweeping continental w a t e r s. There is abruptness also in the changes in nature of the sands, much of which is too coarse and too sharp for river sedimentation in that delta. There is nothing like it in the present Mississippi delta.

*Humphreys on the Age of the Delta.* Only the small lower end of the delta has a depth of 100 feet, and this lessens gradually all the way up to the other end. At New Orleans, about half way up to the head, the depth

46 Hilgard, E. W.: *loc cit.*, pp. 361.
47 Trowbridge, Arthur C.: *loc. cit.*, pp. 874-876.
48 Hilgard, E. W.: *loc. cit.*, pp. 354, 357, 359.

is 41 feet. Therefore, Humphreys chose 40 feet as the average depth of the delta.

Humphreys, with his background of thorough knowledge and vast data, offered several corrections to Lyell's estimate of the amount of sediment carried annually in the waters of the river. He found that more sediment is carried than Lyell has allowed, and especially that large amounts of solid matter are being constantly rolled along on the bottom of the river-bed, of which Lyell had taken no account.

Humphreys also brought more accurately into calculation the bayous, the outlets, and the subsidiary rivers, as well as the delta itself. He made different estimates from different conditions, using alternative sets of figures, in one set taking into account rivers and territory not included in the other, thus providing a scientific countercheck on each estimate. He had all territories and rivers involved carefully platted on maps and charts by the engineers in his department. In a letter to Lyell, he said:

"Now, using the red curves of No. 1, and adopting 40 feet as the mean depth of the alluvium inside of the 10-fathom curve, we have 4,900 years as the age of the delta. [The Tansus river bottom is included in this computation, and in the one following.]

"Using the red curves of No. 2 and the mean thickness of 40 feet for the alluvium inside the 10-fathom curve, we have 5,400 years for the age of the delta.

"The first agrees better than the second with the age computed (4,400 years) from measurements upon the progress of the river into the Gulf, which afforded a means of determining the age of the delta independently of any knowledge of the quantity of earthy matter held in suspension by the river water or that moved along the bottom of the river."[49]

This next method referred to (the result being 4,400 years) is very much simpler than the other, and supplies a countercheck. Humphreys

averaged *the yearly rate of advance of all of the mouths of the river into the Gulf,* and then *divided that rate per year into the total number of miles up to the head of the delta to get the age of the delta.* He said: "It is assumed that the rate of progress has been uniform to the present day . . . and there are some considerations connected with the manner in which the river pushes the bar into the Gulf each year, which tend to establish the correctness of that position . . . the number of years which have elapsed since the river began to advance into the Gulf can be computed. The present rate of progress of the mouth of the river may be obtained *by a careful comparison with the progress of all of the mouths of the river,* as shown on the maps of Captain Talcott, U. S. Engineers, 1838 and the U. S. Coast Survey in 1851—the only maps that admit of such a comparison. They give 262 feet for the mean yearly advance of all the passes (mouths)."[50] Therefore, the 262 feet, divided into the total distance to the head of the delta, (1,-152,800 feet) gives 4,400 years as the age of the delta.

The writer might be inclined to add two or three feet to the 40, because possibly New Orleans might not be quite far enough down the river to represent the cite of average depth. Two more feet would make it 4620 years.

Still another estimate based on Lyell's figures of annual discharge of sediment and area of delta, by which he produced 60,900 years, is offered by the writer, discarding Lyell's depth figure of 528 feet, and using Humphreys' more reasonable figure of 40 feet for the depth of the delta. This 40 feet is about 7½% of 528 feet, and the result would be 7½% of Lyell's

49 Humphreys and Abbot: *loc. cit.,* p. 649.
50 Humphreys and Abbot: *loc. cit.,* p. 466.

age estimate of 60,900 years, or 4,567 years. This is not too far from Humphreys' 4,400 years, and almost equal to his other estimates, and the two additional feet in depth would make it remarkably close.

*Is This the Total Age of the River?* Humphreys said: "The age of the delta has been estimated at 4,400 years, upon the asumption that the river was of equal magnitude during the whole of the period of its delta-forming condition. This assumption implies that the river was suddenly brought into existence with its present condition, or was suddenly converted into that condition. The rapid, simultaneous upheaval of the whole basin of the river would have brought that river suddenly into existence with very much the same characteristics that it now possesses; but geologists do not admit the possibility of such a rapid upheaval."[51]

Humphreys then defeats the geologists' theory of supposed very slow uplift. He had previously cited the constant presence of the pre-river "Blue Clay" at the river's low water mark; now he says that no such alluvium is found higher than the high water mark in the present river. Therefore, he asserts, no delta was uplifted, as in such case its remains would have been cut into, with remnants left. This sound conclusion gives expert confirmation to other evidence submitted against the theory of general upheaval and subsidence.

He then postulates the condition of the possible river before it was delta-forming, saying that it must have been a clear river with no floods and therefore no sediments. He proposed the possibility that the 300-foot gorge between St. Louis and Cairo could for a time have impounded the river behind it while it was being cut down, thus depleting the water of its sediments. He reasoned that the 300-foot fall to the Gulf from the bottom of this cut would not be sufficient to cause a muddy stream.

As to the length of time involved, that would depend upon the hardness of the material in the cut and the depth of the water that was doing the work. From modern and recent detailed observation, geologists are in possession of very surprising data as to the rapid cutting power of water.[52] It is likely that this particular formation is only soft sandstone and shales, with possibly parts consisting of unhardened materials. Postulating the Genesis flood, and that this cut was made during the run-off of the waters before much hardening of materials in those strata had taken place, a comparatively short time only was necessary to make this cut.

A SURVEY OF THE EVIDENCE

After about a century of diligent geological study of the Mississippi river and its delta, much of it devoted to various features bearing on the age of the river, reasonable conclusions based on acceptable facts now seem to be justified. Sir Charles Lyell had estimated its age at 60,900 years. But General Humphreys, who, with his staff of engineers and geologists, had charge of the delta for twenty-five years, and Hilgard, studying it until thirty-five years later, accumulated vast data which have apparently never been superceded by subsequent discoveries. Their basic evidence appears to prove that the river has been in existence only 4,400 to 5,000 years. Facts developed since then seem only to strengthen this conclusion.

The main features may be stated briefly as follows:

1. *The Pre-River Formation.* Recent oil geologists find the deepest

---

[51] Humphreys, Gen. A. A.: *loc. cit.*, pp. 446, 447.
[52] Price, George McCready: *New Geology*, pp. 142, 143.

layers to consist of fine land sediments apparently deposited far from land but somewhat interlayered with ocean sediments, a phenomenon totally unknown to present geological processes, though fitting remarkably well with Deluge mud settling in deep waters during that postulated catastrophe.

Tending to show the erratic and at times extremely violent nature of those waters thus in commotion, there is that great layer of gravel some 3,000 feet beneath the whole region of the north Gulf coast, underlying the delta and well out into the Gulf. Another witness to that overspreading torrent is the bed of gravel and clay nearer the surface, also spread out as widely, far wider than any river could spread it, into which the river has cut its channel for hundreds of miles. The source of this gravel is thought to be the glacial region of the north, the size of the gravel decreasing as the Gulf is approached. All of this, including the ice and water as the source of the gravel and the clay, is well in line with Deluge Geology.

Upon this bed of gravel and clay was deposited a great mantle of wind-blown material, a feature of almost world-wide occurrence. And this, too, coming as it did late in the Deluge period, and possible only in a world barren of vegetation and subject to extremes of temperature which could produce the wind, is acceptable to the catastrophic theory. The original investigation of the pre-river foundation of the Mississippi apparently demonstrated that this wind-blown material fell into the supposed pre-river estuary and settled without being extensively transported. Still above this came the "Yellow Loam," a fine loamy clay brought in by supposed *estuarian* waters, and still prior to the birth of the river. All of these layers were called the "antecedent bed" of the river which subsequently appeared and cut down through them

all and into the layer of gravel and clay.

2. *The Deposits Impossible by River, Estuary, or Normal Ocean.* No river of the gradient of the Mississippi could have transported or deposited such underlying strata as the gravel. The lack of speed and power to transport and spread out such material, much less distribute it so evenly over such a wide area, appears to rule out river action. But very much less could such deposition have been accomplished by an estuary, not only because of a lack of sufficient gradient, but because of the constant buffeting of tides with river flow. The ocean in normal behavior is also out of the question. The finer materials, especially the loess, apparently fell from the atmosphere into standing water periodically in commotion and at rest but not of a river.

3. *Only Oversweeping Ocean Capable of Forming the Deposits.* Waters not now acting anywhere in the world are demanded, waters covering the whole region, at varying depths and at various speeds. The extremes between coarse gravel layers and the finest clay, sand, etc., all equally spread out, seem to demand these variations and this agency. The beds of gravel mingled with clay do not so much represent gravel alone carried along by torrential waters as they do the whole being forced along *as a single viscous mass* by deep waters oversweeping these wide areas in great force. This type of deposit is common throughout the world and diligent study should be given it. The heavy material pushed bodily along the bottom of all deep and rapid streams is a feeble example, the best that nature now affords in operation at present. For nearly a century certain geologists have freely granted that, should the earth be suddenly disturbed in its rotation, the crust would convulse and the waters would

produce just such a debacle as Deluge Geology postulates.

4. *The Size of the Delta.* There was no marked difference between Lyell and Humphreys as to the size of the delta, the main point at issue being the depth. But later geologists, ignoring the findings of these early workers, have gone to extremes in both. Some, while still retaining Humphreys' shallow depth averaging about 40 feet, would spread it out all over the southern Mississippi valley and north Gulf coastal plain. They claim an area of 200,000 square miles instead of the 12,600 to 13,500 of Lyell and Humphreys. Others would retain the small area, or even narrow it down still more, but make a veritable "bottomless pit" syncline of it, 30,000 to 40,000 feet deep. But for such sink-hole no proof whatever is offered, and in fact, oil-well logs bear out Humphreys' figures as to the depth and as to the utter lack of any such syncline.

5. *The Theory of Changes in Level.* The most potent obstacle to any dependable basis for the depth and therefore the age of the delta has been the theory of subsidence and upheaval, especially the theory of general subsidence by the weight of deltaic sediments. But the identical "Blue Clay" found at the water's edge up-river was found 40 feet deep at New Orleans and on the Gulf bottom on each side of the delta, and this fact seems to defeat that theory. Again, if the theory were true, the delta *as a whole* would subside, *and the subsidence would be greatest at the center of gravity of the delta as a whole.* Instead, the most rapid subsidence is wherever the most rapid deposit of fresh sediments happens to be going on.

The theory of the swamp origin of coal is urged by those who hold the general subsidence theory, *and they point to this theory of the origin of coal as proof of the general subsidence of the deltas.* But this theory of coal is very vulnerable and easily disproven and is not held by European geologists generally.

Lava flows, though often thousands of feet thicker and much heavier than delta sediments, do not depress the crust of the earth, and do not even depress sedimentary layers. Conversely, the most deeply eroded areas on earth have never been known to rise on account of that erosion.

For all of these reasons the general theory of subsidence is rejected in estimating the age of deltas.

6. *The Depth of the Delta.* Having disposed of the theory of general subsidence as applied to deltas, the many simple facts of the delta of the Mississippi adjust themselves easily as to its depth. At New Orleans it is 40 feet deep, and 100 feet at its outer edge, and this is well in agreement with official topographical surveys of the Gulf bottom on each side of the delta, and with the "Blue Clay" in the river at corresponding depths. Considering these facts it is difficult not to accept the 40 foot *average* depth chosen by the Humphreys group. (The author would perhaps deepen this estimate two or three feet, inasmuch as New Orleans is apparently not quite far enough south to represent the place of average depth. But this would not greatly lengthen the age of the delta.)

7. *Age Estimates.* Except in the matter of his chosen depth of 528 feet, Lyell's final estimate of 60,910 years was otherwise based on fairly acceptable data. With the 40-foot depth instead of his 528-foot depth, the age of the delta by his calculations is well within range of that of the Humphreys group. The two methods used by Humphreys form a balancing check on each other that lends confidence to the results.

## CONCLUSIONS

That the age of the Mississippi river is within the general range of 4,500 to 5,000 years, in view of all of the facts and principles thus far brought out, now seems beyond much doubt. How it could be substantially increased or decreased is difficult to see. Suppose it were doubled, or quadrupled, such a period would still not be a start toward the immense ages required by the uniformitarians. Even Lyell's estimate, though satisfying the requirements of the geologic age theories of his day, would have to be multiplied several fold for the standard doctrines of today, which demand millions of years instead of thousands. Therefore, any changes in the estimates which would lend any comfort to the evolutionary theorists are almost unthinkable.

The question at once presents itself as to how a great river system like the Mississippi *could thus suddenly come into being except by a geological revolution practically continent-wide.* Since there is no sign of any other river system having previously occupied that vast area, or any part of it, such a cataclysm seems to be demanded, a complete and profound reworking of the crust of the earth to great depths. Furthermore, it is a river system eroded on a surface which was itself the obvious result mostly of water action but *vastly different from river action or any other geological work by water action known today.*

A mere glance at the size, depth and character of the other deltas of the world should impress anyone that they may well be virtually the same age as the Mississippi delta. All of the facts and principles developed in this present study will be of vital application to the other deltas and rivers, and these remarkable results for the Mississippi delta form the basis for age estimates of other rivers of the world.

Labors on several other natural chronometers involving geological processes, besides the growth of river deltas, are apparently developing, each with considerable capacity for accuracy, and they will be of utmost value in correlating and counterchecking. Altogether, there appears to be some promise of satisfying all reasonable doubts *not only that the Flood of Noah was universal,* but that *it occurred well within the range of dates set by sacred writings and archaeological evidences.*

## DISCUSSION

*Dr. Courville*: If, as some geologists claim, the Mississippi delta is 30,000 to 40,000 feet deep (having supposedly subsidided that much in the course of many millions of years as it was pressed down into the earth by its own weight), at what depth are stumps and trees found which must have grown on its surface during this interval and which would be covered up and carried down with it?

*Mr. Allen*: This is a legitimate question. There is abundant proof of the settling or compacting of the sediments in the delta. But this occurs predominantly where the sediments are being freshly deposited. It has practically ceased in the upper portion of the delta. The six or seven miles of subsidance was postulated by Trowbridge, but, strangely enough, he is the one who gives the following information, which answers your question:

*"Stumps Deep Below the Surface*: In these sediments are many undecayed stumps, some of which are at least as low as 12 feet below sea level. The trees grew on swamps much as they do today, and later the sediments settled, carrying the stumps down with them." (Trowbridge, Arhur C., Building the Mississippi Delta, *Bulletin American Petroleum Geologists,* Vol. 14, Pt. 2, 1930, p. 874).

Twelve feet of settling, especially over the lower portion of the delta, is easily accounted for, and is fully in harmony with many other independent facts. But if Trowbridge's six or seven miles of subsidance were a fact, a gradually decaying or carbonizing series of stumps, logs, and other vegetation should appear in position of growth much of the way down, certainly as far down as the postulated top-set beds should extend, many thousands of feet instead of only twelve, according to that theory.

*Dr. Courville:* You cite data from the Humphreys group of geologists that there is no bending down of strata that should indicate that the Mississippi delta has subsided, despite the theories of Trowbridge and others. Is this true of deltas generally and can you present positive and authoritative statements to this effect?

*Mr. Allen:* Let the following from Grabau answer your question: "The numerous (20 or more) well borings made in the confluent deltas of the Po, the Etch and the Brenta, in the region of Venice, have revealed the fact that the structure of the delta is an extremely heterogenous one. *While the beds are, in general, horizontal, with only minor undulations,* the succession is scarcely the same in any two bore holes. This proves that the beds of the delta form a succession of lenticular masses [shaped like lenses] of very limited extent. Only two sandy layers, carrying water, have proved to be in any way constant; all other layers quickly wedge out latterly." (Grabau, A. W., *Principles of Stratigraphy,* 1924, p. 613).

*Question by member:* Both the six-or-seven mile deep but small delta, as inferred by some, and the extremely large but shallow delta favored by others, seem grossly inadequate to contain the vast amount of sediment which would necessarily be deposited during the many millions of years which both of these groups of geologists postulate. Isn't there a serious discrepancy here?

*Mr. Allen:* You are correct. These geologists leave this matter all too vague, and unnecessarily so. The fact is that the Mississippi sediment would fill the whole Gulf of Mexico in less than the time which they postulate for the present dela only, as pointed out by Dana as follows:

"While the land loses through erosion, the gain to the depressions of the ocean, or their borders, is exceedingly small. C. S. Forshey states that the Gulf of Mexico has an area of 600,000 square miles, an average depth of 4,920 feet, and is about 85 quadrillions of cubic feet in content. Its whole drainage area is 2,161,890 square miles, and it receives from this area annually 37.78 trillion cubic feet of water. He adds that, if empty, it would take its tributary rivers at this rate 2,250 years to fill it with water, or the Mississippi alone 4,000 years. Consequently, if all of the rivers contribute on an average of 1/2600 of their bulk in detritus [sediments] it would take nearly 6,000,

000 years to grade the depression [ie., the Gulf of Mexico] up to sea level. *The Mississippi alone would fill it in about* 10,400,000 *years."* (Dana, James G., *Manual of Geology,* 1896, p. 191.)

These pointed figures from Dana bring into sharp relief the vague presumptions and inferences of the more recent writers on the amount of time taken by the Mississippi to build its present delta. At the rate which they themselves allow, one square mile per year to a depth of 268 feet, (which is the approximate rate used by Lyell, by Humphreys and Abbott, and by Hilgard) not only the whole bed of the river from Cairo downward could be filled during the many millions of years which they postulate, but also the entire north Gulf coastal area, and still have several times too much sediment left, or enough to fill up the entire Gulf of Mexico.

*Question by member:* What are the sources and character of the information on the age of the other rivers of the world?

*Mr. Allen:* For a sufficiently large number of rivers to be considered representative, we have geological and historical data repeated by many investigators which supply the age estimates of these rivers. What one author omits another gives, till sufficient facts are accumulated for the age estimates of a large number of rivers. Though the data for a few other important deltas are not complete enough for a full estimation of age, the facts which are at hand about them are still fully in harmony with those of the rivers whose ages are known, so much so that their ages cannot be far out of line.

The following details from Grabau are of the sort which, when supplemented from other sources, form the basis for the age estimates for many other rivers:

"The rate of growth of deltas varies greatly and is often considerable. Thus the Jaxartes increased by 13 3/4 square miles between 1847 and 1900. The delta of the Rhone is said to have lengthened more than 26 kilometers since 400 B. C. The Southwest Pass of the Mississippi delta grew, according to Captain Talcot, 104 meters in length in 1838, the South Pass 85 meters, the Northeast and Southheast Passes each 40 meters, and the Pass a l'Outre 92 meters, giving the average of 80 meters per year for each pass. While this holds true for the year in question, it is not possible to consider that such an increase occurrs in all years. Indeed, often one year destroys what is built in the preceding year. The Po has increased between the years 1200 and 1600 at an average rate of 25 meters per year, but from 1600 to 1804 its rate of increase was 70 meters per annum. One of the most rapidly growing deltas is that of the Tereck on the Caspian. Within a period of 30 years the water has been pushed back 15 kilometers by the growth of the delta, which increased thus at the rate of half a kilometer per year. The other extreme is shown by the delta of the Danube, which at one of its mouths is not over 4 meters per year, though somewhat more rapid at another. The average increase of the Nile is about 4 meters per year, while the delta of the Tiber is estimated at the low rate of 1 meter per year. According to Pumpelly, the Huang-ho [Yellow] has increased on the average at a rate of 30 meters per year between B. C. 220 and A. D. 1730." (Grabau, A. W., *Principles of Stratigraphy*, 1913, p. 609.)

Consider also the following from Tarr: "The delta of a stream from the Hidden Glacier in Alaska was built forward 1600 feet between 1899 and 1910, but this was a heavily loaded stream. Temporarily and locally, as between distributaries [off-branching mouths of a delta], delta growth may be exceedingly rapid. Thus the Mississippi delta advanced about 2,000 feet in Garden Island Bay in the spring of 1912. What even slow, normal growth of deltas means in the course of time may be inferred from the fact that Pisa, in the Middle Ages an important seaport, is now back from the sea on the Arno [some 6 or 7 miles]; the ruins of Ostia, the ancient seaport of Rome, lies three miles inland as a result of the outward growth of the delta of the Tiber, while Adria, a seaport at the head of the Adriatic 1800 years ago, is now 14 miles inland, and scores of other cases are known." (Tarr, Ralph S., *College Physiography*, 1921, pp. 158-159.)

As to the *volume* of solid matter carried by the various rivers, the following statement from Grabau is a fair example. Other writers supply more data, much of it of a supplementary character.

"*Volume of Material Transported by Rivers*: The total amount of material transported by rivers is surprisingly great, and also varies much with different rivers. Taking some of the larrge rivers of the earth, we find that the Mississippi, with a flow of 17,500 cubic meters of water per second, carries 211,300,000 cubic meters of material per year; while the La Plata, with a flow of 19,820 cubic meters per second, carries only 44,000,000 cubic meters of material per pear. Again, the Huang ho or Yellow river in China, with a flow of only 3,285 cubic meters of water per second, carries the enormous quantity of 472,500,000 cubic meters of material per year, its waters being turbid with sediment. The Mississippi actually carries more than 400,000,000 tons of sediment into the Gulf of Mexico each year, or more than 1,000,000 tons a day. The exact volume of material, according to the measurement of Humphreys and Abbott, is 7,471,411,200 cubic feet (211,273,000 cubic meters), a mass sufficient to cover an area one square mile to a depth of 268 feet. The amount carried into the sea by all the rivers of the earth in one year has been estimated to be about 40 times this amount." (Grabau A. W., *A Comprehensive Geology*, 1920, p. 462.)

*Question by member*: Is there any relation between the structure of a modern delta and the major strata of the earth?

*Mr. Allen*: You have now touched upon a matter even more important than the age of the deltas. To Deluge Geology there are many striking differences between the making, the structure, and the materials composing deltas and those of the major strata of the earth. To Deluge Geology the major strata were laid down by the over-sweeping waters of the Deluge, continent-wide, of varying depths, speeds, directions, temperatures, and sources of sediments. But uniformitarian geology, lacking everything in the nature of a catastrophe capable of laying down such sediments, is forced by its own doctrine into the extreme position of attempting to prove that puny deltas such as we have today could and did form the major strata. This profound subject demands further critical attention. (Allen, Benjamin Franklin: "The Significance of the Major Strata of the Earth," *Bulletin of Deluge Geology and Related Sciences*, Vol. 1, 1941, No. 4.)

# BULLETIN

OF

# DELUGE GEOLOGY

### AND RELATED SCIENCES

| Volume 2 | October | Number 3 |
|----------|---------|----------|

## WHAT CHRISTIANS BELIEVE ABOUT CREATION

### GEORGE McCREADY PRICE

#### INTRODUCTION

I have been asked to state specifically what intelligent Christians, in this scientifically trained age, believe about Creation. Necessarily I can give only my own views on these subjects; yet when a man has devoted forty of the best years of his life to a study of all the various aspects of this problem of the origin of things, perhaps even his personal opinions may be regarded with some respect. But I hope I may also be able to give what the majority of this Society believe, and what multiplied thousands in all parts of the civilized world believe. For contrary to the loud boasts of those who deny this doctrine, there are still many who are tremendously encouraged by the modern scientific discoveries to believe what the Bible has revealed to us, that this little speck of rotating matter called the earth, as well as the rest of the entire universe, must have been created by the will or decree of an intelligent and all-powerful Creator.

We all admit three sources of our knowledge of this subject:

1. The divine revelation on this subject, as given in the Sacred Scriptures.

2. Whatever we have been able to learn from nature, or perhaps it would be more accurate to say, what God has revealed to us from the natural world concerning its origin.

3. What we have been able to learn by inference or reasoning upon the two original sources just mentioned.

We all humbly acknowledge that we cannot hope to arrive at rock-bottom truth in any of these three ways without the enlightenment of the Spirit of Wisdom; and so we all crave and expect enlightenment on this profoundly important subject as we proceed.

Moreover, it should be stated here at the outset that we have only very limited objectives in this paper. Necessarily I cannot be expected to give any exhaustive statement of the proofs of the beliefs here to be set forth. In

The BULLETIN is published by, and is the official organ of the "Society for the Study of Deluge Geology and Related Sciences." The Editorial Board is comprised of Professor George McCready Price and Dr. Cyril B. Courville. It is printed at the Collegiate Press, Arlington, California. For members the BULLETIN is free, and extra copies 30 cents each (each number priced according to size); for non-members it is $2.00 per year; and this number is 40 cents. All correspondence should be directed to the Managing Editor, Mr. Ben F. Allen, 219 North Grand Avenue, Los Angeles, California.

two recently published works,[1] I have given some of these supporting proofs. Here I can do little more than to state *what* we believe, without always attempting to present the reasons for this belief.

However, even with these very limited objectives, it will be needful to give some attention to the two chief *wrong* doctrines about Creation (as we regard them), the day-age theory, and the ruin theory. Both of these will be examined in due course.

## DIFFICULTIES IN PROVING CREATION FROM A STUDY OF THE PRESENT ORDER OF NATURE

All are familiar with the sublime statement at the beginning of our Bibles: "In the beginning God created the heaven and the earth" (Gen. 1:1). This is an example of what we Christians call a revealed truth. Other truths come to us through our observational senses, while we also discover new truths by reflecting and reasoning upon those facts or truths with which we are already acquainted. These are the only available sources of all that we know and all that we can ever hope to know concerning such subjects as we are here discussing.

The second and third of these sources unitedly compose what we term natural science. And many persons have claimed that the study of nature alone, with reflection and reasoning upon what we thus discover, constitutes our only source of knowledge about the origin of things. But this method is hopelessly inadequate, and cannot give us any clear conception of an original Creation. The clever Greeks, with all their intensive study of the natural world, never got beyond a vague and hopeless pantheism; and modern scientists who discard the Bible have never been able to get any further. Utter agnosticism, or the cruel fatalism of the great *ALL*, without love and without hope of anything beyond the grave, seems the most that mankind can learn about the universe from nature alone, and apart from a divine revelation from the only Being Who really knows. Any intelligent concept of an original Creation can come only through a divine revelation.

Presently we shall study just what the Bible has told us on this subject. But here at the beginning of our study I want to inject a caution against any undue expectation that the truths of an original Creation can be demonstrated in the same clear, Euclidean fashion that we use to prove such scientific facts as that lead is heavy, or that the earth is globular in form. The former fact is probably not denied; but the latter is being denied every day, and by people who wish to be regarded as intelligent. Why they deny this easily demonstrable scientific truth, need not be considered here. They probably have some mental quirk in their subconsciousness which is fed or flattered by their campaign against the idea that the earth is shaped exactly like all the other astronomical bodies which we can see with our eyes are globular in form.

That the universe was originally created by an intelligent Being is revealed in the Holy Scriptures, but it is not objectively provable by science alone. It is a truth which belongs to a realm of ideas remote from objective demonstration. For one thing, it involves profound moral implications which such a fact as the rotundity of the earth does not involve. Even a slow witted man can see that if the earth and the rest of the universe were actually created by a transcendent Creator, then he and

[1] *Genesis Vindicated*, 313 pages; Review and Herald Pub. Assn., Takoma Park, Washington, D. C., December, 1941. *If You Were the Creator*, 170 pages; Pacific Press, Mountain View, California, August, 1942.

everyone else must forever be morally accountable to this Creator; and this is an idea which very many people are not willing to face. Accordingly, the human mind is so perverse and uncertain in its manoeuvrings that it tends to evade or to deny facts or truths which it does not relish; and hence mental evasions or defense mechanisms are worked up by which this great truth of an original Creation is ignored or even openly denied.

For after all, *the will* is the governing factor in the entire life of man. Man is not by any means pure intellect alone. He does not let cool, calm reason alone tell him what is true with regard to any matter about which his personal interests or inclinations are remotely involved. The will to believe or to disbelieve will always intrude itself into every such problem as this about the origin of the universe. So universal is this condition that no man or set of men seem ever to have been able, apart from a divine revelation, to find out anything worth while about the origin of the material universe.

But there are other reasons for this failure to read nature aright besides what E. A. Hooton, of Harvard, so picturesquely terms "the aboriginal cussedness of human nature," and which the Bible calls the taint of sin or the carnal mind. For in order for us to reason correctly about the original condition of the universe, we must have some assurance that the conditions now prevailing on the earth are very much like those which prevailed at the beginning. For if the earth and the conditions upon it have very materially *changed* since the beginning, either in their general appearance or in their methods of operating, then not even the best informed scientist could judge correctly what the world was like originally.

But the Bible tells us that *two* very profound changes have taken place since the beginning, changes which render it impossible for us to discern the original condition of things from the present conduct of nature.

One of these changes is the profound transformation which has overtaken the plant and animal life of the world. Both plants and animals have degenerated, and in many instances have become so out of control that they are a curse instead of a blessing. The peace and harmony which originally prevailed, have become the tooth-and-claw condition which, as Tennyson expresses it, shrieks against the Christian creed that God is love and love the original law of all the universe. In other words, the present condition of nature makes it difficult to believe (without the revelation of the Bible) that an all-wise and beneficent Creator can be the author of a world with so many marks of evil upon it. And if the Creator is not wise and kindly, we cannot become interested in learning more about Him and His original Creation.

Another profound difficulty in understanding what the earth was like when God first made it, is due to the revealed truth that a completely universal Flood took place several thousand years ago, this universal Flood having completely changed the face of the globe, and having wrecked the genial climate which the earth enjoyed from pole to pole at the first. These profound changes in the face of the globe effected by the Flood have so far been misinterpreted that they have even been used as the chief grounds for working out a burlesque on the original Creation, by which the origin of everything is interpreted in terms of a gradual growth or development. This theory of growth or development, commonly called the evolution theory, has already been considered by this Society under many aspects, and need not now detain us.

But in still another way do we ex-

271

perience a difficulty which precludes us from interpreting the original Creation from the present operation of natural laws and present-day processes. For we also have the revealed truth, a truth which we could never have discovered without a special revelation, that the original Creation was completed at a definite period in the past, that there the work of Creation ceased absolutely, and that ever since other methods or processes have prevailed, though it is still the same God who now controls and manages the universe. For in Genesis 2:2, and repeated more than once subsequently, we are told that God, after finishing His work of Creation, not only "rested" as an attorney does when he has completed his case, but actually erected a memorial of this manner of ending the work of Creation, so that forever afterwards the men and women whom He had created would always be obliged to keep in mind this distinction and radical difference between that original work of Creation and the equally necessary but different work of Jehovah in keeping His universe in good working order. In other words, this primal rest day, the seventh-day Sabbath, was ordained by the Creator to memorialize the radical difference between the method of originally creating the world and this same Creator's present activity in maintaining the world today under the regime of what we term natural law.

But this suggests that the present system of natural law is radically different from the methods of the original Creation. Thus it is impossible for us to evaluate the methods of the original Creation by the processes which we now see going on in nature; for the two are incommensurable. In other words, we cannot project the present order of nature, or natural law, backward into the past, and say that thus and so the world and its animals originated. The revealed truth about the divine resting after Creation, and the institution of the Sabbath to keep in mind this rest and the entire change in the divine method of conducting the world, preclude the possibility of our discovering the method of Creation by the natural processes now going on.

But all this furnishes us the key to a strictly scientific method of proving the reality of a Creation as the only possible origin of things. For when natural law fails to explain how anything originated in the first place, the only method left by which they could have originated must have been by some method different from natural law, that is by some supra-natural method; and this we call Creation.

For example, when our utmost researches in physics and chemistry fail to show us any method by which matter can be brought into existence, we have a right to conclude that the stuff of which the sidereal universe is composed must have been created. Then when we learn from cytology that nobody has ever seen any living thing originate de novo, or from inorganic matter, either in the laboratory or in the field, in spite of all the ingenious experiments of hundreds of years, then we have to own that the first forms of life must have been created at some time in the long ago. Life now comes from antecedent life of the same kind; hence all the distinct kinds of life must have been created, probably simultaneously, just as Genesis declares. For neither Mendelism nor an other branch of biology has ever shown us how one kind of living thing can become changed over into something distinctly different. And all this suggests an original Creation, and an approximately simultaneous Creation of all the distinct kinds of plants and animals.

But I have already expanded on these ideas in several of my books, and need not here go into these matters further.

## WHAT THE BIBLE TEACHES

In the book of Genesis no argument is attempted to prove the existence of God; His existence is assumed, and the writer of the first chapter then proceeds to show the order of events in the original Creation. However, in the book of Isaiah we are pointed to the stars in the heavens, and are asked: "Who hath created these things?"[2] The implication is that the very existence of the sidereal universe is unanswerable proof of a Creator.

Nearly twenty years ago, when Sir James H. Jeans was a comparatively unknown astronomer, I wrote him asking if the then new theory about the disintegration or annihilation of matter, by which the radiation of the stars was sought to be explained, did not imply an original creation of the matter composing the universe. His answer was that the *very fact that matter exists* ought to be regarded as proof of its creation at some time in the long ago. Another recent writer declares that this act of calling matter into existence *ex nihilo*, or from nothing, "is an act for which there can be no formula,"[3] and therefore is a work that only Jehovah can do.

I have not always been able to agree with the statements of the late Sir Oliver Lodge concerning the religious implications of nature, but I most heartily agree with what he says in the following:

"I claim that the material universe with its variously designed atoms, and the way they have been used in the construction of all the objects, mineral, vegetable, and animal, that we see around us, is a sign also of gigantic design and purpose, and is a glorious work of art. . . . We cannot understand the existence of ourselves or of an external world unless we postulate some kind of Creation. Creation involves design and purpose and mental activity, and necessarily implies a Creator of some kind."[4]

It has long been assumed that the stars of the sidereal universe started their careers indiscriminately, at all sorts of times. Dr. Henry Norris Russell, the eminent astronomer of Princeton University, has recently subjected this theory to examination, and he declares that "its consequences disagree violently with the observations. Hence it must be false."[5]

The natural conclusion from this is that the various parts of the sidereal universe must have started their careers simultaneously. And this means a genuine Creation.

Here we should put on record the very clear and positive words of an astronomer whose books have become best sellers on both sides of the Atlantic:

"Everything points with overwhelming force to a definite event, or series of events, of Creation at some time or times, not infinitely remote. The universe cannot have originated by chance out of its present ingredients, and neither can it have been always the same as now."[6]

Two views are held among Creationists regarding the time referred to in the first sentence of Genesis: "In the beginning God created the heaven and the earth."

Some hold that God created the materials of our solar system, together with the entire rest of the material universe, all at this one time, "in the beginning;" but that afterwards He worked on this part of the universe and made it up into the earth and the solar system, as described in the rest of this chapter of Genesis.

---

[2] Isaiah 40:26.

[3] *Evolution in the Light of Modern Knowledge*, p. 452; A Collective Work. London, 1925.

[4] Sir Oliver Lodge, in *The Great Design*, p. 231; (Edited by Frances Mason), The Macmillan Co., New York, 1934.

[5] Henry Norris Russell, *The Scientific Monthly*, September, 1942, p. 237.

[6] Sir James H. Jeans, *Eos, or The Wider Aspects of Cosmogony*, p. 55; Kegan Paul, London, 1928.

Others hold that the earth and the rest of the solar system were created *de novo* at the beginning of the six days, though all the rest of the sidereal universe had been created long before and had been running for uncounted ages previously.

Both of these groups are sincere believers in a literal Creation, and neither group should doubt the integrity and sincerity of the other. For twenty years I believed with the first group; but about twenty years ago I became convinced that the second position is more logical. I can only briefly state the case for each side.

Both sides have to acknowledge that there were intelligent beings, probably many millions of them, constituting an on-looking universe who rejoiced at seeing the creation of this new world. For in Job we are told that at the laying of the foundations of this earth, "the morning stars sang together, and all the sons of God shouted for joy."[7] Clearly this means that a large part of God's universe, with many beings as its intelligent inhabitants, were already in existence when this world was created.

But all this is consistent with either view. Clearly it is a very narrow notion, and contrary to both the Scriptures and good science, to suppose that the entire universe was first brought into existence during the six-day period spoken of in the first chapter of Genesis.

The first view mentioned above, namely, that God used some of the stock material already on hand with which to make this world and solar system, is supposed to be more in accord with modern science or a broad view of things. But I cannot see any such advantage in these respects. Absolutely everything in the universe must have been created out of nothing at some time, and God might as well

and could just as easily create the very material *as needed*. The old Neo-Platonistic doctrine of a primitive "chaos," or the idea of there being somewhere in the universe a vast reservoir of disorderly or half-formed primitive material, on which God could draw as a sort of reserve stock whenever He wished to proceed with some further acts of creating, seems very grotesque to me. For God as the Creator, has only to *wish* or *will* anything into existence that He desires. The Bible represents Him as *speaking* everything into existence, which is the same thing. And in reality this is the only scientific or philosophical method by which a genuine Creation can be thought of or imagined. Accordingly, it is unreasonable to say that the Creator has to rely upon some stock of primitive material already on hand, when He wants to create a new world.

Nor can we be impressed with the objection that the Creation of a new world or a new solar system would disturb the gravitational equilibrium of that part of the universe near by. There is nothing near by. Any one acquainted with the facts of astronomy knows what a minute speck of a world this is, and how prodigious are the distances from our solar system to the nearest of the fixed stars. Thus this objection is of no account.

After a consideration of everything involved, it is my carefully considered view that in this first verse of Genesis the writer is dealing only with this earth as the future abode of man, though of course the rest of the solar system is probably also involved; for the entire solar system, and not merely the sun, is required to keep the earth going in its varied motions.

The words used in the fourth commandment seem decisive in teaching that the very material composing this earth must have been created *ex*

---

[7] Job 38:7.

[8] Sir James H. Jeans, etc., *The Wider Aspects of Cosmogony*, p. London, 1928.

*nihilo*, at the commencement of the six days. For they read: "In six days the Lord made heaven and earth, the sea, and all that in them is."[8] If we take these words at their full face value, we have to believe that at the time here spoken of, and not millions of years previously, the very materials of which this earth is composed were called into existence. No other conclusion seems permissible.

The word "heaven" as here used and also used in the first verse of Genesis, may need some attention to get at its true meaning. Clearly it does not here mean what we now commonly mean by the word; that is, it cannot mean the sidereal universe. For in the eighth verse of this same chapter the term is clearly defined: "And God called the firmament heaven." In the sixth verse this word "firmament" is partly explained: "Let there be a firmament in the midst of the waters, and let it divide the waters from the waters." While in the seventh verse it is stated that this firmament, which in the Hebrew means literally *expanse*, "divided the waters which were under the firmament from the waters which were above the firmament." Thus these two words, *heaven* and *firmament*, as here used mean the very same thing. It has been commonly supposed that they are about equivalent to what we term the *atmosphere*. But recent discoveries indicate that this idea may need some modification.

We now know that there are distinctly different layers to the atmosphere, with quite different characteristics. The total atmosphere may extend upward for a hundred or more miles, but it is only the lower layer up to about seven and a half miles that contains clouds and is the region of convection currents and storms. The name *stratosphere* is given to the next

layer, from about seven and a half miles up to about nineteen miles, or some twelve miles thick. This stratosphere layer is intensly cold, but it has no convection currents and no storms. Above this again is a region which contains large quantities of ozone, an activated form of oxygen which tends to absorb heat and thus is warmed by the passage of the sun's rays through it.

The existence of this ozone layer above the stratosphere is well establiished; and some eminent scientists, including Dr. Fred L. Whipple of Harvard observatory, have recently (1940) announced that there are various lines of evidence to prove that this layer above the stratosphere is *warm*, probably as warm as boiling water. If this high temperature of the layer above the stratosphere should be further confirmed as an unquestionable fact, certain very interesting inferences would necessarily follow, one of which would be the large capacity for holding invisible water vapor which this warm layer, about twenty miles thick, would possess. This would apply to the present conditions; but by inference we would also seem to have some new light on the conditions of the high upper atmosphere which may have prevailed previous to the time of the Flood.

Hence if we consider the *expanse* or firmament to be about equivalent to what we now call the *stratosphere*, it would accurately be described as dividing the waters which are under the firmament from those (invisible) waters which are above it. And since this heated region of the high upper atmosphere is thought to be about twenty-one miles thick, extending from a height of twenty-five miles up to a height of forty-six miles, it is obvious that a prodigious quantity of heated and invisible water vapor could here be held suspended above

[8] Exodus 20:11.

the stratosphere or the firmament.

To speak in terms of modern science, the firmament may signify what we now call the stratosphere; for this cold, dry layer, with no vertical air currents, acts as an effectual barrier between any mixing of the waters in our ordinary atmosphere with those vast quantities of water vapor in the heated regions above.[8a]

The second verse of Genesis says that when first created the earth "was un-formed and void" (Jewish version), which clearly means that at this stage the earth had not yet taken on the form of oceans and dry land, and that it was empty of living things, for no plants or animals had yet been created. For the word *void* means *empty* and nothing else; it does not in the least imply that the earth had been made *desolate* by some unknown cause, as the "ruin theory" taught by the Scofield Bible would have us believe. This "ruin theory" will be examined in due order. This idea of the earth's having been made desolate is not extracted from this verse, it is read into it by a vain, preconceived theory which has no foundation in either science or the Bible.

Throughout this first chapter of Genesis the record states that each successive day of Creation was marked by an evening and a morning, like all subsequent days; for the Bible always reckons the day from sunset to sunset. Thus the obvious meaning of this record is that these days of Creation were ordinary days of twenty-four hours. That the word "*yom*," here translated "day," sometimes in other parts of the Bible may mean something else, or may be used to signify

an indefinitely long period of time, just as the English word "day" may occasionally be used, is nothing to the point. The only question is, What does it mean here? And the obvious answer is that it seems to mean a literal day, like those of the present time, and nothing else. But about a hundred years ago, when the fossils were becoming widely known and were being exploited by skeptics as visible proof that the earth must be vastly older than a literal Creation of only a few thousand years ago would seem to indicate (of course, ignoring the record of the Flood), some theologians who wished to "harmonize" the Bible with that kind of science, invented the "day-age theory" of Creation, which is that these days were immense periods of time, corresponding to the geological "ages." A discussion of this "day-age theory" must be postponed for the moment, but will be taken up presently.

Here it may suffice to note that this "day-age theory" does not treat the "day," as here used, in a clear, straightforward manner. For any day that is bounded by an evening and a morning cannot be an indefinite period of time. And if the grass and the other land-plants, including the fruit trees, were created on the third of these immense periods of time, it is absurd to say that they had to wait until the fourth of these long periods before they got any light from the sun, which was created, or at least came into visibility only on the fourth day. Other objections to this theory will be considered when the topic is discussed later.

Also the record of the making of the

---

[8a] Since air heated above the boiling point of water will hold an indefinite quantity of water vapor, it becomes an interesting speculation to consider what vast quantities of *liquid water* would necessarily be released, if the cold air of the stratosphere were to become violently mixed with this heated upper air. For this would be exactly what would happen, if the disturbance which took place at the time of the Flood extended also to the upper atmosphere. The prodigious quantities of water thus precipitated would indeed make it seem as if the very "floodgates" of heaven were opened (Gen. 7:11, margin).

Sabbath rules out any notion that the days of Creation were different from those with which we are now acquainted. For it is nonsense to ask men to observe every seventh day in memory of a Creation which was accomplished during six indefinitely long periods of geological time.

The Genesis record is that the vegetation of the land, including not only the grass but also the seed-bearing herbs and the fruit-bearing trees, was all created on the third day, and these high-grade land forms were among the very *first* living things created. Only on the *fifth* day were the water animals brought into existence. But the "day-age theory," which is in reality only the evolution theory in disguise, has to make the first forms of life originate *in the sea,* with many millions of years all passing away before any such high-grade land plants appeared. This complete reversal of the order in which these things were created shows the brazen boldness with which this "day-age theory" treats the inspired record.

The record is that Jehovah decreed that the land should "bring forth" the land vegetation and the land animals, while man also was formed "of the dust of the ground," or out of the chemical elements composing the earth. Thus these forms of life, including man, may in one sense be spoken of as a *secondary* creation, in contrast with the *primary* creation of the *stuff* or the elements composing the earth, which in the beginning must have been called into existence from no previously existing material, or out of nothing. Yet a creation of man and these other forms of life was a true *fiat* creation, or a creation by divine fiat or decree, and not a growth or development from the inorganic elements. For nothing like it has since occurred, and nothing of the sort is now taking place anywhere on earth. Thus it was a truly supra-natural

work, or a work wholly unknown to our modern natural law. It was a genuine creation, in sharp contrast to the ways in which new vegetation and new human beings are now being made. It is the same almighty Jehovah in both cases; but for wise reasons God saw fit to register this sharp and everlasting contrast between the original Creation and the present regime under what we call natural law.

One further point needs to be noticed here before closing this section. For the obvious meaning of the inspired record is that many at least of all these forms of life were created fully formed or in a mature state. For the world was created *a going concern,* with all the various forms of plants and animals at least sufficiently mature to be able to take care of themselves. The long period of helpless infancy which characterizes man precludes the supposition that he was created otherwise than fully mature. And the same principle holds for most of the other forms of animal life. But they all needed food from the very first day, and their food was the fruits or seeds or other parts of the various kinds of plants. Hence at least some of these plants must have been sufficiently mature to furnish the appropriate food for man and the various animals. In other words, the entire world was a complete, *going concern,* very beautiful from end to end, including the polar regions and what are now dreary wastes and barren deserts. And the great Jehovah, looking upon it all, pronounced everything "very good."

## OBJECTIONS TO THE DAY-AGE THEORY

For a full century, from 1700 to 1800, practically all persons in England who knew anything about the subject believed that the Flood of the Bible was the cause of the burial of the fossils. And this was not an age of scientific ignorance; for it followed

close after the death of Sir Isaac Newton, who taught the world the true
views about physics and astronomy,
and whose centenary the entire scientific world is celebrating this year. In
France and in other parts of the Continent they had less confidence in the
Flood theory, not because they knew
any more about the rocks and the fossils, but because they had less confidence in the Bible in other respects.

But by 1830 a more skeptical age
had set in even in England. Lyell
began publishing his books denying
the Flood and teaching present-day
changes as the real cause of the fossils.
Lyell's books won their way among
the scientifically minded, but some
one was needed to popularize this uniformitarian theory of the fossils and
the rocks among the common readers.
Hugh Miller, a self-educated stone
mason of Cromarty in the north of
Scotland, first made these subjects
popular just about a hundred years
ago now; but he taught Lyell's theory
of the long geological "ages," and incidently, because he had been piously
brought up, he undertook to show that
these geological "ages" may be understood as harmonizing with the days
of Creation as mentioned in Genesis.

Miller died by shooting himself
two days before Christmas in 1856; but
by this time his "day-age theory" had
become widely known, and was being
advocated by Agassiz and other professional scientists. Such religious
minded men of science here in
America as James D. Dana of Yale and
Sir William Dawson of Montreal
added to its reputation for orthodoxy,
while in England such heavyweight
theologians as the Duke of Argyll and
W. E. Gladstone added the prestige of
their names to the popularity of the
theory.

The net result was that, when Darwinism took the intellectual world by
storm in the closing decades of the
nineteenth century, this day-age period

was almost universally regarded as the
only religious answer to the Darwinian theories of organic evolution. So
it has taken only a few more decades
for the entire civilized world to accept
the theory of evolution; for the day-
age theory is no answer to evolution;
it is a Quisling theory, which betrayed
the Church from within, and handed
over the rising generation intellectually chloroformed and hogtied to the
enemy.

The reason why no modernly educated person of any standing advocates this theory today is very clear
and very simple: they have all become evolutionists. In the whole wide
world probably nobody could now
be found (under fifty years of age)
who would seriously undertake to
do the job of "harmonizing" the
days of Creation with the geological
"ages," as was so glibly and persistently done one or two or three generations ago. I mean, he does not try
to do this, if he knows anything about
the facts of geology. For under this
sort of juggling and twisting the record
of Genesis has steadily and completely
lost its standing in the eyes of the
scientific world, while a consistent
theory of development or evolution
has gradually replaced the jerky and
paroxysmal geology of a century ago,
which was the style of geology that first
became popular. Thus an out-and-
out theory of evolution has by now
completely replaced and displaced the
"day-age theory" of the latter part of
the nineteenth century. "By their
fruits ye shall know them."

When the theory of many geological
ages first came before the world, it
was as a system of successive desolations or catastrophes, each of the
"ages" having been terminated by a
world-convulsion in which practically
all forms of life, both in the ocean and
on the land, were exterminated. At
first less than a dozen of these cataclysms were spoken of; but the number

soon grew to several dozen, and finally well on toward a hundred. Agassiz always taught this view; James D. Dana, who died in 1895, never discarded it; while Sir J. W. Dawson, who lived until 1899 and had a very wide influence, was a strong advocate of catastrophism, and was an outstanding advocate of the "day-age theory." And all of this school of geologists always taught that Noah's Flood was just the last of the long series.

It was this theory of many successive world-convulsions which the Protestant Church adopted under her attempt to harmonize this sort of geology with the days of Creation.

But Lyell and his followers never admitted these successive desolations; they wanted to explain *all* the past in terms of the present. Gradually they won the day with the public; the violent floods were replaced by more orderly methods of changing the face of the earth, on the specious principle that by stretching out the total time involved the same results could be accounted for as by many sudden destructions. It was a case of time versus energy, they said. Lyellism gradually replaced catastrophism, and then evolution replaced both.

Thus the Protestant Church, by the end of the nineteenth century, found that her "day-age theory" of trying to harmonize the days of Creation with the popular geology was becoming very ridiculous. For the lines of demarkation between the successive "ages" had become very dim or almost obliterated; there remained only the long total of organic evolution, the painful climb from the slime of the primordial ooze to the so-called "primitive" man of Trinil, Java, and the Neanderthal monstrosities. It would be a very hardy "harmonizer" indeed who would now have the courage to show any similarity between the modern fully developed evolution theory

and the record of Creation, as given in Genesis.

Accordingly, while nobody with any scientific standing today teaches this "day-age theory" seriously, except a few octogenarians who belong to a previous generation, it may not be amiss to record here the evidences against such a system. And in such an evaluation we are obliged to consider it as it would be today, with the modern teachings of geology, not what geology was supposed to teach a century ago, when Hugh Miller first beguiled the Church into the primrose path of dalliance with the evil spirits of unbelief.

1. In an earlier part of this paper I mentioned that the use of the words "evening" and "morning" in the Genesis account indicates that the word "day" is used there in its ordinary meaning, not as a long period of time. The institution of the Sabbath carries the same implications.

2. In Genesis the grasses, seed-bearing herbs, and the fruit trees were the very first kinds of life created. But in the geological scheme these are among the very *latest* forms of plant life, appearing only long after the coal plants of the Carboniferous and the almost equally abundant plants of the Cretaceous.

3. In Genesis the birds were created contemporaneously with the first ocean animals. But in the day-age arrangement the birds appear only many millions of years after the first forms in the ocean.

4. In Genesis the high-grade land plants were the first to be created; while in the geological scheme every invertebrate phylum was produced in profusion during the Cambrian and the Ordovician, the Silurian, and the Devonian "ages," or uncounted millions of years before even lowly plants appeared on the land, and then these were only such kinds as equiseta, lycopods, and ferns.

5. In Genesis man was made in the image of God; in the scheme of evolutionary geology man was made in the image of apes.

6. In Genesis the first man was made only a little lower than the angels; in evolutionary geology the first man was even lower than the lowest savages to-day.

7. In the Genesis record we read of man's sin and degeneration; but in the theory of evolutionary geology we are taught on the contrary that man has been constantly progressing upward.

8. In Genesis there never was any suffering and death even among the animals until after man had sinned. But in the geological scheme suffering and death reigned supreme among all the animals for millions on millions of years before man appeared at all. This one violent contrast alone is sufficient to show that the "day-age theory" can never be harmonized with an honest treatment of the Bible record.

9. After God had completed the entire work of Creation, He contemplated every thing that He had made, "and, behold, it was very good."[9] This would have been violently untrue if at that time, as geology would have us believe, millions of square miles of the earth's strata were packed with skeletons of animals that had died violent deaths, and even the surface of many parts of the globe was cluttered up with the bones of uncounted millions that had similarly suffered and died.

A good example of the evil results of believing this day-age theory is the way in which it resulted in the stultification and defeat of of William Jennings Bryan in the famous Scopes' trial of 1925, in which poor Bryan, with his day-age theory of Genesis, was so piteously overwhelmed and defeated by the battery of evolutionary scientists under the clever leadership of the atheist Clarence Darrow.

For many months before this trial, which may be regarded as a turning point in the intellectual and religious history of mankind, Bryan had been traveling up and down the country as the militant champion of the Bible against atheism and evolution. He had met with me and talked over some of these matters more than once; he also had read (or at least had in his possession) more than one of my books. And a few months before this trial was to take place he wrote me begging me to come to the trial and help him.

I was then in England, and was myself under written contract to meet in debate with the most prominent advocate of the evolution theory in England. This contract on my part, as well as the distance and the financial expense of coming to America for only a brief trip, for I was also teaching in a college, made it impossible for me to comply with Mr. Bryan's request. But I wrote him at considerable length, pointing out how flimsy and easily refuted were the evolutionary arguments, when the Flood is taken as the cause of the fossils. And I urged him to adopt this policy or strategy, and *to be sure to put the opponents or the evolutionists on the defensive,* and make them prove their case, as he and his side clearly had a right to do. If he had done this, the history of the trial would certainly have been different. And although this trial might not have contributed so much to the hilarity of the unbelievers in all the nations of the civilized world, the subsequent history of all human thinking would inevitably have been radically different.

But Bryan rejected my advice. He committed himself to the day-period theory of interpreting Genesis, and

[9] Genesis 1:31.

needlessly allowed himself to be cross-examined by Darrow, in which he conceded the entire geological argument to the evolutionists, with the pitiful results now known to all the world. No wonder he died a sad and disappointed man. But his is a good example of the outcome of every form of argument which does not take the record of Genesis at its full face value.

## THE RUIN THEORY

A Scotch clergyman, about the year 1810, propounded the theory that the fossils found in the rocks can be accounted for by supposing that the second verse of Genesis first chapter may be understood as meaning that, after the world had been created and had been running for a long time, something happened by which the earth *became* desolate and empty. This is sometimes called the *ruin and reconstruction theory*, because it holds that the present population of the earth in the way of plants and animals originated *after* this postulated ruin had been reconstructed by a new creation, as detailed in the remainder of this chapter of Genesis. It is sometimes called the *interval theory*, and also the *pre-Edenic ruin theory*. But the shorter form of name is more convenient, and so we shall here speak of it as simply the *ruin theory*.

At that time geology as a formal science could hardly be said to exist. But the capital of Scotland was buzzing with many diverse forms of mental activity, and the many discoveries of fossils and other geological phenomena were highly disturbing to those with a skeptical turn of mind who had lost faith in the Flood as the cause of the changes recorded in the earth's surface. And it seems that Thomas Chalmers, the Scotch clergyman mentioned above, with his friends, supposed he could dismiss the entire set of geological phenomena as having no direct bearing upon the present order of the earth. All these, he declared, be-

long to this *interval* implied in the second verse of Genesis 1, "and the earth *became* waste and void," which is the translation advocated by the friends of this theory.

Of course, there is no scholarly Hebrew authority for this word "became." The original word simply corresponds to the verb "was," as all reliable translations give it. But the advocates of the theory also try to put meanings into the adjectives "waste and void," or "without form and void" (A. V.), or "unformed and void" (Jewish version) which these words do not contain. The original words mean only that the earth had not yet been completely formed, as soon took place by the separation of the seas and the dry land (verses 9 and 10), and had not yet been stocked with plants and animals. For the word "void" means simply "empty." It means nothing else and never did mean anything else. It needs to be stated with positiveness that the original language of this verse gives not the slightest hint of a ruin or desolation which had overtaken the earth. Such a meaning is read into this verse and not extracted from it.

This theory of a ruin or a desolation in the early days of our earth, has had a curious history. About a century ago, or soon after being propounded, it became quite popular through the publication of two or three books which taught it in a popular style. It never obtained any standing among scientifically trained men, though it was at one time advocated by Cardinal Wiseman and a few other clergymen. It then dropped out of sight for over half a century, but in recent years it has been revived here in America, chiefly by being taught in the Scofield Bible, the notes of which many people regard as furnishing additional theology and science almost equal to the text of the Bible itself. The result has been that this pre-Edenic ruin theory is now being taught in dozens of Fundamentalist Bible schools all over the country. A pseudo-scientific book appeared in 1940 to defend the theory and to add to the mental and scientific confusion of all who read it.

There are many and serious objections to this theory, besides the primary objection that it is built entirely out of thin air, without any scriptural or scientific foundation whatever. Some of these objections are theological, some are scientific, while others are a mixture of both science and theology. I shall deal with them here only briefly, directing the interested reader to a recent volume of mine where they are given in more detail.[10]

1. One major objection to this ruin theory is essentially the same as one that I have presented against the "day-age theory," namely, that it makes cruelty, suffering, and death the universal condition among the animals for long ages before man's sin, or before there was a man on earth. We can easily account for these conditions now, as a result of the derangement of all nature through man's rebellion against his Creator. But it is contrary to every principle of justice and benevolence for cruelty, suffering, and death to prevail universally among even the animals for ages before man was created. When the advocates of the ruin theory try to dodge this objection by saying that Satan had been made the first ruler of this world, and that this suffering and death among the pre-Edenic animals was caused by Satan's apostasy, they show that they do not require any *proof* for their theories — apparently any plausible fancy is sufficient to support their theory. What could one not "prove"

by always being able to add more and more imaginary conditions?

The apostle Peter sets before us the promise of "the times of restoration of all things."[11] But surely, if this pre-Edenic condition of cruelty, suffering, and death was the genuine primitive condition of this earth under Satan's rule, long before the time of Adam, then these would be the conditions which would prevail by any such has never been known to be in the "times of restoration of all things." There must be something radically wrong with a theory of primitive conditions which thus makes little better than nonsense this statement of the apostle, which is in reality one of the most precious promises of the Bible.

2. My second objection to the ruin theory is also similar to one already presented against the former one. For they both have many features in common, since they both are built upon the tacit denial of the Flood as the cause of the fossils and the geological changes, but that the alleged long-drawn-out geological "ages" really prevailed before the time of the Creation recorded in the first chapter of Genesis, or at least before the creation of any human beings.

The objection is this: At the close of the week of Creation, Jehovah made a survey of everything that He had made, "and, behold, it was very good."[12] Obviously, on the basis of either theory this would involve the preposterous idea that the all-wise, all-loving Creator could contemplate the unnumbered millions of dead animal skeletons packed into the strata of every part of the world, as well as the countless millions of skulls and skeletons lying exposed and cluttering up the surface of half the continents and *pronounce them all "very good."* I

---

[10] *Genesis Vindicated*, pp. 292-297. Review and Herald Pub. Assn.. Takoma Park. Washington, D. C., 1941.

[11] Acts 3:21. A. R. V.

[12] Genesis 1:31.

really do not know how to state in polite language my opinion of a theory which involves such an implied charge of untruthfulness against the Creator.

3. My third objection is related to the one just mentioned, but is based on the words used in a part of the fourth commandment: "In six days the Lord made heaven and earth, the sea, and *all that in them is.*"[13] Now on the basis of either of the two theories we have been examining, uncounted millions of fossils were in the rocks of all the earth *when* these words were proclaimed from Sinai. But on the ruin theory at least these remains of the pre-Edenic animals were *not* made during the six days. For the ruin theory assigns all these fossils to another creation long anterior to the one mentioned in this text and with which this present condition of affairs had nothing to do. Thus we have in this theory another direct contradiction of the language of the Scripture. Further comment on my part would be superfluous.

4. My fourth argument concerns both the day-age theory and the ruin theory, for both take for granted the scientific accuracy of the geological theory of long successive ages. But the members of this Society have had their eyes opened to the fact that the accepted geological ages are replete with mistakes of observation and especially with fallacious reasoning. For in my geological books I have shown conclusively that it is a highly questionable practice for geologists to date the strata by their enclosed fossils, when nobody has ever been able to justify this *differential dating* of the fossils themselves except as a pure, bald assumption. And then it is clearly preposterous, first to date the strata by means of their contained fossils, and then claim to build up a reliable history of organic development by

means of the alleged historical sequence in which the fossils occur. All this is mere whirligig reasoning, and is worthless as a foundation for any scientific theory.

But the ruin theory has less excuse for depending implicity upon the accuracy of the geological ages; for the leading scientific advocate of the theory in this country, the man whose book was published in 1940, as already mentioned, has repeatedly declared, both in correspondence with me and in his published writings, that Price's facts and arguments have destroyed his confidence in the chronology of the fossils. He claims that all the fossil forms of life may have lived contemporary with one another, though he sticks to it that they probably occupied the earth for a long time previous to their destruction by the ruin which his theory postulates.

But persons who are not tied up with any preconceived theory and who look at all these matters in a mood of plain common sense, have extreme difficulty in understanding how such a man can refuse to accept the Flood as the cause of the burial of the fossils, instead of this hypothetical pre-Edenic ruin. For every Bible believer *knows* that the Flood actually took place, while the previous ruin is only a matter of supposition. And since the Flood comes in *between* us and everything that may have happened previously, how can we be so sure that it did not do what we see as the obvious effects of some great world destruction, the killing off of great numbers of animal and plant forms and their burial in aqueous sediments? It is arbritrary and unscientific to ignore what this known Flood did in the way of killing off the animals and plants and burying them in sediments, and to say that all these phenomena that we find were due to this hypothetical pre-

---

[13] Exodus 20:11.

vious ruin. In other words, why should we be asked to assign the fossils to a ruin which is never once expressly mentioned in the Bible, instead of assigning them to the Flood of Noah, which is so clearly and fully described in the Bible?

In God's prediction of what He was going to do by the Flood, He declared that He would "destroy all flesh, wherein is the breath of life, from under heaven;"[14] and also "I will destroy them with the earth."[15] And in the record afterwards of what the Flood accomplished we are told that it did exactly what had been predicted: "And all flesh died that moved upon the earth, both birds, and cattle, and beasts, and every creeping thing that creepeth upon the earth, and every man: all in whose nostrils was the breath of the spirit of life, of all that was on the dry land, died. And every living substance was destroyed that was upon the face of the ground."[16]

I do not see how human language could be put together to express a complete and universal destruction more clearly and positively. And yet the advocates of this ruin theory tell us to ignore all this, to say that the exterminated animals which we do find, which obviously were destroyed and buried by just about such an aqueous catastrophe, were not destroyed by this Flood of Noah, but by another hypothetical ruin which occurred before the present animals and plants were created, though this ruin is never once expressly mentioned anywhere between the lids of the Bible.

5. The arbitrary and unreasonable character of this ruin theory is further seen in the utter impossibility of showing any dividing line between the animals and plants of our present order of

Creation, which must on any reasonable view have been destroyed and buried by the Flood, and those (presumably) quite different kinds which had lived in the pre-Edenic world and were buried by the ruin with which it was terminated.

In all the early days of the science of geology, while the ruin theory was being first advocated, indeed until quite recent years, it was always stoutly maintained that all the fossils belong to *extinct* species, or even to extinct *genera* and *families*. It was always taught that it was a sort of phantom world, all dead and gone, which we find buried as fossils in the rocks.

But we know that this is all wrong. Thousands of kinds of fossils, both of plants and of animals, seem to be identical with kinds now living in various parts of the world. And in multiplied other thousands of instances the differences between the fossil kinds and the living ones is not more than the markedly different environment would lead us to expect. Without a single exception, all the great orders and families of animals and plants have their easily recognized representatives among the fossils somewhere in the strata. And so close is the identity that it takes a finical expert to distinguish the fossil kinds from the modern, except that the fossils usually seem larger and more thrifty looking than their modern representatives.

How completely arbitrary and unscientific it is for the believers in this ruin theory to assure us that the modern living kinds are never the lineal descendants of the kinds found as fossils in the rocks, though the two seem to be identical. Why should we be asked to believe that all these fossil kinds belong to a phantom world which was absolutely wiped out of existence, leaving no possible descend-

---
[14] Genesis 6:17
[15] Genesis 6:13.
[16] Genesis 7:21-23. A. R. V.

ants; but that afterwards the Creator made *exact duplicates* of those buried as fossils, and that our modern ones are the descendants of these recreated duplicates?

6. The last argument which we shall consider here has to do with what is the best or the correct scientific method of investigating such a problem as this of how the fossils were buried. My claim is that by a correct method of study in this case, we will be led to believe in the reality of something very like the universal Flood of Noah, and can then confidently assign it as the cause of the burial of the fossils and of the accompanying changes in the surface of the earth, but that by such a correct scientific method we will never be able to get back of this known Flood to another previous ruin which is purely hypothetical. If a notorious burglar is known to have been loose and near the scene of the crime, it is going to be difficult for him to convince a judge and jury to accept his alibi, and to place the blame on some wholly unknown person who vicinity.

All trustworthy research into the long past history of our earth must always begin with the present and proceed thence backward into the past, from the known to the less known, as is always recognized in all modern archaeological work. I have discussed this principle of methodology in a current geological journal.[17] When we proceed by this which is the only safe method, and are willing to treat the Bible's records of the earth's past with any proper respect, we encounter the account of the destruction of the earth's living things by the Flood of Noah. Then common sense and intellectual honesty tells us that this cataclysm must have accomplished an immense amount of geological change, in the way of shifting vast quantities of gravel, sand, and clay, as well as in the killing off of species and then burying them in these deposits.

And surely it is most arbitrary and unscientific to ignore all this, as the friends of the ruin theory have to do, and to tell us that Noah's Flood either did no geological work of importance, or at least has left us nothing in the way of scientific records of what it did, but that the pre-Edenic ruin did everything of the sort that we find around over the earth. Not only so, but we also find that this pre-Edenic ruin is never once expressly mentioned in the Bible, but has to be read between the lines by injecting meanings into the Scriptural words which the original will not sanction.

All this is not good science, nor is it good and safe theology.

## THE SIGNIFICANCE OF THE DOCTRINE OF CREATION FOR OUR DAY

The strange things taking place around the world have impressed many of us with the settled conviction that some radical change must be about to take place in the Creator's method of dealing with the entire race of mankind. Often in the past, cities and nations have come to the end of their probation, and have gone out in a debacle of blood and ruin. Then why not a world? Those of us who have outgrown the Pollyanna nonsense that every day in every way the world is getting better and better, and who are determined to see the present situation realistically and see it whole, realize fully that the world has almost completely accepted the evolutionary view of the origin of things. This theory has captured the world, and there is not the slightest reason for supposing that this theory will even become less popular than it is today.

But we of this Society believe in a

[17] "Methodology in Historical Geology," in *The Pan-American Geologist*, March, 1937, pp. 117-128.

genuine Creation. This paper has stated some of the reasons for this belief. Accordingly, since the all-wise Creator must have foreseen this present state of affairs, it is an inevitable conclusion that He must have made all the necessary provisions to take care of the situation. How this will be done is not our present concern.

On the other hand, one who studies closely the Bible record of the original Creation can hardly fail to be impressed with the way in which the Creator seems to have deliberately planned some features of His work of Creation in such a way as to forestall what He saw would arise in the end of time in the shape of an evolutionary philosophy.

For evolution is simply *naturalism* applied to "explain" the origin of things. To appear reasonable to scientifically educated men, the theory must conform to rather restricted methods to account for the origin and growth of succesively developing forms of plants and animals. It must start with very small forms, either as one-celled or as simple-celled organisms. And these must necessarily begin in the water, presumably in the ocean. There is no other possible way to make the beginning of life appear plausible.

In radical contrast with all this, Genesis tells us that the first living things to be created were *on the land*, and consisted of the *Graminaceae*, and the seed-bearing herbs and fruit trees, all belonging to the Angiosperms, the very highest class of the plant kingdom.

Now, humanly speaking, it would have seemed far more "natural" to begin with some of the water animals mentioned in the twentieth verse, which were not created until the fifth day. And especially would it seem more "natural" to have the sun and moon created (or brought into visibility) *before* the land plants were

formed, instead of afterwards, and necessarily so if these days were really immensely long periods of time. But no; all these "reasonable" or "natural" sequences were deliberately defied; and the high-grade land plants were created on the third day, the sun and moon on the fourth, and the first of the water animals *on the fifth*. Who cannot see in all this a planned disregard of the only possible sequence in which the gradual development of living things by purely natural process could be made reasonable? It takes a great deal of skillful casuistry to make even a moderately good fit between the Genesis record and the scheme of evolutionary development, even if the days of Creation are stretched out indefinitely.

But there is an even more important respect in which the Creation seems to have been deliberately planned so as to forestall any possible form of natural development or evolution.

For *naturalism* is the very essence of the evolution scheme. Its advocates are constantly boasting that they are only projecting the present-day natural law backwards into the past, and they claim that in this way they are able to explain the origin and gradual development of all living forms. They try unceasingly to show how the earth itself may have originated by some ordinary astronomical process. They mix chemicals in test tubes and retorts in the hope that thus they may be able to produce something like a living cell which will show true metabolism and will reproduce others like itself. Above everything else they have sought endlessly to show how man and the other higher animals have grown up *naturally* from some of the older forms. In other words, evolution means what we call natural law projected backwards indefinitely into the past, thus explaining the origin of every thing in terms of present-day processes. And this is the only basis on which a scheme of evolution could possibly be built up. There could be no other way.

Would it not seem that the Creator must have had this contingency in mind when he set a definite termination to all His work of Creation, and then went on to manage His created world in a radically *different* way, this latter or different way being what is now prevailing all around us and is known to us as "natural law"? I do not see how any thoughtful person can evade the conclusion that the divine foresight of what unbelievers would say in a perverse attempt to "explain" everything in a "natural" way, must have been one of the reasons for making this radical and sharp distinction between the methods of Creation and those now prevailing as natural law.[18]

Every formal statement of truth may be regarded as having been given us as a divine means for protecting us against harmful and dangerous errors. And since our day is strongly characterized by certain forms of error, we should regard as especially timed for our day those revealed truths which forewarn us against these errors.

But besides the evolution doctrine, there are other modern errors against which the doctrine of a genuine Creation ought to forewarn and protect us. One of these is the feeling of dark, helpless pessimism which has seized the so-called "liberal" thinkers of the world. It is only a reaction to the boundless and unreasonable optimism which prevailed up to the very eve of the first World War. The latter was based on the visible progress of a materialistic "civilization" which left God entirely out of account; and the present pessimism is due to the same cause: for unbelievers see their admired "civilization" collapsing all around them, and they have no Creator at their side to reassure them of guidance and protection.

But if God actually created the world in the first place, why not give Him credit for being able to take care of it? When we readjust our scale of values and get a true perspective for estimating all the affairs of life from the point of view of eternity, our gadget-based "civilization" may not seem so important and hardly worth "saving." But if the Creator still lives, and if we are on His side of the controversy, what else can matter?

In the third place, the doctrine of a literal Creation ought to protect us from the modern form of Deism which is so widely held today. The old form of Deism pictured the universe as having been started in the first place by God, who loaded up the various stars and worlds and the smaller pieces of matter with so-called "properties," and then left the great machine to run itself, without any external "interference." This older form of Deism has long since had its day, it has had its day and has ceased to be, like the dodo and the dinosaur. But the new or modern form of Deism pictures the atoms and electrons and photons and quanta about as the older deists pictured the stars and planets. The theory of inherent "properties" of matter is just as deistic as were the older views of Voltaire and Lord Herbert. And it is just as absurd and false. For the modern scientific discoveries, especially such as show the absolute *unity* of the "laws" of matter and of motion, such as that of the conservation of energy, when united with the belief in a genuine Creation by an all-wise and omnipotent Being, preclude any such deistic notion as that of even the modern form of Deism.

In the fourth place, a belief in a

[18] In the first chapter of the author's *Genesis Vindicated* (December, 1941) other reasons are also suggested for making this radical distinction between Creation and present-day natural law. Most divine acts are multifold in purpose.

genuine Creation would protect the modern world from the desolating effects of modern Pantheism, which is fast becoming almost universal.

Pantheism is the form of philosophy which denies any personal God, independent of His created works and superior to them all, because He is the absolute Creator of them all. But Pantheism identifies God with the universe, and says that the universe, or the great ALL, is the only God there is.

But this has a blighting effect upon every phase of human thinking and human conduct. For if the entire universe is God, how can we pray to the universe? We might as well pray to the cyclone or the moonshine. And as for morals or conduct, the bad as well as the good are parts of the great ALL. Hence there is no distinction between the bad and the good; for both are equally an aspect of God.

All this is ruinous to ethics as well as to theology. And the only protection against these desolating ideas is the belief in an absolute Creation by a personal Being, the Jehovah of the first chapter of Genesis.

This basic doctrine of a primal Creation is one of the most precious and most important truths, and its value is especially appropriate for our day.

---

"If all the processes of nature were of the same order, or of the same kind as the beginning of things; that is, if the present processes of nature were but a continuing or a prolonging of the creation or of the ways by which they came into existence, it would be difficult or impossible for man to recognize any difference. But it is reasonable to think that God planned the present order of what we term natural law to be radically different from those ways in which He started the world and the plants and animals upon it. It is obvious that God, by planning the ordinary precesses of nature to go on according to a definite routine of fixed 'laws' or regularities, and by beginning the world *in some other way*, might enable man to recognize the difference, and thus by man's own scientific discoveries he might arrive at the understanding of the great primal truth of an original creation, and might thus be led to adore and honor his Creator."—*Genesis Vindicated*, p. 18, Review and Herald, Takoma Park, Washington, D. C., December, 1941.

"No enlightened Christian can for a moment suppose that the greatly increased knowledge of nature which the world has seen during modern times has come about by mere chance, or by the unaided cleverness of man. But in the light of recent developments it is easy to see why God did not allow this greatly increased knowledge of nature a thousand or two thousand years ago. As I have remarked, there is a dark side to the picture as well as a bright side; for submarines and aerial bombs, to say nothing of the clever tricks of the gangster, are as much the product of modern science as are the automobile and the radio. And since man is what he is, a fallen being, it would not have been for the best of all concerned if this increased command over the forces of nature had been allowed to take place in the days of ancient Greece or Rome. What would the race be like today, if the ancients had acquired a command of these modern discoveries and inventions?

"Man being what he is, it was inevitable that grossly wrong interpretations of nature would arise; for theophobia is not cured by merely acquiring skill in the technique of the test tube, the microscope, the clinometer, or the interferometer. His theophobia is bound to work up intellectual defence mechanisms against the divine lessons which naturally come to any soul who thus gains a close-up view of the works of the great Creator. Accordingly, we may look upon the modern spread of the evolution philosophy as an almost inevitable by-product of man's mind, if God were to allow and foster the greatly increased knowledge of nature which we see prevailing in our modern world."— *Genesis Vindicated*, pp. 32, 33.

THE

# BULLETIN

OF

# DELUGE GEOLOGY

## AND RELATED SCIENCES

| Volume 2 | November, 1942 | Number 4 |

## COMMENTS ON THE EVOLUTIONARY THEORIES
## OF THE EARTH'S ORIGIN

### Dudley Joseph Whitney

It is the purpose of this study to point out certain facts which suggest that the theories that have been proposed for the origin of the earth by evolutionary processes are untenable and in consequence all conceptions as to the geologic history of the earth based upon them must be insecure. The importance of this conclusion is self evident to the students of the problem.

Every thinking person will doubtless agree that the kind of history which the earth has had is dependent upon the way it came into being. If it came into being through purely evolutionary processes, it may be assumed that the processes which operated after its origin and brought it into its present condition were doubtless purely evolutionary also. On the other hand, if the earth came into being by the special exercise of divine power, its history would presumably be far different from that which has been worked out on the postulate that the theory of evolution is correct.

If, too, the earth came into being and has operated by purely evolutionary processes, as is assumed by scientists and has been assumed by them for more than a century, it would seem as though the nature of these processes which brought it into being should be known by now. If they are not known, seeing what great advancement has been made in science in the last century, it would certainly seem reasonable to assume that the earth did not start by evolution. In mathematics, when there is no direct way to solve certain kinds of problems, they may be solved by the elimination of all solutions but one. So in the question of evolution versus creation, if every imaginable evolutionary process for the origin of the earth (or for life, or for the eye, or the human species, or anything else) is studied and found wanting, creation as its method of origin is inferentially indi-

The BULLETIN is published by, and is the official organ of the "Society for the Study of Deluge Geology and Related Sciences." The Editorial Board is comprised of Professor George McCready Price and Dr. Cyril B. Courville. It is printed at the Collegiate Press, Arlington, California. For members the BULLETIN is free, and extra copies 30 cents each (each number priced according to size); for non-members it is $2.00 per year; and this number is 40 cents. All correspondence should be directed to the Managing Editor, Mr. Ben F. Allen, 219 North Grand Avenue, Los Angeles, California.

cated, at least until a theory which looks more plausible can be submitted.

On this point it can be said that every theory that the mind of man has been able to devise to account for the origin of the earth, except that of creation, has been weighed in the balances and found wanting. When the theory of geologic history was worked out, which has been standard belief by geologists for more than a century, the astronomers and geologists thought that they knew how the earth evolved into being. But they had some very false beliefs regarding the original nature of the earth, and their theory of geologic history was based in large part upon those beliefs. For example, the early geologists believed as do some present day geologists that the earth began in a molten state and that the water of the present ocean covered the surface of the globe with a thick blanket of hot, acid steam. Vivid word pictures have been drawn of water condensing from such an atmosphere and falling with hissing sounds upon the hot surface of a newly hardened crust only to be turned immediately into steam again. If the earth formed under such conditions, there would be an extensive and definitely saline ocean from the beginning, and a considerable atmosphere.

On the other hand, other geologists have theorized that the earth was never molten, but began much smaller than at present, that it grew by accretion, and that the ocean and atmosphere came from within the earth by volcanic action. Clearly the history which the earth would have after developing in one of these ways would be far different from what it would have been after originating in the other. Moreover, the nature of the early earth would obviously depend upon the kind of process by which it came into being. Nevertheless, the same kind of geologic history, at least its greater part, is still assumed by those who believe that it probably started in a molten state as by those who assume that it started as a small, cold solid mass.[1] Such a conclusion is bound to be erroneous. In considering the problem of the geologic history of the earth it is well to keep in mind that the early geologists thought that they knew how the earth started and what it was like in the beginning, but that they were wrong on both counts.

### THE NEBULAR HYPOTHESIS

The theory of origin which was standard in the formative period of modern geology was the Nebular Hypothesis and this theory was believed for more than a century. While it has been rejected by every

---

[1] On the difference it would make to the earth whether it started small and cold or molten hot and full size, what the authors of a prominent textbook in geology (Schubert and Dunbar, pp. 1 and 2) say may prove instructive.

"On the physical side, the Earth has, we believe, cooled from a molten to a solid state. As it solidified, the water vapor of its heavy primal atmosphere condensed into rain and fell upon the hot crust, rose as steam over and over again, and finally came to lie in the depressions and to fill the ocean basins. Geologic time, properly speaking, began when the Earth had a cold exterior, and when rain and wind commenced their ages-long task of wearing down the high places and transporting the debris into the low ones."

"According to the hypothesis we have sketched [The Gaseous-Tidal Hypothesis of Sir James Jeans, astronomer, and Harold Jeffreys, geophysisist], the Earth was first gaseous and self-luminous, gradually cooling through a molten stage to solidity. It was thus full-grown at birth and molten until just before the beginning of geologic time."

In the early stages, when the globe was very hot "the molten Earth was surrounded by a vast atmosphere largely of free oxygen, probably a thousand miles deep, and exerting a pressure of 15 to 20 tons per square inch at the surface." (Cont. on next page.)

intelligent astronomer or geologist, as have been substitute theories which have been suggested in its place, the Nebular Hypothesis is so important in considering theories about the history of the earth that some detailed attention to this can well be given. Although creationists assailed this hypothesis as being unworthy of acceptance long before the scientists themselves awoke to the seriousness of its faults,[2] it was not until the closing years of the last century that scientists of standing decided to reject it and managed to get a hearing from other scientists.

The theory is that the sun started as a large cloud of "fire-mist" which rotated so rapidly that it had assumed a disk-like rather than a globular form. As it contracted, rings of matter separated from the central mass and in time these rings became condensed into planets. The central mass was held to have contracted to form the sun. The planets as well as the sun were believed to have been fiery hot in the beginning.

This Nebular Hypothesis was accepted as sound science for more than a century as the result of the calculations of the French mathematician Laplace, and remained standard belief until detailed investigations toward the close of the last century showed that it had so many faults that its rejection became necessary. The story goes that Laplace explained the hypothesis to Napoleon who listened with interest and then asked what place God had in it, and Laplace is said to have replied, "Sire, in this system there is no need of God." His reply was correct. In the Nebular Hypothesis the actions of matter were held to be purely automatic and the only place for a deity would be at some hypothetical starting point untold millions of years ago. In accord with this theory the universe would have to be considered as a self-winding clock which would operate until it was worn out. If that position is taken, it would seem more logical to consider the universe as an eternally existing self-winding clock rather than a product of divine creation.

RELATION OF THE NEBULAR HYPOTHESIS TO GEOLOGIC HISTORY

It seems evident that if the sun and the rest of the solar system began in a purely natural manner, rather than by the direct ordering of matter by the Creator, the history of the earth after its origin would doubtless be purely automatic also. It was natural

"As soon as the temperature had fallen below 374°C. the vapors could condense, and rain fell in torrents beyond human conception, quickly lightening the atmosphere, covering the Earth with its ocean waters and initiating the geologic processes of erosion." (pp. 60, 61.)

On the other hand if the earth started by the accumulation of planetesimals it would start small and cold. "If the Earth was formed by slow accretion of solid particles, it could have no atmosphere until it attained a diameter of more than 2000 miles. With greater mass, it should have retained gases gathered from its path and those generated by volcanoes within. At first its gaseous envelope must have been thin and rare, increasing gradually to its present condition. . . ." (p. 57.)

The book goes on to say that by this way of starting the earth nearly 2000 miles of the earth's crust would have suffered weathering, and sodium far in excess of the amount in the ocean would have been leached from the rocks, and this, among other things tends to discredit the hypothesis that the earth started in this way. Nevertheless many geologists still favor the theory that the earth started small and cold and attained its ocean and atmosphere from within the earth. Clearly the kind of history the earth would have after starting hot and with a large ocean and atmosphere at the beginning would be different from what it would have if it started small and cold and with little or no ocean and atmosphere, yet holders of each theory accepted the same system of geologic ages and the same methods of estimating geologic time.

[2] Patterson, Robert: The Errors of Evolution, Bible Study Library, 1884.

on this basis to conclude that everything came to be as it is by the operation of evolution, and scholars did
come to this conclusion. This conclusion in favor of universal evolution
was aided by two situations—by the
supposedly harmonious (though mistaken) way that the origin of the
earth by the Nebular Hypothesis fitted into evolutionary geology, and
further by the assumed harmony of
the Nebular Hypothesis with the
Genesis account of creation, which
induced many theologians to accept
it as sound science.

According to this hypothesis the
earth was believed to have started as
a fiery globe which cooled until
geologic processes much like those
which operate at the present time
could begin. Mountains supposedly
would be worn away by weathering
and the sediments deposited in valleys or shallow seas. Then new mountains would be uplifted as the earth
lost internal heat and shrunk in cooling. Geologic processes like those
which operate now were presumed
to have continued for millions upon
millions of years, through geologic
epoch, period and era. Thus the current theory of geologic history in its
leading aspects was based upon the
belief that this hypothesis was sound.

Thus James D. Dana, one of the
well known American geologists of
the last century, wrote: "For these
grander phenomena in the earth's
history the only explanation is found
in the fact that the Earth has always
been, and still is, a cooling globe.

"That the Earth was once liquid
is now generally admitted. If so, the
cooling is a fact, and contraction, the
attendant of cooling, is a necessary
consequence."[3] This view was standard among early geologists and still
exercises a great influence among

persons who are not familiar with
recent developments.

Note particularly in the quotation
the statement that the only explanation for "these grander phenomena
in Earth's history" comes through the
assumed cooling and shrinking of the
globe. This illustrates the relation
between the assumed origin and
nature of the early globe and its later
history. Yet the earth is no longer
generally believed to have been
molten at the start nor is it generally
believed to be cooling and shrinking.
T. C. Chamberlain, who with his col-
league F. R. Moulton, overthrew the
Nebular Hypothesis by showing some
of its many faults and by providing
a temporarily satisfactory substitute
for it in the Planetesimal Hypothesis,
proved to his own satisfaction and to
that of most other geologists that the
earth did not begin in a molten state.
There is also good reason to believe
that the interior of the earth is not
cooling and shrinking, but rather may
be gaining in heat through radioactivity,[4] which leaves the problem of
the uplift of mountains completely
unsolved. Therefore, the only evolutionary explanations for "these
grander phenomena in earth's history" have been cancelled by the
advance of knowledge.

GENESIS AND GEOLOGY

Some of the faults of the Nebular
Hypothesis which caused it to be
rejected will be mentioned shortly.
But first the way that the hypothesis
and the kind of geologic history based
upon it were supposed to correspond
to the Genesis account of creation may
well be pointed out. The assumed
harmony between Genesis and old
line geology had much to do with
the acceptance of evolutionary geology
by theologians and geologists alike.

The first chapter of Genesis, after

[3] Dana, James D.: *New Textbook of Geology*, 1877, p. 116.

[4] Holmes, Arthur: *The Age of the Earth*, 1927, p. 48.

stating the fact of the initial creation, tells of the ordering of the earth in six periods of time which are termed *days*, although certain scholars who favor evolutionary geology insist that they should be considered as periods of indefinite length.[5] The initial condition of the earth is described in Genesis as having been unordered, dark and seemingly covered with water. The first step in its development is given as the coming of light; the second the organization of the firmament, or atmosphere; the third the separation of land areas from seas and the creation of plants; the fourth the creation, or at least the appearance, of the heavenly bodies; the fifth the creation of water creatures and birds; and the sixth the creation of beasts and creeping things and, last of all, Man. This course of events was once said to be in a general way what evolutionary geology set forth; so the theologians thought that of course the geologists were correct, that Moses had recorded in the first chapter of Genesis what geologists three thousand years later believed to be fact.

The initial darkness over the face of the deep was assumed to have been due to a deep dense atmosphere of water vapor and other substances over the face of the earth. This would be the result of the supposedly high temperature of the surface of the earth, which would be so high that the water now in the ocean would be in the form of vapor, and in dense clouds which would prevent the light of the sun from reaching the earth. Thus the earth would be "without form and void; and darkness would be over the face of the deep." On this basis, it was therefore thought that the initial condition of the earth according to the Nebular Hypothesis was as Genesis described.

The events of the six periods of Creation Week would then supposedly correspond in a general way at least to the findings of geologic history. Day One according to Genesis brought light, and according to evolutionary geology the loss of heat from the atmosphere would cause water to be precipitated upon the earth, thinning the covering of clouds enough to allow the light to penetrate to the face of the earth, though in diffused form, as in a cloudy day at present. Thus day and night could start on the earth.

Further cooling and precipitation of parts of the dense cloudy covering would bring the atmosphere into a condition approaching its present condition, though with certain important differences in composition, and this would be the making of the firmament, which was the work of Day Two in Genesis.

The surface of the earth would then be covered with water, but the elevation of land areas would bring the continents into existence. This would make possible the coming of vegetation, a necessary prelude to the appearance of animals, which was the work of Day Three. Here, however, a serious uncertainty developed in the effort to fit Genesis to geology. The fossil record, as based on the kind of history developed after belief in the Nebular Hypothesis became common, suggests that the seas teemed with shell fish and numerous other kinds of marine creatures long before there was any land plants at all, except bacteria or other lowly organisms. The harmonizers of Genesis and geology therefore were compelled either to content themselves with the knowledge that plants by necessity had to come before animals, or to decide that the luxurient vegetation of the Carboniferous period, as

---

[5] Price, George McCready, "What Christians Believe About Creation," *Bulletin of Deluge Geology*, Vol. 2, 1942, pp. 66-84.

geology had it, was an important feature of creation of Day Three of Genesis.

## THE SECOND HALF OF CREATION WEEK

The Fourth Day of creation according to Genesis is puzzling in several ways. It says nothing about any advance in life forms on the earth but records the making of the two great lights of heaven, the sun and moon. Theologians often believe that these only *appeared* first on that day, that their light first shown clearly, rather than in diffused form, on the earth at that time. On this basis the harmonizers of Genesis and evolutionary geology thought that the great quantities of carbon dioxide removed from the air in the great coal beds of the Carboniferous period so cleared the atmosphere that the light of sun, moon and stars could finally reach directly, rather than in diffused form, the surface of the earth. This hypothesis, whether valid or not, at least appeared to sustain the harmony between Genesis and geology up to the end of the fourth day of Creation Week.

The simple fact is that no matter where a person decides to place the appearance of birds and animals in the scheme of geologic ages, the fifth and sixth days will not correspond with the Genesis account of creation except in a most general way. According to Genesis, birds and sea animals followed plants in the order of life forms on earth, and beasts and "creeping things" were made on the sixth

day, after birds. But in the scheme of geologic ages, "creeping things" and even animals which the ancient Hebrews would call beasts preceded the appearance of birds. However, since the Scriptures recorded the coming of most of what we call the higher animals after the lower, with man the latest of the great kinds of creatures to appear, there seemed to be a general harmony between Genesis and the theory of geologic history which was built upon the belief that the earth started through the Nebular Hypothesis.

Once the belief in the system of geologic ages was firmly established among scientists and theologians, such serious inconsistencies between Genesis and the geologic ages became apparent that geology was used to assail, not to sustain, the Genesis account of creation. Early geologists, like Dana and Sir J. W. Dawson emphasized the supposed correspondence between Genesis and geology, but only a rare individual will do so now and theologians and geologists alike admit that the correspondence does not exist.

## WHERE THE NEBULAR HYPOTHESIS FAILED

If geologists still believed in the Nebular Hypothesis, there would be reason to show how false it is, but since they now acknowledge their helplessness in devising any explanation for the origin of the solar system that has any real merit, there is no occasion to go into this matter in detail.[6] However, a few leading fea-

---

[6] Statements indicating the inability of scientists to decide how the solar system came into being are so frequent the last few years that citations of them should be unnecessary. Possibly the most thorough discussion of the subject is in H. N. Russell's *The Origin of the Solar System.* However, one or two quotations may be in order. These are taken from the recently published Harvard Books on Astronomy:

"All of the hypotheses so far presented have failed, when physical theory has been properly applied." (p. 231) "There appear to be damning arguments against every theory so far proposed for the origin of the planets." Whipple, F. G., *Earth, Moon and Planets,* p. 238.

"We might say that comets represent the debris left over when the solar system was formed. But that is no answer for we do not know how the solar system was formed." Watson, F. G., *Between the Planets,* p. 85.

tures of the case may well be mentioned.

In the first place, there are no nebulae in the heavens as far as is known like the nebula that was postulated in the Nebular Hypothesis. Those which resemble them in appearance are now known by better telescopes and photography to be galaxies of distant stars and not masses of star dust which would condense into individual stars. Although there are shapeless clouds of star dust in parts of the heavens, these are not rotating, nor disk-shaped, nor contracting to form stars, for all that can be seen.

The essential feature of a nebula which would contract into a solar system would have to be such rapid rotation that it would be disk-shaped, and it is practically inconceivable that gaseous matter could come together in the heavens in such form. A disk-like, rapidly rotating nebula composed of solid particles like those which compose the rings of Saturn might conceivably exist, though only the miracle of creation could bring it into being as far as is known. However, this kind of a nebula is not what was assumed, nor would it possibly contract to form a solar system.

There are stars which are gigantic masses of very rarefied gases in the heavens, but they are globular, not disk-shaped, and while they may in time contract into stars resembling our sun, it is most unlikely that they can contract into solar systems.

However, when we go back still farther in hypothetical time to the origin of either nebula or star, creation of some sort is ultimately necessary. Stars which send forth light are intensely hot, but space distant from stars is intensely cold, so that matter existing there would have a temperature little, if any, above absolute zero. Cold matter will not accumulate, naturally, in cold space to form a hot star. Therefore, regardless how we may theorize, a beginning creation is absolutely demanded.

The one fault above all others which convinced scientists as to the inadequacy of the Nebular Hypothesis is the relative amounts of angular momentum[7] in the sun and other parts of the system. If a nebula rotated so rapidly that it assumed the form of a disk in order that the planets could separate from a central mass, this central mass would have to rotate rapidly, with much angular momentum. Instead, the sun rotates lazily, while the planets have a far greater amount of angular momentum in proportion to their masses, which keeps them traveling in circular orbits around the sun instead of falling into it.

There are other obstacles to belief in the Nebular Hypothesis, only one more of which needs be mentioned. In certain of the outer planets there are satellites which rotate in reverse to the normal direction, the normal direction being from west to east, in the direction the moon travels around the earth. Seemingly this could not occur if the solar system took form through the Nebular Hypothesis, and it would be hard to explain under any alternative theory of evolutionary

---

[7] "The angular momentum of a planet moving in a circular orbit at a given distance from the sun is the product of the mass, distance and speed." (Expressed informally, it can be said to be the force which keeps it moving around the sun instead of falling into it. The angular momentum of the sun is the force which keeps it rotating.)
"Jupiter, with its great mass, carries about six-tenths of the entire angular momentum of the whole system. The four giant planets contribute about ninety-eight per cent, and the terrestrial planets a fifth of a per cent. The sun, with a thousand times the mass of Jupiter, rotates so slowly that its angular momentum is only two per cent of the whole."
Whipple, Fred L., The Earth, Moon and Planets, 1941, p. 233.

origin which had merit enough to make it obtain favor.

## THE ENCOUNTER THEORY AND ITS DEFICIENCY

Although creation as an explanation of the origin of the earth and the rest of the solar system was rejected because of the assumed truth of the Nebular Hypothesis and the supposed merits of the system of geologic ages, it only needed a detailed examination of the data to show that the Nebular Hypothesis was wrong. This was given toward the close of the last century by T. C. Chamberlain and F. R. Moulton who showed that there were so many faults in the Hypothesis that it had to be discarded.

In its place they proposed the theory that a star passing near the sun long ago caused matter to leave the sun and become the earth and other planets. This is now called the "Encounter Theory." It has had several forms, the first of which, devised by Chamberlain and Moulton, was called the Planetesimal Hypothesis. According to this hypothesis the earth was believed to have started, not as a molten hot mass, but as a solid globe much smaller than at present and to have grown by the fall of "planetesimals," or as we might say, meteors and meteorites. The ocean and atmosphere were believed to have come mainly from within the earth through volcanic activity, rather than to have existed at the surface from the beginning.

While the first form of the Planetesimal Hypothesis had to be modified all subsequent modifications also proved to be too much at fault to merit acceptance. The Tidal Theory, developed in Great Britain as another form of the Encounter Theory, also had its brief day of favor before it too was rejected. It is now generally admitted that no naturalistic method by which the solar system could take form is acceptable though belief in some undiscovered and undefined form of Encounter Theory is generally expressed.

Scholars still tend to favor in a general way the Encounter Theory as a means of accounting for the origin of the earth and the rest of the solar system, but every attempt to decide how it could operate fails. In addition to many minor difficulties, two outstanding difficulties exist. One difficulty is that if a great mass (or several smaller masses) shot out from the sun, this matter, instead of remaining together until it could condense into planets or their nuclei, would, on account of its extremely high temperature, explode and spread out into space. This is one of the most damaging objections ever brought against any and all forms of the Encounter Theory. This feature also leaves unsolved and apparently beyond solution all explanations based upon the dogma of evolution for the presence on the earth of the gaseous elements, oxygen, hydrogen, nitrogen, and so on, which make up the ocean and atmosphere of the earth.

The second outstanding objection to the Encounter Theory to which special attention should be directed is the difficulty which matter, having been thrown off from the sun, would have in attaining circular orbits like those of the planets. This matter, losing its momentum as it proceeded away from the sun, would tend to be pulled back into the sun. Or, if for some reason it passed to one side of the sun without falling into it, the orbit would be extremely elliptical, like that of many comets. One part of the path would be close to the sun and the distant part far from the sun, whereas the paths of the planets, though slightly flattened, are nearly circular.

This difficulty has received some attention, with a lack of success which is quite apparent. Speaking of the earth, the authors of a current textbook in geology write: "Its original course must therefore have been highly elliptical, and the present nearly circular orbits of the planets require an explanation. For this Jeans and Jeffreys invoke the interference of the gases that leaked away from the filament—(the explanation goes with the Tidal Theory by the two men mentioned)—formed a vast atmosphere prevading the whole system, and rotated as a unit with the sun. For a time this gaseous medium may have been relatively dense. . . ."[8] There is no need to give the complete explanation. The resistence of the gas is presumed to have rounded out the orbits of the planets.

The explanation, such as it is, provides a striking example of the unscientific reasoning done by scientists of the highest rank in their efforts to explain, naturally, what can be explained only on the basis of the divine ordering of the universe by the Creator.

For one thing, a filament drawn from the sun, as the Tidal Theory has it, would, by the high temperature of the gases composing it, explode and be scattered through solar space instead of having gases leak from it. Moreover, there would be no prospect of it rotating "as a unit with the sun" except perhaps to a very small extent. Again, instead of such gas being relatively dense, it would be extremely rarefied, particularly if it extended out as far as the orbits of Uranus, Neptune and Pluto. The latter is more than 19 times the distance of the earth from the sun, and the earth is 93 million miles from that body. By the time that this hypothetical gaseous atmosphere rounded out the orbit of Pluto, to say nothing of Jupiter, Saturn, Uranus and Nep-

tune, it would accomplish a most astounding miracle. Finally, if there was such a gaseous medium to round out the orbits of the planets, Pluto certainly would have picked up a great amount of the gas, whereas it holds no atmosphere at all and has no frosty covering. Astronomers are therefore helpless in explaining how the planets could attain their nearly circular orbits by any form of the Encounter Theory.

The general situation can perhaps best be understood by viewing the Nebular Hypothesis and the Encounter Theory together. The view that the system began by the contraction of a rotating Nebula would explain the orbits of the planets fairly well, but not the orbits of some of their satellites, and it has too many faults in other ways to allow it to be accepted. The only known alternative to this, outside of *creation* is some form of the Encounter Theory, but every form of this fails completely when studied in detail. One of the serious failures here is in finding a way that the planets could attain their nearly circular orbits. Minor difficulties with both Nebular Hypothesis and Encounter Theory need not be mentioned. It is enough to say that not only are astronomers and geologists at a loss to work out any satisfactory evolutionary explanation for the origin of the earth and the rest of the solar system, but they also admit this deficiency.

COMPARATIVE COMPOSITION OF
THE SUN AND EARTH

Aside from the failings of the Nebular Hypothesis and all forms of the Encounter Theory that have yet been suggested from a mechanical or dynamic standpoint, there is another fundamental weakness in all efforts to account for the origin of the earth by evolution. This concerns the

[8] Schuchert, Charles, and Dunbar, Carl O., *A Textbook of Geology*, Part 2, *Historical Geology*, 933, p. 60.

composition of the earth and of the sun.

It is generally stated that the earth and the other planets are the offspring of the sun, that is, that they were formed from material which came (in some unknown way) from the sun. Formerly no special problem seemed to exist in this connection, for the elements composing the earth seemed to be found in the sun, also in meteorites, and presumably the proportion of the different elements in the sun was of a kind which would reasonably give the earth, Venus, Mars, Jupiter and the other planets the kind of composition they have.

Recently, however, a serious difficulty in this connection has developed which seems to be the outgrowth more of the problem of the manufacture of heat in the sun than of the actual observation of that body.

Lord Kelvin pointed out many years ago that a serious problem existed in trying to figure how the sun could provide heat and light to keep the solar system going for more than a few million years, and the kind of geologic history generally believed cannot be reasonably crowded into that period of time. A solution to this problem seemingly was suggested by the discovery of radioactivity and the apparent relationship between energy and matter. Physicists thought for a while that heat could be produced for untold millions of years in the sun by the destruction of the atom, only to find that apparently they were wrong. Then by degrees they decided that the transformation of hydrogen into helium by several intermediate steps could keep the sun producing heat much as at present for billions of years. This is their current explanation for the assumed very great age of both sun and earth.

However, to make this hypothesis reasonable for the production of heat in the sun for billions of years, it was found necessary to assume a very high hydrogen and helium content of the sun both now and in the past. If, therefore, the sun had anything like such composition when the solar system formed, the earth and the rest of the planets would almost certainly contain immense quantities of helium and even be composed mainly of hydrogen and helium. But the earth is not so constituted, nor are the other planets. In other words, the earth has not the kind of composition it should have if it were derived from the sun, as the geologists believe. This difficulty might possibly be avoided by deciding that the sun has not this high hydrogen and helium content, but in that case both astronomic and geologic theory would be demoralized by the inability of the sun to produce heat for more than a brief period, as astronomers and geologists estimate time.

Recent calculations made on the assumption that the sun is very old and that it manufactures heat by the transformation of hydrogen into helium give the sun a hydrogen content of 51 per cent and a helium content of 42 per cent, with only seven per cent of the heavier elements. These rsults are only thought to be approximate, though not far from correct.[9] Going far back in time to the origin of the solar system, the hydrogen content would be somewhat greater than that named and the helium content somewhat less. However, the helium content would still be high.

The problem then would be to get the earth and other planets from a sun which had that composition, but with so little of both hydrogen and helium in the earth and other planets

---

[9] Russell, H. N., *Present State of the Theory of Stellar Evolution*, Scientific Monthly, Sept., 1942, p. 236.

the thing seems impossible. The earth, for example, is composed almost entirely of metallic and stony materials. There is almost no hydrogen on earth except in water, of which it comprises about one part in nine, and helium exists as a mere trace in both rocks and atmosphere. If the sun from which the earth was made contained much helium, say a fourth or a third, both earth and the other planets should contain great quantities of that element. The practical absence of helium from the planets discredits the hypothesis that the planets were made from the sun.[10] Or, the astronomers can go back to the conclusion (which the writer believes more sound) that there are comparatively small quantities of both helium and hydrogen in the sun. But if this is done, the theory that the sun and the earth are untold millions of years old will have to be discarded and geologic history rewritten on an entirely different basis from that believed and taught by geologists.

## ORIGIN OF THE OCEAN AND ATMOSPHERE

Other serious difficulties exist in accounting for the composition of the earth by any evolutionary theory of the origin. For example, geologists have long been uncertain regarding the source of ocean[11] and atmosphere on the earth. When the problem of their origin is studied, it would seem impossible that the earth would have the ocean and atmosphere it has if the material composing it came from the sun.

The temperature of the sun is thousands of degrees higher than that of the earth. Material shot out from it into space would be fiery hot so that it would be dissipated through space and by the time the metallic and stony material assembled to form solid particles, little, if any, oxygen and hydrogen to form water would be present upon those particles; and when these solids gathered together to form the earth, it would be a hot, dry earth. The planet Pluto, far out in space, is about the size of the

---

[10] This matter of the amount of helium in the sun and the rest of the solar system in relation to the possible age of the sun and of the solar system as a whole is of basic importance in considering the possible history of the earth, and a few details in connection with this problem should prove instructive.

Whipple (*Between the Planets*, p. 201) writes: "In interplanetary and interstellar space are atoms of hydrogen, sodium, calcium, titanium and probably other elements." Note that helium is conspicuous by its absence. If it were there in appreciable amount it doubtless would have been mentioned. Also physicists try to account for the mere trace of helium in the atmosphere of the earth by the escape of helium from the atmosphere. If it escaped from planets so readily, presumably it would be more abundant in space.

On its possible escape from the earth he writes, "For helium it is about the mass of the Earth. . . ." "The values apply for a surface temperature of 2,000 degrees F.—corresponding to liquid volcanic lava." He is dealing with the temperatures necessary for helium and other gases to escape into solar space from the earth and other planets. (p. 241.)

On the constitution of the major planets he writes: (p. 241) "The giant planets possess huge quantities of hydrogen and perhaps helium," while these elements are rare on the earth." Note that the presence of helium in appreciable quantities is asserted with the qualification of a *perhaps*. The "huge quantities" of hydrogen still leave it much less in amount than that of the heavier elements.

On page 243, *probably* has to be used in asserting the presence of much helium in the sun. This would not be necessary if observation showed great quantities of helium there. The statement goes, "The overwhelming abundance of hydrogen and probably helium on the sun . . ."

[11] Whitney, Dudley Joseph, *The Age of the Earth*, Bulletin of Deluge Geology, Vol. 1, 1941, pp. 120-132.

earth, but has neither atmosphere nor icy covering.[12] Evidently no material has separated out from it to form ocean or atmosphere. It is therefore difficult to see why the earth on forming should develop an ocean or atmosphere from within itself. It is also difficult to understand how it could attain it from solar space other than by the express wish and act of the Creator.

There seems also to be an insurmountable problem in getting an ocean of anything like the composition of the present ocean naturally, or except by the express wish and act of creation. This is particularly true when the sulphur and chlorine content of the ocean is considered. From the material available for making an earth it would seem that, naturally speaking, the ocean should contain very little chlorine but have an enormous amount of sulphur. In fact, by any purely naturalistic origin, the earth should be so rich in sulphur on its surface that life for common plants and animals would be impossible.

The earth has often been compared to a gigantic meteorite, the material of which has been sorted by heat. But meteorites normally contain great amounts of sulphur and comparatively little water or chlorine, though chlorine is often present in appreciable quantities. Since the average amount of sulphur in meteorites i estimated as being not far from 1.87 to 1.9 per cent,[13] on this basis about one part in 53 to 55 of the earth would be sulphur if the earth were made from material like that composing meteorites, and that sulphur would now be concentrated mainly on its surface.

Sulphur is easily vaporized by heat and the earth is very hot within and

has generally been believed once to have been molten. If it were molten, the sulphur should be gathered mostly at the surface, but it is not. There is little in the surface rocks and comparatively little in the salts of the ocean.

Sulphur also is known to exist abundantly in the earth as metallic sulphides, that is, united directly with certain metals and other elements. A layer of the earth from 750 to 1800 miles down is believed to be composed in large part of sulphides.[14] These also exist in great quantity in parts of the earth's crust in certain ores, and volcanoes often emit great quantities of liquid sulphur and various sulphur compounds. As has been said, with so much sulphur as part of the earth, only *creation* seemingly could start an earth with so little sulphur at the surface.

Meanwhile the chlorine of the earth seems to be concentrated mainly in the ocean where it exists in several times as great amount as sulphur.

If the earth were originally molten, or if the material of the earth has in some way been sorted by heat, as appears to be the case, this is where most of the chlorine should be; only heat should have driven the sulphur to the surface too, and it is not there. Thus no naturalistic system for starting the earth will seemingly account for the condition of the surface of the earth, for the presence of ocean and atmosphere, and for the abundance of chlorine in the ocean and yet for the comparatively small quantity of sulphur compounds there.

If necessary we could continue this study of details connected with the composition and nature of the earth and show how inadequate are all naturalistic theories to account for

[12] Whipple, Fred L., *loc. cit.* p. 190
[13] Longwell, Knoph and Flint, *A Textbook of Geology,* Part 1 *Physical Geology,* 1932, p. 370.

[14] Watson, F. G., *Between the Planets,* 1941, p. 177.

them. An example is the way that volcanic eruptions are accompanied by the emission of enormous quantities of water vapor and other gases. How did that water vapor get within an earth whose internal temperature seems to be very high? Heat tends to turn water into a gas and make it spread out in space. While the material of the earth was assembling to make the globe, apparently the water would remain a vapor and part of the atmosphere. It would not be likely to enter the earth. Geologists simply do not know how to account for the origin of the ocean, or of the atmosphere, or the water within the earth. Their theories on the origin of the earth and the rest of the solar system fail when viewed in the larger aspects, as in the theories like the Nebular Hypothesis and the Encounter Theory. And they fail when viewed from the standpoint of special problems like that of the source of the water of volcanism. Studies of features such as these, however, deserve a place by themselves. Certainly until the scientists can present a reasonable and consistent naturalistic hypothesis for the origin of the earth, and a reasonable explanation for its nature at the start, which will make the kind of history they assert for it seem probable, they have no right to set forth a kind of history of the earth which they can ask the public to believe.

## FITNESS OF
## ENVIRONMENT FOR LIFE

Closely related to the problem of the origin of the earth is the matter of the fitness of the earth for life. Only a most harmonious combination of chemical and physical conditions make it possible for the numerous life forms of the earth to exist and prosper. Plants, animals, and men may be said to live on a kind of a 'knife edge" of environment, and if the earth were only a little warmer, or colder, or a little different in several other ways, life would either be impossible or could exist in only the most simple forms. Now, even if we agree on the possibility that a solar system with one or more planets of the approximate size of the earth might evolve into being, the chances that conditions on them would be suitable for life such as exists on this earth are almost infinitesimally small. On this basis the theory of divine creation of the earth is infinitely superior to the theory of evolution. This can be seen when the case is examined in some detail.

The matter of temperature is generally held to be of prime importance when a suitable environment for plants and animals is investigated. Water is very important in the make up of plants and animals. The temperature cannot be so low that the water will be a solid rather than a liquid, and in fact for most plant and animal life the temperature must be at least several degrees above freezing, for appreciable lengths of time at least. When warm blooded animals endure colder temperatures it is because internal processes supply them with heat.

On the other hand temperatures approaching the normal boiling point of water are such as to make most life processes impossible, though inactive spores of some organisms can endure fairly high temperatures. As far as man is concerned, he can endure a dry heat ten to twenty, or even more degrees above blood temperature, but a moist heat at blood temperature or a little greater is almost unendurable, if the condition continues for any length of time. This is true with many animals as well as man. There is thus a very narrow range of temperature at which life can prosper, and the chemical nature of the elements is such that it is inconceivable that at some other higher or lower belt of temperature other substances could act like water, carbon compounds and the other substances which are so important in life processes. The temperature suitable for life on earth is the only temperature possible at which highly varied forms of living organisms could thrive. This narrow range of temperature is hard to find in the universe. The stars that we see are fiery hot, so that life could not exist upon them, and out from the stars in dark space the temperature approaches absolute zero, or far below the freezing point of water, and life could not function there.

A world that evolved into being, in order to be fully satisfactory for plants and animals, should rotate at about the same rate as the earth. More rapid rotation would give days and nights of short length, which might not be harmful, but slow rotation would give long days and nights. Long nights would tend to allow too much escape of heat into space and they would likely be too cold, while long days would tend to be too hot. The evolved world could not be too distant from its sun, for then the years would be long and the summers too hot, and the winters too cold. The distance of such a world from its sun would be goverened by the amount of heat and light received from that sun, and this brings us back again to the problem of temperature. If too far from the sun, the temperature would be too low, and if too close to the sun, it would be too high.

An absolute necessity for life is therefore some body which is not hot and glowing, but one which would be dark and cold unless it received both heat and light from some larger body like the sun, and this would have to be at the proper distance to supply enough heat and not too much, and enough light but not too much.

This other world, if it existed, could not be too large because then the force of gravity would be too great for most kinds of organisms to function well; they would weigh too much. On the other hand a much smaller globe could not contain sufficient atmosphere for successful plant and animal growth and for the control of temperature. The moon contains no atmosphere because it is too small to hold one, and Mars contains only a small atmosphere, too small altogether for plant life of any but the most simple kind, and even that probably does not exist.

The atmosphere of an other world could not be much less dense than that of the earth, otherwise the days would be too hot or the nights too cold. The atmospheric pressure on earth of 14.7 pounds per square inch at sea level seems about ideal for human welfare and for the proper control of temperature. While the human body might stand a higher pressure, the air, when moist, at such an higher temperature would contain far more moisture than at our sea level and make human life almost unendurable at anything like blood temperature, for air can contain far more moisture at a high pressure than at a lower one. That is why rain falls when moist air rises and expands.

On the other hand a materially reduced atmosphere would make living conditions difficult. Since a light atmosphere can take up far less moisture than now, the raifall would be less, though evaporation from the ground and from leaf surfaces would be greater, provided moisture was available to evaporate. Also a lighter atmosphere would blanket the ground less against the escape of heat and the days would be hotter and the nights colder. An earth which evolved into being ought to have an atmosphere of approximately the present size, and of course, composition.

The composition of the atmosphere in the nature of the case is extremely important. The two main gases of the atmosphere are oxygen and nitrogen. There are also some minor, inert gases, such as argon and neon, which we need not consider. Nitrogen in the atmosphere is almost chemically inert, but in combination with oxygen, hydrogen and carbon, it is one of the four most important elements in plant and animal nutrition. We hear much about protein these days and proteins are nutrients in which nitrogen is abundant. In the atmosphere there are about four parts of nitrogen to one of oxygen.

If the oxygen were very much less, animal life would have difficulty in functioning. It is needed to "burn" the carbon compounds of the blood and so produce heat and energy. If it were much greater in amount it would doubtless stimulate animal activities too much, and if it were in much less amount they could hardly function. Yet we have seen that the problem of the oxygen of the air is one of the most puzzling to geologists in their theorizing about the nature of the earth. They do not even know whether there was any free oxygen at the start in their theorizing about the origin of the earth. From a naturalistic standpoint the presence in the atmosphere of sufficient free oxygen—and particularly the right amount of oxygen and no great excess—is one of the most puzzling problems of geochemistry.

The carbon of the atmosphere is likewise all essential in the problem of life, for without carbon dioxide in the air there could be no plant growth and so no food for animals, yet the carbon dioxide content of the air is only 3/10,000 of one percent, a trivial amount it would seem. It amounts to only a small fraction of an ounce over each square inch of the earth's surface, yet this amount proves satisfactory for plant growth. More might provide satisfactory conditions for plant life, but much less would make plant and animal life almost impossible. The amount and composition of the atmosphere is amazingly suited for both plants and animals: but delicately balanced.

In the ocean one of the marvels is the abundance, but not the excess, of sodium chloride, common table salt, and the comparatively small amount of sulphates (compounds of sulphur and oxygen with other elements).This is somewhat paradoxical because sulphates are known to be added to the ocean in far greater excess than chlorides and, naturally speaking, this should apply to the past. Nevertheless, for satisfactory marine life the present balance between sulphates and chlorides is what is best. That this could occur naturally, rather than by divine ordering, seems unbelievable.

In the rocks there are many elements which exist in soils in extremely small amounts, and in certain cases in insufficient amounts and yet they are necessary for plant and animal life, or for certain kinds of living forms at least. In some instances, as with arsenic, an excess would be very injurious, but without traces of it certain plants and animals could not prosper. Boron, from which comes borax, is another necessary element, though more than a very little of this element would be very harmful.

Of selenium, which may not be necessary for most plants, it can be said that there are certain areas in which there is so much of the element that plants growing there are poisonous to stock. Fortunately such areas are rare, but this shows how easily an earth might evolve, if solar systems did evolve, in which life, at least of everything but the most simple kinds, could not exist.

The thing is particularly noteworthy when we consider the nature of meteorites, which presumably are typical of the stuff of which worlds are made. These, it has been pointed out, normally contain on an average from 1.87 to 1.9 percent sulphur, and this sulphur naturally would tend to accumulate at the surface of the planet as it took form. Theoretically it would cover such a planet deeper than the ocean covers the earth, but if it did life would be impossible.

Whether we consider the size of the earth, or its surface temperature, or the size and nature of the atmosphere, or the composition of the ocean and of the land, everything proclaims such an amazing and delicately balanced fitness of the environment as seemingly to demand the work of the Creator.

"O Lord, how manifold are thy works! In wisdom hast thou made them all."[15]

### SUMMARY AND CONCLUSION

A system of geologic history has been proposed by scientists at large which has been generally accepted by scholars as fact for more than a century on two false assumptions. (1) That they knew how it started. And (2) the conditions which they assumed at the start they believed, erroneously, would account for "the grander phenomena of earth's history."

---

[15] Psalm 104:24.

Yet in one important detail after another the advance of knowledge has been in conflict with their early conclusions and made unreasonable a belief in the kind of history which they have assumed for the earth. Long after the Nebular Hypothesis should have been rejected it was still taught as fact. When finally it was weighed in the balances and found wanting, a substitute was put forth in its place which was also found to be altogether unsatisfactory. The nature of the earth itself is in conflict with this kind of history. The next logical step should be to cast aside these beliefs and teachings regarding the history of the earth and with an open mind to examine anew the problem.

By logical deduction, which should characterize all genuine scientific thought, the failure of evolution, or purely naturalistic processes in accounting for the origin of the earth and the rest of the solar system, should suggest the possibility of a special *creation* for its origin, and a history after creation very different from that which has been believed and taught for more than a century.

THE

# BULLETIN

OF

# DELUGE GEOLOGY

### AND RELATED SCIENCES

Volume 2         December 1942         Number 5

## THE CONFLICT OVER THE EVOLUTION THEORY

### A REVIEW OF CERTAIN DEVELOPMENTS IN BIOLOGY IN THE LAST TWENTY-FIVE YEARS

#### MOLLEURUS COUPERUS, M. D.

To review, even briefly, all the important events in the controversy over evolution during the last quarter of a century would constitute a major piece of work, entirely beyond the scope of a paper such as this. Instead, we will confine ourselves to a consideration of certain important trends in the biological aspects of the controversy, and in addition call attention to a number of events, personalities, and statements which, to the author at least, seem important.

Twenty-five years in retrospect takes us into the closing days of the first World War. Without hesitation it may be said that this inhuman struggle brought keen disillusionment to many an evolutionist who had subscribed to a belief in an ever better world, a world which, by its own inherent powers, inevitably would rise above such things as war. Many of these sadder and wiser men had no doubt failed to realize that the very doctrines of the "survival of the fittest" and the "struggle for existence" had something in them that might be seed for war, as was exemplified by the interpretation of these doctrines in the teachings and philosophy of Friedrich Nietzsche and his "superman."

### FAILURE OF THE BIOGENIC LAW

One of the most disillusioned of militant evolutionists was Ernest Haeckel. He had been the most ardent champion of Darwinism on the European continent, an uncompromising monist, who had attempted to solve the riddles of the universe through the application of evolution to both the inorganic and organic world, as well as to the fields of psychology, philosophy, and religion. During the latter years of his life, Haeckel, though a materialist, occupied himself more and more with a peculiar sort of mysticism which even his closest admirers had difficulty in understanding. Haeckel died in Jena in 1919, and although his semi-popu-

The BULLETIN is published by, and is the official organ of the "Society for the Study of Deluge Geology and Related Sciences." The Editorial Board is comprised of Professor George McCready Price and Dr. Cyril B. Courville. It is printed at the Collegiate Press, Arlington, California. For members the BULLETIN is free, and extra copies 30 cents each (each number priced according to size); for non-members it is $2.00 per year; and this number is 40 cents. All correspondence should be directed to the Managing Editor, Mr. Ben F. Allen, 219 North Grand Avenue, Los Angeles, California.

lar books, such as the *Natural History of Creation*, were still read by many laymen, his theories of recapitulation and those of man's ancestral tree had already been severely attacked by outstanding biologists. Among these critics was Oscar Hertwig (1849-1922), Professor of anatomy at the University of Berlin, who overthrew the Natural Selection theory and criticized the Recapitulation theory severely. The main point in his criticism of the latter was that the ovum, or germinal cell, is as specialized as the adult organism, and that one could not really accept the idea that such an ovum recapitulated the stage of the first primitive one-celled organism which was supposed to have started on the road of evolution.

"Who therefore wants to continue to believe in the theory of a gradual development of the more highly organized forms of life from the lowest, primitive forms, must say farewell to the claim that the germinal cell recapitulates the first stage of phylogenesis, that is, of the unicellular organism at the beginning of the ancestral chain. Both of the objects here compared and paralleled are in their nature just as different as the fully developed organisms of our day are from their unicellular ancestors. . . . Today the ontogenesis of every form of life has to start with a cell only because it is the elementary, basic form on which organic life is dependent in its reproduction process. . . . The germinal cells of the present-day forms of life and their unicellular ancestors at the beginning of their developmental history—may we call them amoeba or something else—are only, as far as they fall under the common concept of the cell, comparable with each other, but are in their essential character as organized objects of nature so different from each other that one in no wise can speak of a recapitulation of the unicellular ancestral form in the development of an organism living today."[1]

If Hertwig had followed this thought to its logical conclusion, it would seem that he should have discarded the entire hypothesis; as it was, he held fast to a modified, less pretentious version of the theory. Others, however, showed the full fallacy of Haeckel's so-called Biogenetic Law. The views of such is illustrated by the following statement of Shumway,[2] of the University of Illinois:

"A consideration of these biological developments, utterly foreign to the biological background of the early Haeckelians, taken with the many observational departures from the embryological sequences demanded by the theory of recapitulation, as well as the logical difficulties arising from an examination of the theory itself, seems to demand that the hypothesis be abandoned."

It may be said that with the death of Haeckel in 1919 a definite period had come to an end in the history of the theory of evolution, the Neo-Darwinian period. The beginnings of a new period date back to the birth of the twentieth century, although it is not quite possible to date the start of this new phase in the history of the theory by any definite year; in fact, the roots of a new movement in the old theory silently came into being many years before such a movement itself became evident. Many scientists began to revolt against unfounded and speculative theories of evolution, and turned their attention to exact and fundamental research which showed so many of the favored theories in the field of evolution to be untenable, and caused a number of outstanding workers to adopt an agnostic attitude towards the entire subject of evolution, while still others rejected the hypothesis completely. All this, however, did not prevent the great majority of scientists from subscribing to the words of Bateson: "Let us then proclaim in precise and unmistakable language that our faith in evolution is unshaken."

[1] Hertwig, O.: *Das Werden der Organismen*, 1916, 2 Ed., 1918, Jena, p. 205.
[2] Shumway, W.: "The Recapitulation Theory," *Quart. Rev. of Biol.*, Vol. 7, 1932, pp. 93-99.

The new science of genetics especially, which followed the work of Gregor Mendel, brought many facts to light which proved to be difficult to harmonize with any theory of evolution. We have no space to enumerate the many illustrous names which are connected with this work since the beginning of this century, but recall Hugo de Vries, Wilhelm Johannsen, Erwin Baur, William Bateson, L. Cuenot, and Thomas Hunt Morgan, whose untiring labors contributed so much to the progress of the new science.

## GENETICS AND EVOLUTION

There soon seemed to come a definite and deep breach between geneticists and paleontologists, since the facts uncovered by the first contradicted the deductions made by the latter from the fossils. This is clearly seen in an article written by the paleontologist William K. Gregory,[3] of the American Museum of Natural History, from which we take the following:

"Yet such is the skepticism which sometimes results from modern studies in genetics that I have known graduate students who seriously doubted the reality and value of the principle of progressive and retrogressive adaptation, on the ground that, as natural selection and the inheritance of 'acquired' characters had both been disproved, there was no conceivable means whereby adaptation could be brought about! . . . The second idea which seems to be implied by Professor Bateson, and which I have heard certain university students express, is that phylogenetic 'speculations' are unverifiable, because 'control experiments' are not possible. By similar reasoning geological theories concerning the history of the earth . . . are equally untrustworthy. . . . Professor Morgan makes a serious and important criticism of the comparative anatomical and paleontological doctrine that structures have been derived by progressive continuous stages."

## JOHANNSEN AND HEREDITY

After the neglected findings of Gregor Mendel had been resurrected, it was especially the work of Wilhelm Johannsen, professor of plant physiology at the university of Copenhagen, which brought facts to light that discredited the views of the Darwinians. Born in 1857, he was in the prime of his life when the new science of genetics arose, and when many began to investigate hereditary laws and processes he saw the importance of working with as pure strains or lines of genetical material as possible in order to study variation in animals and plants. His investigative work with pure lines of beans was done during the first years of this century, and its influence was far reaching. He found that in such pure lines there were certain characteristics which remained unchanged from generation to generation, and he classified such characters as belonging to the *genotype,* which is hereditary; other characteristics of these beans he found to be variable, depending on soil, climate, and other factors, which characters Johannsen designated with the name *phenotype,* and which are not hereditary.

Of the true influence of Darwinism and other evolutionary theories on biological science Johannsen[4] had the following to say:

"What disturbed the calm development of the science of heredity the most was the great breach in biology caused by the appearance of Darwin. As the evolutionary doctrine and even the whole developmental philosophy revolutionized the science of natural history after the middle of the last century, one might have believed that of necessity the science of heredity should have become more thorough, deeper. It happened, however, entirely different . . . the *exact study of the problems of heredity* was neglected, in order that they might devote themselves in more or less speculative manner to the study of the problems of descent.

---

[3] Gregory, W. K.: "Genetics Versus Paleontology," *Amer. Nat.,* Vol. 51, 1917, pp. 625-626.
[4] Johannsen, W.: *Elemente der exakten Erblichkeits-lehre,* 3 Ed., 1926, Jena, p. 5.

... For the time being the victorious theory of descent had little need of the support of a more thorough science of heredity; for that reason investigations on heredity were destined to stagnation—it being much more inviting to philosophize about developmental problems, to construct 'ancestral trees', to search for 'missing links' and the like, instead of giving oneself to the very sober, much more circumscribed, laborious and in any case at that time thankless mission of determining in exact manner the relationship between the characteristics of parents and children in animals, plants, and human beings."

Johannsen saw clearly the fallaciousness of confusing similarity among plants and animals with proof of relationship. Few scientists have expressed themselves as forcefully on this point as he:

"Genealogical relationship, external similarity and internal fundamental hereditary equipment are certainly in part so independent of each other that it is unreliable to arrive at conclusions of one for the other. The fundamental biological mistake of many speculations about heredity and descent are to be found right here: *the false conception* that similarity must be unquestionably an expression of relationship—or even that 'heredity' can be expressed by 'the degree of similarity between relatives'. . . . It is an unfortunate use of language to employ the word 'related' as being identical with 'similar'."[5]

Johannsen conceived of evolution as a philosophy, and not as an exact branch of the sciences. He definitely stated that the chief question of evolution, whether or not the selection of individual variants could change the genotypical constitution and create new biotypes, was being answered with an always clearer "No."

## FAILURE OF PHYLOGENETIC SPECULATIONS OF PLANT ORIGINS

Working as a botanist and geneticist at the same time as Johannsen, was Jan Paulus Lotsy, born in Dordrecht, Holland, in 1867. He was an indefatigable worker, who labored in many parts of the world, at one time

being lecturer at the Johns Hopkins University in Baltimore. He finally became director of the Dutch Government Herbarium at Leiden and Secretary of the Holland Society for Sciences. He died in Holland in 1931. Early in his career he became actively interested in evolution, and while connected with the University of Leiden he undertook a monumental work on the phylogeny of the plant world. After he had completed three volumes of this work, each one of nearly a thousand pages, he had to choose between two dangerous bridges, as he says, which could lead from the evolution of the gymnosperms to the dicotelydons. He concludes the third volume as follows:[6] "As long as this principal question can not be decided, one cannot think of a phylogenetic presentation of the higher dicotyledons. It is therefore useless to try and construct the phylogenetic tree any further. . . ."

One must certainly honor a man who had spent as much labor on a project as the average individual could give to it in a life time, and who then was willing to confess the uselessness of the project. He definitely turned his back on this type of work after the above lines were penned, and considered phylogeny a hypothesis with a purely speculative basis. He also saw that mutations and natural selection could not explain the multiplicity of organic forms, and he became therefore the champion of hybridization in nature, on which he wrote many articles and books. His last paper was read by him at the Fifth International Botanical Congress at Cambridge in 1930, in which he said:

"When a boy, who has learned foreign languages at school, travels in a country, the language of which he has been taught and finds that he can make himself more or less understood, he is apt to imagine that he knows that language.

[5] Johannsen: *loc. cit.*, p. 233.
[6] Lotsy, J. P.: *Vortrage über Botanische Stammesgeschichte*, Vol. 3, 1911, p. 951.

"The longer he remains in the country, however, the more he realizes how little he knows, so that he will very likely reach a stage in which he despairs of ever mastering the language in question. Yet this period of despair is the crisis, is the time which decides whether he shall succeed or fail.

"In many respects the evolutionist is in the same boat as that school-boy; in the Darwinian period we imagined to know quite a little bit of evolution, while now those among us, who have continued to study the subject, will—if they dare to face the truth—have to acknowledge that they are in a period of despair, of which they fondly hope that it shall be the crisis, which—when it can be overcome—will lead to enlightment. To open the discussion at such a moment, in which everything is in the melting-pot, might be an attractive task for a young fellow, who imagines that decisive effect must result from a discussion in so distinguished an audience as I have the honour to address; it has less attraction for an old hand, who—taught by experience—cherishes no such illusions.

"The real problem of evolution therefore is: from where did these great phyla come, and why do they, after a shorter or longer time, fade out and are replaced by others?

"It is a regrettable fact that we know practically nothing of this momentous question: there is no evidence of any of the great phyla having sprung from a pre-existing one; on the contrary, more and more evidence is accumulating of the extreme antiquity of all of them."[7]

## BIOLOGY AND EVOLUTION

A third worker in the genetical field, of international reputation, is Nils Heribert-Nilsson, of the Botanical Institute at Lund, Sweden. He was the first to prove conclusively that the *Oenothera Lamarckiana*, which De Vries had considered a mutation, was but a hybrid. His paper dealt with the species in the willow family, and was one of the finest pieces of experimental work in botany ever done. He concluded this paper as follows:[8]

"Many of the facts contained in the experimental part of this work, and the dis-

cussion of the last pages, may indeed show that the evolutionary theory can not be harmonized with the results of experimental investigation, which have been brought to fruition through Mendelism. . . . Since one *cannot deny the inductive results of Mendelian investigation*, it seems to me that we have come to the point in the theory of species formation where one must seriously consider if the only consistent solution of the contradiction would not be that we *give up the deductive theory of evolution*."

In a similar vein Nilsson wrote in 1935:[9]

"It is obvious that the investigations of the last three decades into the problem of the origin of species have not been able to show that a variational material capable of competition in the struggle for existence is formed by mutation. Further, as it has also been impossible to demonstrate a progressive adaptation by means of the transmission of acquired characters (all the numerous experiments made have yielded negative results), we are forced to this conclusion that *the theory of evolution has not been verified by experimental investigations of the origin of species*.

"There is, I think, at present as little inclination to give ear to this result as there was seventy years ago to the conception of organic evolution. It is declared to be quite simply unreasonable and also perhaps immaterial. The theory of evolution has been adequately, and more than adequately, proved in its historical form, it is said. But are we so sure that what rises before our eyes, but has not been proved to grow, has really once had an exuberant power of growth? Are we quite certain that evolution is a natural process like the growth of an organism from seed to a many-branched and blossoming tree? May it not be so that evolution is a stately edifice that we ourselves have erected, laid stone on stone and is now completed—and like every other building, dead? It is perhaps not a process that has been going on and is still going on in nature. This is a question that we shall be compelled to take up, whether we will or not The situation demands it. For as scientists we cannot rest content with a *credo, quia absurdum*.

"But is then biology without evolution conceivable? In that branch of science which

[7] Lotsy: "On the Species of the Taxonomist in its Relation to Evolution," *Genetica,* 1931, Vol. 13, pp. 1, 8.

[8] Heribert-Nilsson, N,: *Experimentelle Studien über Variabilitat, Spaltung und Evolution in der Gattung Salix, Acta Univeritatis Lundensis,* N. S. xiv:2. No. 29:143, 1918.

[9] Heribert-Nilsson, N.: *Hereditas,* 1935, xx:236-237.

I myself now represent, systematics, is not here the evolutionary theory an indispensable cornerstone? Do we not classify everything according to relationship? Yes, that is how we express it. But we classify however only according to *likeness*, and we cannot maintain that likeness denotes more than a *constitutional likeness*, the presence of the same genes, *isogenesis*, as it may be correctly formulated. It is at any rate in accordance with isogenesis that we have always classified and will always classify our systematic series. In this respect nothing will be changed, and here no danger threatens. If we call them evolutionary series it is perhaps only a—*sit venia verbo*—poetical periphrasis of the result of research.

"For the theory of evolution is surely, if we think a little more deeply on the matter, nothing but the last remnant of our anthropocentric conception. When Darwin pulled Man from his unique position into the evolutionary series he placed him at any rate at the head, and Nietzsche had Man followed by Superman. Nietzsche's Superman lies crushed by the Great War, and Darwin's Evolution has been proved to be lifeless, and probably, what is worse, to have been a fiction. What then is the trend of Biology? Are we moving towards a new *"ignoramus"* conception? Certainly not. *We are advancing to Biology as an exact Science*. Just as affinity in Chemistry or Mineralogy need not be based on the assumption that the elements have evolved from one another, from hydrogen to uranium, there is no more need of our basing the related series of biology on an evolution from amoeba to Homo and so on."

### VARIATION OR EVOLUTION

To somewhat similar conclusions, although not going as far as either Johannsen or Nilsson, came the geneticist William Bateson (1861-1926). Early in his career he became interested in the phenomena of variations, and for nearly a decade he served on a special committee appointed to study evolution. He held fast to a faith in evolution to the end, but as a student of heredity and a scientist he knew of no mechanism by which evolution could have taken place, and his intellectual honesty compelled him to admit this. In 1913 Bateson[10] wrote:

"The many converging lines of evidence point so clearly to the central fact of the origin of the forms of life by an evolutionary process that we are compelled to accept this deduction, but as to almost all the essential features, whether of cause or mode, by which specific diversity has become what we perceive it to be, we have to confess an ignorance nearly total. The transformation of masses of population by imperceptible steps guided by selection, is, as most of us now see, so inapplicable to the facts, whether of variation or of specificity, that we can only marvel both at the want of penetration displayed by the advocates of such a proposition, and at the forensic skill by which it was made to appear acceptable even for a time.

"In place of this doctrine we have little teaching of a positive kind to offer."

A year later Bateson[11] expressed himself again on this same subject, at the Melbourne meeting of the British Association for the Advancement of Science.

"As the evidence stands at present all that can be safely added in amplification of the evolutionary creed may be summed up in the statement that variation occurs as a definite event often producing a sensibly discontinuous result; that the succession of varieties comes to pass by the elevation and establishment of sporadic groups of individuals owing their origin to such isolated events; and that the change which we see as a nascent variation is often, perhaps always, one of loss. Modern research lends not the smallest encouragement or sanction to the view that gradual evolution occurs by the transformation of masses of individuals, though that fancy has fixed itself on popular imagination. The isolated events to which variation is due are evidently changes in the germinal tissues, probably in the manner in which they divide. . . . New species may be now in course of creation by this means, but the limits of the process are obviously narrow. On the other hand, we see no changes in progress around us in the contemporary world which we can imagine likely to culminate in the evolution of forms distinct in the larger sense. By intercrossing dogs, jackals, and wolves new forms of these types can be made, some of which may be species, but I see no reason to think that from such material a fox could be bred in indefinite time, or that dogs could be bred from foxes. . . .

---

[10] Bateson, W.: *Problems of Genetics*, 1913, p. 248.
[11] Bateson, W.: *Rep. Brit. Assoc. Adv. Science*, Vol. 84, 1914, pp. 20-21.

"Somewhat reluctantly, and rather from a sense of duty, I have devoted most of this Address to the evolutionary aspects of genetic research. We cannot keep these things out of our heads, though sometimes we wish we could. The outcome, as you will have seen, is negative, destroying much that till lately passed for gospel."

A few days later, at the Sydney meeting of the same Association, he stated again:[12]

"At Melbourne I spoke of the new knowledge of the properties of living things which Mendelian analysis has brought us. I indicated how these discoveries are affecting our outlook on that old problem of natural history, the origin and nature of Species, and the chief conclusion I drew was the negative one, that, though we must hold to our faith in the Evolution of Species, there is little evidence as to how it has come about, and no clear proof that the process is continuing in any considerable degree at the present time."

## FAILURE TO DEMONSTRATE THE METHOD OF EVOLUTION

In spite of the great strides which biology made during the next eight years, especially in the field of genetics, evolutionary processes did not become any clearer to Bateson. At the Toronto meeting of the American Association for the Advancement of Science, in 1921, he stated his position once more.[13]

"Standing before the American Association it is not unfit that I should begin with a personal reminiscence. In 1883 I first came to the United States to study the development of Balanoglossus at the Johns Hopkins summer laboratory, then at Hampton, Va. . . . At that time one morphological laboratory was in purpose and aim very much like another. Morphology was studied because it was the material believed to be most favorable for the elucidation of the problems of evolution, and we all thought that in embryology the quintessence of morphological truth was most palpably presented. Therefore every aspiring zoologist was an embryologist, and the one topic of professional conversation was evolution. It had been so in our Cambridge school, and it was so at Hampton.

"I wonder if there is now a single place where the academic problems of morphology which we discussed with such avidity can now arouse a moment's concern. . . . So we went on talking about evolution. That is barely 40 years ago; today we feel silence to be the safer course.

"Systematists still discuss the limits of specific distinction in a spirit, which I fear is often rather scholastic than progressive, but in the other centers of biological research a score of concrete and immediate problems have replaced evolution.

"Discussions of evolution came to an end primarily because it was obvious that no progress was being made. Morphology having been explored in its minutest corners, we turned elsewhere. Variation and heredity, the two components of the evolutionary path, were next tried. The geneticist is the successor of the morphologist. We became geneticists in the conviction that there at least must evolutionary wisdom be found. We got on fast. So soon as a critical study of variation was undertaken, evidence came in as to the way in which varieties do actually arise in descent. The unacceptable doctrine of the secular transformation of masses by the accumulation of impalpable changes become not only unlikely but gratuitous. An examination in the field of the interrelations of pairs of well characterized but closely allied 'species' next proved, almost wherever such an inquiry could be instituted, that neither could both have been gradually evolved by natural selection from a common intermediate progenitor, nor either from the other by such a process. Scarcely ever where such pairs co-exist in nature, or occupy conterminous areas do we find an intermediate normal population as the theory demands. The ignorance of common facts bearing on this part of the inquiry which prevailed among evolutionists, was, as one looks back, astonishing and inexplicable. . . . When students of other sciences ask us what is now currently believed about the origin of species we have no clear answer to give. Faith has given place to agnosticism for reasons which on such an occasion as this we may profitably consider."

## EVOLUTION AS A FAITH

In the remainder of the article Bateson discussed some of the evidence which modern genetics had brought to light on the problem of the origin

[12] Bateson, W.: loc. cit., p. 21.
[13] Bateson, W.: Science, Vol. 55, 1922, pp. 55-61.

of new species. The following sentences reveal his position:

"We cannot see how the differentiation into species came about. Variation of many kinds, often considerable, we daily witness, but no origin of species. . . . We no longer feel as we used to do, that the process of variation, now contemporaneously occurring, is the beginning of a work which needs merely the element of time for its completion; for even time can not complete that which has not yet begun."

At the close of the article Bateson once more reiterated his position of both agnosticism and faith.

"I have put before you very frankly the considerations which have made us agnostic as to the actual mode and processes of evolution. . . . Let us then proclaim in precise and unmistakable language that our faith in evolution is unshaken."

### THE BATESON-OSBORN CONTROVERSY

It is evident from Bateson's article that the one thing which probably kept his *faith* in evolution strong was the so-called paleontological evidence; most of the other lines of argument for evolution he practically dismissed in the first part of his paper. Bateson's address caused quite a bit of discussion in both the secular and scientific press, but one of the most interesting objections came from the paleontologist Henry Fairfield Osborn. He pointed out in *Science* that Bateson's address had given rise to such newspaper headlines as *The Collapse of Darwinism,* and the like, and he suggested that Bateson probably had not followed a written text when he made his speech. Then he added,[14] in direct contradiction of Bateson:

"It is not true that we do not know how species originate. The *mode* of the origin of species has long been known—in fact, it was very clearly stated by the German paleontologist Waagen in the year 1869, a statement which has been absolutely confirmed beyond a possibility of doubt in the fifty years of subsequent research. It is also true that we know the modes of origin of the human species; our knowledge of human evolution has reached a point not only

where a number of links in the chain are thoroughly known but the characters of the missing links can be very clearly predicated. The *cause* of the origin of species is another matter and has been sought in all branches of biology and biological research without an adequate solution having been found."

To this Bateson[15] replied:

"Professor Osborn has expressed great vexation at the tenor of my address. After considering his remarks, I do not know that I can add much to what I have said. The divergence between the conceptions to which genetical analysis introduces us and the doctrines of which Professor Osborn has been so long a distinguished champion, is indeed wide. Paleontological observations have served a useful purpose in delimiting the outline of evolution, but in discussing the physiological problem of interspecific relationship evidence of a more stringent character is now required; and a naturalist acquainted with genetical discoveries would be as reluctant to draw conclusions as to the specific relationship of a series of fossils as a chemist would be to pronounce on the nature of a series of unknown compounds from an inspection of them in a row of bottles. The central tenet of Darwinism that species are merely the culmination of varietal differences, such as we find contemporaneously occurring, is not easily reconcilable with the new knowledge. It was my purpose once more to direct the attention of naturalists, especially geneticists, to this deficiency in the evidence, by no means without hope that it may be supplied."

When Bateson speaks thus of paleontological evidence, we must wonder what he had left to base his faith on; his agnosticism certainly is more apparent than his faith in any argument for evolution which he discusses.

We have dwelt rather at length on the works of Bateson because we believe that he voiced clearly the conflict which was going on at that time between the various *theories* of evolution and the *facts* which biological research was bringing to light. Today, as in Bateson's time, there are scientists who would disagree with Bateson's position concerning the contemporaneous origin of species, while others would staunchly support him:

---

[14] Osborn, Henry Fairfield: *Science,* Vol. 55, 1922, p. 195.
[15] Bateson, W.: *loc. cit.,* p. 373.

their difference would be accounted for partly by their individual definition of "species." Most of them, we think, would be willing to confess that science knows nothing of the present-day origin of truly new species, species sufficiently different in important characteristics that they could no longer be classified with the species-group from which they originated. Bateson was fully aware of such variations as races, sub-species, and even so-called new species within a species-group; but he could see no evolutionary significance in such diversification of existing biological material. (See also the discussion on micro- and macro-evolution at the close of this article.)

## GENETICS AND THE TRANSMISSION OF ACQUIRED CHARACTERS

The outstanding American representative among the world's great geneticists has been Professor Thomas Hunt Morgan, whose experiments on heredity with the fruit fly (Drosophila) during the last quarter of a century or more have added an almost unbelievable amount of information on the processes of inheritance and variation. Morgan has been very outspoken in his criticism of a number of theories held by evolutionists, mainly because his genetical experiments forced him to the conclusion that they were untenable.

"It is not as generally known as it should be that the new work in genetics has struck a fatal blow at the old doctrine of the inheritance of acquired characters. The old doctrine held that a modification of the body-cells, produced during development or in adult stages by means of external agencies, is inherited. In other words: a change in the character of the body-cells causes a corresponding change in the germ-cells. A few examples will serve to show how genet-

ics has undermined this already frail and mysterious doctrine."[16]

Earlier Morgan had demonstrated by his experiments on eyeless Drosophila that the blind or eyeless fish and other animals in the dark interior of caves did not become eyeless because of disuse of their eyes for many generations, but that they had found these caves a suitable environment because they were blind already.

Morgan showed at length that the arguments so often derived from comparative morphology and systematics to prove evolution are not above criticism. In 1925 he said:[17]

"When we study animals and plants we find that they can be arranged in groups according to their resemblance. . . . We find similarities in the skull and backbone of these same animals; in the brain; in the digestive system; in the heart and blood vessels; in the muscles. Each of these systems is very complex, but the same general arrangement is found in all. Anyone familiar with the evidence will, I think, probably reach the conclusion either that these animals have been created on some preconceived plan, or else that they have some other bond that unites them; for we find it difficult to believe that such complex, yet similar, things could have arisen independently. *But we try to convince our students of the truth of the theory of evolution not so much by calling their attention to this relation as by tracing each organ from a simple to a complex structure. I have never known such a course to fail in its intention. In fact, I know that the student often becomes so thoroughly convinced that he resents any such attempt as that which I am about to make to point out that the evidence for his conviction is not above criticism.*

"Because we can often arrange the series of structures in a line extending from the very simple to the more complex, we are apt to become unduly impressed by this fact and conclude that if we found the complete series we should find all the intermediate steps and that they have arisen in the order of their complexity. For example, there have appeared in our cultures of the vinegar fly, *Drosophila melanogaster*, over four

[16] Morgan, T. H.: *The Scientific Basis of Evolution,* 1935, p. 187.

[17] Morgan, T. H.: *Evolution and Genetics,* Princeton University Press, 1925, p. 19-21. (The sentences in italics, omitted in the 1925 edition, were present in the first edition of this work, published in 1916, then called *A Critique of the Theory of Evolution.*)

hundred new types that breed true. Each has arisen independently and suddenly. . . . If we arrange the latter arbitrarily in the order of their size there will be an almost complete series beginning with normal wings and ending with those of apterous flies. . . . The order in which these mutations occurred bears no relation to their size; each originated independently from the wild type.

"Mutations have occurred involving the pigmentation of the body and wings. . . . If put in line a series may be made from the darkest flies at one end to the light yellow flies at the other. These types, with the fluctuations that occur within each type, furnish a complete series of gradations; yet historically they have arisen independently of each other."

## SHALL EVOLUTION BE REJECTED AS A SERIOUS SCIENTIFIC THEORY?

From the mind and pen of a number of well known zoologists have come some very elucidating contributions to the evolutionary controversy. At the opening of the eleventh International Congress of Zoology at Padora, in 1930, Professor Maurice Caullery,[18] of the University of Paris, made the following statements in his address:

"Certain eminent geneticists are even beginning to think that the conclusions of their scientific studies, being based on precise and methodical experimentation, should force us to abandon the idea of evolution whenever their work contradicts it. Others, without going so far, conclude that evolution should only be accepted to the extent that it is in strict conformity with genetical laws, that all conclusions to which zoology and paleontology lead should be deliberately excluded. I do not flatter myself that I have any solution of the difficulty to offer, nor even a new point of view. . . .

"The beliefs held when the generation to which I belong did its apprenticeship in science were very different from those of today. Then the problem of evolution seemed much nearer solution than it does now. The theory itself was no longer seriously contested, nor did we hesitate to reconstruct the phylogeny both of larger and smaller groups by means of genealogical trees and a general application of the fundamental biogenetic law. Haeckel was the prophet of

those days which have now begun to be remote. Today we are far more cautious in this matter.

"In regard to the mechanism of evolution, too, we believed ourselves to be much nearer the truth. . . . Knowing that mutations are hereditary variations, which represent distinct typical forms of a species, we are led naturally to look upon them as the processes by which new and lasting forms have come into being. Admitting, on the other hand, that variations due to the environment are individual and not transmissible, and that phenotypical modifications can not be repeated by the genotype, mutations appear to be the principal if not the only form of evolutional change. . . . However, I do not believe that mutations and genetical laws are sufficient to account for evolution, as it is accounted for by morphological and paleontological data."

Professor Caullery then goes on to show that mutations are perhaps not new developments in the descent of a species, that they may be rarely occurring combinations of normal elements in the genotype of that species. He further points out that mutations are considered modifications of already existing genes, and that almost always these modifications have been degradations or losses. He asks: "Is it necessary to see an essential and elementary process of evolution in a phenomenon which appears to our eyes, in the majority of cases at least, to be sub-pathological?" In the next paragraph he asks the question whether mutations are really evolutionary processes, capable of giving rise to distinct species, and he answers this question by the statement that mutational variants "remain strictly within the frame of the stock species." After having discussed adaptations in relation to evolution, and the failure of mutations to explain evolution in general, Professor Caullery says:

"If the genetical mutationist can give no account of evolution, and evolution is a mere hypothesis, then there is no alternative but to sacrifice this hypothesis. Such is the conclusion at which certain eminent geneticists such as Mr. Heribert Nilsson are

[18] Caullery, M.: *Science*, Vol. 74, 1931, pp. 254-260.

arriving. Evidently there would be no disposition to accept such conclusions on the part of the majority of zoologists and botanists. For them evolution, as a fact, obviously results from all data of comparative anatomy, embryology and paleontology. Naturally I shall not enumerate the arguments, which are classic, that support this statement. Nevertheless, we are clearly unable to avoid taking account of the positive results of experimentation. . . . I am not concealing from myself the fact that it is very improper to imagine that the causes known at present are insufficient to explain the past, and I ask pardon. But I still prefer to adopt such a supposition rather than to deny evolution or to confine myself to a statement of the contradictions between the results of our inadequate experimentation and the facts attested to by the past."

In connection with the above, it is interesting to note that Professor Caullery[19] said at a lecture at Harvard University some fourteen years earlier:

"In any case, we do not see in the facts emerging from the study of Mendelism, how evolution, in the sense that morphology suggests, can have come about. And it comes to pass that some of the biologists of greatest authority in the study of Mendelian heredity are led, with regard to evolution, either to more or less complete agnosticism, or to the expression of ideas quite opposed to those of the preceding generation; ideas which would almost take us back to creationism."

### LACK OF EVIDENCE OF TRANSFORMATION

The unique position of Dr. Albert Fleischmann, Professor of Zoology at the University of Erlangen, as an outright anti-evolutionist in the zoological world, is well known. At the beginning of this century he wrote two books against evolution (*Die Descendenztheorie*, 1901; *Die Darwinsche Theorie*, 1903), and ever since that time Fleischmann has been known for his uncompromising position in respect to that theory. He is the author of many other publications besides those mentioned, among which is a very successful text-book of zoology.

In 1922 Fleischmann[20] was the chief author of a book which contained a series of lectures given during 1921-22 at the University of Erlangen. After having discussed the interdependence of all organs and functions of the animal body, and the impossibility of groups of organisms to have originated in past ages from other groups with an entirely different body construction, Fleischmann states:

"In answer to the question what she has to say concerning the marvelous perfection of function and construction in the four great groups of animals, living under entirely different conditions, evolutionary teaching says: 'Previously there were no mammals, reptiles, or birds on earth. They developed gradually from fishes, which alone were present in the waters of the Silurian period.' . . . One may read through all the publications concerning the evolution of animals, and one will hardly encounter even an attempt seriously to tackle the problem. One hears continually the phrase repeated that the animal remains which are buried in the older strata are proof that the younger remains are the remnants of their descendants. The central question, how prehistoric animals were able to change their body structure to one of different form and function, is in all this not even touched upon."

In 1922 there also appeared a book on the problem of evolution by a member of the zoological faculty of the University of Zurich, S. Tschulok, entitled *Die Deszendenzlehre*. Tschulok was quite perturbed that the evolutionary theory was not more prominently featured in the university curicula of central Europe, and thus wrote his book both as a stimulus to this end and perhaps as a text-book. In spite of this burden for evolution, Tschulok took a sharply critical attitude towards a number of problems often lightly passed over in such books. He devoted considerable discussion to the arguments of Fleischmann, whom he accused of having confused evolution with the problems

---

[19] Caullery, M.: *Science*, Vol. 43, 1916, p. 557.
[20] Fleischmann, A.: *Der Enwicklungsgedanke in der gegenwartigen Natur- und Geisteswissenschaft*, Leipzig, 1922, pp. 71-72.

of phylogeny, species formation, etc. Evolution as such Tschulok considered a fact. Fleischmann[21] has the following to say concerning his critic:

"In spite of all this S. Tschulok adheres to the doctrine of evolution as an 'unavoidable demand of the intellect.' . . . The contrast in the thinking of two specialists comes here clearly to the foreground. We both survey the same field. But one of us (S. Tschulok) is so strongly dominated by evolutionary thought that he is willing to forego experimental evidence. He follows the call of his intellect for a unified concept, and he views the past evolution of life, in spite of its vagueness of thought, as a concluded fact, while I accept the fossil and living species as an unexplainable fundamental phenomenon in zoology and reject as valueless every concept that cannot be confirmed by experience."

## No Evolution of Larger Animal Groups

Another zoologist who disturbed the quiet of evolutionary literature was Austin H. Clark,[22] of the United States National Museum. He was the author of numerous scientific contributions in the field of zoology, and he became a world authority on Crinoidea. The views which he developed on the origin of the great divisions of the animal kingdom were quite revolutionary to the mind of most evolutionists, and stirred up much discussion. In 1928 he published in the *Quarterly Review of Biology* an article entitled '*Animal Evolution*', in which the following sentences typify his position:

"This long list of animal types represented by the fossils in the Cambrian and immediately succeeding rocks, can have only one meaning. It shows conclusively that as far back as Cambrian time in the state of the animal world it was, in its broader features, just what it is today. So we see that the fossil record, the actual history of animal life upon the earth, bears us out in the assumption that at its very first appearance animal life in its broader features was in essentially the same form as that in which

we know it now. . . . Thus so far as concerns the major groups of animals, the creationists seem to have the better of the argument. There is not the slightest evidence that any of the major groups arose from any other."

About two years later Clark published the book "The New Evolution: Zoogenesis," in which he expanded the views laid down in the above mentioned article. In spite of the fact that Clark grants that the creationists seemingly have the better of the argument concerning the origin of the major groups of animals, he remained an evolutionist, as his book well demonstrates. But it is a different, and far more moderate brand of evolution than is generally held by evolutionists.

## Paleontology Offers No Solution to the Problem of the Origin of Species

Paleontology has long been one of the branches of science from which evolutionists have claimed to derive much support. In the United States it was Henry Fairfield Osborn who during his entire scientific career exerted every effort to prove and defend evolution through the findings of paleontology, more so, perhaps, than anyone else. He had formulated, in 1912, his law of *tetraplasy*, which he believed to be revealed through the study of the Titanotheres, and in which he included the following "four inseparable factors of evolution": environment, ontogeny, heredity, and selection. By 1931 Osborn had added to this some twenty "biomechanical" principles, which he deduced from anatomy, embryology, and paleontology. However, Osborn found little acceptance for his elaborate theory, as he confesses.[23]

"This tetraplastic principle which seeks to combine the elements of truth in preced-

21 Fleischman, A.: *loc cit.*, p. 95.
22 Clark, A. H.: *Quart. Rev. Biol.*, Vol. 8, 1928, pp. 523-541.
23 Osborn, H. F.: *Nature*, Vol. 128, 1931, pp. 894-897.

ing hypotheses and theories has, thus far, won no acceptance. . . . We can affirm that we can demonstrate beyond refutation the adaptive biomechanical response, whether in ontogeny or in phylogeny. While we know infinitely more about the principles of evolution than did Charles Darwin, and while it is the essential living principle of biomechanical reaction which calls forth the prevailing twenty principles of biomechanical adaptation discovered in ontogeny and phylogeny, *we are more at a loss than ever before to understand the causes of evolution.* One after another the Buffonian, Lamarckian, Darwinian, Weismannian, and De Vriesian theories of causation have collapsed; each, however, contains elements of truth. All that we can say at present is that Nature does not waste time or effort with chance or fortuity or experiment, but that she proceeds directly and creatively to her marvelous adaptive ends of biomechanism."

The last article on evolution which Osborn[24] wrote gives "Creative Aristogenesis" a lion's share among the forces of evolution. In this we read:

"Like a moth to the flame we are attracted to the eternal problem of the causes of adaptation. The nearer we get to adaptation the more our intellectual wings are singed until we end in agnosticism or despair. In the recent language of Bohr: 'On this view, the existence of life must be considered as an elementary fact that can not be explained, but must be taken as a starting point in biology, in a similar way as the quantum of action, which appears as an irrational element from the point of view of classical mechanical physics and, taken together with the existence of the elementary particles, forms the foundation of atomic physics.' A very sharp distinction must be drawn between the *modes of adaptation* which paleontology reveals with unique fullness and the *causes of adaptation* which paleontology still leaves an inexplicable blank. . . . If, in Bohr's opinion, life cannot be explained, the adaptive evolution of the geneplasm is infinitely more inexplicable."

One can almost discover a note of sadness, disillusionment in these quotations of Osborn. Not only was he no nearer understanding the *causes* of evolution than when he started his life

work, but many workers in biology were also claiming that the *modes* of evolution, which Osborn had so frequently claimed as being firmly established by paleontology, were also unknown. Osborn finally took refuge in the above mentioned creative principle to escape agnosticism. In the *Biographical Memoir of Henry Fairfield Osborn*, (who died in 1935), it is interesting to note what is said about him by Gregory.[25]

" 'One of his last views on evolution was, if I correctly understood it, a belief that life contains within itself a creative power which leads it to adapt itself to its external surroundings and to create such new forms for itself as are required for its existence.' He . . . regarded evolution as an expression of the 'firm and undeviating order' conceived by the divine creative mind. That he was a deist . . . there is no doubt."

It must be said that it was not always evident that Osborn believed in a "divine creative mind."

## EVIDENCE FROM ANTHROPOLOGY

In connection with the many elaborate reconstructions of past life which have been made by paleontologists, especially when attempting to demonstrate a complete series of evolutionary development, or a missing link in the supposed ancestry of man, it is of interest to note here what Marcellin Boule,[26] Professor in the Museum of Natural History in Paris, and Director of the Department of Human Paleontology, has said:

"The fact having been taken for granted that the Trinil (Java) remains belonged to one and the same creature, attempts at restoration were undertaken. Dubois and Manouvrier published reconstructions of the cranium and even of the whole skull. These attempts, coming from medical men, and being based principally on human anatomy, are far too hypothetical, since we possess no data for the reconstruction of the base of the skull, the whole face, and all the apparatus of the lower jaw. It is astonishing

[24] Osborn, H. F.: "The Dual Principles of Evolution" *Science*, Vol. 80, 1934, pp. 601-605.
[25] Gregory, J. W.: *National Academy of Sciences Biographical Memoirs*, Vol. 19, 1938, pp. 53-119.
[26] Boule, M.: *Fossil Man*, Edinburgh, 1923, pp. 105, 227.

to find a great palaeontologist like Osborn also publishing attempts of this kind. . . . Can we present a portrait of Neanderthal Man as he was in life? The artist is at full liberty to attempt to produce works of imagination, original in character and striking in appearance; but men of science—and of conscience—know too well the difficulties of such attempts to regard them as anything but pastimes and recreations. Certain accredited experts have published portraits in the flesh, not only of Neanderthal Man, whose skeleton is now sufficiently well known, but also of Piltdown Man, whose remains are so fragmentary; of Heidelberg Man, of whom we have only the lower jaw; and of *Pithecanthropus,* of whom we only possess a fragment of skull and two teeth. At the best, such productions might find a place in works aiming at extreme popularity, but they singularly mar the books, estimable in other respects, in which they have been introduced."

Following this statement of Professor Boule it is pertinent to add what the American anthoropolgist Ernest Albert Hooton[27] has said on this subject:

"Some anatomists model reconstructions of fossil skulls by building up the soft parts of the head and face upon a skull cast, and thus produce a bust purporting to represent the appearance of the fossil man in life. When, however, we recall the fragmentary condition of most of the skulls, the faces usually being missing, we can readily see that even the reconstruction of the facial *skeleton* leaves room for a good deal of doubt as to details. The various reconstructions of the skull of Piltdown man by Smith-Woodward, Keith, and other experts, differ widely one from another. To attempt to restore the soft parts is an even more hazardous undertaking. The lips, the eyes, the ears, and the nasal tip, leave no clues on the underlying bony parts. You can with equal facility model on a Neanderthaloid skull the features of a chimpanzee or the lineaments of a philosopher. These alleged restorations of ancient types of man have very little if any scientific value and are likely only to mislead the public. To model a bust of *Pithecanthropus erectus* from the skull cap and the two or three teeth is a palpable absurdity. We do not know anything of the minutiae of the appearance of the Pithecanthropus, Heidelberg, Piltdown, or Neanderthal types. We have no know-

ledge of their hair form, hair distribution, pigmentation and the details of such features as I have mentioned. So put not your trust in reconstructions."

It is a regrettable fact of contemporary evolutionary history that such "palpable absurdities" as the reconstructions of Pithecanthropus are still exhibited in such halls of learning as the Museum of Natural History in New York and other institutions.

### THE CONTROVERSY OVER MICRO- AND MACROEVOLUTION

Before closing this review we must not neglect to mention the controversy that has arisen concerning so-called micro- and macro-evolution. Goldschmidt apparently credits Dobzhansky with the first use of these terms, although, as we shall see below, Philiptschenko employed them as early as 1927. For many years a number of workers contended that the mutations with which we are acquainted are not sufficient to account for any such changes as are required by the theory of evolution. Some of these men became entirely agnostic towards evolution, as we have seen earlier, while others simply recognized the difficulties of the situation, were willing to call them to the attention of the scientific world, and let it go at that. Doubtless belonging to the latter class is J. Philiptschenko, Professor of Genetics at the University of Leningrad. He says:[28]

"In this manner has modern genetics doubtlessly removed the veil from the evolution of biotypes, jordanons and linneons (a kind of microevolution), but in contradistinction the evolution of the higher systematic groups (a kind of macroevolution), which has always especially occupied our minds, lies entirely beyond the horizon, and this fact seems to us but to underline ou above introduced deliberations concerning the absence of an internal connection between genetics and evolution."

His previous deliberations included the following:

---

[27] Hooton, E. A.: *Up From the Ape,* New York, 1931, p. 332.
[28] Philiptschenko, J.: *Variabilität und Variation,* Berlin, 1927, pp. 83, 93-94.

"Genetics is an exact science. . . . In contradistinction the theory of evolution has been and will always be only a hypothesis, and one of the best definitions of this idea until now is the one by 'Driesch: 'The evolutionary theory is the hypothetical assertion that the organisms, in spite of their differences, are in blood relationship with each other.' "

Of late micro- and macroevolution have come to the foreground especially through Richard Goldschmidt,[29] Professor of Zoology at the University of California. He says:

"This term (microevolution) has been used by Dobzhansky (1937) for evolutionary processes observable within the span of a human lifetime as opposed to macroevolution, on a geological scale. It will be one of the major contentions of this book to show that the facts of microevolution do not suffice for an understanding of macroevolution. The latter term will be used here for the evolution of the good species and all the higher taxonomic categories."

In concluding the section on microevolution, Goldschmidt says:

"A survey of the facts relating to microevolution; i.e., evolution within the species (or whatever two different, nearly related forms separated by 'an unbridged gap' may be called severally), has led us to reaffirm the conclusions which we have drawn in former papers: Microevolution within the species proceeds by the accumulation of micromutations, in addition to occasional upshoots of local macromutations, or polymorphic recombinations of such. . . . The subspecies do not merge into the species either actually or ideally. . . . Microevolution by accumulation of micromutations— we may also say neo-Darwinian evolution— is a process which leads to diversification strictly within the species, usually, if not exclusively, for the sake of adaptation of the species to specific conditions within the area which it is able to occupy. This is the case for microevolution on the subspecific level of formation of geographical races or ecotypes. Below this level, microevolution has even less significance for evolution (local mutants, polymorphism, etc.). *Subspecies are actually, therefore, neither incipient species nor models for the origin of species. They are more or less diversified blind alleys with-in the species. The decisive step in evolution, the first step toward macroevolution, the step from one species to another, requires another evolutionary method than that of sheer accumulation of micromutations.*"

In the conclusion to the section on macroevolution in his book, he says:

"There is no such category as an incipient species. Species and the higher categories originate in single macroevolutionary steps as completely new genetic systems. . . . The facts of development, especially those furnished by experimental embryology, show that the potentialities, the mechanics of development, permit huge changes to take place in a single step."

On the basis of facts, Goldschmidt here simply overthrows the neo-Darwinian theory of evolution, and presents us instead with another theory, or better, a hypothesis, in which he can not give any proof showing that such higher taxonomic groups as he is dealing with, ever arose in these macroevolutionary steps. His attack on the generally held neo-Darwinian form of the evolution theory is one of the most fearless criticisms ever offered against that theory, and as might be expected, quite a controversy has arisen concerning Goldschmidt's views. Theodosius Dobzhansky,[30] Professor of Zoology at Columbia University, reviewed Goldschmidt's book in *Science* under the tile "Catastrophism versus Evolutionism," and from this we take the following lines:

"This book contains the only basically new theory of organic transformation propounded during the current century. . . . Lamarckianism has become obsolete owing to its basic assumption having fallen short of experimental verification. Autogenesis has always been in conflict with the principles of causality in vogue in the materialistically-minded modern science. Darwinism underwent great changes because of the forward strides of genetics, but the unbroken continuity of ideas between the 'neo-Darwinism' and Darwin's original theory is evident.

[29] Goldschmidt, R.: *The Material Basis of Evolution,* Yale University Press, 1940, pp. 8, 181-183, 397.

[30] Dobzhansky, T.: "Catastrophism Versus Evolution," *Science,* Vol. 92, 1940, pp. 358-359.

The appearance of Goldschmidt's book connotes an at least temporary end of the undivided reign of neo-Darwinian theories. For Goldschmidt not only relegates natural selection to a place of relative unimportance, but in effect rejects evolution beyond the narrow confines in which it has been admitted to exist by Linnaeus and many creationists. His theory belongs to the realm of catastrophism, not to that of evolutionism; his break with the Darwinian tradition is almost complete. . . . Although, in the reviewer's opinion, Goldschmidt's theory is invalid, it must be admitted that Goldschmidt has marshalled an impressive array of evidence in its favor. . . . It must, nevertheless, be recognized that Goldschmidt's keenly critical analysis has emphasized the weaknesses and deficiencies of the neo-Darwinian conception of evolution, which are numerous, as even partisans ought to have the courage to admit."

Another reviewer, Dr. F. B. Sumner,[31] of the Scripps Institution of Oceanography, discusses Goldschmidt's book as follows:

"For he (Goldschmidt) contends that 'macroevolution' (*i.e.*, *real* evolution) comes to pass through single, abrupt genetic changes ('macromutations'), capable of bringing about phenotypic alterations of specific, generic or even much greater magnitude. . . . We should surely need the guiding hand of an entelechy here, if not the direct intervention of the Creator himself. . . . Only the wave of a magician's wand could have transformed the scales of a reptile forthright into the plumage of a bird. . . . If Professor Goldschmidt can point to any one case in which a new, complex, adaptive structure has arisen through a single genetic change, and if this same genetic change is shown to have involved the necessary correlative changes in many other parts of the body, he will have gone a long way toward proving his main contention. But he will, at the same time, have left naturalistic biology in a most embarrassing position."

Doctor A. Franklin Shull,[32] of the University of Michigan, seems to take the side of Goldschmidt on the most important question:

"The thing which microevolution is unable to explain, according to Goldschmidt, is the origin of species. Mere accumulation of small genetic differences is not enough to make them different species. Here he takes issue with innumerable evolutionists both present and past. In this contention we should agree with Goldschmidt. . . ."

In this controversy of micro- and macroevolution the scientific world has come to one of the fundamental issues of the entire evolution theory. Both sides in this controversy claim that the other side is factually unable to account for evolution, and, historically speaking, the evolutionary concept has reached its most critical hour since Darwin's day.

It is no doubt appropriate here to refer briefly to an address by the zoologist W. P. Pycraft,[33] in which he joins the now fairly large group of men which have called for a re-examination, or critical analysis, of part or the whole of the theory of evolution. He said:

"Organisms, simple or complex, from amoeba to man, are not the sport of chance variations after this fashion, dragooned, and 'licked into shape' by external conditions. They, in short, are not to be regarded as so much clay molded into shape by the great potter, 'environment'. . . . So long as we insist on regarding biology as a crystallized creed, requiring no more than a possible rectification of some of its tenets, so long shall we continue groping in the dark to get an insight into the mysteries we are professedly trying to solve. But I venture to hope that some, at least, who will read this address, will do so without bias, in the hope that, perhaps, they may really find new angle from which to survey their beliefs. Hostile criticism, like abuse, is no argument. A review of our position today, as biologists, is undoubtedly called for. I feel that I shall not have written in vain if I induce at least some to endeavor to make that review."

---

[31] Sumner, F. G.: "Is Evolution Inscrutable?" *Science*, Vol. 93, 1941, p. 522.

[32] Shull, Dr. A. Franklin: "Two Decades of Evolution Theory," *American Naturalist*, Vol. 76, 1942, p. 171-178.

[33] Pycraft, W. P.: "Some New Aspects of Evolution," *Annual Report Smithsonian Institution*, 1936, p. 217-241.

THE

# BULLETIN

OF

# CREATION, the DELUGE

AND RELATED SCIENCE

| Volume III | January, 1943 | Number 1 |

## CONCERNING SPECULATIONS

as to the

## VOICE AND VOICE ORGANS OF EARLY MAN*

*By* LLOYD K. ROSENVOLD, M.D., M.SC.

[For lay readers the Editors have appended a non-technical synopsis.—Ed.]

"Facts are desirable possessions, so are theories, but the two should not be confused. Facts should be kept in one pocket and theories in another. One should never forget that diagram, classification, symbolism, and hypothesis are but temporary expedients. They are good servants but poor masters."[1]

In conducting a study of the comparative anatomy and physiology of the larynx the writer has noted the apparently unscientific presumptions in which some writers have indulged in their attempts to substantiate certain theories concerning the evolution of the voice and larynx. Especially noticeable are evidences of wishful deductions in speculating on the softer parts, long since decayed and even in life sometimes bearing but little relationship to the few uncertain, often incomplete and controversial bone fragments which have been assembled in a questionable manner in some instances and made to stand for whole sub-races of man. In this preliminary report, the writer will call attention to several well known bone fragment creations and then analyze the writings concerning the larynx, voice, and speech of these creatures.

### FOSSIL MEN

*Eoanthropus.* Among discovered bones some are easily identified as those of animals, some are human, and other bones become the subject of much controversy as to their human or simian origin. A classical ex-

---

* From the Department of Otolaryngology, College of Medical Evangelists, Los Angeles, California.
1 Streeter, George L., *Science*, April 29, 1927.

---

The BULLETIN is published by, and is the official organ of the "Society for the Study of Creation, the Deluge, and Related Science." The Editorial Board is comprised of Professor George McCready Price and Dr. Dell D. Haughey. It is printed at the Collegiate Press, Arlington, California. For members the BULLETIN is free, and extra copies 20 cents each (each number priced according to size); for non-members it is $2.00 per year and this number is 30 cents. All correspondence should be directed to the Managing Editor, Mr. Ben F. Allen, 219 North Grand Avenue, Los Angeles, 12, California.

ample is the Piltdown Man or Dawn Man (*Eoanthropus dawsoni* Smith Woodward), described in 1912. Miller[2] states that, "The original 'find' consisted of four pieces (reconstructed from nine fragments) of a cranium and an imperfect lower jaw bearing two molar teeth. Afterward a pair of nasal bones and a canine tooth were found and described and still later two more fragments of skull and a third molar made their appearance." The fragments were found in an English gravel bed and were collected over a period of years. During certain months seasonal waters flooded the pit. Besides the alleged human remains, teeth of an elephant, mastodon, hippopotamus, beaver and horse and a deer's metatarsal bone and antlers were found in the gravel pit. Much dispute has occurred concerning these finds. Miller states that there is only one point upon which all authors agree and that is that the fragments of brain case and nasal bones are all human, but that there are at least twenty points of disagreement. The latter center largely on the jaw fragment and teeth which are declared to be simian in origin by many authors. Thus on fragmentary and disputed evidence a whole race has been postulated.

*Neanderthal Man.* In 1857 there was discovered a skull vault, thigh bones, portions of a shoulder blade, pelvis, and ribs in the valley of the Dussel, a tributary of the Rhine. These remains were assembled and named the Neanderthal Man. Later, fragments said to belong to the same race were found in Jersey, France, Belgium, Spain (Gibraltar), Czechoslovakia, and distant Palestine.[3] Great significance has been assigned to the Neanderthal "race," since the discovery of the several remains but it may

be that the Neanderthal Man instead of representing a precursor race of modern man, if indeed he existed as a race, may only have been a degenerate race. Even Sir Arthur Keith has found it necessary to state that ". . . we were compelled to admit that men of the modern type had been in existence long before the extinction of the Neanderthal type."[4]

*Rhodesian Man.* The Rhodesian Man was discovered in a cave in Northern Rhodesia and consisted of a large skull without the mandible and some bones from the lower extremities. This "race" is believed by Keith to have arisen later than the Neanderthal race but to have existed at least for a long time simultaneously. On the other hand, in 1931 Keith wrote that an ". . . acromegalic skull (enlarged by disease) has certain resemblances to the Rhodesian skull" and that ". . . the reader will see that I Keith anticipated the possibility of an acromegalic skull being mistaken for that of an early type of man."[5] In further quoting an earlier statement by himself he says, "There still lurks in the body of modern man the machinery which fashioned the ample features of Rhodesian man and which can be awakened under conditions of disease." Keith of course believed that the Rhodesian Man acquired his somewhat prominent upper jaw and large skull in a normal physiological manner, but may we not ask if possible the original owner of the skull was not simply an acromegalic individual? If then the Rhodesian skull was enlarged by disease it undoubtedly belonged to an unfortunate member of *Homo sapiens*, possibly even a negro, and could therefore be of quite recent origin. Since the skull is the only sample of *Homo Rhodesiensis* that race could no longer be postu-

2 Miller, G. S., Jr., The Controversy Over Man's Missing Links, *Ann. Report Smith. Inst.*, 1928, pp. 413–465.
3 Ency. Brit., 14th Ed., Art. "Neanderthal Man."
4 Keith, A., *Antiquity of Man*, 1915, p. 498, Williams and Norgate, London.
5 Keith, A., *New Discoveries Relating to the Antiquity of Man*, 1931, Williams and Norgate, London.

lated if the skull was truly acromegalic. If the modern conception that acromegaly is associated with an acidophilic adenoma (a tumor) of the posterior lobe of the pituitary gland is correct then we cannot say that the disease as now seen is an atavism, a regression to an ancestral type. Keith's deduction or inference that the "condition of disease" which is now called acromegaly was in ages past a normal physiological state is wholly untenable.

## THE VOICE OF PRIMITIVE MAN

In 1938 there appeared a report by V. E. Negus of London[6] on the evolution of the speech organs in man. One of his diagrams depicts sagittal sections (side view of middle section) of the head and neck of a gorilla, a Rhodesian Man, a Neanderthal Man, and a modern man. The order named is supposed to illustrate degrees of evolution. Concerning Rhodesian Man Negus states that, "There was marked prognathism, (protrusion of lower jaw) almost to the degree seen in the gorilla." Yet the facts are that no lower jaw was found with the acromegaloid Rhodesian skull and therefore there is no factual knowledge as to whether the skull in its living form had a protruding mandible or a receding one. Even if the upper jaw did protrude to some extent the lower jaw might have been recessive or normal. Present day individuals are commonly seen with mal-occluded (mismatching) upper and lower jaws and surely the present century possesses no monopoly on jaw deformities. If the living skull had a protruding lower jaw to complete the picture of acromegaly, then as shown previouly the individual no longer belonged to *Homo Rhodesiansis,* and further speculation concerning his voice organs would be a waste of time. The palate was described and pictured by Mr. Negus as long, yet the skull possessed no soft palate in its fossil state. Every laryngologist, yes, almost every layman, knows that the soft palate varies in thickness, length, and other physical characteristics in most individuals. Various writers, including Keith in his "Antiquity of Man," make much of the size and shape of the bony palatal arch in comparing various fossil men with modern man. If anyone doubts that many and great variations occur in the palatal arches of 20th century individuals all such doubts will be quickly dispelled by a brief visit to the private plaster museum of any up-to-date dentist who specializes in the straightening of teeth, who can even change the form of a human palatal arch in a few months by his dynamic appliances. Negus next describes some more soft tissues—tissues which had decayed and disappeared long before the skull was found. The tongue is pictured as flat in comparison to that of modern man, and again the reader is asked to recall that in 20th century individuals and races may be found tongues of various sizes, shapes, and relations. The larynx and the epiglottis which are also essentially non-bony structures were represented as to their relations to the spinal column and soft palate. Yet the facts are that no larynx and no spinal column were found in the Rhodesian remains. The shape and size of the larynx were described and compared to that of the higher apes. The mouth cavity having long since disappeared was characterized as being larger than that of modern man.

Negus next describes a Neanderthal woman as a higher development than the Rhodesian Man. His diagram is said to be a composite figure "made up from a vault from Gibraltar and a mandible and spine from Palestine." It is common knowledge that a skeleton can be made to have a receding or protruding chin by the simple ex-

6 Negus, V. E., *Evolution of the Speech Organs of Man,* Arch. Otolaryn. Vol. 28, pp. 313-328, Sept., 1938.

pedient of finding the proper size and type of lower jaw (mandible) to produce the desired effect. But in spite of this fact, Negus, on the basis of a Palestinian mandible placed below the vault of a Gibraltean skull states that as compared with earlier men, "The jaws have receded somewhat." As in his description of the Rhodesian Man he goes on to picture theoretical changes in the now non-existent tissues such as the tongue and larynx. Even the size of the pharynx is discussed.

In concluding his report, Negus described the voice of early man. Since the vocal cords were postulated to be larger than those of present human beings, the voice was described as stronger and more harsh. He is said to have been able to execute consonants but he produced less variations in the quality of the voice. Osborne[7] speculated similarly and in the case of the much disputed *Pithecanthropus erectus* on the evidence of one *apelike* thigh bone asserted that the Trinil or Java Man ". . . probably spoke as a man although his vocabulary was limited." Osborne even records that a psychiatrist ". . . has been studying the psychology of Trinil Man . . ." and that "modern intelligence tests" were applied to the Javanese bone fragments. Tilney[8] is reported to have believed that "The brain structure indicated by the cast of the inner surface of the skullcap shows that the animal had actually learned to speak," whereas Symington[9] believed that the inner cast of the skullcap ". . . gives no positive information about the creature's mental capacities." Negus[10] too has theorized on the voice of the Trinil Man. He considered that in

man's "remote ancestors and even perhaps in Javan Man" the vocal cords were more sharp-edged than those of present-day man. Elliott Smith[11] believed he had grounds to state that the "Javan Ape-Man" possessed true articulate speech. Concerning *Eoanthropus*, Keith believed that he "probably ha[d] mere potential ability to speak,"[12] yet in estimating the brain volume of Eoanthropus, he Keith gave him a capacity of 1,400cc. which is almost exactly the average brain volume of present-day man.[13]

Inasmuch as articulate speech depends upon an intact and properly functioning brain the question of mental capacity or power naturally is of interest in this connection. Negus[6] recently wrote, "There is no doubt that in the evolution of the race intelligence progressed in advance of speech, but once the necessity for inter-communication arose the human being found himself provided with a mechanism eminently adapted for vocalization." His position is not based on fact since there are of course no historical records to support his views nor do we have any fossil larynx or brain to lend sustenance. Likewise his statement[14] that, "the brain evolved before the muscles of speech, from the evidence of the Piltdown skull" represents pure imagination since the facts are that the fragments numbered none of the facial bones except a small portion of the left upper orbital margin and two nasal bones. No neck or throat structures were found in the remains. The lower jaw fragment is so much like that of an ape that relatively few authorities assign it a human origin.[2] Therefore, we have no factual knowledge what-

---

7 Osborne, cited by Miller2.
8 Tilney, cited by Miller2
9 Symington, cited by Miller2.
10 Negus, V. E., *The Mechanism of the Larynx*, 1941, p. 405, C. V. Mosby Co., St. Louis.
11 Smith, Elliott, Jr., cited Negus10, p. 335.
12 Keith, A., cited by Negus10, p. 335.
13 Keith, A., *Antiquity of Man*, 1915, p. 339, Williams and Norgate, London.
14 Negus, V. E.10, p. 335.

ever about the muscles of speech and their attachments or the larynx in the instance of the Piltdown Man and as previously noted, anything to the contrary represents pure imagination. The various writers base their estimates of the linguistic abilities of the fossil finds, at least in part, on the estimated or measured volume of the cranial cavity and on the appearance of the internal table of the skull fragments even though some of these fragments may have been assigned a simian origin by certain accredited observers.

This is indeed a very limited yardstick with which to judge the absence, presence or degree of speech. Each human brain has its speech area on one side (usually the left) but examination of a brain will not reveal which cerebral hemisphere controlled speech, nor do the convolutions usually involved in speech necessarily leave their imprints on the inside of the skull.[15] The plight of rash speculators is further illustrated by the words of Huxley[16] when he pondered the ancient human skull from the cave of Engis. Said Huxley, "It might have belonged to a philosopher or it might have contained the thoughtless mind of a savage." If fossil skull fragments are of human origin the living subject undoubtedly used articulate speech. Speech or language both simple and complicated is an indelible stamp upon all known races including even the savage tribes. The writer knows of no historic reference to a speechless race of men. If the living animal represented by fossil finds was an ape there was no speech. There is no evidence to support a middle ground.

## SUMMARY AND CONCLUSIONS

It is not within the province of this preliminary report to delve deeply into the various arguments and disagreements concerning the bones of primitive man in relation to fossil finds. Sufficient of the contested circumstances and features have been reviewed to demonstrate that agreement does not exist even concerning the bones.

From the present study it becomes evident that theorization concerning the detailed anatomy and physiology of soft and non-fossilized structures involved in the production of voice and speech in fossil man is pure theory—theory often based on the scantest of evidence that is often not true evidence but only points in controversy. When such theories are passed on in books and learned treatises as fact, it is evident that gross and regrettable errors are being propagated. It is quite impossible from a few not necessarily related and often controversial bone fragments to postulate the size, shape, and relationships of certain soft tissues that have to do with the production of voice and articulate speech. Attempts to appraise in detail, from a few bone fragments, the voice and vocabulary (not to mention intelligence) of a creature living centuries or millenniums ago would seem to represent evidences of wishful thinking.

15 Personal communication from Dr. C. B. Courville, Director, Cajal lab. of Neuropathology.
16 Huxley, cited by Keith,4 p. 401.

---

## A Synopsis by the Editors

Dr. Lloyd K. Rosenvold, specialist in ear, nose and throat, shows on what limited and even imaginary evidence certain theorists have attempted to postulate the origin of man's voice and vocal organs from brute ancestry. He shows in detail how few and fragmentary the bones are, and how controversially gotten together, to form the Piltdown Man, which was then made to stand for a whole race. He exposes the same fallacies concerning the Rhodesian Man. In neither case were there any cartilages or bones of the throat or neck which could give any clue to the character of the voice or the voice organs. He shows that this is equally true of all other fossil skulls which were considered in the studies on the origin of man's voice.

The extra large skull of the Rhodesian Man Dr. Keith attempts to explain away by asserting that it was caused by disease. But Dr. Rosenvold shows that such an explanation is inconsistent. This is one of the many large fossil human skulls which are embarrassing to these theorists. Fossil man was as large, proportionately, as the larger than modern animals with which he was associated in life.

The lower jaw of Rhodesian Man was presumed as affecting the voice, but no lower jaw was found with that skull. In efforts to construct the palatal arch in ancient man, protruding and recessive lower jaw bones were assumed to match the upper jaws, a thing not recognized as a fact today as occurring generally. The larynx of Rhodesian Man was given a definite relationship to his lower jaw and to his spinal column, though none of these was found with that specimen.

Dr. Rosenvold quotes several well-known theorists in their really extravagant guesses about the quality of the voice of early man. The vocal cords were supposedly larger than at present, with the voice stronger and more harsh, said one. Man "was able to execute the consonants, but he produced less variation in the quality of the voice," said another. "He spoke, but his vocabulary was

limited," ventured another. Some had been studying the psychology of early man, and had actually attempted to apply the late I. Q. tests to the Javanese fragments. The brain casts "showed that man had actually learned to speak," though some of the bones involved in this skull had been declared by accredited investigators to be those of speaking apes. One said that man's voice "was more sharp-edged" than it is today. Some said he had speech, while others said "he had mere potential ability to speak."

All of this was built up, Dr. Rosenvold says, though no fossil larynx has ever been found, and neither records nor tradition exist that man was ever speechless. (On the contrary a leading tradition from Central America says that the first men "talked too much, and were irreverent and lawless," and had to be destroyed.) It seems wholly incongruent with their theory that no races of men, at the present time, however low in development, lack speech in the least, that all have well-developed grammar, and that the oldest languages are invariably the most perfect and capable of the most delicate and accurate shades of meaning.

The doctor closes his paper by calling attention to how all of these facts and speculations constitute "a very limited yardstick with which to judge the presence, the absence, or the degree of speech." He presents this case as an extreme example of "wishful thinking."

## DISCUSSION

By DR. LELAND R. HOUSE

Negus admittedly does not make any allowance for the possibility that the larynx was originally provided for phonation. He has made a masterly study of the function of the larynx in animals, but he assumes that each additional function of the larynx in proceeding from the simple amphibious to the scale of mammals and human beings evolved by a process of necessity.

In speaking of birds, and "their highly evolved organisms," and "social life," he says, "Therefore, it is not surprising to find that as their intelligence increased they found that it was necessary to evolve some mechanism of sound production more efficient than that furnished by the larynx by means of which they might be able to produce sounds of wider variation in pitch and of more powerful volume than the monotonous hisses executed by their reptilian ancestors." (The Mechanism of the Larynx, 1940, p. 350) Because of this "necessity,"

the birds "evolved," as if by their own intelligent choice, the syrinx, a specialized organ in their tracheas by which they produce their songs.

He believes that the larynx in man was evolved by various stages for other purposes than phonation, and that when man's intelligence increased, a means of communication was needed. The larynx was then put into use for phonation and speech, simply because it was the organ most conveniently adapted to take up this function. Its use required a highly developed intellect, and coordination of many already existing functions to produce speech. But F. W. Mott as quoted by Negus himself (p. 437) defeats this position by saying: "Between the vocal instrument of the primitive savage and that of the most cultured singer or orator there is little or no difference; neither by careful naked-eye inspection of the brain nor by the highest power of the microscope, should we be able to discover any sufficient structural difference to account for the great difference in the powers of performance of the vocal instrument of the one as compared with that of the other; nor is there any sufficient difference in size or minute structure of the brain to accomnut for the vast store of intellectual experience and knowledge of the one as compared to the other." How, then, could the hypothecated non-speaking sub-human have been the mastermind of speech invention?

Would it not be more logical and scientific to account for these organs and their functions as being provided for by the Creator who alone could foresee the needs and was alone able to make the necessary manipulations, rather than assume that men, the lower animals, and even involuntary organs could "evolve" some new organ or features because of a sense of need?

*By* BENJAMIN FRANKLIN ALLEN

Some hold that, in the development of man from beasts, thought and speech evolved together, in parallel. Dr. Thorndike, famous psychologist of Columbia University, in *Science* (July 2, 1943, pp. 1-6), gave a typical expression of this conception as he launched a new theory of speech origin. He insists that not even sound preceded thought. However, hosts of lowly creatures with no sound facilities at all display intelligence rivalling man's with marked ability to learn by experience, and even showing individual personality differences. Common earth worms, wasps, ants (which the Bible calls "a people"), bees, the palolo worm of the South Seas, and countless others could be cited. Therefore the claim that thought and speech in man developed in parallel finds no example in nature as a whole, and lowers the intelligence of the so-called speechless sub-humans below that of these more lowly creatures. Besides, horses, dogs, etc., have been taught to communicate with man by code, even themselves forming whole sentences, and birds to use even human words. Horses have learned to spell words with letters on blocks. But the simians seem too dull to star in these feats, though their brains, speech organs, and mouth parts have long been exploited to the utmost in efforts to foster the impression that they are the nearest of kin to man.

A list of the several theories of how man acquired speech seems more comic than scientific. The Editor of the science section in *Time* (July 12, 1943, p. 88), in starting his review of the Thorndike theory, said: "Nobody knows how man began to talk, but plenty of scholars have advanced strangely nick-named theories about it." The theories are either flatly contradictory or merely different ways of stating the same supposed processes. (1) Groups came together and selected certain sounds to express certain meanings—conceivable only among people already having speech. This has been called the "pow-wow" theory. (2) Man imitated certain sounds in nature, called the "bow-wow" theory. But this is rejected because, in the thousands of languages, the same sound in nature is generally represented by far different words. (3) The "ding-dong" theory is that man struck certain objects and imitated the sound of the impacts, but the same objections are urged against this as against the "bow-wow" conception. (4) Instinctive cries were associated with situations that produced them, called the "pooh-pooh" theory. But the same objections apply to this, and besides, such situations would be far too numerous and varied to make possible any standardization of expressions.

*The Encyclopedia Americana* (1939, pp. 382-384), gives a concrete example of the main objection to all of these theories by asking how "dog" could have originated as "canis" in Latin, "hund" in German, "chien" in French, "sobaka" in Russian, etc., etc., on any basis of these theories? It is true that there are many words with the same or related sounds and meanings common to a strikingly large number of languages in all parts of the world. But all too many of these words are purely subjective, rather than objective, thus defeating their objective origin by all of the theories that have been proposed by evolutionists. Objectivity of all origins is, of course, the basic philosophical viewpoint of evolutionists. Besides, there is a large number of words like "father," "mother," etc., having similar forms common to many languages, but which bear no relation to the form or character of the objects named. These words also tend to defeat the theories proposed, their origin seeming to be entirely subjective, and demanding a common source. Abundant data point to a common source for all language groups, but this source stands directly in the way of these theories.

Dr. Clarence L. Meader, in the article referred to in the Encyclopedia Americana, said, "All of these theories must be regarded as attempts to conjecture how speech might conceivably have arisen instead of as anything even remotely approaching a scientific demonstration of how speech actually did arise." Thorndike, in proposing his new theory in 1943, opened his discussion in this manner: "Nobody knows when, where, or how speech originated, and I am stepping in where wise scholars in linguistics and psychology fear to tread." He said of all of the foregoing theories: ". . . for various reasons students of language have decided that the attachment of meanings to the hearing or making of these sounds of instinctive nature is not adequate to originate articulate speech. So-called animal language plus the power of thinking meanings would not produce human language." But does not he thus destroy all of the evolutionary theories of speech origin, including his own, by this statement?

Thorndike kept up the comedy of nicknames by dubbing the new theory which Sir Richard Paget proposed in 1930 (Human Speech, pp. 133-138, 149), as the "tongue-tied" theory, because in Paget's theory "the tongue is yoked with the body by subtle bonds of mimetic kinship," that is, the tongue and the voice Paget presumed to have mimicked the hands or feet as they worked and played. This is number five in our list, as viewed by a competing rival. He said of Paget's proposal: "Personally, I do not believe that any human being before Sir Richard Paget ever made any considerable number of gestures with his mouth parts in sympathetic pantomime with gestures of his hands, arms, and legs, still less that any considerable number of men in any local community made the same oral gestures in such pantomime."

Then Thorndike proposed what he calls the "babble-luck" theory, in which he relies entirely on the chance that a sub-human in meaningless prattle would just happen to repeat the same sound for the same act or event or object and repeat it often enough to make it a fixed habit. He supposes that a man would just happen to utter "kuz" when he found a clam, somehow come to say that every time he found one, and finally his fellows would acquire the habit from him. This is number six in the passing parade.

But now let Paget (Science, July, 1944, pp. 14-15), say what he thinks of the Thorndike idea: "How can this theory account for the fact that many simple [but totally different] sounds are found to bear closely related meanings in nearly all of the language groups—?" Then he explains how his own theory might account for such a correlation, and says: "Such a correlation could surely not occur if the meaning of the words were due to chance." After further defending his theory he quotes a professor as saying "there is something in the method."

One turns from these efforts with a feeling of their futility, even absurdity. Yet the Encyclopedia Americana seemingly went out of its way to class as the "most absurd" of all the theory that man was endowed with speech by his Creator. One suspects philosophical bias in this statement. But, absurd though it seems to evolutionists, this theory has a strong scientific basis.

Concerning the site of the common source of man and his languages, the noted archeologist Melvin Grove Kyle said in his book The Deciding Voice of the Monuments (1924, pp. 44, 231): "The theory of this location of the point of departure for the dispersion of the race, as indicated both by the record of the Bible and by facts ascertained through research, is all but universally held. It cannot be said that it is yet definitely substantiated, but it is receiving cumulative corroboration along theological and philological lines." "Wherever it is possible," he said, "to trace back lines of migration of the various peoples, or to gather notes of direction from the traditions of various peoples, or discover indications of the derivation of languages, it is always found that the ultimate direction is toward a comparatively small area in western Asia."

"Of the first dispersion of the human race over the surface of the earth [before the Deluge] we know absolutely nothing aside from statements in the Bible. Of speculation, scientific theory, there is much that is reasonable; but of real historical statement there is nothing else that presents even a reasonable claim. The second dispersion, however [after the Deluge], as recorded in the Bible, is being exactly, and, as investigation progresses, more and more fully confirmed by results of archeological research. That from a central point, somewhere in Mesopotamia, the Hematic branch of the race migrated to the southwest, the Japhetic branch to the northwest, and the Semitic branch 'eastward' toward 'the land of Shinar,' is indisputable. As the details of these race movements emerge from obscurity the meager account in Genesis 10 is not discredited; rather, little by little, it is being confirmed."

That this is the practically unanimous opinion among archeologists, philologists, and ethnologists, is well known. It would therefore seem that this theory of the origin of speech, number seven in the list, but much the oldest, is based upon far more scientific premises than are the evolutionary theories.

THE

# BULLETIN

OF

# CREATION, THE DELUGE

## AND RELATED SCIENCE

| Volume III | March, 1943 | Number 2 |

## SOME CYCLIC PHENOMENA IN STRATIGRAPHIC GEOLOGY

### By GEORGE McCREADY PRICE

#### PURPOSE

The aim of this paper is to consider certain duplications or repetitions in the strata and their meaning. Both inorganic sediments and the fossils (organic sediments) are involved, and the problem needs to be considered in the light of the two contrasting hypotheses, that of organic evolution and that of a universal Deluge. Some salient points in the history of the discoveries of these phenomena will be presented, with the century-old controversies which these duplications or repetitions have generated, and the conclusions now suggested.

#### OUTLINE

1. In thousands of localities we find that the strata were deposited in sets or in cycles, these cycles of deposition having been repeated many times, when a total vertical section in any specific locality is considered.

2. If the fossils were originally all living contemporaneously, they would naturally be buried like any other sediments, and then we should expect to find them also arranged in cycles of deposition, like the other sediments.

3. But the evolution theory denies that the fossils all lived contemporaneously and postulates that they lived in succession during many millions of years; hence on this theory it would be impossible for the "index fossils" or time-markers to repeat themselves. Any cyclical repetition of the fossils would be absurd. Some other explanation must be postulated.

4. The physical evidence from *conformity* has a bearing upon the problem of when and how the strata were deposited. When strata are conformable over a considerable area, it is good evidence that they must have been deposited in comparatively quick succession. But many examples occur of genuine conformity between beds which, on the evolution theory, were made many ages apart. These "deceptive conformities" are good evidence against this theory; but many *reversed conformities* are also found in various parts of the world, and these are deadly for the theory, for they constitute examples of duplication or repetition of key fossils.

5. In Scotland *five* such repetitions of key fossils were reported over half a century ago, thus initiating the famous "Highland controversy." In the Alps *six* repetitions have been reported. In other places the number of such major repetitions varies, and many diverse explana-

The BULLETIN is published by, and is the official organ of the "Society for the Study of Creation, the Deluge, and Related Science." The Editorial Board is comprised of Professor George McCready Price and Dr. Dell D. Haughey. It is printed at the Collegiate Press, Arlington, California. For members the BULLETIN is free, and extra copies 55 cents each (each number priced according to size); for non-members it is $2.00 per year and this number is 70 cents. All correspondence should be directed to the Managing Editor, Mr. Ben F. Allen, 219 North Grand Avenue, Los Angeles, 12, California.

*329*

tions of these phenomena are offered by evolutionary geologists.

6  Examples are given in which eminent scientists admit the queer methods of reasoning which are adopted to "explain" these repetitions of the fossils.

7. If we postulate a world completely stocked with all kinds of plants and animals, and then assume that this ideal world was suddenly overtaken by a major cataclysm, all the known facts could be readily explained, without any such incredible theories as "deceptive conformities," "thrust faults," "pioneer colonies," "recurrent faunas," etc.

## CYCLES IN THE DEPOSITION OF SEDIMENTS

Every student of the stratified rocks is familiar with cycles which frequently appear in the deposition of the rocks which he examines. The principle of superposition tells us that the lowest of a series of beds must have been deposited before those above. Thus every vertical sequence tells a history of the sequence in which the deposits were made; but whether this history was long or short is too often determined by evolutionary theory quite external to the objective facts of the strata themselves. In other words, many writers on geology seem to have the habit of reading long ages into the record, where the plain physical evidence indicates that the beds must have followed one another in quick succession. But waiving for the present any consideration of this point, the cycle here referred to consists, in its more complete or typical form, of conglomerate, sandstone, shale, and limestone, in ascending order, this series being repeated over and over again, each cycle being bounded both above and below by a more or less marked hiatus. Any member of this typical cycle may be missing, and other sequences are sometimes observed. The various constituent members may be distinctly marked off, or they may grade gradually into one another; any of them may be

thick or thin. But one or more examples of such a cycle, or a considerable portion of it, may be found occurring almost wherever any of the ancient deposits are found, that is, among the Paleozoic or Mesozoic beds, though less commonly among the Tertiary.

This cyclical repetition is spoken of by Sir Archibald Geikie, for so many years the head of the Geological Survey of Great Britain:

". . . among the thickest masses of sedimentary rocks—those of the ancient Paleozoic systems—no features recur more continually than the alternations of different sediments."[1]

I am not here concerned in trying to assign the cause or the method of this cyclic deposition. Those who believe in the uniformity-ages theory (which for convenience, we shall in this paper call *the evolution theory in geology*), commonly assign this deposit in cycles to something like rhythmic marine invasions and retreats; while believers in Deluge Geology usually attribute these phenomena to tidal action. While the former assigned cause is something entirely esoteric, or wholly outside any human experience, tidal action is familiar enough, and is typically rhythmic in its behavior.

Endless examples might be given. As any member of the series, conglomerate, sandstone, shale, limestone, may contain fossils, a coal region might be given for typical examples. Here as many as 50 or 100 or even more repetitions of the cycle may be seen, while ten or a dozen repetitions are exceedingly common in other regions.

J. S. Newberry, about 1873, seems to have been one of the first to call attention to these "Cycles of Deposition," as he named them. But he wanted to expand the local, objective phenomena, as shown in the Appalachians, so as to make them apply to a universal comparison of the geologic

---

1 Quoted by J. W. Gregory, *The Making of the Earth*, p. 99, London, 1925.

"systems." He thought that each of the great systems of the Paleozoic could be shown to begin with a conglomerate or sandstone, followed by a shale, and then by a limestone, from which he deduced certain theories about their formation. These major geological systems, as we now know, are considerably constructive or artificial, being idealized totals resulting from assembling local sections from here and there. Nevertheless, while these major cycles of Newberry may be considered as largely constructive or artificial, it is worth remembering that he was one of the first to emphasize this cyclical arrangement of the sedimentary beds, which we now know to be found occurring in every part of the world.

CONTRASTING ATTITUDE OF THE TWO THEORIES

So much then for the purely mechanical cycles of deposition. But the fossils may be regarded as also mere mechanical sediments, for specimens of plants or animals are picked up by moving water and are deposited in exactly the same way as pebbles or sand. And innumerable examples of fossils occur in the ordinary repetitions of sand or clay or lime. In the coal beds, brachiopods and crinoids and other invertebrates from the deeper parts of the ocean are continually found alternating with the plant remains from the dry lands; fifty or a hundred beds of coal, alternating with usually a much larger number of beds containing the deep-sea invertebrates, being of very common occurrence.

But there is still another aspect of the problem in connection with the fossils. For when the latter are considered in the larger way as a series of successive forms of life for the world as a whole, the believers in the uniformity-ages theory hasten to caution us that there can *never* be any real

repetition of these typical forms of life. For they say that life in its various aspects has during the long geological ages kept steadily forward, with *no repetitions;* and it is a great mistake to look for any cyclic repetition of any of the typical fossils, or what are called "index fossils"; for each of these types of life lived only for a brief period, and was succeeded by other and distinctly different kinds. As Richard M. Field[2] has expressed it:

". . . fossil faunas and floras are never stratigraphically repeated, regardless of how they originated."

Professor Field was for many years the head of the International Summer School of Geology, which used to tour the country every year from Princeton University. He goes on to explain *why* there can never be any cyclic repetitions among the fossils, or why the typical fossils are never repeated. And his *reason* is the *evolution theory.* Under this view of the past of our earth, it would be absurd to talk of a cyclical arrangement of the fossils. And this explains why convinced evolutionists have always taken such pains to explain away all instances where anything like a repetition in the larger sense seems to endanger the steady progress or evolution of life for the world as a whole. "Pioneer colonies," "recurrent faunas," "emigrant faunas," "overturned folds," "thrust faults," or a bodily jerk of the earth from under a mountain mass, inertia thus leaving the mountain sitting on a distinctly "foreign" base—these are some of the fantastic explanations which have been proposed, all necessitated by this most vital evolutionary idea, that the fossils cannot possibly be found repeated.

This is how Field explains the situation:

"While physically each [lithic or petrological] type of formation may be repeated over and over again throughout the history of the earth, the paleontological record

2 Field, Richard M., *The Principles of Historical Geology form the Regional Point of View,* p. 5, Princeton University Press, 1933.

changes [only] according to the laws of evolution. Hence, whether or not we may be able to determine the continuity of the evolutionary record, the continuous change in every branch of the organic kingdom is expressed from time to time by the fossils which occur in the sedimentary rocks. Under the definition of evolution the different species of fossils are never repeated from the older to the younger formations."[3]

To appropriate some lines used by Eddington, the evolution theory means that nature has built the gears of the universe in such a way that they can never get into reverse.

Certainly, if the evolution theory be true, it would be utterly absurd to think that any of the great types of plants and animals would reappear after they had once become extinct. Least of all, they never could reappear *five times over*, as we shall see they do in the Highlands of northern Scotland, or *six times* in the Alps. All of which illustrates the all-important influence of a cosmical theory upon what is supposed to be the strictly objective and empirical science of geology.

And this helps to bring out the fact that there are at least *three* fairly distinct meanings which attach to the phrase, "the sequence of the fossils."

The *first* sense in which this phrase is used is its primary sense, the actual sequence from the bottom to the top of the strata in any specific locality. This is an objectively real sequence which can be verified by anyone. In this sense the sequence is real and cannot be denied. But it is very far from being the same in one locality that it is in another. In some localities Cambrian beds are at the bottom or next to the granite, but in other places Carboniferous, or Cretaceous, or even Tertiary are in this bottom position. In thousands of cases, too, the fossils at the top are identical with those at the bottom, so there is no progressive sequence whatever. But this local,

verifiable sequence is *not* what geologists mean by the expression, and it certainly could never have been used as the outline on which to construct the theory of organic evolution.

The *second* meaning given to the term is as a generalization from many local instances. As early as 1795, in the first scientific treatise on the Deluge as the cause of the burial of the fossils, John Woodward, a friend of Sir Isaac Newton, in the Preface to his "Essay Toward a Natural History of the Earth," mentioned the fact that the fossils are not scattered indiscriminately through the strata, but that they often seem to be arranged according to their specific gravity, the heaviest occurring deepest down in the earth and the lighter sorts shallower and nearer to the surface. While this is not accurate as a universal rule, it seemed to have a certain plausibility for the people of that day. Another somewhat similar generalization, though also subject to many notable exceptions, is that the animals which live on the floor of the ocean, or the bottom-feeders, such as the crinoids, trilobites, and brachiopods, are more often found deep down in the strata, while the fishes and other free-swimming creatures are less deeply buried, and the land mammals occur in the more superficial beds. Count de Buffon called attention to this generalization a century and a half ago, though in our day we know that the rule is far from being universally true. And this second sense in which the term "sequence of the fossils" is used is *not* what every modern scientist means when he uses the expression.

It is in a *third* and still more abstract sense in which the term is universally used today. Buffon's generalization gradually became lengthened and enlarged by filling in thousands of details from here and there all over

3 *Id.*, p. 24.

the world, until today absolutely all the fossils of the entire world are thought of as arranged in their appropriate places in the so-called "geological column," this mental construct of a complete series from the Cambrian to the Pleistocene being what is now always meant when geologists use the term, "the sequence of the fossils."

This is the sequence which we are told is never repeated, and to save which from being repeated here and there all over the globe the most extraordinary devices are invented. And it is upon this total geological column, artificially constructed by assembling in a series what are regarded as key fossils from "typical" localities scattered all over the globe, that the theory of organic evolution has been built up during the period from Count de Buffon to Charles Darwin. This, too, is the alleged "invariable sequence" of the fossils which I have been proclaiming for over forty years to be inherently false and directly contradicted by numerous examples from various parts of the world.

At the risk of being wearisome by repetition, I wish to try to make myself clear by a simple illustration. The evolutionist assumes that the fossils were not contemporary but successive; and he tells us they may be compared to the successive human civilizations. He argues accordingly that it would be absurd to think that the Babylonian civilization reappeared after the period of the Greeks, then after the empire of Rome, and then again several times later. And when he finds in the strata conditions which he thinks appear to indicate something similar to this absurdity, he feels so very sure of his original theory that he is willing to postulate any physical impossibility, rather than admit that there can possibly have been a repetition or duplication in the original deposits. It never seems to occur to him that he ought rather to ask him-

self *just how he originally arrived at the concept* of an invariable sequence of the fossils from the little and less organized types to the larger and more highly organized.

Contrastedly, however, the believer in a universal Deluge sees nothing absurd in any relative order or sequence whatever of the fossils which he may discover. For he says that the plants and animals of the ancient world were contemporary, and were buried like any other sediments, sometimes in one relative sequence and sometimes in another. The ancient ecological setting in which they lived would have something to do with where and how they were buried, but this would be only in the most vague and general way; for since they were *not* buried exactly where they lived, and since in so many cases we find very diverse kinds alternating in a locality, the *in situ* hypothesis will not apply. No, the fossils were washed into their final positions, and were thus treated by the waters exactly like other sediments.

## THE TWO THEORIES CONCERNING CAUSES

At this stage of our study it will be well for us to keep clearly in mind the sharp contrasts between the evolution theory and the theory of the Deluge as to the *cause* of the burial of the fossils.

One of the most prominent ideas of the evolution theory, as already stated, is its denial that the fossils of all the strata were originally contemporary with one another. It always pictures them as having come into existence in a long series, only a few kinds of them having lived at any one time, these having finally become extinct and having been succeeded by distinctly different kinds. But there was no balanced or complete world of *all kinds* at any particular period, only a few kinds at a time, at least in all the early ages of the world's history. During the entire Palaeozoic Era, for example, which geologists tell us lasted for nearly four hundred million years, there were no forest trees or shrubs, as we understand these terms, no whales or land mammals, no game fishes, no grasses, no birds, no flowers.

We have no need to consider here the extremely slender evidence for this queer, unbalanced world. But the next great era, the Mesozoic, which is said to have lasted about a hundred and fifty million years, was also very unbalanced, with seemingly no regard for the interdependent web of life, such as we know our modern world to be. During the Mesozoic there were still no birds or flowers, no whales or land mammals, no grains or fruits.

The evolutionary picture is unbalanced and inconsistent in another way. For not only do geologists deny the existence of biological districts and zones in the remote past, giving us instead one and the same assemblage of life-forms all over the globe at any one time, but they disregard another and very elementary principle. For necessity tells us that the Mesozoic formations ought to contain, in addition to their own new or characteristic species, all the forms also from the Paleozoic which are *now* to be found alive in our modern world. The Tertiary also ought to give us plenty of specimens not only of the Paleozoic but also of all the Mesozoic kinds which still survive. In other words, every "new" formation ought to contain *representatives of all the older forms which still survived, plus its own distinctively new kinds.*

But every student of the rocks knows that this eminently reasonable principle has been completely disregarded—either by nature herself or by those who concocted the evolutionary scheme. The Tertiary beds, for example, never contain the slightest traces of the Paleozoic brachiopods and crustaceans, or of the Mesozoic cephalopods, amphibians, sponges, pelecypods, or even of the foraminifera, though swarms of all these are found today living in all the oceans of the world. Why did these multitudes skip so many millions of years, leaving no trace of their existence then? Or to turn the problem around, why may not these Paleozoic and Mesozoic rocks be just as modern as the Tertiary beds, since they contain representatives of so many forms living today, and especially since they are required to furnish the complimentary forms to make even the Tertiary something like the balanced or interdependent world of our time?

In marked contrast with all this, the Deluge theory tells us that it was a well balanced world, one completely stocked with the complementary forms of plants and animals, which was overtaken and buried by the waters of a great catastrophe. Thus while all the animals and plants would be living contemporaneously, they would be well segregated off into ecological groups, and might even be buried more or less as distinct floras and faunas, these groups being now known as the geological "formations."

But these ancient forms of life, when picked up and buried by the waters, were subject to the very same laws as any other sediments, including the law or principle of superposition. But in thousands of instances *the lithic materials* composing many successive beds in any particular locality were very likely all in existence contemporaneously, I mean the sand grains, the pebbles, and the clay of which these beds were made must *all* have existed in fragmental form before the waters picked them up and redeposited them. Hence it would be obvious nonsense to assign to different ages the pebbles of two beds, merely because the lower bed must have been deposited first. The principle of superposition can give us a difference in time *for the process or act of laying down* the two successive beds, but in any system of clear thinking this principle of superposition must not lead us to think that we can assign relative dates for the stones or other materials of which the beds are composed. And this is just as true regarding the fossils which happen to occur in any of these beds. They were buried like other sediments, but their relative position in a series of beds cannot tell us a single thing about when they existed; for they like the stones very probably were all in existence contemporaneously.

In other words, there could be no scientific grounds for assigning different sizes or shapes of pebbles to distinct successive ages, merely because they now happen to occur at different levels in the same vertical section. Obviously, it would be dogmatic and incapable of proof to say that the pebbles at different levels could not all have been in existence at the same time, the mere accident of the varying currents having placed them in different beds one above another. But on the same principle of reasoning, if we should find a trilobite, a dinosaur bone, and the bone of an elephant at different levels in the same section, on what grounds can anyone say that all these three kinds of animals could not possibly have been living contemporaneously? An unprovable dogmatism like this should have no place in natural science.

These facts and principles are at the real basis of the sharp contrast between the two theories in their attitude toward the possible duplication or repetition of the fossils. The Deluge theory *expects* to find the fossils repeated here and there at different levels, or duplicated perhaps several times in the same vertical section, just like other kinds of sediments. But

such a repetition of the fossils is anathema to the evolutionist.

THE ECOLOGY OF THE FOSSILS, AS VIEWED BY THE TWO THEORIES

For the believer in the Deluge, one of the surprising facts about the fossils is that the waters did not churn everything up into one indistinguishable mixture. On the contrary, in most places the various rock materials now composing the sandstones, shales, and limestones are quite distinct from one another, especially in those layers near the bottom of the series, the upper layers showing much more of a mixture of materials.

In these respects too the fossils resemble other sediments. The kinds are very distinctly segregated, at least in the more deeply buried beds. It is surprising, for instance, how seldom plant remains are mingled with animal fossils. This principle too is more marked in the case of those fossils which are classed as Paleozoic and Mesozoic, the Tertiary beds showing more often a mixture of kinds.

As was pointed out by Woodward and other early writers, much of this segregation, both of the rock fragments and even of the fossils, was probably due to the assorting power of moving water, which in handling bodies of different weights, always separates and drops the heavy ones first, then those next in weight, the the lightest being carried furthest and dropped last. Some recent writers who are inclined to overwork their knowledge of ecology seem to ignore this differential sorting power of flowing water, and mistakenly ascribe to ecology many segregations of the fossils which cannot possibly be due to their having been buried in their original habitats.

For example, on the shores of Bear Lake, Wyoming, after a heavy storm, immense numbers of modern shells are found in layers three or four inches deep and nearly two feet wide, all so completely separated from sand and mud by the action of the waters, that they can be scooped up in double handfuls with practically no sand whatever, as reported by J. Henderson of the University of Colorado.[4] And this writer concludes that such facts help us to understand many astonishing collections of fossils in the ancient beds. But anyone familiar with the shores of the ocean or any large lake will remember similar phenomena.

The bottom-feeding animals, such as the crinoids, brachiopods, and trilobites,[5] many of which were sessile or permanently attached to the bottom of the ocean, seem to have been among the first victims of the disturbed waters of the Deluge. For they are now frequently (but not always) found in the deeper layers, often with thousands of feet of other deposits above them, these upper layers containing in many instances the fossils of fishes and other free-swimming animals which could much longer survive the convulsions of the waters.

It is well known that the carcasses of vertebrate animals, within a few days after death, become distended with the gases of decomposition and tend to rise and float on the surface of the water, much like logs of wood. Thus the bodies of all land animals would often become buried in the superficial deposits, where indeed we usually find them.

And it is this rough outline of the taxonomic life of the ancient world, from the lowly organized forms on the bottom of the ocean to the more highly organized land animals, which for two hundred years has been exploited as the skeleton doctrine of a definite sequence of the fossils for all the world, thus giving rise to the evolution theory. Of course, it was a highly abstract idea to begin with, being based on a few examples from Western Europe which were supposed to be genuinely typical for all the rest of the world; and this first rough outline has since been filled in by still more artificially assembling selected sets of fossils from here and there all over the world, and by resolutely ignoring all the many notable exceptions.

Since temperature and other environmental conditions change with depth in the ocean, just as they change with similar differences in height above sea level, we find that the kinds of life change also with depth in the waters and with height on the mountain side. And though these ecological differences are more noticeable in the fossils from different depths in the ocean than in those (presumably) from the different elevations on the lands, these faint traces of distinct floras and faunas in their ancient ecological niches have given rise to the hope that we might yet be able to trace out where and how these ancient animals and plants really lived in the antediluvian world.

In the large way we are able to do this. For when we find magnolias, grape vines, sequoias, breadfruit trees, and other semi-tropical plant fossils away up in Greenland, far within the Arctic Circle, we rightly conclude that the Polar regions must have been warm, since these fragile plant remains could not possibly have been washed up from the Tropics without all going to pieces, and hence must have grown not very far from where we find them. Similar testimony is presented by the coral limestones of both the Arctic and the Antarctic regions; for corals could not have been carried any great distance by the waters, and corals always require warm

4 Science, Nov. 28, 1930, p. 559.

5 Footnote. The trilobites used to be considered much like our crabs and lobsters, with habitats in the shallow waters off shore. But this is now regarded as a mistake, since many trilobites have large saucer-like eyes and some have no eyes at all, characteristics now recognized as belonging to deep-ocean forms. See Evolution in the Light of Modern Knowledge, pp. 75, 99; London, 1925.

water in which to live. A few outstanding facts like these give us a faint outline of ecological conditions in the ancient world. But we are keenly disappointed when we attempt to fill in the details of the picture. With much care it would, I suppose, be possible to tell the direction of the current, by a close examination of the stratum in which any specific fossils are found, and thus judge in a rough way where they came from; but this has never yet been done in one case out of millions. Hence we know little or nothing as to the localities where the various kinds of ancient life really lived. We know their *provenience,* or where we find them as fossils; but we have no means of knowing where they came from, and can conclude very little about their ecological environment, except by uncertain comparisons with their living representatives, which at best may be very misleading.

But the two theories, evolution and the doctrine of a universal Deluge, give us very different attitudes toward this problem of the ecology of the ancient world.

In the evolution theory, we have to suppose that each of the fossil types was buried in a "natural" way not far from where it lived. But since in our modern deep oceans there are no currents whatever, nothing to disturb the most impalpable ooze, it seems very strange to find brachiopods, crinoids, and trilobites embedded in sandy shales or even coarser strata. These abnormal conditions are rendered still more astonishing by finding crinoidal limestones in direct contact (above or below) with a bed of coal, the latter of course being composed of plants from the dry land.

On the basis of the Deluge theory, all these kinds of fossils must have been washed into their present localities. And although no organic sediments could have been carried very far by the ocean currents, yet we do not know anything about where they came from. But when we find a coal bed with a crinoidal limestone above it, the evolution theory tells us that this locality was successively occupied by a swamp and then covered by the deep ocean; for this theory assumes that both the coal and the limestone were accumulated *in situ,* instead of having been washed into their positions. Accordingly, this theory assumes that this locality was successively the habitat of the coal plants and the deep-ocean crinoids, and it has to assume further that this locality underwent a tremendous depression of a mile or more between the deposition of these two beds, with a time interval of perhaps a million years, though the physical evidence of the beds would seem to indicate that both kinds of life were washed into their present positions, and in comparatively rapid succession.

From all this it is clear that the evolution theory has definite localities as the ancient habitats of the plants and animals now found as fossils, these habitats being the localities where the fossils now occur; for this theory represents all the ancient forms of life as having lived essentially where we now find their remains. On the other hand, the Deluge theory denies that either the plants composing the coal or the animals composing the limestones lived where we find them, since all were brought here by the abnormal currents of that catastrophe, probably from considerable distances. True, the distance could not have been five thousand miles, probably not one thousand, but it might easily have been one hundred, or possibly several hundred.

We conclude, therefore, that the evolution theory tries to give us definite habitats for the fossils, while the Deluge theory cannot be said to do this.

One more important feature of this subject of ecology needs to be considered in this connection, as showing the contrast between the two theories.

There are many places around over the globe where the stratified beds extend for a depth of five thousand or more feet below the surface, that is, we have a mile or more of thickness for the fossiliferous strata. Let us suppose ourselves in a coal-mine region, with many layers of true coal alternating with shales and limestones, the latter containing brachiopods and crinoids.

The evolutionary explanation for all this is that each coal bed represents a period when this area was above sea level, for (we are told) the plant material of the coal grew where we find it, in something like a swamp or a marsh. Then this area settled beneath the waters, and a bed of shale or limestone was slowly deposited upon it, after which it rose again for another accumulation of plant material in another swamp. This process of alternating depression and elevation of this area, we are told, went on for many millions of years, for it is a common thing to find fifty or seventy-five beds of coal, thick or thin, in a vertical series one above another, with the total thickness of a mile or more.

On the basis of the Deluge theory, however, neither the material of the coal beds nor that of the limestones represents a growth *in situ*, but all were brought here by the varying currents of the waters. As to exactly how it took place, there would seem to be three possibilities, which will need to be considered. And in order to visualize the situation, it may be advisable to give names to the localities involved. Let us call the area where the coal beds and limestones are situated *the settling basin,* and let us designate it by *A*. The area to the left, from which the plant material came, we shall call one of the *supply areas,* and

shall name this area *B*. To the right will be another *supply area,* to be called *C*.

Since there is a mile or more of thickness of the combined strata, it is clear that this settling basin *A* must have sunk down about as rapidly as the materials from the two supplying localities were deposited; for otherwise it would soon have become filled up and no more currents would have flowed into it. This is alternative *one*. The second alternative is that first one and then the other of the two supply areas, *B* and *C*, became sufficiently elevated to promote a current bringing in a supply of material to deposit over the bottom of the settling basin *A*. The third alternative is that the whole process of transportation was accomplished by the flood and ebb of tidal action, which would bring materials first from *B* and then from *C*, in each case dropping their loads upon the bottom of the settling basin *A*. Yet unless we are to suppose that this central area *A* was a mile or more deep to begin with, it would seem necessary that this area must have settled about as fast as the material was deposited upon it. Or some suitable combination of deep water and some settling may be imagined. Finally, after a mile or more of sediments was deposited, the area became elevated to the height above sea level where it now is.

But no matter how we explain this set of coal beds, shales, and limestones, a mile or more in thickness, we have here a genuine alternation or cycle of deposits. Hence we cannot speak of any real sequence of the fossils in this particular locality. For no matter how thick the total deposit may be, it is always the case under such circumstances that the *plants in the bottom coal bed are exactly like those in the top bed,* and the same usually holds true for the brachiopods and crinoids as well. Thus there is nothing like a progression from lower-organization forms to higher-organization forms, and thus nothing to correspond to what is meant by the progressive sequence of evolution. On the basis of the evolution theory, with the coal plants *in situ*, we might speak of the geological formations as representing former ecological habitats; but on the Deluge theory it is little better than nonsense to speak of the coal beds and the limestones in this one locality as representing the ecological setting in which both these former plants and animals lived. To be sure, the localities where these materials came from, *B* and *C*, as described above, would be the ecological habitats in which these fossil plants and animals lived and grew; but nobody knows where they were located, not within probably hundreds of miles.

So much, then, for the principles of ecology in the light of Deluge Geology.

THE SIGNIFICANCE OF CONFORMITY

One more important general principle calls for attention here, before we take up specific examples of what we are considering. When a bed of shale or limestone or whatnot is found agreeing perfectly with the bed below it, so that the two fit like hand and glove, with no signs of erosion on the surface of the lower one before the next was laid upon it, and with no sign of disturbance of the lower one, so that the two beds are parallel in their bedding, then the two strata are said to be *conformable,* and they show *conformity* in their deposition. Hence conformity indicates continuity of deposit, that is, the two beds *followed one another in quick succession.* They show some interval, for there are two beds, not one; but since nothing of importance happened in this interval, it could not have been of long duration.

Now the point where conformity comes into the general picture which we are here studying, is that on the Deluge theory we are to take all examples of conformity at their full face value, while there are innumerable instances where, according to the evolution theory, we have to imagine a vast hiatus, though every physical evidence is against it and the conformity is perfect. For these cases W. B. Scott coined the expressive term "deceptive conformity," for the evolutionists prefer to trust to their theory of the invariable sequence of the fossils, and because a vast number of the fossils of their long series are here absent, they think that the mere physical evidence is liable to deceive us and so it cannot be trusted. For whenever a Cretaceous bed, let us say, is found in seemingly perfect conformity upon a Cambrian, with the larger part of both the Paleozoic and the Mesozoic eras entirely wanting, it would never do to admit a genuine case of comparatively quick succession. Hence the name "deceptive conformity."

Literally thousands of such instances are known, and they are in every part of the globe and involve every imaginable pair of formations. As James D. Dana puts it,—". . . a stratum of one era may rest upon any stratum in the whole of the series below it . . . the intermediate being wanting."[6] Without doing any violence to the facts, we might insert the word "conformably" into this sentence, making it read ". . . a stratum of one era may rest *conformably* upon any stratum of the whole series below it . . . the intermediate being wanting."

In a conversation with E. O. Ulrich, a leading authority on this and related subjects, he told me that he supposed he had seen and examined a thousand such instances, some of them covering an area nearly equal

6 Dana, James D., *Manual of Geology*, p. 399; New York, Fourth Edition, 1894.

to an entire state. Of course, since all stratified beds tend to be lens-like and thus to thin out at the edges, there is probably no place on earth where any bed is perfectly conformable to either the bed above it or the one below throughout its entire extent. Hence when any one wants to quibble about such cases, and if he hunts long enough, he can always find some place where the strict conformity apparently fails, and he is able to point triumphantly to a "hiatus" between them, and thus avoid embarrassment to the theory.

But in the innumerable instances where the so-called break or hiatus occurs in what appears to be *one continuous formation,* the very same kind of limestone or whatnot being both above and below, and the whole looking like one continuous deposit, it is difficult to take seriously a theory which tells us many millions of years are here unrepresented by anything that nature did in the way of deposition or erosion. A conformity must be terribly "deceptive," if it has no means of warning us that nature somehow must have served an injunction on the action of the elements, and they had to continue in the *status in quo,* neither wearing away nor depositing anything, until they were ready to lay down an *identically similar shale or limestone on the very same spot in the same horizontal sequence,* after millions and millions of years.

But on the basis of the Deluge theory, with no necessity for trying to read an interval of millions of years, a "deceptive conformity" is exactly like any other conformity. And there is no need to imagine difficulties where none exist. Let the plain physical evidence be true, though every theory founded on the supposed sequence of the fossils be proved a liar. Thus "deceptive conformities" are

to be expected in the Flood theory. But so also would *reversed* conformities be reasonably looked for, I mean conformities with the fossils in the reverse of the *standard* or evolutionary sequence. And the believer in the Deluge is not disappointed. For plenty of these reversed conformities are now known, only they pass under such misleading names as "wedges," or "slices," "thrust faults," "imbricate structure," etc. And the reader should constantly keep in mind that of course every such reversed conformity implies a real repetition or duplication of some of the key fossils.

But we remember that inorganic sediments tend to go in cycles, the same kind of material recurring again and again in the strata. Now if the fossils were treated by the currents exactly like other sediments, we might expect that occasionally at least they would be found repeated or duplicated in the same vertical section. And plenty of such instances are also known, both in the classes known as "deceptive conformities," and in those which I have named "reversed conformities." In his well-known paper on the Paleozoic strata,[7] Ulrich gives one locality where the same special fossils reappear *three* times and another where they are repeated *five* times. These would come under the general heading of "deceptive conformities," as spoken of above. Ulrich called them examples of "periodic emigrants," while others have named them "recurrent faunas," "pioneer colonies," etc. Many cases of the milder forms of reversed conformities have been given similar names. For there are many places where the age of the beds is in dispute because of the incongruity of the fossils they contain, as compared with those above or below, and yet for various reasons it has not been thought important enough to invoke the theory of thrust

[7] *Bull. Geol. Soc. of Amer.,* Vol. 22, 1911, pp. 298, 299.

faults; so some milder term is used to adjust the difficulty. And the theory of "pioneer colonies" or of "recurrent faunas" is much easier to manage, since it does not require any physical explanation through some gigantic displacement of the strata, and thus nobody is obliged to hunt around to find some alleged slickensides of microscopic extent, or to find crystallines or deformations above the so-called thrust plane.

By all these various expedients or subterfuges (and I am here including the whole kit of thrust faults, and the various kinds of "folds," usually measured in tens of miles, sometimes in scores of miles), the plain, objective physical proofs of repetition of the fossils can be explained away and their obvious meaning evaded. And thus the scientific world can still go on believing in the evolutionary fable of a standard or invariable sequence of the fossils for the world as a whole, a sequence which their theory demands must never be reversed. Barnum was surely right after all; and scientists are no slower than other people in their desire to be fooled, whenever anything even remotely involving their dogma or religion or personal interests is concerned.

These two great sets of facts, deceptive conformities and reversed conformities, though seemingly quite different from each other, are in reality both only different aspects of one and the same set of phenomena, namely, the seemingly haphazard manner in which the sediments (including the fossils) were deposited by the waters of the Deluge. Both are to be expected, if the Deluge deposited the fossils; but both are deadly as evidence against the evolutionary theory of a definite sequence of the fossils.

THE GROWTH OF THE CONTROVERSY

A little more than a hundred years ago, when Lyell's books were first appearing in England, he and the small handful of men who were then interested in geology thought they had discovered the exact order in which the fossils would always be found occurring throughout the entire world. I have elsewhere given this part of the history with some detail, and need not repeat it here. With their scanty knowledge of the strata in only a few corners of western Europe and eastern North America, it could be only by the most amazing good luck that they could be expected to know exactly how the fossils would some day be found arranged in Australia, or Patagonia, or New Guinea. But the previous methods of classifying the rocks, as taught by Werner, were becoming inadequate and absurd, and the new method of classifying them by their fossils soon proved so elastic and convenient that it was found that the discoveries from far distant places could be pigeonholed with the greatest ease; and the great utility of the new method soon led them all to believe that they had actually hit upon the precise sequence in which the first living things had appeared upon the earth. Accordingly, with great enthusiasm they hurried around over Europe and eastern America, so far as the slow and clumsy methods of travel then permitted, and like Werner's devoted disciples before them, they always thought they found everything just as their theory had taught them to expect.

The three little green peas in the little green pod observed that their little world was all green, and they themselves green likewise; and by a real induction, though hasty and partial, they concluded that the entire universe must be green. But we are not told that they travelled abroad and persisted in interpreting everything they saw in terms of their theory.

But after this standard sequence of the fossils had become well established, it became apparent soon after the middle of the century that some very troublesome exceptions would have to be reckoned with. The Alps very naturally were the first mountains to be examined geologically, and in many places the apparent contradictions to the established sequence are visible many miles away. By 1870, Prof. Albert Heim of the University of Geneva was publishing diagrams of gigantic folds, miles high and many miles in horizontal extent, to explain why Triassic and Jurassic (Mesozoic) strata occur above the Tertiary in so many parts of Switzerland, and why in other instances Permo-Carboniferous (Paleozoic) are sometimes similarly situated.

At first the colossal scale of the displacements thus involved almost took away the breath of even veteran speculators; but they gradually became accustomed to the concept of gigantic arcs of circles miles high in the air, as the places where the mountains once were. For when one is merely making diagrams on paper in the quiet of a library, the stern requirements of mechanics and engineering can often be disregarded.

Some forty years later than this, when Heim had become an old man and famous all over the world, while I was only a beginner in the study of these subjects, I had some very interesting correspondence with him from Southern California. In one of his communications he candidly explained the compelling evolutionary philosophy behind all these incredible theories of folds and overthrusts:

". . . the most incredible mechanical explanation is more probable than that the evolution of organic nature should have been inverted in one country as compared with another."

The actual meaning of this seemingly wise statement is that, so far as he was concerned, his theory of the evolutionary sequence of the fossils was absolutely paramount, and he was ready to accept any mechanical explanation, no matter how impossible, when confronted on any mountain side with physical, objective evidence of fossils in the reverse of his theory. And apparently all modern geologists agree with him.

This is the way in which they get their invariable sequence of the fossils.

In another letter he dwelt with emphasis on the fact that in Switzerland the fossiliferous strata are visibly in an order directly contrary to the long recognized evolutionary order. This contradictory sequence, he said, "is a fact which can be clearly seen—only we know not yet how to explain it in a mechanical way."

This last statement is still just as true as ever it was. In Switzerland, as might be expected, geology is taught in the high school as well as in the college; and for two generations the students have been encouraged to be very original in drawing their diagrams of how they think the strata got where we find them. I came away with dozens of such diagrams, all of them mechanically absurd and impossible; but the most experienced geologists cannot agree among themselves as to how it all happened.

One of the leading present-day writers on the geology of the Swiss Alps is Leon W. Collet, Albert Heim's successor in the University of Geneva. His teaching is that *six* great sheets or "nappes" have *successively* been pushed over what is now central and eastern Switzerland, so that essentially every mountain of the high calcareous Alps has travelled to its present position,—but not all at once, in *six* successive invasions.[8] Of one of the most conspicuous peaks to the east of Lake Lucerne, Collet says:

8 Collet, Leon W., *The Structure of the Alps*, p. 60, and *passim*. London, 1927.

*"The Mythen represents an outlier of Africa resting on Europe."*[9]

He puts this sentence in italics, as I have done, for he evidently was very certain of his theory. If he had the record of a moving-picture camera when it all happened, he could hardly be more confident or dogmatic. But not all Alpine geologists agree with him. One of them in another Swiss university was quite incredulous; but he admitted that he didn't know where the top of this mountain had come from, "unless it came down from the moon." That this and the other mountains of Switzerland are just ordinary examples of erosion, with the strata having been *deposited in the order in which we find them,* though subsequently slightly disturbed here and there like most other mountains, seems never to have occurred to these good people, because of their dominating obsession, that there is a standard or world-wide sequence of the fossils, and that this sequence is never repeated.

While Albert Heim and the other geologists on the Continent were still disputing over the theories of overturned folds and flat-lying pushes or thrusts, the geologists in Great Britain seemed to settle the case in favor of the flat-lying thrusts, from a study of the mountains in the extreme north of Scotland. Here only *five* duplications or repetitions are involved, instead of the *six* in the Alps; but like the latter, the theory is that these Highlands of Scotland arrived where we now find them in five successive pushes or thrusts. But all the early geologists who were familiar with the rocks in this locality had thought the strata were perfectly normal. Says Richard M. Field:[10]

". . . the pre-Cambrian and Paleozoic formations have been repeated several times. Some of the contacts (mechanical) between the underlying and overlying formations are clean-cut thrusts. The lines of demarcation between the formations are such as to have misled the earlier geologists, including Sir Charles Lyell [also Murchison and A. Geikie], who believed that he was dealing with a normal, or successive, series in which the gneisses and schists were interbedded with the Paleozoic sandstones and limestones."

We may rest assured that when such veteran geologists as Lyell, Murchison, and Geikie had regarded the strata here as perfectly normal, the alleged physical evidence of thrusting could not be very obvious. It was only after the anti-evolutionary fact developed that some of the formations "have been repeated several times," and that wholly "strange" strata are "interbedded" with the Paleozoics, that these veteran geologists became convinced that gigantic thrusts must have taken place. Murchison held out against the new theories for several years. He became partly convinced in 1857, upon "the discovery of additional and better preserved fossils"[11] than were before available; but he still denied the duplication of the formation, which alone would necessitate (for evolutionists) such a drastic theory as several colossal "thrusts."

The "Highland Controversy," as it has been called, was "finally settled upon paleontological evidence," as Field[12] naively tells us. And he goes on to give his students a lesson from the history of this affair to prove that fossils are "the best and safest criteria" for determining the relative age of formations, for correlation by lithology or structural makeup is "a dangerous procedure." Thus it was from the outcome of this "Highland Controversy" that *we can date the final triumph of fossil evidence over every other consideration,* when the relative age of formations is to be determined.

9 *Id.,* p. 103.
10 Field, Richard M., *The Principles of Historical Geology,* p. 171; 1933.
11 *Id.,* p. 192.
12 *Id.,* p. 194.

Today every instructed geologist knows that the fossils are the supreme court in all stratigraphical controversy, and from them there is no appeal. And it is solely because of the fossil evidence that we are asked to believe that *five* successive sheets have overrun the northern part of Scotland, and *six* in the Alps. Also it is solely because of the iron law of the evolutionary sequence of the fossils that flat-lying thrust faults are invoked in any other part of the world.

It was in connection with these conditions in the Highlands that Geikie[13] wrote his picturesque descriptions of how perfectly natural the strata appear; this he says is why he and Lyell and Murchison were so mistaken in their former examination of this region. The thrust planes, Geikie tells us, can only with difficulty be

"distinguished from ordinary stratification planes, like which they have been plicated, faulted, and denuded. Here and there, as a result of denudation, a portion of one of them appears capping a hilltop. One almost refuses to believe that the little outlier on the summit does not lie normally on the rocks below it, but on a nearly horizontal fault by which it has been moved into its place."

He then speaks of some similar conditions in Ross Shire, about which he had previously reported as being naturally conformable, and gives us the revealing admission:

"Had these sections been planned for the purpose of deception, they could not have been more skillfully devised, . . . and no one coming first to this ground would suspect that what appears to be a normal stratigraphic sequence is not really so."

All this confirms what our American veteran geologist, James D. Dana,[14] said about these conditions in Scotland:

"The thrust planes look like planes of bedding, and were long so considered."

And of course *they are true bedding planes,* and nothing but a highly speculative *a priori* theory could ever in-

duce anyone to think otherwise, or to hunt around for some supposed physical evidence for gigantic thrusts, five of them, one after another over the same ground.

The final settlement of the Highland Controversy, by everybody accepting the view that there have been five repetitions of the fossils, marked a very important turning point in the history of geology. Werner's methods of correlating the strata by means of lithology and the other common-sense criteria, had long proved disappointing for what had become the all-absorbing aim of uniformitarian geologists, namely, the working out of a history of earth-changes during many long millions of years. *But from this time onward the fossils were made the supreme criteria for determining the age of any rock deposit;* the color and texture of the rock, and even its stratigraphic position, must all be disregarded, if or whenever they seem to be contradicted by the so-called fossil evidence. It marks a strange chapter in the history of the human mind. For to make a highly speculative theory about the history of the plants and animals on the globe during many millions of years the absolutely supreme guide in studying the rocks of all the world, and to make this a *priori* theory so infallible as to override the plainest physical evidence and all logic, must have caused many qualms of the scientific conscience for great numbers of investigators during the past three-quarters of a century. Verily, the evolution theory, when fully accepted, imposes heavy tasks on the intellect of man. To quote again the revealing statement of Albert Heim in one of his letters to me:

". . . the most incredible mechanical explanation is more probable than that the evolution of organic nature should have been inverted in one country as compared with another."

13 *Nature,* Nov. 13, 1884, pp. 29-35.
14 Dana, James W., *Manual of Geology,* p. 534; fourth edition, 1894.

Like all the others who long stood out against the theory of great thrusts, so contrary to all the visible physical evidence and reason, Sir Archibald Geikie finally learned the lesson, that the theory about the invariable sequence of the fossils must be considered true, though every objective physical evidence is against it. And so, when writing his large college "Textbook" about the turn of the century, he gave this choice bit of scientific reasoning:

"We may even demonstrate [?] that in some mountainous ground the strata have been turned completely upside down, if we can show that the fossils in which are now the uppermost layers ought properly to lie underneath those in the beds below them."[15]

This is a very candid and revealing statement of the mental processes behind all the modern fashionable theories about overturned folds and thrust faults; and I suppose that those who fully believe the evolution theory will see nothing wrong or unscientific in this method of reasoning. Elsewhere in this same textbook Geikie gives us another candid statement about the actual condition of the stata in some parts of the Alps:

"The strata could scarcely be supposed to have been really inverted, save for the evidence [sic] as to their true order of succession supplied by their included fossils. . . . Portions of Carboniferous strata appear as if regularly interbedded among Jurassic rocks, and indeed could not be separated save after a study of their enclosed organic remains."[16]

I confess I don't know how to comment on such statements as these two from this illustrious author, without seeming to use unparliamentary language. But why should an *a priori* theory thus compel otherwise qualified and reasonable men to play—

". . . such fantastic tricks [of logic] before high heaven,
As make the angels weep"?

Occasionally some tyro in geology, zealous for the good reputation of his science, will indignantly deny that the fossils are used in the way described above. And he will point to the many practical ways of identifying the strata and of tracing them across the country for many miles. He may even emphasize the principle of superposition, and ask if the relative age of the strata, as determined by superposition, has anything whatever to do with the fossils.

But all this is mere eye wash, and is put forward by those only who are not familiar with the larger aspects of geology and paleontology. For the methods of identification and correlation by means of lithic composition or even by stratigraphy are of only local use and local importance. Whenever one attempts to correlate these local formations with others elsewhere, or whenever one wishes to *date* these local formations, or to assign them to some definite pigeonhole in the standard geological "column," that is, whenever one wishes to *name* these local beds and *classify* them, as one might name a new bird or a flower, then the fossils become the one and only means of deciding the name and the classification.

At the risk of becoming wearisome, I shall present two quotations from reliable authorities. The first is from Grabau, and has to do with the larger *Groups* (Paleozoic, Mesozoic, etc.):

"The primary divisions of the geological time-scale are, as we have seen, based on the changes in life, with the result that fossils alone determine whether a formation belongs to one or the other of these great divisions."[17]

But fossils are the only criteria also for the subdivisions of the Groups, which are the *systems* (Cambrian, Devonian, Cretaceous, etc.) as is stated by Williams:[18]

15 Geikie, Sir Archibald, *Textbook of Geology*, Ed. of 1903, p. 837.
16 *Id.*, p. 678.
17 Grabau, A. W., *Principles of Stratigraphy*, p. 1103; New York, 1913.
18 Williams, H. S., *Geological Biology*, pp. 37, 38.

"These systems, although actually arbitrary groupings of the stratified rocks of particular regions, have come into common use as the primary divisions of the rocks whenever chronological sequence is considered. In describing any newly discovered fossiliferous strata in any part of the earth, the first step to be taken in giving them a scientific definition, is to assign them to one or other of these systems upon evidence of the fossils found in them. The character of the rocks themselves, their composition, or their mineral contents have nothing to do with settling the question as to the particular system to which the new rocks belong. The fossils alone are the means of correlation."

Now there would be no harm in all this, *if time-values* were not assigned to these classifications. I mean, that if it were merely a question of a convenient method of classifying the strata of all the world, nobody would object to the rule that the character of the rocks themselves or their lithic composition should have nothing to do with it, but that the fossils alone should be the basis of correlation. But the history of the science shows that in actual practice geologists have gone one step further, and have decided *that stratigraphic position also* should have nothing to do with the classification, or in other words, that the fossil evidence shall overrule the stratigraphic evidence. But stratigraphic position above or below another bed obviously involves the *time* element; and since time-values have also been (arbitrarily) attributed to the *systems* to which the strata are being assigned in classification, it is evident that the two methods, both involving the time element, are bound to come into conflict. Hence all this furor about "overturned folds," "thrust faults," "recurrent faunas," "wedges," "slices," "imbricate structure," etc.

The logical and the scientific way out of this impasse, would of course be to give stratigraphy the right of way over the fossils, or in other words, to let the visible stratigraphic position

overrule the *time-element* in the classification, and to say that the long recognized sequence of the fossils is. a purely arbitrary affair, with no time-values in its subdivisions. But *this would make all the fossils contemporary with one another;* and this is of course unthinkable for the evolutionist. And so it remains that the fossil evidence, though denying the obvious common sense of stratigraphic position, still rules as the supreme court of geological classification, overruling not only the character of the strata themselves, but even their stratigraphic position, thus creating the need for "deceptive conformities," "thrust faults," and all the other subterfuges of a theory which has its back to the wall and is fighting for its very life.

The Ptolemaic astronomy also had its "epicycles" and other devices, by means of which it fought a delaying action against the opposing forces of a better and truer science. It remains to be seen how long the current evolutionary geology can maintain its position by employing similar tactics.

In the case of the Rocky Mountains, the physical evidence is even plainer and simpler than in the Alps or the northern Highlands of Scotland. In the Rockies the general fact is that the strata are more generally horizontal throughout long distances than in any other comparable mountain region of the globe. Then, too, the so-called overthrust is on so vast a scale, involving an area of more than one hundred thousand square miles, all astonishingly similar in appearance and structure, that it ought to appeal to the logic of geologists, and lead them to ask themselves if there can not be some better way to account for the conditions as we find them. Around Banff there has been, it is true, some disturbance, but throughout the greater part of this immense area in Alberta and Montana, the strata both above and below the so-called "thrust plane" are parallel to one another in bedding and all are still essentially horizontal. In dozens of localities throughout this wide area, where the contact line is not obscured by talus, the two sets of strata look exactly like any normal sequence and even seem perfectly conformable, thus resembling the cases in Scotland, of which Dana honestly states: "The thrust planes look like planes of bedding, and were long so considered."

Of course, the evolutionary geologist believes there is here at least one duplication or repetition, and on a most colossal scale. Nobody can have any possible doubt about the classification of the underlying Cretaceous beds; for they comprise all the plains region, running out in front of the mountains for hundreds of miles, and extending almost from the Arctic Ocean to the Gulf of Mexico, making it one of the largest areas of these rocks in the entire world. And although the evolutionary geologist can see that all the mountains of this region are Paleozoic, he is also just as confident that if we could only examine the rocks deep down under his feet, he would find these Paleozoic *repeated a mile or two deep;* for in his estimation that is where the Paleozoic naturally belong, and he argues that Paleozoic rocks must be down there, in order to have furnished the massive beds comprising the mountains high above his head. Thus on the evolution theory there just *has to be at least one duplication* of the Paleozoic rocks, and on a most gigantic scale. For in the eyes of the evolutionist every reversal of the sequence of the fossils means a duplication, and the latter he will not tolerate.

Of course, nobody has yet proved

that Paleozoic strata do occur deep down under the Cretaceous. Oil drillings and coal mines have explored the Cretaceous to a depth of several thousand feet, but without any signs of Paleozoic underneath. Personally, I very much doubt if any such deep Paleozoic will ever be proved objectively. On the basis of the Flood theory, the Cretaceous beds are probably the bottom fossiliferous strata for all this region; it just happened that here the Cretaceous were deposited first and the Paleozoic afterwards, though in other localities the deposition was often in the reverse sequence. We all know that in the Thames region in the south of England, geologists long expected to find Carboniferous beds deep down under the Chalk (Cretaceous) ; but it is now admitted that this guess was wrong. But whether or not the massive Paleozoic of these Rocky Mountains are actually physically duplicated in the way the evolutionist expects, everyone knows that here the Paleozoic occur on top of the Cretaceous; and *for the evolutionist that is an obvious repetition or duplication of the order in which he declares the fossils always occur;* and this is all that is required to prove my point.

But there is also duplication or repetition on a small scale here and there, or actual interfingering, as so often occurs when the strata are perfactly conformable. This would be expected on the basis of the Deluge theory, and it is implied by the naive acknowledgement of one of the highest authorities that in more than one locality in this Rocky Mountain region the same texture of beds occurs both above and below the so-called thrust plane, so that the Paleozoic and the Cretaceous cannot be separated except by fossil evidence.[19] All this is

---

[19] See McConnell, R. G., Canadian *Annual Report,* 1886, Part D, p. 17. Some are now saying that in the vicinity of Banff there are seven colossal repetitions or so-called "thrusts," each composed of four layers, these four component layers being about the same in each of the repetitions or cycles. If this situation is confirmed by further investigation, we would have another strong confirmation of the thesis of this paper.

perfectly natural; for similar areas always give us such instances of interfingering or repetition on a small scale. And it should be remembered that this whole region is still comparatively unexplored geologically. It has only been sampled here and there, so to speak, its situation on the international boundary line adding to the difficulties; for neither the Canadian nor the American geologists have become much acquainted with the area as a whole.

The main features of this vast area are very simple; the Cretaceous is underneath and the Paleozoic above; and this is a sufficient challenge to the entire theory of geological evolution to induce its devoted followers to start hunting for every possible scrap of deformation or disturbance which they can possibly find and exploit, to furnish some seeming excuse for saying that this entire area of over a hundred thousand square miles was lifted up from deep down underneath, and then pushed bodily eastward for a score or more of miles, to where we now find these mountains. It is also highly probable that, upon further exploration and examination, more than one gigantic thrust will need to be invoked, just as *five* successive "nappes" or sheets are postulated for Scotland and *six* in the Alps.

In terms of the Deluge theory, this means that the Cretaceous beds of the plains, which can be seen extending under the Rockies just as the soil extends under a building, and which contain coal beds and chalk, with fossils of dinosaurs and ammonites, were deposited fairly early in the history of the Deluge. Afterwards these Cretaceous beds were lowered very deeply (or the adjacent areas were correspondingly elevated) , so that thick deposits from the very depths of the ocean, now comprising the masses of the mountains and several thousand feet in thickness, were spread out over these Cretaceous strata. Later, the entire region was strongly elevated, and enormous quantities of the upper beds were eroded away, this erosion eating down to the underlying Cretaceous in hundreds of places, leaving the latter exposed and thus capable of being worked for the splendid coal they contain, the Bankhead mine near Banff furnishing a good quality of anthracite.

The evolutionist has himself described hundreds of similar methods of rock formation in all parts of the globe; so he can hardly object to this description, except in the matter of the order in which the deposits were made. But he declares with much vigor that the Cretaceous could not possibly have been laid down first, for the Cretaceous animals and plants did not live until many millions of years after the Paleozoic. But *how does he know all this*? And how does he know it so positively that he can confront these conditions in Alberta and Montana, and tell us with a sober face that the rocks are deceiving us, for they could not possibly have been deposited in this order?

I do not feel called upon to discuss here the true principles of empirical scientific investigation. Nor do I think I need to dwell at length upon the absurdities involved in the theory of the Rocky Mountains having been pushed twenty or thirty or forty miles into their present position. A miracle could do it; but evolutionists do not believe in miracles. What conceivable *natural* force could possibly push the top layers for this distance, without the soft underlying shales having also been pushed, or gouged, and disrupted enormously by the process? But the soft underlying Cretaceous shales do not show the slightest trace of any such movement.

Then, too, what must have been the rigidity of the upper layers, which could stand such a push from behind twenty or thirty miles away? A friend of mine has compared the process to that of pushing a freshly rolled-out piecrust across a table, by pressure on one side. How far could one push it this way?

The entire concept of gigantic overthrusts is full of absurdities and mechanical impossibilities. But all these count for nothing in the eyes of the convinced evolutionist, when confronted with such a flat contradiction of his theory as Paleozoic mountains standing on a Cretaceous base. In such circumstances his is a faith which literally has to move the mountains. He knows no other way.

SOME GENERAL CONSIDERATIONS

It is well for us all to remember that the trivial "evidence" for a great overthrust is not the real reason for their believing it. No indeed. It is only the proffered excuse. The real reason, of course, as every geologist knows in his soul, is that slogan which has been so thoroughly learned by every one of them, namely, that the fossils never occur in the reverse of the standard order or sequence, and hence whenever they seem to do so, some mechanical displacement must be sought for as the cause. In the revealing words of Albert Heim, "the most incredible mechanical explanation is more probable than that the evolution of organic nature should have been inverted in one country as compared with another." How can any mere objective, physical facts withstand such a creed?

But this present situation among geologists should not seem strange to any one who has studied the history of science and is acquainted with the vagaries of human reasoning. For it is a law of the human mind that in all scientific research men usually find what they are looking for. In other words, men usually try to test out a definite hypothesis, and they get an answer of *yes* or *no*, but very seldom anything else. Now, since the rocks for a hundred years have been interrogated always in terms of the theory that the fossils occur in an invariable sequence, and are never repeated or duplicated, it is not strange that an affirmative answer has been extracted from the strata sooner or later, though often the methods employed to elicit such an answer remind us of those employed to get the proper answer from obstinate heretics. This is the true explanation for all such fantastic theories as gigantic overturned folds and thrust faults extending for scores of miles.

Additional light is cast upon this phase of the subject by the statements of some modern teachers of logic, like F. C. S. Schiller of Oxford University, that even the best-established "facts" always contain theories or interpretations in their recording or reporting by poor, fallible human beings. In the words of Alfred North Whitehead, of Harvard:

"Every scientific memoir in its record of the 'facts' is shot through and through with interpretation."[20]

The same author tells us further:

"The history of thought shows that false interpretations of observed facts enter into the records of their observation. Thus both theory, and received notions as to fact, are in doubt."[21]

Now it is easy to see that it is these unconsciously assumed theories or latent interpretations which cause all the trouble, or which get scientists into trouble, when these students of nature are confronted with objective facts which are not provided for in their theories, or which perhaps flatly contradict these theories.

Whitehead in his clear-thinking way tells us how to arrive at rock-bottom truth, whenever we find ourselves confronted with just such an *impasse* as the modern situation, when

---

[20] Whitehead, A. N., *Process and Reality*, p. 22; New York, The Macmillan Co., 1929.
[21] *Id.*, p. 13.

the evolutionary theory of the invariable sequence of the fossils finds itself confronted with such phenomena as the six repetitions of the standard order in the Alps and five in the Scottish Highlands. Says Whitehead:

"When you are criticising the philosophy of an epoch, do not chiefly direct your attention to those intellectual positions which its exponents feel it necessary explicitly to defend. There will be some fundamental assumptions which adherents of all the variant systems within the epoch unconsciously presuppose. Such assumptions appear so obvious that people do not know what they are assuming, because no other way of putting things has ever occurred to them."[22]

The theoretical Jonah which is causing all the trouble, and which needs to be thrown overboard in order to bring calm to the troubled sea of modern science, is this evolutionary assumption that the fossils were not contemporary with one another, but lived in a long series of successive ages, and thus could not possibly be duplicated or repeated in the strata. For if the fossils represent the floras and faunas of a contemporary world, then the necessity for gigantic thrust faults does not arise.

As might be expected, there is by no means full agreement among geologists as to how these troublesome phenomena in the Alps and elsewhere should be interpreted. Field tells us "There has been, and still is, a strong antipathy to the nappe theory," especially on the part of American geologists. Many challenge the mechanics and the common sense involved in six successive sheets pushed from Africa over into Switzerland. But Field protests that few if any Americans are familiar with the practical exploratory work of examining the Alps,[23] and warns that for any one to dispute this "nappe" theory of Collet and the

others, "would require years of hard climbing under the expert guidance of those who are used to geologizing in the Alps."[24] But he admits that this "nappe" theory does not agree with other important geological theories commonly believed:

"The mechanics called for in the hypothesis appear incompatible with the diastrophism of a shrinking globe. The tangential forces called for could not possibly be derived from radial contraction, and do not as yet appear to be related to the theory of isostasy!"[25]

Another criticism of this theory appears in an editorial in the English journal *Nature*, which is rightly regarded as one of the foremost scientific publications of the entire world:

"The attractiveness of the *nappe* theory depended upon its seductive simplicity. The alternative explanations [which still assume the evolutionary sequence of the fossils] are often complex. When, however, the theory is followed into details, the simplicity disappears, owing to rapid changes in the hypothesis, extreme differences among its supporters, its evasiveness of crucial tests, and fantastic explanations introduced to explain special cases."[26]

The well known English geologist, W. W. Watts, has this to say about these new developments in geology:

"The problem of the overthrust 'nappes' of mountain regions is one of our greatest difficulties, and all explanations hitherto proposed are so hopelessly inadequate that we have sometimes felt compelled to doubt whether the facts [of repetions of the fossils, etc.] really are as stated. But the phenomena have now been observed so carefully and in so many districts [all over the world, for that matter] that any real doubt as to the facts is out of the question, and we must still look for some adequate method by which the overthrusting could have been brought about."[27]

Of course this author would never admit that it is the basic evolutionary theory of the fossils which is causing all the trouble, and that when this is discarded, all further difficulty completely disappears.

22 Whitehead, A. N., *Science and the Modern World*, p. 71. The Macmillan Co., 1929.
23 Field, R. M., *The Principles of Historical Geology*, p. 217, Princeton, 1933.
24 *Id.*, p. 231.
25 *Id.*, p. 234.
26 *Nature*, June 29, 1929, p. 975.
27 Smithsonian Annual *Report*, 1925, p. 283.

We might pursue this subject indefinitely. In every part of the globe —and often not in any mountainous region—examples are appearing of the fossils in some sequence flatly contradicting the supposedly universal or evolutionary sequence, which has become a sacred cow and must be saved at all costs. How long this absurd farce is to continue, of adjusting the newly discovered facts to fit the traditional theory, is anybody's guess. Since Barnum was right in his estimate of human nature, it might continue indefinitely.

Even a few professed believers in Deluge geology have become confused, and seem to think there must be something right after all in this theory of the traditional sequence of the fossils. And such people seem willing to accept the fantastic theories about thrust faults, to help account for the contradictory conditions in the field. For it requires no independent thinking to follow implicitly the opinions of the evolutionary geologists, when they report alleged "evidences" for the displacement of whole mountain chains. It is always easier to follow the line of least intellectual resistance.

It is a much more difficult task, it requires a distinctly higher order of thinking and of moral force, to analyze critically a set of reported "facts," to discover the real truth behind them all. But this is exactly what every believer in the Bible must do, and must do constantly, unless he is to become a false signboard, pointing his pupils and his fellow workers in the wrong direction, perhaps to their eternal ruin.

REASONING IN A CIRCLE

From the entire discussion of the preceding pages it will be seen that the basic ideas of evolutionary geology are in a very peculiar situation. The prime idea that life has come into existence - in a series of successive forms, each differing from those which preceded and from those following, is not proved objectively by anything in the sciences of paleontology and geology. It is first assumed as an indisputable fact, and is then read into the record of the rocks and the fossils, with every other idea about the rocks and the fossils, even stratigraphy, made subordinate and contributory to this assumed succession of life in a definite sequence. Then the entire scheme of organic evolution is built up around this succession of life as its historic outline.

It should be unnecessary for me to point out that all this is a glaring example of reasoning in a circle. For it first assumes the essence of the idea which one wishes to prove, and then uses this major premise to prove the conclusion.

In any system of clear thinking, it is obvious that the doctrine of organic evolution must have some supposedly reliable *history* of many successively advancing types of life during immense periods of time, with the theory built around this supposed history. This history of life is what is meant by the invariable sequence of the fossils, which is the chief theoretical idea of geology, as currently taught; and this idea is far more important logically than are any conclusions from the variations of present-day organisms, which may be supposed to tell us about the origin of species. The latter idea may serve to put the finishing touch upon the main structure, but a history of life and how it has appeared in successive phases during long periods of time, is far more important logically than any biological theory about change of species. In other words, Lyell's geology was far more important logically, and in its historical influence, than Charles Darwin's biology, in changing the intellectual climate of the world from a belief in Creation to a belief in evolution.

As we study critically this aspect of the subject, we see that the entire idea of a historical succession of life during long geological eras has been assumed *en bloc* and then read into the record of the fossils, and thereafter every physical fact has been made to help support it, often at the cost of a flagrant disregard of scientific logic. All this has been explained in detail by the present writer in previous publications,[28] and need not be further dwelt upon here. It may suffice to point out how other writers have candidly admitted this vicious reasoning in a circle, though in their discussion of the situation they remind us of the famous advice: When you meet with an insuperable difficulty, look it squarely in the face, but don't let it stop you; just pass onward. Long ago, that prince of pedants Herbert Spencer looked at this logical difficulty in his essay on "Illogical Geology."[29] But Spencer followed faithfully the rest of the advice quoted above; for after looking the illogical methods of geology squarely in the face, he then proceeded onward to establish his major thesis of evolution, just the same. Thomas Henry Huxley also looked the situation in the face in an address before the Geological Society in 1862.[30] And his verdict was: "All that geology can prove is local order of succession . . . one verdict, 'not proven and not provable,' must be recorded against all the grand hypotheses of the paleontologist respecting the general succession of life on the globe." But he also, as Spencer had done before him, proceeded forthwith to aid and abet the strong conspiracy then prevailing to establish the theory of organic evolution, logic or no logic.

I must content myself with presenting only two more modern writers in support of my charge that evolutionists are reasoning in a circle, when they invoke geology and the fossils (and they cannot possibly do without them), in support of their theory.

Prof. Robert Heron Rastall is the author of an article in the most recent edition of the *Encyclopaedia Britannica*,[31] in the course of which he takes occasion to consider the logical basis of this idea of a succession of life on the globe. And he makes the following candid admission:

"It cannot be denied that from a strictly philosophical standpoint geologists are here arguing in a circle. The succession of organisms has been determined by a study of their remains embedded in the rocks, and the relative ages of the rocks are determined by the remains of organisms they contain."

Like Spencer and Huxley before him, this author tries to justify this reasoning in a circle by squarely assuming the evolution of organisms, and then saying that this whirligig reasoning is the best that can be done to establish the details of this organic evolution from the fossils and the rocks.

The second and final witness which I shall present here is Johannes Walther, the illustrious professor of Halle University, Germany, in a review of Grabau's *Principles of Stratigraphy* (New York, 1913). The following are the candid words of Walther:

"We have indeed been reasoning in a circle when we attempted to correlate the strata of the earth by their content of some index fossils, and inferred the index value of these particular species from their occurrence in rocks of the same age."[32]

28 See especially *Evolutionary Geology and the New Catastrophism, passim*; Pacific Press, 1926.
29 Spencer, Herbert, *Illustrations of Universal Progress*, pp. 328-380; D. Appleton and Co., 1890. This chapter entitled, "Illogical Geology," was first published as an essay in the *Universal Review*, July, 1859, which it will be noticed was several months before the publication of Charles Darwin's *Origin of Species*.
30 Huxley, T. H., *Lectures and Lay Sermons*, pp. 22-40; edition of 1910; New York, E. P. Dutton.
31 *Encycl. Brit.*, 14th edition, Vol. 10, pp. 167, 168.
32 I take these words from an announcement of Grabau's book, *Principles of Stratigraphy*, put out by the New York Publishers, and presumably with the approval of A. W. Grabau himself.

I do not think that any further comment of mine is needed here, save to say that the geological situation has not changed in the least, since these strictures were written. Geology does not *prove* the succession of life on the globe, or what has been termed in the preceding part of this essay, the sequence of the fossils; it merely assumes it, and then by a glaring case of reasoning in a circle it proceeds to declare in pontifical style the relative dates of every fossiliferous deposit it may henceforth discover, according to this assumed sequence of the fossils. and it invents all sorts of absurd physical theories and impossibilities, to explain away any contradictory facts it may encounter in any part of the world.

And it is upon this illogical geology that the entire superstructure of organic evolution has been erected.

### SUMMARY OF THE FACTS

One of the most common phenomena among the ancient strata is a cyclical repetition of different sediments. In the words of the best-known Director of the Geological Survey of Great Britain: ". . . no features recur more continually [among the Paleozoic formations] than the alternation of different sediments."

While this is universally acknowledged concerning the lithic or inorganic deposits laid down by the ancient waters, we might expect the same to be true regarding the fossils or the organic deposits, for the latter might be expected to behave like other sediments. This is indeed the case; but evolutionary geologists deny that the typical fossils or key fossils are ever found repeating themselves. But to maintain this idea many strange devices are resorted to by evolutionists.

When the repetition of the fossils does not involve specimens very far apart in the standard sequence in the geological "column," minor devices, such as "pioneer colonies," or "recurrent faunas," are used to account for the difficulty.

But when any major duplication is found, or when entire formations are found in some "wrong" position in the standard sequence, thus seeming to present a repetition or a cycle in the fossils, drastic theories are resorted to, and some gigantic mechanical movement is postulated to "explain" how the beds happen to be in this position. For the recognized evolutionary sequence of the fossils is always regarded as true, no matter what the physical or stratigraphic evidence may seem to indicate. Almost every region of the globe which has been carefully examined, is now found to furnish examples, often on a gigantic scale, of strata which would seem to contradict the theory that the fossils never repeat themselves; and modern stratigraphic studies seem to be largely employed in trying to explain the physical evidence in such a way as to save the theory.

### CONCLUSION

The theory that the fossils lived in a series during many long successive ages, has long been held as a basic geological truth; but it breaks down hopelessly under critical examination.

The only possible alternative is that the fossils were contemporary, not successive. The theory that they were contemporary, and that they were overwhelmed by a sudden cosmic cataclysm, fits all the major facts as we now know them.

# DISCUSSION

At the request of Professor Price, the questions were answered by Benjamin Franklin Allen.

*Question by member*: The state of New York has been held up as a model where the geologic time-table fits, and as having served as a pattern for applying the system to North America. Is the sequence well established there?

*Mr. Allen*: No, it is not at all well established. Price[33], having cited cases of geologic time missing without trace in Tennessee and elsewhere, says: "A somewhat similar double case of disconformity occurs at Buffalo, New York, the upper of the two being where the Onondaga (Middle Devonian) rests conformably on the Manlius (Upper Silurian), the lower Devonian being absent. The second disconformity in this same section is a few feet lower down, and a considerable part of the Silurian is missing."

Grabau[34], perhaps the leading authority on the strata, points out two more areas in New York and says ". . . a disconformity has been assumed but not supported by evidence of erosion." In the first area Series 9, 10, and 11 (the Silurian) would be missing without trace unless erosion at the contact can be proven. He says that at the contact where others had supposed the missing ages had elapsed the sandstone is "too intimately related to the shale, and is of the same age." He denies that any hiatus exists there, *but doubtfully*, by saying: "The hiatus, known to exist in this area, occurs at a lower level, unless, indeed, as has been *recently suggested by Ruedman and others, the Brayman shale is Upper Ordovicic.*" Of his second example he says: "The Oriskany-Esopus contact of the Helderberg *also has the aspect of a conformable one*. This conformity, if fully established, *has even more far reaching significance.*" (emphasis ours.)

*Question by member*: What is this significance to which he alludes?

*Mr. Allen*: This "time table" is so constructed that each "age" MUST be either present and where it belongs, or a hiatus there MUST be proven, or else the WHOLE SYSTEM IS DISPROVEN. Suppose a group of astrologers should attempt to drop the year 1492, or the year 1776, out of history, *without a trace?* It is just as simple as that! It cannot be done.

But in some areas there are some series of strata *actually in an order in reverse to that in the schedule.* Suppose some historians should try to *reverse* a few score or a few hundreds of years here and there throughout human history, *or even the greater part of it in certain restricted parts of the world?*

*Question by member*: Have any leading geologists made a critical study of these matters?

*Mr. Allen*: Yes, at this point Grabau refers to reports of increasingly large numbers of such occurrences, and cites Ulrich[35] in his very remarkable 400 page attempt to patch up the system. In his opening remarks Ulrich says: "These schemes do not fit the known conditions. Not only were they founded on a mere fraction of the mass of data now available, but also the criteria used were frequently misinterpreted. . . . But the weakest feature in these classifications is that their original framers availed themselves almost exclusively of a single kind of evidence, namely, that afforded by the fossil faunas and floras. . . ."

*Question by member*: What other irregularities in the New York strata can be cited?

*Mr. Allen*: Perhaps several, but only one more will be mentioned, that in the eastern section, extending into Massachusetts to include the Tectonic Mountains. Here for 50 years the leading geologists of North America hotly debated the sequence of more than a dozen formations. These strata are slanting at various steep angles, somewhat like books in a shelf, and supposedly, on theory, *in series*. But geologists for more than one hundred years have never been able to decide permanently *which end is which*. This was called the "Tectonic Question." Finally at the 1888 meeting of the Geological Congress[36], a group of leaders demanded that this name be dropped as applying to those strata. "Dana objected to the retention of the name, thinking it would be regarded as only 'a reminder of Emmons' blundering work—a succession of unstudied assumptions that brought only evil to the science.' " It was finally dropped, but the new data offered by Wolcott, which had stirred up the old conflict, *Wolcott himself finally changed*. And there are still other points that have since turned around in opposition to the views of Dana and his partisans, so that the old moot question was never really

33 Price, George McCready, *Evolutionary Geology*, 1926, p. 99.

34 Grabau, A. W., *Principles of Stratigraphy*, 1924, pp. 823-824.

35 Ulrich, E. O., *Revision of Paleozoic Systems*, Bulletin of the Geological Society of America, Vol. 22, 1911, pp. 281-680.

36 Merrill, S. P., *The First One Hundred Years of American Geology*, 1924, pp. 594-614.

settled, but only arbitrarily dropped. Many more such debates were never settled, but only forgotten because some other more pressing debates came up.

*Question by member*: Referring back to Professor Price's quotations from Huxley[37] and Spencer[38], how could they logically assert that geology could not prove any but local order of sequence and still hold that world-wide geologic ages are possible?

*Mr. Allen*: That is just what many straight thinking people would like to know. It seems a strange paradox that they would be able to see the one point without seeing the other.

*Question by member*: If the sequence of the strata is fixed by the sequence of the fossils, what determines the latter?

*Mr. Allen*: It is the famous but now abandoned recapitulation theory. This theory is that the embryo, during its growth, rapidly changes in form in a manner illustrating or *recapitulating* its supposed long evolutionary history from the one-celled original form of life on earth. This theory held almost absolute sway during the formative years of the geologic-age system of using only the fossils as the indices of the different ages. As the long ages passed, while life-forms were evolving, the two were supposed to have synchronized, the life forms being buried and preserved as fossils, marking the progress of both evolution and sedimentation.

However, Dr. Cyril B. Courville[39] has shown that the real specialists in embryology have abandoned the theory of recapitulation. At present it is being kept alive by those who must have it as a string for their rosary of evolution, especially the paleontologists and geologists, who procede as though they were still unaware of its abandonment. Price[40] wrote a sequel to the work of Courville, in which he proved the vital connection between this theory and the making of the geologic-age system. Thus, to many scientists, the situation is embarrassing, for they are now caught riding a dead horse, whether they know it or not.

*Question by member*: Are students of geology instructed on these points? Are they given a clear understanding? Will you show what one of the latest textbooks now being used in colleges and universities gives on these evolutionary features?

*Mr. Allen*: One of the latest texts is "Geology, Principles and Processes."[41] It is apparently more completely permeated with evolutionary doctrine than any text ever written. Its most basic thesis is the modern philosophy that nature has through eons created itself by means like the natural processes now going on. The Preface to the First Edition (1932) starts this theme right off in the first sentence: "It is intended to give the student some knowledge of the materials of the earth, and of the processes that operate at the earth's surface, and have *operated in the past to form the earth*." In the second sentence in Chapter I the geologic ages are mentioned thus: "It [geology] is the interpretation of the sequence of events from the beginning of the earth as a definite planet in the solar system, *through its many changes during the long geologic ages, to the present time*." Again on page 1 the uniformitarian theory is presented: "He [the geologist] assumes that these processes have been in operation in the past as well as at present, although perhaps in different degrees, and *he seeks to explain the present earth as the result of processes which have been acting through long ages of time. Thus the present, which is the outgrowth of the past, is also the key to the history of the past*."

Pages 6 to 12 present erosion, deposition, disastrophism (crustal movements like mountain-making), as now working, *as they have always worked*, as having produced present conditions. On page 13 this is emphasized: "Methods of study: *The geologic history of the earth should be interpreted in the light of the processes that are observed to be operating on the earth today. . . . as a means of interpreting the geologic past. This principle was developed chiefly by the British geologist Lyell*." (emphasis ours.)

On page 14 at the close of Chapter I (in the First Edition) is shown the famous time-table of the geologic ages, showing their sequence and index fossils, after more than a century of terrific unsettled conflicts such as the old "Tectonic Controversy."

On page 283 of the Second Edition is a discussion of "FOSSILS and Their Significance." "Such remnants of ancient life," it says, "show its development through the long ages of earth history. Not only are the more primitive forms of life found to characterize the earlier periods of earth history,

37 Huxley, Thomas H., *Discourses: Biological and Geological Essays*, 1894, pp. 274-288.

38 Spencer, Herbert, *Illustrations of Universal Progress*, Article, *Illogical Geology*, 1890, pp. 339-340.

39 Courville, Dr. Cyril B., *The Recapitulation Theory, Some Notes on Its History and Present Status*, BULLETIN OF DELUGE GEOLOGY AND RELATED SCIENCE, Vol. 1, 1941, pp. 21-60.

40 Price, George McCready, *Geology and the Recapitulation Theory, a Study in Circular Reasoning*. BULLETIN OF DELUGE GEOLOGY AND RELATED SCIENCE, Vol. 1, 1941, pp. 61-76.

41 Emmons, Thiel, Stauffer, and Allison, *Geology, Principles and Processes*, 1932 (Second Ed. 1939).

but the developmental changes of modern forms are recorded in the fossils that may be formed in the succeeding time-intervals of that history." "Developmental changes" means evolutionary changes.

Under the heading "Age Relations," page 384, is the following: "Since fossils show the development from the more primitive to the more complex forms of life, it follows that fossil-bearing rock is dated by the character of the life existing during the deposition of the rock that contains it. Thus geologists have come to recognize certain fossil forms as indices or guides to certain formations. Some of these are called horizon markers, because they are found only within certain horizons, or groups, of beds. If, then, the fossils occurring in sedimentary rocks of two widely separated areas are alike, it follows that these sediments were forming at the same time; hence the rocks are of the same age. The sediments that were deposited continuously under similar conditions constitute a formation, and in an undisturbed series of such beds it is evident that the older beds lie at the bottom and the younger at the top. Formations therefore succeed each other in the order of life development. The fossils in one formation differ, therefore, from those in another, and a formation may be traced over wide areas, even through changing types of sediments, by the fossil fauna and flora which it contains."

Most anyone can see the assumption of evolution at the start of this statement, and that therefore certain forms serve as key fossils for each age, as though only certain kinds of life predominated over the whole earth during each age, regardless of the many radically differing environments. Why should life not always have varied as much as at present? Indeed, Clark[42] of the Smithsonian proclaimed almost this very thing—that all leading forms of life originated separately and developed in parallel by evolution, (hence his word "Zoogenesis" in the title of his book) instead of the orthodox view of the one-celled origin for all life. This, though still evolution, would work serious havoc with the present system of index fossils.

The statement that "in an undisturbed series of such beds it is evident that the older beds lie at the bottom and the younger at the top" is full of pitfalls for the unwary student, because of the violence to fact and logic resorted to in efforts to uphold it. Beneath the statement: "The fossils likewise succeed each other in the order of life development" is hidden the fatal chasm of the famous abandoned recapitulation theory. This theory is the basis for the opening statement that "the fossils show the development from the more primitive to the more complex." This theory is often called "the developmental theory," or the "theory of the changes in life," the "biogenetic law," etc. Its obsolete syllogisms still resound in institutions of learning.

For the long periods of geologic time, evolutionists now appeal to the theory of the slow rate at which uranium becomes lead.

But this is only a recent method, the original source of geologic time being the attempted calculation of the time needed at estimated present rates to deposit the vast thicknesses of the sedimentary strata of the earth. Schuchert[43], however, confesses that only estimates for local time can be depended upon—that no world-wide basis for such estimates exists. The rate of erosion, which must also be considered, is a still worse stumbling block. The radio-active method, however, has even more obstacles. Two requirements demanding absolute and continuous stability of mineralogical conditions are laid down by Holmes,[45] but these can be shown to be impossible in nature. Far too many seepages of minerals, transferances, exchanges, replacements, and other metamorphisms have taken place in all mineral ore bodies and deposits to permit of the conditions he specifies, and especially under the theories of the many major recurring periods of disastrophism postulated by evolutionary geology. However, the theory is extremely vulnerable in many other ways. (Besides, Deluge Geology is showing that all of these sedimentary strata and these disastrophes are only the geological work of the Deluge period, including the dating of that event by various geological processes.[46]

The text then goes into details on each geologic age, from the Archeozoic to the Recent, but enough has been given in this BULLETIN and other BULLETINS of this Society, and in the various geological works of Professor Price, to expose the many inconsistencies of these supposed periods.

42 Clark, Austin H., The New Evolution, Zoogenesis, 1932.
43 Schuchert, Charles, Chronology, or the Age of the Earth on the Basis of Sediments and Life, The Age of the Earth, Physics of the Earth IV, National Research Council, No. 80, 1931, p. 36.
44 Holmes, Arthur, The Age of the Earth, Physics of the Earth IV, National Research Council, No. 80, 1931, p. 154.
45 Whitney, Dudley J., The Age of the Earth: Comments on Some Geologic Methods Used in Its Determination, BULLETIN OF DELUGE GEOLOGY AND RELATED SCIENCE, Vol. 1, 1941, pp. 120-132.
46 Allen, Benjamin Franklin, The Geologic Age of the Mississippi River, BULLETIN OF DELUGE GEOLOGY AND RELATED SCIENCE, Vol. 2, 1942, pp. 37-64.

# BULLETIN

OF

# CREATION, THE DELUGE

AND RELATED SCIENCE

| Volume III | May, 1943 | Number 3 |

## THE MEANING OF THE ORIGIN AND ACTIVITIES OF THE HUMAN BODY

---

## I. THE ORIGIN AND DEVELOPMENT OF PRENATAL MAN

### By Hubert O. Swartout, M.S., M.D., Dr.P.H.[*]

In the oldest written story of the way in which all plant and animal life came to be we find the words: "God said, Let Us make man in Our image, after Our likeness." Genesis 1:26. No human being saw how the first man was made, so there has never been a man or woman who could from first-hand knowledge explain how the work was done. But there are scientists to-day who know almost the whole story of how all human bodies except the first pair came to be. They have written and told the story often, but too often in words hard to understand. It is told here in simpler words, except for certain names for which no simpler words have yet been invented.

### THE BEGINNING

In discussing the "Origin and Development of Prenatal Man," the first of the series "The Meaning of the Origin and Activities of the Human Body," the following topics will be considered: (1) the origin of the new individual by fertilization; (2) the formation of the embryonic disk; (3) the sources of the earliest formed organs; (4) the beginnings of the prenatal face; (5) physiological questions of deep scientific and philosophical significance; (6) chance is not the source of orderly processes or of methodical development in nature; (7) the true source of design in prenatal man pointed out.

[*]County Health Officer, Los Angeles County, California; Clinical Professor of Public Health, College of Medical Evangelists, Los Angeles, California.

The BULLETIN is published by, and is the official organ of the "Society for the Study of Creation, the Deluge, and Related Science." The Editorial Board is comprised of Professor George McCready Price and Dr. Dell D. Haughey. It is printed at the Collegiate Press, Arlington, California. For members the BULLETIN is free, and extra copies 20 cents each (each number priced according to size); for non-members it is $2.00 per year and this number is 30 cents. All correspondence should be directed to the Managing Editor, Mr. Ben F. Allen, 219 North Grand Avenue, Los Angeles 12, California.

Your body began as a single *cell*. For many years — perhaps twenty, thirty, or even forty—it lay living but quiet in your mother's body, a *female* cell with a layer of smaller cells wrapped around it. Then, over a period of a few months, it grew to become large enough to be seen by a keen eye without a magnifying glass. While the female cell was growing in this way, the cells around it rapidly increased in number and became a thin-walled sac, about the size of a large pea and filled with fluid. Such a sac is called a *Graafian follicle*. Finally the sac or follicle burst, the female cell inside it was set free, and within a few days, or perhaps hours, it met and united with a male cell which came from the body of your father. This union of male and female cells is called *fertilization*.

Fertilization made a great change in the quiet life of the cell which by and by was to become your body. Rapid changes began at once within its wall, and it soon divided into two cells, each much like the first one. Soon the two cells divided and became four cells, then more and more until there was a mass of cells looking much like a mulberry and called a *morula*.

The cells of the morula were all so much alike that no one could have told any two of them apart. Nor could he have told that morula from another morula that was to become a pig or a sheep, if the two had been taken away from the bodies in which they were growing and had been looked at by his naked eye or through the lens of a microscope. Later, fluid collected in the center of the growing morula, its outer cells arranged themselves into a sac, and its inner cells formed a clump or cluster with one edge attached to the inside of the sac and the other floating free in the fluid in the sac. The cells forming the sac itself are called the *outer cell mass*.

## THE EMBRYONIC DISK

Important changes soon appeared in the cluster of cells inside the sac, the *inner cell mass*. Its free-floating edge became flattened and grew out into a membrane which loosely lined the inside of the sac composed of the outer cell mass. The rest of the cells of the inner cell mass remained rounded for a time, but fluid began to collect among them, gradually pushing them out to form a second sac with fluid in it. Thus there came to be a spot where the flat-celled lining of one sac was attached to the round-celled wall of another sac inside the first. Then a third group of cells began to grow between the two sac walls at this spot of contact, forming three layers of cells. This three-layered spot or area is called the *embryonic disk*. The flat-celled layer of the embryonic disk has been given the name *endoderm*, the middle layer *mesoderm*, and the third layer *ectoderm*. The whole of the structures already described taken together are called the *blastodermic vesicle*. From the embryonic disk alone came all the parts of your body. The rest of the vesicle grew into structures which nourished and protected your body until it was born.

## THE PRIMITIVE ORGANS

The embryonic disk soon lost its rounded shape, became oval, and then elongated. The endodermic side curled its edges forward to make a tube, the early or *primitive intestine*. Meanwhile, the ectodermic layer was wrapping itself around outside the endodermic layer or tube and forming a covering for the body. While this was taking place, a groove appeared down the middle of the back of the ectodermic layer. This groove deepened and then folded its edges together to form a second tube called the *neural tube*, the upper end of which began to grow rapidly larger and form a short chain of hollow bulges, the *primitive brain*, or *encephalon*, near which the mesoderm had already formed the *primitive heart*. Thus the developing body became essentially a pair of parallel tubes, one small and composed entirely of ectoderm, and the other larger, lined with endoderm, and covered with ectoderm.

At this stage we should no longer speak of an embryonic disk, but call the partly developed body an *embryo*. It looked somewhat like the trunk of a body, without limbs but with the head end showing plainly enough so that no one could mistake which end was which. Soon, however, swellings like buds appeared at each side of the trunk, both near the head and near the lower end. These buds grew in thickness, but grew more in length, and their ends began to split into five parts, the promise of arms and hands, legs and feet.

All that has already been described took place within less than five weeks from the time when the original cell was fertilized, and this is only a small part of the story. The further development of organs and body structures, covering a period of nearly thirty-six weeks, must be told in even less detail. To tell the whole story would fill a large book by itself. The most important parts of it will be told by describing more about what came from each of the three layers of the embryonic disk, which, you remember, are the *endoderm*, the *mesoderm*, and the *ectoderm*.

It has already been said that the endoderm, which literally means "inner skin," folded inward and formed a tube, the primitive intestine. Near the upper end of this tube a bud grew from its front side and turned downward, finally becoming the *lining* of the voice box, or *larynx*, of the windpipe, or *trachea*, and of the *lungs*. Farther down, other buds grew out to form the active parts of the *liver* and *pancreas*. The upper quarter of the tube remained narrow and became the lining of that part of the throat called the *pharynx*, and of the *esophagus*, or gullet. A short part of the tube broadened out to form the lining of the *stomach*. The lower half or a bit more of the tube grew rapidly in length and folded upon itself again and again, forming the lining of the *intestines*.

The main part of the ectoderm, "outer skin," became the outer layer of the skin, the *epidermis*. You have already been told that it formed the *neural* tube and the *encephalon*. These became the *spinal cord* and the *brain*, and from them grew out the *nerve fibers*.

The mesoderm, "middle skin," not only formed many entire parts of the body by itself, but also helped to form or to protect nearly every structure of which either endoderm or ectoderm formed a part. It became *bones, cartilages, tendons, muscles, heart, blood vessels, blood,* and many different kinds and shapes of fibrous membranes. It formed the deeper layers of the skin. It formed the muscle layers, where there were any, also the framework and covering of all the organs mentioned above as being lined with endoderm. It formed itself into the jointed, bony canal and tough membranes which grew around the spinal cord, the *spinal column,* also into a strong, rigid, bony, membrane-lined box for the brain, the skull, or *cranium*. It grew into a network between and around the nerve fibers, binding them into bundles and protecting them from injury.

On their part, the nerve fibers grew out farther and farther from the brain and spinal cord until they had reached every other part of the body except the surface layer of the skin and of the membranes that had been formed from the endoderm.

There will be no further mention of other developments except two special cases, which are of more interest than the others.

The kidney is one special case. It came from two sources. About the beginning of the fifth week after the fertilization of the original female cell, or about the time when the developing body began to be called an *embryo*, two buds, one for each kidney, appeared at the back part of the lower end of a mesodermic tube which had earlier joined itself to the lower end of the primitive intestine. Each bud was hollow and grew backward and upward, branching more and more as it grew, until a bundle of thousands of tiny straight tubules was formed. Meanwhile, up in the mesoderm of the middle part of the trunk, a mass of cells had been developing in a special way. Many small coiled tubules had formed within this cell mass. When the bundle of straight tubules grew near the middle of the trunk, the mass of coiled tubules formed itself into a cap to cover the end of the tubule bundle; and the end of each straight tubule joined itself to a coiled tubule. During this time the lower end of the original tube had been moving around the side and toward the front of the primitive intestine, finally attaching itself to a part of this structure which split off to form the *bladder*.

## THE PRENATAL FACE

The other special case is the face. It is hard to understand the development of this part of the body from a

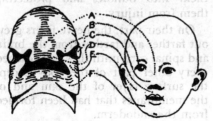

word description. One part of the diagram in the left column shows what your face looked like at the beginning of the fifth week of embryonic life, and the other part shows how the various structures had re-arranged themselves by the time you were born. The names of the various parts are rather unfamiliar words, but no one has yet thought of simpler ones. They have been marked' by letters. If you will refer to the diagram from time to time as you read what follows, it will be easier to understand. If the *frontonasal process* (A) and the *lateral nasal processes* (C) had not grown into the right positions and attached themselves to each other and to the other structures in a normal way, you would have had an unsightly nose, would perhaps not have been able to breathe or swallow properly, and would have suffered lifelong embarrassment and distress. If the *maxillary process* (E) had not grown inward far enough, or had not joined as it should with the *globular process* (D), a cleft palate or a harelip, or both, would have resulted. If the *maxillary process* (E) and the *mandibular arch* (F) had failed to grow together, your mouth would have extended back almost to your ears. If they had grown together too far, you might have had no mouth at all.

## PHYSIOLOGICAL QUESTIONS OF DEEP SIGNIFICANCE

The above sketchy account of your body's beginning has given you but a few samples of the countless interesting truths about the way your body came to be, but it has surely been long enough to raise many questions in your mind if you care much about the "why" of things. And who does not?

Why, for instance, should fertilization cause that original cell to show more activity every minute from that instant onward than it had shown in almost any whole year before? Why should the cells of the morula, at first all alike, begin to become different? Why should a human morula, looking like a morula from a pig or a sheep, develop into a human body instead of the body of a pig or a sheep? Who would think that such a complex structure as the blastodermic vesicle could come from a simple morula in a few days' time? Why should the embryonic disk have three layers of cells, and only three? Why should the disk, at first round, become long as it grows? Why should it curl itself into a tube with the endoderm always inside and the ectoderm always outside? Why should a neural tube develop at all? How is it that the endoderm lines organs, but never forms coverings for them? Why does the ectoderm cover the body, but never line organs?

In the development of your kidneys, the failure of the original tube to migrate properly around the lower end of the primitive intestine would have left the kidneys with an outlet into the intestine instead of to the outside of the body. Why didn't this happen to you, and why do you almost never hear of such a condition?

Consider your face. Since there were so many chances in its development for something to go wrong, how did you ever come to have a face like that of a human being? You may not always be satisfied with it, but are you not glad that it is no worse than it is?

CHANCE NOT THE SOURCE OF SYSTEM

Why did all the development and activity that has been related above, and very much more, go forward in such an orderly way and at such an orderly rate that within only forty weeks after the fertilization of the original female cell you had a normal body ready to be born, the progress being so rapid that your body weighed more than a hundred million times as much at birth as did the original cell from which it grew? If things came by *chance,* the odds would have been billions to one against such an outcome. Instead of being surprised when you see a deformed person, you have much more reason to be surprised when you see one who is not.

Such questions and thoughts bring you face to face with a great mystery—the mystery of the origin of life itself —a mystery the depths of which no man has ever fully understood.

THE TRUE SOURCE OF DESIGN

Since prophets and other Bible writers did not write simply out of what was in their own minds, and especially since the instruments of modern science were unknown in ancient times, David probably understood but a small part of the full meaning of the words which he was inspired to say: "I will praise Thee; for I am fearfully and wonderfully made: marvelous are Thy works; and that my soul knoweth right well. My substance was not hid from Thee, when I was made in secret, and curiously wrought in the lowest parts of the earth. Thine eyes did see my substance, yet being unperfect; and in Thy book all my members were written, which in continuance were fashioned, when as yet there was none of them." Psalm 139:14-16. As you study these words carefully, you can understand them better than David did, even though you know no more embryology than you have learned from this article. Can you, then, be less ready to believe in an all-wise and loving Creator than he was?

# THE SOURCE OF CONTROL IN EMBRYONIC DEVELOPMENT*

## By THE DUKE OF ARGYLL

To know the work which a machine does is a fuller and higher knowledge than to know the nature of the materials of which its parts are composed, or even to perceive and follow the kind of movement by which its effects are produced. And if there be two machines which, in respect to structure and movement and material, are the same or closely similar, but which, nevertheless, produce totally different kinds of work, we may be sure that this difference is the most real and the most important truth respecting them. The new aspects in which we see their likeness are less full and less adequate than the old familiar aspects in which we regard them as dissimilar.

But the mind is apt to be enamored of a new conception of this kind, and to mistake its place and its relative importance in the sphere of knowledge. It is in this way, and in this way only, that we can account for the tendency among some scientific men to exaggerate beyond all bounds the significance of the abstract and artificial definitions which they reach by neglecting differences of work, of function, and of result, and by fixing their attention mainly on some newly discovered likeness in respect to form, or motion, or chemical composition. It is thus that because a particular substance called "protoplasm" is found to be present in all living organisms, an endeavor follows to get rid of life as a separate conception, and to reduce it to the physical property of this material. The fallacy involved in this endeavor needs no other exposure than the fact that, as the appearance and the composition of this material is the same whether it be dead or living, the protoplasm of which such transcendent properties are affirmed has always to be described as "living" protoplasm. But no light can be thrown upon the facts by telling us that life is a property of that which lives. The expression for this substance which has been invented by Professor Huxley is a better one—the "physical basis of life." It is better because it does not suggest the idea that life is a mere physical property of the substance. But it is, after all, a metaphor which does not give an adequate idea of the conceptions suggested by the facts. The word "basis" has a distinct reference to a mechanical support, or to the principal substance in a chemical combination. But at the best there is only a distant and metaphorical analogy between these conceptions and the conceptions which are suggested by the connection between protoplasm and life. We cannot suppose life to be a substance supported by another. Neither can we suppose it to be like a chemical element in combination with another. It seems rather like a force of energy which first works up the inorganic materials into the form of protoplasm, and then continues to exert itself through that combination when achieved.

We call this kind of energy by a special name, life, for the best of all reasons, that it has special effects different from all others. It often happens that the philosophy expressed in some common form of speech is deep and true, whilst the objections which are made to it in the name of science are shallow and fallacious. This is the case with all those familiar phrases and expressions which imply that life and its phenomena are so distinguishable from other things that they must be spoken of by themselves. . . . Every phenomenon or group of phenomena which is clearly separate from all others, shoud have a name as separate and distinctive as itself. The absurdity of speaking of a "watch force" lies in this—that the force by which a watch goes is not separable from the force by which many other mechanical movements are effected. It is a force which is otherwise well known, and can be fully expressed in other and more definite terms. That force is simply the elasticity of a coiled spring. But the phenomena of life are not due to any force which can be fully and definitely expressed in other terms. It is not purely chemical, nor purely mechanical, nor purely electrical, nor reducible to any other more simple and elementary conception. The popular use, therefore, which keeps up separate words and phrases by which to describe and designate the distinctive phenomena of life, is a use which is correct and thoroughly expressive of the truth. There is nothing more common and nothing more fallacious in philosophy than the endeavor, by mere tricks of language, to suppress and keep out of sight the distinctions which Nature proclaims with a loud voice.

It is thus, also, that because certain creatures which, when adult, are widely separate

---

* Argyll, Duke of, *The Unity of Nature*, 1883, pp. 20-26. Though the Duke of Argyll spoke so clearly on the source of control in embryology sixty years ago, his statement still stands, and is now of much historic interest. All subsequent research has only confirmed his conclusions arrived at so long ago.—EDITORS.

in the scale of being, may be traced back to some embryonic stage, in which they are undistinguishable. it has become fashionable to sink the vast differences which must lie behind this uniformity of aspect and of material composition under some vague form of words in which the mind makes, as it were, a covenant with itself not to think of such differences as are latent and invisible, however important we know them to be by the differences of result to which they lead. Thus it is common now to speak of things widely separated in rank and function as being "the same," only "differentiated," or "variously conditioned." In these, and in all similar cases, the differences which are unseen, or which, if seen, are set aside, are often of infinitely greater importance than the similarities which are selected as the characteristics chiefly worthy of regard. If, for example, in the albumen of an egg there is no discernible differences either of structure or of chemical composition, but if, nevertheless, by the mere application of a little heat, part of it is "differentiated" into blood, another part of it into flesh, another part of it into bones, another part of it into feathers, and the whole into one perfect organic structure, it is clear that any purely chemical definition of this albumen, or any purely mechanical definition of it, would not merely fail of being complete, but would absolutely pass by and pass over the one essential characteristic of vitality which makes it what it is, and determines what it is to be in the system of nature.

Let us always remember that the more perfect may be the apparent identity between two things which afterwards become widely different, the greater must be the power and value of those invisible distinctions—of those unseen factors—which determine the subsequent divergence. These distinctions are invisible, not merely because our methods of analysis are too coarse to detect them, but because apparently they are of a nature which no physical dissection and no chemical analysis could possibly reveal. Some scientific men are fond of speaking and thinking of these invisible factors as distinctions due to differences in "molecular arrangements," as if the more secret agencies of nature gave us the idea of depending on nothing else than mechanical arrangement—on differences in the shape or in the position of the molecules of matter. But this is by no means true. No doubt there are such differences—as far beyond the reach of the microscope as the differences which the microscope does reveal are beyond the reach of our unaided vision. But we know enough of the different agencies which must lie hid in things apparently the same, to be sure that the divergences of work which these agencies produce do not depend upon or consist in mere differences of mechanical arrangement. We know enough of those agencies to be sure that they are agencies, which do, indeed, determine both arrangement and composition, but do not themselves consist in either.

This is the conclusion to which we are brought by facts which are well known. There are some simple structures in nature which can be seen in the process of construction. There are conditions of matter in which its particles can be seen rushing under the impulse of invisible forces to take their appointed places in the form which to them is a law. Such are the facts visible in the processes of crystallization. In them we can see the particles of matter passing from one "molecular condition" to another; and it is impossible that this passage can be ascribed either to the old arrangement which is broken up, or to the new arrangement which is substituted in its stead. Both structures have been built up out of elementary materials by some constructive agency which is the master and not the servant—the cause and not the consequence of the movements which are effected, and of the arrangement which is their result. And if this be true of crystalline forms in the mineral kingdom, much more is it true of organic forms in the animal kingdom. Crystals are, as it were, the beginning of nature's architecture, her lowest and simplest forms of building. But the most complex crystalline forms which exist—and many of them are singularly complex and beautiful—are simplicity itself compared with the very lowest organism which is endowed with life. In the wonderful processes by which bone is formed, the foundations or the moulds of the structure are first laid down in cartilage or gristle. This is a compound substance purely organic, whereas bone is a substance in which the mineral element, calcium or lime, is imported into the structure for the purpose of giving it solidity. The movements and changes under which this importation of what may be called comparatively foreign material is effected, have been watched and described. They are changes and movements in the cartilage—that is to say, in the form and arrangement of the mould, which are suggestive of almost conscious anticipation. The mould can be seen in the process of being moulded. "The cells of the cartilage, with their cell-spaces, become larger—flatten out—and usually show a tendency to arrange themselves in parallel rows; between which, if the change has already been in progress for some time, the lines of calcification may be seen advancing."[1]

This is only one example out of thousands in which similar processes have been observed. In all living organisms, therefore, still more than in the formation of crystals, the work of "differentiation"—that is to say, the work of forming out of one material different structures for the discharge of different functions—is the work of agencies which are invisible and unknown; and it is in these agencies, not in the molecular arrangements which they cause, that the essential character and individuality of every organism consists. . . . In that mystery of all mysteries, of which biologists talk so glibly, the living "nucleated cell," the great work of creation may be seen in actual operation, not caused by "molecular condition," but determining it, and, from elements which to all our senses, and to all our means of investigation, appear absolutely the same, building up the molecules of protoplasm, now into a seaweed, now into a cedar of Lebanon, now into an insect, now into a fish, now into a reptile, now into a bird, now into a man. And in proportion as the molecules of matter do not even seem to be the masters but the servants here, so do the forces which dispose of them stand out separate and supreme. In every germ this development can only be "after its kind." The molecules must obey; but no mere wayward or capricious order can be given to them. The formative energies seem to be as much under command as the materials upon which they work. . . . This involves a vast cycle of operations, as to the unity of which we cannot be mistaken—for it is a cycle of operations obviously depending on adjustments among all the forces both of solar and terrestrial physics—and every part of this vast series of adjustments must be in continuous and unbroken correlation with the rest.

Thus every step in the progress of science which tends to reduce all organisms to one and the same set of elementary substances, or to one and the same initial structure, only adds to the certainty with which we conclude that it is upon something else than composition, and upon something else than structure, that those vast differences ultimately depend which separate so widely between living things in rank, in function, and in power. And although we cannot tell what that something is—although science does not as yet even tend to explain what the directive agencies are or how they work—one thing, at least, is plain: that if a very few elementary substances can enter into an untold variety of combinations, and by virtue of this variety can be made to play a vast variety of parts, this result can only be attained by a system of mutual adjustments as immense as the variety it produces, as minute as the differences on which it depends, and as centralized in direction as the order and harmony of its results. And so we come to understand that the unity which we see in nature is that kind of unity which the mind recognizes as the result of operations similar to its own—not a unity which consists in mere sameness of material, or in mere identity of composition, or in mere uniformity of structure, but a unity which consists in the subordination of all these to similar aims and to similar principles of action—that is to say, in like methods of yoking a few elementary forces to the discharge of special functions, and to the production, by adjustment, of one harmonious whole.

---

[1] On the Ossification of the Terminal Phalanges of the Digits, by F. A. Dixey, B.A., Oxon. Preceed. Ro. Soc., Vol. XXXI. No. 207.

# BULLETIN

OF

# CREATION, THE DELUGE

## AND RELATED SCIENCE

Volume III    September, 1943    Number 4

## CONTENTS

## DOES RECENT BIOLOGICAL RESEARCH DISPROVE CREATION?

### By William J. Tinkle, Ph.D.*

During the last century, few words have made a greater impact upon Christian faith than the word evolution. Like many another English word, however, it is used with several different meanings. Many a person at present is quite at sea as to which mean ings he should accept, or even considers denying any validity in the idea. A certain interpretation of evolution has become a dogma and is very widely taught as a scientific law in colleges, high schools, and even in grade schools; while scientists in the universities discuss recent discoveries and frankly state their doubts.

The following discussion will be presented: 1. Darwin's definition of evolution of animal life. 2. Darwin's conceptions now turned aside. 3. Genetics points to the Creator. (1) Mutations, generally degenerative, the opposite of evolution. (2) Likewise the non-living universe is degenerative. 4. Darwin's evolutionary claims for animals improved by man now discredited. (1) Because this only proves that unaided nature is degenerative, and (2) Because its upper limits are soon reached, and thus now cut off Darwin's speculations. 5. Anthropology now disproves man's evolution.

* Professor of Biology, Taylor University, Upland, Indiana. Author of *Fundamentals of Zoology*, a textbook for colleges (Zondervan, Grand Rapids, Mich., 1939) and *Look Again Before You Doubt*, a pamphlet, and other works.

The BULLETIN is published by, and is the official organ of the "Society for the Study of Creation, the Deluge, and Related Science." The Editorial Board is comprised of Professor George McCready Price and Dr. Dell D. Haughey. It is printed at the Collegiate Press, Arlington, California. For members the BULLETIN is free, and extra copies 20 cents each (each number priced according to size); for non-members it is $2.00 per year and this number is 30 cents. All correspondence should be directed to the Managing Editor, Mr. Ben F. Allen, 219 North Grand Avenue, Los Angeles 12, California.

(1) Changes either horizontal or degenerative. (2) *Laissez faire* not evolution. 6. Conclusion: Biology now raises no barrier to a literal view of Genesis, though those who claim evolution as their cosmic religion may not yield.

## DARWIN'S DEFINITION

Charles Darwin's idea of evolution was that all of the species of plants and animals in the world, including man, have descended by slow changes from one or a few simple forms. His theory did not explain the origin of those original ancestral forms. Some modern writers state that evolution is the doctrine that present plants and animals arose from earlier forms by a long process of descent with change. This might mean the same as Darwin's definition or it might not. It is much less exacting. Others state that any fluctuation or change in animals or plants represents evolution. The definition by Darwin is the only one of the three that is definite enough to attempt to prove or to disprove, and is the version that has been fought most vigorously by theologians.

## HIS CONCEPTIONS NOW TURNED ASIDE

A few years ago we often heard the statement that evolution (Darwin's definition) must be true because all of the biological scientists accepted it. The statement is not heard so often now, and never is made by one who knows the facts. Darwin's theory as to how evolution came about has been very widely discredited. At the same time it has been the custom to say that while we do not know how such a process could come about, it is a fact. Thus the tottering frame has been propped up. But since Darwin was the first man to convince any large body of people of the truth of evolution, to discredit him is to leave quite a vacant gap.

## GENETICS POINTS TO THE CREATOR

Among the biological sciences none has made more rapid or valid progress than genetics. Founded upon the careful observations and tests of hundreds of investigators, it lists and describes the characters that are involved in any change. This scrutiny has revealed but one type of phenomenon that brings about a lasting change in a species. This is a mutation. A young animal out of a thousand or a million will have an organ that is different from all of the others. Examples are white eyes, short wings, hairlessness, short legs, crooked legs. In the offspring of this animal, this mutation is inherited like any other character.

So far, the reader might say that the mutation idea supports evolution. But mutations are never in the upward direction. This statement is not dogmatic, but is based upon wide research by a number of geneticists. Only two mutants have ever been claimed to be superior, viz., a change in the shape of a cotton leaf, and a change in the venation of a fruit fly's wing. But they have not been confirmed by other investigators, and can not be proven to confer an advantage. They do not make the animal better fitted to survive independently of man, but usually make it weaker. The animal may be better from man's standpoint, like the Ancon ram, born with crooked front legs, so that it cannot jump fences. Seedless oranges and stringless beans are other examples. But mutations never make plants or animals stronger, more complex, or more symmetrical. Then how can they be the material of a transmutation of a one-celled animal to man?

Some of us are wondering why the supposed evolution of the animal and plant kingdoms should be considered the exception to the rule of degeneration in nature. In astronomy and geology we study a universe that is slowly running down. The rate of the earth in its orbit around the sun is slowing enough to measure; the sun is becoming either cooler or smaller; the deposits of coal and petroleum are being used faster than they are being replenished. For a long time it has been apparent that some species of animal have degenerated; now we cannot find that any of them change in the upward direction.

### DARWIN'S CLAIMS NOT VALID NOW

Darwin had much to say about the improvement of animals by man. Since his time it has been proved that there is a definite upper limit to this improvement. If the owner uses only the best animals for breeding, this selection is effective at first, but when a "pure line" is reached, further selection does not result in improvement. When I first learned this fact, proved by Johannsen of Denmark, it struck me with sledge-hammer force.

A common kind of improvement of animals by man is crossing to combine desired characters already present but in different breeds. This combination is not true evolution, since nothing new is developed. But it is true that MANY new characters, better ones, would have to be added to change a bit of protoplasm to man.

### ANTHROPOLOGY DISCREDITS UNBELIEF

The bones of early man do not help us greatly, for many of them are single specimens or even fragments. In our homes for the feebleminded are types which may cause the anthropologists of the future to puzzle their brows. Only two types of ancient man are represented by an ample number of skeletons. Of these the Neanderthal men were peculiar but had normal cranial capacity. Cromagnon men were superior to modern man in cra-

nial capacity and stature, and made paintings and carvings which we behold with highest admiration.

Scholars have been debating as to whether man arose by special creation or by evolution. Since it seems to be proved that the observed changes are always horizontal or downward in nature, evolution cannot be regarded an alternative to creation. The theory, which has been cited by atheists as one of the strongest proofs of their position, no longer is a stumbling block. Nor can it be used to justify the doctrine of *laissez faire*, with the expectation that superior varieties will arise by natural selection. The average may be shifted by the loss of the individuals least fit to survive, but the ones that remain are not changed; experimenting has taught us that the next generation will not be different from the present one. This experimentation has employed millions of plants and animals.

### BIOLOGY NOW NO BARRIER TO GENESIS

The subject is not exhausted, but if the reader desires more he should consult recent books on the subject. We may summarize by saying that if the thoughtful man believes the Bible to be the word of God, science can present no facts to rob him of his faith. The Bible does not devote many pages to science, but its statements never have been successfully denied. It is gratifying to note that the progress made in biology in the last twenty years, rightly interpreted, leads men to a greater faith in God's word.

However, the scientists who say that evolution is their religion, and those who say that they believe in evolution in order that they may not have to believe in anything supernatural, doubtless will hold on to the theory to the bitter end.

# THE RELATION OF GEOLOGY TO THE CHRISTIAN REVELATION

## By GEORGE McCREADY PRICE

Many believers as well as non-believers in Genesis seem to have very confused ideas about the relationship between the findings of natural science and the Bible. The tumult and the shouting of Darwinism, as heard during the latter part of the nineteenth century, has somewhat died away; yet the claims of evolutionists are still made with much insistence. And it is well for every one to have clear ideas regarding these claims and their relationship to the Christian religion.

### THE CLAIMS OF DISCREDITED PALEONTOLOGY AND GEOLOGY

The theory of evolution professes to give a history of how man and the other forms of life have developed through many hundreds of millions of years to their present condition. Since it professes to tell the history of the organic part of the world, it must of necessity have some reliable documents on which to base this history. It professes to find this history in the rocks. In fact, the current teachings of geology have always been relied upon by all clear thinkers as the main outline of any possible scheme of organic evolution. Botany and zoology may furnish evidence that organisms have changed considerably within historic times. But only by going far back into the history of living things can any large or important changes be discovered. Geology is the only science which can furnish us any clue to the history of animals and plants in the long ago; and by most persons the facts of geology are thought to confirm very decidedly the claims of the evolutionists that animals and plants have existed on the earth for very many mil-

lions of years, and that there has been a progress or advancement from the little to the big and from the simple to the complex during all this immense period. And this alleged history of animals and plants is always the outline to which evolutionists appeal as the strongest confirmation of their theory.

Within recent years, however, this general view of the theory of geology has been challenged in two ways:

(a) It is claimed that, even if we accept the geological succession of life as usually given, this allegedly historical order of the fossils does not by any means correspond to what the theory of evolution would lead us to expect.

(b) It is further claimed that the ordinary arrangement of the fossils in the familiar sequence from the Cambrian, Ordovician, Silurian, etc., up to the Tertiary and the Pleistocene, is a purely artificial arrangement; that there are many facts which show that this is not a real historical sequence; and that the general facts of geology can be far better understood as having been due to a great world-catastrophe, like the Deluge of the Bible, than in the other way as a series of deposits made a little at a time throughout untold millions of years.

It will be in order for us to study in a very brief way some of these facts gathered from the rocks which thus tend to throw serious doubts upon the commonly accepted views. The detailed proofs of many of the statements here to be given will be found in the present writer's various books on these subjects.

*The Geological Arrangement of the Fossils Does Not Correspond to What the Theory of Evolution Would Lead Us to Expect.*

Darwin himself recognized that the fossils, as arranged by geologists, do not present anything like a smooth, graded advance from one of the "ages" to the next, as we should expect. And he admitted that this fact was a very serious objection to his theory. However, he and his immediate followers cheerfully appealed to future discoveries in the rocks, and adopted a waiting attitude. They said that the geological record is so very, very imperfect (forgetful of the fact that, in affirming that only certain kinds of life lived in the Cambrian age, in the Carboniferous age, etc., they were in effect assuming that they had an essentially complete record of *all* the kinds living in these respective ages). And they confidently expected that every new fossil would help to confirm their theory.

But these fond hopes have not been realized. Millions of fossils have been discovered in all parts of the globe since Darwin's day; but it must be confessed that they tend to create more problems for the evolutionists than they solve, even accepting at par the time-values of these fossils.

(1) Contrary to expectation, the so-called lowest or oldest beds (the Algonkian and Cambrian) are not by any means limited to a few of the very lowest type, the invertebrates. Every single one of the great groups of animals (phyla) is represented, except the vertebrates; and the invertebrates are represented, not by small, stunted kinds, but by splendid specimens of their kind, several of which are identical with kinds which have survived unchanged to our own day.

(2) When new classes and orders do appear in the "later" formations, they do not appear as single species (as the theory calls for), but in a profusion of kinds, often showing a most astonishing break with all the preceding classes and orders. Within small groups, as for example, within the great families or sub-orders, such as the horses, the elephants, the camels, the ammonites, the trilobites, etc., it has been possible by cleverly manipulating the fossils to arrange them in an alleged historical order which seems to be a very convincing evolutionary order, if one does not know it to be a purely artificial arrangement of the evidence.

(3) But not a single fossil has been discovered which has helped to bridge the chasm between the great phyla, or even between the classes or orders. Instead of the ten or twelve phyla, as used to be the method of classifying the animals, Austin H. Clark,[1] of the National Museum in Washington, makes them twenty. Clark not only stresses the abrupt differences between the phyla, but in only somewhat lesser degree the similar gaps between the classes and orders. For instance, he says, "the whales and the seals are always whales and seals, and show little or no approach to any other type of mammal." (The New Evolution, p. 167.) "There are no intermediates between turtles and snakes, or turtles and lizards, or snakes and lizards, all of which are reptiles." (p. 182.) And he declares: "From the very first beginnings of the fossil record, the broader aspects of the animal life upon the earth have remained unchanged" (p. 100).

(4) No fossil has been discovered which can be shown to be the direct ancestor of any class, sub-class, or order of animals. According to the evolution theory, there must have been uncounted millions of intergrades between these great natural groups of animals. But no such intergrades are found among the fossils. Why should we be asked to suppose that all these intermediate types have been hidden

from us off in some part of the world not yet explored? The very significant fact is that the more countries which are explored and the more fossils found, the sharper and more distinct become the breaks between all the great groups of life.

Thus far we have been taking the fossils in their accepted order, at the full time-values which are customarily assigned to them. It will be in order now to consider the second major line of objections to the validity of the fossils as evidence for organic evolution.

*It Is Now Known That the Familiar Sequence of the Fossils from the Cambrian, Ordovician, Silurian, etc., Up to the Tertiary and the Pleistocene Is a Purely Artificial Arrangement, Without any Adequate Evidence That They Represent Successive Ages Rather Than One Age.*

What is meant is that there is no scientific evidence that what are called "Cambrian" fossils really lived in an age of the world before such other types as the Carboniferous, the Cretaceous, or the Tertiary. The pioneer geologists of a hundred years ago *assumed* this to be the case, but never attempted to prove the point. The evidence now strongly shows that these groups of fossils do not really mean any true historical sequence; they have been made to resemble a historical order by means of a purely artificial arrangement, by selecting special sets of fossils from here and there all over the globe. Hence it is quite permissible for us to suppose that all these various types of life now found as fossils may have all been living contemporaneously in the same "age" of the world, all of them having (on this supposition) been overtaken by some sudden world-catastrophe, such as the Deluge spoken of in the Bible.

(1) There is no place on earth where a half or even a quarter of the dozen-odd series or sets of rocks are ever found together one above another. The total thickness of the fossiliferous series is alleged by evolutionists to be about 100 miles, or some 500,000 feet. But I don't know of any place where we actually find much more than about ten or fifteen thousand feet of strata, and in most places there is not half this thickness of stratified beds. The great thickness given above is made in a purely artificial way by adding together "type" sections from here and there all over the globe.

(2) There are no bottom (or oldest) fossils for the world as a whole. Every type of fossil, that is, representing any of the "ages," may occur at the bottom of the series or next to the granite. Similarly, such so-called old rocks as Cambrian and Ordovician occur around the Baltic in Europe perfectly unconsolidated, consisting of sands and clays as young looking as anything deposited last year; but because they contain typical trilobites and brachiopods they have to be called Cambrian or Ordovician, and are reputed to be a thousand million years old.

But if there are no real bottom fossils for the world as a whole, how are we going to fix on any particular set of animals which we can confidently say are older than others?

(3) In many localities we find physical evidence at the contact-line between the two successive beds that the traditional "ages" were never represented, but that these beds followed one another in quick succession, whereas the theory says that they were deposited millions of years apart. A case of this sort is called a "deceptive conformity." Let me explain.

---

1 Clark, Austin H., *Zoogenesis, The New Evolution,* 1930, p. 167.

It is a common thing to find that the upper surface of a bed must have been soft and undisturbed when the next layer was deposited upon it. There was evidently just enough of an interval to make two beds instead of one; but the physical evidence shows that the upper bed followed the lower in comparatively rapid succession. If the fossils in such a case happen to agree with the evolution theory, such an instance is called a true "conformity," and the two beds are said to be "conformable." But in case the fossils are such as ought to be widely apart in the geological series, if for instance a Carboniferous occurs thus conformably upon a Silurian, with the Devonian missing, it is called a "deceptive conformity."

Thousands of such instances occur. Often two or three or more of the "ages" are thus missing; and yet the upper bed not only fits perfectly upon the lower one, but may even *be made of exactly the same kinds of clay or sand or limestone,* the two differing solely in the kinds of fossils they contain. Is it reasonable to suppose that in such cases ten or twenty or thirty millions of years elapsed between these exactly similar sandstone layers or limestone layers as the case may be, with absolutely nothing having occurred in the way of erosion or deposition throughout hundreds of thousands of square miles of area?

Common sense tells us that in such cases these long "ages" alleged to have intervened without any physical record of any kind never really took place in these localities. But if not in this locality, they did not take place at all.

(4) In very many instances, and often covering wide areas, the "ages" occur in reverse order. Though the physical condition of the rocks may be perfectly normal, though the upper set of beds may appear to be in perfectly natural conformity upon the lower ones, yet because the accustomed sequence of the typical fossils is reversed, geologists have invented the name "thrust fault" to apply to such cases. And they say that the upper beds were once deep down below, perhaps two or three miles, but were lifted and pushed bodily forward over the others into their present position.

Such is the power of a theory to lead its advocates to deny every physical evidence and invent incredible contortions of the earth to explain away obvious facts.

In a large district which comprises all the Rocky Mountain region in Alberta and Montana, Cambrian and other Palaeozoic rocks occur in apparently normal sequence on top of Cretaceous. In other words, dinosaurs and ammonites and modern-looking plant remains are down underneath, while on top are trilobites and other "ancient" fossils. The district thus involved is some 500 miles long and from thirty to fifty miles wide, comprising all the front range of the Rockies and several other parallel ranges.

Obviously, if we are to accept the physical facts as we find them, we must say that in this region the remains of dinosaurs and other Cretaceous forms were laid down first, and the trilobites and other "ancient" kinds were deposited afterwards.

In the Salt Range of India remains of mammals are found underneath and trilobites on top. As all such fossils frequently occur the other way around, it is quite evident that we must suppose that all these kinds of life were in the long ago living contemporaneously in the same "age" of the world's history. Similar instances of the fossils in an order directly contradicting the evolutionary order are found occurring in all parts of the world that have been carefully explored geologically.

## A World Catastrophe Proposed

The lesson from these facts is not ambiguous or difficult. Clearly, the hypothesis of a world with a wonderful climate and with a marvelous flora and fauna which was overtaken by a sudden change, so that the ocean in repeated inundations overflowed the lands and buried land and marine forms in deep sets of alternate beds, is the best explanation of the facts as we find them.

The catastrophic nature of these changes is attested by the fossils themselves. Such animals as fishes and other marine organisms were obviously buried alive or before decomposition took place; for the soft parts are shown in full outline. Tell-tale facts associated with the shellfish tell the same story. A similar record is to be read from the vast numbers of fossil elephants which occur away within the Arctic regions, often in such splendid condition that the dogs and wolves and bears greedily eat the meat which has been kept in cold storage all these thousands of years. The dinosaurs tell a similar story. Their remains occur on all the continents; and one scientist speaks of the "dramatic extinction of this mighty race," while another tells us that the cutting off of this race of animals was nearly if not quite "simultaneous the world over."

I can well believe this last statement. But what ordinary cause could have killed all these monsters off around the entire globe? Reptiles are notoriously tough and hard to kill, being not subject to ordinary diseases or parasites. What was it that killed them all off?

From all the facts given above it is evident that the theory of many long successive ages, some kinds of life living in one age and others only long

afterwards, will not fit the facts. While the hypothesis—to which we hold—of all the fossils having existed contemporaneously in an older state of our world and having been destroyed together in one big world-catastrophe, fits the facts completely.

## A Poor Apology for Evolution

But if these geological "ages" are all a mistake, there is no scientific reason for assuming a long pre-Adamite age and world-desolation before the creation described in the first chapter of Genesis. Whatever may be imagined as having taken place during or before the second verse of Genesis 1, there is not the slightest hint in all the Bible that a single animal or plant ever existed on this earth before the creation described in some detail in the rest of this chapter. In the opinion of the present writer, this theory of a pre-Adamite age or ages is wholly unnecessary and misleading. The moral difficulties involved in thus supposing that suffering and death at least among the animals took place for long ages before man's sin, ought alone to rule this pre-Adamite theory out of court. Now, when the scientific evidence is all proving the unity of the fossil world and the oneness of the age in which they lived, it is very clear that the Deluge of Noah must have been a vastly bigger and more important event than most people have supposed.

As for the evolution theory, who that believes in a real world-catastrophe as described in the Bible can have any place for such a theory? The real record of the Bible, when consistently applied and at its full face value in all respects, makes the evolution theory simply ridiculous.

Verily the Bible is an anvil that has worn out many a hammer.

# BULLETIN

OF

# CREATION, THE DELUGE

## AND RELATED SCIENCE

Volume III                     DECEMBER, 1943                     Number 5

## CONTENTS

---

## THE CAUSAL SIGNIFICANCE OF EMBRYONIC DEVELOPMENT*

### *By* CYRIL B. COURVILLE, M.D.

No other phenomenon of biology is so remarkable as the development of a new being in the animal or plant world. In all nature a provision has been made for the perpetuation of the various forms of life, "each after his kind." The process designed for the continuance of this chain of life is called *reproduction*. In the one-celled plants and animals this result is achieved in an economic and efficient way by simple division, the parent cell dividing its life potencies and protoplasm between two daughter cells. In the more complex animal and plant forms, so simple a process is not applicable. While various methods are found for the reproduction of plant species, in the animal world it is usually accomplished by the union of two sex cells or gametes, one from the male, the other from the female. This infinitely more complex process is called sexual reproduction.

From the single fertilized cell, the result of fusion of the two sex cells, the new individual is produced. This cell promptly divides into two, then four, then eight, and so on, until the adult individual is formed of millions of separate cellular elements forming a wide variety of tissues, structures, and organs, each with diversified, highly specialized function. This process of forming a new individual from a single cell comes as close to a "new creation" (DeBeer) as man is privileged to witness.

The question which a study of this bit of fascinating biologic history

* Presented at the Symposium of Bible Science, Los Angeles, California, November 26, 27, 28, 1943.

The BULLETIN is published by, and is the official organ of the "Society for the Study of Creation, the Deluge, and Related Science." The Editorial Board is comprised of Professor George McCready Price and Dr. Dell D. Haughey. It is printed at the Collegiate Press, Arlington, California. For members the BULLETIN is free, and extra copies 30 cents each (each number priced according to size); for non-members it is $2.00 per year and this number is 40 cents. All correspondence should be directed to the Managing Editor, Mr. Ben F. Allen, 219 North Grand Avenue, Los Angeles, 12, California.

tends to provoke in one of reflective temperament is, "What do these things mean?" For an answer to this fundamental question, man has explored the realms of living matter from the times of Aristotle to the present. It is the purpose of this brief essay to review a bit of comparatively recent history of this search, to scan the outstanding philosophic pronouncement on the question, and to point out a few features of embryonic development which seem pertinent to the discussion.

## PHILOSOPHY IN SCIENCE

In the first place, it will be well for us to consider whether or not it is a legitimate exercise of one's intellectual faculties to indulge in such philosophic exploration, for such it must prove to be. While some individual scientists who have been more inclined to delve into the technical phases of investigation may frown on such an ethereal project, scientists as a group, however, by their voice and example say "Yes, the effort is legitimate and worth while." To the point is the contention of Gengerelli:

"It is clear that there is no place where science stops and philosophy begins. If we insist upon creating an artificial dichotomy of this sort we do ourselves a great deal of mischief: it can only result in bad scientific method and worse theory. If we would gain an insight into the problem of the relationship between science and philosophy, we have but to ask ourselves this question: what does the human mind attempt to do in its efforts to understand the universe? The answer is that it tries to embrace as many experiences as possible under the fewest possible rubrics with the minimum number of contradictions. This is the basic impulse behind the efforts of all thinking men, be they physicists, biologists or metaphysicians. If we do not keep this fact clearly in mind at all times, we are likely to create for ourselves no end of silly problems and misleading convictions."[1]

Without an investigation into the implications of natural phenomena,

the scientist reduces himself intellectually to the level of the peon making *adobes,* and cannot become a builder and construct a usable edifice, to say nothing of an architect to rear a lofty structure of the materials of his own and others' making.

## EVOLUTION'S PROPOSAL: RECAPITULATION

In answer to the question as to the significance of embryonic development, Biologic Science of the 19th century proposed the recapitulation theory. Building on the theory of evolution brought to a focus by Darwin in his philosophies of survival of the fittest, otherwise referred to as "natural selection," the German biologist Haeckel reared the structure of his biogenetic law which he asserted was the fundamental law of all living things. Following the lead of Agassiz and Darwin, he called attention to the fact that all embryos begin their existence as a single cell and follow a parallel course of development, with the early stages in particular resembling one another very closely. The biogenetic law, as he enunciated it, was to the effect that "the developmental history or ontogeny of every multicellular organism recapitulates the various stages of its evolutionary ancestry, and thereby every organism resembles roughly at each stage of its development the form of one of its ancestors." In other words, he was convinced that each "stage" of development of the human embryo was a rough counterpart of some evolutionary ancestor. He divided this period of development into first 22, then 30 and finally 32 stages each of which was presumed to resemble one of man's evolutionary forbears.

Two years ago the present writer reviewed the history of the recapitulation theory.[2] As a result, it became obvious that the more critical embry-

---

1 Gengerelli, J. A. Facts and Philosophers, *Sc. Monthly* 54:431-440 (May) 1942.

2 Courville, C. B.: The Recapitulation Theory. Some Notes on Its History and Present Status, *Bull. Deluge Geol.* 1:21-59 (Aug.) 1941.

ologists no longer pay any attention to this theory as an explanation of development. The essential reasons why the theory is now rejected may be briefly stated as follows:

1. The logic of the theory is false since it presumes the truth of the theory of evolution which is in itself deductive. 2. The embryonic record is not coordinately condensed in its parallelism to assumed evolutionary history. 3. The order of presumed ancestral history is too seriously altered in embryonic development, and also has many features of development which have no relative meaning whatever to evolution. 4. The biogenetic law is fundamentally insecure because it is based upon resemblances now shown to be merely superficial. 5. Certain major details of embryonic development which obviously run counter to the concept are ignored, hence the theory is inconsistent with fact. 6. The recapitulation theory does not apply to anatomic detail even in closely allied forms. 7. Supposed "transitional stages" cannot be reproduced by natural or experimental retardation. Since, as Thomas Hunt Morgan has so aptly said, "If the recapitulation theory is a 'law,' it has so many exceptions that it has become useless and often misleading,"[3] the only thing that any logical investigator can do is to reject it completely as an explanation of embryonic development.

As recently as 1940, an effort was made to exhume the long-since defunct theory, redress it, and give it another name. The best that its proponent DeBeer could say for it was:

"Clearly, phylogeny (evolution) does not explain ontogeny (embryonic development) at all. Even if we had a complete phylogenetic series of adults ancestral to any given descendant, it would not help us to understand the processes of fertilization, cleavage, differentiation, organogeny, etc., which take place in the ontogeny of that descendant. The historical descriptive study of evolution has no bearing on the causal analytic study of embryology. . . . Conversely, if we knew all the processes involved in the events of ontogeny, such knowledge would not of itself provide an explanation of phylogeny."[4]

It seems clear therefore that at the present time evolution has nothing to offer as an explanation or interpretation of the phenomena of development of the embryo.

## WHAT THEN DOES "PARALLELISM" MEAN?

Although one can, with a clear conscience, discard the recapitulation theory, one cannot ignore the fundamental fact upon which this theory rests, viz., that embryos of even widely different forms of animal life begin as a single cell and follow a roughly parallel course in their external form and internal structure. This parallelism is too striking to be without significance. If not recapitulation, what does it mean?

In attempting to answer this question, the present writer proposed seven postulates to account for this similarity in the course of development.[5] Briefly stated, they are as follows:

1. In embryonic development, of necessity there must be a progression from the simple to the complex which in itself allows of variable degrees of parallelism. 2. This parallelism tends to become more and more "inexact" or "divergent," as far as individual organs or organ-systems are concerned. 3. There is a remarkable identity of structure and function of individual organs and tissues of animals widely separated in the scale of life, indicating stabilization on a successful solution of a functional problem. 4. While temporary function and structure are often similar in different embryos,

3 Morgan, T. H.: *Embryology and Genetics*, New York, 1934, p. 149.
4 DeBeer, G. R.: *Embryos and Ancestors*, London, 1940, pp. 97 and 98.
5 Courville, C. B.: The Causal Significance of Parallelism. An Inquiry into Certain Fundamental Principles of Embryonic Development, *Bull. Deluge Geol.* 2:1-35, 1942.

neither are absolutely parallel even in closely related forms of life. 5. In the development of comparative structure or organs, the embryo does not always use the same material in accomplishing the task, nor does it utilize the same potencies (organizers) in doing so. 6. In the attainment of their individual goals (i. e., the adult forms) , comparative embryos take the most efficient courses in the development of their individual structures and organs. 7. Back of all embryonic development there is a controlling force, a guiding principle which directs in the formation of each separate part as well as of the coordinated whole.

This analysis serves to emphasize that this comparative "parallelism" does not signify what the recapitulation theory would have us to believe; it is due instead to the influence of similar powers inherent in each embryo. Moreover, in its internal and external development of the embryo, there is a coordination of developmental factors which reach the adult stage in the most direct and efficient manner. If the Creator of the universe were a mathematician, as Sir James Jeans avers, then the designer of the embryo must indeed be an efficiency expert.

### EVIDENCES OF FORETHOUGHT AND DESIGN IN THE EMBRYO

There have been only two philosophies proposed to account for the origin of man — evolution and special creation. There are likewise only two possible causal explanations for the phenomenon of embryonic development, the recapitulation theory (which is the offspring of the theory of evolution) on one hand, and that these phenomena have their origin in a Creator, on the other. The evolutionist has long contended that his theories are to be accepted as fact. However, since almost a century of research has not only failed to support,

but rather to nullify, the recapitulation theory, it is only reasonable to investigate the possibilities in that "outworn and completely refuted idea of special creation, now retained only by the ignorant, the dogmatic and the prejudiced," to see what it holds as an explanation of embryonic development.

As an evidence of forethought and design in embryonic development, suggesting an orderly and planned, not a haphazard process, the present writer proposes the following postulates:

1. The genetic system for the transmission of characters must have been placed as a functioning system in all original life forms, because all living entities, no matter how small or simple, have it. Furthermore, no one has offered any adequate theory for the origin or evolution of such a system. 2. The synchronism of development of organs or structures indicates a basic plan of integrated development which in itself has no possible phylogenetic interpretation. The variations in rate and plan of development of closely related organs depend upon *present* embryonic demands of the situation and *future* adult function of the organ concerned, not upon any assumed past history. 3. The provisions in structure and function for transient needs are such as to indicate a minimum expenditure of energy and materials. If there were any implication in embryonic development of a haphazard, hit-or-miss past history, the embryo should be full of the relics of his ancient past. Such is not the case. 4. Important ultimate functions are foreshadowed by prominent early development, a sequence entirely out of harmony with any phylogenetic scheme. The development of the brain, for example, far outstrips any embryonic demands. 5. The anticipation of the order of required vital functions suggests a preconcep-

tion of the needs of the embryo, rather than any history of its presumed ancestry. The heart of the chick develops precociously because an efficient circulation is the one vital prerequisite to any embryonic growth. 6. The principle of terminal perfection indicates purposive development, a foreordinated design for an ultimate, usually highly specialized use. If this obvious fact is to be analyzed on a causal basis, the evolutionist must assume that the process of evolution was begun with the specific end of the evolution of man, a rather undesirable conclusion in a theory in which all forms of life are but biologic accidents. 7. The development of certain cellular mechanisms for only rare and uncertain needs indicates an intelligent forethought beyond any phylogenetic interpretation. For example, brain injury with survival is rare among vertebrate animals and yet in all animals and in man there is a highly developed system of cellular elements (microglia) which are provided for possible injury (or other physical damage) to the nervous system. According to phylogenesis, such a system should never have developed in the first place.

Thus we have ample evidence that the embryo shows forethought in the details of its development. Any system of causal interpretation of the embryo which ignores this fact cannot be wholly correct. The least that one can conclude in any such interpretation of embryonic development is that there is design and purpose behind the process. If one chooses to obscure this purpose and design by a noncommittal title of "vitalism" or anything else, he resorts to about the same kind of reasoning which accounts for the origin of life on the earth by saying that it came from some other planet. It is far simpler and more satisfying to acknowledge a wisdom

higher than our own to account for these phenomena than to continue to shake our agnostic heads in a confession that we do not know what the significance of such manifestations might be.

## NEED FOR A CAUSAL CONCEPT OF EMBRYONIC DEVELOPMENT

In reviewing the story of the recapitulation theory, the well-known scientific historian, Nordenskiöld, said that "time has dealt hardly with Haeckel's ontogenetical theories," adding that in these passing years. Haeckel "produced nothing to increase his reputation but detracted much from it."[6] Haeckel's decision to turn from his earlier interests of pure science to wandar afar as a wool-gatherer in the false philosophy of recapitulation, doubtless contributed largely to his retrograde course. The accumulating evidence in embryology drove him from one defensive position to another, until after almost fifty years the best argument he could muster in defense of his thesis was that his opponents had nothing better to put in its place, a charge which incidentally was entirely true.

The fact remains that embryologists today have nothing to substitute for the recapitulation theory. The rebaptized version of the theory advocated by DeBeer fills the bill no better than does the original thesis. There are those who have realized this deficit. As long ago as 1909 Sedgwick wrote: "If after 50 years of research and close examination of the facts the recapitulation theory is still without satisfactory proof, it seems desirable to take a wider sweep and to inquire whether the facts of embryology cannot be included in a larger category."[7] In this same vein comes the plea of Needham who writes:

"But this strictly evolutionary dominance did not last on into the twentieth century. The unfortunate thing is that nothing

---

6 Nordenskiold, E: *The History of Biology*, trans. by L. B. Eyre, New York, 1928, p. 517.
7 Sedgwick, A.: *Darwin and Modern Science*, New York, 1909, pp. 175 and 176.

has so far been devised to put in its place. Experimental embryology, morphological embryology, physiological embryology and chemical embryology form today a vast range of factual knowledge, without one single unifying hypothesis, for we cannot dignify the axial gradient doctrines, the field theories, and the speculations on the genetic control of enzymes, with such a position. We cannot doubt that the most urgent need of modern embryology is a series of advances of purely theoretical, even mathematicological, nature. Only by something of this kind can we redress the balance which has fallen over to observation and experiment; only by some such effort can we obtain a theoretical embryology suited in magnitude and spaciousness to the wealth of facts which contemporary investigators are accumulating day by day."[8]

In our attitude toward the possible causal significance of embryonic development we are therefore faced with four possible choices. We may stubbornly remain in the "mental straight-jacket" of the recapitulation theory, ignoring all the evidence which has accumulated to destroy it. We may turn back to wander once more in the wilderness of evolution in the vain hope of finding there some other interpretation for the phenomena of development. Or we may just content ourselves with picking and sorting the facts of embryology, adding our bit "to the wealth of facts which contemporary investigators are accumulating day by day." Or finally, one can turn to the only remaining admitted possibility, that living creatures were once actually created *de novo*, and see whether the facts are in accord with this postulate. This last alternative would of course imply that today the growth of each embryo is actively supervised by the same sleepless Power which in the beginning brought its first ancestor into existence.

Which course will Embryology and its followers choose?

## EVOLUTION AND PRENATAL DEVELOPMENT

A REVIEW

*By* Benjamin Franklin Allen

Since the theory of evolution from a biologic viewpoint rests to no small degree on the interpretation of the features of the developing embryo, a clear understanding of this subject is very important. During the past few years a number of studies on this relationship have been given to our Society by Dr. Cyril B. Courville. In order to present this material clearly to the lay reader, the present writer has made an effort to review the studies in a brief way.

Dr. Courville's first paper, "The Recapitulation Theory,"[1] recounts the origin, the significance, and the final abandonment of that theory. On its validity or falsity rests not only its own fate, but largely those of evolutionary geology and paleontology (the study of animal fossils,) and it is therefore doubly important.

The pre-natal animal changes from the simple to the complex as new parts and functions develop. This fact was seized upon by evolutionists to account for the origin of animals from a supposed one-celled beginning, countless changes being condensed into the brief period before birth. The old syllogism was: "Ontogeny (pre-natal growth) recapitulates phylogeny (evolutionary history)."

Early began the attempt of the paleontologists to show that the changes in the embryo parallel the evolution of the supposedly primitive fossil animals. Courville quotes one authority as saying that "If the embryologists had not forestalled them, the paleontologists would have had to invent the theory of recapitulation." Through paleontology, recapitulation entered into the making of the system of geologic ages, the sequence of the key fossils being agreed upon as the sequence of the strata and the ages, these fossils being adopted as the "time markers" of geology. Indeed, the strata being conceived of as having been deposited

---

8 Needham, J.: Limiting Factors in the Advancement of Science as Observed in the History of Embryology, *Yale J. Biol. & Med.*, 8:1-18 (Oct.) 1935.

1 Courville, Cyril B., The Recapitulation Theory, Some Notes on Its History and Present Status, *Bulletin of Deluge Geology and Related Science*, Vol. 1, 1941.

in that order, they were duly "discovered" to be in that order, and this gave a strong impression not only of confirming the efforts of paleontology, *but of recapitulation as well.*

Hence we have the three-legged pedestal of evolution: *recapitulation, paleontology,* and the *geologic-age system.* Growing up together, most intricately interwoven at all stages, and *interdependent,* yet each of these soon came to be very erroneously considered as *separate* and *independent proofs* of evolution, *and are still so accepted.* Fancy now the absurd predicament of the paleontologists and geologists, the *embryologists* having abandoned recapitulation! They are riding a dead horse. Besides, years ago Professor Price proved on a purely geological basis that the strata are not in the order necessary to the "age" system.

The following are Dr. Courville's main propositions: (1) The recapitulation theory is invalid because it is based on a false system of logic. (Before it was at all tested, Darwin seized upon it, and forced it to fit his thesis, and Haeckel went to extremes in this.) (2) It is unreliable because the embryonic "record" is not coordinately condensed. (Some parts of the "story" are abbreviated almost or entirely out of existence, while others are disproportionately long-drawn-out.) (3) The "record" is too seriously altered to be relied upon. (4) It rests on fundamentally insecure superficial resemblances. (5) It does not take into account anatomic details, even in cases of closely allied forms. (That is, it always fails in actually detailed anatomical tests.) (6) It ignores certain other major details of development which run counter to it. (7) Natural or experimental retardation cannot produce the supposed transitional parts necessary to the theory. (Abnormalities generally bear no relation to the theory, and far outnumber the few chance cases which appear to support the theory.)

Then turning to the work of a group of experimental embryologists who shut out all philosophical conceptions and considered only objective facts capable of actual physiological demonstration, Dr. Courville showed that they produced nothing favorable but much that is unfavorable to the theory. In fact, these specialists practically ignore recapitulation.

Dr. Courville's summary contains these potent words: "It is now believed by modern embryologists that the embryo has more important things to do than to reminisce on its presumed ancestry." He closed by repeating Haeckel's famous challenge that nothing had been proposed to take the place of the theory, and asked the question, "What, then, does parallelism mean?"

His second paper, "The Causal Significance of Parallelism,"[2] discusses this question under the following propositions: (1) In the pre-natal growth there is an obvious parallelism which must of necessity occur, as many forms pass from the simple to the complex. (Taken alone this might be either for or against the theory, but other features place it on the opposing side.) (2) During growth, this parallelism tends to become more and more inexact or divergent in external form, but may continue relatively exact in certain organs or organ systems. (The eye is relatively alike in all vertebrate and some invertebrate animals, while parts like the head and limbs differ extremely.) (3) The remarkable similarity of structure and function of certain organs in such widely different animals can be more against than for the theory, and favor not only design, *but stabilization thereof.* (4) Of the temporary similarities, which soon differentiate, there is no exact parallelism. (5) In forming similar parts or functions, the same material is not used in all cases, nor do the same organizers perform the work, thus still further emphasizing the lack of identity, indicating that the *processes,* as well as the end results, differ at all stages according to *contemplated* ends. (6) Similar embryos are similar only because they take the same most efficient course to attain their goals, and parallelism is a mere inevitable incident in this economy, and *nothing else.* (7) Back of the whole process there is a guiding principle which pervades it all, coordinating and supervising, but which cannot be located objectively in any of the parts.

Dr. Courville applies to these, processes the profound "principle of least action," which is the basis of changes in the material universe. The least possible time and energy are used, the product of energy multiplied by time always being the least possible amount. In this, he enters the field of physics, in which a most amazing philosophical revolution has been in progress for about fifteen years, all toward the scientific and logical necessity for a creative and directive Mind, the Maker of the laws of nature, permeating the universe. *A similar revolution is overdue in biology.* But the catch-phrases of recapitulation still resound in halls of learning, and millions of youth are still indoctrinated with them.

---

2 Courville, Cyril B., The Causal Significance of Parallelism, An Inquiry into Certain Fundamental Principles of Embryonic Development, *Bulletin of Deluge Geology and Related Science,* Vol. 2, 1942.

Dr. Courville's third paper, "The Causal Significance of Embryonic Development,"[3] starts with a brief outline of his other two papers, but it primarily deals with evidences of forethought and design in the embryo. He proposes: (1) That the origin of the system of reproduction has neither basis nor explanation in the current theories of the embryo, and no one has even offered an adequate evolutionary explanation. (2) The necessarily accurate synchronizing of the development of the parts and functions has no evolutionary interpretation, but strongly indicates overall design and coordination in accord with future functional demands, rather than any historical hangover. (3) Only a minimum of time and material are used in accomplishing this result. If vague evolutionary history were being recapitulated, one would expect on the other hand a haphazard development full of odd relics of the past. (4) Functions far beyond the embryonic needs are foreshadowed, long before they could be of use, such as the brain, which far outstrips any possible embryonic demand. (5) Early embryonic needs, however, are also anticipated. For example, the early growth of the heart provides the obviously needed blood circulation for the growth of the embryo. (6) Logically, the highest and most specialized result, *man*, would have to be the original end of evolu-

tion, but this is a conclusion incongruous to a theory depending wholly upon biologic accidents. (7) The development of certain cellular resources for rare and uncertain needs, such as a special system of cells for possible injury to the brain or nervous system, is inexplicable by the theory, and demands forethought.

Stressing the need for a new concept of embryology, Dr. Courville offers four possible choices: We may stubbornly remain unconvinced of the errors of recapitulation. We may turn back to wander in the wilderness of evolution in the generally recognized vain hope of finding some other causal explanation of pre-natal growth. We may content ourselves with merely picking and sorting the facts of embryology. Or we may turn to the only remaining admitted possibility, that living creatures were once actually created *de novo*, testing this postulate to the utmost to see if it is in accord with all of the facts.

The net result seems to be that now in biology, as already in physics and astronomy, biologists are face to face with the clear necessity of acknowledging the origin and maintenance of life by the Creator. And Dr. Courville appropriately closes his discussion with the very timely question whether embryologists and their followers will candidly face this situation.

---

## DISCUSSION

[The discussion following this paper had to take into consideration also the two very important previous papers by Dr. Courville dealing with other aspects of embryonic development and the recapitulation theory. For this present paper is only the third of a series, and when they are all taken together and considered as a unity, they can confidently be said to be one of the most important contributions to this subject in modern times. Henceforth no one lecturing or writing on the recapitulation theory or on the philosophic aspects of embryonic development, can afford to ignore these profoundly important contributions by Dr. Cyril B. Courville, no matter which side of the controversy he may take. They must be reckoned with, and many will say that they are final and conclusive. It is to be hoped that they can soon be published in book form.—THE EDITORS.]

The discussion of this paper, as the third of Dr. Courville's series, was conducted by George McCready Price and Benjamin Franklin Allen.

*Question.* Why was it that a hundred years ago, when geology and embryology were both in their infancy, the embryonic development of the individual animal was taken as furnishing the key to the sequence in which the fossils would be found occurring in the strata of the long ago?

*Answer by Prof. Price.* It is an incontrovertible fact of history that Louis Agassiz and others of his time did thus appeal to the embryonic development as the true guide to the sequence of the fossils in their long-drawn-out scheme of geological history. Some very definite statements by Agassiz have already been given in the former papers by Dr. Courville and in my paper on "Geology and the Recapitulation Theory" (BULLETIN, Vol. 1, No. 3; October, 1941); and it is quite certain that further research in the historical literature of those times will bring to light other important facts and statements along the same line.

But we should remember that often some of the most profound and important guiding principles in a scientific discussion are only vaguely realized by those even most intimately connected with the rise and growth of a large scientific idea. This is because the growth and shaping up of all the larger aspects of what we term modern sci-

---

3 Courville, Cyril B., The Causal Significance of Embryonic Development, *Bulletin of Creation, the Deluge, and Related Science*, Vol. 3, 1943.

ence have always been quite beyond any human planning; they seem to be conducted by unseen forces entirely beyond our control. During the first half-century after the rise of embryology and geology, it is now clear that not even the leaders in these sciences realized quite what they were doing, or how the results of their work would shape up in the end. The scientists of the preceding century had quite generally accepted the view that the Noachian deluge was the cause of the burial of the fossils and the geological changes; but Cuvier and Agassiz, with the more decided uniformitarians, such as Charles Lyell, discarded the idea that the fossils could possibly have lived contemporaneously in a world which was destroyed by a sudden cataclysm. Agassiz and his associates seem to have had the conviction that in the stratified rocks they would find relics of the stages in which living things had been created on the earth during long periods of time. Then they reasoned that this original creation must naturally have followed the same order in which a new individual is now developed in the embryo from the one-celled stage onward. So they enthusiastically applied this embryonic measuring rule first to the fossil fishes, then to the ammonites, to the trilobites, and to all the other fossils. Agassiz, who was a man of very pronounced religious ideas, became the leading exponent of the idea that the so-called "sequence of the fossils" really represents the history of the successive stages of creation. And in his famous essay on "Classification," published in 1857, or two years before Charles Darwin's "Origin of Species," he claimed that the true taxonomic or classification series, the geological series, and even the modern geographical distribution series, are all parallel to or essentially similar to the embryonic series.

*Question.* But Agassiz was a definitely religious man. And he used all these comparisons to contribute to his theism, and to what he considered the Divine Plan of Creation. How did it happen that this same idea of a parallelism between the development of the embryo and the long-drawn-out history of life on the globe as shown by the fossils, was picked up by militant atheists, like Haeckel, and exploited by them in so forceful a way as to become the most effective argument in favor of their scheme of materialistic evolution?

*Answer.* That's very easy. If the so-called "laws of comparison," as enunciated by Agassiz, had been founded on truth, they never could have been thus exploited by atheists in the interests of atheism. But the members of this Society are fully convinced

that Agassiz and his associates were working along false and misleading lines. Only by much wishful thinking and by brazenly manipulating the evidence can the fossils be arranged in anything resembling a definite historical sequence for the world as a whole. They show instead clear and incontrovertible evidence that they represent the ruins of a world, not its ideal creation. And since Agassiz was working along wholly unsound lines, and was, moreover, flying in the very face of the plain teachings of the Bible in several respects, his work could very easily be made use of for a further extension of falsehood. Scientific problems, like apples, have a time for ripening; and their value can best be estimated after they have ripened. In the anti-Christian use to which Agassiz's theories finally developed under Haeckel, and indeed in the entire modern theory of organic evolution, we can best evaluate them and thus judge their real character. If they had been sound and true, they could never have been thus exploited by atheists in the interests of the great modern apostasy and the war again the Bible. It is said of Agassiz that most of his students later became atheists.

*Question.* How was it that Haeckel first came into possession of this plausible and seductive idea that the embryo repeats or recapitulates the geological history of its remote ancestor?

*Answer.* The genealogy of an idea is often of enlightening importance toward its true evaluation. Matthew Arnold said that there is a power not ourselves which makes for righteousness; but it is just as true that there is a power not ourselves which works for devilishness or falsehood. And in science, as in so many other phases of human activity, the evil that men do often appears most strongly long after they are dead and gone. And in this matter of the supposed relationship between the growth of the embryo and the supposed geological sequence of the fossils, we have an unusually clear example of what we may term an apostolic succession of evil, which has come down to our day, and which though long discarded by all clear thinkers is still here to plague and muddle the elementary student of these subjects, as is shown by the need for and the timeliness of these papers by Dr. Courville in this late date of 1944.

Charles Darwin had never had any training in embryology. But in his "Origin of Species," in 1859, he made use of Agassiz's so-called laws of comparison based on the growing embryo as some of his chief arguments for his theory of organic evolution. Then in 1864, or five years later, the German-born Fritz Müller, then living in Brazil, had a paper entitled "Für Darwin" presented before a scientific gathering in Germany, in which he expanded on this idea that the embryonic development of the individual is a "historical document," and in which he went to considerable lengths in illustrating this idea from the early stages of some of the crustaceans.

This theory of recapitulation, as expounded by Fritz Müller's paper, "aroused Haeckel's ardent enthusiasm," to use the words of Erik Nordenskiold, the leading historian of biology, (History of Biology, New York, 1928, p. 517). From this time onward, Haeckel became a flaming evangelist of this theory of recapitulation as the key to what he termed the Riddle of the Universe. And while his books have now long declined in popularity, we should remember how, about the beginning of the present century, his anti-Christian works and those of a similar style and object were best sellers both in Germany and in translation in such countries as Japan and even here in America. Indeed, it is only sober truth to say that the teachings of such works were at bottom one of the chief factors in bringing about those conditions in the Old World against which the democratic nations are now waging war.

Haeckel, the great propagandist of the recapitulation theory, lived until 1919, or until after the first World War. But even during his lifetime, the trained embryologists, like Wilhelm His of Switzerland and the two Hertwigs of Germany, repudiated his theories about recapitulation, and showed how much more natural and truly scientific it is to explain the development of the embryo on purely physiological grounds. Such rejections of his pet theory, however, always made the Jena professor furious, and

called forth from him a torrent of personal abuse for his opponents. But soon from various parts of his native country and elsewhere arose other eminent scientists who bluntly accused him of flagrant inaccuracies and even of deliberate falsification of many of his diagrams (always made by his own hands) in his illustrated books.*

The last days of the prophet of recapitulation do not make pleasant reading. But still more sad were the desolating intellectual and moral results following inevitably from the militant atheism and the utter misrepresentation of the laws and processes of nature to which he had dedicated the larger part of his life.

Reflective and informed people know that there was a definite and logical connection between the triumph of Darwinism in Germany under Haeckel and his followers, and the arrogant boasts of world conquest taught and put into practice by the next generation of those who had been brought up on these ideas. Usually the false ideas which infect one generation bear their baneful fruit in the following ones. Two world wars within one lifetime have been sprung on an unsuspecting world by the children of those who so eagerly accepted the morally disintegrating theories of such men as Darwin and Haeckel; for it is a well known fact that in no other country did these theories take such deep and permanent root as in the land beyond the Rhine.

When we think of the moral and religious condition of such a country as Germany, or even of its political condition, let us remember the scientific and philosophical reasons behind it all. Only something extremely horrible could have so debauched the land of Luther and Melanchthon as to bring it to the condition in which it is today.

*Those who wish to investigate further into this unsavory subject may consult: *Haeckel's Frauds and Forgeries*, by J. Assmuth and E. R. Hull, The Examiner Press, Bombay, India, 1915.

---

## GILL ARCHES AND VESTIGIAL REMAINS STILL TAUGHT

### By PROFESSOR GEORGE McCREADY PRICE

[Were it not for the deplorable hangover of admittedly erroneous 19th century biology still being taught in our educational institutions, the following excerpt from "The Phantom of Organic Evolution," 1924, pp. 157-163, by Professor George McCready Price, would seem uncalled for. But, even at this late date, this statement is almost as timely as when first published, and this fact is so impressive that it more than justifies the repetition.—THE EDITORS]

"Close in front of the bulb which marks the cerebellum [of the human embryo], under the bulb composing the forebrain, are seen several incomplete arches with a corresponding number of clefts or depressions between them, these structures arising from the sides and uniting at the median line in front. When the embryo becomes more developed, the upper one of these arches forms the upper jaw; the second forms the lower jaw; between them, when the two sides of the organs have united is the oral or mouth cavity. The others eventually go to form the organs of the neck, the roots of the tongue, and the larynx.

"These parts have been called branchial arches, because of their fancied resemblance to the arches of certain fishes which support the gills. By Haeckel and others the clefts or depressions between them were called 'gill-slits,' though actual openings into the pharynx are never formed in the human embryo; and evolutionists never become tired of pointing to them as proof that man in the long ago passed through a stage resembling that of a fish. But it should be expressly noted that these embryonic arches do not take any part in producing the respiratory organs in man, as the true branchial arches do in the fish. In the light of what is now known about this part of embryology, it may be stated with confidence that these so-called arches and clefts are the very natural and necessary structural preparation for the growth of the organs which ultimately develop from them. Any fancied resemblance between these structures and the gill-slits of elasmobranch fishes is merely the product of a highly inventive imagination. Inaccurate or even deliberately false diagrams of these parts have been peddled around from one textbook to another, materially assisting in this misconception, Haeckel's inventions having been one of the chief supports of this propaganda.

"Frankly, it is quite discouraging to see that Vernon Kellogg, in his latest work, *Evolution the Way of Man* (1924), dwells long and earnestly on this argument from 'recapitulation,' gill-clefts and all, and says that these 'recapitulation' features of the embryo constitute 'one of the strongest of the evidences of evolution' (p. 54). I had thought that modern science had definitely outgrown this whimsical explanation of the structures found in the human embryo, and that the exposure of the methods used by Haeckel in this connection had brought the whole thing into a state where common sense and accuracy would again have the right of way over whimsicality and misrepresentation.

"*Vestigial organs.* Many of the alleged instances of vestigial organs in man, as abduced by the evolutionists, are trivial and childish, while others are completely false as to fact. I do not know of a single instance that ought not properly to be classed under the one head or the other.

"Among the trivial ones may be mentioned the muscles of the ears, of the scalp, and of the coccyx, with the coccyx itself, which has been asserted to be the relic of a tail. Arguments based on such examples are trivial in the extreme; and would never have been used in this connection, if Charles Darwin had not set the example. If the theo-

logians of the Middle Ages were addicted to hair splitting and word twisting, the evolutionists have merely changed the form, but not the habit.

"Among the organs which were once said to be useless relics of the past, may be mentioned the thyroid gland, the pineal gland, and the vermiform appendix. The thyroid used to be called a useless heirloom; but with the advance in a knowledge of physiological processes, we now know that it serves a very essential function in keeping us all from becoming cretins. Indeed, the mistake made by evolutionists regarding the thyroid was recognized by Huxley, who said: 'The recent discovery of the important part played by the thyroid gland should be a warning to all speculators about useless organs.'

"But this warning was unheeded; for in 1919, Sir Arthur Keith, in his presidential address before the Anthropological Section of the British Association for the Advancement of Science, had this to say:

'We have hitherto regarded the pineal gland, little bigger that a wheat grain and buried deeply in the brain, as a mere useless vestige of a median or parietal eye, derived from some distant human ancestor in whom that eye was functional; but on the clinical and experimental evidence now rapidly accumulating we must assign to it a place in the machinery which controls the growth of the body.' (Smithsonian Report, 1919; p. 448).

"Another portion of the human anatomy which is often spoken of as a vestige or relic from some previous form of animal life, is the vermiform appendix, a tubular structure about the size of a short lead pencil. Evolutionists claim that this worm-like appendage is the vestigial remains of the much elongated caecum of the herbivorous animals. This vermiform appendix is found also in the anthropoid apes and in most other herbivorous animals; but in man it has often been regarded as a useless or even a dangerous relic of the past. Among civilized peoples this organ often gives a good deal of trouble; but it is significant that among people who live more naturally, the organ never gives any trouble whatever; and we may well suppose that it has a useful function to perform, though it is not well understood just what its function really is. The appendix is composed largely of lymphoid tissue, in common with the spleen, the thymus, and the tonsils; and any of these can apparently be removed without causing any particular harm to the rest of the body. However, we do know that all of these organs serve as the factories or points of origin of large quantities of the white blood-cells.

"It also appears that these lymphoid tissues, including the appendix, act as filters or obstructions to foreign particles, such as disease germs, and even to chemical poisons, in their passage toward the general circulation system. It may be safely asserted that the appendix has a useful work to perform, and that in the normal condition of the body it not only would never be of any trouble necessitating its surgical removal, but would assist in maintaining the normal tone of the body. The old notion that it is a

relic of a former stage of man's existence, a useless and dangerous heirloom which has persisted in man's body when it is not wanted and not needed, is merely a part of the alleged evidence in favour of the evolution theory which has no substantial foundation in actual fact."

## EMBRYOLOGY, THE BIBLE, AND CHRISTIANITY

### By Dr. Cyril B. Courville

*Creation at Last Appealed to.*—The false philosophy of Evolution has attempted for the past century to obliterate the concept of a Creator and a creation by the introduction of the Recapitulation Theory. It now becomes doubly significant that, after viewing the results of more than a century of study of the details of embryonic development, two outstanding present-day embryologists (and evolutionists) were impelled to say:

"The inevitable conclusion is that development involves a true increase of diversity, a *creation* of differentiation where previously none existed, and that *the interpretation of embryonic development must be sought along the lines of some epigenetic* [literally *new formation* or *creation*] theory." G. R. DeBeer, in "Elements of Experimental Embryology," 1934 (italics by the writer).

*Embryology and Salvation.*—Creation, natural birth and the new birth are indissolubly linked together in the Creator's plan for humankind. If there was no action of creation in bringing man into existence in the first place, then it is impossible to account for the scientific phenomenon of natural development and birth, and all hope of salvation by a new birth is in vain. When man was created (Isa. 43:1, Mal. 2:10) God did

not speak him into existence but formed him from the dust of the ground (the word *Adam* means 'red earth') and breathed into his nostrils the breath of life. In natural birth, which the Scriptures imply is also a form of creation (compare Ps. 22:31, Isa. 43:21, and Ps. 102:18), the new individual is formed from pre-existing material (germinal cells), and this process of development is considered to be the handiwork of the Creator (Ps. 139:14). Life, in its full sense, begins when the new-born babe begins to breathe (Job 33:4). So in the new birth there is created a new heart (Ps. 51:10) in which act God takes pre-existing material (our natural human heart), cleanses it from sin, and activates it by his (creative) spirit (Jno. 3:5) which is spoken of as being "breathed" upon us (Jno. 20:22). Just as the unborn individual is not perfect in the sense of being fully developed (Ps. 139:16), just so in the spiritual birth, the new creature (creation) (2 Cor. 5:17) is not perfect but must "grow up" unto "the stature of the fullness of Christ" (Eph. 4:15, 13), when, in his perfection, he will be the handiwork of the Master Craftsman (Eph. 2:10), being made anew in the image (the character) of God (Compare Gen. 1:26, first part, and Eph. 4:24).

THE

# BULLETIN

OF

# CREATION, THE DELUGE

AND RELATED SCIENCE

| Volume IV | JANUARY, 1944 | Number 1 |

## THE ORIGIN OF THE RACES*

*Its Significance in Man's Origin, in Early Chronology,*

*and in Present World Problems*

A PRELIMINARY SURVEY

*By* VARNER J. JOHNS, J.D.

Ethnology, Philology, Archeology, Chronology, and other related sciences, which are concerned with ancient peoples and civilizations, contribute much to our knowledge of origins. Ethnology embraces:

(1) Ethnology, the study of races and racial characteristics.

(2) Sociology, the study of the origin and history of society,

(3) Linguistics, the study of the origin and signification of words,

(4) Ethnotechnics, the study of arts in their relation to races,

(5) The study of comparative religions, in seeking their common origin.

It is readily seen how large a place the science of Ethnology holds in the fascinating field of origins. In this study, reference will be made to an ethnological chart found in an ancient Book. The book of Genesis—Beresheth—is a book of origins. While its primary purpose is to teach Soteriology, the Science of Salvation, this Book makes incidentally many interesting assertions connected with racial origins and relationships. *Is the chart of Genesis chapter ten an accurate ethnological and chronological record? Does it contain trustworthy clews to guide the scientist along the ancient trail of racial and national origins?* The origin of races, the dispersion, the analogies found in various languages, are a captivating study for those who are interested in Creation and the Deluge. The science of Ethnology, in very fact, is a positive and essential contribution in evidence to the study of origins. *What data on man's origin can Ethnology supply?*

* Presented at the Symposium of Bible Science November 26, 1943, at Los Angeles, California.

The BULLETIN is published by, and is the official organ of the "Society for the Study of Creation, the Deluge, and Related Science." The Editorial Board is comprised of Professor George McCready Price and Dr. Dell D. Haughey. It is printed at the Collegiate Press, Arlington, California. For members the BULLETIN is free, and extra copies 30 cents each (each number priced accordoing to size); for non-members it is $2.00 per year and this number is 40 cents. All correspondence should be directed to the Managing Editor, Mr. Ben F. Allen, 219 North Grand Avenue, Los Angeles, 12, California.

The discussion follows this outline:

1. Ethnology and the Racial Problem:
   (a) The *one* solution essential for a program of world betterment and racial amity and understanding and, indeed, of world evangelism, as opposed to the evolutionary conception of the survival of the fittest and the ruthless struggle of race against race, and nation against nation, for their very existence.
   (b) Genesis and Four Fundamental Facts:
      (1) The site of man's original home,
      (2) The essential unity of the race,
      (3) The common origin of languages,
      (4) The time element in the history of man.
2. Philology and the Sons of Noah:
   (a) The three main divisions of human speech.
   (b) Recognized language groups evidence the tri-parte division, of the race and the post-Deluge Mesopotamian origin of man.
3. The Dispersion:
   (a) Putting to the test Genesis, chapter 10, as an Ethnological chart,
   (b) Iran as the center,
   (c) The scattering of the three distinct branches of the Noachian family.
4. Evidence from Chronology:
   (a) The three vital points of agreement with the Bible, viz., racial unity, language unity, and Iran as the center of origin,
   (b) The marked disagreement in chronology,
   (c) Earliest dates assigned to historical peoples not far removed from the Bible dates.
   (d) Exaggerated and uncertain estimates of the pre-historic periods.
5. Man Began Civilized:
   (a) The earliest civilization acknowledged to be the highest,
   (b) Post-Deluge time estimates from population growth.
6. Summary and Conclusion:
   Post-Deluge man emigrated from Mesopotamia, from the family of Noah, as proved by history, archeology, language affinities, and chronology. All men are united by the blood-ties of racial relationship; they are bound together in a double kinship when "born again" into the family of God. The time element is established within reasonable range of Bible chronology.

## THE RACIAL PROBLEM, ITS ONE SOLUTION

The most perplexing of world problems have their source in deep-seated racial antagonisms. The story of history is the story of the ceaseless clash of race against race, nation against nation. Modern history is a repetition of the past, but with rivalries and antagonisms and wars, more bitter, more intense, more disastrous than were ever known in the past. Through the inventive genius of modern man, the world has been narrowed to a neighborhood. No longer do the "seven seas" or the "snow-covered peaks" act as barriers. Crowded peoples gaze upon green fields across the neighborhood fence. While boundaries have been narrowed, the problems of race have been multiplied and intensified.

We talk much of universal brotherhood and of world peace. The actualities speak louder than our words. Pious platitudes avail nothing while the flash of fire is in the eyes of men of different color or conflicting creed. While great industries are paralyzed in wartime because of the hiring or firing of a man of different race or color, it is folly to dream of peace and prosperity. With pogroms in the Old World, and racial discrimination and race riots in the New World, and racial antagonisms in all the world—what hope is there for permanent peace?

If peace prevails, there must be solution of our problems of race. There must be a common understanding of mutual interests. The deep roots of racial hate and fear and distrust must be severed. Race must be studied, not only from its biological aspects, but especially in its sociological applications. Indeed, as Dr. Redfield, Professor of Anthropology, University of Chicago, says, "The biological differences which enable us to classify the human species into races are superficial differences. There are few racial differences deep inside our bodies. Racial differences are mostly in the outermost layer."[1] The racial differences may be overemphasized, yes, *are* overemphasized, to the prejudice of peace among races and between nations. "The beliefs of people about the physical features of race become a sort of false science. Or we might call them a modern mythology."[2] We must face the factual, and forget the mythical. The fact of human brotherhood needs emphasis and application.

It was said in days of old, "God that made the world and all things therein . . . hath made of one blood all nations of men."[3] The race is merely an enlarged family group, and the racial family group is but a part of the whole family of earth. Millenniums ago, a man by the name of Moses declared: "The life . . . is in the blood."[4] That statement, repeated four times in the book of Leviticus, is in strict harmony with modern medical science. It is no less true, scientifically, that it is the same blood and therefore the same life that is shared by every descendant of the common ancestor. Let us ever remember this fact, in our study of origins, that our enlarged vision of the essential unity of the human race may lead us to a more active interest in the problems of postwar peace.

Our plea in this study is not only for an enlarged vision but also for the essential love and respect of man for man, without which there can be no understanding, no agreement, no peace. With Joseph Le Conte, late Professor of Geology and Natural History, University of California, we would say: " 'It is impossible to know a man unless you first love him.' There is a profound truth in this re-mark. You cannot be a wise philanthropist unless you deeply sympathize with human nature, unless you love your fellow men. . . . Indifference shuts the door of the mind as well as of the heart. Hate not only shuts but double-locks it, and throws away the key. Only Love can open it."[5]

From an article entitled "What Do We Know About Race?" by Prof. Wilton Marion Krogman of the Department of Anatomy and Physical Anthropology of Chicago University, the following statements are gleaned:

"In this general morphological pattern all mankind is truly one; one genus, one species. In all important and major bodily details we are one—in brain, in peripheral nerves, in heart, in blood viscera, in muscles, and in skeletal architecture.

"Biologically the knowledge of these four genetic patterns is important because the mechanism is identical for all human beings; the inherited traits cut straight across stock and race; e. g., all blood groups and their genes are found in Whites, Yellows, and Blacks, though in varying percentage combinations. It is possible that these combinations may have some value in racial distinction, just as does skin, color, etc., but as far as transfusibility is concerned (allowing for blood groups) all human blood is alike.

"Much is being made these days of 'race superiority' and 'race inferiority.' In words of one syllable, there is no such thing."[6]

The textbooks on Biology recognize but one species, the Homo sapiens; organic chemistry recognizes but one blood (allowing for blood groups) for men of all races. The expression, "The brotherhood of man" is more than a mere gesture of friendship. "We are all brothers under the skin" is more than a mere token of fellowship.

A textbook entitled "A Popular Zoology,"[7] written by two professors of Brown University, was daring enough

---

1 Redfield, Dr. Robert, *Scientific Monthly*, Sept., 1943, p. 193.
2 *Id.*, p. 194.
3 Acts 17:24, 26, "One blood"; 20th Cent., "One stock"; Moffatt, "One origin"; Weymouth, "One Father." "The great majority of manuscripts have the word 'blood.'" Jamieson; Fausett; Brown, *A Critical and Experimental Commentary*, 1870, Vol. 6, p. 126.
4 Leviticus 17:11, 14.
5 Le Conte, Joseph, *Religion and Science*, 1891, p. 11.
6 Krogman, Wilton Marion, *Scientific Monthly*, Aug., 1943, 97-101.
7 Steele, J. Dorman, and Jenks, J. W. P., *A Popular Zoology*, 1887, pp. 276-278.

in independent thinking to classify man in a different *order* from the orang-utan and the ape. The lower order of lemurs, gibbons, gorillas, etc., were classified as "Order Quadrumana." Then, under the heading, "Order Bimana," were the words: "This order comprises only one genus and a single species; thus,

| Order | Genus | Species | Example |
|-------|-------|---------|---------|
| Bimana | Homo | sapiens | man" |

Describing the common origin of man, this textbook continues:

"While in the human race there is but a single species, zoologists are accustomed to speak of several very distinctly marked varieties. . . . We therefore agree with Dr. Prichard 'that no other differences occur than may fairly be attributed to the differences of external circumstances; and hence it may safely be concluded that the different races are all members of the same family, and the offspring of one common stock.'"
—Pages 276-278.

*Three Fundamental Facts*

Three fundamental facts in the field of origins are acknowledged by most students of the history of civilization. Furthermore, these fundamental facts are in harmony with the book of Genesis. Let us notice three of the fundamentals. First: it is generally agreed that Mesopotamia is the cradle of civilization. An illustration of this point is the statement by Will Durant:[8] "As the spades of archeology, after a century of victorious inquiry along the Nile, pass across Suez into Arabia, Palestine, Mesopotamia, and Persia, it becomes more probable with every year of accumulating research that it was the rich delta of Mesopotamia's rivers that saw the earliest known scenes in the drama of civilization." The very heart of the story of origins as told in Genesis is the fact that from Mesopotamia the races emigrated to other parts of the earth. Secondly, the unity

of races is a fundamental fact of general agreement. According to John D. Baldwin, "The essential unity of mankind in all the peculiar characteristics of humanity is an incontestable fact, which cannot be affected by any differences of race or language."[9] Thirdly: all acknowledge the unity and common origin of languages as well as the unexcelled perfection of the earliest languages. Where the evolutionist expects development he acknowledges decadence. The earliest languages are the most perfect. Says Ridpath:[10] "The oldest languages with which we are acquainted were the most perfect of their kind."

PHILOLOGY AND NOAH'S SONS

There were three sons of Noah and from these three have come the three distinct branches of the human race. How interesting to find that from these three have come the three distinct root languages, the mother languages of the world. In the similarity of languages is an invaluable aid in tracing the origin of races. For example, Will Durant in speaking of the ancient Sumerian says: "There is much in their language that resembles the Mongol speech."[11] This similarity of speech helps to confirm the other evidence of the Sumerian or Hamitic origin of the Chinese peoples. There is the Aryan or Indo-European group of languages. Says Whitney, "It [the Indo-European family of languages] is known also by various other designations: some style it 'Japhetic' as it appertains to the descendants of the patriarch Japheth, as the so-called Semitic tongues to the descendants of Shem."[12] And so with the other language relationships. The dispersion followed the confusion of tongues, and in tracing the lines of dispersion

---

8 Durant, William James, *The Story of Civilization*, 1935, p. 109.

9 Baldwin, John D., *Prehistoric Nations*, 1896, p. 16.

10 Ridpath, John Clark, *History of the World*, 1894, Vol. 1, p. 379.

11 Durant, Will, *loc. cit.*, p. 117.

12 Whitney, William D., *Language and Study of Language*, 1869, p. 192.

of the Hamitic, Semitic, and Japhetic peoples, we may follow with interest the speech trails. How wonderful it is for the student of the Bible to find in his study of origins that the language groups follow the Bible division in the dispersion.

## The Recognized Language Groups

"Philologists recognize groups of related languages or language-stocks, the most important of which (genetically speaking) are the Aryan or Indo-European, the Semitic, and Ural-Altaic, Scythian or Turanian, the monosyllabic or isolating, or southeastern Asian, and the Hamitic. These groups of languages may be roughly classified, according to the morphological character as agglutinative, incorporating, inflectional or isolating."[13] Notice how closely the language affinities follow the picture which we shall later draw of the dispersion of races. Says our dictionary authority:

"The chief families of agglutinative languages are:

| | |
|---|---|
| Bantu | Malayan |
| Dravido-Munda | Polynesian |
| Hamitic | Ural-Altaic |

and they also include:

| | |
|---|---|
| Ainu | Basque |
| Japanese | Hottentot |
| Korean | Negrito |
| Linkiu | Native Australian |
| Caucasian | Tasmanian" |
| Georgian | |

Of the Chinese inclusion with this group our authority says: "It would also appear that certain languages, once agglutinative and inflectional, have reverted to the isolating type through a process of phonetic decay, as in modern Chinese."

Included under the Indo-European in this dictionary chart are:

| | |
|---|---|
| Aryan | Celtic |
| Armenian | Italic |
| Hellenic | Teutonic |
| Illyrian | Slavo-Lithuanian |

And under the Semitic classifications are:

| | |
|---|---|
| Aramaeo-Assyrian | Himyaritic |
| Canaanitic | Abysinnian |
| Arabic | |

This chart or table is based on a work of T. G. Tucker.[14] We must remember that many of the languages of earth cannot be classified as distinct groups because of the mingling of races and the consequent mingling of language.

That the "agglutinating speech spread over a vast region from Turkey to the sea of Okhotsk and from the Mediterranean to the Arctic Ocean" is clearly indicated. Philologists detect a relationship between the Accadian or Sumerian and the Ural-Altaic. Modern Finnish is related to this group. This helps us to realize how wide was the Hamitic or Cushite migrations in the dispersion of the races.

Much could be said of the similarities of languages. Take serial words as an example, from the Aryan or Indo-European group, the oldest of which is the Sanskrit: Sanskrit, pitri; Persian, padar; Greek, pater; Latin, pater; German, vater; English, father, and again Sanskrit, tri; Greek, treis; Latin, tres; Portugese, tres; English, three.

## SCIENTIFIC EVIDENCE OF THE DISPERSION

Let us now take our proposed Ethnological chart—Genesis chapter 10— and attempt to apply it to the origin and distribution of the race. There were only five families on earth after the Deluge. Convenience—centralization—organized tyranny has ever been the greatest of perils for freedom and religion. Nimrod, the grandson of Ham, the son of Cush, made a daring attempt to unite the people together in apostasy. Nimrod was more than a hunter of wild beasts. The word "tsayed" which is translated "hunter"

---

13 Funk and Wagnalls, *New Standard Dictionary*, article "Languages."
14 Tucker, T. G., *Introduction to the Natural History of Languages*, 1908, as cited in Funk and Wagnalls Dictionary, Article, "Languages."

signified "prey," and is applied in the Scriptures to the hunting of men by persecution, oppression, and tyranny. (Jer. 16:16) The Jewish Targums, which are paraphrases in Aramaic of the ancient Hebrew text, help to illuminate many Bible texts. The Jerusalem Targum reads:

"He was mighty in hunting and in sin before God, for he was a hunter of the children of men in their languages; and he said unto them 'depart from the religion of Shem; and cleave to the institutions of Nimrod.' "

The Targum quotes I Chron. 1:10: "Nimrod began to be a mighty man in sin, a murderer of innocent men, and a rebel before the Lord."

In the Septuagint the expression "before the Lord" is translated "against the Lord."

Nimrod was the originator of a systematic and ordered opposition to the religion of the true God, an opposition that took shape in a mighty kingdom, whose authority, reaching out to the ends of the civilized earth, was destined to shape the history of the world. This empire, established by Nimrod, threw all its influence around idolatry, and in so doing, subverted every truth of God. The seeds of rebellion, sown in Babylon of old, multiplied through succeeding ages into iniquitous fields of tyranny and oppression, and the harvest is being reaped by the men of today and will continue to be reaped by the men of tomorrow.

After his death Nimrod was deified and worshipped as Bel (Bilounipru) the "hunter-lord." In Babylon sunworship had its inception with Nimrod as its center.

"Until comparatively recent years it has been commonly assumed that what we call our 'western civilization' had its origin in the valley of the Nile. Ancient Egypt was commonly credited with being the cradle of civilization. . . . Many standard textbooks on the subject have been completely antiquated

by information gleaned at the point of the spade by modern scientific investigators. The unearthing of the ruins of ancient Chaldean cities reveals that much of the civilization of ancient Egypt was borrowed from a much older and much broader civilization which flourished in the Tigris-Euphrates valley at a time when the Nile valley was inhabited by tribes of wandering nomads."[15]

### DISPERSED FROM IRAN AS A CENTER

Something happened to disrupt the plan of the rebel Nimrod. Was that something the confusion of tongues? In Genesis 9:19 we read, "These are the three sons of Noah: and of them was the whole earth overspread." And in Genesis 10:32, "These are the families of the sons of Noah . . . and by these were the nations divided." It is interesting to note that one man was given his name because of this division. Of the elder son of Eber (Gen. 10:25) the "name of one was Peleg [division]; for in his days was the earth divided." This was in the land of "Shinar" or "Sumer" in Mesopotamia. From thence came the dispersion.

"It is no longer probable only, but it is absolutely certain, that the whole race of man proceeded from Iran as from a center, whence they migrated first in three great colonies; and that these three branches grew from a common stock, which had been miraculously preserved in a general convulsion and inundation of this globe."[16]

Nimrod was the builder of the city-kingdoms of "Babel, and Erech, and Accad, and Calneh, in the land of Shinar" (Sumer). The earliest inhabitants of this lower Mesopotamian valley were the Sumerians, and the Sumerians were descendants of Ham, the Cushites. The descendants of Ham are listed in Genesis 10:6-20, and it is interesting to find in this list the origin of many of the great nations of antiquity. The name Cush is preserved in the name Kish, the ancient Egyptian name for Ethoipia. Mizraim, another son of Ham, is the common name for Egypt in the Bible. From

15 Muir, James C., His Truth Endureth, 1937, pp. 29, 30.
16 Jones, Sir William, The Origin of Families and Nations, 1807, Vol. 3, p. 194-197.

Canaan, another son of Ham, came the warlike and wicked Canaanites, who are mentioned so frequently in the Bible. Of the sons of Canaan, Sidon gave his name to the city of Sidon in Phoenicia, and from Heth came the great Hittite empire, whose very existence, and the Biblical authority in mentioning them was questioned by historians a generation ago, but who are now known to have been a mighty but iniquitous people.

The Sumerians were the earliest inhabitants of Mesopotamia. They were the children of Cush and established themselves in a number of small city-kingdoms each with its own ruler. The names mentioned in the Bible— Erech, Accad, Calneh—are all recognized by the historian as belonging to this Sumerian period, as follows:

"The earliest inhabitants of Mesopotamia in times approaching the historical period are known as the Sumerians. The earliest Sumerian monarch who exercised dominion as far as the Mediterranean is Lugalraggizi, king of Erech, 2775-2750 B.C."[17]

The Encyclopedia continues: "According to the actual figures of the records, the first capital was founded at Kish 3768 B.C., *which is clearly a mythical date.*" The first Sumerian monarch is dated between 2775 and 2750 B.C., which is most conservative when compared with the wild chronological guesses of some ethnologists.

The fact is: the Nimrod Cushites built upon the ruins of a civilization that existed in Shinar before the Flood. They were the inheritors of the pre-Flood civilization of the descendants of Cain. Says Johns: "They glorified their ancient cities by ascribing to them a foundation in the ages before the Flood."[18] A Babylonian inscription now in the British Museum reads: "These are the kings after the Deluge." From the Encyclopaedia Britannica, article Babylonia, we read:

"(1) The prehistoric age, a period without written historical records before 3500 B.C.
"(2) The early Sumerian period, from before 3000 B.C. to about 2500 B.C."[19]

Every student of the Bible acknowledges a pre-Flood period reaching back approximately from 4000 to 5500 B.C. The Bible dates the Deluge and the early Sumerian period at about 2500 B.C., (the Alexandrian Septuagint dates the Deluge at 3246 B.C., with 2263 years back to Creation), the Encyclopaedia at about 3000 B.C. Not much discrepancy here! And so it is with other Babylonian dates.

The Sumerians were overrun by the Semites. Just how long the Sumerian period continued, it is impossible to estimate. Professor Clay and other chronologists find the names of one hundred kings in early Babylonia and lengthen their chronologies to conform to a consecutive rule of these one hundred kings. They forget that in these early days, all the kingdoms were small city-kingdoms, and that the kings were, many of them, contemporaries. Back of Hammurabi's day the nations were mere tribes and their wars were merely wars between these city kings. Even in the days of Hammurabi, a contemporary of Abraham, we have the record in Genesis 14 of the battle of the Kings. Here is a long list of kings, four against five, who formed a confederacy in their warfare. That Abraham was able successfully to war against them in rescuing his nephew, Lot, proves that they were not much more than feudal kings.

*Wanderings of the Three Branches*

For some reason, the Cushites in Babylon, all at once, swarmed out all over the earth. The historian Ridpath says, "We don't know what caused the Hamites to leave Chaldea."[20] The Bible

17 *Ency. Brit.*, 14th Ed., Vol. 15, p. 294.
18 Johns, Dr. C. H. W., *Ancient Assyria*, 1912, p. 3.
19 *Ency. Brit.*, 14th Ed., Vol. 2, p. 843.
20 Ridpath, John Clark, *Loc. cit.*, Vol. 2, p. 450.

account of the confusion of tongues gives a definite reason for the dispersion. Going east, these Cushite tribes overran the Semites in Elam, then continued their eastern trek. Under the name of Dravidian they settled all along the coast of India and Ceylon. When pushed on by the later Aryans, they peopled the islands of the Pacific. A branch of these early Cushites from Chaldea became the Mongols who peopled China and Japan and later crossed over into America and became the American Indians.

Baldwin says: "If, as I believe, and as the antiquities show, these ante-Sanskrit civilizers were Cushites, the Dravidian speech must have been a very ancient form of the Cushite tongue."[21] Again he says on page 265, "The ancient Malayan civilization, like that of India, came originally, we may suppose from the old Arabian."

Du Halde says: "The posterity of the sons of Noah, spreading themselves over the eastern parts of Asia, arrived in China about two hundred years after the Deluge."[22]

Ridpath says: "The first trace of the Mongols is just east of Cush in Beluchistan."[23]

Encyclopaedia Britannica says: "It seems reasonable to assume that the Australian natives are Dravidians exiled in remote times from Hindustan."[24]

These quotations could be multiplied. C. J. Bell[25] says there is no doubt that the Chinese are descendants of the Sumerians, and he devotes several pages to showing the similarity between Chinese words and Sumerian words. In Anderson's "The Story of Extinct Civilizations," we read:

"The earliest civilized race possessing this country 'Between-the-Rivers' [Mesopotamia], as the Greeks long afterward called it, appear from the inscriptions to have been the Akkads—'Mountaineers,' in their own language—who at an unknown period, had descended from the highlands on the east and northeast. This wonderful people, who have recently been presented to history for the first time, are proved, by their language in the inscriptions, their features as shown in many sculptures, their art and religion, to have been Turanian by descent, that is, they belonged to the yellow or Mongolian family, which have already been mentioned.[26]

The Hamitic peoples occupied the continent of Asia and the continents of North and South America. So also their footprints are found in the sands of Africa. Of the Egyptians, Ridpath says: "These Egyptians were descendants of the older Hamites in Asia."[27] Mizraim is the Bible name for Egypt and Mizraim was the son of Ham. Ethiopia is an interesting word, reaching back into remote Bible times and forward to the days in which we live. The words Cush and Ethiopia are identical as used in the Scriptures, so that in a very special sense Ethiopia is Cushite in its origin, though strongly Semitic in its later development and in its language. As to the Africans south of Ethiopia, it is presumed that they are a mutated race, springing from the Hamitic peoples of North Africa.

The Cushites went everywhere after the dispersion. The other branches of the Noachian family followed, and it is easy to trace their pathway into various parts of the earth. The very names are significant. From Madai, son of Japheth, came the Medes. From Javan, another son, the Grecians were descended. The Greeks were called Ionians by the Persians and Hebrews. It is not difficult to see the connection between Javan and Ionian. The Celts

21 Baldwin, loc. cit., p. 200-242.
22 Du Halde, Jean B., Description of China, 1738-1741, p. 130.
23 Ridpath, loc. cit., Vol. 1, p. 176.
24 Ency. Brit., 11th Ed., Vol. 2, p. 956.
25 Bell, C. J., The Witness of the Monuments.
26 Anderson, Robert E., The Story of Extinct Civilizations, 1912, pp. 24-25.
27 Ridpath, John Clark, Great Races of Mankind, 1893, Vol. 2, (Book 4) p. 447.

are the ancient Cimmerians. From Togarmah came the Armenians. In the names Tubal and Meshech we find the "Rosh, Meshech and Tubal" of Ezekiel 39, and the Tobalsk and Moscow of today remind us of these Bible names.

The Semitic peoples are of greater interest to Bible students than are the others, for it was through them that the worship of Jehovah was continued through the centuries. In the word Elam, one of the sons of Shem, we have the ancient name for Persia. In Asshur we find Assyria. From Aram came the Syrians; from Lud the Lydians; and from Arphaxad we have Abraham and his descendants. The chronological dated line of the Bible is traced through Shem, then Abraham and Judah, and finally to Jesus. While the Bible mentions various peoples and nations, it is concerned primarily with the blood-line from Adam to Jesus. It is this line that gives us a continuous chronology. And by this line we are enabled to assign dates to the various monarchs of other nations. Instead of going to the uncertainties of the records of nations which had no chronological systems, we find our certainty in the Bible record and make our comparisons with this record as our rule.

### THE PROBLEM OF TIME EXAGGERATION

Sargon I was the first king of Semitic Babylonia. Says Myers, "The first prominent monarch is called Sargon I, a Semitic king of Agade, one of the great early cities. An inscription recently deciphered makes this king to have reigned as early as 3800 B.C."[28] The Encyclopaedia Britannica dates the Agade period at 2500 B.C. There is a great difference between 3800 and 2500. The Encyclopedia is 1300 years nearer to the Bible dates than is Professor Myers. There is extreme uncertainty in any chronological dates for the nations of antiquity. That the historian estimates and guesses and conjectures is proved by the immense difference in their dates. When Breasted gives the year 3400 B.C. for Menes, the mythological king of the first dynasty of Egypt, and Myers gives 4500, and Mariette, Bey gives 5004, and Böckh gives 5702, and Josephus gives 2350, and Bunsen in one edition gives 3623 and in a later edition gives 3059, and Wilkinson puts it at 2691, and Rawlinson dates it between 2450 and 2250, we know that there must be a little game of guessing being played by historians.

"It is a patent fact, and one that is beginning to obtain general recognition, that the chronological element in the early Egyptian history is in a state of almost hopeless obscurity. Modern critics of the best judgment and the widest knowledge, *basing their conclusions* on identically *the same data*, have published to the world views upon the subject which are not only divergent and conflicting, but which differ in the estimates that are most extreme, to the extent of about *three thousand years!*"[29]

### THE PASSION FOR EXAGGERATION

Will Durant, who loves to play with immense eons of time, recognizes exaggeration in others. He says: "In 1907 Pumpelly unearthed at Ana, in southern Turkestan, pottery and other remains of a culture which he has ascribed to 9000 B.C., with a possible exaggeration of 4000 years."[30] If Mr. Durant admits a possible exaggeration of 4000 years, we may be pardoned for putting 3000 more years into the shrinkage.

Rawlinson adds his testimony to uncertainty in these words:

"Probably we shall do best to acquiesce in the judgment of Dr. Birch: 'Menes must be placed among those founders of monarchies whose personal existence a severe and en-

28 Myers, P. V. N., *General History*, 1895, p. 42.
29 Rawlinson, George, *History of Ancient Egypt*, 1880, Vol. 2, p. 1.
30 Durant, Will, loc. cit., p. 108.
31 Rawlinson, George, *The Story of the Nations*, 1891, pp. 53, 54.

lightened criticism doubts or denies.' . . . If the great Menes . . . be a mere shadowy personage, little more than *magni nominis umbra,* what shall we say of the twenty or thirty successors of the first, second, and third dynasties? What but that they are shadows of shadows? . . . The kings, if they were kings, have left no history."[31]

These quotations are given merely to show the folly of building our chronology upon the quicksands of human speculation. The man who glibly ascribes a date of origin that is away out of line with the Bible record is not bringing sound scholarship into his history. What is true of Babylon and Egypt is true also of China. The Encyclopaedia Britannica in commenting upon the "Three Emperors" of China, the mythical first kings, says: "Whether these emperors ever existed is uncertain. At best they are but legendary figures. . . . Even the historicity of the three is to be viewed with some doubt."[32]

How ridiculous, after all, are the supposed gradations from barbarism to civilization with thousands of years in between. As far back as we can measure time, the age of stone and the age of metal have been contemporaneous. The North American Indian was living in the conditions of the so-called "Stone Age" thousands of years after Babylon had reached her zenith and crumbled in the dust. His implements were like the implements of the "Stone Age"; the flint arrowheads, the gouge-shaped stone tools, the grooved hammer-head for lashing to a handle, the same shapes and ornaments in pottery—and yet he was found in the 16th century of our era! It would be as reasonable to date the American Indian of 1600 A.D. at 25,000 B.C. as it is to assign some bones found in a cave in Europe to 25,000 B.C. because stone implements are found by the side of them.

Will Durant even admits that, "It may be but a jest of time that only those of them who lived in caves, or died in them, have transmitted their bones to the archeologists."[33] How do we know they were cave-men because their bones were found in caves?

## MAN BEGAN CIVILIZED

Archeology speaks with finality in regard to the antiquity of man and the beginning of civilization. How remarkable to find that the earliest culture in Mesopotamia and Egypt is the highest. The story of civilization, as far as Egypt and Babylonia are concerned, is a story of retrogression. There is degeneration, not evolution. The tide of culture rises and falls with the centuries, but the earliest is the highest.

"Instead of proving a process of evolution, the history of man as found in the archeology of Egypt is a consistent record of degeneration. . . . Indeed, we can no longer start Egyptian culture with the beginning of the dynastic ages. . . . Instead of finding the dawn of a developing humanity, we see mankind already in the high noon of cultural accomplishments. Instead of nomadic dwellers in shaggy tents, we look upon the works of enduring stone. Instead of brutish, Egyptian ancestral artifacts, we find a pottery culture that is really superb. It almost seems that the farther back we go into Egyptian antiquity, the more perfect was their culture and learning . . . stone knives have handles of beaten gold. At once we are impressed with the anomalous fact that the stone age was thus synonymous with the age of metal. The golden handles on these stone weapons are engraved with scenes common to the lives of the people . . . a high development of the engravers art. . . . The culture of Egypt starts on a magnificently high level and is later reduced to a tremendous degree by a consistent record of degeneration."[34]

Modern discoveries have revolutionized our ideas of ancient civilizations. The Spade of Archeology has proved to be more mighty than the pen of history. Many books on antiquity must be re-written, for apparently

32 *Ency. Brit.,* 14th Ed., Vol. 5, p. 531.
33 Durant, Will, *loc. cit.,* p. 29.
34 Rimmer, Harry, *Dead Men Tell Tales,* 1939, pp. 41-45.

there was no "savage life" or "stone age" in ancient Mesopotamia. Let the Magazine *Asia* tell the story:

"They are so rich and so old, their wealth of material is so surprising, that they revolutionize our ideas about Mesopotamian civilization in the fourth millennium before Christ. The treasures of Agamemnon at Mycenae or those of the palace of Minas at Crete cannot compare with them. . . . Once again human culture looks toward Asia as its source and the spring whence it spread over the rest of the world. . . . The Ur cemetery belongs to a period when Menes was establishing the first dynasty in Egypt, and already, writing is here no less advanced than on the Nile, and the technique of the arts and crafts is definitely superior.

"How comfortable to find that the distant ancestors of six thousand years ago like so many things that we like—games and music, gold and silver plate, jewels and fine garments, works of art, engraving, stone and metal relief, painting! Where shall we look for a beginning of that savage life from which we are told we are descended? Is it too much to say that these beautiful works of art revolutionize our ideas of Mesopotamian civilization? The history of the city of Ur and of the land has been carried back into periods for which there existed no records. What is truly surprising is the wealth, with the high level of culture, of that remote age and the further we go back the more finished seems to be the art of Sumeria. Old Asia is coming into its own as the traditional source of the best in humankind."[35]

Dr. Sayce, one of the leading authorities, has this to say on this MOST IMPORTANT matter:

"Neither in Egypt nor in Babylonia has any beginning of civilization been found. As far back as Archeology can take us, man is already civilized, building cities and temples, carving hard stone into artistic forms, and even employing a system of picture writing; and of Egypt it may be said, the older the country the more perfect it is found to be. The fact is a very remarkable one in view of modern theories of development and of the evolution of civilization out of barbarism. Whatever may be the reason, such theories are not borne out by the discoveries of Archeology. Instead of the progress we should expect, we find an advanced society and artistic perfection. Is it possible that the Biblical view is right after all, and that civilized man has been civilized from the outset?"[36]

*How Far Back with Certainty?*

How far back do these ancient civilizations go? In the center, Mesopotamia, we cannot trace them even to 2500 B.C. The great mounds with their successive pavements have been preserved in the sands of time through thousands of years, awaiting the spade of the archeologist. The graveyards of past civilizations are uncovered; one by one the reign of the kings is opened before us. How far back do they go? Where does the lowest pavement begin? Whose name is inscribed on the ancient sun-dried bricks? While Babylon had no chronology, there is an occasional date that can be set with certainty. There is Hammurabi, for instance, the sixth king of the first dynasty. He was a contemporary of Abraham. The historians all agree that his reign must be placed not earlier than 2100 B.C. If there were only five kings reigning between Hammurabi and Sargon, the period of this dynasty would reach back to about 2200 B.C. Before these Semitic peoples, the Sumerians were in Mesopotamia. They list their kings to the Flood and before the Flood. Why, then, is such an effort made to date Sargon at 3800 B.C. and the Sumerians still earlier?

What is true of Babylon is true of Egypt. Says the McClintock and Strong Cyclopedia, "Egyptian technical chronology gives us no direct evidence in favor of the high antiquity which some assign to the foundation of the first kingdom. The Egyptians themselves seemed to have placed the beginning of the first dynasty in the 28th century B.C."[37]

35 *Asia*, March, 1929, article "Wonderful Discoveries from Ur of the Chaldees."
36 As quoted by Dawson, W. Bell, *The Bible Confirmed by Science*, 1936, p. 141.
37 McClintock, John, and Strong, James, *Cyclopedia of Biblical, Theological, and Ecclesiastical Literature*, 1874, Vol. 3, p. 90.

## Time Estimates from Population Growth

But someone says: "Does the date 2500 B.C. [the Deluge] give us time enough for the inhabiting of the earth?" It has been estimated that 250 years after the Flood, the population of the earth could have been several millions. The race was hardy in those early days.

The children of Jacob and their children and followers, numbering 80 people, after 215 years in Egypt, part of the time in slavery, increased to more than a million, and possibly two or three million.

At the present time the population of the earth approximates two billion. It is not difficult to prove that the approximate Biblical date for the Deluge is the only date that is possible with our present population. Were the race 10,000 years old, the earth could scarce contain the multiplied billions of people. Allowing for war and famine and pestilence, our present population demands a date of origin for the race that coincides with a period approximately 5000 years ago. Mathematics disproves and makes absurd the wild guesses of 100,000 years, 50,000 years, even 10,000 years for the time of man's origin.

## SUMMARY AND CONCLUSION

"Hath made of one blood all the nations of men." According to the science of Biometry, "The statistical study of variation and heredity," the human race is a unity. We are all brothers — black, brown, and white —we are blood relatives. And for the great body of believers in Christ, the redeemed of earth, there is a double relationship—the natural birth and the spiritual birth. The whole family in heaven and earth are one spiritually in Christ Jesus. We are interested in the Bible story of the origin and relationship of the races; we are more concerned with its marvelous story of salvation, of the nation of the saved, and their unity in Christ.

The Bible record is true. The cradle of civilization is Mesopotamia; the Semitic, Japhetic and Hamitic origin of the races is sustained; the unity and blood kinship of all the races is a scientific fact, demonstrated in the laboratory as well as in history; the unity of languages in their three-fold origin is indisputable; and the chronology of the Bible is in line with the findings of archeology and the facts of history.

"That precious document, the 'Toldoth Beni Noah,' or 'Book of the Generation of the Sons of Noah,' well deserves to be called 'The most authentic record that we possess for the affiliation of nations!' " "The Mosaical narrative conveys the exact truth—a truth alike in accordance with the earliest classical traditions, and with the latest results in modern comparative philology."[38]

Archeology gives the final word to Ethnology. The Bible is confirmed by the spade. Let the books on antiquity be revised—the Bible needs no revision. "The scientific investigations of many cities, . . . has antiquated many standard histories. . . . Many scholarly works of Biblical criticism have also been rendered obsolete by the material evidence recovered at the point of the spade of the scientific investigator. . . . The early history of accounting, of architecture, and of transportation will have to be revised, but it is worthy of note, not 'one jot or one tittle' of the Bible will have to be revised."[39] Thank God for such a testimony and for His Wonderful Word, wherein we find not only the records of human life, but the Life of the Ages, Jesus Christ our Lord.

---

38 Rawlinson, George, Seven Great Monarchies, 1884, pp. 29, 34.
39 Muir, James C., His Truth Endureth, 1937, p. 5.

THE

# BULLETIN

OF

# CREATION, THE DELUGE

## AND RELATED SCIENCE

| VOLUME IV | MARCH, 1944 | NUMBER 2 |

## HIGHLIGHTS OF THE SYMPOSIUM OF BIBLE SCIENCE*

* NOTE: The Symposium was held in Los Angeles, California, November 26, 27, and 28, 1943, under the auspices of this Society. Seventeen papers were submitted and seven formally assigned addresses were given. Nine of the papers were on the *"Species Question,"* which, because of unfinished study, have not yet been published. Prof. L. M. Ashley of the College of Medical Evangelists, Loma Linda, California, read a still unfinished paper on *"Species in Relation to Paracitism and Degeneration."* Two papers and two formal addresses were given on the topic *"Science in Evangelism,"* but the Board of Editors are as yet releasing for the BULLETIN *only material on objective science.* Already published in the BULLETIN are *"The Causal Significance of Embryology,"* by Dr. Cyril B. Courville (No. 5, 1943), and *"The Origin of Races,"* by Varner J. Johns, J.D. (No. 1, 1944). A paper on *"The Silicification of Fossils,"* by Dr. R. E. Hoen of the Department of Chemistry, Pacific Union College, is still being studied and developed, as is a paper on *"Geologic Time and the Removal of $CO_2$ From Air and Land,"* by D. J. Whitney. There was an extensive field report on fossil human footprints, with casts, photographs, and several written statements collected by E. E. Beddoe; and C. L. Burdick and Ben F. Allen participated. But lest this research project be hindered, the details will not be published at this time.

—THE EDITORS.

The BULLETIN is published by, and is the official organ of the "Society for the Study of Creation, the Deluge, and Related Science." The Editorial Board is comprised of Professor George McCready Price and Dr. Dell D. Haughey. It is printed at the Collegiate Press, Arlington, California. For members the BULLETIN is free, and extra copies 50 cents each (each number priced according to size); for non-members it is $2.00 per year and this number is 65 cents. All correspondence should be directed to the Managing Editor, Mr. Ben F Allen, 219 North Grand Avenue, Los Angeles 12, California.

## I. THE DELUGE ON THE SCREEN, A SYNOPSIS

### A System of Visual Lectures of the Most Pictorial Features of the Deluge

*By* HERBERT C. WHITE AND BENJAMIN FRANKLIN ALLEN

"The Deluge on the Screen" was only a preview of fragments of four lectures which are still unfinished. This is the work of the Committee on Visual Lectures. Herbert C. White, the Chairman, was in charge of the meeting. He opened with a clear and challenging portrayal of the need and the opportunity of the visual method today. He is widely known in this country and in China as a master of the screen in lecturing and as a rare artist in photography. He told of his thrills in actually recording on film not only the very plants and animals supposedly entombed by the Deluge, but also the mighty upheavals and the work of the angry waters. He declared, "My faith has been changed to knowledge." He said that "the Deluge seemingly was purposely conducted in such a way that the results could be conclusively and strikingly demonstrated by photography. It would be utterly impossible for an event like that described in Genesis to occur and not leave abundant and overwhelming proof, from hundreds of points of view, involving all of the physical sciences, many of them aided by photographic methods. It is high time for those who really believe the Genesis account of the Deluge to cooperate in our efforts to demonstrate it in the earth, as this is the only scientific reply to its denial by agnostic scientists."

Mr. White introduced Mr. C. L. Burdick of Arizona, an experienced technical mining engineer and geologist, a member of this society and a graduate geologist from a leading state university. Mr. Burdick had made slides of some fossil human footprints associated with dinosaur tracks, and had assisted Mr. E. E. Beddoe in making casts. He explained the vast difference in the supposed geologic age of the two creatures and how devastating to evolution is their association in the same strata. He also showed on the screen some footprints carved in rock by Indians, illustrating the marked differences from fossil footprints.

The present writer was then introduced to give the geologic data as the Deluge pictures were screened. He prefaced by reading several of the more than twenty Scriptures on the Deluge outside the Genesis account describing the upheavals of the surface of the earth, the skies blackened by volcanic smoke and dust, the heat from below, and the action of the waters, all of which wrecked the former surface of the earth and completely transformed it, *as postulated by this Society for scientific investigation.*

*Four Outstanding Visual Features of the Deluge* were screened in beautiful nature color: (1), river and ocean terraces left by the receding waters, and the subsequent cutting and eroding away of the basic land surface left by the Deluge; (2), the catastrophic burial of fossils illustrated by some very choice specimens; (3), the vivid and beautiful rock coloration resulting from the solution and distribution of coloring minerals while the great mass of sediments were still wet; (4), the extreme bending of the sediments during their necessarily brief wet state.

*The River and Ocean Terraces* ("raised beaches") are very striking and easy to photograph. They are offered as records of where the mighty waters stood and raged for a brief time, as they declined by stages. This subject was treated by Prof. George McCready Price in a paper for this

Society.[1] Another leading geologist collected a vast array of data from many geologists in all parts of the world tending to show that all of the terraces of oceans and lake basins, seas, etc., *incline upward from the equator to the poles as compared to present sea level.* He postulated, as we do (along with many leading geologists from the present back 250 years), that the earth was disturbed in its rotation, causing the waters to become unbalanced, overslop the lands, and to seek the poles. The Deluge evidently was over all for a time, partially filling with sediment the lower places and in fairly level areas smoothing off great plains in many parts of the world.

Since then, *exactly the opposite* has been in progress. Streams are now cutting, grooving, and eroding sharply and deeply into the deposits of that smooth surface. At the Symposium, river terraces and plains along the St. Francis River in Southern California were shown, and the upper reaches of Piru Creek, a tributary, were shown to be even yet in process of cutting the original over-all surface. In these and all regions of slight rainfall, these features give a strong impression of the marked recency of the Deluge.

One of the striking evidences of *"the one event"* and a disproof of the geologic ages is the fact that all land surfaces whatsoever, regardless of the millions and billions of years which are assigned to some of them by evolutionists, have been eroded exactly the same, to the same extent, even where the extremely "young" is intersprsed with the extremely "old." Also, in all regions of mountains, the small irregularities incident to the action of the uplifting processes are just as little erased or smoothed out in the extremely "old" mountains as in the extremely "young" mountains. All of these features lend themselves very forcibly to photography, and they can be easily explained to all. These and other features were treated in a Bulletin of this Society by the present writer.[2]

*The Catastrophic Burial of the Fossils* is also easy to demonstrate on the screen. Big, little, old, and young are all mingled together as fossils, while in nature they are seldom found that way alive. The large numbers of closed shells, many of which are now empty, testify to the live burial also, as no such shells are found on beaches in this condition, as they open immediately at death. *The enormous masses of shells, merely as such,* prove catastrophic burial, because so very few dead shells are ever now found in any water or beach owing to their rapid solvency in the water. Almost none in these large masses show any work of this water solvency before burial. Vast climatic change is universally demonstrated by shell life, especially reef corals, and almost exact former temperatures of the air and the waters can be known. Most beautiful nature-color pictures of shells were screened.

Fish, for instance, can be shown scarcely ever to be preserved as fossils today, and they only as a few stray bones or vertebrae. But we threw on the screen fossil fish complete in every detail, even showing the soft lobes at the end of the tail and fins, and in some cases the rainbow colors on the scales. The vast quantities of these is one of the most famous legends in all geology, but also one of the greatest paradoxes to evolutionary geology, completely baffling to the uniformitarians. Cataclysm seems to be demanded by these facts.

In plant life the perfect preservation of the most delicate forms are often found in the shale or sand be-

1 Price, George McCready, "Visible Proofs of the Flood; Its Universality and Its Recency," BULLETIN OF DELUGE GEOLOGY AND RELATED SCIENCE, Vol. 1, 1941, No. 5, pp. 110-119.
2 Allen, Benjamin Franklin, "Significance of the Strata of the Earth," BULLETIN OF DELUGE GEOLOGY AND RELATED SCIENCE, Vol. 1, 1941, No. 4, pp. 93-108.

tween the coarser and more massive layers, even in areas containing coal from the same plants. It would seem that the waters were in tidal or other periodic rushes, and, during the brief lull between each on-rush, while the finest sand and mud were settling to the bottom, the lighter plant remains had a chance to spread out in natural form and settle in more perfect condition. Layers of different assorted earthy materials run in cycles everywhere, and this is world wide in occurrance, whether there were any plants to be saved with the fine material or not.

Perhaps one of the strongest proofs of catastrophic burial of animal life was its chemical effect on the surrounding minerals. They immediately formed many acids, such as carbon dioxide, and these actively dissolved many minerals. When the decay was complete, and the chemical action re-spent, these dissolved minerals re-christalized and cemented the whole large mass, including the fossils, into a hard rock. Gigantic strata or thin layers of hard rock were thus formed by the chemical action of the fossils. If calcium were plentiful enough, and if some heat was formed by the chemical reactions (or from volcanic or other earth-sources), then the recrystalization was often complete enough so that *marble* (instead of mere limestone) was formed.

Especially in remains of animal life were formed a group of very strong solvents called "albuminoids," capable of dissolving silica and all other minerals which were nearly insoluble in the acids, as these albuminoids act like alkalines. The brevity of these actions of course is obvious. The solvents seeped out in all directions, and the final result was often a crust on a thick mass of rock around one or more fossils, called a *concretion*. Needless to say that this can be well shown by photography, especially as rich colora-

tion was often caused by the chemical action. But leached bones, old shells, or rotten wood could have no such effects. Life still alive or fresh, often with the flesh still on, is demanded. Placer gold miners in arctic regions continually find specimens still fresh, *hide, hair, and flesh*. Uniformitarian theories are thus put to rout. Cataclysm is indicated.

*Rock Coloration Can Be Best Accounted For* on the basis of a brief period of universal wet sediments. Under present conditions, with negligible amounts of wet sediments and nearly all hard rock or dry fragile shale, etc., the even coloration and even change of color could not be possible, as the water carrying the mineral colors cannot now penetrate the rock except in cracks. Neither could coloring minerals be brought near the surface and evenly distributed in great masses of sediments under present conditions. This all apparently had to be done during the necessarily brief mud stage. Heat from below also at that period, (and from chemically formed heat within the mass itself), could also only have been of brief duration. *These processes coincided*, a fact that is very pertinent.

Most of the landscape coloration, on a large scale, was shown to be due to different degrees of oxidation of iron, the colors resulting being variously influenced by white, black, or blue colors in non-metallic material. Local areas are often influenced by small amounts of silver, copper, sulphur, manganese, carbon, etc., various chemical compounds of these with other elements. But iron, being by far the most abundant, and perhaps forming the largest number of colors by its varied degrees of oxidation and its other chemical compounds, has by far the most influence on the coloration of the rocks and soil. Carbon (mostly black) prevents iron from oxidizing, forming a dark carbonate, and in this way prevents it from forming brilliant colors. But where there is an excess of iron, the excess oxidizes, changing the color. When clays containing carbon and iron are burned, as in brick-making, the carbon is burned up, thus freeing the iron to oxidize; and it forms its vivid yellow, brown, and red colors. Vast geological areas have been thus heated (metamorphosed), with this result, affording every degree of oxidation and coloration of the most beautiful hues. The colors of such masses were changed from black, blue, or green to yellow, brown, or red, or combinations of these. As iron takes on more oxygen, its color becomes yellow, then brownish, then red. Over vast areas, such as the great Painted Desert of northeastern Arizona, where much of the coloration is from clays, the colors are almost entirely on the surface, and this is because of surface oxidation from the chemical action of surface water and air. The desert rocks, too, are generally much more richly colored on the outside than inside, for the same reason; but in wetter climates these minerals are washed away by excess of moisture and penetrate the rocks more.

*The Main Sources of the Primary Colors* are as follows:

*White:* lime (in chalk or white limestone), sodas, borates, magnesiums, potassiums, quartz, diatomacious shale, alumina, kaoline, talc,— (all of these of course in the pure state).

*Black:* Carbonaceous material from vegetation, manganese oxide, and other mineral compounds.

*Blue:* carbonaceous material, some copper-sulphur combinations, some silver compounds, and many minor sources.

*Yellow:* from sulphur in many forms, from the first step in iron oxidation, etc.

*Browns:* mixtures of greens and reds, also second step in iron oxidation.

*Red:* from complete oxidation of iron, and from many other mineral oxides and other compounds, all very much less in amount than iron.

*Greens:* mixtures of yellows with blues, silver chloride, and blue carboniferous material tinged with yellow iron oxidation, etc.

*Purples:* reds and blues mixed.

Naturally, there is every gradation of each of these color influences, resulting in everything the most gifted painter can possibly do, *and more.* The writer is acquainted with a color expert who gathers 100 separate colors in and around the Painted Desert of Arizona. Question: Did anyone ever see rock and soil coloration form an unharmonious color scheme in a landscape? The writer never has seen such a thing.

Rock coloration of course we have treated in a special paper somewhat thoroughly and technically, and it is the plan of the Visual Lecture Committee to publish this and other full and thoroughly tested and documented data to accompany all of its screen lectures. The extremely rich coloration screened for the Symposium was from the famous Calico Mountains and Rainbow Canyon, both in Southern California.

*The testimony of Contorted Layers* to the brief mud stage of the great mass of sediments is positive, proving the same brief period as do the fossils and the coloration. Whole ranges of hills and mountains and even mountain systems were crumpled like old-fashioned ribbon candy, but without a break, *for a brief period only.* Escarpments a thousand or more feet thick can be photographed which waved almost like the waves of the ocean. Considerable breakage occurred as the material hardened, and later, and this again *gives force to the argument* that the mass was all soft at first. This is one of the most striking evidences that the crust of the earth was being heaved and shaken about during the Deluge, calling for earth-motions which were evidently connected with mountain-making and the disturbance of the ocean in overslopping the lands.

It is by detailed data like these that we get proper conceptions for comprehending the work of the waters of the Deluge, and for recognizing in the strata proper subjects for the work of the Committee on Visual Lectures. Quite profound work has to be done, both in the library and in the field, before pictures with a message can be taken.

To sum up, the erosion since the Deluge, especially in dry climates, makes us realize how *very recent* that event was. The ocean, lake, and river terraces picture the decline of the over-all waters, and indicate something of the postulated disturbance in the earth's rotation. The catastrophic burial of the fossils, *alive,* is demonstrated by both physical and chemical

data of many kinds. The vivid rock coloration demands universal mud conditions for a short period, as do the bent and crumpled sedimentary layers.

The present members of the Visual Lecture Committee are Herbert C. White, and Evangelist R. R. Spear. Dr. Roy A. Falconer (just moved away) was formerly chairman, and was very active. C. M. Platner, a talented photographer for the screen, is another member. The writer is assisting with the geological features. The plan is to develop several lectures for distribution at near cost, including strong written textual material dealing with all scientific facts. All ambitious college instructors, public speakers dealing with nature or science, all evangelists who are looking for something as beautiful as it is scientific, should be interested. A very large field of work is this, with great possibilities. "Speak to the earth, and it shall teach thee . . ." Job 12:7-10.

## II.  DELUGE SEDIMENTS AND CANYONS ON THE CONTINENTAL SHELVES, A SYNOPSIS

### By BENJAMIN FRANKLIN ALLEN

The present writer submitted a paper (as yet unfinished) to the Symposium on the recent discovery, on a world-wide basis, of sediments all around the continents on the bottom of the ocean *which are much too coarse and many times too far from shore to be explained by means now in operation.* They are not only coarser, but many times farther from shore, and in many times deeper waters than the ocean can now transport even fine sediment. The "continental shelf" was formerly defined as the ocean bottom out from shore to a depth of 600 feet. But these coarse materials are found more than twenty times that depth, and often several

hundred times farther from shore than would now be possible. Statements from geologists were read that the tides, the greatest storms known, the ocean currents, and ocean bottom animals are all totally inadequate to solve this mystery.

In the discussion, it was brought out that present ocean shore deposits of the world as a whole *average less than a mile in width,* though of course at the mouths of the largest rivers they are much wider. This is a far cry from an explanation of the far-flung coarse sediments, and a far cry from what was necessary in laying down the wide level plains regions of the world now on land. (Evolutionary geology is restricted for the origin of the latter to shore deposits and to river deposits.) Authority was cited, however, that "the deposit of rivers is negligible" at present.

The writer offered as the explanation of the coarse sediments beneath the ocean waters around the continents, the violent oversweeping of the ocean *as a whole,* having been unbalanced by some sudden catastrophe, as yet not well defined, which affected the whole earth. Several geologists of note have postulated causes for such a catastrophe, generally some sudden disturbance in the earth's rotation.

Speaking further on the predicament of evolutionary geology in accounting for the great land plains, the speaker cited an instance in geological literature of a dumbfounded geologist who saw, by cross-bedded layers, *that the waters had flowed alternately both ways,* in back and forth sweeps. And, furthermore, *it flowed,* not merely was agitated on the mere surface as is the ocean today. It is a fact generally accepted that almost all sedimentary deposits were laid down in comparatively shallow *moving* water, not over 600 feet deep. But the bottom of the ocean is by no means moving at all, in that sense, and besides, even in the greatest storms, it cannot influence or disturb sediments below "60 to 70 meters." Moreover, the investigators point out that only in a few spots in the oceans can anything like this depth be reached by any *present* agitation. And these figures apply even to the lightest muds on the bottom. However, coarse sediments are found as deep in the ocean as 18,000 feet. The necessity for catastrophe is apparent.

Add to this the statements of the geologists who recently reported the widespread and sporadic ocean floor deposits of coarse material around the continents and islands, *that the surface features on these shelves are exactly like those on the adjacent coastal plains on land,* and we get a point closer to a better conception of the great marginal off-washing that apparently formed the present coastal plains *at the same time and manner in which the continental shelves were formed.* This is only a brief statement of our working theory.

Recently, and even since the Symposium, tremendous attention has been devoted by the world's leading geologists to the problem of the origin of the submarine canyons. Two geologists in one of the most prominent universities proposed for the origin of these canyons exactly what a late geologist had proposed for the ocean terraces ("raised beaches"), that the rotation of the earth had been suddenly unbalanced, for a time shifting much water toward the poles, during which the submarine canyons were cut. That late geologist found that the raised beaches all incline upward toward the poles. A leading museum of science publishes the picture of a large and very accurate model of a part of the continental shelf from New Jersey northeastward, including one of the deepest submarine canyons in the world, off the mouth of the Hudson river. This canyon is steeper and a little deeper than the Grand Canyon. The whole phenomenon tends to confirm the present writer's impression (which he is investigating) that the deductions of these men need no unreasonable changes to fit our conceptions, or postulations, of the most fundamental dynamical features of the Deluge.

THERE ARE NO CONCLUSIONS AS YET

No conclusions can be drawn as yet, owing to the incompleteness of the data. There may be some relation between the coarse bottom sediments, found too far off shore and too deep for any present or uncatastrophic processes, and the action of the waters as we postulate for the Deluge. The data seem to indicate that most of the features of the continental shelves are similar to those of the coastal plains, in materials, in surface, in slope, and in other ways indicating a common origin. Owing to the extremely sparce present deposits of the ocean shores, the old theory of the origin of the continental plains and coastal plains by present means or by any process known to geology, is open to grave doubt. Perhaps we should investigate the conception that the continental plains, the coastal plains, and the continental shelves all had their origin in the same manner and at the same time. But how?

One eminent geologist (Barrell) proposed catastrophic motion of the oceans as a whole, by violent earthquake action, as having eroded out the "hacked" outer edge of the continental shelf, and the submarine canyons.

Further research may reveal the possibility that the unbalancing of the oceans by a rotational disturbance of the earth *might set in motion the great body of the oceans as a whole.* This might overslop the lands as a whole, even the highest plateaus, and this bodily sweeping motion might be able to erode and deposit material to a depth of thousands of feet below sea-level on the continental shelves and beyond. During such a disturbance there would be no shore lines, and the coastal plains and continental shelves might be undergoing approximately this same erosion and deposit, giving them a common origin in both time and manner.

If the rotational disturbance should be of the most probable sort, a wabbling motion, it is commonly thought that the ocean waters would seek the polar regions, to an extent depending on several factors. This would lower it in the equitorial regions, and perhaps allow for the cutting of the submarine canyons.

However, at present we lack sufficient data to form even theories, to say nothing of proposing or attempting to prove a definite thesis concerning these great problems of the continental shelves and the submarine canyons. If any large number of people are able to see the main outlines of the problems from this brief synopsis, the purpose will have been accomplished. Adequate conclusions may have to wait indefinitely.

## III. THE QUEEREST THEORY OF EVOLUTION ABANDONED*

### The Abandonment of the Theory That Changes During Prenatal Life Recapitulate Evolutionary Ancestry Leaves Evolutionists In Serious Predicament

#### *Reported by Benjamin Franklin Allen*

The queerest theory in all the realms of evolution finally has been abandoned by those who are supposed to know the real facts in the case, and this concept happens to be the scaffolding for a whole group of other postulates still more important. This was the freak theory that the animal, as it develops before birth, evolves rapidly through such progressive changes as to recapitulate the changes during the supposed hundreds of mil-

*Though the paper on which this synopsis is based has been published in the BULLETIN, an exception is being made in including a synopsis here owing to the importance of the subject.

lions of years of evolution from the one-celled form of life which "chanced" to form of itself as the first of all life. Dr. Cyril B. Courville, who had written two previous papers for this Society on this subject, gave a third at the Symposium, "The Causal Significance of Embryonic Development."

He reviewed briefly his other two papers,[1] explaining the basic ideas of the theory and touching upon its history, then outlining the steps by which its abandonment has come about. For nearly one hundred years that theory had formed the main background of the supposed biological basis of evolution, as firmly as did the now abandoned nebular theory. Both of these old theories reigned supreme in the realms of science, *with a high hand,* as supremely as does now the most fundamental of all modern scientific conceptions, *the theory of uniformity in nature.*

Dr. Courville gave many examples of the growth of the unborn animals of radically different kinds (though seeming to the casual observer to be parallel for a time), yet they proceed from the first to pass by the shortest possible route, by the most economical and efficient processes, each to its own specific destination.

The evolutionary interpretations appear to be based on superficial implications, as there actually is no time or process or change in its prenatal life when any animal takes a single false, supernumerary, "historical," or unnecessary step or shows any essential relationship to any other animal either before or after birth. Though an elephant and a mouse may be outwardly similar at first, the chromosome numbers and other marked differences can always be discerned, and the difference in these and the direc-

tive powers at work lend no aid to any theory of relationship. Trains running out of a grand central terminal may run on parallel tracks for a time, but each engineer has his own separate orders, and we all know the results. The resemblance of embryos is only superficial, and no one can furnish any evidence that any form of pre-natal life spends any time, energy, or material reminiscing on its supposed evolutionary ancestry.

We might well ask WHY, if recapitulation be a law of nature, it is not manifested in plant life also? But instead, we hear nothing of it from evolutionary botanists. We hereby further press this matter upon them by reminding them that the law of Mendel works in exactly the same mathematical proportions and principles in both plants and animals. Therefore, *why not recapitulation also?*

We see going on the skillful organization of a new being *necessitating design,* and the impressions gained lead to no other conception than that there is guidance of a higher order than is within the province of mere protoplasm to supply. In fact, we may well ask: Is there any such thing as MERE protoplasm? Dr. Courville gave biological illustrations which seem to permit of no other explanation than guidance of a higher order.

So far as the chemistry is concerned, or the routine physiological processes of growth as such, it might be granted, for the sake of discussion, that these operate within what is *commonly considered* the realm of natural law. But natural law can never be anything but mere routine behavior. Physics now describes natural law as governing only in the grosser processes, *not in the infinitesimal.* It has no initiative in itself, whereas the prenatal growth is seen to possess or be acti-

---

1 Courville, Cyril B., M.D., "The Recapitulation Theory," BULLETIN OF DELUGE GEOLOGY AND RELATED SCIENCE, Vol. 1, 1941, No. 2, pp. 21-60, and "The Causal Significance of Parallelism," Vol. 2, 1942, No. 1, pp. 1-35. His third paper is published in the BULLETIN OF CREATION, THE DELUGE, AND RELATED SCIENCE, Vol. III, No. 5, 1943.

vated by initiative, a directive of constant creative construction. Biology manifests countless examples of this. In fact all biological processes are manifestations of it. Several well-known doctrines have been built up to account for this, such as holism, vitalism, life as a separate entity, cell intelligence, entelechy, etc. Mutations, for instance, utterly defy natural law in their origin (or at least cannot be reduced to the routine of law), but, once they appear, they reproduce and hybridize according to the law of Mendel. Leaders of physics, in dealing with the atom and with all sub-atomic features, have found that the same utter flouting of law goes on, though, as in the mutation, once an event has been initiated, the behavior henceforth conforms to law. These facts have led physicists (dealing with non-living matter) to decide *that an initiating Mind, back of natural law, permeates the universe.* Surely no one will be able to deny by proof that this conclusion may be applied even more strongly to the realm of life.

THE RESULTING DILEMMA OF EVOLU-
TIONARY BIOLOGY AND GEOLOGY

In his two previous papers Dr. Courville had shown that specialists in the study of prenatal life have practically all abandoned the old idea of recapitulation. But still it lingers in the minds and textbooks of thousands of teachers of biology *who do not know or who ignore the fact that it has been abandoned.* It was long thought to be one of the main if not the main foundation of biological evolution. The recapitulation theory of prenatal life still vitally influences

millions of people toward evolution, especially students. Its syllogisms are still pounded into their minds like those of Newton's laws of motion. Also, very few specialists in other sciences than that of pre-natal life even among biologists, know that it is now thoroughly discredited, and they still contend for it and use it in their thinking. The situation is full of contradiction and confusion.

The geologists are one important group of this kind. In geology, the supposed sequence in which the evolving forms of life appeared on earth was largely taken from this theory of recapitulation. Through paleontology (the study of the history of life by the fossils) it helped to supply the present standard sequence of the supposed geologic ages, as Professor Price has described in a Bulletin of this Society.[2] Each major layer of fossils, supposedly (according to the theory) in regular sequence from bottom to top, was and is considered to be synchronized with the development of the leading fossil life as illustrated in its pre-natal state. But, now that this old theory of the prenatal changes recapitulating a billion years of evolution is abandoned, *with the evolutionary geologists still using this system of geologic ages,* these geologists seem to be left "riding a dead horse" without knowing it.

In this discussion, the attention of the group was given to the urgent need of getting this very important information before the scientific world, and before the millions of students, teachers of biology, and educated people generally.

2 Price, George McCready, "Geology and the Recapitulation Theory," BULLETIN OF DELUGE GEOLOGY AND RELATED SCIENCE, Vol. 1, 1941, No. 3, pp. 61-76.

## IV.  SUBSURFACE TEMPERATURES AND DENSITIES
## OF THE EARTH

*Reported by Benjamin Franklin Allen*

Data on underground temperatures, pressures to the center of the earth, ocean temperatures at all depths, temperatures of glacial ice with depth, and the freezing point of water at various pressures—all were discussed at the Symposium by Mr. H. L. Transtrom, research engineer at the Los Angeles Bureau of Power and Light.

The rate of increase of heat from the surface of the earth is so great that, were this rate to continue to the earth's center, the heat would be inconceivably high. The earth could not exist as a solid body. Test holes show great irregularity between areas in near-surface heat of the earth. Though recent estimates of this excessive near-surface heat are slightly less than former estimates, *still this is a mystery to evolutionists.* It bears no relation whatever to the heat which certain theories say begins to increase very moderately at a much greater depth and continues to increase to the earth's center.

Mr. Transtrom ventured no opinion to account for this condition, but the writer suggests, *for consideration only,* that the excessive near-surface heat is a remnant of the heat developed near the surface by the intense friction of the crumpling of the crystalline crustal rocks during the Deluge period. The subsequent world-wide dying out of volcanism (which started apparently as a world-wide sudden initial outburst due primarily to this cataclysm), accompanied by the decline in all surface heat, like hot waters, seem to point to such an explanation. The very rapid rate of heat radiation from molten lava is fast enough to permit this view. Mr. Transtrom presented evidence indicating that, outside of volcanic radiation of heat,

the amount of heat radiated from the earth at present is negligible, and that the surface and near-surface warmth is supplied by the sun.

Another view taken by many geophysicists is that the earth 40 to 60 miles down is much above the melting point at surface pressure, though prevented from melting by high internal pressure, and that, *should the surface be broken or fissured by some sudden event,* somewhat relieving the pressure at near-surface depths, the material would at once melt, start expanding and rising, and even reaching and rising far above the surface in favored locations, as molten granite, basalt, etc. The writer sees no necessary conflict between these two views, and even offers a third possible source of heat, *that of chemical formation.* Geologists and geophysicists have suggested this as a source of heat. Such a terrific and sudden catastrophe, *aqueous, dynamic, and thermal,* including the mingling and burial of a world of plants and animals perhaps hundreds of times more abundant than at present, seemingly could not avoid the production of large amounts of heat from chemical sources in certain localities. However, these are all *research projects,* not conclusions.

Mr. Transtrom cited data showing that the temperature of the ocean at the surface has a seasonal variation of not more than 30 feet in depth; that from 1000 feet down to 2000 the temperature rapidly decreases to near freezing, and from 2000 to the bottom it is constant at about 2 degrees C. above freezing. The heat content of the ocean is due almost entirely to the heat of the sun, and heat from radioactive elements in the sediments on the ocean floor is said to be negligible.

These facts are urged in denial of any heat radiating from the earth on the ocean bottom. The present writer has obtained data indicating how very slowly the *undisturbed* surface of water radiates heat but how *very rapidly* it gives it off *when agitated.* This feature should be investigated in an effort to discover how rapidly the warm pre-Deluge ocean could have given off its heat during the terrific agitation of the ocean and the extreme cold postulated for that event.

Like the constant temperature in ocean depths, Mr. Transtrom cited field test-hole data that showed the temperature of deep glacial ice on land to be constant at about 2 degrees C. below freezing, after only a comparatively few feet of temperature fluctuations near the surface. These facts on ice have a bearing on the possible depth to which glacial ice could accumulate without melting on the bottom by its own pressure, a point raised by Prof. George McCready Price. It is true that *compression,* with decrease of volume, raises the temperature. However, *static pressure alone* does not increase or maintain temperature. Some contend that the flow of ice is not caused by any change of temperature but by pressure alone. One experimenter buried some lead bullets in a chunk of ice near the top. Then he subjected that ice to 40 long tons of pressure per square inch. The ice did not melt, nor did the bullets sink deeper into it. However, data are still being sought, and are still insufficient to draw conclusions.

Mr. Transtrom noted some laboratory discoveries that the freezing point of ice declines as pressure increases, to a given point. Several different forms of "heavy" ice are thus produced. Then the freezing point rises as pressure continues to increase, till under 291,600 lbs. per sq. in. pressure, ice is formed at 176 degrees F., (and perhaps at higher temperatures under greater pressure). But these facts have not yet been fitted into nature, and few if any such high pressures could be reached by natural ice. These data may or may not be of value in our field, but absolutely no such facts should be overlooked.

After Mr. Transtrom presented these features, the writer gave some of the results of temperature tests in drill holes all over Siberia in the perpetually frozen subsurface areas. There are many very pertinent details, but the main contention among those in charge of the tests is whether this condition was and is caused by current climatic conditions, or was produced by the abnormal chill of the so-called "last ice period." Frozen ground is found far too deep to be at all affected by present climates, however, and unfrozen layers are found sandwiched in between. Water is occasionally found between two frozen starta. These Siberian researches are highly potential for Deluge Geology, in several respects, and must be watched with care.

## V.  HYDROLYSIS OF MOLTEN GRANITES
### Its Possible Significance in Deluge Geology
#### *Reported by Benjamin Franklin Allen*

That granites and all plutonic and magmatic rock which have risen to the earth's surface in the molten condition is well known. Inasmuch as Deluge Geology postulates that almost all of this action coincided with the Deluge, and had the same or a closely related cause, the question arises as to the chemical and physical effects of the overflowing waters upon these molten and convulsing masses, many of which occupied large areas. If hydrolysis did thus occur, and on such a grand scale, the position is taken that this can be demonstrated beyond any doubt.

In our field research in granite areas we have given some attention to this subject. At the Symposium, Mr. Harry Hurlbut showed by chemical equations the alteration of granite constituents into the common metamorphic and granitoid rock by the addition of $H_2O$ and $CO_2$, the two substances which from various sources were abundant at the cataclysm of the Deluge. He showed that the end products are metamorphics or decomposed granite, *or they are merely sand and clay.*

There is a large mass of geo-chemical data on the decomposition of granites, and much of it is very encouraging to our labors. No researches from our viewpoint have ever been published, though considerable work has been done by members of our Society in all fields of mineralogy. All evidence tends to confirm the theory that the derivatives of granites resulted from the addition to and the reaction of the mineral-carrying waters rich in $CO_2$ with granite magma (molten granite).

Even pure water, overflowing and mingling with seething and convulsing molten granite uplifts, or volcanoes, or with outpourings of basalt, would soon be saturated with countless substances. Intense heat causes extreme saturation, but the intensely cold atmosphere would force quick precipitation. Mr. Hurlbut added $CO_2$ in harmony with its well known volcanic sources, and from the postulated but much more abundant source, the sudden destruction of a world of plants and animals perhaps hundreds of times more abundant than at present—both sources being a part of the "movie" of the catastrophe now being investigated. (This may be a start toward accounting for certain tremendous beds of clay, lime, etc., *apparently precipitated from solution* as saturated warm waters were exposed in shallows and shoals to the extreme cold and on contact with floating ice.)

It was formerly thought by some, Dana for instance, that there was but one route or process for granitic decomposition, one set of metamorphic steps. But since his day it has been learned that the countless varieties of granite, and the varied chemical and physical environments of the metamorphic process, *provided many different means and varieties of metamorphosis,* and this fact is now abundantly established by laboratory experiments.

All of these chemical and field investigations take on greater significance for the truly catastrophic standpoint because, for each increase of 10 degrees C. (or 18 degrees F.), *the rate of chemical reaction doubles and sometimes trebles.* When 2000 or 3000 degrees are involved, or even 1000 or 500, as in molten rock, in the presence of water and unlimited minerals and decaying life for solution, *the possibility of extreme rapidity of decomposition by hydrolysis during a thermal-magmatic-aqueous cataclysm is brought forcibly to mind.*

Therefore, this project is of first importance to Deluge Geology. The chemical and physical facts of hydrolysis may not only prove that the great heat outpouring coincided with the Deluge, but that these features are fully as essential in explaining the present condition of that material as were the mere physical work of the waters of the Deluge in laying down the sedimentary layers and the fossil deposits.

Through color-photography, some of it microscopic, all leading features of this subject are being prepared for demonstration on the screen.

## VI.  SPECIES BEFORE AND SINCE THE DELUGE

*A Conference, Reported by Benjamin Franklin Allen*

This was one of the most important discussions, and was participated in by more specialists, with more papers sent in by absent workers, than on any other topic. Bible teachings seem to call for groups of plants and animals which bring forth only after their "kind." Can biology define these groups scientifically and demonstrate the truth of those definitions? Papers were read from biologists presenting some extremely marked variations within what has been supposed to be the original Genesis "kinds." Because of these it was questioned whether it is now possible to recognize the original kinds in all cases. The late "splitter" practice of calling all or even many of these variations "good species" was not favored in the discussion. It was admitted that some of the most extreme variations which have occurred, as plants and animals have spread over the earth, are difficult to distinguish from what are commonly known as true species, as conservatively interpreted. It was concluded that, although under natural conditions now obtaining variations occur which seemingly approximate the true species, these are relatively few. Most of the experimentally produced "species" are not comparable to the "good" species, and certainly not to the Genesis kinds.

Moreover, serious defects of these so-called "new species," which have been artificially produced, were presented in detail, from original records. The publicity given these so-called "new species" has been misleading, when checked with the original data, as many unfavorable details have been ignored by the evolutionists. This type of species was discredited. It was also shown that high authorities are of late turning away from the fad of multiplying the number of species described. There is a marked "shakedown" going on. They are turning to the *principles* on which Linnaeus worked in classifying the species (of course some of his species as he defined them, have been justly modified in the light of more modern data). No evidence of crossings between these original kinds has ever been demonstrated, provided, of course, that "kind" is properly defined.

The problem was stated that, though some marked changes have occurred which are still confusing, and which approach rather closely to the original conception of true species in some extreme cases, no methods or causes now operating as proposed by biologists are apparently adequate to produce them. This part of the problem was left open, with plans for systematic written exchanges and group conferences. Much progress was made on definitions of terms, in adjusting viewpoints, and new common grounds and agreements were discovered.

---

## VII.  THE CURRENT REVOLUTION TOWARD CREATIONISM AMONG PHYSICISTS*

*By* BENJAMIN FRANKLIN ALLEN

The present writer reviewed the very significant trend among physicists toward admitting the scientific necessity for a central, initiating, mathematical Mind as permeating and governing the material universe. Physics

* This paper is still in course of preparation and only the briefest synopsis can be given here.

had long been the rock-ribbed stronghold of determinism under the mechanistic theory that *matter* is all there is in existence, and that *it alone* has self-developed into all its present manifestations. But lo, only about fifteen years ago a most revolutionizing movement started within the inner chambers of this fortress of atheism. Determinism had seized upon the laws of gravity and of motion, as discovered by the devout Newton, and attempted to convert them into its tight, purely materialistic philosophy, though never once daring to consider the true character of natural law and its necessary source, as Newton had done.

Determinists had gone so far as to deny the free will of man, denying that man is responsible for his choices in behavior, or in any other aspect of life, since man, according to this conception, is only a part of the rocks and soil, with no more responsibility for his activity than they. Of course, it might have been well recognized by liberal thinkers, and it was so recognized, that such a conception would sooner or later run afoul as scientific research continued.

After research in the atomic and sub-atomic world had developed for twenty or thirty years, the scientists finally got down to the seemingly ultimate forces and bodies constituting matter. *It was found that the old mechanistic view does not apply*. It is now admitted by all but a few that in sub-atomic affairs, natural law takes effect only after events are initiated, and regulates only routine processes of the grosser sort. The initiation of sub-atomic events appears to occur entirely unregulated by natural law as commonly understood, that is, natural law cannot be credited with the initiation of events in the sub-atomic realm.

These facts are extremely technical, and cannot be amplified in this brief; but it was soon seen that they explain a great mass of problems and puzzling phenomena in nature. No two snowflakes are alike, though Bentley photographed 15,000 of them, and the whole subject has been given exhaustive research. Scientists are apparently at last sure of this physical paradox, which portrays a complete flouting of natural law, demanding a separate preconceived plan or pattern for each flake (though the actual crystallographical growth of the flake, *a mere process*, proceeds according to physical laws). But whence the plan? And prior to plan, there had to be a purpose. Whence the firm and decisive and constant power and skill and extreme mathematics and artistry which sees to it that the plan is carried out amidst perhaps *the most tumultous environment known in all nature, the conditions under which snowflakes are formed?* "Hast thou entered into the treasures of the snow?" Job 38:22.

Profound statements from doctors, biologists, embryologists, botanists, and from the whole realm of sciences dealing with the ultra minute, show strikingly similar phenomena all through nature. The living cell and its various activities is a case in point, as is crystallography in mineralogy, *for who guides the cells and the molecules?* A personal friend of the writer holds the highest degrees in science and mathematics from the world's leading universities, and *is a firm determinist of the old school*. He occupied a chair of mathematics for 25 years. When the writer asked him how mere accident (which is his only means of origin of progress or system or law), could bring any order at all, *let alone universal order*, out of *complete disorder*, he replied: "You are asking me some difficult questions." The writer asked him how mere mathematical probability could reasonably be looked to to produce *universal* and *complete order, inasmuch as this result completely transcends every principle and concept of mathe-*

*matical probability?* He could make no definite reply. He had rested his entire case for systematization in nature on mathematical probability.

ILLUSTRATIONS FROM RADIOACTIVITY

The physicists use as an example the well-known fact that each radio-active element, like radium, is disintegrating to lower elements at a fixed mathematical rate. The maintenance of this rate is one of the things that has upset the mechanistic philosophy. The exact sequence or order of the break-down of each atomic nucleus must be regulated with absolute precision. In other words, the break-down of each nucleus must be individually dated with unthinkable precision *in advance* (either that or there is a continual ordering of each event going on), in order to maintain the absolutely steady process. The age or source of the atoms or chemical changes have nothing to do with it, and nothing man can do can alter the fixed rates in the least. *Where and what is the governing directive?* How could each nucleus, in and of itself, know when, even at all, let alone the exact instant, when it is to make the change? We seem to be again facing the same all-permeating Intelligence which previously designs and then carefully governs the formation of each snowflake, cell, crystal, etc.

Eddington, the great physicist, says of this problem: "Anything which depends upon the relative location of electrons in an atom is unpredictable more than a minute fraction of a second ahead. For this reason, the breakdown of an atomic nucleus, such as occurs in radio-activity, is not predetermined by anything in the existing scheme of physics." This brings to mind Newton's famous statement that the sources of behavior in the physical world "are certainly not mechanical." *Physics is returning to Newton.*

The famous physicist Jeans says in his late book, "Physics and Philosophy," 1943, ". . . the radio-active break-up appeared to be an effect without a cause, and suggested that the ultimate laws of nature were not even causal [the cause of the process]." Elsewhere he said, "This being so, it was almost a foregone conclusion that either *causality* or *continuity* [the continuous causes as though from the operation of natural laws] would have to be renounced, and there was no special reason for surprise when it was found necessary to renounce both." (Emphasis ours.) These are tremendous words, and they should be deeply pondered. If they are true, then the real "cause and continuity" are behind, and prior to, natural law, the latter being only a manifestation of the governing power of that source.

WHAT IS REALITY?

Radio-activity, however, is only one objective example of the failure of the old philosophy. Examples run through the whole of sub-atomic physics, and inasmuch as the whole material universe is composed of these very particles (which after all are only centers of electric energy, that is, *power and energy*, and not at all what has been commonly thought of as solid matter), the fundamental, all-inclusive importance of these discoveries is at once apparent to all. As might be expected, since matter is seemingly not "real" after all, but only energy under the absolute control of an intelligence higher than natural law, the physicists have been asking, "Then where and what is 'REALITY'?" And they have been conceiving of this transcendent Mind, or wherever conscious mind might be, as the only reality, and trying out this conception of the problem as a postulation.

Accordingly, leading physicists are making such declarations as this one from Jeans: "Again we may think of the laws to which phenomena conform . . . the laws of nature as the laws of thought of a universal mind. The uniformity of nature proclaims the self-consistency of this mind. This concept of the universe as a world of pure thought throws a new light on many of the situations we have encountered in our survey of modern physics . . . there must have been a 'creation' at a time not infinitely remote. If the universe is a universe of thought, then its creation must have been an act of thought."

What more can be expected of pure physics and honest research? What more can any or all scientific research do than this? If there is a Creator, it is certain that He is as much concerned with, and as much manifested by the material as by the mental or spiritual.

## PHYSICS NOW GRANTS FREE WILL TO MAN

This is one of the philosophical by-products of the current revolution. Eddington said: "The revolution of theory which has expelled determinism from present-day physics has therefore the important consequence that it is no longer necessary to suppose that actions (of man's mind) are predetermined. . . . To me it seems that responsibility is one of the fundamental facts of nature." The great physicist Compton recently said: "For the purposes of religion, God without intelligence would be as good as no God at all. Thus, if religion is to be acceptable to science, it is important to examine the hypothesis of an Intelligence working in nature. That such higher powers exist, cannot be denied." He stated his reason for his profound interest in the new revolution in physics thus: "It is rather that I find reason to believe in freedom [free will as opposed to the mechanistic philosophy], and wish to find whether the recognized laws of physics are consistent with such freedom." (This Society, likewise, chooses to believe in a literal view of Genesis, and wishes to find whether the recognized laws of physics are consistent there-

with. Thus we have a celebrated scientist, whom none can gainsay, who is activated by kindred motives.)

Dr. Robert Andrews Millikan, in a strong plea for the new revolution, recounts in detail and in sequence some two hundred years of the "failures of materialists" (determinists) to explain nature. This is his famous broadside of "brute fact" statements of how the materialists have been driven along from one deterministic position to another as each of the really outstanding discoveries of physics has enabled it step by step to arrive at its present revolutionized position. The problem has been to reconcile free will with the difficulty *and error* of an all-governing system of natural law, *the source of which no determinist will consent to consider* (because this takes him out of his cocoon of complete objectivity), which seems to leave no leeway for freedom of the will. *Government was confused with mere law alone,* as though *only the law* constituted all government and is self-creative and self-sustaining. Millikan says: "Now if anybody here is bothered by the reconciliation of free will with determinism, I shall be glad to state for him my own position as follows: Practical free will, or the sense of responsibility, is to me a brute fact given by direct experience," (and this is the climax of his famous "brute fact" discourse).

It would seem inevitably logical, apparently, that free will in all creatures is a gift from the great Source of free will, the only being capable of exercising it without limitations. It would seem equally logical, and in harmony with nature, to ascribe not only natural law to that Will, but its much more immanent manifestations as seen in living cells, as well as in the instincts of ants, etc., instinct being invariably associated with more or less free will, but a part of animal inheritable function.

This deeply significant revolution is amazing in that it seems to be proceeding from Z toward A, as though man has been mostly having to "crawfish" out of a vast amount of his own self-created overburden of philosophic dogma. George Bernard Shaw characteristically stated this well in November, 1943: "Today, people know the XYZ of everything, but they don't know the ABC."

## CONCLUSION

The present writer, in giving this lecture to the Symposium, read many statements from many leaders in physics, showing that this science no longer erects any bar to a literal Bible faith. Some approach nearer to the Bible than do others. Most of this may be deism, but, even at that, deism is a long leap toward the light from the dismal darkness of atheism and pantheism based on mechanism and a stubborn refusal to consider real origins, *ultimate origins*, for fear of getting away from *purely objective data*. In dealing with such thinkers, the writer has found many of them *personally resentful* toward any conception of any power higher than man, very much as is portrayed in Romans from the 19th verse to the end of the chapter (though Paul is here writing of a people who do, *partially, believe*). But we must seek them out, search them out, become perfectly well informed on their viewpoints, that we may know how to help them. And remember, they have amassed a vast amount of factual data which we can use, and we can interpret it to them in ways that will at least form a very profitable line of contact with them. *Thus they can do much for us.* For these reasons, and for many others, we must make the most of this great revolution now in progress revealing to the scientific world the Creator as described in the Bible, making known to millions, especially young people, these profitable facts.

## VIII. RECENT PHILOSOPHIC TRENDS TOWARD CREATIONISM*

### By PASTOR JOHN F. HUENERGARDT, PH.D.

One of the interesting and almost inexplicable things in the history of mankind is the fact that human beings began to deal, first of all, with what has since become the subject-matter of philosophy and theology, with wonder about their religion and about the power which governed and controlled them, and about their ultimate destiny and about what was possible or conceivable after death. Men were concerned with those thoughts and those speculations long before they took the very first steps to study definitely and precisely the nature which surrounds them or to examine and attempt to understand the institutions, social, political, and economic, under which they lived. In other words, religion, in the largest sense of the word, has accompanied human life from its earliest reflective consciousness and is older than philosophy, older than science, and there is no part of human activity and human interest which it has not at one time or another held in its grip.

However, in the history of the last one hundred or one hundred and fifty years, science—modern scientific inquiry—came to occupy the center of the intellectual stage. Since then,

* NOTE: This section of the Symposium was led by Pastor John F. Huenergardt, who finished in the graduate college of philosophy in a leading state university. For many years he labored in Europe, and collaborated with the famous Kepler Bund in defense of Bible faith.

there has been a distinct schism between science and religion, and between ordered and tested knowledge and the field of faith, and much that once seemed so obvious, so natural, and so necessary, has now, for well night two hundred years, taken a very different form.

But some very interesting things are happening. After all that science has done, after all that physics has discovered, after all that chemistry has revealed, what do we find? We find now that the physical sciences begin with a hypothesis and end with a conjecture. The area of observation is accurate, definite, and mathematically exact, but the great physicists of Germany, of France, of England, or of America today find themselves asking the precise question which earliest man asked so many many ages ago: Where did human life begin, and where will it end? And the physicist, the chemist, the mathematician, despite the absorbingly important content of his field of observation, is no better off to start that inquiry than were the earliest of mankind.

In other words, faith in a power underneath, behind, above, is *more than* coming back, with fewer objections from leading scientists, to be the ruling hypothesis when you ask from where did we come, to what are we indebted for control and order and direction, and where are we going. The physicist cannot tell you, the chemist cannot tell you, the mathematician cannot tell you. The scientist is no wiser when he faces that question than was Adam in the Garden of Eden, but he has made it perfectly plain to you, in very significant ways, which have absorbed the attention of mankind, that those questions are still there, pressing for an answer. The consequence is that religion again naturally rules not only the life of man, but particularly every effort he makes in the field of letters. We are

getting away from the materialistic absurdities of a science falsely so-called, and mankind is called to worship again at the altar of creationism.

Today we are safe to say that we are acquiring a more just estimate of the time required for geological and human changes; *and a more careful* reading of the early narrations of Genesis, with an honest *appreciation* of the geological history of early man, will yet convince the thinking world that man *did* appear suddenly on this planet about six thousand years ago; that he *was* the product of special creation and not the outcome of a process of evolution.

If man be that product of special creation, and not the result of a process of evolution, then, if it does not follow of necessity, it becomes more than probable that his religion, the bond which binds him to the unseen Deity, who called him into existence, *was communicated to him.*

Recent contribution to philosophy has saved us from catastrophe. We were near thinking of the world as a finished and predetermined show, in which our initiative was a self-delusion and our efforts a devilish humor of the gods, but we now more and more come to see the world as a stage, and the material of our own originative powers. Before, we appeared to ourselves as cogs and wheels in a vast and dead machine; now, if we wish it, we can help write our own parts in the drama of creation.

Mr. President, the religious aspect of civilization is the original aspect, the most long-continuing and the one which no matter what happens can never be escaped. Religion holds in its hands the comfort, the satisfaction, and the destiny of the human race. Strike it out, and what becomes of tomorrow? Dark, black, comfortless! Strike it out, and what beomes of the whole doctrine of unselfish human service? Why trouble to serve one's fellows? As so many animals, they are coming and going like the crops of the field. Why trouble? But the moment you are seized *and powerfully seized,* by the religious insight and instinct, and by the religious feeling, then you give a very different answer to these searching questions. Then you have something for which confidently to hope, then you have something in which truly to believe. Materialistic evolution is not science, it is a philosophy, the philosophy of despair.

---

## DISCUSSION
### Reprted by Benjamin Franklin Allen

In the discussion that followed, many questions were asked Pastor Huenergardt as to the specific *fields* of philosophy and their changing attitudes. The attention was finally centered on the field of psychology. "A hundred years ago or more this science was called by many 'soul psychology'," he said, "but soon many psychologists ceased to believe in the 'soul.' Psychology lost its soul, and it was called 'psychology of the mind.' But it lost its 'mind' also, and it finally was dubbed 'behaviorism.' It has had its baptism in the oceans of evolutionary philosophy, like all of the sciences. But, still like some of the other sciences, the day came when men began to feel impeded by the barnacles of philosophical interpretations, and began to study psychology *objectively, for its own sake.* This led to the study of behavior on the basis of research.

The result is that today psychology not only erects no or few barriers against Bible faith, but some of its leaders are finding in the spiritual teachings of the Bible much of the true basis of that science."

When asked to give a list of such leaders and their works, he complied, and has consented to give the Society a paper or papers dealing with his fields of the science of psychology relating to materialism and Bible faith, and to philosophy. The science of the mind, and the psychology of the Scriptures, and their bearing on the underlying philosophies, are of course fully as important in the discovery of the Creator and His works as are the physical sciences. They are indispensable in the necessary discernment of truth and error in the uncertain space between objective science and the tangled webs of philosophy.

---

## IX.  WHY ARE CREATION AND THE DELUGE IMPORTANT TODAY?
### By BENJAMIN FRANKLIN ALLEN

Our purpose is to help large masses of people to understand the purport of our labors.

For example, the most spectacular single item at the Symposium was a report of the discovery of several new sites containing fossil human footprints, some of them of giants, and some of them associated with dinosaur tracks and even in strata much older

(?) than the age of the dinosaurs—on the reckoning of the evolutionists. In one leading scientific journal, a paleontologist said that if these things can be fully established, geologists and paleontologists "may as well quit and get a job driving a truck." He meant that his science would be scrapped; however, our view is that it would be just coming into its own.

But many otherwise well informed people do not understand. They ask "Why?" and "How could this final proof about the fossil footprints substantiate belief in a literal version of the Genesis account of Creation and the Deluge?" They wish to understand more of the significance of Creation and especially the Deluge today in science and Bible faith. Many can see no reason whatever for any special attention to the Deluge, and especially do evolutionists spurn all reference to it with extreme loathing (that is, the Deluge as a world-wide *geological* event, or anything but a mere legend).

In the minds of Bible believers, the great modern increase of scientific knowledge should have pointed man to his Creator. And this it did, up to less than two centuries ago, when Bible believers began to give way to unbelievers in the development of science, and Bible believers began to lose control of education, and especially scientific education, because they failed to see its importance to Bible faith. The study of science then soon began to be conducted as though nothing except that which can be tested in the laboratory existed. The modern science revolution became one of the greatest obstacles to Bible faith. Largely owing to tremendous *industrial* progress, science gained great prestige. It developed an all-inclusive philosophy of its own which would completely supplant Bible faith or deny its leading features.

Unbelief today simply points to the earth and its life as self-creative (or at least capable of unlimited change), which it claims has progressed in harmony with present processes through about two billion years. During much of that time these changing and supposedly evolving life-forms are conceived as having been buried in water-laid sediments which now form the major sedimentary layers, and thus a supposed progressive record of evolving life was kept. (This is the basis of the concept of uniformity in nature— *that present processes have continued to create for billions of years and will never be interrupted by any "unnatural" events.*) This is the most fundamental creed of modern philosophy, eduation, social progress, and, among many educated groups, of religion itself, for many excluding all moral or spiritual forces or events from sources external to man himself. Of course, all beliefs (and unbeliefs) have to be based on a cosmogeny of some sort. In a sense, TIME is the most important factor of belief as well as of unbelief.

But the Bible, read straightforwardly, we submit, teaches that the Creator created the earth and its life only a few thousand years ago, and completed it in six literal days. In a few centuries the surface was disrupted and destroyed by a world-wide catastrophe of water and crustal convulsions which buried and fossilized the life then flourishing, leaving ill-adapted remnants for the most part.

This Society takes the position that the reality of the Creation and of the living Creator are the crucial features of the controversy. Many lines of research, involving all of the sciences, are under way to prove, as far as may be possible, that the Creator acted substantially as recorded in Genesis (though the mechanics of the process may not now be definable in terms of science). And vital data are being assembled to show that the continuing presence of the Creator, both personally and through His laws of nature, is logically and scientifically necessary.

In order to account for the present disrupted condition of the earth and the degenerative condition of its life (so vastly different from its first state), a study of the Deluge and of the life-forms which it supposedly interred is necessary. From this viewpoint the nearest possible approach to an understanding of the earth and its life as created, and especially life, is to study the fossil life. Geologically, evidence is being offered that the main basis of evolutionary theories is a mere misinterpretation of the layers of sediment and other effects of the Deluge. *What could strike more fatally at the very heart of the theory of uniformitarianism?* Belief in a universal Deluge and belief in uniformitarianism are *mutually exclusive.* Thus the Deluge, merely as a geological event, becomes of supreme importance. In fact, next to Creation itself and the present world, it should be the most important scientifically, and the focal point between the two.

## MORE REVOLUTIONARY THAN NEWTON'S DISCOVERIES

Deluge Geology is making rapid strides toward demonstrating the truth of the former Edenic condition as described in Genesis. It is doing this by showing the very superior quality of the life not many centuries after creation, as indicated by the fossils buried by the Deluge. The former ideal Edenic climatic conditions in all parts of the earth can be shown with surprising accuracy by a study of the temperature and other requirements of similar forms of life today. The indications of the sudden character of the destruction, too, its brief duration, its very sudden climatic change, and how every foot of the earth's surface (and often many thousands of feet) demand just such a catastrophe, are being shown in many ways. Even the famous theories of the origin of the earth, and of the solar system, are shown to be now mostly abandoned by scientists. The origin and deposit of mineral ores, and of the rocks themselves, all of them, we are now reasonably capable of being attributed to the processes and events of the Deluge or to conditions resulting from them. But the concept of uniformity in nature as the basis of the origin of the present world now practically dominates the educated classes, especially those influenced by scientists. This is as firmly fixed in their minds as are Newton's discoveries. *But that the Creator described in Genesis is the God of nature, and that Creation and the Deluge can possibly supplant uniformity as the basis of cosmogeny—* THAT is the most revolutionary conception in both science and religion perhaps ever to be offered. (Is this the counter-revolution of the great modern apostate science revolution?)

For nearly two hundred years philosophy and education have been increasingly adapting themselves to the theory of continuous and uniform creation in nature (the geologic ages) till that adjustment is practically complete. The springs of knowledge such as libraries, schools (from kindergarten to graduate college), the press, the radio, and practically all scientific research, are permeated with it. Popular education and social science proceed from that viewpoint as a foundation. Even the popular churches and ministry have bowed to or compromised with it, building up a huge system of faith pretending to be Biblical, but neither scientific nor Biblical. It is a case of over-science-mindedness resulting in blindness both scientific and spiritual.

One of the saddest and darkest nights of the Christian faith was a period of about 100 years when Christianity seemed to have no scientific escape from the geologic-age system, the basis of uniformitarian philosophy. THAT, more than anything else, first forced itself upon the church leadership, and there it is to this day, in the form of various compromises, or in no compromise form at all. "Modernism" arose holding more boldly to it than do the others. One compromise is that the geologic ages correspond to the six literal days of creation week as recorded in Genesis. A still more odd compromise is that the geologic ages elapsed before creation week, and this is the one held even by most Fundamentalists today. None of these positions will stand the scrutiny of the Bible, let alone of science, *and none is capable of more than a feeble resistance to the uniformitarian theory and its philosophy.* Indeed, they lead right into its camp.

However, for 40 years Prof. George McCready Price has been completely refuting the geologic ages, (1), by proving that the strata are not in the order or sequence proposed by that system, and (2), by indicating that the Deluge was responsible for the deposit of the strata. But large numbers of religious leaders, through the neglect of science, are not capable of comprehending the facts involved, while others lack the courage to break away from the overwhelming prestige of the established dogma. Before this method of interpreting geology was discovered, the camel had already gotten into the tent of Israel, *and there it stays.* Millions of sincere Christians, brought up in this system, still struggle on, in vain opposing agnosticism and certain details of evolution, or intending to do so, but still ignorantly embracing the most fundamental basis of evolution. These struggles, though valiant, are often inco.isistent, and cannot lead to victory.

As Price pointed out, *the Deluge is the cause of the chief geologic changes since Creation, and it is the only possible scientific reply to the uniformitarian system.* However, the vast superstructure rolls on, like the giant juggernaut that it is, carrying pyramided and repyramided upon it, like a new Tower of Babel (but already accursed with a confusion of tongues), most of the religious people of today, and nearly the whole educated world.

But, for all of these vast superstructures *to be found wanting by the unanswerable proof of the simple Genesis narratives*—that would eclipse all records of scientific, philosophical, and spiritual revolutions! *It would perhaps be the most drastic dissolutionment in the history of the world since the Deluge itself!*

And can Bible believers now conceive of a more needed shift of faith in the minds and hearts of men? If God is going to judge mankind, as the Bible declares, will He not at least show man these things in time for escape? God's love still yearns for man's salvation, and His yearning makes evangelists of all of His children, *even the most highly specialized scientists.*

## UNIFORMITY IN NATURE VS. CHRIST'S SECOND COMING

There are many people to whom the Old Testament is very sacred, and they have just as high regard for the Genesis cosmogeny as do Christians, but they do not accept the New Testament. To them the work of this Society should appeal strongly, and they are fully eligible to participate, *along with all who take literally the Genesis account of the origin and history of the earth and its life.* The relation of these issues to the Christian doctrines, like the second coming of Christ, though strongly appropriate for Christians, are only the personal views of some Christian members of the Society, *and do not bind or exclude any non-Christian believer in Genesis* from the work of this Society. This Society has erected no sectarian barriers whatever. It asks no questions as to creeds other than its own, and its own it holds only to insure adequate unity of effort.

One of the leading themes in the Old Testament (as well as in the New from the Christian viewpoint), is Christ's second coming and the resurrection, accompanied by great physical events affecting the earth. But, of all of the despised miracles to which present-day philosophy objects, THAT is the most objectionable. Nothing could be invented to render man less expectant and less prepared for that event than the great modern system of uniformity. Doubtless the same theory was used to talk down Noah's warning, and it swept away the belief of all but eight people. It is a supreme counterstroke, manifestly the working of a mind or minds in direct opposition to the mind of the Creator. And it is apparently back of the whole controversy to discredit the Creator in the minds of men, and to blind them to His just character, His laws, His announced judgment upon all, and even of His existence.

The doctrine of uniformity in nature is not only the leading conception about nature today, *but it is the spearhead of the opposition to the Bible message of the second coming of Christ.* The Bible itself foretells that this would be the case. It also repeatedly compares the events of the Deluge with those of the time of the second coming, and the significance of the Deluge and of the Creation are both foretold as an essential part of the message of the second coming and of the judgment. Proof of the Deluge as an actual event would not only put "teeth" into the warnings, but it finds a huge class of highly educated and scientifically minded people who are fully able to comprehend all scientific aspects of the situation. Thus that event is now indispensable as a means of demonstrating the actual physical effects of God's judgment and wrath, and to serve as an understandable message to scientific classes and a cutting edge to the warning message. While we have every resource of science at our command, Noah had no recourse to such aid, for the hitherto undisturbed Edenic conditions tended to argue against all catastrophism.

What more logical and appropriate approach could now be had to instill a reasonable faith in the physical aspects of the second coming, in the events foretold us affecting the condition of the earth, and for the earth made new, than the actual scientific demonstration of the Deluge? The best way to get some idea of what the prophets picture for the life and climate of the new earth is the study of the life and climate before the Deluge. Perhaps the most pointed single passage in the New Testament revealing some of these things is found in 2 Peter 3, and Weymouth's rendition of it is recommended.

MILITANCY'S SUPREME OPPORTUNITY

This Society holds it imperative that believers present physical proof or reasonable evidence from nature in support of Bible statements to meet the just demands of science and the spiritual needs of sincere seekers after truth. With all available facts of nature before us, and even the promised guidance and wisdom of the Creator to aid us, we are obligated to present this evidence, and have no excuse whatever for not doing so. The modern science revolution is not necessarily an evil in itself. It may well be only the result of the neglect or default of believers to keep pace with the needs of man in his intellectual and scientific progress. Believers are merely far behind with the present truth. The situation should be regarded as a supreme opportunity awaiting a more militant Christianity.

God's ministry in nature should be used to free man's mind and unlock an entrance to God's ministry in the heart. The extreme peace of heart, joy of mind, and love for man which personally experiencing the presence of God in our inmost souls brings to us—*these are the well-springs from which all of the activities of our Society start*—and the whole purpose is that others might be drawn into that marvelous state, without which life is not worth living.

THE

# BULLETIN

OF

# DELUGE GEOLOGY

## AND RELATED SCIENCES

| VOLUME IV | JULY, 1944 | NUMBER 3 |

## CONTENTS

## PHYSIOLOGICAL EVIDENCES OF DESIGN IN THE HUMAN BODY*

### *By* ARCHIBALD W. TRUMAN, M.D.**

Physiologists, anatomists, and other scientists have only begun to get vital glimpses of the wonders of the human body temple. I wish to try to offer this evening a few evidences that only an all-wise Creator could design, construct, and operate that marvelous mechanism, "fearfully and wonderfully made."

The body has been compared to a machine, but is this only contrast and not comparison? What machine can grow? What machine can think? What machine can reason? What machine can choose? What machine can love? What machine can develop character?

What machine can repair itself while running? Will investigation reveal a miraculous mechanism, or a machine?

And now, *to the facts.* We shall throw on the screen, and study, the blood and blood vessels, the heart, the lungs, the ribs, the cranium, the eye, the ear, and the larynx, according to the following plan:

1. *The Blood:* "The life is in the blood", now an established scientific fact; the marvel of single-file blood cells in capillaries and its logical explanation; the purpose behind the large vessels in protected areas; the

---

*A screen lecture stenographically reported.
**Medical Superintendent Glendale Sanitarium, Glendale, California.

---

The BULLETIN is published by, and is the official organ of the "Society for the Study of Deluge Geology and Related Sciences." The Editorial Board is comprised of Professor George McCready Price, Dr. D. D. Haughey and Ben F. Allen. It is printed at the Collegiate Press, Arlington, California. For members the BULLETIN is free, and extra copies 20 cents each (each number priced according to size); for non-members it is $2.00 per year; and this number is 30 cents. All correspondence should be directed to the Editors, Box 1030, Glendale, California.

ultimate secret of blood-clotting; the miracle of the red cells.

2. *The Heart:* the proportion of size to work done unequalled; why does it beat?; heart disease and the violation of natural law, as an evidence of the Law Maker.

3. *The Lungs:* the enormous total space; the exchange it affords; the cilia.

4. *The Nose:* the acuteness of the sense of smell; design in its location, pleasure and safety during food intake and its relation to taste.

5. *The Ribs:* a combination of geometrical and dynamical design; collapsible chamber, planned co-ordination.

6. *The Cranium:* how the brain is protected.

7. *The Eye:* equal to the instant focussing of any one of 3000 lenses; the pupil of man may increase light intake 25 fold; the several detailed features in cross-section; the eyes of insects.

8. *The Ear:* features impossible of pre-use or self-origin; how do we hear?; the 24,000 strings prove design.

9. *The Larynx:* the origin of the voice; the "order" for 2 billion two-stringed instruments, each with all of its tones individually distinct from those of any other instrument.

As we study each of these organs, we shall apply the logic to the facts and point out in detail the evidences for design. It would be strange if there is a person living or who ever lived who would not sincerely desire to know if there are any actual facts in their body which unmistakably point them to the Creator. Poor indeed is the soul that would disdain such a line of investigation.

### "THE LIFE IS IN THE BLOOD"

"The life is in the blood." From here on I want to take up those nine specific features of the structure of the human body and try to discover whether a Creator, an all-wise Designer, must have conceived and constructed the human body.

If we take the foot of a living frog and stretch it across the stage of a microscope and view the circulation in motion you see the arterial blood moving in one direction and the venous going in the other. Then you see the capillaries, the little hair tubes connecting the two. You see the red blood cells and the white blood cells in motion passing through these tubes single file. *How and why single file, except by design?* When I first saw that picture I felt like Herschel, the great astronomer, when he peered into the starry heavens and said, "The undevout astronomer is mad." I think the undevout physiologist is mad, for he is confessedly without any other scientific or logical explanation. God has written His name in large characters everywhere, but particularly in the structure and function of the human body, and then for scientists and doctors to study this marvelous body temple and pretend they can't find God anywhere!

You know in the olden days those ancient Egyptian sorcerers, soothsayers, miracle workers essayed to duplicate the miracles performed by Moses and Aaron but there came a time when even these heathen magicians said, "This is the finger of God." However, somehow today there are many supposedly educated, would-be wise men that will not recognize the finger of God even though it is so clearly seen.

It is interesting that the large blood vessels have all been placed in the protected areas. You know violence usually comes from the front, and if we stand in the anatomical position, you would have to cut clear through the thigh, including the bone, the femur, before you would strike any large vessels. The same is true down in the leg. You would have to go through the tibia and the fibula to get to the large vessels. The same is true here in the arm. The arteries are behind the bones in protected areas. This is one of the countless examples of design in the human body and in all life having blood vessels.

Then, just for a moment let us think of the clotting of the blood. Isn't it interesting that just as soon as the blood is exposed to any foreign condition, it will change automatically from a liquid into a solid stage, forming clots, natural stoppers that plug up the injured blood vessels and thus preserve the life current. The clotting of the blood is in itself a miracle.

Do you know that in each tiny drop of blood, a cubic millimeter (a millimeter is one twenty-fifth part of an inch) there are 5,000,000 on the average of these living, growing, functioning oxygen carriers, the red blood cells, and that that same tiny drop of blood will contain eight or ten thousand of these white blood cells, the body defenders, the policemen of the body? They attack and actually engulf and digest and destroy living bacteria and thus become our longest and strongest line of defense, that is, together with the liquid part of the blood, the plasma. Forty per cent of the blood is the solid part, the corpuscles, and sixty per cent is liquid or plasma. We have wonderfully protective bodies, immune bodies that protect us from diseases, that destroy bacteria and thus save us from their ravages.

There is an interesting point or two further that I would like to mention in regard to these red blood cells. Now they are so tiny—they are 7½ micromillimeters in diameter. A micromillimeter is a thousandth part of a millimeter, and a micromillimeter is one twenty-five thousandth of an inch, so that one of these cells in diameter is seven twenty-five thousandths of an inch. They are so small that you can't see them, and yet if those cells were placed side by side the number of red blood corpuscles in one human body would have a square surface area of 3,000 square yards, nearly the size of four city lots 50 x 140 feet.

What are these cells for? They pick up oxygen and carry it to the body, the life-giving oxygen, which enables all of the chemical changes of combustion by which our food is oxidized and energy is liberated for heat and work.

## WHAT MAKES THE HEART BEAT?

The blood could not circulate unless it were under differences of pressure, and we call that blood pressure. It is the business of this pressure pump to create blood pressure, high pressure in the arteries, very low pressure in the veins, even negative pressure as they empty the blood back into the heart. The heart weighs from eight to ten ounces. How much work do you think this little organ does in a day? It can be computed.

We can measure the blood pressure in anyone, and it is just the measure of the resistance to the force of this pump and to the circulation of the blood. We know how fast the heart beats. We can count the pulses and, therefore, it is a mathematical problem, and I am quoting good authority when I say that the average adult human heart in an ordinary day does an amount of work equivalent to lifting thirty tons, 60,000 pounds, one foot high; 60,000 foot pounds of mechanical work is accomplished by this little engine that weighs less than a pound. Talk about efficiency! If you want to put it in other terms, we will take the weight of an average man, say 150 pounds. The work that little muscle does in one day is equivalent to lifting a human body 2½ miles into the air. Isn't that interesting? Who made it? Was it accidental?

Why does it beat? Now it was my privilege to teach physiology for a number of years in a medical school. I went away and tried to get prepared for it. There is no part of the human anatomy which is more intriguing than the study of the heart, to me. What causes it to beat? I am going to quote from one of the standard physiologies and you can find a similar statement in many of the standard texts on why the heart beats. "The origin and maintenance of the heart beat are best explained by assuming an inherent automatic rhythmicity of the heart muscle." May I repeat it? "The origin and maintenance of the heart beat are best explained by assuming" [what can you explain upon assumption?] "an inherent," in itself automatic—runs itself—"rhythmicity of the beat of the heart muscle."

It reminds one of a question asked of Job by the Lord, the Creator,— "Who is this that darkeneth counsel by words without knowledge?" When you puncture that bombastic statement, you haven't anything but a bubble. It is euphonius, high sounding, but what does it say? Nothing. The heart runs itself. It is an automatic organ.

Well, in that same chapter this question is asked of Job, "Who hath put wisdom in the inward parts, or who hath given understanding to the heart?" The heart acts as though it had a brain. You know, friends, we have two contending theories in the realm of scientific study and investigation as to why the heart beats. One attributes the heart beat to nerves, the "neurogenic theory." The other attributes the sequences of the beats to the muscle, the "myogenic theory." When anatomists were studying the heart they cut it up into thin serial sections. They found groups of nerve cells. They thought the nerves they found there kept the heart beating.

They said the heart had a brain of its own, a governor within itself. That is what keeps the heart going. Then they cut it into large sections and they discovered that the apex of the heart beats the longest and the strongest of any portion *and it doesn't have a nerve cell in it.*

They were again at sea so they decided there was nothing left but the muscle, the myogenic theory, that the origin of the heart beat is attributed to some strange automatic impulse arising within the heart muscle. Science does not really know the cause, but revelation through Job points to God as the cause.

I am not talking on health and how to care for the human body, but I am just tempted to pause and say that death from organic diseases of the heart leads the list of all mortality statistics in the United States. And these people that are dropping down are not 80 years of age. They are 45, they are 50, and friends, there is one major reason. The heart is being poisoned. It is sensitive to poisoning. It is being poisoned. The Mayo Foundation a few years ago published some very interesting papers on angina pectoris, coronary sclerosis, and they found them at that time ten times as common in men as in women, and six times as common in smokers as non-smokers; while recognizing that there are other causes of coronary disease, heading the list is the poisoning of the heart by nicotine. The laws of nature (the laws of the Creator) cannot be ignored without penalty.

(A series of diagrams of the heart beat.) The first pulse tracing represents the normal beating of the heart. Each one of these little curves represents a beat. Note the uniformity of the curves both in force and in rhythm. There is a time of four tenths of a second for contraction and four tenths for rest. The heart takes a rest after each beat. Here we have different types of pulse variations, and underneath this very irregular malformed tracing is written, "a smoker's pulse."

### THE LUNGS, A MIRACLE OF PHYSICAL NEED SERVED BY CHEMICAL LAWS

If we should take a pair of human lungs and spread them out over a flat surface they would cover 1,800 square feet. The millions of little, tiny air sacs spread out over a flat surface would cover 1,800 square feet. On one side of those air sacs we have air that may be pure or not. It may be laden with poisonous fumes. On the other we have the finest network, finest labyrinth of capillaries. The blood goes through these in order to give off through the thin membranes the carbon dioxide from the body tissues and other wastes, and to take in the life-giving oxygen. Design, rather than accident, arranged the delicate adjustments to physical need and chemical affinity.

In the laboratory we used to take a living frog and lower his head and put a piece of lead in the trachea, opening it up part way. Then we would watch that lead go up hill at a 45 degree angle. It was wonderfully interesting. How does that come about? The trachea and these bronchial tubes are lined with cylinder-shaped epithelial cells. On the free ends of the cells lining these tubes there is a little tuft of hair called cilia, and those hairs have whip-like motion. They fall back gently and then they whip out. You can see them under the microscope. They remove coal dust, or anything that is foreign from the lungs, moving it up toward the exit. Who designed that? Is that a matter of chance or accident? Chance or accident would destroy them, instead of producing and maintaining them.

### THE NOSE SHOWS DESIGN WITH NEEDS AND LOCATION

The olfactory sense—the sense of smell—is said to be but "tasting at a distance." Do you know that if you can't smell, you can't taste? At least the taste is very obtuse unless the sense of smell is acute, and it is one of the most acute senses in the human body, and, perhaps fortunately, one of the most easily fatigued. You can pass down through the slaughter house section, where odors are so obnoxious and in just a few minutes the olfactory sense is fatigued and you are not conscious of the presence of these odors; but you can take camphor and dilute it four hundred thousand times, and you can still detect its odor. It is a wonderfully acute sense.

The nose is placed just above the chief gateway to the body, above the mouth. What for? What was the design? It is one of those marvelous mechanisms of defense by smelling the food that enters the mouth, by its location affording both pleasure and protection. We breathe through the nose and in case of poisonous fumes or gas we are enabled to detect them.

### THE RIBS, A GEOMETRIC-DYNAMIC CORRELATION

I want to say a word about the ribs. I am thinking now of evidences of design. I want you to think of the ribs as forming the bony encasement for the lungs, and how we breathe. Do you know that in the arrangement of these ribs they increase in length from above downward, and when this cage is lifted during inspiration a longer rib takes the position of a shorter one, and they are attached in front to the sternum or breastbone? Now when you lift this cage by muscular action, what is going to happen if a longer rib takes the place of a shorter one? Well, it pushes the breast bone outward and enlarges the antero-posterior diameter of the thorax. It is interesting that these ribs are like half barrel staves and they drop down during expiration, and when they are lifted they swing outward. Now what is that going to accomplish? Well, it greatly enlarges the lateral diameter of the chest and also, because the ribs are flat when elevated, there is further widening. When these have dropped down into the resting posture, their lower margins are inward and when they swing out, the position of the rib is straight up and down instead of at an angle and so the diameter of the chest is further increased by the dimension of the rib.

Then, of course, we have the muscular partition — the diaphragm — between the thorax and the abdomen. During inspiration this is depressed and thus we greatly increase the depth of the thorax as we breathe.

It would seem foolhardy to contend that mere chance designed all of these complicated geometrical and dynamical niceties, and adjusted them all in such perfect and undeniably contemplated harmony, *and did it though the unborn child has no use whatever for them till birth.*

### THE CRANIUM, BRAIN PROTECTION, FORETHOUGHT

The cranium, containing the brain, is a bony encasement. It is not capable of enlarging, increasing in capacity. What is to prevent that soft, semigelatinous substance, the brain, from becoming seriously injured from a fall or a blow on the head? Sometimes we do get concussion, but ordinary accidents do not injure the brain. It is very interesting to observe in passing that running down between the two hemispheres of the brain there is a strong supporting membrane, and the brain is swung upon a hammock of membranes and then jacketed with fluid, at least two layers of it. The

brain is swung in a hammock, and to prevent lateral motion between the two hemispheres there is a deep furrow and there is a membrane that goes right down there to keep the brain poised laterally. The hammock supports it from below, and it is all jacketed with fluid. Who designed this protective mechanism?

### "SHALL HE NOT SEE" WHO DESIGNED THE EYE?

There is a question in the ninety-fourth Psalm, "He that formed the eye, shall he not see?" Now, I want you to think for a few moments about the eye. It is the size of a marble, less than an inch in diameter. Think of the pictures it can take and register on the brain through the optic nerves. Wouldn't it be a difficult thing if we had to carry around with us about three thousand lenses of different focal strength and when you wanted to see something four inches away you would hunt around until you got the right lens? And if you were looking off six feet you would have to find a lens for that. Friends, isn't it a marvelous thing that this eye can focus instantly upon objects four inches away, four feet away, ten feet away, and then is optically adjusted for infinity? "He that formed the eye, shall He not see?"

It we should turn the lights out here and someone should come into this hall, it would be very dark, black. But after he had been in here a short time, he might be able to discern roughly the outlines of furniture. He could see much better. How did that happen? How does that occur? "Well," you say, "it is the pupil, that little aperture which admits light, that dilates in the darkness and admits more light." That is true, but it is only a fraction of the truth. Back here on this visual screen in the back of the eye, that visual screen called the retina, there is a certain sensitive photographic material called rhodopsia or "visual purple" and it has the marvelous property of becoming twenty-five times as sensitive to light if the light is very dim. It increases its sensitiveness to light in the presence of darkness. Who designed that? "He that formed the eye, shall He not see?"

A cross-section of the eye shows the marvelous little lens by which light rays are focused upon the retina. This bi-convex lens in the front of the eye is connected all the way around to a muscle, the ciliary muscle, and when that muscle contracts, it pulls the choroid coat of the eye forward, thus relaxing the ligaments that surround the lens, which now, by its elasticity, becomes more bi-convex. Now the flatter the lens is, the more parallel the rays of light go through it, but make it bi-convex, and depending upon the convexity, the more bi-convex, the more the light rays are bent, and the shorter the focal distance. Thus this little lens body, half the size of a split pea in the front of your eye is able, automatically, (you do not know when it happens), to focus rays of light and thus present a clear, well-defined image of an object upon the retina at varying distances.

Leuwenhoek said, "The beetle has on one side 3,180 eyes. The house fly has 4000. (No wonder we cannot swat them!) The dragon fly has 13,500. I adjusted the eye of a common house fly and could see distinctly in each tiny lens the whole steeple of a church 299 feet high and 750 feet distant. I could see the doors and windows and could even discern whether the windows were open or shut." H. W. Morris, naturalist, wrote: "The most singular eye is that of the analepx, a fish of Eastern Asia. The ball of each eye is divided into two hemispheres and each half is a perfect eye. The two lower halves are nearsighted and the two upper halves are farsighted. Thus the little animal can at the same time see its enemies at a distance and its food near at hand." What do you think of that? Is not that interesting? Who designed an eye like that? Is that a matter of chance, evolution? I think it is evidence of a divine Creator.

### How Do We Hear?

In a cross section of the ear, we have the outer ear of cartilage, the pinna, and the auditory canal leading into the drum, which is in position here, and here are these three little bony ossicles, the hammer, the anvil, and the stirrup—the "malleus," the "incus," and the "stapes." These form a bridge across the middle ear which is a cavity connected with the throat by the eustachian tubes. That is why a child with a sore throat might get an abscess in the ear. It is only a little way to the brain and it is only a little way to the mastoid cavity. Then there is the internal ear which is the hearing part of the ear and is made up of three canals, the semicircular canals. How do we hear? "He that planted the ear, shall He not hear? He that formed the eye, shall He not see?"

"The human ear has 24,000 strings" and I am quoting from Professor Howell of John Hopkins. No two strings are of the same length. The actual hearing part of the ear, the internal ear, occupies much less space than the last joint of your little finger. There are 24,000 strings stretched across this tube, which as you see varies in width and is filled with fluid. Standing on top of those strings are the most marvelous little end organs for perception of sound imaginable. Now, how do we hear? These strings are stretched across this tube in the fluid. Sound waves are picked up by the outer ear, turned down the auditory canal, strike that drum and the very sensitive drum vibrates. As it vibrates those vibrations are carried through this little chain of bones to the fluid in the inner ear. The movement of the fluid disturbs those strings, causing them to vibrate, and resting on those strings are thousands of little end organs which are connected directly with the auditory nerve. The impulses are carried to the brain and are there interpreted, all the way from the low base of 16 double vibrations per second, to the high tenor of 90,000.

## "THE VOICE IS JACOB'S"

In the few moments that remain I want us to think about the voice. I am going to suppose that we go to a manufacturer of musical instruments and we say to him, "Sir, we want you to make us 2,000,000,000 musical instruments. These are all to be stringed instruments. I want you to make each instrument so as to have a voice so distinctive that you can detect it from every other instrument. In each of these we must have only two strings, and these less than an inch long." What would you think of such a problem for this musical manufacturer? He is to make 2,000,000,000 stringed instruments, each to have only two strings and no string in any of them to be more than an inch long, and each instrument is to have a voice so distinctive that it can be detected from all others (there being some 2 billion people living today).

Now, I am talking about your voice and mine. Do you know your friend's voice? Remember the old story in the Bible, "The voice is Jacob's voice but the hands are the hands of Esau." They couldn't deceive the old blind father by the voice. "Who hath made man's mouth?" Each voice has but two vocal cords. These are less than an inch in length and in any one individual are exactly alike yet different for each person.

I was in a city not long ago where a brother of mine lives. I hadn't seen him for several years. He didn't know I was coming through the city. I called him on the telephone and I said, "Hello, Carl." "Hello, Archie, where are you?" How is that possible on the telephone? "The voice is Jacob's voice."

## CONCLUSIONS

I think, friends, that to say: "That is an accident, or has developed by some process of selection" is to deny the evidences that are uncontrovertible that there is a great Creator who has formed these body temples of ours and has left the evidence written large upon every structure and function of the human body.

The very name of this Society and its purpose leads me to feel free to read a verse or two from the most authoritative Book as to creation that we have. I shall read a few verses from the 139th Psalm.

"O Lord, Thou hast searched me, and known me. Thou knowest my downsitting and mine uprising, thou understandest my thought afar off. . . . I will praise thee; for I am fearfully and wonderfully made." Who made us? God. "Marvelous are Thy works; and my soul knoweth right well."

That reminds us of the first five words of the Bible which read, "In the beginning God created"—the first great cause. "My substance was not hid from thee, when I was made . . . Thine eyes did see my substance, yet being imperfect; and in thy book all my members were written, which in continuance were fashioned, *when as yet there was none of them.*" Here is clearly expressed the Creator's forethought. Those of us who have had a little introduction to the study of embryology can see a volume in that, can't we? "In thy book all my members were written, which in continuance were fashioned . . . How precious also are thy thoughts unto me, O God." Ps. 139:15-16. It appears that the Creator even *drew plans* and made specifications *in writing*.

I wish to refer to two or three other texts on the origin of the body features: Job 33:4, "The spirit of God hath made me, and the breath of the Almighty hath given me life"; Psalm 119:73, "Thy hands have made me and fashioned me"; Psalm 100:3, "Know ye that the Lord he is God: it is he that hath made us and not we ourselves."

Now, I brought along a watch. I am going to suppose that someone of you and I were walking along the street and we find this watch and you say to me, "I wonder who made that watch."

And I say, "No one."

"Oh yes. What is it, an Elgin, a Waltham, a Gruen? Who made that watch?"

"Oh, no one made it. You see, there was just going to be a watch, and the iron in the mainspring came from the iron mines of Spain. The gold there came from the Yukon up in Alaska. These jewels came from the crystal mines of Czechoslovakia. And all these minerals decided that there was to be a watch and they all got together and organized themselves and now we have a timekeeper." Friends, what would you think? What would anyone think of that kind of reasoning? And how long would this watch be of any value if it couldn't be regulated by that master watch, the clock of the heavens?

Who made the stars? Well, star dust came from nowhere and got somewhere and organized itself and life appeared. Isn't it strange that anyone in our day should go that far in trying to rule God out of His created universe? "If there is a God," they say, "we are responsible to Him, and

we don't wish to be; therefore, we'll rule Him out of the universe," by such lack of reasoning as that!

(Picture of the Bible) Yes, the Bible, God's great book of truth. If we do not know the origin of the human race, how can we know its destiny? If one does not know where he came from, how can he know where he is going? "In the beginning God created," "which was the son of Adam, which was the Son of God."

If anyone can get any real consolation in believing *that*, (picture of ape) is his grandfather, that that represents the origin of the human species, we won't deny him that privilege; but, friends, shall we go back to the slimy ooze of some prehistoric pool in our search for the origin of the human race in some amoeba, some single-celled animalcule—and rob man of the dignity of his origin—"which was the son of Adam," "which was the Son of God"?

This statement is from Virchow: "The attempt to find the transition from animal to man has ended in total failure. The missing link has not been found and will not be found. Man is not descended from the ape. [Friends, without the book of Genesis there are a thousand missing links, and they never will be found.] It has been proved beyond the shadow of a doubt that during the past five thousand years there has been no noticeable change in mankind."

I like this, too, from Lord Kelvin in the *London Times* of May 4, 1903: "Was there anything so absurd as to believe that a number of atoms by falling together of their own accord could make a sprig of moss, a microbe, a living animal? It is utterly absurd. Here scientific thought is compelled to accept the idea of creative power. Forty years ago I asked Liebig, [also a famous scientist] if he believed that the grass and flowers which we saw around us grew by mere mechanical force. He answered, 'No more than I believe that a book of Botany describing them could grow by mere chemical force.' "

Sometime ago I was in a strange city waiting for a train. I had to lay over two hours, so went into a bookstore. I picked up an old volume entitled "In My Father's House." I opened the volume and the first sentence read, "There are 20,000 species of grass." And when we think there are no two leaves alike, no two sprigs of grass alike, no two faces alike, surely somewhere there is a marvelous infinite Creator that planned, designed, and constructed the human body and

all the forms of nature. *Only a designer could prevent duplications.*

In the Bible in a number of places the human body is likened to a temple; not to an old broken-down shack, but a temple, something more costly, something more enduring, something more beautiful, something more serviceable. "What? know ye not that your body is the temple of the Holy Ghost which is in you, which ye have of God, and ye are not your own? For ye are bought with a price; therefore glorify God in your body, and in your spirit, which are God's."

*The Saviour tabernacled in a human body. He carried it through the portals of the tomb and to the morning of the resurrection.*

---

# MAN AS THE REPRESENTATIVE OF THE SUPERNATURAL

## By THE DUKE OF ARGYLL[*]

The denial and exclusion of what is called "The Supernatural" in our explanations of Nature, is the same doctrine in another form as the denial and exclusion of Anthropopsychism. The connection may not be evident at first sight, but it arises from the fact that the human Mind is really the type, and the only type, of that which men call the Supernatural. It would be well if this word were altogether banished from our vocabulary. It is in the highest degree ambiguous and deceptive. It assumes that the system of "Nature" in which we live and of which we form a part, is limited to purely physical agencies linked together by nothing but mechanical necessity. There might indeed be no harm in this limitation of the word Nature if it could possibly be adhered to. But it is not possible to adhere to it, and that for the best of all reasons, because even inanimate Nature, as we habitually see it, and are obliged to speak of it, is not a System which gives us the idea of being governed and guided by mechanical necessity. No wonder men find it difficult to believe in the Supernatural, if by the Supernatural they mean any agency which is nowhere present in the visible and intelligible Universe, or is not implicitly represented and continually reflected there. For indeed in this sense no Christian can believe in the Supernatural—in a Creation from which the Creator has been banished, or has withdrawn Himself. On the other hand, if by the Supernatural we mean an Agency which, while ever present in the material and intelligible Universe, is not confined to it, but transcends it, then indeed the difficulty is not in the believing of it, but in the disbelieving of it. No man can really hold that the Material System which is visible or intelligible to us is anything more than a fragment or a part. No man can believe that its existing arrangements of Matter and of Force are self-caused, self-originated and self-sustained. It is not possible, therefore, so to "crib, cabin and confine" our conceptions of Nature as to exclude elements which essentially belong to what is called the Supernatural. And there is another reason why it is impossible to adhere to such conceptions of the Natural, and that is, that it would compel us to exclude the Mind of Man, and indeed the lesser minds of all living things, from our scientific definition of Nature, and to establish an absolute and rigorous separation be-

---

[*]Argyll, Duke of, THE UNITY OF NATURE, 1883, pp. 163-166. This excerpt is presented as an example of teleological reasoning on man's place in the unity of nature, and of the illogic of efforts that have been made to escape it.—Editors.

tween all of these and the world in which they move and act. We have seen not only how impracticable such a separation is, but how false it is to the facts of science. The same condemnation must fall on every conception of the Universe which assumes this separation as not only important but fundamental. Yet this is the very separation on which those philosophers absolutely depend who condemn what they call the Supernatural in our conceptions and explanations of the world. And in the interest of their own argument they are quite right in keeping to this separation as indispensable for their purpose. In order to exclude fom Nature what they call the Supernatural, it is absolutely necessary that they should in the first place exclude Man. If Nature be nothing but Matter, Force, and Mechanical Necessity, then Man belongs to the Supernatural, and is indeed the very embodiment and representation of it.

Accordingly this identification of Man with the Supernatural is necessarily and almost unconsciously involved in language which is intended to be strictly philosophical, and in the most careful utterances of our most distinguished scientific men. Thus Professor Tyndall, in his Belfast Address to the British Association, uses these words: "Our earliest historic ancestors fell back also upon experience, but with this difference, that the particular experiences which furnished the weft and woof of their theories were drawn, not from the study of Nature, but from what lay much closer to them—the observation of men." Here Man is especially contradistinguished from Nature, and accordingly we find in the next sentence that this idea is connected with a condemnation of the error of seeing ourselves—that is, the Supernatural in Nature. "Their theories," the Professor goes on to say, "accordingly took an anthropomorphic form." Further on, in the same Address, the same antithesis is still more distinctly expressed, thus: "If Mr. Darwin rejects the notion of creative power acting after human fashion it certainly is not because he is unacquainted with the numberless exquisite adaptations on which the notion of a supernatural artificer is founded." Here we see that the idea of "acting after human fashion" is treated as synonymous with the idea of a "supernatural artificer"; and the same identification may be observed running throughout the language which is commonly employed to condemn what is sometimes called Anthropomorphism and at other times is called the Supernatural.

The two propositions, therefore, which are really involved in the thoroughgoing denial of Anthropopsychism and the Supernatural are the following: 1st, that there is nothing except Man which is above or outside of mere Matter and Force in Nature as we see and know it; 2nd, that in the System of Nature as thus seen and known, there are no phenomena due to Mind having any analogies with our own.

Surely these propositions have been refuted the moment the definition of them has been attained. We have only to observe, in the first place, the strange and anomalous position in which it places Man. As regards at least the higher faculties of his mind, he is allowed no place in Nature, and no fellowship with any other thing or any other Being outside of Nature. He is absolutely alone—out of all relation with the Universe around him, and under a complete delusion when he sees in any part of it any mental homologies with his own Intelligence, or with his own Will, or with his own Affections. Does this absolute solitariness of position as regards the higher attributes of Man—does it sound reasonable, or possible, or consistent with some of the most fundamental conceptions of science? How, for example, does it accord with that great conception whose truth and sweep become every day more apparent—the Unity of Nature?

How can it be true that Man is so outside of that Unity that the very notion of seeing anything like himself in it is the greatest of all philosophical heresies? Does not the very possibility of science consist in the possibility of reducing all natural phenomena to purely natural conceptions, which must be related to the Intellect of Man when they are worked out and apprehended by it? And if, according to the latest theories, Man is himself a Product of Evolution, and is, therefore, in every atom of his Body and in every function of his Mind a part and a child of Nature, is it not in the highest degree illogical so to separate him from it as to condemn him for seeing in it some image of himself? If he is its product and its child, is it not certain that he is right when he sees and feels the indissoluble bonds of unity which unite him to the great System of things in which he lives?

This fundamental inconsistency in the Agnostic philosophy becomes all the more remarkable when we find that the very men who tell us that we are not One with anything above us, are the same who insist that we are One with everything beneath us. Whatever there is in us or about us which is purely animal we may see everywhere; but whatever there is in us purely intellectual and moral, we delude ourselves if we think we see it anywhere? There are abundant homologies between our bodies and the bodies of the beasts, but there are no homologies between our minds and any Mind which lives and manifests itself in Nature? Our livers and our lungs, our vertebrae and our nervous systems, are identical in origin and in function with those of the living creatures round us; but there is nothing in Nature or above it which corresponds to our Forethought, or Design, or

Purpose—to our love of the Good or our admiration of the Beautiful—to our indignation with the wicked, or to our pity for the suffering and the fallen? I venture to think that no system of philosophy that has ever been taught on Earth lies under such a weight of antecedent improbability; and this improbability increases in direct proportion to the success of science in tracing the Unity of Nature, and in showing step by step how its laws and their results can be brought more and more into direct relation with the Mind and Intellect of Man.

# BULLETIN

OF

# CREATION, THE DELUGE

## AND RELATED SCIENCE

| Volume IV | September, 1944 | Number 4 |

## THE VICTORIA INSTITUTE TRANSACTIONS*

677th Ordinary Meeting

Held in Committee Room B, the Central Hall,

Westminister, S. W. I., on Monday, April 20th, 1925

At 4:30 P. M.

Sir George King, M.A., in the chair

## REVELATION AND EVOLUTION: CAN THEY BE HARMONIZED?**

### By George McCready Price

Being the Langhorne Orchard Prize Essay for 1925

### I

The Evolution doctrine has its astronomical and cosmic aspects; but for our present purpose the term may be narrowed down to that portion of the general theory which deals with the origin of the plants and animals of our globe. The latter theory is more generally termed "Organic Evolution"; and such is the sense in which the term *Evolution* is used in the present essay. By "Revelation" we mean the Bible, the embodiment of those facts and doctrines upon which Christianity has been built. So that our subject may be more specifically stated: "Can the theory of Organic Evolution be harmonized with the teachings of the Bible?"

The Bible describes the origin of our plants and animals by what may be termed a *fiat creation*, that is, a creation brought about by the fiat or directly exercised will of God. The

---

*Reprinted by special request especially for American readers, and to indicate the trend of thought at that time.

**Presentation of the silver medal and the cash prize.

The BULLETIN is published by, and is the official organ of the "Society for the Study of Creation, the Deluge, and Related Science." The Editorial Board is comprised of Professor George McCready Price, Dr. Dell D. Haughey, and B. F. Allen. It is printed at the Collegiate Press, Arlington, California. For members the BULLETIN is free, and extra copies 30 cents each (each number priced according to size); for non-members it is $2.00 per year and this number is 40 cents. All correspondence should be directed to the Editors, Box 1030, Glendale, California.

question of how long ago this creation took place is not important, neither is the question of how much time was occupied in this original creation; though on both of these points the Bible has made very interesting and important declarations. But for our present discussion, that is, with regard to the aspects of the subject which are related to the theory of Organic Evolution, the chief feature of the Biblical account of Creation is that this Creation is very definitely stated to have been *a finished work,* something very different from those processes of natural law by which the present order of Nature is perpetuated or reproduced. Not only is this aspect of the case very clearly stated in the first and second chapters of Genesis, but, in addition, we have the record of the institution of the Sabbath, which was primarily designed as a memorial of a *completed* Creation, thus emphasizing the idea that this original Creation was something quite different from those processes now prevailing under which the organic kingdoms are perpetuated or sustained.

In marked contrast with this, we have as the prime idea of Organic Evolution the notion that our plants and animals have come about by a long process of development under precisely those processes of Nature which now prevail round us. In other words, the Evolution theory measures all events in the past by the present; it says that the present is the real measure of the past, and the measure of all the past, including the so-called origin of life and of all organic existences. In explaining this theory, the emphasis is always placed on such present-acting processes as variation, heredity, and environment; and we are constantly impressed with the idea that these present-acting processes or

laws of organic nature are quite sufficient to explain how our present complex array of plants and animals have arisen by purely natural process from simple beginnings, and ultimately from the inorganic or the not-living.

In short, the theory of Evolution is only a special form of the general theory of *Uniformity,* the latter being a view of the Universe which denies that there is any real contrast between the beginnings of things and the present order of Nature under which the world around us is being sustained and perpetuated. In contrast with this idea, we have the Bible picture of a real beginning, a real Creation, distinctly different both in the degree and in the character of the Divine power then manifested, from the present exercise of God's power in sustaining and perpetuating what He then originated.

Practically all scientific writers who have dealt with this aspect of the question have emphasized the marked contrast between Evolution and Creation. It is only some very modern theologians who, by an utter confusion of thought, have tried to smooth out all difference between the two ideas.

Erasmus Darwin, the grandfather of Charles Darwin declared: "The world has been evolved, not created; it has arisen little by little from a small beginning, and has increased through the activity of the elemental forces embodied in itself, and so has rather grown than suddenly come into being at an almighty word."[1]

Henry Edward Compton has also spoken very clearly of the emphasis which the theory of Evolution places on the philosophic concept of uniformity:

"The doctrine of Evolution is a body of principles and facts concerning the present condition and past

1 Darwin, Erasmus, quoted in READINGS IN EVOLUTION, GENETICS, AND EUGENICS. University of Chicago Press, 1921, p. 3.

history of the living and the lifeless things that make up the Universe. It teaches that natural processes have gone on in the earlier ages of the world as they do to-day, and that natural forces have ordered the production of all things about which we know."[2]

On the other hand, the Bible teaches that the things which are seen, that is, the material things around us, "were not made of things which do appear" (Heb. xi, 3); or in other words, they did not come into existence by any process which we could call a "natural" process. Creation is the term applied to this beginning of things; and the Bible always speaks of it as a completed work, not as something now going on. It may likewise be borne in mind, that when arraigned by the Sanhedrin for exercising miraculous powers of healing on the Sabbath Jesus declared: "My Father worketh hitherto, and I work" (John v, 17); thus intimating quite plainly that the continued exercise of miraculous power on the part of God or Christ is perfectly consistent with the primal fact that the Sabbath was given to mankind as a memorial of a *completed* Creation.

It is thus very evident that there is no similarity between the idea of Evolution and that of Creation; it is all contrast. The two terms are antonyms; they are mutually exclusive; no mind can entertain a belief in both at the same time; when one notion is believed, the other is thereby denied and repudiated.

II

A similar relationship of contrast and mutual exclusiveness is seen when we consider the bearings of Creation and Evolution toward the problem of sin, or moral evil.

The Bible has a clear and understandable explanation of sin, or moral evil, as having been brought about by the free choice of a created being, or beings. We may not be able to explain entirely the origin of sin; for to "explain" it, in the sense of showing a cause for it, would be to defend it, and then it would cease to be reprehensible. Sin is due to an abuse of freedom; it has no other explanation. But God has permitted it for the sake of teaching essential lessons to the Universe. And the risk of sin occurring is a risk inseparable from the endowment of free moral choice, which the Creator bestowed on angels and men. But the Bible clearly teaches that God from the beginning made provision for this desperate emergency, whenever it should arise; and the whole history of God's dealings with mankind is simply the record of God's method of dealing with this situation which has arisen because of the abuse of that freedom, or the power of free moral choice, which the Creator bestowed on some of the higher orders of His created existences.

From this it follows that sin is an intruder, an anomalous situation; its essential nature is that of a revolt, a rebellion against the established order of the Universe, as the latter is an expression, and a perfect expression, of the will of the Creator. Thus, sin is not a primal or an original condition; it is wholly secondary, in point of time. From this it follows further that suffering and death, (on the part of animals and man) are also wholly secondary, and are not a part of God's original design in Creation. "God saw everything that He had made, and behold it was very good" (Gen. i:31). God created man "upright" (Eccl. vii: 29), "in His own image" (Gen. i:27), with no bias whatever toward evil. But "by one man sin entered into the world, and death by sin; and so death

---

2 Compton, Henry Edward, THE DOCTRINE OF EVOLUTION, 1911, p. 1.

passed upon all men, for that all have sinned" (Rom. v:12).

All this is the uniform and absolutely unanimous testimony of the Bible from Genesis to Revelation. The Bible gives no sanction to Manichaeism, or the doctrine that evil has existed from the very beginning of things, that it is coeval with the good.

But the latter, however, is exactly the teaching of the Evolution doctrine. Evolution gives us no solution of the problem of the origin of evil; it merely pushes the problem back into the shadow, where we cannot see anything distinctly. In the last analysis, Evolution either makes evil the deliberate work of God, in forming beings with a bias toward evil; or it makes evil an inherent property of matter, beyond the reach of God's power, something in the very nature of things, which God Himself could not help or overcome when He started the Universe evolving. This theory of a "finite God," as taught by J. S. Mill, William James, and others, seems to have become very popular with modern philosophers who have accepted the Evolution theory; but it certainly is not in accord with the Bible. It is a sort of modern Manichaeism, wholly antagonistic to the Christian religion.

This is the testimony of Le Conte: "If Evolution be true, and especially if man be indeed a product of Evolution, then what we call evil is not a a unique phenomenon confined to man, and the result of an accident (the 'fall'), but must be a great fact pervading all nature, and a part of its very constitution."[3]

But anyone who will take the pains to compare this view of evil with that taught by Celsus, the Neo-Platonist, and the first pagan writer to devote an express work to attacking Christianity, will see that this modern evolutionary philosophy is identical with the ancient pagan view of the world in this respect. There is certainly nothing Christian about such a view; it is paganism, pure and unmixed.

We have been considering the primary or the more remote cause of sin, evil, suffering and death. If we consider briefly the nearer or the proximate cause of these things, we find that, according to Evolution, sin is simply inherited animalism. It appears to make no difference to the advocates of this view that many very evil propensities, such as pride, envy and rebellion against God, seem to have no possible connection with animalism; there really is nothing else in the Evolution view of the case to which we may trace the multitudinous propensities of what the Bible calls the "carnal heart."

As John Fiske expresses it: "Theology has much to say about original sin. This original sin is neither more nor less than the brute-inheritance which every man carries with him."[4]

Dr. E. W. MacBride, at the Oxford Conference of Modern Churchmen, expressed himself on the same point as follows:

"If mankind have been slowly developed out of ape-like ancestors, then what is called sin consists of nothing but the tendencies which they have inherited from these ancestors; there never was a state of primeval innocence, and all the nations of the world have developed out of primitive man by processes as natural as those which gave rise to the Jews."[5]

On the same occasion, Dr. H.D.A. Major made a similar declaration:

"Science has shown us that what is popularly called 'original sin' ... consists of man's inheritance from his brute ancestry."[6]

---

3 Le Conte, Joseph, EVOLUTION AND RELIGIOUS THOUGHT, 1899, p. 365.
4 Fiske, John, THE DESTINY OF MAN, 1884, p. 103.
5 MacBride, Dr. E. W., THE MODERN CHURCHMAN, Sept., 1924, p. 232.
6 Major, Dr. H. D. A., Id., p. 206.

From these statements by representative Evolutionists, we are safe in concluding that the teaching of the Evolution doctrine is in vital and complete antagonism with the historic teachings of Christianity. If it should be objected that the Bible does not use the expression, "the fall of man," it may be replied that the idea of a fall, as an explanation of the great fact that man is a sinner, runs like a scarlet thread through the entire Bible from beginning to end.

From the profusion of references which might be cited on this point, the following from John Wesley may suffice to show the place which this doctrine of the fall of man occupies in Christian theology:

"The fall of man is the very foundation of revealed religion. If this be taken away, the Christian system is subverted, nor will it deserve so honorable an appellation as that of a cunningly devised fable."[7]

Also the following from the same author:

"All who deny this, call it original sin, or by any other title, are but heathens still in the fundamental point which differentiates heathenism from Christianity."

We may safely conclude from all these testimonies that the theory of Organic Evolution is in hopeless antagonism with the teachings of the Bible regarding the subject of the origin of sin. I cannot see how this direct antagonism can be reconciled. The Bible gives us an account of the beginnings of sin which makes sin the result of a deliberate wrong choice on the part of the parents of the human race. Because of this first disobedience, the nature of mankind has become degenerate and depraved; man is naturally a sinner, out of harmony with his Creator and the fundamental laws of the Universe. But the Evolution theory says that man's "sinful" tendencies are simply his inheritance from his brute ancestors; man is not a fallen being, but a rising being; sin is but the "growing pains" of the race, something which impedes and hinders us, it is true, but something which the race is gradually outgrowing. As for the origin of these "sinful" tendencies, Evolution has no explanation, except to make them an inherent part of the very Universe itself, something which God Himself could not avoid or eliminate when He started the process of an evolving Universe—if, indeed, we can suppose any such deliberate or purposive beginning of the Universe on the part of a personal God. In this respect, the Evolution theory seems to be merely reverting to the crude pagan ideas which had long occupied the mind of the world when Christianity came with the light of its Divine Revelation.

III

As Christianity and Evolution are in direct contrast in the matter of the origin of sin, so also we may notice next, they are in the same diametric opposition when they come to deal with the problem of the remedy for the sin and evil of our world.

The Bible treats of sin as a desperate condition, something ensuring eternal death, eternal separation from God, unless it is remedied. And it offers that unique remedy for sin which is called the Atonement. The desperateness of the situation called sin can be estimated only in the light of the amazing remedy for it, namely, the death of a Divine Sacrifice. In the very nature of things, this awful remedy would not have been required if mankind could have been saved from sin in any other possible way. Indeed, Peter declared that there is no salvation in any other way (Acts iv:12).

---

7 Wesley, John, WORKS, Vol. 1, 1825, p. 176, and Vol. 5, p. 195.

But what conceivable place is there for a substitutionary Atonement in the scheme of Organic Evolution? Not only is there no room for such a remedial system through the death of the Son of God, but almost to a man Evolutionists and "advanced" theologians seem to exhibit a strong antipathy to any such idea. The following from Sir Oliver Lodge is quite typical of this class:

"As a matter of fact, the higher man of to-day is not worrying about his sins at all, still less about their punishment. His mission, if he is good for anything, is to be up and doing; and in so far as he acts wrongly or unwisely he expects to suffer. He may unconsciously plead for mitigation on the ground of good intentions, but never either consciously or unconsciously will any one but a cur ask for the punishment to fall on someone else, nor rejoice if told that it already has so fallen."[8]

The implacable hatred shown towards the Bible doctrine of the Atonement on the part of Evolutionists, may be further illustrated by the following from Durant Drake:

"What sort of justice is it that could be satisfied with the punishment of one innocent man and the free pardon of myriads of guilty men? The theory seems a remnant of the ancient idea that the gods need to be placated; but by the side of the pagan gods, who were content with humble offerings of flesh and fruit, the Christian God, demanding the suffering and death of His own Son, appears a monster of cruelty."[9]

These two quotations sound very strange as coming from men who call themselves Christians, Durant Drake even being a well-known teacher of a certain form of "advanced" religion.

But we can better understand the logic of the situation from the following pungent statement of Robert Blatchford:

"But—no Adam, no Fall; no Fall, no Atonement; no Atonement, no Saviour. Accepting Evolution, how can we believe in a Fall? *When* did man fall; was it before he ceased to be a monkey, or after? Was it when he was a tree man, or later? Was it in the Stone Age, or the Bronze Age, or in the Age of Iron? . . . And if there never was a Fall, why should there be any Atonement?"[10]

There is surely no need of multiplying testimony on this point, to prove that Evolution and Christianity are as far asunder as the poles in their attitude toward the remedy for sin. The Bible, as the Divine Revelation of Christianity, comes to a focus in its remedy for sin, through the vicarious death of the divine-human Sacrifice on the Cross of Calvary. The utter repudiation of this provisional remedy for sin has long been familiar to the historian, from the writings of Celsus and Porphyry, down through the long line of skeptics and atheists, such as Hume, Voltaire, Paine and Ingersoll. But in our day this rejection of the basic idea of Christianity finds its chief support in that widespread theory of the origin of man which makes the doctrine of the Atonement meaningless, through its explanation of sin as mere inherited animalism, and nothing really very bad after all. As R. J. Campbell has expressed it—If there ever was a "fall" it was a fall "upward!"

Surely, there is no possible method, consistent with logical and honest thinking, by which this inherent teaching of Organic Evolution can be harmonized with the historic form of

---

8 Lodge, Sir Oliver, MAN AND THE UNIVERSE, 1920, p. 204.
9 Drake, Durant, PROBLEMS OF RELIGION, 1916, p. 176.
10 Blatchford, Robert, GOD AND MY NEIGHBORS, Chicago, 1917, p. 159.

Christianity, as represented by the Bible.

## IV

Evolution's forecast of the future of the human race is by no means cheering. Until the outbreak of the World War, its picture of the future was roseate and glorious, like that of a bright summer morn. Man was a rapidly rising being; he had already progressed so far that the future was assured. Soon the war-drums would throb no longer, and the battle-flags would be for ever furled, in the parliament of man, the federation of the world! But the sad and grim reality of the past ten years has changed all this. Today the most hopelessly pessimistic of the world's prophets, for example, H. G. Wells, are those who most completely adopted and assimilated the doctrine of Organic Evolution. The more enthusiastic followers of Marxian Socialism, with its programme of the dictatorship of the proletariat, are, so far as I know, about the only Evolutionists who take at all a cheerful view of the world's future. The others all paint the picture in dark shadows: the collapse of civilization, the utter extinction of the race of mankind, are the favourite titles.

The future of mankind is made a biological fate, grim and ineluctable, after the example of the extinction of the trilobites, the dinosaurs, the dodo, and the great auk. "Our little systems have their day; they have their day, and cease to be." True, each of these Evolutionary prophets has his infallible remedy which, if the world would but adopt it, would long postpone, perhaps entirely avert, the impending doom. But the stubborn race goes on, heedless of suggested panaceas; and accordingly these world-forecasters have become, almost invariably, preachers of world disasters and oblivion.

On the other hand, the Bible does not give a bright or hopeful picture of the world's future, so far as the present age or the present order of things is concerned. True, it has a bright future in store, when "there shall be no more death, neither sorrow, nor crying, neither shall there be any more pain" (Rev. xxi:4). But it treats the present condition of the world as being hopelessly diseased; and only by the abrupt end of the present age, and the supernatural replacement of the present by the direct reign of Christ as King of kings and Lord of lords, can that reign of eternal joy and happiness be ushered in. But between this and that lies a dark shadow, like the death of the race; only on the other side of which can the vision of faith discern the tearless eye, the fadeless cheek, and a social state unmarred by sin, hatred, or oppression.

The Evolution doctrine, even at its highest level of hopefulness, never had any such outlook. At best, it promised a sort of salvation of the human race through the alleged perfectibility of mankind as a whole, and tried to cheer us with the hazy hope, as Philip Mauro expresses it, that the world might at some time "become a more comfortable place for the man of the future to sin and die in." But such a hope is pitifully inadequate as a message for those who, here and now, under this hideous handicap of sin, fail in the sad conflict with inherited animalism. Certain is it that Evolution has no message of salvation for the moral failures of our day, nor for those of all past ages, unless it may be supposed that, at some future time, such beings are to be reincarnated at a higher stage of the racial development, and provided with another chance under less hard conditions. And, of course, in the minds of those Evolutionists who hold such views, the programme of racial development, reincarnation, and all, is to be accomplished fatalistically, quite without the intervention of any Divine Mediator and the death of a Divine Sacrifice.

Most Evolutionists, however, have not been able to cheer themselves with any such hope, feeble and uncertain though it may be. Most of them would probably express themselves in the pathetic language of Bertrand Russell:

"Brief and powerless is man's life; on him and all his race the slow, sure doom falls pitiless and dark." . . . "The life of man is a long march through the night, surrounded by invisible foes, tortured by weariness and pain, toward a goal that few can hope to reach, and where none may tarry long. One by one, as they march, our comrades vanish from our sight, seized by the silent orders of omnipotent Death."[11]

Are we as Christians asked to surrender our hope of immortal life, a hope that has been confirmed by the Resurrection of our Lord, that has cheered an innumerable company of the saints of all ages, in loneliness, in torture, at the stake, or in toil while proclaiming it in distant lands—are we asked to surrender this hope for such a gospel of despair as this, now offered us in the name of Organic Evolution?

The Christian view is that the present order is but a temporary condition; the time is coming when a great world-change will occur, when the world will come under the direct and special rule of the Lord Jesus Christ. This change is not a gradual kind of transition; it is sudden and abrupt. In the Christian view of the matter, it is utterly unthinkable that the present order—involving innumerable births and deaths, with incomputable suffering and misery in the interim—should continue throughout eternity, world without end. Thank God, the Bible gives no countenance to such a hopeless world-nightmare; there is to be a change, and by many it is thought

that the change is not far distant. However this may be, the chief point is that there is to be a change; and that ultimately the long reign of sinning, and suffering, and dying will become but a memory, if indeed even the relic of a memory will remain to fret and annoy those who are so happy as to become partakers of that bright immortal life. But the Evolution doctrine has nothing as a substitute for this hope of the world, as revealed in the Christian's Bible.

The utter futility of the Evolutionary programme for the future is well stated by Dr. Joseph A. Leighton, of Ohio State University. Even if we may suppose that moral and humane progress goes on through the welter of industrialism, commercialism, and war, who, he asks, are to enjoy the final fruits of this progress? Is humanity, as it toils in history, "engaged in an endless and goalless task"? Or is the goal to be reached only by some far-off generation, while "all the preceding generations will have been mere 'hewers of wood and drawers of water' to serve the welfare of the final happy one"? "Is it the lot of the living members of each generation simply to toil, and suffer, and achieve somewhat, in order to hand on to the following generation a nest of problems, with (and at) which that generation, in turn, will labour, to pass to the grave, and be forgotten after a brief toil at an endless task—one which is never done, but continues and changes throughout the centuries and the aeons without final goal?"[12]

There is no need for us to dwell on the utter inadequacy of such a system of philosophy, with its endless round of birth, struggle and death, world without end, or until our earth finally tumbles into the sun, or becomes frozen up by the exhaustion of the central heating-plant of the solar system.

11 Russell, Bertrand, MYSTICISM AND LOGIC, 1916, p. 56.
12 Leighton, Dr. Joseph A., THE FIELD OF PHILOSOPHY, 1923 Ed., p. 501.

The one thing pertinent to our present discussion is to point out that such a scheme of cosmic despair is completely at variance with that portrayed in the Christian's Bible. And unless the latter is completely false, the former is merely the invention of ingenious unbelievers, who refuse to accept that warm, joyful, inspiring solution of the enigma of life which has been revealed to mankind directly by the only Being in the Universe who can really know what the future is to be.

### V

If in our consideration of the question before us, we should confine ourselves strictly to its narrower and formal aspects, there would be no need of our considering the contingency of the truthfulness of the theory of Organic Evolution. Yet, unless we are content to leave our discussion in a very unsatisfactory state of incompleteness, we must consider, even though in the briefest way, the problem of whether or not the theory of Organic Evolution is an accurate and truthful explanation of the origin of the plants and animals of our world. The Christian may feel so confident of the Revelation which has been given him that he can say, "Yea, let God be true, and every man a liar," for it is certain that the theory of Evolution is not to-day any more confidently or more universally believed than was that old pagan view of the world in the Augustine age, against which Paul and a handful of fishermen pitted themselves in seemingly futile array. Again, the scientist may feel similarly confident that the results he has obtained by his research are to be trusted implicitly, regardless of what the Church may think has been revealed to her. It seems to me, however, that the modern world has been deadlocked in this fashion quite long enough. The time has fully arrived for those who think for themselves, and who do not entrust the keeping of their opinions to any set of supposed experts, to dismiss once for all the idea that man may possibly have arisen by a long-drawn-out process of development from preceding animal ancestors. Confident I am that in this year 1925 sufficient facts are available to settle this long-debated problem in a way entirely satisfactory to the believer in the literal truthfulness of the first chapters of Genesis.

Much water has gone under London Bridge since Darwin's theory of Natural Selection captured the imagination of the world, by appearing to give a materialistic (and incidently a very hideous) explanation of how a species could become so modified in the course of descent as to be changed over into some very different type of life. To-day Darwinism is as dead as the dodo, so far as its being regarded as a *vera causa* of the origin of species is concerned.

Mendelism has shown us how new types of animals and plants may arise by means of hybridization; and in this respect the results of experimental breeding constitute a valuable and permanent addition to our knowledge of the behaviour of living things. But its chief value lies in the fact that it shows how, by concentrating our attention on the "species" concept, as the crucial unit of Organic Existence, we have been looking at things too narrowly; we need to enlarge our ideas about the fixed units of life, and make the *genus*, or in some cases the *family*, the unit of biological work, so far as the discussion of origins is concerned. So far from showing us how really new kinds of plants or animals can originate by natural process, Mendelism has proved that in all our breeding experiments we are just milling around on the same old ground, merely marking time, so far as our being able to produce any types which could be spoken of as really new. In the light of our modern knowledge, we can substitute the word "family" for the word "species," in the famous aphorism of Linnaeus, so that it will now read, *"Familiae tot sunt diversae quot diversae formae ab initio sunt creatae."* That is, there are as many families to be listed and spoken of by natural science as there were of different kinds originally created. And in the light of modern biological research, this statement appears to be literally and scientifically true.

Some little time before he died, Alfred Russel Wallace left us the following very illuminating remarks:

"On the general relation of Mendelism to Evolution, I have come to a very definite conclusion. That is, that it has no relation whatever to the Evolution of species or higher groups, but is really antagonistic to such Evolution. The essential basis of Evolution, involving as it does the most minute and all-pervading adaptation to the whole environment, is extreme and ever-present plasticity, as a condition of survival and adaptation. But the essence of Mendelian characters is their rigidity. They are transmitted without variation, and, therefore, except by the rarest of accidents, they can never become adapted to ever-varying conditions."[13]

But one of the foremost of American biologists, Edwin Grant Conklin, of Princeton University, has told us that: "At present it is practically certain that there is no other kind of inheritance than Mendelian."[14] Accordingly, if we put this fact alongside the statement given above from A. R. Wallace, we are safe in concluding that all our modern knowledge regarding breeding and heredity "is really antagonistic" to the theory of Organic Evolution.

We may draw a similar conclusion from the following words of Dr. E. W. MacBride:

"I well remember the enthusiasm with which the Mendelian theory was received, when it was introduced to the scientific world in the early years of this century. We thought that at last the key to Evolution had been discovered. As a leading Mendelian put it, whilst the rest of us had been held up by an apparently impenetrable hedge, namely, the difficulty of explaining the origin of variation, Mendel had, unnoticed, cut a way through. But, as our knowledge of the facts grew, the difficulty of using Mendelian phenomena to explain Evolution became apparent, and this early hope sickened and died. The way which Mendel cut was seen to lead into a *cul-de-sac.*"[15]

But since Mendelism seems to give us rock-bottom facts in all this field of variation and heredity, why is not the suspicion very naturally suggested, that any theory of origins which finds itself in a *cul-de-sac,* or a blind alley, because of these Mendelian facts, must itself be wholly wrong and unscientific? Certainly, no other conclusion seems to me to be adequate to the present situation.

It is safe to say that many modern scientists, if not going quite so far as this, are at least becoming much less confident regarding the general subject of how our animals and plants have become what they are. For example, in his Presidential Address before the Botanical Section of the British Association, at the Liverpool Meeting, in 1923, Dr. A. G. Tansley stated that in the light of recent developments in botany, the search for common ancestors among the great groups of plants would appear to be "literally a hopeless quest, the genealogical tree an illusory vision."[16]

13. Wallace, Alfred Russel, LETTERS AND REMINISCENCES, 1805, p. 340.
14 Conklin, Edwin Grant, HEREDITY AND ENVIRONMENT, 1920, p. 99.
15 MacBride, Dr. E. W., SCIENCE PROGRESS, Jan., 1922, pp. 450-451.
16 Tansley, Dr. A. G., NATURE, Mar. 8, 1924, p. 356.

In commenting on these declarations of Tansley, Prof. F. O. Bower, of the University of Glasgow, declared:

"At the present moment we seem to have reached a phase of negation in respect of the achievements of phyletic morphology and in conclusions as to descent. . . . I believe that a similar negative attitude is also to be found among those who pursue zoological science."[17]

Similar statements could be given from such leading scientists as Dr. William Bateson and Dr. D. H. Scott. These men still cling to the general idea of Evolution, but they expressly tell us that they do so only as "an act of faith," for they cannot see any scientific explanation of how this process of organic development has come about. The former spoke as follows in his Toronto Address:

"We cannot see how the differentiation into species came about. Variation of many kinds, often considerable, we daily witness, but no origin of species. . . . Meanwhile, though our faith in Evolution stands unshaken, we have no acceptable account of the origin of species."[18]

Similarly, Dr. D. H. Scott has declared that he still holds to the general theory of Evolution, "even if we hold it only as an act of faith"; but he tells us expressly that we do not know *how* the process of development came about:

"For the moment, at all events, the Darwinian period is past; we can no longer enjoy the comfortable assurance, which once satisfied so many of us, that the main problem had been solved. . . all is again in the melting-pot."[19]

In his work, *Extinct Plants and Problems of Evolution*, issued in 1924, Scott, gives an admirable statement of the utter perplexity now confronting those who are face to face with the biological knowledge now available, who nevertheless feel that they must still hold to some form of Organic Evolution.

Up until recent years, the last stronghold of every form of a philosophic belief in Organic Evolution has been the Lyellian or Uniformitarian Geology. For if life has been appearing in various successive forms, age after age, with a more or less steady advance in the grade of life thus represented; and if this scheme of geology can scientifically prove this relative sequence of the great groups of living things, both plants and animals, the human mind will instinctively say that the higher and later kinds have probably grown by some natural development out of the lower kinds, which were earlier in point of time. Thus the Lyellian or Uniformitarian Geology might well be called an Evolutionary Geology; for some form of Organic Evolution would seem to be inevitably implied by this long-popular serial arrangement of the fossils in what was supposed to be a true historical sequence.

It may be permitted to add that, in works given to the world during recent years the present writer has placed a big question-mark after the evolutionary scheme of the fossils, and the gauntlet which has thus been thrown down has not so far been taken up by those whose opinions have come under undisguised attack. The question asked has taken the following shape: If the Cambrian and the Ordovician forms of life are not actually older than the Cretaceous and the Tertiary, might we not reasonably expect to find some localities where the Cretaceous or Tertiary animals and plants were buried first, and the Cam-

17 Bower, Prof. F. O., Id.
18 Bateson, Dr. William, SCIENCE, Jan. 20, 1922, p. 57.
19 Scott, Dr. D. H., NATURE, Sept. 29, 1921, p. 154.

brian and the other Paleozoic laid down afterwards? Certainly; and I have pointed to the famous area in Alberta and Montana, where, over an area some 500 miles long and 40 or 50 miles wide, *Cretaceous beds are below and Cambrian and other Paleozoic rocks on top, with every physical evidence that they were actually laid down in this relative order.* In the Salt Range of India, *Tertiary beds were manifestly laid down before the Cambrian.*

From these and many similar examples found in various parts of the world, I have drawn the conclusion—surprising, but seemingly inevitable—that intrinsically, and as of necessity, no particular type of fossil life is older or younger than any other. In other words, what we have in the rocks as the geological formations are merely the buried floras and faunas of the world before the great world-cataclysm of the Deluge, all of which were once living contemporaneously together. It is a purely arbitrary and artificial scheme by which the evolutionary geologists have arranged these buried floras and faunas, found in widely scattered localities such that no possible stratigraphical relationship can be made out for them, in an alleged chronological sequence. In a word, there are absolutely no solid scientific facts to hinder us from believing that these buried floras and faunas really represent the life of the Antediluvian world, which was destroyed and buried by this great world-cataclysm. That is, there is nothing to hinder·us from believing this explanation of the riddle of Geology, except the sheer incredibility of there ever having been such a tremendous world catastrophe, and that mankind and the present surviving animals and plants must have lived through it. If the latter is admittedly possible, as the Sacred Scriptures seem to declare, the long popular scheme of Evolutionary Geology is a myth.

Here is, at least, a wholly new method of meeting the arguments of the Evolutionists. Whether or not it will be accepted by the scientific world, or even accepted by believers in the Bible, remains to be seen. Certain it is, this New Catastrophism, with Mendelism and the new light on Biology in support, stands alone between Christian people and the logical necessity of accepting the scheme of Organic Evolution, with its theory of man's animal origin, and all that this latter idea implies.

## DISCUSSION

Mr. H. Owen Weller said that he was embarrassed by being called upon to open the discussion, as he was not in sympathy with the paper. At first sight it might attract people by its superficial orthodoxy, but actually it was dangerous. He contested the opinion that "only very modern theologians by an utter confusion of thought" had tried to smooth out the difference between the two ideas of Evolution and Creation. He, and many others, did it by seeing God working by some such gradual process as Evolution. A man of science might still be Christian. Further, he refused to accept the author's alternative between his "New Catastrophism" and "the logical necessity of accepting the scheme of Organic Evolution." And he deplored the intention, or effect, of the paper to drive a wedge between Christians and scientists. This had been done, or was being done, in America; he hoped that the quarrel would not be brought across the Atlantic.

Lieut.-Colonel G. Mackinlay said: I fully agree with the author in believing in the strict truth of the Bible in the subject of the origin of man, and I think the first pages of his address are admirable, and that he has quite proved his point; but, if I understand all his arguments aright, I cannot follow him in his last few pages—for instance, I cannot agree with his statement on p. 16, that "no particular type of fossil life is older or younger than any other." I should be glad if he would give his reasons for these words in his reply.

Rev. J. J. B. Coles said: The Professor's valuable essay should be circulated among those who attempt to use the doctrine of Evolution to exclude the equally true doctrine of Special Creation. Gen. i and ii should not be amalgamated.

"My Father worketh hitherto and I work." God's rest had been broken by the introduction of sin, and so God and Christ in long-suffering grace and mercy are "working" still.

Mr. Theodore Roberts remarked that, strictly speaking, the Bible was the divinely given record of the Revelation rather than the Revelation itself, just as the fossils were claimed to be the record of the Evolution which had taken place.

He did not feel vitally concerned in the question of whether the theory of Organic Evolution up to man was true, as many believed it could be reconciled with Gen. i, but he pointed out that the thrice-repeated statement that God created man (twice adding "in His own image" (verse 27), and the more detailed record of chap. ii, 7, that He "formed man of the dust of the ground and breathed into his nostrils the breath of life" clearly indicated an immediate link between man and his Creator) which led to the Creator being described as "the Father of our spirits" (Heb. xii, 9) in contra-distinction to our natural parents. When God thus imparted to man's body—whether formed instanta-neously of the actual soil or out of it gradually through some evolutionary process—an immortal spirit, He to some extent limited His own future action by thus creating a moral agent, capable of rebelling against Him, and therefore free to choose between right and wrong. Having endowed such a being with a spark of His own life, God in future could only influence that being by moral motives, and, in the sacrifice of Christ and His present Resurrection activity, He had brought the mightiest moral forces to bear upon the man He had thus created. If that man deliberately rejected all God's gracious pleadings, there remained nothing but eternal misery for him. The love of God revealed in the Gospel assured us that none would be in the lake of fire that God could by any means save out of it.

Mr. Hoste said: I think the lecturer may fairly claim to have proved logically that a belief in Organic Evolution, as usually understood, with its dogmatic denials of acts of Creation, any fall of man, and, therefore, the need or fact of atonement, is not consistent with belief in the Scriptural account of such matters.

Of course, there are dilettante evolutionists who are better than their creed; they have never faced the fair deductions of the theory in question, and so retain their general faith in the Scriptures. Some yield to the clamour of the second-rank evolutionists, who ignore the fact that their theory is as far as ever from being proved and that the Darwinian theory (which in the closing decades of the last century was as loudly asserted to be a scientific fact as the parent doctrine to day) is now bankrupt. If Evolution be reduced to "an act of faith" to such men as Dr. W. Bateson and Dr. D. H. Scott, how can it be scientific to acclaim it victor all along the line, as the Bishop of Birmingham,

D.Sc., is said to do? No doubt it is convenient to unload our moral delinquencies on a putative anthropoid ancestry, but how can this be righteous when, as the Professor notes, the most patent of these evils are not found in any of these lower "ancestors"?

There is one point I would venture to ask the learned lecturer to reconsider, and that is the passage on p. 16, where he seems to ascribe the present geological formations to the great world-cataclysm of the Deluge. I have no desire to minimize this catastrophe, but what authority have we for associating with it the deposition of the great fossil-bearing strata, with all the tremendous upheavals and reversals implied? How could the ark have fared in such a general condition of topsy-turvydom, except by a perpetual miracle? Even Ararat would not have been safe. Is there any hint in the biblical narrative of such a stately cataclysm?

Rather the mountains are spoken of as already existing in stable form, and can they be dissociated from geological formation? The Cretaceous deposits, known as the Dover Cliffs, took more than the months of the flood to be laid down. Is it not safer, then, to associate the geological formations with the interval which, as has before been noticed from this platform, is believed by many to exist between the first and second verses of Genesis, whatever conclusions one may come to as to the Professor's general theory?

Mr. Sidney Collett said: Mr. Chairman, I most heartily welcome the paper we have listened to this afternoon as a very fine contribution to the subject under discussion, because it goes to the very root of the matter, and shows that the evolution theory denies the statements made in the Word of God concerning the creation of man.

The very essence of the evolutionary theory is that man was evolved from a lower animal—a monkey.

Not only, however, does the Bible give no countenance to this, but its teaching concerning the origin of man is entirely different.

In Gen. i, 27, we read, concerning man's *spirit*, that God created man *in His own image.* Surely any attempt to reconcile that with Evolution is nothing short of blasphemy.

Then, in Gen. ii, 7, we read, concerning man's *body*, "The Lord God formed man of the dust of the ground." Now, if man was formed from the dust of the ground, how can it be true to say he was formed from an ape?

Again, in Luke iii, 38, where the *genealogy* of the *Man Christ Jesus* is traced back to Adam, we are distinctly told that Adam was the *son of God!* Will any evolutionist, in view of this verse, dare face the logical result of their theory and say that our blessed Lord, in His Holy Human Nature, was really descended from an ape?

Ladies and gentlemen, the position is perfectly clear. The two teachings are absolutely incompatible and irreconcilable. So that if Evolution on this subject is right, then the Bible is wrong, and we had better throw it aside as being unworthy of our confidence. But if the Bible is right, then Evolution is utterly and entirely wrong, and deserves to be cast aside and rejected for ever.

Pastor W. Percival-Prescott writes: Last year the general criticism of the members of the Institute upon Prof. McCready Price's paper, "Geology and its Relation to Scripture Revelation," was the sparse references it contained to the Bible. This year on the Langhorne Orchard Prize Essay, "Revelation and Evolution," Prof. Price merits no such criticism. He has clearly shown from the Bible that Evolution is entirely out of harmony with Revelation.

However, perhaps more space could have been devoted to the biological aspect of Evolution and the doctrine of the unity of type. The Darwinian theory is still held by many people to-day, among them leading religious lights like Bishop Barnes. The argument centres around the questions of Special Creation and the process of Evolution supposed to be proved by the similiarity of type. In spite of the fact that the missing link has not yet been discovered, many still have faith in the Darwinian theory.

Now, it must not be supposed that this similarity of type is an argument in support of Darwin's theory of Evolution.

The fact that a unity of type is adopted where a unity of function is aimed at, and that increasing complexity of type is associated with increasing complexity of function, does not necessarily suggest that C is derived from B, or B from A, but much more forcibly that they were all derived from the same source—the master mind of God.

Lieut.-Colonel F. Molony writes: I have edited your *Transactions* for some years now, but I do not think I have ever passed a discussion with so many misgivings as to its effects as I feel about this one.

In 1921 I had the privilege of reading a paper before this Society on "Predictions and Expectations of the First Coming of Christ." The main object of that paper was to prove the reality of inspiration, and our Secretary was so good as to say that I had proved my thesis up to the hilt.

We all know that the historicity of Genesis has been established as far back as the fourteenth chapter inclusive. And I myself believe in the inspiration of the whole book, but hold that we have no right to assume that inspiration includes infallibility.

May I, then, be permitted to point out that, although whole libraries of books have been written on the subject, Christian apologists need be very little concerned in defending the inspiration of the early chapters of Genesis.

Most of us believe that Moses wrote the Pentateuch: but how? Surely he wrote Genesis as an editor of older documents, but the other four books as a witness. It is his reliability as a witness that is important for the defence of Revelation; and it is very little affected by the trustworthiness of his judgment as an editor. To hold Moses responsible for all that is said in Genesis would be almost as unfair as to hold me responsible for all that is said in this discussion.

Our lecturer has offered us new ground for distrusting Evolution. But his geological theories are by no means accepted as yet on this side of the Atlantic. Yet, on the strength of them, we are apparently invited to open a new crusade against Evolution!

I think this would be a foolish thing for us to do, and beg to associate myself with Mr. Weller's remarks.

Author's Reply.—I fully sympathize with our worthy Hon. Secretary in his incredulity about all the great geological changes of the past having been caused by the world-catastrophe of the Deluge. For one who has at all travelled about the world, it does seem preposterous to say that all the tremendous phenomena which we see were produced by one great world-convulsion.

But I have never affirmed this. I do not wish to dogmatize on this point. I don't know.

But one thing I do know. There is no method worthy of being called scientific by which we can affirm that the trilobites, for example, lived and died long before the ammonites and the mastodons came into existence. There is no way to prove logically that the trilobites and the graptolites may not have lived contemporaneously with the dinosaurs, or that the dinosaurs may not have been contemporary with the mastodons and the other elephants, or with man himself. Fortunately, I have already discussed this topic at some length in a paper read last year before the Victoria Institute; hence I need not go into the matter further here. I would also refer the interested reader to my College Text-book, "The New Geology," where this subject is dealt with quite fully. This book may be obtained in this country through The Stanborough Press, Watford, Herts.

On this point we now have a very interesting recent discovery. *The Illustrated London News,* of May 9, 1925, gives a reproduction of a drawing of a dinosaur which has been found on the walls of a canyon in Arizona, U. S. A. This drawing was made by prehistoric man; and it proves conclusively that, either the one who made this drawing, or some of his ancestors, must have been familiar with the form of the Diplodocus or some similar dinosaur in real life. An accompanying drawing found on the same canyon wall shows a man fighting with a mastodon or a similar kind of elephant, perhaps a Mammoth.

Thus we have objective proof that man was contemporary with both the dinosaurs and the ancient elephants. The latter were thus living side by side in the same world; and thus we have one further proof from objective fact of that great principle of the contemporaneity of these ancient faunas, a principle which we have already found to be demanded by strict scientific logic.

Now, the problem before any common-sense view of geology is this: *How did all these great animals (and many other kinds could be included) become extinct?* No doubt we can easily work ourselves up into a feeling that any world-catastrophe sufficient to bring about such an extinction would be quite "impossible." I have little faith in such *a priori* methods of reasoning in the face of objective proof, such as we now possess. At any rate, How did all these animals become exterminated from all over the world, and exterminated apparently at once?

This, I claim, is the great outstanding problem of Geology—or of all natural science, for that matter. A very large amount of new evidence has come to light which tends to support the views of the New Catastrophism in Geology. A re-examination of this entire subject is the next thing in order. In the meantime, it should be remembered that the strictest logic must be applied to all these studies regarding the early days of our world, the same hard rules of logic which we would apply to a problem in physics or chemistry or astronomy. For it is already as clear as sunlight that very many ideas now confidently held in the name of Geology will not stand critical inspection. The geological theory of the successive forms of life is without doubt the weakest point in the theory of organic Evolution. How long are we going to retain this part of the Evolution theory in our orthodox discussions of the problems of science and religion?

THE

# BULLETIN

OF

# CREATION, THE DELUGE

### AND RELATED SCIENCE

| VOLUME IV | DECEMBER, 1944 | NUMBER 5 |

## THE MEANING OF THE ORIGIN AND ACTIVITIES OF THE HUMAN BODY

### II. Control of Growth and Aging in the Human Body

*By* HUBERT O. SWARTOUT, M.S., M.D., Dr.P.H.

#### Part 1. HOW DOES YOUR BODY GROW?

Think of yourself as an average-sized person who has reached full growth. That means you are about five feet seven inches tall, and that you weigh about one hundred fifty pounds. At birth you were about twenty inches tall and weighed about seven pounds, so you are now more than three times as tall and more than twenty times as heavy as you were then. This growth covered a period of eighteen or twenty years.

Your growth, however, was not simply an increase in height and weight. The poet who said, "Men are only boys grown tall," was wrong. Not only in mind, but in body as well, are you merely a one-hundred-fifty-pound baby. If the proportions of the various parts of your body were the same now as they were at the time of your birth, you would be a monstrosity to be pitied instead of a normal human being.

Long years of study of the way in which the normal human body grows have not only confirmed the old idea that diet supplies the materials which enable the body to grow, but also have revealed the fact that the *trophic* nerves, several minerals and vitamins, and the secretions of certain glands are all of great importance in guiding and controlling growth. It is knowledge of these facts that enables the physician or wise parent to cooperate with nature in insuring normal growth. The wisdom of nature, however, is still beyond that of the wisest physician, but of the source of that wisdom much can be learned by physiological studies.

This study will include the following topics: *Part 1, How does your body grow?* 1, The extreme complexity of body growth, beyond explanation on a physiological basis; 2, Bone growth regulation a special challenge to evolution; 3, Questions of teleology; 4, Other cases of growth regulation, certain internal organs; 5, Growth and life span of cells; 6, Cell

The BULLETIN is published by, and is the official organ of the "Society for the Study of Creation, the Deluge, and Related Science." The Editorial Board is comprised of Professor George McCready Price, Dr. Dell D. Haughey, and Mr. Ben F. Allen. It is printed at the College Press, Arlington, California. For members the BULLETIN is free, and extra copies 50 cents each (each number priced according to size); for non-members it is $2.00 per year and this number is 65 cents. All correspondence should be directed to the editors, Box 1030, Glendale, Calif.

*449*

differentiation a special case of teleology; 7, Rate of production of blood cells.

*Part 2, How does your body age?* 1, The "energy charge" unaccountable; 2, Special cases of teleological regulation; 3, Life chart of five vital functions; 4, Three wise provisions of nature; 5, Mental power need not abate with age.

### GROWTH REGULATION BEYOND PHYSIOLOGICAL EXPLANATION

When you were born, the distance from your chin to the back of your head was about one fourth of your height, and the distance around your head was nearly two thirds of your height. Your head was larger around than your chest, and your chest was larger than your hips. There was not much difference in the length and thickness of your arms and your legs, and your legs made up scarcely one third of your height.

Now that you are grown, the distance from your chin to the back of your head is only about one sixth of your height, and the distance around your head is one third of your height. Your head is much smaller around than your chest, which in turn is somewhat smaller around than your hips. Your legs are much thicker than your arms, also much longer. They make up about half of your height.

The changes in these proportions did not all take place at a regular rate. For instance, while your chest grew faster than your head did, it did not gain much in the race before you were ten years old. In fact, fully half of the growth of your head took place before you were three. By the time you were ten, your head was nearly as large as it is now; but you were not much more than four feet tall; and you weighed less than seventy pounds.

Your increase in height was not steady either. During the first year, you gained eight or nine inches. Growth at that rate for twenty years would have made you at least fifteen feet tall. The second year you gained about four and a half inches, the third year three and a half, the fourth year two and a half, and after that about two inches each year up to the age of twelve. Then you grew faster for three or four years, later slowing up rapidly as you approached your full height. When you think of it, don't you think it strange that people do not differ more in height than they do, and that there is so little difference in the time it takes different persons to reach their full growth?

### DETAILS OF BONE GROWTH

The growth of your bones was an interesting process, especially the growth of your long bones, such as those of your arms and legs. Each of these bones has two broadened ends, which help to form joints, and a long, slender, hollow *shaft* between the ends. The whole bone, except the end sections which touch other bones, is covered with a tough membrane called the *periosteum;* and the hollow shaft is filled with *marrow.* During your growing years there was a thin layer of tough *cartilage* extending across the entire width of the bone at each region where the shaft joined a broadened end section.

All the growth in length of the bones took place at these cartilage layers. On the one side, they constantly added a little to the length of the end section, and on the other they added much more to the length of the shaft. Some cells on the inner surface of the periosteum kept building the bone out and increasing its thickness, while other cells on the outer surface of the marrow kept eating away at the bone and increasing the size of the cavity to keep it in correct proportion. When you reached your full height, the bone-building and bone-eating cells both stopped working, except a few in the cartilage layers, which took up the job of changing the cartilage itself into solid bone.

## QUESTIONS OF TELEOLOGY

Bone growth, such as has just been described, raises many difficult questions for those who do not acknowledge the existence of an intelligent Planner and Controller of everything in nature. Why, for instance, should the cartilage layers keep adding to the length of the long bones for eighteen or twenty years and then stop forever? Why should they remain cartilage for that length of time and then turn to bone? Why should corresponding bones in limbs on opposite sides of the body grow at the same rate and stop growing at the same time? Why should the bones in the lower limbs grow faster than those in the upper? What keeps the periosteum cells working just fast enough to preserve the proper outward shape and proportions of the bone? Why should the cells in the marrow cavity eat away bone at the same time that the cells outside the shaft build bone? Why should these two opposing processes stop at the same time? Why should the eating-away process proceed at a rate that keeps the shell of the shaft from becoming either too thick or too thin?

A tendency to vary from the normal in growth and development must be assumed by the believer in organic evolution in order to explain the origin of different kinds of plants and animals. If there were even one chance in ten of any considerable variation in each of the many phases of bone growth, a majority of all human beings would be dwarfs, giants, or deformed monstrosities; and a large proportion of those who were of normal size and shape would have bones so heavy as to make them awkward, or so light and fragile as to be in constant danger of fracture.

## GROWTH CHANGES IN CERTAIN ORGANS

When you were born, many of your internal organs, as well as your head, were larger in proportion to the size of your body than they now are; but some were smaller. At birth, your *liver* probably weighed one twentieth as much as your entire body. Now it weighs scarcely one fortieth. You had an active *thymus gland* under your breastbone. It grew for a year or two, and then began to shrink. Now it is inactive, and probably much smaller than it was when you were born. Your tonsils grew as your throat grew until you were about seven years old; but unless they became inflamed and swollen, they grew little, if any, after that. At present you have large, air-filled cavities, or *sinuses*, in the bones of your face and forehead. When you were born, these openings had not appeared, or were tiny.

Some changes of great importance took place in your lungs, heart, and blood vessels at, and soon after your birth. Before that time your lungs were heavy and soggy, and contained no air. Your body was supplied with blood through vessels in a thick cord attached to the front of your abdomen, but your heart was at work keeping your blood in circulation. There was an opening between the upper two chambers of your heart, so the blood could go from the right to the left side without having to go through the blood vessels of your lungs, as it has to do now. There was a short cut or sidetrack between the two large arteries coming from the two lower chambers of your heart, and another between two large blood vessels in your abdominal cavity.

These special passages were necessary because your lungs and most of the organs in your abdomen were not yet busy at the work they were to do after you were born. Within a few minutes after your birth, however, your lungs were working normally and the circulation in the cord vessels had stopped. A few days later the doorway between the right and the left side of your heart had grown shut, and both of the sidetrack blood vessels had shrunken to fibrous cords, forcing your blood to take the route through your lungs and abdominal organs that it has followed ever since.

## Growth and Life Span of Cells

At birth, nearly every kind of cell that will ever form a part of your body was already present in it, but the life histories of these cells have varied widely. Some of them have lived for many years with little change in size —such as bone cells, cartilage cells, tendon cells, and others. No one knows how long they may live. Other cells have a very short life. Some cells grow much in size, but increase little, if any, in number. Other cells increase greatly in number, but do not grow in size.

The cells of most of your muscles were present when you were born, have grown in proportion to your body, are still alive, and will live as long as you do. Some of them are thick enough to be seen with the naked eye, and are five or six inches long. Your nerve cells have a somewhat similar life story. They are composed of cell bodies with fibers extending out from them. Probably no human eye is keen enough to see even the largest of these cell bodies without the aid of a magnifier, and certainly not keen enough to see any of the fibers; but we have ways of knowing that cell bodies in the spinal cord sent out fibers that grew in length as your body grew and that have endings in your toes, making the entire cells

nearly four feet long. It is probable that many of the fibers can increase in number and become more and more branched. We know that they can regenerate when damaged or destroyed. The cell bodies do not increase in number, and when destroyed they cannot be restored.

The cells of the outer layer of your skin and those that form the lining of many of your organs are constantly being formed deep beneath the surface, pushed upward by cells formed later, gradually becoming less and less active, and finally dying and being cast off or rubbed off from the surface. Their lives are measured in weeks, or months at most. Such cells were as large in your body when you were born as they are now, but you have many more of them now than you did then. When damaged or destroyed, they are soon replaced.

## Special Examples of Cell Differentiation

Right here it is interesting to recall that cells so different in history and nature, as well as in structure, as are nerve cells and the cells that form the outer layer of the skin came from the same original germ layer, the *ectoderm*. If there were not some allwise Planner behind all this, how could this particular kind of differentiation take place time after time in the same way as each new human being develops?

Your blood cells, as well as your skin cells, were as large when you were a baby as they are now, but their number depends chiefly upon the amount of blood you have. You should know also that these cells are among the smallest in your body. It would take more than a hundred thousand of them placed side by side to make a row as long as one of the longest nerve cells. Ten of them side by side would not reach across the width of one of the largest muscle cells, and ten thousand of them side by side would not measure as long as such a muscle cell. In other words, the bulk of a single large muscle cell may be more than a million times as great as that of a red blood cell. Yet both kinds of cells developed from the same kind of germ-layer cells in the *mesoderm*.

As an average-sized, full-grown person, you have five or six quarts of blood, every pinhead-sized drop of which contains about seven thousand white cells and about five million red cells. The total number would be represented by twenty-five to twenty-eight with twelve zeros added. One can hardly conceive of the real meaning of such large numbers. Yet, many as these cells are, within a short time, —averaging between twenty and thirty days,—every one of the red ones will have been destroyed and replaced by a new cell; and few of the white cells will last as long as a week.

### RATE OF PRODUCTION OF BLOOD CELLS

Probably all the red cells and most of the white cells grow to maturity in the bone marrow. You may have thought of the marrow simply as something to fill the hollows in the bones; but how amazing must be the growth activity in this tissue to enable it to produce many more new cells every ten minutes of time than there are people on the whole face of the earth!

Thus you see that at one extreme of the growth and life history of your body cells you have large muscle cells and nerve cells, whose life is measured by your own life, and which will never increase much in number, if any at all; while at the other extreme you have tiny blood cells that live but a few days, but are produced so rapidly that if each new cell were a person, the entire city of New York could be repopulated in a single second of time.

### Part 2. HOW DOES YOUR BODY AGE?

As the latter end of life approaches, some of the earlier growth processes tend to reverse themselves. Changes in body and mind are constantly taking place, and these all call for adjustments in our attitudes, programs, and activities. The better our understanding of the changes, the more perfect our adjustments can be, and the more easily and naturally we can enter and pass through old age.

Somebody has said that a man begins to die as soon as he is born. The fact is that he begins before that. As the female sex cell comes to maturity, it has about it three small structures that are already marked for death; and at the moment the male and female cells unite,—the great moment when a new life begins,—a part of the male cell is cast off to die. The dictum: "Thou shalt surely die", is in operation every moment.

The following are the topics in this part of the study: 1, The "energy charge" is an unaccountable gift; 2, The tonsils are a special case of teleological regulation; 3, A life chart of five vital functions; 4, Three wise provisions of nature; 5, Man's mental powers need not abate with age.

Conclusion: Job pointed out the Designer and the Source of regulation of cell and body growth.

### THE "ENERGY CHARGE" UNACCOUNTABLE

The essential features of the aging process, whether for a single cell or for the whole human organism, may be stated in a few sentences. It seems as if each new individual at the very beginning of his existence, as well as each newly formed cell in his body forever afterward, receives a certain, definite "energy charge". This heritage may be expended in growth or in the performance of various other functions; but, however used, it is used most rapidly at first and less and less so as time goes on, until there is none of it left, and death occurs.

Outwardly, and viewed without a real understanding of fundamentals, it may seem as if the early part of life represents a constant gain, because the individual is growing. This growth itself, however, is at the expense of some of the original energy heritage, and really goes on at a constantly decreasing rate. The original fertilized cell becomes two cells, each as large as the first, probably in much less than an hour. Later doublings in body size take longer. Soon each doubling takes days, then weeks. For a baby to double its birth size requires about five months, and it is approaching its second birthday before it weighs twice as much as it did at five months. Five or six years pass before the next doubling is complete, and eight or nine before the next, which brings the young person to the age of fifteen or sixteen. Few people ever grow to twice the size they were at these ages, no matter how long they live; and near the end they not only do not gain weight, but lose it.

While some cells grow, many do not begin their separate existence until they are full size. The life history of these cells is a simpler example of the aging process than is that of the whole body, because the growth feature does not obscure the picture. At first, all the structures within the cell wall are virtually liquid, and vital functions proceed at a rapid rate; but the liquid gradually becomes thicker and thicker until it sets into a solid, while the activity of the cell steadily decreases. Finally the whole cell dries and shrinks and all activity ceases.

A SPECIAL CASE OF TELEOLOGICAL
REGULATION

The tonsils have a life history that is significant. Healthy tonsils grow from five to seven years, then remain about the same size while their owner goes on growing. Soon after he reaches his full size, they begin to shrink; and by the time he is forty or fifty years old his tonsils are so small they can hardly be found. Tonsils are composed chiefly of tissue like that of lymph glands, whose purpose is to fight infection. You are familiar with the infectious diseases that people have but once in a lifetime, the reason being that one attack causes the body to build up a resistance or *immunity* to them. Children begin life with very little immunity, but it rapidly increases after they are large enough to run about and come in contact with various sources of infection. By the time they are seven years old, the need for help from the tonsils is less; and when adult years have been reached it is practically nil. Here you see an illustration of the fundamental principle that when any part of the body become useless it develops the characteristics of old age, while the body as a whole may be still in its prime.

The skin shows its age by decreasing elasticity and consequent inability to smooth out wrinkles, and hangs in a baggy manner on the shrunken trunk and limbs which it covers. Muscles, including those of the heart, shrink and grow flabby as they become drier and stiffer. Fat partly wastes away and is partly replaced by water. Ligaments in the chest and abdomen lose their tone and begin to stretch, allowing the organs to sag. Bones become drier and more brittle. The cartilages between the vertebrae become thinner and harder. The walls of the blood vessels harden, and may have lime and fat deposited in them. Hardening of the arteries is not necessarily a disease, but to a considerable degree a mark of age,—everybody has it more or less, or will have it if he lives long enough. Vital organs show a slowing up of activity and an inability to handle loads as great as those they could easily manage in earlier years. The circulation becomes sluggish, and it is harder to keep the hands and feet warm. The pulse is slower, the digestion weaker, and there is more tendency to constipation. All the senses grow less keen. By the age of forty-five, the lenses of the eyes become solid, set for far vision, so that glasses are often needed for reading. Repair

cannot be much improved, study is well worth while up to sixty. After thirty-five, one should not expect to be able to do as heavy work as before, or to stand up under as strenuous play.

THREE WISE PROVISIONS OF NATURE

The curve of reproductive power (referring to chart) shows that the time when people are more likely to have children is between the ages of twenty and forty. Careful scientific

## LIFE CHART OF FIVE VITAL FUNCTIONS
### (Partly after charts of Stratz and Warthin)

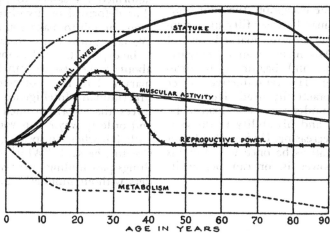

processes are retarded, — wounds and broken bones take longer to heal, and it requires more rest and sleep to recover from fatigue.

LIFE CHART OF FIVE VITAL FUNCTIONS

(Partly after charts of Stratz and Warthin)

As you read on from this point, make a careful study of the accompanying chart of five vital functions. This chart, indicating as it does the time that old age begins to attack the various vital functions, leads to some interesting conclusions. It shows that the best time to study and to develop a good musculature is before twenty; but, though after twenty the physique

study has proved that the reproductive power of men, on the average, does not last more than five or ten years longer than that of women, and that the "sex urge" often dies out with it unless unnaturally stimulated. The decline and disappearance of reproductive power is a perfectly natural process. Men are foolish, then, to worry or be ashamed about it, and to waste their money on quacks who promise to "restore lost manhood."

Not only is the curve of reproductive power interesting because it is so different from the other curves, but it shows three wise provisions of nature. First, the power is dormant until the prospective parents are at least physically able to. care for their off-spring. Second, the fruitful period is short enough to insure that all the children will be near enough of the same age to be able to work and counsel together as people of the same generation. This makes for a more harmonious group of brothers and sisters. Third, reproductive power ceases while there is still a good prospect that the parents will live to bring up their youngest children to maturity.

### MENTAL POWER NEED NOT ABATE WITH AGE

With one exception, the vital functions of a man between fifty and seventy show more or less marked signs of old age. His metabolism is comparatively low, and beginning to drop still lower. His reproductive power may be practically dead. He cannot stand up under a physical load as he once did, and his ability to do so is steadily decreasing. He is probably not quite as tall as he once was. But his mental power is, or can be, at its height.

### CONCLUSION

However, most of you who are reading these words are not yet aged. You have much of your life before you, and growth and development mean more to you than does the way in which the body goes through its period of decline.

Think of the multitude of ways in which, and the rates at which, the various parts of your body have grown to make it what it is today. Only one or at most a few of these growth details getting out of balance would have deformed or disabled you, yet a person thus deformed or disabled is uncommon enough to make you notice him. We take normal growth as something to be expected, but the more we know about it the less we can fathom the marvel of it. Is it not evident that a superhuman Intelligence rules the forces that work in such wonderful and orderly ways? Can you not agree with Job when, in speaking about the Creator, he said: "Which doeth great things past finding out; yea, and wonders without number"? Job. 9:10.

THE

# BULLETIN

OF

# CREATION, THE DELUGE

### AND RELATED SCIENCE

| VOLUME V | JANUARY, 1945 | NUMBER 1 |
| --- | --- | --- |

## CONTENTS

---

### THE PRESENT STATUS OF GENETICS AND THE ORIGIN OF SPECIES
#### By FRANK LEWIS MARSH, Ph.D.*

##### THE PROBLEM STATED

The student of the problem of what processes of change occur in plants and animals and to what extent they are effective, finds himself faced today with a serious situation. Extensive research in this field, both in America and in Eurasia, has resulted in such a tremendous bulk of records and discussions that in most instances he is unable to find the time necessary to familiarize himself with even the majority of these findings. It is, therefore, with sincerest gratitude that he receives the second edition, revised, of *Genetics and the Origin of Species*, by Dr. Theodosius Dobzhansky, Professor of Zoology, Columbia University.[1]

Since the rediscovery of Mendel's principles in 1900, the history of genetics has been the story of the development of methods to study the agencies which brought about and maintained the diversification of plants and animals into their present groups. In the words of L. C. Dunn, editor of the Columbia Biological Series, "It is possible now to take stock of what these methods have done to improve our understanding of what has been, in spite of all research, so great a mystery— the origin of species." This is what Dobzhansky's present volume attempts to do.

In studying Dr. Dobzhansky's summarization of the discoveries of genetics in the field of speciation, one is impressed with the author's sincerity, analytical power, and nearly faultless logic. Although

---

*Professor of Biology, Union College, Lincoln, Nebraska.

1. Dobzhansky, Theodosius, *Genetics and the Origin of Species*; Columbia University Press, New York City, 1941; 446 pages.

The BULLETIN is published by, and is the official organ of the "Society for the Study of Creation, the Deluge, and Related Science." The Editorial Board is comprised of Professor George McCready Price, Mr. B. F. Allen, and Dr. Dell D. Haughey. It is printed at the College Press, Arlington, California. For members the BULLETIN is free, and extra copies 30 cents each (each number priced according to size); for non-members it is $2.00 per year and this number is 45 cents. All correspondence should be directed to the Editors, Box 1030, Glendale, California.

the author is completely sold to the conception of organic evolution, still he has brought together a wealth of facts presented in a fair way so that his volume becomes a valuable sourcebook for evolutionists and creationists alike. Of course, it is necessary for the reader to bear in mind constantly that Dr. Dobzhansky is an evolutionist, and as such, often, perhaps unconsciously, marshals purely subjective matter in the direction of evidence which he feels favors evolution only. But by giving careful attention, the reader is able to distinguish scientific facts from subjective interpretations, and to find in this volume what is doubtless the best existing summarization of what the science of genetics, the only science which studies those processes of change which can or cannot produce evolution, has to offer in the field of explanation of variation in organisms.

The following is an outline of our discussion:

1. Darwin, at first a special creationist, erred in his conception of fixity of species as well as in the real teachings of the Scriptures.

2. Examining Darwin's problems on his voyage of the Beagle, the variation and distribution of life on islands and on isolated land areas.

3. Interpreting Darwin's problems according to the facts as known at present, and on the basis of the Deluge as a world-wide geological cataclysm.

4. The limitations of variation by mutation.

5. The limitations of variation by changes in the number of chromosomes and in the number and distribution of genes in the chromosomes.

6. "Variation within the kind," the only evolution (if it can be so designated) known to biologists.

7. The threefold problem for Creationists.

## WHY DARWIN'S ORIGINAL BELIEF IN CREATION FAILED HIM

At the time that Charles Darwin made his five-year voyage around the world with a group of map makers on the British cruiser *Beagle*, he was a special creationist. Furthermore, he was a creationist of the most conservative order, holding that the plants and animals of his day had, in all their wealth of variation, been created by God and placed in the niches they then occupied. However, on this leisurely voyage of circumnavigation he had the rare opportunity of employing his marked ability of keen observation in noting the real distribution of organisms over the face of the earth. What he saw troubled him very greatly. He found that the actual distribution of organisms was not as it would most likely be if they had been created and placed in their specific areas. The different "species" of a genus were most commonly not found inhabiting the same area but were more frequently separated by some natural barrier. Two races of a "species" rarely lived in the same region but were almost invariably isolated from each other by some mountain wall, desert, large body of water, or by mere distance alone. Continental islands were usually populated with forms obviously related to those on the mainland, while the organisms of oceanic islands differed in marked external characters from those of either mainlands or continental islands. Added to this fact of mosaic distribution of organisms which apparently were blood related, was the fact of populations which existed on volcanic islands which had without doubt arisen since Creation week.

These facts of distribution were not in harmony with Darwin's belief in the absolute fixity of "species"; and his conception of the individuals of successive generations being as like as parts from a single mold in an automobile factory, of necessity broke down. It would appear that Darwin was a creationist, not in his own right as the result of careful study of the Scriptures and nature, but rather merely because he had been taught it by his professors at Cambridge. Due to his misunderstanding of the basis principles of the theory, he was unable to harmonize natural facts of distribution with his unnatural conception of creationism. Tragically, he turned away from the theory of special creation and became the champion of one of the most unscientific theories of modern science, the theory of organic evolution.

Darwin's professors at Cambridge University taught this ultraconservative type of creationism because they were ignorant of the actual state of affairs in the distribution of living things over the earth. Just to the extent that creationists today ignore the geographical distribution of organisms, when they fill in the details of their philosophy, will they likewise be in danger of drawing unjustifiably narrow lines in nature.

### DARWIN'S BEAGLE VOYAGE
### PROBLEMS EXAMINED

At this point, with the use of a few modern illustrations, I will sample the type of distribution which so greatly troubled Darwin. The Atlantic ocean serves as a common barrier to a whole group of forms. The faunae of Europe and America have a great similarity of composition, without being exactly identical. Thus in Europe the American beaver, the elk, the moose, the caribou, the bison, and the Canada lynx are replaced respectively by the European beaver, the red deer, the elk, the reindeer, the wisent, and the European lynx. Each species, though bearing a different "species" name, is crossfertile with its vicar on the other side of the Atlantic, e.g., the European beaver with the American beaver, the European red deer with the American elk, the wisent with the American bison, etc.

The Hawaiian Islands are the most completely isolated archipelago in the world. They form a group of volcanic islands which have very possibly appeared since the Noachian flood. The individual islands are well separated. Unique groups of forms consisting of large series of "species", and some "genera", and even "families", of birds, insects, and land snails are found here which appear nowhere else in the world.

In contrast with this fauna is that of the Galapagos Islands. The nearest member of this group is about 585 miles west of Ecuador, while a distance of about 300 miles lies between the most widely separated islands in the group. In contrast with the situation in the Hawaiian Islands, a large percentage of the "genera" of animals in the Galapagos group are also found in Central or South America. It is of interest here to note that the ocean currents in this part of the world favor a migration from that direction. Upon nine of the widely separated islands in the Galapagos group are fourteen "species" of the giant land tortoise, and a single "genus" of lizard is represented by separate "species" or "subspecies" on each of the twelve islands of the group.

The Hawaiian Islands are purely oceanic, and the Galapagos Islands partake somewhat of the nature of oceanic islands and somewhat of that of continental islands. It would be well here to see what faunal conditions prevail on a purely continental island. Trinidad, a short thirty miles from Venezuela, would classify here, and we find that it is zoogeographically indisstinguishable from the adjacent mainland.

Contrasting with the widely isolated land areas of the Hawaiian and Galapagos Islands with their abundance of different "species", "genera", and "families", is the great area of Africa south of the Sahara. This vast expanse is not broken by high mountain chains, and it is profitable to observe that the fauna is strikingly uniform. The principal groups and even a great number of "species" of reptiles, birds, mammals, insects, and land isopods have an unusually wide range from east to west and from north to south.

Rising above the general level of this great area in Africa, simulating islands in an ocean, are the two mountain peaks, Kilimanjara and Kenya, respectively 19,000 and 17,000 feet high. A vicariation of "species" similar to that observed between America and Europe is found on these two peaks which stand a mere two hundred miles apart. The monkeys, lemurs, shrews, squirrels, various mice, hyraces, elephants, river hogs, and antelopes are represented on the two mountains by corresponding "species" and "subspecies". Such vicariation is demonstrable in eighteen pairs of forms.

Another interesting case of isolation on mountains is found in the distribution of the wild goats known as ibex. Seven different "species" of ibex now live respectively in the Pyrenees, in the Alps, in the Caucasus, in the Himalayas, in Sinai, and in Abyssinia. Although these forms now remain separate on their lofty "islands" in this interrupted series of mountain ranges, and have been assigned different "species" names, still they are distinguishable only by the shape of their horns, being otherwise closely similar and still completely fertile with each other.

In America an illustration of this typical mosaic pattern of distribution is furnished by the American reindeer or caribou. Ignoring the Scandinavian Reindeer which has been thriving in Labrador and Alaska since its introduction there over thirty years ago, there are eleven "species" and one "subspecies" of native caribou in America. A study of the regions occupied by these "species" as given in H. E. Anthony's *Animals of America* (Doubleday, Doran and Company, New York City, 1938. 335 pages), reveals that in no place do the distributions of these caribou overlap. Each group is isolated from all others and differences between the "species" are chiefly size of horns, general size of body, and coloration.

The fact that different "species" and "subspecies" almost invariably occupy adjacent regions and are not found living together in the same area, is well illustrated in our own country by the distribution of the twelve to fourteen "species" and "subspecies" of coyotes, by the sixteen "species" and "subspecies" of red foxes, and by the fourteen "species" and "subspecies" of gray foxes. The coyotes of different regions vary in size, length of ears, and coloration. The red foxes of one area differ from those inhabiting other areas by some variation of the color pattern or in size. The gray-fox mosaic is built upon differences that the layman cannot always readily distinguish. These differences lie in type of hair, coloration, length of ears and tail, and in body size. As the distribution of these "species" of caribou, coyotes, and foxes is studied it is obvious that the topography of the country has much to do with the number of "species". Concerning this matter Dobzhansky (p. 342) remarks, "It appears that, at least in the temperate and subtropical zones, the maximum diversity of species and races of land forms is found usually in mountainous countries rather than on plains." The abundance of "species" and races appears in direct proportion to the abundance of natural barriers which break up the large region into more or less isolated areas.

In the realm of birds many interesting mosaics occur. In the case of the titmouse in Eurasia an area of distribution exists which is roughly of a hollow oval pattern. *Parus major*, the European form, also extends eastward across Siberia. In the south it reaches Iran where it is cross-fertile with *P. bokharensis*. The latter extends eastward in its range through Turkestan to India. In India it is cross-fertile with *P. minor*. The range of the latter includes southeastern Asia and Japan. In the region of Amur, *P. major* and *P. minor* occupy the same territory but for some unknown physiological or psychological reason do not cross.

In the case of two Eurasian crows, *Corvus corone* and *C. cornix*, their geographical areas are apposed along a line nearly 2,000 miles in length. Hybrids between the two "species" occur only in a zone from seven to sixty-five miles wide. In the United States a similar situation exists between the bronzed and the purple grackles. The latter occupies the eastern seaboard while the former occurs throughout the interior of the United States. Along a line from Lousiana to New England where these two areas converge hybrid forms are common.

In plants the same type of vicariation is even more common than in animals. Many of our modern economically valuable forms have been developed as hybrids between vicarious groups brought together from different continents. Upon any continent the distribution of plants presents much the same mosaic type of pattern, often with integrades appearing in areas of overlap. A specific illustration of larger mosaic units is furnished by the distribution of the spiderwort, *Tradescantia occidentalis,* from the Rockies east over the prairie states to the Mississippi. The range of *T. canaliculata* lies mostly east of that of *T. occidentalis.* In a fairly broad strip west of the Mississippi the ranges of the two "species" overlap. The members of this same "genus" often display a distribution pattern of extremely small units. In the Ozark region *T. caniculata* grows mostly on exposed locations at the top of cliffs, and *T. subaspera* on rich shaded soils at the foot of the same cliffs. Hybrids are produced along the ravines formed by erosion in the cliffs.

DISTRIBUTION IN THE LIGHT OF TODAY

It was this type of distribution of organisms which so greatly troubled Darwin on his voyage around the world. His interpretation of the theory of special creation called for no variation among organisms, but the actual testimony of nature at least *appeared* to indicate instead that in many cases groups of "species" and sometimes even "genera" and "families" had arisen from common ancestors. In the face of what appeared to him to be clear evidence for development with change, he forsook his impossibly *narrow* conception

of creation and adopted one of *unlimited variation.* Today we marvel that he should refuse one unscientific theory for another which was equally unscientific. He merely shifted his position from one impossible extreme to the other.

In the light of this type of distribution how shall a special creationist build his philosophy of speciation so that it will harmonize with facts? Three basic facts of Genesis apply here: (1) The fact emphasized by ten repetitions in Genesis 1 that each organism brings forth only after its kind; (2) The fact expressed in Genesis 7 that every dry-land animal, except those in the Ark, died during the Flood; and (3) The fact recorded in Genesis 8 that after the Flood all dry-land animals spread out over the earth from the mountains of Ararat.

Occasionally a creationist is met who does not believe that *all* land animals outside the Ark died during the Flood. Such an opinion, it seems to me, is difficultly defensible in the light of the very simple and clear statements in Genesis 7:21-23. It seems to me that no clearer statements are to be found in the Bible than are found in these verses, and I believe that they say that around the entire circle of the globe all dry-land forms, including "every creeping thing," i.e., land snails, which were outside the Ark, died in the Flood. This means that the modern land snails of Hawaii must have descended from ancestors which were in the Ark. (It should be remembered that it is possible that the Hawaiian Islands did not even exist before the Flood.)

The difficulties which lie in the way of holding the view that all modern land animals have come from Ararat, along with existing situations with regard to distribution of land animals, e.g., the wingless Kiwi in New Zealand and the tree sloths in South America, have led a few creationists to adopt a resurrection theory. This theory holds that after all animal life was destroyed in the Flood, God brought certain forms back to life in the same parts of the world in which they died.[2] However, at the present time the theory has few adherents. It is an intriguingly simple theory from the standpoint of explanation of present-day distribution; but the fact that such a revival of antediluvian forms would make Noah's herculean task of building an Ark sufficiently commodious to hold representatives of *every* created kind (Gen. 6:19, 20) a farce; and the expressed purpose of bringing the animals forth from the Ark, "that they may breed abundantly in the earth, and be fruitful, and multiply upon the earth" (Gen. 8:17), lead most creationists to hold to the view that modern land animals have descended from ancestors which debarked in the mountains of Ararat. These problems of distribution offer the creationst, as well as the evolutionist, a tremendous and stimulating challenge.

The actual situation with regard to distribution which was illustrated in Section III above is not that which would be found if a state of fixity of species had existed since the Flood. It is very obvious that any one generation of the slow moving animals in particular would not get much farther out over the surface of the earth than did the generation which preceded them. Forms which continued to survive would of necessity reproduce. This outward dispersal accompanied with reproduction, and probably caused by it, would, if "species" were fixed, result in long lines of identical individuals extending all the way from Ararat to the farthest present distribution point. Granted that all of the individuals of any "species" may have vanished from many areas after the pioneer wave passed, if post-flood fixety governed, we still should find identical "species" at widely removed points. But actually, the only cosmopolitan "species" are those comparatively few which have great powers of locomotion, or of being moved, and which today continually shift about over wide areas. The vast majority of the smaller taxonomic groups of organisms present the mosaic, definitely local,

type of distribution referred to above. Of the several "species" of a single "genus", the individuals composing the population of one niche may differ from those of the adjacent unit of mosaic by no more than slightly longer ears and tail, but differ from them they invariably do. The establishment by the taxonomic "splitters" of thousands of modern species is made possible because of this very fact of variation within geographically isolated groups.

## LIMITATIONS OF VARIATION BY MUTATION

In view of this obvious variation, the question naturally arises, Is there any limit to the amount of change which these processes of variation may produce in organisms? Darwin decided that these very forces could produce a man from a one-celled organism, if given sufficient time. Was he correct in his opinion? What processes of change in organisms do actually exist? Are they capable of erecting races, "species", "genera", and "families" within a single group since the Flood?

It is in the answering of these questions that Dobzhansky's *Genetics and the Origin of Species* serves as a veritable godsend. Geneticists are agreed that changes in the line of heredity come from within. Environment apparently fails to effect any heritable changes in the germ line. It is therefore to the geneticists that we must turn in order to learn what processes of change in inheritance are known at the present time.

In his summary of these causes of change Dobzhansky (p. 13) lists two processes, mutations and chromosomal changes. Mutations are (1) chemical changes within hereditary units, called genes, which are thought to be extremely complex organic molecules, situated in a linear order in the chromosomes; and (2) changes which involve physical destruc-

2. Only in rare chance occurrances do living forms coincide with fossil forms in the same locality. Tropical and subtropical fossils are equally abundant in polar and in temperate regions as in the tropics, and this is only one of the difficulties this "resurrection" theory. Geology and paleontology vote "No" on this proposition.—*The Editors.*

tion, multiplication, or spatial rearrangements of the genes.

Dobzhansky devotes seventy-eight pages of his book to a very profitable discussion of mutations and of differences due to mutations. The student of speciation eagerly studies this summarization of what is known about mutation to learn if this process could possibly erect new "species". Dobzhansky directs attention to the fact that the only known method of origin of genic differences is through mutation (p. 51), and that mutation affects only a single gene at a time (p. 42). On pages 80 and 222 he states that systemic mutations have never been observed. That is to say, no new "species" arises suddenly from a single mutation. Specific differences are due always to cooperation of *many* genes and hence cannot arise through the mutation of a single gene (p. 24).

Dobzhansky is of the opinion that if it were possible to demonstrate that the differences between two good "species" can be resolved into gene changes, then there would be a possibility that new "species" could arise through mutation. However, he makes it clear (p. 82) that it is impossible so to break down a "species". He states (p. 81) that even between two good "species" of a single "genus" there is always left a residue of differences which cannot be dissolved into constituent genes. (He contradicts himself on this point on page 151.) Thus it cannot be shown in the laboratory that even *all* the differences between two good "species" of a "genus" could arise through mutation. In the final analysis, evolution of one good "species" from another through mutation is impossible. Furthermore, if not even the gap between two good "species" can be bridged by mutation, how entirely beyond the realm of possibility would be the development through mutation of the great discontinuity which appears between "genera" and still higher categories of our modern taxonomic system!

Even if it were possible to resolve the differences between good or valid "species" into constituent genes, there still remains the almost certain fact that sufficient mutations of the necessary sort could never occur as a result of natural forces. Mutations most commonly are of the nature of deteriorations. It is not in harmony with natural facts to assume that sufficient mutational changes appearing in the usual chance manner could occur which would erect a new valid "species" before a resultant chaotic state within the protoplasm would cause the death of the living substance.

However, although at the present stage of genetical progress there appears to be no mutational mechanism in nature which can erect even a new, valid "species", it should be borne in mind that it *is* entirely within the realm of possibility that new *races* may develop through mutational change within isolated groups. In other words, it may be *scientific* to assume that the "species" of caribou, ibex, coyotes, and foxes referred to above, which are in fact but geographical races of a single kind, have arisen since the Flood. The very greatest service of mutation appears to be merely the production of variation *within the kind*. Nothing really new has ever been known to result from this process. However, the changes which mutation *can* produce in conjunction with isolation are sufficient in many cases, at least, to explain the mosaic distribution of organisms. Many of the known "species" of today are without doubt but geographical races of a single large polytypic species or kind. An example of such a group is found in the modern "species" of tapirs in South America and in the Dutch East Indies, now living on opposite sides of the earth.

## LIMITATION OF VARIATION BY CHANGES IN CHROMOSOMES AND GENES

The other known process of variation is that of chromosomal change. Dobzhansky devotes eighty-six pages of his book to a consideration of this subject. To this group belong those changes which involve (1) variations of the number of chromosomes, and (2) those which alter the number or the distribution of genes in separate chromosomes. In such changes the chemical structure of the hereditary units themselves, i.e., the genes, is supposedly not affected.

According to Dobzhansky, the sort of chromosome change called a translocation is known to have produced different strains in the evening primrose, in maize, and in the Jimson weed (p. 114). He states that in the case of the primrose, many of the "species" are permanent translocation products (p. 115). However, the most "powerful tool" in the origin of "species" is, according to Dobzhansky, to be found in the type of chromosome change known as polyploidy. This process, according to him, may cause "a rapid, sudden, cataclysmic emergence of new species" (p. 223). But the candid observer is struck with the fact that in no single instance has chromosomal change produced *evolutionary* change. The theory of evolution demands that *new kinds* be produced. The very most that this type of change can do is to give rise merely to variants which but add to the delightful diversity of such kinds as maize, Jimson weed, and primrose. In each separate case the bounds of the kind is never crossed by chromosomal change. This process helps to explain dispersion with variation but is neither quantitatively nor qualitatively capable of producing evolution.

### VARIATION WITHIN THE KIND

Dobzhansky states on page 13 that "Mutations and chromosomal changes arise in every sufficiently studied organism with a certain finite frequency, and thus constantly and unremittingly supply the raw materials for evolution." According to his own summarization of the work of geneticists, this statement would be scientifically correct, i.e., in harmony with demonstrated facts, if he were to substitute the phrase "variation within the kinds" for the word "evolution." The only sort of evolution that has ever been demonstrated is the evolution of new varieties within a

kind which already existed. This type of evolution would never shape a man from a one-celled organism in a billion billion years, because it can never give rise to anything basically new. But in the case of our modern land animals, if we assume one center of distribution for all and conceive of these forms possessed of an inward urge to wander out over the earth, we can find abundance of laboratory proof that these processes of change, in conjunction with the necessary condition of geographical isolation which would exist under such circumstances, would produce the very mosaic type of distribution so evident on the earth today.

### THE THREEFOLD PROBLEM FOR CREATIONISTS

The question that naturally arises here is, Could mutation and chromosomal change produce so much variation in organisms in the brief span of approximately forty-three to fifty centuries which have elapsed since the Noachian flood? Some creationists have let this supposed obstacle so fill their minds as to cause them to ignore the fact of the present-day mosaic distribution of "species", "subspecies", and races. In the light of facts of distribution it is absolutely essential to recognize that variation *has* occurred as organisms have dispersed over the earth. If it be assumed that modern species are fixed or practically nonvariable, just as they came from the Ark, there would be no way of explaining how they got from Ararat to their present niches without leaving others of their peculiar sort somewhere along their distribution paths. Variation since the Flood, at least to the extent of the production of modern races, "subspecies", and "species", must be recognized. The only escape theory would be that of resurrection of forms where they died in the Flood—and few creationists can harmonize such a possibility with the facts recorded in the Scriptures which bear upon this point and with those furnished by geology and paleontology.

Thus the creationist finds himself in the center of a three-way squeeze, i.e., (1) the Scriptural position of but forty-three to fifty-odd centuries since the Flood, (2) the fact that variation since the Flood most certainly *has* occurred, and (3) the present manifest slowness of mutation and chromosomal change in producing appreciable variation. The first two cannot be breached. The last may or may not, depending largely upon the opinion of the one who is discussing the point. For instance, there is a possibility that the rate of these changes was more rapid at one time than now. On this point Dobzhansky says (p. 163), "A finite population left to its own devices must, therefore, suffer a progressive decay of its hereditary variability and sooner or later must reach a complete genetic uniformity." Wherever the truth may lie here, I would like to express it as my personal opinion that this variation within the kinds since the Flood has taken place in natural ways which are recognized today or which may still be unrecognized. Such an opinion does not rule out any supernatural speeding up of natural processes, but it does preclude the entire brushing aside of natural processes in order that a miracle might here be accomplished. It seems to me that the type of distribution which we find over the earth must have been achieved through the operation of natural processes alone.

In conclusion I will say that this unsurpassed summarization and discussion of processes of change which Dr. Dobzhansky has made from the point of view of genetics, is a first necessity for every student of speciation. Other chapters to which I have not referred, particularly the one on isolating mechanisms, are essential if the student would gain a clearer picture of the mechanisms in nature which have produced the present wealth of variation, and which have, in conjunction with geographical isolation, resulted in the present-day mosaic pattern of distribution of animals and plants over the earth.

---

## AN UNREGIMENTED BIOLOGIST
### By GEORGE McCREADY PRICE

I am frequently asked for the name of the best book dealing with the theory of evolution. My reply now is that the one by Dr. Frank L. March, recently issued in Washington, is the best one now before the public. It is entitled: "Evolution, Creation, and Science,"* and the author is head of the department of biology in Union College, Lincoln, Nebraska. The only one of my books attempting to cover similar ground was published about twenty years ago, and has long been out of print. This new one by Professor Marsh covers the entire field; it is well thought out and well written; more than that, it gives a reliable summary of the latest discoveries which bear upon these controversial problems in the relationship between science and religion. So this is the book to get, if you want to read the latest and best in this large and perplexing field.

But how can I possibly review so good and important a work within the very limited space here available? I might give an outline of its eighteen chapters; but this would not be acceptable to my readers; they would want to see the book itself, not my outline. Or I might use the occasion of this book as a sort of mental springboard, from which to launch off in a discussion of some of the most recent developments in biology or geology. Also, any adequate or full review might involve some mention of a few very minor points where there may be room for a difference of opinion. And how could I expect to get anywhere with all this within the compass of a thousand or twelve hundred words?

Besides, I am not competent to discuss the recent developments in biology; for that is not my field. And Doctor Marsh himself has already discussed these recent

*Marsh, Frank Lewis, *Evolution, Creation, and Science*; Review and Herald, Washington, D. C., 1944, 304 pages. $2.25.

trends in the preceding pages of this issue of THE BULLETIN. As for any recent trends or developments in the field of geology and its fundamental principles, to be frank about the matter, there have been none. Oh yes, many new observational facts have been added to the already swollen accumulations of data; but I mean that in the field of fundamental geology there has been no progress whatever for more than a hundred years; just a repeated milling around in the same old tracks, assuming evolution to start with, and then "proving" this major premise by means of selected "facts" to fit it. If that is progress, then it is progress in a circle. Some of my readers may be aware that I have already discussed this circular reasoning in geology so many times that I have become tired of the subject. And seemingly very few even among professional scientists are much interested in examining strictly logical processes in the basic sciences, at least not those in geology and biology.

But one thing I can do in the very limited space here available. I can invite my readers to consider for a brief minute the present position of the entire evolution theory. In its Darwinian form, the theory of organic evolution has now been before the world for about 85 years. For the first half of this period, like all new heresies or aggressive falsehoods in either science or religion, it was extremely aggressive, and fostered discussion in season and out of season in every part of the world. Today, however, the theory has become ensconced in all the places of prestige and power throughout the civilized world. It has now become conservative, for it is now an orthodoxy, and like all orthodoxies, it is running true to form, and has become very much opposed to any further discussion of its basic ideas. Its bid now is for unity and harmony. These basic ideas about biological development (in contrast to the doctrine of Creation) have been settled long ago, so we are told; then what is there to discuss further among modernly educated people?

Thus in our modern world we have reached another stage of standardized thinking, of an entrenched dogmatism, this time with the evolution theory almost universally in the places of power as a scientific orthodoxy. Hence, with this form of standardized thinking in charge of all the modern methods of publicity, every one who wishes to be thought of as a "reputable" man of science must be careful not to offend the unwritten code of the dominant fashionable theories, at least not to the wholly unthinkable extent of publishing a book attacking any of the sacred cows of evolution. For those in places of power in the universities and the publishing centers have ways of very effectually dealing with any one who is not careful to keep up the lock step of the intellectual parade; and Professor Marsh will learn about these matters before very long.

For this book which I have mentioned is clearly not the product of a standardized mind. It gives evidence of original, independent thought, based on a logical and fearless evaluation of the available data about the origin of things, as we know these data in this the middle of the fifth decade of the twentieth century. And this independent thinking is in spite of the fact that Doctor Marsh took his advanced work in no less than three of the leading universities of America, and thus may be presumed to have passed under the personal training of many of our top-ranking men of science.

It certainly takes real intellectual and moral courage to come out in open opposition to the almost universally accepted dogmas of the modern scientific world. I wish I had the space to give some of the hard experiences of other intellectual pioneers or innovators, such as Galileo and Harvey; of Jenner, Pasteur, and Lister. These and many others had to endure the ostracism and open abuse which has too often been the lot of those who have been unwilling to follow the crowd; and today a similar ban is being experienced by those who have been compelled by the logic of hard facts to believe in a literal Creation and a universal Deluge, in opposition to the prevailing theories. Doctor Marsh will undoubtedly have personal experiences of

his own before long. But I have confidence that he is quite able to take care of himself.

## EXCESSIVE ASSIGNMENT OF SPECIES RANK

"There is, however, a systematic category which, in contrast to others, has withstood the changes in the nomenclature with a singular tenacity. This is the category of species. To be sure, some of the species described by Linnaeus have been split into two or more new ones, and yet a majority of the Linnaean species are still treated as species, not as subgenera, genera, or anything else. In animal and plant groups which are taxonomically well understood, and excepting the so-called 'difficult' ones (which constitute a special problem to be discussed below), the delimitation of species usually is subject to no dispute at all (May, 1940). To be sure, a few taxonomists have from time to time succumbed to the temptation of assigning the species rank to any local race distinct enough to permit every speci-

men to receive a determination label. Excesses of this sort were frequent, for example, among mammalogists and specialists on certain genera of butterflies, but a salutary reaction has apparently started against them. The notion, entertained by some biologists unfamiliar with the subject, that species are arbitrary units like all other systematic categories is unfounded. In fact, no category is arbitrary so long as its limits are made to coincide with those of the discontinuously varying arrays of living forms. The category of species has certain attributes peculiar to itself that restrict the freedom of its usage, and consequently make it methodologically more valuable than the rest."

Theodosius Dubzhansky, *Genetics and the Origin of Species,* p. 365-366 (Second Edition, Columbia University Press, New York, 1941)

## MUTATIONS POWERFULLY INJURIOUS ABNORMALITIES, WEAKNESSES, AND IMPERFECTIONS

"The discovery of agents producing mutation brings us squarely to the question in which these lectures are primarily interested. Both the known agents are powerfully injurious. Both kill a large proportion of the individuals exposed to them; both leave many of the others abnormal or imperfect. Both damage the genetic system, producing changes that make it impossible for the individuals to develop. And both produce inherited changes that

are manifested mainly as abnormalities, weaknesses and imperfections.

"Are these the type of changes on which evolution is based? Amid the carnage engendered by blighting radiation and unbearable heat, do we find produced the changes that mean progressive evolution? The gene mutations produced by radiation and by heat are of the same types as occur spontaneously."

H. S. Jennings, *Genetic Variations in Relation to Evolution,* p. 56 (Princeton University Press, Princeton, 1935)

## THE "UNKNOWN FACTOR" IN EVOLUTION

"If this is the situation, where are we left as to the source of the variations in genic materials that must underlie evolution in higher organisms?

"Some investigators have expressed the

opinion that such variation is not required; that mere change of combination and grouping, without alteration in the nature of any gene, can in some way give rise to progressive evolution; can have produced the seeming differentiation among genes now existing. To most, however, this appears unintelligible.

"Possibly a type of gene change that is in the nature of developmpent rather than in that of disintegration and abnormality will eventually be detected. When

this is demonstrated, the road for progressive evolution will be open; until this is demonstrated genetic science appears to be left with the task that Osborn has called The Search for the Unknown Factor in Evolution."

Id., p. 138.

THE

# BULLETIN

OF

# DELUGE GEOLOGY

AND RELATED SCIENCE

| VOLUME V | APRIL, 1945 | NUMBER 2 |

## CONTENTS

THE MEANING OF THE ORIGIN AND ACTIVITIES OF THE HUMAN BODY

### PART 1

III. DESIGN AND USE OF FRAMEWORK AND TRUNK

Engineers are today using the same principles in the construction of modern edifices as used in the framework of man.

*By Hubert O. Swartout, M.S., M.D., Dr.P.H.*

Your body has many different parts and organs, which will be discussed in due time; but for some purposes it is preferable to think of it as a whole, or to let the discussion take a more general course. The general shape and posture of your body, which more than anything else distinguish it from the body of a lower animal, depend chiefly on its framework, commonly called the *skeleton.* When you read or hear this word, it naturally makes you think of *bones,* but the living skeleton includes *cartilage* and *ligaments* also. Cartilage is somewhat like bone, but not nearly so hard. That part of meat which we call "gristle" is really one kind of cartilage.

Ligaments are sheets or cords of tough, fibrous material. They bend, but do not stretch unless injured or overloaded. The fascinating story of bone growth has been told elsewhere,[1] and will not be repeated here; but the peculiar fitness of each part of the skeleton for its own work is a subject no less interesting.

This study consists of two parts. Part 1 is a description of engineering skill in designing the bones themselves and in their assembly and use. Part 2 describes, as an example, the structural design of the trunk and its use in housing vital organs.

[1] BULLETIN OF CREATION, THE DELUGE, AND RELATED SCIENCES, Sept., 1944, No. 4.

The BULLETIN is published by, and is the official organ of the "Society for the Study of Creation, the Deluge, and Related Science." The Editorial Board is comprised of Professor George McCready Price, Dr. Dell D. Haughey, and Mr. Ben F. Allen. It is printed at the College Press, Arlington, California. For members the BULLETIN is free, and extra copies 20 cents each (each number priced according to size); for non-members it is $2.00 per year and this number is 30 cents. All correspondence should be directed to the Editors, Box 1030, Glendale, California.

In Part 1 the topics will be: 1, Expert engineering design in bone structure; 2, The studies of engineering in the human skeleton; 3, The bones used for protecting vital organs; 4, Evidence of design in our joints; 5, The regulation of chemical changes in bones; 6, Bone repair is clearly teleological; 7, None of these things could result from chance.

Bones serve three chief purposes, though few of them serve all three. They support weight; they protect organs; they make possible properly directed and controlled motion, both of the whole body and of many of its parts. Their structure and shape differ widely, but always in such a way as to suit the special work which they have to do.

### EXPERT ENGINEERING DESIGN

The long bones of the thigh and leg are outstanding examples of bones built to support weight; and their outer solid part has weight-bearing strength far beyond any ordinary need, being stronger, weight for weight, than mild carbon steel and twice as strong as granite. All these bones have tube-shaped *shafts*. The shaft of a bone is the long, slender, rounded part. Engineers have long known that a given amount of material provides more stiffness and useful strength in the form of a tube than in the form of a solid bar or rod. They have also known that if the walls of the tube are fairly thick, no inside bracing is necessary; but if the walls are thin, the tube is liable to buckle and give way without such bracing.

The ends of these long bones need to be considerably enlarged or broadened to make a broad bearing surface so the joints will be strong. These enlarged ends would be much heavier than necessary, however, if their bony shell were as thick as that of the shaft. You have probably seen such a bone end that has been sawed or split open, and know that there is a thin shell of solid bone on the surface and a fine network of bony plates inside, cross bracing it in all directions.

There are scores of places in the skeleton that would prove to be good examples of expert engineering if carefully studied from that point of view, but the part of the body framework in which there is the most easily understood need for proper proportions in the thickness of the different parts of the bony shell and in the arrangement and strength of inside cross braces is the upper end of the thigh bone, or *femur.* Here the weight bearing is not in a straight line with the shaft, but at an angle, because the joint ball at the upper end of this bone extends at least as far sideways as it does upward. Such an angle makes necessary some intricate engineering so as to balance strains, stresses, pressures, and tensions to make sure that the bone is strong enough at every point without being any heavier than necessary.

### KOCH'S STUDIES

The medical scientist, Robert Koch, made a careful study of the engineering principles shown by the bony structures in this region. Anyone who will look in Gray's *Anatomy,* probably the most widely used textbook of its kind in medical schools, can find pictures, diagrams, and discussions based on Koch's study, showing that every scientific theory of engineering that one would expect to see worked out in this part of the skeleton if it were perfectly built to serve its weight-bearing purpose, is actually found there. Truly, there was a Master Engineer long before the laws and principles of engineering were even dreamed of by any man.

### BONES FOR PROTECTION

Some of the vital organs are so delicate that they need special protection. The most delicate of all is the *brain,* but it is one of the few organs that do their work without any noticeable change in size. Quite fittingly, therefore, the brain is enclosed in a solid box of bone, the only opening of any considerable size in this box being in the base, where it is well away from ordinary danger. The walls of this box, which is called the *skull,* consist of two moderately thick layers of solid bone, the outer layer being a bit thicker than the inner, with a layer of cross bracing plates between. The whole box, in shape and structure, is a fine example of the economical use of material to serve a needed purpose.

The *heart* and *lungs* are also delicate organs, but they must expand and contract several times a minute to keep the body alive. It would not do for them to be encased in a solid box. They are protected by a somewhat flexible bony cage, narrow above and broad below, with the breastbone and the backbone as posts in front and behind, the ribs as bars around each side, the floor of the cage being a sheet of tissues that can move up or down with considerable freedom.

### DESIGN IN OUR JOINTS

The skeleton permits and directs motion by means of its joints. A typical joint is composed of the broad ends of two bones, with a layer of smooth cartilage covering each bone end where it comes in contact with the other bone end; bands of ligament that extend from one bone to the other, attached to both bones, forming a tough, strong, more or less complete sac around the joint; and a membrane which completely lines the sac and produces a fluid to lubricate the joint.

Ligaments are not elastic; and wherever the joints need to move freely, as the shoulders, the elbows, the hips, the knees, the ligaments are slack to allow for this motion without stretching them. In other joints, good examples of which are those between the sacrum and the hipbones, where but little motion is needed, the ligaments are heavier and stronger and have little or no slack.

In such joints as those of the backbone, so little motion is needed that pads of tough, fibrous cartilage lying between adjoining sections of bone and firmly attached to each of them have enough "give" to allow for all necessary motion. Here also the ligaments are strong and have little or no slack.

It is an advantage to have more or less free motion in some joints and to have restricted motion in others. Such free motion is characteristic of the hips and shoulders, and is made possible by one bearing surface being a ball and the other a socket. The normal motion of knees and elbows consists of bending backward and forward in one direction only, like a hinge; and the peculiar shapes of the bone ends concerned is the chief reason why this is the only normal motion they have. Think how awkward one would be if his hip and shoulder motions were no more free than those of his knees and elbows! On the other hand, free motion in all directions at his knees would not only lead to awkwardness, but would also make his legs a much less firm support for his body.

### BONE CHEMISTRY REGULATION

When one begins to study how to care for the body's framework, he must take account of other things besides the size, shape, structure, and arrangement of bones, cartilage, ligaments, and joints. Their chemical composition, the changes which they undergo during growth and afterward, and what happens to them under various unfavorable circumstances all have an important bearing on this subject.

Grammar-school textbooks used to carry the simple teaching that bones are composed of "animal matter" and "mineral matter." This is still known to be a fact, though we often use different words to express the idea now. The hardness, stiffness, and weight-bearing strength of bones depend on the "mineral matter"; and their toughness depends on the "animal matter." The "animal matter" consists largely of certain special kinds of protein; and these are also found in cartilage and ligaments, which contain little "mineral matter." While bones are growing, both types of structural material constantly increase in amount; but all through life from birth to death the proportion of "mineral matter" to "animal matter" increases. In other words, the bones grow larger for from fifteen to twenty years; but they keep on growing harder, stiffer, and less elastic as long as one lives. The ligaments also become firmer and less pliable with age.

### REPAIR CLEARLY TELEOLOGICAL

When a bone is broken, the bone-building and bone-eating cells that have lain dormant for many years, wake up and go to work again, producing and shaping new bone to repair the break. You no doubt remember the interesting story of the work of these cells as given in the article, "Your Body's Growth," that appeared in the BULLETIN referred to. If the bone is properly "set" and put at rest, the repair will in most cases finally make the bone as strong and shapely as before. If not, a more or less severe permanent deformity will result.

### BLIND CHANCE IMPOSSIBLE

Having read thus far, you have learned, if you did not already know it, that the normal human body has a framework marvelously well adapted for the work it has to do. One cannot help wondering how anyone can think that blind chance put all these varieties of bones and joints, with their remarkable fitness for their work, into a single human body, and in the same way and with so few and such slight exceptions, put the same number of similar bones and joints into corresponding locations in the framework of every other human body.

Blind chance, as used in ordinary language, is what the scientist means when he speaks of mathematical probability. This principle, as any mathematician knows, would never result in a series of so nearly indentical human bodies, or bodies of any species of the lower animals for that matter. To ascribe the origin of the natural laws according to which these bodies develop to mathematical probability would be contrary to every scientific application of this principle.

---

## PART 2
### STRUCTURAL DESIGN AND FUNCTIONS OF THE TRUNK

The largest part of your body, in fact all of it except its head, neck, arms, and legs, is called the *trunk*. This name was probably given to it because of some slight resemblance between the body and a tree, which has a trunk, roots, and branches, and not as a little girl said, because a trunk has so many things packed inside it; but her idea was not so far wrong, at that. At any rate, the trunk is a central mass or frame to which the above-named parts of the body are attached; and its walls surround two large cavities in which most of the vital organs are located.

The bony framework of your trunk must be strong, but not rigid, for it must allow a considerable amount of motion. You need to be able to bend your back forward, backward, and sideways, and to twist it slightly. Your chest must expand and contract if you are to breathe freely.

In walking and in many other activities you would be quite awkward if you could not raise one hip a little higher than the other. As to shoulder motion, someone has jokingly said that if all mankind's shoulders should turn rigid the people in certain countries would hardly know how to talk. But, all joking aside, your shoulders do need great freedom of motion.

The following features will be described: 1, The extreme adaptability of the backbone; 2, The bones and organs of the upper part of the trunk; 3, The mechanisms of chest expansion; 4, The organs of the lower part of the trunk; 5, The Designer and Sustainer.

### THE BACKBONE

Your backbone presents a remarkable combination of strength and flexibility. It is made up of twenty-four sections, called *vertebrae*, seventeen of which belong to your trunk. Each vertebra has a *body*, a thick disc of bone, with outgrowths, or *processes*, extending sideways and backward, all together forming a ring surrounding an open space. Between each two adjoining discs there is a layer of tough, but somewhat elastic, cartilage, firmly attached to both. Certain of the processes form sliding joints with corresponding processes of the vertebrae above and below, thus helping to hold the vertebrae in place. When you consider the column of seventeen vertebrae and their processes and cartilages as a whole, you can understand how your backbone can be flexible, yet how hard it is for one of your vertebrae to slip out of line with the others, and how the process-enclosed open spaces, set one above another, form an armored tube to hold and protect your spinal cord.

BONES AND ORGANS OF THE UPPER PART OF THE TRUNK

At the upper end of your trunk you have a bony ring, the *shoulder girdle*. Since the upper vertebrae of the trunk have ribs attached to them, the flexibility of this part of your backbone is limited. The free motion of your shoulders, therefore, must depend on the arrangement of the bones of your shoulder girdle. They do not form a complete ring, but each half of the girdle is composed of two bones, a collarbone, or *clavicle*, in front, and a shoulder blade, or *scapula*, behind. Each clavicle has a joint which connects it to the side of the upper end of the sternum. At its outer end an another joint attaches it to the corresponding scapula. Both of these joints allow considerable motion. Neither scapula is joined to any other bone in your trunk except its corresponding clavicle, but each is loosely held by muscles and ligaments against the back part of your chest. It can slide about so freely that its edge can be brought almost into contact with that of its mate in the middle of the upper part of your back or these two edges can be drawn apart from six to ten inches. The up-and-down motion of these bones is al-

most as free as their side-to-side motion. These facts about your shoulder girdle should help you to understand how both of your shoulders together, or either of them separately, can be freely moved upward, downward, forward, or backward.

The organs of the upper half of your trunk are arranged inside a bony cage, formed behind by the upper twelve of the seventeen vertebrae, on each side by twelve *ribs*, and in front by the breastbone, or *sternum*. The spaces between all these bones are filled in by muscles, ligaments, tendons, and membranes, the whole forming an airtight cavity, called the *chest* or *thorax*.

The largest organs in your thorax are your lungs and heart. You know, of course, that breathing depends on lung action, the circulation of the blood on heart action, and that both are necessary to life. In a narrow, vertical space between your two lungs, however, there are several smaller organs or structures, all of great importance. They are your windpipe, or *trachea*, carrying air into and out of your lungs; your *esophagus*, a large tube carrying food from your throat to your stomach; your *thoracic duct*, a small tube carrying lymph and digested fat from a pouch in the upper part of your abdomen to a large vein at the base of your neck; the shrunken remains of your *thymus* gland, which served a good purpose in the early years of your life; many lymph glands; several important nerves; and parts of all the large blood vessels that connect directly with your heart.

MECHANISMS OF CHEST EXPANSION

The mechanisms that cause your chest to expand and take in air are interesting. There are three phases to this mechanism of expansion, which we will now discuss in detail. I. A special group of muscles contracts and pulls your sternum and its attached rib ends upward. Lines drawn from the rear, or vertebral attachments, of your ribs to their front, or sternal attachments, slant downward markedly; so when your sternum is raised, it is forced forward by the leverage of your ribs, thus making your chest deeper from front to back. II. The short-fibered muscles running from rib to rib along your sides contract at the same time. Your ribs are not straight lines, but are strongly curved; and the central part of the curve, corresponding to your sides, droops considerably below the line joining the front and rear attachments. When the front end of a rib is raised, this drooping part of the curve is raised still more, making your chest wider from side to side. III. The dome-shaped floor of your chest flattens. This floor is composed of a broad sheet of tissues, mainly muscle, called the *diaphragm*. It is attached all the way round to the wall of your chest on a line corresponding in general to the lower margin of the cage formed by your ribs. It is the contraction of its muscle fibers that flattens it and increases the depth of your chest from top to bottom. Thus you see three instances of the paradoxical fact that the *contraction* of muscles in the wall of the chest cavity makes that cavity *larger*.

### ORGANS OF THE LOWER PART OF THE TRUNK

The lower half of your trunk is called your *abdomen*. The only bones that have to do with this part of your body are the lower five vertebrae behind and a broad, bony basin that forms a partial support below. The sides and front are closed in by several layers of broad, flat muscles, with their fibers running in various directions.

The bony basin or ring that helps to form the floor of your abdominal cavity is made up of three bones, a *hipbone* on each side and the *sacrum* set between them behind. The entire ring is called the *pelvic girdle*. The joint between your two hipbones in front allows almost no motion at all, and those between your hipbones and sacrum behind very little more. This arrangement gives you a firm foundation for your trunk and a secure attachment for your legs, which must bear the weight of your body. Your lowest vertebra rests on

the top of your sacrum; but the joint between the two bones permits practically no motion, so it is the flexibility of the lower part of your backbone that allows you to raise one hip higher than the other, rather than any joint in, or adjoining, your pelvic girdle itself.

There are many important organs in your abdominal cavity. Your *liver* is close up under your diaphragm on the right side, with your *gall bladder* lying close beneath it near its front edge; and your *spleen* lies close beneath your diaphragm to the left. Your *stomach* lies between your liver and spleen, while your *pancreas* is situated behind your stomach, lying against the back wall of the abdominal cavity. Partly below and partly behind the liver on the right side, and near the spleen on the left side, are your *kidneys*, which also lie in contact with the back wall of the cavity. Perched on the upper end of each kidney, there is a small, cap-shaped organ or gland. These two glands are your *suprarenals;* and, while you may never have heard much about them, they are vital organs. You would die if you lost them. Your *bladder* is in the lower, front part of your abdominal cavity, close to its front wall. Your *large intestine* begins low down on the right side, passes upward until it reaches the level of your liver, then curves downward, to the left, and upward again to the region of your spleen, and finally passes downward on the left side of the cavity in a series of irregular curves. Your *appendix* is a small, wormlike tube attached to your large intestine near its beginning. Nearly all of the remaining portion of your abdominal cavity is occupied by your *small intestine*, most of which is loosely hung to the back wall of the cavity by a ligament called the *mesentery*. Several of the largest blood vessels in your body are also located in your abdominal cavity.

All your abdominal organs are partly held up by ligaments, but many of these ligaments are neither strong nor tight; so it is fairly easy for the organs they hold to sag downward more or less. You must depend on the muscles of your abdominal wall to help the ligaments hold the organs in place. If these muscles become weakened by sitting or standing with wrong postures, or by lack of exercise, there will be three undesirable results: Your abdomen will protrude, its organs will hang too low, and your diaphragm will not be held as high as it should to favor easy breathing.

### THE DESIGNER AND SUSTAINER

The discussion in this article has been largely of a general nature. Some of the paragraphs must have made you think of a section from the dictionary—one name after another; but you will hear more about many of these names in later articles, as the work of the various organs is described in greater detail. It is hoped, moreover, that you have been interested in the ingenuity of several of the mechanisms of your trunk, and that you have been impressed with the logical necessity of a Designer and Sustainer of infinite wisdom and power, to account for the design and harmonious activities of these various parts of the human body.

---

## TELEOLOGICAL LANGUAGE USED BY DARWIN[*]
### By the Duke of Argyll

Mr. Mivart has remarked in a very able work,[1] as Mr. Wallace had remarked before him, that the teleological language used so freely by Mr. Darwin and others is purely metaphorical. As I have already elsewhere[2] dealt with this criticism, I need only repeat here, what cannot be insisted upon too firmly, that even if it were strictly accurate, it had no adverse bearing upon the evidence which this language of so-called metaphor involves. It is not strictly accurate because there is no real element of metaphor except where the outward forms of the human Personality are ascribed to Nature. Nature has no hands and no brain; but these members, even in Man, are regarded as "Organs," and as nothing else—the visible representatives of invisible powers: and where the names of these organs, and of such like, are not figuratively used in respect to Nature,— where nothing is expressed but the facts of teleological adaptation, there is not, properly speaking, any metaphor at all. But putting this aside for the moment, and granting that in the description of the invisible phenomena of Mind it is difficult to avoid all reference to the outward and visible forms in which these phenomena are manifested in us—even so, this metaphorical element does not affect the evidence supplied by the inevitable phraseology of all natural philosophers when it is their business to describe what they see in Nature. For what purpose are metaphors used? Is it not as a means of making plain to our own understanding the principle of things, and of tracing amid the varieties of phenomena the essential Unities of Nature? In this sense all Language is full of metaphor, being indeed composed of little else. That is to say, the whole structure and architecture of Language consists of words which transfer and apply to one sphere of investigation ideas which have been derived from another, because there also the same ideas are seen to be expressed, only under some differences of form. Accordingly, when naturalists, describing plants or animals, use the language of Contrivance to describe the Adaptations of Function, they must use it because they feel it to be a help in the understanding of the facts. When, for example, we are told that flowers are constructed in a peculiar manner, "in order that" they may catch the probosces of Moths or the backs of Bees, and that this

[*] Argyll, Duke of, The Unity of Nature, 1883, pp. 173-174.
[1] "Genesis of Species."
[2] Argyll, Duke of, The Regin of Law, 1866, pp. 1-27.

adaptation again is necessary "in order that" these insects should carry the fertilizing pollen from flower to flower, nothing more may be immediately intended by the writer than that all this elaborate mechanism does as a matter of fact attain this end, and that it may be fitly described "as if" it had been arranged "in order that" these things might happen. But this use of language is none the less an acknowledgment of the truth that the facts of Nature are best brought home and explained to the Understanding, and to the

Intelligence of Man, by stating them in terms of the relation which they obviously bear to the familiar operations of our own Mind and Spirit.

And this is the invariable result of all physical inquiry. In this sense Nature is essentially anthropopsychic. Man sees his own Mind everywhere reflected in it—his own, not in quantity but in quality—his own fundamental attributes of Intellect, and, to a wonderful and mysterious degree, even his own methods of operation.

THE

# BULLETIN

OF

# DELUGE GEOLOGY

AND RELATED SCIENCE

| VOLUME V | AUGUST, 1945 | NUMBER 3 |
|---|---|---|

## CONTENTS

### ESSAYS ON CREATION

By ROBERT W. SHINN

---

## NEW FACTS IN GEOLOGY ABOUT CREATION*

### By Robert W. Shinn

This article is written with the intention of presenting an entirely new approach to the old and greatly disputed question of just how life on this planet has developed. The facts presented here are revolutionary in their nature, and yet they are still unheralded in many scientific circles. This article is based upon the works of Professor George McCready Price, an accredited research worker in the field of geology. This man's observations and conclusions are worthy of the thoughtful consideration of anyone who is truly a seeker after truth.

The theory of evolution is generally considered to be the best explanation of the development of species, and some scientists regard it as a proven fact or an organized science of its own. In order to avoid confusion in terminology, we shall define organic evolution as the progression of life in past ages from the simpler forms to the

more complex; from "Amoeba to Man." Upon thoughtful reflection, we believe that it will be agreed that the primary evidence in support of evolution must come from geology. The geological succession of fossil forms is really the framework of evolution. Supplementary evidences, such as embryology, assume the progression of life from the simple to the complex. Let us now examine in detail this geological "proof" of evolution. The reader is undoubtedly familiar with the geological series so widely accepted. The geological series, or any subdivision of it, is always read from the bottom upward. From this

NOTE—The following two articles by the same author are reprinted by permission from *Sigma News*, Autumn, 1944, and Winter, 1945; Philadelphia College of Pharmacy and Science, Lansdowne, Pa. The Editors do not wish to be held responsible for all the views here expressed; but they have thought that the readers of THE BULLETIN may like to see how these matters are viewed by one on the other side of the continent. It may seem quite remarkable that this article is from an undergraduate only twenty years of age.—THE EDITORS.

The BULLETIN is published by, and is the official organ of the "Society for the Study of Creation, the Deluge, and Related Science." The Editorial Board is comprised of Professor George McCready Price, Mr. B. F. Allen, and Dr. Dell D. Haughey. It is printed at the College Press, Arlington, California. For members the BULLETIN is free, and extra copies 30 cents each (each number priced according to size); for non-members it is $2.00 per year and this number is 50 cents. All correspondence should be directed to the Editors, Box 1030, Glendale, California.

classification chart we may readily enumerate the *assumptions* that form its basis.

(1) The fossils in the Cambrian age constitute the more simple forms of life. The fossils in the Pleistocene age represent an advanced or more complex development of life.

(2) The great assemblage of life found in any particular set of rock beds represents a group which at some remote time occupied the world exclusively and universally.

(3) Each geological system represents a universal condition and, therefore, the rocks furnish a time gauge for past ages. The trilobites lived before the dinosaurs, and the dinosaurs and man were not contemporary.

(4) Since the rock systems and the fossils contained in them were universal, the fossil record must be a true HISTORICAL order; an order which is the basis of the evolutionary claim that life has evolved from the simple to the complex.

The assumptions listed above embodied in the geological chart are a vital basis of the lines of descent formulated for many species of plants and animals. In order for this chart to have any historical value for evolution, the sequence of rock layers would have to be invariable. But exactly the opposite is true. The rocks are not found in this order any place on the globe. Here are some specific examples.

Through the states of Tennessee, eastern Mississippi, and Alabama, the Cretaceous layer rests on the Paleozoic. This means that the Jurassic and the Triassic layers are simply not there. In Georgia, the Cretaceous rests upon the Archaean. In the Rocky Mountain region, the Triassic beds are found directly upon the Archaean. Looking on our chart, we see that the whole Paleozoic age has been omitted. This same condition also exists in Mexico and Central America. The Carboniferous may occur directly above the Archaean as is the case in other parts of the Rocky Mountains. In Cuba and Jamaica, the

Cretaceous is above the Archaean. In California, the Eocene layer is in this position. In Saxony and Bohemia, the Mesozoic rests upon the Archaean. In northern Russia, the Pleistocene beds are found directly above Permian deposits.

When strata are found parallel to one another in bedding, as originally laid down upon one another, the geologist calls the strata CONFORMABLE. But if the two sets of strata are not parallel to each other, due to tilting, erosion, or some other natural agency, they are said to be UNCONFORMABLE. In cases of conformity, the physical evidence is strong that the one stratum followed the other in quick succession. Thus, the Cretaceous may rest in conformity on the Devonian, the whole of the Jurassic, Triassic, Permian, and Carboniferous being omitted.

Reverse conditions of strata order are also common. Not only may Cambrian or Silurian or Devonian beds be ABOVE Triassic, Cretaceous, or Tertiary, but with a degree of conformity giving every physical evidence that vast areas were deposited in exactly the order in which the geologist finds them. Glacier National Park and sections in Alberta, Canada, are composed of Paleozoic rocks resting in a perfectly normal position upon the Cretaceous layer. In the Appalachian region of the southern United States, the Cambrian or Lower Silurian lie conformably upon Carboniferous. The Highlands of Scotland, the Alps, a Scandinavian district, and northern China all have vast areas which are upside down, geologically speaking. A multitude of other examples might be culled from almost every quarter of the earth.

If we correlate all the information that we have, we would find that we have examples of the strata occurring in practically every order of serial relationship. Professor George McCready Price sums up the facts about geological strata in his Law of Stratigraphic Sequence. This law states:

"Any kind of fossiliferous rock, 'young' or 'old,' may be found occurring conform-

## CHART OF THE GEOLOGICAL "AGES"

| GROUP | SYSTEM | SERIES | DOMINANT TYPE OF LIFE |
|---|---|---|---|
| Cenozoic | Quaternary or Post-Tertiary or Pleistocene | Recent<br>Terrace<br>Drift (Glacial) | Man |
| | Tertiary | Pliocene<br>Miocene<br>Oligocene<br>Eocene<br>Paleocene | Mammals |
| Mesozoic | Cretaceous | Upper or Cretaceous Proper<br>Lower or Comanchean | Reptiles Conifers and Palms |
| | Jurassic | Upper (Malm)<br>Middle (Dogger)<br>Lower (Lias) | |
| | Triassic | Upper (Keuper)<br>Middle (Muschelkalk)<br>Lower (Bunter Sandstein) | |
| Paleozoic | Permian | Upper<br>Lower | Amphibians and Coal Plants |
| | Carboniferous | Pennsylvanian<br>Mississippian | |
| | Devonian | Upper<br>Middle<br>Lower | Fishes and Insects |
| | Silurian | Upper—Monroan<br>Middle—Salina<br>Lower—Niagara | Profuse Marine Invertebrates |
| | Ordovician | Upper—Cincinnatian<br>Middle—Champlainian<br>Lower—Canadian | |
| | Cambrian | Upper (Saratogan)<br>Middle (Acadian)<br>Lower (Waucobian) | |
| Primary or Primitive | Algonkian<br>Archaean | | Few Fossils or None |

ably on any other kind of fossiliferous rock, 'older' or 'younger.' "

This law puts an end to these evolutionary speculations about an invariable "historical" order of rock sequence. The new facts of geology show that it cannot be proved that one type of life in past ages lived before any others. The puerile procedure of constructing lines of descent of pigs, horses, camels, and elephants in an "historical" order to prove evolution is not any credit to trained scientific research. If the creature that evolved out of a diminutive ancestor millions of years after that ancestor died out, really lived with that ancestor side by side, the supposed demonstration becomes a joke. If we realize the fact that any kind of fossiliferous rock may occur above the Archaean, different kinds in different parts of the world, we are faced with the imminent possibility that the various types of life may have lived contemporaneously in scattered localities all over the world.

The geological chart is purely an artificial arrangement with no more scientific value than if the Shetland pony, the western desert burro, the African zebra, the ass, the western bronc, the saddle horse, the Arabian racer, the Percheron, and the giant Clydesdale were arranged in an ascending order from the small to the large in order to demonstrate their "evolution." It cannot be proved that Cretaceous dinosaurs were not contemporary with the late Tertiary mammals. There is no evidence that the trilobites were not contemporary with more complex marine life.

In summary we may say our further knowledge in geology shows us that the various fossiliferous beds have never been universal, never more than of local occurrence, and that this phenomenon is evidenced in many numerous and important instances. When the beds were found to occur in many orders of sequence very different from the assumed "invariable" order, the theory of evolution lost the one bit of evidence essential to its proof. The theory of organic evolution, as defined at the beginning of this article, stands today positively disproved. A subsequent article in the *Sigma News* will bear out the philosophical implications of this refutation, and describe an alternative hypothesis to take the place of evolution.

All we ask is an unbiased and careful consideration of the evidence presented. It is purely a case of dogmatism against facts. Let us discard methods and assumptions so manifestly unscientific, and conduct research where FACTS will have the right of way over baseless theories. This writer having had a real intellectual conversion to the work of Professor Price, is anxious to receive any comments, criticisms or correspondence concerning the subject matter in this article.

## BIBLIOGRAPHY

Works of George McCready Price:
(1) *The New Geology*. Pacific Press Pub. Association.
(2) *Evolutionary Geology and the New Catastrophism*. Pacific Press.
(3) *Some Scientific Stories and Allegories*. Zondervan Pub. House.
(4) *The Geological-Ages Hoax*. Fleming H. Revell Co.
(5) *How Did the World Begin?* Fleming H. Revell Co.

# THE MODERN DOCTRINE OF SPECIAL CREATION

## By ROBERT W. SHINN

In the Autumn issue of the *Sigma News* it was shown that organic evolution, in the sense that all animals and plants have descended from a common ancestor, was predicated on the assumption that geological strata will always be found in the same sequence all over the world. But subsequent investigation has failed to confirm this invariable sequence, and hence the entire argument in favor of organic evolution from the viewpoint of geology was shown to be without any scientific foundation. A definite chronological order cannot be established from the present-day evidences which are culled from all parts of the world. If a correct view of geology forever puts the evolution theory out of possible consideration, then the philosophical implications must be studied and an alternative hypothesis be put forth. This article is written with the intention of presenting the scientific basis of the true philosophy of the origin of life.

Let us examine a typical case of how the new facts of geology refute the old fallacies of evolution. Have you read or been taught that the Cambrian beds are the oldest fossiliferous strata? Do you know that in the Middle West of this country, the upper and lower Carboniferous are found in the position where the Cambrian should be, if we accept a definite "historical" sequence of rocks? In Georgia and the southeastern United States, the upper and lower Cretaceous are the oldest strata; in Southern California the Tertiary rocks (occupying a "recent" position on the geological timetable) occur in this position. In Central Europe the Jurassic and Triassic strata are found in a similar condition. From these and other examples we learn that there are no definite bottom or oldest fossils for the world as a whole. Any of the fossils might be found in this bottom position. This is true of all rock strata,

and examples are found of the strata occurring in practically every order of serial relationship. The evidence is clear and conclusive that the fossils of past ages lived contemporaneously.

Not only do the facts of geology refute evolution, but important evidence is being brought forth from research work in biology, morphology, embryology, anthropology, archaeology, chemistry, physics, astronomy, bacteriology, medical science—facts are being piled upon facts to overthrow the dogma whose basis is prejudice. A comprehensive study of the evidences in each of these fields is beyond the scope of this article, but the reader is directed to the bibliography at the end of this article to obtain this new information. It is becoming more and more evident that the "facts" which are said to prove evolution are really the arbitrary conclusions of those who propose the theory without honestly considering all the evidence that can be gathered. The general public has been kept in great ignorance concerning the validity of organic evolution. When the new facts of science cease to be suppressed, and research is no longer bridled by assumptions which dictate the conclusions reached in experimental work, the people of the world will see the mighty fall of a delusion which has permeated every branch of knowledge, and influenced the thinking and conduct of civilized man.

Science has often had long periods of intense intellectual adherence to popular dogma. The theory of spontaneous generation in biology, A. G. Werner's "onion-coat" theory in mineralogy, and the reign of the phlogiston theory in chemistry might be mentioned. Each theory had its advocates and defenders who tenaciously upheld their position in the presence of all criticisms and obstacles. Yet they were wrong. Trained scientific research finally brought about the downfall of these theories.

So today, those who hold to the unorthodox view of critically examining the basis of evolution are in danger of the most ruthless kind of ostracism. But those who have had their eyes opened are working toward the day when facts will have the right of way over baseless theories, even though these theories may have the acceptance of great men throughout the world. It will be extremely difficult to make this transition, since many men of the old school will seek to repudiate new truth for the sake of clinging fast to old theories. But in the next few decades, the younger men who are free from blind prejudices of former generations will bring the scientific world to new and truer vistas of knowledge concerning the world in which we live.

The only other present alternative to organic evolution is the old, but newly re-established fact of special creation. One has only to read the voluminous works of noted evolutionists to observe the misconceptions, often grotesque and unbelievably remote from the truth, which are supposed to represent the concept of special creation. It is hoped that this article will make clear the basic principles of the Modern Doctrine of Creation. The Modern Doctrine of Special Creation, whose foundation is the Creation narrative in the book of Genesis, does NOT maintain that:

1. Organisms were created as they appear to us now.
2. Organisms do not change.
3. Nature is static.
4. The universe was created 6000 years ago.
5. Spontaneous generation has ever occurred.
6. Man was created on "October 23, 4004 B.C., at nine o'clock in the morning."

These and other misconceptions are due to opinions formulated by the church of the Dark Ages, Linnaeus, Agassiz, and others. These opinions are NOT found in the Genesis record. Many scientists today erroneously confuse the interpretation of special creation, made during the Dark Ages, with the true scientific interpretation that we have today. The record found in Genesis gives no support to these medieval interpretations, but rather it is in harmony with established scientific facts.

Essentially, evolution means transmutation, or the transformation of one kind of organism into another kind. The meaning of the word "kind" will be discussed later in this article. The question of whether evolution is occurring today must be answered by genetics, the science of heredity. In genetics, the process of mutation (changes in an organism which appear abruptly without transitional steps) has been the subject of intensive investigation. Drosophila melanogaster, the fruit fly, is a typical case. Under controlled laboratory conditions, hundreds of interesting mutations have been accomplished, yet there is never any doubt that the resulting mutant is still a fruit fly. The attempt to demonstrate organic evolution has failed. Until mutation of the Drosophila actually results in a creature that is no longer a fruit fly, the theory of evolution is not sustained in these genetic experiments.

It can now be understood why the proponents of evolution, who realize the impossibility of their ever establishing their case in modern research, flee to the dim ages that are so far past no adequate check can ever be made on their vaunted findings; and there, in the mists of antiquity, they postulate the "demonstration" of evolution. With our modern knowledge of the order of rock strata showing that animals and plants of past ages were contemporary, it is impossible to see how the forces of change could accomplish the formation of an entirely different kind of life, even given a time period of billions of years.

Modern creationists believe that the "kind" mentioned in Genesis probably refers to what is known in our taxonomic classification as the "family." Examples of these "kinds" are men, apes, dogs, cats, horses, rabbits, squirrels, oak trees, maple trees, violets, sunflowers, roses, beans, and others which make up the tremendous diversity of life upon our planet. The cat family *Felidae* includes such well-known members as the lion, tiger, leopard, lynx, jaguar, Siamese, Persian, *et. al.*, but this wide variation has not proceeded to the stage where an individual would be formed which was NOT a cat. Likewise we have as representatives of the family *Canidae* the greyhound, bulldog, newfoundland, pekinese, great dane, bloodhound, spaniel, *et. al.*, as well as the diverse forms of foxes, wolves, and coyotes. Variation has not produced a new individual which cannot be recognized as a representative of the family *Canidae*. Therefore, the family is a unit whose boundaries have not been crossed by any amount of variation, either in nature or under laboratory conditions. The creationist believes that the members of a family are all descended from an original pair which were created at some time in the past.

The creationist does not say that in twenty-four hours God covered the entire earth with pine forests in their present profusion, with wild ducks by the millions, with humans by the myriads; but He only inaugurated on each day of creation the origin or beginning of a particular kind. There has been plenty of time since the original act of Creation for the multitudinous life of today to have developed. The family still retains its distinctiveness in obedience to the Creator's command that all life should multiply and reproduce, each always after its own kind.

This law of kind producing kind is so obvious to us today that we commonly overlook it. We know that from sparrow's eggs only sparrows will emerge, not bees or elephants. The study of the structure of the cell gives support to this law. Different kinds of animals are composed of different kinds of protoplasm. The protoplasm of the cat family is one type of protoplasm, and the dog family has a distinct type of protoplasm, that differs from that of the cat. Each kind of organism has its own chemical individuality, implying a specific molecular composition. There are probably specific proteins for each genus at least. It has been found that there is an incredible variety in the groupings and proportions of the amino acids and diamino acids which constitute the complex protein molecules. It must be recalled that many of the constituents of protoplasm exhibit the phenomenon of stereoisomerism. An albumin molecule, only one of the many complex constituents present, with 40 carbon atoms could have about 1,000,000,000 stereoisomers, and some albumins have more than 700 carbon atoms. There must be an infinite number of possibilities of combination, enough for all the plant and animal kingdoms.

The creationist sees in a new theory, propounded by Dr. J. C. Willis, a plausible and scientific explanation of the development of life from the first ancestral representative of each family. Dr. J. C. Willis, an evolutionist, rejects the principle of natural selection, and instead postulates the theory of Divergent Mutation. According to his theory, the family is the oldest unit; whereas according to the Darwinian theory the family is a later appearance. The essential feature of the theory of Divergent Mutation is that evolutionary change goes downward from the family toward the species and the earliest mutations gave rise to or differentiated into the chief divisions of the family, the genera and species. In summary, the special creationist believes in a real creation of a vast number of ancestral progenitors from which the widely divergent forms of today have descended by processes of variation imperfectly known, but which are the subject of intense research in the science of genetics.

Here then is the crux of the matter. The position of the creationist has been grossly misrepresented. Likewise our intellectual vision has been clouded by evolutionists' defining evolution as the production of increased complexity through the origin of varieties within the limits of established kinds, instead of the transmutation of one kind of life into an entirely different kind of life. The creationist does not dispute the fact that animals and plants change; he is concerned with the EXTENT of these changes. If there has not been discovered one instance, in nature or in the laboratory, of the transmutation of one kind of animal or plant into another kind, how can we accept the theory which states that the extremely complex systems of higher organisms have evolved from the one-celled system of some primitive ancestor, which requires transmutation at every major stage of transition.

Variation is a law of nature, but no organism can produce an individual which is sufficiently different to constitute the member of an entirely different kind. The creationist points to the various genetical experiments, and proclaims that these do not demonstrate organic evolution, but rather that they emphasize the amazing capacity for variation within the limits of the particular kind of organism. These experiments in genetics prove the scientific accuracy of the Genesis record when it states that organisms reproduce after their own kind. The creationist believes in descent with limited change, the limits being the boundaries of the created kinds. If it can be shown that new kinds are formed under the influences of natural forces, then special creation is disproved. The ultimate answer given by nature is that natural forces do not give rise to new kinds, but each kind is fixed in relation to other kinds.

ALL variation is within the limits of the particular kind. By this fact evolution stands refuted, and the Doctrine of Special Creation has been vindicated.

The theory of evolution has been met on the very grounds of science. We have before us the pathetic picture of scientists working for decades, and spending all their energy to find "missing links" and evidences to bolster their pet theory. All science has been sidetracked in the vain attempt to prove a fantastic idea that all life has arisen from a simple one-celled form. The false trail of evolution has SLOWED progress in science. The Bible contains only the bare facts necessary to direct the course that research must take if truth is to be unveiled. Long years of a scientist's life will be utterly wasted in searching for evidence and proof of that which the Bible clearly says does not exist. We cannot enter a new day handicapped with ancient ignorance, and the fallacies of past generations. Let us conduct ourselves with scientific intelligence in a scientific age, and discard baseless theories which are out of harmony with the facts of the world about us.

## BIBLIOGRAPHY

Works of Harry Rimmer, Sc.D., LL.D.:

(1) *The Theory of Evolution and the Facts of Science*. Wm. Eerdmans Pub. Co.

(2) *Modern Science and the Genesis Record*. Wm. B. Eerdmans Pub. Co.

(3) *The Inquiring Student and the Honest Professor*. Research Science Bureau.

(4) *The Harmony of Science and Scripture*. Wm. B. Eerdmans Pub. Co.

(5) *Monkeyshines*. Research Science Bureau.

(6) *Modern Science and the Youth of Today*. Research Science Bureau.

(7) *Dead Men Tell Tales*. Wm. B. Eerdmans Pub. Co.

Works of George McCready Price:

(8) *Some Scientific Stories and Allegories*. Zondervan Publishing House.

(9) *The Phantom of Organic Evolution*. Fleming Revell Co.

(10) *Modern Discoveries which Help Us to Believe*. Fleming Revell Co.

(11) *How Did the World Begin?* Fleming Revell Co.

(12) *God or Gorilla*. McCann, Alfred W., Devin-Adair Co.

(13) *Fundamentals of Zoology*. Tinkle, William J., Ph.D., Zondervan Pub. House.

(14) *Evolution, Creation and Science*. Marsh, Frank L., Ph.D., Review and Herald Pub. Assn.

(15) *The Course of Evolution*. Willis, J. C., Sc.D., Macmillan Co.

(16) Various authors in the BULLETINS of the Society for the Study of Creation, the Deluge, and Related Science. 1941-1942-1943.

THE

# BULLETIN

OF

# DELUGE GEOLOGY

## AND RELATED SCIENCE

| VOLUME V | DECEMBER, 1945 | NUMBER 4 |

## METHODOLOGY IN HISTORICAL GEOLOGY[*]

### By PROF. GEORGE McCREADY PRICE
### *Walla Walla College, College Place, Washington*

In the history of all the natural sciences we see three aspects: First, a hit-and-miss gathering of facts; second, a formulation of theories to "explain" these facts; and third, intelligent criticism to revise and improve the accepted theories to bring them into better accord with new discoveries. These three aspects do not always develop in this order; indeed they all react with one another endlessly, though ultimately a state of stability is reached where the science rests on facts and theoretical explanations as definite and settled as any human knowledge can become.

By methodology we mean the study of the best methods of arranging the facts of the science so as to bring out their true meaning, and the elimination of all logical flaws in the theoretical aspects of the science. In other words, a study of the methodology of a science is a study of logic and clear thinking as applied to the subjects under consideration. And no science can afford to scoff at admonitions to put its house in order, when these admonitions come in the name of that mentor of all good science, Methodology.

Geology has always labored under several severe handicaps. In the first place, it

is largely a historical science, for it deals with events long past, and endeavors to interpret these long-past events by means of records engraved on the rocks. As Louis Agassiz used to say, "The crust of our globe is a great cemetery, where the rocks are tombstones on which the buried dead have written their own epitaphs." Since it is thus almost wholly beyond the possibility of experimental methods, the reading of these epitaphs is rendered a thousand times more difficult than the reading of cuneiform, or hieroglyphic, inscriptions, because the geological records require a knowledge of essentially all the biological and physical sciences, plus an unusually persistent attempt to think clearly and without bias of any kind. Again, the student of the Earth's long-past history has as his guide only those processes and facts which he sees around him in the modern world; and too often these modern conditions seem to give but meager help in interpreting those scanty, mysterious, and oftentimes astonishing records which he finds in the rocks. Another handicap, and not the least of them all, is that hasty,

[*] Reprinted from *The Pan-American Geologist*, Vol. 67, March, 1937, No. 2; pp. 117-128.

The BULLETIN is published by, and is the official organ of the "Society for the Study of Creation, the Deluge, and Related Science." The Editorial Board is comprised of Professor George McCready Price, Dr. Dell D. Haughey, and Mr. Ben F. Allen. It is printed at the College Press, Arlington, California. For members the BULLETIN is free, and extra copies 40 cents each (each number priced according to size); for non-members it is $2.00 per year and this number is 50 cents. All correspondence should be directed to the Editors, Box 1030, Glendale, California.

rule-of-thumb theories had to be framed a hundred years or so ago, when as yet but a scanty beginning had been made in a few small localities of western Europe; yet these temporary, or *ad hoc* theories have tended to cling to the science like a Nessus' shirt in the subsequent study of all the rest of the world. With the result that these one-time working theories have long since acquired the prestige of classical authority which cannot be disregarded, or even questioned, even though a multitude of newly discovered facts cry loudly for a revision of the older theories.

For example, Adam Sedgwick found certain kinds of invertebrate remains in the lowest beds, or just above the primitive crystallines in Wales; and these are still regarded as index fossils of the oldest formations wherever they are found occurring, in spite of the fact that fossils of many of the other formations have since been found somewhere in this same bottom-position. Cretacic Beds occur thus in Georgia, Cuba, and Jamaica; early Carbonic strata occur at the bottom in many parts of the Middle West; while in the Tehachapi and the Coast Range of California, Tertic deposits lie directly upon the old granites and gneisses, and are themselves as highly consolidated and crystalline as any of the Paleoziocs. From these facts we now know that there are really no bottom-fossils for the world as a whole; and if we are still to call certain Cambric, or pre-Cambric, older than all others we shall have to find reasons for so doing which are quite independent of their stratigraphic position.

In the early days of the science the phenomena of conformity were observed, and were judged, to be evidence of rather rapid succession; the lower bed had not had time to consolidate before the next was deposited upon it; and conformity was regarded as proving almost continuity of deposition. But presently beds were found in perfect conformity which, by their fossils, were classed as many millions of years

apart. For example, Cretacic strata occur in seeming conformity on Devonic rocks around Lake Athabasca, in northwest Canada; Carbonic beds lie upon the Ordovicic throughout several provinces of northeastern China, where Richthofen actually reported them as forming an unbroken sequence; while Pleistocene is spread out in perfect conformity upon Permian beds throughout northern Russia. Thousands of such obvious anachronisms have now been reported; yet the traditional sequence in which the fossils ought to be found occurring is so strong that the physical evidence of real continuity is vigorously denied, and the term "deceptive conformity" has been invented to fit these cases.

But we go much further than this. For the traditional order in which the fossils may be expected to be found has become so strong within our souls that when we find Permian, or Carbonic lying upon Tertic, as in much of the Alps; or Cambric upon Carbonic, as in eastern Tennessee and northern Georgia; or Cambric and other Paleoziocs upon Cretacic, as in Montana and Alberta, we invent the term "thrust-fault," and with sober faces we tell our students how huge areas of ten thousand or more square miles were lifted up from deep underground, and then pushed bodily forward for many miles across the soft underlying beds, without scratching or disturbing the latter in any way, so that they now lie in what look exactly like true conformity upon them.

Geikie's classic description of similar conditions in northern Scotland might serve to describe the actual physical appearance of all these incredible thrust faults:

"Had these sections been planned for the purpose of deception, they could not have been more skilfully devised, . . . and no one coming first to this ground would suspect that what appears to be a normal stratigraphical sequence is not really so."

The canons of methodology cry aloud that there must be something wrong with such a state of affairs. But before we try to put a finger on the exact place which is in need of remedying, we ought to consider a somewhat different aspect of the stratigraphic evidence which has also been much misunderstood.

Instead of looking at the world as a whole, let us focus for the moment, our attention upon the phenomena of ordinary superposition, which have always been thought to present a very simple problem with regard to time. This problem, however, proves to be somewhat complex; and it may be advisable to examine it in some detail.

We may distinguish three distinct aspects of the time-element in every case of superposition:

(1) The time-factor shown by the mere sequence in which the beds were deposited;

(2) The time-factor attaching to the materials composing the successive beds;

(3) The time-factor attaching to the fossils contained in the beds.

I. Regarding the first of these factors, it is obvious that a genuine time-element is shown by the sequence of the beds, that is by the obvious process of depositing the one bed above the other. The lower one of any specific pair of undisturbed beds is obviously the older. Whether the time-interval between these two successive depositions was long, or short, is not so self-evident. There must have been some interval; else there would be one continuous bed, not two. Some clue to the length of this interval may be surmised from a study of the physical aspects of the two beds, their lithic characters, and their contact surfaces at the plane of separation; but at best we can do little more than guess as to the possible length of time between the two beds. Of course, if we detect any sign of erosion in the lower bed, or notice any tilting of its surface so as to make the upper bed not exactly parallel with it, we

have a right to speak of an unknown additional time-interval. But where there is genuine conformity between the two beds throughout a considerable area, the physical evidence alone would indicate that the interval was not very long. Only as we bring in external factors, such as the time-element supposed to be shown by the different kinds of fossils found in the two beds, can we arrive at any very extended interval of time between two strictly conformable strata; for true conformity means almost a continuity of deposition.

II. The time-elements shown by the materials composing two or more successive beds are not so self-evident. Let us suppose that we have three beds, limestone, sandstone, and conglomerate in ascending order. Now, who is ready to affirm that these various materials represent genuine time-values? That is, who will categorically say that the sand of the second bed was not already in existence when the limestone was deposited, or that the gravel in the third bed could not have been in existence when the underlying sand was laid down? Obviously all three classes of materials might very probably have been already in existence contemporaneously in separated localities, the shifting currents having merely brought here into a vertical relationship these diverse materials which had previously existed in separated geographical relationships. To deny the probable contemporaneity of the materials composing these beds would seem to require a hardy dogmatism which is quite foreign to natural science. We thus reach the very important conclusion that no real time-values can be read legitimately from the materials composing any set of superposed strata.

III. Thus far I think all students of the science must be in agreement. It is the problems presented by the fossils contained in the beds which may give rise to doubt or debate. And yet how are the fossils which may be found in these beds one whit different from the lime-silt, the sand, or the gravel of which these beds are composed? Unless we already know from some outside sources of information that the different fossils found in these beds are of very different ages, it is logically inevitable that we are not at liberty to assign these fossils to three distinct ages on the mere fact that they happen to occur here in three successive strata.

This may sound like a very strange conclusion; but I do not see how it is to be avoided. And yet it really means that if the first bed contains trilobites and graptolites, if the sandstone bed contains dinosaur remains, and the conglomerate at the top contains elephant bones, we ought to be honest enough with ourselves to own that, so far as their occurrence here in this section of successive beds is concerned, we do not have sufficient facts to assign these three types of fossils to three very distinct ages in the Earth's history. If we are to keep on affirming very distinct time-values for these representative fossils, we ought to acknowledge that we must have received this idea of their relative time-values from some other sources besides their mere occurrence in a vertical sequence of strata. For obviously, we outrage every principle of scientific proof if we assign time-values to these fossils which we dare not assign to the lithic materials composing the beds. We may, of course, feel sure that we have other and outside sources of information which tell us that these trilobites, and dinosaurs, and elephants, did live in very distinct ages; but we merely bemuse ourselves if we think that we got this information from geological records such as these.

We do not here have the space to follow out this very enticing problem of what other or extraneous sources of information, such as taxonomy, or embryology, may be supposed to have furnished us with this idea of intrinsic time-values for such fossils as trilobites, dinosaurs, and elephants. This detour would lead us too far afield. We must confine ourselves to the facts and the logical principle here developed, namely, that the mere occurrence of distinctly different fossils in a vertical series of successive beds does not itself furnish the slightest proof that these fossils belonged to distant ages. The principle, of course, will help us to understand the very common phenomenon of an alternation or recurrence of typical fossils. In such instances we, of course, say that these fossils which are repeated over and over again in the same vertical section cannot possibly represent successive ages, but are merely local, topographical faunas.

But this principle may do much more than this. For, since it shows us a logical fallacy which has been woven into the very warp and woof of all the current teachings about historical geology, it may help to explain the *impasse* which we have reached in such matters as there being no bottom fossils for the world as a whole, the deceptive conformities, and the thrust-faults which have been mentioned in the first part of this article. Major difficulties which arise in any science are always admonitions that something must be wrong with the primary assumptions, or with the methodology employed in this phase of the scientific inquiry. But we have already discovered one fallacy in the common custom of transferring to the fossils in two successive beds time-values which properly pertain only to the mere process of forming these beds, and never inhere in the materials composing the beds nor in the fossils which they may contain. Who can doubt that this fallacy about stratigraphic position will go far to account for the predicament in which the science now finds itself regarding such phenomena as thrust-faults and deceptive conformities?

But we have now progressed two stages in the present paper. We first found many facts from the field which are very difficult to explain on the basis of the current theories. Then we discovered a logical fallacy which seems to pervade all notions of time-values inhering in two distinct sets of fossils from the mere position in which they happen to occur in successive beds.

It will now be in order for us to return to the study of the methodology of the science in its cosmopolitan, or world-wide, aspects.

In the early days of the science the findings of certain types of fossils at the bottom of the stratigraphic series in Wales, gave rise to the theory that these types of ancient life must be of world significance, and indeed must represent an age of the world when such types and only such types were universally spread around the globe. In this conclusion it has long been recognized that there was a considerable element of the then-current false Wernerian notion, and that Sedgwick and his fellow-workers were merely substituting onion coats of index fossils for onion coats of index minerals. But we have now learned from the preceding discussion that there was also present in this conclusion the further fallacy of attributing time-values of world significance to these fossils in the bottom of the fossiliferous series in Wales. And in confirmation of the error in this conclusion we have learned in modern times that every other type of fossil life in the entire geological series is somewhere found in this same bottom position. From this series of facts we seem obliged to draw the inevitable conclusion that there are no specific types of fossil life that we can point to as intrinsically older than all others.

Yet, a century or so ago these Cambric fossils were selected as, if not absolutely the oldest forms of life that ever lived, at least older than any others which had then been discovered. From these Cambric beds as a starting point, the science has endeavored to navigate its way up through the long ages to the Present, trusting to its skill in cosmic dead-reckoning and hoping to arrive at the present with a cargo of so-called "living" species unaccounted for that would be sufficiently small in number to splice on with the modern world smoothly and easily on the basis of uniformity among rock-processes and transformism among the plants and animals.

What a method for a science which aspires to rank with such others as physics and chemistry!

Surely there must be a better way. Since by this method we have been accustomed to start from some guess-work place in the Earth's long past, and from this hypothetical starting-point have endeavored to work up toward the present, how would it do to reverse this method and start from the present state of the world and work backward by recession into the past? The latter method would at least have the scientific merit of starting from the known and proceeding to the unknown; whereas the former method has always started from the unknown and worked toward the better known. And by doing so it has developed all kinds of difficulties with recent discoveries which have been made in the field all over the globe. What a commentary on our boasted scientific progress that this strange hypothetical method has stood unquestioned for over a hundred years!

What do I mean by starting from the present state of the world and proceeding backward into the past? Remember this is a methodology of interpretation; it has nothing whatever to do with the methods of making field-surveys, or of gathering data of any kind by field-observations. Probably it will always be convenient to start from the base in any specific section and follow the beds upwards; and very likely it will always be convenient to employ such names as Cambric, Ordovicic, Siluric, and Tertic to designate the stratified deposits of the Earth. A name is only a convenient handle to enable us to work with large masses of facts; and some names will always be necessary to group together various types of strata for our mental convenience. And probably the long-familiar names will always be convenient as labels, for they represent groups of beds from all over the globe which are alike in containing similar fossils. But in the light of what we now know it will be necessary for clearness of thinking that we try to forget the time-value so long associated with these names.

Since this article is not meant as a reconstruction of the science of geology, but as only a brief statement of a new methodology for explaining what has actually taken place in the earth's long-past history, it will be necessary only to show what is meant by this new methodology, leaving for some other occasion the further development of this new method.

One of the outstanding features of the surface of the globe is the great number of basins of interior drainage, with either no outlet to the ocean, or with only a long-unused outlet. Such interior basins are scattered around over all the continents, and some of them, like the Great Basin, which comprises most of Nevada and Utah and parts of several other states, are very large. Taking the large and small together, these interior basins are estimated to occupy nearly one-fourth of the entire land-surface of the globe.

Many of these interior basins give visible evidences that they were once full of water, full to the very brims, as admirably set forth lately by O. E. Meinzer. Old shore-lines circle them around on the inside, these former beaches being sometimes a thousand feet, or so, above the levels of the dwindling little bodies of water which now occupy the lower levels of these basins. I am not affirming here dogmatically that all these interior basins of all the continents were full of water at the same time; but in any unbiased examination of the world as a whole, if we are to work from the present backward into the past without any theories whatever, all these basins with their tell-tale marks of having been once full of water would be among the first sets of facts which we would have to take into consideration; and the burden of proof would certainly rest on him who wished to deny that these great masses of water were all contemporary. Certainly they seem to have been contemporary; and we shall have to treat them as having been contemporary until

we find very positive evidence to the contrary.

Another related set of facts would be the high-terraces of many of the rivers of the world. These high-terraces, some of them several hundred feet above the present levels of the streams, are also a set of phenomena which are found over the globe; and, as in the case of the shore-lines of the great interior basins, the burden of proof must rest upon the man who seeks to affirm that they do not represent contemporary conditions, similar and due to the same causes in every land on earth.

Then, too, as we trace these high river-terraces down to the mouths of the streams, where they empty into the ocean, we find that these terraces blend with old shore-lines on the ocean. Many of the rivers of Europe and of America have had their terraces thus traced downwards to raised beaches on the shores of the ocean; and while a similar correlation has not yet been worked out for all the rivers of the world, it is undoubtedly true that similar conditions must prevail with all rivers which enter the ocean.

Obviously, if we are to start from the present condition of the world and work backward into the past, these world-wide conditions of interior basins, full of water, and of rivers of enormous size running at levels hundreds of feet above their present banks, will be the first great set of facts to stare us in the face. They tell us in no uncertain words that all the lands must at that time have been but recently emerging from the ocean, or that the oceans were then going down from off the lands, which would be the same thing. (See R. A. Daly's recent essays.) We cannot escape this conclusion, if we employ the new methodology and read the clear and undeniable records written in every quarter of the globe.

But all this means a world cataclysm of some kind. And if such a world cataclysm did really happen to our world some time in the past, its probable effects in killing off animals and plants of all kinds must be taken into consideration. Such an event must have stirred the oceans to their very bottoms; it must have destroyed and buried in sediments naturally all living things, both those living on the lands and those living in the seas. And a reasonable allowance must be made for all this whenever we try to deal with the fossiliferous deposits in any part of the globe and to any depth in any specific locality.

For this reason, the favorite method of classifying the Tertic beds in all parts of the world is by the percentages of living and extinct species which they contain, the beds the fossils of which are said to be mostly extinct are listed as older, and those with a high percentage of living species among their fossils are listed as "late" Tertic. And these Tertic beds occur so largely in isolated patches here and there around on all the continents that this classification can be carried out without running much risk of stratigraphical facts interfering with any juggling, or shuffling, of the classification thus made.

But if we are working from the present backward into the past history of the globe, and if we are confronted with something of a world-cataclysm which blocks our way in any consideration of the problem of the fossils, what possible value could such a percentage system have as indicating the relative ages of these Tertic deposits? How do we know that the fossils of a Pliocene set of strata, 90 per cent of the mollusca of which are classed as living, were not merely the lucky survivors of this world cataclysm, in which essentially all of the creatures of another set of strata called Eocene were destroyed? This classification of the superficial strata of the world may still be a convenient way of handling and distinguishing them from one another; but such a system can have no value as telling us the relative ages of the beds, if we are tracing our way by sound scientific principles from the present back into the past.

And all this is true whether we know the approximate magnitude of this world cataclysm or not. We do not need to know its magnitude; if there has been a world convulsion of any magnitude intervening between us and that ancient world of plant and animal life, it becomes sheer folly to classify the beds which we think lie back of this event as if such an event had never happened. Possibly by careful and extended study we might, at some future time, be able to separate those deposits and species-extinctions which were caused by this world-convulsion from others which were due to some previous causes. But at present nobody is able to do this; and so, while it would be rash to say dogmatically that this one established cataclysm produced all the fossiliferous deposits, the burden of proof must always be upon the one who would seek to assign some of these deposits to previous geological causes, whether we think them to have been mild, or catastrophic, in character. If a dozen burglaries have been taking place, and a fellow is caught redhanded in the act of doing one such "job," the natural inference would be that he was probably connected with the others.

I have tried to point out in brief outline some of the ways in which the new methodology would work and some of the conclusions which would follow the application of this method to the problems of historical geology. But it is very important that we carefully distinguish the method itself from its results. After all, it is the method which is important. We may not like the results which it seems to bring; but there can be no shadow of doubt that the method itself is the only safe and soundly scientific method of studying the problems of the Earth's past. The prevailing methods of beginning at a hypothetical point of time in the past, and attempting to unroll a uniformitarian behavior of the agencies of geologic change from that time to the present, has been tried now for over a hundred years, but it has developed scores of logical difficulties and sheer impossibilities, until it is breaking down before our very eyes. As a method of attacking the problems of the Earth it never could stand the inspection of intelligent criticism; and the logical atrocities of deceptive conformities and thrust-faults and the "skipping" of species have long cried aloud for a reconstruction of the methodology of the science.

It would be unreasonable for any one to feel alarm at the suggestion of this new methodology, or to say that it would destroy all that the science has accomplished in a hundred years. Nothing that has been suggested here can have the slightest effect on the ordinary methods of gathering facts from the field, or even on the methods of tabulating the discoveries thus obtained into the accepted geological classifications. Cambric beds will still be identified by the familiar brachiopods and trilobites; the Tertiaries will still be identified by their mammals and other specific index fossils. The new methodology has nothing to do with all this; it has to do only with the point of approach to the interpretation of the causes of the stratigraphic changes, and the general interpretation of geological processes. It suggests a completely new method of attacking the problem of geological causes; but if the method be sound, if it conforms strictly to the most rigid of scientific principles, no one ought to be afraid of the results thus to be obtained. "Let us not fight against facts," said one of the wise old Greeks, "for they can do us no harm."

Undoubtedly this method of proceeding from the modern world by direct regression into the Earth's past has its distinct limitations. It will never permit us to beguile ourselves with thinking that geology gives us the data for a scientific cosmogony; we shall never by this method discover how the world was made, or how its plants and animals began their careers. This may prove a great disappointment to some people. But in reality these limitations are the limitations inherent in all sound objective science. The latter must start with correct logical methods, and it can proceed only so far as the verified facts permit; when it runs out of such facts true science must call a halt and say, "Thus far and no further."

But this method has one very important advantage: it can be sure of its results, so far as it is able to go. It will not need to revise its "assured results" every so often, contradicting today what it declared yesterday. And this promise of results which will be able to withstand the severest criticism ought to be something which appeals to all seekers after truth.

## INDUCTIVE METHODS[*]

### By GEORGE McCREADY PRICE

In the First Part of this book I tried to examine into the facts and methods which are commonly supposed to prove that there has been a succession of life on the globe. We found that this life succession theory has not a single fact to support it; that it is not the result of scientific research, but wholly the product of an inventive imagination; that no one kind of fossil has even been proved or can be proved to be intrinsically older than another, or than Man himself; and hence that a complete reconstruction of geological theory is imperatively demanded by our modern knowledge.

In the Second Part I have brought out the following additional facts:

1. The abnormal character of much of the fossiliferous deposits.

2. A radical and world-wide change of climate.

* The following is taken from the book *Illogical Geology*, by George McCready Price, published in 1906 at Los Angeles, Calif. Since this was written forty years ago the editors believe that it will be of interest to the readers of the BULLETIN as indicating the position which George McCready Price had taken at that time regarding the subjects which he discusses.

3. The marked degeneration in passing from the fossil world to the modern one.

4. The fact that the human race, to say nothing of a vast number of living species of plants and animals, has participated in some of the greatest of the geological changes—we really know not how to limit the number or character of these changes.

Surely a true spirit of scientific investigation would now begin to inquire, HOW DID THESE CHANGES TAKE PLACE? Discarding the use of stronger language, it is at least utterly unscientific to begin somewhere at the vanishing point of a past eternity and formulate our pretty theories as to how this deposit was made, and how that was laid down, and the exact order in which they all occurred; while these "recent" deposits, in which our race and the plants and animals living about us are acknowledged to be concerned, are left over till the last, and we then find that they admit of absolutely no explanation. We ourselves, to say nothing of thousands of living species of plants and animals, have participated in some of the very greatest of the geological changes—we know not how many or how great. THESE THINGS MUST BE FIRST EXPLAINED. Has anything happened to our world that will explain them? Are there known forces and changes now in operation which, granting time enough, will amply and sufficiently explain these facts, as simply one in kind with those of the present day?

To this last question we must admit that our historic experience, prolonged over several thousand years, utters a thundering NO! Volcanoes are every now and then breaking forth; but volcanoes and mountain ranges have nothing in common with one another as to structure and origin. No one claims that a single mountain flexure is now being formed or has been formed within the historic period. There are indeed "creeps" in the rocks in certain places, but these are not such as to contribute to the height of the mountains in which they occur, but rather the reverse. Sudden changes of level within small areas have occurred, but neither in extent nor in kind do they furnish any key as to past changes of level; while the so-called "secular" changes are so microscopic in extent and so doubtful in character that they are utterly unworthy of consideration in view of the stupendous problems which we are trying to explain. The well-known work of Eduard Suess is a standing protest that such geological changes are NOT NOW IN PROGRESS; for, in speaking of how the land and ocean have exchanged places in the past, Zittel represents him as teaching that their "cause of origin until now HAS NOT YET BEEN DISCOVERED."—"History," p. 320.

Or, to quote the expressive words of Suess himself, with which he concludes his discussion of this very subject:

"As Rama looks across the ocean of the universe, and sees its surface blend in the distant horizon with the dipping sky, and as he considers if indeed a path might be built far out into the almost immeasurable space, so we gaze over the ocean of the ages, but NO SIGN OF A SHORE SHOWS ITSELF TO OUR VIEW." —"History," p. 294.

As for climate, I never heard anyone suggest that cosmic changes of climate are now known to be going on, much less that SUDDEN changes of the kind indicated by the North Siberian "mummies" are in the habit of occurring. In fact, we must all own that the mountains, the relative position of land and water, as well as the climate of our globe, are each and all now in a state of stable equilibrium, and have been in this state since the dawn of history or of scientific observation.

Accordingly I ask, HOW MUCH TIME IS NEEDED to account for the facts before us on the basis of Uniformity? In common honesty will a short eternity itself satisfy the stern problem before us? I cannot see that it holds out the slightest promise of solving it; while, on the other hand, I am sure that, in dealing with the past of Man's existence (theories of evolution and all other theories of origins whatever cast aside), we are not at liberty to make unreasonable demands of time. The evidence of history and archaeology is all against it.

From the latter sciences it can be shown that at their very dawn we have, over all the continents, a group of civilizations seldom equalled since save in very modern times, and all so undeniably related to one another and of such a character that they prove a previous state of civilization in some locality TOGETHER, before these scattered fragments of our race were dispersed abroad. We can track these various peoples all back to some region in Southwestern Asia, though the exact locality for this source of inherited civilization has never yet been found, and it is now almost certain that it is somehow lost in the geological changes which have intervened.

For when we cross the well marked boundary line between history and geology, we have still to deal with men who apparently WERE NOT SAVAGES, men who with tremendous disadvantages could carve and draw and paint as no savages have ever done, and who had evidently domesticated the horse and other animals. But as to time, history gives no countenance to long time, i.e., what geologists would call long. Good authentic history extends back a few score centuries, archaeology may promise us a few more. As for MILLIONS of years, or even a few HUNDRED THOUSANDS, the thing seems too absurd for discussion, unless we forsake inductive methods, and assume some form of evolution *a priori.—Illogical Geology*, pp. 81-83.

## REFLECTIONS ON GEOLOGY AND THE DELUGE

### I.

In the preceding pages I have tried to give a purely scientific argument, firstly against the traditional theory of successive types of life, and secondly against the dogma of uniformity. The two lines of thought are intimately connected; and it is obvious that if the successive-ages theory is discredited, uniformity becomes utterly unthinkable. In that case, a catastrophic interpretation of the chief geological phenomena becomes quite inevitable. What things are further implied because of this, may well be worthy of a little attention.

For if there really has been a world-catastrophe, such as seems to be indicated by the geological evidence, this fact can never be permitted to stand as an isolated fact in our thinking, with absolutely no further influence upon our other ideas of nature and of the universe. If we are to act as rational creatures, this fact of the great world-cataclysm must be given its proper place and be allowed its proper influence on the rest of our thinking. That is, we must make a proper adjustment of

our philosophy; for philosophy is only a general view of the problems of nature and their correlation with human values and human destiny. Every man has some sort of philosophy, adequate or inadequate; but the philosophy of the man who is convinced of the catastrophic interpretation of the geological phenomena will be vastly different from the philosophy of the one who believes in an absolute uniformity of nature; yes, very different,—as different as creation is different from evolution.

The bearings of the catastrophic theory of geology upon the doctrine of creation have been discussed by the present writer in various publications, particularly in "Q. E. D."[1] This phase of the matter need not be repeated here. It remains to consider briefly the various possible alternatives of a strict system of natural science toward the facts brought out in the previous pages.

Personally, I can see only two possible methods of adjustment, in view of the facts of geology as we now know them:

----
[1] "Q. E. D., or New Light on the Doctrine of Creation," New York, 1917.

1. Scientists may adopt an agnostic attitude, and say that, although they have been disappointed in tracing out the beginning of things by means of the fossils, nevertheless they still believe that somehow life has been on the globe for an immensely long time, and that it may have come about by progression from crude or scanty beginnings. Of course, this cannot be proved, and the more candid will readily admit this; but rather than face the other alternative, many will probably adopt this attitude.

To do this, they will have to shut their eyes to any real candid or philosophical explanation of the general facts of the rocks. But these people may refuse to attempt any explanation of the general facts. They may simply say, as a leading state geologist once said to me, that he had done with general theories about the past of the world; he was simply noting the facts in the field, and trying to explain them locally, caring nothing whatever about a world philosophy of geology. This may be an easy way out of the difficulty for some people, but it seems very inadequate to me.

2. The only other alternative, as it seems to me, is to say that this world-cataclysm, so clearly indicated by the new geology, must correspond to the Deluge spoken of in Genesis. But on this basis, this deluge must have been a much vaster and much more important event than it has usually been considered. It would seem that nothing but a specially planned event, that is, what we understand as a "supernatural" event, must be indicated both by the Scriptural record and also by the geological. Conceivable, if there were enough loose materials on hand in various parts of the earth, that is, enough clay, sand, and gravel, etc., a huge world-convulsion might pick them up here and there and rearrange them in strata or layers, much as we find them now, their present consolidated condition being easily accounted for by the subsequent "setting" of the materials, due to chemical and mechanical action.

—Price, G. M. *Evolutionary Geology and the New Catastrophism*, California, Pacific Press, 1926, pp. 338-341.

## II.

In a preceding section we gave some facts regarding the deposits on the bottom of the ocean, showing how different the deposits now forming are from the ancient deposits found in the rocks of the land. These rocks often contain fossils of various kinds of creatures which now live only in the deeper waters of the ocean; but modern investigation has revealed the surprising fact that nothing like a stratified formation of gravel or sand or clay is now being formed anywhere over the deep ocean floor. Hence, we now realize that the rocks composing our hills and mountains must have been formed by some quite abnormal action of the waters of the ocean.

We also showed that there is no evidence that the ocean and the land are now gradually exchanging places around any of our coasts. Small, sudden displacements due to earthquakes have occurred in modern times; but there is absolutely no scientific evidence of those slow, enormous movements up and down of the sea or land, which have so long been the theme of much geological teaching. We conclude from this fact also that the great movements of the waters which are recorded in the rocks, must have been due to some action of the waters which is not going on at the present time.

In other pages we have mentioned evidences of a sudden and world-wide change of climate,—a change as great in difference of temperature as it must have been in suddenness of action. A climate which must have been mild and delightful, was changed suddenly into the arctic frosts of the polar regions, with no moment of relaxation of this terrific cold since that time; for the carcasses of the animals then destroyed have been kept in the cold storage of a perfect refrigerator even to our own day. Other considerations also give evidence of the suddenness and enormous extent of the changes which then took place in our world.

By correlating all these scattered facts, we have arrived at the general conclusion of a great world catastrophe which at some time in the long ago overtook our earth. This is a truly scientific induction from these many facts; and the abundance of the evidence and its perfectly consistent and unambiguous character, make this conclusion as certain as any other of the conclusions of science. In view of these facts, and in view of the uniform traditions of every race of men on earth,—even leaving out of consideration the history in the Bible,—the Deluge, or Flood, becomes as certain a historical event as any other fact of history—as certain, for instance, as the conquest of Egypt by the Hyksos, or as the fall of Carthage.

This light which we now have on the reality of the universal Deluge, inevitably clears away a great deal of fog with which the popular evolutionary teachings have surrounded the subject of the early days of our world. We have ample evidence that the world before the Flood enjoyed a climate like that of perpetual spring. It is easy for us to enlarge on the picture, and catch glimpses of that Eden home of our first parents in which the Bible and tradition alike have taught us to believe.

But these new facts of geology also destroy with one sweep all evolutionary schemes of the long-drawn-out development of one kind of animal into another, a kind of idle dreaming which has been the diversion of nearly two generations of scientists. If there has really been a great world catastrophe, like a universal Deluge, there is no more chance to construct a scheme of Evolution based on the fossil remains found in the earth (and it can never have any other foundation), than there would be to construct a sky-scraping office building on the top of an ant hill. As the mists and fogs of evolutionary speculations clear away, the great truth of a real Creation at some time previous to this world catastrophe, becomes as clear and inevitable as any other fact of existence.

—Price, G. M., *Science and Religion in a Nutshell*, Washington, D. C., Review & Herald Pub. Assoc., 1923, pp. 34-36.

# The Forum

## For The Correlation of Science And The Bible

## Vol. I and II

1946 - 1948

Society For The Study of Natural Science, 1801 New Jersey
Street, Los Angeles 33, California

Printed by Glendale Academy Press, Glendale, California

# TABLE OF CONTENTS

## VOLUME ONE

## VOLUME TWO

# TABLE OF CONTENTS

## VOLUME ONE

## VOLUME TWO

# *The Forum*

## FOR THE CORRELATION OF SCIENCE AND THE BIBLE

Volume I                                                                    1946 - 47

# ANNOUNCEMENT

With this first issue, THE FORUM for the Correlation of Science and the Bible takes its place with the already overwhelming amount of scientific and religious periodical literature of our age. What excuse or reason do we then have for adding yet another journal to these almost countless publications? We believe that THE FORUM will fill a need which is not now being filled by any other existing periodical. There will be afforded an opportunity to discuss freely and reverently such problems and questions as have come and will come out of the relationship of the Bible to science. Such problems and questions nearly always result from a lack of knowledge regarding either one or both of these fields.

It is the purpose of this publication to provide a medium for the exchange of thoughts and facts regarding such subjects relating to science and the Bible which merit discussion and clarification. The plan adopted is a "forum" in which several individuals will discuss at length a certain problem, to be followed by such arguments and comments as will be precipitated by these discussions. In this way, the subject under study will be quite thoroughly covered, and the material thus brought together should be invaluable to many. Such discussions should also promote unity of thought regarding important subjects which lie within the fields of both science and the Bible.

The first general subject for THE FORUM is that of The Creation Record of the First and Second Chapters of Genesis, but will deal especially with The Creation of the Earth, or particularly Genesis 1:1-2, and its relation to the creation of the rest of the universe. After the completion of this study on creation, it is planned that THE FORUM will take up other subjects dealing with the relation of science and the Bible as may be suggested by its readers.

Ordinarily THE FORUM contains material that will make it primarily useful and interesting only to teachers of biblical or scientific subjects, to ministers, and to other workers in science or theology. It is for these groups that THE FORUM is intended.

It is quite evident that the views expressed by various writers in THE FORUM do not necessarily reflect the opinion of one or all of the editors. Such articles as set forth the viewpoint of one of the editors will be written and be signed by the editor in question.

The editors of THE FORUM hope that its readers will feel free to contribute to the discussions on each subject as it is presented. Although they can make no promise that all comments which are received will be published, they will make a sincere effort to include all the worthwhile discussions that are sent in. When several readers submit comments which are of a similar nature, the one best suited for THE FORUM will be selected by the editors. After the discussion of a subject is completed there will be added a summary, which will be prepared by one of the editors or someone selected by them.

THE FORUM will not be published at designated intervals, but whenever the necessary material for a number is in the hands of the editors it will be issued. Usually several numbers dealing with the same subject will form a volume, although occasionally a single large number may be issued as a complete volume, or two volumes may be issued together. The subscription price for THE FORUM is two dollars a volume, but it is not expected that this will cover the cost of publication. It is hoped that many will voluntarily contribute an additional amount to the publication fund of THE FORUM.

---

## SCIENCE AND THE BIBLE

"God is the author of science. Scientific research opens to the mind vast fields of thought and information, enabling us to see God in His created works. Ignorance may try to support skepticism by appealing to science; but instead of upholding skepticism, true science contributes fresh evidences of the wisdom and power of God. Rightly understood, science and the written Word agree, and each sheds light on the other. Together they lead us to God, by teaching us something of the wise and beneficent laws through which He works.

Ellen G. White
Counsels to Teachers, p. 42

THE FORUM FOR THE CORRELATION OF SCIENCE AND THE BIBLE is published by the Society for the Study of Natural science. THE FORUM will be issued whenever sufficient material for publication is available. The subscription price is two dollars a volume. All correspondence and manuscripts should be sent to THE FORUM, 1801 New Jersey Street, Los Angeles 33, California.

# THE CREATION OF THE EARTH
## A SYMPOSIUM
### INTRODUCTION

A discussion of Genesis 1:1-2 was requested by more individuals for early publication in the FORUM than any other subject, and this indication of general interest caused the editors to select THE CREATION OF THE EARTH as the first topic for consideration in this new publication. It might be well to discuss briefly at the outset what is involved in this subject, and what conclusions can or cannot be drawn.

There seem to be several possible interpretations of the first two verses of Genesis, and each of these has its champions. The first possibility is that the creation mentioned in Genesis 1:1 occurred on the first day of the six days of creation. If one takes this position, there is still left to be decided what is meant by "the heavens," and so we find that some hold this creation of Genesis 1:1 refers only to the earth and its atmosphere. Others believe that by "heavens" is to be understood the sun and the rest of our solar system, while still others hold that on this first day the entire astronomical heavens, the universe, was created.

The second view on these verses is that the creative act here mentioned was not a part of the six days of creation, but that it occurred some time *prior* to it. The word *beginning* would not refer then to the beginning of the creation week, but to some other beginning, such as that of the earth, the solar system, the universe, etc. The word "heavens" in this second view also is interpreted in the various ways mentioned above.

How can we decide which of these possibilities is the one which corresponds to the truth? The evidence upon which our decision must be based can come from only two sources: the revelation of God in His written Word, and the revelation of God in the book of Nature. It is possible that both these sources have information on this subject, or that one of them has the preponderance of evidence. In addition, we must also remember that it may be possible that sufficient evidence cannot be gathered from either of these sources to form a final opinion. For that reason it behooves us to be tolerant of the other person's opinion, and not to develop an exaggerated view of the importance of our own ideas. This, in turn, should make us willing to weigh the evidence presented by those who hold an opposing view, and to discuss freely the merits of each case.

Finally, let us note what is *not* involved in this subject. In none of the above views is there any limitation of God's creative power; all of the interpretations mentioned equally recognize the creation of the earth as being entirely due to the creative will and power of God, the only difference being the *when* of that creation. There is no doubt in the minds of the advocates of any of these views that God could have created the earth at any time He desired, and that He was not dependent in His creation on pre-existing material. There is no leaning towards evolution to be read in the views of those who hold that the earth might be older than six thousand years, but simply an attempt to ascertain from the Bible and sciences what God has revealed to us on this question as to when the earth was created.

M. Couperus, M.D.

# "IN THE BEGINNING'

## By George McCready Price

Those who wish to solve any major problem about the universe, such as its age, or how it started, may take their choice of either of two methods, or a combination of the two. They may decide to work out the problem by themselves, that is from the objective facts which are available and which they think are pertinent. This would be the scientific method. Or they may appeal to some one who knows, which would be the theological method; for God is the only being who really knows all the answers.

Any scientific investigation of the problem of how old the universe is leads without fail to the conviction that it is very, very old. Some twenty or more years ago, Jeans and other astronomers were teaching that the universe must have been created; and then still more recently, by at least two independent lines of investigation, the conclusion has been reached that the entire physical universe,—our solar system, our entire galaxy, and all the other galaxies,—is all of the same age, and that all must have started together about 2,000 million years ago. In other words, it is now being taught, not universally, but by many astronomers and atomic physicists, that the entire sidereal universe, including our own solar system, started off with a bang, as it were, by a miracle of creation about two billion years ago.

Now I am not going to present the scientific evidence for all this: some one else can do that later. Nor am I going to discuss the mystical, pantheistic theories which have become so fashionable as the outcome of the new views about the interchangeableness of matter and energy. These discussions can wait for some future time. What I am concerned with here is simply the relationship of the smaller problem of the age of our earth to this larger problem of the age of the rest of the universe. I mean, How old should we regard the body or matter of our earth to be?

On this point two very different views are held by Adventists and others who believe in the Bible record of a literal creation only a few thousand years ago. All those whom I call creationists believe in the creation of the first plants and animals, including man, about six or seven thousand years ago. But one group thinks that the body of the earth itself, that is, the inorganic elements of which it is composed, was also created or spoken into existence at the same time, just a few thousand years ago; while the other group thinks that the substance of the earth was created long before that, or at the same time all the rest of the universe was created, and that Creation Week, as recorded in the first chapter of Genesis, had to do only with the secondary aspects of creation, or the making of the first plants and animals as the inhabitants of the earth.

I may say in passing that there are good, sincere Creationists in both groups; and no charges of heresy or of unbelief should be hurled by any one against those on the other side. Personally, I do not know of any clear statements of Scripture which positively settle the matter either one way or the other. I used to think that the wording of the fourth commandment was decisive in favor of the short chronology for the age of the earth; but now I do not believe that this view can be maintained.

Accordingly, I am inclined to let the scientific evidence decide the matter. There can be no denying that the scientific evidence is overwhelmingly in favor of the greater age of the body of the earth, I mean, exclusive of the stratified rocks and the volcanic eruptions upon its surface. Since we know that extensive masses of rocks have been metamorphosed by heat and pressure, it will probably be impossible positively to separate all the changes effected by the universal Deluge from those geological processes which may have preceded, and thus be impossible to differentiate among the so-called "primitive" rocks between those belonging to the age preceding Creation Week and those belonging to those formed afterwards.

No enlightened Creationist will be reckless enough to deny that innumerable other worlds already existed and were inhabited by rational beings, when the foundations of the present order of things on this earth took place, "when the morning stars sang together, and all the sons of God shouted for joy" (Job 38:4-7). There is plenty of Scripture to prove the pre-edenic existence of not only the sidereal universe of suns and galaxies, but of great numbers of other inhabited worlds for long ages before our earth's Creation Week.

And there is very cogent scientific evidence that our sun and all the other planets must all have been created at the same time as the earth. They all belong together, and must all have been created together. But astronomy tells us of many dark suns now scattered through our galaxy; hence it is reasonable to say that our sun may have existed for a long period as a dark body, and that it was only lit up or made incandescent at the beginning of Creation Week, the first three days thereafter being cloudy or dark days, and the sun, moon, and stars only becoming visible from the earth on the fourth day. From Gen. 1:16 it would seem plain that whatever we say about the stars must also be affirmed about the sun and moon; and since it is palpably erroneous to say that the stars were not in existence until the fourth day, we should be able to say the same about the sun and moon. That is, all of them must have been in existence long before this, and all came into visibility or were able to be seen on the fourth day.

The Bible certainly does *not* affirm that the sun and moon were created on the fourth day. In the Revised Version of Gen. 2:4-6 we also seem to have a statement of conditions on this earth *before* the beginning of Creation Week, thus indicating that the earth had existed for some time previously.

As stated above, the scientific evidence is overwhelmingly in favor of the view that the body of the earth had existed long before Creation Week, though of course it was not then stocked with any plants or animals. There is neither science nor Scripture to favor the pre-edenic ruin theory. But many scientific facts seem to indicate that the body of the earth is very much older than the brief six or seven thousand years since the beginning of plant and animal life. And while scientific evidence should never be allowed to contradict plain Bible statements, yet it is not sound Christian policy to ignore entirely the scientific evidence, or to brush it all aside as unworthy of any consideration. All the evidence from nature must be considered in our attempts to form true views about the early days of our world. Only when the evidence from nature, from Scripture, and from sound reasoning and good common sense all agree, can we feel safe and confident concerning our views concerning the early conditions of our world and the living things upon it.

*Loma Linda, California.*

# IN DEFENSE OF THE ULTRA-LITERAL VIEW OF THE CREATION OF THE EARTH

Harold W. Clark

Professor of Biology, Pacific Union College
Angwin, California

## A Basic Principle

In any disputed question of interpretation of Scripture there is one principle that should always be kept clearly in mind, namely, that we should choose the *simplest, most obvious, most literal* interpretation, unless it can be proved to be based on a wrong translation of the original or to be out of harmony with well-established scientific principles. For instance, we refuse to believe that God actually brought the stars into existence on the fourth day of creation, for well-established scientific data shows most of them to be much older than 6000 years. In like manner we object to the idea that the thief on the cross would be with Jesus on that very day, because we believe such an interpretation of the Scripture to be based on wrong translation, the punctuation having been placed in the wrong place as the result of certain theological doctrines held by the translators. But when we come to the Genesis record of creation and the Flood, we maintain a simple, literal interpretation because we do not believe that the scientific facts make it necessary to take any other view.

## In Six Days

When we come, however, to the question of the *time* of the creation of the substance of the earth, we find a difficult problem, and one on which there seems to be a wide diversity of opinion. The Bible says: "For in six days the Lord made heaven and earth, the sea, and all that in them is." Exodus 20:11. Does this mean the substance of the earth, or only the finished forms of land and sea and air and of living creatures?

The ultra-literal view of the question is that the matter composing the earth was spoken into existence as the first step in the six-day creation process. Another view maintains that the record of creation week refers only to the organization of the matter and the formation of living creatures. This position varies in considerable degree. Some of its advocates hold that there is evidence for great age of the earth. Others do not accept this evidence as valid, but believe that the substance of the earth was created at a comparatively short time preceding the events of creation week.

Three main reasons are advanced for the idea that the substance of the earth was in existence before the first day of creation week: (1) that the radioactive minerals prove the earth to be very old, (2) that the language of Genesis 1:1, 2 refers to a "beginning" different from the creation process of the rest of the chapter, and (3) that certain astronomical facts make such a position necessary. We shall discuss each of these in order.

## The Radioactivity Theory

Extensive discussion of the evidence on this point is not necessary, since the readers are probably more or less familiar with the general principles on which the radioactivity theory is based. If one wishes full detail, he can find it in the reports of the National Research Council on the age of the earth. In brief, the whole question turns on the validity of the theory that the ratio of uranium-lead to uranium indicates the time it has taken to produce such a ratio. In other words, uranium is known to decompose through a series of intermediate products until finally it becomes an isotope of lead which can be distinguished from ordinary lead because of its different atomic weight. The U/Pb ratio is checked against the amount of helium found in the rock sample, since helium is a by-product of the same disintegrative process.

At first glance the radioactivity theory appears to be invulnerable, and many have been led to accept the evidence as conclusive. But a critical examination shows several flaws in the argument. Let us notice them one by one.

The method by which the U/Pb ratio is determined is open to question. The amount of uranium is not determined by chemical analysis, but by its effect on the electroscope. Now between uranium and lead there are 14 intermediate substances, each with a different rate of disintegration, some very rapid, some very slow. The radiations which effect the electroscope are the combined discharge of this mixture.

If pure uranium, radium, actinium, or thorium are tested, their disintegration rates are found to be constant, and no changes in physical surroundings can alter these rates. But it is one thing to test a pure sample and another to test a mixture, for the simple reason that a mixture is changing its proportions of intermediate products, and since each one has its own rate, the sum total at a given time will be different than at another time.

Furthermore, the statement that it is not possible to change the disintegration rate of a pure substance is now open to challenge. The invention of the atomic bomb is a $2,-000,000,000 demonstration that the rate of uranium disintegration can be changed. And this opens up several possibilities well worth consideration.

In the first place, how do we know that God created the earth with uranium, radium, etc., in pure form? Might He not have made mixtures at the beginning? To some, this suggestion is unwelcome, for, they say, other minerals are pure. But are they? How do we know that iron was isolated? Or copper? Or any other mineral? Today we often find them in a mixture. There is no valid reason for assuming that all minerals, including the radioactive ones, were in separate masses at the creation.

Let us assume, however, that God may have made uranium pure. How do we know but what those terrific changes going on during creation week may not have produced physical conditions that would cause or allow a much more rapid uranium decay than we now observe? Or how do we know but what conditions prevailing at the

time of the Flood may not have been responsible for more rapid changes?

There is a more serious aspect to this question than anything yet mentioned, and that is the apparent correlation between the U/Pb ratio and the supposed geological sequence of the rocks. According to figures given in the reports of the National Research Council, the pre-Cambrian rocks are of the order of 1,400,000,000 years old, and the succeeding members of the geological series respectively less. Thus it would appear that if the radioactivity of these rocks means anything in terms of age, it shows that the supposed geological "ages" are valid. Such a conclusion would make it necessary to accept the theory of the evolutionary sequence of the stratified rocks, and leave no argument against popular evolutionary geology.

The reader should understand the method by which samples are taken. In each portion of the geological "column" are both sedimentary and igneous rocks. The igneous rocks which accompany any certain group of sediments are assumed to have lost their lead content by volatization when they were poured out. Thus there would have begun a new uranium disintegration series, whose U/Pb ratio would vary according to the time when the igneous rock was extruded.

Several possibilities might be suggested to show why these figures do not necessarily indicate relative ages for the samples tested. For one, the temperature at which lead volatizes and that at which granitic rocks melt is about the same,—something of the order of 800° C. There is, therefore, the possibility of an irregularity due to partial volatization of the lead. Added to this is the chance that the nature of the materials may have varied, as they came from different depths where pressure and temperature conditions were different. All in all, it seems that there are so many possibilities aside from that of long ages, that the radioactivity theory cannot be taken as proof of the great age of the rocks of the earth.

### The Language Problem

"In the Beginning" (Genesis 1:1) reads in the original as simply *in beginning,* which connotes *at first*, or *originally*. The argument that there was *the* beginning as distinct from the other events of creation week cannot be maintained in the light of the original text.

It has been asserted that the fact that the narrative form of the Hebrew verbs does not begin until verse 3, indicates that verses 1 and 2 have reference to a separate event. Such a position is entirely uncalled for, for another meaning can be just as readily attached to this fact. Verses 1 and 2 are merely preliminary statements to prepare the way for the narrative that begins in verse 3.

Moses wrote his record of creation at a time when the theory of the eternality of matter was universally accepted. All nature was regarded as automatic in its action. The gods, even the Supreme God, were personifications of natural forces, and these forces were as eternal and automatic as matter itself. When God revealed Himself to Moses, He characterized Himself as the "I Am," the self-existent One. Thus the creation record is a direct blow at the pagan concept of a self-operating nature. The fundamental truth that was given as the introduction to the creation story was that *in beginning*, or *at first*, God created. To read more than this into the record is to insert pagan concepts.

The first two verses of Genesis constitute a series of preliminary statements,—(1) God created, (2) the earth was not brought into existence in a finished state, (3) the work of creation was a sequence of events. After these statements the record proceeds to give a detailed narrative of the events of creation week.

It is held by some that after He began the creation, God was obliged to cease the work for a time in order to give attention to the rebellion of Satan. But to assume that the record of verses 1 and 2 refers to a time previous to the rebellion is a purely subjective conclusion. If Satan found his spirit of rebellion, which had doubtless been stirring for a long time, brought to a focus at the time of creation, he would have been influenced by the plans for creation rather than by the actual process. For if God had brought the matter of the earth into existence millions of years ago, that would not have had any bearing on the events of creation week. If on the other hand, we hold that the matter of the earth was brought into existence instantly at the beginning of creation week, Satan would have had no time to bring his rebellion to a head. It seems, therefore, that the only reasonable position to take is that Satan was led to open rebellion by his jealousy of Christ at the time of the council in which the plans for the creation of this earth were consummated.

A strict creationist view of creation, especially in view of the modern knowledge of the dynamic nature of matter, would be that the creation of the substance of the earth would take place instantly, and at the time when that substance was needed for the creation process. To take any other position requires that we postulate the existance of matter lying for millions of years, or at least for long periods of time, in total darkness, until the command came, "Let there be light."

Let us now take the expressions in verses 1 and 2 and consider them in detail.

"In the beginning God created the heavens and the earth." This is a simple principle that at first God created,—the earth did not come about by any natural process.

"And the earth was without form, and void." The earth was not created in a fully organized state at first, but was chaotic, and lacking those refinements of nature that make life possible.

"And darkness was upon the face of the deep." As the watcher views the creation scene, he sees only blank space, the darkness of the abyss.

"And the Spirit of God moved upon the waters." Whether the Hebrew idiom "the face of the waters," really meant the ocean or was synonymous with "face of the deep," is not fully agreed upon by writers. The concept of the ocean surrounding the lands and forming the base upon which they rested was so firmly imbedded into ancient thought that it was a part of their common speech, just as we say today that the sun rises, when we know very well that it does not move at all. It would be perfectly consistent with the meaning of the rest of the text to take this expression as referring to the action of the Spirit of God upon the great abyss of space (and possibly also to the great expanse of waters that covered the earth as it came into existence.)

"And God said, Let there be light." Light is not a substance that can exist by itself. It is a radiation from a luminous body or else a reflection. But the light of the first day did not wrap itself around the earth like a garment, for it was separated into two parts, the light part and the dark part. To anyone viewing the creative process the great blank of heaven, dark and empty one moment, would show a body reflecting light and rapidly being organized. As the globe takes form, and begins its rotation, it establishes the daily cycle of "evening and morning."

### Astronomical Evidence

Why should God bring matter into existence, only to leave it lying around unfinished for long ages? Some have declared that this is apparently God's manner of creation, for, they say, do not masses of nebulous matter throughout the universe indicate that such unorganized material exists? There may be matter in the universe that is not organized into bodies like the sun or planets. But to assume that such matter ever will be used to form systems of worlds, or that our system came from such a mass of matter, is placing ourselves on very dangerous ground. The idea that masses of nebulous matter are solar systems *in embryo* is derived from the nebular hypothesis. Which is not only unscientific, but wholly foreign to any literal view of creation. Anything that identifies the creative process with masses of nebulous or inert matter introduces confusion into the whole issue.

It is claimed by some that since the solar system is a unit, it must have been created as such, all at one time. There is a question as to whether God could create the planets at different times. We do not know enough about God's methods of celestial mechanics to be positive one way or another.

But if we feel that it would not be possible to insert the earth into the system, let us consider this possibility. Suppose God

had created the sun first, then the major planets one by one, beginning at the outer one and coming inward. After the first one had been formed, it would undergo so little movement by the time that the next one would be created that no upset of its motion would be involved. Thus one by one the whole line of planets could be slipped into place without any noticeable disturbance in the balance of the solar system. I am not even suggesting that God did do this, but only showing how it could have been done, in order to point out that it is not necessary, even from this viewpoint, to assume the matter of the earth to be even a day older than the first day of creation week.

### Origin of the Idea of Great Age

The idea of the great age of the earth came from ancient pagan philosophy. To all the ancients matter was an eternal reality, existing even before the gods themselves. Even those peoples that believed in a Supreme God did not believe he was the creator; they regarded him simply as a more powerful spirit than the other gods or else as a builder or former who used the matter already in existence. When pagan concepts were introduced into Christianity in the early centuries, this idea of great age for the earth came with them. Augustine, whose theology has been studied more than any other of the early fathers, and has been influential in molding the doctrines of nearly all Protestant churches as well as that of the Catholic church, taught that creation was at a far distant time. God created matter and imparted to it certain properties, by which it was enabled to carry on its processes. If we study the course of theology and philosophy throughout the centuries since the time of Augustine, we shall see that there has been a continual conflict between this pagan concept and the literal view of creation.

### What Is the Safe Position?

In conclusion, let us assert again that the *simplest, most obvious, most literal* interpretation is that the matter of the earth was spoken into existence as the first step in the events of creation week. The radio-activity theory, the language problem, and the astronomical evidence—the three main arguments against this position,—while they may seem significant to some, do not afford any positive arguments that cannot readily be answered, for they can all be interpreted in harmony with the ultra-literal view.

Since there is no positive evidence that cannot be harmonized with the simple interpretation suggested, it is in line with sound principles of logic to believe that the Bible statement, "in six days God made the heaven and earth, the sea, and all that in them is," must refer to the material particles as well as the finished organic and inorganic forms.

## THE UNITY OF TRUTH

"We therefore cannot accept the dualism that there are two Gods—one of grace and another of nature. There is one God, and He is the author of both. Christ revealed in His own person and life the laws underlying the universe. What is covert in the universe became overt in Him. He is the revelation of God, and of the universe that God created. Reality is shot through and through with Christ. He is woven into the very texture of its being, the soul of its soul.

"If that is true, then it has important implications: go far enough with the facts, whenever you find them, and they will bring you out at the place of Christ. That is my profoundest conviction. If I did not believe that, I could not be a Christian with the consent of all my being. But does life verify it? I believe that the discovery of the facts, when they are facts and not half-truths, is leading in one direction and in only one

direction—in the direction of Christ. Let the scientist, therefore, begin with the facts, and let him go far enough with those facts, and he will come out at the fact of Christ. He may not get to Christ; he may stop short, but at least his facts will be pointing in the direction of Christ as their fulfillment." E. Stanley Jones, *The Christ of the American Road*, p. 159, 1944.

"Divine wisdom, infinite grace, were made plain by the things of God's creation. Through nature and the experiences of life, men were taught of God. 'The invisible things of Him since the creation of the world,' were 'perceived through the things that are made, even His everlasting power and divinity.' "

Ellen G. White
Christ's Object Lessons, p. 22

# GOD'S PRIMARY AND SECONDARY CREATIONS*
## By John Lowell Butler

There has existed for some time a need for a more complete exegesis of the first chapter of the book of Genesis and several other related statements in the Bible relative to God's two very different kinds of creative work, namely, His Primary and Secondary Creations. By careful examination it has been found that when *the astronomical evidences* which are involved in these subjects are given more emphasis, many of the dark mysteries and unsolved problems are readily solved, and we see a distinct picture of two great creations: and we also see God as the author of two great ages, namely, (1) the age of primary time, which is notable for its long duration, and (2) the age of secondary time, which is remarkable for its many living forms on the Earth.

### Many Inhabited Worlds

In beginning this study it is interesting to observe that the great Christian apostle Paul, in beginning his remarkable epistle to the Hebrews said:

"God, who at sundry times and in divers manners spake in time past unto the fathers by the prophets, hath in these last days spoken unto us by his Son, whom he hath appointed heir of all things, by whom also he made *the worlds.*" Hebrews 1:1, 2. And later in this document he said, "Through faith we understand that *the worlds* were framed by the word of God." Hebrews 11:3.

These statements make it very clear that we must take into consideration more than just one world, our own.

The leading Levites who returned from the Babylonian captivity regarded many of the worlds in starry space as inhabited worlds, for they said in their praise of God, as recorded by Nehemiah:

"Thou, even thou, art Lord alone; thou hast made heaven, the heaven of heavens, with all their host, the earth, and all things that are therein, the seas, and all that is therein, and thou preservest them all; and

the host of heaven worshippeth thee." Nehemiah 9:6.

In one of the oldest books of the Bible, the book of Job, we find the following statements:

"Then the Lord answered Job out of the whirlwind, and said, . . . Where wast thou when I laid the foundations of the earth? . . . When the morning stars sang together, and *all the sons of God shouted for joy?"* Job 38:1, 4, 7.

Who was it that shouted for joy when our Earth was created? The Lord said it was "all the sons of God." And who were these people?

According to the genealogy of Christ's foster father, Joseph, Adam was called "the son of God." Luke 3:38. But there was only one such son of God on our planet when its creation was finished. Therefore, since many "sons of God" shouted for joy at that time, *we must conclude that there were at that time many other inhabited worlds in the starry heavens:* and when the news of the creation of Adam and Eve reached those worlds, *many other Adams and Eves rejoiced.* Knowing what a good job the Creator did each time he made a planet habitable and stocked it with living forms, the original parents on each of these other inhabited worlds had good reason to "shout for joy" at the news that the planet named "Earth" had also been made habitable and stocked with many living plants and animals and a pair of human beings, who, like themselves, were capable of being the happy rulers of another wonderful world. People live on worlds, and worlds are lighted by suns, and suns are called stars, some of which we call "morning stars." Therefore both worlds and suns were in existence *before* our planet's special week of Secondary Creation.

And who carried this good news to all these other inhabited worlds? It must have been the angels, because they are a higher order of people (Ps. 8:4, 5) who travel as messengers from God's throne to the Earth, and, no doubt, to other inhabited worlds also. (Compare the following references: Daniel 9:20-23; Matthew 4:11; 18:10; 26:53; 25:31; 13:41-43; Hebrews 1:7, 14; Job 1:6-12; 2:1, 2, 7; Revelation 12:7-10; Jude 1:6; Psalm 34:7; Revelation 3:5 Hebrews 12:22; Revelation 5:11; etc.) And since the number of angels is so great that the are called "innumerable" (Heb. 12:22), we may conclude that there are almost innumerable inhabited worlds in the starry heavens.

As a passing suggestion it might be said, if there is an average of one inhabited planet for each shining sun that the astronomers can photograph, then there would be no less than 30 billions of inhabited planets in our Milky Way galaxy. Within the range of the 100 inch telescope on Mount Wilson there are approximately 100 million similar galaxies out beyond our Milky Way system, and no doubt there are still more beyond that range waiting to be photographed by the 200 inch telescope on Mount Palomar![1] Even if the percentage of inhabited planets is only a small fraction of this total number of shining suns, still the total number of inhabited worlds would be *very great!* A closer estimate will be given later on.

### Two Kinds of Creative Work

There is clear evidence that God performed two different kinds of creative work by the time that each of these inhabited worlds was finished and inhabited by living begins. The first need was to bring into existence the elements and substances of these worlds. That this was done is indicated in the following quotation:

"Through faith we understand that *the worlds* were framed by the word of God, so that things which are seen *were not made of things which do appear.*" Hebrews 11:3.

In other words, when "the worlds" were created, which might include all the stars or astronomical bodies, they were *not* formed out of visible substances that were already in existence. This, then, shows that the visible substances of which they are composed were brought into existence at the same time that those worlds were brought into existence. *This is a clear picture of the nature of the Primary Creation.* When God performed His primary kind of creative work *He created the elements and the stars at the same time.* The elements had to be put somewhere and the most logical place to put them would be where they were wanted, namely, in the many kinds of astronomical bodies. And, as the astronomers know so well, all astronomical bodies must move in orbits of some kind of preserve them from destruction by gravitating into one huge mass. Therefore we may include in the Primary Creation the motions of the stars and all their planets and satellites, etc.

Had the elements been in existence before the making of the stars, or worlds, then it might be said that the worlds were made out of visible things, because, even though the individual elements are invisible because of their smallness, yet their collective mass is very visible, especially when sufficient in amount to constitute a satellite, planet, or sun.

If the worlds, of which ours is only one, "were *not* made of things which do appear," then how could the Earth or any of the planets which are members of our solar system be aggregations of visible fragments, or, as the astronomers would say, worlds made by the planetesimal method?[2]

The Bible consistently presents a different method of the original creation of the astronomical bodies. The details of that primary method are still a deep mystery, but may be understood someday. He who understands that method will know all the secrets of all the atoms. In this great original Primary Creation of the elements and the stars there seems to be one great principle of design, so that we may either liken the individual elements to the astronomical systems, or liken many of the astronomical systems to the various kinds of chemical elements. This

---

[1] W. T. Skilling, and R. S. Richardson: "Astronomy," p. 521, 551, 1939.
[2] W. T. Skilling, and R. S. Richardson: "Astronomy," p. 311-313, 1939.

comparison is frequently made today by our leading scientists. It seems reasonable to observe that He who could invent and make, or "create," a chemical element originally could also invent and make, or "create," an astronomical system, provided he had a large enough supply of power. The making of countless numbers of well organized galaxies of stars would be no more difficult, given enough power, than the making of countless numbers of many kinds of elements and chemical compounds. And while making the class of midgets, the other class of giants might as well be created simultaneously. There is evidence that all this was done during the time of the Primary Creation. And the method by which it was accomplished is releaved in the following quotations:

The great scholar and logician, Paul, concluded that "the worlds were framed *by the word of God.*" Hebrews 11:3. In this statement he is backed up by several statements of other Bible writers. Elsewhere we read:

In the Psalms: *"By the word of the Lord* were the heavens made; and all the host of them by the breath of his mouth. . . . For *he spake, and it was done; he commanded, and it stood fast."* Psalm 33:6, 9. "Praise him, ye heavens of heavens. . . . for *he commanded, and they were created."* Psalm 148:4, 5. "O give thanks unto the Lord; . . . that *by wisdom made the heavens."* Psalm 136:1, 5. "He telleth the number of the stars; he calleth them all by their names. *Great is our Lord, and of great power: his understanding is infinite."* Psalm 147:4, 5.

In the book of Isaiah: "I have made the earth, and created man upon it: I, even my hands, have stretched out the heavens, and *all their host have I commanded."* Isaiah 45:12. "Lift up your eyes on high, and behold who hath created these things . . . *He is strong in power; not one faileth."* Isaiah 40:26.

In the second epistle of Peter: *"By the word of God the heavens were of old."* 2 Peter 3:5. (See also John 1:1-3; Colossians 1:16.)

This method of creating was used in both the Primary and the Secondary creative acts of God. The Genesis detailed account of our planet's Secondary Creation is full of such expressions as: "And God said, . . . and there was." (Genesis 1:3, 6, 9, 11, 14, 20, 24, 26, etc.)

But aside from this similar method used in both creations, there was a decided difference in the two creations themselves, because *God in every instance in every creative act performed during our planet's week of Secondary Creation used substances already in existence* in making light, heat, a clear atmosphere, the Earth's geography, and its plants and animals and human beings.

Of the parents of the human race it is written: *"And the Lord God formed man of the dust of the ground,* and breathed into his nostrils the breath of life; and man became a living soul . . . And the Lord God caused a deep sleep to fall upon Adam, and he slept: and he took one of his ribs, and closed up the flesh instead thereof; and the rib, which the Lord God had taken from man, made he a woman, and brought her unto the man. And Adam said, This is now bone of my bones, and flesh of my flesh: she shall be called Woman, because *she was taken out of Man."* Genesis 2:7, 21-23. And later in the story it is recorded: "In the sweat of thy face shalt thou eat bread, till thou return unto the ground; for *out of it wast thou taken:* for dust thou art, and unto dust shalt thou return." Genesis 3:19; (Eccl. 3:19, 20; Job 33:6.)

This is also true of the animals that God created on the Earth. Of them it is written: "And God said, *Let the waters bring forth abundantly* the moving creature that hath life, and fowl that may fly above the earth in the open firmament of heaven. And God created great whales, and every living creature that moveth, which the waters brought forth abundantly, after their kind, and every winged fowl after his kind: and God saw that it was good . . . And God said, *Let the earth bring forth* the living creature after his kind, cattle, and creeping thing, and beast of the earth after his kind: and it was so. And God made the beast of the earth after his kind, and cattle after their kind, and every thing that creepeth upon the earth after his kind: and God saw that it was good." Genesis 1:20, 21, 24, 25. *"Out of the ground* the Lord God formed every beast of the field, and every fowl of the air; and brought them unto Adam to see what he would call them." Genesis 2:19.

This is also true of the plants that God created on the Earth. Of them it is written: "And God said, Let the earth bring forth grass, the herb yielding seed, and the fruit tree yielding fruit after his kind, whose seed is in itself, upon the earth: and it was so." Genesis 1:11. "And out of the ground made the Lord God to grow every tree that is pleasant to the sight, and good for food; and the tree of life also in the midst of the garden, and the tree of knowledge of good and evil." Genesis 2:9 (Ps. 104:13, 14; Isa. 55:10)

This is also true of the geography of the Earth. Of this it is written: "And God said, Let the waters under the heaven be gathered together unto one place, and let the dry land appear: and it was so. And God called the dry land Earth; and the gathering together of the waters called he Seas: and God saw that it was good." Genesis 1:9, 10.

Likewise this is true of our clear atmosphere. Of this it is written: "And God said, Let there be a firmament (or expansion) in the midst of the waters, and let it divide the waters from the waters. And God made the firmament, and divided the waters which were under the firmament from the waters which were above the firmament: and it was so. And God called the firmament Heaven. And the evening and the morning were the second day." Genesis 1:6-8.

It will be shown later that the light of the first day came from our Sun, and that the first three days were cloudy days. This is why none of the astronomical bodies out in space were seen from the ground until the fourth day.

In the light of all these evidences it seems proper to ask, Why did the Creator consistently refuse to bring new elements into existence during our planet's week of Secondary Creation? or, Why did He always use substances that were already in existence, and had been in existence from the time of His great Primary Creation of all the elements and all the stars?

When God created the elements He gave them physical power to attract each other slightly, and when He made the stars He gave them power to attract each other with great force—the power of gravity. And in designing the astronomical heavens He chose to depend upon certain balanced forces to perpetuate their existence, and to make their individual suns and planets safe from collisions throughout the long ages of eternity. These very important balances would be somewhat disturbed by the creation of more weight in the Universe at later times. Therefore this may be the principal reason for the chief difference between God's Primary Creative work and His subsequent Secondary Creative work. God was wise enough to recognize in advance the importance of such little things as this when He exercised His creative power in a secondary manner.

The following quotation seems to be related to this phase of our study. "Who hath measured the waters in the hollow of his hand, and meted out heaven with the span, and comprehended the dust of the earth in a measure, and weighed the mountains in scales, and the hills in a balance?" No one had done so in Isaiah's day; but today our astronomers and other scientists can do so, and have even gone so far as to weight the entire Earth! And they know the importance of its weight. But who anciently could have told the truth of these things? So the prophet continues, "Who hath directed the Spirit of the Lord, or being his counsellor hath taught him? With whom took he counsel, and who instructed him (made him understand), and taught him in the path of judgment, and taught him knowledge, and shewed to him the way of understanding? Behold, the nations are as a drop of a bucket, and are counted as the small dust of the balance: . . . " Isaiah 40:12-15.

This phase of our study is somewhat complicated when we take into consideration the fact that the Earth and Moon, and our planets and their moons, are constantly collecting meteorites, or star dust, and that the yearly total runs into many tons. These collected meteorites make these members of our solar family weigh more as the years come and go. And a large percentage of this star dust comes to us from all directions of space and at speeds which show that it does not move in orbits around our Sun, but comes to us from the wide open spaces of the distant stars. However, astronomers are agreed that these meteorites, or star dust, are confined to our Milky Way galaxy, and that there is nothing of this nature between the many galaxies in space to hinder the free passage of light.[3]

Therefore our galaxy is not becoming heavier as the ages of eternity come and go. But if new elements were created within its limits, then it would be made heavier and would be thrown off balance, somewhat, with the millions of other huge clusters of stars, or nebulae, and might lead ultimately to interference on a much larger and more disasterous scale. Within our galaxy there seems to be plenty of space for its suns and planets and satellites to make adjustments in their orbits without any disaster resulting. And since all the astronomical bodies in our Milky Way galaxy are subject to increase of weight from meteorites, the balances within this system may thus be preserved. However this may be, whether we understand it fully or not, we may be sure that nothing is too small or too big to escape the notice and calculations of the Inventor of the Universe.

## Two Kinds of Heavens

In studying the general subject of creation it should also be observed that the Bible speaks of more than one kind of "heaven." Apart from the heaven that is often referred to as the capital of the Universe and a place of rewards, two other heavens are mentioned, that is, two different kinds of heavens. One is the astronomical heaven of the stars, and the other is the atmospheric heaven of the Earth.

In the book of Nehemiah we find the following statements: "Thou, even thou, art Lord alone; thou has made heaven, *the heaven of heavens, with all their host,* the earth and all things that are therein, the sea

and all that is therein, and thou preservest them all; and the host of heaven worshippeth thee." Nehemiah 9:6. There can be no doubt about this meaning the astronomical heaven, with its host of stars and worlds, etc. This is true of the following statements also: "By the word of the Lord were the heavens made; and all the host of them by the breath of his mouth." Psalm 33:6. "Praise him, ye heavens of heavens . . . for he commanded, and they were created." Psalm 148:4, 5. "I, even my hands, have stretched out the heavens, and all their host have I commanded." Isaiah 45:12. "He telleth the number of the stars; he calleth them all by their names." Psalm 147:4. "Lift up your eyes on high, and behold who hath created these things." Isaiah 40:26. "For by him (Jesus) were all things created, that are in heaven, and that are in earth." Colossians 1:16.

Both kinds of heavens are evidently included in Peter's statement that "By the word of God the heavens were of old," because of the context and because he mentions more than one heaven. (2 Peter 3:5.) Also in the first chapter of Genesis two different kinds of heavens are mentioned, the first being the astronomical heaven and the next being our planet's atmospheric heaven. In describing the detailed work done on each day of our planet's week of Secondary Creation, our *atmospheric heaven* is mentioned several times. (See Genesis 1:6-8, 14, 15, 17, 20, 28, 30; 2:19.) But *before* our planet's atmospheric heaven was made on *the second day,* another heaven is mentioned in verse 1 as being *in existence before the first day.* Therefore *this must be the heaven of stars, or the astronomical heaven.* It could *not* be our planet's atmospheric heaven, for that was not made until *the second day.* (Genesis 1:6-8.) This conclusion agrees with all the other evidences that the astronomical heaven, with its countless number of stars and worlds, etc., was in existence *before* the first day of our planet's special week of Secondary Creation.

[3] C. P. Olivier: "Meteors," p. 198, 1925. G. P. Merrill: "Minerals from Earth and Sky," p. 61, 1934. H. S. Jones: "Worlds Without End," p. 248, 1935. A. Holmes: "The Age of the Earth," p. 230, 1937. F. R. Moulton: "Astronomy," p. 422, 1931.

## The Earth as an Astronomical Unit

Very significant, indeed, is the following statement of God through the prophet Isaiah. God said of Himself, "I am the first, I also am the last. Mine hand also hath laid *the foundation of the earth,* and my right hand hath spanned *the heavens:* when I call unto them, *they stand up together."* Isaiah 48:12, 13.

This Scripture may be taken to mean that the substance of the Earth—its "foundation"—was created, or "laid," when God created the astronomical "heavens." *Both stood up "together,"* that is, *both were created simultaneously.* In other words, when God created the astronomical heavens He included the Earth as one of its astronomical units.

This agrees perfectly with the statement in Genesis 1:1 that "In *The* Beginning God created the [astronomical] heaven *and the earth."*

Therefore the Earth as an astronomical unit possessed all its astronomical qualities of weight and proper relative motions in our solar system *before* Creation Week. Its astronomical motions include its rotation on its axis, its travel around the central large sphere of our solar system, that is, around our Sun; and also other movements in space as our entire local system moves in its place among other such systems; and they in turn move around the center of our Milky Way galaxy, which in turn has its orbit among the millions of similar giant galaxies. And since "seasons" existed on the Earth from Creation Week onwards after light and heat were supplied to the Earth from its "two great lights" (Genesis 1:14-16), we may say that the axis of our planet's rotation was inclined about 66.5° to the plane of its orbit (the ecliptic), instead of being at right angles to it as some have supposed. And this astronomical factor must have existed from the time of the Earth's Primary Creation "In *The* Beginning."

Since the substance of the Earth as an astronomical unit was created at the same time that the astronomical heaven was created, namely, "In *The* Beginning," that time would mark the beginning of all chemical and radioactive time, and the beginning

of all astronomical time. Consequently it should be possible to show scientifically that all of these natural clocks of primary time agree on the approximate date of the zero hour.

## Condition of the Earth During Primary Time

It will doubtless come as a surprise to most readers to learn that the Bible gives us a picture of the condition of our planet during Primary Time, that is, *before* Creation Week—which week ushered in our planet's inhabited history, and which we may refer to as our planet's Secondary Time.

When speaking to Job the Creator said, "Where wast thou when I laid the foundations of the earth? . . . when I made *the cloud* the garment thereof, and thick darkness a swaddlingband for it." Job 38:4, 9.

In the Genesis account of God's Primary Creation it is also stated, "These are the generations of the heavens and of the earth when they were created, *in the day that the Lord made the earth and the heavens,* and every plant of the field *before* it was in the earth, and every herb of the field *before* it grew: for the Lord God had not caused it to rain upon the earth, and *there was not a man* to till the ground. But *there went up a mist from the earth,* and watered the whole face of the ground." Genesis 2:4-6.

In quoting Genesis 1:2, which gives us a little more description of the condition of our planet after its original Primary Creation and *before* its week of Secondary Creation, it is proper to supply in brackets a few words which the brevity of this statement omits, and which the context and contrast indicate. Verse 2 then reads as follows:

"The earth was without [geographical] form, and void [of life]; and darkness was upon the face of the deep [ocean]. And the Spirit of God moved upon the face of the waters [of the ocean]." Genesis 1:2.

These three Scriptures in Job and Genesis give us brief descriptions of our planet, the Earth, after its original Primary Creation and *before* its week of Secondary Creation. During this primary time, or at least during the latter part of it, the Earth was enveloped with dense clouds which made a "thick darkness" everywhere on its surface. And as "the Spirit of God moved upon the face of the deep water," which evidently did not cover all the land, "there went up a mist from the earth, and watered the whole face of the ground." Mark this well, this was, as the Genesis account explicitly states, "before" (Gen. 2:5) there were any plants or human beings created on the Earth! or, in other words, *before our planet's special week of Secondary Creation.*

Have you ever noticed that the story of the work done by God *during* the seven days of our planet's special week of Secondary Creation *does not contain any such expressions as the following:* "And God said, Let there be earth," or "Let there be water," or "Let there be rotation of the Earth," or "Let there be clouds," or "Let there be a Sun," or "Let there be a Moon," or 'Let there be stars," etc. Stars are mentioned as being *seen* in, or through, the firmament on the fourth day, and God is given credit for making them; but the record does *not* say that God made the stars on the fourth day. It merely says, "He made the stars also." Thus He is given credit for the making of everything that is seen. Other Scriptures show *when* the stars were really brought into existence, namely "in *The* Beginning" of all the astronomical heavens, which was a long time before the first day of our planet's week of Secondary Creation.

The reason why there is no mention of the creation of the dust of the Earth, its water, its clouds, etc., or the Sun and Moon, during the seven days of our planet's special week of Secondary Creation is *because all those things were already in existence from the time of the Primary Creation,* which was "In *The* Beginning" of the astronomical heaven—which is referred to in Genesis 1:1 and many other Scriptures, such as: Hebrews 11:3; 1:2; Colossians 1;16; Isaiah 48:12, 13; Psalm 33:6, 9; 148:4-6; 147:4, 5; etc. All these things rightfully belonged to God's astronomical creative work, for their creation involved the making of weight and astronomical motions.

## First Three Days of Creation Week Were Cloudy Days

When Creation Week began, our planet was enveloped in clouds, mist and thick darkness. (Job 38:4, 9; Gen. 2:4-6; Gen. 1:2) The light of the stars was unable to penetrate those clouds. At the surface of the Earth the darkness was "thick" because of the heavy fog and mist. Under such astronomical conditions as this, the turning on of the light of the Sun for the first time would produce only a diffused "light" at the surface of the Earth. Therefore, when "God said, Let there be light; and there was light" *on one side of the Earth only,* so that "evening and morning" were produced by the continued rotation of the Earth (Gen. 1:5), it is no stretch of our imagination to say that when God said, "Let there be light" He then made our Sun radiate visible light and much heat. (Gen. 1:3-5, 16; Ps. 136:7-9) Anyone who knows the details of our Sun's behavior knows that a vast amount of properly directed power would be required to warm up a huge dark sun as large as ours and make it radiate light and heat. Whether or not our Sun was a *brief* "nova" when first turned on may be only conjecture; but the thought is at least intriguing. At any rate, in making our Sun begin to shine with visible light on the first day, our Creator did a big day's work: in fact, in that one creative act alone He expended more energy than in the creative acts of all the other days combined! The creation of the light that produced the first day, and all the other days too, was no trivial matter. And because the Sun was not seen when that light shone on one side of the Earth only, we are justified in concluding that *the first day of Creation Week was simply a cloudy day.*

In connection with the second day of Creation Week reference is made to the moisture, or "water," in the clouds that still enveloped the Earth, namely, in the expression "the waters which were *above* the firmament." Genesis 1:7. The word "firmament" means "expansion" (margin of verse 6), and was finally given the name of "Heaven." (Gen. 1:8). Proof that these words refer to the air or atmosphere of the Earth is found in verses 20, 26, 28, 30; 2:19, 20, wherein occur the following expressions: "and fowl that may fly above the earth in the open firmament of heaven" (v. 20), and the "fowl of the air." On the second day of Creation Week God said, "Let there be a firmament [or atmosphere of clear air] in the midst of the waters, and let it divide the waters from the waters." (v. 6) "And God made the firmament [of clear air], and divided the waters which were under the firmament [of clear air] from *the waters which were above* the firmament [of clear air]: and it was so. *And God called the firmament {of clear air} Heaven.* And the evening and the morning were the second day." Genesis 1:7, 8.

If the clouds and mist that formerly rested on the surface of the earth had remained at the surface after God made the firmament of air, then the firmament of air *would not have divided or separated them* from the waters of the ocean. Therefore we may conclude that since the waters in the clouds were actually separated from the waters in the ocean on the second day, *the coluds were lifted and a clear air was formed below them.* In other words, the dense fog lifted and became a high fog on the second day. Heat from our Sun could have played an important role in helping to accomplish this; especially if the Sun shone much brighter for a brief period, like some new stars, or "novae."

Proof that the third day of Creation Week was a cloudy day is found in the fact that the Sun, Moon, and stars were not seen until the fourth day, together with the evidence that the preceding days were cloudy days. (Gen. 1:14-19)

It is significant, indeed, that all of these were seen for the first time on the fourth day. Since the stars and Sun and Moon were *all* seen on the fourth day for the first time by one who in vision was watching the events of Creation Week, we see that *the first three days of Creation Week must have been cloudy days,* and that on the fourth day those clouds became transparent water vapor. Fog and clouds are transformed into transparent water vapor when they are warmed up sufficiently by the heat of the Sun. *By taking the astronomical view point* of these evidences they all fit together beautifully and easily into a sensible and logical picture, with none of the parts of the picture left out or distorted.

Have you ever noticed *the point of view of the writer* of the Genesis record of Creation Week? It was not away off in space, where he saw the Earth as a huge sphere, and as one of many astronomical bodies in space; but *his point of view, or position of observation so to speak, was very close to the surface of our planet.* In fact, *it was beneath the clouds that enveloped the Earth.* Otherwise he could not have seen the clear air which was formed below them on the second day. He was close enough to the surface of the Earth to see the geography and the plants that were made on the third day; and to see and recognize the birds and animals and even the fish in the water when they were brought into existence. He was close enough to see man and his companion when they were created, and to observe the details. This close point of view of the writer of the Genesis account of our planet's special Week of Secondary Creation shows why he saw only "light" on the first day, when God made our Sun to shine; and *why* he did not see the Sun or Moon or any of the stars until the fourth day. *The first three days were simply cloudy days, and his point of view was beneath those clouds.*

This justified and greatly simplified conclusion harmonizes with the previous conclusion based on still more evidences that God created *all* the elements, suns, planets, satellites, etc., at the same time; namely, in the beginning of all chemical and astronomical time, which was a long time before our planet's special Week of Secondary Creation. The chief reasons why the writer of the Genesis record of Creation Week did not see any of the stars or our Sun and Moon during the first three days was because they were simply cloudy days, and he was looking at the earth and sky from below those clouds in his point of view. It is remarkable how all the details of the record of God's Secondary Creation *allow of a great Primary Creation previously, and a long time previously.*

## What Was Done on the Fourth Day

"And God said, *Let there be lights in the firmament* of the heaven to divide the day from the night; and let them be for signs, *and for seasons,* and for days, and years: and let them be for lights *in the firmament* of the heaven to *give light upon the earth:* and it was so. And *God made TWO GREAT LIGHTS:* the greater light to rule the day, and the lesser light to rule the night: he made the stars also. And God set them *in the firmament* of the heaven to *give light upon the earth,* and to rule over the day and over the night, and to divide the light from the darkness: and God saw that *it was good.* And the evening and the morning were the fourth day." Genesis 1:14-19.

It will be observed that no less than three times the expression occurs, *"in the firmament* of the heaven." (v. 14, 15, 17) We have previously observed that this means the lower atmosphere, or air, in which the birds fly. (v. 7, 8, 20, 26). Now we know that the Sun and the Moon themselves are not located this close to the surface of the Earth; consequently the language of the writer is trying to convey to us his viewpoint, namely, that as he was looking at the Sun and Moon from his ground location they looked as if they were up there in the air, because he was seeing them *through* the air, or *"firmament* of the heaven." He himself was located *"in* the firmament," and they appeared to be in its upper regions.

It will also be observed that twice the expression occurs, "to give light *upon the earth."* (v. 15, 17). In other words, on the fourth day the light from the Sun and the light from the Moon (Ps. 136:7-9) *shone directly upon the ground.* The word "earth" frequently means dirt or ground. (Gen. 1:10, 24; 2:19; 3:19). When the light was *not* shining directly upon the ground, but upon

the clouds instead, the light was a diffused light, and its *sources* could not be seen. But when, on the fourth day, the light from the Sun and Moon and stars shone *directly upon the ground,* then *the sources* of all that light could be seen in the sky, and each astronomical object that produced some of that light could be recognized! The fact that they were seen by one whose point of view was "in the firmament" of the heaven shows that *on the fourth day the high clouds disappeared, or became transformed into transparent water vapor*—just as high fog does after the Sun comes up in the morning and warms the air sufficiently.

In this connection it is also valuable to observe that the writer saw *"two* great lights;" one of which was brighter than the other and ruled the day, while the other less brilliant source ruled the night. These are now called the Sun and the Moon, respectively. (Gen. 1:16 with Psalm 136:7-9). And if we may use here a statement by the prophet Isaiah, in which he predicted how bright the light of the Sun and the light of the Moon will be when our planet is *restored* to its Edenic conditions, as an index of how brilliant the sunlight and moonlight were made to be at the time of the Week of Creation, then we can agree that, indeed, God did create "two GREAT lights," and that *both* of them actually *gave* light. At the present time our Moon does not "give" light, but it merely *reflects* light—only about 7 per cent of the sunlight that falls upon its surface. The wording in Genesis indicates that our Moon used to actually "give light" just as our Sun does today. (Gen. 1:15, 17). The statement referred to in Isaiah reads as follows:

"Moreover *the light of the Moon shall be as the light of the Sun,* and the light of the Sun shall be seven-fold, as the light of seven days; in the day that the Lord *bindeth up* the breach of his people, and *healeth the stroke* of their wound."—Isaiah 30:26.[4]

---

[4] These two Bible statements are substantiated by an abundance of evidence in archaeology and astronomy, and even in geology. For some of this evidence read the following publications: *Popular Astronomy,* Vol. 40, No. 4, p. 200-215, Aprid, 1932; *Bibliotheca Sacra,* Vol. 89, No. 353, p. 68-86, January, 1932; *Bibliotheca Sacra,* Vol. 90, No. 357, p. 49-69, January, 1933; also a series of four articles by J. L. Butler in *The Watchman Magazine,* February, March, April, May, 1932.

Sunlight today is at least 465,000 times brighter than our brightest moonlight. When our present sunlight is made to be seven times brighter than it is today, then, if our Moon only *reflected* sunlight, the light of the Moon would be only seven times brighter. For the light of the Moon to be "as the light of the Sun," that is, at least 465,000 times brighter, our Moon must actually "give light," as suggested in the Genesis account of Creation Week.

What we should observe further of the work done on the fourth day is the fact that *"good* seasons" were established on that day. (Gen. 1:14, 18)

Recurring seasons are the sum total of several astronomical and meteorological forces. (1) First of all there must be a source of heat and light for the entire Earth; (2) the axis of the Earth must be inclined less than 90° to the Sun; (3) the Earth must travel around the Sun, so that the northern and southern hemispheres will be alternately exposed to the more direct rays of the sunlight; (4) the surface of the Earth must be protected against the most intense solar radiations by a filtering atmosphere, that is, if the resulting seasons are to be "good" for the plants and animals of the Earth.

At the present time our planet is blessed with all these cooperating factors. Nevertheless, there are places on the Earth today where the seasons are *far from being good*. In the polar regions of the Earth, and even in the temperate zones, the winter season is frigid and destructive of life: and in the more equatorial regions the summer season is too hot and dry for vegetation to flourish, so that great deserts have resulted where very little life is found. Therefore, *originally there must have been some other astronomical and meteorological forces at work* in combination with those that are now operative; otherwise God certainly would not have pronounced the seasons of the Earth "good."

As we have just noticed, there is the possibility that our planet was blessed with another great source of heat and light in addition to the Sun. Without going into all the scientific details which fully substantiate this suggestion which we find in the Bible, we can here notice briefly that *if our Moon was once an active midget sun, its orbit is adjusted perfectly to help it prevent the occurrence of frigid winter seasons in the arctic and antarctic lands and their adjoining temperate belts.*

The Moon does not go around the Earth directly above its equator, like some of the satallites of Mars, Jupiter, Saturn, and Uranus, but instead the plane of its orbit is inclined 28° 35' 40" to the Earth's equator. This means that when the Moon is in its northermost position in the sky its light shines 28° 35' 40" beyond the North Pole,— which is 5° 08' 40" farther than the direct sunlight shines in midsummer. And likewise when the Moon is in its southermost position in the sky its light shines the same distance beyond the South Pole. In other words, *the Moon's highest position in the sky* in those lands that now experience bad winter seasons *is over five degrees higher than the Sun's highest position in midsummer.*

Now put with this the additional astronomical fact that the Moon travels completely around the Earth in its greatly inclined orbit *in only 27.3217 days,* which is less than a calendar month and just a little less than four weeks, and we can see why it could have prevented the winter season from being bad anywhere on the Earth. For about two weeks *each month* the arctic lands and antarctic lands were warmed and lighted by the Moon *more effectually* than they are now by the Sun in summertime. During the absence of the Moon for about two weeks each month, the warm atmosphere and the warm ground and the warm ocean waters and the other warm bodies of water *did not have time to become freezing cold.* Suppose our winters were *only two weeks long today,* from autumn to spring, would they be freezing cold? Indeed not. *They would be very mild and "good."* Had the Earth been warmed and lighted *by our Moon only,* than the mild winter season would have come every 27.3217 days, or *over thirteen times a year* (13.3651 times a year). In fact, there would hardly be any noticeable difference in the seasons, but practically *one continuous warm climate.* But because "God made

TWO great lights . . . to give light upon the Earth," this otherwise almost steady warm climate resulting from the Moon's solar radiation *was amplified by the Sun into yearly seasons,* none of which were freezing cold. Therefore under those astronomical conditions the winter season was always a *"good season."* In this connection it is interesting to notice that in Psalm 104:19 we are told that God "appointed the Moon for seasons," that is, *good winter seasons.* It most certainly did have a lot to do in making that season of the year "good" anciently.

But how about the other seasons of the year: would they be scorching hot? No, not if the transparent water vapor high in or above the stratosphere was sufficient in amount to filter out the excessive heat rays coming from our "two great lights." This combination of astronomical and meteorological factors of climate and seasons helps us to understand *why the Creator was careful to preserve the water in the clouds that previously enveloped the entire Earth, and why they were lifted to a position "above" the air,* instead of being put back into the ocean. Water vapor is known to be a very effective filter of the heat in sunlight.

If this water vapor above the air or in its upper rare regions was of considerable thickness, then the rotation of this vapor with the Earth would cause it to have centrifugal force within itself, which would cause this vapor to bulge outward over the equatorial regions and be drawn into a thinner filter above the polar lands. Thus it would help to *equalize* the temperature at the surface of the Earth—filtering out the excessive heat rays in the equatorial regions, and letting more reach the ground in the polar lands where it is needed. This possibility is illustrated several times by

the present huge atmospheres of the planets Jupiter, Saturn, Uranus, and Neptune, whose equatorial diameters are *greater* than their polar diameters, by the following number of miles, respectively, 5760, 7800, 2314, 774. This means that Jupiter's atmosphere, which is in a cloudy condition like the others, is about 2,880 miles *thicker above its equator* than above its poles; Saturn's atmosphere is 3,900 miles thicker above its equator; Uranus' atmosphere is 1,157 miles thicker above its equator, and Neptune's atmosphere is only 387 miles thicker above its equator than it is above its poles. It seems reasonable to conclude that *the Earth also had a large oblate atmosphere originally and until the time of Noah's Deluge.*[5]

While considering this meteorological factor of the Earth's ancient climate and seasons it is very interesting to observe that *the results of the creative work that was done on the second day are not pronounced "good."* The results of the creative work that was performed during all the other days were pronounced "good" (Gen. 1:4, 12, 18, 21, 25, 31); but not so the results of the work of the second day. (Gen. 1:6-8) And why?

On the second day the clouds were lifted and a clear air formed below them. But this arrangement of our atmosphere was not yet ideal for the living things that were to inhabit our planet. Many of them would need *direct* solar radiations; and continual cloudy days would not be good for them. Even today there are many human beings who object to cloudy days. Yes, even human psychology needs some bright cheery sunlight. And most certainly God would not want to deprive the human race of an opportunity to *study astronomy.* If He did, then it could become very much self-centered and egotis-

---

[5] When studying the Earth's original meteorological factors we are led to wonder why the *new* Earth is to have a "new heaven" also, when "the light of the Moon shall be as the light of the Sun, and the light of the Sun shall be sevenfold, as the light of seven days." (Isa. 65:17; 66:22; 2 Pet. 3:13; Rev. 21:1; Isa. 30:26.) It must be that the original large atmosphere of our planet *collapsed* when "the windows of heaven were opened" at the time of Noah's Deluge, *because* at that time the Creator suddenly chilled the entire Earth by turning off all the solar activities of our Moon and by turning down the Sun's brilliance. (Compare also Gen. 7:11, 12; 8:21, 22; Isaiah 60:20.) The very fact that the *new* Earth, which is predicted in the Bible prophecies, is to have a *"new* heaven," lends support to the Genesis story that *the Earth was originally protected by a huge oblate atmospheric heaven,* which is no longer in existence.

tical—and ignorant beyond measure. *It was not until the fourth day that our planet's entire atmosphere was in the condition that God wanted it. It must be made transparent from the ground to its upper limits and be kept in that condition,* so that the stars could be seen and studied, and so that the direct sunlight and moonlight would reach the ground. Temporary clouds could easily form in the lower layers of the air without thwarting these objectives. But the high clouds that completely enveloped the Earth during the first three days and even before that, must be warmed up sufficiently to transform them into *transparent* water vapor. *When this condition of our atmosphere was achieved on the fourth day than it was pronounced "good," but not before that.* (Gen. 1:17, 18)

It is easy now to see where the additional heat may have come from that warmed those upper high clouds enough to make them transparent and also to *keep them transparent.* Our Moon supplied the entire Earth with that greatly needed additional heat: it actually gave, or radiated, both heat and light, so that "the light of the Moon" *was* "as the light of the Sun" today, and it was distributed over the entire Earth in an ideal manner. *Evidently the creative work of the fourth day consisted mainly in turning on the solar activities of our Moon,* so that from then on there were two active suns in our sky, or "two great lights" that actually "gave light" upon the earth, that is, *directly upon the ground.*

### The Events of Creation Week Summarized

As interesting as is all this astronomical aspect of our study, we must not overlook other details that belong in our study of God's two creations. We are now in a better position to see just what the Creator did on each day of our planet's special Week of Secondary Creation. In brief summary the outstanding events were as follows:

1. On the first day God created sunlight by turning on the solar activities of our Sun; and within about eight minutes there was light on one side of the Earth only; and the Earth's continued rotation produced the first of our twenty-four hour days. But this day was a cloudy day. (Gen. 1:3-5, 16; Ps. 136:7-9, Gen. 2:6, 4, 5; Job 38:1, 4, 9.)

2. On the second day God made a clear atmosphere next to the surface of the Earth, and raised the clouds to a great height. (Gen. 1:6-8; 2:4-6)

3. On the third day God made the geography of the Earth by rearranging the land and water and making the soil dry enough for vegetation: and he created vegetation of all kinds, using the elements of the land and water. This, too, was a cloudy day. (Gen. 1:9-13; 2:8-14; etc.)

4. On the fourth day God caused the high clouds, that had enveloped the entire Earth long before Creation Week, and during its first three days, to become transparent water vapor, by turning on the solar activities of our Moon: then the Sun, Moon, and stars were all seen from the surface of the Earth, and direct sunlight shone upon the ground: and under these astronomical conditions the seasons of the entire Earth were mild, and God pronounced them "good." (Isa. 30:26; Ps. 104:19; Gen. 1:14-19). These astronomical conditions remained in force until the time of Noah's Deluge.

5. On the fifth day God created fish and birds, using the elements in the land and water. (Gen. 1:20-25; 2:19).

6. On the sixth day God created land animals and man, again using the elements in the land and water. (Gen. 1:24-31; 2:7, 18-25; 3:19; 5:1, 2.)

7. On the seventh day God made the first Sabbath and designated it as the birthday of the Earth, to be observed to remind us of our Creator. (Gen. 2:1-3; Ex. 20:8-11; 31:13-18; Col. 1:16; Mark 2:27, 28; Rev. 1:10; Heb. 4:3, 4, 9-11; Isa. 66:22, 23.)

This is a brief summary of the record which we have of the work which our Creator did during the Earth's special Week of *Secondary* Creation. And one prominent thing is noticeable in all these creative acts, namely, *in every instance God used substances already in existence.* He used the Sun and Moon to produce light and heat for the Earth; He rearranged the contents of our atmosphere to make it ideal for plant and animal life; He rearranged the land and water of the Earth to make suitable habitats for the plants and animals and man; and He used the elements in the land and water and air when making the plants, animals, and man himself. And after man sinned, He told him plainly, "In the sweat of thy face shalt thou eat bread, till thou return unto the ground; for out of it wast thou taken: for dust thou art, and unto dust shalt thou return."—Genesis 3:19.

This means, then, that *when God exercised His creative power in a secondary manner He did not increase the weight of our planet, or the weight of our solar system.* During Creation Week He did not create any new elements: this was not necessary, because all the elements that were needed He had formerly created at the time of the great Primary Creation of *all* the elements and *all* the astronomical bodies and systems. That original creation marked "THE Beginning" of all chemical and astronomical time. By the time that Adam and Eve were created on our planet, there were in existence *many* other inhabited worlds in starry space; and their Adams and Eves rejoiced when they learned of the creation of another pair of human beings on another beautiful world, —our Earth. God's *many* secondary creations did not disturb in the least the important astronomical balances that were established during his great Primary Creation.

### The Fourth Commandment of the Decalog and the Creation Record

Some people have thought that the statement in the fourth commandment of the Decalog included *both* the Primary and the Secondary creative acts of God; for it is stated there:

". . . for *in six days the Lord made heaven and earth, the sea, and all that in them is,* and rested the seventh day."—Exodus 20:11.

Let us examine the words used, and compare them with the same words that are used in the Genesis record, where more details are given.

The words "heaven," "earth," and "sea" are used in the Genesis record of Creation Week in the following places: Genesis 1:8,

10, 11, 12, 14, 15, 17, 20, 24, 25, 26, 28, 29, 30; 2:1, 7, 19; 3:17-19. In these many instances the word "Heaven" means *only the atmospheric heaven* in which the birds fly and the clouds float; the word "Earth" means *the dry land or ground;* and the word "Sea" means *the ocean and large bodies of water.* All these are specifically mentioned in the Genesis account as being made *during the Week of Creation,* and *not before it!* The atmospheric heaven was made on *the second day;* and the earth and sea were made, or formed, on *the third day.* But the wording of the story shows clearly that *before* the "seas" and "dry land" were formed, *their chemical contents were already in existence!* The exact wording of the Genesis story is as follows:

"And God said, Let the waters under the heaven be gathered together unto one place, and let the dry land appear: and it was so. And God called the dry land Earth: and the gathering together of the waters called he Seas: and God saw that it was good . . . And the evening and the morning were the third day."—Genesis 1:9, 10, 13.

(Parenthetically it should be remarked, for the sake of those who might be a little confused over the use of capital letters in this quotation, wherein the words "Earth" and "Sea" are capitalized, that this was done by the printers of the Bible because they never anywhere in the Bible used quotation marks, but wished in some way to emphasize those two words. When used subsequently in the story they are not capitalized. However, when the *name* of some *astronomical* body is used in this exegesis it should begin with a capital letter, for it is then a proper noun. Therefore, since the word *earth* in the last quotation does not refer to our planet's name, but to the dirt or ground, it should not be capitalized. Its capitalization does not make this quotation refer to our planet as an astronomical unit.)

In other words, the "earth" and "sea" referred to here *were not in existence as geographical components of our planet until after the water and land were rearranged,* so that more of the land stood above the waters where it could be dry. But *before* this rearranging was done, that is, before this part of the geography which was called "earth" existed, and before the "seas" existed on our planet, the mud and rocks of the land were in existence and the water of the seas was in existence. In fact, *they* are described as being in existence *before the first day*. (Gen. 1:2) Therefore the fourth commandment of the Decalog does *not* refer to the water and the mud and rocks that compose our planet; but *it refers only to the geography, or special arrangements of the water and land, which were created or formed on the third day.*

The fourth commandment is *not* concerned with any of God's creative acts before and after the Earth's Week of Creation. When that special week was finished our planet experienced its first real birthday. It was conceived as a potential inhabited world at the time of the Primary Creation. But the Sabbath of the fourth commandment is in commemoration of its birthday only.

Previously we have observed that the Genesis record mentions more than one kind of "heaven," namely, the astronomical heaven and our planet's atmospheric heaven of air. Since the fourth commandment is concerned with what was done *during* Creation Week, it is clear that the "heaven" to which it refers is *our atmospheric heaven of air only*. It does not refer to the astronomical heaven of stars, which are mentioned as being in existence *before* the first day. (Gen. 1:1; etc.)

The expression "all that in *them* is" refers *briefly* to all the plants, fishes, birds, animals, creeping things, human beings, etc., that are mentioned more fully in the Genesis detailed record of Creation Week. This is the obvious meaning of such an expression, "all that in them is." *The fourth commandment of the Decalog was not the place to give all the details of Creation Week.*

When the expression in this brief summarizing statement "all that in them is" is stretched until it includes things that are *not* mentioned in the Genesis record of the creative acts of God that were performed *during* the Week of Creation, and made to include, for instance, "all the primitive rocks, with all their contents, including their radioactive metals, etc.," it is

not only a breach of rhetoric and good logic, but it is contrary to many evidences on this subject. What is meant by the expression, "all that in *them* is," are all the *living* plants and creatures which inhabited our atmospheric heaven, dry land areas, and bodies of water at that time. And that is all that it means.

The fourth commandment of the Decalog does *not* refer to God's Primary Creation: and therefore it does not refer to the astronomical heaven, or to the Earth as an astronomical body. Therefore *it does not even hint* that all the stars and our Sun and Moon were brought into existence during the six working days of Creation Week. It merely refers us briefly to the Genesis record of Creation Week, where the details are given. And there we learn that Creation Week was a series of *secondary* creative acts of God, in which he always used substances that were already in existence from the time of his great Primary Creation in "THE Beginning."

One of the chief objects of the fourth commandment of the Decalog is to perpetuate the observance of the seventh day of each week in commemoration of the Earth's birthday—an event which can never be changed, anymore than we can change the date of our own birthday. And the reason given for specifying the seventh day of each week—and for the existence of a seven day week—is the history of Creation Week as recorded in Genesis. And when we study this history in detail we find that it is a history of a *secondary kind* of creative work, which never created elements or astronomical bodies. We should keep this fact in mind, and not misuse and abuse the wording of the fourth commandment. Its improper use can furnish cause for rejection of the entire Genesis record of Creation Week, and also furnish cause for scoffing at the law of God itself! Ignorance of the law is not "bliss": it is disaster, in this sense.

## Dark Suns

We have now come to realize that the Bible indicates that suns can be dark as well as intensely brilliant. All suns are easily under God's control.

According to the testimony of Isaiah, when the Earth is restored to its former Edenic condition, our Moon will again give light that is as bright as our present sunlight, and our present sunlight will be as bright as it was before Noah's Deluge, namely, seven times brighter. (Isaiah 30:26; 60:20; Gen. 8:22; Psalm 136:7-9) And another instance, yet future, which *shows that the Creator can control suns* and do with them what he wants to, is connected with the seven last plagues; indeed, it is to be one of them, at which time more power will be given to the Sun, and men will learn what it is like to have a brighter Sun without a literal new atmospheric heaven to protect the Earth from being scorched. And the prophecy says, "And men were scorched with great heat."—Revelation 16:8, 9.

Yes, the omnipotent and omniscient Creator can do what he wants to do with any of the suns in starry space. He invented them: therefore he should understand them perfectly. And it is interesting to study astronomy and see what a great variety of suns he has designed and has had in operation for a long, long time. He has not made all of them alike, for he loves variety,—as is evidenced in all his created works. Some suns are very small, and some of them are very large, with many different sizes between. Some are very light in weight, while others are extremely heavy for their size. And there are different colored suns, radiating a predominance of such colors as blue, white, green, yellow, orange, and red. And within the last few years astronomers have discovered suns which radiate only invisible infra-red light, and therefore they are called dark suns, because we cannot see them; but special photographic plates which are sensitive to the infra-red rays can see them.

In a book published in 1939 by the Dial Press, New York, entitled "The Story of Astronomy," written by Arthur L. Draper and Marion Lockwood, Assistant Curators at the Hayden Planetarium, is a chapter on "Queer Kinds of Stars." The following quotation is from this chapter.

"No account of strange stars would possibly be complete without some mention of the dark or black stars which have recently been discovered. Until 1938 astronomers were ignorant of the fact (not yet having learned to see in the dark) that space was more thickly peopled with stars than they had believed it to be.

"In the spring of 1938 Dr. Otto Struve of Yerkes Observatory and his colleagues, Dr. Gerald P. Kuiper and Dr. Bengt Stroemgren, discovered that the star Epsilon Aurigae, which we have met before as one of the Algol-type variables, is accompanied in space by an enormous and black ghost-companion, a star so large that if placed with its center at the center of the Sun it would extend out almost to the orbit of Uranus—with a diameter of about 1,782,800,000 miles. The discovery of this star, invisible to the human eye, but visible when photographed by infra-red light, raises an entirely new problem for the astronomer—how to detect the presence of, and how to measure these dark bodies. It raises many interesting questions, also, as to the possible close proximity of such unknown dark stars to the Sun."—pp. 291, 292.

Whether or not our Sun was similar to this "black star" but smaller, or whether it was of such a nature that it radiated no infra-red radiations to space just before Creation Week we cannot say. There probably are many kinds of dark or black suns which do not radiate any visible light, and many which may not even radiate infra-red rays. But what is interesting in this connection is the fact that modern astronomy has again verified the Bible, when the Bible is understood more fully and correctly.

There is some astronomical evidence which indicates that the dark suns and their families of planets may be very numerous in the Universe. Those who have studied carefully the eclipsing variable stars (which are often binary groups of two visible suns that revolve around a common center) have found some evidence which indicates the presence of a third invisible body in the system. According to the astronomers Leon Campbell and Luigi Jacchia, in one of the Harvard books on astronomy—"The Story of Variable Stars,"

1946—we are told that "The presence of a third body has been suspected in the systems of RT Persei, SW Lacertae, and VW Cephei because of slight periodic variations in period that can not be caused by a displacement of the apsidal line, since we find that the relative positions of the primary and secondary minima remain unchanged."—p. 192. And, referring to the numerous dark nebulae, the astronomers Russell, Dugan, and Stewart say, "There appears to be little doubt that the main obscuring agent in these clouds is *fine dust*. This does not mean that the clouds are composed entirely or mainly of such dust. They may contain particles of all other sizes, from separate molecules *to masses as large as planets or even stars*."—"Astronomy," vol. 2, p. 822; 1938.

Many of the great spiral galaxies of stars are in an edgewise position to us and show a peripheral dark band of obscuring matter, such as those listed in the New General Catalog as numbers 891, 4565, 4594, and 5128. Other galaxies give us a side view, such as the southern Magellanic Clouds and the Gerat Nebula in Andromeda (also cataloged as Messier 31, or NGC 223). Referring to the Magellanic Clouds of stars, which are extra-galactic systems that are from 75,000 to 84,000 light-years distant, Doctor Harlow Shapley of Harvard said, "Actually the Clouds are much closer together than on first inspection they appear to be. Special photographic plates, and a detailed counting of the faint stars, as well as diligent searching for outlying variables and open clusters, have greatly extended the recognized boundaries of both systems. In fact, each Cloud now appears to be a concentrated irregular mass of stars surrounded by a lightly populated envelope. That is, *a haze of stars surrounds* the main body which contains most of the mass of the system."—"Galaxies," p. 49; 1944.

And in commenting on the recent investigations of the Great Nebula in Andromeda through use of the microdensitometer, Doctor Shapley said, "The area on the sky now recognized as covered by the Andromeda Nebula has in consequence been increased ten times, to about fourteen square degrees, equal to approximately seventy full moons or one third the area of the bowl of the Big Dipper. In appearance, as in fact, it is a gigantic galaxy, if one looks deep enough. . . . It is, indeed, if these preliminary measures are fully verified, an odd structure—a flat wheel with conspicuous hub enveloped by a large spheroidal haze that is composed of something that yields a faint glow—*presumably composed of stars* that lie beyond the limits of our present powers of resolution and isolation, stars too faint for individual registering, but able, when shining in unison, to contribute feebly to the chemical disturbance on the photographic plate."—id. p. 127, 128. However, in view of all the evidences now available on dark suns and cloud-enveloped planets, it seems reasonable to suggest that *these* may be largely responsible for the "faint glow" in the outer regions of these galaxies, *because they are numerous enough to reflect in unison enough light* to be detected by the sensitive electric microdensitometer. However, when they are seen against a much brighter background they appear darker by contrast, as in the spirals that are seen edgewise.

### Records of Primary Time

It is now evident that the subject of creation is composed of two kinds of creative work: namely, (1) the Primary kind which brought into existence all the elements in the Universe and placed them in the major astronomical bodies, which were set in proper motions and proper groups at that time; and (2) the Secondary kind which always used elements and substances already in existence, and transformed dark suns and moons into light and heat giving bodies, and planets into ideal habitats for life, and brought into being many kinds of living plants and animals, and human beings.

And in addition to this it is also evident that there were many shining suns and inhabited planets in existence *before* our planet, the Earth, was transformed into a beautiful world and stocked with many kinds of life. Furthermore, it is now evident that the substance of our planet itself was in existence *before* the first day of its Week of Secondary Creation, and that it was already performing its proper astronomical motions in space. Likewise, it is now evident that our Moon and our Sun were in existence as astronomical bodies *before* the first day of Creation Week.

And, on the authority of the Bible itself, we may say that the Earth, as an astronomical unit, was brought into existence *at the same time* that God created all the astronomical heaven and its host of stars, planets, moons, etc. In other words, there was a definite and supernatural beginning for *all* the major astronomical bodies and systems, and for *all* the elements and basic substances of which they are made. That time is called *"THE Beginning."* It was the beginning of all chemical time, all radioactive time, and all astronomical time. And if these natural clocks of Primary Time could all be read correctly and fully, they should agreed on the date of the zero hour.

However, it is probably not yet within the ability of mankind to take into consideration all the natural forces that were set in operation immediately after the initial Primary Creation. There is plenty of evidence in the oldest rocks of our planet that they were molten hot at some time in their early existence. And the billions of meteorites that come to use from space tell us a similar story, though quite different in some respects from the surface rocks of the Earth. There certainly can be no objection to the view that some of the astronomical bodies in God's great Universe were left in a hot, molten condition, at the time of the Primary Creation, and some may have been created originally in a gaseous state, so that their dimensions were enormous. And what objection can there be to allowing some natural modifications of the original astronomical bodies and systems subsequent to their Primary Creation? Personally, I cannot think of any except those theories which seek to crowd the Creator entirely out of His Universe, or which seek to hide the great facts of the Primary and Secondary Creations, or their clear distinction.

It is evident that some time did elapse between God's Primary Creation and his special week of Secondary Creation that was performed on *our* Sun, Moon, and Earth. Naturally we are now interested in finding out *how much time elapsed between these*

*two creations.* And it seems proper to refer to this period of time as Primary Time. It is *not* "pre-Genesis time," but *pre-creation-week time.*

The Bible does not say how much time elapsed between these two creations; but it does indicate that some time did elapse. Therefore we cannot say that the Bible is opposed to a long interval of time prior to Creation Week.

In this connection perhaps a Biblical illustration might be of some value. Just as telescopes magnify an apparent single dot of light in the sky into two or more individual lights, so also the properly focused evidences in all the Bible magnify the subject of Creation into more than one event. Some subjects of prophecy are also magnified in this same way, such as the subject of the Resurrection. In some places it is briefly referred to as a single event, as for instance in Acts 4:2, 17:32; 24:15; etc. But with the help of all the evidences on this subject it is magnified into several events, two of which are separated by a thousand years (Revelation 20:6, 5). This is also true of some of the Biblical discussions of Creation. *Both* the Primary and the Secondary Creations are referred to in such Scriptures as: Isaiah 45:18; Job 38:1-11; and Genesis 1:1-31. It is sometimes difficult to magnify a single statement into a clear and distinct view of God's two creations, and probably is not always necessary when the object of the writer is given proper consideration. However, we should not let any such brief statements on the subject of Creation blind our understanding of the many additional details that are revealed elsewhere.

Since the Bible does not reveal how much time elapsed between the Primary Creation of the elements and the stars and the Secondary Creation of our Sun, Moon, and Earth, we may feel at liberty to accept any amount of time which God's great natural clocks have recorded.

Some natural clocks give us records of time that extend back only a few hundred years, such as tree rings; while other natural clocks, such as river deltas or carved-out canyons, may record time that reaches back several thousand years. But even this last mentioned time-recorder, or time-meter, is easily misunderstood: and to assume that during all the life of such rivers or canyons erosion and deposition have been as slow as at the present time, may be a serious mistake. When Secondary Time includes Noah's great Deluge, which had mighty astronomical forces assisting it, then the historical scientist must reckon with deep layers of newly formed strata which would be soft and subject to rapid erosion, and more rainfall, for some time before our modern climatic conditions and slow erosion would prevail. Therefore he who studies Secondary Time has some real problems on his hands in trying to measure it.

But forunately God has provided us with at least two very good meters of Primary Time. These are the radioactive rocks and the light-years of astronomy.

We cannot include the fossils of geology among the clocks of Primary Time, for two or more very good reasons. The great majority of the fossils, both plant and animal, show that they all enjoyed our former age of ideal climate, when there were "two great lights," or brilliant suns, in our sky. Furthermore, they show that they were brought to a dramatic death and burial by rapidly acting tidal waves, etc., which buried most of them before decay set in, so that their skeletons and shells are articulate, and so that millions of the leaves of the plants were preserved instead of reduced to leaf mould. Knowing now that Noah's Deluge was assisted by great astronomical forces, which were sufficient to make it absolutely earth-wide and very destructive and capable of producing the major sedimentary strata of the Earth, we must first of all assign as many of the fossils and sedimentary strata to that cataclysm as we can—and that leaves out none but a few that have been formed since that time.

If the fossils should be regarded as clocks of Primary Time, then we would be obliged to ignore God's special week of Secondary Creation, and assume without sufficient proof that all differences in design were developed very slowly in tandem style. Instead, we feel justified in saying that the fossils merely give us *a cross-sectional view of our world as it was when the former age of dual sunlight with its ideal climate came to a sudden and dramatic end,* and that they do *not* give us a record of millions of years of life history on our planet, reaching back beyond the Biblical date of Creation Week.

Among the fossils, however, are some marine deposits, such as accumulated sea shells, ocean oozes, corals, etc., which may be regarded as clocks of early Secondary Time, provided they were buried in an undisturbed condition and not washed together into layers of unnatural thickness. But most certainly none of the fossils were in existence before God's Week of Secondary Creation on our planet.

### Radioactive Rocks

In the study of the radioactive rocks we find records of time that reach far back of the beginning of Secondary Time. And we also soon discover that not all specimens record the same amount of time. This difference in specimens is explained by saying that a radioactive rock records only the time which has passed since it crystallized from a molten, or igneous, state. In other words, it records "solid" time. Whether or not physical splitting or crushing of a specimen would also have to be considered as affecting the time records of the radioactive rocks is not altogether clear. On the basis that the products of decomposition (helium gas and lead) would *not* accumulate in the immediate vacinity of the radioactive elements while they were floating in a molten mass, and that only after the mass cooled and crystallized would deposits of lead and helium gas remain associated closely with the radioactive elements, such as Uranium, Thorium, and Radium, we are compelled to acknowledge that some rocks remained hot longer than others, or were re-melted one or more times since their primary crystallization.

Herein, then, are to be recognized some records of an event or a series of events since the Primary Creation, which event or series of events resulted in melting some of the igneous rocks of the Earth on large or small scales; or possibly we should regard them as evidences of occasional volcanic action through craters or dykes from the depths of the Earth. In any of these instances where the time recorded reaches back of the beginning of Secondary Time, we have some rock records of actions of some kind *during* Primary Time. It may be very difficult or impossible to determine the outlines of that dark history. However, we may be able to ascertain either the approximate time of the crystallizing of the majority of the surface rocks of the Earth from a molten state, or, if they were created in a crystallized state originally, the approximate date of the zero hour of Primary Time.

Whether or not the earth-movements which occurred on the third day of Creation Week, and again during Noah's Deluge, would alter in a recognizable way some of the radioactive rocks remains to be found out.

In a book entitled "The Age of the Earth," by Dr. Arthur Holmes, and published in 1937 by Thomas Nelson & Sons, New York, are two chapters on "The Radioactive Timekeepers of the Rocks." One chapter gives many excellent details of the "Helium Method," and the other the details of the "Lead Method" of determining the age of rocks. (Read pages 93-179) The samples of radioactive rocks referred to by Dr. Holmes give us dates that range from a few million years to several hundred million years. A few of the oldest radioactive rocks exceed a thousand million years, and even approach the 2,000 million year date.

### Radioactive Meteorites

It has been found that meteorites, which come to the Earth constantly from interstellar space and from disintegrated local comets, contain radioactive minerals. And it is therefore possible to read their internal records of the amount of time which has elapsed since they congealed from the molten state or were originally brought into existence in a cool crystallized state at the time of the great Primary Creation. Doctor Holmes gives a very interesting list of several sample meteorites. The ages of these meteorites were determined by F. A. Paneth, W. Koeck, and W. D. Urry. The ages of the 22 samples listed range from 100 million years to 2,800 million years. (See pages 232-233.)

### Light-Years

In astronomy there is another very reliable time-recording clock: it is the speed of light itself through the vast distances of the starry heavens. The speed of light was first discovered in 1675 by a Danish astronomer, Roemer, who has been referred to as "a man almost a century in advance of his day."[6] He noticed that the eclipses of Jupiter's satellites "show a peculiar variation in their times of occurrence, which he explained as due to *the time taken by light to pass through space*." "The observed times of the eclipses of Jupiter's satellites are affected by the change in the distance of the Earth from Jupiter. From such observations it is possible to find the time required for light to traverse the diameter of the Earth's orbit,—about 16½ minutes."[7]

But the most accurate speed of light has been determined by special experiments with mirrors located on Mt. Wilson and Mt. San Antonio, about 22 miles apart. Dr. Michelson found in this way in 1926 that the speed of light in vacuum is 186,285 miles per second (or 299,796 kilometers per second).[8] The distance that light travels in a year has been appropriately called the *light-year*, which is 5,880 billion miles (or 63,310 astronomical units, or about one-third of a parsec).

If a map were made in which the Earth was placed one inch from the Sun, then a mile would almost exactly represent the distance that light travels in one year. On this map the *nearest* of all the other visible suns in space would be about 4.3 miles away! And the farthest in our Milky Way galactic

[6] Russell, Dugan, & Stewart, "Astronomy," Vol. 1, p. 375, 1926.
[7] Id. p. 375-376.
[8] Id. vol. 2, p. 480, 481.

system would be about 83,000 miles distant. Remember, we are using a mile to represent a light-year.

But out beyond our slowly whirling island galaxy, or Milky Way nebulae, which contains about 30 billion suns, there are many other similar huge groups of stars which are usually called *nebulae,* but are more properly called *galaxies.* The very *nearest* such neighborhood of stars is the one in Andromeda called Messier 31: and *it has taken light about 750,000 years to travel across the intervening distance to us.* Incidentally, this is the farthest distance that you can see with your naked eyes. All that lies beyond that distance must be seen with the telescopes and photographs.[9] Out in the vast distances of the starry heaven there are many of these huge galaxies of stars. The 100-inch telescope on Mount Wilson has photographed galaxies which are about 500 million light-years distant: and within the field of observation of this powerful telescope it is believed on the basis of good evidence that there exist "approximately 100 million extra-galactic nebulae."[10]

The astronomers tell us truthfully that "when we observe a celestial body, we see it, not as it *is* at the moment of observation, but as it *was* at the moment when the light which we see left it."[11] In other words, *the farther we see out into space, the farther back we are observing in time.* This being so, it is then only necessary to study a series of progressively distant stars or groups of stars to study many periods of solar history and astronomical motions. This fact seems to have been somewhat overlooked by our pseudo-scientists, the evolutionists.

## An Epoch of Creation

In summarizing the evidences which we have on the subject of Primary Time, the following quotation is highly significant, and it comes as a surprise to most of us.

While some of the lines of argument upon which Dr. Holme's final conclusion is based are subject to question or elimination, nevertheless those which are drawn from the radioactive minerals, the iron meteorites, and many of the spiral nebulae, are valid within reasonable limits. In final summary of the subject of the age of the Earth, Dr. Holmes said,

"This highly significant convergence—quite unexpected a few years ago—strongly indicates that Earth, solar system, meteorites, stars, and galaxies *all came into existence about the same time,* some 2,000 million years ago. *This natural zero of time* possesses, 'to an overwhelming degree of probability,' as Professor Milne has claimed, 'the properties of *an epoch of creation.*"[12]

The "epoch of creation" referred to in this connection would be God's Primary Creation, when he brought into existence all the elements and all the astronomical systems. How wonderful it is that the evidences in the Bible and the evidences in God's Universe of created things both indicate a great original Primary Creation of all the elements and all the stars *simultaneously.*

Whether or not any of the astronomical systems, such as the galaxies, or nebulae, have been expanding and also moving farther apart, like a "growing" universe (or "expanding universe"), we do not know for certain; but such a growth by large-scale movement and preserved balances seems possible and reasonable. However, the progressively greater shift of the spectrum of light toward the red in the light coming from the more and more distant galaxies may be due entirely to the weakening of the light with increased distance, so that light waves actually get tired and travel more slowly the farther they go. Even if we allow for an expanding universe, with its outer portions moving fastest away from the center (which sounds like another and bigger geocentric philosophy), we may be erring

---

[9] Draper & Lockwood, "The Story of Astronomy," p. 360, 1939.
[10] Id. p. 363; and Skilling and Richardson, "Astronomy," p. 551, 1939.
[11] Russell, Dugan, & Stewart, "Astronomy," p. 375-376, 1926.
[12] Dr. Arthur Holmes, D.Sc., A.R.C.S., M.R.I.A., F.G.S., etc., Professor of Geology in The University, Durham; published in his book "The Age of the Earth," page 242, 1937.

seriously if we *begin* this expanding universe with a single huge lump of materials or a single very dense sphere of hot exploding gases. It would be as easy and sensible to suggest that each galaxy existed in wonderful complexity and beauty separate and distinct from the very beginning of all astronomical and chemical time, just as all the great phyla and families of plants and animals have existed together on the Earth since its Secondary Creation.

## God During the Ages of Primary Time

It matters not to the well informed Christian how far back into Primary Time God's natural clocks register the Primary Creation. Those long stretches of time in no way weaken our faith in the Creator of the elements and the stars.

There is a Scripture which says, *"Before the mountains were brought forth, or ever thou hadst formed the Earth and the [inhabited] world, even from everlasting to everlasting, thou art God."*—Psalm 90:2.

The prophet Micah shows that this is also true of the Messiah of the Jews, the Saviour of the world, Jesus Christ, the only begotten Son of God, for he said, "But thou, Bethlehem Ephratah, though thou be little among the thousands of Judah, yet out of thee shall he come forth unto me that is to be ruler in Israel, whose goings forth have been from of old, *from everlasting (the days of eternity)."* —Micah 5:2, margin.

And in another place we read: "But the mercy of the Lord is *from everlasting to everlasting* upon them that fear him and his righteousness unto children's children; to such as keep his covenant, and to those that remember his commandments to do them."—Psalm 103:17, 18.

## God's Throne, or the Capital of the Universe

*"The Lord hath prepared his throne in the {astronomical} heavens; and his kingdom ruleth over all.* Bless the Lord, ye his angels, that excell in strength, that do his commandments, hearkening unto the voice of his word. Bless the Lord, all ye his hosts; ye ministers of his, that do his pleasure. Bless the Lord, all his works in all places of his dominion; bless the Lord, O my soul."—Psalm 103:19-22. (Read also Psalm 93:2; Prov. 8:22, 23; Isaiah 63;16; Hab. 1:12; Psalm 11:4 Isa 66:1; Heb. 8:1; etc.)

There are many Scriptures which give us some descriptions of God's throne. But in some instances the early writers of the Bible had difficulty in comprehending its magnitude, even though they realized that it was important, and that it symbolized the Creator's sovereignty. Perhaps all these descriptions when combined are very inadequate, and merely outline some of the most prominent features. If we may regard these descriptions as "surveyors' stakes," which are preliminary to a lot of detailed work, then we may very profitably do a lot of mental work within the limits of these Biblical facts, and then be better prepared to comprehend greater revelations.

The prophet Ezekiel was given a vision of God's throne, and he was shown how it is exalted in its relation to the starry heavens. The revelation was so startling and new that he had difficulty in describing it. To him the Creator's throne seemed to be exalted above wheels within wheels that turned not. Today we may apply this description to the galaxies of stars which revolve so slowly that they seem not to turn at all. Some of the stars looked to Ezekiel like eyes—"their rings were full of eyes." (Ezek. 1:18; 10:12)

Daniel was given a vision of God's throne, which appeared to be above some wheels also; and the power which radiated out from that throne was likened to "a fiery stream." God is here called "the Ancient of days": and "thousand thousands ministered unto him, and ten thousand times ten thousand stood before him."— Daniel 7:9, 10.

John saw still more of the details as they are today: he saw 24 smaller thrones near God's throne, on which sat 24 elders; and "round about the throne were four beasts full of eyes before and behind. And the first beast was like a lion, and the second beast like a calf, and the third beast had a face as a man, and the fourth beast was like a flying eagle. And the four beasts had each of them six wings about him; and they were full of eyes within: and they rest not day and night, saying, Holy, holy, holy, *Lord God Almighty; which was, and is, and is to come* . . . Thou art worthy, O Lord, to receive glory and honour and power: *for thou hast created all things, and for thy pleasure they are and were created.*"—Revelation 4:6-11.

These "four beasts full of eyes before and behind" evidently are four large groups of people who have arranged themselves in those shapes. This is frequently done even today by university students: they arrange themselves in their amphitheaters in the shape of the animals they have chosen as their emblems. This, coupled with a careful study of the Bible subject of the "firstfruit people" whom Jesus took to Heaven when he ascended ten days before the Feast of Firstfruits, or the Feast of Pentecost, leads us to the conclusion that there are now in Heaven four great universities, or one great university composed of four great colleges; and that they now include those firstfruit people, who are performing and will perform some very important work in behalf of our planet, the Earth. This great fact of revelation may have been foreshadowed by the orderly arrangement of the twelve tribes of the children of Israel in four camps around the wilderness tabernacle.[13]

John also saw "ten thousand times ten thousand, and thousands of thousands" of angels in the Capital of the Universe. And he described God's throne as "the great white throne." It is pictured by him as having a beautiful rainbow over it: and a clear river of water of life flowing out from it, on whose banks grow a huge tree called the "Tree of Life." And farther out from this immediate area is a beautiful "sea of glass." There are also many mansions in that great metropolis, which is 375 miles square. (Read, Rev. 5:11; 20:4, 11; 4:1-6; 22:1-6; 15:2-4; John 14:1-4; Rev. 21:9-27.)

It would be wonderful, indeed, if we could find out which large planet in the starry heavens is the one on which is located the Capital of the Universe. Is it in our Milky Way galaxy? Is it in a nearby galaxy? Or is it in one of those distant galaxies that are still beyond the range of our most powerful telescopes? Perhaps it does not remain in the same place through all the ages of time. Perhaps it is in one galaxy awhile, and then in another. Ezekiel and John seemed to get this impression. (Ezek. 1:19-21; Rev. 21:1-3.)

But, best of all, the Bible reveals to us that God's throne is a place where righteousness, judgment, justice, and mercy dwell: and where problems can be taken and solved.[14]

Since the Father and the Son are so perfect that they are "the same yesterday, and today, and for ever," we may project these descriptions of them, and most of the descriptions of their supreme place of abode, back to the beginning of Primary Time.[15] In fact, it may be that God's throne was in existence long before the Primary Creation. (Ps. 93:2.)

## Many Secondary Creations, Past and Future

Reflecting back a little we see that our planet was transformed into an inhabited world a very long time after the Primary Creation and the beginning of Primary Time: and we see also that God had transformed other planets into inhabited worlds before Primary Time ended for our planet. This, then, leads us to suggest that the Creator exercised his creative power in a secondary manner *many times* throughout Primary Time. There is no proof in astron-

13 Compare Numbers 2:1-34; Revelation 4:6-8; Hebrews 8:1-6; Revelation 5:8-10 with context; Ephesians 4:8 margin; Matt. 27:50-53; Jn. 5:25, (28); Rev. 14:1-5; etc.
14 Read Psalm 9:4, 7-10, 16; 94: 14, 15; 97:2; 103:17-19; Isa. 9-7; Exodus 20:6; Revelation 22:12-17; 20:4; 5:10; etc.
15 Jer. 17:12; Heb. 8:1, 2; Mal. 3:6; Heb. 13:8; Matt. 5:48; Heb. 1:12; 5:9.

omy or the Bible that God performed many of His *secondary creations* simultaneously.

Consider the estimated total number of stars or shining suns, which there are in the known Universe. Our Milky Way Galaxy is composed of about 30,000,000,000 shining suns: and within the seeing radius of the 100-inch telescope on Mount Wilson, which range is 500,000,000 light-years, there are approximately 100,000,000 galaxies like our own.[16]

Our Sun has nine planets and fragments of a tenth traveling around it. If every sun, or star, in known space has this many planets (which is doubtful), then the astronomical heavens contain about 30,000,000,-000,000,000,000 planets! (Which is 30 quintillion.) This is 30 raised to the 18th power of ten, written $30 \times 10^{18}$,—which is 30 followed by 18 ciphers. We may also call it 30,000,000 trillion! If only one-tenth of these planets are inhabited, then there would be 3,000,000 trillion inhabited worlds in the known Universe. But because of the very nature of many of the suns in starry space, it is very doubtful if all of them have planets revolving around them, and most certainly no inhabited worlds anywhere near them.

If we allow half of the suns in known space to be for other purposes than lighting and heating nearby inhabited worlds, and allow only one inhabited world for each of the other suns, we would still have in the known Universe about 1,500,000 trillion *inhabited worlds* (or $15 \times 10$,[17] which is 15 followed by 17 ciphers).

In addition to a vast number of inhabited worlds in the Universe, which we may regard as being the result of an equally vast number of weeks of Secondary Creation, there is evidence that there may be a larger number of uninhabited planets waiting for their special weeks of Secondary Creation in the future. Astronomers know that there are many dark

suns in space, in addition to those that are shining and we should remember that our Sun was a dark sun before the Earth's special Week of Secondary Creation. When, therefore, we consider that our Sun has a family of nine planets, and that *only one of these is inhabited,* we begin to wake up and realize what a vast number of potential inhabited worlds there may be in God's immense Universe; and *how much of this secondary creative work remains to be done,* if all the planets in the Universe are ultimately to be inhabited. The Bible also has something very denite to say about this subject; but its comments are limited almost exclusively to telling about the Earth's next Secondary Creation and the regular, normal, sinless life of its inhabitants, when our experiment with sin is forever past.[17]

*One thing is very certain, indeed, that by now God has watched the civilizations of a large number of inhabited worlds for a very long time.* The knowledge that the God of the Bible has witnessed the progress of human beings on many worlds for a very long time *should instill into our souls a confidence in Him that cannot be eclipsed by any other being, living or dead.* Most certainly He is our most reliable Guide and Counselor. It will pay us to get better acquainted with Him. How fitting is the title which He holds, namely, *"The Faithful and True Witness."* Anyone who has observed history as long as He has, certainly should know something about the problems of mankind. *He should know what is most essential in the lives of individuals and nations for the permanent establishment of a kingdom of peace and happiness.*

The prophet John was instructed to write, "These things saith the Amen, *the faithful and true Witness, the beginning of the creation of God;* I KNOW THY WORK . . ."—Revelation 3:14, 15[18]

16 W. T. Skilling of the San Diego State College, and R. S. Richardson of the Mount Wilson Observatory, "Astronomy," p. 521, 551, published by Henry Holt & Co., New York, in 1939; also Russell, Dugan and Stewart, "Astronomy," Vol. 2, p. 625, 813; 1938.

17 Compare: Isa. 45:18; 48:18, 19; Matt. 5:5; Zeph. 2:3; Isa. 65:17-25; 66:22, 23; 2 Pet. 3:13; Isa. 60:14-22; 62:1-9, 11:5-9; 66:9, Jer. 3:14-17; Rev. 21 and 22; 2:28; Isa. 64:4; 1 Cor. 2:9, 10; Jn. 16:13, 14; Mark 12:18-25 with Rev. 20:4-6.

18 Compare also these references: Revelation 19:11-16; Deuteronomy 7:9; Proverbs 14:5; Jeremiah 42:5; I Thessalonians 5:24; 2 Thessalonians 3:3; Hebrews 2:17; 10:23; 1 Peter 4:19; Revelation 1:5; Romans 11:33-36.

# THE RADIOACTIVE TIME THEORY AND RECENT TRENDS IN METHODS OF RECKONING GEOLOGIC TIME

## By Clifford Leslie Burdick

One of the most notable philosophical and scientific efforts of man has been the attempt to determine by means of natural processes the age of the earth. It is believed that few scientific subjects of our time can lay more legitimate claim to our attention and study than this topic, because it affects so vitally our concepts concerning the origin and history of the earth and its life.

In this brief survey the following seven aspects of this subject will be discussed: 1. The earliest speculations, how they foreshadowed modern theories; 2. The evolution of the Playfair-Lyell-Darwin-Kelvin conceptions; 3. Geologic age from ocean salts; 4. Denudation and deposition of sediments as age criteria; 5. The Varve theory; 6. The situation supposedly saved by the radioactive time theory; 7. The effect of the failure of all these theories upon the position of sacred chronology.

### The Earliest Speculations

As early as 450 B.C. Herodotus was laying the foundation for present-day Uniformitarianism by trying to estimate the age of the earth through study of the rate of deposition of silt in the delta of the Nile. Later during the Dark Ages, interest in geology and objective science was at low ebb, because such interest was largely stifled by "Authority," and fossils were looked upon as "freaks of nature." The Renaissance revived interest in science, and we find Leonardo Da Vinci studying fossils about the time that Columbus was discovering America. But it was not until about 1800 that William Smith in England was using the fossils as age markers, thus laying the foundation for modern evolutionary paleontology.

At the beginning of the nineteenth century the prevailing view on biology was the Creationism of Linnaeus and Agassiz, and

from Steno, (1669), until Cuvier, in the early part of the nineteenth century, the true spirit of geology was bound up in Catastrophism. Then James Hutton, in 1795, speaking before the Royal Society of Edinborough proclaimed: "They (geological phenomena) are the processes of nature and of the weather, as the land erodes and as the sediment is deposited just as we observe it in the world about us. The changes of the earth are orderly, always and everywhere orderly. They are slow. The results are traceable in the layers of the earth's crust."

### The Playfair-Lyell-Kelvin-Darwin Conceptions

Geology really became a science when Playfair in 1800 published an interpretation of Hutton's observations. Lyell lent his influence to back up Hutton and Playfair, and by the time that Charles Darwin came along, uniformitarian geology had about replaced Bible Catastrophism, and it was not long before the evolution of Darwin and his co-workers, Huxley, Spencer, and Wallace, had supplanted Special Creationism.[1]

Darwin admitted that such processes of evolution or variation as could be observed in living species were so very slow that if his hypothesis were true he would need time, lots of time.

It is interesting to note that up to the time of Darwin about the only really scientific attempt to compute the age of the earth was that of Lord Kelvin who was working on the Nebular Hypothesis that the earth was a mass that was ejected from the sun, and had cooled sufficiently to support life. He estimated the age of the earth from its rate of cooling, which age he placed at from 20 to 40 million years. Darwin complained that that was too short a time for his complete evolutionary process to have taken

---

[1] Marsh, Frank L. Evolution, Creation and Science, 1944. Ch. 3.

place. He refused to settle for less than a hundred million. Subsequent discoveries showed that Kelvin was on the wrong track, and his theory and conclusions were dropped with dramatic suddenness. From then on evolutionary science has claimed "room enough in which to turn around." One cannot help wondering at times, however, at the ease with which these multi-million year periods are "pulled out of the hat" when needed, but when the method is proved wrong, *just as mysteriously they disappear.* Let us note in passing that Kelvin's method was disproved scientifically, but Bible Creationism and Catastrophism never were disproved.

Darwinism had taken deep root, but it sorely lacked a confirmatory science to give it the time it needed. Biology in itself had little to offer. Charles Schuchert concluded that from the rate of organic evolution there can be no way of determining the length of geologic time. He said, "Students of the living world see little or no change going on, and for this reason have *assumed* (emphasis ours) that the present organic world must have taken far more than one hundred million years for its evolution."[2]

If, as Schuchert admitted, that students of biology can see no present-day evidence of evolutionary activity, then the more obvious and logical assumption would seem to be that there had never been any evolution.

Since Lord Kelvin's attempt astronomy has had little to offer. This is shown by the words of Ernest W. Brown, the astronomer: "There are no known methods derived from astronomical data alone for estimating the age of the earth."[3] There was however a presumptive inference in the minds of some, from the recent discoveries in astronomy that the earth must indeed be very old. Modern high powered telescopes have been able to reach out into space and photograph stars so distant that it has required hundreds of millions of years for the light, traveling at 186,000 miles per second, to reach the earth. The minimum age of these blazing suns could thus be determined. According to the nebular hypothesis, so popular a few years ago, all cosmic matter was presumed to have the same age, and if this presumption were correct, then the earth must be hundreds of millions of years old at least, so they reasoned. Spurred on by this conception, men of science believed that some means could be found to determine the age of the earth as the minimum age of the stars had been demonstrated.

## Geologic Age from Ocean Salts

As a last resort evolutionary biologists turned to geology for the answer, and not entirely in vain, for considerable work was being done along the lines suggested by Herodotus more than two milleniums before. It was about two hundred years ago that Edmund Halley first suggested the possibility of ascertaining the age of the earth by measuring the rate at which rivers delivered salt to the ocean.[4] There were no data available at that time, but more recently work has been done along that line by many scientists. Their results ran all the way from fifty to one hundred million years.

It is important to note that these computations are based upon three unproved assumptions: (1) That the water of the ocean was originally fresh. Some German scientists believe that the ocean has always been saline, and the science of paleontology was built on that assumption in classifying paleozoic fossils, for example, as marine or fresh water. (2) That all sodium carried by the rivers to the ocean remains in solution. Many scientists insist that much of the sodium is removed by absorption and base exchange with the newly deposited sediments, the sodium thus leaving the solution and combining with the sediments. (3) That the principle of *uniformity* has been in effect in delivering sodium to the oceans at a uniform rate. Becker has shown that the rate has been anything but uniform.[5] This system of computing time has now largely fallen into dis-

---

2 Schuchert, Charles, Physics of the Earth, National Research Council, 1931. Bulletin 80, p. 59.
3 Brown, Ernest W., Physics of the Earth. National Research Council, 1931. Bulletin 80, p. 460.
4 Halley, Edmund. Philos. Trans., vol. 29, 1715, p. 296.
5 Becker, G. F., Age of the Earth, Smithsonian Misc. Coll. vol. 56, No. 6, 1910.

repute. Whitney deals at greater length with this subject in a former Bulletin of the Deluge Society.[6]

## Denudation and Deposition of Sediments as Criteria

Referring again to the river delta method of time measurement, as first suggested by Herodotus, it will be recalled that Allen, in a former Bulletin of this Society showed that, according to an outstanding piece of work by army engineers and leading geologists, the age of the Mississippi River, adjudged by the delta, is from 4500 to 5000 years. What little work has been done on other major rivers, tends to confirm these results.[7] It is believed that this is the measure of time since the mountain-making movement during and at the close of the Deluge period, at which time the present principal physiographic features and river systems were established.

Perhaps more dependence for time reckoning during the past hundred years has been placed on the denudation and sedimentation method than any other. Many gelogists have attempted to compute the average rate of denudation of the continents and the consequent deposition of the sediments. It was found that there was such a serious discrepancy in rates of deposition from place to place and from age to age, that the law of uniformity practically became a dead issue. Furthermore, the tremendous difference in results between investigators is sufficient to neutralize any claim to credence which this method might make. As one leading geologist remarked, that sedimentary computations were little more than rough guesses.

A little examination of the variations in estimations of rates of deposition will suffice to show how ludicrous is the attempt to estimate geologic time from the sediments. Some stratigraphers have claimed that one foot of sediments in 100 years was about the average, whereas others placed the figure as high as one foot in 2350 years in the case of limestone, one foot in 1000 years for shale, and one foot in 750 years for sandstone. Others have said that in some places it required 87,100 years to deposit one foot, a variation of 871 to 1.

On the island of Timor in the East Indies, the upper Triassic is only 2.1 meters thick, but this thickness is claimed to represent millions of years of time. The Tertiary of the Ventura quadrangle of California is 9000 meters thick, but this thickness is assumed to represent about the same lapse of time as the two meters of Timor. According to this assumption the California rate of sediment deposition was about 4000 times that of Timor. Thus we see an enormous variation in rates of deposition in various times and places, even though comparative uniformity is postulated, according to the standard geological conception. But according to the new Catastrophic Geology of the Deluge we can easily conceive of 9000 meters or more being deposited in a very short time during the Deluge period.

It is little wonder, therefore, that such a leading stratigrapher as Charles Schuchert should say, "We do not yet know the mean rate at which any kind of deposit accumulates; that local rates in sedimentation vary immensely among themselves is well known from the accumulations *now going on.*"[8] Note that he says NOW. The present is a time, of course, of comparative uniformity. As mentioned above there have been times in the past, even from the evolutionist viewpoint, when sedimentation was not as uniform as at present. Twenhofel sums this up very nicely as follows, "The thickness (of the strata) is not a measure of the rate of deposition or of time. A thin layer of sediments of any kind may have taken as long a time to deposit as many meters of the same or some other kind of sediment at a different time or place."[9] What consistency

---

[6] Whitney, D. J., Age of the Earth, Bulletin of Deluge Geology, vol. 1, No. 5, Dec. 1941, pp. 120-131.

[7] Allen, Ben F., Age of the Mississippi River, Bulletin of Deluge Geology, vol. 2, No. 2, 1942.

[8] Schuchert, Charles, Physics of the Earth, National Research Council, 1931, Bulletin 80, p. 33.

[9] Twenhofel, W. H., Principles of Sedimentation, 1939, p. 496.

can be gathered from all this confusion of figures, unless it be that the death-knell has been sounded for the principle of uniformity?

Holmes summarized this conclusion as follows: "Most of these estimates are little more than rough guesses. We do not know how much of the story is lost to us, or how much is hidden away."[10]

Just to the extent that sedimentary figures have varied, so has opinion among stratigraphers, but in general it might be said that there were two schools of thought. Until about 1925 when the radioactive age calculations began to impress the scientific world, one hundred million years was regarded by geologists as about right for the age of the earth based both on the sediments, and on the sodium content in the ocean, as T. C. Chamberlin stated in 1922, "The mean of the four estimates on the basis of the sediments was 90,000,000 years, on the basis of the ocean 95,000,000 years."[11]

Soon afterward the influence of the radioactive time estimates began to be felt, and gave the earth an age of from ten to twenty times as much. This terrible age discrepancy was most embarassing to scientists and especially purely geological scientists interested in estimating the age of the earth. Manifestly one system or the other must be wrong, but the tendency was to accept the findings of the radioactive workers.

The first school of thought considered the age differences too great to be reconciled, and abandoned all sodium and sedimentary estimates as a *big mistake*. Charles Schuchert, selected by the National Research Council as a leading spokesman for the geologists, stated: "Now from the known rate of disintegration of uranium and thorium, *all our previous estimates have been set aside*, (emphasis ours) and we believe with Barrell and Holmes that the duration of geologic time is of the order of 1,600,000,000 years."[12] Thus to sweep aside with a single

gesture the fruitage of years of scientific research in pure geology would seem to indicate what slight confidence these geologists had in their own calculations. They were ready to "scrap" the whole system.

The other school of geological thought believed that the way out of the dilemma was to try to harmonize the various age estimates. The National Research Council sponsored such a program. They sought out data from all corners of the earth on exceptionally thick formations from all geological ages, which very materially increased the total to about 400,000 feet. Then they decided that the average estimated rate of deposition of sediments was too high. This was cut away down. Limestone, sandstone, and shale all have different rates of deposition in these calculations and occur in different average proportions in the sedimentary crust of the earth. These factors were all taken into consideration and 25,000,000 years were added for unconformities (the main breaks in the deposition) and 40,-000,000 more for diastems (short breaks in disposition). Chamberlin's 95,000,000 years had been stretched to 536,000,000 years. At least some semblance of harmony between various age estimates was arrived at which was apparently satisfactory to those theorists, but to many it merely emphasized a vital weakness in a system of age calculations that could *be stretched* at will to cover any gap. In this effort it seemed that the "wish was the father of the thought."

In arriving at these estimates for the age of the earth, whether it be the 95,000,000 years of the first school of geological thought, or the 536,000,000 years of the second school, an amazing bit of mental gymnastics was indulged in which professor George McCready Price has called "reasoning in a circle."[13] Or it might be thought of as calling upon the conclusion to help prove the premise. The average thickness of sedimentary rocks the world over has been estimated

10 Holmes, Arthur, Physics of the Earth, National Research Council, 1931, Bulletin 80, p. 18.
11 Chamberlin, T. C., Age of the Earth From a Geological Viewpoint, Proc. Am. Phil. Soc., 61 (1922), p. 249.
12 Schuchert, Charles, Physics of the Earth, National Research Council, 1931, Bulletin 80, p. 16.
13 Price, George McCready, Geology and the Recapitulation Theory, Bulletin of Deluge Geology, vol. 1, No. 3, 1941.

at about 2,500 feet, although one authority places it as high as one mile. Instead of using those figures in the equation for computing the age of the earth, geologists have used the 400,000 foot figure. And how did they arrive at that immense total? By calling upon the fossils for help. In using *the fossils as interpreted on the evolutionary basis and its supposed sequence of changing forms of life, many layers of sediments were in theory set apart into different periods.* By the time these "sedimentarians" got around to add into the total a sample of each layer (and, as mentioned previously, they chose the thickest they could find) that staggering total was created.

As previously brought out, biological evolution was calling upon geology to prove that sufficient time had elapsed for evolution to take place. If such proof were not forthcoming, then the only remaining generally acceptable record of time, that contained in sacred history, of from six to seven thousand years, would fall far short of providing the necessary time for biological evolution, and the evolutionary hypothesis would fall of its own weight.

It is here submitted that the logical figure to use, then, for the thickness of the sediments is the average of 2,500 feet. But geologists preferred the sedimentary time scale "build up" figure of 400,000 feet. The only logic that would permit the use of that immense total was the *assumption* that evolution involving many separate periods was true. They apparently forgot that they set out to prove it, not to *assume* it. Therefore, if assumption is necessary, then the sedimentary "build up" system of age-reckoning falls like a house of cards. Little wonder, then, that many leading geologists charge that the science of geology stands ready for "a good house cleaning."

R. H. Rastall makes some pertinent suggestions on how to start cleaning house. He claims there never was any excuse for naming the Permian age, for it was identical with the Pennsylvanian. It is believed that further study will reveal many more duplications, and as fast as they are eliminated, geological time will undergo a great shrinking process. As Price has pointed out, it may be that most or all of the geological ages or formations were contemporaneous rather than consecutive. Rastall also believes that it was "a major geological disaster" when geological time was divided into three major divisions, the Paleozoic, Mesozoic, and Cenozoic. Only technically skilled geologists can fully grasp the tremendous import of this. The sole justification he sees in retaining them is for purposes of identification.[14] There is of course a tendency to retain all the old landmarks once established, even though later discoveries suggest revision.

A far worse fault, as mentioned before, has been to over-emphasize the fossils as age markers, *while practically ignoring lithological or physical evidence.* Hensen cites many cases where clear-cut non-confirmities cut across the single index fossil age formations when followed out laterally.[15] Theoretically when non-conformities do occur they always separate different age formations, but never the same age formations. The fossil life above the break is supposed to be quite distinct from that below it since the break is supposed to represent a long period of time when the land was elevated above the ocean and folding of the strata and orogeny took place, with a period of erosion before the other stratum was laid down on top of the non-conformity caused by that orogeny and erosion.

Formerly these index fossil age observations were probably made only locally, and one type of index fossil would be found in a locality below a non-conformity, while in another locality some other observer would unknowingly report the same type of fossil as occurring above a *supposedly different* non-conformity. No incongruity suggested itself until these two exposures of non-conformity were traced out *and found to be one and the same.* How could the same age-index occur on both sids of a break of from 1,000,000 to 100,000,000 or more years apart?

---

14 Rastall, R. H., Geological Magazine, July 1944, p. 162.
15 Hensen, F. R. S., Geological Magazine, July 1944, p. 166.

These recurring discoveries have had the practical effect of jumbling the formations. The same fossil formation, belonging perhaps to the Mesozoic age in one locality would become Paleozoic in another place, (many millions of years apart, from the evolutionary viewpoint) further condensing the geologic ages and confusing the taxonomists. Evolutionary geology may try to explain fossils in the wrong order in some places by illogical and presumed "thrust faults," as Price has pointed out, *but it is not clear just how the intersections of the fossil formations with the lithological non-conformities can be explained on the basis of evolutionary paleontology.* The theory, it appears, has headed straight into a "cul de sac."

In review of the sedimentary evidence, such as it is, we see that the age of the earth has been placed all the way from 90,-000,000 years to 536,000,000 years, based upon the evolutionary hypothesis. But if we use the only logical measurement of sediments, the average of 2,500 feet, this would, at the average present rate of deposition, reduce geologic time to the order of 4,000,000 years, *which no evolutionist will concede is enough. It is submitted that this is nevertheless the correct figure for the age of the earth on the basis of uniformitarian deposition.* One geologist claims a mile for the average thickness of the world sediments, which would raise the age of the earth to 8,000,000 years, but the practical effect is the same; evolution would be ruled out. However, with a highly accelerated rate of deposition during and for a time after the Deluge, this 4,000,000 year age of the earth could be reduced to a few thousand.

There are many other geological methods of lesser importance that are sometimes employed to help build up the general impression of a grossly exaggerated antiquity for this terrestial globe. Guides who introduce the visitors to the natural wonders of our land perhaps feel that the tourists will think that they are really getting their money's worth if they are duly impressed with awe and wonder at the immense age of the phenomena of nature which they behold. Personal friends of the writer were conducted through the beautiful Louray Caverns in Virginia. The guide was pointing to the tall, graceful stalactites suspended from the vaulted ceilings and almost touching the stalagmites below. This great pillar he explained was 300,000 years in process of formation. Most of the observers gasped and marveled, all but one man "from Missouri." He demanded to know what justification the guide had for assigning such an age for the pillar. The guide explained that geologists from the university had made observations and marked the lower limit of the stalactite just twenty years before, and had returned after that time and measured the amount by which the structure had lengthened, and by measuring the total length of the statlactite and by a simply problem of arithmetic had computed an age of 300,000 years. This seemed convincing enough to everyone but our friend "from Missouri." He was not so easily convinced and proceeded to ask an embarrassing question or two: (1) Was there any proof that throughout the period of formation of the pillar, that the same amount of lime-laden water was always supplying mineral to the stalactite as during the past twenty years? The guide had to confess that there was no proof. (2) Was there any proof that the water of the past had the same percentage of lime in solution per unit of water as now? Again there was no proof. (3) Did he know that the temperature and other environmental factors were uniform throughout the period of its formation? And again the admission of ignorance on these vital points. Thereupon our friend "from Missouri" suggested to the guide that he refrain from drawing any more unwarranted conclusions until he had sufficient data upon which to premise them. Parenthetically we might add "ditto" to some of these other age-of-the-earth estimations.

### The Varve Theory

Some geologists place as much confidence in the varves to count the years as the botanist does in the rings of the trees. The varves are alternations of two kinds of sediment, the theory being that one kind is deposited in the summer, and the other in the winter.

On this hypothesis the Green River formation of Colorado, Wyoming, and Utah, representing about one third of Eocene time, covers from five to eight million years, which agrees well with accepted evolutionary time estimates. The varve theory therefore is based upon the assumption that one couplet of laminations represents one year. But recent laboratory experiments have demmonstrated that even with controlled constant supply of water and sediment it is almost impossible to prevent laminations. It has been further demonstrated that variations in direction and intensity of the wind cause variation in the competency of the flowing water that deposits the sediments.[16] Furthermore, inasmuch as every possible gradation and variation from only two parts of the varve to many parts occur, how shall we be sure just what are true varves and what are not? There is ample evidence that the strata were laid down to the accompaniment of powerful and variable air currents. Observers in Siberia in the frozen tundra find laminations of ice and silt in which imbedded air bubbles are elongated. Probably many varve-like laminations were deposited in a single day or an hour.

One glaring abuse of the varve theory has been the persistent custom of adding together the varves from different localities to make staggering totals. They base the count of the varves on the geologic age system by presuming that the varves in each of the thirty-two or more geologic ages must represent separate periods of time.

Let us test out the varve theory again in Siberia where whole mammoths with flesh, hair, and all were dug out of the melting banks of laminated mud. Some were in upright position, stomachs filled with undecayed food, and some had food in their mouths. Digby tells of how one of the beasts was stuck in the mud and buried with a series of varves or alternating laminations. If we are to believe the varve theory, it took a good many hundreds or even thousands of years to get this big fellow finally buried. Why did his flesh not decay, or why did the wolves not devour him?[17]

Digby also describes the carcass of a wooly rhinoceros that was exposed in the surface of the bank of the river Vilui in northeast Siberia. He said: "The animal appears to have been drowned, for the blood vessels of the head were found by Professor Brandt, to be filled with red, coagulated blood, such as would be produced by suffocation through drowning. Probably it was caught suddenly in a flood of rushing water, from which it had no opportunity to escape. At one moment the animal was standing on firm ground, peacefully browsing, and in the next was overwhelmed by a roaring flood, the tumultuous waves of which bore along masses of mud and gravel in their sweeping course so that it was drowned and buried almost instantly. Then an intense cold set in, the body was frozen up, and the ground never thawed until the day when it fell down on the banks of the river."[18]

The fallacy of uniformity underlying all these time estimates is apparent with the mammoths, and in fact with all fossils as well. If the principle of uniformity were true, then many fossil trees would have had to stand erect in water or air before being fossilized, for hundreds of thousands of years. Actually they had to be buried suddenly to be preserved at all. Geologists are slowly discovering that it is impossible to explain all geological phenomena of the past on the basis of uniformity or present-day geological action. Schuchert recognized this when he said, "At these slow rates of accumulation it is evident that no fossils could be preserved, since they would not be covered by sediment before being dissolved away by the acid of the water or effaced by the wear and tear on the shallow sea bottoms. The accident of sudden burial alone could entomb them."[19] It sounds as though Schuchert were describing the Bible Deluge.

Our present information confirms the fact

16 Twenhofel, W. H., Principles of Sedimentation, 1939, p. 500.
17 Digby, Bassett, The Mammoth and Mammoth hunting in N. E. Siberia, Chap. 9.
18 Digby, Bassett, The Mammoth and Mammoth Hunting in N. E. Siberia, p. 54.
19 Schuchert, Charles, Physics of the Earth, Natl. Research Council, 1931, Bulletin 80, p. 14.

that there is little opportunity for dead marine life to be buried naturally on the bottom of the ocean at the present time. Scavengers are almost everywhere, and as fast as animals die they are broken up and eaten, and it is believed that nothing edible escapes these scavengers of the deep. In zones where scavengers cannot live, aerobic bacteria take their place and decompose the soft tissues of the carcass, and this decomposition process produces ammonia, hydrogen sulfide, and hydro-carbons that dissolve the shells.[20] A most embarrassing question for uniformitarians is: How could the fossil deposits be duplicated by present-day processes?

## Review of the Purely Geologic Time Measurement Theories

From earliest times there has been a strong desire to know the age of the earth. The Greek Historian, Herodotus seems to have been the first to go about this inquiry in a scientific manner by studying the rate of deposition of the delta of the Nile. Until the last 150 years, the Deluge was vaguely held to be responsible for the burial of the fossils and their enclosing strata. By some, a series of Creations and Catastrophies was postulated, a sort of stepping stone or compromise between Genesis Creation, and the Deluge, on the one hand, and modern Evolution and Uniformity on the other. With Darwin's precedent-upsetting theory requiring long ages for the earth's history, an accelerated and intensive study was organized in many sciences to provide this time. During the latter part of the nineteenth century geological uniformity seemed to be the key that would unlock the secret.

Study was given to the time required to carry the sodium from the land to the oceans; also the time required to deposit all the consolidated sediments at the present rate of deposition. Both results added up to about 100,000,000 years, the amount Darwin said was needed for the generalization of biologic evolution. It seemed to be a "closed case" until further study revealed that there was no definite rate of deposition. New variable factors were discovered that threw the whole sedimentary time scale into confusion and caused some of the leading geologists to make some startling statements that supported the Deluge explanation for the burial of the fossils and their enclosing strata. Others were still looking for some "face-saving" new evidence when the radioactive science appeared about the beginning of the present century. When the principle of geologic uniformity was thrown overboard, purely geologic evidence was no more. Confusion reigned supreme.

## Rescued by the Radioactive Time Theory?

Most geologists knew that they were riding a sinking vessel as far as time estimates were concerned but could not abandon ship until a better one put in an appearance. Like a rescue boat appearing on the horizon, the new science of radioactivity, developing in the early part of the twentieth century gave promise of fixing the age of the earth with more exactness. Once the geologists had accepted the new radioactive time clock they were quick to expose the fallacies of the old ways.

Arthur Holmes, the eminent geologist declared: "The convergence toward harmonious results will come about by setting aside the PRINCIPLE OF UNIFORMITY. That is the root of the difficulty."[21] Thus by the simple process of elimination, it would appear that the way is left wide open for the NEW CATASTROPHISM and DELUGE GEOLOGY to step right in and assert its rights.

Charles Schuchert also admitted that he too had jumped onto the radioactive bandwagon by saying, "One stratigrapher at least has wholly gone over into the camp of the radioactive workers."[22] This frank confession on the part of a leading geologist seemed to sound the signal for a general stampede away from all the older methods of estimating the age of the earth, and of a general

---

[20] Twenhofel, W. H., Principles of Sedimentation, 1939, pp. 478, 479.
[21] Holmes, Arthur, Age of the Earth, An Introduction to Geological Ideas, 1927.
[22] Schuchert, Charles, Physics of the Earth, Natl. Research Council, 1931, Bulletin 80, p. 15.

rallying around the new more promising radioactive system.

Adolph Knopf also joined the parade and expressed himself thus: "The methods of age determination based on radioactive disintegration involve the least number of *assumptions*" (emphasis ours).[23] Let us examine the true import of this last statement. Mr. Knopf makes no claim that the radioactive time-table is yet to be classed as a demonstrated scientific principle, but that it is preferred over the former methods *because it contains fewer guesses*. When any new scientific discovery is made, even while in the experimental state, it is bound to get publicity, and there is always a tendency on the part of the general public to accept it at fuller face value than its proponents ever intended. It might be well therefore to withhold acceptance of the radioactive time-system until *all* the assumptions are eliminated, or at least until it is brought into some semblance of harmony with the generally acceptable chronology of sacred history.

But as a matter of fact the divergence is increasing rather than decreasing. Besides the conceded assumptions, one cornerstone of the system that was thought to be fact has now turned out to be just another assumption. Holmes, also one of the leading investigators in radioactivity, made this statement about fifteen years ago, "The quantum theory provides a reason for the *fact* (emphasis ours) that the rate of radioactive decay cannot be increased or decreased by such methods as can be applied in the laboratory."[24] What Holmes called a "fact" has now been proved to be a fallacy. The bomb that fell on Hiroshima, Japan, profoundly impressed that upon the world and left the radioactive time-clock about as badly wrecked as Hiroshima.

It may be said that that was merely a laboratory phenomenon, that it could not happen in nature. Any thoughtful observer will concede however that nature's laboratory has produced far more and greater feats than man. Once it has been demonstrated that the rate of radioactive disintegration is not necessarily constant, the further use of it for estimating geologic time is meaningless.

It was Madame Curie who opened up this new epoch in scientific advancement when she discovered radium and its characteristic of disintegration into elements of lesser atomic weight, with release of energy; but her daughter Madame Curie-Joliet made a discovery scarcely less epochmaking at about the opening of the twentieth century. She made two outstanding contributions to science: (1) She found that if she took a small amount of radium and a small amount of beryllium, that the radium knocked slow neutrons out of the beryllium in the form of radiant energy; that these were easily picked up by a chemical element that was near and converted into weight. In other words energy became mass. In the case of the decomposition of the radium, mass became energy. The interchangeability of matter and energy was thus demonstrated. Albert Einstein, the mathematician, who propounded the theory of relativity, was also the first to work out a mathematical formula or equation to express this interchangeability between mass and energy. This has been called the most important equation ever devised by man: $E=mc^2$. This means simply that energy is equal to mass multiplied by the square of the velocity of light (186,000 miles per second). One pound of matter therefore is equal to 10,000,000,000 kilowatt-hours of energy.

(2) Madame Curie-Joliet's second contribution to science was a corollary of the first, that the disintegration process can be a double track line with travel in either direction. This discovery was of the utmost importance to the later application of radioactivity to time calculations of the age of the earth, because it foreshadowed the later demonstration that the disintegration process can be reversed. Astronomical computations can be made with some degree of accuracy because heavenly bodies maintain their unvarying motions, but a radioactive mineral, it seems, is like the family car, it can speed up, slow down, or be shifted into reverse.

[23] Knopf, Adolph, Physics of the Earth, Natl. Research Council, 1931, Bull. 80, p. 5.
[24] Holmes, Arthur, Physics of the Earth, National Research Council, 1931, Bulletin 80, p. 147.

### Outline of Radioactivity as a Means of Estimating Geologic Time

Thus having introduced the subject of radioactive time, let us consider it in detail under the following headings:

1. The rate of disintegration is not necessarily constant.
2. There is too great a discrepancy between the estimates from the same mineral specimens, and from the same geologic formations.
3. Chemical instability, an outstanding characteristic of radioactive mineral ores.
4. The supposed radioactive time-clock can be accelerated, or it can run either backward or forward, neutralizing its value as a measure of geologic time.
5. Contamination of the by-products of radioactive disintegration vitiate time calculations.
6. Dating of individual geologic formations impossible by this method.
7. The relation between the fossils and the radioactive ores of the enclosing strata.
8. Radioactivity and the principle of uniformity.
9. Metamorphism.
10. Geologic time by radium disintegration.
11. The age of the sun.
12. Extinct elements.

Let us state clearly at the outset, that the atom bomb features are not the crucial points offered in presenting the failure of the radioactive time theory. The geo-chemical and mineralogical data, involving the extreme solubility of the radioactive ores and their consequent transitory and fickle nature, together with the same characteristics of the by-products of radioactive disintegration, are considered the more vulnerable or basic objections to the theory. But the purely geological features, as well as the paleontological, are strikingly important, and these tend to give the theory much the same objections as have been raised to the purely geological methods of measuring time.

### 1. The Rate of Disintegration Is Not Necessarily Constant

As early as 1925 Dr. A. Glashler stated that he had succeeded in accelerating the change of uranium to uranium X, the first step in the disintegration series, by submitting uranium oxide to strong rushes of momentary high-tension electric currents.[25] The work of both Gillette and Joly seemed to indicate that the older the rock the more rapid the disintegration.[26] As the laboratory work progressed along this line, Watson Davis wrote that, *"The radioactive time-clock method of determining the age of the earth may be proved wrong if uranium can be split up in the strange new fashion."*[27] (Emphasis ours) Recent events bear mute testimony to the truth of that statement. Writing thus in 1939 Davis attempted to allay fears that these developments might prove destructive to life. The extent to which he underestimated the ultimate outcome of radioactive research, recent events will testify. It would appear that the principle of uniformity is no more applicable to radioactive minerals than to other geological processes.

Now that the radioactive system has been introduced, it might be in order again to refer to the varve method of estimating geologic time with special reference to the Oligocene and Miocene of Burma. The varve system is the only phase of the sedimentary method of time reckoning that is even claimed to be somewhere near exact. Here the varve theory comes to deadly grips with the radioactive time system. Stamp has done considerable work on those formations, and by carefully counting the varve laminations he deduced the age of the Oligocene and one half of the Miocene at 2,500,000 years. Gillette, as already referred to, says that computations from the radioactive ores of these formations multiply these figures many

25 Glashler, A., Nature, Sept. 12, 1925, p. 397.
26 Gillette, Halbert P., Pan American Geologist, Nov. 1939, p. 270.
27 Davis, Watson, Science News Letter, Feb. 11, 1939.

times.[28] Furthermore, the most complete figures obtainable for the varve age of all sedimentary formations of the world put the age of the earth at only 56,000,000 years, as against the radioactive time estimate of 1,600,000,000 years so much used. Which system is at fault, or are both wrong?

## 2. Too Great a Discrepancy in Different Calculations of the Same Rocks or Formations

For the Ceylonese thorite overlying the Archean, using the thorium-lead ratio, Joly calculated the age as 130,000,000 years, whereas by using the uranium-lead ratio he got an age of 512,000,000 years.[29] Note that these tests were from the same geologic stratum, the same mineral specimen, and by the same scientist. Discrepancies of that magnitude can mean but one thing, that the system is wrong in principle. A difference of 382,000,000 years between two computations of pre-Cambrian rocks may not seem serious to one who strongly favors that time system, but to others it makes the computations appear as little better than "rough guesses." Using the uranium-lead ratio alone, Becker found a variation in age of rocks from *the same formation, and same hill*, in Llano County, Texas, between 1,671,000,000 years, and 11,470,000,000 years, a slight variation of some ten billion years. And so on "ad infinitum, ad absurdum."[30]

## 3. Instability Is One of the Outstanding Characteristics of Radioactive Ores

This is perhaps the most important defect of the theory. Uranium is found in many minerals, such as phosphates, arsenates, sulphates, carbonates, and silicates, which are of secondary origin. It is associated with such unstable ores as copper, lead, zinc, bismuth, and silver ores. It is leached very easily and enters into many chemical combinations. Every time this occurs, that particular time cycle comes to an end and a new one is started. But this is going on all the time, at

infinitely varying rates and combinations. Therefore, how can any definite stability be counted on with any assurance whatever? How can a start be made with any accuracy at all without a definite starting point?

According to the best authorities on sedimentation and mineral ore formation, this erosion, leaching, transportation, and re-deposition cycle takes place numerous times in the history of minerals and their elements. Twenhofel throws a flood of light on this question when he says, "If an environment always remained constant at the conditions that permitted a mineral to form, there would be no changes. There are probably no places on the earth's surface, or in the outer crust, where immutability is possible. Environments are constantly changing."[32] He then enumerates environmental factors, such as temperature, pressure, light intensity, humidity, precipitation, contents of the underground water, character of the soil and rock, nature of the surface and life.

Whether therefore in igneous, metamorphic, or sedimentary rocks anywhere in the crust of the earth, most all ores are subject to chemical transformation, and to transportation. Therefore the likelihood of the especially soluble uranium ores remaining unaffected by their environment for a billion plus years, or even a few years, is so remote as to be negligible.

Much new light is now being thrown on the radioactive elements by the reports published by the government of the hitherto secret war operations. These atom bomb features, however, are not the most important defects in radioactive time. We are informed how the rare uranium 235 was separated from the uranium 238. This was done by the centrifuge or "cream separator" method based on the principle that one element was heavier than the other. But in order to make this separation the elements or minerals had first to be volatilized or transformed into the gaseous state.

This would serve to reemphasize what has

[28] Stamp, L. D., Geol. Magazine, vol. 62, p. 515, 1925.
[29] Joly, J., Nature, vol. 109, 1022, p. 480.
[30] Becker, G. F., Bull. Geol. Soc. America, vol. 19, 1908, p. 134.
[31] Knopf, Adolph, Physics of the Earth, National Research Council, 1931, Bulletin 80, p. 8.
[32] Twenhofel, W. H., Principles of Sedimentation, 1939, p. 6.

already been stated, that these radioactive elements or minerals are not particularly stable. They are leached, enter into new chemical combinations, and recrystallize. Each time this occurs, the *continuity of the time calculations is upset,* and a new start must be made. Now add to these conceptions of the element, the above mentioned fact that uranium is volatilized. When this occurs in nature, of course most of the gas escapes, and time calculations are again upset. If uranium were a comparatively inert element, such as gold, there might be more basis for assuming sufficient stability to endure unaffected by its environment for sufficient time to estimate at least a small portion of supposed geologic time.

Another startling revelation came out of these same reports. When volatilized, the uranium elements or minerals were so terribly corrosive and poisonous that only gold containers would resist the corrosion—further witness, if any were needed, that radioactive minerals are very unstable. A corrosive element is one that has a powerful affinity for other elements, and such elements seek to make new chemical combinations, which naturally neutralize their value as time markers.

What chance, therefore, would there be that the exact original mass could remain unaffected for a billion years, a million, or even a short time? Mineral ores far more stable than uranium have been known to be seriously affected within the lifetime of one man.

So far we have been describing how outside environments alter the mineral, but there is a logical inference that in the case of the radio-active minerals additional internal forces would help to hasten the breakdown of the mineral crystal, and expose it to the processes of leaching. As the helium and lead replace the original uranium, they are bound to require a rearrangement of both crystal structure and space, so that we might expect a radioactive mineral to be far less stable than any *other.* Norman B. Keevil expresses this view by saying, "The crystal structure of radioactive minerals must be badly shattered by radioactive decay, for a mineral . . . will have disintegrated, liberating a large amount of energy and leaving in its place eight helium atoms and one lead atom for every uranium atom. This crystal break-up renders the mineral susceptible to alteration and selective leaching of lead and radioactive atoms and permits a partial escape of helium, especially if metamorphism takes place."[33]

Mr. Keevil mentions metamorphism as a potent cause of the loss of the products of decay, and thus vitiating the age calculations. This is a major topic in itself, but important enough to take note of briefly here. As suggested by Clarke and Rutherford, the enormous pressure and heat of metamorphism might cause a reversal of the decay process, but one thing is certain, that the crystals are melted and re-formed, and there is every opportunity for loss of much of the by-products of decay. In 1927 Spitzen showed that radium emanation is removed from radioactive minerals by flowing water.[34]

Koszy has done recent work on isotopic lead, and places the age of the earth or of the oldest sedimentary rocks at five billion years. Then he infers that, before this, the parents of our present radioactive elements had just completed a long disintegration series *from some unknow parent* to become uranium, thorium, etc.[35] The presumptive philosophical conclusion from the radioactive theory therefore leads on back toward infinity. The further back the beginnings of things on earth can be pushed, in the opinion of some, the further the Creator is excluded from their thinking.

Further proof of the instability and solubility of these minerals is evidenced by the 20,000 or more metric tons of radium believed to be in solution in the oceans. Obviously the source of most of this was the rocks on the continents, whence it was leached and carried in solution by the rivers

---

[33] Keevil, Norman B., Am. Acad. Arts and Science, Proc. 1940, p. 349.
[34] Spitzen, V., Physics of the Earth, National Research Council, 1931, Bulletin 80, p. 431.
[35] Koczy, F. F., Nature, Jan. 2, 1943, p. 24.

to the ocean (though Deluge Geology attributes much of this to the waters of that catastrophe). It simply puts too much of a strain upon scientific credulity to believe that these unstable, soluble minerals in the rocks could withstand *perfectly* the processes of erosion and leaching even for a few years, let alone several billion.

### 4. This Time-Clock Can Be Accelerated, or Can Run Backward or Forward

Clarke, Rutherford, and others early recognized the influence of changing environments on radioactive ores, to the extent that they admitted of the possibility that under certain conditions of enormous pressures and high temperatures existing within the earth, the reaction of decay might be reversed, and uranium might *integrate* from the lead and helium, and the helium found free in the rocks might be left-over material from these reactions, instead of products of decay.[36]

Their suggestions were made some years ago. Now it appears that their conceptions were not so visionary as they may have seemed at that time. Just now the first full comprehensive story is appearing in many publications giving the background of the secret governmentally sponsored research since the beginning of the war to develop atomic power. It will not be necessary in this paper to give that story, but one or two points should be noted. Uranium ore was the basis of the bomb. In the Hiroshima bomb the explosive power was generated from the rapid disintegration of the rare form of uranium 235, but to obtain material for the Nagasaki bomb, the regular uranium 238 was bombarded with neutron particles. They did not break down the uranium but the atomic core captured the neutrons and built up a new element not previously in existence with atomic weight of 239, and given No. 93 in the family of elements and named Neptunium. Thus we now see Clarke's and Rutherford's predictions fulfilled although in a slightly different way. The process has now been reversed, and an element has been created by synthesis rather than by disintegration.

This new element disintegrated into still another new element, Plutonium, with an atomic weight of 235, the same as the rare form of uranium which occurs with uranium 238 in proportion of one pound in 140. The synthetic plutonium was easier to produce in quantity and when bombarded with slow neutrons, it split and liberated enormous quantities of energy.

Thus we see that the radioactive time-clock was more like an electric clock than the old fashioned type; it could be run either forward or backward. Although in nature it is observed to be running forward it cannot be dogmatically stated that in the geologic past, under stress of catastrophic physical conditions not now obtaining, that the time-clock may not have been running in reverse. Since it has been demonstrated that such a possibility does exist, the value of radioactivity as a geological time-clock, has very largely been neutralized.

The past hundred years have seen new scientific horizons opened up with kaleidoscopic drama, but none with more dramatic suddenness than the smashing and synthesis of atoms. The close of the war has ushered in a new age scientifically, and new discoveries and uses of them in the atomic world will doubtless follow one another with breath-taking rapidity. Some scientists have long contended that mass and matter were merely inert forms of force and energy. We may have to make many new readjustments of our concepts as to the nature of created entities. Thomas Edison aptly remarked that we don't know a millionth part of the truth on any subject.

### 5. Contamination

*All workers admit that this is one of the weakest links in the whole radioactive time system.* This fault too is perhaps more vital than any recent revelations of the atom bomb. Until recently most scientists ignored contamination. They believed that all the lead found with uranium was radiogenic. They ignored the possibility that common lead might be associated with uranium too at the time of crystallization. Including com-

---

[36] Clarke, F. W., Data of Geochemistry, U. S. Geol. Bulletin 770, p. 321.

mon lead in the calculations would of course make age computations too great. Another source of contamination is primordial or fossil helium. It was formerly assumed that all helium in the mineral was a by-product of disintegration, and entered into the equation. Recent investigations have disproved that assumption. *There is much helium in the sun, but no sign of uranium, radium, or thorium has been detected.*\* There would seem to be no evidence therefore that radioactivity is now going on in the sun, therefore radioactivity of these minerals could not be called upon to explain how the sun retains its temperature in view of the fact that it is constantly losing heat by radiation. This has been a mystery to some scientists, if they would attempt to explain it on the basis of naturalism.

Much helium has been found in minerals where no supposed radioactive parent exists. Helium is found in some spring water, and in some natural gas helium is present up to as much as 2%, but no one has yet suggested the oil and gas fields as sources of Uranium. The world's greatest supply of helium gas is from locations in Texas where there are no signs of unusual amounts of radioactive elements or any of their derivatives. This is another case of the same order as the sun, and is equally destructive to the theory of radioactive time.

Horwood's very recent work in Canada has shown that the helium retentivity of different minerals varies over wide limits and that the loss of helium is pronounced in the more highly altered rocks. Horwood also admits of the possibility of contamination with magmatic helium.[37] From all these criteria it would seem that we might safely conclude that the presence of helium in a mineral is no indicator of its age.

The Handbook of Physical Constants[38] enumerates five rigid requirements which each mineral to be tested for age must meet:

(a) The mineral must be fresh and un-adulterated and show no signs of leaching.

(b) The isotopic constitution of the lead must be determined.

(c) All chemicals must be checked for lead content.

(d) All analyses must be made on the same sample.

(e) Primal radiogenic lead must be absent.

Francis Birch states in this handbook that for accuracy, the minerals must pass these preliminary requirements, but he adds, "No radioactive mineral has been found that satisfies all these requirements." This is the latest authority put out by the National Research Council and should carry some weight. According to the above statement there has as yet been no accurate measurement of geologic time by this method, and accuracy is demanded where we are asked to substitute one school of thought regarding origins for another. Astronomy as a whole can lay some claim to acceptance on the basis of proven accuracy as to astronomical motion, time, and the speed of light, especially after discarding the nebular and planetary hypotheses. Astronomical science can predict the exact day, hour, minute, and second of an eclipse a century or more in advance, but for accuracy or dependability the radioactive time-clock can make no such claim for our acceptance.

## 6. Dating Each Geological Formation Impossible by This Method

Another edition of the Bulletin of the National Research Council adds a further preliminary requirement for a mineral to be tested for age, as follows: *"The geologic age of the mineral should be known."* If the purpose of the test is to determine the age of the mineral ore or formation it might not be out of place to inquire why the age of the mineral deposit must be known in advance?[39] Is the radioactive system unable to stand on its own feet?

---

\*Thorium has recently been reported to be present in the Sun. Editor.

[37] Horwood, H. C., Journal of Geology, Jan. 1943, p. 18.

[38] Birch, Francis, Handbook of Physical Constants, National Research Council, Jan. 31, 1942, p. 274.

[39] Knopf, Adolph, Physics of the Earth, National Research Council, 1931, Bulletin 80, p. 6.

If the radioactive time-scale were merely applied vaguely to the age of the earth as a whole the difficulties might be less than by attempting to affix an age for each geological formation. Although the ages of the formations as computed by the radioactive formula are much greater than by the older methods, *they are strangely proportional.* (One naturally wonders and questions if this is because "the geologic age of the mineral should be known in advance?")

The theory is that when each separate geologic-age formation was laid down, with its index fossils, the radioactive minerals were crystallized at that time. (Incidentally, the extreme solubility of the uranium ores is taken for granted.) Let us suppose that it was an early paleozoic formation such as the Taconic, age about 500,000,000 years, according to the radio-active time table. But the earth was supposed to be of the order of two billion years. Therefore the mineral ore would at the time of the Taconic deposition show an age of 1,500,000,000 years, and in order now to show us the true age of the Taconic formation, it must have had all the radiogenic lead and helium ACCURATELY removed 500,000,000 years ago, and have made a fresh start at that time. Every time a new formation is laid down a new chemical metamorphosis must take place, according to the theory, *with absolutely NO left-overs.* This is not only an admission of the extremely unstable or soluble nature of the radioactive mineral ores, but it confronts the theory with some still more difficult problems, as follows:

(a). If the strata were laid down as clastic rock fragments broken from the parent rocks and carried by running water by traction, or by suspension, and redeposited, how did the minerals get a chance to recrystallize and *eliminate with ABSOLUTE accuracy ONLY the accumulated products of disintegration and thus re-set the time-clock?* Yet this would be required.

Many formations such as conglomerates and breccia are coarsely broken from the older parent rock formation and carried comparatively short distances before being redeposited as a younger formation. Fossils might be found in either or both of the formations. According to the old theory, a long period of time could separate the two formations, involving a radical change in geologic age, and if true, all of the formerly accumulated by-products of radioactive decay must have been removed after the conglomerate and breccia had been severed from the parent rock formation and before being laid down in the new one. But if the rock fragments were too coarsely broken to release the products of decay, how could the time-clock be reset? And yet the radioactive scientists insist that the radio-active minerals tell a story of millions of years between the times of laying down of the two formations. Since there are supposed to be some thirty-two separate age formations in the geologic column, these difficulties are multiplied about thirty-two times.

(b). If we take the other alternative and admit that these minerals were all leached and re-crystallized in absolutely pure state, they must have been carried from the parent rocks to the new formations as solutions in the waters that carried the sediments to the sea, and, according to the accepted evolutionary conception, deposited very slowly as marine strata. In such a case, how could the very soluble radioactive solutions crystallize in the sediments instead of remaining in solution in the ocean? Their present abundance in the ocean water demostrates this difficulty.

(c). Or, granted that they were crystalized out of solution, and the Taconic uplift brought the strata above sea level, what would prevent fresh surface ground waters from re-leaching the soluble minerals long before the 500,000,000 year interval had elapsed? As explained before, all soluble minerals on or near the surface within reach of percolating ground water are continually subject to leaching, transportation and redeposition, and this zone may reach a depth of ten miles.

## 7. Paleontology and Radioactive Ores

(a). It was with considerable show of triumph some years ago when radioactive workers announced that the age of the separate formations could be ascertained, thus corroborating biological evolution and the geologic ages. The case for evolution seemed to be complete, but this seeming security was short lived. Many of these time estimations were based upon radioactive ores found in intrusive dikes in the strata. These dikes are of pegmatite material, meaning large crystals. The molten magma, or granite, or quartz and felspar was forced up into and filled these fissures in the formations or granite already in place. Slow cooling of the molten dikes caused the large crystals. This would reset the radioactive time-clock. (But water and the intense heat and pressure generally caused a great deal of mineral solution, with much exchange, altering both the dike and the rock content on each side— all known as metamorphic action. If the material cut by the dike had its own radioactive ores, this metamorphic action caused by the dike would *remineralize those ores, but in varying degrees,* thus *in part* resetting the time-clock *near the dike, and introducing confusion.*)

Generally speaking, however, there could of course be no demonstrable time relation between the sedimentary formation as a whole and the dike. All that could be known is that some time after the strata were deposited, folding or some form of dynamics took place which fractured or fissured the formations. These fissures were subsequently filled with this intrusive molten material. In such a case the proof would seem to be conclusive that the *radioactive ores were younger than the fossils.*

(b). In other cases where the fossils were found in coarse conglomerate formations there is a possibility that the radioactive ores could give a false reading indicating an age greater than that when the fossils were deposited. The ores could have been crystallized in the prior, or *parent formation,* and not disturbed when coarsely broken and transported and redeposited as conglomerate with the inclusion of the fossils. (However, *in some parts* of almost every such formation, *more or less metamorphism* would introduce hopeless confusion, the same as in (a) above.)

(c) Still another possibility confronts us. As has been indicated previously, at some

time *subsequent* to the original deposition of the fossil strata with its radioactive ores, under the influence of percolating ground water the ores are generally leached and the crystals entirely or partly dissolved, some of the disintegration products removed (inaccurately of course), and the chemicals redeposited and the time-clock re-set. *Even if this could happen without discrepancies* it would give a false time reading, making the fossils appear "younger" than they really are if judged by the radioactive minerals. But, on the contrary, the fossils would in fact be *older* than the radioactive crystals. What comfort therefore can biological evolution gather from radioactivity?

(d) Viewing the fossil problem from another angle, that of speed of deposition, we will recall that Schuchert came to the conclusion that the *fossils were buried suddenly,* which accords with the view of Deluge Geology. This would of course mean that catastrophic violence eroded, transported, and deposited the sediments very swiftly and in a short space of time. There could therefore be but slight lapse of time between the deposition of one fossil formation and another.

Speed of deposition of fossils being therefore a demonstrated fact, the multi-million years eras assumed for the sedimentation, and supposedly corroborated by the radioactive time-table, must be fictitious. It is *self-evident* that the time needed to bury the fossils could not differ from the time required to deposit the sediments with their radioactive minerals in which the fossils were buried. But, while the fossils retain their identity, *dozens of causes change the ore ratios.* This line of evidence alone should suffice to throw the whole radioactive case out of court.

## 8. Radioactivity and Uniformity

There is one glaring weakness in the radioactive system of measuring geologic time that many have completely overlooked. It is the same old weakness that wrecked the sedimentary time system, *uniformity,* and it is doing the same for the radioactive time system. The best brains in this field of research have been quick to admit this, too. Referring again to an earlier statement by

Adolph Knopf, that the radioactive method involved fewer *assumptions* than the sedimentary method, we will note that he did not enumerate said assumptions. We are not left in the dark on this matter long however, for that brilliant radioactive worker, Arthur Holmes, put his finger on the sore spot when he said: "The only assumption that can reasonably be called in question is that of uniformity, *and it is involved equally in both calculations.*"[40] (Emphasis ours.) He meant both the sedimentary and radioactive calculations. Holmes had already denounced the principle of uniformity as applied to the sedimentary time system. Other authorities have agreed with him that the mirage of geological uniformity was exploded. Holmes went so far as to infer that the validity of the radioactive time method might reasonably be called in question on the same basis as had the sedimentary time system, that of supposed uniformity. That statement was made prior to the recent new developments in atom splitting. Today his statement would be a thousand times as forceful as when he made it.

We will remember that Watson Davis intimated that if present attempts at atom splitting were successful (1939), then we might have to cast aside the radioactive time method for geological time measuring. Since he wrote that, these attempts were fully successful. Davis, like Holmes, *was referring to the principle of uniformity as applied to radioactivity.* Dr. Glashler, it will be recalled, did succeed experimentally in disrupting the principle of uniformity when he succeeded in accelerating the disintegration process of Uranium. This was done in the laboratory, but both Joly and Gillette, above referred to, claimed its occurrence in nature under certain conditions.

If radioactive uniformity has thus been disrupted under more or less normal conditions, on what basis therefore could we safely assume radioactive uniformity during the catastrophic period of this earth's history that Schuchert and other leading paleontologists postulate, and which Deluge Geol-

ogy corroborates? We were formerly inclined to agree with Holmes, that the assumption of radioactive uniformity could reasonably be called in question; but according to the most recent information, radioactivity uniformity is a dead issue. Since uniformity was the foundation of radioactive time estimation, this system has now become obsolete.

### 9. Metamorphism

Here the topic of Metamorphism should logically be mentioned. Physical forces are continually at work in the crust of the earth. Nothing is fixed for long. All is in a state of flux. Diastrophism raises a range of mountains. No sooner are they established than the "Eternal Hills" begin to erode through the constant application of the elements. The mountains are worn down and the valleys are filled up.

The mineral composition of any given rock represents the adjustment to the environment in which the rock was formed. The minerals were in stable equilibrium under the conditions then prevailing. Under changed conditions they cease to be stable. As the forces of diastrophism, volcanism, and peneplanation are directed toward the crust of the earth, the minerals of the rocks become out of adjustment to their environment, and new minerals are formed. Metamorphism is the result of this tendency of the rocks to adjust themselves to their environment. The factors determining this adjustment are temperature, pressure, and composition. A change in any one of these factors causes internal changes in the mineral crystals.

Evidence is mounting that the entire crust of the earth was radically altered during a Cataclysmic convulsion of nature not many thousands of years ago. At or soon after this time probably most of the pagmalite dikes in which are found most of the radioactive samples that are tested, were intruded. The chances of finding mineral crystals undisturbed by that mighty Cataclysm would indeed seem remote.

---

40 Holmes, Arthur, Physics of the Earth, National Research Council, 1931, Bulletin 80, p. 11.

## 10. Geologic Time by Radium as a By-Product in the Disintegration of Uranium

Let us consider Radium as a step in the chain of disintegration products. Most of these links in the chain have a half-life of very short duration as compared with the half-life of Uranium which is about five billion years.

Radium has another notable parent, Thorium, whose half-life is about thirteen billion years. Furthermore, Thorium seems to be more abundant in the crust of the earth than Uranium; therefore in considering the time element we must take into account the relative proportions of thorium and uranium in the crust of the earth, and also their relative half-periods. Therefore any computations arrived at by this method are merely rough estimates, but sufficiently accurate to demonstrate the method.

The latest information would indicate that the total amount of radium in the crust of the earth amounts to some one billion tons. The total amount of Uranium plus Thorium is computed at about five quadrillion tons.

For the sake of this estimation, we will take the average half-life of Uranium plus Thorium, or about nine billion years. Therefore according to the theory, in about nine billion years from now we will have only about two and one half quadrillion tons of Uranium plus Thorium in the crust of the earth. At some stage of the disintegration process we will have radium.

But in the half period of Uranium and Thorium just past we might have expected the production of nearly five quadrillion tons of Radium. However most radio-active physicists give the earth an age of only about two billion years.

In that time we could expect the production of about one quadrillion tons of Radium. The actual estimated amount of Radium in the world is only about one billion tons. The actual length of time required to produce this one billion tons of Radium from a parent stock of five quadrillion tons of Uranium and Thorium can be easily computed:

$$\frac{5,000,000,000,000,000}{1,000,000,000} = \frac{9,000,000,000}{X}.$$

X = 1800 years, the time required to produce the present amount of Radium in the crust of the earth. Upon the hypothesis of a possible earth-age of about 6,000 years, there could have been produced about three and one half billion tons of radium. However, the loss in Radium could be explained by the disintegration of the Radium itself into its by-products, during the approximately six thousand years of earth history.

## 11. The Age of the Sun Disagrees with Radioactive Time Estimates

There is one school of thought, possibly related to the group known as the proponents of Pre-Adamic Time, who maintain that the actual age of the matter of which the earth was created at the beginning of Creation Week, some six thousand years ago, was brought into existence simultaneously with all other matter in the universe, generally computed by radioactive time as about two billion years ago, or possibly a little less.

It is interesting to note in this connection that Sir James Jeans has done a great deal of recent research work with the mass spectroscope, studying the light from the sun. He has computed the age of the sun as about seven trillion years, thus placing the age of the sun about four thousand times as great as even the radioactive scientists compute the age of the earth.

It would appear therefore, if the conclusions of Sir James Jeans mean anything at all, that the school of thought referred to above, is proceeding along the wrong line.

## 12. Extinct Elements Discovered?

As predicted, the arrival of the atomic bomb inaugurated a new day for scientific research. Already, this country is offering the world the medical, healing aspects of atomic discovery. The new, synthetic element, Neptunium, was assigned a place in the periodic system of elements, and it is now claimed that the secret is out as to why that element was missing or extinct since it fitted so perfectly into the empty pigeon-hole assigned to it. The reason given for Neptunium having become extinct was that it had a comparatively short half-life, about two million years, as against the assumed age of the earth of two billion. Therefore no trace was left.

Probably it is too early to get the full significance of this problem; more discoveries may be made that will completely change the whole picture, but two or three observations might not be out of order:

(1). The synthetic production of an element that seems to fit into an empty space in the periodic table does not necessarily prove the case for the previous existence of an element, any more than an artist's creation of a man-ape would prove the missing link.

(2). If this "extinct" element had a half-life of two million years, according to the half-life theory, some small remnant at least should still be in existence. The only Neptunium in existence so far as known is the laboratory synthetic product.

(3). If such an extinct element ever did exist, possibly its extinction could well have the same explanation as extinct animal species, namely the Deluge. There appears now to be ample evidence that conditions of metamorphism greatly accelerated the disintegration of some radioactive elements.

### General Summary of Attempts to Measure the Age of the Earth

Let us recall, therefore, that for almost all of recorded history man's principal clue to the age of the earth was taken from the pages of Sacred History, the Genesis account, a matter of a few thousand years. Within the last one hundred and fifty years the idea gained force that the Genesis account was unscientific, and Creationism was replaced with biological evolution, suggesting millions of years.

Lord Kelvin's astronomical computations of from 20 to 40 million years was the first supposedly scientific expression of the age of the earth. Later scientific discoveries caused an abandonment of this method. Other investigators claimed about 100,000,000 years as the age of the earth based on the amount of sodium in the oceans and the rate of annual addition of sodium to the seas by the streams. This was about the amount of time the evolutionists were hoping for, but further studies proved that the principle of uniformity could not apply in this method, and other unproved assumptions made this system untenable.

A more elaborate and promising system of age computation was the measurement of the sum total of all rock strata divided by the annual rate of deposition. At first this method agreed very closely with the sodium method, and the case for evolutionary science seemed established; however, as in the case with sodium, further study soon disclosed that "a little knowledge is a dangerous thing," and often leads to wrong conclusions. Leading geologists finally agreed that there was no such thing as an average rate for sedimentation. The principle of sedimentary uniformity had to be discarded, which simply meant that sedimentation was valueless as an age marker.

Recently, the new science of radioactivity has given estimates of the age of the earth of the order of 1,600,000,000 years, so much greater than former measurements that it practically destroyed or made obsolete all of the older, shorter estimates. Now Holmes has raised the estimate to three billion years. There have been attempts to harmonize all the age calculations by stretching the shorter ones to match the very much longer radioactive ones, but such efforts were wasted in a lost cause. When radioactive time estimates were compared with purely geological time estimates, there was a general abandonment of the latter method, because it had been compromised beyond scientific respectability.

Radioactivity seemed to be just what the doctor ordered to put new life into the project of adding years to the age of the earth, and most scientists were quick to jump onto the radioactive band-wagon, at which time they were dogmatic in their statements that the rate of radioactive disintegration was as unchangeable as the speed of light. This cornerstone of their faith was soon undermined however in the development of the atom bomb, when radioactive minerals were made to disintegrate almost instantaneously. It was demonstrated that the disintegration process could be reversed and integration or synthesis take place. The principle of uniformity was as inapplicable to the radioactive method as to the sedimentary method. It had been demonstrated that the radioactive time-clock could run backward. The cornerstone of this method has been undermined.

But long before the atom bomb, hurdle after hurdle, and obstacle after obstacle had been presenting themselves *that were still more damaging to the system.* After all, *the failure of the radioactive time theory does not depend on the atom bomb features.* Contamination is one of the most serious. Accuracy in computations can be expected only when all the lead and helium present are radiogenic. All workers agree that no common lead or helium could be present, *but they also admit that no such uncontaminated radioactive ore has ever been found.* Therefore no radioactive calculation can be accurate.

Almost as serious an obstacle to the radioactive time-system is the marked chemical instability of all radioactive ores. They are so susceptible to leaching, removal, loss, and recrystallization of remnants or "what have you?" that the probability of these ores remaining stabilized long enough to measure geologic time as estimated by evolutionary science approaches zero. The very process of radioactivity causes a disruption of the mineral crystal from within, and opens it up to the processes of erosion by solution from without even faster than other minerals. Mineralogically, they are all too fickle to serve as time markers.

These weaknesses perhaps account in some measure at least for the amazing discrepancies, amounting in some cases to billions of years between the age estimates of different samples of the same locality and formation. And if these discrepancies exist in estimates of the same formation, what dependance if any could be placed on time calculations designed to show age differences between one formation and another, and to set the age relations of many individual geological formations?

The fossils themselves disprove these great age differences between formations. Leading historical geologists admit that the fossils had to be buried suddenly to be preserved

at all, and the rapidity of erosion and deposition would in itself destroy the radioactive time-table, as well as the principle of uniformity upon which it is based.

A state of catastrophe of the surface of the earth to cause this quick process of erosion and subsequent deposition of the sediments and their enclosed fossils seems a foregone conclusion. It is probable that unprecedented environmental factors also at the same time, such as intense heat and pressure, caused such sudden, unpredictable changes in the radioactive elements that present attempts to interpret them in terms of time only lead to misleading results. As leading radioactive workers admit, all radioactive time calculations are based on the principle of uniformity, which principle was non-operative, at least during the time of the Deluge, which factor most radioactive workers ignore. An admission of the Deluge, thus negates the principle of uniformity, which in turn knocks the foundation out from under all sedimentary and radioactive calculations. The net result: Total bankruptcy for all earth-age estimates.

### Conclusion

Time has become the crux of belief and of unbelief. The astronomical, chemical, geological, and physical sciences have joined hands with biology in the attempt to provide sufficient time for the evolutionary hypothesis, as well as to throw a cloud of doubt over much of the early history of this world as outlined in the book of Genesis, and to attack the integrity of Creation Week.

All of these methods have proved to be hopelessly inadequate. There would seem to be no logical reason, therefore, to accept the radioactive time-scale, or any of the others for that matter, in preference to the chronology of Sacred History. The two alternatives obviously are diametrically opposed and mutually exclusive.

Therefore, with the way cleared of all pseudo-scientific time speculations, and the natural sciences unshackled from all such dead weights, it may well be that the unimpeded scientific research will be directed more toward the fostering and development of TRUE SCIENCE.

# *The Forum*

## FOR THE CORRELATION OF SCIENCE AND THE BIBLE
**VOLUME II**          **1947-48**

The articles in the second volume of THE FORUM are a continuation of the subject which was started in the first volume, namely "the Genesis Record of Creation." Letters from people all over the world have been received by the editors of THE FORUM, expressing their interest in and appreciation of the articles which were published in the first volume. Some have expressed their disappointment in the position taken by one writer or another, and have criticized the publication of some of the material, because the conclusions of the author were out of harmony with their personal viewpoints. The name of this magazine, THE FORUM, indicates that in its very nature it must contain matter which is open to discussion, matter which is controversial, on which there is as yet no unanimity of opinion. Not all the subject matter in either volume one or two is of this nature, but in practically every article there are one or more issues raised on which the opinion of many of the readers will vary, as it does evidently among the authors who have contributed the various articles to THE FORUM. Even among the editors of THE FORUM there is a difference of opinion regarding some of the points at issue, and there are even some suggestions or theories in these articles which all the editors very definitely question, but which they considered worthwhile to retain in the particular paper for the sake of completeness and discussion. The editors hope that in such a spirit all readers will approach the articles of this and the previous volume.

The Editors

# GOD BEFORE PRIMARY TIME *

### By John Lowell Butler

### Three Major Divisions of Time

As we have seen in the previous discussion of evidence, the term *secondary time* applies to all the time which follows God's secondary creations: and the length of secondary time varies for any given planet, sun, or satellite, depending on how long ago God chose to exercise on them his creative skill and power in a secondary manner. Secondary time for the Earth, the Moon, and the Sun can be measured by only a few thousand years; but for some worlds and suns their secondary time can be measured by millions of years, or possibly by many billions or trillions or more years.

The term *primary time* applies to all the astronomical and chemical time before God's many secondary creations, and likewise varies for many of the astronomical bodies, and reaches back to God's great Primary Creation of all the elements and all the major astronomical bodies and systems simultaneously.

Just as each of the many secondary creations was a series of orderly and logical events extending over a brief week of time, so it may be that the great Primary Creation was also a series of orderly and logical events on a grander scale extending over some longer appropriate period of time. Just what event would mark the close of the universal week of the Primary Creation is not clearly evident to us as yet. Perhaps the beginning of that week was more important than its close, since all natural time began at the beginning of the Primary Creation.

And, just as the Earth's secondary creation has been followed by some limited modifications of its living "kinds," and its climatic environments and geography, so likewise the great Primary Creaton may have been followed by some subsequent and limited modifications of the rocks, the stars, and the astronomical systems.

When primary time is measured from the Earth it reaches back into astronomical and chemical history many millions or billions of years: and even then we are not certain that we have measured all of the time that has been spun off this side of the Primary Creation. It makes no difference how long primary time has been for the Earth and our local family of astronomical bodies. If we understand the inspired Scriptures correctly, the stars were created to endure throughout an endless eternity yet to come! It makes no difference how long ago the great Primary Creation occurred; for when it occurred our great Creator was there supervising it all. And if we find ourselves a long way down the stream of a natural eternity; well, that gives us greater confidence in a very great future ahead, with no ending.

Back of the beginning of the present order of the stars and the elements, that is, before primary time, there was an eternity which we can never measure. Three names have been suggested for all the time prior to primary time, namely: *primary eternity,* or pre-Genesis time, or *tempus Dei* (that is, God's time).

The only hint in the book of Genesis of the existence of an eternity before The Beginning of the present order of the stars and the elements is found in the opening sentence, "In The Beginning God created the [astronomical] heaven and the Earth."— Genesis 1:1. In other words, God was in existence before the stars and the Earth were created as astronomical units: and *He was at that time great enough to make all of them!*

Subsequent writers of the Bible have meditated upon this condensed hint in Genesis and have written many inspired and expanding statements which reveal more of the actual greatness of the Creator of the elements and the stars long before they were brought into existence.

Also in the great realms of astronomy and in the wonderful minute perfection of the various chemical elements there exists an abundance of evidence which reveals to the open minds of sincere scientists the existence of a great Inventor who had the present order of the Universe *well planned before it was brought into existence.*

The three major divisions of time are, therefore, characterized by three major differences in which time is only incidental. (1) First in order was the planning or blueprinting of the Universe structurally and historically. This was done by the Trinity during the primary eternity, before primary time began. (2) Next in order was the actual construction or creation of all the elements and all the major astronomical bodies and systems simultaneously throughout the Universe, according to the perfected plan. This was the Primary Creation of the Universe, and it provided means for systematically measuring and recording time. Primary time began with the Primary Creation of the Universe. (3) And later it was proper to transform planets into suitable abodes for myriads of living things, and to create many kinds of life on them. This work was a secondary kind of creative work, which brought no new elements into existence; but it required definite previous planning and intelligently directed supernatural power. It was not necessary that the secondary creative work be performed simultaneously on all the planets and satellites and their nearby suns. This could be whenever a planet or sun reached a certain more desirable stage of natural curing, or whenever the Creator deliberately chose to perform more secondary creative work on them. Secondary time began at different times for the many inhabited worlds. It began for the Earth, Moon, and Sun only a few thousand years ago.

## Intelligently Directed Power

When we take time to consider thoughtfully the magnitude of the Primary Creation of all the elements and all the stars in the Universe we are amazed at *the unmeasurable amount of power which was in action then,* even if the Primary Creation was a series of orderly and logical events extending over some appropriate period of time, just as the secondary creations were during subsequent weeks of time.

And when we consider more thoughtfully

*the results* of that almighty creative force in the realms of chemistry, physics, and astronomy, we are filled with unlimited gratitude by realizing that *this prodigious amount of energy was definitely under control,* and that *it was directed* into the accomplishment of results which have been *highly beneficial* in almost numberless ways to all subsequent sciences, industries, and civilizations.

It is now evident that the Primary Creation had a Cause which was something more than the sum total of all the energy in the Universe. That Cause must have included the supreme qualities of intellectual understanding, wisdom, *and forethought.* Aided today by our exact sciences of astronomy, chemistry, and physics, in which remarkable research work is being constantly done, we are able to see more and more clearly the great overwhelming reality of this truth of the Primary Creation.

Throughout human history, more or less, there have been individuals who have looked upon the results of God's Primary and Secondary Creations thoughtfully and compared them, on the one hand, with the results of haphazard chance, or forces that expand themselves without being directed by some intellectual forces or minds; and, on the other hand, they have compared those results with the results of intellectually directed forces. The results of the intellectually directed forces are more useful, more beautiful, and more efficient, than those which are not thus directed. Finding, therefore, many useful and beautiful and efficient things in the Earth and in the starry heavens beyond its horizons, it has been quite natural for those people with honest minds and sincere affections to recognize in these things of nature *evidences of an intellect which designed them,* even though subsequent conditions may have altered them somewhat. If these examples were few in number, or if they were of such a quality that they revealed a low inventive intelligence, they would excite no admiration. But since the examples are very many in astronomy, in chemistry, and in physics, in biology, and in geology, showing that they were all produced by great forces that were directed by a coordinating and designing mind of superior intelligence, it has been natural and very proper for honest men and women to recognize the existence in the Universe of *a supreme Creator who is both omniscient and almighty.*

On the other hand, there are, of course, people who *do not want to see* anyone who is actually that great; nor do they want to admit the possibility of someone somewhere in the Universe who knows and understands everything. This class of self-centered, bigoted, geocentric people prefer an evolution which exalts *our* wretched civilization as the best that is to be found on any planet! They *like* to begin with a dark past in their thinking, proceed along an uncertain trail of warring animal ancestors, reach the caves of human morons or poor early pioneers, then excuse the greed and injustice and killing of their own generation as necessary evils in human progress, and finally end their thinking in a dark uncertain future and an eternal annihilation. If there is any gain in such a dark philosophy, it certainly is temporary.

Then about midway between these two groups of people are others, especially our compromising modernists, who *try to give us the impression that the God of the Bible was not very great anciently.*

For instance, they like to begin their talk about Him as though He were merely a storm God on a desert mountain: and they like to make it appear that there was a time when He was only a God of the Ark and tabernacle, and was only a tribal war God of the Hebrews. Then they like to proceed to an enlarged view of Him as the God of all the promised land of Palestine, who then cared only for his chosen people: and later as a God of the sky, who was interested in righteousness; and, because these are not limited to Palestine, they then like to place emphasis on the writings of those prophets which saw God as the God of the whole Earth, everywhere accessible to prayer and a saviour of all mankind. And finally they prefer to emphasize the fact that He is one universal God who needs no temple or altar, a fatherly God who wants all people to live as though they really believed He existed, a Christ-like God, and the God of a worldwide kingdom of righteousness and peace.

(See: Harry Emerson Fosdick, "A Guide to Understanding the Bible," pages 1-55; 1938.)

Right here it should be said that regardless of numerous examples of human ignorance which can be cited from the pages of history, *there never has been a time when the God of the Bible was no greater than man's comprehension of Him.* The fact is that regardless of the progress of human knowledge and experience and man's ability to appreciate more of the many qualities of the Supreme Creators of the Universe, the one great God who was paramount in Old Testament times was far greater in reality, character, and plans for His creatures than people of that time realized. Even today we cannot limit His actual greatness to the combined intelligence of our theologions and scientists. We are still learning more of His greatness and probably always shall. Nevertheless, even though certain periods of human history required emphasis of certain phases of God's character, power, and plans, He has been through all these centuries and millenniums as great as He is today, as great as He was during Creation Week, and as great as He was even before the great Primary Creation of all the elements and all the stars.

## More Than One God

In reading the Genesis account of Creation Week it is interesting to notice that more than one God had something to say about what was created at that time. This is clearly evident in the following quotation: "And God said, Let *us* make man in *our* image, after *our* likeness. . . . So God created man in *his own* image."—Genesis 1:26, 27. This quotation reveals the fact that one God of at least two was the active one during Creation Week, and that He looked just like His partner. When one person is made to look like two previous individuals, those two must have been very similar. In subsequent Scriptures this early revelation is magnified and made plainer.

The gospel according to St. John begins by saying, "In the beginning was the Word, and *the Word was with God,* and *the Word was God.* The same was in the beginning *with* God. All things were made by him; and without him was not any thing made that was made. In him was life; and the life was the light of men. . . . He was in the world, and the world was made by him, and the world knew him not. . . . And the Word was made flesh, and dwelt among us, (and we beheld his glory, the glory as of the only begotten of the Father), full of grace and truth."—John 1:1-14. This is a clear picture of at least two Gods who were in existence at the time of "The Beginning" of all created things. Both cooperated to such an extent that one of these Gods is referred to as the Word of the other. And John refers to them as *the Father and the Son.* "No man hath seen God [the Father] at any time; the only begotten son [Jesus Christ, v. 17], which is in the bosom of the Father, he hath declared him."—John 1:18.

In his letter to the Colossians, written about A.D. 64 or about forty years before John wrote his version of the gospel, Paul wrote more at length concerning the everlasting gospel in the following words:

"For this cause we also, since the day we heard it, do not cease to pray for you, and to desire that ye might be filled with the knowledge of his will in all wisdom and spiritual understanding; that ye might walk worthy of the Lord unto all pleasing, being fruitful in every good work, and *increasing in the knowledge of God;* strengthened with all might, according to his glorious power, unto all patience and longsuffering with joyfulness; *giving thanks unto the Father,* which hath made us meet to be partakers of the inheritance of the saints in light: who hath delivered us from the power of darkness, and *hath translated us into the kingdom of his dear Son:* in whom we have redemption through his blood, even the forgiveness of sins: *who is the image of the invisible God,* the firstborn of every creature: for *by him were all things created, that are in heaven, and that are in Earth,* visible and invisible, whether they be thrones, or dominions, or principalities, or powers: *all things were created by him, and for him:* and *he is before all things,* and by him all things consist.

'And he is the head of the body, the church: who is the beginning, the firstborn

from the dead; *that in all things he might have the preeminence.* For it pleased the *Father that in him should all fulness dwell;* and, having made peace through the blood of his cross, *by him to reconcile all things unto himself,* by him, I say, *whether they be things in Earth, or things in heaven."*—Colossians 1:9-20.

This shows that Paul recognized the existence of two supreme Gods before primary time began, before the Primary Creation, and who were related to each other as closely as father and son, and who cooperated perfectly with each other in all the creative work, and later in the redemption of sinners in our world, and in settling thereby some much larger problem which involved their accepted supremacy over the other inhabited worlds, wherein are organized governments, or "dominions" with "thrones," etc. These two supreme Gods are referred to elsewhere also as God the Father and God the Son. (Compare, John 1:1, 14, 17, 18; 8:14, 23, 42, 58; 10:29, 30; 17:5, 24; Hebrews 1:1-14; Revelation 1:1, 2, 5, 6, 8, 11; etc.)

When Jesus said, "I and my Father are one" (John 10:30), he evidently referred to their character and to their complete cooperation in all things. They were one in their plans for the Universe, they acted as one being in all their activities, and both upheld the same principles of life. They were united in all their plans and endeavors. That may be why in Old Testament times and even in our time they have been often referred to as "one" God. But in reality there were at least two supreme Gods throughout secondary time and throughout the long ages of primary time and even before that during the eons of primary eternity.

Near the close of his redemptive work on our world the Son of God, Jesus, comprehended his former complete equality with God the Father, when he said, "I have glorified thee on the Earth: I have finished the work which thou gavest me to do. And now, O Father, glorify thou me with thine own self with *the glory which I had with thee before the world was.*

"I have manifested thy name unto the men which thou gavest me out of the world: thine they were, and thou gavest them me;

and they have kept thy word. . . . Sanctify them through thy truth: thy word is truth. . . . Neither pray I for these alone, but for them also which shall believe on me through their word; *that they all may be one;* as thou, Father, art in me, and I in thee, that they also may be *one in us"* (Read also, Eph. 2:11-22; 4:1-7, 11-16; 1 Cor. 12: 4-20): "that the world may believe that thou hast sent me. And *the glory which thou gavest me I have given them; that they may be one, even as we are one:* I in them, and thou in me, that they may be made perfect in one. . . . thou hast loved them as thou hast loved me.

"Father, I will that they also, whom thou hast given me, be with me where I am; that they may behold my glory, which thou hast given me: for *thou lovedst me before the foundation of the world."*—John 17:4-24.

### Perfect Before Primary Time

When Jesus said, "The glory which thou gavest me I have given them," he must have referred to the glory of a righteous character. And Jesus also declared that he had this glory "before the world was." At that time, before the beginning of primary time, love was one of the attributes of the Father and the Son. Jesus said of his heavenly Father, "thou lovedst me *before* the foundation of the world." The chemical and astronomical foundation of the world was brought into existence during the Primary Creation. But *before* that great and very ancient event there were two supreme Gods who possessed perfect characters and loved each other. They were not enemies battling each other for the supremacy of absolute power; but they were the closest of friends, working together in their plans and deeds.

In his much honored sermon on the mountain, that is, given from a mountain side, Jesus said, "Ye have heard that it hath been said, Thou shalt love thy neighbor and hate thine enemy. But I say unto you, Love your enemies, bless them that curse you, do good to them that hate you, and pray for them which despitefully use you and persecute you; *that ye may be the children of your Father which is in heaven:* for he maketh his sun to rise on the evil and on the good, and sendeth rain on the just and on the unjust.

For if ye love them which love you, what reward have ye? do not even the publicans the same? And if ye salute your brethren only, what do ye more than others? do not even the publicans so? Be ye therefore perfect, even as *your Father which is in heaven is perfect."*—Matthew 5:43-48. (Compare Deuteronomy 10:12-19; Hebrews 13:21)

The psalmist wrote, "For as the heaven is high above the Earth, *so great is his mercy* toward them that fear him. As far as the east is from the west, so far hath he removed our transgressions from us. Like as a father pitieth his children, so the Lord pitieth them that fear him. For he knoweth our frame; he remembereth that we are dust. . . . But *the mercy of the Lord is from everlasting to everlasting* upon them that fear him, and *his righteousness* unto children's children; to such as keep his covenant, and to those that remember his commandments to do them. The Lord hath prepared his throne in the heavens: and his kingdom ruleth over all."—Psalm 103:11-19.

Of the perfection of God, other writers said, "As for God, *his way is perfect".*—2 Samuel 22:31. *"The law of the Lord is perfect,"*—Psalm 19:7. *"His work is perfect:* for all his ways are judgment: *a God of truth* and without iniquity, *just and right is he."*—Deuteronomy 32:4.

Because the supreme Father and Son are perfect in character, perfect in their ways of doing things, perfect in their plans and work, and perfect in their appropriate laws for the material and intellectual Universe, they cannot improve; they are at the top of all excellent attainments, of every science. Therefore we read in both the Old and New Testaments of the Bible the following statements: *"I am the Lord, I change not;* therefore ye sons of Jacob are not consumed."—Malachi 3:6. *"Jesus Christ the same yesterday, and today, and for ever."*—Hebrews 13:8. "Every good gift and every perfect gift is from above, coming down from *the Father* of lights, *with whom can be no variation,* neither shadow that is cast by turning."—James 1:17, American Standard Version. This does not mean, however, that the Father and the Son do not adapt their plans and instruction to man's changing needs as the human race grows from its infancy to a responsible world-wide civilization. No perfect father would talk to an infant or child in the same way that he talks to a senior in a university. This adaptation is evidence of perfection of understanding of each situation. And yet the character and all the abilities of the father are not altered by his wise handling of each different situation. And his larger objectives may be unaltered. (Compare, Jer. 17:10; 2 Cor. 12:8-11; Matt. 25: 14-30; 2 Sam. 22:21; Matt. 9:29; Rom. 2:1-11; Isa. 59:1-21; Matt. 16:27; etc.)

In this connection we should read again the first chapter of Paul's epistle to the Hebrews. In this chapter we find the following excellent summary statements: "God, who at sundry times and in divers manners spake in time past unto the fathers by the prophets, hath in these last days spoken unto us by his Son, whom he hath appointed heir of all things, by whom also he made the worlds; who being the brightness of his glory, and the express image of his person, and upholding all things by the word of his power, when he had by himself purged our sins, sat down on the right hand of the Majesty on high; being made so much better than the angels, as he hath by inheritance obtained a more excellent name than they. . . . Unto the Son he saith, Thy throne, O God, is for ever and ever: a sceptre of *righteousness* is the sceptre of thy kingdom. *Thou hast loved righteousness and hated iniquity;* therefore God, even thy God hath anointed thee with the oil of gladness above thy fellows.

"And thou, Lord, in the beginning hast laid the foundation of the Earth; and the heavens are the works of thine hands: they shall perish; but thou remainest; and they all shall wax old as doth a garment; and as a vesture shalt thou fold them up, and they shall be changed: *but thou are the same* and thy years shall not fail."—Hebrews 1:1-4, 8-12. (Compare, Psalm 102:24-27)

## From the Days of Eternity

In the book of Micah is found a remarkable prophecy of the Messiah, which proves that He was to be one of the two supreme Gods who lived before the Primary Crea-tion, and that he was to be born in Bethlehem, a small town in the tribe of Judah in the land of Palestine. This prophecy said, "But thou, Bethlehem Ephratah, though thou be little among the thousands of Judah, yet out of thee shall he come forth unto me that is to be ruler in Israel; whose goings forth have been from of old, from everlasting (or "the days of eternity")."—Micah 5:2, margin. (Compare, Hab. 1:12)

The prophet Isaiah used somewhat similar words when he said, "For thus saith *the high and lofty One that inhabiteth eternity,* whose name is Holy; I dwell in the high and holy place, with him also that is of a contrite and humble spirit, to revive the spirit of the humble, and to revive the heart of the contrite ones."—Isaiah 57:15.

From the pen of Jeremiah we have the following statements: "But the Lord is the true God (or "the God of truth"), he is the living God, and an everlasting king (or "a king of eternity"): at his wrath the Earth shall tremble, and the nations shall not be able to abide his indignation. Thus shall ye say unto them, The gods that have not made the heavens and the Earth, even they shall perish from the Earth, and from under these heavens. He hath made the Earth by his power, he hath established the world by his wisdom, and hath stretched out the heavens by his discretion."—Jeremiah 10:10-12, margin.

In one of the Psalms that is attributed to Moses we read: "Lord, thou hast been our dwelling place in all generations. *Before* the mountains were brought forth, or ever thou hadst formed the Earth and the world, *even from everlasting to everlasting, thou art God.* . . . For a thousand years in thy sight are but as yesterday when it is past, and as a watch in the night. . . . So teach us to number our days that we may apply our hearts unto wisdom."—Psalm 90: 1-4, 12. And in another Psalm we read, "Thy throne is established of old: thou art from everlasting."—Psalm 93: 2. In the book of Deuteronomy Moses wrote, *"The eternal God* is thy refuge, and underneath are the everlasting arms."—Deuteronomy 33:27. (Compare, Gen. 21:33; Isa. 40:28; Rom. 16:26)

In writing to the Romans, Paul said, "The

invisible things of Him from the creation of the world are clearly seen, being understood by the things that are made, even *his eternal power and Godhead;* so that they are without excuse." And then he continued, "Because that, when they knew God, they glorified him not as God, neither were thankful; but became vain in their imaginations, and their foolish heart was darkened. Professing themselves to be wise, they became fools. . . . Who changed the truth of God into a lie, and worshipped and served the creature more than the Creator."—Romans 1:20-22, 25.

The Psalmist declared, "How excellent is thy loving-kindness, O God! . . . For *with thee is the fountain of life:* in thy light shall we see light."—Psalm 36:7, 9. And a New Testament writer added, "Who is the blessed and only Potentate, the King of kings, and Lord of lords: *who only hath immortality,* dwelling in the light which no man can approach unto; whom no man hath seen, nor can see: to whom be honour and power everlasting."—1 Timothy 6:15, 16.

When the Father and the San worked together in planning and making the Universe they were assisted by *"the eternal Spirit."* (Compare, Hebrews 9:14, 8; Psalm 104:30; Genesis 1:2). There still remains much mystery about this third person of the God-head. Paul mentioned "the mind of the Spirit," (Romans 8:27); the Psalmist said, "Whither shall I go from thy Spirit?" (Psalm 139:7-12), indicating that He is omnipresent, or always present everywhere: and many writers have said more about Him. (Isa. 34:16; Jn. 15:26; Eph. 3:16; 2:22; 1:13; 1 Cor. 12:4-14; 2 Thess. 2:8; Rev. 11: 11; 22:17; etc.)

Perhaps the best illustration which can be used to show the intimate relationship between these three eternal supreme Beings is that of a builder who supplies the materials, a contractor who helps make the blueprints

and supervises the construction, and the workmen who do the actual work of construction: these may represent the Father, the Son, and the Holy Spirit, respectively. (See also John 14:28)

## What Was Done During Primary Eternity?

In view of the fact that God the Father, with the help of his Son and the Holy Spirit, performed so much work during the Primary Creation of all the elements and all the stars: and in view of the fact that all three have been very busy throughout the long ensuing ages of primary time and the few thousand years of the Earth's secondary history, it is absolutely unthinkable that *before* primary time began they said nothing and did nothing and were as inactive as three stone idols. Primary eternity could have been much longer than primary time: in fact, it seems unorthodox to speak of it as having any beginning. What, then, was done during that time?

Has divine inspiration given us any hints about what was done by the Trinity during the eons of primary eternity?

Yes, it has. The information may be meager; but it is like a window opened into the great council chamber of the supreme Trinity of the Universe at the time that the blueprints and plans for our present Universe were being formed. What preceded that time we are not told: we can only guess and conjecture and surmise.

The following quotation from the Bible is indeed remarkable. *"I wisdom,* dwell with prudence, and find out knowledge of witty inventions. . . . I lead in the way of righteousness, in the midst of the paths of judgment: that I may cause those that love me to inherit substance; and that I may fill their treasuries.

563

*"The Lord possessed me in the beginning of his way, before his works of old. I was set up from everlasting,* from the beginning, *before* the Earth was. When there were no depths, I was brought forth: when there were no fountains abounding with water: *before* the mountains were settled, *before* the hills was I brought forth: while as yet he had not made the Earth, nor the fields, nor the beginning of the dust of the world: *when he prepared the heavens I was there:* when he set a compass upon the face of the depth: when he established the clouds above: when he strengthened the fountains of the deep: when he gave to the sea his decree, that the waters should not pass his commandment: *when he appointed the foundations of the Earth: then I was by him, as one brought up with him: and I was daily his delight,* rejoicing always before him; rejoicing in the habitable part of his Earth; and my delights were with the sons of men."—Proverbs 8:12, 20-31. (Authorized and Revised Versions)

From the following quotation can be gleaned some idea of the perfection of the eternal Holy Spirit. It was prophesied that when the Son would come to live on the Earth as a human being, to show us more fully the way of eternal life and to redeem us from sin, that *"the Spirit of the Lord shall rest upon him, the spirit of wisdom* and understanding, *the spirit of counsel* and might, the spirit of knowledge and of the fear of the Lord; and shall make him of quick understanding in the fear of the Lord: and he shall not judge after the sight of his eyes, neither reprove after the hearing of his ears: but with righteousness shall he judge the poor, and reprove with equity for the meek of the Earth: and he shall smite the Earth with the rod of his mouth, and with the breath of his lips shall he slay the wicked. And righteousness shall be the girdle of his loins, and faithfulness the girdle of his reins."—Isaiah 11:1-5. Keeping in mind the previous quotation from Proverbs we can conclude that the above descriptions set forth some of the chief characteristics of both the Holy Spirit and the Son of God during not only the years of Jesus' life on the Earth but also before that, even before the beginning of primary time. (Read also, Galatians 5:22, 23 and Ephesians 5:9) It should be noticed that the Spirit of the Lord is a "spirit of counsel", as well as a spirit of wisdom and knowledge, etc. Evidently, then, the Father, the Son, and the Holy Spirit talk things over in council.

From the pen of Isaiah we have this interesting series of questions: *"Who hath directed the Spirit of the Lord,* or being His counsellor hath taught *Him? With whom took He counsel, and who instructed Him,* and taught *Him* in the path of judgment, and taught *Him* knowledge, and shewed to *Him* the way of understanding?—Isaiah 40: 13, 14. Perhaps these questions of the prophet have remained unanswered for a long time. Most certainly the Spirit of the Lord did not seek counsel and instruction from the nations of the Earth, for the next verse proceeds to say, "Behold, the nations are as a drop of a bucket, and are counted as the small dust of the balance." (v. 15). By contrast the implication is that the Spirit of the Lord did sit in counsel with the Lord himself and with his Son, and that He received instruction from them as to what to do and when and where to do it. And the quotation from Proverbs shows that this was also done before the beginning of primary time, during the eons of primary eternity.

Then the prophet Isaiah proceeds to put another great question, "To whom then will ye liken God? or what likeness will ye compare unto him?" And then he reminds us of his great astronomical works, which may very fittingly represent his work throughout the Universe. "It is he that . . . stretcheth out the heavens as a curtain, and spreadeth them out as a tent to dwell in: . . . To whom then will ye liken me, or shall I be equal? saith the Holy One. Lift up your eyes on high, and behold who hath created these things, that bringeth out their host by number: he calleth them all by names by the greatness of his might, for that he is strong in power; not one faileth. . . . Hast thou not known? hast thou not heard, that *the everlasting God, the Lord, the Creator* of the ends of the Earth, fainteth not, neither is weary? there is no searching of his understanding."—Isaiah 40: 18-28.

Indeed, it is very difficult to find any illustration to which we can liken God. However, regardless of the magnitude of his astronomical work at the time of the great Primary Creation, to which the prophet refers, we can very fittingly liken the Father to a mighty king or ruler who decided to erect a wonderful city and domain, which would be appropriate for himself, his family, his friends, and his servants; and who had the assistance of the best informed and experienced contractor, and the help of the best skilled craftsmen. God the Father had the cooperating help of God the Son and God the Holy Spirit in planning and creating our present wonderful Universe. And, of course, all the actual construction of the Universe was preceded by many and prolonged discussions of all the details that would be involved and the purposes for which every part was planned.*

---

* *Notice:* The two articles entitled "God's Primary and Secondary Creations" and "God Before Primary Time," which have appeared in THE FORUM, form a part of a book entitled "God's Primary and Secondary Creations" by J. L. Butler which will shortly appear. The readers who are interested in this larger work are advised to write directly to the author at Route 2, Box 110-A, Troutdale, Oregon.

# THE INTEGRITY OF CREATION WEEK

By J. F. Huenergardt

## The Beginning of Creation Week

"In the beginning God created the heaven and the earth."[1]

This opening sentence tells the story primarily of the Creation of our globe and its solar system. We are informed that *with* this first act of Creation, time, apart from eternity, began for our planet, and that this Creation which began "in the beginning" on the first day, was completed on the sixth day and pronounced "very good". Contrast the labored formula of the scientists, contrast the writings of the poets, contrast the meaningless cosmogonies of the ancients and the foolish mythologies of the heathen, and the uniqueness of this Divine account of Creation will be very evident.

The Scriptural account of Creation bears in some respects a close resemblance to the heathen cosmogonies. But as soon as we begin to examine them, we find great and essential differences. The Bible alone gives us the pure theistic conception of God, as the absolute Being, the self-existent Creator. The heathen traditions all contain some radically wrong and unseemly conceptions of God and of His relation to the world. Anamistic, pantheistic, or dualistic elements are present in almost all of them. Generally the starting-point of Creation is the pre-existing chaos, out of which all things came. The gods themselves are created. Only this account of Genesis puts first the self-existent God. The universe is due to his fiat. There is no pre-existent material and no blind process of development.

Physical science, when it deals with past history of the universe, is concerned wholly with secondary causes. Quantitative exactitude is its great end. Such facts are of more value to it than ultimate origins. If there are spiritual beings higher than man, science has nothing to do with them. It admits the presence of original causes in nature only grudgingly.

Not so the Bible. It is essentially a religious book. Only incidentally does it touch upon the subjects with which science is concerned, and when it does, its motive is religious. It aims to describe the beginning of our world, so far as it is necessary to the understanding of redemption and the establishment of God's kingdom. Those are the great ends at which the cosmogony of Genesis aims, and it is in the light of these facts that the opening sentences of Genesis must be considered.

In commenting on Genesis 1, 1. Dr. Murphy says:

"This great introductory sentence assumes the existence of the Creator. It assumes his eternity: for he is before all things. It implies his absolute freedom, for he begins a new course of action. It implies his infinite wisdom; for a *Kosmos,* an order of matter and mind, can only come from a being of absolute intelligence. It presumes him to be beyond all limit of time and space, as he is before time and space.

"This simple sentence denies atheism; for it assumes the being of God. It denies polytheism, and among its various forms, the doctrine of two eternal principles, the one good and the other evil, for it confesses the one eternal Creator. It denies Materialism; for it asserts the creation of matter. It denies pantheism; for it assumes the existence of God before all things, and apart from them. It denies fatalism, for it involves the freedom of the eternal being."[2]

It is therefore laden with physical and metaphysical, with ethical and theological instruction for the first man, for the contemporaries of Moses, and for all the succeeding generations of mankind.

This first verse forms an integral part of the narrative, *it is not a mere heading*. This is evident from the following reasons:

1. It has the form of a narrative.

2. The conjunctive particle connects the second verse with it; which could not be if it

[1] Genesis I, 1.
[2] Murphy, G. James, LL.D., T.C.D., Commentary on the Book of Genesis, 1873, page 28.

were a heading.

3. The very next sentence speaks of the earth as already in existence, although in a very imperfect form, and therefore its Creation must be recorded in the first verse, with the beginning of the first day of time. No time interval is mentioned.

This creating is the omnipotent act of giving existence to things which before had *no existence*. This beginning is the great mystery of things, as their end is the second. Natural science observes things as they are, when they have already laid hold of existence. It extends into the past as far as observation will reach, and penetrates into the future as far as experience will guide, but it does not touch the *beginning* or the *end*. This first sentence of revelation, however, records the beginning of our globe, in time and space. At the same time it narrates the progressive acts of Creation of that which was spoken into existence at the beginning of the six days of Creation,[3] and so contains within its bosom the whole of what is revealed in the Book of God. It is thus historical of the beginning and prophetical of the whole time, recording its Creation, and anticipating the end also. This sentence is the testimony of revelation, and actual world in us and around us is the reality. Faith takes the account of the one, observation of the other.[4]

It bears on the very face of it the indication, that it was written by inspiration, and solely for man; for it divides all things into the heaven and the earth.[5] Such a division evidently fits only those who are inhabitants of the earth. We can safely say, that this sentence is the foundation stone of the history, *not* of the universe at large, of the sun, of any other planet, but of our earth, and of man, its rational inhabitant. In any discussion of Genesis this one fundamental fact must not be overlooked, namely that this creation record has to do *solely* with the beginning of our own planet and its solar system, and that it is not supposed to give us any information on the rest of the universe. For this information we must rely on other Bible passages which, although very brief, give us a general conception of the immensity of the plan of the Creator. In fact the Bible as a whole must be regarded as a book which deals exclusively with the nature and destiny of man on this earth. It was given solely for the purpose of securing and substantiating the complete salvation of the human race, and does not primarily concern itself with the fall and redemption of created beings, called angels, apart from man. The book of Hebrews states it thus: "For assuredly it is not to angels that he reaches a helping hand, but it is to the descendants of Abraham."[6]

---

[*] At any rate, the wording of the fourth commandment of the Decalogue is what seems convincing to us, that there must have been an absolute Creation *ex nihilo*, (from nothing) of the material of our earth at this beginning of the six days: "For in six days the Lord made heaven and earth, the sea, and all that in them is, and rested the seventh day: Wherefore the Lord blessed the Sabbath day, and hallowed it." Exodus 20, 11. If we take these words at their full face value, we must believe that the very materials of which the earth is composed, were brought into existence within the time here spoken of. No other conclusion seems possible. The integrity of Creation Week, as the basis of the fourth commandment, apparently demands this conception.

[*] Hebrews 11, 3.

[*] The word heaven here used, and also in Exodus 20, 11, does not mean the sidereal universe; for it is expressly defined in Genesis 1, 8 as meaning the firmament, or what we would now call the atmosphere, or that part of it which was under the firmament from the waters which are above the firmament. Genesis 1, 7.

[*] Hebrews 2, 16. Weymouth's translation. If the Creator has given us information on the origin of the rest of the universe, it was solely to help humanity to comprehend his greatness, power, and love. If he withheld anything, which he undoubtedly did, it was for a kindred purpose. Deut. 29, 29.

Bible passages, such as Col. 1, 16; John 17, 5; Hebr. 1, 2; Psalms 33, 6; and Job 38, 7, deal with parts of the universe brought into existence long before our solar system was created. These Creations took place before time began to be registered for our earth, in eternity, and must therefore stand apart from the Creation of our heaven and earth, our solar system of which Genesis 1, 1, speaks.

The sons of God, which Job speaks of, are an order of rational beings created before the Creation of man, and joining in the symphony of the universe when the earth and all that was in it, were called into being.

It is thus evident, that Genesis 1, 1 is not supposed to deal with anything *before* or outside the Creation of man on this our planet. It marks the beginning of time for man, and will never cease to engage the attention of the reflective mind.

## A Step in the Creative Process

We now turn to the second verse of the Genesis record, and again observe that it simply describes the original condition of matter as it came directly from the hand of the Creator, at the beginning of the first Creation day. The "without form and void" spoken of here is itself of his own making, and his spirit sat dove-like brooding on the vast abyss. From the first God is represented as freely creating by the word of his power.

Let us glance for a moment at this "primeval chaos", as some love to call it. All the elements, which now exist, were doubtless there, but all out of relation, a form of matter utterly unknown to science. As far as the eye could reach, not a thing of life or beauty or definite form redeemed a single point of the monstrous waste. And over this wild structureless desolate abyss rested the pall of blackness. In what other condition, we ask, could the substance that God had just created be, since God was immediately to continue the actual Creation of the substance into objects, into an earth? This all was not to be finished completely simply by the first creative act. Logically, this was only a momentary step in the process of Creation. The substance from which the earth and everything in it was to be made in six days, was still in the raw, as it were. Then step by step God takes the earth material he had just

created and continues his creative work during the six days. He tells us in just so many words what was done, but not *how* it was done. The newly created material would logically be without form and void. What other description could there be given? The water and the land were all comingled in one mass until the creative acts separated them thus shaping this state of matter into a cosmos.[7] So far the process of Creation had advanced along the line of the divine plan of the Creator. Why should it become waste and void, or without form and void, when it already was that after the first act of Creation? This condition was the first step in the process and served the purpose well, for at the close of the first day of Creation the Creator pronounced it "very good". To insist that a fall of man or some phantom creature caused a desolation at this point, seems to belie this plain statement of the Scriptures. More than that, it is opposed to God's usual method of working. That method is orderly, although yet incomplete in itself, it is God's method of progress, from small to vast, from embryo to fruition, from stage to stage, through diversity to unity in diversity. For these reasons we are compelled to believe that the so called "chaos" of the original elements, not less than the Creation of them, was the direct issue of the creative Will; that is to say, God created the atoms of our solar system, starting with them in a chaotic state from man's standpoint, for all progress seems to man to begin in chaos. We have the word of the scientist for this, who states it thus: "All life begins chaotically. This is true of physical life. Look at this bioplast; the most powerful microscope fails to detect in it much sign of system or structure; the most

---

[7] No such state of matter is known in nature or in science, because all existing matter is known to be *very definitely non-chaotic*. Those who advocate some chaotic state lasting billions of years, during which they suppose radioactive mineral ores, recorded such eons of time, must face this and other very serious obstacles. Whether the chaotic state continued a moment or a billion years, even those with little technical knowledge of mineralization can easily see the absurdity of the idea that ores could form under such conditions. It can be seen also that, even though such ores should be thus formed, to imagine that they and their extremely delicate records could survive the tremendous geological events at the opening of Creation Week (not to mention the devastating and all-pervading minerological transformations during the Deluge period), *is unthinkable*. Therefore it is impossible to reconcile any supposed period of time, based on the formation and preservation of mineral ores, with either a long or a short period of chaos, if we at all respect Bible events. The condition described was essentially one of the processes of Creation and therefore is utterly beyond man to understand, *even now*. But the terms used, are apparently sufficient for man, and cover the case amply *from man's standpoint*. This is typical of the language used throughout the Bible.

that it detects is a tiny grouping of seemingly unarranged chaotic material, in fact, so structureless does it seem, that the microscope declines to prophecy whether it will unfold into a cedar, an elephant, or a man."[8] Let the reader take note, that he said "seemingly".

In conclusion we repeat, that this second verse of Genesis 1. simply describes the unarranged state which existed the very instant after the Creation of matter, *when everything in our own solar system was void,* when darkness enveloped its Creation, and hovered over the abyss, when the Divine Spirit brooded over the process marshalling, organizing its shapeless desolate immensity by his own energy of movement, advancing step by step, creating unity and beauty.

Strangely enough this very verse, as we will see later, has been made the basis of a so-called ruin and restoration theory by a forced rendering. There is nothing in the original to give even a hint of a ruin or desolation of some previously inhabited pre-Edenic, pre-Adamic world. It requires a great deal of imagination to say that this second verse "carries a tremendous suggestion of collapse", and another still greater stretch of imagination to conclude, that this "chaotic" upheaval took place, *prior* to the first week of Creation, and nothing in the text indicates such conclusions. Why, we ask, do people indulge in them?

## Time Theories the Crux of Belief and Unbelief

We invite the candid reader to follow us closely in our discussion of pre-Genesis time theories which will, we hope, reward him with a satisfactory answer to some of those questions involved.

Until near the commencement of the 19th century it was the opinion, sanctioned by Holy Scripture, that the earth dated from an epoch of about six thousand years ago, and that previous to that period the matter of which it is composed was not in existence. But modern science has questioned these opinions, by pointing to innumerable wrecks

of a supposed former state of nature, wonderfully preserved, which have been brought from the deepest caverns of the earth and the bottoms of the mountains, to prove the immeasurable antiquity of our globe.

The celebrated French naturalist Cuvier was the first to establish an order of theories pointing to the above conclusion. Since his time, the various strata of the earth and their imbedded contents which had been for centuries the occasion of wonder and perplexity, have been laboriously investigated by the ablest scientific minds. This has led to still other assumptions which in turn have again been gravely questioned on the ground that the postulations of science are constantly changing and assumptions are continually revised and altered by new discoveries as we progress.

It must be granted that there is a wide difference between the teachings of evolutionary geology and the statements of the Bible. Inspired by the necessity of vindicating the truth of Scripture, numerous attempts have been made to overthrow the interpretations which evolutionary geology has attempted to give to the records found in the stone book of nature. The most popular counter explanation has been the effect produced by the Deluge of Noah. That mighty catastrophe, both non-geologists and geologists have maintained is sufficient to account for all the deposits of fossil remains in the rocks without resorting to such incalculable periods of time as are postulated. This is Deluge Geology, which is now rapidly developing into a science. Its data go to show that the very layers of sediments, the fossils and all geological features are the result of the Deluge. And, since these are all that evolutionary geology has to stand on, with its theory of vast ages between the various strata, therefore Deluge Geology does away with all the vast time periods of evolutionary geology. Thus evolutionary geology and Deluge Geology are absolutely incompatible and mutually exclusive, because they both deal with the same set of facts in nature.

---

[8] Boardman, D. George, Studies in the Creative Week, 1878, page 59.

But for those who are unable to understand Deluge Geology, or who have not as yet had access to it, there still remains the difficulty of reconciling the supposed vast antiquity of our globe (which the various geological phenomena seemed to have suggested) with the chronolgy of the mosaic record, the latter teaching that the earth is nearly coeval with the appearance of man. In order to harmonize the Creation record with evolutionary geology several other schemes by which this objection is met and supposedly overcome, have been offered.

The first outstanding and most accepted scheme supposes that the opening verse of the first chapter of Genesis refers to the original fiat, which called our material solar system into existence—after which an undefined and enormous interval of time took place; and that our globe was then cast into the chaotic state of emptiness and waste supposed to be described in the second verse as preceding the six days, each of 24 hours of duration, in which it was fitted and arranged as a habitation for man. According to this theory, Genesis 1, 1, speaks of the orriginal Creation, and Genesis 1, 2. is supposed to describe the condition of the earth six days before Adam was called into existence. To what remote point in time Genesis 1, 1. is supposed to conduct us, or as to how long an interval passed before the earth "became" a ruin, we are told we have no means of knowing. We are, however, assured that if the surmises of the evolutionary geologists could be conclusively established, there should not be any conflict at all between the findings of science and the teachings of the Scripture.

It is further claimed for this hypothesis, that there is nothing in it which is not entirely consistent with the discoveries of popular theories of geology. Its advocates claim to have found a beginning, old enough for all ages that geology can require. According to them, this opening sentence of Genesis, which they separate off from the rest of Genesis, implies no date whatever; and therefore does not fix the antiquity of the globe. Between them and the subsequent narrative there is ample duration for the supposed discoveries of geology to intervene. All the pre-Adamic formations may be allowed to follow this first opening statement.[9]

This theory was for a long time thought to meet all requirements of evolutionary geology. It has numbered among its advocates many who were anxious to harmonize language of Scriptures with discoveries of science, and is still advocated by some who have no first hand knowledge of geology.

It was later contended by eminent geologists, many of whom were earnest friends of Revelation, that this scheme of reconciliation was no longer adequate. These critics insisted that it requires, in order to maintain its ground, that there should be a "break" or "chaotic" period, just previous to the Creation of man. But it was further asserted that all the facts of geology go to show that there was no such universal catastrophe at that epoch, and this latter suggestion fell into disrepute.

Some time later, however, it was announced that the required "break" or catastrophe had been found, and that there really existed a complete break just before the Creation of man. Whether this supposed evidence was produced by geologists or theologians, is not clearly stated, but we antici-

---

[9] When—how far back in the past—"the beginning" was, could not be known from this text alone, but we are told in the fourth commandment of the Decalogue that this Creation came to pass in six days. Viewed in the light of the fourth commandment which refers to this Creation, it is wrong to conclude on the basis of Gen. 1, 1, that it stands as an independent sentence and relates a separate creative act distinct from and long prior to the work of the six days. Neither does the sacred historian, in passing from the event announced in the first verse to the state of things described in the second, say anything about an interruption, of a period of indefinite, and supposedly incalculable length of time. The second verse simply describes the condition of the created earth which came to being at the beginning of the first day. Exodus 20, 8-11. These pre-Adamic advocates force the following rendering of the text of the fourth commandment: "For, *before* six days the Lord made heaven and earth . . ." (Here "bara" and "asah" have the same meaning.) Thus we see that this verse does fix the date of our globe. Bear in mind that these words refer all the way back to, and *include* the first verse of Genesis.

pate that it was by the latter, for the theory was "revived a generation or so ago by C. I. Scofield and others, chiefly among people who know nothing first hand about geology. No geological references are found to point to any such discussion by geologists. It is the theory taught in the notes of the Scofield Bible, and is very enthusiastically defended by some who call themselves fundamentalists and who seem to regard the notes of Mr. Scofield on a par with the Bible."[10]

This theory is, that God had formerly created a world, before he created Adam, vast and beautiful, an abode of angels, that these reared against the Almighty the standard of rebellion, that the legions of Satan were vanquished and this globe of ours *became* a total wreck without form and void, and darkness settled on the face of the deep —a wreck and ruin, and then after six successive fiats of restoration (not Creation) the Creator completed His work, bestowing upon all of it His benediction, "very good".

Research has fully revealed beyond doubt, that this theory is nothing more than a modernized version of a very ancient tradition of certain Synagogues, held by some learned Jews, long before the dawn of Christianity. Originally a pagan and Jewish and not a Christian doctrine at all, it was first borrowed by the Church Fathers and writers, accepted by the mediatory gnostics, and it is now eagerly seized upon by some of our modern would-be theologians in their attempt to harmonize their theology with the ever varying claims of evolutionary geology and speculative evolution, which strangely, they otherwise reject.

It is now over a hundred and twenty-five years ago since Dr. Chalmers called attention to this idea that the word "was" in Genesis 1, 2. should be translated "became", and that between the first two verses of Genesis 1., some terrible catastrophe must have intervened. This catastrophe was attributed to the apostacy of Satan by the theolgians, who based this assumption upon Isaih 14, 12-14 and Ezekiel 28, to give it a scriptural basis. To fortify this "ruin and interval" theory by

Holy Writ, these expositors make much of different renderings of Gen. 1, 2. upon which they base their theory. They tell us, that the phrase Tohu v' bohu of the original text, which the American revision translates "waste and void", the Authorized "without form and void", the modern Jewish version, "unformed and void", should literally read: "but the earth had *become* desolate, ruined and unfurnished . . .", as Dr. Chalmers suggested more than a hundred years ago. They justify this rendering by claiming that the Hebrew language lacks a word for "became", so the word "was" is always used to carry out the sense of "became", though of course, there is not the slightest authority in the field of Hebrew Scholarship for any such translation. It also tries to put into the adjectives "waste" and "void", meanings which the original words do not carry, the meaning of the Hebrew words being merely that the earth was still unformed and empty, and had not yet been stocked with plant and animal life, and had not yet even been separated into ocean and dry land.

We have already shown, that the correct understanding of the second verse of Genesis 1. completely ignores all such suppositions. Since we know what it really says, we can easily discard all such theories.

In the face of this plain language of the Scriptures, these theorists still insist that the first and second verses of Genesis 1, stand as two separate and independent statements. They maintain, that the first verse relates a creative act distinct from, and long prior to the work of the six days. Then they claim, that in passing from the event announced in the first verse to the state of things described in the *second,* the sacred historian passes over another period of indefinite, and perhaps incalculable length. Of the condition of our planet during that period, what changes or revolutions it underwent, nothing is said; but the second verse is supposed to describe the conditions immediately before the commencement of the Adamic Creation, the history of which would then begin in the third verse.[11]

---

[10] Price, McCready George, M. A., Genesis Vindicated, 1941, page 291.
[11] Pink, W. Arthur, "Gleanings in Genesis," 1922, page 11.

Thus they imagine a vast gap in the Mosaic narrative, between the Creation of the earth, as stated in the first verse and the condition mentioned in the second verse, where they believe that a long and indefinite period of time must have elapsed, a chasm of unnumbered ages and of unrecorded events. They frankly admit that, about what was supposed to have happened, what was done, or what existed, during this immense interval, the Scripture is *entirely silent*. Their frank admission is of the greatest importance for it is an acknowledgment coming from them that the above mentioned suppositions, are without any biblical ground whatever, and that we vainly look for scriptural proof for them.

We have seen that this idea of a pre-Adamic chaos introduces an unwarrantable and arbitrary break between the first and second verses, that is to say—between Creation and the chaotic state in which all matter naturally found itself at that given moment. Again: instead of being sustained by the geologic records, it is in direct conflict with them.

Interpreted in the light of Exodus 20, 8-11 the first chapter of Genesis plainly reveals that the six days of Creation can neither be understood as days of renovation nor as acts of "secondary Creation," but as an unbroken record of Creation plain and simple, to be reckoned from the moment our solar system was spoken into existence to the close of the sixth day, all of which falls within the scope of the six Creation days.

## "Create" and "Make" Interchangeable

However, in the effort to gain their point, the defenders of this pre-Adamic theory inject a strange and uncalled-for element into the discussion by insisting that there is a fundamental difference between "creating" and "making". "Bara", they claim, is always used where something is made out of nothing and the word "asah" is used only where something is made or formed out of already existing matter, which was brought into existence in the beginning by what they term a "primary Creation".

This is what they say: "The Bible does say, that in six days the Lord *made* heaven and earth, but there is a difference between the words 'made' and 'created.' 'To create' is to bring into existence out of nothing. 'To make' is to take pre-existing matter and change its form. The latter is what the Lord did in six days."[12]

However, the fact in the matter is, that the Creation record does not bear them out in the above statement. From verses 21 and 28, where the word "bara" (create), is used, we plainly see that the Lord did create during the six days: "And God created (bara) sea-monsters, and every living creature that moveth wherewith the waters swarmed after their kind, and every winged bird after its kind." Verse 21. "So God created (bara) man out of the dust of the earth in his own image . . ." Verse 27. Thus we see that the Lord *did create during* the six days, and the author of Genesis speaks plainly of this "forming out of already existing matter" as Creation (bara), and uses the two words "bara" and asah" interchangingly. Therefore this attempt to *differentiate* between the "primal Creation" and the work of the Creation Week is without scriptural foundation.

Thus it becomes very plain that the above mentioned scheme, and all similar efforts of reconciliation, are not tenable without positively resorting to a forced construction of the language of Scripture. Only by ignoring the simple record of the progressive work of Creation as the inspired writer narrates it,

---

[12] Pink, A. W., "Gleanings in Genesis," Vol. I, Chap. 1, page 9. Bible Truth Depot, Swengel, Pa.

[12] Talbot, Louis T., "God's Plan of the Ages," Second Edition, 1943, page 12.

and by a gross encroachment of the Text, is it possible to find even a ghost of a chance for such assumptions.

This word "bara" (create) appears in the Hebrew text 55 times,[13] and although it suggests instant and miraculous Creation of something out of nothing, it also expresses the making or forming of something out of already existing matter. But whatever does come into existence is in itself original, and as such is a Creation, something that did not exist before.

The President of the United States sits in the White House and touching an electric button he opens the doors of the world's fair in Chicago hundreds of miles away. How did that come to pass? By a choice and a volition setting free and directing the energy in a few molecules of the brain. The physical force, we grant, was not created; it was only directed. But what was that spiritual energy which has the wonderful power of directing physical energy? Was it not a new thing? Did not the free will act creatively, and have we not here an analogy, true so far as it goes, even though it may not get very far, of the infinite creative activity of the Creator by which matter and energy were first brought into being and the human soul itself called out of non-existence into reality?

The other operation of the soul to which we ascribe a creative quality is the imagina-tion. It is illustrated in some of its highest exercises by the artist's work. He has indeed, to a certain extent, the material of his constructive thought in the things of the external world and the ideas which are the common property of man. But artistic genius does more than taking pre-existing matter and arranging or changing its form. The common language of the race expresses a real truth when it declares that the *artist creates*. Forms of beauty expresive of noble ideals make their appearance under the magic touch of his brush or chisel. *They had no previous existence.* There is in all of them an element that is new. So the poet or the writer sets new ideas before us, of characters which live and move in the world of thought. We readily admit that all this is but a far-off imitation of what the Creator has done in His infinitely higher and better way. Those who have felt the glow and sense of power which the creative work of art brings into existence, know that they can be rightly termed Creations, *because something is produced which never existed before.*[14]

In their attempt to differentiate between the words "bara", to create, and "asah", to make, our fundamentalist friends attempt to inject a new meaning into the Text which in reality does not exist in the Bible. The fact of the matter is that these two words are used interchangingly where and whenever the

---

[13] For the benefit of the reader, we give these texts:
Gen. 1, 1.27. Chap. 2, 3. Chap. 5, 2. Chap. 6, 7.
Deut. 4, 32.
Psalms 89, 12 (13), 47 (48) verses.
Isa. 4, 5. Chap. 40, 28. Chap. 41, 20. Chap. 43, 7. Chap. 45, 8. Chap. 45, 12.18.
Isa. 54, 16.
Jeremiah 31, 22.
Mal. 2, 10.
Infinitive: Gen. 5, 1.
Imperative: Psalm 51, 10 (12).
Future: Gen. 1, 21, 27. Numbers 16, 30.
Participle: Eccl. 12, 1. Isa. 40, 28. Chap. 42, 5. Chap. 43, 1. Chap. 45, 7.18.
        Isa. 57, 19. Chap. 65, 17.18. Amos 4, 13.
Preterite: Exod. 34, 10. Ps. 148, 5. Isa. 48, 7. Ezek. 21, 30 (35).
Infinitive: Gen. 2, 4. Chap. 5, 2. Ezek. 28, 13.15.
Future: Psalm 104, 30.
Participle: Psalm 102, 18 (19).
Treterite: Isa. 17, 15.18.
Infinitive: Ezek. 23, 47. I. Sam. 2, 29.
Imperative: Ezek. 21, 19 (24).
Englishman's Hebrew and Caldec Concordance Vol. I, p. 270—bah-rah.
Longmann & Green & Co., 1843.
[14] See Webster's unabridged Dictionary: Creation.

Scriptures speak of the great drama of Creation. For proof of this, we quote the opinion of the noted Hebrew scholar Benjamin Marcus in his book, published by the Dublin University Press in 1851, "Mycur Hayem", Mistranslations and difficult passages of the Old Testament, corrected and explained from the Caldaic Reading. Referring to the first verse of Genesis 1., he says:

"I shall now give you the opinion of Aben Esra on *bara* (created). He says that bara signifies, 'God created the world out of nothing'. This opinion is certainly an undeniable fact, as will be seen by referring to Numbers 16, 30. Jeremiah 31, 22. 'A new thing' (which never existed before.) This is the interpretation of *bara*.

"It is very remarkable that the word *bara* (which signies 'created out of nothing') occurs but three times in the first chapter of Genesis, verses 1. 21. 27., from which I infer, that in these verses, where this word bara occurs, we are to understand that there was no previous existence of the things mentioned; hence it follows, that in the first verse, by the word 'created', I understand to be included the materials of the different works which appeared successively. . . . In the 21. verse another Creation is mentioned, great whales, which includes serpents, dragons, etc., and in the 27th verse we have the noblest of the three Creations mentioned: God created man. The opinions concerning this verse are so many, that I feel a difficulty in making a selection. I shall, therefore, merely make a few remarks on a question which has been sometimes proposed to me: 'If bara signifies a making out of nothing, does it not contradict what we are expressly told, "that man was *made* out of the dust of the ground?"' To many this question may appear to carry some weight, or perhaps to be unanswerable. . . . Had not the Lord breathed into his nostrils, his body would have continued a lifeless mass of clay, and this fact proves, I think of itself, and that beyond a doubt, that the view which has been taken in reference to the word bara or

*created*, even as regards the origin or Creation of man, does not contradict, but on the contrary fully coincides with the Scriptures; for as there is an evident distinction made between the formation of Adam's body and the animation of the body by the Lord's *breathing into it the breath of life*, it follows, that though God made, or formed man out of the dust of the ground, still the living principle which animated him not only was, but must have been created out of nothing. In conclusion I would merely refer to Isaiah 43, 7: 'For I have created him, I have formed him, yea I have made him.' "[15]

This shows conclusively, that both Revelation and also Jewish Scholarship do not make any distinction between the word "bara" (create) and "asah" (to make or form), creating, making or forming something out of nothing, or out of the material already at hand. Both stand for Creation in the truest sense of the word.

This point is also substantiated by the "Englishman's Hebrew and Caldee Concordance of the Old Testament, an attempt at a verbal connection between the original and the English translations."[16] Here we find all the texts containing the word "bara" in the original Hebrew translated sometimes into "create", oftentimes into "made" and "formed" alternatively.

The earth was created (bara).

Man was made (bara).

*All things* were created (bara).

Psalms 148, 1-5.

It is therefore misleading and out of harmony with the Scriptures to claim that "bara" is used only when the primal Creation of matter or the work of origination is spoken of. With the disproval of this claim also falls the assumption that the first week of time was a week of reforming and reconstruction, which some are willing to accept as a "secondary Creation" which to our mind is not only equally erroneous and absolutely without scriptural foundation but also in open contradiction to many plain statements of the Bible. According to this theory the week

---

[15] Marcus, Benjamin, Mykur Hayem, Mistranslations and Difficult Passages of the Old Testament, 1851, pages 15-17.

[16] The Englishmans Hebrew and Caldec Concordance, Vol. I, p. 270 bah-rah. Longmann & Green & Co., 1843.

of Creation was not a week of Creation at all, but "a week of restoration and renovation", if you please. At least that is what they say: "How long the earth remained in this chaotic state we do not know—many years, perhaps possibly millions of years. . . . From verse four to the close of the chapter one, we have the account of the renovation in which God made the earth, reformed it, and placed man upon it. The order of this reformation is thus stated: 1. Light; 2. Firmament; 3. earth and sea; 4. sun, moon, and stars; 5. fish and fowl; cattle, creeping things, beasts and man."[17]

To prove some of their claims, much is made out of different translations of these verses. Right here we would like to call attention to a translation of Gen. 1, 1. 2. made directly from the Caldee, strictly *ad literam,* which preserves the idiomatic characteristics of the original, the Targum of Onkelos and which possesses an intrinsic philological and critical worth, from its close adherence to the Hebrew Text. The translation reads: "In the first times the Lord created the heavens and the earth. And the earth was waste and empty, and darkness was upon the face of the abyss, and a wind from before the Lord blew upon the face of the waters."[18]

This rendering can be considered as good as any and perhaps more accurate, for it preserves the idiomatic characteristics of the original. It most certainly does not contain any ground for the supposition of a wreck of an earlier world or worlds, as assumed by some of the ancient Church Fathers we have already referred to, who at that early age knew nothing about our modern science, but who were prone to build on the foundation of heathen philosophers and writers. Since it was mainly from among the heathen that converts to Christianity were obtained, we know from early Church History that in many instances they allowed heathen ideas and customs to enter the church. And why should they not in their zeal to please the popular mind, also in this respect attempt an adjustment to the "Chaos of the Ancients" in Greek and Latin literature."[19]

The modern theologians of this school of thought now even claim to have found scriptural proof for this wreck and ruin theory in texts like Isa. 45, 18. which, to their opinion, "expressly declares, that the earth was not originally created in the condition in which Genesis 1, 2. views it." Furthermore they say, since God is not the author of confusion, therefore some terrible catastrophe must have intervened, and that this catastrophe may have been connected with the apostacy of Satan at this time, etc. However, if these and other texts thus inter-

---

[17] Talbot, Louis T., "God's Plan of the Ages," Second Edition, 1943, page 14.

[18] Etheridge, J. W., M.A., The Targums of Onkelos and Jonathan Ben Uzziel on the Pentateuch, 1862, page 35.

[19] "A lifeless lump, unfashioned and unframed,
Of jarring seeds, and justly Chaos named.
No sun was lighted up, the world to view;
No moon did yet her blunted horns renew;
Not yet was earth suspended in the sky,
Nor poised, did on her own foundation lie;
Nor seas about the shores their arms had thrown:
But earth and air and water were in one
Thus air was void of light, and earth unstable,
And water's dark abyss unnavigatable,
No certain form on any was impressed;
All were confused, and each disturbed the rest."

"Chaos of the Ancients,"—Ovid's Metamorphos, 5. Translation by Dryden. Quoted in "Library of the World's best Literature." Vol. XIX, page 10925, *Creation.*

We are all familiar with the Greek myth of Creation which Hesiod has preserved—how at first there was only Chaos and Eros or Love, how under the influence of the latter, as the principal of order and harmony, Chaos was divided into Tartarus and Earth, and the Earth gave birth to heaven and the sea. Quoted in "Present Day Theology," by L. F. Stearns, page 248.

See also: "The Two Babylons," by A. Hislop, page 26.27 and "Fathers of the Catholic Church," by E. J. Waggoner, page 9, Pacific Press Pub. Co., 1888, Oakland, Calif.

preted and applied, are carefuuly read and not forced out of their relationship with the context, it will easily be seen, that they refer exclusively to *our present state of the world.* They are not to be applied to some imaginary past of which, according to the admission of these theorists, Holy Writ has nothing to say whatever, as to the events or details of that vast period.[20]

## Lucifer and the Ruin and Reconstruction Theory

At this point of discussion we kindly ask the reader to bear with us if we give the theological aspect of this pre-Genesis theory a little more attention from a biblical viewpoint. As a reward for his patience he will have the satisfaction of seeing that this pagan-Jewish-gnostic doctrine can never be reconciled with the Bible which they claim to follow so faithfully in their effort to harmonize their theories with those of science. Let us follow them closely and note how they attempt to prove this "tremendous collapse of the earth" even before the Adamic Creation began. They first ask the question as to whether there really is any hint in the Scriptures that warrants us to conclude an "interval" or a "break" in the second verse of the Creation story, and then instantly answer that there is, but very modestly admit that it is a *hint only.* But this "hint" is not to be found in the text of the Creation story, but in the prophetic books of Ezekiel 28, and Isaiah 14. There they mean to find proof of what they term a "primal Creation", a Creation different from, and prior to the Creation week of Genesis 1.

The 28th chapter of Ezekiel does speak of the Creation of Lucifer, the morning star, a covering angel in the immediate presence of God, second only to Michael, the Arch-Angel, the Son of God.

But when was this covering angel created? While it is impossible to construct a definite chronological history of the career of Lucifer who became Satan, since he was created before time began for our planet, we can say, that the Scriptures are clear on the following

1. He belongs to the angelic order of beings. He is one of the created sons of Elohim.[21] Of his person we read: "Thus sayeth the Lord God: thou sealest up the sum, full of wisdom, and perfect in beauty. Thou hast been in Eden the Garden of God; every precious stone was thy covering."

2. He was a covering cherub, in the presence of God, around the throne of God. Of this we read: "Thou are the anointed cherub that covereth; and I have set thee so: thou wast upon the holy mountains of God. . . . Thou wast perfect in thy ways from the day, that thou wast created, till iniquity was found in thee."[22]

3. His Fall did not occur on our little planet, remote from the Throne of God. He began his revolt against God in the presence of God in heaven. Of his fall we read: "Thou hast set thine heart as the heart of God." "Thou hast said . . . I will exalt my throne above the stars of God; I will sit down also upon the mount of congregation . . . I will ascend above the heights of the clouds; I will be like the Most High."[23] Coveting the honor which the Father had bestowed upon his Son, this prince of angels aspired to power which it was the prerogative of Christ alone to wield.

Leaving his place in the immediate presence of God, Lucifer went forth to diffuse the spirit of discontent among the angels, and not without success, for we read in the book of Revelation, that, after the "war in

---

[20] See A. W. Pink, "Gleanings in Genesis," Vol. I, Chap. I, Sec. 1, p. 9, Bible Truth Depot, Swengel, Pa.

[21] Job 1:6.

[22] Ezek. 28, 12-15.17. He was a covering cherub around the throne of God, in the third heaven which is also called the paradise of God, 2. Cor. 12, 2.4. This is the paradise referred to by Jesus on the cross, Luke 23, 42.43. When Jesus returned to his Father he passed, according to Paul "through all heavens," Eph. 4, 8-10. He crossed the atmospheric heavens, the starry heavens and sat down at the right hand of God "in the most ancient heaven." Hebr. 8, 1.

[23] Ezek. 26, 6. Isa. 14, 13.14.

heaven, between Michael and his angels and the dragon and his angels, he drew the third part of the stars of heaven (the angels) after him".[24]

These passages give us a complete history of the origin of Satan and how such an incarnation of evil came to exist. But let us remember that this revolt started in the presence of God, and not on this little planet of ours.

Satan and his angels were cast out of heaven after their rebellion had come to a crisis.[25] The Tartarus into which he and his angels were cast, according to Peter, is defined by leading lexographers as meaning the dark, void interplanetary spaces, surrounding the world, but not the world itself. Only later did he appear right after Creation in the abode of men, using the serpent as a medium, seducing them also into rebellion. The dominion which was given to Adam (Gen. 1, 28.) he thus alienated to Satan by becoming his servant. Now, consequently such scriptural titles as "prince of this world", "prince of the power of the air", "God of this world", etc. are applied to him, because he has by fraud usurped that place.[26]

On what biblical ground can we believe that assumption that he already had once before ruled on this planet, and suffered a defeat, turning this earth into a "chaos" before the Creation of Man, and then for the second time becomes prince of this world? Bible history knows but one fall on this earth, the fall of Man, and for this fall the plan of Salvation had already been provided, to make good what had been spoiled by Satan. This is the plain simple language of the Scriptures. What we have found in the

books of Ezekiel, Isaiah and Jeremiah, plainly shows that these texts are misapplied and misinterpreted. The facts are that Satan started his rebellion in heaven, near the throne of God. He fell in heaven and was cast out of heaven long before the fall of Adam took place. You may search the Scriptures from Genesis to Revelation and you will not find the least foundation of the notion that there were two falls on this earth, or that Satan in consequence of his fall, turned this world into a chaos. We read of the fall of Man, and how it was brought about. It was thus understood by all men of God during the past milleniums. It was likewise interpreted by the great geniuses of universal literature, by von Eschenbach when he wrote his "Parseval", so by Dante, the most commanding literary figure of the middle ages, of which fact his "Divine Comedy" testifies. It inspired Milton to write his "Paradise Lost", and Shakespeare to create his "Hamlet", and Goethe to write his "Faust", and last, but not least the great Hungarian writer Emerich Madacs thus pictured the fall of Lucifer in heaven, his expulsion from paradise, from the presence of God, in his "Tragedy of Man."[27]

From what has been said above it will be clear why we cannot acept the assumption of these theologians as to the time and place of the fall of Satan, but insist, that it happened before earthtime began, and in heaven, near the throne of God.[28]

The Bible texts referred to by the theologians, who defend this wreck and ruin theory, can only consistently be understood as we have explained above, and not as these

---

[24] Rev. 12, 4.7.8.
[25] John 14, 30. Eph. 2, 2. 2. Cor. 4, 4.
[26] 2. Peter 2, 4. Jude 6. The meaning of Peter's words correspond with the language of Paul, who styles Satan the "prince of the power of the air." Again, "we wrestle not against flesh and blood, but against principalities, against powers, against the rulers of the darkness of this world, against spiritual wickedness of high places." Eph. 6, 12.
[27] There is a special place which is called the "heaven of Jehovah," where God's throne is located. (Psalms 115, 16.) This is a definite area in the vast fields of unlimited space. God's throne is in the north, in a position north from this earth. Psalms 75, 5-7. See also Isaiah 14, 12-14. The "holy mountain of God" is in the uttermost parts of the north: God's Throne.
[28] Since time is "measured duration" it is incorrect to speak of "pre-Genesis time," before the beginning of the six days of Creation, for man and our earth. Before "in the beginning" we can only speak of eternity, limitless, unmeasured, incessant duration. We must use the same terms in describing the future. We cannot avoid the conclusion, that a period will come when "measured duration" shall again cease. Eternity in the past never had any beginning neither will it have any ending in the future. Hebr. 7, 3. John 3, 36.

theologians have interpreted them. This being true, it deprives them of even the "hint" they claim to have found in support of their theory.[29] Thus, strictly speaking from a biblical point of view, this "pre-Edenic, pre-Adamic" ruin theory clearly dissolves into a mere unfounded supposition, disproved by the very authority it appeals to. It is a guess found in the books of certain students of theology, who are anxious to reconcile the Genesis record with their ever varying theories of geology and etymology.

Let us once more briefly sum up what has been said, in the following manner: The first five verses of Genesis 1. relate what was accomplished on the first Creation day, which began with "in the beginning, God created the heaven and the earth", introducing the Creation of the substance of our solar system, the imparting of motion, the production of light. It ends with the first night and day on our planet: "And the evening and the morning were the first day." See also Exodus 20:11.

### Scientific Aspects of Leading Time Theories

Thus far, there has not yet been given any positive reason to warrant us in going back on our conviction that "in the beginning", about 6000 years ago, God created our heaven and earth (our solar system) out of nothing, and that our earth, immediately after its Creation was in a state of incomplete Creation, seemingly without law and order as man now understands them, until a further act of Creation divided light from darkness, after which the Creator called the light day, and the darkness he called night, and that all this was done on the first Creation day.

The world has always believed that this record of Creation referred to events which occurred with relation to our earth about 6000 years ago. The Bible gives its own chronology in the ages of the Patriarchs, it was written for that purpose. The sacred Scriptures contain the most ancient geographical, historical, and chronological records extant.[30] "In the beginning, (when earth time began, on the first Creation day), God created the heavens and the earth." Gen. 1, 1. On the sixth day God created man. What logical proof have certain others to say that it refers to matters a thousandfold more distant? Time is measured by motion. The swing of a clock pendulum marks seconds. The revolutions of the earth mark days and years. The earliest measure of time is the day, which began with primeval Creation. Its duration is strikingly indicated by the marked contrast and succession of light and darkness.[31] Then too the story moves on without break from day to day from the first to last; what right have they to separate statements so joined, and to place between them intervals of thousands if not billions of years?[32]

---

[29] David L. Cooper, in his recent book: "What Man Must Believe," on page 181 speaks of "a few echoes here and there in the Scriptures of that far off disaster, when the earth became a desolation and waste (Genesis 1, 2.)" He then quotes Job 9, 5-12 and Psalms 74, 12-17 where these "far off echoes" are supposed to be found. We must confess, that it is beyond us to find any traces of these "echoes" in these texts.

[30] "We assume, as we have every reason to do, the trustworthiness of the Bible records, which have been corroborated in countless instances; and we shall follow their guidance in preference to any other." See "Chronology" of the Int. Standard Bible Encyclopedia. 1915, Vol. I, p. 636. Chicago, Howard Severence Co.

[31] The week, another primeval measure, is not a natural measure of time. It was originated by Divine appointment at the Creation. "The week is a period of seven days, having no reference whatever to the celestial motions,—a circumstance to which it owes its unalterable uniformity . . . It has been employed from time immemorial in almost all eastern countries."

[32] The long "chaotic state" of matter which some claim between verses 1 and 2 of Genesis I (which of late they have hit upon the radio-active theory to prove) is totally defeated because the mineral ores depended upon for such time calculations *could not form in that state*. Besides, such a great catastrophe as the ruin and reconstruction theory supposes *would entirely disrupt and remineralize all of the rocks and minerals* and thus reset the supposed time-clock, *starting it with the origin of man—which would ruin the theory*. To see this does not require a profound knowledge of minerals or of radio-activity. Besides, somewhat equally disrupting the minerals were the tremendous minerological transformations of the Deluge period.

On top of all these different calculations of the age of our planet now comes this new science of radioactivity which also gives promise of fixing the age of our globe with still more unerring exactness.[33] As soon as the majority of the scientists had accepted this new radioactive time-table, they followed the usual formula of exposing the "fallacies of the old theories." This has been done over and over again, as the last hundred years have seen new scientific horizons opened. The close of this war has brought in an age of new discoveries, which will compel our "scientists" to make many more readjustments in the near future. It has already been demonstrated in more than one way, that the radio-active calculation is equally inaccurate. Present attempts to interpret radio-active elements in terms of time can only lead to further unfounded and incorrect results. Why, then, accept this radio-active time scale or any other method to figure out the age of our world in preference to the chronology of the Holy Scriptures: "In the beginning God created the heaven and the earth"? Gen. 1, 1. Exod. 20, 11. "He spoke and it was done. He commanded and it stood fast." Psalms 33, 9. Should we not rather be cautious and hold ourselves by a sane reserve before we accept the liberal estimates of scientists regarding the age of our earth? That should safeguard us from many rash conclusions and disappointments.

The Genesis record bears in itself evidence of being the work of One who exhaustively understood the import and the order of all phenomena and from an infinite abundance selected those suited to his purpose. These he recorded in accurate language. He says that once the earth was without form and void; and then he places the beginning of motion between the primordial darkness and the first light; and he names the fact that marks the close of one condition and the beginning of the other, a fact that fits in no where else. In short, every word and every phrase indicates a knowledge not cramped within the narrow limits of scientific formulas, but as free and suggestive as nature herself.

Apostles of theistic evolution and theologians of the liberal school, have monopolized the sciences in their attempt to provide sufficient time for their evolutionary hypothesis, but in this their attempt they have also brought doubt and dispute over much of the Genesis account of Creation and have undermined the faith in the integrity of the Creation Week.

## Examination of the Day-Age Theory

To do justice to our subject, we hold it necessary to give some attention to the day-age theory first advocated by Hugh Miller, although it was held by some previous to his day and even dates back to the age of St. Augustine. The support of Origen is also claimed for it. This scheme of reconciliation differs from the ruin and reconstruction theory already discussed above in prefixing the opening sentences of Genesis to the geologic periods. According to its interpretation of the sacred text, these days were periods of great and indefinite extent instead of being natural days of 24 hours each. By this theory sufficient time is supposed to be afforded for any duration which is required by geological theories. In his "Testimony of the Rocks", Hugh Miller gives us the following division of creative time:

The "First Day" of Moses stands for the *Azoic Period;* the "Second Day" *the Silurian* and *Old Red Sandstone Period;* the "Third Day" the *Carboniferous Period;* the "Fourth Day" the *Permian* and *Triassic Period;* The "Fifth Day" the Tertiary Period.[34]

While this author is acknowledged to be an intentional friend of the Bible, it must be admitted by all who fairly examine the above division of time, that it is arbitrary, that it has no foundation in nature, and is irreconcilable with Scripture. And not only this, but

[33] Peter F. Stoner, Professor at Pasadena Junior College, refers to this new method to determine the age of the earth, which has been developed within th last few years, according to which "the earth is perhaps not younger than two billion years." Quoted in "What Men Must Believe," by D. L. Cooper, page 176.

[34] Quoted in "Testimony of the Rocks," by Hugh Miller, Boston, 1857; p. 196.

the Days of Moses will not fit into or coincide with these periods, nor can the works recorded in them be made to harmonize with the fossils found in these geological formations.

Sir Charles Lyell divided the crust of the globe into thirteen principal systems of rock, and subdivided these into *thirty-eight* classes of distinct fossiliferous strata. To compound and reduce all these into six, therefore, is obviously an arbitrary proceeding. There is nothing in the crust of the earth to indicate such a division. Hugh Miller appears to have felt these difficulties himself when he made the acknowledgement: "Respecting the work of at least the *first* and second days, more especially the *second*, we can still but vaguely guess, . . . at present we can indulge in but doubtful surmises regarding them."[35]

This theory of interpretation, a further attempt to reconcile the history of Creation with geology, plainly indicates how irreconcilable both as to order and phenomena the Mosaic Days of Creation are with such arbitrarily assumed periods. The Author of "Workdays of God" aptly concludes: "Had a reconciliation been possible, in this way, no one would have been more successful in effecting it than Hugh Miller. His thorough acquaintance with geological science, his clear perception of Divine Truth, his powerful logical mind together with his admirable vigour and perspicuity of expression, qualified him beyond most men for such a task. His failure therefore, is the best proof, that the theory is untenable."[36]

It is especially common in geology for bias or mere hypothesis to be embodied in the very wording of the records of the facts observed in the field. "What geological memoir has been written in the last hundred years, which did not show the facts in the field colored by Lyell's and Darwin's spectacles?"

### Comparing the Sequence of Events in Genesis I with That of Geologic Age System

About the only point in the sequence of the origin of the forms of life that can be harmonized with the sequence given in the day-age time table *is the origin of man on the sixth day*. Man is a mammal, and the mammals are supposed by all the evolutionary theories to have been the latest to evolve. (Consult the table or chart of geologic time in most any text book on geology, and in other works on geology. (See the Geologic Time Chart in our text, p. 32 aa.) That was in Post-Tertiary time, and not more than one million years ago, as per evolution. "Creeping things" are also included by the text in this "day-age," but perhaps practically all of these would be geologically "age-tagged" far, far back in the time-scale, perhaps a billion years, so few if any of them are mammals and many of them belong to the so-called "primary" or "primitive" forms of life on earth. By the evolutionary sequence of events, most of such creatures being invertebrates are dated hundreds of millions of years prior to the fishes and insects, or any of the other forms of animal life, especially such creeping things as inhabit the water, as this would include the worms, etc., of the so-called "lowest" classes. This is a gross and troublesome disagreement. Again, the whale is classed as a mammal, and therefore evolutionary theory places the whale in Day 6. But Genesis 1, 21 puts the whale back in Day 5., perhaps hundreds of millions of years prior, another serious disagreement. However, the entire business of Day 5 is shockingly out of place, evolutionarily, because the fish, perhaps most of them, belong far and away far back, *before the plants*, and certainly before the land plants. Evolutionary sequence would place the fish in Day 3, nearly a billion years earlier than Day 5 where Genesis places them.

Moreover, the fish would have to evolve at the earliest possible time in Day 3, just after the waters were separated from the lands, (as they could not live at all till then, and they *must* come before the plants, at least the land plants described for Day 3.) Therefore to place the origin of the "primitive" sea

---

[*] Quoted in "Workdays of God," by H. W. Morris, D.D., page 101.
[**] Morris, Herbert W., A.M., D.D., Ibd., page 105.

worms and the fish at their proper times in the day-age plan, the evolutionist day-age theorist would be compelled to insert another verse of Scripture between verse 10 and 11, as verse 10 describes the separation of the land from the water and verse 11 tells of the Creation of plant life. The "primitive" sea worms are supposed to have started so long prior to the fish, however, that they really should be at least one day-age earlier. The day-age people, the *geologists at least*, know all these things well. Even at this, however, the close proximity in time of fish evolution and evolutionary date for the evolution of land plants "yielding seed" is extremely embarrassing to the evolutionists. Moreover, this predicament is still more serious in that verse 11 also speaks of "trees" whose seeds "was in themselves," because in evolution such trees did not appear till long after the so-called carboniferous age, perhaps half-billion years later. And many of these trees did not come into being till Tertiary time, the last major "age" prior to that of man. This last feature is perhaps more out

of line with the apperance of the trees in Day 3 than is anything else in the whole theory.

Came Day 4, and still the discrepancies multiply, because here we have a whole Day (consisting of perhaps a quarter of a billion years or so) devoted only to the formation of the sun and the moon. Did life utterly quit evolving during that day? How can the day-age people avoid this dilemma? Besides, it would have been impossible for such a period to elapse, with only plant life in existence, without laying down tremendous fossiliferous deposits, the very earliest on earth, *and all of plant life only*, and much of those deposits consisting of the "highest" forms of trees and other plant life!!! (Nothing could be more absurd, and contrary to the "facts", as held by the day-age geologists, than this, yet this is the position in which they themselves have placed themselves by their own theory. Nothing could be more absurd *to them* than that these plant fossils antedate all other forms of life on earth!)

# SUPPOSED "TIME TABLE" OF SEQUENCE OF EVOLUTIONARY LIFE WITH THE STRATA OF THE GEOLOGIC AGES*

| Group | System | Series | Years from the Present | Dominant Types of Life |
|---|---|---|---|---|
| | Quarternary or | 34 Recent | 10 Thousand Years | |
| | Post-Tertiary or | 33 Terrace | 1 Million | |
| | Pleistocene | 32 Drift (Glacial) | 1 Million to 2 Million | Man |
| Ceno- | | 31 Pliocene | 12 Million | |
| zoic | | 30 Miocene | 30 " | Mammals and |
| | Tertiary | 29 Oligocene | 30 " | many modern Trees |
| | | 28 Eocene | 55 " | |
| | | 27 Paleocene | 60 " | |
| | Cretaccous | 26 Upper or Cretaccous Proper | 130 Million | |
| | | 25 Lower or Comanchean | | |
| | | 24 Upper (Malm) | | Reptiles |
| Meso- | Jurassic | 23 Middle (Dogger) | 168 Million | Conifers and |
| zoic | | 22 Lower (Lias) | | Palms |
| | | 21 Upper (Keuper) | | |
| | Triassic | 20 Middle (Muschelkalk) | 200 Million | |
| | | 19 Lower (Bunter Sandstein) | | |
| | Permian | 18 Upper | 235 Million | Amphibians and |
| | | 17 Lower | | |
| | Carboniferous | 16 Pennsylvanean | 315 Million | Coal Plants |
| | | 15 Mississippian | | |
| | | 14 Upper | | |
| | Devonian | 13 Middle | 350 Million | Fishes and Insects |
| Paleo- | | 12 Lower | | |
| zoic | | 11 Upper—Monroan | | |
| | Silvrian | 10 Middle—Salina | 375 Million | Fishes |
| | | 9 Lower—Niagara | | |
| | | 8 Upper—Cincinnatian | | |
| | Ordovician | 7 Middle—Champlanian | 445 Million | Higher Invertebrates |
| | | 6 Lower—Canadian | | |
| | | 5 Saratogan | | |
| | Cambrian | 4 Acadian | 550 Million | Lower Invertebrates |
| | | 3 Waucobian | | |
| Primary | Algonkian | 2 Proterozoic | 1 Billion, 200 Million | Primitive Sea Worms |
| or | Archaen | 1 Archeozoic | 2 Billion | Few fossils or none |
| Primitive | | | | |
| Azoic | | | 3 Billion | No fossils |

*NOTE: This so-called "TIME TABLE OF EVOLUTION AND GEOLOGY" is the tabulated form of the most important conceptions of the whole theory of evolution and time. Indeed, it is the crux of modern evolutionary cosmology and parallel philosophy.

One of the outstanding features of the Genesis account is the repeated statement of alternating darkness and light, as day and night. But the day-age theory, and all theories of the geologic ages whatsoever, are utterly wanting in a single feature to correspond with these periods. HALF of all geologic time would have to be darkness! And the dark periods would have to alternate with the light periods! Geology or Astronomy have never mentioned such a thing. Life of any kind would be impossible under conditions of long periods of darkness.

And where are the various Ice Ages in the Genesis account? Most evolutionary geologists insist on four Ice Ages. Some high authorities insist that there were Ice Ages in certain parts of the earth during almost all of the "ages", because rocks and debris which are classed as belonging to those "ages" show unmistakable evidence of it.

That only plant life, or any other life, for that matter, could be so many hundreds of millions of years, (or even a few days) on earth without the sun is also profoundly out of harmony with the day-age theory, and with all scientific theories whatsoever as to the origin and early history of the earth and its life. Immediate freezing of all water and earth would have occurred, and not one step concerning the very elaborate placing of the waters could have been taken, as described for Day 1 to Day 3. Not even the 24-hour day could have fit these events without the special care of the Creator, in ways now utterly unknown to science. All scientific theories would be compelled to clip Day 4 out of its place, and insert it even before verse 1, as no scientific theory has ever been offered which allows the earth to be created prior to the sun. It would be difficult to imagine a wider discrepancy than this! Is there no end?

Again we say that about the only point of agreement is that man was formed last! The day-age theory is a most blunderous paradox of error and illogic.

From all this it should be clear that the intelligent layman dare not trust even the statements of reputed experts in matters in which any phase of the evolutionary theory is involved; and what set of scientific data on origins is wholly clear from such involvement?

"We believe most firmly," says the learned Dr. Kurtz, "that were this record explained merely on its own merits and with the aid of other Scriptures, and were there no outside, no foreign influence at work, the Days could only be regarded as *natural days*. . . . The first day came to a close with 'darkness', and the second day was introduced with 'light'. We therefore believe with Rosenmuller, whose authority as a Hebrew philologist and critic is entitled to the highest respect, 'that it could scarcely be more clearly expressed than by this formula, that the natural day is to be understood, and not a space consisting of more days or years.'"

Professor Kurtz, whose words we have quoted above, makes this additional statement: "Now there is no question but that the division of time which is here called *day*, was conditional and limited by the presence of *natural light*; consequently, the 'evening' which followed such a day and the 'morning' which preceded the next day, must in like manner be understood as parts of an *ordinary, natural* whole day; and the latter can only be measured according to the natural, every day standard still in use—the occurrence of one regular natural change of light and darkness (of day and night). The days of Creation were thus measured by the natural advent and departure of the light of day, by the occurrence of evening and morning. This standard of measurement is given by the record itself, and must be applied alike to each of the six days of Creation."[37]

All of these oft repeated statements in the account of Creation Week about the evening and the morning and the coming and going of light and darkness (day and night), are not only perfectly useless and senseless in the Day-Age theory, they are a fatal rebuke and refutation of the theory, because, if they are given any meaning at all, both such long days and such long nights would be fatal to much of the life, *if not all life*, in many ways.

---

[37] Scholia, Gen. 1, 5.

"Defined throughout the chapter," says Dr. John Kitto, "as the term *day* is to its natural meaning by the recurring phrase of 'morning and evening' as if with the very object of excluding any such signification (as immense periods), we cannot but fear that the latter explanation does considerable violence to the plainest principles of scriptural interpretation."[38]

Dr. H. Rimmer, in his recent work "Modern Science and the Genesis Record", gives quite a detailed discussion on the time element implied in the days of Creation. In this discussion he touches on the different interpretations of the Hebrew "yom" for day which appears in the Hebrew text of the old Testament almost fifteen hundred times, and which is translated into the English Scripture by no less than fifty-four different meanings. It may mean a figure of speech covering a long period of time, or it may be a collective word covering a definite number of years, or time itself, it may mean a solar day. The latter is true, when a definite day of the month, or for that, of the week is referred to. Then finally, while admitting that there are arguments favoring the era theory, he gives seven conclusive and convincing reasons, why he believes that these days of Genesis were literal twenty-four-hour days.[39]

For the sake of brevity we give the following thought from these convincing reasons:

He notes that each of these days in Genesis is divided into periods of darkness and light, exactly as a solar day is. Some may say, that the first three days could not have been solar days, but we must not forget that the earth revolved around its own axis from the very beginning. There was evening and morning from the first day on. The stability of the earth's axis and the uniformity of the earth's rotation has not changed. This uniformity has been preserved. Calculation has shown that for two thousand years it could not have varied the one hundredth part of a second of time. And God's covenant of time is thus brought forward in Scripture as the peculiar emblem of His faithfulness. We cannot get away from the idea of a solar day, when we read this Creation Record carefully and the eternal order of night and day upon this earth will not be changed.[40]

The Sabbath would be meaningless as a memorial of Creation, if this Creation was really accomplished during six long periods of time.

Dr. James G. Murphy, whose "Commentary on Genesis" was produced at a time when the controversy between evolution and Creationism was at its height, both in America and England, and who as a Hebrew and English scholar was "fully persuaded, that no independent version more adapted to the genius of the English language will ever be produced," was a firm believer in the literal twenty-four-hour days of Creation. In his Critical and Exegetical Commentary on Genesis 1, he says: "The days of this Creation are natural days of twenty-four hours each. We may not depart from the ordinary meaning of the word without a sufficient warrant either in the text of Scripture or in the law of nature. But we have not found any such warrant. . . . Scripture, on the other hand, warrants us in retaining the common meaning, by yielding no hint of another, and by introducing 'evening' night, 'morning' day, as its ordinary divisions. Nature favors the same interpretation."[41]

Otherwise Dr. Murphy is a believer in the ruin and restoration theory according to which, as we have already seen, all geological changes are antecedent to the state of things supposed to be described in the second verse, hence it is logical for him not to require another lengthened period for the creative act during the six Creation Days. In defense of this view he appeals to Scripture and urges us to accept its literal meaning and not depart from the ordinary meaning of the word. We ask ourselves, whether it is not better to follow his advise throughout the

---

[38] Quoted in "Workdays of God," by H. W. Morris, D.D., pages 105, 106.
[39] Rimmer, Harry, D.D., ScD., "Modern Science and the Genesis Record," 1945, pages 11-23.
[40] Jeremiah 31, 35-37.
[41] Murphy, G. James, LL.D., T.C.D., "Critical and Exegetical Commentary on The Book of Genesis," 1873, page 45.

whole text, including the second verse also, and not depart from its ordinary meaning. His interpretation of this second verse seems inconsistent with his own advice. It thus becomes a question of whether the Doctor really practiced what he preached, when he yielded to this pre-Genesis theory of ruin and reconstruction.

Much ingenuity and learning have been exercised in attempts to make the Divine Record countenance the day-age idea. While we regard the well established facts of geology, we are constrained to say that the method pursued to establish their evolutionary-age interpretation does not appear to us to be plain and fair dealing either with the geologic facts or with the Word of God.

More than 40 years ago Prof. George McCready Price began a series of geological discoveries which culminated in breaking the spell of the geologic age system so essential to all theories of evolution. (See especially his Evolutionary Geology and the New Catastrophism, 1926, Pacific Press Pub. Co., Mountain View, Calif. and his New Geology, the latter now out of print.) He found vast areas in which the supposedly never-failing sequence of the evolutionary ages, as represented by the strata, were not at all in the sequence required by that system. Over large areas he found one or more of the supposed "ages" missing without trace, not even an eroded line or surface at the levels where these "ages" belong to account for them. There is no material at the proper place, with its fossils supposedly indicating that it belongs there (according to the theory of evolving life), but there is no sign that any time at all elapsed there during that "age" at that place. How could absolutely NOTHING happen for millions of years?

Then Professor Price found some of the "ages" not only missing without trace in large areas, but, even in these same areas and elsewhere he found some of the missing "ages" *where they did not belong* in the geologic column of strata as defined by the geologic time table. And he found that in some cases an "age" divides itself more than once, *and in the wrong places in the column* in the same area. One or more of these may not be in the proper position in the geologic

column, as called for by the theory itself. How could million-year ages hop, skip, and jump irregularly in such a manner, so frequently in the wrong places? Could evolution have so abruptly changed its sequence from place to place?

Lastly he found that all too often in huge areas parts of the geologic column are up-side-down, *often the greater part of it,* with no acceptable theory as to how this could have occurred. How could evolution have worked in reverse gear in certain areas and not in others? In other words, not only evolution but time itself?

Therefore it is not at all hard to see that the geologic age system has been utterly exposed as a gross error by the work of Professor Price. No longer do thologians have to struggle with that terrible juggernaut facing them in their dealings with the Genesis sequence of events.

It has turned out that the strata are just about in the sequence to be expected if they had been the result of the catastrophic Deluge period, as understood and described by workers and writers on Deluge Geology. The work of the Deluge, which God teaches was the result of His wrath, has thus in modern times been turned completely around by the deceptive development of the influence of evolutionary philosophy during the growth of the science of geology. The work of the Deluge has been given grossly false appearance, that there never was such an event as the Deluge nor even a Creation at the time and manner stated *in Genesis,* and "certainly" no foundation at all for the least semblance of a Creation Week. Creation Week, as the basis of the 4th Commandment, becomes the grossest of myths. But this gross deception, the geologic age system (the most basic foundation of all theories of evolution) has thought to do much more than that. It stands today as the basis for almost all atheism, and is the source of almost all forms of unbelief, doubt and difficulty of Bible faith. Disturb the cosmogony underlying the Scriptures, and it is like blasting the foundation out from under the throne of God.

If the first chapter of Genesis can be made to mean what these theories express, then other portions of Scripture can, with equal ease, be made to mean almost anything that the whim of man may desire, or his imagination invent. Here the point to be decided is, not what the Scripture can be *made* to mean but what *does* it mean; what idea was it intended to convey?

By giving "yom" the signification of a geological period these liberal theologians defend this day-age theory with the Scriptures and cite for authorities Augustine, Josephus, Philo Judaeus, Taylor, Lewis, McCausland, besides an array of scientific judges, as Whiston, Descartes, Cuvier, De Luc, Parkinson, Jameson, Silliman, Miller, Dana, etc. They add, that the events described could not have transpired in six literal days, according to all we know of the order of nature. They admit that the Creator was able to create this world in six days, but they seem to find evidence that he did not, and wrench the Bible to make it fit their theories, excusing their alterations of the text on the basis of inadequate and incomplete renderings of the original.[42]

In the "Question Box" (New Edition 1929) for non-Catholics by B. L. Conway, on pages 69, 70, in the discussion of the six Creation Days, the question is asked: "Are Catholics bound to believe that the world was created in six days of twenty-four hours each?"

The answer is "no". The author then continues: "A careful examination of the account of Creation in Genesis shows that it is given in a more or less poetical form . Catholics are perfectly free to adapt any theory that does not deny the historical character of the first three chapters of Genesis.

"The literal view, commonly held by the Fathers and the Schoolmen, interprets the six days as literal days of twenty-four hours each. This general concensus has no binding dogmatic force, because it has against it the authority of St. Augustine and St. Thomas Aquinas."[43]

In a book recently published by the Devin-Adair Company, New York, R. Elliott Ross, in defending the Catholic religion, in creed and life, says: "Though the Catholic Church is irrevocably committed to the biblical account of Creation, it is not committed to a literal interpretation of that account. A Catholic may believe that God created the universe in six days of twenty-four hours each; but on the other hand, he may believe in any theory of evolution which safeguards the spirituality of the human soul and the idea of God as the ultimate First Cause. Likewise he may believe in Archbishop Usher's chronology of the Bible or in the latest scientific estimate of the age of the earth and the human race."[44]

From this we see, that the Roman Catholic Church, in trying to play safe does not commit itself by taking a definite stand in the question of creationism versus evolution. It is ready to compromise in one of the most clearly expressed Bible Truths. This can easily be understood if we remember the attitude this religious body has always taken toward the Holy Scriptures, when it openly declares that it does not consider the Bible the sole rule of faith.[45]

Those, however, who choose to follow the clarion call of God in His sacred Word, believe that this Genesis record of Creation

---

[42] Right here it may be proper to refer to some general rules which bear on translations of ancient texts:
1. Only that translation bears the stamp of accuracy, which truly expresses the original meaning of the author, and the current meaning of the times when it originated.
2. The rendering must be in harmony with the usage of speech as far as can be known.
3. It must absolutely refrain from injecting modern notions into the text.
4. It must not be out of harmony with the interpretations given by those who stand nearest the times when the communications in question, were given. With reference to the texts in question, we do well in turning to Israel, "to whom were committed the oracles of God," and note first what they have to say.
[43] Conway, B. L., "Question Box," new edition, pages 69, 70.
[44] The Religion of Democracy, *Catholocism*, 1943, page 116. See also *"Whence and How the Universe,"* by J. Guibert and V. A. Best, Ph.D., chapter on Biblical Cosmogany, Article IV, pages 91-119. Published by St. Mary's Seminary Press, Baltimore, Md.
[45] Conway, B. L., "Question Box," new edition, page 76.

really speaks of literal and natural days for the following reasons:

1. No language could have been chosen more explicit, nor any terms found in the Hebrew more definite, to express literal days, than those here employed. There was a first day, a second day, a third day, etc., each opening and closing with a definite evening and morning—literally rendered. There was evening, there was morning, day two, etc.

2. Moses, who penned the record, we have every reason to believe understood these days, and meant that his readers should understand them as literal days; for we cannot suppose for a moment that he ever had in his mind anything like the ideas suggested by modern evolutionary geology.

3. God Himself refers to them as literal days in the commandments given from Sinai: "Remember the Sabbath day to keep it holy; for in six days the Lord made heaven and earth, the sea, and all that in them is, and rested on the seventh day." No impartial mind can read these words and come to any other conclusion than that the *six days* as well as the *seventh* were literal days.[46]

On this first day it was said, "let there be light; and there was light." Now, which is the more natural and consistent to suppose that this fiat was followed by instant obedience?

The history of the second day reads, "let there be a firmament dividing the waters from the waters, and it was so." What is there in all this to forbid our believing that, as soon as it was said, it was done? The Creation was continued on the third, fourth, fifth, and sixth days, and we repeat, what is there in all the domain of nature to hinder us from believing what this record of Creation claims? What difficulty is removed, or what advantage is gained, by supposing that their production occupied immense periods of time? By forsaking the more simple and natural interpretations of this chapter nothing is gained, but much is lost. We therefore hold the six days of Creation to be days

measured by so many revolutions of the earth on its axis.

"By what rule of Grammar, or by what rule of Biblical interpretation can we make the six periods set apart for work, natural days, and the period set apart for rest, that follows the working days, a vast period? How can this be done? To attempt to do this, would be a clear violation of every rule of logic, and grammar, and of Biblical interpretation.—'The Sabbath of the Lord thy God.'—*This is God's Sabbath. It is a natural day of twenty-four hours.* And there is no word in the Bible, from Genesis to Revelation, to show, that God has two Sabbaths or that God's Sabbath is an extended period.[47]

God founded the Sabbath by three distinct steps. After the six days of Creation God rested upon the 7th day making it God's *rest* day. And then He blessed and sanctified or set apart the rest day for all time to come. That day was a seventh of a cycle of days. It was the maker of the week, because all days were numbered with respect to that one day. It is one of God's choicest gifts to man.

Attacks upon the Sabbath throughout the ages have been numerous and persistent. And they have not come from unbelievers, but also from ministers and theologians. But the most effective and far-reaching attack upon the Sabbath has come as a bi-product of the theory of organic evolution, accepted by many scientists. We can only give it passing attention here.

Theistic Evolutionists deny that God created this world in six days, substitute these days with six periods of undetermined length, each probably hundreds of millions of years. It is clear to the reader that in any such scheme a twenty-four-hour Sabbath recurring weekly finds no place. If the theory of evolution is true, then the ground of the Sabbath as presented in the fourth commandment is untrue and irrelevant. These two oppositions cannot be harmonized, nor will they allow any compromise.

Some theologians think they can clear the way for the evolutionists by adjusting their

---

[46] Morris, W. Herbert, A. M., D.D., "Work-Days of God," page 110.
[47] S. A. Hodgman, M. J. C., quoted in "The Terrible Catastrophe," 1885, by Rev. G. C. H. Hasskarl, pages 305-306.

theology to science, but they should realize that this is an impossibility. The consistent evolutionist cannot accept a fall. For him man is on the upgrade.

We are far from condemning individually adherents of the evolutionary theory, or any-one else for that matter; we believe that there are thousands of sincere, honest Chris-tians who are influenced by this fatal philosophy. Some do not realize the implica-tions of their belief. Evolution constitutes one of the most serious challenges to Bible Christianity, a challenge that must be met, or Christianity is doomed. Since the Sabbath is closely bound up with Christianity, it is also doomed. If Evolution is true, there is no Sabbath.

Let us be frank, no man can believe in the word of God and also believe in Evolution. They are mutually exclusive. It is impossible to straddle the question, as the Roman Catholic Church attempts to do.

Did God give a false basis to the Fourth Commandment, and leave a hoax behind the seeming straightforwardness and integrity of Creation Week on which it was based? This is unthinkable!

On the integrity of Creation Week the following excerpt is offered not as a purely scholastic authority, but as expressing in a very clear manner the true issues *involved*. Our object is also to use these statements as a summary and a partial conclusion of the matter of the Day-Age theory thus far presented.

## Summary and Conclusion

### 1. The Literal Week

"Like the Sabbath, the week originated at Creation, and it has been preserved and brought down to us through Bible history. God Himself measured off the first week as a sample for successive weeks to the close of time. Like every other, it consisted of seven literal days. Six days were employed in the work of Creation; upon the seventh, God rested, and He then blessed this day, and set it apart as a day of rest for man.

"In the law given from Sinai, God recog-nized the week, and the facts upon which it is based. After giving the command, 'Re-member the Sabbath day, to keep it holy,' and specifying what shall be done on the six days, and what shall not be done on the seventh, He states the reason for thus observ-ing the week, by pointing back to His own example: 'For in six days the Lord made heaven and earth, the sea, and all that in them is, and rested the seventh day; where-fore the Lord blessed the Sabbath day, and hallowed it.' Ex. 20, 8-11. This reason ap-pears beautiful and forcible when we under-stand the days of Creation to be literal. The first six days of each week are given to man for labor, because God employed the same period of the first week in the work of Crea-tion. On the seventh day man is to refrain from labor, in commemoration of the Crea-tor's rest.

"But the assumption that the events of the first week required thousands upon thou-sands of years, strikes directly at the founda-tion of the fourth commandment. It repre-sents the Creator as commanding men to observe the week of literal days in com-memoration of vast, indefinite periods. This is unlike his method of dealing with His creatures. It makes indefinite and obscure that which He has made very plain. It is infidelity in its most insidious and hence most dangerous form; its real character is so disguised that it is held and taught by many who profess to believe the Bible.

"'By the word of the Lord were the heav-ens made; and all the host of them by the breath of his mouth.' 'For he spake, and it was done; he commanded, and it stood fast.' Ps. 33, 6.9. The Bible recognizes no long ages in which the earth was slowly evolved from chaos. Of each successive day of Crea-tion, the sacred word declares that it con-sisted of the evening and the morning, like all other days that have followed. At the close of each day is given the result of the Crea-tor's work. The statement is made at the close of the first week's record, 'These are the generations of the heavens and of the earth when they were created.' Gen. 2, 4. But this does not convey the idea that the days of Creation were other than literal days. Each day was called a generation, because that in it God generated, or produced, some new portion of His work.

"Geologists claim to find evidence from the earth itself that it is very much older than the Mosaic record teaches. Bones of men and animals, as well as instruments of warfare, petrified trees, etc., much larger than any that now exist, or that have existed for thousands of years, have been discovered, and from this it is inferred that the earth was populated long before the time brought to view in the record of Creation, and by a race of beings vastly superior in size to any men now living. Such reasoning has led many professed Bible-believers to adopt the position that the days of Creation were vast, indefinite periods.

"But apart from Bible history, geology can prove nothing. Those who reason so confidently upon its discoveries, have no adequate conception of the size of men, animals, and trees before the flood, or of the great changes which then took place. Relics found in the earth do give evidence of conditions differing in many respects from the present; but the time when these conditions existed can be learned only from the Inspired Record. In the history of the flood, inspiration has explained that which geology alone could never fathom. In the days of Noah, men, animals, and trees, many times larger than now exist, were buried, and thus preserved as an evidence to later generations that the antediluvians perished by a flood. God designed that the discovery of these things should establish faith in inspired history; but men, with their vain reasoning, fall into the same error as did the people before the flood,—the things which God gave them as a benefit, they turn into a curse by making a wrong use of them."[48]

From all this please do not conclude that we are casting reflections upon the findings of true science. We question only the philosophic interpretation of science. Facts are facts by whomsoever found and propagated. Bible-believers do not deny facts. Science has a right and a duty to find and present facts, that is its legitimate field. But science cannot enter the field of religion, and it is prone to wander into the field of philosophy.

On the other hand it was no part of the design of the sacred writer of Genesis to communicate scientific truth as such. The mission with which he was charged was of a far different character. It was to announce the claims and declare the will of God as the moral Governor of the universe and to prepare a chart whereby a man might be guided in reference of his eternal destiny.[49] It was to unfold the mysteries, not of nature but of grace. Yet its statements on nature must not be untrue, and science is slowly discovering its truth in nature.

## Final Causation and the Story of Creation

Those who are so anxious to harmonize the Genesis record with their theories of theology and evolutionary geology will be sorely disappointed. They sell out to evolution without counting the costs. They encourage theories which lead away from a plain "so sayeth the Lord." They undermine faith in the Word of God. They encourage belief in evolution which when followed to its logical conclusion rules out the first cause—God, the Creator.

Dudley Joseph Whitney concludes his splendid paper on his "Comments on the Evolutionary Theories of the Earth's Origin," with the following words:

"By logical deduction, which should characterize all genuine scientific thought, the failure of evolution or *purely naturalistic* processes in accounting for the origin of the earth and the rest of the solar system, should suggest the possibility of a special *Creation* for its origin, and a history after Creation very different from that which has been believed and taught for more than a century."[50]

But materialistic philosophy does not believe in a Creation, nor in regeneration. It seeks to make men happy, by changing their environment. They say: "Improve your surroundings, and you yourself will improve."

---

[48] White, E. G., Patriarchs and Prophets, 1913, pages 111-112.
[49] Psalm 51, 10. 2. Cor. 5, 17.
[50] Whitney, D. J., published in the "Bulletin of Deluge Geology," Vol. II, Nov., 1942, No. 4, page 100.

*Christianity* says: "Change the heart of the individual and he will change his surroundings." This idea of improving the individual by improving his environment is as old as the hills. It was the idea advanced by ancient philosophy. It was embodied into Jewish ceremonialism and legalism. It was revived in the middle ages, when the medieval church built high strong walls and convents to keep sin out. And now it is again presented by these modern would-be reformers, who tell us that sin, in the last analysis, is not a personal, but a social evil, the result of improper social conditions, placing all responsibility on society, not on the individual, who is excused. But when the sense of sin and responsibility is brushed aside, the idea of right and wrong becomes merely relative, resting on nothing more substantial than personal opinion and inclination.

Jesus approached the social order from *within*, teaching, that the main fact about a man is not his outer wealth or wisdom, but his *inner worth;* not his external position, but his *internal disposition.* He thus spiritualized the social order without revolutionizing it. For him the individual is the social unit, and the regeneration of the individual must ever precede the regeneration of society.

The change of the heart of the individual and through the individual the change of society, is the process Jesus followed. That is not primarily an outward work, brought about by legislation, or by violence or force, but inward and spiritual, eventually the reform of character, not of institutions. Doubtless with the reform of character, institutions will also change.

We must first get a better people before we can get a better world. "The soul of improvement," said Horace Bushnell, "is the improvement of the soul." If the owner of a business is regenerated, his business will be regenerated. If the teachers are born again, their principles of education will be in line with the teachings of Jesus. Society cannot be saved until its units are saved, a truth which

the "saviours of society" commonly forget.

Perhaps we owe an apology to the reader for this lengthy discussion of our theological objections of the above theories, but to our mind it seems that the moral bearing is so great, that not enough can be said. We must call the attention of the reader to something which has often been overlooked by most of us, and especially by our scientist friends. It is this: Science will never be able to solve these problems alone. They are primarily questions for religious philosophy. Allow us to give our reasons.

"Children often ask their parents questions about when things were made, where they came from, which the parents are unable to answer, or do not wish to answer. This shows that the human mind is naturally curious about these matters. In fact this curiosity about the origin of things is one of the very foundation stones of both science and religion."[51]

Some of us perhaps remember the story in Rousseau's "Emil" of the little boy, in the care and training of an atheist, who saw to it that no one approached him with religion. However, after reaching the stage of judgment, he put the question to his unbelieving tutor: "Sir, who made the sun, the stars, the moon, and this beautiful earth?" His common sense demanded an answer.

Gazing at all those wonderful things in our world, man's mind is eagerly concerned, not with their proximate constitution, but with their *ultimate* origin, their spiritual import *for him.* What do they mean in relation to his own soul and life and destiny? *Who made them?* That is the mood in which he approaches the subject, and through it, as through an open door, the eternal spirit enters, sheds His light on all things and prepares his heart and mind to accept this fadeless psalm of Creation. And the writer of this record of Creation is dealing in no sense with the scientific *but with the* religious aspect of things.

Science can only take note of secondary causes. It has nothing to say about a First Cause. That is a question *solely* for religious

---

[51] Price, Geo. McCready, "How Did the World Begin?," 1942, p. 7.

philosophy. Science takes for granted force, order, matter, motion, and all other inter-relations; and on these postulates it builds up the order and sequence of things in detail. How one thing follows another; how cause produces effect, and the same cause always the same effect; how physical phenomena and organic life are interdependent,—*these are the problems of science.* Science asks: *When? Where? How?* And when it has obtained a satisfactory answer to these questions, it sinks back satisfied, having no more questions to ask, its function as an instrument of inquiry being completed. But when the scientific faculty—the intellect—has done its work, or rather, in point of time and importance, *before* it has begun it, the human soul with its deeper and more ultimate inquiries comes forward and passionately inquires: *Whence? Why? Whither?* What is the ultimate source of all these things? Why are they here, thus, and so? What moral or purposeful plan is being developed by their means? What is the great end toward which they tend? These are the questions of religion, of religious philosophy. And it is to these questions that the first chapter of Genesis gives a reply.

It is not merely science, it is religion, everything is viewed in relation to the eternal cause and source of all things—a consideration which has, strictly speaking, no place whatever in a strictly scientific argument. Final causation—God, is reached by the act

of faith: "For he that cometh to God, must believe that He is." In the thought of an all-creating Deity that is back of us, I rest with a degree of mental comfort. Yet it is, after all, by my heart that I perceive and know God, rather than by my thinking. Indeed, to *know* God is a gift of God and has to be given, not learned.

The simple narrative, in tracing the origin of all things in six literal days to the creative work of God, does not conflict with anything that may yet be discovered by science as to the actual method or sequence of Creation. Whatever may be said of the outward form of the narrative, one has only to look at the great ideas which the first chapter of Genesis is intended to teach to see that it conveys those great truths on the origin and ordering of things which are necessary as the basis of a true religious view of the world, no matter to what stage knowledge or science may attain. This chapter standing at the head of the Bible, lays the foundation for all that follows in the view of the relation of God to the world. The story of Creation, therefore remains for all time of the highest religous value.

In closing let us state that there is no conflict between true science and true religion, but that sound science cannot be irreligious nor true religion unphilosophical. Above all let us ever remember, that science takes the world apart, philosophy puts it together again, religion gives it a meaning.

# THE CREATION OF THE EARTH

By Molleurus Couperus, M.D.

The problem of the creation of the earth would seem to present at least two aspects, namely the creation of the earth itself (its origin as an astronomical body), and the creation of life upon the earth. If one does not believe in creation these same two problems are still present, except that the evolutionist substitutes the word origin for the word creation. The creationist, of course, may fuse these two aspects of the problem into one, and say that the earth and all life upon it was created simultaneously. If one questions such creationists more closely, however, one finds that they actually do separate the two problems, and that they believe that the earth was created some time previous to the creation of its animal and plant life, at least three days previous. The Creator, of course, could easily have created both the matter of the earth and the life upon it in the same instant, if He had so chosen, but the question is: Did He? And from the evidence which He has given us we can conclude that He did not. There are other questions connected with the problem of the creation of the earth which are not as easily answered, and in which the answer can not be as positive; there are still other questions which can not be answered at all, at present.

As indicated above, few actually believe in the simultaneous creation of the earth and the life it bears. The creationists may be divided into two large groups regarding the creation of the earth, namely those who believe that the earth and all its life was created very recently, during six literal days, only six to ten thousand years ago, and those who believe that the earth was created a long time ago, much longer than ten thousand years ago. Among those who hold the latter belief, there are several views regarding the time of the creation of life. One group holds that the creation of life occurred and was completed a long time (perhaps many millions of years) ago; their creation week lies far in the past. Another group holds that life was created in successive steps or periods, beginning also a long time (many millions

of years) ago. A third group holds that life was created only comparatively recently during six literal days on an earth which had been created a long time previously. The question arises now: How can we choose between these varying opinions, and upon what must our choice be based?

## The Creation Record in Genesis

Most of what we know about creation is found in the first two chapters of the book of Genesis, and most of the rest of our knowledge is derived from various scattered statements throughout the Bible. Among those who believe in the divine inspiration of the Bible, very little difference of opinion exists concerning the interpretation of the creation record of Genesis, except that of the first and second verses of the first chapter, and the meaning of the word *day* in the rest of the chapter.

"In the beginning God created the heaven and the earth. And the earth was without form, and void; and darkness was upon the face of the deep. And the Spirit of God moved upon the face of the waters."

Some claim that the phrase "in the beginning" refers to the beginning of the six literal days of creation; others claim that this phrase has no reference to the subsequently mentioned week of creation, but refers to a creative act long preceding the week of creation, namely the beginning of heaven and earth, or even to the begining of the universe. Those who hold the latter view start the creation week with the divine Word: "And God said, Let there be light: and there was light." They also point out that the Genesis record speaks of *created* in the following verses: 1, 21, 27; while in the other references to the creative work of this first week the word *made* is used. In Hebrew the word used for *creation* in the above named verses is *bara*, and the word for *made* is *a:ah*. To these folks holding the view that the phrase "in the beginning" does not mean the first day of the earth's creation week, the use of the word *bara* in Genesis 1:1 indicates the absolute creation of the matter of the earth and the heavens, following which the earth was "without form and void, and darkness was upon the face of the deep" until God spoke: "Let there be light." This word *bara* is used again then in connection with the creation of animal life, and the creation of man "in the image of God." They also point out that the use of the word *bara* in the Scriptures is always connected with a new creation, while the use of *asah* is adequately expressed by *made;* asah is the word used when we are told in Exodus 5:16 that the Israelites made bricks for the building of store-cities in Egypt; it is also the word used in Exodus 20:4 where we are commanded not to make any graven images unto ourselves.

Those who hold the view that "in the beginning" means the beginning of the week of creation refer to the words of the Sabbath commandment, which says: "For in six days the Lord *made* heaven and earth, the sea, and all that in them is." This means to them that heaven and earth were created during the six days of creation. Those holding the other view, however, point out that the word used here is the word *asah*, which refers to the actual work as is described in Genesis 1:3 and on, but that it does not include the *de novo* creation of the earth itself.

It is probably worthwhile at this time to present several of the well known translations of Genesis 1:1-2.

"In the beginning God created the heaven and the earth. Now the earth was unformed and void, and darkness was upon the face of the deep; and the spirit of God hovered over the face of the waters."—The Holy Scriptures According to the Masoretic Text. A New Translation . . . of Jewish Authorities. Philadelphia, 1917.

"In the beginning God made the heavens and the earth. But the earth was unsightly and unfurnished, and darkness was over the deep, and the Spirit of God moved over the water. And God said, Let there be light, and there was light."—The Septuagint Version of the Old Testament, with an English Translation. Bagster and Sons, London. (n.d.)

"In the beginning God created the heavens and the earth. And the earth was waste and void; and darkness was upon the face of the deep: and the Spirit of God moved upon the face of the waters."—American Revised Version (1901), Thomas Nelson & Sons, New York.

"In the beginning God created heaven, and earth. And the earth was void and empty, and darkness was upon the face of the deep; and the spirit of God moved over the waters. And God said: Be light made. And light was made."—Douay Version (Translated from the Latin Vulgate)

"When God began to create the heavens and the earth, the earth was a desolate waste, with darkness covering the abyss and a tempestuous wind raging over the surface of the waters. Then God said, Let there be light."—An American Translation—The Old Testament, by J. M. Powis Smith. University of Chicago Press, 1939.

"In the beginning created God the heaven and the earth. Now the earth was waste and empty, and darkness was over the abyss; and the Spirit of God hovered over the waters."—Dutch Translation of the Bible (National Synod, 1618-19), British and Foreign Bible Society, London, 1928.

If one reads these and other translations it would seem that the most evident thought expressed here regarding the time of the earth's creation is that it occurred *at some beginning* prior to the creative work described further on in the record, and that the earth, following this original creation, was left in a condition which is described as desolate and empty. One might go a little further and state that from the plain wording the "beginning" here described is the creative origin of the heavens and the earth, the beginning of the universe. As to *how long* before the rest of the creative work as it is described in Genesis 1 and 2 this earlier creation took place, we are not told in these verses.

As mentioned before, the Hebrew word translated in our Bible as *created* in Genesis 1:1 is the word *barah,* and it is found in addition to this in the first two chapters of Genesis only in relation to the creation of the great whales (1:21), and the creation of man (1:27; 2:3, 4). I do not want to base the interpretation of Genesis 1:1-2 solely on a shade of meaning which one word may have above another, but if the best translation of a word used in the Bible bears out what the rest of the text seems to convey, we should accept such evidence. Certainly, if we believe in the divine inspiration of the Bible, there was some reason in the mind of God why certain words were used to express the inspired thought instead of some other word, and if we are to get as perfect as possible a picture of what God intended us to learn through His word we must study as fully as possible the meaning and usage of the word in question. There seems to be almost a unanimity of opinion among biblical scholars that the word *barah* carries a special significance in regards to creation which is not carried by any other word in the Old Testament, and that for the same reason such other words as *asah* and *yatsar* are not translated as create but as *make, form,* etc. There are, of course, instances where the word *barah* may be used in addition to one or more of the other words, such as occurs in Isaiah 43: 7, but in this instance it is quite clear that all three words apply, each with its own individual meaning.

"*Bara* is confined to God's acts; the other two verbs are used also of man's acts. Though *bara* extends to other acts of God besides the original creation, it is only in a secondary application, without reference to preexisting materials; still, except in the original creation, they are not excluded." Cannon A. R. Fausset, Bible Cyclopaedia, p. 140.

"In the first two chapters of Genesis we meet with four different verbs to express the creative work of God, viz. 1, to create; 2, to make; 3, to form; 4, to build. The first is used of the creation of the universe (v. 1); of the creation of the great sea-monsters, whose vastness appears to have excited special wonder (v. 21); and of the creation of man, the head of the animated nature, in the image of God (v. 27). Everywhere else we read of God's *making,* as from an already created substance, the firmament, the sun, the stars, the brute creation (vv. 7, 16, 25, etc.); or of His *forming* the beasts of the field out of the ground (ch. ii. 19); or lastly, of His *building up* (ii. 22, margin) into a woman the rib which He had taken from man." E. Harold Browne, D.D., in: The Holy Bible With An Explanatory and Critical Commentary, Edited by F. C. Cook, Vol. 1, Comments on Genesis 1: 1.

"It may be proper here to treat briefly of the meaning of *bara,* create, in Genesis ch. 1 ... As the act of creation was in the nature of the case but *once* performed, the term could only be used infrequently with reference to that event, just as 'create' with moderns etymologically and even practically refers rather to production in a subordinate sense than to absolute origination. In both words, however, the higher and full sense is never lost sight of, and thus they appear as nearly synonymous in actual usage as any two in different and widely remote languages could well be. The translators of the Auth. Vers. have therefore done well by invariably (except in the single passage above noted) rendering bara (in Kal and Niphal at least) and no other Heb. term, by *create.* That this absolute sense is the true one in Gen. 1:1, at least, is demonstrable from the association there with the term 'beginning'. For if matter had existed eternally, there would have been no proper 'beginning' at all of its existence." Cyclopedia of Biblical, Theological and Ecclesiastical Literature, by J. McClintock and James Strong, Vol. II, pp. 554-555.

"I shall now give the opinion of Aben Esrah on Bara *(created)*; he says that Bara signifies, 'God created the world out of nothing'; this opinion is certainly an undeniable fact, as will be seen by referring to Numbers xvi. 30, and Jerm. xxxi. 22, 'A new thing' (which never evisted before). This is the interpretation of Bara. He further says that ... Gen. i. 1 denotes that God in the beginning had created, not merely the heavens, but everything therein, a view which will, I think, satisfactorily account for the omissions of Moses, who has given no record of many things of God's creation, as Angels, Seraphim, etc.

"It is very remarkable, that the word Bara (which signified, 'created out of nothing') occurs but three times in the first chapter of Genesis, verses 1, 21, 27, from which I infer, that in these verses, where this word Bara occurs, we are to understand that there was no previous existence of the things mentioned; hence it follows, that in the 1st verse, by the word 'created', I understand to be included the materials of the different works which appeared successively, until we meet with the word again in the 21st verse." Benjamin Marcus, Mistranslations and Difficult Passages of the Old Testament, Comments on Genesis 1:1. Dublin, 1851.

We may now ask the question: If the record in Genesis 1 and 2 does not indicate *how long* prior to the six days of creation the earth and the heavens were created, does the Bible elsewhere give us any indication if this original creation occurred shortly before or a long time prior to the creation week? I believe that there are texts in the Bible which shed some light on the above question. Others in this symposium have discussed many of these at length, and I will confine myself here to mentioning only the following. "Before the mountains were brought forth, or ever thou hadst formed the earth and the world, even from everlasting to everlasting, thou are God." Psalms 90:2. "Of old hast thou laid the foundations of the earth: and the heavens are the work of thy hands." Psalms 102:25. "Where wast thou when I laid the foundations of the earth? declare, if thou hast understanding. Whereupon are the foundations thereof fastened? or who laid the cornerstone thereof; When the morning stars sang together, and all the sons of God shouted for joy?" Job 37:4, 6-7. "Jehovah possessed me in the beginning of his way, Before his works of old. I was set us from everlasting, from the beginning, Before the earth was. While as yet he had not made the earth, nor the fields, Nor the beginning of the dust of the world." Proverbs 8:22-23, 26. (Rev. Vers.) 'God . . . hath in these last days spoken unto us by his Son, whom he hath appointed heir of all things, by whom also he made the worlds; And, Thou Lord, in the beginning hast laid the foundation of the earth; and the heavens are the works of thine hands." Hebrew 1:2, 10. "Through faith we understand that the worlds were framed by the word of God, so that the things which are seen were not made of things which do appear." Hebrew 11:3.

"For this they willingly are ignorant of, that by the word of God the heavens were of old, and the earth standing out of the water and in the water." II. Peter 3:5.

In these and other texts there are several facts which are repeated over and over again by the various writers of the Holy Scriptures. First, there is repeated reference to a creation of the world or worlds, of which the creation of the earth formed only a part. Secondly, there is reference in other texts to an act which may be called *laying the foundations of the earth*, and from its association with the first group of statements, this act would seem to be identical with the creation of the worlds. Thirdly, this part of the creative work of God is frequently referred to as occurring "of old," "in the beginning." None of this, of course, fixes the time of earth's creation, it simply indicates that the belief in a creation of the earth which took place a long time ago, long before the well known creation week, is not incompatible with the words of Holy Scripture.

There is one text, however, which has led many to take a positive stand that the creation of the substance of the earth prior to the creation week of Genesis 1 is unbiblical, even though they agree that from the reading of Genesis 1:1-2 such a prior creation of the earth would be acceptable. This text which gives many so much difficulty in relation to this subject is Exodus 20:11, part of the fourth commandment, where it says: "For in six days the Lord made heaven and earth, the sea, and all that in them is, and rested the seventh day: wherefore the Lord blessed the sabbath day, and hallowed it." In reviewing the difference of opinion which exists regarding the first part of this verse, I want to emphasize that this difference of opinion has no bearing or relation to the divine command to keep the seventh day holy, which command stands as grand and immutable as before. The only point where there exists a difference of opinion here is regarding the exact creative work of God for which the Sabbath is a permanent memorial. Some take the position that "heaven and earth" mentioned in the above verse refers to the entire universe, all matter and life having been created during earth's creative week. Others limit "heaven and earth" to our solar system, and point to the fact that sun, moon and stars are mentioned in Genesis 1. Still others believe that what is meant here is only the earth and its atmosphere. Finally there are those, including the present writer, who believe that "heaven and earth, the sea, and all that in them is" refers to making the earth and atmosphere ready for the sustenance of life, and the subsequent creation of that life in its various forms; it presupposes the previous creation of the matter of the earth, as revealed in Genesis 1: 1-2. Those who believe that the body of the earth (its matter) was also created during the six days of Genesis 1, refer to the positive language, as they see it, of the above text: "For in six days the Lord made heaven and earth, the sea, and all that in them is." They feel that no difference of opinion can exist here, that the earth in its totality was brought into being during these six days, according to this verse.

It seems to me that there are several facts here which must not be lost sight of. First of all, this verse is part of the fourth commandment, which announces to man the holiness of the seventh day, and that this Sabbath took its origin in that fact and in the resting of the Creator on that day after He completed a six-day period of creative work. The primary purpose then of this commandment is not to go into detail as to all that which was done during this six-day period, but *to call to remembrance* that such a creative period had occurred in which Jehovah had worked, and that the sacredness of the Sabbath took its origin in that fact and in the fact that He rested on the seventh day following this creative period, and that He had set apart the seventh day of every week after that as a sacred memorial. Secondly, the word used here is the word *made*, in harmony with what we find in the creative record after Genesis 1:1-2. Thirdly, if the interpretation of an all inclusive creation is accepted, then we must also accept, it would seem, the creation of heaven to mean the creation of the universe. This would then not be in harmony with other bible statements, such as the one in Job 38:4-7, where the morning stars are described as rejoicing when

the earth was created, indicating their prior existence. Fourthly, it would also seem that in order to get an accurate and detailed picture of what the creative work involved which was done during the six days, we should have to go to the original record of that creation, to which the commandment of course refers. That record is found in Genesis 1 and 2, and our interpretation of what is meant by the phrase "heaven and earth, the sea, and all that in them is" in Exodus 20:11 should be based on what is said in the Genesis record. Here in the original account of creation we find also the denfiition of the words "heaven, earth, sea, and all that in them is", as it relates to that event, and we discover that it means the making ready of the earth and atmosphere for the advent of life, and the formation of the myriads of forms of living organisms on and in that earth, in its heaven, and in the sea.

To me it seems that "in the beginning" refers to a time which preceded the six days of creation, and that the Bible gives us no information as to when this beginning was. The beginning referred to in Genesis 1:1 could very well be the creation of our universe, preceding by an unknown period of time the creative work of God in making the earth habitable and establishing life upon it, which was accomplished in six days; it could, however, also be a creation which was more limited in scope than that of our entire universe. If the Bible does not give us a definite time for the creation of the heavens and the earth, it is still possible that God's other book, nature, may give us this information. Astronomers and physicists claim that they have found several independent methods of arriving at such a date of primeval creation, and we should be aware at least that such claims have been made.

One problem that is often thrown up to the creationist is the apparent age of the earth based on radioactive disintegration studies. By this method the age of the earth is claimed to be in the neighborhood of some 1600 million to two billion years. If we take for granted that the technical analyses and the complicated mathematical calculations are reasonably correct, there remain two positions open for the creationist to take. First, that the earth was indeed created that long ago, and that the apparent age of the earth as indicated by the radioactive disintegration is also its true age; in this case the phrase "in the beginning" refers to the creation of the earth as a planetary body a long time ago, say some 1600 million years. Secondly, one may take the position that at the time of creation the radioactive series were created in such a proportional relationship that the age of earth on the day of creation seemed to be much greater than it really was, that the apparent age of the earth was much greater than its true age; in this case the phrase "in the begining" could refer to an act of creation immediately preceding the six days of creation, or even be part of the first day, and the earth would be very young indeed. Though this second possibility must be kept in mind, one should not reject the first one as false unless there is definite evidence compelling us to do so.

## Pre-Adamic Ruin Theory

Two theories in relation to the work of creation have become widely accepted among professed Christians of today, and these are the so-called pre-adamic ruin theory and the day-age theory.

The advocates of the pre-adamic ruin theory believe that Genesis 1:2 indicates a condition of ruin following a previous creation of life upon this earth. No proof of such previous life on earth is found in the Bible record, but the adherents of this theory bring together a number of texts which, they say, indicate such a creation. An example of such evidence as they give is Isaiah 45:18, and Ezekiel 28, which certainly does not require such an interpretation. They also state that Genesis 1:2 should read: "The earth *became* waste and void" instead of "*was* waste and void." But practically all Greek and Hebrew scholars insist that the correct translation here is *was*.

There seem to be two main reasons why these folks desire to advocate such a theory.

1. The long geological ages, as indicated by the fossils (they believe), require such a theory.

2. God could not create anything chaotic or imperfect, and that therefore the condition described in Gen. 1:2 was the result of a catastrophe, of evil.

To the first argument we would answer that no such necessity exists to require a long age of life before the biblical week of creation; the deluge explains the fossil-bearing strata. To the second argument we answer that in this instance man tries to impute to the Creator the same thoughts, standards and views as man has; who are we to say that the Creator should or should not create or use a condition which we call chaotic, or waste, or void? Astronomy reveals to us that indeed such condidtions as described in Gen. 1:2 are found in our universe today, and that the phraseology of the biblical record may justly be applied to heavenly bodies now in existence; such conditions are one of the ways of God's working. This pre-adamic ruin theory necessitates the belief that before the fall of man death and suffering befell the animal world previously created. At the close of the week of Creation we are told that "God saw everything that he had made, and, behold, it was very good" (Gen. 1:31), which would hardly seem fitting for a world which was then a great grave-yard, acording to the ruin-theory.

## The Day-Age Theory

The reason for adopting this theory seems to be the same as the first one cited under the ruin-theory, namely the mental difficulty created by the claims of the evolutionary geologists and paleontologists that very long ages must be allotted to certain forms of life upon the earth, each age at least a hundred thousand years long, probably many millions of years.

The day-age advocates point out that the word *day*, as used in the first chapter of Genesis, is translated from the Hebrew word *yom*, and that although this word is usually translated as day, it is also used in the sense of age, time, etc., and that it should be translated as age in Genesis 1. To this viewpoint the following objections may be raised:

1. Whenever the word *yom* is used with a definite number, such as first, second, etc., it is always used in the sense of *day* in the Bible; the addition of evening and morning

with the use of yom in every instance in this chapter has the same implication, and makes it inexcusable to translate *yom* as *age* here.

2. If these days of Genesis 1 were long ages instead of twenty-four hour periods, then each age was divided into a period of light and one of darkness, evening and morning.

3. On the third day plant life was created, while the sun did not become visible until the fourth day. It would be impossible for most species of the plant kingdom to carry on very long without the aid of sunlight, certainly not for an entire geologic period of some hundred thousand years.

4. Nature as we know it is balanced, and it would seem impossible for the plant kingdom to exist for any great length of time without the mutually adapted animal kingdom. Many plants, for instance, are dependent on insect pollination for their reproduction.

5. The phraseology used in the creation record: "And God said, Let there be . . . and it was so," would indicate an instantaneous action, and not a long period of gradual evolution, as is held by at least some of those believing in the day-age theory.

6. Adam was created on the sixth day, rested on the seventh, and lived beyond the seventh for many a year. If these days were ages, then we must believe that Adam existed through part of the sixth age, the entire seventh, and part of modern time!

7. In the fourth commandment, the seventh day or Sabbath is a memorial of the six days of creation, a solar day in commemoration of what are also called days in the same commandment.

In order to keep our thinking clear, it should be stated that neither the pre-adamic ruin theory or the day-age theory has any connection with evolution as such, since in both of these the Creator is the originator of life in its various forms. Some of the adherents of the day-age theory (as mentioned before) hold to a form of evolutionary development during the long ages after the Creator had formed certain basic forms. The pre-adamic ruin theory and the day-age theory are therefore not evolutionary theories (though probably inspired by evolution) but

unscriptural and unscientific creationist' theories.

## The Six Days of Creation

The earth was enshrouded in darkness and covered with water when God said, Let there be light. From Genesis 1:6 it seems clear that the whole earth was covered with a thick blanket of water vapor, which probably extended through the entire atmosphere of the earth (See Job 38:4, 9). Just what this light or its source was which God created on this first day is impossible for us to say with certainty. Many explanations and theories have been offered, some of which seem quite plausible, while other are very far-fetched. Although it is quite permissible to try and discover in just what way God worked His wonders to perform, it is not at all *necessary* to know any more than that God on this first day caused light to shine upon this earth. From the record we do know that this light alternated with darkness, thus instituting day and night, and forming the first day. The sequence of day and night depends on the rotation of the earth on its axis, and its exposure to a point-source of light. Some have believed that God caused some diffuse cosmic light to lighten the earth on this first day; or light of purely local, earthly origin, but this could hardly be harmonized with the day and night sequence. Others hold that the sun was the source of this light, and that one of three things happened on this first day: First, that God actually created the sun on this first day. Secondly, that the sun had previously existed as a *dark* sun, and that on this first day God caused the sun to become a new sun or nova. Thirdly, that the sun was already a luminary body, whose light had been unable to penetrate to the surface of the earth, due to the blanket of water vapor, but that God brought about a change in the atmospheric conditions of the earth so that the light of the sun was able to reach in some degree to the surface of the waters which covered the earth. I believe that this last possibility is a reasonable one when one considers the other texts which have to do with the condition of the earth and compares this with what happened on the fourth day of creation.

On the second day of creation the water vapors which rested upon the universal ocean that covered the earth were separated from it by a firmament or expanse, which was called *Heaven* (singular). On the third day of creation, God first gathered the waters on the earth together in one place, (which He called *Seas*), thus letting the dry land appear (which He called *Earth*.) After the dry land had thus been made available, God caused the earth to bring forth the plant kingdom, with its myriads of forms of grasses, herbs, and trees, each bringing forth seed after its kind. This completed the work of the third day.

On the fourth day God said, "Let there be lights in the firmament of heaven to divide the day from the night; and let them be for signs, and for seasons, and for days and years: and let them be for lights in the firmament of heaven to give light upon the earth: and it was so. And God made the two great lights; the greater light to rule the day, and the lesser light to rule the night; *he made* the stars also. And God set them in the firmament of heaven to give light up on the earth, and to rule over the day and over the night, and to divide the light from the darkness: and God saw that it was good." Gen. 1: 14-18. Just as the creation of light on the first day is understood in more than one way, so the record of the work of the fourth day of creation is interpreted in various ways by different bible students. Let me hasten to say that none of these various interpretations in any way reflect upon the interpreter's faith in the word of God or the creative act of God; there is only a difference of opinion as to what actually was done by the Creator on that particular day. It may be impossible to glean from the biblical record the exact details as to how God brought the described results about, and, on the other hand, it may be possible that this can be done by comparing this text with other texts dealing with the same subject.

The main views which are held by creationists on the work of this fourth day may be divided into two groups: those holding that the sun and moon (and some include the stars as well) were created on this day, and that they had no existence in any form prior to this day. The second group represents those who believe that the sun, moon and stars had been created previously by God, but that on this fourth day their light was made completely available for the surface of the earth. In either case they were created by God. At first glance the bible student may come to a quick support of the view that these heavenly bodies were first brought into existence on this fourth day. A careful study of these texts and of what has gone before may make him change his views, however. From God's answer to Job we learn that the morning stars sang together, and all the sons of God shouted for joy when He laid the foundations of the earth (Job 38: 4-7). There was then a creation which had taken place prior to the laying of the foundations of the earth, and thus prior to the fourth day of the creation week when God set lights in the firmament of heaven. Now, in Genesis 1:1 we are told that God created the heavens and the earth in the beginning; whenever this beginning may have been, it certainly was before the fourth day of the creation week. What did God create when He created the heavens? It was not the firmament-heaven, for this was made on the second day, and God called it heaven (singular). The heavens (plural) designated in Genesis 1:1 could hardly be anything but the astronomical heavens. It is also worthy of notice that the lights which were set in the firmament on the fourth day were to divide the day from the night, light from darkness, and for seasons, and for days and years. Yet the light which was brought forth on the first day also alternated with darkness or night, and evening and morning formed the first day. In both verse 4 and verse 18 it is said that God divided the light from the darkness. Taking all this together with what we are told was the condition of the earth during the first few days of the creation week, it seems altogether in harmony with the bible record to believe that God did not create the sun, moon and stars on the fourth day of the creation week (the word *create* is not used for the work of this day), but that on this day God made fully available the light of these heavenly bodies for the earth's surface. Just how He did this is again another question. Keeping in mind what we have been told about the atmospheric conditions surrounding the earth at the beginning of creation week, it is at least very plausible that on this fourth day by the word of God the obstructing vapor bank which was above the firmament was completely removed, thus allowing the light of sun, moon and stars to fall upon the earth's surface. If we consider the logical sequence of events for the second, third and fourth day from the biblical record, such an interpretation of what occurred on the fourth day is also logical. On the second day the heavy, thick layer of vaporized water which surrounded the earth was separated from the waters below, thus forming an expanse between the two; the waters above the firmament were still there, however, as the text expressly states. On the third day God separated the waters on the earth, so that the dry land appeared; we may well believe that this act was accompanied by a mighty convulsion on this earth when thus the continents were born in a single day. The following day, the fourth of the creation week, the lights of the astronomical heavens appeared for the first time in the firmament: God had taken away the interference of 'the waters above the firmament,' and man, who was soon to be created, would be able to receive and study rays of light which had been on its way for millions of years. It is further of interest that evening and morning make a day, and the unobstructed availability and visibility of this light from the astronomical heavens probably started at the close of the third day, after the plants were created; the great changes in the physical condition of the earth were then completed. The moon and stars shone that night, and the following day the sun poured forth its rays upon the newly created plant world.

On the fifth day God created the animal life of air and water, after its kind. On the sixth day God made the multitude of land animals, all after their kind, and He then created man in His own image from the dust of the ground.

Some believers in creation hold that the Creator made only one pair of all the various animals He created (also of the plants?), just as He created only one pair of the human species. Why they should take this view is hard to understand. When speaking of the creation of life in the waters, it is said: "The waters brought forth abundantly," which would seem to indicate that enormous numbers of the same species were created. (The Revised Version reads: "Let the waters swarm with swarms of living creatures.") It seems reasonable to believe that when the work of the Creator was finished that the earth was in its entirety a harmonious and beautiful picture of life, the various animals and plants distributed over the entire earth into those regions to which they were adapted.

Some also hold that only very few forms of animals were created, so that Adam on a part of the sixth day was able to see and name them all. This is, I believe, an unwarranted interpretation of Genesis 2:18-23, where God brought certain forms of life before Adam to demonstrate to him that he also needed a 'help meet for him.' These same folks argue from this that this experience of Adam shows how few basic forms were really created, and that subsequently the multitudinous forms of life have 'developed' from these original kinds of Genesis. It seems clear from the scriptural record that God brought animals of various kinds to Adam for his observation, which Adam gave names, and which caused him to arrive at the conclusion which God intended for him, namely that of all creatures he was the only one who was alone. We know of no scientific explanation which could satisfactorily account for the changing of so few original kinds into the almost innumerable species of today, and on biblical grounds also it seems difficult to defend.

Thus was completed the work of the six days of creation, and God "rested on the seventh day from all His works which He had made. And God blessed the seventh day and hallowed it."

1930 Wilshire Boulevard
Los Angeles 5, Calif.

# LETTERS AND COMMENTS

## COMMENTS ON THE FIRST VOLUME OF THE FORUM

### By George McCready Price

I believe that the articles in the previous number of THE FORUM have done much to clarify the hitherto hazy ideas which most Creationists have held regarding the meaning of the opening verses of Genesis I. It is now clear that some among us believe that the body or substance of the earth may have been created long before the beginning of what we term Creation Week, while others are very sure that the entire earth was spoken into existence only at the first of this latter period. This second class hold that the opening verse of the bible has nothing at all to do with the origin of the sidereal universe, while the former group hold that this first verse is concerned entirely with the origin of the universe as a whole, and only incidentally with that of the earth. Both sides admit that the starry universe had been in existence long previous to Creation Week.

Particularly clear and convincing (to me at least) is the distinction which John Lowell Butler makes between the *primary* and *secondary* creations. No one can deny that the vast majority of the suns and galaxies were probably created at one time, "in the beginning," and created by this primary method, or "*ex nihilo*," out of nothing, as the philosophers express it. Similarly, no one can deny that all the plants and animals of our world (including man) were created in the *secondary way*, or out of the previously created materials. And if this distinction holds true in the complete and absolute way that Butler contends, then his case is won without further argument.

Butler is absolutely right in showing the two distinct meanings for the word "heaven," as used in this chapter and elsewhere, the astronomical heaven and the atmospheric heaven. This clear distinction is also helpful in understanding its possible meaning in the first verse. Of course, this distinction may be admitted by Clark and his side without their having to admit also that in this first verse

it means the heaven of the stars or the sidereal universe as a whole. But by remembring this very clear and important distinction between the two meanings of the word "heaven," we can help to narrow down the discussion.

It seems to me that Butler is also correct in interpreting Isa. 48: 12, 13 as meaning that the "foundations" of the earth were laid simultaneously with the spreading out of the sidereal heaven. The clear and positive statement is: "When I call unto them, *they stand up together.*" It is certainly a clear and obvious interpretation of this passage, to say that it means that the universe of he stars and the earth were created simultaneously. This is a primary and very strong argument for Butler's similar interpretation of the first verse of Genesis: "In the beginning God created the [astronomical] heaven and the earth." It is going to be very difficult for the other side to explain away this text in Isaiah 48.

Butler's astronomical argument also appears to me very clear and convincing. He has devoted many long years to the study of astronomy; and when he reminds us that there are even now many dark stars throughout our galaxy, it seems highly probable that our sun may well have been like one of these dark stars for a long period, and that only at the beginning of Creation Week it was lit up by the fiat of the Creator, when the word went forth concerning our little world: "Let there be light."

So I repeat, Butler's argument is convincing to me. As for Clark's argument, I shall leave to someone else the work of dealing with it in detail; but this much may be said here, that in probably more than half of it the standard bearer of the "Ultra" party is dealing with straw men, whom he creates for the purpose of knocking them down. For example, in the first column on page 14 he deals with the idea that the matter of our earth, when first created, was in a nebulous or widely diffused state. As a matter of fact, I do not know of any intelligent Creationist who holds this view. As Butler so well expresses the matter, when God created the substance of our earth, he naturally placed its elements or component parts exactly where they would be wanted to compose the inhabited planet. Or in other words, he made the entire body of the earth exactly where it would at the proper time be ready to be fitted up as the home of the plants and animals which He planned to create upon it. He always sees the end from the beginning, and plans accordingly. God never made a "chaos" among the stars, any more than he makes a jumble of "unformed" protoplasm for the beginning of the embryo of an animal.

The problem of God's non-indebtedness to "pre-existing matter" is frequently brought up in the discusisons of our present subject. Butler and all the rest of us believe that no such thing as "pre-existing matter" was involved in the formation of our world. We all believe that it was created "*ex nihilo,*" or spoken into existence. The only question is, *When* did this occur? Was it at the beginning of Creation Week, or was it away back at the beginning of all the rest of the astronomical universe?

As the discussion now stands, Clark has given us nothing but his *opinion,* or his *credo,* with absolutely no text from the Bible to prove it; while Butler has at least given one very clear and seemingly conclusive text for his belief.

Does any other person have further light to shed on the subject?

---

# THE VALUE OF DISCUSSION

"DISCUSSION!—It is through candid discussion, the untrammeled expression of conviction, and the summoning of every available argument and pertinent fact, that the truest and soundest conclusions are reached. A sound position has nothing to fear from investigation. Especially does it court the questions of friends. It is through freedom of discussion that all the facts are brought out. In this way weak points come to light that can be remedied. Repression is the method of the weakling, the refuge of the intolerant. Let freedom of discussion ever prevail in our committees, councils, and conferences."

L. E. Froom
THE MINISTRY,
October, 1945.

"The fact that there is no controversy or agitation among God's people, should not be regarded as conclusive evidence that they are holding fast to sound doctrine. There is reason to fear that they may not be clearly discriminating between truth and error. When no new questions are started by investigation of the Scriptures, when no difference of opinion arises which will set men to searching the Bible for themselves, to make sure that they have the truth, there will be many now, as in ancient times, who will hold to tradition, and worship they know not what . . . .

"God will arouse His people. If other means fail, heresies will come in among them, which will sift them, separating the chaff from the wheat . . .

"Our brethren should be willing to investigate in a candid way every point of controversy. If a brother is teaching error, those who are in responsible positions ought to know it; and if he is teaching truth, they ought to take their stand at his side."

Ellen G. White
"Gospel Workers," pp. 298-300

# A REBUTTAL

## To THE FORUM:

May I be allowed a few words in rebuttal on the points discussed in the first volume of THE FORUM.

I think we are all agreed that there are "many inhabited worlds," and that some of them have been inhabited for mililons of years. This point is well taken by Butler.

But the assumption that the "primary creation,"—the origin of matter,—of *all* the worlds, was simultaneous, and took place, as Price suggests, somewhere about 2000 million years ago, is based on very slim evidence, if not entirely on conjecture. Let us remember that the force of gravitation is inversely proportional to the square of the distance. Imagine a world next to ours, with equal volume and mass. The centers of the two worlds would be 8000 mile sapart. Let us take this as our unit of comparison. Now let such a world be placed at the distance of the nearest fixed star, 4½ light-years away. This would be roughly 26⅓ trillion miles away. The square of this equals 685 septillion miles (24 ciphers). This is the ration to 8000 of 8 sextillion to 1. Therefore at that distance the pul of gravity of a planet the mass of ours would be 1/86,000,000,000,000,000,-000,000 that at the surface of our earth. Who dares say that God could not create new matter and slip it into the universe because there would be danger that He could not make the trifling adjustment these figures call for? In 1918 all the planets were lined up on the same side of the sun, and yet this seeming maladjustment was cared for somehow. Surely God has power to make the necessary balance to keep the universe running. I do not believe we are justified in assuming He must have made all the matter simultaneously in order to keep it balanced.

Butler is absolutely right in saying that God used substances already in existence during the week of creation. But to assume that the matter was in existence *long ages* before that week is beyond the realm of proof. The expression in Isaiah 48, "they stand up together," is read as if it said, *they stood up together.* The idea of simultaneous creation is read into the text by those who wish it to mean that. It can just as well be read to mean that all these works consist, or hold together by the power of God, as is expressed in Colossians 1:17.

Furthermore, the contention that *the* beginning was distinct from creation week is unfounded, since the article *the* does not occur in the original, neither in Genesis 1:1 nor in John 1:1. In both these places the literal translation would be *in beginning,* or *originally,* and would be wholly without any implication as to the length of time involved.

Price, in the editorial remarks, makes the statement that the "scientific evidence is overwhelmingly in favor" of a great age for the earth. "Many scientific facts," he says, lead, "without fail," to the same conclusion. This is very positive language, and should be supported by unequivocal proof. If there is any such proof, such overwhelming evidence, it has escaped my notice completely. The data in support of these statements should be presented in an early issue of THE FORUM. At least, the advocates of the long age of the earth should state clearly all the reasons why they believe in such an interpretation, so that it may be seen whether that belief is founded on facts or on opinions deduced from certain facts that are open to more than one interpretation.

H. W. Clark

# "IN THE BEGINNING"

### Elmer Wm. Pruett

The first issue of THE FORUM has been read with interest, mingled with both pleasure and disappointment. Comments were invited, and this response has been delayed sufficiently to assure that the ideas herein expressed shall not be hasty, first reading impressions, but the sober attempt to discuss the question on its merits.

For the purpose of discussion, let it be granted that the words, "made heaven and earth," *may* refer only to the events of Genesis 1:3-31, so far as the limiting factor of "in six days," is concerned; and that therefore, it does not (or *may* not), apply to the opening statement of Genesis 1:1. Just as when we say that a carpenter "made" a house and all the furniture in it,—we refer to the construction of those articles, and not to the actual production of the raw materials which he used.

There being no really conclusive *proof* either way, it would seem that the wisest course would be to say so, and let it go at that, rather than get into another Arian-Athanasian controversy over a subject that none of us know anything about.

But since both Mr. Price and Mr. Butler have essayed to present "evidence" in support of a prior creation of the *substance* of the earth, it seems to me fitting that their arguments be answered. And in harmony with the principle stated in the preceding paragraph, we shall content ourselves with giving our reasons for considering their evidences unsatisfactory, without any attempt to "prove" the opposite view from theirs.

Both of the above gentlemen try to bring in Genesis 2:4-6 as applying to the earth *before* the events of Creation Week. I believe that this is utterly erroneous. It would seem clear that the first connected account of Creation Week, ends with Genesis 2:3, rather than with Genesis 1:31; and that the whole of Genesis 2:4-25 is in the nature of a supplement or appendix, giving additional interesting details which would have marred the continuity of the first brief record. But it is definitely erroneous to try to go farther back than Creation Week to find their application. Genesis 1:2-10 records two full days and part of the third *before any plants grew*, and the following verses to the 26th, record two

more full days during which there was "not a man to till the ground," and then goes on to tell what the Lord did about it. This passage certainly could not be talking about Pre-Creation ages, for there was no ground to be tilled prior to the events of the third day.

And for a long time *after* Creation it still remained true that there were no human inhabitants to till the ground of the earth anywhere except in the one locality of the Garden of Eden.

As to the passage: "for the Lord God had not caused it to rain upon the earth,—But there went up a mist from the earth, and watered the whole face of the ground," this too could *not* be applicable to any time prior to the third day, for there was no *ground* to be watered before that time.

Mr. Butler asks, "Why did the Creator consistently refuse to bring new elements into existence during our planet's week of (Secondary?!) Creation?" I find no record of any such *refusal*. It would be more to the point to ask, "Why should He bring new matter into existence, when He had already provided the raw material as the first act of Creation Week?" The first thing any good builder does, after his plans are completed, is to get the materials before he starts to build. Then he does not need to be continually interrupting his work to go for more nails, or lath, or whatever;—*Why* should it be so hard for us to credit the Creator with at least equal intelligence? The record says that God first made the raw elements, and then organized them into an orderly world, complete with plants, animals, and people.

Let us dispense with further wondering as to whether or not the Creator had to create the substance of the entire Universe at one time, or whether He *could* with perfect ease introduce new planets at any time He saw fit.

The argument from radio-activity seems to me to contain entirely too many unknown factors to be of any value in proving the age of the Earth. To use the argument we have to *suppose* a large measure of that same *supposed uniformity* on which the evolutionist counts so heavily.

To recapitulate: I do not *know* that the substance of this Earth was *not* Created prior to the events of Creation Week recorded in Genesis, and at the same time as the whole Universe; but the arguments so far presented to show that it was so created, seem to me very unsatisfactory. I am definitely in agreement with the position taken by Professor Clark on this question.

Route 1, Box 98<br>
Romoland, California

---

# WHEN WAS THE EARTH CREATED?

*"Was this earth made and in the condition of Genesis 1:2 any time before creation week?*

Candidly, this is a question over which there is considerable difference of opinion among even the best of Bible scholars. Some hold there was absolutely nothing here until the first day of creation week, nothing but emptiness. Others believe that the matter from which the earth was made was here in a formless state long before creation week began. On this latter view it may be interesting to observe the following:

Genesis 1:1 seems to be cut off from the six days which follow by the passage which intervenes. It is not said, 'In six days the Lord *created* heaven and earth;' but, 'In six days the Lord *made* heaven and earth.' The first verse of Genesis carries us back to the beginning, whenever that was, as the time when God began His creation. 'In the beginning God created the heavens and the earth.' The book of John begins in the same way. 'In the beginning was the Word, and the Word was with God, and the Word was God. The same was in the beginning with God. All things were made by Him; and without Him was not anything made that was made.' This may pertain to the very material out of which the heavens and the earth were made,—the finishing of many things and the calling into existence of our own solar system with others. Then we read that 'the earth was without form, and void; and darkness was upon the face of the deep.' See the Revised Version, 'The earth was waste and void.' It was in a chaotic condition. Out of that chaotic condition the creative and formative power of God brought the earth into the condition it was at the close of the six days' work."

Milton C. Wilcox,
*Questions Answered*, p. 177-178;
Pacific Press Publishing Association,
Mountain View, Calif., 1938.

# FOR THE RECENT CREATION OF THE EARTH

Dudley Joseph Whitney

The general position taken by writers in the first issue of the FORUM was that there was a first creation of the earth and the rest of the universe, and that later there was the making over of the earth at the time of the Edenic creation. (This view evidently does not require one to believe that the earth was created at the same time as the first part of the material universe.) Clark, on the other hand, believed it probable that the actual creating of the earth occurred as the first step in the Edenic creation, the first act of Creation Week, so to speak, and this is not an uncommon view, nor is it unreasonable.

The special feature that this writer wishes to uphold is that of Clark, that the earth is a recent creation, though he believes, with the other writers, that the earth was created *before* the Edenic creation started. In other words, it is unreasonable to believe that God made the sun, moon, earth and stars, perhaps two billion years ago, and let the earth remain unordered and uninhabited, or without form and void, until about six thousand years ago, and then prepared it as the home for man and made our first parents upon it. From the standpoint of reason—which is not evidence in a problem like this—it seems more probable that He made the earth and then, without unnecessary delay, finished its creation as Genesis 1 records. The sun evidently existed at the start of the earth's ordering, and, for all we know, it may have been made long before the earth, as most of the stars seem to have been.

However, there is also evidence that the earth cannot be millions of years old. It is to be believed that if God made the whole solar system millions of years ago, the sun would have shone upon the earth and caused earth processes to operate much as at present, save for the absence of life; the rains would have fallen on lands, rocks would have been weathered and soluble substances carried into the seas, and so on. At this rate then enormous quantities of sulphur compounds would have been brought into the sea, and enormous quantities of helium emitted from the rocks and mineral springs.

Volcanoes, if they operated in a long pre-Edenic time, would have sent out enough sulphur compounds to make the ocean an unfit home for all but a few, simple marine organisms.

Comets also testify that the solar system is not old. Nearly all writers upon the subject comment upon the way they loose substance, are broken into streams of meteors, or have their orbits changed so that they no longer become visible from the earth again. If God had created the earth long ages ago, with the rest of the solar system, few, if any, comets would now exist, instead of thousands of them. For instance, a writer in the Outline of Science in the Pocket Library of the World's Essential Knowledge gives the probable age of comets as 50,000 to 100,000 years, a period that is far too long considering the number that have been lost to view or destroyed since the rise of modern astronomy. Also, H. N. Russell has pointed out that comets cannot have been picked up by the solar system as it passed through space. While they are not an important part of the solar system they at least testify strongly to the newness of the solar system as a system, and therefore to the recent creation of the earth. Much other evidence to this effect has been given by the writer in The Bulletin of Deluge Geology, Vol. 1, No. 5; December, 1941.

One other observation on the subject of the original condition of the earth might seem to be in order: the darkness that covered the earth at the start of Creation Week evidently came from a cloudy covering, not because the sun did not exist or was dark and cold. Surely the material of our oceans was here once the substance of the earth was formed. If the sun was cold, the earth would be cold and all the water at the surface of the earth would be ice. Light from the stars would then shine upon the earth's surface and it would not be shrouded in darkness. On the other hand, a very hot surface of the earth would turn all the water of the earth into vapor through which the sun's light could shine clearly. Therefore at the beginning of Creation Week the earth cannot have been fiery hot, and it cannot have been so cold that clouds would be thin or non existent.

Radioactivity cannot be held to provide any measure of the age of the earth. Reasons for this belief were given in the FORUM, and also discussed at some detail in the paper by this writer referred to earlier. It should be noted that investigations along this line have dealt with the age of definite rocks, or formations, from which finding the supposed age of the earth is inferred. If these findings have value, some rocks must be held to be 1,800 million years old; others 270 million years old, and other rocks of lesser

age, indicating that the earth was going along with normal earth processes for millions of years before the Edenic Creation. Aside from the inherent flaws of radioactivity estimates, this kind of history for the earth would certainly make the ocean far richer in sodium, mangnesium, sulphate and some other substances than it is, and the air far richer in helium. Of course, the Creator might remedy all this in the Edenic ordering of the earth, but it is surely far more simple and reasonable to believe that God first made the earth and then, with little delay, made it in the way Genesis describes. That was only a few thousand years ago.

Exeter, California

# TWO CREATIONS

### Klemis A. Offermann

I have been much interested in the questions relating to the creation of the universe and our globe. Years ago the present writer found in a German edition of Josephus' works, published 1838 in Philadelphia, Pa., on the subject of creation an interesting note of which we give here an English translation:

"The reader would perhaps appreciate it to find here a short note concerning the well known difficulty relative to the Mosaic record of creation. The question has been asked how could there be light three days before the sun; how the variation of day and night could have started before there was a sun on which it depends; how there could be plants on the earth before the creation of the sun. From the many answers only one should be given. Some say: Everything that Moses relates from verse 2 onward refers only to the finishing of our own globe. That happened perhaps as follows: On the first day there arose a strong wind which began to disperse the thick vapors ascending from the waters, so that it could begin to brighten up on the earth. Thus there began immediately the variation of day and night. The difficulty, therefore, from whence the light came before the sun, disappears at once according to this explanation. On the third day the waters which were left upon the earth gathered in certain regions, and the dry land arose. This could be clothed at once with plants, since the earth was somewhat warmed up from the first day on. On the fourth day all the vapors and mists had been dispelled in such a way that sun, moon and stars could be clearly seen and the mild influence of their warmth and light could be distinctly perceived.—So Reinhard and many others."

In the old edition of Uriah Smith's work on the book of Daniel we find on page 331 the following remarks:

"Astronomers tell us of nebulae lying on the farthest outposts of telescopic vision, whose light in its never ending flight would consume five million years in reaching this planet. So ancient are these stellar orbs."

For certain reasons the last sentence is left out in the latest revised edition. But the author obviously believed and taught that the universe is millions of years old.

This great age of the universe as a whole can only be explained, it seems, by taking the view that there must have been a primary and a secondary creation. The Father, by his own will expressed through his Son, created the entire material universe by simply speaking it into existence, *ex nihilo*, as the theologians say. The atoms of this material universe, as we are now discovering, seem to be endowed with gigantic power; but their seeming power is only the endowed power bestowed upon them by their Creator, who is also the active Manager of the universe. Then the Father, through the Son, in the second creation, completed our planet with its teeming life by the power of His word. See Colossians 1:15, 16; John 1:1-3.

Only the Father and the Son have the "know-how" of the created things. No created being will be able to understand fully the mysteries of the atom and the secrets of the living cell, the fundamental building blocks of all creation. These mysteries are known fully only by the divine Creators, and everything is subject to their will, to the power of their word. They do not need any cyclotron or betatron to change the atom; they command, and everything exists.

# GENESIS AND ASTRONOMY

## By John L. Butler

When more and sufficient consideration is given to *the astronomical aspects* of the Universe, while studying the subject of origins as revealed in Genesis and other portions of the Bible, it is possible to rise above the confusing fog and clouds and to see clearly much more of the grand perspective of history and its beginnings in the many secondary creations of many worlds that are now inhabited in God's majestic Universe: and even to glimpse the resplendent Primary Creation of the Universe itself, long, long ago.

Professor Clark has shown some interest in the astronomical facts that are related to the subject of origins, and has called our attention to an important and basic part of it by reminding us of the law of gravity and just how it operates out to a distance of 4½ light-years. This is the approximate distance to the *nearest* of all the shining stars in our Milky Way galaxy. And because the figures indicate a very weak gravitational force at this short astronomical distance, he has suggested that God could create new matter, even as much as all the elements of the Earth, "and slip it into the Universe" as a trifling deed that would bring no serious consequences, or that would require only "trifling adjustment" of all the other parts of "the Universe." Such an argument is to be expected, sooner or later; and the sooner the better.

In my articles on God's Primary and Secondary Creations I did not intend to give the impression that God "could not" create new matter during any of the weeks of secondary creative work, or that He "could not" make adjustments throughout the Universe each time more weight was introduced into it. It is not a question of what He could or could not do; but, instead, *what did He do?* And *why did He choose to do it this way?*

The Bible says, "As for God, *His way is perfect;*" and *"the law of the Lord is perfect;"* and *"His work is perfect;"* and He himself *"is perfect."* (2 Samuel 22:31; Psalm 19:7; Deuteronomy 32:4; Matthew 5:48; also Deut. 10:14, 17, and Heb. 13:20, 21.) Because of this perfection in everything that He does, God can say, "I am the Lord, I change not." (Malachi 3:6) This is especially true of the Son of God, Jesus Christ, the Creator of the Universe. Of Him one writer said, "Jesus Christ the same yesterday, and today, and for ever." (Hebrews 13:8) And another writer said, "Every good gift and every perfect gift is from above, coming down from the Father of lights, with whom can be no variation, neither shadow that is cast by turning." (James 1:17, American Standard Version) God the Father and God the Son are so perfect in all their plans and work and methods of working that they cannot be improved.

Evidently, then, whichever way would be the most perfect way, would be God's way. Since God is the Author of all astronomy, He is the greatest astronomer. When planning the entire Universe as an astronomer, certainly the most perfect plan would call for the rapid creation of all the elements and all the astronomical bodies and all the astronomical systems simultaneously. Then everything throughout the entire Universe would be in perfect balance, with no "trifling adjustments" necessary time after time subsequently. In this way His *astronomical* work would be "perfect."

Let us consider a few moments the other way that Clark has suggested, namely, that of repeatedly creating new matter and slipping it into the Universe each time another inhabited world was created. What would be the ultimate cumulative effect upon the Universe if this was done a great many times?

He has agreed that "there are 'many inhabited worlds,' and that some of them have been inhabited for millions of years." This basic information needs more consideraton. During the many millions of years that have passed since the beginning of the Universe, God has made many inhabited worlds, which may total a vast number far beyond our ordinary thoughts or ideas of such things. There are well over 30 billions of *shining* suns in our Milky Way galaxy, and well over 100 million giant galaxies within the range of the 100-inch telescope, with millions more to be photographed by more powerful instruments. The entire Universe of which we are speaking may be very large, indeed, and it may contain as many inhabited worlds as all the suns whose light we now see or photograph! When the cumulative effect is considered of the gravitational pull of something like 3 quintillion planets (3 and 18 ciphers) —many of which may be much larger than the Earth—the effect upon the Universe is not trifling, and the amount of adjustment throughout the Universe would be no trivial affair if it had to be done that many times!

In studying astronomy we should remember that *both* light and gravity vary inversely with the square of the distance. Therefore *where light goes gravity goes also.* And light has gone much farther than 4.3 light-years. It has gone over 500,000,000 light-years! And light tells us the amazing story of billions of far flung suns obeying the gentle and steady law of *gravity,* and also the fact that millions of galaxies likewise influence each other. This shows the tremendous importance of some "little" forces, and how God uses them throughout his vast Universe. After all, the Universe is made up of its many parts: without its parts there would be no majestic Universe. Consequently there is nothing too small or too big to escape the notice and the calculation of the Designer and Maker of the Universe.

God sees the end, or fruition, from the beginning. And since the Genesis story records the fact that God chose to *always* use substances that were already in existence when performing a week of the secondary kind of creative work on our planet, we may regard this as a sample of the manner in which He had worked many times previously when making other inhabited worlds in the Universe. *This of itself would indicate that the Creator had planned originally to have a vast number of inhabited worlds in the Universe ultimately:* and because of this fact it would be best to bring into being the substances of *all* those planets in the beginning of the Universe. In this way His work as an astronomer would be perfect, and would prove Him to be **perfect as an**

Architect and Creator of the Universe of astronomical bodies and systems. The proved existence of many dark suns in space now, likewise indicates that *all* of the astronomical bodies, and *all* of the matter, that was ultimately to compose the Universe *was all created by a great primary method simultaneously in the beginning of the Universe.* There are still many dark suns and lifeless planets waiting for their weeks of secondary creation.

In Mr. Whitney's comments I noticed with pleasure that he has been doing some advanced thinking about the logical possibilities that would follow the creation of the substance of the Earth and all our local solar system a long time before the Week of Creation. Many of his comments are excellent, and should be taken seriously and constructively. The admission that the Sun and the stars may have been made long before the Earth's special week of secondary creation agrees with the evidences which indicate the existence of many inhabited worlds before that time and the evidences in the light-years of astronomy that most of the shining stars have been shining longer than the Earth's secondary time. The evidence indicates, as Clark admits, that some of the worlds "have been inhabited for millions of years," because their light-and-heat-giving suns have been shining steadily for millions of years.

However, it is utterly wrong to use a true statement such as this, namely, "Radioactivity cannot be held to provide any measure of the age of the Earth," meaning "any *exact measure,*" for the purpose of giving the impression that *none* of the time actually recorded by the radioactive rocks of the Earth reaches back beyond the beginning of the Earth's special week of Secondary Creation. We do not need to hide the main truths behind obscuring clouds of prejudiced words and phrases or statements of partial truth. We are sincerely seeking truth, the whole truth, and nothing but the truth on any particular subject.

The repeatedly proved fact is that many samples of the radioactive rocks and radioactive meteorites do contain records of time that reaches far back of the Earth's special Week of Secondary Creation, and must be

measured in millions of years! Some variations in the time recorded by the various
samples has very little significance, in this
respect—it does not negate all of the evidences at all. Such dates do not have to be
exact to within a thousand or a hundred
years or a year or a day to have overwhelmingly important scientific value in measuring time before Creation Week. The speed-
ed-up chain reaction in the atomic bombs
(which is witnessed elsewhere in Nature in
the gigantic solar eruptions only, but never
in geology), seems to have wrecked the
logic of more than one recent writer. They
forget that *any marked speeding up of the
radioactive process is always accompanied by
the liberation of an immense amount of
energy,* which would either re-melt the ores
or produce an explosion that would utterly
destroy all the involved radioactive minerals
and records of long preceding ages of time.
We must admit that primary time is only
partially recorded by the radioactve rocks
and meteorites, and therefore the original
Primary Creation of all the elements and all
the stars and astronomical bodies and systems of the Universe was *more* than a mere
2,000 million years ago. Actual time has
been much *longer* than recorded radioactive time.

In addition to these considerations, there
are a few other remarks that need answering. On page 13 of the first issue of THE
FORUM, Prof. Clark has endeavored to explain some of the details of how the first
day of Creation Week was produced. It
should be noticed, however, that "the light
of the heavenly bodies" (the stars) *would
not* produce "distinct day and night sides"
of the Earth; but, instead, they would produce only a starlit night all around the
Earth, because the Earth is surrounded at all
times by shining stars, and has been for
millions of years—ever since the Primary
Creation of the Universe.

On the other hand, Mr. Whitney has suggested that "the darkness that covered the
Earth at the start of Creation Week evidently came from a cloudy covering, not
because the Sun did not exist or was dark
and cold." To this I wish to reply that if
the Sun was already shining just before
Creation Week, then there would have been
a light and dark side to the Earth, and therefore day and night before the first day of
Creation Week. The planets Jupiter, Saturn,
Uranus, and Neptune are now surrounded
by huge oblate atmospheres of clouds; nevertheless because the Sun is shining they
show distinct day and night sides. The
planets include their atmospheres. Before
Creation Week the Earth was not only dark
at its ocean and ground levels, but there
were no day and night sides at higher levels.
Not until God said, "Let there be *light*,"
and thus turned on the visible solar activities of our Sun, was there a regular twenty-
four hour day, composed of "Day" and
"Night." Please notice that when God wanted
days and nights to begin on the Earth He
did not say, "Let the clouds disappear." Instead, he performed a more basic work by
creating a great source of light on one side
of the Earth only—by turning on the visible solar activities of our Sun. Instead of
thinking of only one factor, such as "a
cloudy covering" about the Earth, we need
to think of all the factors that combined
to produce the results that God wanted.

I read with interest Mr. Pruett's observation that "Genesis 2:4-25 is in the nature of
a supplement or appendix, giving *additional*
interesting details." I agree that this is what
we have in this supplement to the first chapter of Genesis. But the "additional interesting details" given in Genesis 2:4-6 are not
necessarily limited to Creation Week. They
may also describe some details of the condition of the Earth before God exercised
any of His secondary creative work on the
Earth. The brief mention in verse 5 of *only
plants and man* may be taken to be a *brief*
reference to all of the things that were created during Creation Week. *This supplement
is talking mainly about the condition of the
Earth "before" any of these things existed
on the Earth.* In fact, it is talking about the
great Primary Creation of the Universe in
verse 4, when "the Lord God made the
Earth and the heavens." Please notice that
the word "heavens" is in the plural form
twice in this verse. As I have shown, God
created two kinds of heavens, namely, the
astronomical heaven of stars and the atmospheric heaven of the Earth. And the
record indicates that the atmospheric heaven

of the Earth was in a cloudy form at the beginning of Creation Week, and was partially clear on the second and third days; but was not clear enough for the Sun and Moon and stars to be seen from the ground until the fourth day. Before the first day of Creation Week our planet had an atmospheric heaven, but it was in an embryonic condition, similar, no doubt, to the present huge oblate atmospheres of Jupiter, Saturn, Uranus, and Neptune. When God created "heavens" (plural) he created the Universe of astronomical bodies and gave atmospheres to many of those astronomical bodies. That was during the great original Primary Creation of matter and the Universe.

Some people have hastily concluded that all of the book of Revelation is limited to events which were yet future in the author's day, because they read in verse 1 the expression "things which must shortly come to pass." But even though most of this book is concerned with such events, it does refer briefly to the origin of sin in Heaven where God's Capital is located, and to the war there that caused "that old serpent, called the Devil, and Satan," and his angels to be cast out into the Earth. The story of the temptation of Eve in the garden of Eden shows that sin began on the Earth very soon after its Week of Creation, and after there was a devil to tempt her through the medium of the "serpent." Therefore we may conclude that some of the book of Revelation, such as Rev. 12:7-9, *does refer to previous history.* We may also regard Genesis 2:4-6 as a brief description of some of the Earth's dark physical history *before* Creation Week, even though Genesis is mainly concerned with the details of Creation Week.

And because Genesis 2:4-6 *is a supplement,* and because it evidently describes the condition of the Earth as it was *a long time before* any plants or human beings existed on the Earth, we may accept its statement that "the Lord God had not caused it to rain upon the earth, . . . but there went up a mist from the earth, and watered the whole face of the ground," to *prove* that there was *some* ground somewhere above the levels of the waters of the ocean before

Creation Week began. This higher ground must have been on the other side of our planet or *far away from the viewpoint of the author of the story in Genesis 1.* From his close viewpoint beneath the cloudy atmosphere of the Earth he saw only water beneath him for as far as his eyes could see on the second day. And as the day progressed, *he moved along with its surface,* otherwise he would not have experienced day and night! Had he remained stationary with regard to space and the stars, he would have seen the Earth turn around under him, and would have seen, no doubt, those areas where there was ground above the level of the ocean waters—but he would not then have noticed any change from day to night, but only a steady continuous day for a long time. Just as our planet, when it is made new again, will have more land areas above the level of the waters of the Earth, so it was similarly transformed during its first week of secondary creation. Perhaps this detail is disconcerting to some theologians; but to those who are studying the book of Nature, where many more details are found, and especially to those who have learned to include the astronomical factors, all this detail is of real importance.

I like the following statement of Mr. Pruett very much, "The first thing any good builder does, after his plans are completed, is to get the materials before he starts to build. Then he does not need to be continually interrupting his work to go for more nails, or lath, or whatever;—*Why* should it be so hard for us to credit the Creator with at least equal intelligence? The record says that God made the raw elements, and then organized them into an orderly world, complete with plants, animals, and people."

However, we must always remember that our Creator is also the Creator of the entire Universe, and that whatever He does is done for the best good of all. I have contended that the Creator of the Universe *did* supply *all the materials for all the Universe first,* instead of "continually interrupting his work to go for more" materials each time he made an inhabited world.

# SOME REMARKS REGARDING THE RADIOACTIVE TIME ESTIMATION OF THE AGE OF THE EARTH

Molleurus Couperus, M.D.

Much has been written during the last twenty-five years regarding the age of the earth from radioactive data, most of it by those who hold that from such data the age of the rocks and indirectly the age of the earth can be determined. Many of the articles written by advocates of the validity of this theory have been very critical of the methods employed, of the data collected, and of the inferences drawn from this data. Such criticism has usually been followed by an improvement in method and more critical evaluation of the data obtained by the various analyses.

If one believes that from a biblical standpoint the earth can not be older than about six thousand years, than one can not accept the conclusions reached from radioactive disintegration. If, however, one believes that the Bible does not limit the age of the earth to a few thousand years, then one may examine the claims of the radioactive time estimation theories, and accept or reject them on their own merit. As indicated by the various articles which are contained in the first and second volume of the Forum, there is no unanimity of opinion regarding the age of the earth from a biblical viewpoint. For the sake of argument, let us accept for the time being that from evidence supplied by the bible an undetermined period of time elapsed since its creation, and that there is nothing in the bible to indicate that this period of time which has elapsed since its original creation may not have been a very long period of time, even billions of years. If we can take such a position we may then examine the claims of various theories of science purporting to give us an answer regarding the age of the earth. Without going into any details at the present time, such an examination soon leads to the conclusion that practically all the theories proposed for estimating the age of the rocks of the earth are scientifically unacceptable. An exception to this generalization may be found in the age estimation based on radioactive disintegration which is going on in the earth. That this theory is practically the only one which is considered worthy of the careful attention of scientists interested in the age of the earth and its geological strata is clearly indicated by the fact that all other methods and theories have been almost completely abandoned by them.

There is no question that the fundamental premise of the physicist and geologist in this theory of radioactive time estimation is a sound one. This basic assumption is simply that from the proportional relationship of the disintegration products of the radioactive series the elapsed time of that disintegration process can be determined. In carrying this premise over into the age determination of a crystal, a piece of rock, geological strata, and the age of the earth, there are a number of factors which must be known in order to obtain an accurate answer. Accepting the basic premise of the theory of radioactive time estimation as sound is a far cry from agreeing to all the deductions which the proponents of the theory may wish to build upon this premise, nor should the acceptance of the basic assumption be any reason why one should close one's eyes to the various factors which may make the application of the theory impossible to part or all of the problem under investigation. Without going into detail at this time, it is the weighing and critical examination of these various factors which has been going on for many years. As a result of such work the method of dating mineral crystals by the radium-lead method has been superseded, at least for the present, by the helium method, the latter being considered as more dependable. It is agreed by nearly all workers in this field that this method has also a number of factors which require careful study, and it is possible that this method may also be rejected as not giving a dependable answer, although the results of this method are generally accepted at present as being reasonably accurate. There are at least half a dozen different methods of measuring various radioactive disintegration processes, some of which have as yet been very poorly evaluated.

In conclusion, I would say that radioactive time estimation has not given a final or wholly reliable answer to the question: How old is the earth? The preponderance of the evidence thus far, however, suggests that the earth is quite old, probably older than two billion years. The estimation of the age of the various rock strata is an entirely different problem, involving other factors which have to be known in order to obtain a reliable answer, particularly as it applies to sedimentary rocks. Only careful study and painstaking work will determine how much, if any, reliance may be placed upon radioactive time estimations of the age of the earth, meteorites, and the various rocks of the earth.

results of this method are generally accepted at present as being reasonably accurate. There are at least half a dozen different methods of measuring various radioactive disintegration processes, some of which have as yet been very poorly evaluated.

In conclusion, I would say that radioactive time estimation has not given a final or wholly reliable answer to the question: How old is the earth? The preponderance of the evidence thus far, however, suggests that the earth is quite old, probably older than two billion years. The estimation of the age of the various rock strata is an entirely different problem, involving other factors which have to be known in order to obtain a reliable answer, particularly as it applies to sedimentary rocks. Only careful study and painstaking work will determine how much, if any, reliance may be placed upon radioactive time estimations of the age of the earth, meteorites, and the various rocks of the earth.

# STREAMLINING STRATIGRAPHY

*By* CLIFFORD L. BURDICK, M.A.

### Introduction

Stratigraphy has been called the "Highest category of Geology to which all other divisions are subsidiary."[1] But even so it is also admitted that it is not as exact a science as Physics or Chemistry, and as such it is only natural that some speculations should be offered to explain geologic phenomena where as yet not all of the laws governing the dynamics of earth movements are evident.

Charles Lyell was the father of the principle of Uniformity as applied to geologic processes, and this law or supposed law has been basic since his day in the development of the science. Even though the progress of geology has been flavored by subjective reasoning, it is reassuring to note that it has not been in vain that some have pointed out certain of these excursions into "a priori" reasoning. Speaking of Uniformity, R. H. Rastall,[2] admits that in modern times this principle has had to be qualified to some extent by the reservation that processes may have been more active in the past than at present. Possibly here we can perceive some influence being brought to bear by a new revitalized Deluge Geology.

If this be the case, perhaps these and other like-minded geological "non-conformists" should take courage in keeping up the good fight to further "streamline" other phases of the science where speculation has appeared to out-run the evidence.

Since we are dealing with Stratigraphy, it might be in order to note in passing that the father of this branch of the science was William Smith in England about 1800. He was the first to announce that the age of the strata can be determined by means of their included fossils, assuming the succession of life much as evolutionists do today, from the less organized types to the more organized, from the lower to the higher forms of life.

Smith, along with subsequent stratigraphers, first assumed that evolution or the succession of life was true, before they could logically use that means to prove which strata were older.

On the other side of the fence, in the field of biology, scientists were marshaling lines of evidence to prove the correctness of their evolutionary assumptions. More recently, as further research has tended to undermine some of these lines of evidence such as comparative anatomy, recapitulation, etc., biologists have fallen back on their "trump card," geology to hold up the hypothesis. It reminds one of the man who got tired and leaned on his friend for support; finally his friend got tired too and leaned on the first fellow.

This strange anomaly or logical contradiction has been pointed out for years by some geologists, and at last some top-flight scientists have taken note. We will again refer to Rastall,[3] who said, "It cannot be denied from a strictly philosophical standpoint geologists are here arguing in a circle. The succession of organisms has been determined by a study of their remains embedded in the rocks, and the relative ages of the rocks are determined by the remains of the organisms that they contain."

Perhaps this paradox is the present bottleneck that most needs attention at the present time. Logically a conclusion is not worth much if the premise is assumed, nor is a premise worth any more if it looks to the conclusion for proof. What is proving what? One of the definitions of SCIENCE engraved on the Hollywood, California high school is that it is ORGANIZED KNOWLEDGE, and that in the attaining of it, REASON is the guide. In the case of geological science, and some biological for that matter, much of this reasoning has been in a circle. Surely

---

[1] Encyclopedia Britannica, vol. 10, p. 167.
[2] Rastall, R. H. Encyclopedia Britannica, vol. 10, p. 167.
[3] Rastall, R. H. Encyclopedia Britannica, vol. 10, p. 167.

the science as a whole cannot progress as it should until the "dog quits chasing its tail."

It is with the hope that these defects may be corrected that we will deal with the following divisions of Stratigraphy.

(1). Disconformities.
(2). Interbedding.
(3). Mechanical Contacts.
(4). Inertia.
(5). Isostasy.
(6). The mechanics of low angle faults.

## 1. Disconformities

The explanation of disconformities or as some call them, "Deceptive Conformities," as ordinarily given by stratigraphers is such as to severely strain the credulity of some logical scientists. Something should really be done about this, before the explanation can be called scientific. As Geike[4] has pointed out, "fossil evidence may be made to prove the existence of gaps which are not otherwise apparent." Here he makes geological evidence bend to fit the biological concept. He goes on to describe how the index fossils suddenly change during an apparently continuous episode of sedimentation, and thus we are asked to believe there existed an hiatus of possibly a million years, when any schoolboy can discern that there was no interruption at all, that the two kinds of life co-existed and the water brought first a batch from one quarter, then from another where the type of sediment was the same. Were it not for certain pre-conceived ideas, we might more easily get the picture of geographical distribution of life in the ancient world as in our own.

Then there is that other type of cause for wonderment: when we find a radical change in type of formation, such as from limestone to shale, which is regarded as evidence of a change in environment and, according to Darwin, would bring on a different form of life. But we oftentimes find the same fossils on either side of the lithological break. It is said that the exception proves the rule, but it

would seem that such a formidable array of exceptions and inconsistencies would in time prove embarrassing to those who advance theories that do not fit the observed facts.

In certain places in the Grand Canyon in Arizona the Red Wall limestone (Mississippian) rests both upon the Devonian and Cambrian, forming a double disconformity. These are all parallel strata, and if such million year periods of hiatus of erosion did exist, the physical evidence should be so evident it could be seen at a distance, but Field[5] explains, "without the aid of *fossils* disconformities are usually very difficult to determine—the physical evidence of an hiatus between the Pennsylvanian and the Permian periods, is, therefore, not represented by a well defined plane of erosion."

The region about Heart Mountain, Wyoming, is also full of contradictions and inconsistencies when interpreted from the biological succession of life point of view. But at this juncture we will merely take note of the disconformities. Several geological systems are misisng, such as the Silurian and Devonian, representing an hiatus of millions of years according to geologists, and yet the strata appear in perfect conformity. But let us have it in the words of Field,[6] who said: "We realize that what at first appears to be a perfectly gradational contact between the Big Horn and Madison represents a considerable stratigraphical hiatus, measured by the total absence of the Silurian and probably the Devonian sediments and fossils. This experience serves to remind us of the value of fossils in helping to determine the age of formations, for it is extremely difficult to discover any physical evidence of even a disconformity between the sediments which were deposited in the Ordovician and those which were deposited in the Mississippian periods." It surely looks as if Stratigraphy were bound up in an evolutionary "straight jacket."

A person does not have to be a trained scientist to see the point that if there were an intermission from deposition of a million

---

[4] Geike, Sir Archibald, Encyclopedia Britannica, vol. II, p. 667.
[5] Field, Richard M. The Principles of Historical Geology from the regional point of view. 1933. p. 102.
[6] Field, Richard M. The Principles of Historical Geology, Princeton University Press, 1933. page 242.

years, the various forces of erosion would so cut up that surface of rock that the casual observer could not miss the contact of angular non-conformity. "The very stones would cry out." Such stratigraphical inconsistencies should be sufficient to cause logical scientists to re-examine the evidences that the evolutionary succession of life has been proved.

Since the modern science of Stratigraphy was born in England, it is only natural that the most intensive study of the strata should start in Western Europe, and that the order in which the fossils were found in that small segment of the globe should be set up as a sort of guide for the order in which fossils should be found everywhere, much as Werner had earlier formulated the "onion skin" theory, that stratified rocks should occur all over the earth in the same order he found them in that section of Germany he studied. His theory was based upon the mineralogical characteristics of the rocks, rather than upon the type of fossils they contained. Although wider observation did not substantiate his theory, still, later stratigraphers, such as Smith and others following him, applied Werner's idea to the fossils.

Some of the earlier observations in America were made in New York State, and at first these observations seemed to bear out the European observations, but as this ideal order of fossil succession was applied to wider fields both in America and in other parts of the world, the exceptions soon accumulated to such an extent that they no longer proved the rule, but proved very embarrassing to it.

But even in New York State, the strata do not always fit the pattern. A case of double disconformity occurs at Buffalo. In the upper case, the Devonian is missing, in the lower one, most of the Silurian is missing, all without structural evidence of a break. Grabau,[7] one of the leading stratigraphers, mentions two other New York disconformities, and says, "a disconformity has been assumed but not supported by evidence of erosion."

## 2. Interbeddings

Repetition or alternations of similar kinds of strata is one of the most common phenomena to be seen in the rocks. In some places are to be seen regular alternations of red and white layers like the stripes in the American flag. There are similar exposures in Topanga canyon, near Santa Monica, California, where layers of red conglomerate alternate with layers of white limestone. Geologists who have made observations along the new Alcan highway from Canada to Alaska have noted as many as 150 such alternations or repetitions of similar strata. In fact these types of formations are so common the world over as to elicit no special wonderment, especially for those versed in the principles of Deluge Geology.

The Bible can in no sense be considered a textbook of geology, but the few things it does say about geological processes in the past are highly illuminating to say the least. Some worthy commentaries have gone so far as to state that even the best geological intellects are bound to come to wrong conclusions when interpreting events of the past in the light of processes now going on, if they refuse to be guided by what the Scriptures have to say on the subject.

Two of the most notable examples of repetition of similar strata occur in the Highlands of Scotland, and in the Alps. At least these regions have attracted more publicity on account of long drawn out geological controversy centering in these two regions. Not only have there been repetitions of the strata, judged from a lithological standpoint, but the fossils have also been repeated, and this violates a cardinal principle of paleontology, and calls for plenary action; as Field[8] has enunciated the code, "It makes little or no difference whether the geologist believes in evolution or not. All that is essential is to prove that fossil faunas and floras are never stratigraphically repeated, regardless of how they originated." The inference is clear, that for the health and well being of biological evolution, no such repetitions must be observed; such would prove a deadly wound to the theory.

But these very repetitions that were so greatly feared, have popped up in Scotland

---

[7] Grabau, A. W. Principles of Stratigraphy, 1924, pp. 823, 824.
[8] Field, Richard M. Principles of Historical Geology. 1933, p. 9.

and in the Alps, five such repetitions having been recorded in the former, and six in the latter. There seemed to be but two horns to this dilemma: (1). Biological Evolution must die a horrible death, or (2). Geologists must discover or invent some principle of earth dynamics to explain how the original conformable order of the strata was so distorted that any one formation could be sliced up like a block of cheese and sandwiched in between other formations. In our next section we will endeavor to show how geologists have tried to solve this.

Murchison and Lyell wrestled with this problem of interbedding or repetition in the Highlands of Scotland, where gneisses and schists were interbedded with Paleozoic sandstones and limestones. They were convinced that they were dealing with a conformable series because they failed to discover any physical evidence to the contrary. But because the fossils were repeated, it was finally decided on fossil evidence alone that some earth movement had taken place to upset the order of the formations.

Field[9] summed up the lesson to be learned from this experience, "Geologists all over the world began to realize that—correlation by lithology alone was a dangerous procedure . . . fossils were the best and safest criteria."

Here is another case where geologists have made a comparatively simple matter complex or impossible mechanically. If scientists would read what the Word of God has to say on this subject, light might break through, and the "Highland Controversy" might never have arisen. In the assuaging and drying up of the Flood waters Genesis tells us that God caused a strong wind to blow, first, from one direction, then from another. This tidal action served a two-fold purpose, (1) it eroded away the mountains and elevations, and, (2) it deposited the sediments in the low places, and in the process buried the dead fauna and flora which blanketed the earth. Since this tidal action of the waters changed direction rythmically it would deposit first a layer of one type of sediment, then a different kind. This is just what was found in Scotland, the Alps and in fact all over the world.

But the state of scientific confusion was not to be wondered at when such stratigraphers as Field[10] expressed a view quite generally held among scientists, "While the Protestant Reformation helped to encourage interest in geologic research, Christianity had unfortunately included in its 'Sacred Writings' the Mosaic account of the origin of the earth as well as the deluge." By refusing to accept the account of the Creation and the Deluge by the One who was present at these events, scientists have hopelessly tangled themselves up in the web of their own spinning.

### 3. Mechanical Contacts

(Otherwise known as Low Angle Faults, Thrust Faults, or Overthrusting.) The inference is that the contacts between the strata are not as originally laid down, but by some mechanical movement one formation or series of formations have been superimposed upon another. Simple thrust faulting is called upon to explain single repetitons, and a series of repetitions by a series of overthrusting. However, this multiple overthrusting imposes a far greater degree of credulity than simple overthrusting, because some of the repeated strata sliced in between other formations are far too thin to have the mechanical strength to be pushed so far, and in the case of the giant thrusts of the Alps, or Nappes, this calls for great slices of North Africa to be shoved over into Europe. This imposed too much on the credulity of even American geologists and they decided there must have been some mistake in the observations made by the European geologists. The high and pointed Matterhorn is supposed to be "upside down" stratigraphically. All because fossils that taxonomists have decded are older, are found in the upper layers and fossils considered younger are found lower down. Even Field[11] seemed a bit doubtful. "IF this be true, it represents one of the most

---

[9] Field, Richard M. The principles of historical geology, p. 194.
[10] Field, Richard M. Principles of Historicall Geology, p. 12.
[11] Field, R. M. Principles of Historical Geology, pp. 224, 231, 234.

astonishing and impressive features in the structures of the Alps.—But what caused such a tremendous translocation as to move a portion of North Africa (Hinterland) toward and finally over Switzerland (Foreland)? The question still remains unanswered. Like any other outstanding hypothesis, even when built on careful and critical research, it must be open to discussion—What caused the western jaw to move is not known. Some geologists are skeptical of the whole interpretation of the structure of the Alps because they are unable to visualize the cause."

The usual mechanical explanation of Overthrusting is that a compressional force is applied by some cause possibly shrinking, or wrinkling, and the fold thus formed breaks in the pinched and thus the weakest section, and the upper layer of formations is pushed over the lower series, in many cases for miles, and in the Alps for hundreds of miles.

In another section we shall endeavor to examine the laws of Physics as applied to the science of the dynamics of the earth. Such men as B. N. Peach and J. Horne settled the controversy of the Scottish Highlands by advancing this same theory of overthrusting, before it was proved mechanically possible. And so likewise in all sections of the world where fossils are found in the reverse order from what is expected according to the biological theory of evolution and the geological theory of the succession of life in the geological ages as evidenced by the remains or fossils found in the strata, this same thrust fault or low angle fault or mechanical contact is invoked to save the theory.

One might suppose that physical evidences would be found of thrust faulting to bear out the contention, but strange as it may seem, such physical evidences of thrusting on a large scale are seldom found. As already pointed out, such great geologists as Lyell, Murchison, Geike, etc., who studied these thrust fault areas failed to discover any evidences of great mechanical displacement. They thought they were looking at perfectly

conformable series. Dana[12] says the same thing: "The thrust planes look like planes of bedding and were long so considered." Geike said,[13] "Had these sections been planned for the purpose of deception they could not have been more skillfully devised," and in his textbook we read, "The strata could scarcely be supposed to have been really inverted save for the evidence as to their true order of succession supplied by their included fossils."[14] Apparently it never occurred to them that the deception might have been the evolutionary succession of life theory.

And so as observations accumulate, the exceptions multiply. We can not go into detail here; suffice it to mention an area in eastern Tennessee and northern Georgia where the fossils are supposed to be in the wrong order, and thrust faults are again invoked to plug the leak in the evolutionary conception.

We previously mentioned Heart Mountain, Wyoming, as showing disconformities. It also has strata in the wrong order. It is capped with Paleozoic limestone, and lower down is "younger" Jurassic and Tertiary sediments. The same is true of near-by Sheep Mountain, and last but by no means least is the great thrust fault area extending from Montana in Glacier National Park and extending northwest for at least five hundred miles along the Rockies wherein an area covering several thousand square miles is supposed to have been pushed from the west toward the east from thirty to sixty miles, all to keep the good ship Evolution from capsizing. The caps of the Rocky Mountain Range in this section is composed of Cambrian, pre-Cambrian, or Paleozoic strata. This mighty Rocky Mountain Cordillera rests upon a base of Cretaceous rocks, in some places showing dinosaur remains. The fossil flora of the mountain capping is mostly an algae.

Uniformitarian geologists generally object when Deluge geologists offer to explain any of the phenomena of stratification or fossilization by the cataclysm of the Flood, but here

[12] Dana, James W. Manual of Geology, p. 534; fourth edition, 1894.
[13] Nature, Nov. 13, 1884, pp. 29-35.
[14] Geike, Sir Archibald, Textbook of Geology, Ed. 1903, p. 837.

they are offering an equally cataclysmic event when they speak of Giant thrusts. Field[15] summed this up as follows, "The last support of the cataclysmic idea was destroyed by the proof of the glacial drift, and the doctrine of uniformitarianism so ably championed by Charles Lyell finally supplanted the unnatural, and to many, the *irreligious* theory of Catastrophism."

It appears that here Mr. Field may have got his wires crossed up just a bit, perhaps, for thrust faulting is surely just as catastrophic as anything postulated by Deluge geology. In fact no Deluge geologist, I think, would object to thrust-faulting if it could be proved objectively. On the other hand it is hard to harmonize thrust-faulting on a giant scale with the law of Uniformity, that processes of the geologic past are to be interpreted in the light of present-day geologic action. The fact is that most of the leaders in geologic thought have now cast aside the idea of Uniformity. The eminent geologist, Arthur Holmes,[16] in discussing the discrepancy between time estimates of the age of the earth, declared, "The convergence toward harmonius results will come about by setting aside the PRINCIPLE OF UNIFORMITY. That is the root of the difficulty."

But the theory of Overthrusting is to the evolutionary geologist what water is to the desert prospector. If you question that explanation of fossils in the wrong order, you are delivering to him a solar-plexus jab. In reviewing George McCready Price's NEW GEOLOGY, Field[17] has this to say, "James McCready Price has recently written a textbook called THE NEW GEOLOGY in which he not only attempts to refute the paleontological record of evolution, but even insists that the reversal of formations due to low-angle overthrusts is impossible, and that paleontological proof, as cited by the stratigrapher, is merely a subterfuge when he discovers the original stratigraphic sequence of his faunas and floras to be inverted."

THE NEW GEOLOGY is a textbook of about 700 pages, and in it Price devotes only about ten pages to this subject of low-angle faults, about one-seventieth of the book, and yet Field picks out that subject to bear the brunt of his criticism. Proof enough it would seem that the explanation of thrust-faulting is one of the most closely guarded pillars in the evolutionary temple, and adherents of that faith greatly fear lest some modern Samson buckle the pillar, and bring down the entire building about their heads.

Perhaps "faith" is not quite the proper term to use, but Bateson[18] in reviewing the reaction that had set in against Darwinism, said that all methods of proof of evolution had failed, but they were still holding on BY FAITH, believing that the real proofs would show up most any day. That was over twenty years ago, but they are still looking, although certainly not in the direction of geology, for geology looks to evolution to prove the overthrusts, in the absence of any objective evidence of its own.

For those who live in Western North America, Glacier Park in the U. S. A., and Banff and Jasper National Parks in Canada are the best and most scenic places to study these alleged thrusts. The scenery is so gorgeous that one may forget to study geology. In Glacier Park beautiful St. Mary's lake has water so blue that it is almost indigo. Lake MacDonald is perhaps more popular as a resort. The continental divide is known as the Garden Wall, composed of level, apparently undisturbed strata which contain algal fossils, classified as Cambrian or pre-Cambrian. These Proterozoic "Dawn of Life" strata are claimed to be the oldest rocks on earth that contain recognizable fossils.

Geologists have assigned an age to these formations of half a billion years, and then are astonished that they are so slightly changed in character since they were originally laid down. Other rocks of this same age, they say, are so greatly altered that they retain very few of their original characteristics.

If this Belt series of Proterozoic age, furnishing the cap rock of the continental

---

[15] Field, R. M. The Principles of Historical Geology, 1933. p. 12.
[16] Holmes, Arthur. Age of the Earth, an introduction to Geological Ideas, 1927.
[17] Field, Richard M. The Principles of Historical Geology. p. 11.
[18] Nature, Nov. 15, 1924.

divide, could be conceived of as actually being the youngest of the present strata, as its topmost position would suggest, then most of this wonder and astonishment would fade away. These formations of the Garden Wall are so level and undisturbed, that it is hard to believe that they represent the mobile unit of the great Lewis Overthrust as postulated by standard geologic interpretation.

The contact between the older rock and the underlying Cretaceous has been examined on Chief Mountain and shows no slickensides, as would be the case if a thrust had occurred.

The same type of "inverted" formation extends on north for hundreds of miles. It is to be observed to good advantage in Crowsnest Pass across the continental divide north of Waterton Lakes Park. Around the beautiful resort city of Banff is to be seen a good variety of scenery where there has been much diastrophism, tilting, folding and blockfaulting. It has been assumed that the blockfaulting of the Palliser, Cascade, and Sulphur Mountain ranges took place subseqently to the overthrust, for five hot springs now flow up through these fractures and around one is built the famous Banff Hot Springs resort. The physical evidences of tilting, folding and block-faulting are easily observed, but where are the physical evidences of thrusting, apart from the fossil data?

A few miles to the north of Banff are Pilot and Eisenhower Mountains, composed of the same "ancient" rock formations, floating on a "sea" of younger Cretaceous. Although these mountains are assumed to have traveled or to have been pushed over the Cretaceous for thirty to fifty miles, strangely enough the strata appear perfectly level and undisturbed, except for erosion, both glacial and by water.

A few more miles north and we find that world famous and beautiful Lake Louise, set as a gem in a mountain and glacier setting unsurpassed anywhere. Near-by Emerald Lake in Yoho National Park, although not quite as famous, is almost as beautiful, the water perhaps more beautiful, if the mountain setting falls a bit short.

And so on north, past the great Columbia snow fields with its seven glaciers, clear up to Jasper. There is massive, imposing Pyramid Mountain, with its slightly tilted strata as a part of the great overthrust, so catalogued by the discovery of so-called primitive fossil algae in the upper mountain, and resting on the "younger" Cretaceous base.

This long overthrust occupies an area of several thousand square miles. As Professor Leith once remarked, "One wonders what great lubricator enabled the great mass to be translated forward many miles with no unconformity or brecciation?" Indeed the whole theory of overthrusting is so loaded with physical and mechancal incongruities, that it seems strange that the stratigraphers who propounded that explanation did not first call in the science of Physics for consultation to see if such an earth movement were possible before going on record in its favor. In our next topic we will call in that branch of science to see if it will throw any light on the problem.

## 4. Inertia

The theory of Inertia is a variation of the Overthrust theory, in that forces are assumed to be applied to the lower portion of the earth's crust suddenly and to have moved it out from under the upper segment of the thrust. Thus the force is not directly exerted as pressure against the upper layer. It is as if a brick were lying on the table, and the table were suddenly moved by a lateral blow. The brick would find itself in another position on the table. The table was moved out from under it.

However this is as yet but an interesting hypothesis, with little field data to back it up. It would be hard to imagine a sudden lateral thrust of the earth's crust which would move a mass thousands of miles in area over another mass, and yet leave undisturbed all of the surrounding territory.

E. H. Stevens[19] of the Colorado School of Mines, in a paper on the subject, says, "This paper attempts to evaluate the importance

---

[19] Stevens, E. H. Bulletin, Geol. Soc. of America, vol. 49, No. 8, pp. 1233-1266.

of inertia in the mechanics of the large low-angle thrust faults. Because of a lack of precise information, many assumptions have been necessary, involving both the mechanics of thrusting, and the numerical values of the factors involved. Further field data will have to be obtained before it can be determined to what extent these principles can be applied in nature."

This statement speaks for itself. Due to lack of exact data, and the number of assumptions, the theory of Inertia can not be taken seriously.

## 5. Isostasy

The modern science of Isostasy as developed by Lawson, Bowie, and others, is now considered to throw considerable light on the theory of Low-Angle faults, and is fundamental in the science of dynamic geology. It is even claimed now that most Orogeny of mountain ranges takes place vertically, rather than horizontally. Isostasy claims that the earth always tends to adjust itself to uneven loads on the surface caused by erosion and deposition of sediments. Part of this adjustment takes place superficially through faulting and earthquakes. It is axiomatic among geologists that the region of greatest faulting and imbrication of structure takes place in regions of heaviest sedimentation. The surface movement therefore is mostly vertical. But since the movement of the sediment was largely lateral, there must be a lateral adjustment somewhere. This is assumed to take place at or near the zone of isostasy, probably within a depth of 75 miles. Thus if the Andes were to be eroded away, and the sediment dumped in the Pacific Ocean, this would create an isostatic unbalance which would be equalized by a deep flow or movement eastward.

When the earth is in isostatic balance, it is believed that drill borings taken anywhere from the surface to the center of the earth would weigh the same, although the borings taken on top of Mount Everest would be longer than one taken in the Pacific Ocean. It is believed, however, that the material

under Everest would be of less density, such as acidic rock, granite, syenite, rhyolite, etc., whereas the bedrock under the oceans would be basic.

Isostasy would seem to make unnecessary if not impossible any large scale overthrusting on the surface of the earth.

## 6. The Mechanics of Low-Angle Faults

It is interesting to note that both Butcher and Lawson came to the same conclusions when applying the laws of physics to Overthrusting. There was a limiting factor on the theoretical size of overthrust blocks, beyond which no rock was strong enough to withstand the stress without crushing. They found that the active force required at the back of the thrust plate or block to overcome the friction alone would exceed the crushing strength of the strongest rock when the thrust plane reaches an extent of 28 miles in the direction of movement. But to let Lawson use his own words,[20] "This estimate can not be exact, but it serves to indicate an approximate limit to the extent of a thrust plane in the direction of slip. This conclusion was reached without considering the effect of the inertia of the upper block which would tend to still further limit the extent of the thrust plane. It is apparent that the mechanics of an overthrust are not well understood, or that *these thrusts are not overthrusts.*"

Lawson was certainly speaking candidly when he admitted that the mechanics of overthrusts are not well understood, that we might be mistaken entirely in considering them overthrusts at all.

With Lawson's and Butcher's theoretical limit of 28 miles, let us consider further limiting factors that would greatly reduce the possible size of overthrusts:

(1). They disregarded entirely the effect of inertia, which would considerably reduce the 28-mile maximum.

(2). They used the hardest rock as their basis of calculations. Evidence is accumulating that much of the strata folding was done while the rocks were yet soft. This factor would still further reduce the numeri-

[20] Lawson, A. C. "Isostatic compensation as a cause of Thrusting." Bull, Geol. Soc. of America, 1922, No. 33. p. 341.

cal calculation, almost to the vanishing point in fact.

(3). If the thrust planes were wet instead of dry, as seems to have been the case, that factor in itself doubles the coefficient of friction, further reducing the theoretical distance a block could be thrusted.

But in the Nappes or giant thrusts of the Alps, portions of Northern Africa are supposed to have been pushed over into Europe. No wonder that even the American overthrust geologists refused to swallow that.

Furthermore, remember that in the Alps as well as the Scottish Highlands there is an interlacing of relatively thin thrust slices; far too thin to have the internal stiffness to withstand such pressures as needed to push these slices so far. The same anomaly was observed in Heart Mountain, Wyoming. And so on, "ad infinitum, ad absurdum."

Lawson[21] sums up his thesis thus: "It seems therefore, mechanically impossible (a priori) that a single intact prism of the earth's crust could move more than *a small fraction of a mile* by real overthrusting as a mobile block past a passive underlying block. It appears therefore that in the case of a real overthrust, there can be no large relative displacement of any single block owing to the fact that strain is relieved by a succession of limited ruptures and the development of an imbricated structure."

William Bowie,[22] of the U. S. Coast and Geodetic Survey, has spent much time in the study of Isostasy and the mechanics of earth movements, and is perhaps as well qualified to speak as anyone. It seems that he has summed up this whole question beautifully, and we will quote at length from him, "The theory that a mountain system has been caused by lateral thrusts originating from a distance supposes a very anomalous condition. The theory implies that the earth's crust is competent to carry thrusts that would squeeze up mountains and plateaus, and at the same time that it is so weak that it can undergo the distortion incident to the movement causing the uplift,—this it seems is an inconceivable situation because no structure

that is so weak as to be distorted to this extent (folded mountains of the Appalachians), could possibly transmit the stresses necessary to hoist the mountains.—From an engineering standpoint we can not conceive of horizontal movements originating outside of the area occupied by the mountains as the cause of a mountain uplift. It seems illogical to suppose that the necessary forces could have originated in vast areas which were quiescent at the time, apparently, that the mountain masses were formed. Tremendous forces are required to throw up a mountain mass, and these forces must be developed in some way.

"It is very difficult to conceive of a disk of *viscous* material buckling in parallel ridges from regional lateral pressure through surface strata. If a disk were subjected to excessive lateral stresses it would undoubtedly fail along some one line, and further exertion of pressures would exaggerate this initial failure. It is inconceivable that the disk would fail in such a way as to make its surface corrugated.

"If the earth's outer strata were strong enough to throw up mountain masses, then they would certainly be too strong to buckle locally into low parallel ridges. It seems probable that the folded parallel ridges are caused by horizontal thrusts and movements of a local character."

And that was precisely the writer's impression of the whole Canadian Rocky Mountain system. The folding, faulting and distortion was of a local character. Evidences of major thrust-faulting simply were lacking.

## Summary

We have reviewed some of the major disconformities or "breaks" where whole systems involving alleged millions of years were missing, with no apparent physical evidences. The only criteria was the lack of index fossils. We believe it is time to let the rocks speak first when it comes to geology, then see if the fossils want to corroborate the physical evidence, if not throw out the

---

[21] Lawson, A. C. Bull. Geol. Soc. America, 1922. p. 340. Bull 33.
[22] Bowie, Wm. Isostatic investigations, etc. Spec. Pub. 99, 1924. U.S. Coast and Geodetic Survey.

succession of life in the geological ages theory.

Interbedding as we have seen corroborates the Genesis account of the Deluge, and negates Evolution, unless we accept the successive overthrusts, which possibly it now appears is remote. Interbedding, with its thin slices is one of the toughest nuts for biological evolutionists to crack.

To explain fossils in "the wrong order," we see how scientists have resorted to developing the theory of Overthrusts or "mechanical contacts." Starting with the Alps and Scottish Highlands in Europe, we now find these barriers to evolution in every land where geologic observations progress. We have seen how the Canadian Rockies are just too big to have been pushed forty miles or such a matter.

Inertia, or "underthrusting" was thought by some possibly to be a saner way to explain these alleged earth movements, but it is admitted that field evidence is lacking, as well as the logic of it.

The science of isostasy believes that all or most of the lateral adjustments in the earth's crust due to transfer of sediments takes place deep in the earth, near the isostatic shell, that most of the mountains are formed vertically.

Lastly come the highly important studies in the mechanics of earth movements, by Lawson, Bowie, and others. The results of these studies seem to prove quite conclusively that overthrusting on a scale necessary to explain how the fossils got in the "wrong order" is a physical impossibility;

that a fraction of a mile is the limit before the fault block would fracture and relieve the stress.

## Conclusion

With the theory of Overthrusting disproved and soon possibly entirely discredited, evolutionists are set back a whole generation in discovering an explanation for the numerous exceptions to the order in which the fossils "must" be found. If *true science* is "organized knowledge," and in science "reason is the guide," then cold logic demands that there is no fast rule or order in which fossils must be found. Deluge geology believes that most of the rock strata were deposited during the Flood Epoch, and then as now fauna and flora were distributed about the earth according as the various forms of life were adapted to their own environment. Therefore strata in one locality might have a different type of life to bury from that of another locality. As the contributing water currents came from differing localities, a different type of fossil would naturally be found in the top strata from that in the lower ones, all life being of the same age, the order of burial being accidental, except that life in the lower basins as the seas would be filled first, and marine life might more often be found in the lower strata. Truly, as Bateson and others have said, Evoluton is now held only as a FAITH. Might we suggest a better FAITH, that found in the Bible account of CREATION?

# SOME RECENT BOOKS

Miracles of Science, by Arthur L. Brown. Pages: 287. Price: $2.00. 1946? Published by the Fundamental Truth Publishers, Findley, Ohio.

The New Diluvialism, by Harold W. Clark. Pages: 222. Price $3.25. 1946. Published by Science Publications, Angwin, Calif.

Evolution: The Root of All Isms, by Dan Gilbert. 2. Edition. Pages: 128. Price $2.00. Danielle Publishers, San Diego.

Social Darwinism, by Richard Hofstadter. Pages 191. 1945. University of Pennsylvania Press, Philadelphia, Pa.

Lot's Wife and the Science of Physics, by Harry Rimmer. Pages: 160. Price $2.50. 1947. Eerdmans Publishing Company, Grand Rapids, Mich.

The Bible in the Age of Science, by O. E. Sanden. Pages: 141. Price $1.75. 1946. Moody Press, Chicago, Ill.

Evolution, Creation and Science, by Frank L. Marsh. Pages: 304. Price: $2.00. 1944. Review and Herald Publishing Association Washington, D. C.

The Moral Theory of Evolutionary Naturalism, by William S. Quillian, Jr. Pages: 154. Price: $3.75. 1945. Yale University Press, New Haven, Conn.

That You Might Believe, by Henry M. Morris. Pages: 155. Price: $1.50. 1946. Good Books, Inc. Chicago 6, Ill.

Common-Sense Geology, by George McCready Price. Pages: 239. 1946. Price: $2.00. Pacific Press Publishing Association, Mountain View, California.

# SOME RECENT BOOKS

The Bible in the Age of Science, by G. D. Sanden. Pages 141. Price $1.75. 1945. Moody Press, Chicago, Ill.

Evolution, Creation and Science, by Frank L. Marsh. Pages 304. Price $2.00. 1944. Review and Herald Publishing Association, Washington, D. C.

The Moral Theory of Evolutionary Naturalism, by William S. Quillian, Jr. Pages 154. Price $2.75. 1945. Yale University Press, New Haven, Conn.

That You Might Believe, by Henry M. Morris. Pages 155. Price $1.50. 1946. Good Books, Inc., Chicago 6, Ill.

Common-Sense Geology, by George McCready Price. Pages 239. 1946. Price $2.00. Pacific Press Publishing Association, Mountain View, California.

Miracles of Science, by Arthur I. Brown. Pages 297. Price $2.00. 1946. Published by the Fundamental Truth Publishers, Findlay, Ohio.

The New Diluvialism, by Harold W. Clark. Pages 222. Price $3.25. 1946. Published by Science Publications, Angwin, Cauf.

Evolution, The Root of All Isms, by Dan Gilbert. 2. Edition. Pages 128. Price $2.00. Danielle Publishers, San Diego.

Social Darwinism, by Richard Hofstadter. Pages 191. 1945. University of Pennsylvania Press, Philadelphia, Pa.

Lot's Wife and the Science of Physics, by Harry Rimmer. Pages 160. Price $2.50. 1947. Eerdmans Publishing Company, Grand Rapids, Mich.

# ACKNOWLEDGMENTS

*The Creationist* 1–2 (1937–8). Courtesy of James White Library, Andrews University.

*The Bulletin of Deluge Geology and Related Sciences* 1–2 (1941–2). Courtesy of James White Library, Andrews University.

*The Bulletin of Creation, the Deluge and Related Science* 3–5 (1943–5). Courtesy of James White Library, Andrews University.

*The Forum for the Correlation of Science and the Bible* 1–2 (1946–8): 1–131. Courtesy of James White Library, Andrews University.

# ACKNOWLEDGMENTS

The Creationist 1-2 (1937-8). Courtesy of James White Library, Andrews University.

The Bulletin of Deluge Geology and Related Sciences 1-2 (1941-2). Courtesy of James White Library, Andrews University.

The Bulletin of Creation, the Deluge and Related Science 3-5 (1943-5). Courtesy of James White Library, Andrews University.

The Forum for the Correlation of Science and the Bible 1-2 (1943-5): 1-131. Courtesy of James White Library, Andrews University.